WITHDRAWN
UTSA Libraries

RENEWALS 458-4574

FORENSIC PSYCHOLOGY

FORENSIC PSYCHOLOGY

Emerging Topics and Expanding Roles

Edited by

ALAN M. GOLDSTEIN, PhD, ABPP

John Wiley & Sons, Inc.

This book is printed on acid-free paper. ∞

Copyright © 2007 by John Wiley & Sons, Inc. All rights reserved.

Published by John Wiley & Sons, Inc., Hoboken, New Jersey.
Published simultaneously in Canada.

No part of this publication may be reproduced, stored in a retrieval system, or transmitted in any form or
by any means, electronic, mechanical, photocopying, recording, scanning, or otherwise, except as
permitted under Section 107 or 108 of the 1976 United States Copyright Act, without either the prior
written permission of the Publisher, or authorization through payment of the appropriate per-copy fee to
the Copyright Clearance Center, Inc., 222 Rosewood Drive, Danvers, MA 01923, (978) 750-8400,
fax (978) 646-8600, or on the web at www.copyright.com. Requests to the Publisher for permission should
be addressed to the Permissions Department, John Wiley & Sons, Inc., 111 River Street, Hoboken, NJ
07030, (201) 748-6011, fax (201) 748-6008, or online at http://www.wiley.com/go/permissions.

Limit of Liability/Disclaimer of Warranty: While the publisher and author have used their best efforts
in preparing this book, they make no representations or warranties with respect to the accuracy or
completeness of the contents of this book and specifically disclaim any implied warranties of
merchantability or fitness for a particular purpose. No warranty may be created or extended by sales
representatives or written sales materials. The advice and strategies contained herein may not be
suitable for your situation. You should consult with a professional where appropriate. Neither the
publisher nor author shall be liable for any loss of profit or any other commercial damages, including
but not limited to special, incidental, consequential, or other damages.

For general information on our other products and services or for technical support, please contact our
Customer Care Department within the United States at (800) 762-2974, outside the United States at
(317) 572-3993 or fax (317) 572-4002.

Wiley also publishes its books in a variety of electronic formats. Some content that appears in print
may not be available in electronic books. For more information about Wiley products, visit our web site
at www.wiley.com.

Library of Congress Cataloging-in-Publication Data:

Forensic psychology : emerging topics and expanding roles / edited by Alan
M. Goldstein.
      p.   cm.
  ISBN-13: 978-0-471-71407-1 (cloth)
  ISBN-10: 0-471-71407-0 (cloth)
  1. Forensic psychology.   I. Goldstein, Alan M.
  RA1148.F5572   2006
  614′.15—dc22
                                                    2005032274

Printed in the United States of America.

10 9 8 7 6 5 4 3 2 1

Library
University of Texas
at San Antonio

To my family with love,
admiration, and appreciation:
Paula
Naomi and Josh
Marion and Jon

Contents

PART VII
Forensic Psychological Consultation

PART VIII
Special Populations

PART IX
Special Topics in Forensic Practice

Foreword

SO, YOU REALLY WANT TO PRACTICE FORENSIC PSYCHOLOGY?

Forensic psychologists are by nature an argumentative bunch, with abundant self-confidence and strongly held opinions. Why else would they readily subject themselves to the high degree of scrutiny and challenge that goes along with presenting oneself as an expert in the legal system (e.g., challenging cross-examination, withering criticism of peers consulting to the opposing side, and increased risk of ethical complaints)? I believe that one answer lies at the intersection of their strong commitment to both behavioral science and the public interest. Forensic psychology at its best brings well-founded scientific methods and behavioral research to bear on important social and legal questions, shedding important light on cases in which triers of fact must render critical judgments.

As Alan Goldstein describes in his opening chapter, the half-century since the *Jenkins* decision (*Jenkins v. U.S.,* 1962) has seen a growing acceptance of behavioral science expertise in the courtroom. Reaching back even further, social advocates called on behavioral science experts to address matters of juvenile and mentally disordered offenders. As respect for the so-called mental sciences and public acceptance of psychology have grown, our legal system has increasingly welcomed behavioral science experts. The downside of this welcome parallels the rapid evolution of other forensic sciences in several respects, not the least of which involves emerging standards of care.

How do we discriminate between valid and junk science (*Daubert v. Merrell Dow Pharmaceuticals,* 1993)? What constitutes adequate training and credentials to provide expertise? How do we integrate the different cultures, ethics, and modes of inquiry that clash when behavioral scientists and attorneys interact? How can we assure that the opinions we offer flow from sound scientific principles, appropriately collected and interpreted data, and the most current research? Such questions will continue to provide fodder for professional debate and consensus seeking; however, it has become increasingly clear that mental health professionals cannot expect to wander into forensic work without specialized education, training, and credentials and remain unchallenged.

Alas, the lure of forensic work can prove seductive to the self-absorbed or naive practitioner. A client in need or earnest attorney calls the office seeking your expertise, posing a question seemingly easy to resolve (i.e., "I need someone to evaluate me and tell them I'm a really good mother" or "My wrongly convicted client had a miserable childhood. Don't you think that ought to mitigate his sentence?"). The fact that the work will not involve dealing with a managed care case reviewer also seems a definite plus. In a moment of superficial insight, it seems unimportant that you really do not know the relevant state laws, legal procedures, or current state of case law on such matters. You do, after all, have a license, you know how to do testing as well as any other psychologist, and you have years of clinical experience; plus, you can count on your client's lawyer to fill you in.

The courtroom seems very impressive. As you walk to the witness stand, all the attention focuses on you. You swear to tell the truth. Your curriculum vitae is presented and the judge declares you an expert. Under friendly questioning by the client's attorney you expound on your findings and opinions. All the while a court reporter diligently records your every word. The sequence and trappings that brought you to this point are all very seductive. Will you be prepared, however, for the withering cross-examination informed by experts consulting to the opposing counsel? Will you be surprised by the complaint to the ethics committee or licensing board that you practiced beyond your area of competence or gave opinions unsupported by data or expertise? Will a malpractice lawsuit follow? Will your words, so carefully recorded, come back to embarrass you or betray your ignorance on some key points?

Aside from sexual intimacies with clients, incompetent entanglements with the legal system form the most frequent basis of ethics and licensing board complaints against psychologists. I hope to have illustrated how some of these situations come to pass. More important, I hope to have demonstrated that psychologists increasingly find themselves held to a standard of care and competence when practicing in the forensic arena. This book will help both to teach and elaborate on that standard.

Alan Goldstein has gathered together an impressive array of experts to focus not only on established areas of forensic practice, but also on emerging and rapidly evolving areas. The topics cover material from the traditional civil and criminal content to the content that seems drawn from today's headlines: abuse of children by teachers and clergy, abuse of the elderly, forensic issues at the end of life, and workplace violence. The contributors have provided a current snapshot with fine-grained detail in subspecialty areas of forensic practice. In addition, readers will come away with a comprehensive view of the field that affords a sense both of the past and of the future potential of the field, grounded (as it should be) in rigorous behavioral science and professional integrity.

GERALD P. KOOCHER, PhD, ABPP

Boston, Massachusetts

REFERENCES

Daubert v. Merrell Dow Pharmaceuticals, Inc., 509 U.S., 579 (1993).

Jenkins v. U.S., 307 F.2d 637 U.S. App. D.C. (1962).

Preface

FORENSIC PSYCHOLOGY: EMERGING TOPICS AND EXPANDING ROLES

Four years ago, I shipped a carton containing the manuscript of *Forensic Psychology,* the 11th volume of the *Handbook of Psychology,* to the publisher, John Wiley & Sons (Goldstein, 2003). In that carton were twenty-eight chapters, addressing such topics as forensic ethics, the nature of expert testimony, methodological approaches to forensic assessment, and those psycholegal issues that most frequently serve as sources of assessment referrals for forensic mental health professionals. Topics that are covered in that book represent the mainstream of forensic psychology and psychiatry practice and research. They include chapters focusing on jury selection, eyewitness memory, child custody, personal injury, employment discrimination, trial competence, criminal responsibility, juvenile offenders, child sexual abuse, sexual predators, and violence risk assessment. As the editor of that volume, among the most difficult tasks was limiting the topics that were to be addressed there. Initially, the plan called for 25 chapters, but when the outline of the book was presented to Irving Weiner, the editor-in-chief of the 12-volume series, he spared me the pain of eliminating three topics. As a board certified forensic psychologist, he, too, recognized that describing the state of knowledge of the field of forensic psychology at that time required the inclusion of all the proposed topics.

Even with 28 chapters and more than 600 pages, I recognized that a number of topics reflective of the field of forensic psychology research and practice were not included. Some represented what many would consider to fall within the mainstream of forensic psychology and psychiatry: civil commitment, termination of parental rights, and federal sentencing evaluations. Others, though not frequent sources of referrals, nonetheless occasionally generate requests for assessments and had a published knowledge base: postconviction evaluations, psychological independent medical evaluations (IMEs), and workplace violence. Over the past decade, a number of other psycholegal topics have emerged and have begun to serve as the source of referrals to forensic mental health experts; they are psycholegal topics about which very little has been published integrating their broad knowledge base: clergy and teacher sexual abuse, abuse of the elderly, and end-of-life issues such as physician-assisted suicide and the legal capacity of terminally ill patients to initiate do-not-resuscitate orders. In addition, few publications have addressed the appropriate application of instruments frequently used in clinical psychology to address psycholegal issues: the Minnesota Multiphasic Personality Inventory 2, the Personality Assessment Inventory, and, a source of considerable controversy and debate, the Rorschach.

Forensic Psychology: Emerging Topics and Expanding Roles has, as its primary goal, the thorough, objective presentation of these and other topics, including, where appropriate, a consideration of relevant statutes and case law, ethical issues, research, and assessment methodology. Because statutes and case law, the driving force behind every forensic evaluation, continue to evolve, forensic mental health practitioners must remain up to date on the most recent developments in the law. Two chapters provide a legal update, focusing on statutes and landmark cases in both the civil and criminal arenas. This volume is designed to present the current state of the field in terms of law, ethics, research, and practice. It is hoped that this book proves to be of significant value to forensic mental health professionals, civil and criminal attorneys, and advanced graduate students and forensic postdoctoral fellows.

The working title of this book was *Forensic Psychology: Advanced Topics*. However, I was never convinced that there are "advanced" topics in the field. *All* forensic assessments require a reasonable knowledge of: the statutes and case law that drive each evaluation; a thorough recognition of the ethics that govern our profession as mental health professionals and as forensic experts; an understanding of and the ability to apply relevant research to each evaluation when appropriate; and specific knowledge of and the ability to utilize appropriate methodology in conducting forensic mental health assessments. If all forensic assessments, not just "advanced" areas of practice, draw on this identical knowledge base, it appears more appropriate to consider these topics in another light. As this book developed, it became obvious that, for the most part, the chapters that compose this volume represent emerging areas of forensic mental health research and practice and in many ways reflect the expanding roles for competent forensic experts. I believe that the title of this book accurately reflects this perspective.

A standard of care, what the reasonably prudent professional would do, is rapidly emerging in the field of forensic psychology. From an ethical perspective, it exists in terms of the enforceable principles stated in the Code of Ethics for psychologists and as an aspiration model in the *Specialty Guidelines for Forensic Psychologists*. These documents are discussed at length in Chapter 7, and their specific applications are included in other chapters of this volume. In terms of practice issues, the standard of care is evolving. The concept of a standard of care in forensic psychology is considered in detail in the first chapter of this volume. It is hoped that this book provides a basis for practitioners to conduct forensic mental health assessments consistent with the state of the field as it currently exists and the standard of care that is emerging.

This volume contains the work of 49 contributors, each a recognized expert in his or her area of research or, practice, or the law (and for many, both law *and* forensic practice). Most are friends and colleagues, board certified forensic psychologists of the American Board of Professional Psychology. Many have conducted national workshops on behalf of the American Academy of Forensic Psychology (AAFP), the continuing education division of the American Board of

Forensic Psychology. Every contributor submitted outstanding first drafts of their chapters, requiring little in the way of editorial changes other than those designed to create a uniformity of style and voice. I am most grateful to them for their major contributions to this book and to the field and for their friendship and tolerance of my numerous e-mails and letters "subtly" reminding them of deadlines long before they approached. They have shared their knowledge and experience in the most professional way and I will be forever appreciative.

For almost 18 years, I have chaired the continuing education program of the AAFP. During that time, more than 120 different experts—practitioners and researchers, lawyers and forensic mental health experts—have presented postdoctoral seminars to more than 14,000 forensic mental health professionals and attorneys. The topics of these workshops have served as the foundation for most of this volume and for the majority of chapters covered in Volume 11 of the *Handbook of Psychology*. Even though I have edited both books, I am unable to find words to express my gratitude to these wonderful, generous people for the major contribution each has made to those in forensic practice and research, to graduate students, and to me. Although mine is an unpaid position, I have been more than compensated by what you have taught me and by your friendship, not to mention the great food and wine.

My involvement in the field of forensic psychology began thanks to Marvin Reznikoff, PhD, ABPP, who was the director of clinical psychology at Fordham University. Marv was my mentor, chairing my dissertation committee. He continues to be my mentor, a constant source of guidance, support, and, most important, friendship. He referred me my first forensic case, and I thank him for shaping my career and allowing me to earn a living! I am grateful to others at Fordham who made major contributions to my professional and personal life, especially Peggy Mackiewicz and Anne Anastasi. At John Jay College of Criminal Justice, I have been fortunate to work with a group of very special colleagues. My students in the master's and doctoral programs, present and former, are a pleasure to teach and to learn from. The college continues to be a wonderful place to work, even after all these years.

I want to thank my friend and colleague Kirk Heilbrun for his insightful comments. As always, his levelheaded thinking and his ability to quickly grasp complex issues contributed greatly to the second chapter in this book. Martin Stolar, a practicing attorney who specializes in federal criminal cases in New York City, reviewed the draft of Chapter 14. His comments were, as always, concise and on target, and I and my coauthor of that chapter, Daniel Krauss, thank him for his suggestions, all of which are incorporated in that chapter.

This book is a direct outgrowth of Volume 11, *Forensic Psychology*. Were it not for Irving Weiner, the editor-in-chief of that series, who invited me to edit the first book, this volume would never have been written, at least not by me. Irv serves as a model not only for how to put together a book of this nature, edit it, and see it through to completion, but as a practitioner; his sense of ethics and professional competence serve as a source of inspiration.

At John Wiley & Sons, Margaret Alexander, vice president and publisher, has always been receptive, encouraging, and highly supportive of this project. Patricia

(Tisha) Rossi, senior editor for psychology, and Ester Mallach, editorial assistant, did everything and more to ensure the completion of this volume. Each responded immediately and cheerfully to my calls and e-mails for advice and assistance, and because of their efforts, this book was completed before the deadline.

This book could not have been written without the support, encouragement, and understanding of my family. My wife, Paula, more than tolerated the time I spent working on it. In our tiny summer home, she spent the summer stepping over journals, books, legal pads, notes, and stacks of index cards. She accepted this major inconvenience with good humor (most of the time), never complained (well, almost never), and went beyond the call of duty as both a wife and my best friend, using her skills as an English teacher to edit material I authored. As my mother used to say, "Paula could have done better." I am very lucky, a view shared by anyone who knows us. Naomi Sevin Goldstein, my daughter and a forensic psychologist at Drexel University, was a major source of help when I was deciding on topics and authors to include in this volume. Her wisdom, her solid and consistently sound judgment, and her good humor helped significantly in the development of this book—as it does throughout my life. Her husband, Joshua Sevin, an urban planner, is one of the most well-rounded, intelligent people I know; his suggestions were right on target. Marion Goldstein, my nonforensic psychologist daughter, always manages to keep everything in perspective for me (and, I suspect, for everyone in her life). She provided help (along with Jon Feldman, her husband and, coincidentally, a PhD in computer science), when I encountered computer glitches while working on this book. Her words of advice, her cheerfulness, and her optimism played a major role in the completion of this book and represent a major contribution to my life.

This book represents the hard work, effort, and contributions of many. My deepest gratitude to all.

ALAN M. GOLDSTEIN

Hartsdale, New York

REFERENCE

Goldstein, A. M. (Ed.). (2003). *Handbook of psychology: Vol. 11. Forensic psychology.* Hoboken, NJ: Wiley.

Contributors

Jorge C. Armesto, PhD
Department of Psychiatry
Harvard Medical School
Boston, Massachusetts

Steven C. Bank, PhD, ABPP
Board Certified Forensic Psychologist
Center for Forensic Psychiatry
Ann Arbor, Michigan

Curtis L. Barrett, PhD, ABPP
Board Certified Forensic Psychologist
University of Louisville School of
    Medicine
Louisville, Kentucky

Randy Borum, PhD, ABPP
Board Certified Forensic Psychologist
University of South Florida
Tampa, Florida

Stanley L. Brodsky, PhD
Department of Psychology
University of Alabama
Tuscaloosa, Alabama

Don Condie, MD, ABPN
Board Certified Forensic Psychiatrist
Massachusetts General Hospital
Boston, Massachusetts

Lois Oberlander Condie, PhD, ABPP
Board Certified Forensic Psychologist
Harvard Medical School
Boston, Massachusetts

David DeMatteo, JD, PhD
Treatment Research Institute
University of Pennsylvania
Philadelphia, Pennsylvania

Eric Y. Drogin, JD, PhD, ABPP
Board Certified Forensic Psychologist
University of Louisville School of
    Medicine
Louisville, Kentucky

Joel A. Dvoskin, PhD, ABPP
Board Certified Forensic Psychologist
University of Arizona College of
    Medicine
Tucson, Arizona

**Charles Patrick Ewing, JD, PhD,
    ABPP**
Board Certified Forensic Psychologist
School of Law
State University of New York
Buffalo, New York

Stephen R. Feldman, JD, PhD
Department of Psychiatry and
    Behavioral Sciences
University of Washington
Seattle, Washington

William E. Foote, PhD, ABPP
Board Certified Forensic Psychologist
University of New Mexico School of
    Medicine
Albuquerque, New Mexico

Alan M. Goldstein, PhD, ABPP
Board Certified Forensic Psychologist
John Jay College of Criminal Justice
City University of New York
New York, New York

Stuart A. Greenberg, PhD, ABPP
Board Certified Forensic Psychologist
University of Washington
Seattle, Washington

Roger L. Greene, PhD
Pacific Graduate School of Psychology
Palo Alto, California

Thomas Grisso, PhD, ABPP
Board Certified Forensic Psychologist
University of Massachusetts Medical
    Center
Worcester, Massachusetts

Kirk Heilbrun, PhD, ABPP
Board Certified Forensic and Clinical
    Psychologist
Drexel University
Philadelphia, Pennsylvania

Christopher J. Hopwood, MS
Texas A&M University
College Station, Texas

Colleen McClain Jacobson, PhD
Columbia University
New York State Psychiatric Institute
New York, New York

Michele J. Karel, PhD
Department of Psychiatry
Harvard Medical School
Boston, Massachusetts

Susan C. Knight, PhD
Keck School of Medicine
University of Southern California
Los Angeles, California

Daniel A. Krauss, JD, PhD
Department of Psychology
Claremont McKenna College
Claremont, California

Paul D. Lipsitt, LLB, PhD, ABPP
Board Certified Forensic Psychologist
Boston University Student Mental
    Health Center
Boston, Massachusetts

Jenette Mack-Allen, PhD
Department of Psychology
Widener University
Chester, Pennsylvania

Geoffrey Marczyk, JD, PhD
Department of Psychology
Widener University
Chester, Pennsylvania

Robert G. Meyer, PhD, ABPP
Board Certified Forensic Psychologist
University of Louisville
Louisville, Kentucky

Collin Middleton, JD
Middleton & Timme, PC
Anchorage, Arkansas

Leslie C. Morey, PhD
Department of Psychology
Texas A&M University
College Station, Texas

Jennifer Moye, PhD
Department of Psychiatry
Harvard Medical School
Boston, Massachusetts

David F. Mrad, PhD, ABPP
Board Certified Forensic Psychologist
Drury University
Springfield, Missouri

Daniel C. Murrie, PhD
Department of Psychology
Sam Houston State University
Huntsville, Texas

Erik Nabors, JD, PhD
Federal Bureau of Prisons
Yazoo City, Mississippi

Randy K. Otto, PhD, ABPP
Board Certified Forensic Psychologist
University of South Florida
Tampa, Florida

Ira K. Packer, PhD, ABPP
Board Certified Forensic Psychologist
University of Massachusetts Medical
    School
Worcester, Massachusetts

Michael L. Perlin, JD
New York Law School
New York, New York

John Petrila, JD, LLM
University of South Florida
Tampa, Florida

Richard E. Redding, JD, PhD
Villanova University and Drexel
    University School of Law
Villanova, Pennsylvania

Beth N. Rom-Rymer, PhD, FICPP
Diplomate in Psychopharmacology
Rom-Rymer and Associates
Chicago, Illinois

Barry Rosenfeld, PhD, ABPP
Board Certified Forensic Psychologist
Fordham University
Bronx, New York

Louis B. Schlesinger, PhD, ABPP
Board Certified Forensic Psychologist
John Jay College of Criminal Justice
City University of New York
New York, New York

Daniel W. Shuman, JD
Southern Methodist University
Dedman School of Law
Dallas, Texas

Christopher Slobogin, JD, LLM
Fredric G. Levin College of Law
University of Florida
Gainesville, Florida

Erin M. Spiers, PhD
Louisiana State University School of
    Medicine
New Orleans, Louisiana

Harley V. Stock, PhD, ABPP
Board Certified Forensic Psychologist
Incident Management Group
Plantation, Florida

Wilfred G. van Gorp, PhD, ABPP
Board Certified Clinical
    Neuropsychologist
College of Physicians and Surgeons
Department of Psychiatry
New York, New York

David A. Vore, PhD, ABPP
Board Certified Forensic Psychologist
Swiss Re Life & Health American, Inc.
Southfield, Michigan

Megan B. Warner, PhD
Texas A&M University
College Station, Texas

Irving B. Weiner, PhD, ABPP
Board Certified Forensic Psychologist
University of South Florida
Tampa, Florida

PART I

Expanding Roles and Emerging Areas of Practice

CHAPTER 1

Forensic Psychology: Toward a Standard of Care

Alan M. Goldstein

INTRODUCTION

In his groundbreaking book, *On the Witness Stand* (subtitled *Essays on Psychology and Crime*), Hugo Münsterberg (1908) was highly critical of judges, attorneys, and jurors. He wrote, "The lawyer and the judge and the juryman are sure that they do not need the experimental psychologist. They go on thinking that their legal instinct and their common sense supplies them with all that is needed and somewhat more" (p. 11). Without citing a single reference, Münsterberg indicated that the "strong strides" (p. 10) made in experimental research had profound implications for new roles for psychologists—as expert witnesses in court. He described the potential contributions psychologists could make in addressing issues such as inaccurate perceptions and faulty memories of witnesses, the use of reaction time and visible "traces of emotions" to distinguish truth from lying and to establish guilt, the role of suggestion in contaminating witness recall, the use of hypnosis as a possible contributing factor to false confessions, and the role of posthypnotic suggestion as a potential motivating factor in some crimes. Furthermore, Münsterberg explained that psychologists not only possessed the skills to treat those who committed crimes, but, at the turn of the twentieth century, had the knowledge and expertise to prevent crime as well.

Münsterberg's advocacy for these new roles for psychologists did not, unfortunately, fall on deaf ears. Rather, as described by Ewing (2003), John H. Wigmore (1909), a leading scholar on the laws of evidence, attacked Münsterberg's assertions in a scathing article in the *Illinois Law Review*. Consequently, Münsterberg's somewhat grandiose proposals for new roles for psychologists were rejected by attorneys. Unless called as fact witnesses (or as defendants or plaintiffs), psychologists rarely saw the inside of a courtroom. Yet, over time, some of Münsterberg's ideas proved to be, at least in part, valid. Psychologists assumed some of the roles envisioned by him. For example, empirical research abounds on eyewitness memory for people and events (see Castelli et al., 2006; Wells & Loftus, 2003) and factors contributing to false confessions (see Oberlander, Goldstein, & Goldstein, 2003). Although none of what Münsterberg foresaw as valid indicators of malingering was ever empirically validated, psychologists have developed reliable and valid methods to assess response style (see Rogers & Bender, 2003). The use of hypnosis in a range of forensic settings has become almost commonplace (Scheflin, 2006; also see Chapter 28).

Almost 100 years after the publication of Münsterberg's book, forensic psychology has been recognized as a field unto itself. *Jenkins v. U.S.* (1962) held that psychologists could serve as experts in federal court. The American Psychological Association (APA) frequently submits *amicus* briefs to appeals courts and to the U.S. Supreme Court on those matters for which relevant empirically based research is available. The APA formally recognized forensic psychology as an area of specialization in 2001 (A. M. Goldstein, 2003b; Heilbrun, 2000). Journals devoted to forensic psychology research and practice are plentiful. Forensic assessment instruments, designed to assist forensic mental health professions in conducting evaluations in a wide range of civil and criminal settings, continue to be developed and researched (Grisso, 1986, 2003a). Graduate courses at the master's and doctoral levels continue to proliferate, and new clinical-forensic doctoral programs have been developed (e.g., Sam Houston State University in Texas; John Jay College of Criminal Justice in New York; see Krauss & Sales, 2006). Postdoctoral continuing education in forensic psychology is regularly offered by professional organizations such as the APA and the American Academy of Forensic Psychology (listings of representative forensic training workshops can be found at www.abfp.com). The American Psychology-Law Society now schedules its national meetings annually, as opposed to biannually, to accommodate the increased interest and research in this field. Postdoctoral training programs receive a steady stream of applicants seeking formalized training in the field (Grisso, personal communication, 2005). The APA, the Association of State and Provincial Psychology Boards, and the National Register of Health Service Providers formally recognize board certification in forensic psychology, awarded by examination through the American Board of Professional Psychology. (For a thorough description of the origins of the field of forensic psychology, see Bartol & Bartol, 2006; Brigham & Grisso, 2003.) The state of the field of forensic psychology has evolved such that a standard of care is emerging in selecting forensic assessment methodology, conducting ethical forensic assessments, and in presenting opinions in written reports and in courtroom testimony.

Forensic Psychology (A. M. Goldstein, 2003a), a volume of the *Handbook of Psychology* (I. B. Weiner, 2003), consisted of 28 chapters, each of which was written by an expert or experts on a different aspect or area of forensic psychological practice. The topics included what is generally thought of as the "meat and potatoes" (or, if a vegetarian, the "bread and butter") of forensic practice (i.e., trial competence, mental state at the time of an offense, eyewitness memories, child custody, personal injury, and violence risk assessment). Limiting that book to only 28 chapters and 606 pages was a challenge. A number of emerging psycholegal issues that forensic mental health experts may be called on to address were not included. This volume, in many ways, represents a continuation of that book.

In 28 new chapters, the latest research on a number of assessment techniques and methods commonly used in the field of forensic psychology is considered, the most recent and significant case law in the areas of civil and criminal forensic mental health practice is described, and ethical issues, research, case law, and methodology in emerging areas of forensic mental health practice are presented. As such, this book describes expanding roles for forensic experts—not only beyond those fantasized by Münsterberg, but also beyond those psycholegal areas covered in the 2003 book. The forensic assessment methodology and the models for assessment described by the authors of these chapters should be considered in light of the emerging standard of care in the field: what the reasonably prudent professional should do in conducting similar evaluations. Although specific methodology must be determined on a case-by-case basis, forensic mental health practitioners should consider the material in those chapters that address methodology as a template in designing their own evaluation methodology on similar psycholegal issues.

Definition of Forensic Psychology

Although many definitions of forensic psychology exist (e.g., Committee on Ethical Guidelines for Psychologists, 1991; Hess, 2006), most share common characteristics. In the successful petition submitted to the APA to designate this field as a specialty in professional psychology, Heilbrun (2000) defined forensic psychology as

> the professional practice by psychologists within the areas of clinical psychology, counseling psychology, neuropsychology, and school psychology, when they are engaged regularly as experts and represent themselves as such, in an activity primarily intended to provide professional psychological expertise to the judicial system. (p. 6)

The definition of this expanding area of practice proposed by this author (A. M. Goldstein, 2003a) in *Forensic Psychology,* Volume 11 of the *Handbook of Psychology* (I. B. Weiner, 2003), proposes that forensic psychology "involves the application of psychological research, theory, practice, and traditional and specialized methodology (e.g., interviewing, psychological testing, forensic assessment and forensically relevant instruments) to provide information relevant to a legal question" (p. 4).

Forensic psychologists may conduct *research* on topics related to the civil and criminal legal systems or may focus on specific questions that these institutions of justice consider; such findings may take the form of expert testimony, whose goal is to educate a jury or judge about a specific legally relevant topic (i.e., issues related to eyewitness identification; factors that may contribute to false confessions). Those in the *practice* of forensic psychology typically conduct individual assessments of defendants, plaintiffs, or parents involved in child custody cases; the product of these evaluations has a similar goal: to educate jurors and judges by providing them with information they may not otherwise have known when they consider making a legal determination (i.e., the impact of mental retardation or mental illness on the ability of a defendant to assist an attorney in defending the client in court; the possible role that duress or coercion may have played in a defendant's involvement in a criminal act to be considered by a federal judge at the time of sentencing; the effects of Alzheimer's disease on a patient's ability to make an informed decision about consenting to or refusing medical treatment). The chapters in this book reflect the perspective that an element of the evolving standard of care in the field of forensic psychology involves the integration of practice and research to reach ethical, relevant, informed forensic opinions.

TOWARD A STANDARD OF CARE

Over the past 20 years, there have been considerable advances in forensic mental health assessment involving research that has supported the theoretical underpinnings of psycholegal evaluations, the development of valid, reliable forensic assessment instruments (A. M. Goldstein, 2003a, 2005; Grisso, 1986, 2003a; Heilbrun, 2001; Heilbrun, Marczyk, & DeMatteo, 2002; Melton, Petrila, Poythress, & Slobogin, 1997; I. B. Weiner & Hess, 2006), and a dramatic increase in the number of criminal and civil issues that forensic mental health experts are retained to address. Because of this growth, the need for a standard of care— those steps the reasonably prudent forensic mental heath expert should take to ensure quality, ethical, relevant opinions, reports, and testimony that are data-based—is even more critical.

In his landmark text, *Evaluating Competencies: Forensic Assessments and Instruments,* Grisso (1986) described some of the common criticisms leveled against forensic mental health experts. These focused on the lack of relevance of opinions to the legal issue, incredibility as to the opinions reached, and opinions that were based on inadequate sources of information. With the recognition of forensic psychology as a specialty by the APA in 2002 (A. M. Goldstein, 2003b; Heilbrun, 2000), the APA acknowledged that as a field, forensic psychology has, among other characteristics, unique educational and training requirements, its own theoretical orientation, a specialized knowledge base (including research and journals devoted to the field), and its own methodology to ensure the credibility of the field and to protect the public from uninformed or unqualified practitioners. The recognition of these characteristics or factors that contributed to the APA's approval of forensic psychology as a specialty in many ways serves as a foundation for the premise that a standard of care for conducting forensic mental health assessments is emerging. The acknowledgment that there is an expected threshold for the quality of forensic psychological assessments should be not merely an aspirational goal or theoretical concept, but a reality.

The standard of care in forensic psychology is composed of a number of elements: ethical conduct; knowledge of the legal system and the statutes and case law that drive forensic assessments; use of appropriate methodology, including, when appropriate, traditional psychological tests, forensic assessment instruments, and forensically relevant instruments; the integration of information from a variety of data sources to formulate opinions; an awareness of empirical research relevant to the psycholegal issue being evaluated and the use of results of such studies to inform the forensic decision-making process; and the preparation of written reports and presentation of expert testimony in court that is objective and thorough and that honestly reflects *all* findings, not only those advanced by the retaining attorney. These elements of the standard of care are also areas of knowledge and practice that are considered when applicants for board certification in forensic psychology are examined by the American Board of Forensic Psychology.

It is expected that the reasonably prudent forensic psychologist practices in a manner consistent with the APA (2002) ethical principles, follows the aspirational guidelines established in the "Specialty Guidelines for Forensic Psychologists" (Committee on Ethical Guidelines for Forensic Psychologists, 1991), and adheres to other guidelines such as those related to record keeping (APA, 1993) and those focusing on specialized areas of forensic practice such as child custody evaluations (APA, 1994). Weissman and Debow (2003) argue that adhering to these ethical principles and guidelines serves to enhance the competence of the expert. These documents stress that, from an ethical perspective, the standard of care includes practicing within one's area of competence, presenting credentials in court that are honest and without "puffery," rendering an opinion based on sufficient information and data, and considering alternative opinions and being able to explain why they have been rejected. Some of these documents describe the methodological steps that should be followed in conducting a forensic assessment (APA, 1994) and thus suggest a standard of care to be followed by practitioners in terms of expected methodology.

As advanced by Grisso (1986) and reinforced by other experts in the field (A. M. Goldstein, 2003a; Heilbrun, 2001; Heilbrun et al., 2002; Melton et al., 1997; I. B. Weiner & Hess, 2006), forensic mental health professionals must understand those legal concepts that serve as the basis for their evaluations. The standard of care must include not only a reasonable familiarity with the relevant statutes and case law that shape the forensic assessment and any report and testimony that flow from them, but, in addition, experts are expected to know the rules that govern expert testimony in those jurisdictions in which the assessments are conducted. Forensic psychologists must be familiar with the nature of expert testimony, including rules of evidence and limits placed on the content of such testimony (Ewing, 2003).

The standard of care includes the recognition that any forensic referral may result in courtroom testimony. As such, forensic mental health experts are expected to memorialize their interviews by recording sessions (where permissible) or by keeping thorough, contemporaneous written notes (Committee on Ethical Guidelines for Forensic Psychologists, 1991). Experts should not rely on their memory when preparing written reports or testifying. Rather, the reasonably prudent expert documents the content of interviews, maintains these records, and relies on them as a source of information in formulating, explaining, and defending opinions.

Part of the emerging standard of care in the field is the reliance on multiple sources of information to arrive at opinions. Shapiro (1991) urges forensic mental health experts to integrate data from numerous sources to arrive at informed, credible opinions. Unquestioned acceptance of an examinee's presentation of his or her background, history, or rendition as to what occurred at the time of a crime or how well qualified he or she is as a parent (and how poor a parent an ex-spouse would be) is naive at best. It ignores the obvious motivation to deceive and does not meet acknowledged practice standards in the field. Malingering and exaggeration are coping strategies used by examinees to make the best of a bad situation and, thus, should be expected in forensic evaluative contexts (Rogers, Salekin, Sewell, Goldstein, & Leonard, 1998; Rogers, Sewell, & Goldstein, 1994). The assessment of response style is considered by many to be a fundamental element, a cornerstone of any forensic assessment (i.e., A. M. Goldstein, 2003a; Heilbrun, 2000; Rogers, 1997; Rogers & Bender, 2003; see Chapter 2), and must be considered in all forensic evaluations. It is at least partially addressed by incorporating third-party information into the assessment process to corroborate information provided by those who have much to gain or lose by successfully deceiving the evaluator (Heilbrun, Warren, & Picarillo, 2003; see Chapter 8). Forensically relevant instruments that address issues of response style related to claimed symptoms of memory loss, Schizophrenia, and other cognitive disorders (including intellectual deficits and neurological symptomatology) are part of the evaluation process (Rogers & Bender, 2003), and their appropriate use is part of the evolving standard of care.

Reliable and valid forensic assessment and forensically relevant instruments provide information relevant to a determination of legal competency and address issues related to response style. Grisso (1986, 2003a) describes a wide range of forensic assessment instruments developed by experts to provide information of direct relevance to specific legal questions and competencies. When used with other sources of information, forensic assessment instruments may help determine whether or not the examinee's performance suggests competence or incompetence. Forensically relevant instruments may serve to evaluate the credibility or genuineness of an examinee's responses to other tests and thus address the significant issue of malingering. However, these techniques do not explain *why* an examinee is not competent. The use of traditional psychological tests (i.e., those that measure cognitive functioning or personality characteristics) as part of the forensic assessment battery may contribute to an understanding of the source of an examinee's lack of competence. Forensic psychology experts should consider the use of instruments from all three categories when conducting evaluations, and if testing is not included in the evaluation protocol, there should be a clearly stated rationale for omitting this element of the forensic assessment. Consistent with the evolving standard of care, information derived from these instruments must be integrated into the written report and testimony.

Numerous high-quality peer-reviewed journals are devoted to research on a broad range of topics relevant to forensic mental health practice (i.e., *Law and Human Behavior, Behavioral Sciences and the Law, Criminal Justice and Behavior, Journal of Forensic Psychology Practice*). The results of empirical studies appearing in these and other journals often provide the foundation on which forensic assessment and forensically relevant instruments are based. Research findings relating to specific demographic groups are of prime significance when practitioners must interpret data and present opinions in court, and results of such studies must be considered in formulating opinions about those from minority populations (a group overrepresented in the criminal justice system and, thus, among examinees in criminal forensic evaluations). Studies that consider factors that may serve to increase or decrease the risk of future violence must be familiar to forensic mental health practitioners conducting risk assessments. As such, part of the developing standard of care involves a reasonable familiarity with current research to inform forensic opinions and testimony. Forensic experts are expected to integrate published research results with their findings to formulate informed opinions and present them in an accurate and meaningful manner to the trier of fact.

In preparing reports and offering testimony, there is a recognized standard, most clearly articulated in the "Specialty Guidelines" (Committee on Ethical Guidelines for Forensic Psychologists, 1991; also see I. R. Weiner, 2006). Forensic mental health experts are ethically obligated to present opinions in an objective manner, independent of the spin hoped for by the retaining attorney. It is expected that experts will bring to the stand all material they relied on to reach the opinions that are the subject matter of the testimony, including detailed notes that serve to memorialize interviews. The report and testimony should focus solely on the specific legal issue in question (Heilbrun et al., 2002). In presenting findings based on a forensic evaluation, whether in a written report or on the witness stand, the emerging standard of care from an ethical and practice perspective requires the expert to serve an educative function rather than adopt an advocacy role.

SELECTION OF TOPICS

As previously described, there was a dilemma in limiting topics covered in *Forensic Psychology* (A. M. Goldstein, 2003a) to a total of 28 (and 606 pages). For practical reasons, including the fact that the 2003 book was part of a 12-book series, certain topics were purposefully omitted, even though some in the field may have considered them as in the mainstream of forensic mental health practice. This text includes those areas of forensic psychological and psychiatric assessment. Also, forensic mental health experts may have been referred cases for assessment involving somewhat uncommon psycholegal questions with only a modest research and practice literature to which they can refer. These areas of forensic assessment are addressed in this volume as well. In addition, over the past decade, a number of new, unique areas requiring forensic evaluations and expert opinions have emerged. The range of psycholegal questions for which attorneys seek expert opinions from forensic mental health professionals has expanded. Some of the chapters included in this work focus on these emerging topics, areas of forensic involvement about which few if any chapters or books have been written that integrate an appropriate research-practice knowledge base. As such, this book provides practitioners with a foundation and perspective to consider when accepting (or rejecting) a referral for a specific assessment and to assist them in selecting appropriate evaluation methodology and to familiarize them with representative case law and research. In short, this volume is designed to assist forensic mental health practitioners in acquiring a clearer understanding of the legal, ethical, research, and methodological issues related to each topic—elements of the evolving standard of care in the field.

Chapter authors are nationally recognized experts in their specific areas. Most are board certified in forensic psychology by the American Board of Professional Psychology. (For information on board certification in forensic psychology, readers are referred to the web site of the American Board of Forensic Psychology, www.abfp.com.) Many of these authors have conducted national workshops on behalf of the American Academy of Forensic Psychology and are noted for their clarity of thought and teaching abilities. Others are legal scholars, many of them law professors, who have published extensively on the topics they were invited to cover in this text. Still others are authors of tests commonly used in the fields of clinical and forensic psychology, or they are considered to be among the field's leading experts on these instruments. In short, the authors of these chapters were selected because of their specific expertise, national reputation, and familiarity with the most up-to-date case law, ethical issues, research, and methodology in their specific area of expertise.

ORGANIZATION OF THIS VOLUME

The field of forensic mental health assessment is rapidly expanding, and forensic experts are retained by attorneys to address an increasing number of psycholegal questions. The topics included in this volume are organized into eight major areas: (1) forensic assessment methodology, (2) ethical issues in forensic practice, (3) civil forensic psychology, (4) criminal forensic psychology, (5) forensic mental health experts in court, (6) forensic psychological consultation, (7) special populations, and (8) special topics in forensic practice.

Forensic Assessment Methodology

Forensic experts must rely on multiple sources of information when conducting forensic mental health assessments. In this section, a general model for designing and conducting these evaluations is described. The application of psychological tests commonly used in clinical psychological practice to forensic cases, including the Minnesota Multiphasic Personality Inventory-2 (MMPI-2), the Personality Assessment Inventory (PAI), and the Rorschach, is presented by authors and coauthors who are nationally recognized experts on each of these instruments. Because forensic cases in both civil and criminal settings may raise questions about the presence and implications of underlying neurological disorders, a section addressing the use of neuropsychological tests in forensic mental health assessment is included.

A Principles-Based Approach to Forensic Mental Health Assessment: Utility and Update

There are *many* incorrect and inadequate ways to conduct a forensic psychological evaluation. But is there only *one* correct way to perform a thorough, ethical, and credible forensic assessment? The answer to this question is somewhat complex because each forensic case is different. Experts must design assessment methodologies based not only on the referral question (i.e., the psycholegal issue to be addressed), but also on the individual characteristics of the examinee (i.e., language, culture, age, reading level). However, there are agreed-on components that constitute a thorough forensic psychological assessment that will meet the emerging standard of care in the field, and experts should select from among these elements in light of each examinee's characteristics. In his book *Principles of Forensic Mental Health Assessment,* Heilbrun (2001) described those elements that forensic mental health practitioners should consider when conducting psycholegal evaluations. In many ways, the principles advanced by Heilbrun (see also Heilbrun, DeMatteo, & Marczyk, 2004) reflect, in part, an emerging standard of care in forensic psychology practice.

In their chapter in this volume, Kirk Heilbrun, Geoffrey Marczyk, David DeMatteo, and Jenette Mack-Allen present 29 principles that guide effective and acceptable practice in performing forensic mental health assessments. Their goal in providing these principles is to promote and improve the quality and consistency of forensic evaluations. According to Heilbrun and his colleagues, these principles "should help minimize arbitrariness in the legal decision-making process through promoting thoroughness, consistency, and impartiality" (Chapter 2). Their principles-based approach has significance for (a) the education and training that those entering the field of forensic practice should receive (see Packer & Borum, 2003, for a discussion of forensic psychology training and education); (b) research and theory in the development of forensic assessments; and (c) shaping of public policy regarding the development of legal standards, interpreting legislation, and applying and developing administrative codes (Heilbrun, 2001). Heilbrun and his coauthors propose, among other areas, the need to correctly identify, understand, and focus assessment strategies on appropriate statutes; the requirement that reliable, valid, and appropriate data sources be used in forming opinions; the need to rely on third-party sources of information (for more information on this topic, see Heilbrun et al., 2003; Chapter 8); the inclusion of strategies to address issues related to response style (malingering, exaggeration, and defensiveness; see Rogers & Bender, 2003, for additional information on this topic); avoidance of responding to the ultimate issue; and the need to rely on "scientific reasoning" in forming opinions. Although the specific steps required to conduct an individual forensic assessment must be determined on a case-by-case basis, these principles should serve to increase the quality of forensic mental health assessments, a view presented by Heilbrun et al. (2004).

Forensic Applications of the Minnesota Multiphasic Personality Inventory-2

In conducting forensic psychological assessments, the need to rely on objective, valid, and reliable sources of data is well established (Grisso, 1986, 2003a; Heilbrun, 2001; Melton et al., 1997). There is little controversy from mental health experts that the MMPI-2 fulfills this need. Developed by Hathaway and McKinley (1940), the MMPI became the most researched and most frequently administered instrument in mental health practice (Lubin, Larsen, Matarazzo, & Seever, 1985). For a number of reasons, including the outdatedness of item content, this instrument was restandardized (Butcher, Dahlstrom, Graham, Tellegen, & Kaemmer, 1989, 2001), and the MMPI-2 gradually replaced the initial version of this instrument. The MMPI-2 is used in a wide range of forensic settings when behaviors relevant to psycholegal issues are in question.

Roger Greene (Chapter 3) describes the use and limitations of the MMPI-2 in a number of forensic settings. In his chapter, Greene cautions that, despite the voluminous research on the MMPI and MMPI-2, individuals involved in legal cases (e.g., defendants, plaintiffs) have rarely, if ever, been represented in research studies. He reviews the literature related to the effects of the context in which the MMPI-2 was administered (e.g., personal injury versus custody evaluations) and its impact on MMPI-2 results. In forensic contexts, especially those involving criminal cases, those tested are typically younger and less educated and frequently come from minority culture backgrounds. Greene reviews the effects of age on MMPI-2 results (there is a substantial effect for those under the age of 20; Greene, 2000), level of education (affecting a number of scale scores; Caldwell, 2000; Dahlstrom & Tellegen, 1993), and the role of ethnicity (there is no consistent pattern of differences between scale scores for any two ethnic groups; Greene, 2000; Timbrook & Graham, 1994; Zalewski & Greene, 1996). Among the issues addressed by Greene are questions of validity, item omissions, consistency of item endorsement, and research and interpretation of scales related to response style as reflected by malingering, exaggeration, defensiveness, and social desirability. Because those who are evaluated in a legal context have much to lose (e.g., freedom, custody of a child) or to gain (e.g., acquittal by reason of insanity versus incarceration, financial award in a personal injury case), Greene discusses the effects of "coaching" on MMPI-2 results. Because those involved in forensic cases may be retested some time in the future with the MMPI-2 (e.g., by opposing counsel, the result of successful appeals), he discusses the stability of MMPI-2 performance over time. In his chapter, Greene also reviews research on content-based interpretation of the MMPI-2.

The Personality Assessment Inventory: Issues in Legal and Forensic Settings

As described in the introduction to this chapter and by Heilbrun et al. (Chapter 2), it is essential that, whenever possible, experts in forensic psychology include valid, objective tests as sources of data on which to rely in formulating opinions. Many of the instruments used in conducting forensic assessments provide essential information relevant to diagnostic issues and personality dynamics and address a major area of concern in forensic assessments: response style (see Rogers & Bender, 2003, for a thorough description of issues and instruments related to the assessment of malingering). In forensic psychological practice, examinees, especially in criminal settings, may have difficulty with both reading and comprehending questions on paper-and-pencil personality tests, making the administration of many of hese instruments inappropriate. Similarly, under *Frye v. United States* (1923) and *Daubert v. Merrell Dow Pharmaceuticals* (1993), instruments used by experts may be challenged in court as to their admissibility. Experts must carefully select methods in terms of their relevance to the psycholegal issue under scrutiny and choose tests that are appropriate for the demographics of the examinee, including reading level; test also must possess the properties delineated in *Frye* and *Daubert* that will convince the trial judge that testimony based on such instruments meets the legal standard for admissibility.

Leslie Morey (1991), the author of the Personality Assessment Inventory (PAI), and his coauthors, Megan Warner and Christopher Hopwood (Chapter 4), describe the development of this frequently used instrument, its structure, its psychometric properties, and studies that support its use in a wide range of forensic settings. In their chapter, they review those PAI scales designed to assess profile validity and its clinical scales and several treatment consideration scales of this 344-question self-report measure. A brief consideration of those legal issues relevant to the admissibility of expert testimony is included. This review is followed by a description of the empirical literature with which forensic psychologists should be familiar so that they may respond to evidentiary challenges that may arise regarding the use of the PAI in court. Studies on the PAI that address the criteria for admissibility are organized in terms of legal questions: (a) Is the method based on scientifically tested or testable theories?; (b) Has the method been subjected to peer review and publication?; (c) Is there a known error rate and standards for drawing conclusions from the method?; and (d) Is the method accepted within the field? Morey, Warner, and Hopwood describe the relevance of the PAI as part of an overall forensic assessment strategy to evaluate the genuineness of claimed symptoms of mental illness, emotional damages, and self-reports of physical pain, risk to self, and risk to others. They further describe its use in addressing psycholegal issues relevant to criminal culpability, competence to confess, and fitness for trial and its role in custody evaluations and assessments designed to screen for high-risk occupations. Because of the length of this instrument, its fourth-grade reading level (Morey, 1991), and the empirical research supporting its reliability and validity in a range of settings, the authors of this chapter emphasize the value of the PAI as part of a forensic mental health assessment battery.

Rorschach Assessment in Forensic Cases

Psychologists frequently use psychological tests, both objective and projective, as part of the methodology relied on to address psycholegal issues that involve personality characteristics and functioning (Borum & Grisso, 1995). Over the past decade, criticism has been leveled at projective techniques, much of which has been specifically aimed at the Rorschach Inkblot Method (RIM). Questions have been raised regarding its reliability, validity, norms, and tendencies to identify psychological dysfunction where none exists and whether Rorschach-based evidence meets the legal standard for admissibility in a court of law (Grove, Barden, Garb, & Lillenfeld, 2002; Wood, Nezworski, Gard, & Lillenfeld, 2001; Wood, Nezworski, Stejskal, & McKinzey, 2001). As such, the RIM has been viewed as a controversial technique.

Citing research published in peer-reviewed journals, Irving Weiner (Chapter 5) addresses these issues and criticisms. His chapter serves to educate experts about the proper use of this instrument in a wide range of forensic cases, including those involving child custody issues, personal injury claims, Posttraumatic Stress Disorder, and assessments to determine mental state at the time of the crime. Weiner presents empirically based data to prepare experts to effectively present Rorschach-based evidence in reports and in court testimony in an ethical, scientifically grounded manner. In his chapter, Weiner reviews research that supports the use of a number of criteria of the Rorschach Comprehensive System (CS; Exner, 2003; I. B. Weiner, 2003). He describes studies that establish interrater reliability, short- and long-term stability, and validity of the CS. He describes the proper use of the Rorschach to address issues of malingering and defensiveness and its use with culturally diverse populations. In addition, Weiner discusses the role of computer-based printouts, such as the Rorschach Interpretation Assistance Program (Exner & Weiner, 2003) and the forensic edition of this instrument (I. R. Weiner, 2004). The information presented by Weiner should help experts explain the nature of the RIM to judges and juries, to establish its admissibility if challenged, and to prepare the expert for questions focusing on its norms, validity, and reliability.

Neuropsychology for the Forensic Psychologist

Whether in criminal or civil areas of forensic practice, it is somewhat common to encounter defendants or plaintiffs whose history, presentation, or test results unexpectedly suggest the presence of an underlying neurological disorder. At times, the referral question itself may require an assessment for brain dysfunction. The APA's (2002) *Ethical Principles of Psychologists and Code of Conduct* requires that psychologists limit their practice to those areas that fall within the boundaries of their expertise. Clinical and forensic psychologists may appropriately *screen* for neurological impairments, but if they do not possess the required background, skills, training, experience, and knowledge required by the law to qualify as experts (and to engage in this specialized area of work consistent with the APA ethics code), practitioners should refer cases whose screens are found to be positive (and cases in which referral questions require a specific focus on the assessment of neurological dysfunction) to those properly qualified in this specialized area of practice. At other times, forensic experts may need to consult with trained neuropsychologists and incorporate their findings into their forensic reports and testimony.

Wilfred van Gorp (Chapter 6), a board certified neuropsychologist by the American Board of Professional Psychology (ABPP), describes the training and qualifications of neuropsychologists. In his chapter, he describes the role of the forensic psychologist in screening for neurocognitive impairments and in integrating neuropsychological findings into forensic expert opinions and testimony. He distinguishes between a process-oriented and a fixed battery approach to neuropsychological test selection and reviews the basic principles of test interpretation. Of specific relevance to forensic psychologists is a section on the use of screening instruments that may be of value in detecting the presence of cognitive impairments in forensic cases. The appropriate use of normative data in interpreting neuropsychological tests and batteries is described. Van Gorp provides a description of commonly used measures to evaluate neuropsychological dysfunction in a number of domains: motivation (including malingering), intelligence, attention, language, learning and memory, visuospatial abilities, motor functioning, and, of most relevance in forensic cases, executive or decision-making functioning. The use of neuropsychological tests and batteries with children and adolescents and with culturally and ethnically diverse populations is considered.

Ethical Issues in Forensic Practice

Those working in the field of forensic mental health assessment are aware of the conflicts that routinely develop when professional ethics collides with the demands of the legal system. Experts are under close scrutiny not only because of the high profile nature of their work but also because their adherence to the code of ethics of their profession may be a major topic of cross-examination during testimony. This section considers both the nature of those common ethical dilemmas facing forensic mental health experts and the legal and ethical issues that arise when accessing and utilizing third-party information and when conducting forensic evaluations.

Ethics and Forensic Psychological Practice

As previously noted, it is inevitable that ethical issues and conflicts will arise whenever psychologists enter the legal arena. The realties of a legal system, adversarial in its approach to achieving justice, inherently place demands on forensic mental health experts who, by training, professional orientation, and ethics, approach evaluations and the formation of opinions in an objective, empirical manner. Experts are exposed to cross-examination and potential ethics complaints because of the methodology they employed in conducting an evaluation, the opinions they reached, how they were reached, statements made in court, and cases that end with unhappy litigants; all these circumstances increase the potential for allegations of unethical conduct. As such, the expert's entire participation in the legal process receives close scrutiny. Because, with very few exceptions, forensic psychologists have not received degrees from forensically oriented programs and because specialized knowledge, training, and skills are required to practice in a competent fashion, consistent with the *Ethical Principles of Psychologists and Code of Conduct* (APA, 2002), the need to appropriately address ethics issues and conflicts as they arise is paramount. As Weissman and DeBow (2003) have described, following the *Ethical Principles* and adhering to the aspirational guidelines set forth in the "Specialty Guidelines for Forensic Psychologists" (Committee on Ethical Guidelines for Forensic Psychologists, 1991) not only serve to decrease the chances of ethics complaints, but enhances professional competence as well.

In his chapter, Paul Lipsitt (Chapter 7), an attorney and practicing forensic psychologist, analyses those sections of the *Ethics Code* that relate to the practice of forensic psychology. He approaches ethics from both legal and practice perspectives. Lipsitt discusses the legal origins of the notion that individuals have a right to privacy (*Bowers v. Hardwick,* 1986; *Griswold v. Connecticut,* 1965; *Roe v. Wade,* 1973; *Schloendorff v. The Society of New York Hospital,* 1914). He describes the relationship between legal privilege and the ethical principle of confidentiality and emphasizes the obligation of forensic psychologists to understand and appropriately address the delicate balance that exists between these two concepts. Among those conflicts described by Lipsitt that psychologists encounter because of their involvement in the legal system are those related to dual relationships, informed consent, fees, and the nature of courtroom testimony (including legal evidentiary issues). Strategies for negotiating these conflicts are presented.

Legal and Ethical Issues in Accessing and Utilizing Third-Party Information

In conducting forensic evaluations in criminal and civil contexts, the expert must rely on multiple sources of information. In part, the need to integrate data from a number of different sources is attributable to the distinct differences between clinical and forensic assessments (A. M. Goldstein, 2003b; Greenberg & Shuman, 1997) and the demand characteristics associated with evaluations that, inherently, encourage deception because of the possibility of secondary gain. Whereas mental health experts can generally rely on the truthfulness of an examinee's responses to interviews and psychological tests in the *clinical* setting, the need to consider response style (i.e., malingering, exaggeration, and defensiveness) in *forensic* settings is obvious. As described by Heilbrun et al. (2003), third-party information serves as a major source of corroboration of information provided by forensic examinees and contributes to the validity of opinions reached by forensic experts (and the perception of credibility of those opinions by judges and juries). In fact, authorities agree that reliance on third-party information is part of the standard of care in forensic psychiatry and psychology (Grisso, 2003a; Melton et al., 1997; Shapiro, 1991; Simon & Gold, 2004; see Chapter 2).

In their chapter, Randy Otto, Christopher Slobogin, and Stuart Greenberg (Chapter 8) describe the essential role third-party information serves in forensic mental health assessment. They discuss a number of reasons why experts must consider information contained in written records (school, mental health, employment, military, and legal documents) and provided through interviews conducted with those other than the examinee. Although such data are relied on by forensic mental health experts and are necessary to formulate opinions, nonetheless, this information falls within the hearsay category, and, as such, it is normally inadmissible for consideration by the jury for any purpose other than to establish the credibility (or lack thereof) of the expert's opinions. Otto, Slobogin, and Greenberg review relevant statutes and case law, including federal rules of evidence, related to the admissibility and use of third-party information. They consider the nature of the expert's appointment in a case (i.e., examinee-retained experts, adverse party-retained experts, and court-appointed experts) and its effect on the process of obtaining third-party information. The authors describe a range of practice issues that forensic mental health experts must address in obtaining, considering, and testifying about third-party data and the relationship of these issues to the *Ethical Principles of Psychologists and Code of Conduct* (APA, 2002), the "Specialty Guidelines for Forensic Psychologists" (Committee on Ethical Guidelines for Forensic Psychologists, 1991), the model codes of professional responsibility and professional conduct of the American Bar Association (1969, 1983), and the Health Insurance Portability and Accountability Act. A model for conducting interviews with third parties is included, with a focus on the notification that should be provided to the third-party interviewee, the need to assess the relationship between this person and the examinee, content areas to be covered in third-party interviews, and how to bring closure to the interviews.

Civil Forensic Psychology

Forensic mental health experts are frequently called on to evaluate cases that involve civil psycholegal issues. In this section, emerging topics for forensic assessment are considered. Recent landmark decisions are reviewed and a number of areas of civil forensic practice are covered, including: (a) the role of the psychologist in civil commitment, (b) evaluating capacity to consent to treatment, and (c) termination of parental rights.

Recent Civil Legal Decisions: Implications for Forensic Mental Heath Experts

In conducting forensic mental health assessments, experts recognize that such evaluations are always legally driven, fueled by statutes and case law that define the psycholegal issue under consideration. As such, competence as a forensic expert is enhanced and, in part, defined by knowledge of up-to-date federal and state statutes and case law relevant to the psycholegal issue that is the focus of the evaluation (Weissman & DeBow, 2003). Legal decisions help to determine the nature of the questions asked of the examinee, the types of records that are reviewed, the focus of the information gleaned from those records, and, ultimately, the focus of the report and testimony. In the civil arena, there have been significant changes in case law in areas related to civil commitment, duty to protect, and advanced directives for health care created by psychiatric patients. A familiarity with these changes and their implications for forensic mental health practice is essential for experts working in these areas of civil forensic practice.

John Petrila (Chapter 9) considers significant recent developments in civil laws that have a direct impact on forensic mental health assessments. In his chapter, he summarizes the history of civil commitment laws and describes a shift in such laws to a more medically oriented model (Wisc. Stat. § 51.20 (1)(a)(2e)). A specific focus is on the application of civil commitment laws to sexually violent predators (*Kansas v. Crane,* 2002; *Kansas v. Henricks,* 1997). In the wake of *Tarasoff v. Board of Regents* (1976), issues of confidentiality and privileged communication are foremost on the minds of clinical and forensic mental health petitioners. Petrila describes two recent California cases, *Ewing v. Northridge Hospital Medical Center* (2004) and *Ewing v. Goldstein* (2004), whose holdings may serve to broaden the doctrine of duty to protect to those situations in which a therapist is informed of a possible danger to others presented by his or her patient through a relative or other third party (in this case, the father of the patient). Changes in the application of advanced directives created by psychiatric patients to express their wishes for future mental health care are described as well (*Hargrave v. Vermont,* 2003).

The Role of the Psychologist in Civil Commitment

The criminal justice system grants defendants accused of crimes due process rights. If convicted of an illegal activity, such people may be segregated from society—incarcerated for the main purpose of punishing them for their past actions. They are deprived of their freedom, in part, to protect others from future criminal acts. In the mental health system, those who are believed to be at risk of violence to themselves or others are also guaranteed their constitutional rights. At a hearing, if a judge concludes that they represent a likely risk, as required by law they may be involuntarily civilly committed to a mental hospital, deprived of their right to freedom, and to self-determination. These people have committed no crimes, but they have been found to need protection from themselves, or society requires protection from them. Civilly committed individuals are not recipients of punishment; rather, it is assumed that they will receive appropriate treatment for their mental condition. The process of civil commitment of those found to be mentally ill is traceable to colonial times (Harvard Law Association, 1974). In many states, forensic psychologists may serve as evaluators, conducting assessments of individuals to determine the presence or absence of those criteria legally required to involuntarily hospitalize a patient; these experts may then present their findings in court.

In their chapter, David Mrad and Eric Nabors (Chapter 10) describe the historical foundations of civil commitment laws, which have their basis in the *parens patriae* doctrine. Under this principle, the state assumed the power and responsibility to serve as guardian for those deemed unable to protect themselves. Mrad and Nabors review landmark cases, in the main, addressing procedural and due process issues (e.g., *Baxstrom v. Herold,* 1966; *Lessard v. Schmidt,* 1972), and those cases attempting to delineate the treatment to which civilly committed patients are entitled (e.g., *O'Connor v. Donaldson,* 1975; *Wyatt v. Stickney,* 1971). The authors consider the application of civil commitment laws to special populations, including children, those diagnosed with mental retardation, and criminal offenders, and they discuss the concept of outpatient commitment. Current procedures for civil commitment are described. Mrad and Nabors review risks for suicide, including research findings related to demographic factors associated with suicide and the management of such risk. Ethical issues involved in assessing individuals who may be denied the right of self-determination and deprived of their freedom are considered.

Evaluating Capacity to Consent to Treatment

Grisso (1986) described a model applicable for conducting forensic psychological assessments. He proposed that psychologists asked to conduct forensic assessments of a specific legal competency must first understand the legal constructs that define that competency. They must then operationalize those legal constructs—translate them into psychological concepts and terms that can be objectively evaluated—using valid and reliable forensic assessment instruments and available research. This approach to forensic psychological evaluations described by Grisso has been embraced by those in the field and in many ways represents the standard of care in forensic psychology. At times, questions are raised as to the capacity of a patient "to make informed, reasoned judgments in his or her best interests and that accurately respect the individual's intentions" (A. M. Goldstein, 2003b, p. 13; see Stanley & Galietta, 2006). Referrals for evaluations related to this general issue may address situations involving living wills, health care surrogacies, conservatorships and guardianships, and durable powers of attorney (Drogin & Barrett, 2003).

Jennifer Moye, Michele Karel, and Jorge Armesto (Chapter 11) focus on the capacity of adults to provide consent to medical treatment. Specifically, they consider a range of issues related to whether those with psychiatric and neurodegenerative disorders can make autonomous decisions about their treatment in health care settings. In their chapter, they describe the legal basis for assessing the components of this capacity: understanding, appreciation, reasoning, and the ability to express a choice. Moye, Karel, and Armesto review a range of statutes and case law on surrogate health care decision making. They discuss the role of a patient's personal values as a factor to be considered in assessing consent capacity. A model based on Grisso's (1986, 2003a) approach to forensic psychological assessment is described; it integrates legal standards (i.e., statutes and case law), including those addressing proxy consent and guardianships, with forensic assessment methodology. Factors such as the individual's functional capacity and judgment, complexity of the decision to be made, and those factors unique to the situation itself are described. The authors review the research literature on the capacity to provide consent for treatment for a number of groups, including those with Schizophrenia, those with dementia, and patients who are institutionalized and hospitalized. A range of forensic assessment instruments, including tests and semistructured interviews used to assess capacity to consent, are reviewed and compared to evaluations based on the clinical judgment of the evaluator. Moye and Karel present information on those factors that forensic evaluators should consider when evaluating this issue, including concepts involving the patient's expectation of quality of life and the impact of the treatment decision on family members. They conclude with specific suggestions for future research on a number of topics related to capacity to consent to medical treatment.

Termination of Parental Rights

Most, if not all, societies expect parents to meet certain minimum requirements in caring for and protecting their children. Beyond providing food, clothing, and shelter, it is anticipated that parents will provide for their children's emotional, moral, and educational needs. Beyond commonly held expectations, public policy, in the form of statutes and regulations, delineate this requirement, define the behaviors associated with the capacity needed to parent, and authorize the termination of parental rights under severe, specified circumstances. In cases in which allegations have been filed alleging maltreatment or neglect, forensic mental heath experts may be retained to evaluate parental fitness and to submit reports to the court, which will be used, in part, to determine whether there is a pattern of neglect, abuse, or maltreatment. In other cases, judgments may be made by the court about the suitability of returning the children to the custody of their parent(s).

In their chapter, Lois Oberlander Condie and Don Condie (Chapter 12) address the legal and practical issues that are involved in assessing termination of parental rights. The authors describe the organization of the legal and administrative systems for child protection intervention from historical and legal contexts, including an 1864 landmark case reviewed by Shelman and Lazoritz (2005) that affords children the same protections granted to animals. They include a discussion of U.S. Supreme Court cases specific to parental rights termination (*Lassiter v. Department of Social Services,* 1981; *Santosky v. Kramer,* 1982). In the context of this topic, Oberlander Condie and Condie review child development theory and research, focusing on issues of linguistic capacity, accuracy of children's memories, and suggestibility. They address the methodology that forensic mental health experts should consider when conducting evaluations of both adult caregivers and children. Also included in this chapter is a comprehensive review of the scientific literature related to factors associated with maltreatment, cognitive development of children, risk of child maltreatment (physical and sexual abuse), and amenability to treatment.

Criminal Forensic Psychology

Criminal psycholegal evaluations have long been a major area of focus of forensic mental health assessments. This section provides readers with an update on recent landmark legal decisions and their implications for experts conducting criminal forensic evaluations. Two emerging areas of criminal forensic assessment are considered: (1) the role of experts in federal sentencing proceedings and (2) postconviction assessments.

Recent Criminal Legal Decisions: Implications for Forensic Mental Health Experts

Forensic mental health evaluators are keenly aware of the essential relationship between the structure, methodology, and focus of their assessments and the driving force behind such assessments: statutes and case law. In cases involving criminal psycholegal issues (e.g., competence to stand trial, evaluating sexual predators, death penalty assessments, sentencing reports), case law is rapidly changing and evolving. As Perlin (1996, 1999) has noted, the U.S. Supreme Court has demonstrated a "fascination" with mental health disability law, accepting cases and issuing decisions on a wide range of criminal issues, holdings that have a direct impact on the work of forensic mental health experts. Since 2001, the Court has issued decisions involving mental retardation and its relationship to the death penalty (*Atkins v. Virginia,* 2002); involuntarily medicating those adjudicated as unfit to stand trial in order to establish trial competence (*United States v. Sell,* 2003); involuntary civil commitment of sexually violent predators following expiration of their criminal sentence (*Kansas v. Crane,* 2002; *Kansas v. Hendricks,* 1997); and the unconstitutionality of the once mandated federal sentencing guidelines (U.S. Sentencing Guidelines, 2003, in *United States v. Booker & Fanfan,* 2005). Each decision has important implications for criminal forensic mental health evaluators.

In his chapter, Michael Perlin (Chapter 13), an attorney specializing in criminal mental health law, describes the historical background of issues that serve as precedents for these recent landmark cases and discusses both the legal implications of these holdings and their impact on forensic practice. Perlin focuses primarily on the *Atkins* (2002) and *Sell* (2003) decisions, noting the profound effects both are likely to have on forensic mental health evaluations. In *Atkins v. Virginia* (2002), the Court barred the execution of those people found to be mentally retarded. Questions raised by this case, as presented by Perlin, include defining mental retardation, a criterion left entirely up to each state; problems in assessing the level of intellectual functioning of those for whom English is a second language; application of this decision to those found to be functioning within the borderline range of intelligence; and the proper role of experts in addressing issues related to subnormal intellectual functioning. In *United States v. Sell* (2003), the Court held that if specific conditions are met, those defendants adjudicated as incompetent to stand trial might be medicated against their will for the sole purpose of establishing or restoring trial competence. Perlin describes why the *Sell* decision may prove to be of tremendous importance both from legal and forensic mental health practice perspectives, and the impact *Sell* is likely to have on expert witnesses (e.g., side effects of "typical" versus "atypical" medications, issues related to least restrictive alternative). In his consideration of *Atkins* and *Sell,* Perlin provides the legal historical background for these cases, and he discusses the reasoning behind both the majority and dissenting opinions. In this chapter, Perlin reviews two other areas involving mental health law addressed by the Court in recent decisions: sexual violent predator laws (*Kansas v. Crane,* 2002; *Kansas v. Hendricks,* 1997) and the status of the federal sentencing guidelines (*United States v. Booker & Fanfan,* 2005; see also Chapter 14). Again, the likely implications of these decisions for forensic practitioners are described.

The Role of Mental Health Experts in Federal Sentencing Proceedings

To be convicted of a crime, two elements must be proven: (1) The defendant actually committed the proscribed behavior, *actus reas;* and (2) at the moment of the crime, the actor possessed the requisite mental state legally required to be held responsible, *mens rea.* A number of different mental states may be associated with the same criminal act, and the degree of responsibility and punishment relates, in part, to the degree of evilness associated with a particular act, or, as A. M. Goldstein, Morse, and Shapiro (2003) have stated, "Moral responsibility depends crucially on the mental state with which a person acts" (p. 382). In most state jurisdictions, forensic mental health experts may be asked to evaluate and proffer testimony during sentencing proceedings related to a convicted defendant's level of emotional maturity, intelligence, mental health history, substance abuse, or history of abuse—the purpose of which is to persuade the court to take mitigating factors into account when imposing a sentence. In the past, such factors were not typically relevant in federal court (Lutjen, 1996). Judges were constrained by the federal sentencing guidelines (U.S. Sentencing Commission, 1987), which for almost 2 decades limited the ability of federal judges to exercise discretion in sentencing and instead required a relatively rigid set of factors to be applied in a formulaic manner to reach a sentencing determination. However, U.S. Supreme Court decisions in *U.S. v. Booker & Fanfan* redefined the role of the guidelines from mandatory to advisory status. Because the federal sentencing system is responsible for the largest population of the nation's prisoners, this dramatic change in the role of the guidelines has important implications for the use of expert opinions as information a federal judge may choose to consider before the imposition of sentence.

In their chapter, Daniel Krauss (an attorney and forensic psychologist who served as a U.S. Supreme Court Fellow assigned to the U.S. Sentencing Commission in 2002 to 2003) and Alan Goldstein (Chapter 14) describe the purpose, development, and structure of the federal sentencing guidelines. They consider categories in the guidelines that permit judges to grant downward departures in sentencing, including diminished capacity, aberrant behavior, and coercion and duress. Case histories are included to illustrate the role that forensic mental health professionals may play in providing the court with relevant data to consider at the time of sentencing. They review a series of U.S. Supreme Court decisions that paved the way for the shift in the guidelines from mandatory to advisory (e.g., *Appredi v. New Jersey,* 2000; *Blakeley v. Washington,* 2004; *Jones v. United States,* 1999), as well as the historic *Booker & Fanfan* (2005) holdings. Krauss and Goldstein describe the potential impact of these discussions and the relevance of these changes on forensic mental health practice and research.

Postconviction Assessment

In the criminal justice arena, forensic mental health experts may be asked to conduct a range of assessments, starting from those involving pretrial hearings (i.e., the validity of *Miranda* rights waivers, Oberlander et al., 2003; competence to stand trial, Stafford, 2003; Zapf & Roesch, 2006); questions raised at trial (i.e., the trustworthiness of a confession; Oberlander et al., 2003; a defendant's mental state at the time of the offense, A. M. Goldstein, Morse, et al., 2003; Zapf, Golding, &

Roesch, 2006); and presence or absence of mitigating and aggravating factors that may impact sentencing decisions (Cunningham & Goldstein, 2003; Chapter 14). If a trial ends with a finding of guilt (or the defendant entered a plea of guilty), Article I of the U.S. Constitution provides the prisoner the right to seek relief by filing a writ of *habeas corpus*. Petitioners are granted the right to appeal the findings of guilt; in many cases, the basis for such claims is ineffectiveness of counsel. To be granted an appeal in such cases, the petitioner must meet a two-pronged test: (1) It must be established that the attorney's performance was "deficient" in that "counsel made errors so serious that counsel was not functioning as the 'counsel' guaranteed the defendant by the Sixth Amendment"; and (2) these errors rose to a level so "as to deprive the defendant of a fair trial, a trial whose result is reliable" (*Strickland v. Washington,* 1984, p. 687). Petitioners may claim that the forensic mental health expert retained by counsel was, in fact, not an expert in the area in which an assessment was conducted or that the evaluation itself was substandard in terms of scope, methodology, and opinions reached. In some cases, the basis for relief may be that the attorney failed to obtain the services of a mental health expert when information was available to indicate that a forensic evaluation should have been pursued. As such, forensic mental health experts may be retained to both examine the data, reports, and testimony of trial experts and to conduct a forensic evaluation of the petitioner for submission to an appeals court for review and as a possible basis for future testimony if a new trial is granted. Although referrals for postconviction assessments are increasingly requested by attorneys, little has been written in the professional literature on this topic.

Eric Drogin (Chapter 15), a forensic psychologist and attorney, examines the legal, ethical, and methodological issues involved in postconviction assessments. He reviews the legal background that serves as the foundation for these evaluations, including recently decided U.S. Supreme Court cases on this topic (*Dodd v. United States,* 2005; *Mayle v. Felix,* 2005; *Rompilla v. Beard,* 2005). He describes legal guidelines promulgated by the American Bar Association and the National Legal Aid and Defender Association designed to address requirements for attorneys practicing in this area. Drogin presents a model based on the integration of data from numerous sources, which may serve as guidance for forensic mental health experts conducting postconviction relief assessments. Relevant ethical considerations involved in peer consultation, obtaining data, and reporting obligations are discussed. Because postconviction assessments may arise in a number of legal contexts, Drogin describes the application of these evaluations to cases involving criminal responsibility, trial competence, prison programming, parole board reviews, release of insanity acquittees, competence to confess, and competence to be executed. The emphasis of this chapter is not on second-guessing juries (Bodenhausen, 1990) or criticizing the work of colleagues, but on providing methodologically reliable and ethical assessments that serve the interests of justice.

Forensic Mental Health Experts in the Courtroom

When forensic mental health experts testify, their ethical conduct, the methodology they relied on, the opinions they have reached, and their demeanor and ability to respond to questions on both direct and cross-examination are closely scrutinized. Is the expert likely to be considered an objective, credible source of information by the trier of fact, or merely a hired gun? In this section, authors and coauthors address issues related to courtroom testimony, including: (a) ways in which credibility may be enhanced by presenting testimony in a balanced, thorough, fair manner; and (b) issues that should be considered by testifying experts related to potential malpractice lawsuits that may arise from their testimony.

Expert Witness Testimony: Law, Ethics, and Practice

When forensic mental health experts accept a referral to conduct a forensic assessment, it should be done with full recognition that the case may eventually result in a hearing or trial before a judge or jury. As such, the preparation for expert testimony, including *voir dire,* direct examination, and cross-examination, should begin not days or weeks before the expected date of testimony but at the moment the decision is made to participate in the legal process. Experts should ask themselves if involvement in a specific case will conform to all *ethical* standards (APA, 2002): Is the subject matter within the expert's boundaries of expertise? Is there a dual relationship or a possible perception of such? When selecting methodology to be used in conducting the evaluation, are multiple sources of information being used? Are tests and instruments appropriate for the individual(s) to be assessed? Are tests being used for the purposes for which they are intended? Do they have established reliability and validity? When writing a report, are there sufficient reliable data on which to base an opinion? Does the report present information from an objective, balanced perspective (i.e., are positive as well as negative findings of the assessment included)? Are issues related to response style such as malingering, exaggeration, and defensiveness addressed? Are alternative hypotheses or opinions considered or addressed, either directly or indirectly in the written document? Ewing (2003) has traced the development of the field of forensic psychology and the acceptance of psychologists as experts in court, describing the contribution and, ironically, the negative consequences of Münsterberg's 1908 book (*On the Witness Stand*) for his "undoubtedly, premature, if not grandiose [claims for the benefits of lawyers retaining psychologists as experts in court]" (p. 56). Ewing discussed the reaction to this book by law professor John Henry Wigmore (1909), who discouraged law students from employing psychologists as courtroom experts. He traced those events, starting some 15 years after the Münsterberg/Wigmore publications, which contributed to the acceptance of psychologists as expert witness (i.e., Guttmacher & Weihofen, 1952; *Jenkins v. United States,* 1962).

In their chapter, Steven Bank and Ira Packer (Chapter 16) trace the historical roots of the advocacy trial process back to the medieval period and early Saxon "ordeals," which were designed to determine guilt or innocence. They describe how the current role of the expert has evolved. Bank and Packer discuss the steps forensic mental health experts should follow to present testimony in a legally relevant, ethically consistent manner, including the proper role for forensic mental health experts in court. Of particular significance to forensic experts, the authors present a courtroom communication model (Bank, 2001) designed to maximize clarity, effectiveness, and credibility of experts in presenting their findings to a judge or jury. This model emphasizes witness characteristics, such as expertise and presentation style; the content of the testimony itself, such as emotional and logical appeals and addressing counterarguments; and factors that may affect jury receptivity to the testimony, including heterogeneity of the jurors and maintaining their attention. In their chapter, Bank and Packer present representative questions that may be asked of experts by both the retaining and the opposing attorneys during *voir dire* (or qualification process), direct examination, and cross-examination. Sample responses to such questions are analyzed in an effort to lessen the likelihood that either attorney distorts or misuses the expert's findings and with the hope that the expert can best express his or her opinion in the most accurate, ethical light.

Lessons for Forensic Practice Drawn from the Law of Malpractice

Forensic mental health professionals are highly visible in their role as experts; in legal terms, they have a high degree of exposure. Reports they submit are carefully scrutinized for even minor, often inconsequential, errors and omissions, not only by the retaining attorney, but also by opposing counsel and possibly by other forensic experts retained by opposing counsel as trial consultants (see Chapter 18). On the witness stand, their credibility will be questioned during cross-examination, designed to decrease the weight the judge or jury will give to their testimony and opinion. Some of these questions may focus on the appropriateness of the methodology used, failure to employ specific techniques to complete the assessment, possible scoring errors on tests, misinterpretation of data, and suggestions that the expert deviated from the ethics of his or her profession and the standard of care in conducting the forensic evaluation. In trials, there is typically a winner and a loser. Litigants on the losing side are, understandably, angry, may feel that they were treated unfairly, and may look for someone, in addition to their attorney, to blame. With or without adequate justification and support, litigants and attorneys may not only file ethics complaints against mental health professionals because of their actions in a specific case but, in many states, are free to file malpractice actions against retained experts.

Stuart Greenberg, Daniel Shuman, Stephen Feldman, Collin Middleton, and Charles Patrick Ewing (Chapter 17) review the laws of malpractice, specifically cases that address the liability of experts for their professional activities. In their chapter, they describe the fundamental differences between therapeutic and forensic roles, as previously delineated by Greenberg and Shuman (1997). Arguments both for and against the granting of expert witness immunity from malpractice actions related to their work are presented along with legal decisions that both recognize and deny immunity for forensic mental health professionals. Some decisions have granted absolute immunity to experts (e.g., *Bruce v. Byrne-Stevens,* 1989); other holdings, acknowledging some immunity for experts, have noted exceptions to this rule (such as destruction of records that were relied on to reach opinions; *Ingham v. United States,* 1999). The authors emphasize that most successful malpractice suits against experts address issues of negligence. In such cases, a duty must exist to the party who retained the expert's services, there must be a breach of that duty, and damage or harm must occur to that party as a result of the breach of duty (e.g., the retaining party loses his or her case) for it to constitute actionable negligence. Based on these holdings and legal principles, Greenberg and his colleagues suggest ways for forensic mental health professionals to reduce the likelihood of successful malpractice actions in those jurisdictions where absolute immunity is not granted to experts. They contend that by following the suggested guidelines (many of which are necessitated by the differences between therapeutic and forensic roles), experts' credibility and effectiveness are increased.

Forensic Psychological Consultation

Not all experts are retained with the expectation that they will offer sworn testimony in court. Forensic mental health professionals may be asked to assist attorneys in trial preparation and in jury selection or may be hired to conduct evaluations for insurance companies or by businesses. In this section, the role of the forensic psychologist in a range of emerging consultation capacities is considered. Topics include: (a) consulting for attorneys "off the witness stand," (b) conducting disability psychological independent medical evaluations (IMEs), and (c) assessing and consulting in cases involving potential or actual workplace violence.

Off the Witness Stand: The Forensic Psychologist as Consultant

Watching rebroadcasts of episodes of *Perry Mason,* a television series popular decades ago, a naive viewer would have the impression that all witnesses, whether lay or expert, come to court, take the stand, and answer questions they have heard for the first time. Mr. Mason, a defense attorney, always managed to catch witnesses off guard, asking unanticipated questions and ultimately winning the case. The district attorney, Hamilton Burger, consistently failed to prepare his witnesses for the difficult questions put to them by Mr. Mason during cross-examination, and viewers watched as his "airtight" case fell apart before their eyes. Any person who has been to court in the role of witness quickly discovers that unanticipated questions are few and that any negative or embarrassing material is dealt with on direct examination. Lawyers prepare witnesses as to what will be asked of them on the stand. But how does an attorney unversed in forensic psychological theory, research, methodology, ethics, and practice know what questions to ask on direct or cross-examination? For that matter, how do attorneys know how to locate, identify, and work with forensic mental health experts?

In their chapter, Eric Drogin (a practicing attorney and forensic psychologist) and Curtis Barrett (Chapter 18) consider the roles of the forensic expert as court consultant. They describe the history of the use of consultants, first in medicine in the thirteenth century (Brown, Pryzwansky, & Schulte, 1998), then in psychiatry, and finally in forensic psychology, involving such well-established activities as jury selection (see Kovera, Dickinson, & Cutler, 2003) and the roles of trial or courtroom consultant (Boccaccini & Brodsky, 2002; Nietzel & Dillehay, 1986), litigation support (Friedman & Klee, 2001), and forensic consultant (Drogin, 2000, 2001). Legal and ethical considerations related to the roles played by forensic consultants are described, including the caution that consultants must avoid serving as both expert witnesses and as consultants in the same case. Among the specialized areas of involvement for forensic psychological consultants reviewed by Drogin and Barrett are case analysis and development, review of reports and files, identification and retention of expert witnesses, assisting in the development of direct and cross-examination strategies, and preparing witnesses, both lay and expert, for trial. They offer concrete advice for forensic psychological consultants in the identification of appropriate expert witnesses, reviewing mental heath records, entering into a contract to provide consulting services to attorneys, and preparing experts to offer sworn testimony in court.

The Disability Psychological Independent Medical Evaluation Case Law, Ethical Issues, and Procedures

With increasing frequency, forensic psychologists are being called on by insurance carriers to address issues related to mental health disability claims filed by an insured party. Typically, the insured has requested benefits, claiming that symptoms of a mental disorder are such that it is no longer possible to continue employment at his or her own occupation or in any occupational capacity. Referral questions from carriers may focus on a number of issues, and the opinion of the expert may serve as a basis for denial or discontinuation of benefits. Forensic experts may be asked to determine the claimant's diagnosis or to comment on the diagnosis provided by the treating mental health professional. An opinion may be sought on the appropriateness of the treatment the claimant is currently receiving and for a prognosis as to if or when the claimant may be capable of returning to work. Of greatest significance are questions focusing on the nature of the claimant's symptoms and their impact on the ability of that person to function in his or her specific occupation (or any occupation). In addition, the independent medical examiner may be asked to assess the claimant's response style, focusing on issues of malingering and exaggeration of symptoms (Rogers & Bender, 2003).

In his chapter, David Vore (Chapter 19) defines and explains the relevant terms and concepts usually contained in disability contracts. As Grisso (1986, 2003a) has indicated, forensic experts must operationalize these legal concepts to conduct relevant forensic evaluations that address the specific psycholegal issues in question. For example, to select appropriate methodology for the IME, the expert must understand such terms as short- and long-term disability, partial and total disability, and own and any occupation. Vore describes the components and methodology involved in conducting IMEs, including the need to rely on multiple sources of information and issues related to the weight to be given to videotapes of the claimant provided to the examiner by the carrier. The issues of response style, including malingering, defensiveness, irrelevant responding, feigning, suboptimal effort, and dissimulation, are addressed, as are those situations in which a claimant is unwilling to cooperate in the IME process. Case law addressing a range of legal issues is reviewed and the application of the relevance of the holdings from these cases to IMEs is described. For example, Vore describes cases related to definitions of disability (e.g., *Gates v. Prudential Insurance Company of America,* 1934; *Massachusetts Mutual Life Insurance v. Ouellette,* 1992; *Wright v. Paul Revere Life Insurance Company,* 2003), substance abuse as a basis for disability claims (i.e., *Adams v. Weinberger,* 1977; *Gaines v. Sun Life Assurance Company of Canada,* 1943; *O'Connor v. Sullivan,* 1947), and relapse potential as a basis for the continuation of disability benefits (e.g., *Hinchman v. General American Insurance Company,* 1998; *Kupshik v. John Hancock Mutual Life Insurance Company,* 2000; *Massachusetts Casualty Insurance Company v. Rief,* 1962). He discusses legal issues related to the admissibility of testimony and potential liability of experts conducting IMEs (see also Chapter 17, for a through discussion of the issue of liability of experts). Vore describes and provides potential solutions to a range of ethical conflicts that independent medical evaluators may encounter, focusing on identification of the client, informed consent, and boundaries of expertise.

Workplace Violence: Advances in Consultation and Assessment

Referrals to forensic mental health experts to conduct violence risk assessments arise in a number of contexts. In considering job applications for high-risk positions (e.g., law enforcement) or in performing fitness-for-duty evaluations, a major focus of the assessment is on the propensity of that person to act in an inappropriately impulsive, aggressive manner when under stress (Borum, Super, & Rand, 2003; Inwald & Resko, 1995). In some jurisdictions, states may conduct a hearing to determine whether a juvenile's case should be transferred from family or juvenile court, where the stated goal is rehabilitation or treatment, to criminal court, where the major purpose is punishment (Grisso, 2003b); the assessment of the likelihood of future violence may be one of the factors considered at such hearings. If a capital case proceeds to the penalty phase of the trial, an aggravating factor a jury may consider in deciding if the defendant is "death-worthy" may be the risk of future aggression if not sentenced to death; testimony by experts on this issue may be requested (Cunningham & Goldstein, 2003) and considered by the jury in reaching the decision. Many states now have statutes allowing courts to determine whether an inmate who has completed his or her maximum sentence for a sexually violent crime can be civilly committed as a sexually violent predator. In such cases, risk assessments to inform the court of the level of risk the individual presents may be ordered (Conroy, 2003). A major factor addressed in civil commitment proceedings, designed to determine whether an individual can be involuntarily committed to a mental hospital, is the likelihood of imminent harm to self or others (see Chapter 10). Judges assign considerable weight to expert opinions on violence risk in reaching opinions on this legal issue (see Chapter 26). Judicial focus on the potential for future violence also occurs in cases involving termination of parental rights (see Chapter 12) and sentencing decisions in federal (see Chapter 14) and state criminal cases. Questions about the risk of violence an inmate may present if released into the community are considered by parole boards at inmate hearings for those applying for early release from prison (see Chapter 15). In recent years, there has been a marked increase in referrals to forensic mental health experts from corporations and government and private agencies for evaluations of employees who, they believe, pose a threat of violence to fellow workers, supervisors, other third parties, and themselves.

In his chapter, Harley Stock (Chapter 20) focuses on organizational, legal, ethical, and methodological issues involved in the assessment of risk of violence in workplace settings. He provides various incidence rates for workplace violence (including surprising data on violence at U.S. postal facilities) and the financial consequences of workplace threats and violence. He reviews those factors associated with increased risk of violence in the workplace. He describes the legal theories and contexts that underlie lawsuits arising from workplace aggression (i.e., negligent action, respondent superior, negligent hiring, negligent retention, negligent supervision, and negligent training). Stock reviews the history of violence risk assessment and the acknowledged validity (or lack thereof) of such evaluations over the past 2 decades, including the legal status of risk assessments reflected in case law. Current risk assessment practices are analyzed and the author presents a model for conducting workplace violence risk assessments (Stock, 2000). This model includes consideration of those variables, factors, and questions that forensic mental health experts must consider in providing opinions to businesses and agencies about an employee whom they consider to be a potential threat.

Special Populations

In recent years, new demographic groups have been identified as a focus of forensic mental health evaluations. Because of research, the development of new forensic assessment instruments, and the expanding psycholegal areas for which forensic assessments are requested, a number of special populations have emerged as forensic evaluees, each group requiring specialized knowledge and methodology. The topics presented in this section include: (a) forensic assessment from a development perspective, focusing on children and adolescents as clients for evaluation; (b) psychological evaluation and testimony in cases of clergy and teacher sex abuse, focusing on children who may have been sexually victimized; (c) correctional psychology, a field that provides a range of evaluations of and services to prison inmates; (d) evaluating the psychological sequelae of elder abuse; and (e) forensic issues at the end of life.

Forensic Assessment from a Developmental Perspective

Although at first glance, Piaget's (1953) theory of cognitive development and forensic psychological assessment appear to have nothing in common, changes in the law and recent research on the competency of juveniles have established a strong connection between these seemingly disparate areas of psychology. In the past, delinquent youths were viewed as youngsters who were in need of understanding and treatment, and such cases were handled in juvenile courts. However, many states have instituted "get tough" approaches to juveniles who commit crimes, and these changing attitudes have resulted in legislation that calls for the transfer of some juveniles, especially those accused of committing violent crimes, to adult courts, exposing them to adult punishments (Grisso, 1998, 2003b, 2004; Grisso & Schwartz, 2000; Otto & Goldstein, 2005). As such, because these youths may receive long sentences in adult prisons (rather than a limited course of "treatment" at a juvenile detention facility), defense attorneys and judges now question whether these young defendants are competent in terms of their ability to waive *Miranda* rights, to stand trial, and to make other legal decisions about the handling of their cases. Research on juvenile legal competencies reinforces what has always been known: juveniles are not miniature adults; competence is a developmentally related process (Grisso, 1981, 1998; Grisso & Schwartz, 2000). Other research shows that substantial numbers of juveniles are susceptible to providing false confessions to crimes they might not have committed (N. E. Goldstein, Condie, Kalbeitzer, Osman, & Geiger, 2003). Had forensic psychology been an established field in the 1940s and 1950s, Piaget could well have proposed a stage in his theory of cognitive development that follows the formal operations stage: the legal competence stage. Forensic mental health professionals may be asked to evaluate the competence of juveniles, and familiarity with the theory and research on legal competence as a developmental process appears to be an important, emerging area of knowledge such experts should possess.

Randy Borum and Thomas Grisso (Chapter 21) provide the legal and research background that supports the relevance of a developmental perspective to forensic assessment in delinquency cases. Drawing on concepts from developmental psychopathology (Cicchetti, 1984, 1990), they present a framework for considering juvenile maladaptive behavior as it relates to factors involving physical, cognitive, and psychosocial domains. In their chapter, Borum and Grisso consider the relationship between biological development (i.e., brain structures and functions, related physical changes), cognitive development (i.e., mental and intellectual functioning, including reasoning), and psychosocial maturation (i.e., responsibility, perspective, and self-restraint), and the impact of these maturational processes on a number of adjudicative capacities. They review the research on the effects of the developmental process on such issues as culpability, risk appraisal, impulse control, resistance of peer pressure, and the ability of juveniles to empathize with potential victims. The authors describe the relationship between the developmental perspective and law and public policy, research, and forensic mental health practice.

Psychological Evaluation and Testimony in Cases of Clergy and Teacher Sex Abuse

In the past 2 decades, increased attention has been paid to claims made by adults that as children, they were sexually abused by clergy and teachers who had been entrusted with their care. In a study commissioned by the U.S. Conference of Bishops (2004) of the Catholic Church conducted by John Jay College of Criminal Justice, between 3% and 7% of ordained priests have been accused of sexual abuse, and it was estimated that between 1950 and 2002, a total of 10,505 victims had been abused. Teachers have not fared much better, according to the research. Studies found that 9.7% of students in the 8th to 12th grades had reported sexual misconduct with educators, involving either contact or noncontact (American Association of University Women, 1993, 2001). Children who have been sexually abused may face a number of emotional, social, and vocational impairments as a direct or indirect consequence of their abuse (Beitchman et al., 1992; Neumann, Houskamp, Pollock, & Briere, 1996; Paolucci, Genuis, & Violato, 2001). Thus, forensic mental health experts may be called on to address issues that arise in cases involving allegations of clergy and teacher abuse. Evaluations and testimony may focus on a number of questions, including the presence or absence of those factors established in the professional literature that tend to support or refute the nature of the specific allegations, the impact of the abuse on the victim, the assessment of the severity of such harm, and what would be required to restore the victim to his her premorbid level of functioning.

William Foote (Chapter 22) presents an overview of the history of allegations of sexual abuse by clergy and educators and reviews data indicating the scope of this problem. In his chapter, he considers legal issues related to liability of church organizations, school boards, and municipal entities because of the activities of their employees; causes of action; claims of immunity; and statutes of limitation. Research on the impact of clergy and teacher child sexual abuse on its victims (both during childhood and later, as adults) is reviewed. Based on his extensive experience as an evaluator in these cases and the published literature (Finkelhor, 1984; Foote, 2002; U.S. Department of Education, 2004), Foote discusses typical patterns of abuse used by perpetrators to identify, isolate, and abuse children in their care, and ensure their cooperation and silence. Methods designed to establish a link between the abuse and the presence of symptoms and behavioral dysfunctions (proximate cause) are provided, including guidelines for evaluating the severity of the trauma. In his chapter, Foote describes the need for mental health professionals to distinguish between genuine symptoms and those that may be malingered or exaggerated or are related to traumas a victim may have been exposed to other than or in addition to sexual abuse by the clergy or teacher. The chapter includes a consideration of the impact these forensic mental health assessments have on those who conduct these emotionally charged evaluations.

Correctional Psychology: Law, Ethics, and Practice

Roles for forensic psychologists who work in the criminal justice system encompass not only evaluations of behavior that relate to a specific crime (i.e., validity of *Miranda* rights waivers, Oberlander et al., 2003; insanity assessments, A. M. Goldstein, Morse, et al., 2003; Zapf et al., 2006); they are also concerned with evaluations that relate to hearings or the trial itself (i.e., trial competence; Stafford, 2003; Zapf & Roesch, 2006), address posttrial issues (i.e., sentencing reports, postconviction evaluations; Nussbaum, 2006; Chapters 14 and 15), and issues arising from prisoners' incarceration. In the 1930s and 1940s, psychologists employed in prison settings focused primarily on administering psychological tests (i.e., Wilson, 1951) and providing treatment to inmates (i.e., Lindner, 1944, 1954). Over the years, as a result of successful lawsuits that have created a legal responsibility for prisons to address the mental health needs of inmates, there has been a significant expansion of roles for psychologists working in correctional settings. However, because of the nature of this special population and the unique demands of the prison environment (including the need to maintain safety for staff and other inmates), ethical conflicts frequently arise when psychologists perform these various roles.

Joel Dvoskin, Erin Spiers, and Stanley Brodsky (Chapter 23) provide a summary of the history of the expanding role for psychologists in prison and jail settings. In their chapter, they attribute this growth to a number of factors, including the development of graduate training in departments of correctional-clinical psychology, successful class action suits filed on behalf of prisoners (Metzner, 2002a, 2002b), the formation of professional associations for psychologists working in corrections, and the publication of peer-reviewed journals devoted to or including research on correctional psychology. They review landmark cases that established the obligation of prisons to address the medical needs (*Estelle v. Gamble,* 1976) and psychiatric needs (*Bowring v. Godwin,* 1977) of inmates and cases related to the responsibility of prisons to meet the general mental health needs of residents (i.e., *Langley v. Coughlin,* 1989; *Ruiz v. Estelle,* 1980). The authors consider the consequences that may follow the failure of correctional institutions to fulfill these obligations. These include lawsuits, investigations, and the effects on other prisoners and staff. Dvoskin et al. describe a number of roles for psychologists employed in prison settings, with a focus on providing treatment for those with serious mental illness, conducting reception and classification assessments, screening for potential suicide risk and suicide prevention, managerial and administrative positions in the institution, designing and conducting training programs, and consulting with prison boards and external committees. A range of mental health programs relevant to correctional settings is considered, including outpatient clinical services, residential treatment, and discharge and prerelease planning. The authors consider problems encountered when working with special populations of inmates: women, ethnic and cultural minorities, "manipulative" prisoners, and those placed in long-term segregation.

Evaluating the Psychological Sequelae of Elder Abuse

Much has been written about the aging of America. In the past 100 years, the percentage of Americans who are age 65 or older has tripled (to 12.3% of the population), and those between the ages of 75 and 84 have increased more than 16-fold (Greenberg, 2003). According to projections, by the year 2020, those age 60 or older will constitute approximately 18% of the world's population (Daly, 2002). Accompanying the increase in this segment of our population is a greater reliance on caregivers: family, in-home providers, and staff in nursing care or residential facilities. Because of the nature of this population (i.e., declines in physical condition, cognitive abilities, neurological functioning), they are highly vulnerable to physical, sexual, and psychological abuse, and the effects of physical and psychological neglect.

In her chapter, Beth Rom-Rymer (Chapter 24) considers the psychological sequelae associated with elder abuse. She reviews statutes that address mandatory reporting requirements and civil and criminal sanctions that arise from such claims. She reviews representative case law, focusing on statutes of limitation, procedural protections, levels of neglect, the causal link between the alleged abuse and harm to the individual, emotional damages, damages related to pain and suffering, and punitive awards. Rom-Rymer describes the multiple sources of information that experts should consider when conducting these assessments and the need for evaluators to determine or rule out the presence of a causal link between any impairment found and the alleged abusive incident. She summarizes relevant ethical issues that arise in these assessments, the standard of practice, and expert testimony. Her chapter concludes with an illustrative case, one that alleges sexual abuse and medical malpractice occurring in a nursing home setting.

Forensic Issues at the End of Life

Most forensic mental health assessments focus on the evaluation of competencies, a legal construct (Grisso, 1986, 2003a) delineated by statute and defined most often in case law, that identify those cognitive abilities and skills necessary to waive *Miranda* rights, stand trial, be held criminally culpable, adequately parent, exercise a duty to protect others, and make autonomous decisions, to name just a few psycholegal competencies commonly addressed by experts. The role of the forensic mental heath evaluator is to assess a defendant, plaintiff, or other party in order to assist the trier of fact in determining when a significant disparity exists between that individual's cognitive abilities and those the law mandates are necessary to establish a finding of competence. In the case of terminally ill patients who seek to have their life prematurely ended either by physician-assisted suicide (where legal) or by withholding life-sustaining treatment, forensic experts may be asked to evaluate their competence to elect such a drastic, irreversible course of action. As in the evaluation of any psycholegal competence, the forensic expert must be familiar with relevant federal and state statutes, case law, appropriate forensic assessment instruments, and the standard of care in the field, including, as always, the need to rely on and integrate information obtained from a number of sources (see Chapter 2).

Barry Rosenfeld and Colleen McCain Jacobson (Chapter 25) review issues that arise when forensic mental experts are asked to conduct end-of-life evaluations. In their chapter, they describe the historical roots of the concept of the right to die, summarizing a number of recent, high-profile cases that have focused attention on this topic (i.e., *Cruzan v. Director, Missouri Department of Health*, 1990; *In re Quinlan*, 1976; and the Jack Kevorkian and Terri Schiavo cases); they further describe the prevailing legal standards. Physician-assisted suicide, advanced directives, and do-not-resuscitate requests may all serve to trigger the need for a forensic assessment of the decision-making competency of the patient. Rosenfeld and McCain Jacobson review the empirical research on decision-making capacity in this psycholegal context and focus on the effects of depression and cognitive impairment, conditions that frequently accompany terminal illness and pain. They describe the methodology that should be used when conducting end-of-life evaluations, including the role of patient interviews, interviews with third parties, and record reviews and the use of such forensic assessment instruments as the Macarthur Competence Assessment Tool-Treatment (Grisso & Appelbaum, 1998) and the Hopkins Competency Assessment Test (Janofsky, McCarthy, & Folstein, 1992). The authors explain how these varied sources of information contribute to a forensic opinion and caution that the forensic expert must avoid imposing his or her own personal, cultural, and religious values on the process of assessing the patient's decision-making ability.

Special Topics in Forensic Practice

In addition to the traditional and emerging roles for the forensic mental health professionals described in this volume and in Goldstein (2003a), a number of other roles and topics have emerged within the field of forensic mental health practice. In the final section of this chapter, these special topics are considered, including: (a) judicial decision making about forensic mental health evidence, (b) the psychopathology of homicide; and (c) forensic hypnosis.

Judicial Decision Making about Forensic Mental Health Evidence

Although most research on legal decision making has focused on juries, recent attention has been devoted to the decision-making process of judges. In juvenile court, the judge is the sole trier of fact, and in some states, the judge rules on issues related to the transfer of juveniles to adult court. In civil cases, judges are involved in civil commitment proceedings (see Chapter 9), child custody cases (Otto, Buffington-Vollum, & Edens, 2003), and cases involving parental abuse and neglect petitions (see Chapter 12). In criminal cases, judges are the sole decision makers for questions raised at pretrial hearings (i.e., validity of *Miranda* waivers, Oberlander et al., 2003; trial competency, Stafford, 2003; competence of a witness to testify during trial; e.g., admissibility of evidence), and posttrial sentencing (see Chapter 14). At times, courts have seemingly distrusted and ignored input provided by mental health experts in the form of reports, testimony, and amicus briefs aimed at providing information to judges that they might not otherwise have available (Fradella, Fogarty, & O'Neill, 2003; Tanford, 1990). In still other cases, including those decided by the U.S. Supreme Court, social science research has been cited in holdings in support of the Court's ruling (*Atkins v. Virginia,* 2002; *Roper v. Simmons,* 2005). As such, the question has been raised, "Do judges listen?" (A. M. Goldstein, Thomson, Redding, & Osman, 2003).

Richard Redding and Daniel Murrie (Chapter 26) review the current empirical research on judicial decision making for a number of legal issues frequently raised in juvenile, civil, and criminal cases. The authors focus on decision making about forensic mental health evidence in these cases, the receptivity of judges to forensic reports and testimony on these issues, judges' ability to understanding this testimony, and the process by which judges reach decisions about such evidence. In their chapter, they describe the successes and failures of forensic mental health professionals to influence the courts. Redding and Murrie discuss research that sheds light on judges' perceptions of forensic mental health evidence and the ability of judges to grasp and apply the *Daubert* standard (*Daubert v. Merrell Dow Pharmaceuticals,* 1993) when considering the admissibility of forensic psychological and psychiatric testimony. They present the argument for judicial education on social science methodology in adjudicating individual cases.

Psychopathology of Homicide

In forensic psychology education and training, and as reflected in texts recognized as authorities in these fields (A. M. Goldstein, 2003a; Heilbrun, 2001; Melton et al., 1997; I. B. Weiner & Hess, 2006), major emphasis is placed on the relevance of legal statutes and case law and the use of appropriate assessment methodology in formulated criminal psycholegal opinions (e.g., mens rea, diminished capacity, extreme emotional disturbance, insanity). Very little, if any, attention is devoted to psychopathological disorders and the psychodynamics that may be associated with crimes such as homicide. An increased understanding of the motivational aspects and psychopathology of homicide may assist forensic experts in formulating psycholegal opinions related to criminal culpability and in conducting risk assessments on the likelihood of similar violent behavior by the offender in the future. Opinions as to the psychopathology that fueled a specific homicide may provide important information to the court, probation and parole boards, and those agencies involved in the management and disposition of the offender.

In his chapter, Louis Schlesinger (Chapter 27) offers an approach to the evaluation of homicide designed to complement the traditional model of assessment (see Chapter 2), which may assist forensic mental health experts in understanding the psychopathology of homicide. He presents a model for the classification of homicides based on the motivational dynamics of the offender (Revitch & Schlesinger, 1978, 1981, 1989; Schlesinger, 2004b) and focusing attention on the behavioral crime scene characteristics, rather than relying on the defendant's rendition and explanation as to what occurred. He describes and provides illustrative case histories of homicides that fall along a motivation spectrum: environmentally stimulated homicides, situational homicides, homicides that are impulse driven, catathymic homicides, and compulsive homicides. Schlesinger (2004a) explains the connection between the psychodynamics and underlying psychopathology of a homicide offender to violence risk prediction.

Forensic Hypnosis

Initially barred as expert testimony more than 100 years ago (*People v. Ebanks,* 1989), the use of forensic hypnosis as an investigative tool to refresh memories of crime victims and witnesses gained notoriety and acceptability in the 1970s because of its role in solving the Chowchilla kidnapping case. A school bus was hijacked, and the children in it virtually disappeared, unable to be found by investigators. Although the driver of the bus escaped, he was unable to provide useful information to assist in locating the missing children. He underwent forensic hypnosis and was able to recall new details of the kidnapping, including the license plate number of the car driven by the kidnappers, and investigators eventually located the bus and children, hidden from view in a cave. Suddenly, the use of forensic hypnosis became popular. Numerous explanations have been proposed to explain the phenomenon of hypnosis, tending to view it either as an altered state of consciousness or as a behavior having psychological and sociological explanations (Hilgard, 1992; Scheflin & Shapiro, 1989; Spanos & Coe, 1992). The impact of hypnotically refreshed memories on a jury is potentially considerable, and as such, questions as to the accuracy of hypnotically recalled memories are significant.

Susan Knight and Robert Meyer (Chapter 28) define and distinguish between clinical and forensic hypnosis. In their chapter, they review research related to the trustworthiness of hypnotically refreshed memories and describe the arguments advanced in support of or discouraging their use in court. They focus on issues related to suggestibility, reliability, and believability, and they consider the topic of pseudomemories. The role of forensic hypnosis with crime victims and witnesses is described, along with relevant case law addressing the admissibility of testimony that has passed through the sieve of forensic hypnosis. Knight and Meyer consider the legal issues and practical use of forensic hypnosis with those claiming they were sexually abused as children, defendants in criminal cases, and those who may seek to provide additional information (i.e., investigative leads, details that might assist in a defense against the charges). They also consider the use of forensic hypnosis by investigators seeking to obtain confessions from defendants. Research on behavior that may have been coerced while in a hypnotic state and on the detection of mimicked hypnotic states is described. The authors review those criteria, based on case law (*State of New Jersey v. Hurd,* 1981) and guidelines prepared by a number of organizations and agencies, that describe the proper use of forensic hypnosis. They consider ethical issues involved in performing forensic hypnosis, qualifications and training of those serving as experts in this area, and methods to reduce legal liability from claims arising from information gleaned through forensic hypnosis.

CONCLUSION

Forensic psychology has evolved to the point that a standard of care in conducting forensic psychological assessments is emerging. Each forensic referral is different, and methodology must be determined on a case-by-case basis, yet there is general agreement that forensic evaluations are legally driven, fueled by statutes that are defined by case law. Before accepting a case, experts must familiarize themselves with the applicable statutes and case law that will then determine what questions to ask the examinee; what tests to administer (including traditional, forensic assessment, and forensically relevant instruments); what records to request and review; what third parties should be interviewed; and how to write a relevant, focused report that will assist the trier of fact. It is accepted in the field of forensic psychology that multiple sources of information must be considered in arriving at opinions, that opinions should be based on sufficient data, and that issues related to response style, including malingering, defensiveness, and exaggeration, must be addressed. It is agreed that forensic psychological evaluations must conform to the principles of the APA (2002) Code of Ethics and should follow the aspirational "Specialty Guidelines" (Committee on Ethical Guidelines for Psychologists, 1991).

A standard to care, not an unreasonably high threshold to meet from a legal perspective (what the *reasonably* prudent profession would do—and who among us would chose to have the reasonably prudent neurosurgeon operate to remove a brain tumor?), should guide forensic mental health experts in their decisions to accept or reject referrals, in designing and conducting forensic assessments, in preparing reports, and in offering expert testimony in court. It is hoped that the information contained in these chapters contribute to the understanding that practitioners should possess in their efforts to meet the emerging standard of care when working in the land-mined field of forensic mental health assessment.

REFERENCES

Adams v. Weinberger, 548 F. 2d. 239 (1977).

American Association of University Women. (1993). *Hostile hallways: Bullying, teasing and sexual harassment in school.* Washington, DC: Author.

American Association of University Women. (2001). *Hostile hallways: Bullying, teasing and sexual harassment in school.* Washington, DC: Author.

American Bar Association. (1969). *Model code of professional responsibility.* Washington, DC: ABA Press.

American Bar Association. (1983). *Model code of professional conduct.* Washington, DC: ABA Press.

American Psychological Association. (1993). Record keeping guidelines. *American Psychologist, 48,* 984–986.

American Psychological Association. (1994). Guidelines for child custody evaluations in divorce proceedings. *American Psychologist, 47,* 677–680.

American Psychological Association. (2002). Ethical principles of psychologists and code of conduct. *American Psychologist, 47,* 1597–1611.

Apprendi v. New Jersey, 530 U.S. 466 (2000).

Atkins v. Virginia, 536 U.S. 304 (2002).

Bank, S. (2001). From mental health professional to expert witness: Testifying in court. *New Directions for Mental Health Services, 91,* 57–66.

Bartol, C. R., & Bartol, A. M. (2006). History of forensic psychology. In I. B. Weiner & A. K. Hess (Eds.), *Handbook of forensic psychology* (3rd ed., pp. 3–27). Hoboken, NJ: Wiley.

Baxstrom v. Herold, 383 U.S. 107 (1966).

Beitchman, J. H., Zucker, K. L., Hood, J. E., daCosta, G. A., Akman, D., & Cassavia, E. (1992). A review of the long-term effects of child sexual abuse. *Child Abuse and Neglect, 16,* 101–118.

Blakeley v. Washington, 124 S. Ct. 2531 (2004).

Boccaccini, M. T., & Brodsky, S. L. (2002). Believability of expert and lay witnesses: Implications for trial consultation. *Professional Psychology: Research and Practice, 33,* 384–388.

Bodenhausen, G. V. (1990). Second-guessing the jury: Stereotypic and hindsight biases in perceptions of court cases. *Journal of Applied Social Psychology, 20,* 1112–1121.

Borum R., & Grisso, T. (1995). Psychological test use in criminal forensic evaluations. *Professional Psychology, 26,* 465–473.

Borum, R., Super, J., & Rand, M. (2003). Forensic assessment for high-risk occupations. In I. B. Weiner (Editor in Chief) & A. M. Goldstein (Vol. Ed.), *Handbook of psychology: Vol. 11. Forensic psychology* (pp. 133–148). Hoboken, NJ: Wiley.

Bowers v. Hardwick, 478 U.S. 186 (1986).

Bowring v. Goodwin, 551 F.2d. 44 (1977).

Brigham, J. C., & Grisso, T. T. (2003). Forensic psychology. In D. K. Freedheim (Ed.), *History of psychology* (Vol. 1, pp. 391–412). Hoboken, NJ: Wiley.

Brown, D., Pryzwansky, W. B., & Schulte, A. C. (1998). *Psychological consultation: Introduction to theory and practice* (4th ed.). Boston: Allyn & Bacon.

Bruce v. Bryne-Stevens, 776 P.2d 666 (Wash. 1989).

Butcher, J. N., Dahlstrom, W. G., Graham, J. R., Tellegen, A., & Kaemmer, B. (1989). *MMPI-2: Manual for administration and scoring.* Minneapolis: University of Minnesota Press.

Butcher, J. N., Dahlstrom, W. G., Graham, J. R., Tellegen, A., & Kaemmer, B. (2001). *MMPI-2: Manual for administration and scoring* (Rev. ed.). Minneapolis: University of Minnesota Press.

Caldwell, A. B. (2000). *MMPI-2 data research file for clinical patients.* Unpublished raw data.

Castelli, P., Goodman, G. S., Edelstein, R. S., Mitchell, E. B., Alonso, P. M. P., Lyons, K. E., et al. (2006). Evaluating eyewitness testimony in adults and children. In I. B. Weiner & A. K. Hess (Eds.), *Handbook of forensic psychology* (3rd ed., pp. 243–304). Hoboken, NJ: Wiley.

Cicchetti, D. (1984). The emergence of developmental psychopathology. *Child Development, 55,* 1–7.

Cicchetti, D. (1990). An historical perspective on the discipline of developmental psychopathology. In J. Rolf, A. Master, D. Cicchetti, K. Nuechterlien, & S. Weintraub (Eds.), *Risk and protective factors in the development of psychopathology* (pp. 2–28). New York: Cambridge University Press.

Committee on Ethical Guidelines for Forensic Psychologists. (1991). Specialty guidelines for forensic psychologists. *Law and Human Behavior, 15,* 655–665.

Conroy, M. A. (2003). Evaluation of sexual predators. In I. B. Weiner (Editor in Chief) & A. M. Goldstein (Vol. Ed.), *Handbook of psychology: Vol. 11. Forensic psychology* (pp. 463–484). Hoboken, NJ: Wiley.

Cruzan v. Director, Missouri Department of Health, 497 U.S. 261, 110 S. Ct. 2841 (1990).

Cunningham, M. D., & Goldstein, A. M. (2003). Sentencing determinations in death penalty cases. In I. B. Weiner (Editor in Chief) & A. M. Goldstein (Vol. Ed.), *Handbook of psychology: Vol. 11. Forensic psychology* (pp. 407–436). Hoboken, NJ: Wiley.

Dahlstrom, W. G., & Tellegen, A. (1993). *Socioeconomic status and the MMPI-2: The relation of MMPI-2 patterns to levels of education and occupation.* Minneapolis: University of Minnesota Press.

Daly, E. (2002, April 9). U.S. says elderly will soon outnumber young for the first time. *New York Times,* p. 6.

Daubert v. Merrell Dow Pharmaceuticals, Inc., 509 U.S. 579 (1993).

Dodd v. United States, U.S. (2005).

Drogin, E. Y. (2000). Evidence and expert mental health witnesses: A jurisprudent therapy perspective. In E. Pierson (Ed.), *New developments in personal injury litigation* (pp. 295–333). New York: Aspen.

Drogin, E. Y. (2001). Utilizing forensic psychological consultation: A jurisprudent therapy analysis. *Mental and Physical Disability Law Reporter, 25,* 17–22.

Drogin, E. Y., & Barrett, C. L. (2003). Substituted judgment: Roles for the forensic psychologist. In I. B. Weiner (Editor in Chief) & A. M. Goldstein (Vol. Ed.), *Handbook of psychology: Vol. 11. Forensic psychology* (pp. 301–314). Hoboken, NJ: Wiley.

Estelle v. Gamble, 429 U.S. 97 (1976).

Ewing, C. P. (2003). Expert testimony: Law and practice. In I. B. Weiner (Editor in Chief) & A. M. Goldstein (Vol. Ed.), *Handbook of psychology: Vol. 11. Forensic psychology* (pp. 55–66). Hoboken, NJ: Wiley.

Ewing v. Goldstein, 120 Cal. App. 4th 807 (2004).

Ewing v. Northridge Hospital, 120 Cal. App. 4th 1289 (2004).

Exner, J. E. (2003). *Rorschach: A comprehensive system: Vol. 1. Basic foundations and principles of interpretation* (4th ed.). Hoboken, NJ: Wiley.

Exner, J. E., & Weiner, I. B. (2003). *Rorschach interpretation assistance program.* Lutz, FL: Psychological Assessment Resource.

Finkelhor, D. (1984). *Child sexual abuse: New theory and research.* New York: Macmillan.

Foote, W. E. (2002, August). *The Inuit project: Forensic evaluation of a large group of sex abuse survivors.* Paper presented at the annual meeting of the American Psychological Association, Chicago.

Fradella, H. F., Fogarty, A., & O'Neill, L. (2003). The impact of Daubert on the admissibility of behavioral science testimony. *Pepperdine Law Review, 30,* 403–444.

Friedman, R. S., & Klee, C. H. (2001). The roles of expert and litigation support consultants in medical-legal claims. *Neurorehabilitation, 16,* 123–130.

Frye v. United States, 292 Fed. 1013 D.C. (1923).

Gaines v. Sun Life Assurance Company of Canada, 306 Mich. 192, 196 (1943).

Gates v. Prudential Insurance Company of America, 270 NYS 282 (1934).

Goldstein, A. M. (Ed.). (2003a). *Forensic psychology* (Vol. 11). Hoboken, NJ: Wiley.

Goldstein, A. M. (2003b). Overview of forensic psychology. In I. B. Weiner (Editor in Chief) & A. M. Goldstein (Vol. Ed.), *Handbook of psychology: Vol. 11. Forensic psychology* (pp. 3–20). Hoboken, NJ: Wiley.

Goldstein, A. M. (2005, September 12). *Best practices: Standards for forensic evaluations.* Invited seminar, National Association of State Mental Health Program Directors, annual forensic division conference, Lake Tahoe, NV.

Goldstein, A. M., Morse, S. J., & Shapiro, D. L. (2003). Evaluation of criminal responsibility. In I. B. Weiner (Editor in Chief) & A. M. Goldstein (Vol. Ed.), *Handbook of psychology: Vol. 11. Forensic psychology* (pp. 381–406). Hoboken, NJ: Wiley.

Goldstein, A. M., Thomson, M. R., Redding, R. E., & Osman, D. (2003). The role of research in forensic psychological testimony: Do judges listen? *Journal of Forensic Psychology Practice, 3,* 89–101.

Goldstein, N. E., Condie, L. O., Kalbeitzer, R., Osman, D., & Geiger, J. (2003). Juvenile offenders' Miranda rights comprehension and self-reported likelihood of offering false confessions. *Assessment, 10,* 359–369.

Greenberg, S. (2003). *A profile of older Americans: 2003.* Washington, DC: U.S. Department of Health and Human Services, Administration on Aging.

Greenberg, S. A., & Shuman, D. W. (1997). Irreconcilable conflict between therapeutic and forensic roles. *Professional Psychology: Research and Practice, 28,* 50–57.

Greene, R. L. (2000). *The MMPI-2: An interpretive manual* (2nd ed.). Boston: Allyn & Bacon.

Grisso, T. (1981). *Juveniles' waiver of rights: Legal and psychological competence.* New York: Plenum Press.

Grisso, T. (1986). *Evaluating competencies: Forensic assessments and instruments.* New York: Plenum Press.

Grisso, T. (1998). *Forensic evaluation of juveniles.* Sarasota, FL: Professional Resource Press.

Grisso, T. (2003a). *Evaluating competencies: Forensic assessments and instruments* (2nd. ed.). New York: Kluwer Academic/Plenum Press.

Grisso, T. (2003b). Forensic evaluation in delinquency cases. In I. B. Weiner (Editor in Chief) & A. M. Goldstein (Vol. Ed.), *Handbook of psychology: Vol. 11. Forensic psychology* (pp. 315–334). Hoboken, NJ: Wiley.

Grisso, T. (2004). *Double jeopardy: Adolescent offenders with mental disorders.* Chicago: University of Chicago Press.

Grisso, T., & Appelbaum, P. S. (1998). *Assessing competence to consent to treatment: A guide for physicians and other health professionals.* New York: Oxford University Press.

Grisso, T., & Schwartz, R. (Eds.). (2000). *Youth on trial.* Chicago: University of Chicago Press.

Griswold v. Connecticut, 381 U.S. 479 (1965).

Grove, W. M., Barden, R. C., Garb, H. N., & Lilienfeld, S. O. (2002). Failure of Rorschach-Comprehensive-System-based testimony to be admissible under the *Daubert-Joiner-Kumho* standard. *Psychology, Public Policy, and Law, 8,* 216–234.

Guttmacher, M. S., & Weihofen, H. (1952). *Psychiatry and the law.* New York: Norton.

Hargrave v. Vermont, 340 F.3d 27 (2003).

Harvard Law Association. (1974). Developments in the law: Civil commitment of the mentally ill. *Harvard Law Review, 87,* 1190–1406.

Hathaway, S. R., & McKinley, J. C. (1940). A multiphasic individuality schedule (Minnesota): Illinois. Construction of the schedule. *Journal of Psychology, 10,* 249–254.

Heilbrun, K. (2000). *Petition for the recognition of a specialty in professional psychology.* Submitted on behalf of the American Board of Forensic Psychology and the American Psychology-Law Society to the American Psychological Association.

Heilbrun, K. (2001). *Principles of forensic mental health assessment.* New York: Kluwer Academic/Plenum Press.

Heilbrun, K., DeMatteo, D., & Marczyk, G. R. (2004). Pragmatic psychology and forensic mental health assessment: Applying principles to promote quality. *Psychology, Public Policy, and Law, 10,* 31–70.

Heilbrun, K., Marczyk, G. R., & DeMatteo, D. (2002). *Forensic mental health assessment: A casebook.* New York: Oxford University Press.

Heilbrun, K., Warren, J., & Picarello, K. (2003). Third party information in forensic assessment. In I. B. Weiner (Editor in Chief) & A. M. Goldstein (Vol. Ed.), *Handbook of psychology: Vol. 11. Forensic psychology* (pp. 65–87). Hoboken, NJ: Wiley.

Hess, A. K. (2006). Defining forensic psychology. In I. B. Weiner & A. K. Hess (Eds.), *Handbook of forensic psychology* (3rd ed., pp. 28–58). Hoboken, NJ: Wiley.

Hilgard, E. R. (1992). Dissociation and theories of hypnosis. In E. Fromm & M. R. Nash (Eds.), *Contemporary hypnosis research* (pp. 69–101). New York: Guilford Press.

Hinchman v. General American Insurance Company, IP-96–0578-C-B/S, J. D., IN. (1998).

Ingham v. United States, 167 F.3d 1240 (9th Cir. 1999).

In re Quinlan, 355 A. 2d 647 (N.J. 1976), *cert. denied,* 429 U.S. 922 (1976).

Inwald, R., & Resko, J. (1995). Pre-employment screening for public safety personnel. In L. VandeCreek & S. Knapp (Eds.), *Innovations in clinical practice: Vol. 14. A sourcebook* (pp. 365–382). Sarasota, FL: Professional Resource Press.

Janofsky, J. S., McCarthy, R. J., & Folstein, M. F. (1992). The Hopkins Competence Assessment Test: A brief method for evaluating patients' capacity to give informed consent. *Hospital and Community Psychiatry, 43,* 132–136.

Jenkins v. United States, 307 F.2d 637 U.S. App, D. C. (1962).

Jones v. United States, 526 U.S. 277 (1999).

Kansas v. Crane, 534 U.S. 407 (2002).

Kansas v. Hendricks, 521 U.S. 346 (1997).

Kovera, M. B., Dickinson, J. J., & Cutler, B. L. (2003). Voir dire and jury selection. In I. B. Weiner (Editor in Chief) & A. M. Goldstein (Vol. Ed.), *Handbook of psychology: Vol. 11. Forensic psychology* (pp. 161–175). Hoboken, NJ: Wiley.

Krauss, D. A., & Sales, B. D. (2006). Training in forensic psychology: Training for what goal? In I. B. Weiner & A. K. Hess (Eds.), *Handbook of forensic psychology* (3rd ed., pp. 851–872). Hoboken, NJ: Wiley.

Kupshik v. John Hancock Mutual Life Insurance Company, 1, 98-CV-3-CAM, M. D., Ga. (2000).

Langley v. Coughlin, 888 F. 2d 252 (1989).

Lassiter v. Department of Social Services, 452 U.S. 18 (1981).

Lessard v. Schmidt, 349 F. Supp. 1078 (1972).

Lindner, R. (1944). *Rebel without a cause.* New York: Grune & Stratton.

Lindner, R. (1954). *The fifty-minute hour: A collection of true psychoanalytic tales.* New York: Holt, Rinehart and Winston.

Lubin, B., Larsen, R. M., Matarazzo, J. D., & Seever, M. (1985). Psychological test usage patterns in five professional settings. *American Psychologist, 40,* 857–861.

Lutjen, K. (1996). Culpability and sentencing under the mandatory minimums and the federal sentencing guidelines: The punishment no longer fits the crime. *Notre Dame Journal of Law and Ethics, 10,* 389–432.

Massachusetts Casualty Insurance Company v. Rief, 227 MD. 324, 176 A. 77 (1962).

Massachusetts Mutual Life Insurance Company v. Oullette, 617 A. 2d. 132 Vt. (1992).

Mayle v. Felix, 125 S. Ct. 2562 (2005).

Melton, G., Petrila, J., Poythress, N., & Slobogin, C. (1997). *Psychological evaluations for the courts: A handbook for mental health professionals and lawyers* (2nd ed.). New York: Guilford Press.

Metzner, J. L. (2002a). Case action litigation in correctional psychiatry. *Journal of the American Academy of Psychiatry and the Law, 30,* 19–29.

Metzner, J. L. (2002b). Prison litigation in the USA. *Journal of Forensic Psychiatry, 13,* 240–244.

Morey, L. C. (1991). *The Personality Assessment Inventory manual.* Odessa, FL: Psychological Assessment Resources.

Münsterberg, H. (1908). *On the witness stand: Essays on psychology and crime.* New York: Doubleday.

Neumann, D. A., Houskamp, B. M., Pollock, V. E., & Briere, J. (1996). The long-term sequelae of childhood sexual abuse in women: A meta-analytic review. *Child Maltreatment: Journal of the American Professional Society on the Abuse of Children, 1,* 6–16.

Nietzel, M. T., & Dillehay, R. C. (1986). *Psychological consultation in the courtroom.* New York: Pergamon Press.

Nussbaum, D. (2006). Recommending probation and parole. In I. B. Weiner & A. K. Hess (Eds.), *Handbook of forensic psychology* (3rd ed., pp. 426–486). Hoboken, NJ: Wiley.

Oberlander, L. B., Goldstein, N. E., & Goldstein, A. M. (2003). Competence to confess. In I. B. Weiner (Editor in Chief) & A. M. Goldstein (Vol. Ed.), *Handbook of psychology: Vol. 11. Forensic psychology* (pp. 335–359). Hoboken, NJ: Wiley.

O'Connor v. Donaldson, 422 U.S. 563 (1975).

O'Connor v. Sullivan 938 F.2d 542 (1947).

Otto, R., Buffington-Vollum, J. K., & Edens, J. F. (2003). Child custody evaluations. In I. B. Weiner (Editor in Chief) & A. M. Goldstein (Vol. Ed.), *Handbook of psychology: Vol. 11. Forensic psychology* (pp. 179–208). Hoboken, NJ: Wiley.

Otto, R. K., & Goldstein, A. M. (2005). Juveniles' competence to confess and competence to participate in the juvenile justice process. In K. Heilbrun, N. E. Goldstein, & R. Redding (Eds.), *Current perspectives on juvenile delinquency: Prevention, assessment, and intervention* (pp. 179–208). New York: Oxford University Press.

Packer, I. K., & Borum, R. (2003). Forensic training and practice. In I. B. Weiner (Editor in Chief) & A. M. Goldstein (Vol. Ed.), *Handbook of psychology: Vol. 11. Forensic psychology* (pp. 21–32). Hoboken, NJ: Wiley.

Paolucci, E. O., Genuis, M. L., & Violato, C. (2001). A meta-analysis of the published research on the effects of child sexual abuse. *Journal of Psychology, 135,* 17–36.

People v. Ebanks, 117 Cal. 652, 49P. 1049, 40 L. R. A. 269 (1989).

Perlin, M. L. (1996). "No direction home": The law and criminal defendants with mental disabilities. *Mental and Physical Disability Law Reporter, 20,* 605–613.

Perlin, M. L. (1999). "Half-wracked prejudice leaped forth": Sanism pretextuality and why and how mental disability law developed as it did. *Journal of Contemporary Legal Issues, 10,* 3–31.

Piaget, J. (1953). *The origins of intelligence in children.* London: Routledge & Kegan Paul.

Revitch, E., & Schlesinger, L. B. (1978). Murder: Evaluation, classification, and prediction. In I. L. Kutash, S. B. Kutash, & L. B. Schlesinger (Eds.), *Violence: Perspectives on murder and aggression* (pp. 138–164). San Francisco: Jossey-Bass.

Revitch, E., & Schlesinger, L. B. (1981). *Psychopathology of homicide.* Springfield, IL: Charles C. Thomas.

Revitch, E., & Schlesinger, L. B. (1989). *Sex murder and sex aggression.* Springfield, IL: Charles C. Thomas.

Roe v. Wade, 410 U.S. 113 (1973).

Rogers, R. (Ed.). (1997). *Clinical assessment of malingering and deception.* New York: Guilford Press.

Rogers, R., & Bender, S. (2003). Evaluation of malingering and deception. In A. M. Goldstein (Ed.), *Forensic psychology* (Vol. 11, pp. 109–133). Hoboken, NJ: Wiley.

Rogers, R., Salekin, R. T., Sewell, K. W., Goldstein, A. M., & Leonard, K. (1998). A comparison of forensic and nonforensic malingerers: A prototypical analysis of explanatory models. *Law and Human Behavior, 22,* 353–368.

Rogers, R., Sewell, K. W., & Goldstein, A. M. (1994). Explanatory models of malingering: A prototypical analysis. *Law and Human Behavior, 18,* 543–552.

Rompilla v. Beard, 545 U.S. _____ (2005).

Roper v. Simmons, 125 S.Ct. 1183 (2005).

Ruiz v. Estelle, 53 F. Supp. 1265 (1980).

Santosky v. Kramer, 455 U.S. 745 (1982).

Scheflin, A. W. (2006). Forensic uses of hypnosis. In I. B. Weiner & A. K. Hess (Eds.), *Handbook of forensic psychology* (3rd ed., pp. 589–630). Hoboken, NJ: Wiley.

Scheflin, A. W., & Shapiro, J. L. (1989). *Trance on trial.* New York. Guilford Press.

Schlesinger, L. B. (2004a). Classification of antisocial behavior for prognostic purposes: Study the motivation not the crime. *Journal of Psychiatry and the Law, 32,* 191–219.

Schlesinger, L. B. (2004b). *Sexual murder: Catathymic and compulsive homicides.* Boca Raton, FL: CRC Press.

Schloendorff v. The Society of the New York Hospital, 211 NY 125 (1914).

Shapiro, D. L. (1991). *Forensic psychological assessment: An integrative approach.* Boston: Allyn & Bacon.

Shelman, E. A., & Lazoritz, S. (2005). *The Mary Ellen Wilson child abuse case and the beginning of children's rights in nineteenth century America.* Jefferson, NC: McFarland.

Simon, R. I., & Gold, L. H. (2004). *American psychiatric publishing textbook of forensic psychiatry.* Washington, DC: American Psychiatric Press.

Spanos, N. P., & Coe, W. C. (1992). A social-psychological approach to hypnosis. In E. Fromm & M. R. Nash (Eds.), *Contemporary hypnosis research* (pp. 102–130). New York: Guilford Press.

Stafford, K. P. (2003). Assessment of competence to stand trial. In I. B. Weiner (Editor in Chief) & A. M. Goldstein (Vol. Ed.), *Handbook of psychology: Vol. 11. Forensic psychology* (pp. 359–380). Hoboken, NJ: Wiley.

Stanley, B., & Galietta, M. (2006). Informed consent in treatment and research. In I. B. Weiner & A. K. Hess (Eds.), *Handbook of forensic psychology* (3rd ed., pp. 211–242). Hoboken, NJ: Wiley.

State of New Jersey v. Hurd, 414 A.2d 291 (1981).

Stock, H. V. (2000, August). *Pathological organizational affective attachment: Why some people threaten to kill in the workplace.* Paper presented at the annual convention of the American Psychological Association, Presidential Miniconvention on Law, Psychology and Violence in the Workplace, Washington, DC.

Strickland v. Washington, 466 U.S. 668 (1984).

Tanford, J. A. (1990). The limits of a scientific jurisprudence: The Supreme Court and psychology. *Indiana Law Journal, 66,* 137–173.

Tarasoff v. Board of Regents, 551 P.2d 334 (1976).

Timbrook, R. E., & Graham, J. R. (1994). Ethnic differences on the MMPI-2? *Psychological Assessment, 6,* 212–217.

United States v. Booker & Fanfan, 125 S. Ct. 738 (2005).

United States v. Sell, 539 U.S. 166 (2003).

U.S. Conference of Catholic Bishops. (2004). *The nature and scope of sexual abuse of minors by Catholic priests and deacons in the United States: 1950–2002.* Washington, DC: Conference of Catholic Bishops.

U.S. Department of Education. (2004). *Educator sexual misconduct: A synthesis of existing literature.* Washington, DC: U.S. Department of Education.

U.S. Sentencing Commission. (1987). *Federal sentencing guidelines manual.* Westlaw.

U.S. Sentencing Guidelines 5K2.20, 5K2.22 (2003); 18 U.S.C. 3553(b)(2) (amended 2003).

Weiner, I. B. (Editor in Chief). (2003). *Handbook of psychology.* Hoboken, NJ: Wiley.

Weiner, I. B., & Hess, A. K. (Eds.). (2006). *The handbook of forensic psychology* (3rd ed.). Hoboken, NJ: Wiley.

Weiner, I. R. (2004). *Rorschach Interpretation Assistance Program: Forensic report (RIAP5 FE)*. Lutz, FL: Psychological Assessment Resources.

Weiner, I. R. (2006). Writing forensic reports. In I. B. Weiner & A. K. Hess (Eds.), *Handbook of forensic psychology* (3rd ed., pp. 631–651). Hoboken, NJ: Wiley.

Weissman, H. N., & DeBow, D. M. (2003). Ethical principles and professional competencies. In I. B. Weiner (Editor in Chief) & A. M. Goldstein (Vol. Ed.), *Handbook of psychology: Vol. 11. Forensic psychology* (pp. 33–54). Hoboken, NJ: Wiley.

Wells, G. L., & Loftus, E. F. (2003). Eyewitness memory for people and events. In I. B. Weiner (Editor in Chief) & A. M. Goldstein (Vol. Ed.), *Handbook of psychology: Vol. 11. Forensic psychology* (pp. 149–160). Hoboken, NJ: Wiley.

Wigmore, J. H. (1909). Professor Munsterberg and the psychology of testimony: Being a report in the case of *Cokestone v. Munsterberg*. *Illinois Law Review, 3*, 399–445.

Wilson, D. P. (1951). *My six convicts: A psychologist's three years in Fort Leavenworth*. New York: Rinehart.

Wood, J. M., Nezworski, M. T., Garb, H. N., & Lilienfeld, S. O. (2001). The misperception of psychopathology: Problems with the norms of the Comprehensive System of the Rorschach. *Clinical Psychology, 8*, 350–373.

Wood, J. M., Nezworski, M. T., Stejskal, W., & McKinzey, R. (2001). Problems of the Comprehensive System for the Rorschach in forensic settings: Recent developments. *Journal of Forensic Psychology Practice, 1*, 89–103.

Wright v. Paul Revere Life Insurance Company, 294 F. Supp. 2d 1104, C. D. Cal. (2003).

Wyatt v. Stickney, 325 F.Supp. 781 (1971).

Zalewski, C., & Greene, R. L. (1996). Multicultural usage of the MMPI-2. In L. A. Suzuki, P. J. Meller, & G. Ponterotto (Eds.), *Handbook of multicultural assessment: Clinical, psychological and educational applications* (pp. 77–114). San Francisco: Jossey-Bass.

Zapf, P. A., Golding, S. L., & Roesch, R. (2006). Criminal responsibility and the insanity defense. In I. B. Weiner & A. K. Hess (Eds.), *Handbook of forensic psychology* (3rd ed., pp. 332–364). Hoboken, NJ: Wiley.

Zapf, P. A., & Roesch, R. (2006). Competence to stand trial: A guide for evaluators. In I. B. Weiner & A. K. Hess (Eds.), *Handbook of forensic psychology* (3rd ed., pp. 305–331). Hoboken, NJ: Wiley.

PART II

Forensic Assessment Methodology

CHAPTER 2

A Principles-Based Approach to Forensic Mental Health Assessment: Utility and Update

Kirk Heilbrun, Geoffrey Marczyk, David DeMatteo, and Jenette Mack-Allen

The past 2 decades have witnessed significant conceptual and empirical advances in the specialty of forensic mental health assessment (FMHA; Grisso, 1986, 2003; Heilbrun, 2001; Heilbrun, Marczyk, & DeMatteo, 2002; Melton, Petrila, Poythress, & Slobogin, 1997). These advances have occurred at the theoretical, research, and applied levels of forensic assessment and result from a number of influences. Examples of such influences include increased recognition of forensic specialization by the legal system, evolving ethical and legal demands consistent with such specialization, interdisciplinary collaboration between subspecialties within psychology, the recognition of forensic psychology as an American Psychological Association (APA) specialization, and programmatic research funded by grants and foundations. Each of these influences has helped to improve the accuracy and effectiveness of FMHA.

NATURE AND DERIVATION OF FORENSIC MENTAL HEALTH ASSESSMENT PRINCIPLES

Forensic mental health assessment refers to psychological evaluations that are performed by mental health professionals (typically psychologists, psychiatrists, and social workers) to provide relevant clinical and functional-legal information to a legal decision-maker. Forensic mental health assessment is distinct from therapeutic mental health assessment, as the latter is performed primarily for diagnosis and treatment planning. There are a number of specific ways in which forensic and therapeutic assessment differ. Understanding these differences helps to explain and justify a broad set of principles that encompass a wide range of legal questions and forensic issues (Heilbrun, 2001, 2003; Heilbrun, DeMatteo, & Marczyk, 2004; Heilbrun et al., 2002, 2005; Heilbrun, Marczyk, et al., 2003; Marczyk, Heilbrun, DeMatteo, & Bell, 2003).

Forensic and Therapeutic Assessment: Relevant Differences

This section summarizes the differences between forensic and therapeutic assessment, which are discussed at length elsewhere (Heilbrun, 2001). The first difference is in purpose. The primary purpose of FMHA is to assist a legal decision maker or litigant's attorney by providing information about an individual's relevant capacities underlying the specific civil (e.g., child custody, personal injury) or criminal (e.g., competence to stand trial, sanity at the time of the offense) legal question at hand. Therapeutic evaluation, by contrast, is usually conducted to facilitate diagnosis and treatment.

The nature of the examiner-examinee relationship is another difference. In FMHA, the evaluator assumes an impartial stance that typically requires a higher standard for both relevance and documentation, with a primary emphasis on accuracy rather than the therapeutic interests of the client. Therapeutic assessment is conducted by an evaluator in a helping role, in which the best interests of the client are paramount and a more collaborative approach may be preferable.

The nature of the examiner-examinee relationship also has a direct bearing on the notification of purpose for the assessment. Forensic mental health assessment evaluations begin with a formal notification that describes the purpose of the assessment and the relationship between the examiner and examinee. This is to convey that the evaluator will be conducting the assessment at the request of a third party, such as the court or an attorney. This notification is particularly important because the evaluator is not representing the individual being assessed, and the results of the FMHA will not always be in the best interests of the examinee. This can be contrasted with therapeutic assessment, in which the evaluation is performed on behalf of the client to provide information intended to facilitate mental health treatment.

The standards used in forensic and therapeutic assessment are also distinct. Standards in therapeutic assessment promote diagnosis and treatment, and serve organizing, condensing, and orienting functions (Heilbrun, 2001). These mental health standards are more circumscribed than those considered in FMHA. Unlike therapeutic assessment, however, FMHA requires the evaluator to address both a mental health and a legal standard. For example, an evaluation to assess competence to stand trial requires the forensic evaluator to consider the capacities relevant to the legal standard: whether the individual understands the nature of the charges and can assist counsel in his or her own defense. Mental health symptoms might also be a factor in this kind of evaluation. The presence of a serious mental disorder, for instance, might have a direct impact on the individual's legally relevant capacities.

Another important difference between FMHA and therapeutic assessment involves the sources of information used in each. The two kinds of evaluation share some common data sources, including clinical data and psychosocial information. The most common sources of such information are self-report, psychological testing, and behavioral assessment (Heilbrun, 2001). Although these sources are typically sufficient for therapeutic assessment, additional information must be used in forensic evaluations. The more rigorous demands of FMHA require the use of collateral information (e.g., document review, interviews; see Heilbrun, Warren, & Picarello, 2003) to assess the accuracy and consistency of response style and other information provided in the evaluation.

Although important to the overall accuracy of the evaluation, collateral information is particularly valuable in assessing the response style of the individual being evaluated in a forensic context. Response style refers to the nature and accuracy of the information provided by individuals being evaluated regarding their own thoughts, feelings, and behaviors (Rogers, 1997). In most therapeutic evaluations, it is not necessary to consider the possibility of deliberate distortion of self-report through exaggeration or minimization of certain symptoms or experiences. In FMHA, however, there is a consistent expectation that the individual being assessed might attempt to dissimulate. This consistent presence of situational incentives, and their potential impact on response style in the context of litigation, further distinguishes forensic from therapeutic evaluation (Heilbrun, 2001).

Clarifying the reasoning and the limits on knowledge also differs between forensic and therapeutic evaluation. Therapeutic evaluations tend to be collaborative and based on the training, theoretical orientation, professional expertise, and knowledge of the evaluator. Given this, there is little expectation that the assumptions and methods used to complete such evaluations will be challenged, except under unusual circumstances. The opposite is true in the FMHA context. Forensic evaluations are conducted in an adversarial legal context, subject to challenge through rules of evidence or by cross-examination by opposing counsel. Accordingly, there is the expectation that relevant assumptions and methods will be challenged, particularly in *Daubert* (1993) jurisdictions.

Differences between forensic and therapeutic assessment are also apparent in the documentation and communication of results, typically through reports and testimony. Given the wide range of theoretical approaches and specializations among clinicians, as well as the variety of available assessment instruments, there are no firmly established expectations about the structure, format, level of detail, and content of the written report documenting a therapeutic evaluation. Conversely, expectations regarding the documentation and communication of forensic evaluation results are far more extensive. Forensic reports tend to be lengthy and detailed because the legal issue being considered, and the demand for material relevant to preparing a challenge, require extensive documentation that clearly describes the procedures, findings, and reasoning used in the assessment (Heilbrun, 2001). There is a comparable distinction between the two types of evaluation in the expectation of expert testimony. Only rarely will a therapeutic evaluation be entered into evidence in a legal proceeding, so the likelihood of having to provide testimony is small (and would more appropriately be presented as fact than expert testimony in the rare instances in which it is introduced into a legal proceeding). By contrast, the forensic evaluator should always anticipate that testimony will be associated with the assessment.

The process that guides forensic assessment also differs substantially from therapeutic assessment. Therapeutic assessments tend to be shaped by the theoretical orientation of the practitioner without the explicit expectation of challenge to the methods employed. In contrast, FMHA is associated with the expectation of challenge, so psychometric considerations such as normative data, reliability, validity, sensitivity, and specificity become more prominent.

Taken independently and as a whole, these distinctions suggest that any set of general principles that guide therapeutic assessment will be insufficient when applied to FMHA (Heilbrun, 2001).

Improving the Quality and Consistency of Forensic Mental Health Assessments through a Principle-Centered Approach

This discussion of the distinction between forensic and therapeutic assessment highlights the need for a principle-centered approach specific to FMHA. We now describe how a set of principles of FMHA can improve the quality and consistency of forensic assessment. Ultimately, the application of these principles should help to minimize arbitrariness in the legal decision-making process by promoting thoroughness, consistency, clarity, and impartiality.

This principle-centered approach to FMHA holds considerable promise for improving the quality of forensic practice; it has value at both a broad and a specific level of analysis. At the broadest level, these principles could serve three important functions. The first concerns the training of mental health professionals in the understanding and practice of FMHA. This "broad principles" model would provide trainees with a generalizable approach to FMHA that would also allow subsequent development of expertise with specific populations (e.g., adult offenders, juveniles, families) and legal issues (e.g., trial competence, sentencing, juvenile transfer, child custody).

Second, the application of core principles should have a positive impact on research and theory development in forensic assessment. Some of the principles described in this chapter have limited empirical support because little or no relevant research has been conducted. Such research could clarify the importance and appropriate application of these principles, and contribute to theory development and refinement in FMHA. Research might provide empirical support for some principles but not for others. In this event, modifications to the core principles would be needed to reflect changing patterns of empirical evidence. Some principles might be amended or dropped, others might be retained intact, and new principles might emerge. However these principles evolve, having a core set of principles can also serve as an essential step in the larger process of theory development.

These principles can also be instrumental in addressing more narrowly focused research questions within the field of FMHA. The rigor of FMHA requires the careful consideration of data sources. Some of the principles focus on the use of idiographic and nomothetic data and the use of scientific reasoning. Research in this area could focus on how such evidence and reasoning are actually applied in the context of FMHA. In addition, these principles could serve as a basis for providing empirical descriptions of normative FMHA practice. This avenue might be especially important given the relative paucity of empirical evidence on how FMHA is actually performed across a variety of settings. On a related note, the principles could be used to investigate and define empirical descriptions of desirable FMHA practice, including approaches that have not yet been discussed in the literature. The establishment of guidelines for normative and effective forensic practice also has research implications for assessing the impact of specialized training and measuring FMHA quality. Finally, the principles could be used in organizational-level research on the quality of reports. For example, the principles might provide a framework for improving the reporting of data to agency administrators, forensic directors, or legislators.

There are two additional points related to report quality: (1) how these principles might relate to a standard of practice in FMHA; and (2) whether such principles can reasonably be implemented in settings with limited resources. There are different kinds of professional standards, some describing the basic minimum needed and others offering an ideal to which evaluators should aspire (Grisso, 2005). In some respects, the FMHA principles described in this chapter seem to document basic minimum standards. Principles 1, 6, 10, 12 through 14, 16 through 17, 20, 25, 26, and 28, in particular, seem to describe procedures absent which an evaluation would not be minimally adequate (see Table 2.1 for a listing of all principles). Other principles, however, can be interpreted across a wider spectrum, the upper part of which would represent the aspirational level of the standard. Those conducting and supervising evaluations in settings with limited resources might reasonably decide to incorporate all basic principles into their assessments and conduct a cost-benefit analysis to decide which remaining (more aspirational) principles should also be used for guidance in that particular setting, given available resources.

Third, such principles are relevant to policy. A broad set of principles could help in shaping or interpreting legislation, legal standards, or administrative code relevant to FMHA. Similarly, a set of general principles could also guide the development and implementation of policy intended to promote consistency and quality in FMHA (Heilbrun, 2001). For example, legislators might consider the particular content of FMHA and associated time expected in specifying what information courts should receive and how much evaluators should be paid when such evaluations are publicly funded.

Theoretically, such principles can improve the quality of FMHA when properly applied. Poorly conducted FMHA in an adversarial context is particularly problematic, given the importance and possible consequences of litigation. Poor assessments may fail to address the appropriate legal standard; exceed the scope of the evaluation and yield opinions that invade the province of the legal decision-maker; or fail to provide adequate, credible information consistent with the conclusions drawn from the results of the evaluation (Grisso, 1986, 2003). A general set of principles would provide guidance for avoiding such problems (Heilbrun, 2001; Heilbrun et al., 2002).

We next briefly summarize each of the 29 principles, which are described in detail elsewhere (Heilbrun, 2001). We then comment on recent applications and developments and elaborate on the utility of a principles-based approach to FMHA.

Deriving Principles of Forensic Mental Health Assessment

Until recently, there was no set of sufficiently broad principles that could be applied to the shared features of different types of FMHA, although some clinical-legal scholars (e.g., Melton et al., 1997) have described principles of forensic assessment applicable to specific types of FMHA. Despite the usefulness of their detailed descriptions and recommendations, a set of general principles broadly applicable to FMHA was still needed. Heilbrun (2001) provided a detailed description of such a set of broadly applicable principles.

The 29 principles of FMHA identified and described by Heilbrun (2001) are organized sequentially around the four broad stages within FMHA: (1) preparation,

Table 2.1   Principles of Forensic Mental Health Assessment

Preparation

1. Identify relevant forensic issues
2. Accept referrals only within area of expertise
3. Decline the referral when evaluator impartiality is unlikely
4. Clarify the evaluator's role with the attorney
5. Clarify financial arrangements
6. Obtain appropriate authorization
7. Avoid playing the dual role of therapist and forensic evaluator
8. Determine the particular role to be played within the forensic assessment if the referral is accepted
9. Select the most appropriate model to guide data gathering, interpretation, and communication

Data Collection

10. Use multiple sources of information for each area being assessed
11. Use relevance and reliability (validity) as guides for seeking information and selecting data sources
12. Obtain relevant historical information
13. Assess clinical characteristics in relevant, reliable, and valid ways
14. Assess legally relevant behavior
15. Ensure that conditions for the evaluation are quiet, private, and distraction-free
16. Provide appropriate notification of purpose and/or obtain appropriate authorization before beginning
17. Determine whether the individual understands the purpose of the evaluation and the associated limits on confidentiality

Data Interpretation

18. Use third-party information in assessing response style
19. Use testing when indicated in assessing response style
20. Use case-specific (idiographic) evidence in assessing clinical condition, functional abilities, and causal connection
21. Use nomothetic evidence in assessing causal connection between clinical condition and functional abilities
22. Use scientific reasoning in assessing causal connection between clinical condition and functional abilities
23. Do not answer the ultimate legal question
24. Describe findings and limits so that they need change little under cross-examination

Communication

25. Attribute information to sources
26. Use plain language; avoid technical jargon
27. Write report in sections, according to model and procedures
28. Base testimony on the results of the properly performed FMHA
29. Testify effectively

Source: From *Principles of Forensic Mental Health Assessment,* by K. Heilbrun, 2001, New York: Kluwer Academic/Plenum Press.

(2) data collection, (3) data interpretation, and (4) communication (see Table 2.1). Each principle was discussed with respect to the support that it received from four sources of authority: ethics, law, science, and practice. The major sources of *ethical* authority were the ethical standards for psychology ("Ethical Principles of Psychologists and Code of Conduct," APA, 1992), the ethical guidelines for forensic psy-

chology ("Specialty Guidelines for Forensic Psychologists," Committee on Ethical Guidelines for Forensic Psychologists, 1991), the ethical standards for psychiatry (*Principles of Medical Ethics with Annotations Especially Applicable to Psychiatry,* American Psychiatric Association, 1998), and the ethical guidelines in forensic psychiatry (*Ethical Guidelines for the Practice of Forensic Psychiatry,* American Academy of Psychiatry and the Law, 1995). Support from *legal* sources of authority was analyzed by examining federal case law (federal appellate and U.S. Supreme Court cases), federal statutes and administrative regulations, and model mental health law (e.g., *Criminal Justice Mental Health Standards,* American Bar Association, 1989). *Scientific* support was assessed by reviewing the relevant behavioral science and medical literature, with particular attention on well-designed empirical studies. Finally, the *practice* criterion considered the extent to which each principle is recognized by various authors, organizations, and other contributors to the professional literature as being important or useful for the practice of FMHA.

Based on an analysis using these sources of authority, Heilbrun (2001) classified each principle as either established or emerging. *Established* principles are largely supported by research, accepted in practice, and consistent with ethical and legal standards; *emerging* principles are supported in some areas, but with mixed or no evidence in others, or partly supported but with continuing disagreement regarding their application (Heilbrun, 2001). Principles 4, 8, 9, 19, and 23 (see Table 2.1) were classified as emerging; the remainder were considered established. The 29 principles can be summarized as follows:

1. *Identify relevant forensic issues.* This principle is concerned with the relevant capacities and behaviors that are to be evaluated as part of the assessment. It distinguishes the broader legal question, which is decided by the court in the course of the litigation, from the more specific forensic issues, which are the capacities and abilities included in the legal question.

2. *Accept referrals only within area of expertise.* This principle underscores the importance of two aspects of expertise in FMHA: (a) clinical and didactic training and experience with populations similar to the individual(s) being evaluated, and (b) previous application of this expertise in a forensic context. More specific indicators such as training, licensure, and board certification may provide additional bases for judging forensic expertise, but it is often important to document experience in the form of the curriculum vitae and a description of comparable forensic cases in which assessment has been conducted.

3. *Decline the referral when evaluator impartiality is unlikely.* This principle stresses the importance of impartiality in FMHA. In this context, impartiality involves the absence of personal beliefs or circumstances that could significantly interfere with the evaluator's effort to be fair and even-handed in collecting data and drawing conclusions. When there are substantial barriers to such impartiality, whether personal, professional, or monetary, this principle would suggest that the forensic clinician decline involvement in that particular case.

4. *Clarify the evaluator's role with the attorney.* This principle addresses the problem of multiple roles and the potentially harmful impact of filling more than one role in a single forensic case. The most common roles played by the evaluator in

forensic assessment are those of court-ordered evaluator, defense-, prosecution-, or plaintiff-requested evaluator, and consultant (Heilbrun, 2001). Playing more than one such role in a single case is potentially problematic; this principle underscores the importance of assuming and retaining a single role from the outset.

5. *Clarify financial arrangements.* Sometimes payment for FMHA is established in law or policy, and the fee is set. However, when there is discretion regarding the source and amount of payment (e.g., payment from a private attorney), it is important to clarify in advance (and in writing, if necessary) who will be responsible for payment, when, at what rate or total amount, and on what schedule.

6. *Obtain appropriate authorization.* There are two different forms of authorization that are obtained in the context of FMHA. The forensic clinician may need to obtain authorization from the court, or from the retaining attorney and client, depending on the role being played and who requested the evaluation. In court-ordered FMHA, the forensic clinician needs only a signed order from the court. Conversely, the forensic clinician needs authorization from both the referring attorney and the individual being evaluated when serving as an expert for the defense/prosecution/plaintiff.

7. *Avoid playing the dual roles of therapist and forensic evaluator.* Simultaneous or even sequential assumption of the roles of both therapist and forensic evaluator with the same individual has the potential to create substantial problems and should, accordingly, be avoided. In cases in which it cannot be avoided, this principle stresses the importance of explicit justification, advance planning, and clear notification to the individual(s) affected.

8. *Determine the particular role to be played within the forensic assessment if the referral is accepted.* Identifying a single role in FMHA and maintaining that role throughout the case are stressed in this principle. The forensic clinician should strive to maintain impartiality in any role that involves submitting a report and possibly testifying, whether that role is court-appointed or as an expert for a referring attorney. Part of maintaining an impartial stance involves addressing only the questions that are asked, thereby avoiding gratuitous opinions.

9. *Select the most appropriate model to guide data gathering, interpretation, and communication.* There are two models, one described by Morse (1978a, 1978b) and the other by Grisso (1986), that are most appropriate for guiding the conceptualization, procedure selection, interpretation of results, and reasoning in FMHA. Both models have a section in which "clinical condition" or "symptoms" are featured prominently; both emphasize the relationship between functional legal capacities and whatever causes deficits (e.g., symptoms of psychopathology, intellectual limitations) in such capacities when communicating the results of the evaluation.

10. *Use multiple sources of information for each area being assessed.* Litigation often increases the motivation of those involved to distort the accuracy of self-reported information. In addition, many psychological tests, structured clinical interviews, and other measures used in FMHA were initially developed and validated in nonforensic contexts. The use of a multimethod, multisource approach to assessing the important symptoms and capacities in forensic assessment is particularly important for these reasons. The use of three particular sources—self-report, formal tests and measures, and third-party information (both records and collateral

interviews)—is suggested. Consistency across sources makes it more likely that the agreed-upon information is accurate, whereas inconsistency across sources suggests the presence of inaccuracy in at least one source of information.

11. *Use relevance and reliability (validity) as guides for seeking information and selecting data sources.* Relevance to the legal question(s) and reliability (in a legal context, meaning both psychometric reliability and validity) are important elements of evidentiary law that are directly applicable to the admissibility and weight of expert testimony. Accordingly, this principle stresses both relevance and reliability in considering sources of information in FMHA. In practice, this principle emphasizes that data sources with demonstrated satisfactory levels of reliability and validity, particularly psychological tests (for which such information is often available), are preferable to poorly validated or unreliable sources (as courts in *Daubert* jurisdictions could, at their discretion, consider).

12. *Obtain relevant historical information.* Relevant historical information about the individual being evaluated is almost always essential in FMHA, and typically in greater detail than that needed in therapeutic evaluation. This varies according to the type of FMHA, however, with some evaluations (e.g., competence to consent to treatment) needing a reasonably circumscribed history, and others (e.g., capital sentencing) requiring a far broader focus.

13. *Assess clinical characteristics in relevant, reliable, and valid ways.* The decision about which clinical characteristics to assess, and how to assess them, is facilitated through the use of relevance and reliability as guides, according to this principle. More specifically, this principle calls for the use of appropriate measures, the results of which are weighed against findings from collateral sources.

14. *Assess legally relevant behavior.* This principle addresses the capacities and behavior related to the specific legal question(s) being addressed by the court, and is used to focus the assessment on these particular capacities. Relevance and reliability are useful in considering how to assess those functional legal capacities and behavior. For some forensic assessments, there are now validated tools that can be used to help the evaluator determine how the individual being evaluated compares with other such individuals on certain relevant legal capacities (e.g., the MacArthur Competence Assessment Tool—Criminal Adjudication for competence to stand trial, Poythress et al., 1999; the MacArthur Competence Assessment Tool for Treatment for competence to consent to treatment, Grisso & Appelbaum, 1998). For the majority of forensic issues that are assessed by evaluators, however, there is not yet a validated tool available to assist in this manner. In such cases, the evaluator must carefully identify the relevant functional demands associated with the legal question and obtain cognitive, affective, and behavioral data on the individual's capacities to meet such demands at the time specified by the parameters of the evaluation.

15. *Ensure that conditions for the evaluation are quiet, private, and distraction-free.* This principle describes the important balance between reasonable evaluation conditions—those in which noise and other distractions are limited, and the communication between evaluator and evaluee cannot be overheard—and other influences such as security. FMHA is sometimes conducted in correctional or secure psychiatric settings in which evaluation conditions in these areas are problematic,

and the evaluator must determine when they become sufficiently problematic to require a change or a postponement of the entire process.

16. *Provide appropriate notification of purpose and/or obtain appropriate authorization before beginning.* The forensic clinician provides a notification of purpose or obtains informed consent before beginning the FMHA. This principle emphasizes that one of these must be provided; which depends on the role being played and the nature of the associated authorization obtained. When an attorney retains a forensic clinician to evaluate the attorney's client, the evaluation is legally voluntary—the client has no legal obligation to participate—and informed consent should therefore be obtained before proceeding. By contrast, when conducting a court-ordered evaluation, the forensic clinician should notify the individual being evaluated about the nature and purpose of the evaluation, its authorization by the court, and the associated limits on confidentiality, including how the evaluation might be used. In a court-ordered context, however, the individual's participation in the evaluation is not voluntary, and the clinician provides notification of purpose but does not seek informed consent.

17. *Determine whether the individual understands the purpose of the evaluation and the associated limits on confidentiality.* The information communicated in the course of providing notification of purpose or obtaining informed consent must be understood for the notification or informed consent to be meaningful. To the extent that it is not, the notification or informed consent process becomes less meaningful. This principle stresses the importance of gauging how well such information has been understood and how the evaluator might proceed if the information was not well understood.

18. *Use third-party information in assessing response style.* Response style—whether an individual being evaluated is deliberately overreporting or exaggerating deficits, underreporting or minimizing such deficits, or trying to report them as accurately as possible—is particularly important in FMHA. This principle addresses the value of collateral interviews and records to help provide a description of history, clinical functioning, and functional legal capacities from multiple sources of information. When information from other sources is not consistent with self-report, then response style must be scrutinized with particular care.

19. *Use testing when indicated in assessing response style.* There are tests and measures that address response style across a variety of contexts and assessment issues. They may have been developed specifically to measure malingering (e.g., the Validity Indictor Profile, Frederick, 1997; the Structured Interview of Reported Symptoms, Rogers, 1992; the Test of Memory Malingering, Tombaugh, 1997) or have "validity indicators" built into their structure (e.g., the Minnesota Multiphasic Personality Inventory-2 [MMPI-2]; Butcher, Dahlstrom, Graham, Tellegen, & Kaemmer, 1989). This principle urges the use of tests and specialized measures whenever they are available and appropriate for the kind of potential distortion in response style that is being considered.

20. *Use case-specific (idiographic) evidence in assessing clinical condition, functional abilities, and causal connection.* Heilbrun (2001) asserted that science can be applied to FMHA in three ways: through using idiographic analysis, by considering nomothetic data, and with scientific reasoning. This principle describes the first: obtaining information specific to the case and present functioning of the individual

and comparing it to that individual's capacities and functioning at other times. This approach is consistent with the law's goal of individualized justice, so developing and presenting FMHA findings in this manner may have particular appeal to judges and attorneys.

21. *Use nomothetic evidence in assessing causal connection between clinical condition and functional abilities.* Science can also be applied to FMHA by considering empirical data applicable to populations similar to that of the individual being evaluated, and by using tests and instruments developed and validated on similar populations. Assessing forensic capacities with norm-referenced tools allows the evaluator and the legal decision maker to compare such measured capacities to those of individuals in "known groups." More specifically, the research supporting such tools allows evaluators to consider base rates, sensitivity, specificity, and the particular percentile at which an individual functions—all valuable aspects of prediction and comparison that are possible only through nomothetic approaches.

22. *Use scientific reasoning in assessing causal connection between clinical condition and functional abilities.* In some ways, FMHA procedures are comparable to those used in a scientific study. The results obtained from one source of information (e.g., interview) can be treated as "hypotheses to be verified" through further information obtained from additional sources of information. Such hypotheses could be generated theoretically, through behavioral observations, from computerized interpretation of actuarial testing, from a review of records, or from other sources. Accepting or rejecting hypotheses depending on whether they account for the most information with the simplest explanation applies the principle of parsimony. This principle suggests that scientific reasoning is a third important way in which science can contribute to the FMHA process.

23. *Do not answer the ultimate legal question.* This principle concerns the unsettled and often debated question of whether forensic evaluators should answer the ultimate legal question (the legal question to be decided by the judge or jury, such as a defendant's liability for a plaintiff's injury, and the associated damages). Some (e.g., Rogers & Ewing, 1989) have argued that many judges and attorneys expect the forensic clinician to offer an ultimate opinion (which, with few exceptions, is permitted by the evidentiary laws in most jurisdictions) and that there is little harm in doing so; others (e.g., Melton et al., 1997) emphasize the importance of the relevant included forensic capacities, but observe that the ultimate legal question, which includes moral, political, and community values, should not be the focus of the evaluation's conclusion.

24. *Describe findings and limits so that they need change little under cross-examination.* According to this principle, FMHA findings should be described carefully and thoroughly, supported by multiple sources of information, and be accompanied by acknowledgment of the limits on data accuracy and consistency. When this kind of critical scrutiny is applied to the results and reasoning that are communicated in the report, and subsequently in testimony, the forensic clinician can expect that the description of findings and conclusions will not change significantly during cross-examination.

25. *Attribute information to sources.* This principle emphasizes the importance of attributing all information in the FMHA report to specific source(s). This allows the evaluator to describe consistency (or inconsistency) across sources; it also

permits the judge and opposing counsel to gauge the credibility of any given information when it is linked to its source.

26. *Use plain language; avoid technical jargon.* It is unusual for consumers of FMHA—judges, attorneys, and jurors—to have specific training in the behavioral or medical sciences. For this reason alone, the communication of results without technical jargon is preferable; technical language may have a specific meaning that is quite different from everyday language. For example, rather than describing a defendant as "delusional," it would be preferable to indicate that one of his or her symptoms involved having false beliefs that are not bizarre (thereby making the further distinction between bizarre and nonbizarre delusions) but are nonetheless very unlikely to be true and appear to be a symptom of his or her disorder.

27. *Write report in sections, according to model and procedures.* The organization of the report into specific sections can communicate the application of many of these principles. The following sections have been suggested (Heilbrun, 2001): (a) *Referral* (with identifying information concerning the individual, his or her characteristics, the nature of the evaluation, and by whom it was requested or ordered); (b) *Procedures* (times and dates of the evaluation, tests or procedures used, different records reviewed, and third-party interviews conducted, as well as documentation of the notification of purpose or informed consent and the degree to which the information was apparently understood); (c) *Relevant History* (containing information from multiple sources describing areas important to the evaluation); (d) *Current Clinical Condition* (broadly considered to include appearance, mood, behavior, sensorium, intellectual functioning, thought, and personality); (e) *Forensic Capacities* (varying according to the nature of the legal questions); and (f) *Conclusions and Recommendations* (addressed to the relevant capacities rather than the ultimate legal questions).

28. *Base testimony on the results of the properly performed FMHA.* The FMHA report should document the substantive basis for an expert's testimony. This allows the referring attorney to present the expert's findings more effectively, the opposing attorney to challenge them, the judge and jury to understand them, and the expert to communicate them in a comprehensible, organized fashion.

29. *Testify effectively.* This principle describes both the substantive (covered by the previous principles) and stylistic aspects of expert testimony. Stylistic aspects concern how the expert speaks, dresses, responds to challenges, and otherwise behaves to make testimony clear and credible. When both substance and style of expert testimony are strong, testimony is maximally effective.

UTILITY OF A PRINCIPLES-BASED APPROACH

As part of this broader discussion, it is useful to consider the advantages and disadvantages of a principles-based approach to FMHA. These are addressed in this section.

The first advantage that may accrue from seeking and successfully identifying broad principles of FMHA involves forcing a consistent focus on all such principles, whether in assessment or research. In some respects, this advantage is comparable to that obtained from using structured approaches to diagnosis, decision making, and prediction. There is a significant amount of evidence from the decision-making literature demonstrating the superiority of structured over unstructured judgment in these tasks (Dawes, Faust, & Meehl, 1989; Grove, Zald, Lebow, Snitz, & Nelson, 2000). One need only review the changes in the *Diagnostic and Statistical Manual of Mental Disorders* from I to IV-Text Revision (American Psychiatric Association, 1980, 1987, 1994, 2000) to find evidence that the field has moved strongly in the direction of more structured approaches to mental health diagnosis, with greatly elaborated and more specific criteria in the areas of history/course of onset and currently experienced symptoms.

It is important to demonstrate that such principles have been derived from sources that are relevant and authoritative. The FMHA principles described in this chapter were obtained from a thorough review of the relevant legal, ethical, scientific, and practice literatures. It would be fair to consider these sources both relevant and authoritative for FMHA. Hence, principles derived from and weighed against such sources should represent constructs that are theoretically valuable, serving as a basis for practice guidance and a basis for operationalizing FMHA research variables to facilitate empirical research.

Given that these principles can provide a structured approach to viewing the FMHA process, and that the components of the structure have the value imbued by their derivation from relevant and authoritative sources, there is a resulting third advantage. This approach is likely to increase consistency in FMHA practice and consistency in research approaches to FMHA quality. Further, when principles are operationalized reliably, the entire core of principles should also provide a reliable tool for research on FMHA quality.

Such operationalization is essential if the FMHA process is to undergo validity testing on a large scale. It is certainly possible at present to develop and validate specific forensic assessment tools, much as it is possible to develop and test the efficacy of manualized therapeutic interventions. However, there may be an interest in the broader question as well. Does psychotherapy work? Is FMHA effective? Such questions create the risk of diluting the research question to a meaningless breadth—unless there is some way of describing the core parameters of the activity, which then would allow research to be conducted on FMHA that fell within those parameters.

Forensic mental health assessment principles may therefore provide a mechanism for systematic research on the larger process of forensic assessment. The questions posed as part of such research are consistent with a broader trend in medical and behavioral science involving empirically validated approaches to assessment and treatment. It should be noted, of course, that broad principles are only one approach to studying larger-scale forensic assessment questions. However, they do offer some real advantages, particularly if many of the needed research steps (discussed in the chapter's final section) can be taken in coming years.

Broad principles, and the principles-based approach involving their application, also have some disadvantages. The clearest disadvantage results from their breadth. Because such principles are necessarily written to apply to a wide range of FMHA, they lack the distinctive specificity that may be needed with a particular kind of assessment. Principles do not serve as the best guide to elicit particular data, describe specifically needed experience or knowledge, or otherwise illustrate the idiosyncratic parameters of certain kinds of evaluations. Rather, they can only prompt the evaluator or researcher to be mindful of these parameters.

Second, it is possible that FMHA principles do not generalize well to certain contexts or specific kinds of evaluations. In the next section, we describe certain populations and legal questions to which the generalizability of these broad principles seems reasonably good. However, there are a number of contexts that have not yet been analyzed in the way that we have considered sexual offenders, or neuropsychological populations, or capital sentencing (see next section). These contexts remain to be considered theoretically. Further, generalizability of broad principles has not yet been considered *empirically,* an important next step.

Related to the second disadvantage, these principles may be specific to the culture and legal systems from which they were derived almost exclusively—those of the United States and Canada. No work has yet been done to consider, either theoretically or empirically, how they might apply in other countries with very different cultures, with associated differences in legal and mental health systems. Until this work is done, such principles should not be considered necessarily applicable outside of the United States and Canada.

Finally, any set of principles (particularly when designed for broad applicability) may implicitly promise more than it can deliver. We are sufficiently concerned about this to caution the reader to consider FMHA principles as valuable only to the extent that they have been developed and discussed in areas that are specifically applicable to an FMHA of interest, and to regard them in some respects as a thorough review and condensation of relevant sources of authority in law, ethics, science, and practice. However, we are also cautiously optimistic that this set of principles can be put through the necessary derivation, theoretically analytic, and empirically validating steps that would allow them greater utility and applicability. The final two sections summarize what has been done to date in the theoretically analytic phase and describe the next steps that are needed to fully address the derivation, analysis, and validation steps.

APPLYING PRINCIPLES IN FORENSIC MENTAL HEALTH ASSESSMENT: AN UPDATE

After Heilbrun (2001) provided an initial description of the 29 principles of FMHA, an effort was made to demonstrate how these broad principles could be applied to various types of FMHA. Heilbrun et al. (2002) demonstrated how the principles could be applied to different types of FMHA across a range of legal questions in criminal, civil, and juvenile/family forensic contexts. Subsequent efforts have focused on demonstrating how the principles can be used to improve the overall quality of forensic practice (Heilbrun et al., 2004) and how they can be applied to specific offender and clinical populations (e.g., sexual offenders and neuropsychological populations; Heilbrun, 2003; Heilbrun, Marczyk, et al., 2003) and specific legal issues (e.g., capital sentencing; Heilbrun et al., 2005; Marczyk et al., 2003).

The following sections summarize the recent discussion regarding the application of the principles of FMHA to various populations and legal issues. As may be seen, the FMHA principles can be readily applied to specialized populations and specific legal questions, and therefore serve as useful guides when conducting FMHA in a variety of legal contexts.

Quality and Guidelines

One of the originally intended functions of the principles of FMHA was to promote the improvement of practice in the field of forensic psychology (Heilbrun, 2001). It was hoped that the description of a core set of principles applicable to various kinds of FMHA could potentially improve the quality of forensic practice by, among other things, providing guidance to forensic clinicians. Because the principles of FMHA are supported from major sources of authority in law, science, professional ethics, and standards for professional practice, we thought it possible that these principles could be used to derive a measure of the quality of the forensic evaluation report.

Accordingly, Heilbrun et al. (2004) recently described how the principles of FMHA could be used to improve the overall quality of forensic reports. In doing so, Heilbrun et al. also demonstrated how the application of the principles of FMHA to specific forensic reports could achieve some of the goals of *pragmatic psychology* (Fishman, 1999), which seeks to integrate both empirical procedures and the interpretations of individual behaviors in producing information that is useful to those who seek guidance from psychology. Fishman (1999, 2000) has advocated applying the pragmatic psychology approach in forensic psychology as a means of improving the quality of forensic practice (Slobogin, 2003).

Heilbrun et al. (2004) demonstrated how the principles of FMHA could serve as a guide to improve the overall quality of forensic practice, thereby achieving a primary goal of pragmatic psychology. Specifically, Heilbrun et al. addressed (a) how the FMHA principles could be used to guide the construction of a single case report, and (b) how the quality of existing forensic evaluation reports could be measured using the FMHA principles as quality indicators. Each of these objectives are briefly discussed.

Constructing Forensic Evaluation Reports

The principles of FMHA are applicable to the entire process of conducting a forensic assessment, from the initial referral to the communication of the results of the assessment in the form of testimony or in the written report. Heilbrun et al. (2004) recently demonstrated how these principles could be applied to writing the forensic evaluation report in a specific case. Each of the applicable principles (22 of the 29 principles are directly applicable to forensic evaluation report construction) was translated into a guideline that can be used to assist clinicians in writing a forensic evaluation report. The resulting guidelines constitute a set of criteria that can then be applied to conceptualizing, teaching, and constructing forensic evaluation reports.

Although a detailed analysis of each of the 22 principles applicable to report construction is beyond the scope of this chapter, we illustrate the application of several of the principles, and the guidelines derived from those principles, to the process of report construction. This section covers the principles that are most important to the process of report construction.

Principle 1: Identify relevant forensic issues. In every FMHA, the relevant forensic issues (i.e., capacities and abilities included within the larger legal question) must be identified in the accompanying report. The guideline associated with this principle would be to cite the legal question and the relevant forensic issues in the first section of the report.

Principle 6: Obtain appropriate authorization. This principle emphasizes the importance of citing the basis for the evaluation. For example, the evaluator should clearly indicate whether the evaluation was court-ordered or attorney-requested. The associated guideline involves citing the basis for the evaluation request and indicating whether informed consent was obtained if the evaluation was not court-ordered.

Principle 10: Use multiple sources of information for each area being assessed. This principle recognizes the importance of using multiple sources of information in ensuring accurate data interpretation and reasoning in FMHA. The associated guideline recommends obtaining data from multiple sources, including self-report, psychological testing, third-party interviews, and collateral records.

Principle 12: Obtain relevant historical information. Historical information provides a valuable context for the information contained in the clinical condition and forensic capacities sections of a report. Historical information relevant to the legal question should be included. The associated guideline recommends documenting the individual's history and previous functioning in areas relevant to current clinical condition and functional legal capacities.

Principle 15: Ensure that conditions for the evaluation are quiet, private, and distraction-free. The guideline associated with this principle recommends that the evaluator note any deviation from reasonably quiet, private, and distraction-free conditions, and describe any impact that the conditions might have had on the data collected. A forensic report should include some statement regarding the conditions under which the evaluation was conducted, even if no problems were encountered.

Principle 18: Use third-party information in assessing response style. In FMHA, the possibility that the individual being evaluated is deliberately overreporting or underreporting deficits must be considered. Therefore, evaluators are advised to gauge and describe the extent to which third-party information is consistent with self-reported information and to be cautious about relying on self-report data when they are significantly different from third-party accounts. Obviously, the presence of a great deal of third-party information facilitates assessing the response style of the individual being evaluated, and the response style should be explicitly addressed in the forensic evaluation report.

Principle 23: Do not answer the ultimate legal question. There is an ongoing debate in the field regarding whether FMHA should address primarily forensic issues or also include an opinion about the ultimate legal issue. Heilbrun (2001) recommended the former approach; evaluators are advised to present conclusions about forensic capacities, but not the larger legal question, whenever feasible.

Principle 25: Attribute information to sources. Virtually every sentence in a forensic evaluation report should indicate the source of the information being presented. In addition to allowing the reader to learn the source of all information contained in the report, it allows the opposing attorney to prepare to challenge the findings. Accordingly, evaluators are advised to describe data so that the sources of information are clear.

Principle 26: Use plain language; avoid technical jargon. Writing a report consistent with this principle certainly makes the findings clearer to those who are not trained in mental health specializations. However, there are additional advantages. Formulating findings without the assistance of technical language, with its built-in assumptions, allows such findings to be expressed more plainly—and perhaps reconsidered or rephrased by the evaluator if such clarity of expression is not supported by consistent evidence.

Principle 27: Write report in sections, according to model and procedures. A forensic evaluation report should typically include sections on referral information, sources of data, relevant history, clinical functioning, relevant functional legal capacities, and conclusions. Writing a report in sections allows the reader to follow the progression from history to current clinical condition and their causal relationship to forensic capacities.

A total of 22 principles are directly relevant to report construction. Because of current space limitations, we have mentioned only some of these. A fuller discussion is available elsewhere (Heilbrun et al., 2004).

Measuring the Quality of Forensic Evaluation Reports

In addition to shaping the construction of a forensic report in a single case, FMHA principles could be applied toward measuring the quality of existing forensic reports (Heilbrun et al., 2004). There are, of course, important methodological issues that would need to be addressed in developing a rating system for forensic reports (e.g., nature of the rating system, interrater reliability for items requiring judgment). However, assuming these methodological issues could be addressed, the principles could be used to provide several different levels of quality ratings for forensic reports. For example, they could yield an overall global rating of the quality of the report, or quality ratings of different aspects of the report. Because these principles are fairly generic, they should be applicable across different types of FMHA evaluations, jurisdictions, and evaluators.

Sexual Offenders

Heilbrun (2003) has also demonstrated how the principles of FMHA can be applied to forensic assessments performed with sexual offenders. Forensic evaluations of sexual offenders may be conducted for a variety of reasons. For example, in many jurisdictions, being classified as a violent sexual predator results in an enhanced sentence, and clinicians are increasingly being called on by courts (or state panels) to assist in these classification determinations. Many jurisdictions also have sexually violent predator laws that provide for the civil commitment and long-term care of certain sex offenders upon completion of a term of incarceration (Boardman & DeMatteo, 2003; Conroy, 2003; see *Kansas v. Hendricks,* 1997). Clinicians may therefore be asked to conduct an evaluation to determine whether postsentence commitment would be appropriate for a particular sexual offender. In the alternative, a clinician may be asked to assess whether a release from postsentence commitment is appropriate in a given case.

The application of the FMHA principles can offer substantial guidance in the forensic evaluation of sexual offenders. In consideration of our finite space for this chapter, we again describe only a subset of the applicable principles, focusing on those that seem most relevant in the context of FMHA with sexual offenders, to illustrate the use of these principles.

Principle 2: Accept referrals only within area of expertise. This principle is particularly important when working with specialized offender populations such as sexual offenders. Forensic expertise is based on training and experience with populations similar to that of the individual being evaluated, and experience applying this expertise in conducting forensic assessments. The associated guideline involves documenting the evaluator's expertise by citing relevant degrees, licensure, and board certification. Evaluators should also ensure that their curriculum vitae includes specific information about clinical and forensic experience with sexual offenders. Finally, the evaluator should provide information describing the basis for the appointment. For example, in some jurisdictions, evaluators are appointed from a panel (as opposed to being attorney-requested or court-ordered), so it may be useful to indicate the basis of one's appointment.

Principle 3: Decline the referral when evaluator impartiality is unlikely. As in any FMHA, an evaluator should avoid involvement in cases in which there is a substantial incentive (personal, financial, or professional) for the evaluator to have a case decided in a particular direction. When conducting an evaluation of a sexual offender, this principle takes on added importance, because sexual offenders may evoke strongly negative reactions. Therefore, evaluators should monitor their own personal and professional reactions to the punishment and treatment of sexual offenders.

Principle 8: Determine the particular role to be played within the forensic assessment if the referral is accepted. Clinicians should choose one role—expert or consultant—in the beginning of the case, and maintain that role throughout their involvement in the case. When working with sexual offenders, this principle emphasizes that evaluators must be careful to avoid addressing treatment needs unless they are among the specific forensic issues being evaluated.

Principle 12: Obtain relevant historical information. When conducting an evaluation of a sexual offender, it is important to include historical information regarding both healthy and deviant sexual behavior.

Principle 13: Assess clinical characteristics in relevant, reliable, and valid ways. In evaluating a sexual offender, "clinical characteristics" must be defined broadly to include patterns of thinking, feeling, arousal, and behavior associated with sexual offending.

Principle 14: Assess legally relevant behavior. This principle refers to the capacities and behavior that are contained within the larger legal question that triggered the FMHA. When conducting a forensic evaluation of a sexual offender, it is crucial to address the individual's reoffense risk. It is important, however, to distinguish between risk of reoffending for any kind of offense, and risk of sexual reoffending.

Principle 17: Determine whether the individual understands the purpose of the evaluation and the associated limits on confidentiality. In evaluations with sexual offenders, there is a danger that the individual may not understand the distinction between a forensic assessment and an assessment done for diagnostic or treatment-planning purposes. This may be particularly true if the individual has a history of involvement in specialized treatment for sexual offending. Therefore, evaluators must be careful to underscore the distinction between forensic evaluations and other evaluations, and document the individual's apparent understanding of the distinction. It is important that the individual understand that the evaluation is being conducted for forensic purposes only.

Principle 18: Use third-party information in assessing response style. When working with sexual offenders, an evaluator should anticipate the potential underreporting of sexual offending by the individual being evaluated because of the private aspect of such behavior and the sensitive nature of the information. Moreover, sexual offending, and its related risk factors, is typically less observable to third parties than the symptoms of mental illness. To address this problem, evaluators should focus on behaviors that are more observable, but still meaningful, in the context of an evaluation with a sexual offender.

Principle 19: Use testing when indicated in assessing response style. The use of psychological tests and specialized measures can be helpful in assessing an individual's response style. The results of such testing allow the evaluator to determine how heavily to rely on self-report data in the course of the assessment. When conducting FMHA with a sexual offender, the evaluator should consider using specialized measures that are particularly applicable to sexual offenders, particularly measures that are sensitive to defensiveness (underreporting of symptoms; see Conroy, 2003).

Principle 20: Use case-specific (idiographic) evidence in assessing clinical condition, functional abilities, and causal connection. When conducting a forensic evaluation of a sexual offender, clinical condition must be interpreted broadly to include all aspects of personality and behavior relevant to sexual offending.

Principle 21: Use nomothetic evidence in assessing causal connection between clinical condition and functional abilities. When conducting a sexual offender evaluation, it is important to use tests and measures that have been specifically validated with sexual offenders.

Principle 22: Use scientific reasoning in assessing causal connection between clinical condition and functional abilities. As with Principle 20, clinical condition should be interpreted sufficiently flexibly to include characteristics and behavior particularly relevant to sexual offending.

As may be seen, the principles of FMHA can be applied to the forensic evaluation of sexual offenders, a specialized type of FMHA. Although it was necessary to slightly modify some of the principles before they could be applied to the forensic evaluation of sexual offenders—for example, broadly interpreting clinical condition to include aspects of sexual functioning and modifying the types of assessment tools used (i.e., using tools validated for sexual offenders)—it appears that the principles can offer substantial guidance when conducting forensic evaluations with this specialized population.

Neuropsychological Populations and Questions

A neuropsychological assessment can be conceptualized as a method of examining the brain by studying its behavioral product (Heilbrun, Marczyk, et al., 2003). As with other psychological assessments, neuropsychological evaluations involve the systematic study of behavior by using standardized tests that provide relatively sensitive indices of brain-behavior relationships. In particular, neuropsychological tests are sensitive to the organic integrity of the cerebral hemispheres, and they are used to pinpoint specific neurological or psychological deficits (Zillmer, 2003).

Because neuropsychological assessments are objective and quantitative, they have proven valuable in litigation by providing information to the judge or jury regarding the determination, effects, and prognosis of brain dysfunction. Neuropsychological assessments provide a comprehensive description of the cognitive, behavioral, and emotional sequelae of a variety of neuropsychological conditions for purposes of legal decision making. As a result, neuropsychologists are increasingly being asked to conduct forensic assessments in personal injury, disability determination, and worker's compensation cases. Forensic neuropsychology is a rapidly growing subspecialty of neuropsychology, with approximately 7% of all neuropsychological evaluations being forensic in nature (Zillmer & Spiers, 2001). Therefore, it would be useful to consider how well the principles of FMHA and their associated guidelines apply specifically to forensic neuropsychological evaluations. Recently, Heilbrun, Marczyk, et al. (2003) applied the FMHA principles to neuropsychological assessments in forensic contexts. A brief summary follows.

> *Principle 2: Accept referrals only within area of expertise.* This principle is particularly important when conducting a forensic neuropsychological evaluation. Evaluators should ensure that their curriculum vitae reflects their training and experience in conducting neuropsychological assessments in clinical and forensic contexts.

> *Principle 11: Use relevance and reliability (validity) as guides for seeking information and selecting data sources.* In the forensic neuropsychological context, it is important that evaluators provide a theoretical and empirical justification for using particular neuropsychological measures to assess specific functions. Neuropsychologists often assess a number of cognitive areas, including orientation, sensation and perception, attention/concentration, visual-spatial organization, memory, and judgment, and there are specialized measures and assessment techniques for each of these functions. It is important that evaluators be aware of the psychometric properties of each of the assessment approaches used.

> *Principle 12: Obtain relevant historical information.* Evaluators should include history that may provide useful information regarding the nature and possible

causes of the brain dysfunction being assessed. Some evaluations may require a pre/postanalysis of symptoms, behaviors, and particular performance (e.g., school, occupational) when there is a specific injury that is the focus of the litigation, so it is particularly important to obtain historical information regarding relevant functioning prior to the event in question. Documenting a decline in functioning in this manner can be valuable in identifying potential cause(s) of an individual's brain dysfunction.

Principle 17: Determine whether the individual understands the purpose of the evaluation and the associated limits on confidentiality. When there are potential deficits in neuropsychological functioning, it is possible that individuals being evaluated will have more difficulty understanding the purpose of the evaluation or providing informed consent. Accordingly, it is particularly important that the evaluator describe and document how such information was apparently understood by the individual.

Principle 18: Use third-party information in assessing response style. Because neuropsychological assessments rely predominantly on testing to measure neuropsychological deficits, it is important to consider whether the assessment instruments have built-in validity indicators sensitive to overreporting and underreporting. If the assessment instruments lack validity indicators, the use of third-party information takes on increased importance as a means of assessing the consistency of self-report and measured functioning with other information regarding such functioning.

Principle 20: Use case-specific (idiographic) evidence in assessing clinical condition, functional abilities, and causal connection. When conducting an FMHA in the context of personal injury litigation, the evaluator should conduct a pre/postanalysis of the nature of the individual's neuropsychological deficits and related functional abilities prior to and following the trauma. In this manner, the evaluator is comparing the individual's present neuropsychological functioning to his or her previous level of functioning.

Principle 26: Use plain language; avoid technical jargon. This principle is particularly important in the context of forensic neuropsychological assessments. The field of neuropsychology necessarily includes a large number of technical terms, and it may be difficult to communicate neuropsychological findings without using some technical language. However, the technical language used in neuropsychology may be difficult to understand for those without neuropsychological training, including most judges, attorneys, and jurors. Therefore, if the use of technical terms cannot be avoided in a forensic evaluation report or testimony, it is important to define the terms in a manner that can be easily understood by laypersons.

The preceding would suggest that FMHA principles appear to fit well within the specialized context of forensic neuropsychological assessments. The majority of principles required little modification to be applicable to forensic neuropsychology, and the application of these principles should provide a useful framework for those conducting forensic neuropsychological evaluations.

Capital Sentencing

In *Atkins v. Virginia* (2002), the Supreme Court of the United States held that executing mentally retarded defendants constitutes cruel and unusual punishment in violation of the 8th Amendment to the U.S. Constitution. The *Atkins* decision underscored the need for mental health professionals to conduct FMHAs of capital defendants to assist the trier of fact in determining whether the defendant is mentally retarded and, therefore, ineligible for the death penalty. In a recent article, Heilbrun et al. (2005) demonstrated how the FMHA principles could be used to improve the quality and consistency of FMHAs conducted post-*Atkins,* and for capital cases more generally in which the presence of mental retardation is not necessarily an issue (or at least not the primary issue).

Of particular importance, the application of the FMHA principles is consistent with the guidelines and substantive criteria for capital mitigation first articulated by the U.S. Supreme Court in *Furman v. Georgia* (1972). In response to the *Furman* decision, which abolished the death penalty on 8th Amendment grounds, modern death penalty statutes typically specify aggravating and mitigating factors designed to assist juries in reaching a sentencing decision in a capital case. The application of the FMHA principles should minimize arbitrariness in the decision-making process by promoting thoroughness, consistency, clarity, and impartiality. We now provide an examination of some of the FMHA principles most relevant to *Atkins* evaluations and to capital sentencing evaluations more generally. (For a discussion of relevant case law and application of forensic assessment to address factors in capital sentencing, see, for example, Cunningham & Goldstein, 2003.)

Principle 1: Identify relevant forensic issues. It is important to cite the capacities and abilities underlying the ultimate legal question. In a capital sentencing evaluation generally, the capacities would be enumerated by the aggravating and mitigating factors that are appropriate for expert mental health evaluation, as opposed to the aggravating and mitigating factors for which forensic clinicians provide no special expertise (e.g., history of offending, heinousness of offense). In an *Atkins* evaluation, however, the focus of the evaluation is exclusively diagnostic, because the presence of mental retardation makes the offender ineligible for a death sentence.

Principle 2: Accept referrals only within area of expertise. Clinicians conducting capital sentencing evaluations should have experience with offenders and individuals with severe mental illness, whereas clinicians conducting *Atkins* evaluations should have experience with individuals who are developmentally disabled. For either type of evaluation, the clinician should have experience applying this expertise in forensic contexts.

Principle 6: Obtain appropriate authorization. There are important distinctions between *Atkins* evaluations and broader capital sentencing evaluations; these distinctions result from the type of information sought in each type of evaluation. The focus of an *Atkins* evaluation is determining whether the defendant is mentally retarded, which requires data on intellectual functioning, adaptive functioning, and evidence of a previous diagnosis of mental retardation. As such, the evaluation is largely present-focused and does not necessarily obtain information about the defendant's thinking, behavior, and functioning at the time of the offense. By contrast, a capital sentencing evaluation typically requires addressing several factors associated with the defendant's mental state at the time of the offense, and is therefore predominantly focused on the past. It is often difficult to obtain information, on a pretrial basis, about the defendant's thinking, emotions, perceptions, and behavior at the time of the offense because many defendants deny or minimize their culpability. In a capital sentencing evaluation, the notification of purpose must distinguish between the defendant's legal right to assert innocence until proven guilty, exercised preadjudication, and the defendant's interest in providing information regarding mental state at the time of the offense, potentially useful in mitigation, which would nevertheless be used only at sentencing if the defendant has been convicted.

Principle 9: Select the most appropriate model to guide data gathering, interpretation, and communication. As noted previously, the Morse (1978a, 1978b) and Grisso (1986, 2003) models are useful in helping to structure the data gathering, interpretation and reasoning, and communication of the results of a forensic evaluation. Two components shared by both models are (a) the functional legal capacities underlying the legal question, and (b) the causal connection between deficits in such functional legal capacities and the potential sources of these deficits. These models apply quite differently to *Atkins* assessments and capital sentencing FMHAs. Because the sole question in an *Atkins* evaluation is whether the defendant meets diagnostic criteria for mental retardation, the diagnostic/symptomatic and functional legal criteria are the same, and there is no demand for a description of the functional legal capacities underlying the larger legal question. (The functional legal criteria should not be confused with the functional criteria that are part of the diagnosis of mental retardation, with the former typically emphasizing areas such as knowing and capacities to conform conduct and the latter describing skills in daily living activities.) By contrast, in a capital sentencing evaluation, diagnostic/symptomatic criteria are distinct from functional legal criteria, and use of the Morse or Grisso model can help to identify these two domains distinctly.

Principle 11: Use relevance and reliability (validity) as guides for seeking information and selecting data sources. The scope of an *Atkins* evaluation is quite circumscribed, and an evaluator relies largely on conventional diagnostic measures, such as IQ tests and adaptive behavior scales, that have been developed and validated for assessing mental retardation (e.g., the Wechsler Adult Intelligence Scale-III, Wechsler, 1997; the American Association on Mental Retardation Adaptive Behavior Scale-Residential and Community, second edition, Nihira, Leland, & Lambert, 1993). By contrast, capital sentencing evaluations require the assessment of data relevant to mental state at the time of the offense and other domains that encompass thinking, perception, and judgment, for which there are fewer well-validated tools available. As a result, the evaluator must employ more sources of information, judge the credibility of sources that have no formal validation (e.g., third-party interviews), and gauge the consistency of findings across sources rather than relying more heavily on fewer but well-validated sources.

Principle 13: Assess clinical characteristics in relevant, reliable, and valid ways. When conducting an *Atkins* evaluation, it is important to use standardized, validated, and reliable measures of intellectual functioning and adaptive behavior that are used to assess mental retardation. In a capital sentencing evaluation, the domain of clinical symptoms and personal characteristics is much broader, but it is still important to use psychological measures that have been developed for the purposes for which they are being used. (For example, when using the MMPI-2, it is important to use the norms applicable to correctional populations.)

Principle 14: Assess legally relevant behavior. There is a substantial difference between the legally relevant behavior that must be assessed in an *Atkins* evaluation versus what must be addressed in a capital sentencing evaluation. The sole legal question in an *Atkins* evaluation is whether the defendant is mentally retarded and therefore ineligible for the death penalty. In the context of a capital sentencing evaluation, however, the evaluator typically must address several factors, such as whether the offense was committed while the defendant was under the influence of extreme mental or emotional disturbance, whether the defendant acted under extreme duress or under the substantial domination of another person, and whether at the time of the offense the capacity of the defendant to appreciate the criminality of his or her conduct or to conform his or her conduct to the requirements of the law was impaired as a result of mental disease or defect. There are few specialized tools that can assist an evaluator in addressing these factors, so an evaluator must typically combine information obtained from multiple sources to reach valid conclusions.

Principle 15: Ensure that conditions for the evaluation are quiet, private, and distraction-free. An *Atkins* evaluation involves an assessment of the defendant's level of intellectual functioning, and performance on relevant assessment measures can be adversely affected by distractions that impair concentration or attention. Moreover, in an *Atkins* evaluation, a small deviation in performance on an intellectual measure could affect the evaluator's conclusion regarding whether the defendant is mentally retarded. Therefore, this principle should be respected carefully in an *Atkins* evaluation. In a capital sentencing evaluation, this principle is important because sensitive information regarding the defendant's mental state at the time of the offense is being discussed while the defendant is still preadjudication. If overheard by another inmate or even jail staff, such sensitive information could potentially be damaging to the individual's case.

Principle 17: Determine whether the individual understands the purpose of the evaluation and the associated limits on confidentiality. The purpose of an *Atkins* evaluation is fairly straightforward and easy to understand when compared to a capital sentencing evaluation. Even if a defendant has significant cognitive limitations, it is possible that he or she can understand the basic purpose of an *Atkins* evaluation and the associated limits on confidentiality (i.e., that the evaluation results could be used at a hearing to help the judge decide if the defendant could possibly be charged with a capital offense). Because of the complexities involved in a capital sentencing evaluation, however, it is important that the evaluator carefully explain the purpose of the evaluation and the associated limits on confidentiality, and then document the extent to which the explanation was apparently understood by the defendant. It is unlikely that an individual who is mentally retarded will meaningfully understand aspects of the evaluation such as how the jury will consider and weigh aggravating and mitigating factors, or the use of the evaluation results only at sentencing but not at the guilt phase (with associated implications for the openness of their discussion of the offense). The level of such understanding, however, should still be assessed and documented as part of the larger evaluation process.

Principle 23: Do not answer the ultimate legal question. The ultimate issue in an *Atkins* evaluation is whether the defendant is mentally retarded and therefore ineligible for the death penalty. There is little reasoning needed between a finding of mental retardation and the conclusion regarding whether the defendant should be excluded from the death penalty. Therefore, an evaluator in an *Atkins* evaluation can draw a conclusion that is well-supported by science and come close to the ultimate issue without injecting political or moral values into the process. By contrast, the ultimate legal question in a capital sentencing evaluation is whether the defendant should be sentenced to death. This determination is based on a consideration of a broad range of aggravating and mitigating factors, some of which are appropriate for expert mental health evaluation and others of which are not (because they are primarily fact-based; e.g., number of prior convictions, heinousness of the offense). Therefore, evaluators should address the applicability of each factor that is part of the FMHA but not combine them in the form of the ultimate legal decision.

The *Atkins* decision created a somewhat different kind of FMHA in the capital context, but the FMHA principles appear to be applicable to both *Atkins* assessments and the more traditional capital sentencing evaluations. Although some of the principles apply slightly differently to each type of evaluation, the application of the principles as a whole seems to fit well in both contexts. Using the FMHA principles can make both types of evaluations more consistent, impartial, and attentive to the demands of law, science, professional ethics, and standards for professional practice.

CURRENT STATUS OF FORENSIC MENTAL HEALTH ASSESSMENT PRINCIPLES

There are three important steps in applying broad principles of FMHA: derivation, theoretical analysis, and empirical validation. The derivation process is complete (see Heilbrun, 2001). Although some principles may eventually be modified, perhaps because the field evolves or because theoretical or empirical evidence suggests that modification is necessary, such modification will not take place for some time. Instead, the important effort during the next decade will be invested in the remaining steps of theoretical analysis and empirical validation.

The consideration of how well these principles may be generalized to different legal questions and different populations has been extended to some populations (e.g., sexual offenders, the neuropsychologically impaired, offenders charged with capital offenses) and their related legal questions. There remain a number of populations and legal questions to be considered, but the approaches used in the theoretical analyses to date (Heilbrun, 2003; Heilbrun et al., 2002, 2004, 2005; Heilbrun, Marczyk, et al., 2003) should be useful in extending consideration to areas not yet covered.

The empirical work on a principles-based approach to FMHA, however, is just beginning. A meaningful research agenda will include operationalizing each principle so that it can be reliably rated by an individual who need not be trained as a doctoral-level psychologist or a psychiatrist. Following that, the selection of principles applicable to the task will exclude some of these principles (e.g., reports typically do not provide information concerning the adequacy of evaluation conditions, nor do they offer data that would allow expert testimony to be rated). Validation of a principles-based approach to measuring quality or effectiveness might proceed using different kinds of outcome measures. The blue ribbon panel involving legal and mental health experts (see, e.g., Petrella & Poythress, 1983) has been used as one measure of report quality and could serve as a validating measure of report quality gauged by operationalized FMHA principles. There are other outcome measures that should be obtained as well, however. Regarding the quality of reports, it would be helpful to have the opinions of judges, practicing attorneys, forensic psychologists, forensic psychiatrists, and participants drawn from a potential jury pool. It is not likely that there would be strong consensus about quality across all such groups, but it would be useful to understand the extent to which a principles-based approach to quality would predict the ratings of those in these different groups. Finally, there should be empirical study of outcomes in addition to quality. Measures of thoroughness, usefulness to the decision maker, and credibility would probably relate to judgments about overall quality but might add some unique variance. As empirical studies in this area begin, we will begin to see the larger utility—both theoretical and empirical—of broad principles of FMHA.

REFERENCES

American Academy of Psychiatry and the Law. (1995). *Ethical guidelines for the practice of forensic psychiatry.* Bloomfield, CT: Author.

American Bar Association. (1989). *Criminal justice mental health standards.* Washington, DC: Author.

American Psychiatric Association. (1980). *Diagnostic and statistical manual of mental disorders* (3rd ed.). Washington, DC: Author.

American Psychiatric Association. (1987). *Diagnostic and statistical manual of mental disorders* (3rd ed., rev.). Washington, DC: Author.

American Psychiatric Association. (1994). *Diagnostic and statistical manual of mental disorders* (4th ed.). Washington, DC: Author.

American Psychiatric Association. (1998). *Principles of medical ethics with annotations especially applicable to psychiatry.* Washington, DC: Author.

American Psychiatric Association. (2000). *Diagnostic and statistical manual of mental disorders* (4th ed., text rev.). Washington, DC: Author.

American Psychological Association. (1992). Ethical principles of psychologists and code of conduct. *American Psychologist, 47,* 1597–1611.

Atkins v. Virginia, 536 U.S. 304 (2002).

Boardman, A. F., & DeMatteo, D. (2003). Treating and managing sexual offenders and predators. In T. J. Fagan & R. K. Ax (Eds.), *Correctional mental health handbook* (pp. 145–165). Thousand Oaks, CA: Sage.

Butcher, J., Dahlstrom, W., Graham, J., Tellegen, A., & Kaemmer, B. (1989). *MMPI-2: Manual for administration and scoring.* Minneapolis: University of Minnesota Press.

Committee on Ethical Guidelines for Forensic Psychologists. (1991). Specialty guidelines for forensic psychologists. *Law and Human Behavior, 15,* 655–665.

Conroy, M. (2003). Evaluation of sexual predators. In I. Weiner (Editor in Chief) & A. Goldstein (Vol. Ed.), *Handbook of psychology: Vol. 11. Forensic psychology* (pp. 463–484). Hoboken, NJ: Wiley.

Cunningham, M., & Goldstein, A. (2003). Sentencing determinations in death penalty cases. In I. Weiner (Editor in Chief) & A. Goldstein (Ed.), *Handbook of psychology: Vol. 11. Forensic psychology* (pp. 381–406). Hoboken, NJ: Wiley.

Daubert v. Merrell Dow Pharmaceuticals, Inc., 113 S. Ct. 2786 (1993).

Dawes, R., Faust, D., & Meehl, P. (1989). Clinical versus actuarial judgment. *Science, 243,* 1668–1674.

Fishman, D. (1999). *The case for pragmatic psychology.* New York: New York University Press.

Fishman, D. (2000, May 3). Transcending the efficacy versus effectiveness debate: Proposal for a new, electronic "Journal of Pragmatic Case Studies." *Prevention and Treatment, 3,* Article 8. Retrieved February 11, 2005, from http://journals.apa.org/prevention/volume3/pre0030008a.html.

Frederick, R. (1997). *Validity Indictor Profile manual.* Minnetonka, MN: NSC Assessments.

Furman v. Georgia, 408 U.S. 238 (1972).

Grisso, T. (1986). *Evaluating competencies: Forensic assessments and instruments.* New York: Plenum Press.

Grisso, T. (2003). *Evaluating competencies: Forensic assessments and instruments* (2nd ed.). New York: Kluwer Academic/Plenum Press.

Grisso, T. (2005). *Evaluating juveniles' adjudicative competence: A guide for clinical practice.* Sarasota, FL: Professional Resource Press.

Grisso, T., & Appelbaum, P. (1998). *MacArthur Competence Assessment Tool for Treatment (MacCAT-T).* Sarasota, FL: Professional Resource Press.

Grove, W., Zald, K., Lebow, B., Snitz, B., & Nelson, C. (2000). Clinical versus mechanical prediction: A meta-analysis. *Psychological Assessment, 12,* 19–30.

Heilbrun, K. (2001). *Principles of forensic mental health assessment.* New York: Kluwer Academic/Plenum Press.

Heilbrun, K. (2003). Principles of forensic mental health assessment: Implications for the forensic assessment of sexual offenders. *Annals of the New York Academy of Sciences, 89,* 1–18.

Heilbrun, K., DeMatteo, D., & Marczyk, G. (2004). Pragmatic psychology and forensic mental health assessment: Applying principles to promote quality. *Psychology, Public Policy, and Law, 10,* 31–70.

Heilbrun, K., DeMatteo, D., Marczyk, G., Finello, C., Smith, R., & Mack-Allen, J. (2005). Applying principles of forensic mental health assessment to capital sentencing. *Widener Law Review, 11,* 93–118.

Heilbrun, K., Marczyk, G. R., & DeMatteo, D. (2002). *Forensic mental health assessment: A casebook.* New York: Oxford University Press.

Heilbrun, K., Marczyk, G. R., DeMatteo, D., Zillmer, E., Harris, J., & Jennings, T. (2003). Principles of forensic mental health assessment: Implications for neuropsychological assessment in forensic contexts. *Assessment, 10,* 329–343.

Heilbrun, K., Warren, J., & Picarello, K. (2003). Use of third party information in forensic assessment. In I. Weiner (Editor in Chief) & A. Goldstein (Ed.), *Handbook of psychology: Vol. 11. Forensic psychology* (pp. 69–86). Hoboken, NJ: Wiley.

Kansas v. Hendricks, 521 U.S. 346 (1997).

Marczyk, G., Heilbrun, K., DeMatteo, D., & Bell, B. (2003). Using a model to guide data gathering, interpretation, and communication in capital mitigation evaluations. *Journal of Forensic Psychology Practice, 3,* 89–103.

Melton, G., Petrila, J., Poythress, N., & Slobogin, C. (1997). *Psychological evaluations for the courts: A handbook for mental health professionals and lawyers* (2nd ed.). New York: Guilford Press.

Morse, S. (1978a). Crazy behavior, morals, and science: An analysis of mental health law. *Southern California Law Review, 51,* 527–654.

Morse, S. (1978b). Law and mental health professionals: The limits of expertise. *Professional Psychology, 9,* 389–399.

Nihira, K., Leland, H., & Lambert, N. (1993). *AAMR Adaptive Behavior Scale-Residential and Community* (2nd ed.). Lutz, FL: Psychological Assessment Resources.

Petrella, R., & Poythress, N. (1983). The quality of forensic evaluations: An interdisciplinary study. *Journal of Consulting and Clinical Psychology, 51,* 76–85.

Poythress, N., Nicholson, R., Otto, R., Edens, J., Bonnie, R., Monahan, J., et al. (1999). *Professional manual for the MacArthur Competence Assessment Tool—Criminal Adjudication.* Odessa, FL: Psychological Assessment Resources.

Rogers, R. (1992). *Structured Interview of Reported Symptoms.* Odessa, FL: Psychological Assessment Resources.

Rogers, R. (Ed.). (1997). *Clinical assessment of malingering and deception* (2nd ed.). New York: Guilford Press.

Rogers, R., & Ewing, C. (1989). Ultimate opinion proscriptions: A cosmetic fix and a plea for empiricism. *Law and Human Behavior, 13,* 357–374.

Slobogin, C. (2003). Pragmatic forensic psychology: A means of "scientizing" expert testimony from mental health professionals. *Psychology, Public Policy, and Law, 9,* 275–300.

Tombaugh, T. N. (1997). *TOMM: Test of Memory Malingering manual.* Toronto, Ontario, Canada: Multi-Health Systems.

Wechsler, D. (1997). *Wechsler Adult Intelligence Scale: Administration and scoring manual* (3rd ed.). San Antonio, TX: Harcourt Brace & Company.

Zillmer, E. (2003). The neuropsychology of 1- and 3-meter spring-board diving. *Applied Neuropsychology, 10,* 23–30.

Zillmer, E., & Spiers, M. V. (2001). *Principles of neuropsychology.* Belmont, CA: Wadsworth.

CHAPTER 3

Forensic Applications of the Minnesota Multiphasic Personality Inventory-2

Roger L. Greene

OVERVIEW

The Minnesota Multiphasic Personality Inventory (MMPI) was developed to provide a self-report means of assessing psychopathology (Hathaway & McKinley, 1940), and it is one of the most widely used and researched self-report inventories in forensic psychology (Boccaccini & Brodsky, 1999). The restandardization of the MMPI resulted in the MMPI-2 (Butcher, Dahlstrom, Graham, Tellegen, & Kaemmer, 1989, 2001), which is the focus of this chapter. The major change at the item level on the standard validity and clinical scales in the restandardization of the MMPI-2 was the deletion of 13 items with objectionable or outdated content (Butcher et al., 1989, 2001). A total of 107 items were added to the item pool (Butcher et al., 1989, 2001), and 106 items from the original MMPI were deleted, resulting in the 567 items on the MMPI-2. A new set of content scales was developed for the MMPI-2 (Butcher, Graham, Williams, & Ben-Porath, 1990). In the ensuing years, content component scales (Ben-Porath & Sherwood, 1993), Personality Psychopathology 5 scales (Harkness, McNulty, Ben-Porath, & Graham, 2002), and restructured clinical scales (Tellegen et al., 2003) have been developed for the MMPI-2. Even with the addition of these new sets of scales and items, the MMPI-2 remains a broadband instrument to assess or screen for Axis I psychopathology and, to a lesser extent, for Axis II psychopathology. It is not a measure of general personality, although some positive personality or emotional factors are assessed, such as dominance (*Do*) and social responsibility (*Re*).

The MMPI-2 can be administered to examinees 18 years of age and older who can read English at the sixth- to eighth-grade level. The MMPI-2 also can be administered by cassette tape or CD; this lowers the reading comprehension level to nearly the third grade and IQ near 70 (Dahlstrom, Welsh, & Dahlstrom, 1972). As long as the consistency of item endorsement on the MMPI-2 is evaluated carefully

The author appreciates the feedback provided by Alex Caldwell and Stuart A. Greenberg on an earlier draft of this chapter.

(described later), the forensic psychologist will have a direct performance measure of whether the examinee could and was willing to read and comprehend the items.

The extant literature that has examined the empirical correlates of MMPI-2 scales and codetypes has been consistent with the correlates reported for their MMPI counterparts (Archer, Griffin, & Aiduk, 1995; Bence, Sabourin, Luty, & Thackrey, 1995; Ben-Porath, Butcher, & Graham, 1991; Boone, 1994; Sieber & Meyers, 1992). Consequently, it appears safe to assume that the correlates of well-defined MMPI-2 codetypes (i.e., those profiles that have the scale defining them at least 5 T points higher than the next highest clinical scale) and the individual validity and clinical scales will be similar to those for the MMPI. The data are less clear for MMPI-2 codetypes that are not well-defined (i.e., those profiles in which there is not at least 5 T points between the scales defining the codetype and the next highest clinical scale), although it still will be safe to interpret the individual scales in any codetypes using MMPI correlates.

CLINICAL EVALUATIONS VERSUS FORENSIC EXAMINATIONS

The forensic psychologist must be aware of and make explicit to the examinee that the process and focus of a forensic examination is different from that of a clinical evaluation (cf. Greenberg & Shuman, 1997). The examinee must clearly understand the purpose of the examination, who is to receive a copy of the results, the limits of confidentiality, and the specific issue(s) to be addressed. There are several issues specific to the MMPI-2 that must be made explicit to the examinee as part of the process of informed consent: (a) The MMPI-2 is being used to assess a standard set of behaviors and symptoms that the examinee may be experiencing; (b) the MMPI-2 is not being used to make a psychiatric diagnosis (unless a diagnosis is specific to the psycholegal question); (c) any statement generated from the MMPI-2 is a hypothesis or probability statement that must be corroborated from the case history or other information; and (d) the MMPI-2 contains a number of validity scales to assess the accuracy of his or her self-description.

The forensic psychologist also must keep in mind that the MMPI-2 is being used to address a specific psycholegal issue rather than as a general screen for psychopathology. Thus, the interpretations provided by the MMPI-2 must be relevant to this psycholegal issue. For example, the mere presence of psychopathology as indicated by elevation of several clinical scales on the MMPI-2 may not be directly relevant to the psycholegal issue of quality of parenting skills in a child custody examination or the ability to understand legal proceedings in a competency hearing.

LIMITATIONS OF THE MINNESOTA MULTIPHASIC PERSONALITY INVENTORY-2 IN FORENSIC CONTEXTS

The MMPI-2 is essentially a self-report instrument with a majority of the items having obvious, face-valid content that can be influenced easily by the accuracy of the examinee's self-report. Any examinee can easily use a general strategy to report more or fewer problematic behaviors and symptoms of psychopathology on the MMPI-2. However, because the specific scale on which any item is scored is much more difficult to discern (Mehlman & Rand, 1960), the task becomes significantly more complicated for examinees trying to simulate specific forms of psychopathology.

The internal states and private behaviors of the examinee are rarely amenable to direct assessment by the forensic psychologist with any psychological test or technique. The only direct performance measures on the MMPI-2 are the Cannot Say (?), Variable Response Inconsistency (VRIN), and True Response Inconsistency (TRIN) scales. These scales are the only scales that yield a direct measure of how the examinee performs on the MMPI-2 as opposed to how the examinee self-reports problematic behaviors and symptoms of psychopathology.

At its most basic level, interpretation of the MMPI-2 is largely based on the inference that an examinee who produces a T score in a specific range on a certain scale will have similar behavioral correlates as the clinical patients in the external correlates research who produced similar scores. However, the forensic psychologist must realize that there were few, if any, forensically involved examinees in these studies of clinical patients. In addition, there are few studies directly demonstrating that, despite any context effects of taking the MMPI-2 in a forensic setting and for a forensic purpose, the behavioral correlates are maintained. One of the few exceptions to this statement is the research that has demonstrated that the correlates of 3-4/4-3 codetypes tended to be similar in clinical patients and prison inmates (Davis & Sines, 1971; Persons & Marks, 1971).

Scores on the MMPI-2 scales are heavily influenced by whether the examinee is willing to report problematic behaviors and symptoms of psychopathology and the ability of the K-correction process to correct for these potential distortions in the willingness or unwillingness to report. The few studies in clinical settings have suggested that the K-correction process does correct for these potential distortions in willingness to report problematic behaviors and symptoms of psychopathology (Jenkins, 1985; Putzke, Williams, Daniel, & Boll, 1999). Scores on MMPI-2 scales in a forensic setting are influenced both by the examinee's own typical willingness to report problematic behaviors and symptoms of psychopathology as well as the demand whether or not to report imposed by the specific forensic setting. Thus, examinees in a parenting evaluation would not be expected to report any type of problematic behaviors and symptoms of psychopathology, whereas examinees who are planning on pleading not guilty by reason of insanity would be expected to report all types of problematic behaviors and symptoms of psychopathology. The K-correction process was developed to correct for the first (i.e., defensiveness characteristic of the examinee), but not necessarily the second (i.e., defensiveness elicited by the forensic context) potential distortion in willingness to report problematic behaviors and symptoms of psychopathology. There is no research that demonstrates the effectiveness of the K-correction process in any forensic setting, so the forensic psychologist needs to be very cautious when making any interpretation of the K scale without consideration of the demands of the forensic context (Greenberg, 2004).

ADMINISTRATION AND SCORING ISSUES

In many respects, the issues that arise in the use of the MMPI-2 in forensic examinations are no different from those in clinical evaluations, although some issues arise more frequently and others less frequently. Thus, the forensic psychologist must administer the MMPI-2 to an examinee who is capable of comprehending the items, score and profile the results accurately, carefully determine their validity, and develop an adequate interpretation of the data in this psycholegal context. The forensic psychologist also must provide ongoing supervision of the examinee taking the MMPI-2 as part of a forensic examination; the MMPI-2 should *never* be sent home with the examinee or left with the examinee to complete in a jail cell or psychiatric unit.

Regardless of whether the MMPI-2 is hand- or computer scored, the scoring must be verified. Errors in hand scoring are more likely to result in lower raw scores because deviant responses are being summed and one or two items were overlooked. Errors in data entry for computer scoring may result in either higher or lower raw scores depending on the error that is made. That is, the error in data entry can result in either a deviant or a nondeviant response being entered for an item. One advantage of having the examinee take the MMPI-2 on the computer is that errors in scoring can be avoided. Computer scoring ensures that all of the more than 120 commonly used MMPI-2 scales and indexes are readily available for the forensic psychologist. Obviously, an evaluation by the forensic psychologist stating that the MMPI-2 was not suggestive of depression because Scale 2 (*D*) was at a T score of 60 could be impeached easily if the Content Depression (*DEP*) scale was a T score of 80. Given the number of scales to be scored (120+), it is neither reasonable nor cost-effective for the forensic psychologist, or any other psychologist, to expect to score and profile this number of scales accurately by hand.

The scoring algorithms, as well as the physical templates for the MMPI-2, are copyright-protected (*Regents of the University of Minnesota and National Computer Systems v. Applied Innovations,* 1987), and any computer program developed for scoring the MMPI-2 without the written authorization of the University of Minnesota is a violation of copyright. Thus, the use of any unauthorized computer scoring for the MMPI-2 would raise impeachment questions about the psychologist's professional judgment and ethic concerns more generally. Caldwell Report and Pearson Assessment are the only companies licensed to score the MMPI-2 at the present time. The copyright for computer interpretations of the MMPI-2, after it has been scored appropriately, is held by the developers of the various available interpretive systems. The "Ethical Principles of Psychologists and Code of Conduct" of the American Psychological Association (2002, 9.09(c)) states that psychologists retain responsibility for the appropriate interpretation of assessment instruments whether they score and interpret such themselves or use automated services.

The forensic psychologist should be ready to provide an adequate scientific foundation for the use of any MMPI-2 scale. Caldwell Report provides scoring for more than 100 scales, and Pearson Assessment's Extended Score Report provides scores on more than 120 MMPI-2 scales. The forensic psychologist must realize that a specific scale as scored on the Caldwell Report or the Pearson Assessment Extended Score Report does not guarantee that it will meet the admissibility standards for trustworthy evidence. Most of the Harris-Lingoes subscales, the Overcontrolled-Hostility (*O-H*) scale and the Ego Strength (*Es*) scale, to provide a few examples, are generally lacking in adequate empirical data to justify their use in forensic or clinical settings. Similarly, omission from the Caldwell Report or the Pearson Assessment Extended Score Report should not be taken as an indication that the omitted scale lacks scientific foundation. There are a number of scales that are not scored on the Caldwell Report or the Pearson Assessment Extended Score Report that have excellent validity, such as Wiggins's (1966) Content scales.

The forensic psychologist will need to review the responses to a number of specific items on the MMPI-2 to determine whether the examinee has endorsed or omitted any of the suicide items (150, 303, 506, 520, 524, 530) because they are not found on any scale or in any set of items in the Pearson Assessment Extended Score Report. Neither the Koss and Butcher (1973) Depressed Suicidal Ideation critical items nor the content component scale of Suicidal Ideation (Ben-Porath & Sherwood, 1993) contains all of these items. Even though the forensic psychologist is unlikely to have clinical responsibility for the examinee's treatment and treatment planning, competent professional care still requires attention to the risk of suicide in any examinee. There is a 20% discordance rate between whether an examinee reports suicidal ideation and behavior in the interview and on the MMPI-2 (Glassmire, Stolberg, & Greene, 2001) that underscores the importance of reviewing these items every time the MMPI-2 is administered in any setting.

DIFFERENT FORENSIC SETTINGS

The different forensic settings in which the MMPI-2 is administered can have a significant impact on the data obtained from an examinee. Items particularly sensitive to this impact are likely to be those about which the examinee is not sure or ambivalent as to how to respond. In civil forensic settings such as personal injury, workers' compensation, and insurance disability claims, this impact is likely to be in the opposite direction from what it is in parenting examinations or personnel selection. For example, portraying oneself as being more impaired in cases for civil damages is likely to benefit the examinee's claim; portraying oneself as being less impaired and more psychologically healthy is likely to benefit the examinee's chances of being selected, or at least not screened out, in personnel selection. Consequently, it behooves the forensic psychologist to know what types of MMPI-2 scores and profiles are to be expected in every forensic setting.

There also are different expectations regarding whether or not to report problematic behaviors and symptoms in criminal cases. Examinees who are being evaluated for competency to stand trial or mitigating circumstances to be introduced during the sentencing phase after a conviction for murder versus probation or parole should have different expectations of the types of problematic behaviors and symptoms of psychopathology that are, or are not, to be reported. For example, examinees in the former forensic contexts would be expected to report any and all problematic behaviors or symptoms that might be in any way relevant to their circumstances, whereas examinees in the latter would not be expected to report any problematic behaviors or symptoms.

Whether it is the prosecution (plaintiff) or the defense (defendant) that has retained the forensic psychologist also may impact the problematic behaviors and symptoms reported by the examinee, but there are minimal empirical data on this

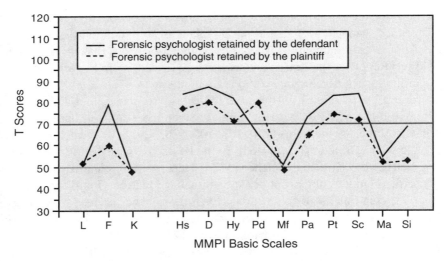

Figure 3.1 Workers' compensation claimants evaluated by defense and plaintiff experts.

point. Hasemann (1997) provided data on workers' compensation claimants who were evaluated by forensic psychologists for both the defense and the plaintiff. There are striking differences between the MMPI profiles that were obtained (see Figure 3.1). The claimant reported more symptoms and distress to the forensic psychologist retained by the defense attorney. Consequently, some of the differences in examinations performed by forensic psychologists on the same examinee may reflect that examinees actually describe their problematic behaviors and symptoms differently depending on whether they believe the forensic psychologist is likely to be sensitive or insensitive to their self-reports. The underlying heuristic of the examinee is likely to be that the "opposing" forensic psychologist will require more proof to be able or willing to perceive and report the examinee as being impaired. These results suggest the possibility that being examined by the plaintiff's expert and then by the defense's expert over the same psycholegal issue should be considered different forensic contexts.

Although the forensic psychologist may go to great effort to be unbiased, examinees may have different expectations or may have been provided with different expectations by their legal counsel. Attorneys may remind their clients about the diagnostic criteria for the disorder they are supposed to have, such as Posttraumatic Stress Disorder, or simply remind them to be sure to tell the forensic psychologist about all of the problems they have experienced and not to forget to report some particularly relevant event or experience. At a minimum, the forensic psychologist should inquire about the examinee's expectations for the examination and about any "suggestions" that may have been made.

Figures 3.2 and 3.3 illustrate the impact that different forensic settings can have on MMPI-2 clinical and content scales, respectively, in the *same* examinee.[1] Figure 3.2a (long dashed lines) was obtained during the initial phase of a forensic exami-

---

[1] This case was provided by Stuart A. Greenberg.

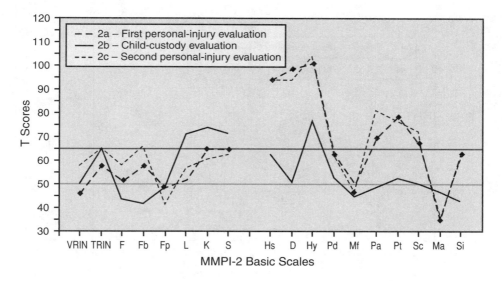

Figure 3.2   MMPI-2 Basic Scales across forensic settings in the same examinee.

nation for a personal injury suit; Figure 3.2c (short dashed lines) was obtained about 2 years later during a reexamination of the examinee as part of the ongoing personal injury litigation; and Figure 3.2b (solid line) was obtained from a child custody examination that occurred between the two personal injury examinations. Figures 3.2a and 3.2c are very similar and are commonly seen MMPI-2 profiles in personal injury examinations (cf. Lees-Haley, 1997), and Figure 3.2b is commonly seen in child custody examinations (cf. Bathurst, Gottfried, & Gottfried, 1997). There is a difference of more than 3 standard deviations (> 30 T points) between Scales 1 (*Hs*), 2 (*D*), and 3 (*Hy*) in Figures 3.2a and 3.2c when compared to Figure 3.2b. In the personal injury context, this examinee is reporting a large number of physical symptoms and significant psychological distress, but in the child custody context, the examinee reports only a limited number of physical symptoms and almost no psychological distress. Obviously, this examinee understood that there were different expectations for reporting, or not reporting, problematic behaviors and symptoms of psychopathology in these two forensic examinations and responded accordingly. Figures 3.3a, 3.3b, and 3.3c illustrate the MMPI-2 content scales at the same three times as those in Figure 3.2, respectively. The pattern of the content scales across all three administrations is fairly consistent, although the overall elevation of the entire profile is significantly lower during the child custody examination. Again, these differences are in the range of 2 to 3 standard deviations (20 to 30 T points) between Figures 3.3a and 3.3c when compared with Figure 3.3b.

POTENTIAL IMPACT OF DEMOGRAPHIC VARIABLES

The importance of demographic variables must not be underestimated in forensic examinations because of the frequency with which differences from the MMPI-2 normative group are likely to be encountered. Particularly in criminal cases, the

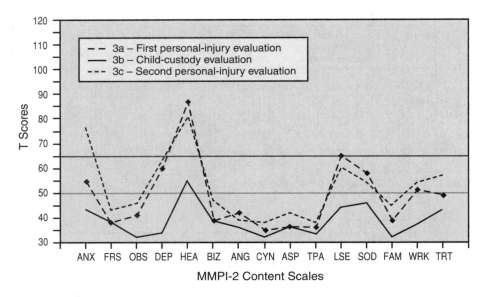

Figure 3.3 MMPI-2 Content Scales across forensic settings in the same examinee.

examinee is more likely to be younger, have fewer years of education, and have a lower socioeconomic status than the MMPI-2 normative group (Caucasian adults, 30 to 50 years of age, who had close to 3 years of college education). The forensic psychologist must be aware of the potential impact of demographic variables for any examinee who differs substantially from the MMPI-2 normative group. When the examinee differs significantly from the normative group, for example, the examinee was born in China and immigrated to the United States about 5 years ago, the forensic psychologist should make this point explicit in the report and describe the examinee's familiarity with English and degree of acculturation. The issue of how well this examinee understood the MMPI-2 items will be assessed directly when consistency of item endorsement is evaluated (discussed later). The examinee should be allowed to have a dictionary to look up any words that are not understood. The potential impact of how acculturated the examinee is will need to be considered as each issue is raised in the forensic report.

Specific norms are not provided by age on the MMPI-2, even though it is well known that there are substantial effects of age below 20 years (Greene, 2000). These age effects are reflected in the development of separate sets of adolescent norms for the original MMPI (Marks & Briggs, 1972) and the restandardization of a different form of the MMPI for adolescents (MMPI-A; Butcher et al., 1992). Several MMPI-2 scales demonstrate differences of nearly 5 T points between 20-year-olds and 60-year-olds (Butcher et al., 1989, 2001; Caldwell, 2000; Greene & Schinka, 1995), with scores on Scales L (Lie; women only), 1 (*Hs*), and 3 (*Hy*) increasing and Scales 4 (*Pd*) and 9 (*Ma*) decreasing with age. Given that these age comparisons involve different cohorts, it is not possible to know whether these effects actually reflect the influence of age or simply reflect differences between the cohorts. Butcher et al. (1991) found few effects of age in older (> 60) men and saw no reason for age-related norms in this group.

The potential effects of education have not been investigated in any systematic manner either on the MMPI or the MMPI-2. Dahlstrom and Tellegen (1993) contrasted men and women in the MMPI-2 normative group with less than a high school education with men and women with a postgraduate education. The differences on the following scales exceeded 5 T points: *L* (women only), *F, K, 5* (*Mf*), and 0 (*Si*). Men and women with less than a high school education had a higher score in all of these comparisons except for Scales *K* and 5. When psychiatric patients with 8 years or less of education were contrasted with patients with 16 or more years of education (Caldwell, 2000), the differences ranged from 4 to 8 T points on all of the standard validity and clinical scales except 3 (*Hy*). The patients with less education had higher scores in all of these comparisons except for Scales *K* and 5.

There do not appear to be any systematic effects of occupation or income within the MMPI-2 normative group (Dahlstrom & Tellegen, 1993; Long, Graham, & Timbrook, 1994). There have been no studies of the effects of these two factors in any other groups.

Dahlstrom, Lachar, and Dahlstrom (1986) and Greene (1987) have reviewed the effects of ethnicity on MMPI performance and concluded that there is no consistent pattern of scale differences between any two ethnic groups. Timbrook and Graham (1994), Zalewski and Greene (1996), and Greene (2000) reached a similar conclusion in their review of ethnicity on MMPI-2 performance.

Multivariate regressions of age, education, gender, ethnicity, and occupation on the standard validity and clinical scales have been reported for the MMPI-2 normative group (Dahlstrom & Tellegen, 1993) and psychiatric patients (Caldwell, 2000 [age, education, and gender only]; Schinka, LaLone, & Greene, 1998). These studies found that the variance accounted for by these factors does not exceed 10%. The one exception to this generalization is Scale 5 (*Mf*), in which slightly over 50% of the variance is accounted for by gender. Such small percentages of variance are unlikely to impact the interpretation of most MMPI-2 profiles.

In summary, it appears that demographic variables will have minimal impact on the MMPI-2 profile in most examinees. It is particularly important to monitor the validity of the MMPI-2 profile more closely in examinees with limited education and lower occupational status because being able to read and comprehend the MMPI-2 items is an obvious prerequisite for its appropriate interpretation. The forensic psychologist must be aware of the possibility that demographic effects seen in examinees with limited education and lower occupational status may simply reflect that the reading level of the MMPI-2 is the eighth grade. That is, what appear to be demographic effects on MMPI-2 scales actually may reflect the higher probability that these examinees are not able to read at the eighth-grade level rather than any real effect of education per se. If the forensic psychologist can demonstrate that the examinee has read and comprehended the MMPI-2 items, the potential impact of demographic variables on the MMPI-2 profile probably is fairly minimal. In examinees in whom there are significant differences from the MMPI-2 normative group, the forensic psychologist should make explicit in the report how these differences may have affected the obtained results. For example, in examinees with less than a high school education, the forensic psychologist should expect that 3 to 5 T points of elevation on most MMPI-2 scales reflect the effects of limited educational opportunity and should adjust any interpretations accordingly.

ASSESSING VALIDITY

Once the MMPI-2 data have been scored and profiled accurately, the forensic psychologist must assess their validity.[2] The validity of the MMPI-2 is a paramount issue in forensic settings, and one of the reasons for the popularity of the MMPI-2 is the existence of the numerous validity scales and indexes as well as extensive empirical data to support their use at least in clinical settings. In the following sections, data are reported separately for examinees in forensic settings who would be expected to be more (criminal forensic, death row, personal injury) or less (parenting; personnel screening such as for police officers, firefighters, clergy) likely to report problematic behaviors and symptoms of psychopathology. Comparable scores for examinees from the MMPI-2 normative group and clinical patients are provided to serve as a benchmark for interpreting these scores in a forensic setting.

Item Omissions

Item omissions evaluate whether the examinee has endorsed enough items so that the MMPI-2 can be scored. Item omissions occur infrequently in all forensic settings (see Table 3.1). If 10 or more items are used as a marker for excessive omissions, which is a very stringent criterion, nearly all of the groups, except for the criminal psychiatric defendants, are at or below the 98th percentile. If 30 or more items are used as a marker, which is a more traditional criterion for excessive item omissions, all of the groups are below the 99th percentile.

One reason for item omissions is that the examinee does not understand the meaning of some word. The forensic psychologist should not personally provide a definition of the word. Instead, the examinee should be provided with a dictionary in which the word can be looked up.

Before ending the administration of the MMPI-2, the forensic psychologist should review the examinee's responses to determine whether any items have been omitted. If items have been omitted, these items should be pointed out to the examinee to make sure that they were not omitted inadvertently. It also may help in these instances to remind the examinee that the instructions for the MMPI-2 ask whether the item is *true or mostly true* or *false or not usually true*.

Consistency of Item Endorsement

Consistency of item endorsement evaluates whether the examinee has the necessary language skills and is willing to use these skills to read and comprehend the MMPI-2 items. The importance of a careful review of the consistency of the item endorsement cannot be overestimated in forensic examinations with the MMPI-2.

---

[2] The examples of cutting scores used in this section are to illustrate their impact across these various forensic settings. They are *not* intended to be used as absolute cutting scores across all forensic settings.

Table 3.1 Descriptive Statistics for Representative MMPI-2 Validity Scales and Indices in Various Forensic Settings

				Percentile						
	N	*M*	*SD*	1	2	34	50	86	98	99
Omissions (?)										
Child custody litigants	2,059	1.48	8.20				0	1	12	19
Police applicants	7,209	0.52	3.01					0	5	8
Clergy applicants	521	1.00	3.09				0	1	9	16
Normal individuals	2,600	0.96	2.95				0	1	11	15
Clinical patients	52,543	1.46	4.51				0	2	14	21
Criminal psychiatric defendants	2,834	3.18	5.67				0	9	24	25
Death row inmates	102	2.24	4.76				0	4	17	20
Personal injury claimants	269	1.53	6.59				0	1	13	21
Consistency of Item Endorsement (VRIN)										
Child custody litigants	2,059	3.56	2.49	0	1	2	3	6	9	11
Police applicants	7,209	3.39	2.50		0	2	3	5	9	10
Clergy applicants	521	3.06	2.31		0	1	2	5	8	10
Normal individuals	2,600	5.05	2.56	0	1	3	5	7	11	12
Clinical patients	5,254	5.33	3.07		0	3	5	8	12	14
Criminal psychiatric defendants	2,834	7.34	4.18	0	1	5	6	11	17	18
Death row inmates	102	5.60	3.05		0	3	5	8	14	15
Personal injury claimants	269	6.19	2.93	0	1	4	5	9	12	13
Accuracy of Item Endorsement										
Increased Reporting of Symptoms (Fp)										
Child custody litigants	2,059	0.90	1.26				0	2	4	5
Police applicants	7,209	0.67	1.43				0	1	3	4
Clergy applicants	521	0.50	0.85				0	1	3	4
Normal individuals	2,600	1.09	1.32				0	2	4	5
Clinical patients	5,254	1.76	2.21			0	1	3	9	11
Criminal psychiatric defendants	2,834	4.67	4.30		0	2	3	9	16	17
Death row inmates	102	3.10	3.51		0	1	2	5	14	15
Personal injury claimants	269	1.81	2.35			0	1	3	9	11
Decreased Reporting of Symptoms										
Impression Management (L)										
Child custody litigants	2,059	5.55	2.55	0	1	4	5	8	11	12
Police applicants	7,209	3.92	2.22		0	2	3	6	9	10
Clergy applicants	521	4.24	2.18	0	1	3	4	7	9	10
Normal individuals	2,600	3.55	2.17		0	2	3	5	9	10
Clinical patients	52,543	4.68	2.54		0	3	4	7	10	11
Criminal psychiatric defendants	2,834	5.25	2.83		0	3	4	8	11	12
Death row inmates	102	4.72	2.29		0	3	4	7	10	11
Personal injury claimants	269	5.00	2.25	0	1	3	4	7	9	10

(continued)

Table 3.1   *(Continued)*

	N	*M*	*SD*	1	2	34	50	86	98	99
							Percentile			
Self-Deception (K)										
Child custody litigants	2,059	19.89	4.33	8	9	18	20	24	26	27
Police applicants	7,209	18.19	4.54	6	7	16	18	23	25	26
Clergy applicants	521	19.88	3.98	9	10	18	20	24	26	27
Normal individuals	2,600	15.15	4.66	4	5	13	15	20	24	25
Clinical patients	52,543	15.74	5.40	4	5	13	15	22	25	26
Criminal psychiatric defendants	2,834	13.48	5.66	3	4	10	12	19	25	26
Death row inmates	102	13.01	4.57	4		10	13	18	21	22
Personal injury claimants	269	15.22	5.06	4	5	13	15	21	25	26

Note: Statistics for child custody litigants provided by Alex Caldwell; for police applicants, provided by Eva Christiansen and Marcia Cohan; for clergy applicants, provided by Don Damsteetgt and Alan Friedman; for normal individuals, from the MMPI-2 normative group; for clinical patients, provided by Alex Caldwell; for criminal psychiatric defendants, provided by Jeffrey Davis, the Center for Forensic Psychiatry; for death row inmates, provided by Michael Gelbort; for personal injury claimants, provided by Stuart Greenberg, Paul Lees-Haley, and Randy Otto.

Source: From *MMPI-2: Manual for administration and scoring,* by J. N. Butcher, W. G. Dahlstrom, J. R. Graham, A. Tellegen, and B. Kaemmer, 1989, Minneapolis: University of Minnesota Press; *MMPI-2: Manual for administration and scoring,* revised edition, by J. N. Butcher, W. G. Dahlstrom, J. R. Graham, A. Tellegen, and B. Kaemmer, 2001, Minneapolis: University of Minnesota Press.

Greene (2000, pp. 51–63) provides an overview of all the scales and indexes that can be used to assess consistency of item endorsement and its interpretation. These scales and indexes include the *VRIN, TRIN,* and the difference between the raw scores on the *F* and F_B scales. If the forensic psychologist can demonstrate that the examinee has endorsed the items consistently, it is apparent that the examinee has understood the instructions for the examination, was able to read and comprehend the items, and was willing to respond appropriately. On the other hand, clear indications of inconsistent item endorsement preclude any interpretation of the MMPI-2. Considerable time can be spent trying to determine whether the examinee can read at the eighth-grade level necessary to complete the MMPI-2. Probably the most expedient solution is simply to ask the examinee whether reading the MMPI-2 items may be a problem in those instances where it may be likely, such as limited educational opportunity, below-average level of intellectual functioning, or limited familiarity with the English language. In these instances, the MMPI-2 can be administered by cassette tape or CD (Dahlstrom et al., 1972).

Table 3.1 provides data on the consistency of item endorsement in a variety of forensic settings in which examinees would be expected to be more or less likely to report problematic behaviors or symptoms of psychopathology. Examinees who are trying to report fewer problematic behaviors or symptoms of psychopathology, such as child custody litigants and examinees (clergy, police) in personnel screening settings, are more consistent (lower raw scores on the *VRIN* scale than any of the other groups). If 10 or more inconsistent responses on *VRIN* are used as a criterion for excessive inconsistency, which is a fairly stringent criterion, all of the groups except criminal psychiatric defendants are below the 86th percentile and most groups are at or below the 98th percentile. Most examinees, regardless of the forensic setting, are able and willing to endorse the MMPI-2 items consistently.

If too many items have been endorsed inconsistently, the forensic psychologist will need to determine the cause(s), correct the cause(s), if possible, and readminister the MMPI-2. The most likely cause for inconsistent item endorsement on the MMPI-2 is that the examinee lacks the necessary skills to comprehend the items. In these instances, the forensic psychologist can acknowledge that reading the items was difficult for the examinee and reiterate the importance of the MMPI-2 results for the examination, and the MMPI-2 can be readministered by cassette tape or CD. If the examinee has the requisite reading skills but did not endorse the items consistently, the forensic psychologist will need to point out to the examinee that the lack of compliance compromises the integrity of the examination and will be noted in the report. The examinee can then be given the opportunity to retake the MMPI-2.

Accuracy of Item Endorsement

In evaluating the accuracy of endorsement of the MMPI-2 items, the forensic psychologist should consider whether the specific forensic setting is one that *increases* or *decreases* the probability that the examinee will be reporting problematic behaviors and symptoms of psychopathology. In both civil and criminal forensic settings, there may be a reasonable expectation for increased reporting of problematic behaviors and symptoms of psychopathology (e.g., monetary compensation for personal injury, competency to be executed) and decreased reporting (e.g., child custody, personnel screening, parole, or probation hearings). These two circumstances of the increased or decreased expectation of reporting problematic behaviors and symptoms of psychopathology on the MMPI-2 are examined sequentially, without regard to the specific setting in which they occur. Although intuitively it makes sense that there may be differences in the types of problematic behaviors and symptoms of psychopathology that are reported in a personal injury case versus competency to be executed, there are limited empirical data that have made direct comparisons of MMPI-2 validity scales and indexes in such circumstances.

Increased Reporting of Problematic Behaviors and Symptoms of Psychopathology

The *Diagnostic and Statistical Manual of Mental Disorders-Text Revision* (*DSM-IV-TR*, American Psychiatric Association, 2000, p. 739) states that malingering is the *intentional* production of *false or grossly exaggerated* physical or psychological symptoms, motivated by external incentives (emphasis added). Rogers (1997) has estimated that the prevalence of malingering is approximately 15% in most forensic settings. Thus, the detection of malingering per se is *not* the most likely task in an MMPI-2 administration in any forensic setting. Rather, the forensic psychologist needs to determine whether the examinee may be expected to have increased the reporting of the actual problematic behaviors and symptoms of psychopathology that are being experienced. The Infrequency Psychopathology (*Fp*) scale (Arbisi & Ben-Porath, 1995) is particularly well suited to provide the forensic psychologist valuable information in making this determination. The *Fp* scale is the only scale reviewed in this section because of space limitations. Greene (2000, pp. 66–88) provides an overview of the other scales and indexes that can be used to assess whether the examinee may have increased the reporting of their problematic behaviors and symptoms of psychopathology and their interpretation. Given the frequency with which the increased reporting of symptoms is to be expected in most forensic settings, the *Fp* scale should be scored routinely. Archer, Handel, Greene, Baer, and Elkins (2001) reported that the *Fp* scale performed well at separating actual psychiatric patients from students attempting to simulate psychopathology. Rothke et al. (2000) have provided normative data across a variety of clinical and forensic settings for the *Fp* scale, and Table 3.1 provides similar information. Very few *Fp* items are endorsed in any forensic setting, even in the groups of criminal psychiatric defendants and death row inmates who might be thought to be highly motivated to endorse these items. If 7 or more *Fp* items are used as a criterion for excessive endorsement of atypical symptoms and behaviors, only the criminal psychiatric defendants exceed that score at the 86th percentile. Forensic psychologists may be somewhat surprised by how infrequently *Fp* items are endorsed in all of these forensic settings.

There are two potential factors that can erroneously result in elevated raw scores on the *Fp* scale: (a) the presence of four *L* scale items and (b) four items inquiring about familial relations. The *L* scale items are particularly troubling because the *L* scale is sensitive to examinees who are less likely to report problematic behaviors and symptoms, the exact opposite of what is being assessed by the *Fp* scale. The relatively small number of *Fp* items that are endorsed in all forensic settings means that the forensic psychologist can easily question examinees about their reasons for endorsing the specific items and can quickly determine whether the endorsement reflects the *L* scale items, the familial items, or a more general excessive endorsement of atypical symptoms of psychopathology and problematic behaviors.

Numerous studies have provided psychiatric patients (Bagby, Rogers, Buis, & Kalemba, 1994; Berry et al., 2001; Graham, Watts, & Timbrook, 1991; Rogers, Sewell, & Ustad, 1995) and correctional/forensic patients (Bagby, Rogers, & Buis, 1994; Iverson, Franzen, & Hammond, 1995; G. D. Walters, 1988; G. D. Walters, White, & Greene, 1988) with general or global instructions to increase their report of the behaviors and symptoms of psychopathology. These studies typically found that those patients who were instructed to increase their reporting of psychopathology could be successfully distinguished from the group taking the test accurately, although the specific scale or index employed and the optimal cutting score tended to vary widely from study to study. This line of research has been criticized because such general or global instructions have little external validity (Rogers, 1988; Sivec, Lynn, & Garske, 1994; Wetter, Baer, Berry, & Reynolds, 1994). To parallel real-world circumstances, it has been suggested that the participants must possess or be provided with specific knowledge of the psychopathology to be simulated.

A series of studies have made disorder-specific criteria available to the participants, who were then instructed to simulate Borderline Personality Disorder (Sivec, Hilsenroth, & Lynn, 1995; Wetter, Baer, Berry, Robinson, & Sumpter, 1993; Wetter et al., 1994), closed head injury (Lamb, Berry, Wetter, & Baer, 1994), paranoia (Sivec et al., 1994), Posttraumatic Stress Disorder (Fairbank, McCaffrey, & Keane,

1985; Wetter et al., 1993), Schizophrenia (Rogers, Bagby, & Chakraborty, 1993; Wetter et al., 1993), or somatoform disorders (Sivec et al., 1994). Two generalizations can be made based on this series of studies. First, the traditional validity scales usually had good success at detecting disorders such as Schizophrenia (Rogers et al., 1993) and Borderline Personality Disorder (Sivec et al., 1995; Wetter et al., 1994) that are characterized by extensive and severe psychopathology. Again, the specific scale or index that was most successful varied by study, as did the optimal cutting score. Second, examinees who were instructed to increase their report of the symptoms of a specific disorder that is characterized by circumscribed and less severe psychopathology were able to do so quite readily and were fairly difficult to detect (Lamb et al., 1994; Wetter et al., 1993).

If the items have been endorsed inaccurately, the forensic psychologist may explain to the examinee about the excessive endorsement of very unusual and unlikely symptoms and to readminister the MMPI-2. If the MMPI-2 is readministered, however, it is fairly common for an examinee to persist in endorsing the items inaccurately. The seeming inability of an examinee to change the reporting of these very unusual and unlikely symptoms when the MMPI-2 is readministered suggests that the cause may not be totally conscious or intentional.

Decreased Reporting of Problematic Behaviors and Symptoms of Psychopathology

The determination of whether an examinee has decreased the likelihood of reporting problematic behaviors and symptoms of psychopathology is limited to the L (Lie) and K (Correction) scales. Greene (2000, pp. 88–108) provides an overview of the other scales and indexes that can be used to assess whether the examinee may have decreased the reporting of the actual problematic behaviors and symptoms of psychopathology and their interpretation. These other scales and indexes include the Superlative (S), Other Deception ($ODecp$), Wiggins's Social Desirability (Sd), and Edwards's Social Desirability (So) scales, and the Gough Dissimulation Index (F—K). The use of the L and K scales is organized by Paulhus's (1984, 1986) model of social desirability responding, a model that distinguishes between impression management and self-deception. In impression management (L scale), examinees consciously decrease the likelihood of reporting problematic behaviors and symptoms of psychopathology to create a favorable impression in others, whereas in self-deception (K scale), examinees are conjectured to believe their positive self-reports that they are not experiencing any form of psychopathology. Thus, impression management (L) reflects that the examinee understands that the nature of the forensic context is not to report any type of problematic behaviors or symptoms of psychopathology and responds accordingly. These examinees would be expected to change their report of problematic behaviors and symptoms of psychopathology in a different forensic setting, as was illustrated in Figures 3.2 and 3.3. Self-deception (K) reflects that the examinee actually believes that he or she does not have any problematic behaviors or symptoms of psychopathology, and consequently there is nothing to be reported regardless of the forensic setting. These examinees would be expected to provide similar MMPI-2 profiles regardless of the forensic setting in which they are evaluated. Greenberg (2004) has made a similar distinction within the K scale by identifying context-sensitive (impression management) and context-resilient (self-deception) items.

Table 3.1 shows that impression management is rather constant across all of these forensic settings. It does not appear that either the child custody litigants or the examinees (clergy, police) in personnel screening settings are more likely to endorse the L scale items. If a raw score of seven on the L scale is used as a criterion for a significant distortion in not reporting problematic behaviors and symptoms of psychopathology, all of the groups are nearly at or below the 86th percentile. That is, impression management as measured by the L scale occurs rather infrequently and to about the same degree in all of these forensic settings.

There are rather substantial differences in the K scale across these various forensic settings (Table 3.1). Those groups who would be expected to decrease their reporting of problematic behaviors and symptoms of psychopathology (child custody litigants, clergy and police applicants) have substantially higher mean scores (> 1 standard deviation) on the K scale than those groups who would be expected to increase their reporting (criminal psychiatric defendants, death row inmates, personal injury claimants). Greenberg (2004) found that there are subsets of items on the K scale that remain unaffected by the forensic setting (83, 157, 158, 290, 365) and subsets of items that are affected (58, 116, 130, 196, 356). These two subsets of items are context-resilient (self-deception) and context-sensitive (impression management), respectively. Because of these differences in scores across forensic settings, the forensic psychologist will need to be cognizant of the specific setting and how it would be expected to affect scores on the K scale. These differences in the K scale also will impact all of the clinical scales that are K-corrected when the K-corrected profile is interpreted.

If the items have been endorsed inaccurately as measured by high scores (T > 70) on the L and K scales, it may be possible to explain to these examinees that they were too cautious in endorsing the items and provided an unrealistic appraisal of their psychological health, and to readminister the MMPI-2. If the MMPI-2 is readministered, it is fairly common for these examinees to persist in endorsing the items inaccurately, suggesting that the cause may not be totally conscious or intentional.

KNOWLEDGE OF VALIDITY SCALES

What examinees know about the validity scales on the MMPI-2 may range widely, from no knowledge whatsoever to factual knowledge. Factual knowledge may range from conversation with others who have completed the MMPI-2 to a formal preadministration orientation to the test and the purposes of the MMPI-2 examination or explicit training or coaching on their purpose along with illustrative items. Web sites exist that provide instructions on how examinees should respond to both the MMPI-2 and Rorschach. Wetter and Corrigan (1995) surveyed attorneys and found that over half of them believed that their clients should be informed of the existence of validity scales on psychological tests. Consequently, the client's attorney may be a potential source of information or provide a referral to a psychologist to "coach" the client about the validity scales.

Several studies have investigated the effects of providing participants with information about the validity scales that would be used to detect increased or decreased reporting of psychopathology (Baer, Wetter, & Berry, 1995; Lamb et al., 1994; Rogers et al., 1993; G. L. Walters & Clopton, 2000), sometimes in combination with information about diagnostic-specific criteria. The more information provided to participants about the validity scales, the better they were able to increase or decrease their reporting of the behaviors and symptoms of psychopathology without being detected (Baer et al., 1995; Rogers et al., 1993). Rogers et al. reported that information about the validity scales was more valuable in avoiding detection of the increased reporting of psychopathology than was information about diagnostic-specific criteria; G. L. Walters and Clopton (2000) found that information about the validity scales and about diagnostic-specific criteria were equally important. Figure 3.4 illustrates the group mean profile for graduate students (Greene, 2001) and undergraduate students (G. L. Walters & Clopton, 2000) who were provided with information about the validity scales and the diagnostic criteria for depression and three groups of psychiatric patients who were diagnosed with Major Depression (Ben-Porath et al., 1991; Munley, Busby, & Jaynes, 1997; Wetzler, Khadivi, & Mosher, 1998). The two student groups were able to simulate the general profile for Major Depression, although the overall elevation was significantly higher in these two groups than in the patient groups.

There appear to be a number of factors that will impact how successful an examinee may be in simulating psychopathology: (a) whether a *specific* form of psychopathology is being simulated rather than an attempt on the part of the examinee to increase the reporting of behaviors and symptoms of psychopathology in a *generic* sense; (b) knowledge of the existence and purpose of validity scales; (c) whether the form of psychopathology being simulated is characterized by a small set of circumscribed symptoms or a larger set of symptoms across multiple domains or areas; (d) the incentive to simulate; and (e) the psychological mindedness of the examinee. When the psychopathology being simulated is fairly specific with a circumscribed set of symptoms, the examinee is aware of the presence of validity scales on the MMPI-2, and the examinee has adequate motivation, it may be nearly impossible for the forensic psychologist to detect this type of distortion with the MMPI-2, or with any other self-report test. It is more likely to become evident when the examinee's presentation during the forensic examination is quite discrepant with the MMPI-2 results. When the converse of these conditions exists, however, it is fairly easy to detect the purposeful distortion because it is so extensive across most MMPI-2 scales.

STABILITY OF PROFILES

There are limited empirical data that indicate how consistently examinees will obtain the same codetype on two successive administrations of the MMPI-2. The research on the stability of the MMPI historically focused either on the individual validity and clinical scales (cf. Graham, 2006; Greene, 2000) or group mean profiles (cf. Lichenstein & Bryan, 1966; Pauker, 1966; Warman & Hannum, 1965), which leaves unanswered whether codetypes have remained unchanged. Graham,

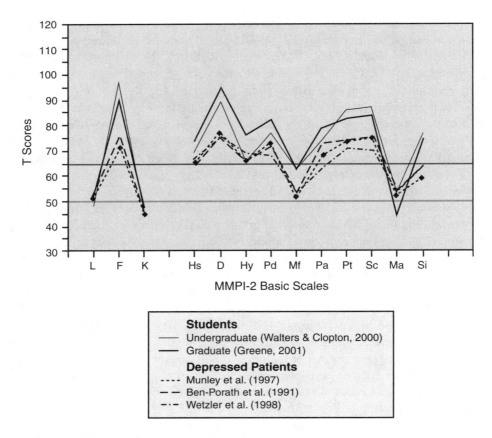

Figure 3.4 Undergraduate and graduate students simulating depression and depressed patients. *Sources:* From "Effect of Symptom Information and Validity Scale Information on the Malingering of Depression on the MMPI-2," by G. L. Walters and J. C. Clopton, 2000, *Journal of Personality Assessment, 72,* pp. 183–199; *MMPI-2 Data Research File for Graduate Students Simulating Specific Diagnostic Groups* by R. L. Greene, 2001, unpublished raw data; "MMPI-2 Findings in Schizophrenia and Depression," by P. H. Munley, R. M. Busby, and G. Jaynes, 1997, *Psychological Assessment, 9,* pp. 508–511; "Contribution of the MMPI-2 Content Scales to the Differential Diagnosis of Schizophrenia and Major Depression," by Y. S. Ben-Porath, J. N. Butcher, and J. R. Graham, 1991, *Psychological Assessment, 3,* pp. 634–640; "The Use of the MMPI-2 for the Assessment of Depressive and Psychotic Disorders," by S. Wetzler, A. Khadivi, and R. K. Mosher, 1998, *Assessment, 5,* pp. 249–261.

Smith, and Schwartz (1986) have provided the only empirical data on the stability of MMPI codetypes for a large sample of psychiatric inpatients. They reported 42.7%, 44.0%, and 27.7% agreement across an average interval of approximately 3 months for high-point, low-point, and two-point codetypes, respectively. Greene, Davis, and Morse (1993) examined MMPI codetype stability for inpatient alcoholics. Approximately 40% of the men and 32% of the women obtained the same high-point scale on two successive administrations of the MMPI. However, these patients had the same codetype only 12% and 13% of the time, respectively. It is even more interesting that almost 30% of these men and women had two different high-point scales when they took the MMPI on their second admission. For example, an examinee with a *4-9* codetype on the first admission might have a *2-7* or *1-3* codetype on the second admission. Thus, it seems imperative that forensic psychologists restrict their MMPI-2 interpretations to a description of the examinee's current situation rather than trying to make long-term predictions based on a specific codetype.

Greene, Greenberg, Davis, Ackerman, and Frederick (2001) provided data on two successive administrations of the MMPI-2 in 63 examinees undergoing child custody examinations and two samples of examinees (*n* = 1,187 and 58) undergoing criminal examinations. There was slightly over an average of 1 year between the two administrations of the MMPI-2 in all of the samples. The specific MMPI-2 codetypes that were found in both the child custody and criminal examinations varied broadly. A total of 17 different codetypes were found in the child custody examinations and 49 in the criminal examinations out of a total of 55 potential two-point and spike codetypes. Thus, there is no specific MMPI-2 codetype that was limited to a single forensic setting. Rather, there appeared to be considerable diversity among these examinees.

The same examinee was unlikely to produce the same MMPI-2 codetype across two successive administrations in either of these forensic settings. The highest frequency of the same codetype being found in the same examinee occurred in well-defined profiles (WNL: all clinical scales less than a T score of 65; 47.6%) in both the child custody examinations and the criminal examinations (7.6%). When the analysis is restricted to well-defined profiles, slightly fewer than half of the examinees had the same MMPI-2 codetype on two successive administrations, even though nearly 60% of the cases had been excluded. Frequently, these examinees produced very discrepant codetypes even in the same forensic setting. For example, one examinee who was being evaluated for allegations of sexual abuse in a family court case produced a Spike 4, a Spike 5 (with Scale 4 at 52), and a *WNL* profile within a time span of slightly less than 1 year.

It appears that forensic psychologists need to be very cautious about making long-term or characterologic interpretations from the single interpretation of the MMPI-2 in *any* forensic setting. Instead, the forensic psychologist should describe how this given MMPI-2 profile reflects the examinee's current circumstances.

CONTENT-BASED INTERPRETATION

Despite the empirical roots of the MMPI that eschewed interpreting the content of the examinee items, interest in item content began with the identification of critical items (Grayson, 1951; Koss & Butcher, 1973; Lachar & Wrobel, 1979). Interest in item content continued with the development of content scales for the MMPI (Wiggins, 1966) and MMPI-2 (Butcher et al., 1990).

Hathaway and McKinley (1940) tried to be quite comprehensive at sampling the domain of self-reported symptoms and complaints of distress in selecting the items for the original MMPI. However, Hathaway and McKinley did not consider interpreting the substantive meaning of the items to be important because of the much greater predictive power of the empirically derived MMPI scales, so there was no need to be exhaustive in selecting potential items. As a result, the growing trend to emphasize content in the interpretation of the MMPI-2 may be impeded by the inherent limitations of the item pool.

The forensic psychologist must score the MMPI-2 content (Butcher et al., 1990) and content-component scales (Ben-Porath & Sherwood, 1993) to be aware of how concordant or discordant these scales are when compared with the basic validity and clinical scales and the empirically based interpretation of the codetype. Concordance between content-based and empirically based interpretations can provide further substantiation to the integrity of the codetype interpretation. However, when these two sources of information are discordant, the forensic psychologist must acknowledge this discordance explicitly and provide a rationale for it. In a similar vein, the forensic psychologist must ensure that the endorsement of specific MMPI-2 items is consistent with the overall interpretation. For example, the forensic psychologist who uses only the MacAndrew (1965) Alcoholism (MAC-R) scale to assess alcohol abuse without examining specific items could be impeached when the examinee endorses items 264 and 489, which ask about a drug or alcohol problem, but does not elevate the MAC-R.

This emphasis on the item content can be problematic for scales that have a relatively limited number of items, such as some of the Harris and Lingoes (1955) clinical subscales and the MMPI-2 content component scales (Ben-Porath & Sherwood, 1993). It is not clear whether these subscales should be interpreted only when the parent scale is elevated above a T score of 65 (Ben-Porath & Sherwood, 1993) or whether any elevation on a subscale of 65 or higher is reflective of a content area of particular importance for an examinee. The former position is more conservative and clearly appropriate given the psychometric limitations of some of these subscales; the latter position holds that this content area is important for the examinee regardless of its psychometric qualities. Most of these subscales have little empirical validation, suggesting that forensic psychologists should be cautious in their use of them.

CONTENT-BASED VERSUS EMPIRICALLY BASED INTERPRETATIONS

The three alcohol and drug scales on the MMPI-2 (Addiction Admission scale [AAS], Weed, Butcher, McKenna, & Ben-Porath, 1992; Addiction Potential scale [APS], Weed et al., 1992; and MacAndrew Alcoholism Scale-Revised [MAC-R], MacAndrew, 1965) can be used to illustrate the potential differences in a content-based versus an empirically based interpretation of the MMPI-2.

Examinees who directly acknowledge their abuse of alcohol or drugs by endorsing the face-valid items on the AAS make the development of the hypothesis very straightforward for the forensic psychologist. However, when examinees elevate the APS and/or MAC-R, which are empirically based (indirect) measures of alcohol or drug abuse, but do not elevate the AAS, the forensic psychologist may have a difficult time justifying the hypothesis that the examinee has a drug or alcohol problem. This point is particularly true if the examinee's history and background provide no suggestion of such problems. That is, the APS and/or MAC-R may suggest that the examinee may be vulnerable to abuse alcohol or drugs, but case history information is needed to corroborate this hypothesis.

COMPUTERIZED INTERPRETATIONS

Computerized interpretations are a potential source of valuable information in forensic examinations. Their advantages, however, must be weighed against their disadvantages in deciding whether they should be used in a specific instance.

The primary advantage of a computerized interpretation is that it provides a rapid summary of the standard interpretation of the MMPI-2 profile that is not biased for or against the examinee by other knowledge that the forensic psychologist might have or by who retained the services of the forensic psychologist. However, a computerized interpretation cannot be used verbatim as a valid description of the examinee because of the limited empirical data on its forensic use in different settings, the lack of specificity for addressing the psycholegal issue for this examinee, and the presence of statements that are erroneous in the midst of an otherwise appropriate interpretation. Every statement in a computerized interpretation must be understood as a hypothesis that must be verified against the case history and interview information. In addition, an explicit rationale must be provided for any specific information that is taken from the computerized interpretation as well as any disconfirmatory information that is not being used. The judgment process of the forensic psychologist in selecting some and not other specific information from the computerized interpretation will be open to examination by other experts and attorneys.

CONCLUSION

The MMPI-2 is well suited for forensic examinations because of the extensive number of validity scales and indexes to assess whether the examinee may have increased or decreased the reporting of problematic behaviors and symptoms of psychopathology. There is a long history of empirical research that validates its use. Such research can be used to provide the scientific evidence needed for specific psycholegal issues that are being evaluated in the forensic examination. The forensic psychologist must be well steeped in this empirical research on the MMPI-2, particularly how this research relates directly to the specific psycholegal issue for which the MMPI-2 has been administered.

REFERENCES

American Psychiatric Association. (2000). *Diagnostic and statistical manual of mental disorders* (4th ed., text rev.). Washington, DC: Author.

American Psychological Association. (2002). Ethical principles of psychologists and code of conduct. *American Psychologist, 57,* 1060–1073.

Arbisi, P., & Ben-Porath, Y. S. (1995). An MMPI-2 infrequent response scale for use with psychopathological populations: The Infrequency Psychopathology scale, *Fp. Psychological Assessment, 7,* 424–431.

Archer, R. P., Griffin, R., & Aiduk, R. (1995). MMPI-2 clinical correlates for ten common codes. *Journal of Personality Assessment, 65,* 391–407.

Archer, R. P., Handel, R. W., Greene, R. L., Baer, R. A., & Elkins, D. E. (2001). An examination of the usefulness of the MMPI-2 *Fp* scale. *Journal of Personality Assessment, 76,* 282–295.

Baer, R. A., Wetter, M. W., & Berry, D. T. R. (1995). Effects of information about validity scales on underreporting of symptoms on the MMPI-2: An analogue investigation. *Assessment, 2,* 189–200.

Bagby, R. M., Rogers, R., & Buis, T. (1994). Detecting malingered and defensive responding on the MMPI-2 in a forensic inpatient sample. *Journal of Personality Assessment, 62,* 191–203.

Bagby, R. M., Rogers, R., Buis, T., & Kalemba, V. (1994). Malingered and defensive response styles on the MMPI-2: An examination of validity scales. *Assessment, 1,* 31–38.

Bathurst, K., Gottfried, A. W., & Gottfried, A. E. (1997). Normative data for the MMPI-2 in child custody litigation. *Psychological Assessment, 9,* 205–211.

Ben-Porath, Y. S., Butcher, J. N., & Graham, J. R. (1991). Contribution of the MMPI-2 content scales to the differential diagnosis of schizophrenia and major depression. *Psychological Assessment, 3,* 634–640.

Ben-Porath, Y. S., & Sherwood, N. E. (1993). *The MMPI-2 content component subscales: Development, psychometric characteristics, and clinical application.* Minneapolis: University of Minnesota Press.

Bence, V. M., Sabourin, C., Luty, D. T., & Thackrey, M. (1995). Differential sensitivity of the MMPI-2 depression scales and subscales. *Journal of Clinical Psychology, 51,* 375–377.

Berry, D. T. R., Cimino, C. R., Chong, N. K., LaVelle, S. N., Ho, I. K., Morse, T. M., et al. (2001). MMPI-2 fake-bad scales: An attempted cross-validation of proposed cutting scores for outpatients. *Journal of Personality Assessment, 76,* 296–314.

Boccaccini, M. T., & Brodsky, S. L. (1999). Diagnostic test usage by forensic psychologists in emotional injury cases. *Professional Psychology Research and Practice, 30,* 253–259.

Boone, D. E. (1994). Validity of the MMPI-2 depression content scale with psychiatric patients. *Psychological Reports, 74,* 159–162.

Butcher, J. N., Aldwin, C. M., Levenson, M. R., Ben-Porath, Y. S., Spiro, A., & Bosse, R. (1991). Personality and aging: A study of the MMPI-2 among older men. *Psychology and Aging, 6,* 361–370.

Butcher, J. N., Dahlstrom, W. G., Graham, J. R., Tellegen, A., & Kaemmer, B. (1989). *MMPI-2: Manual for administration and scoring.* Minneapolis: University of Minnesota Press.

Butcher, J. N., Dahlstrom, W. G., Graham, J. R., Tellegen, A., & Kaemmer, B. (2001). *MMPI-2: Manual for administration and scoring* (Rev. ed.). Minneapolis: University of Minnesota Press.

Butcher, J. N., Graham, J. R., Williams, C. L., & Ben-Porath, Y. S. (1990). *Development and use of the MMPI-2 content scales.* Minneapolis: University of Minnesota Press.

Butcher, J. N., Williams, C. L., Graham, J. R., Archer, R. P., Tellegen, A., Ben-Porath, Y. S., et al. (1992). *MMPI-A (Minnesota Multiphasic Personality Inventory—Adolescent): Manual for administration, scoring, and interpretation.* Minneapolis: University of Minnesota Press.

Caldwell, A. B. (2000). [MMPI-2 data research file for clinical patients]. Unpublished raw data.

Dahlstrom, W. G., Lachar, D., & Dahlstrom, L. E. (1986). *MMPI patterns of American minorities.* Minneapolis: University of Minnesota Press.

Dahlstrom, W. G., & Tellegen, A. (1993). *Socioeconomic status and the MMPI-2: The relation of MMPI-2 patterns to levels of education and occupation.* Minneapolis: University of Minnesota Press.

Dahlstrom, W. G., Welsh, G. S., & Dahlstrom, L. E. (1972). *An MMPI handbook: Vol. I. Clinical interpretation* (Rev. ed.). Minneapolis: University of Minnesota Press.

Davis, K. R., & Sines, J. O. (1971). An antisocial behavior pattern associated with a specific MMPI profile. *Journal of Consulting and Clinical Psychology, 36,* 229–234.

Fairbank, J. A., McCaffrey, R. J., & Keane, T. M. (1985). Psychometric detection of fabricated symptoms of posttraumatic stress disorder. *American Journal of Psychiatry, 142,* 501–503.

Glassmire, D. M., Stolberg, R. A., & Greene, R. L. (2001). The utility of MMPI-2 suicide items for assessing suicidal potential: Development of a suicidal potential scale. *Assessment, 8,* 281–290.

Graham, J. R. (2006). *MMPI-2: Assessing individuality and psychopathology* (3rd ed.). New York: Oxford University Press.

Graham, J. R., Smith, R. L., & Schwartz, G. F. (1986). Stability of MMPI configurations for psychiatric inpatients. *Journal of Consulting and Clinical Psychology, 54,* 375–380.

Graham, J. R., Watts, D., & Timbrook, R. E. (1991). Detecting fake-good and fake-bad MMPI-2 profiles. *Journal of Personality Assessment, 57,* 264–277.

Grayson, H. M. (1951). *A psychological admissions testing program and manual.* Los Angeles: Veterans Administration Center, Neuropsychiatric Hospital.

Greenberg, S. A. (2004, March). *The "Not Me" scale: Forensic implications of K item disavowal.* Master lecture presented at the midwinter meeting of the Society for Personality Assessment, Miami, FL.

Greenberg, S. A., & Shuman, D. W. (1997). Irreconcilable conflict between therapeutic and forensic roles. *Professional Psychology: Research and Practice, 28,* 50–57.

Greene, R. L. (1987). Ethnicity and MMPI performance: A review. *Journal of Consulting and Clinical Psychology, 55,* 497–512.

Greene, R. L. (2000). *The MMPI-2: An interpretive manual* (2nd ed.). Boston: Allyn & Bacon.

Greene, R. L. (2001). [MMPI-2 data research file for graduate students simulating specific diagnostic groups]. Unpublished raw data.

Greene, R. L., Davis, L. J., & Morse, R. P. (1993, March). *Stability of MMPI codetypes in alcoholic inpatients.* Paper presented at the midwinter meeting of the Society for Personality Assessment, San Francisco.

Greene, R. L., Greenberg, S. A., Davis, J., Ackerman, M. J., & Frederick, R. I. (2001, August). *MMPI-2 stability within and across forensic settings.* Paper presented at the annual meeting of the American Psychological Association, San Francisco.

Greene, R. L., & Schinka, J. A. (1995). [MMPI-2 data research file for psychiatric inpatients and outpatients]. Unpublished raw data.

Harkness, A. R., McNulty, J. L., Ben-Porath, Y. S., & Graham, J. R. (2002). *MMPI-2 Personality Psychopathology 5 (PSY-5) scales: Gaining an overview for case conceptualization and treatment planning.* Minneapolis: University of Minnesota Press.

Harris, R. E., & Lingoes, J. C. (1955). *Subscales for the MMPI: An aid to profile interpretation.* Unpublished manuscript, University of California.

Hasemann, D. M. (1997). *Practices and findings of mental health professionals conducting workers' compensation examinations.* Unpublished doctoral dissertation, University of Kentucky.

Hathaway, S. R., & McKinley, J. C. (1940). A multiphasic individuality schedule (Minnesota): Illinois. Construction of the schedule. *Journal of Psychology, 10,* 249–254.

Iverson, G. L., Franzen, M. D., & Hammond, J. A. (1995). Examination of inmates' ability to malinger on the MMPI-2. *Psychological Assessment, 7,* 118–121.

Jenkins, G. (1985). *Response sets and personality measures: The K scale of the MMPI.* Unpublished doctoral dissertation, Texas Tech University, Lubbock.

Koss, M. P., & Butcher, J. N. (1973). A comparison of psychiatric patients' self-report with other sources of clinical information. *Journal of Research in Personality, 7,* 225–236.

Lachar, D., & Wrobel, T. A. (1979). Validating clinicians' hunches: Construction of a new MMPI critical item set. *Journal of Consulting and Clinical Psychology, 47,* 277–284.

Lamb, D. G., Berry, D. T. R., Wetter, M. W., & Baer, R. A. (1994). Effects of two types of information on malingering of closed head injury on the MMPI-2: An analog investigation. *Psychological Assessment, 6,* 8–13.

Lees-Haley, P. R. (1997). MMPI-2 base rates for 492 examinee injury plaintiffs: Implications and challenges for forensic assessment. *Journal of Clinical Psychology, 53,* 745–755.

Lichtenstein, E., & Bryan, J. H. (1966). Short-term stability of MMPI profiles. *Journal of Consulting Psychology, 30,* 172–174.

Long, K. A., Graham, J. R., & Timbrook, R. E. (1994). Socioeconomic status and MMPI-2 interpretation. *Measurement and Examination in Counseling and Development, 27,* 158–177.

MacAndrew, C. (1965). The differentiation of male alcoholic outpatients from non-alcoholic psychiatric outpatients by means of the MMPI. *Quarterly Journal of Studies on Alcohol, 26,* 238–246.

Marks, P. A., & Briggs, P. F. (1972). Adolescent norm tables for the MMPI. In W. G. Dahlstrom, G. S. Welsh, & L. E. Dahlstrom (Eds.), *An MMPI handbook: Vol. 1. Clinical interpretation* (Rev. ed., pp. 388–399). Minneapolis: University of Minnesota Press.

Mehlman, B., & Rand, M. E. (1960). Face validity of the MMPI. *Journal of General Psychology, 63,* 171–178.

Munley, P. H., Busby, R. M., & Jaynes, G. (1997). MMPI-2 findings in schizophrenia and depression. *Psychological Assessment, 9,* 508–511.

Pauker, J. D. (1966). Identification of MMPI profile types in a female, inpatient, psychiatric setting using the Marks and Seeman rules. *Journal of Consulting Psychology, 30,* 90.

Paulhus, D. L. (1984). Two-component models of socially desirable responding. *Journal of Personality and Social Psychology, 46,* 598–609.

Paulhus, D. L. (1986). Self-deception and impression management in test responses. In A. Angleitner & J. S. Wiggins (Eds.), *Personality assessment via questionnaires: Current issues in theory and measurement* (pp. 143–165).

Persons, R. W., & Marks, P. A. (1971). The violent *4–3* MMPI personality type. *Journal of Consulting and Clinical Psychology, 36,* 189–196.

Putzke, J. D., Williams, M. A., Daniel, F. J., & Boll, T. J. (1999). The utility of the *K*-correction to adjust for a defensive response set on the MMPI. *Assessment, 6,* 61–70.

Regents of the University of Minnesota and National Computer Systems v. Applied Innovations No. 3-86 CIV 683 U.S. Dist. (D. Minn. 3rd Div.; 685 F. Supp. 698; U.S. Dist. LEXIS 13539; 1987).

Rogers, R. (1988). Researching dissimulation. In R. Rogers (Ed.), *Clinical assessment of malingering and deception* (pp. 309–327). New York: Guilford Press.

Rogers, R. (1997). Introduction. In R. Rogers (Ed.), *Clinical assessment of malingering and deception* (2nd ed., pp. 1–19). New York: Guilford Press.

Rogers, R., Bagby, R. M., & Chakraborty, D. (1993). Feigning schizophrenic disorders on the MMPI-2: Detection of coached simulators. *Journal of Personality Assessment, 60,* 215–226.

Rogers, R., Sewell, K. W., & Ustad, K. I. (1995). Feigning among chronic outpatients on the MMPI-2: A systematic investigation of fake-bad indicators. *Assessment, 2,* 81–89.

Rothke, S. E., Friedman, A. F., Jaffe, A. M., Greene, R. L., Wetter, M. W., Cole, P., et al. (2000). Normative data for the *Fp* scale of the MMPI-2: Implications for clinical and forensic assessment of malingering. *Psychological Assessment, 12,* 335–340.

Schinka, J. A., LaLone, L., & Greene, R. L. (1998). Effects of psychopathology and demographic characteristics on MMPI-2 scale scores. *Journal of Personality Assessment, 70,* 197–211.

Sieber, K. O., & Meyers, L. S. (1992). Validation of the MMPI-2 social introversion subscales. *Psychological Assessment, 4,* 185–189.

Sivec, H. J., Hilsenroth, M. J., & Lynn, S. J. (1995). Impact of simulating borderline personality disorder on the MMPI-2: A cost-benefits model employing base rates. *Journal of Personality Assessment, 64,* 295–311.

Sivec, H. J., Lynn, S. J., & Garske, J. P. (1994). The effect of somatoform disorder and paranoid psychotic role-related dissimulation as a response set on the MMPI-2. *Assessment, 1,* 69–81.

Tellegen, A., Ben-Porath, Y. S., McNulty, J. L., Arbisi, P. A., Graham, J. R., & Kaemmer, B. (2003). *The MMPI-2 Restructured Clinical (RC) scales: Development, validation, and interpretation.* Minneapolis: University of Minnesota Press.

Timbrook, R. E., & Graham, J. R. (1994). Ethnic differences on the MMPI-2? *Psychological Assessment, 6,* 212–217.

Walters, G. D. (1988). Assessing dissimulation and denial on the MMPI in a sample of maximum security inmates. *Journal of Personality Assessment, 52,* 465–474.

Walters, G. D., White, T. W., & Greene, R. L. (1988). Use of the MMPI to identify malingering and exaggeration of psychiatric symptomatology in male prison inmates. *Journal of Consulting and Clinical Psychology, 56,* 111–117.

Walters, G. L., & Clopton, J. C. (2000). Effect of symptom information and validity scale information on the malingering of depression on the MMPI-2. *Journal of Personality Assessment, 72,* 183–199.

Warman, R. E., & Hannum, T. E. (1965). MMPI pattern changes in female prisoners. *Journal of Research in Crime and Delinquency, 2,* 72–76.

Weed, N. C., Butcher, J. N., McKenna, T., & Ben-Porath, Y. S. (1992). New measures for assessing alcohol and drug abuse with the MMPI-2: The *APS* and *AAS*. *Journal of Personality Assessment, 58,* 389–404.

Wetter, M. W., Baer, R. A., Berry, D. T. R., & Reynolds, S. K. (1994). The effect of symptom information on faking on the MMPI. *Assessment, 1,* 199–207.

Wetter, M. W., Baer, R. A., & Berry, D. T. R., Robinson, L. H., & Sumpter, J. (1993). MMPI-2 profiles of motivated fakers given specific symptom information: A comparison to matched patients. *Psychological Assessment, 5,* 317–323.

Wetter, M. W., & Corrigan, S. K. (1995). Providing information to examinees about psychological tests: A survey of attorneys' and law students' attitudes. *Professional Psychology: Research and Practice, 26,* 474–477.

Wetzler, S., Khadivi, A., & Mosher, R. K. (1998). The use of the MMPI-2 for the assessment of depressive and psychotic disorders. *Assessment, 5,* 249–261.

Wiggins, J. S. (1966). Substantive dimensions of self-report in the MMPI item pool. *Psychological Monographs, 80* (Whole No. 630).

Zalewski, C., & Greene, R. L. (1996). Multicultural usage of the MMPI-2. In L. A. Suzuki, P. J. Meller, & J. G. Ponterotto (Eds.), *Handbook of multicultural assessment: Clinical, psychological, and educational applications* (pp. 77–114). San Francisco: Jossey-Bass.

CHAPTER 4

The Personality Assessment Inventory:
Issues in Legal and Forensic Settings

Leslie C. Morey, Megan B. Warner, and Christopher J. Hopwood

The field of psychological assessment can bring an established body of theory and data to bear on clinical forensic practice and thus holds particular promise for clarifying psycholegal decision making. Unfortunately, standards for the acceptability of data and practice within the legal and mental health professions are not fully overlapping, and their intersection is often marked by controversy (Nicholson & Norwood, 2000). Effective practice in this area is most likely to be realized when professionals maintain a grasp of recent developments in test construction and psychometrics, as well as an understanding of recent developments surrounding the use of such instruments in legal settings. The purpose of this chapter is to provide information on the uses and limitations of one such modern psychological instrument, the Personality Assessment Inventory (PAI; Morey, 1991), in the context of current scientific and legal standards. More detailed coverage than is possible in this chapter can be found in several primary sources (Morey, 1991, 1996, 2003). To orient the reader to the structure of the PAI, brief scales and subscale descriptions are provided, followed by a discussion of legal issues and standards and a consideration of the PAI with respect to those standards.

STRUCTURE OF THE PERSONALITY ASSESSMENT INVENTORY

The PAI includes 344 self-report items that load onto 22 scales named for the constructs they were designed to measure. Scales representing sufficiently broad constructs are additive combinations of subscales designed to measure theoretically and empirically derived facets. These scales and subscales are presented, along with a brief description, in Table 4.1. Responses are made on a 4-point Likert scale for each item with possible responses of false, slightly true, mainly true, or very true.

As shown in Table 4.1, four scales on the PAI were specifically designed to assess profile validity, although several supplemental validity indexes have been developed since the introduction of the PAI in 1991. The Inconsistency (ICN) scale is actually an index calculated by comparing items from various scales that demonstrate high correlations in the standardization sample. Individuals with elevations on ICN respond in different ways to highly correlated items, suggesting that they

Table 4.1   PAI Scales and Subscales

	Scale	Interpretation of High Scores
	Validity Scales	
ICN	Inconsistency	Poor concentration or inattention
INF	Infrequency	Idiosyncratic or random response set
NIM	Negative Impression Management	Negative response set due to pessimistic worldview and/or intentional dissimulation
PIM	Positive Impression Management	Positive response set due to naivete or intentional dissimulation
	Clinical Scales	
SOM	Somatic Complaints	
SOM-C	Conversion	Rare sensorimotor symptoms associated with conversion disorders or certain medical conditions
SOM-S	Somatization	The occurrence of common physical symptoms or vague complaints of ill health or fatigue
SOM-H	Health Concerns	Preoccupation with physical functioning and symptoms
ANX	Anxiety	
ANX-C	Cognitive	Ruminative worry and impaired concentration and attention
ANX-A	Affective	Experience of tension, difficulty relaxing, nervousness, and fatigue
ANX-P	Physiological	Overt signs of anxiety, including sweating, trembling, shortness of breath, and irregular heartbeat
ARD	Anxiety-Related Disorders	
ARD-O	Obsessive-Compulsive	Intrusive thoughts, compulsive behaviors, rigidity, indecision, perfectionism, and affective constriction
ARD-P	Phobias	Common fears, including social situation, heights, and public or enclosed places; low scores suggest fearlessness
ARD-T	Traumatic Stress	Experience of trauma that continues to cause distress
DEP	Depression	
DEP-C	Cognitive	Worthlessness, hopelessness, indecisiveness, and difficulty concentrating; low scores indicate personal confidence
DEP-A	Affective	Feelings of sadness, diminished interest, and anhedonia
DEP-P	Physiological	Level of physical functioning, activity, and sleep and diet patterns

Table 4.1 *(Continued)*

	Scale	Interpretation of High Scores
	Clinical Scales	
MAN	Mania	
MAN-A	Activity Level	Disorganized overinvolvement in activities, accelerated thought processes and behavior
MAN-G	Grandiosity	Inflated self-esteem and expansiveness; low scores indicate low self-esteem
MAN-I	Irritability	Frustration intolerance, impatience, and resulting strained relationships
PAR	Paranoia	
PAR-H	Hypervigilance	Suspiciousness and tendency to closely monitor environment; low scores suggest interpersonal trust
PAR-P	Persecution	Belief that others have intentionally constructed obstacles to one's achievement
PAR-R	Resentment	Bitterness and cynicism in relationships, tendency to hold grudges, and externalization of blame
SCZ	Schizophrenia	
SCZ-P	Psychotic Experiences	Unusual perceptions and sensations, magical thinking, and unusual ideas
SXZ-S	Social Detachment	Social isolation, discomfort, and awkwardness
SCZ-T	Thought Disorder	Confusion, concentration difficulties, and disorganization
BOR	Borderline Features	
BOR-A	Affective Instability	Emotional responsiveness, rapid mood change, poor modulation
BOR-I	Identity Problems	Uncertainty about major life issues and feelings of emptiness or lack of fulfillment or purpose
BOR-N	Negative Relationships	History of intense, ambivalent relationships and feelings of exploitation or betrayal
BOR-S	Self-Harm	Impulsivity in areas likely to be dangerous
ANT	Antisocial Features	
ANT-A	Antisocial Behaviors	History of antisocial and illegal behavior
ANT-E	Egocentricity	Lack of empathy or remorse, exploitive approach to relationships
ANT-S	Stimulus Seeking	Cravings for excitement, low boredom tolerance, recklessness
ALC	Alcohol Problems	Use of and problems with alcohol
DRG	Drug Problems	Use of and problems with drugs

(continued)

Table 4.1   *(Continued)*

Scale		Interpretation of High Scores
	Treatment Consideration Scales	
AGG	Aggression	
AGG-A	Aggressive Attitude	Hostility, poor control over anger and belief in instrumental utility of violence
AGG-V	Verbal Aggression	Assertiveness, abusiveness, and readiness to express anger to others
AGG-P	Physical Aggression	Tendency to be involved in physical aggression
SUI	Suicidal Ideation	Frequency and intensity of thoughts of self-harm or fantasies about suicide
STR	Stress	Perception of an uncertain or difficult environment
NON	Nonsupport	Perception that others are not available or willing to provide support
RXR	Treatment Rejection	Attitudes that represent obstacles or indicate low motivation for treatment
	Interpersonal Scales	
DOM	Dominance	Desire and tendency for control in relationships; low scores suggest meekness and submissiveness
WRM	Warmth	Interest and comfort with close relationships; low scores suggest hostility, anger, and mistrust

may be manifesting poor concentration or inattention. To supplement this information on response consistency, Edens and Ruiz (2005) developed the Correctional Inconsistency (ICN-C) scale, composed of two items regarding illegal behavior found to co-occur highly in their sample of incarcerated individuals that may be particularly useful in correctional settings. The Infrequency (INF) scale is composed of items with extremely low endorsement rates in the standardization sample. Individuals with elevations on INF may be utilizing idiosyncratic or random response sets. Edens and Ruiz divided the INF scale into a front and back section to assess the possibility that individuals responded randomly to only part of the measure. Using a different strategy, Morey and Hopwood (2004) reported a method involving comparisons between the first and second half of other scales (Alcohol Problems and Suicidal Ideation) with the capability of efficiently detecting random responding across various portions of the test and base rates of the phenomenon.

The Negative Impression Management (NIM) scale includes items representing a pessimistic worldview and/or intentional malingering. To supplement this scale, several other negative distortion indicators have been developed. The Malingering Index (MAL; Morey, 1996) is composed of several configural indicators found to co-occur with intentional negative distortion. The Rogers Discriminant Function (RDF; Rogers, Sewell, Morey, & Ustad, 1996) is an empirical model maximized to differentiate individuals who intentionally malinger symptoms from individuals in clinical populations. Because of its low correlation with the clinical scales, RDF is perhaps the best single indicator of intentional malingering free from negative distortion commonly associated with psychopathology (e.g., depression). The Positive Impression Management (PIM) scale was developed to indicate an overly positive response set due to naivete or intentional positive distortion. As with NIM, several indexes can be used to supplement PIM in evaluating positive dissimulation. The Defensiveness Index (DEF; Morey, 1996) is an algorithm composed of several profile configurations that commonly occur when individuals attempt to positively dissimulate. The Cashel Discriminant Function (Cashel, Rogers, Sewell, & Martin-Cannici, 1995) is an empirical model found to differentiate honest responders from individuals faking good in both college student and correctional samples, and indicates intentional concealment of specific problems. Individuals commonly conceal substance use issues, and several indexes have been developed to identify them. Two scales measure substance use problems: Alcohol Problems (ALC) and Drug Problems (DRG). Items composing these scales are face-valid, so that individuals can easily achieve low scores if motivated to do so. Thus, Morey developed regression models composed of several scales, not including ALC or DRG, to predict the ALC and DRG scores. These indexes represent the best guess regarding respondents' substance use based on their personality, as inferred from the other PAI scales. To the extent that an individual's predicted score is greater than his or her obtained score on ALC or DRG, it is likely that the person is concealing use. Edens and Ruiz (2005) used a similar approach to develop the Addictive Characteristics Scale based on correctional norms.

Table 4.1 indicates that the PAI includes 11 clinical scales, two of which (ALC and DRG) were previously described. All of the clinical scales except ALC and DRG include subscales that assist in clarifying the nature of problems indicated by full-scale elevations. Within the neurotic spectrum, the Somatic Complaints (SOM) scale indicates overall health concerns; the Anxiety (ANX) scale assesses the general level of anxiety and the typical mode of anxiety expression; the Anxiety-Related Disorders (ARD) scale was developed to assess symptoms characteristic of anxiety disorders, including obsessive-compulsive, phobias, and traumatic stress reactions; and the Depression (DEP) scale measures core features of a major depressive episode. In the more psychotic spectrum, the Mania (MAN) scale was developed to measure cognitive, affective, and behavioral features of a manic episode; the Paranoia (PAR) scale assesses symptoms consistent with paranoid personality or psychosis; and the Schizophrenia (SCZ) scale measures positive and negative symptoms of that disorder. Finally, two clinical scales assess characteristics of the most commonly researched personality disorders, the Borderline Features (BOR) scale and the Antisocial Features (ANT) scale.

The PAI also includes several treatment consideration scales and indexes. First is the Aggression (AGG) scale, which measures overall level of anger and its typical mode of aggressive expression through its three subscales. In addition, the Violence Potential Index (VPI; Morey, 1996) is a configural algorithm based on several PAI scales that assists in the prediction of violence. The Suicidal Ideation (SUI) scale was developed to assess the frequency and intensity of suicidal thoughts and can be supplemented with the Suicide Potential Index (SPI; Morey, 1996), a configural algorithm comprising suicidal risk factors inferred from the profile. The Stress (STR) scale was developed to measure the degree to which respondents view their environment as unpredictable or difficult, whereas the Nonsupport (NON) scale measures respondents' perception that others are unavailable or unwilling to provide support. The Treatment Rejection (RXR) scale indicates attitudes that represent common obstacles or low motivation for treatment and personal change. To facilitate the assessment of amenability to treatment, Morey developed the Treatment Process Index, a configural algorithm composed of PAI scales related to treatment amenability. Finally, two scales, Dominance (DOM) and Warmth (WRM), were designed to measure normative personality traits associated with interpersonal theory that are helpful in predicting and understanding interpersonal behavior.

THE PERSONALITY ASSESSMENT INVENTORY AND CONTEMPORARY LEGAL STANDARDS

Mental health professionals are responsible for determining the utility of any assessment method they choose to employ in forensic and clinical settings, and they may be asked to defend such decisions in court. Evaluators can take several steps to prepare themselves to defend their choice of methods or the validity of their inferences should the need arise. These steps may include employing a variety of validated assessment methods, being thoroughly aware of current psychological research regarding the methods they choose, and using methods that meet current legal admissibility criteria (see Hess, 1999, for a detailed discussion regarding serving as an expert witness).

The PAI was designed to be used as part of a comprehensive assessment procedure, and clinical or forensic inferences should be based on information that goes beyond a consideration of PAI scores in isolation. However, invalid judgments can occur even in the context of an appropriately broad assessment battery. Inaccurate inferences can also occur due to a misunderstanding of the assessment method or unfamiliarity with the scientific literature. Consider the prediction of suicide within 72 hours of the evaluation based on an elevated score on the PAI SUI scale. In predicting imminent suicide, the odds of being correct are almost certainly lower than the odds of being incorrect, regardless of the prediction method, because of the low base rate of suicide. This prediction would also reflect a misunderstanding of the SUI scale, which was developed to measure suicidal ideation, not to predict suicidal behavior. It would be more appropriate to use the SUI in conjunction with the Suicide Potential Index and other indicators of suicide risk available from the clinical and life history data, rather than using SUI by itself (Morey, 2003).

Individuals may also misuse the PAI, for example by interpreting clearly invalid profiles or administering the measure to inappropriate populations. As the measure has demonstrated validity in a variety of applications, a number of important conclusions can be drawn from the use of the test, but the accuracy of such conclusions must be considered at a level of inference appropriate in light of the available research data. For example, despite the empirically demonstrated validity of BOR in predicting Borderline Personality Disorder (Edens & Ruiz, 2005), and the empirical demonstration that the base rate of childhood abuse is significantly higher in borderline individuals, it would be inappropriate to infer that an individual with a

BOR elevation was abused. Evaluators can buffet themselves from this mistake by discussing the degree of confidence they have in each inference they make and supplementing the PAI with other validated assessment methods.

In the determination of psycholegal assessment batteries, evaluating the source of the data according to existing legal standards may further prevent later legal difficulties. A variety of legal standards exists to assist judges in admissibility decisions. The issue first presented itself in the 1923 case *Frye v. United States,* a case in which a psychologist admitted systolic blood pressure changes as evidence of lie detection. The Court ruled that this technology had not reached general acceptance in the field and thus could not be admitted, setting a precedent for the ill-defined General Acceptance Test. However, many felt that this precedent set the bar too high and unnecessarily limited the potential for new scientific developments to be applied forensically (Hess, 1999). The *Daubert* criteria, which articulated the notion of general acceptance and added three additional criteria 70 years after *Frye,* resulted from the U.S. Supreme Court decision in *Daubert v. Merrell Dow Pharmaceuticals, Inc.* (1993). To determine the admissibility of scientific expert testimony, the *Daubert* criteria advocated a "four-pronged inquiry" (Emmerich, 1994; cited in Rotgers & Barrett, 1996). The criteria are used to evaluate the adequacy of the methods for the data on which the testimony is based, not the conclusions from the testimony itself (Rotgers & Barrett, 1996). Rotgers and Barrett summarize these criteria as follows:

> The *Daubert* (standard) requires (a) that scientific expert testimony be based on scientifically tested or testable theories; (b) that the theories and data-gathering methods on which testimony is based have been "subjected to peer review and publication"; (c) that known error rates in the application of the theory be explicitly stated; and (d) that the theory be generally accepted within the applicable field. (p. 469)

Several cases following *Daubert* have extended this integration, which is a process that appears on course to continue as legal precedent and scientific evidence mounts. In 1999, the U.S. Supreme Court expanded the applicability of *Daubert* criteria beyond scientific expert testimony to testimony that may be described as "technical" or "specialized" (*Kumho Tire Company v. Carmichael,* 1999). They also loosened the *Daubert* criteria by describing them as neither necessary nor sufficient for admissibility decisions, thus expanding judicial latitude with respect to their consideration of data from expert testimony (Medoff, 2003). Finally, in *General Electric Company v. Joiner* (1997), the U.S. Supreme Court emphasized the trial court's role in determining the legal reliability of the method, but not the validity of inferences based on that method. This decision reinforced the role of the court as gatekeeper of evidence, as well as the role of nonjudicial decision makers (e.g., jurors) in assessing the validity of inferences drawn (Medoff, 2003).

Although questions have been raised about the attention judges pay to legal admissibility criteria (Dahir et al., 2005) and the extent to which jurors are likely to be influenced by scientific as opposed to anecdotal data (Bornstein, 2004), the overall consensus appears to be that attempts to integrate scientific and legal standards of admissibility are worthwhile (Faigman & Monahan, 2005). Thus, professionals who use the PAI in expert testimony must be prepared to answer challenges to the admissibility of the instrument. The remainder of this chapter is devoted to a consideration of the PAI in the context of legal and psychometric criteria.

Criterion 1: Method Based on Scientifically Tested or Testable Theories

This criterion suggests that courts consider whether a specific technique is based on theories that have been or are capable of being empirically tested. The development of the PAI as a standardized psychological test was based on a construct validation framework that sampled constructs whose validity had been tested and largely accepted within the field and that utilized a variety of quantitative methods of item and scale development. After the PAI was developed, it went through a series of standard psychometric procedures to test normative responses, reliability, and validity of the scales. This articulation of the scales allowed a series of testable hypotheses to be drawn, and numerous such hypotheses have been tested since the PAI was first introduced. These results are described in more detail in a subsequent section; the following discussion focuses on the scientific and theoretical basis of the construction strategy for the instrument.

As a first step in the development of the PAI, the theoretical and empirical literature for each of the constructs to be measured was closely examined because this articulation had to serve as a guide to the content of information sampled and to the subsequent assessment of content validity. The development of the test then went through four iterations in a sequential construct validation strategy similar to that described by Loevinger (1957) and Jackson (1970) and included the consideration of a number of item parameters not described by those authors. Of paramount importance at each point of the development process was the assumption that no single quantitative item parameter should be used as the sole criterion for item selection. An overreliance on a single parameter in item selection typically leads to a scale with one desirable psychometric property and numerous undesirable ones. Both the conceptual nature and empirical adequacy of the items played an important role in their inclusion in the final version of the PAI.

The construction of the PAI sought to develop scales that provided a balanced sampling of the most important elements of the constructs being measured. This content coverage was designed to include a consideration of the *breadth* as well as *depth* of the construct. The breadth of content coverage refers to the diversity of elements subsumed within a construct. For example, in measuring depression, it is important to inquire about physiological and cognitive symptoms as well as features of affect. Depression scales that focus exclusively on one of these elements have limited breadth of coverage and compromised content validity. The PAI sought to ensure breadth of content coverage through the use of subscales representing the major elements of the measured constructs, as indicated by the theoretical and empirical literature.

The depth of content coverage refers to the need to sample across the full range of construct severity. To assure adequate depth of coverage, the scales were designed to include items reflecting both its milder and most severe forms. The use of four-alternative scaling provides each item with the capacity to capture differences in the severity of the manifestation of a feature of a particular disorder and is further justified psychometrically in that it allows a scale to capture more true variance per item, meaning that even scales of modest length can achieve satisfactory reliability. This item type may also be preferred by clinicians considering particular items (e.g., risk indicators) or clients themselves, who often express dissatisfaction with forced-choice alternatives because they believe that the truth is between the two extremes presented. The items themselves were also constructed to tap different levels of severity. For example, cognitive elements of depression can vary from mild pessimism to severe feelings of hopelessness, helplessness, and despair. Item characteristic curves were used to select items that provide information across the full range of construct severity. The nature of the severity continuum varies across the constructs. For example, severity on the SUI scale involves the imminence of the suicidal threat. Thus, items on this scale vary from vague and poorly articulated thoughts about suicide to immediate plans for self-harm.

One implication of a careful consideration of content validity in the construction of a test is that it is assumed that item content is critical in determining an item's ability to capture the phenomenology of various disorders and traits, and hence is relevant for the assessment of the construct. Empirically derived tests may include items on a construct scale that have no apparent relation to the construct in question. However, research (e.g., Holden, 1989; Holden & Fekken, 1990; Peterson, Clark, & Bennett, 1989) has consistently indicated that such items add little or no validity to self-report tests. The available empirical evidence is entirely consistent with the assumption that the content of a self-report item is critical in determining its utility in measurement. This assumption does not preclude the potential utility of items that are truly "subtle" in the sense that a lay audience cannot readily identify the relationship of the item to mental health status. However, the assumption does suggest that the implications of such items for mental health status should be apparent to expert diagnosticians for the item to be useful. Such expert judgments were used as one criterion in selecting PAI items; as a result, most judges and jurors can clearly recognize the relationship between clinical scale items and criteria for various emotional disorders derived from sources such as the fourth edition of the *Diagnostic and Statistical Manual of Mental Disorders* (American Psychiatric Association, 1994).

Another central psychometric concept in the development of the PAI was discriminant validity. Although discriminant validity has long been recognized as an important facet of construct validity, it traditionally has not played a major role in the construction of psychological tests, and it continues to represent one of the largest challenges in the assessment of psychological constructs. There are a variety of threats to validity in which discriminant validity plays a vital role. One such area involves *test bias*. A test that is intended to measure a psychological construct should not be measuring a demographic variable, such as gender, age, or sex. This does not mean that psychological tests should never be correlated with demographic variables, but that the magnitude of any such correlations should not exceed the theoretical overlap of the demographic feature with the construct. For example, nearly every indicator of antisocial behavior suggests that it is more common in men than in women; thus, it would be expected that an assessment of antisocial behavior would yield average scores for men that are higher than that for women. However, the items should have identical interpretive meaning regardless of the sex of the respondent. The construction of the PAI involved procedures such as bias review panels and differential item functioning analyses (Morey, 1991) that were designed to minimize the likelihood of test bias.

The issue of test bias is one that is particularly salient in light of past abuses of testing and current legislation designed to prevent such abuses. However, such bias is just one form of potential problems with discriminant validity. It is particularly common in the field of clinical assessment to find that a measure that supposedly measures one construct (such as anxiety or Schizophrenia) is, in fact, highly related to many constructs. It is this tendency that makes many instruments quite difficult to interpret. How does the clinician evaluate an elevated score on a scale measuring Schizophrenia if that scale is also a measure of alienation, indecisiveness, family problems, and depression? At each stage of the development of the PAI, items were selected that had maximal associations with indicators of the pertinent construct and minimal associations with the other constructs measured by the test.

Criterion 2: Method Subjected to Review and Publication

The second criterion involves the requirement that the scientific community has had adequate opportunity to uncover flaws in the method. The PAI was published by a commercial test publisher and was subjected to review and revision as part of this publication process. Since its publication, the test has been the subject of numerous reviews and publications in peer-reviewed journals. For example, the PAI has received favorable reviews in volumes dedicated to reviewing psychological procedures, such as the *Mental Measurements Yearbook* (Buros Institute, 1995) and the *Handbook of Psychiatric Measures* (American Psychiatric Association, 2000). The test has also been cited in widely used textbooks on psychometrics as an example of sophisticated strategies in test development (e.g., Anastasi & Urbina, 1997). The test and the professional manual have received favorable reviews in professional journals (Helmes, 1993; Schlosser, 1992; White, 1996), as has the computer version and interpretive report software (Schlosser, 1992). The PAI has been described as superior to widely used alternatives in several respects (Helmes, 1993; Rogers, 2003), and it has been suggested that the PAI has particular utility in forensic contexts as a screener, diagnostic instrument, and descriptive tool for describing offender populations (Douglas, Hart, & Kropp, 2001; Edens, Cruise, & Buffington-Vollum, 2001; White, 1996). Furthermore, numerous articles have been published in peer-reviewed journals that utilized the PAI specifically with forensic populations, as reviewed later in this chapter in the context of the *Daubert* criterion of acceptance in the field.

Criterion 3: Consideration of Error Rates and Standards Controlling Operation

The third *Daubert* criterion is particularly complex. Although vague in implications, two elements appear noteworthy. First, it is important that error rates for the method have been or can be established; second, it is essential that standards have been developed for drawing conclusions from the data. These two aspects are considered in turn.

A variety of potential decisions across a multitude of contexts may occur based entirely or in part on PAI data. The efficiency of the PAI may vary considerably across decisions and across contexts. Thus, it is misleading to discuss the concept of error rate as if it were a single, static number. In some areas, such as the identification of distorted profiles (a categorical dependent variable determined by random assignment), error rates for PAI decisions have been well documented. For example, accuracy rates for a PIM cutting score of $57T$ in identifying individuals instructed to "fake good" have been found to be in the 80% to 85% range in settings ranging from college students to correctional inmates to substance abuse inpatients (Cashel et al., 1995; Fals-Stewart, 1996; Fals-Stewart & Lucente, 1997; Morey, 1991; Morey & Lanier, 1998; Peebles & Moore, 1998).

However, establishing the validity of inferences drawn from any psychological procedure is much more complex than simply establishing an error rate. It is well-known in psychometrics that the efficiency of any procedure will vary across different contexts as a function of the a priori probability of the phenomenon being considered (Meehl & Rosen, 1955). As such, the error rate for any particular procedure may be quite different when applied, for example, in a custody evaluation context as opposed to a maximum security correctional setting. Furthermore, many of the important validating criteria in mental health tend to be continuous rather than dichotomous in nature, and the PAI scales themselves provide continuous scores. For example, considering clients as simply depressed or not depressed would ignore the continuous range of severity of depressive symptomatology, which is why nearly every depression treatment efficacy study uses continuous measures to gauge client outcome. Thus, error for many important mental health concepts must be measured as a continuous association—as in a confidence interval derived from a linear regression prediction—rather than as a percentage or rate. There are many studies that report such correlational evidence of the validity of PAI scales; the test manual alone provides validity correlations with more than 50 widely used markers of clinical constructs (Morey, 1991). Error percentages can be established from correlational data by establishing cutoffs, but selecting a cutoff may be somewhat arbitrary; the cutoff may have different efficiency in different settings, and it may also lose important client information in the process. Thus, for many of the validity studies of the PAI, error rates have not been reported, although it would be possible (although perhaps not always advisable) to calculate such rates. The validity of the PAI across a variety of potential decisions is considered in more detail later in this chapter.

The second element of this *Daubert* criterion involves the existence of clear standards controlling the operation of the method. As required by an objective psychometric instrument, standardization represents an essential feature of the PAI (standardization is described more thoroughly at a later point). Respondents receive the same questions in the same order with the same instructions, regardless of the assessment context, and standardized scores are calculated with reference to a national census-matched sample of community adults. Standards also exist for the professionals using the PAI: Use is restricted to qualified professionals who understand principles of psychiatric diagnosis and theories of personality and psychopathology and who possess knowledge of the appropriate uses and limitations of self-report inventories. Users are required to establish these qualifications before they are allowed to purchase the test materials.

Criterion 4: Acceptance of the Method within the Field

The fourth *Daubert* criterion seeks to ensure that the theory or methodology being used by experts is generally accepted within the scientific and professional field. To a certain extent, this overlaps with the notion of peer review described in the discussion of the second criterion. For example, the positive reviews of the PAI in professional journals related to psychometrics (e.g., Helmes, 1993; Schlosser, 1992; White, 1996) reflect its acceptance by the assessment discipline. The test has also generated a considerable amount of research in forensic settings (see review by Edens et al., 2001). Its acceptance within the professional community is further corroborated by the frequency with which it is used in a variety of settings. Survey data have demonstrated that the PAI ranks among the most frequently used personality measures in clinical training and practice (Piotrowski, 2000); for example, it was ranked fourth in a survey of internship directors as an objective personality instrument used in internship programs (Piotrowski & Belter, 2000). In a survey study of assessment instruments used by forensic psychologists in emotional injury cases, Boccaccini and Brodsky (1999) demonstrated that the PAI was used in 11% of the cases sampled; 17% of those who classified themselves as "frequent assessors" used the PAI, and professionals had used the test in such cases an average of 22 times over the preceding year. Finally, a majority of practicing forensic psychologists surveyed by Lally (2003) characterized the PAI as acceptable for evaluations of mental status at the time of offense, risk, sexual violence, competency to stand trial, and malingering.

One reason for its high rates of acceptability is that the PAI has several administrative advantages compared to similar measures (Rogers, 2003). It was developed and standardized for use in the assessment of individuals in the age range of 18 through adulthood. Items were written to be easily understood and applicable across cultures; the initial reading level analyses of the PAI test items indicated that reading ability at the fourth-grade level was necessary to complete the inventory. A comparative study of similar instruments by Schinka and Borum (1993) supported the conclusion that the PAI items are written at a grade equivalent lower than estimates for comparable instruments, an important issue in forensic settings, where reading ability is commonly lower than average. The PAI is also shorter and thus requires less time to complete than similar measures. Finally, scale names are based on the construct the scale was designed to measure and do not include overlapping items, facilitating discriminant validity and interpretation.

THE PERSONALITY ASSESSMENT INVENTORY AND CONTEMPORARY PSYCHOMETRIC STANDARDS

While the PAI has received considerable attention in the legal context because of its ability to meet the psycholegal criteria reviewed above, its acceptability to mental health professionals is also related to its demonstration of standardization and psychometric characteristics that meet current scientific standards. What follows is a description of the standardization procedures and psychometric properties of the

PAI, with particular emphasis on the demonstrated validity of inferences likely to occur in psycholegal settings.

Standardization

The PAI scale and subscale raw scores are transformed to *T*-scores (mean of 50, standard deviation of 10) to provide interpretation relative to a standardization sample of 1,000 community-dwelling adults. This sample was carefully selected to match 1995 U.S. Census projections on the basis of sex, race, and age; the educational level of the standardization sample (mean of 13.3 years) was representative of a community group with the required fourth-grade reading level. Unlike several similar instruments, the PAI does not calculate *T*-scores differently for men and women; instead, combined norms are used for both sexes. Separate norms are necessary only when the scale contains some bias that alters the interpretation of a score based on the respondent's sex. To use separate norms in the absence of such bias would only distort the natural epidemiological differences between the sexes. In the example discussed earlier, women are less likely than men to receive the diagnosis of Antisocial Personality Disorder, and this is reflected in the lower mean scores for women on the Antisocial Features (ANT) scale. A separate normative procedure for men and women would result in similar numbers of each sex scoring in the clinically significant range, a result that does not reflect the established sex ratio for this disorder. The PAI included several procedures to eliminate items that might be biased due to demographic features, and items that displayed any signs of being interpreted differently as a function of these features were eliminated in the course of selecting final items for the test. As it turns out, with relatively few exceptions, differences as a function of demography were negligible in the community sample. The most noteworthy effects involve the tendency for younger adults to score higher on the BOR and ANT scales and the tendency for men to score higher on the ANT and ALC relative to women.

Because *T*-scores are derived from a community sample, they provide a useful means for determining if certain problems are clinically significant, because relatively few normal adults will obtain markedly elevated scores. However, other comparisons are often of equal importance in clinical decision making. For example, nearly all patients report depression at their initial evaluation; the question confronting the clinician considering a diagnosis of Major Depressive Disorder is one of relative severity of symptomatology. Knowing the individual's score on the PAI Depression scale is elevated in comparison to the standardization sample is of value, but a comparison of the elevation relative to a clinical sample may be more critical in forming diagnostic hypotheses. To facilitate these comparisons, the PAI profile form also indicates the *T*-scores that correspond to marked elevations when referenced against a representative clinical sample. This profile skyline indicates the score for each scale and subscale that represents the raw score that is 2 standard deviations above the mean for a clinical sample of 1,246 patients selected from a wide variety of professional settings, such as inpatient hospitals, outpatient clinics, and private practices. Scores above this skyline represent a marked elevation relative to scores of patients in clinical settings. Thus, interpretation of the PAI profiles can be accomplished in comparison to both normal and clinical samples.

The PAI manual provides normative transformations for a number of different comparisons. Various appendixes provide *T*-score transformations referenced against the clinical sample and a large sample of college students, as well as for various demographic subgroups of the community standardization sample. Although the differences between demographic groups were generally quite small, there are occasions when it may be useful to make comparisons with reference to particular groups. Thus, the raw score means and standard deviations needed to convert raw scores to *T*-scores with reference to normative data provided by particular groups are provided in the manual. Correctional and Personnel Selection norms and scoring software are also available through the test publisher. Although it is appropriate to make normative comparisons to a sample most representative of the individual being assessed, for most clinical and research applications the use of *T*-scores derived from the full normative data is strongly recommended because of its representativeness and large sample size.

In addition, Edens and Ruiz (2005) have recently developed correctional software using normative data gathered from multiple correctional settings to enhance the forensic utility of the PAI. Their normative sample consisted of inmates in a prerelease treatment facility in New Jersey ($N = 542$), a treatment program for convicted sex offenders in Texas ($N = 98$), state prison inmates in Washington ($N = 515$), and forensic inpatients in New Hampshire ($N = 57$). Overall, the sample averaged 33.6 years of age ($SD = 8.9$) and 10.8 years of education. A large proportion of the sample were male (68.1%), and racial/ethnic representation mirrored that of corrections settings (45.2% African American, 37.7% Caucasian, 7.8% Hispanic). As would be predicted, the correctional norm group tended to score higher than the community standardization sample on Antisocial Features ($d = 1.15$), Drug Problems ($d = 1.62$), Stress ($d = .99$), and Borderline Features ($d = .84$), whereas they scored lower on Treatment Rejection ($d = -.96$). The use of these specialized norms may be appropriate in situations where an evaluation is being conducted in a correctional context with an incarcerated individual.

Reliability

The reliability of the PAI scales and subscales has been examined in terms of internal consistency (Alterman et al., 1995; Boyle & Lennon, 1994; Edens & Ruiz, 2005; Morey, 1991; Rogers, Flores, Ustad, & Sewell, 1995; Schinka, 1995), test-retest reliability (Boyle & Lennon, 1994; Edens & Ruiz, 2005; Morey, 1991; Rogers et al., 1995), and configural stability (Morey, 1991). Internal consistency alphas for the full scales are generally found to be in the .80s, whereas the subscales yield alphas in the .70s. Although these numbers are acceptable, internal consistency estimates are generally not the ideal basis for deriving the standard error of measurement (SEM) in clinical measures because temporal instability is often of greater concern than interitem correlations.

For the standardization studies, the median test-retest reliability value over a 4-week interval for the 11 full clinical scales was .86 (Morey, 1991), leading to SEM for these scales on the order of 3 to 4 *T*-score points, with 95% confidence intervals of +/− 6 to 8 *T*-score points. Absolute *T*-score change values over time were quite small across scales, on the order of 2 to 3 *T*-score points for most of the full scales

(Morey, 1991). Boyle and Lennon (1994) reported a median test-retest reliability of .73 in their normal sample over 28 days. Rogers et al. (1995) found an average stability of .71 for the Spanish version of the PAI administered over a 2-week period.

Because multiscale inventories are often interpreted configurally, additional questions should be asked concerning the stability of configurations on the 11 PAI clinical scales. One such analysis involved determining the inverse (or Q-type) correlation between each participant's profile at Time 1 and the profile at Time 2. Correlations were obtained for each of the 155 participants in the full retest sample, and a distribution of the within-subject profile correlations was obtained. Conducted in this manner, the median correlation of the clinical scale configuration was .83, indicating a substantial degree of stability in profile configurations over time (Morey, 1991).

Validity

As suggested earlier, uses and abuses of a psychological instrument can be described in the context of scientific or legal standards. However, evidence of scientific validity can only buttress legal arguments for acceptability. The array of potential assessment issues a mental health professional may encounter in a psycholegal setting are divided in this section into unsystematic, positive, and negative profile distortion; risk to others and to self; criminal responsibility; and competency to perform in a legal situation or in a personal or work context.

Nonsystematic Profile Distortion

The assessment of profile validity is a critical component of any method intended for use in an evaluative context; the issue is compounded in most forensic settings, where incentives for dishonest responding often exist. The PAI validity scales were developed to provide an assessment of the potential influence of certain response tendencies on PAI test performance, including both random and systematic influences. A comparison of profiles derived from normal and clinical participants and random response simulations in the standardization sample demonstrated a clear separation of scores of actual respondents from the random simulations, and 99% of these random profiles were identified as such by the Inconsistency (ICN) or Infrequency (INF) scales (Morey, 1991). To address the potential problem of partially random response sets, Morey and Hopwood (2004) developed an indicator of back random responding (e.g., a respondent discontinues attending to item content midway through the examination), involving front-to-back scaled score discrepancies on two PAI scales (ALC and SUI) with satisfactory positive and negative predictive power across levels and base rates of back random responding. As described earlier, Edens and Ruiz (2005) have recently introduced several validity scales that may prove to enhance the inferences about profile distortion in correctional settings.

Systematic Profile Distortion

Systematic profile distortion can occur in the positive or negative directions (Caruso, Benedek, Auble, & Bernet, 2003; Holden, Book, Edwards, Wasylkiw, & Starzyk, 2003). It can also occur in both directions in the same profile. For example, an individual may wish to emphasize feelings of anxiety and depression (i.e., negatively dissimulate) and also disguise use of alcohol or drugs (i.e., positively dissimulate). Systematic profile distortion can also occur in at least two ways. Individuals may consciously present themselves in a manner that is inconsistent with their experience or historical facts based on their perception of the consequences of their presentation (i.e., malinger or fake good). Conversely, individuals may present themselves in a way that is consistent with their subjective experience, but which most other individuals would see as an exaggeration (if overly negative) or lack of insight (if overly positive). This latter type of profile distortion has been referred to as self-deception and is related to specific forms of psychopathology. For example, cognitive symptoms of depression involve an underestimation of one's own abilities and worth and an overestimation of obstacles to emotional health or achievement. Conversely, narcissistic or manic disorders often involve an expansive approach to life and limited capacity for a critical appraisal of one's real abilities and prospects. Personality Assessment Inventory indexes of systematic profile distortion were developed to assess self- and other-deception in both the positive and negative directions.

The three indexes developed to directly assess *positive dissimulation* have been subjected to numerous empirical studies. In the initial validation studies described in the test manual, individuals scoring above the threshold on the PIM scale were 13.9 times more likely than a community sample to be in the positive dissimulation sample (Morey, 1991). Subsequent studies have generally supported the ability of PIM to distinguish simulators from actual protocols under a variety of response set conditions. For example, the studies described in the test manual found that the point of rarity on PIM between the distributions of the impression management sample (i.e., fake good) and the community normative sample was at a raw score of 57T; application of this cut score resulted in a sensitivity in the identification of defensiveness of 82% and a specificity with respect to normal individuals of 70%. These findings have been replicated in several samples (Fals-Stewart, 1996; Morey & Lanier, 1998; Peebles & Moore, 1998). In addition, it appears as though coaching has minimal effects on the PIM scale (Cashel et al., 1995).

The Defensiveness Index (DEF; Morey, 1996) is a composite of PAI scale configurations that tend to occur more frequently in profiles of individuals instructed to convey a positive impression than in honest respondents from clinical or community populations. Peebles and Moore (1998) reported a hit rate of 83% in distinguishing honest from fake-good respondents with the DEF. However, Cashel et al. (1995) reported that coached dissimulators obtained a lower mean score on the DEF than naive dissimulators, though the coached mean was still roughly 1 standard deviation above the norm for community samples. Cashel et al. developed the Cashel Discriminant Function (CDF) to measure positive dissimulation unassociated with self-deception to indicate the possibility that an examinee is faking good. The CDF is a function composed of weighted scale scores that was found to optimally distinguish defensive and honest respondents in their study. Cashel et al. demonstrated CDF sensitivities ranging from 79% to 87% in identifying the falsified profiles of college students and jail inmates and a specificity of 88%. These results, which have been replicated with naive dissimulators (Morey, 1996; Morey & Lanier, 1998), suggest the ability of the CDF to increment PIM and DEF in the detection of positive dissimulation.

One issue that is particularly prone to positive profile distortion is substance abuse. The PAI contains two scales, ALC and DRG, that inquire directly about behaviors and consequences related to alcohol and drug use, abuse, and dependence. These scales demonstrate a similar pattern of correlates: strong correlations with corresponding measures of substance abuse and moderate associations with indicators of behavior problems and antisocial personality (Alterman et al., 1995; Parker, Daleiden, & Simpson, 1999). The ALC scale has been found to differentiate patients in an alcohol rehabilitation clinic from patients with Schizophrenia (Boyle & Lennon, 1994) as well as normal controls (Ruiz, Dickinson, & Pincus, 2002). The DRG scale has been found to successfully discriminate drug abusers and methadone maintenance patients from general clinical and community samples (Alterman et al., 1995; Kellogg et al., 2002). DRG has also demonstrated strong correlations with the Addiction Severity Index (McLellan et al., 1992) and predicted both involvement with (as measured by urine samples) and negative consequences of substance use in a clinical sample (Kellogg et al., 2002). Another interesting finding from the Kellogg et al. study was that individuals who had been in methadone maintenance treatment for more than 1 year produced lower DRG scores than individuals who had been treated for less than 1 year. The authors attributed this effect to the biological and psychosocial stabilization that occurs as individuals maintain successful methadone treatment. Finally, individuals entering substance abuse treatment often demonstrate elevations on NIM and other indicators of negative dissimulation (Alterman et al., 1995; Boyle & Lennon, 1994), a phenomenon that may be related to state effects associated with intoxication or the detoxification process.

As items on ALC and DRG are face-valid, individuals who wish to avoid disclosing the full extent of their substance use can obtain low scores somewhat easily. Therefore, several empirically derived procedures to assess the likelihood that a profile underrepresents the extent of alcohol or drug problems (Edens & Ruiz, 2005; Fals-Stewart, 1996; Fals-Stewart & Lucente, 1997; Morey, 1996) have been described. Fals-Stewart and colleagues have demonstrated some success using PIM and a combination of PIM, ALC, and DRG in identifying questionable substance use respondents. Additionally, Morey (1996, 2003) described a linear regression strategy that successfully distinguished the groups described in Fals-Stewart's study with greater accuracy than the composite of PIM, ALC, and DRG. In this strategy, a predicted score is derived for both ALC and DRG based on the scores on other scales in the regression model. The difference between the predicted and observed scores is then used to indicate the probability of underreporting. Edens and Ruiz validated a similar strategy in their correctional sample.

The PAI has also received considerable research attention in the evaluation of *negative distortion.* A number of examinations of the utility of the NIM scale in the evaluation of malingering have been reported in the literature. In the initial validation studies cited in the test manual, individuals scoring above the critical level of NIM were 14.7 times more likely to be a member of the malingering group than of the clinical sample (Morey, 1991). Rogers, Ornduff, and Sewell (1993) examined the effectiveness of NIM in identifying both naive and sophisticated simulators (advanced graduate students in clinical and counseling psychology) who were given a financial incentive to avoid detection as malingerers while attempting to feign specific disorders. Rogers et al. found that the recommended NIM scale cutoff (84T) successfully identified 91% of participants attempting to feign Schizophrenia, 56% of participants simulating depression, and 39% of participants simulating an anxiety disorder. In contrast, only 3% of control participants were identified as simulators. Rogers et al. concluded that NIM is most effective in identifying the malingering of more severe mental disorders. As with PIM, there was no effect of subject sophistication: The scale was equally effective in identifying naive and sophisticated malingerers. Gaies (1993) conducted a similar study of malingering, focusing on the feigning of clinical depression, and reported average scores on NIM of 92T for sophisticated malingerers and 81T for naive malingerers. Although both simulation groups were elevated relative to honest responding groups, the results are similar to those of Rogers et al. in suggesting that individuals attempting to simulate milder forms of mental disorder (in this case, depression) will obtain more moderate elevations on NIM. Liljequist, Kinder, and Schinka (1998) reported significant NIM elevations in both clinical (alcohol mean = 62.93 and Posttraumatic Stress Disorder [PTSD] mean = 67.93) and malingering (mean = 92.48) groups relative to college student samples. Calhoun, Earnst, Tucker, Kirby, and Beckham (2000) compared PAI scores among PTSD diagnosed veterans, college student PTSD simulators, and community controls. A NIM score of 80T detected 75% of feigned protocols and demonstrated a hit rate of 59%, whereas a score of 102T detected 44% of simulators and demonstrated a hit rate of 63%. Finally, Scragg, Bor, and Mendham (2000) reported a sensitivity of 54% and a specificity of 100% for distinguishing malingered from true PTSD with the NIM scale.

The Malingering Index (MAL; Morey, 1996), a composite of PAI configural indicators, was introduced to measure malingering more directly than NIM, which is often affected by response styles consequent to psychopathology in addition to overt attempts at negative dissimulation. The MAL has been shown to differentiate individuals in a malingering sample from the community and clinical standardization samples (Morey, 1996). Wang et al. (1997) reported a statistically significant positive correlation between the MAL and two scales of the Structured Interview of Reported Symptoms (SIRS; Rogers, Bagby, & Dickens, 1992): Improbable or Absurd Symptoms ($r = .39$) and Symptom Combinations ($r = .42$). Gaies (1993) reported MAL (cut score = 3) sensitivity estimates of 56.6% and 34.2% in identifying informed and naive malingerers, respectively. Specificity with respect to depressed controls in that study was 89% and with respect to community controls was 100%. Calhoun et al. (2000) reported that a MAL cut score of 3 detected 44% of simulators in their sample and misclassified several individuals with PTSD as malingerers. Scragg et al. (2000) reported sensitivity of 45% and specificity of 94% in distinguishing malingered from true PTSD with MAL. These results suggest both an association with psychopathology, though less so than is the case with NIM, and that sensitivity declines to the extent that less severe forms of psychopathology are malingered.

Rogers and colleagues (1996) developed the RDF, an index that appears able to indicate malingering but that is not associated with psychopathology (i.e., does not systematically correlate with the clinical scales). This research group demonstrated and cross-validated sensitivity and specificity estimates above 80% in distinguishing both coached and naive malingerers from honest respondents. Morey

(1996) replicated these results using naive college student simulators and found RDF to be the most accurate among the PAI negative validity indicators in identifying malingerers. In fact, RDF resulted in positive predictive power estimates > .80 across malingering base rates of 20%, 50%, and 80%. Bagby, Nicholson, Bacchiochi, Ryder, and Bury (2002) compared the PAI validity indexes of individuals drawn from a clinical population to coached and uncoached college students asked to feign a mental disorder. Similar to previous results, coaching had no effect on the ability of research participants to achieve valid profiles. They found that RDF was significantly superior to NIM and DEF as well as every Minnesota Multiphasic Personality Inventory 2 (MMPI-2; Butcher, Dahlstrom, Graham, Tellegen, & Kaemmer, 1989) malingering index, although the MMPI-2 indexes F and $F(p)$ were able to increment the predictive capability of RDF. In a similar study, Blanchard, McGrath, Pogge, and Khadivi (2003) reported that NIM, MAL, and RDF all demonstrated hit rates > .93 in identifying simulators, and that the PAI indicators significantly incremented MMPI-2 indicators of malingering and vice versa. Scragg et al. (2000) reported a sensitivity of 63% and specificity of 94% for the RDF in their study of malingered PTSD. However, Wang et al. (1997) failed to find a relationship between RDF and the SIRS malingering classification in a small correctional sample, and several authors have suggested that the translation of RDF from clinical to forensic settings is problematic (e.g., Edens et al., 2001). Rogers, Sewell, Ustad, Reinhardt, and Edwards (1998) tested the RDF in a forensic setting and observed a classification rate shrinkage to 62%. Based on these results, Rogers et al. recommended using RDF to screen for, but not directly indicate, malingering in forensic settings.

One common context in which response set validity is a particular problem is the area of pain assessment, for example in disability evaluations. The Somatic Complaints (SOM) scale was designed to address the phenomenology of individuals reporting pain or somatic deficits. It includes the Conversion Disorders (SOM-C), Somatic Complaints (SOM-S), and Health Concerns (SOM-H) subscales. The use of SOM in diagnostic formulations is most helpful when used in concert with medical information, reported symptoms, and an understanding of the assessment context. The SOM subscales can be used in combination with the validity indexes and external data to differentiate individuals who are malingering somatic problems, converting psychological problems to somatic symptoms as a characteristic strategy to minimize anxiety, or reporting genuine symptoms and severity. Differentiating among these classes of individuals, all of whom are likely to obtain elevations on SOM, is a common and important forensic issue, particularly in contexts in which there is motivation to exaggerate symptoms, such as disability evaluations. The administration of a multiscale instrument such as the PAI is the industry standard in such cases (Bianchini, Etherton, & Greve, 2004; Slick, Sherman, & Iverson, 1999), and available data support the utility of the PAI in assessing emotional aspects of chronic pain (George & Wagner, 1995; Karlin et al., in press).

Claims of emotional damage are also commonly encountered in forensic assessment. In such cases, the potential for response distortion is high due to the incentive to overreport symptoms. The clinical scales of the PAI were assembled to provide information about clinical constructs relevant in a variety of forensic and clinical contexts. A number of instruments have been used to provide information on the convergent and discriminant validity of the PAI clinical scales. Correlations tend to follow hypothesized patterns; for example, strong associations are found between neurotic spectrum scales such as Anxiety (ANX), Anxiety-Related Disorder (ARD), and Depression (DEP) and other psychometric measures of neuroticism (Costa & McCrae, 1992; Montag & Levin, 1994; Morey, 1991). The ARD scale has also been found to correlate with the probability of experiencing nightmares, with ARD-T in particular being associated with night terrors (Greenstein, 1993). The ARD scale (particularly ARD-T) has also been found to differentiate women psychiatric patients who were victims of childhood abuse from other women patients who did not experience such abuse (Cherepon & Prinzhorn, 1994). Similarly, the DEP scale demonstrates its largest correlations with various widely used indicators of depression, such as the Beck Depression Inventory (Beck & Steer, 1987), the Hamilton Rating Scale for Depression (Hamilton, 1960), and the Wiggins (1966) MMPI Depression content scale (Ban, Fjetland, Kutcher, & Morey, 1993; Morey, 1991). Several indicators have been found useful in discriminating PTSD from Antisocial Personality Disorder among individuals traumatized in motor vehicle accidents (G. E. Holmes, Williams, & Haines, 2001), and the PAI has demonstrated effectiveness in distinguishing true from malingered PTSD in psychiatric (Liljequist et al., 1998) and VA (Calhoun et al., 2000) samples. It has also been suggested that the PAI provides important diagnostic information about individuals with Eating Disorder (Tasca, Wood, Demidenko, & Bissada, 2002) problems. These clinical scales can be used in conjunction with the validity scales, as well as clinical scales tapping more severe types of psychopathology (considered next), to make inferences in the context of emotional injury evaluations.

Risk to Self

The SUI scale was developed to indicate the degree to which the examinee is thinking about suicide as an option. In the initial validation studies (Morey, 1991), the scale was found to correlate positively with the Beck Hopelessness Inventory (.64; Beck & Steer, 1988), the Beck Depression Inventory (Beck & Steer, 1987), and the Suicidal Ideation (.56) and Total Score (.40) of the Suicide Probability Scale (Cull & Gill, 1982), while it correlated negatively with Perceived Social Support (PSS; Procidano & Heller, 1983). Wang et al. (1997) found that SUI had the largest correlation among PAI scales to the number of suicide risk assessments in a large sample of incarcerated men, and that the scale could reliably differentiate individuals who had or had not made suicidal gestures. Rogers, Ustad, and Salekin (1998) found that SUI demonstrated moderate to large correlations with other self-report measures of suicidal ideation in a sample of correctional emergency referrals. Although most individuals who commit suicide tend also to ideate around the issue, the two factors are somewhat independent. Many individuals in clinical samples ideate without acting on their suicidal thoughts, whereas some suicides occur in individuals who apparently spent little time planning or ruminating about the act. The Suicide Potential Index (SPI) comprises 20 configural indexes of suicide potential independent of SUI (e.g., substance use, impulsivity) and was developed to increment SUI in the prediction of suicidal behavior. The Wang et al. and Rogers, Ustad, et al. (1998) studies found significant positive correlations between suicidal behavior and the SPI. Negative Impression Management appears to moderate the relation between SUI and SPI, suggesting that an elevated SPI score with a NIM score in the normal range is worth particular attention (Morey, 2003).

Risk to Others

Several PAI indexes are particularly useful in assessing risk to others. The literature on violence suggests that trait aggression, life stress, history of externalizing or chaotic behavior, and substance use represent risk factors for violence to others, and the PAI provides important information in each of these domains. The most direct measure of aggression on the PAI is the Aggression (AGG) scale. Substantial correlations have been described (Morey, 1991) between the AGG scale and related indicators, such as the NEO Personality Inventory (NEO-PI; Costa & McCrae, 1992) Hostility (.83) scale and the Spielberger State-Trait Anxiety Inventory (Spielberger, 1988) Trait Anger (.75) and Anger Control (−.57) scales. The AGG has also received considerable research attention in forensic settings. Wang et al. (1997) found significant positive relations between AGG and all three of its subscales to the Overt Aggression Scale (Yudofsky, Silver, Jackson, Endicott, & Williams, 1986) in a sample of inmates receiving or requesting psychiatric services. Wang and Diamond (1999) identified the Physical Aggression (AGG-P) and Verbal Aggression (AGG-V) scales as related to institutional misbehavior among mentally ill offenders. Salekin, Rogers, Ustad, and Sewell (1998) found that AGG predicted recidivism among female offenders over a 14-month follow-up. Finally, Walters, Duncan, and Geyer (2003) reported that AGG significantly incremented the Psychopathy Checklist-Revised (PCL-R; Hare, 1985) and demographic variables in predicting disciplinary adjustment in prison inmates.

Personality disorders are common in forensic examinees and represent risk factors for a variety of problematic behaviors common in forensic settings, including violent behavior. Two scales on the PAI directly target personality disorders: the BOR scale and the ANT scale. The choice to include these two constructs on the PAI was based on the fact that the majority of the literature on personality disorders relates to these constructs. Both the BOR and the ANT have been found to relate to other measures of these constructs and to predict relevant behavioral outcomes (e.g., Salekin et al., 1998; Trull, Useda, Conforti, & Doan, 1997). The BOR scale has been found to correlate with the MMPI Borderline scale (Morey, 1991), the Bell Object Relations Inventory (Bell, Billington, & Becker, 1985; Kurtz, Morey, & Tomarken, 1992), and the NEO-PI (Costa & McCrae, 1992) Neuroticism scale. Other studies have supported the validity and utility of this scale in borderline treatment samples (e.g., Evershed et al., 2003; Yeomans, Hull, & Clarkin, 1994) and in predicting general maladjustment in college students (Bagge et al., 2004). It has also been demonstrated that an assessment of BOR increments the information provided by a diagnosis of Major Depressive Disorder (Kurtz & Morey, 2001). The BOR scale in isolation has been found to distinguish borderline patients from unscreened controls with an 80% hit rate and successfully identified 91% of these participants as part of a discriminant function (Bell-Pringle, Pate, & Brown, 1997). Edens and Ruiz (2005) found that BOR was able to classify individuals discharged from an inpatient corrections unit as having Borderline Personality

Disorder with impressive efficiency (*AUC* = .97). Classifications based on the BOR scale have been validated in a variety of domains related to borderline functioning, including depression, personality traits, coping, Axis I disorders, and interpersonal problems (Trull, 1995). These BOR scale classifications were also found to be predictive of 2-year outcome on academic indexes (e.g., grades, academic status) in college students, even controlling for academic potential and substance abuse (Trull et al., 1997).

The ANT scale demonstrated its largest correlations in initial validation studies (Morey, 1991) with the MMPI Antisocial Personality Disorder (Morey, Waugh, & Blashfield, 1985) and the Self-Report Psychopathy test designed by Hare (Psychopathy Checklist-Revised, 1985) to assess his model of psychopathy. Subsequent studies have also supported the validity of ANT. Salekin, Rogers, and Sewell (1997) examined the relationship between ANT and psychopathic traits in a sample of female offenders and found that elevations on ANT among this population were primarily the result of endorsements on Antisocial Behaviors (ANT-A). Also, support was found for the convergent validity of ANT with other measures of psychopathy, including the PCL-R total score and the Personality Disorder Examination (Loranger, 1988) Antisocial scale. Edens, Hart, Johnson, Johnson, and Olver (2000) examined the relationship of the ANT scale to the screening version of the Psychopathy Checklist (PCL-SV; Hart, Cox, & Hare, 1995) and the PCL-R. Moderately strong correlations were found between ANT and the PCL-SV and the PCL-R total score, with the highest correlations with these measures being found on ANT-A. Salekin et al. (1998) demonstrated the ability of the ANT and AGG scales of the PAI to predict recidivism among female inmates over a 14-month follow-up interval. The ANT has also demonstrated validity in predicting violence in a sample of incarcerated mentally ill individuals (Wang & Diamond, 1999) and in predicting treatment course for a sample of borderline females (Clarkin, Hull, Yeomans, Kakuma, & Cantor, 1994). The ANT was shown to both increment and outperform the PCL-R in predicting disciplinary infractions among incarcerated sex offenders over a 2-year follow-up period, demonstrating an overall hit rate of .70 with a cut score of 70*T* (Buffington-Vollum, Edens, Johnson, & Johnson, 2002). Finally, the PAI, and in particular the BOR, ANT, and AGG scales, has demonstrated the capacity to differentiate various types of antisocial individuals, such as generally violent men versus men who abuse family members but are not violent outside the home (DelSol, Margolin, & John, 2003) and individuals convicted of violent versus nonviolent crimes (Edwards, Scott, Yarvis, Paizis, & Panizzon, 2003).

As described earlier, several other PAI scales are particularly useful in assessing risk to others. For example, substance use is associated with impulsivity and a general tendency to violence. Mania (MAN) scale elevations may also cause some concern, as overactivity (MAN-A), grandiosity (MAN-G), and irritability (MAN-I) all represent risk factors for violence in response to frustration. Some of the treatment consideration scales, including Stress (STR) and Nonsupport (NON), may also suggest the possibility that someone is likely to engage in violence. Many of these factors have been incorporated into the VPI, a configural algorithm developed to predict violent behavior (Morey, 1996). The VPI has been found to correlate with the staff-rated Overt Aggression Scale (Wang et al., 1997), and scores on the VPI have been found to be elevated, relative to general psychiatric patients, in groups on current assault precautions and those convicted of violent crimes (Morey, 1996). Caperton, Edens, and Johnson (2004) found the VPI to be related to disciplinary infractions, both general and major, in a sex offender corrections-based treatment program. It is important to remember, however, that this index can be influenced by negative profile distortion, as it comprises several scales that correlate positively with negative dissimulation (Morey, 2003).

Criminal Responsibility

Psychosis and cognitive impairment are perhaps the most common psychological reasons arguing that individuals were not responsible for crimes they admit to having committed. Although a diagnosis of a mental disorder alone is not sufficient in and of itself to provide an opinion supporting an insanity defense, a diagnosis of a mental disorder (e.g., Schizophrenia) or mental defect (e.g., mental retardation) is a prerequisite for such an opinion (see Goldstein, Morse, & Shapiro, 2003, for a description of the legal elements of an insanity defense). Within the psychotic spectrum, PAI scales such as Paranoia (PAR), Mania (MAN), and Schizophrenia (SCZ) have been found to be correlated with a variety of other indicators of severe psychopathology (Morey, 1991). For example, PAR has been found to correlate particularly well with diagnostic assessments of paranoia made via structured clinical interview (Rogers, Ustad, et al., 1998), and the SCZ scale has been found to distinguish schizophrenic patients from controls (Boyle & Lennon, 1994). In that study, the schizophrenic sample did not differ significantly from a sample of alcoholics on SCZ scores, although certain characteristics of their criterion group (patients on medication maintenance) and their alcoholic group (alcoholics undergoing detoxification) may have, in part, accounted for these findings (Morey, 1995). Schizophrenia has also been shown to significantly increment the Rorschach Comprehensive System Schizophrenia Index (SCZI; Exner, 1993) in differentiating inpatients with schizophrenic spectrum disorders from inpatients with other diagnoses, whereas SCZI was unable to increment SCZ (Klonsky, 2004). These data suggest that efforts during the construction of the PAI to enhance discriminant validity on the SCZ scale were justified, as the control group comprised psychiatric inpatients, many of whom met criteria for disorders with symptoms similar to Schizophrenia (e.g., organic psychoses, cognitive deficits). Nonetheless, given the limited research with the SCZ scale, some have suggested it be interpreted as a measure of general impairment rather than as a specific marker of Schizophrenia (Rogers, Ustad, et al., 1998). Combining the PAI profile with information from other assessment sources may be particularly important for differential diagnosis of psychotic disorders (Edens et al., 2001).

Cognitive impairment is suggested by elevations on scales such as ICN, ANX-C, and SCZ-T. However, the PAI is not a measure of cognitive functioning, and indications of cognitive compromise suggested by these scales should be followed up with measures designed to specifically assess that domain.

Competency to Perform in Legal Settings

The capacity to waive *Miranda* rights or to be competent to appear in court are common concerns in psycholegal settings (see Oberlander, Goldstein, & Goldstein, 2003, for a discussion of issues related to evaluations of *Miranda* rights waivers, and Stafford, 2003, for a description of issues relevant to trial competency assessments). Several psychological reasons may exist for a compromised ability to perform such tasks, such as cognitive disruption or severely impaired reality testing, and these are similar to common issues in criminal responsibility cases. Factors affecting competency are also likely to affect the client's ability to complete a self-report instrument such as the PAI, and in many cases, relevant information can be gleaned from validity scales, particularly ICN and INF. In another scenario, individuals may experience comprehension difficulties related to psychosis, as indicated by elevations on SCZ (particularly SCZ-P and SCZ-T), and these scales have demonstrated effectiveness in identifying Schizophrenia (Klonsky, 2004).

Competency to Perform in Nonlegal Settings

The capacity of individuals to perform as parents or as employees is another common assessment issue and is related to overall psychological adjustment. Obviously, elevations on any indicators of severe psychopathology or substance use suggest an increased likelihood for poor outcomes. The PAI profile has been studied in the context of custody evaluations (Colby & Campagna, 2003), and survey data indicate the use of the test for this purpose is increasing (Quinnell & Bow, 2001). The PAI has also been empirically related to various criteria associated with success in sensitive occupations such as in law enforcement (Hays, 1997), including successful completion of a 1-year probationary period as a police officer (Roberts, Thompson, & Johnson, 1999). In addition to clinically oriented constructs, the PAI also has several scales that address environmental and motivational factors in performance. As expected, the Nonsupport (NON) scale was found to be highly (and inversely) correlated with the social support measures: −.67 with PSS-Family, −.63 with PSS-Friends in the standardization studies. It was also moderately associated with numerous measures of distress and tension. The Stress (STR) scale displayed its largest correlations with the Schedule of Recent Events (.50), a unit-scoring adaptation of the widely used T. H. Holmes and Rahe (1967) Checklist of Recent Stressors, and was also associated with various indexes of depression and poor morale. Finally, the Treatment Rejection (RXR) scale has been found to be negatively associated with indicators of demoralization and vulnerability from the MMPI and NEO-PI (Morey, 1991), consistent with the idea that distress motivates treatment utilization and effort. The RXR has been shown to be positively associated with indexes of social support, implying that people are less likely to be motivated for treatment if they have an intact and available support system as an alternative. This scale has predicted treatment noncompliance in a sample of sex offending inmates (Caperton et al., 2004).

CONCLUSION

Scientific and legal standards for the admissibility of psychological assessment data have historically relied on different methods and have come to somewhat different conclusions. Recent efforts to clarify such criteria in legal situations have resulted in a need to integrate methods from both fields and for mental health professionals to be aware of both criteria sets. In particular, professionals who may have to defend the use of particular measures or the inferences they derive from data should choose instruments that meet contemporary standards in both fields and should take care to limit inferences to those that are scientifically defensible. The PAI, a multiscale self-report instrument that is commonly used in psycholegal settings, appears to meet important standards with respect to both legal and scientific methods. The PAI may assist forensic mental health professionals in the assessment of a wide range of both criminal and civil psycholegal issues. In addition, it offers a number of advantages over similar instruments, including reading level, length, interpretive clarity, item response options, and nonoverlapping scales that result in excellent reliability and discriminant validity (Rogers, 2003). However, it is important that additional research continues to assess the utility of the PAI for specific psycholegal assessment decisions, in terms of both replicating previous findings and establishing new ones. In particular, additional efforts to gather prospective data regarding risk and outcome would further the validation process for the PAI when used for this purpose.

REFERENCES

Alterman, A. I., Zaballero, A. R., Lin, M. M., Siddiqui, N., Brown, L. S., Rutherford, M. J., et al. (1995). Personality Assessment Inventory (PAI) scores of lower-socioeconomic African American and Latino methadone maintenance patients. *Assessment, 2*(1), 91–100.

American Psychiatric Association. (1994). *Diagnostic and statistical manual of mental disorders* (4th ed.). Washington, DC: Author.

American Psychiatric Association, Task Force for the Handbook of Psychiatric Measures. (2000). *Handbook of psychiatric measures.* Washington, DC: Author.

Anastasi, A., & Urbina, S. (1997). *Psychological testing* (7th ed.). Upper Saddle River, NJ: Prentice-Hall.

Bagby, M. R., Nicholson, R. A., Bacchiochi, J. R., Ryder, A. G., & Bury, A. S. (2002). The predictive capacity of the MMPI-2 and PAI validity scales and indexes to detect coached and uncoached feigning. *Journal of Personality Assessment, 78*(1), 69–86.

Bagge, C., Nickell, A., Stepp, S., Durrett, C., Jackson, K., & Trull, T. J. (2004). Borderline personality disorder features predict negative outcomes 2 years later. *Journal of Abnormal Psychology, 113*(2), 279–288.

Ban, T. A., Fjetland, O. K., Kutcher, M., & Morey, L. C. (1993). CODE-DD: Development of a diagnostic scale for depressive disorders. In I. Hindmarch & P. Stonier (Eds.), *Human psychopharmacology: Vol. 4. Measures and methods* (pp. 73–85). Chichester, West Sussex, England: Wiley.

Beck, A. T., & Steer, R. A. (1987). *Beck Depression Inventory manual.* San Antonio, TX: Psychological Corporation.

Beck, A. T., & Steer, R. A. (1988). *Beck Hopelessness Scale manual.* San Antonio, TX: Psychological Corporation.

Bell, M. J., Billington, R., & Becker, B. (1985). A scale for the assessment of object relations: Reliability, validity, and factorial invariance. *Journal of Clinical Psychology, 42,* 733–741.

Bell-Pringle, V. J., Pate, J. L., & Brown, R. C. (1997). Assessment of borderline personality disorder using the MMPI-2 and the Personality Assessment Inventory. *Assessment, 4,* 131–139.

Bianchini, K. J., Etherton, J. L., & Greve, K. W. (2004). Diagnosing cognitive malingering in patients with work-related pain: Four cases. *Journal of Forensic Neuropsychology, 4*(1), 65–85.

Blanchard, D. D., McGrath, R. E., Pogge, D. L., & Khadivi, A. (2003). A comparison of the PAI and MMPI-2 as predictors of faking bad in college students. *Journal of Personality Assessment, 80*(2), 197–205.

Boccaccini, M. T., & Brodsky, S. L. (1999). Diagnostic test usage by forensic psychologists in emotional injury cases. *Professional Psychology: Research and Practice, 30,* 253–259.

Bornstein, B. H. (2004). The impact of different types of expert scientific testimony on mock juror's libability verdicts. *Psychology, Crime, and Law, 10*(4), 429–446.

Boyle, G. J., & Lennon, T. (1994). Examination of the reliability and validity of the Personality Assessment Inventory. *Journal of Psychopathology and Behavioral Assessment, 16*(3), 173–187.

Buffington-Vollum, J., Edens, J. F., Johnson, D. W., & Johnson, J. K. (2002). Psychopathy as a predictor of institutional misbehavior among sex offenders: A prospective replication. *Criminal Justice and Behavior, 29*(5), 497–511.

Buros Institute. (1995). *Mental measurements yearbook*. Highland Park, NJ: Gryphon Press.

Butcher, J. H., Dahlstrom, W. G., Graham, J. R., Tellegen, A., & Kaemmer, B. (1989). *Manual for the administration and scoring of the MMPI-2*. Minneapolis: University of Minnesota Press.

Calhoun, P. S., Earnst, K. S., Tucker, D. D., Kirby, A. C., & Beckham, J. C. (2000). Feigning combat-related posttraumatic stress disorder on the Personality Assessment Inventory. *Journal of Personality Assessment, 75*(2), 338–350.

Caperton, J. D., Edens, J. F., & Johnson, J. K. (2004). Predicting sex offender institutional adjustment and treatment compliance using the Personality Assessment Inventory. *Psychological Assessment, 16*(2), 187–191.

Caruso, K. A., Benedek, D. M., Auble, P. M., & Bernet, W. (2003). Concealment of psychopathology in forensic evaluations: A pilot study of intentional and uninsightful dissimulators. *Journal of the American Academy of Psychiatry and Law, 31*, 444–450.

Cashel, M. L., Rogers, R., Sewell, K., & Martin-Cannici, C. (1995). The Personality Assessment Inventory (PAI) and the detection of defensiveness. *Assessment, 2*(4), 333–342.

Cherepon, J. A., & Prinzhorn, B. (1994). Personality Assessment Inventory (PAI) profiles of adult female abuse survivors. *Assessment, 1*(4), 393–399.

Clarkin, J. F., Hull, J. W., Yeomans, F., Kakuma, T., & Cantor, J. (1994). Antisocial traits as modifiers of treatment response in borderline inpatients. *Journal of Psychotherapy Practice and Research, 3*(4), 307–312.

Colby, F., & Campagna, V. (2003, May). *Local norms and the Personality Assessment Inventory*. Paper presented at the meetings of the American Psychological Society, Atlanta, GA.

Costa, P. T., & McCrae, R. R. (1992). Normal personality in clinical practice: The NEO Personality Inventory. *Psychological Assessment: A Journal of Consulting and Clinical Psychology, 4*, 5–13.

Cull, J. G., & Gill, W. S. (1982). *Suicide Probability Scale manual*. Los Angeles: Western Psychological Services.

Dahir, D. B., Richardson, J. T., Ginsburg, G. P., Gatowski, S. I., Dobbin, S. A., & Merlino, M. L. (2005). Judicial application of *Daubert* to psychological syndrome and profile evidence. *Psychology, Public Policy, and Law, 11*(1), 62–82.

Daubert v. Merrell Dow Pharmaceuticals, Inc., 509 U.S. 579 (1993).

DelSol, C., Margolin, G., & John, R. S. (2003). A typology of maritally violent men and correlates of violence in a community sample. *Journal of Marriage and Family, 65*(3), 635–651.

Douglas, K. S., Hart, S. D., & Kropp, P. R. (2001). Validity of the Personality Assessment Inventory for forensic assessments. *International Journal of Offender Therapy and Comparative Criminology, 45*(2), 183–197.

Edens, J. F., Cruise, K. R., & Buffington-Vollum, J. K. (2001). Forensic and correctional applications of the Personality Assessment Inventory. *Behavioral Sciences and the Law, 19*(4), 519–543.

Edens, J. F., Hart, S. D., Johnson, D. W., Johnson, J. K., & Olver, M. E. (2000). Use of the Personality Assessment Inventory to assess psychopathy in offender populations. *Psychological Assessment, 12*(2), 132–139.

Edens, J. F., & Ruiz, M. A. (2005). *PAI interpretive report for correctional settings (PAI-CS)*. Odessa, FL: Psychological Assessment Resources.

Edwards, D. W., Scott, C. L., Yarvis, R. M., Paizis, C. L., & Panizzon, M. S. (2003). Impulsiveness, impulse aggression, personality disorder, and spousal violence. *Violence and Victims, 18*(1), 3–14.

Emmerich, F. R. (1994). The Supreme Court strengthens the discretionary powers of the disctrict courts in admitting expert scientific testimony: *Daubert v. Merrell Dow Pharmaceuticals, Inc. Widener Journal of Public Law, 3*, 1051–1108.

Evershed, S., Tennant, A., Boomer, D., Rees, A., Barkham, M., & Watson, A. (2003). Practice-based outcomes of dialectical behaviour therapy (DBT) targeting anger and violence, with male forensic patients: A pragmatic and non-contemporaneous comparison. *Criminal Behaviour and Mental Health, 13*(3), 198–213.

Exner, J. E. (1993). *The Rorschach: A comprehensive system*. Asheville, NC: Rorschach Workshops.

Faigman, D. L., & Monohan, J. (2005). Psychological evidence at the dawn of the law's scientific age. *Annual Review of Psychology, 56,* 631–659.

Fals-Stewart, W. (1996). The ability of individuals with psychoactive substance use disorders to escape detection by the Personality Assessment Inventory. *Psychological Assessment, 8*(1), 60–68.

Fals-Stewart, W., & Lucente, S. (1997). Identifying positive dissimulation substance-abusing individuals on the Personality Assessment Inventory: A cross-validation study. *Journal of Personality Assessment, 68,* 455–469.

Frye v. United States, 293 Fed. 1013 D.C. (1923).

Gaies, L. A. (1993). Malingering of depression on the Personality Assessment Inventory (doctoral dissertation, University of South Florida). *Dissertation Abstracts International, 55,* 6711.

General Electric Co. v. Joiner, 522 U.S. 136 (1997).

George, J. M., & Wagner, E. (1995). Correlations between the Hand Test pathology score and Personality Assessment Inventory scales for pain clinic patients. *Perceptual and Motor Skills, 80*(3, Pt. 2), 1377–1378.

Goldstein, A. M., Morse, S. T., & Shapiro, D. L. (2003). Evaluation of criminal responsibility. In I. B. Weiner (Series Ed.) & A. M. Goldstein (Vol. Ed.), *Comprehensive handbook of psychology: Vol. 11. Forensic psychology* (pp. 381–407). Hoboken, NJ: Wiley.

Greenstein, D. S. (1993). Relationship between frequent nightmares, psychopathology, and boundaries among incarcerated male inmates (doctoral dissertation, Adler School of Professional Psychology). *Dissertation Abstracts International, 55,* 4119.

Hamilton, M. (1960). A rating scale for depression. *Journal of Neurology, Neurosurgery, and Psychiatry, 23,* 56–62.

Hare, R. D. (1985). Comparison of procedures for the assessment of psychopathy. *Journal of Consulting and Clinical Psychology, 53,* 7–16.

Hart, S. D., Cox, D. N., & Hare, R. D. (1995). *Psychopathy Checklist: Screening version.* Toronto, Ontario, Canada: Multi-Health Systems.

Hays, J. R. (1997). Note on concurrent validation of the Personality Assessment Inventory in law enforcement. *Psychological Reports, 81,* 244–246.

Helmes, E. (1993). A modern instrument for evaluating psychopathology: The Personality Assessment Inventory professional manual. *Journal of Personality Assessment, 61,* 414–417.

Hess, A. K. (1999). Serving as an expert witness. In A. K. Hess & I. B. Weiner (Eds.), *Handbook for forensic psychology* (pp. 521–555). New York: Wiley.

Holden, R. R. (1989). Disguise and the structured self-report assessment of psychopathology: Pt. II. A clinical replication. *Journal of Clinical Psychology, 45*(4), 583–586.

Holden, R. R., Book, A. S., Edwards, M. J., Wasylkiw, L., & Starzyk, K. B. (2003). Experimental faking in self-reported psychopathology: Unidimensional or mulitidimensional? *Personality and Individual Differences, 35,* 1107–1117.

Holden, R. R., & Fekken, G. C. (1990). Structured psychopathological test item characteristics and validity. *Psychological Assessment, 2*(1), 35–40.

Holmes, G. E., Williams, C. L., & Haines, J. (2001). Motor vehicle accident trauma exposure: Personality profiles associated with posttraumatic diagnoses. *Anxiety, Stress and Coping: An International Journal, 14*(3), 301–313.

Holmes, T. H., & Rahe, R. H. (1967). The social readjustment rating scale. *Journal of Psychosomatic Research, 11,* 213–218.

Jackson, D. N. (1970). A sequential system for personality scale development. In C. D. Spielberger (Ed.), *Current topics in clinical and community psychology* (Vol. 2, pp. 62–97). New York: Academic Press.

Karlin, B. E., Creech, S. K., Grimes, J. S., Clark, T. S., Meagher, M. W., & Morey, L. C. (in press). Personality Assessment Inventory with chronic pain patients: Psychometric properties and clinical utility. *Journal of Clinical Psychology.*

Kellogg, S. H., Ho, A., Bell, K., Schluger, R. P., McHugh, P. F., McClary, K. A., et al. (2002). Personality Assessment Inventory drug problems scale: A validity analysis. *Journal of Personality Assessment, 79*(1), 73–84.

Klonsky, E. D. (2004). Performance of Personality Assessment Inventory and Rorschach indices of schizophrenia in a public psychiatric hospital. *Psychological Services, 1*(2), 107–110.

Kumho Tire Co. v. Carmichael, 526 U.S. 137 (1999).

Kurtz, J. E., & Morey, L. C. (2001). Use of structured self-report assessment to diagnose borderline personality disorder during major depressive episodes. *Assessment, 8*(3), 291–300.

Kurtz, J. E., Morey, L. C., & Tomarken, A. (1992, March). *The concurrent validity study of three self-report measures of borderline personality.* Paper presented at the meetings of the Society for Personality Assessment, Washington, DC.

Lally, S. J. (2003). What tests are acceptable for use in forensic evaluations? A survey of experts. *Professional Psychology: Research and Practice, 34*(5), 491–498.

Liljequist, L., Kinder, B. N., & Schinka, J. A. (1998). An investigation of malingering posttraumatic stress disorder on the Personality Assessment Inventory. *Journal of Personality Assessment, 71*(3), 322–336.

Loevinger, J. (1957). Objective tests as instruments of psychological theory. *Psychological Reports, 3,* 635–694.

Loranger, A. W. (1988). *Personality disorders examination manual.* Yonkers, NY: DV Communications.

McLellan, A. T., Kushner, H., Metzger, D., Peters, R., Smith, I., Grissom, G., et al. (1992). The 5th ed. of the Addiction Severity Index. *Journal of Substance Abuse Treatment, 9*(3), 199–213.

Medoff, D. (2003). The scientific basis of psychological testing: Considerations following *Daubert, Kuhmo,* and *Joiner. Family Court Review, 41*(2), 199–213.

Meehl, P. E., & Rosen, A. (1955). Antecedent probability and the efficiency of psychometric signs, patterns, or cutting scores. *Psychological Bulletin, 52,* 194–216.

Montag, I., & Levin, J. (1994). The five factor model and psychopathology in nonclinical samples. *Personality and Individual Differences, 17*(1), 1–7.

Morey, L. C. (1991). *Personality Assessment Inventory professional manual.* Odessa, FL: Psychological Assessment Resources.

Morey, L. C. (1995). Critical issues in construct validation: Comment on Boyle and Lennon (1994). *Journal of Psychopathology and Behavioral Assessment, 17*(4), 393–401.

Morey, L. C. (1996). *An interpretive guide to the Personality Assessment Inventory.* Odessa, FL: Psychological Assessment Resources.

Morey, L. C. (2003). *Essentials of PAI assessment.* Hoboken, NJ: Wiley.

Morey, L. C., & Hopwood, C. J. (2004). Efficiency of a strategy for detecting back random responding on the Personality Assessment Inventory. *Psychological Assessment, 16*(2), 197–200.

Morey, L. C., & Lanier, V. W. (1998). Operating characteristics of six response distortion indicators for the Personality Assessment Inventory. *Assessment, 5*(3), 203–214.

Morey, L. C., Waugh, M. H., & Blashfield, R. K. (1985). MMPI scales for *DSM-III* personality disorders: Their derivation and correlates. *Journal of Personality Assessment, 49,* 245–251.

Nicholson, R. A., & Norwood, S. (2000). The quality of psychological assessments, reports, and testimony: Acknowledging the gap between promise and practice. *Law and Human Behavior, 24*(1), 9–44.

Oberlander, L. B., Goldstein, N. E., & Goldstein, A. M. (2003). Competence to confess. In I. B. Weiner (Series Ed.) & A. M. Goldstein (Vol. Ed.), *Comprehensive handbook of psychology: Vol. 11. Forensic psychology* (pp. 335–358). Hoboken, NJ: Wiley.

Parker, J. D., Daleiden, E. L., & Simpson, C. A. (1999). Personality Assessment Inventory substance-use scales: Convergent and discriminant relations with the Addiction Severity Index in a residential chemical dependence treatment setting. *Psychological Assessment, 11*(4), 507–513.

Peebles, J., & Moore, R. J. (1998). Detecting socially desirable responding with the Personality Assessment Inventory: Positive impression management scale and the defensiveness index. *Journal of Clinical Psychology, 54*(5), 621–628.

Peterson, G. W., Clark, D. A., & Bennett, B. (1989). The utility of MMPI subtle, obvious scales for detecting fake good and fake bad response sets. *Journal of Clinical Psychology, 45*(4), 575–583.

Piotrowski, C. (2000). How popular is the Personality Assessment Inventory in practice and training? *Psychological Reports, 86,* 65–66.

Piotrowski, C., & Belter, R. W. (2000). Internship training in psychological assessment: Has managed care had an impact? *Assessment, 6,* 381–389.

Procidano, M. E., & Heller, K. (1983). Measures of perceived social support from friends and from family: Three validation studies. *American Journal of Community Psychology, 11,* 1–24.

Quinnell, F. A., & Bow, J. N. (2001). Psychological tests used in child custody evaluations. *Behavioral Sciences and the Law, 19,* 491–501.

Roberts, M. D., Thompson, J. A., & Johnson, M. (1999). *PAI law enforcement, corrections, and public safety selection report module manual.* Odessa, FL: Psychological Assessment Resources.

Rogers, R. (2003). Forensic uses and abuses of psychological tests: Multi-scale inventories. *Journal of Psychiatric Practice, 9*(4), 316–320.

Rogers, R., Bagby, R. M., & Dickens, S. E. (1992). *Structured Interview of Reported Symptoms: Professional manual.* Odessa, FL: Psychological Assessment Resources.

Rogers, R., Flores, J., Ustad, K., & Sewell, K. W. (1995). Initial validation of the Personality Assessment Inventory—Spanish version with clients from Mexican American communities. *Journal of Personality Assessment, 64*(2), 340–348.

Rogers, R., Ornduff, S. R., & Sewell, K. (1993). Feigning specific disorders: A study of the Personality Assessment Inventory (PAI). *Journal of Personality Disorders, 60,* 554–560.

Rogers, R., Sewell, K. W., Morey, L. C., & Ustad, K. L. (1996). Detection of feigned mental disorders on the Personality Assessment Inventory: A discriminant analysis. *Journal of Personality Assessment, 67*(3), 629–640.

Rogers, R., Sewell, K. W., Ustad, K., Reinhardt, V., & Edwards, W. (1998). The Referral Decision Scale with mentally disordered inmates: A preliminary study of convergent and discriminant validity. *Law and Human Behavior, 19*(5), 481–492.

Rogers, R., Ustad, K. L., & Salekin, R. T. (1998). Convergent validity of the Personality Assessment Inventory: A study of emergency referrals in a correctional setting. *Assessment, 5*(1), 3–12.

Rotgers, F., & Barrett, D. (1996). *Daubert v. Merrell Dow* and expert testimony by clinical psychologists: Implications and recommendations for practice. *Professional Psychology: Research and Practice, 27*(5), 467–474.

Ruiz, M. A., Dickinson, K. A., & Pincus, A. L. (2002). Concurrent validity of the Personality Assessment Inventory alcohol problems (ALC) scale in a college student sample. *Assessment, 9*(3), 261–270.

Salekin, R. T., Rogers, R., & Sewell, K. W. (1997). Construct validity of psychopathy in a female offender sample: A multitrait-multimethod evaluation. *Journal of Abnormal Psychology, 106*(4), 576–585.

Salekin, R. T., Rogers, R., Ustad, K. L., & Sewell, K. W. (1998). Psychopathy and recidivism among female inmates. *Law and Human Behavior, 22,* 109–128.

Schinka, J. A. (1995). PAI profiles in alcohol-dependent patients. *Journal of Personality Assessment, 65*(1), 35–51.

Schinka, J. A., & Borum, R. (1993). Readability of adult psychopathology inventories. *Psychological Assessment, 5,* 384–386.

Schlosser, B. (1992). Computer assisted practice. *Independent Practitioner, 12,* 12–15.

Scragg, P., Bor, R., & Mendham, M. C. (2000). Feigning post-traumatic stress disorder on the PAI. *Clinical Psychology and Psychotherapy, 7,* 155–160.

Slick, D. J., Sherman, E. M. S., & Iverson, G. L. (1999). Diagnosing criteria for malingering neurocognitive dysfunction: Proposed standards for clinical practice and research. *Clinical Neuropsychologist, 13,* 545–561.

Spielberger, C. D. (1988). *State-Trait Anger Expression Inventory.* Odessa, FL: Psychological Assessment Resources.

Stafford, K. P. (2003). Assessment of competence to stand trial. In I. B. Weiner (Series Ed.) & A. M. Goldstein (Vol. Ed.), *Comprehensive handbook of psychology: Vol. 11. Forensic psychology* (pp. 359–380). Hoboken, NJ: Wiley.

Tasca, G. A., Wood, J., Demidenko, N., & Bissada, H. (2002). Using the PAI with an eating disordered population: Scale characteristics, factor structure and differences among diagnostic groups. *Journal of Personality Assessment, 79*(2), 337–356.

Trull, T. J. (1995). Borderline personality disorder features in nonclinical young adults: Pt. I. Identification and validation. *Psychological Assessment, 7*(1), 33–41.

Trull, T. J., Useda, J. D., Conforti, K., & Doan, B. T. (1997). Borderline personality features in nonclinical young adults: Two year outcome. *Journal of Abnormal Psychology, 106,* 307–314.

Walters, G. D., Duncan, S. A., & Geyer, M. D. (2003). Predicting disciplinary adjustment in inmates undergoing forensic evaluation: A direct comparison of the PCL-R and the PAI. *Journal of Forensic Psychiatry and Psychology, 14*(2), 382–393.

Wang, E. W., & Diamond, P. M. (1999). Empirically identifying factors related to violence risk in corrections. *Behavioral Sciences and the Law, 17*(3), 377–389.

Wang, E. W., Rogers, R., Giles, C. L., Diamond, P. M., Herrington-Wang, L. E., & Taylor, E. R. (1997). A pilot study of the Personality Assessment Inventory (PAI) in corrections: Assessment of malingering, suicide risk, and aggression in male inmates. *Behavioral Sciences and the Law, 15*(4), 469–482.

White, L. J. (1996). Review of the Personality Assessment Inventory (PAI): A new psychological test for clinical and forensic assessment. *Australian Psychologist, 31,* 38–39.

Wiggins, J. S. (1966). Substantive dimensions of self-report in the MMPI item pool. *Psychological Monographs, 80*(22, Whole No. 630).

Yeomans, F. E., Hull, J. W., & Clarkin, J. C. (1994). Risk factors for self-damaging acts in a borderline population. *Journal of Personality Disorders, 8*(1), 10–16.

Yudofsky, S. C., Silver, J. M., Jackson, W., Endicott, J., & Williams, D. (1986). Overt Aggression Scale for the objective rating of verbal and physical aggression. *American Journal of Psychiatry, 143,* 35–39.

CHAPTER 5

Rorschach Assessment in Forensic Cases

Irving B. Weiner

The Rorschach Inkblot Method (RIM) is a personality assessment instrument that frequently facilitates decision making in forensic cases. Rorschach examiners assist triers of fact in arriving at their judgments by translating test findings from the language of personality functioning into psycholegal terminology relevant to the issues in a particular case. Examiners enhance the value of their forensic consultations by becoming proficient in presenting their findings and conclusions in incisive written reports and effective courtroom testimony. Forensic Rorschach experts should also be prepared to defend their testimony, especially with respect to documenting that the RIM is a widely used and psychometrically sound instrument that meets criteria for admissibility into evidence and is largely resistant to malingering and deception.

With these considerations in mind, this chapter elaborates (a) the psycholegal relevance of Rorschach assessment, (b) the application of Rorschach data in various types of forensic cases, (c) guidelines for effective presentation of Rorschach findings, and (d) the evidentiary basis for defending the propriety and utility of Rorschach-based testimony.

THE PSYCHOLEGAL RELEVANCE OF RORSCHACH ASSESSMENT

Rorschach assessment becomes relevant in forensic consultations whenever the applicable law in a case has implications for aspects of personality functioning. Adequately conceptualized bridges between psychology and the law identify psycholegal issues on which forensic psychologists can advise the court. As an example, the competence of a defendant in a criminal case is a legal matter, debated by attorneys and decided by the court. Whether a criminal defendant is psychotic is a psychological matter, assessed by mental health professionals and having little direct relevance to proceedings in the courtroom. However, when criminal defendants are found to have an impairment of reality testing that is preventing them from understanding the charges they are facing, a psycholegal connection is established between trial competence (a legal concept) and psychosis (a psychological term), and the court's decision can be guided accordingly. In like fashion, suggesting that a defendant was unable to appreciate the wrongfulness of his or her conduct at the time of an alleged offense because he or she was out of touch with reality when the crime was committed links the legal concept of sanity with the psychological concept of psychosis.

In personal injury litigation, the legal question of whether plaintiffs have suffered compensatory psychological damages calls for determining whether they are manifesting mental or emotional disturbance or disability that was not present prior to an allegedly damaging tort or breech of duty on the part of a defendant. When psychic injury is part of a claimed disturbance or disability, indications of overwhelming anxiety, incapacitating depression, or inability to think clearly are likely to be relevant in documenting the nature and extent of the damage. Such circumstances make assessment with the RIM and other measures of personality functioning relevant to a forensic consultation.

APPLYING RORSCHACH DATA IN FORENSIC CASES

As just noted, Rorschach assessment becomes relevant in forensic consultation when personality characteristics as measured by the RIM have a bearing on the psycholegal issues in a particular case. Rorschach examiners can assist judge and jury by identifying the personality characteristics pertinent to a case and attending to Rorschach indicators of these characteristics. When adequately conceived in these respects and properly implemented, Rorschach assessment can be applied effectively in forensic cases involving child custody decisions, determinations of trial competence and criminal responsibility, and resolution of personal injury claims. In each type of case, however, Rorschach findings will be just one of many sources of data that contribute to an adequate forensic psychological evaluation. Consistent with general principles of integrative psychological assessment, impressions based on the RIM must typically be considered in light of information from such sources as other test results, interview responses, behavioral observations, collateral reports, and police, medical, military, and school records (see Beutler & Groth-Marnat, 2003; Weiner, 2003a, 2005).

Child Custody Decisions

Family court judges often seek information about the personality characteristics of children and their parents when making decisions about custody and parental rights. Of particular interest to the court in such cases is the general adjustment level of the involved parties and how well the coping skills and interpersonal accessibility of the parents meet the needs of their children (see K. D. Hess & Brinson, 1999; Otto, Buffington-Vollum, & Edens, 2003). With respect to general adjustment level, evidence that the children in a case of disputed custody are functioning adequately typically gives the court reason to be satisfied with the adequacy of their current living situation. On the other hand, indications of serious psychological problems in children, although not necessarily a reflection of poor parental care, can lead the court to ponder whether these children would benefit from a change in environment.

As for the adjustment level of parents, having psychological problems does not necessarily preclude their functioning effectively in the parental role. Greenberg, Shuman, and Meyer (2004) have aptly noted, "Parents with diagnosable disorders may still be quite capable of meeting a child's needs" (p. 10). However, having an active psychosis that diminishes their sense of reality or a severe depression that depletes their energy may be regarded by the court as an impediment to their ful-filling the normally expected obligations and responsibilities of parents.

The coping skills that contribute to effective parenting are generally considered to include being able to exercise good judgment, make decisions carefully, deal with problems flexibly, maintain reasonably good self-control, and manage stress-ful situations without becoming unduly upset by them. By contrast, poor judgment, careless decision making, inflexible problem solving, impulsive behavior, and be-coming distraught in the face of even mildly stressful situations are likely to inter-fere with functioning effectively and responsibly as a parent.

Interpersonal qualities that are likely to promote positive parenting include being nurturing and empathic, interested in people, comfortable in close relation-ships, and able to express feelings and recognize and respond to the feelings of oth-ers. Conversely, being generally self-absorbed, inattentive to what other people are saying and doing, uncomfortable in close relationships, insensitive to the needs and concerns of others, and emotionally unresponsive or withdrawn limits a parent's likelihood of providing the warmth, nurturance, understanding, and guidance that foster positive personality development in young people.

As delineated in basic texts on Rorschach interpretation, the RIM includes mea-sures of each of these personality characteristics (see Exner, 2003b; Weiner, 2003b). With respect to serious psychological disturbance, elevations on the Per-ceptual Thinking Index ($PTI > 3$) usually identify disordered thinking and im-paired reality testing, and elevations on the Depression Index ($DEPI > 4$) often reflect some combination of dysphoric affect, negative cognitions, and depleted en-ergy (see also Kleiger, 1999). Examiners using these indexes must keep in mind that low scores do not rule out psychological disturbance and should not be inter-preted as doing so. As elaborated in the previously referenced Exner and Weiner texts, however, elevated scores on them are a normatively rare event that strongly suggests psychological disorder.

With specific respect to the normative data for these two indexes, a demograph-ically representative sample of 600 reasonably well-functioning nonpatient adults examined in developing the Rorschach Comprehensive System (CS) showed a 0% frequency of $PTI > 3$ and a 5% frequency of $DEPI > 4$ (Exner, 2003b, chap. 12). In a new normative study currently in process, only one of the first 350 nonpatients examined showed an elevation in PTI, and just 11% had an elevated $DEPI$ (Exner, 2003a). As for children and adolescents, a normative reference sample of 1,390 5- to 16-year-olds was found to include only two with $DEPI > 4$ and none at all with $PTI > 3$ (Exner, 2003b, Table A.12).

Among children, adolescents, and adults alike, then, these two Rorschach in-dexes of psychological disturbance ($PTI > 3$ and $DEPI > 4$) rarely occur in the test records of well-functioning individuals. Their presence in a properly administered Rorschach protocol gives probable evidence of some significant cognitive or affec-tive dysfunction that merits careful consideration in the course of a child custody evaluation. Examiners should attend in particular to whether a person with these test findings has ever received professional mental health care or been prescribed psychotropic medication. Should neither be the case, these findings still warrant looking closely at interview and life history data, including the employment records of adults and the school records of children, for possible indications of previously undetected or untreated psychological disorder.

Some critics of Rorschach assessment have alleged that the instrument tends to overpathologize, that is, to suggest psychological disorder where none is present (Wood, Nezworski, Garb, & Lilienfeld, 2001). Regrettably, these allegations may dissuade some psychologists from using the RIM in custody evaluations, and they may discourage some parents from agreeing to take it. As delineated by Meyer (2001) and Weiner (2001b), however, these allegations were based on research studies in which small and unrepresentative samples of participants were tested mostly by inexperienced examiners and sometimes under such unusual conditions as being told not to move while taking the Rorschach or being connected to a set of electrodes. By contrast, the CS normative data were obtained by experienced professionals from a large, nationally representative sample and, as just noted, clearly affirm that elevations in *PTI* and *DEPI*—and the disordered thinking, impaired reality testing, dysphoric mood, negative self-attitudes, and depleted energy they help to identify—rarely occur in well-adjusted respondents.

A variety of other Rorschach variables have implications for the coping skills and interpersonal qualities that are likely to have a bearing on parental care. The adequacy with which people exercise judgment, make decisions, solve problems, exert self-control, and manage stress can often be inferred in part from the *XA%* (Form Appropriate Extended), *WDA%* (Form Appropriate-Common Areas), *P* (Popular), *Zd* (Processing Efficiency), *a:p* (Active:Passive Ratio), *CDI* (Coping Deficit Index), and *D* (Difference) and *AdjD* (Adjusted *Difference*) scores in their record. Level of interest in people, comfort in close relationships, concern about and sensitivity to the needs of others, and capacity to experience and express feelings are often reflected in the *H:Hd + (H) + (Hd)* (Interpersonal Interest), *HVI* (Hypervigilance Index), *T* (Texture), *M−* (Human Movement-Distorted Form), *COP* (Cooperative Movement), *Fr + rF* (Reflections), *3r + 2/R* (Egocentricity Index), *WSumC* (Weighted Sum Chromatic Color), and *Afr* (Affective Ratio) scores. Specific guidelines for the interpretation of these variables can be found in Weiner (2003b, chap. 5).

None of these Rorschach variables suffices by itself to indicate an adult's likelihood of being an effective or suitable parent. Taken together and weighed by knowledgeable examiners in light of the overall configuration of Rorschach findings, other test data, and life history information, however, these variables can identify a variety of parental assets and limitations relevant to the issues in custody cases (see Weiner, in press). For all of these Rorschach variables, moreover, there is little likelihood of inferring significant adjustment difficulties when none is present. On each of them, the score levels customarily taken to signify probable functioning limitations occur with very low frequencies in the CS normative sample of well-adjusted adults (Exner, 2003b, Tables 12.2, 12.3).

Determinations of Trial Competence and Responsibility in Criminal Defendants

Forensic consultation in criminal cases most commonly concerns the competence of defendants to proceed to trial and the extent of their responsibility for the offenses they are alleged to have committed. Competence to proceed consists in legal terms of being able to consult with one's lawyer with a reasonable degree of rational understanding and having a factual and rational understanding of the offenses with which one is charged. Most jurisdictions extrapolate these two basic elements of competence into such considerations as whether defendants can appreciate the nature of the charges and possible penalties they are facing, grasp the nature of the adversarial process and courtroom proceedings, disclose pertinent facts to their attorney, testify relevantly in their own behalf, and conduct themselves appropriately in the courtroom (see Roesch, Zapf, Golding, & Skeem, 1999; Stafford, 2003).

With respect to personality characteristics, inability to satisfy these criteria for competence is most likely to derive from impaired reality testing, disordered thinking, and the poor judgment and peculiar behavior to which these cognitive dysfunctions often lead. Accordingly, Rorschach indexes of difficulty perceiving experiences accurately and thinking logically and coherently about them identify a susceptibility to being unable to demonstrate competence to proceed. Impaired reality testing is dependably measured on the RIM by low scores on the *XA%, WDA%,* and *P* variables, and an elevation on the *WSum6* (Weighted Sum Critical Special Scores) variable constitutes strong evidence of a thinking disorder.

As an indirect measure of personality characteristics, however, the RIM is limited in how much it can reveal about what respondents actually know or can do. Although Rorschach findings of impaired reality testing and disordered thinking identify susceptibility to incompetence, they do not document its presence. Whether defendants have an adequate appreciation of the charges and penalties they are facing, for example, is best determined by asking them directly about these matters (e.g., "As far as you know, what are the charges against you?"; "What do you think the outcome of this situation might be?"), and not from personality test responses. On the other hand, when direct inquiry appears to establish legal incompetence, Rorschach evidence of poor reality testing or disordered thinking can help examiners explain to the court why a particular defendant is having difficulty demonstrating competence.

Determinations of criminal responsibility depend on the sanity of defendants at the time of their alleged offense. Being sane at the time of an offense is most commonly defined as being able to recognize the criminality of one's illegal actions and appreciate the wrongfulness of this conduct (i.e., the M'Naghten test of being able to tell right from wrong). In some jurisdictions, sanity is alternatively defined as having been able, at the time of the offense, to alter or refrain from the alleged criminal conduct (i.e., having sufficient self-control to resist impulses to break the law). These alternatives are often referred to as the *cognitive* and *volitional* prongs of sanity, and jurisdictions vary with respect to whether an insanity plea can be presented solely on the basis of cognitive incapacity on the part of the defendant or can also be based on volitional incapacity (see Golding, Skeem, Roesch, & Zapf, 1999; Goldstein, Morse, & Shapiro, 2003).

The cognitive prong of legal insanity translates, in part, into the previously mentioned Rorschach indexes of poor reality testing and disordered thinking, both of which could have implications for diminished criminal responsibility. With respect to the volitional prong, limited self-control is measured on the RIM by indexes of acute or chronic stress overload (*D* < 0, *AdjD* < 0), which are commonly associated with limited frustration tolerance, intemperate outbursts of affect, and episodes of impulsive behavior. Unlike trial competence, however, criminal responsibility is a matter of the defendant's mental state at some previous time, not at the time of the present examination. Hence, it is essential for examiners formulating opinions about criminal responsibility to supplement Rorschach indications of either cognitive or volitional incapacity with information gleaned from defendants and observers concerning the defendant's mental state and behavior preceding, during, and immediately following an alleged offense.

Although the RIM, together with other personality assessment instruments, is limited with respect to postdicting mental state at the time of an alleged offense, some elements of a test protocol may increase the likelihood that currently measured incapacities were present at some previous time. As one of these elements, test indexes of chronicity can help to estimate previous functioning capacities from presently obtained Rorschach data. More often than not, signs of stability and self-satisfaction increase the likelihood that a currently well-functioning person has been well-adjusted in the past and, conversely, that a psychologically disturbed person has been persistently maladjusted for some period of time. The pertinent Rorschach result in this regard is $D => 0$, which typically indicates stability over time, even when this stability consists of being emotionally unstable on a persistent or recurring basis.

In addition, Rorschach findings can sometimes facilitate an informative diathesis-stress analysis when defendants who appear to be functioning fairly well at present are claiming temporary insanity at the time of an alleged offense. Current indications of characterologically limited resources for coping with stress, combined with obviously stressful circumstances or surroundings at the time of an offense, increase the likelihood that a defendant might have experienced a transient episode of cognitive incapacity or behavioral dyscontrol. Conversely, the better the coping resources shown by a defendant's current test responses, and the less stress the defendant appeared to be experiencing prior to and during the commission of an alleged offense, the less likely the person would have been at that previous time to suffer a psychological breakdown accompanied by loss of cognitive or volitional capacities.

Rorschach findings measure the diathesis component of such an analysis with indexes of psychological resources for managing stress and coping effectively with demands in one's life. Central in identifying a persistent susceptibility to becoming overwhelmed by events, to the point of being unable to think clearly and exert self-control, is a finding of $AdjD < -1$. Other variables that help to identify inadequate coping resources include the occurrence in an unguarded record of a low EA (Experience Actual), an ambient EB (Experience Balance) style, an elevated CDI (Coping Deficit Index), and several indexes of interpersonal discomfort and affective disequilibrium, as elaborated in the Exner and Weiner texts. By contrast, an $AdjD => 0$, a nonpervasive introversive or extratensive EB, a normal-range CDI, and indexes of interpersonal and affective comfort indicate relatively good insulation against psychological breakdown, except in extremely stressful circumstances.

Like all efforts to postdict or predict behavior from Rorschach findings, using presently obtained clues to chronicity and resourcefulness as a basis for commenting on a defendant's prior mental state involves some conjecture. Recognizing that such conjectures will vary in probability, forensic psychologists should neither shrink from venturing estimates when asked to do so nor present them with an unwarranted air of certainty. Preferably, they should use the strength of their overall assessment data as a basis for indicating, as best they can, where a postdiction or prediction falls between being fairly likely or being only a remote possibility that might nevertheless be worth considering.

Resolution of Personal Injury Claims

Personal injury claims consist of complaints alleging that irresponsible conduct on the part of a defendant has caused the plaintiff some compensable damage (see Greenberg, 2003). When such claimed damage includes emotional distress, Rorschach assessment of personality characteristics often assists in evaluating the type and extent of whatever psychic damage the plaintiff may have incurred. Among types of emotional distress claimed in personal injury cases, the two most likely to occur are Depressive Disorder and anxiety reactions, especially in the form of Posttraumatic Stress Disorder (PTSD).

The utility of the Rorschach *DEPI* index in identifying features of depression (i.e., dysphoria and negative self-attitudes) was noted in the earlier discussion of child custody evaluations (see also Ganellen, 2001; Hartman, Wang, Berg, & Saether, 2003). With more specific reference to the components of Depressive Disorder, dysphoric mood is suggested on the RIM by elevations in *C'* (Achromatic Color) and *Col-Shd Blds* (Color-Shading Blends); negative cognitions by numerous *V* (Vista) and *MOR* (Morbid) responses and a low *3r + (2)/R;* and depleted energy by a short, unelaborated record with infrequent Blends and few *DQ+* (Synthesis) responses.

With regard to PTSD, two patterns of Rorschach responses commonly accompany this condition and lead to what Luxenberg and Levin (2004) have termed "biphasic" protocols. In one common PTSD pattern, the Rorschach protocol is flooded with pervasive indications of anxiety. Evidence of such flooding includes (a) apparent preoccupation with intrusive and unwelcome ideation, as reflected in numerous *FM* (Animal Movement) and *m* (Inanimate Movement) responses, especially the latter; (b) considerable stress overload that precludes managing everyday demands without becoming unduly upset by them, as suggested by scores of $D < -1$ and $AdjD < -1$; and (c) particularly troubling concerns about incurring bodily harm, as shown by a Trauma Content Index composed of frequent Aggression, Anatomy, Blood, Morbid, and Sex contents. When appearing in the records of persons who have experienced probable traumatic events, these Rorschach findings are usually associated with stress disorder manifestations of reexperiencing phenomena and hyperarousal (see Armstrong, 1991; Armstrong & Kaser-Boyd, 2004).

In the other PTSD pattern, as reviewed by Armstrong and Kaser-Boyd (2004) and Luxenberg and Levin (2004), respondents give constricted Rorschach protocols characterized by evasion and such hallmarks of guardedness as low *R* (Response Total), high *Lambda* (proportion of pure form responses), low *WSumC* (Weighted Sum of Color Use), low *Afr* (Affective Ratio), numerous *DQv* (Vague) responses, and bland content. A constricted Rorschach protocol given by persons who are suspected of having been traumatized suggests a stress disorder characterized by defensive avoidance. Instead of becoming excitable, easily upset, and troubled by flashbacks, nightmares, and other types of reexperiencing, traumatized persons who are defensively avoidant shut down psychologically by withdrawing from thoughts, feelings, and situations that might cause them to experience an episode of distress.

In actual practice, however, forensic consultants must keep in mind that neither flooded nor constricted Rorschach protocols are specific to anxiety and stress disorders. As one example, depressed persons with primary symptoms of lethargy and depleted energy, in common with stress-disordered persons with defensive avoidance, often produce constricted protocols. In the context of historical and other clinical or test data suggestive of PTSD, flooded or constricted Rorschach protocols increase the likelihood of this condition, but they do not by themselves constitute conclusive evidence that such a disorder is present. Like all personality assessment instruments, the RIM works best when it is interpreted as part of a multifaceted test battery and in the context of a respondent's personal history and sociocultural heritage (see Beutler & Groth-Marnat, 2003; Weiner, 2005).

Finally, of note in this last regard, personal injury assessments, like evaluations of criminal responsibility, must go beyond attention to presently obtained test findings and consider as well the likely origins and history of any psychic damage in evidence. In particular, forensic consultants in personal injury cases must seek answers to the following four questions: To what extent does any present distress or dysfunction apparent in the test data constitute a decline in functioning capacity from some previously higher level prior to the alleged misconduct by the defendant? To what extent did any presently observed distress or dysfunction precede the alleged misconduct? Was the defendant's misconduct of such a nature as to have been a likely cause of the particular distress or dysfunction presently in evidence? Have other events in the plaintiff's life been equally as likely as or more likely than the defendant's conduct to have caused the presently observed distress or dysfunction?

PRESENTING RORSCHACH FINDINGS EFFECTIVELY IN THE COURTROOM

Effective courtroom presentation of Rorschach findings begins with explaining the nature of the RIM, how and why it works, and what kinds of information it provides. In some instances, explanations of this kind may not be expected or required, either on direct or cross-examination or by the trier of fact. Forensic consultants who use the RIM should nevertheless be prepared to talk about the instrument, and they should welcome an opportunity to do so. Speaking knowledgeably about Rorschach assessment allows experts to demonstrate that their testimony has an objective basis in test data, as opposed to reflecting only their subjective opinion, and to enhance their witness credibility with a clear, informative, and well-crafted account of the inkblot method. Rorschach-based testimony can also be strengthened by relying mainly on the structural rather than the thematic features of a protocol, presenting certain kinds of conclusions in nomothetic rather than idiographic terms, making frequent use of qualifiers in framing inferences, avoiding response-level explanations, and managing computer printouts of test interpretations advisedly.

Explaining the RIM

As a general principle in explaining the nature of the RIM in the courtroom, examiners should avoid any implication that the test is a complex and mysterious procedure that can be understood only after years of study. Instead, the inkblot method should be presented as a straightforward way of sampling how people look at their world, in the expectation that how people look at the world conveys considerable information about what they are like and how they are likely to deal with events in their lives. The Rorschach administration, coding, and interpretive procedures can then be described in the following way:

> The Rorschach consists of 10 cards, each with a blot of ink on it. The blots aren't anything in particular, but they look like various things to people, and people taking the test see various things in them. The cards are shown to people one at a time, and they are asked, "What might this be?" On the first card, a person taking the test may use the whole blot for a response, and this response is coded with a *W,* for Whole. Or the person may use just a part or a detail of the blot for a response, which is coded with a *D,* for Detail. A person may say that this first card looks like a bat or a butterfly, which are very common responses, so they are coded with *P,* for Popular.
>
> After going through all 10 cards, the examiner adds up how many of these *W*s, *D*s and *P*s a person has given. People who give a lot of *W*s tend to take a global view of situations. They focus on the big picture, sometimes without paying as much attention as they should to details. People who give a lot of *D*s are likely to focus mainly on details, perhaps being the kind of people who lose sight of the forest for the trees and have difficulty grasping the overall significance of situations. People who give a lot of *P*s are seeing things the way most other people do and are likely to be conventional in the opinions they form and how they conduct themselves. Those who give only a few *P*s are not so conventional and may be nonconformists in their attitudes and behavior.
>
> And that's how it goes, with many other different codes for aspects of how people look at the blots, and more than 100 different summary scores based on the frequencies of the various codes. These summary scores provide information about many aspects of personality functioning, including how people pay attention to what is going on around them, how they tend to think about events in their lives, how they experience and express feelings, how they manage stress, and how they view themselves and other people.

Relying on Structural Data

The preceding explanation of what the RIM is and how it works does not include any mention of thematic imagery. Although the thematic imagery in Rorschach responses can provide clinically useful clues to a respondent's underlying attitudes and concerns (see Lerner, 1998; Schafer, 1954; Weiner, 2003b, chap. 6), there are several reasons why this clinical utility seldom extends to the courtroom. First, the inferences derived from the thematic imagery in a Rorschach protocol are typically more speculative and less conclusive than inferences based on the structural data. This difference derives from the fact that the structural data in a protocol tend to be *representative* of behavior, whereas the thematic data are primarily *symbolic* of behavior.

For example, the kind of people just mentioned who attend almost exclusively to the details of the blot while rarely giving responses involving the entire blot are showing on the Rorschach a representative sample of exactly the kind of behavior that leads to losing sight of the forest for the trees. Suppose, by contrast, a respondent sees the center detail of Card I as "A woman with her arms waving in the air," without any further elaboration. The thematic imagery in this response could symbolize a woman waving "Hello" or a woman waving "Good-bye"; depending on which is the case, the imagery could reflect expectations of reunion and being welcomed, or concerns about separation and being rejected or abandoned; whichever is the case, the woman could symbolize the person's mother, grandmother, daughter, women in general, or, for a male respondent, his wife. In clinical work, such possibilities provide alternative and potentially fruitful speculations, some combination of which may, on further examination of other sources of information, appear applicable in the case of a particular respondent. However, these possibilities do not by themselves warrant any single or generally applicable conclusion, in the way that a predominance of Ds over Ws usually identifies difficulty attaining a global perspective.

Second, because the rationales for thematic interpretations are more symbolic and less representative than the rationales for structural interpretations, and because they are more likely to involve alternative possibilities, they are more complex and difficult to explain in the courtroom. Third, the available validating data for thematic variables are less extensive than those for structural variables, which gives thematic interpretations less of an objective basis than structural interpretations and makes them more subjective. Fourth and finally, the interpretive implications of thematic variables for respondents' underlying attitudes and concerns are typically less relevant to psycholegal issues than the implications of structural variables for a person's functioning capacities, coping skills, and personal style.

For these reasons, Rorschach examiners will do well to base their forensic reports and courtroom testimony primarily on the structural data. Relying mainly on the structural data provides an expert witness a strong foundation with respect not only to the available research support, as reviewed in the next section of the chapter, but also in responding to certain types of challenging cross-examination. For example, to the attorney who is attempting to minimize the import of a psychologist's conclusions by asking "So that's your *opinion,* Doctor?" the witness who has relied on the structural data can respond, "No, that's not my opinion, that's what the test data show." In thus emphasizing the objectivity of their evaluation, examiners who have relied mainly on structural variables can also draw on the normative data to buttress their conclusions, as in the following statement: "The defendant showed a 35% frequency of inaccurate or distorted perceptions in giving responses on the Rorschach. Fewer than 1% of normally functioning people show such a high frequency of poor reality testing, whereas a frequency this high is found in over 60% of persons hospitalized with Schizophrenia."

As an exception to avoiding thematic imagery in forensic presentations of Rorschach findings, repetitive content themes may sometimes be relevant to a particular case and sufficiently compelling to strengthen an expert's testimony. A good example of such imagery can be elaborated from the Trauma Content Index described earlier with respect to evaluating stress disorder in personal injury cases. Should an accident or assault victim see numerous bloody body parts in the inkblots (thus increasing the structural scores for *BL, MOR,* and the TCI), a report of the specific imagery in these responses will have considerable face validity for disturbing preoccupations with incurring bodily harm (e.g., "Somebody's arms and legs, all bloody, like they've been cut up"; "What's left of a person after a bomb exploded, like in the war").

Presenting Conclusions in Nomothetic Terms

Along with emphasizing structural data and their relationship to available norms, Rorschach examiners can bolster their testimony and gain some insulation against cross-examination by presenting certain types of conclusions in nomothetic rather than idiographic terms. Idiographic statements describe a respondent without reference to other people (as in "His ability to think logically and coherently is quite limited"), whereas nomothetic statements compare the respondent to relevant reference groups (as in "She has more difficulty than most people in thinking logically and coherently, and the extent of her dysfunction in this respect resembles what is found in persons with Schizophrenia").

When idiographic statements are describing basic personality characteristics, they may not differ very much from nomothetic statements in their impact. Consider, for example, such idiographic descriptions as "She is more of a reflective than an expressive kind of person and tends to keep her feelings to herself" (inferred from an introversive *EB*), or "He is inclined to be hasty and careless in making decisions" (inferred from an underincorporative *Zd*). Idiographic inferences of this type describe readily observable features of a person's present behavior, which usually makes them no more complicated or difficult to explain than nomothetic statements.

On the other hand, when conclusions address not what a respondent is *like* but what the person is *likely to have done or experienced* or how the person may be *likely to behave* in the future, nomothetic statements have a distinct advantage over idiographic statements. To illustrate this advantage, suppose a 10-year-old child in a custody case has given an average-length record ($R = 20$) with some C' and Y but no T. The absence of T would be an unusual finding, in that almost 90% of the 10-year-olds in the CS nonpatient reference data gave at least one T (Exner, 2001, chap. 11). Customary interpretive guidelines would suggest that this child's T-less performance, particularly in a record containing C' and Y, reflects some difficulty in forming attachments to people, probably as a result of the child's not having received much early life nurturance from his or her caretakers. In court, however, an expert witness would do well to avoid using this test result as a basis for commenting on how the child was likely to have been treated by his or her parents. Doing so, especially in the absence of dependable collateral reports concerning the parents' child-rearing proclivities, would expose the expert to some embarrassing questions, such as "How do you know how these parents conducted themselves years ago?" and "How many hours out of this child's 10-year life have you spent observing the care he or she received?" When such questions are warranted by idiographic statements that overreach the data, they are likely to damage an expert's credibility in the eyes of judge and jury.

Preferable testimony regarding this instance of a T-less record would be the nomothetic observation, "This child shows some patterns of responses similar to those often seen in young people who have not had the benefit of the kinds of experiences that help them come to expect close and caring relationships with other people." If then asked on cross-examination, "Are you saying that my client didn't give her child proper care?" the expert's response can be, "No, I'm not saying that. I don't know what kind of care she gave her child, because I wasn't there to observe. I only know that the child's test responses resemble a pattern often seen in children who have not received much nurturance."

Using Qualifiers

Rorschach examiners can also strengthen their testimony by making frequent use of qualifiers in phrasing their conclusions. Even at their most accurate, Rorschach inferences are not absolute certainties, and the courtroom is not a place for being excessively definitive. As ways of avoiding overstatement, qualifiers consist of stating that the test findings are "usually indicative of," "often associated with," or "typical of" whatever the witness is inferring from them. Other examples of qualified statements are saying that "the test data suggest" whatever is being inferred, or that respondents "appear to be" or "give evidence of having" whatever characteristics are being attributed to them. Using such qualifiers freely does not prevent experts from distinguishing between conclusions with low, high, or intermediate probability, nor does it preclude their being able to satisfy a common courtroom request to affirm that a conclusion has been drawn "with reasonable psychological certainty."

In this regard, qualifiers should not be conceived merely as a hedge against being pinned down or as a way of sidestepping a challenging question on cross-examination. Instead, qualifying statements should be phrased in terms that accurately describe the probability of the findings and correctly reflect the limits of the conclusions being drawn (as in "The test results contain some/considerable evidence that . . ." or "This person appears highly/somewhat prone to . . .").

When judiciously employed, qualifiers do not detract from the effectiveness of test-based testimony, nor do they make an expert witness appear tentative or wishy-washy. Rather, appropriate qualifiers are likely to convey caution, thoughtfulness, and a degree of humility on the part of an expert witness, as opposed to unwarranted self-assurance. Qualifiers also help to spare experts from cross-examination along the lines of "Do your findings *always* mean what you say they mean?" or "Isn't it true that there are *exceptions* to the way you are interpreting the tests or even *other possibilities* for what the findings might mean?" Such questions are not difficult to fend off (e.g., "There are exceptions to just about anything"; "Although anything is possible, other possibilities seem unlikely"). However, the expert who is challenged in this way after eschewing qualifiers in direct testimony risks losing some credibility by appearing given to exaggeration and overgeneralization.

Avoiding Response-Level Explanations

Rorschach examiners should avoid presenting information or answering questions at the level of the individual response. A worst-case scenario will serve to illustrate this caution:

Lawyer: On this first inkblot, he said, "It looks like a bat with damaged wings." What does that response mean, Doctor?

Witness: It means that he has some concerns about his body being harmed or damaged in some way, or that he doesn't like his body very much.

Judge: Let me see that card. [Judge studies Card I] I agree. The wings look damaged to me, too. But I don't have any fears of being harmed, and I like my body just fine. [Snickering in courtroom] Maybe we better look at some more of these.

Having reached this point, the situation can deteriorate quickly, with Rorschach cards and responses being bandied about and serious, research-based consideration of the Rorschach testimony being compromised along the way. There is only one advisable answer to questions about what a particular response means: "It doesn't mean anything by itself." The witness can then elaborate this answer, if invited and permitted to do so, by explaining, first, that Rorschach interpretations are based on the summary scores after all of the codes have been tallied, and second, that each individual response is important for what it contributes to the total scores but cannot be taken out of context and considered the sole basis for inferring anything.

Managing Computer Printouts

The availability of computerized programs for personality tests has produced a conundrum of sorts for forensic psychologists. On the one hand, these programs save time in scoring, they produce data arrays and graphic displays that facilitate interpretation, and they generate narrative reports that take full and systematic account of the test responses in arriving at descriptions of personality functioning (see Butcher, 2002, 2004). Moreover, some of these programs have been developed specifically for application in forensic cases. Relevant to this chapter, the Rorschach Interpretation Assistance Program (RIAP5; Exner & Weiner, 2003) has been expanded to include a Forensic Edition (RIAP5 FE; Weiner, 2004) that applies relevant Rorschach findings to psycholegal issues in child custody, criminal, and personal injury cases.

Along with these potential benefits, on the other hand, computer-generated narrative reports have the potential disadvantage of being discoverable in forensic cases, and they may be cross-examined in detail. This cross-examination can be challenging for forensic examiners in two respects. First, if they have generated a Rorschach report with the RIAP5 or RIAP5 FE, they may be asked to indicate which data in the test protocol provided the basis for various statements in the report. Rorschach assessors who come to court unprepared to answer such questions risk embarrassment on the witness stand. Familiarity with the Exner (2003b) and Weiner (2003b) texts, from which the RIAP personality descriptions are derived, can help forensic examiners avoid such embarrassment by speaking knowledgeably about the content of the interpretive printout.

Second, forensic examiners may be asked to account for computer-generated statements that mischaracterize the person who took the test. At least a few inaccurate statements are almost inevitable in computer-based test interpretations, because these narrative reports describe the test protocol, not the individual respondent. If questioned about such statements, the expert witness should be prepared to explain that the descriptive statements in these computer printouts refer to characteristics shown by a group of people with a test protocol similar to the respondent's test protocol, and that some of these statements will consequently be more applicable than others to the person who has been examined. Most computerized test reports begin with a caveat to this effect. The introduction to the RIAP5 printout, for example, includes the following alert:

> The narrative statements produced by RIAP5 for Windows describe the implications of Rorschach findings among people in general, and do not necessarily apply in all respects to the functioning of any one person. To ensure a thorough and accurate description of a particular individual's personality characteristics and behavioral tendencies, examiners should . . . judge the applicability of RIAP5 interpretive hypotheses in light of information from other sources concerning the person's clinical status and past and present life circumstances (Exner & Weiner, 2003).

Even when clearly expressed, however, these explanations of seeming inaccuracies in a computer printout may have limited impact following a skillful attorney's use of selected parts of the printout to "expose" the RIM as a misleading and undependable source of information—and thereby to raise questions about the dependability of the expert's testimony in other respects as well. As in the case of identifying the data sources of interpretive statements in computer printouts, forensic examiners can minimize the negative fallout from inapplicable statements by anticipating the possibility of challenging cross-examination about such statements and coming to court prepared to explain the caveat as effectively as possible. Additionally, because these interpretive statements are hypotheses to be verified in the process of a psychological assessment with recourse to other relevant data sources, examiners have a clear basis for explaining why some statements may prove more accurate than others.

DEFENDING RORSCHACH TESTIMONY: THE EVIDENTIARY BASIS

The evidentiary basis for defending Rorschach testimony resides in commonly applied legal standards for admissibility into evidence. Jurisdictions and jurists vary in their interpretation of these standards, and the precise implications of the standards for test-based testimony are yet to be determined. By and large, however, decisions from the bench regarding the admissibility of psychological assessment testimony involve consideration of whether the procedures that have been used are scientifically respectable (the essence of the *Daubert* standard; *Daubert v. Merrell Dow Pharmaceuticals,* 1993), generally accepted in the professional community (the essence of the *Frye* standard; *Frye v. United States,* 1923), and likely to yield information helpful to the trier of fact (the essence of Federal Rules of Evidence 702; see Ewing, 2003; A. K. Hess, 1999). This final section of the chapter addresses the scientific respectability, general acceptance, and helpfulness of Rorschach assessment.

Scientific Respectability of Rorschach Assessment

The scientific respectability of an assessment instrument depends on its demonstrated reliability and validity and the adequacy of the normative reference base that is available for it. With respect to its reliability, the RIM has shown substantial retest correlations and good to excellent interrater agreement. In adults, the short-term and long-term stability of most summary scores and indexes in the Rorschach CS exceed .75, and 19 core variables with major interpretive significance have shown 1-year or 3-year retest correlations of .85 or higher (see Exner, 2003b, chap. 12; Gronnerod, 2003; Viglione & Hilsenroth, 2001). The only Rorschach scores that show low retest correlations are a few variables that are conceptualized as measures of situationally influenced personality states, particularly m and Y (Exner, 2003b, chap. 12).

Over the span of a few weeks, children show stability coefficients for Rorschach variables similar to those found in adults. When retested over 2-year intervals, young people age 8 to 16 initially fluctuate considerably in their Rorschach scores but become increasingly more consistent in their responses as they grow older (Exner, Thomas, & Mason, 1985). This increasing stability of Rorschach variables from age 8 to 16 corresponds to the gradual consolidation of personality characteristics that is expected to occur during the developmental years and provides indirect validation of the RIM as a measure of psychological maturation.

As for interrater agreement, two recent studies have confirmed the psychometric adequacy of the RIM in this respect. Meyer and colleagues (2002) examined inter-coder agreement in four samples containing 219 protocols with 4,761 responses. They found a median intraclass correlation coefficient (ICC) of .93 for intercoder agreement across 138 regularly occurring Rorschach CS variables. Of these 138 variables, 134 had correlations in the excellent range for chance-corrected agreement, which is traditionally defined by values between .75 and 1.00 (see Cicchetti, 1994; Fleiss, 1981). Viglione and Taylor (2003) conducted a similar study of coder concurrence with 84 protocols with 1,732 responses. They obtained a median ICC of .92 for 68 variables considered to be of central interpretive significance. Earlier meta-analytic reviews and studies with patient and nonpatient samples had identified mean kappa coefficients ranging from .79 to .88 across various CS coding categories, which for this statistic also fall in the excellent range with respect to their clinical significance (Acklin, McDowell, Verschell, & Chan, 2000; Meyer, 1997a, 1997b; Viglione & Taylor, 2003).

The validity of Rorschach assessment has been documented in a large-scale meta-analysis in which Hiller, Rosenthal, Bornstein, Berry, and Brunell-Neuleib (1999) examined the association of Rorschach and Minnesota Multiphasic Personality Inventory (MMPI) variables with external (nontest) criteria they were posited to predict. In their analysis of research studies published between 1977 and 1997 and including 2,276 Rorschach and 5,007 MMPI protocols, Hiller et al. found un-weighted mean validity coefficients of .29 for Rorschach variables and .30 for MMPI variables. As indicated by these average effect sizes, the validity of the RIM is virtually identical to the validity of the MMPI. For both measures, Hiller et al. concluded, this validity level "is about as good as can be expected for personality tests" (p. 291) and warrants confidence in using both the RIM and the MMPI for their intended purposes. This documented equivalence between the two measures has particular implications for the respectability of the RIM in forensic circles, in which the MMPI is generally regarded as the gold standard of clinical personality assessment.

The Hiller et al. (1999) findings also identified some noteworthy differences between the RIM and the MMPI in their degree of association with different types of criteria. On the average, MMPI variables were superior (mean validity coefficient of .37) to Rorschach variables (mean validity coefficient of .18) in correlating with psychiatric diagnoses. On the other hand, the RIM showed higher effect sizes than the MMPI (.37 vs. .20) in predicting behavioral outcomes, such as whether patients remain in or drop out of therapy. To put these validity coefficients in perspective, correlations emerging from large-scale meta-analyses are generally considered to reflect moderate effect size when they range from .30 to .49 (see Cohen, 1988), which provided the basis for Hiller et al. to conclude that the .29 and .30 averages in the RIM and MMPI research warrants confidence in using these instruments. Moreover, the .37 effect sizes these instruments showed in correlating with psychiatric diagnoses (MMPI) or behavioral outcomes (RIM) are comparable to the effect sizes found for many intellectual measures and widely used medical procedures. Taken from a much longer list of such validity coefficients published by Meyer et al. (2001), the following effect sizes identify the potential relative effectiveness of the RIM and MMPI when they are being used for their intended purposes:

> Sleeping pills and short-term improvement in chronic insomnia—.30
>
> Screening mammogram results and detection of breast cancer within 1 year—.32
>
> Hare Psychopathy Checklist scores and subsequent violent behavior—.33
>
> MMPI scale scores and average ability to detect depressive or psychotic disorder—.37
>
> Rorschach dependency scores and dependent behavior—.37
>
> Viagra and improved male sexual functioning—.38
>
> Rorschach Prognostic Rating Scale (PRS) scores and subsequent psychotherapy outcome—.44
>
> Wechsler Adult Intelligent Scales (WAIS) IQ and obtained level of education—.44
>
> MMPI validity scales and detection of malingered psychopathology—.44
>
> Weight and height for U.S. adults—.44

With respect to the differences between the RIM and MMPI in the kinds of criteria with which they are likely to show moderate effect sizes, these findings probably reflect differences in the nature of the two instruments. As a self-report inventory, the MMPI collects data in much the same way as a psychiatric diagnostic interview, that is, by asking patients directly about their current and past symptoms. By contrast, Rorschach assessment is an indirect, performance-based procedure, and its coded variables have implications mainly for trait dimensions of personality. Hence, the RIM tends to be particularly sensitive to the behavioral dispositions of individuals, and less so to their current symptomatology.

It may be useful to note that the RIM shares its indirect methodology with commonly used tests of intelligence, which are also performance-based measures. Examiners seeking to determine a person's level of intelligence do not ask, "How intelligent are you?" Instead, they give the person a series of tasks to perform, score the person's accuracy or speed in performing these tasks, and obtain an IQ estimate by comparing these scores with normative reference data. This obtained IQ estimate typically proves more dependable than what people might say if asked how intelligent they are. Respondents to performance-based personality tests are similarly likely to reveal characteristics of themselves that they might not fully recognize or would prefer not to disclose if asked about them directly.

Returning to the psychometric foundations of the RIM, an extensive research base supplements the Hiller et al. (1999) meta-analysis in documenting the validity of Rorschach assessment when the instrument is used for its intended purposes. As described in reviews by Hilsenroth and Stricker (2004), Mattlar (2004), Stricker and Gold (1999), Viglione (1999), Viglione and Hilsenroth (2001), and Weiner (2001a), this validation research has also demonstrated that Rorschach findings can show incremental validity as well, by contributing diagnostic and predictive information in addition to what can be learned from self-report inventories and clinical interviews (see Blais, Hilsenroth, Castlebury, Fowler, & Baity, 2001; Janson & Stattin, 2003; Meyer & Handler, 2000; Perry, 2001). A thorough review of the available empirical evidence led Meyer and Archer (2001) to conclude as follows:

> The global and focused meta-analyses clearly indicate Rorschach scales can provide valid information. Like all tests, the Rorschach is more valid for some purposes than for others. Given this evidence and the limitations inherent in any assessment procedure, there is no reason to single out the Rorschach for praise or criticism. (p. 499)

The normative reference base for the Rorschach CS includes the previously mentioned sample of 600 nonpatient adults, who ranged in age from 19 to 69, were recruited in various parts of the country, were informed that they were participating in the standardization of a widely used personality test, and were tested according to usual procedures by well-trained examiners. This volunteer sample closely resembled U.S. Census data with respect to marital and socioeconomic status and urban-suburban-rural residence, and 18% of the respondents were of African American, Latino, or Asian American descent. These 600 persons were relatively well educated (average of 13.4 years), had no significant history of mental health problems, and appeared to be functioning reasonably well socially and vocationally. Reference data are also available for 1,390 nonpatient young people, age 5 to 16, and for three groups of adult psychiatric patients: 328 first-admission inpatients with Schizophrenia, 279 patients hospitalized for depression, and 535 outpatients presenting a diversity of symptoms (Exner, 2001, chap. 11).

Because these CS data were collected more than 20 years ago, questions can be raised concerning whether the findings remain applicable in the twenty-first century. In consideration of this question, Exner undertook the previously mentioned replication of his earlier work, and relatively well-functioning volunteer adults are again being tested by experienced examiners in various parts of the United States. Exner (2002) has published the findings for the first 175 persons in this new normative study and presented data on the first 350 (Exner, 2003a). To the present moment, with the data collection now including 450 respondents (J. E. Exner, personal communication, February 25, 2005), the findings for the new adult nonpatient sample closely resemble the original reference data and do not call for any noteworthy modifications in interpretive guidelines for the RIM.

Raising another issue, Rorschach critics have alleged that norms appropriate to a culturally diverse population have not yet been developed and that Rorschach assessment is therefore inappropriate for minority groups in the United States (Wood & Lilienfeld, 1999). The inclusion of minority group respondents in the normative reference sample and recent research findings refute this allegation. In one relevant study, Presley, Smith, Hilsenroth, and Exner (2001) found a clinically significant difference on only 1 of 23 core Rorschach variables in the records of 44 African Americans and 44 demographically matched Caucasian Americans in the CS nonpatient reference sample. This sole difference consisted of a notably lower frequency of *COP* (Cooperative Movement) responses in the African American than the Caucasian respondents, which Presley et al. suggest may reflect less anticipation in this group of cooperative interactions with members of the broad society.

In another study, Meyer (2002) found no association whatsoever between ethnicity and any of 188 Rorschach summary scores in a multicultural sample of 432 demographically matched European American, African American, Hispanic American, Asian American, and Native American respondents who were consecutively evaluated in a hospital-based psychological testing program. There is no substantial empirical basis for taking issue with Meyer's conclusion that "the available data clearly support the cross-ethnic use of the Comprehensive system" (p. 127), or for disagreeing with Ritzler's (2004) even broader view that "the Rorschach is a major, culture-free assessment method that is likely to yield similar results across a wide range of cultures" (pp. 580–581).

General Acceptance of Rorschach Assessment

The criterion of general acceptance in the professional community does not require a procedure to be universally practiced or endorsed. Few if any assessment or treatment methods in psychology and health care would meet such a standard. In less stringent fashion, general acceptance of a procedure is indicated when a sizable number of professionals are engaged in using, teaching, or conducting research with it. Available survey data indicate that Rorschach assessment is generally accepted in all three of these respects.

Regarding the use and teaching of the RIM, professionals and students responding to surveys over the past 40 years have consistently endorsed Rorschach assessment as a valuable skill to learn and practice (Camara, Nathan, & Puente, 2000; Hogan, 2005). Over 80% of the clinical psychologists in these surveys who are engaged in providing assessment services report that they use the RIM in their work and believe that clinical students should become competent in Rorschach assessment. Just under 80% of reporting graduate programs cover the RIM in required assessment courses (Childs & Eyde, 2002). Survey data indicate that most students in these courses find Rorschach training helpful in understanding personality functioning, approximately 80% want to learn more about Rorschach assessment, and about 60% say they are moderately or very likely to use the RIM in their professional careers (Mihura & Weinle, 2002). Training directors in internship programs commonly assign considerable value to Rorschach assessment, report that the RIM is among the three measures most frequently used in their test batteries (together with the WAIS/Wechsler Intelligence Scale for Children and MMPI-2/MMPI-A), and prefer their incoming interns to have had prior Rorschach coursework (Clemence & Handler, 2001; Stedman, Hatch, & Schoenfeld, 2000).

Survey findings indicate further that Rorschach assessment has gained an established place in forensic as well as clinical practice. Among forensic practitioners surveyed, 30% have reported using the RIM in competency evaluations, 32% in assessing criminal responsibility, 41% in personal injury cases, and almost 50% in evaluating adults in custody cases (Ackerman & Ackerman, 1997; Boccaccini & Brodsky, 1999; Borum & Grisso, 1995; Bow, Quinnell, Zaroff, & Assemany, 2002). Examining the cases of 134 young people evaluated in the course of juvenile court proceedings, Budd, Felix, Poindexter, Naik-Polan, and Sloss (2002) found that over 90% had been given projective personality measures, including the RIM.

As for research with the RIM, a steady stream of Rorschach publications over the years has reflected sustained interest in studying the nature and utility of the instrument. Buros's (1974) *Mental Measurements Yearbook* identified 4,580 Rorschach references through 1971, with an average yearly rate of 92 publications. In the 1990s, Butcher and Rouse (1996) found an almost identical trend continuing from 1974 to 1994. An average of 96 Rorschach research articles appeared annually during this 20-year period in journals published in the United States, and the RIM was second only to the MMPI among personality assessment measures in the volume of research it generated. The major peer-reviewed journals in which personality assessment research articles regularly appear, listed historically according to their initial year of publication, are the *Journal of Personality Assessment* (1936), the *Journal of Clinical Psychology* (1944), the *European Journal of Psychological Assessment* (1984), *Psychological Assessment* (1988), and *Assessment* (1993).

There is also a large international community of Rorschach scholars and practitioners whose research published in languages other than English has for many years made important contributions to the literature (see Weiner, 1999b). The international presence of Rorschach assessment is reflected in a survey of test use in Spain, Portugal, and Latin American countries by Muniz, Prieto, and Almeida (1998), in which the RIM emerged as the third most widely used psychological assessment instrument, following the Wechsler intelligence scales and versions of the MMPI. An international society for Rorschach and Projective Methods has been in existence since 1947, and triennial congresses sponsored by this society typically attract participants from more than 30 countries on five continents. Finally, postdoctoral training and seminars in Rorschach assessment are regularly offered for American Psychological Association-approved continuing education credit by such organizations as the Society for Personality Assessment, the American Academy of Forensic Psychology, Rorschach Workshops, and many state psychological associations.

Helpfulness of Rorschach Assessment

The previously described utility of Rorschach findings in addressing psycholegal issues in child custody, criminal, and personal injury cases bears witness to the ways Rorschach-based testimony can be helpful to triers of fact. Two other features of the RIM enhance its utility as part of a forensic assessment battery: its potential for providing incremental validity and its resistance to impression management.

Incremental Validity

Because the RIM is an indirect, performance-based measure of personality, it often can provide incremental validity by adding information beyond that which can be learned from self-report measures. The information gleaned from self-report measures is limited to what respondents are able and willing to say about themselves. To the extent that respondents choose not to disclose certain facts about themselves or are not themselves aware of certain of their own personality characteristics, these facts and characteristics will not be identified by self-report inventories. On performance-based measures like the RIM, on the other hand, the key data are not what people are able and willing to say about themselves, but the manner in which they perform on tasks that the examiner sets for them.

Research studies confirming this incremental validity of Rorschach assessment in providing information that would not otherwise have come to light were cited earlier, in reviewing the scientific respectability of the instrument. As also intimated earlier, however, adequate evaluation of personality functioning requires an integrated assessment that draws on the strengths of both self-report and performance-based measures. Forensic assessors who limit their test battery to either one or the other type of measure risk failing to obtain information that might be crucial to an accurate formulation of the psycholegal issues that drive a case (see Masling, 1997; Weiner, 1999a).

Impression Management

Respondents' ability to manipulate an assessment instrument tends to be directly related to its face validity: The more obvious the reason for a task or the meaning of a test item, the easier it is for people to respond in ways that suit their purpose. Performance-based measures like the RIM usually provide little opportunity for people to sense the implications of the responses they are giving. The relatively ambiguous nature of the inkblots, combined with the minimal instructions on how to proceed and the absence of clues to what responses might signify, limit the face validity of the RIM and make it difficult—though not impossible—to fake.

Rorschach respondents who are consciously attempting to portray themselves as more disturbed or impaired than is actually the case—which is not uncommon among criminal defendants pleading insanity or personal injury plaintiffs claiming psychic damage—typically overdo their efforts to appear incapacitated. Either by producing patterns of data that are internally inconsistent (e.g., extraordinarily bizarre fantasy elaborations in combination with normal-range structural summary scores) or by showing extremely deviant score levels that are inconsistent with an unremarkable appearance, a coherent and socially appropriate interview presentation, and no history of mental health problems, malingerers rarely succeed in deceiving experienced examiners.

In a real-world study of persons presumably motivated to appear disturbed, Ganellen, Wasyliw, Haywood, and Grossman (1996) administered the RIM and the MMPI during competency or sanity evaluations of 48 persons charged with serious crimes that carried long prison sentences or the death penalty. The MMPI validity scales were used as a basis for dividing these defendants into two groups: one group of 35 who were classified as honest responders, and a second group of 13 who were considered malingerers. On the RIM, the malingerers in this study, despite their probable inclination to fake bad, showed no significant differences from the honest responders—except for a higher frequency of responses containing dramatic content.

Respondents who are attempting to deny or conceal psychological difficulties— which is not uncommon among parents in child custody cases or incarcerated prisoners seeking parole—may be able to keep these difficulties hidden by delivering a guarded record. Examiners who can extract only a few brief, vague, unelaborated, and form-only responses, delivered after long reaction times and following attempted card rejections ("I don't see anything"; "It looks like nothing at all"), will know very little about the personality characteristics of the person they have tested, but they will know that he or she has attempted to mislead them by suppressing potentially revealing responses.

When examinees who are motivated to fake good give unguarded Rorschach records, they are unlikely to succeed in disguising psychological disturbance. In companion research to the Ganellen et al. (1996) study, Grossman, Wasyliw, Benn, and Gyoerkoe (2002) examined 74 accused sex offenders and used their MMPI validity scales to classify 53 of them as "minimizers" and 21 as "nonminimizers." On the MMPI clinical scales, the minimizers in this sample received significantly lower scores than the nonminimizers. On the RIM, however, they were not able to appear better adjusted than the nonminimizers. Instead, these would-be minimizers showed just as much emotional distress, impaired judgment, and interpersonal dysfunction in their Rorschach responses as the nonminimizers, and both groups of defendants showed more of these types of adjustment difficulty than the normative reference sample of nonpatient adults.

Identification of malingering and deception may become challenging if defendants or litigants have obtained some prior information concerning the kinds of Rorschach responses that would serve their purpose of appearing disturbed or making a good impression. This information may have come from basic Rorschach texts, which are available in public bookstores, from web sites and published manuals designed specifically to give guidance in faking the RIM, or from friends and acquaintances who have had some experience with Rorschach assessment as a respondent or student. Nevertheless, because of the complex composition of the Structural Summary and the interactive manner in which responses are interpreted, advice concerning a list of "good" and "bad" responses one should give or avoid does not approach the level of sophistication necessary to deliver a convincingly malingered or deceptive Rorschach protocol.

As an example in this regard, consider a parent in a custody case who wants to appear psychologically effective and well-adjusted on the Rorschach and learns from an Internet source that Popular responses are "good" ones to give. In light of this information, the person memorizes and reports all of the 13 Populars in the CS. What this respondent is unlikely to know is that P in nonpatients ranges from 6 to 10, with a median of 6, and not one of the 600 nonpatients in the CS reference sample gave all 13 of them. No one is likely to give all 13 Ps, then, except for respondents who have been coached and are being deceptive.

Welcome in the Courtroom

Despite this extensive information concerning the scientific respectability, general acceptance, and helpfulness of Rorschach assessment in forensic cases, some critics have asserted that Rorschach assessment using the CS is not sufficiently relevant and reliable to provide an admissible basis for courtroom testimony, and that testimony based on Rorschach findings is therefore unlikely to be admitted into evidence in courts of law (e.g., Grove & Barden, 1999; Grove, Barden, Garb, & Lilienfeld, 2002). To the contrary, however, reviews of the evidence by Hilsenroth and Stricker (2004), McCann (1998, 2004), and Ritzler, Erard, and Pettigrew (2002a, 2002b) concur with the present chapter in documenting how and why a properly conducted Rorschach assessment satisfies applicable legal standards for admissibility.

Specifically in this regard, the evidence documents that the RIM is a standardized, testable, valid, reliable, and extensively peer-reviewed instrument that is associated with a reasonable error rate, accepted by a substantial scientific community, and relevant to a wide range of forensic issues. These characteristics of the instrument clearly satisfy the central thrust of the *Frye* standard that "the thing from which the deduction is made must be sufficiently established to have gained general acceptance in the particular field in which it belongs" (*Frye v. United States,* 1923, p. 1014). The literature likewise indicates that Rorschach assessment satisfies the four cornerstones of the *Daubert* standard, which, in addition to a general acceptance criterion, includes whether the methodology underlying testimony has been or can be tested, whether the method has been subjected to peer review and publication, and whether the method has an acceptable known or potential error rate (*Daubert v. Merrell Dow Pharmaceuticals,* 1993).

Moreover, survey data indicate that Rorschach testimony is in fact welcome in the courtroom and that questions about its admissibility are the exception rather than the rule. In one such survey involving Rorschach-based testimony in 4,024 criminal cases, 3,052 custody cases, and 858 personal injury cases, the appropriateness of the testimony was challenged in only six instances (less than 0.1%), and in only one of these was the testimony ruled inadmissible (Weiner, Exner, & Sciara, 1996). Among 247 cases in which Rorschach findings were presented to courts of appeal, 90% proceeded without the reliability or validity of the RIM becoming an issue (Meloy, Hansen, & Weiner, 1997). When the relevance or utility of the Rorschach findings was challenged in the remaining 10% of these appellate cases, the arguments were typically directed at how the data were being interpreted rather than at the reliability and validity of the instrument itself.

Critics have also maintained that the admissibility of Rorschach testimony is compromised by its being a "controversial" method (Wood, Nezworski, Stejskal, &

McKinzey, 2001). According to these critics, disagreements and unresolved issues concerning the psychometric soundness of the RIM should preclude its being brought into the courtroom. Putting aside the adequate psychometric foundations of Rorschach assessment, as documented in this chapter and in the numerous peer-reviewed articles cited here, the "controversial" critique reveals an inadequate grasp of both scientific and legal perspectives.

From a scientific perspective, there is little justification in attacking the propriety of procedures that are widely endorsed for their utility but may be imperfectly understood or have some margin of error. There are few matters of science that have not at times spurred controversy, and very few procedures currently employed in evaluating the physical and mental status of people approach 100% accuracy. Being controversial, in the sense that some people disagree with a widely held belief or question the validity of a frequently used procedure, does not automatically render the procedure scientifically suspect, nor does it make it legally unacceptable. The admissibility into evidence of testimony based on a personality assessment instrument does not depend on whether the instrument has critics who consider it controversial. Admissibility depends on whether the instrument has proved scientifically respectable, generally accepted, and helpful to triers of fact, all of which define the current status of the RIM.

CONCLUSION

As elaborated in this chapter, psycholegal issues that link legal statutes with psychological formulations of personality functioning establish the relevance of Rorschach assessment in forensic practice. As a multifaceted instrument that provides dependable information about a broad range of personality characteristics, the RIM can assist forensic decision making by elucidating the psychological adjustment and capacities of parents and children in custody cases, by helping to identify mental disturbances that may be contributing to trial incompetence or insanity in criminal cases, and by evaluating the nature and severity of claimed emotional distress or disability in personal injury cases.

This chapter presents several ways that forensic Rorschach examiners can enhance the effectiveness of their expert witness testimony. These include explaining in clear and uncomplicated terms how the RIM identifies a respondent's personality characteristics, basing conclusions mainly on the structural rather than the thematic features of a Rorschach protocol, stating their conclusions in nomothetic rather than idiographic terms, and framing inferences with frequent use of qualifiers that accurately reflect the certainty of the data.

The chapter continues with a discussion of the evidentiary basis for defending the propriety and utility of Rorschach-based testimony. Attention is paid in particular to (a) the scientific respectability of the RIM as a reliable and valid procedure; (b) the general acceptance of Rorschach assessment in the professional community, as documented by the frequency with which it is used, taught, and studied; and (c) the usefulness of the RIM to triers of fact in facilitating decision making in various types of cases, providing incremental information beyond what can be learned from self-report measures, and resisting efforts at impression management. Noteworthy in this latter regard is the usually low susceptibility of Rorschach assessment in real-life situations to conscious efforts on the part of respondents to present a more disturbed or more positive picture of themselves than their actual clinical state may warrant. The chapter concludes with information indicating that Rorschach testimony is in fact regularly admitted into evidence in the courtroom.

REFERENCES

Ackerman, M. J., & Ackerman, M. C. (1997). Custody evaluations in practice: A survey of experienced professionals (revisited). *Professional Psychology, 28,* 137–145.

Acklin, M. W., McDowell, C. J., Verschell, M. S., & Chan, D. (2000). Interobserver agreement, intraobserver agreement, and the Rorschach Comprehensive System. *Journal of Personality Assessment, 74,* 15–57.

Armstrong, J. (1991). The psychological organization of multiple personality disordered patients as revealed in psychological testing. *Psychiatric Clinics of North America, 14,* 533–546.

Armstrong, J., & Kaser-Boyd, N. (2004). Projective assessment of psychological trauma. In M. Hersen (Editor in Chief) & M. Hilsenroth & D. Segal (Vol. Eds.), *Comprehensive handbook of psychological assessment: Vol. 2. Objective and projective assessment of personality* (pp. 500–512). Hoboken, NJ: Wiley.

Beutler, L. E., & Groth-Marnat, G. (2003). *Integrative assessment of adult personality* (2nd ed.). New York: Guilford Press.

Blais, M. A., Hilsenroth, M. J., Castlebury, F., Fowler, J. C., & Baity, M. R. (2001). Predicting *DSM-IV* Cluster B personality disorder criteria from MMPI-2 and Rorschach data: A test of incremental validity. *Journal of Personality Assessment, 76,* 150–168.

Boccaccini, M. T., & Brodsky, S. L. (1999). Diagnostic test usage by forensic psychologists in emotional injury cases. *Professional Psychology, 30,* 253–259.

Borum, R., & Grisso, T. (1995). Psychological test use in criminal forensic evaluations. *Professional Psychology, 26,* 465–473.

Bow, J. N., Quinnell, F. Z., Zaroff, M., & Assemany, A. (2002). Assessment of sexual abuse allegations in child custody cases. *Professional Psychology, 33,* 566–575.

Budd, K. S., Felix, E. D., Poindexter, L. M., Naik-Polan, A. T., & Sloss, C. F. (2002). Clinical assessment of children in child protection cases: An empirical assessment. *Professional Psychology, 33,* 3–12.

Buros, O. K. (Ed.). (1974). *Tests in print II.* Highland Park, NJ: Gryphon.

Butcher, J. N. (2002). How to use computer-based reports. In J. N. Butcher (Ed.), *Clinical personality assessment* (2nd ed., pp. 109–125). New York: Oxford University Press.

Butcher, J. N. (2004). Computers in clinical assessment: Historical developments, present status, and future challenges. *Journal of Clinical Psychology, 60,* 331–345.

Butcher, J. N., & Rouse, S. V. (1996). Personality: Individual differences and clinical assessment. *Annual Review of Psychology, 47,* 87–111.

Camara, W., Nathan, J., & Puente, A. (2000). Psychological test usage: Implications in professional use. *Professional Psychology, 31,* 141–154.

Childs, R. A., & Eyde, L. D. (2002). Assessment training in clinical psychology doctoral programs: What should we teach? What do we teach? *Journal of Personality Assessment, 78,* 130–144.

Cicchetti, D. V. (1994). Guidelines, criteria, and rules of thumb for evaluating normed and standardized instruments in psychology. *Psychological Assessment, 6,* 284–290.

Clemence, A., & Handler, L. (2001). Psychological assessment on internship: A survey of training directors and their expectations for students. *Journal of Personality Assessment, 76,* 18–47.

Cohen, J. (1988). *Statistical power for the behavioral sciences* (2nd ed.). Hillsdale, NJ: Erlbaum.

Daubert v. Merrell Dow Pharmaceuticals, 509 U.S. 579 (1993).

Ewing, C. P. (2003). Expert testimony: Law and practice. In I. B. Weiner (Series Ed.) & A. M. Goldstein (Vol. Ed.), *Comprehensive handbook of psychology: Vol. 11. Forensic psychology* (pp. 55–66). Hoboken, NJ: Wiley.

Exner, J. E., Jr. (2001). *A Rorschach workbook for the Comprehensive System.* Asheville, NC: Rorschach Workshops.

Exner, J. E., Jr. (2002). A new nonpatient data sample for the Rorschach Comprehensive System: A progress report. *Journal of Personality Assessment, 78,* 391–404.

Exner, J. E., Jr. (2003a, March). *An update on the new non-patient sample for the Rorschach Comprehensive System.* Paper presented at the meeting of the Society for Personality Assessment, San Francisco.

Exner, J. E., Jr. (2003b). *The Rorschach: A comprehensive system: Vol. 1. Basic foundations and principles of interpretation* (4th ed.). Hoboken, NJ: Wiley.

Exner, J. E., Jr., Thomas, E. A., & Mason, B. (1985). Children's Rorschachs: Description and prediction. *Journal of Personality Assessment, 49,* 13–20.

Exner, J. E., Jr., & Weiner, I. B. (2003). *Rorschach Interpretation Assistance Program (RIAP5).* Lutz, FL: Psychological Assessment Resource.

Fleiss, J. L. (1981). *Statistical methods for the behavioral sciences* (2nd ed.). New York: Wiley.

Frye v. United States, 293 Fed. 1013 (D.C. Cir. 1923).

Ganellen, R. J. (2001). Weighing evidence for the Rorschach's validity: A response to Wood et al. (1999). *Journal of Personality Assessment, 77,* 1–15.

Ganellen, R. J., Wasyliw, O. E., Haywood, T. W., & Grossman, L. S. (1996). Can psychosis be malingered on the Rorschach? An empirical study. *Journal of Personality Assessment, 66,* 65–80.

Golding, S. L., Skeem, J. L., Roesch, R., & Zapf, P. A. (1999). The assessment of criminal responsibility. In A. K. Hess & I. B. Weiner (Eds.), *Handbook of forensic psychology* (pp. 379–408). New York: Wiley.

Goldstein, A. M., Morse, S. J., & Shapiro, D. L. (2003). Evaluation of criminal responsibility. In I. B. Weiner (Series Ed.) & A. M. Goldstein (Vol. Ed.), *Comprehensive handbook of psychology: Vol. 11. Forensic psychology* (pp. 381–406). Hoboken, NJ: Wiley.

Greenberg, S. A. (2003). Personal injury examinations in torts for emotional distress. In I. B. Weiner (Series Ed.) & A. M. Goldstein (Vol. Ed.), *Comprehensive handbook of psychology: Vol. 11. Forensic psychology* (pp. 233–257). Hoboken, NJ: Wiley.

Greenberg, S. A., Shuman, D., & Meyer, R. (2004). Unmasking forensic diagnosis. *Journal of Law and Psychiatry, 27,* 1–15.

Gronnerod, C. (2003). Temporal stability in the Rorschach method: A meta-analytic review. *Journal of Personality Assessment, 80,* 272–293.

Grossman, L. S., Wasyliw, O. E., Benn, A. F., & Gyoerkoe, K. L. (2002). Can sex offenders who minimize on the MMPI conceal psychopathology on the Rorschach? *Journal of Personality Assessment, 78,* 484–501.

Grove, W. M., & Barden, R. C. (1999). Protecting the integrity of the legal system: The admissibility of testimony from mental health experts under *Daubert/Kumho* analysis. *Psychology, Public Policy, and Law, 5,* 224–242.

Grove, W. M., Barden, R. C., Garb, H. N., & Lilienfeld, S. O. (2002). Failure of Rorschach-Comprehensive-System-based testimony to be admissible under the *Daubert-Joiner-Kumho* standard. *Psychology, Public Policy, and Law, 8,* 216–234.

Hartman, E., Wang, C., Berg, M., & Saether, L. (2003). Depression and vulnerability as assessed by the Rorschach method. *Journal of Personality Assessment, 81,* 243–256.

Hess, A. K. (1999). Serving as an expert witness. In A. K. Hess & I. B. Weiner (Eds.), *Handbook of forensic psychology* (2nd ed., pp. 521–555). New York: Wiley.

Hess, K. D., & Brinson, P. (1999). Mediating domestic law issues. In A. K. Hess & I. B. Weiner (Eds.), *Handbook of forensic psychology* (2nd ed., pp. 63–104). New York: Wiley.

Hiller, J. B., Rosenthal, R., Bornstein, R. F., Berry, D. T. R., & Brunell-Neuleib, S. (1999). A comparative meta-analysis of Rorschach validity. *Psychological Assessment, 11,* 278–296.

Hilsenroth, M. J., & Stricker, G. (2004). A consideration of challenges to psychological assessment instruments used in forensic settings: Rorschach as exemplar. *Journal of Personality Assessment, 83,* 141–152.

Hogan, T. P. (2005). Fifty widely used psychological tests. In G. P. Koocher, J. C. Norcross, & S. S. Hill (Eds.), *Psychologists' desk reference* (2nd ed., pp. 101–104). New York: Oxford University Press.

Janson, H., & Stattin, H. (2003). Predictions of adolescent and adult delinquency from childhood Rorschach ratings. *Journal of Personality Assessment, 81,* 51–63.

Kleiger, M. H. (1999). *Disordered thinking and the Rorschach.* Hillsdale, NJ: Analytic Press.

Lerner, P. M. (1998). *Psychoanalytic perspectives on the Rorschach.* Hillsdale, NJ: Analytic Press.

Luxenberg, T., & Levin, P. (2004). The role of the Rorschach in the assessment of trauma. In J. P. Wilson & T. M. Keane (Eds.), *Assessing psychological trauma and PTSD* (2nd ed., pp. 190–225). New York: Guilford Press.

Masling, J. (1997). On the nature and utility of projective and objective tests. *Journal of Personality Assessment, 69,* 254–270.

Mattlar, C.-E. (2004). The Rorschach Comprehensive System is reliable, valid, and cost-effective. *Rorschachiana, 26,* 158–186.

McCann, J. T. (1998). Defending the Rorschach in court: An analysis of admissibility using legal and professional standards. *Journal of Personality Assessment, 70,* 125–144.

McCann, J. T. (2004). Projective assessment of personality in forensic settings. In M. L. Hersen (Editor in Chief) & M. J. Hilsenroth & D. L. Segal (Vol. Eds.), *Comprehensive handbook of psychological assessment: Vol. 2. Personality assessment* (pp. 562–572). Hoboken, NJ: Wiley.

Meloy, J. R., Hansen, T., & Weiner, I. B. (1997). Authority of the Rorschach: Legal citations in the past 50 years. *Journal of Personality Assessment, 69,* 53–62.

Meyer, G. J. (1997a). Assessing reliability: Critical corrections for a critical examination of the Rorschach Comprehensive System. *Psychological Assessment, 9,* 480–489.

Meyer, G. J. (1997b). Thinking clearly about reliability: More critical corrections regarding the Rorschach Comprehensive System. *Psychological Assessment, 9,* 495–598.

Meyer, G. J. (2001). Evidence to correct misperceptions about Rorschach norms. *Clinical Psychology: Science and Practice, 8,* 389–396.

Meyer, G. J. (2002). Exploring possible ethnic differences and bias in the Rorschach Comprehensive System. *Journal of Personality Assessment, 78,* 104–129.

Meyer, G. J., & Archer, R. P. (2001). The hard science of Rorschach research: What do we know and where do we go? *Psychological Assessment, 13,* 486–502.

Meyer, G. J., Finn, S. E., Eyde, L. D., Kay, G. G., Moreland, K. L., Dies, R. R., et al. (2001). Psychological testing and psychological assessment: A review of evidence and issues. *American Psychologist, 56,* 128–165.

Meyer, G. J., & Handler, L. (2000). Incremental validity of the Rorschach prognostic rating scale over the MMPI ego strength scale and IQ. *Journal of Personality Assessment, 74,* 356–370.

Meyer, G. J., Hilsenroth, M. J., Baxter, D., Exner, J. E., Jr., Fowler, J. C., Piers, C. C., et al. (2002). An examination of the interrater reliability for scoring the Rorschach Comprehensive System in eight data sets. *Journal of Personality Assessment, 78,* 219–274.

Mihura, J. L., & Weinle, C. A. (2002). Rorschach training: Doctoral students' experiences and preferences. *Journal of Personality Assessment, 79,* 39–52.

Muniz, J., Prieto, G., & Almeida, L. (1998, August). *Test use in Spain, Portugal, and Latin American countries.* Paper presented at the 24th International Congress of Applied Psychology, San Francisco.

Otto, R. K., Buffington-Vollum, J. K., & Edens, J. F. (2003). Child custody evaluation. In I. B. Weiner (Series Ed.) & A. M. Goldstein (Vol. Ed.), *Comprehensive handbook of psychology: Vol. 11. Forensic psychology* (pp. 179–208). Hoboken, NJ: Wiley.

Perry, W. (2001). Incremental validity of the Ego Impairment Index: A reexamination of Dawes (1999). *Psychological Assessment, 13,* 403–407.

Presley, G., Smith, C., Hilsenroth, M., & Exner, J. E. (2001). Rorschach validity with African Americans. *Journal of Personality Assessment, 77,* 491–507.

Ritzler, B. (2004). Cultural applications of the Rorschach, apperception tests, and figure drawings. In M. Hersen (Editor in Chief) & M. J. Hilsenroth & D. L. Segal (Vol. Eds.), *Comprehensive handbook of psychological assessment: Vol. 2. Personality assessment* (pp. 573–585). Hoboken, NJ: Wiley.

Ritzler, B., Erard, R., & Pettigrew, G. (2002a). A final reply to Grove and Barden: The relevance of the Rorschach Comprehensive System for expert testimony. *Psychology, Public Policy, and Law, 8,* 235–246.

Ritzler, B., Erard, R., & Pettigrew, T. (2002b). Protecting the integrity of Rorschach expert witnesses: A reply to Grove and Barden, 1999 (Re: The admissibility of testimony under *Daubert/Kumho* analysis). *Psychology, Public Policy, and Law, 8,* 201–215.

Roesch, R., Zapf, P. A., Golding, S. L., & Skeem, J. L. (1999). Defining and assessing competency to stand trial. In A. K. Hess & I. B. Weiner (Eds.), *Handbook of forensic psychology* (2nd ed., pp. 327–349). New York: Wiley.

Schafer, R. (1954). *Psychoanalytic interpretation in Rorschach testing*. New York: Grune & Stratton.

Stafford, K. P. (2003). Assessment of competence to stand trial. In I. B. Weiner (Series Ed.) & A. M. Goldstein (Vol. Ed.), *Comprehensive handbook of psychology: Vol. 11. Forensic psychology* (pp. 359–380). Hoboken, NJ: Wiley.

Stedman, J., Hatch, J., & Schoenfeld, L. (2000). Preinternship preparation in psychological testing and psychotherapy: What internship directors say they expect. *Professional Psychology, 31,* 321–326.

Stricker, G., & Gold, J. R. (1999). The Rorschach: Toward a nomothetically based, idiographically applicable configurational model. *Psychological Assessment, 11,* 240–250.

Viglione, D. J. (1999). A review of recent research addressing the utility of the Rorschach. *Psychological Assessment, 11,* 251–265.

Viglione, D. J., & Hilsenroth, M. J. (2001). The Rorschach: Facts, fictions, and future. *Psychological Assessment, 13,* 452–471.

Viglione, D. J., & Taylor, N. (2003). Empirical support for interrater reliability of Rorschach Comprehensive System coding. *Journal of Clinical Psychology, 59,* 111–121.

Weiner, I. B. (1999a). Contemporary perspectives on Rorschach assessment. *European Journal of Psychological Assessment, 15,* 78–86.

Weiner, I. B. (1999b). What the Rorschach can do for you: Incremental validity in clinical practice. *Assessment, 6,* 327–339.

Weiner, I. B. (2001a). Advancing the science of psychological assessment: The Rorschach Inkblot Method as exemplar. *Psychological Assessment, 13,* 423–432.

Weiner, I. B. (2001b). Considerations in collecting Rorschach reference data. *Journal of Personality Assessment, 77,* 122–127.

Weiner, I. B. (2003a). The assessment process. In I. B. Weiner (Series Ed.) & J. R. Graham & J. A. Naglieri (Vol. Eds.), *Comprehensive handbook of psychology: Vol. 10. Assessment psychology* (pp. 3–25). Hoboken, NJ. Wiley.

Weiner, I. B. (2003b). *Principles of Rorschach interpretation* (2nd ed.). Mahwah, NJ: Erlbaum.

Weiner, I. B. (2004). *Rorschach Interpretation Assistance Program: Forensic report (RIAP5 FE)*. Lutz, FL: Psychological Assessment Resources.

Weiner, I. B. (2005). Integrative personality assessment with self-report and performance-based measures. In S. Strack (Ed.), *Personality and psychopathology* (pp. 317–331). Hoboken, NJ: Wiley.

Weiner, I. B. (2005). Rorschach assessment in child custody cases. *Journal of Child Custody*.2, 99–120.

Weiner, I. B., Exner, J. E., Jr., & Sciara, A. (1996). Is the Rorschach welcome in the courtroom? *Journal of Personality Assessment, 67,* 422–424.

Wood, J. M., & Lilienfeld, S. O. (1999). The Rorschach inkblot test: A case of overstatement. *Assessment, 6,* 341–349.

Wood, J. M., Nezworski, M. T., Garb, H. N., & Lilienfeld, S. O. (2001). The misperception of psychopathology: Problems with the norms of the Comprehensive System of the Rorschach. *Clinical Psychology, 8,* 350–373.

Wood, J. M., Nezworski, M. T., Stejskal, W., & McKinzey, R. (2001). Problems of the Comprehensive System for the Rorschach in forensic settings: Recent developments. *Journal of Forensic Psychology Practice, 1,* 89–103.

CHAPTER 6

Neuropsychology for the Forensic Psychologist

Wilfred G. van Gorp

Because they offer quantification of specific aspects of cognitive functioning, re-sults from neuropsychological assessments and expert testimony of the neuropsy-chologist are often utilized in civil and criminal proceedings in which there are questions about cognitive capabilities. Neuropsychology is the study of the rela-tionship between cognition (e.g., memory, reasoning, judgment, problem solving) and the brain. Clinical neuropsychology applies the known relationships between brain and behavior to conclusions regarding questions of impairment in cognitive functioning, loss of integrity of brain function, and the relationship between neu-ropsychological deficits and daily functioning abilities such as disability, indepen-dent living status, and ability to manage one's own medications and to make independent decisions as applied to an individual case.

There are now training standards in place in neuropsychology, the Houston Conference Guidelines (Hannay, 1998), to guide the pre- and postdoctoral training experience of the clinical neuropsychologist. Related to these guidelines, eligibility for board certification in neuropsychology is offered by the American Board of Professional Psychology. A 2-year postdoctoral fellowship in neuro-psychology is required for board eligibility. Some organizations, such as the National Academy of Neuropsychology (2001), specify credentials required of neuropsychologists.

The clinical neuropsychologist will often conduct an in-depth neuropsychologi-cal examination (described later in this chapter); however, the forensic psychologist is often asked to provide a neuropsychological screening to determine if a more in-depth examination is warranted. This chapter reviews the basic approaches to the examination of brain-behavior relationships and applies them to the forensic arena. The topics addressed are chosen for the forensic psychologist to better understand the utility as well as limitations of neuropsychology in forensic practice.

THE ROLE OF THE FORENSIC PSYCHOLOGIST
IN NEUROPSYCHOLOGY

Clinical and forensic psychologists play an important role in detecting cognitive impairment associated with brain dysfunction. The forensic psychologist is often the first to identify cognitive impairment or the need for a more comprehensive neuropsychological evaluation within the forensic arena. This determination can come from a review of records (e.g., indicating that a litigant has a history of dyslexia or brain injury that has gone unnoticed by other experts) or through an examination of the patient in which the person fails a cognitive screening examination or evidences memory difficulties. Referral to a neuropsychologist for a more in-depth assessment would then be an appropriate action.

The forensic psychologist offers the important function of screening for and therefore identifying neurocognitive impairment when it is present. In the forensic arena, the forensic psychologist also makes the important link between clinical psychological issues (e.g., psychiatric disorders such as Major Depression) and cognitive functioning, as well as forensic issues as they relate to cognition (e.g., legal standards of competency). On the witness stand, the forensic expert can provide this big picture overview and link emotional or other psychological issues with findings from the neuropsychological examination as provided (usually in separate testimony) by the neuropsychologist. The forensic psychologist can also bridge opinions proffered by the neuropsychologist with forensic mental health concepts, such as definitions of insanity, irresistible impulse, competency, and fitness for duty in the workplace. However, the nonspecialist must avoid exceeding his or her knowledge base; this is true for both the forensic psychologist and the neuropsychologist. A generalist, with little training in brain-behavior relationships, was once asked (and agreed) to testify regarding nuances of his memory testing of a litigant who had sustained a subdural hematoma following a traumatic brain injury and the effects of this impairment on discrete cognitive functions. On cross-examination, the attorney established that the expert had represented himself as an expert on brain functioning. When the attorney asked the expert to come to a blackboard placed in the courtroom and draw and label the parts of a neuron for the jury, a "deer in the headlights" stare was the response by the expert, and he was unable to comply. One must be careful not to overrepresent specialization without the requisite training and experience.

APPROACHES IN NEUROPSYCHOLOGY

Most neuropsychologists utilize either a *process*-oriented approach (e.g., selecting neuropsychological tests from a wide array depending on the referral question or unique characteristics of the patient, such as age) or administer a fixed battery of tests such as the Halstead-Reitan Neuropsychological Battery (HRNB; Reitan & Wolfson, 1985) or the Neuropsychological Assessment Battery (NAB; Stern & White, 2003). A *fixed* battery offers the advantage of standardization of a single set of tests, though this advantage is often tempered (in the forensic context) by the fact that most clinicians supplement the battery with other tests (e.g., an IQ test, tests of motivation, personality tests, and/or memory tests). Perhaps most important, the fixed approach offers an overall impairment index score as well as a single set of norms collected on all subtests of the battery (in the case of the NAB). These batteries are discussed in more detail subsequently. Those who utilize a process approach select individual tests based on the referral question and unique patient characteristics and frown on an attempt to administer the same battery of tests to all persons.

PRINCIPLES OF INTERPRETATION

It has been said that test scores by themselves mean very little, and this is certainly true in a vacuum. For example, an IQ score of 65 could represent mental retardation or poor motivation to do well (e.g., malingering) or may be the result of an artificially low score attributable to cultural or language factors. Without important information about the evaluee's history, cultural, and educational background, the clinician is limited in drawing conclusions as to the origins or meaning of specific test scores. All information about the evaluee must be taken into account when interpreting test scores, and the rule of thumb in clinical practice is "The more information, the better." Neuropsychologists usually take into account the evaluee's school records, job history or performance evaluations, collateral informants (if available), hospital/ambulance/ER records, and premorbid baseline ability.

Once norms are selected, clinicians must then determine what constitutes clinical impairment. Though some clinicians consider scores below 1 standard deviation indicative of impairment, most clinicians require performance of 1.5 (or even 2) standard deviations below the normative group on a given measure or group of measures to consider a person clinically impaired on that instrument. Best practice is to examine for a *pattern* of impairment on a range of tests rather than interpreting from a single test score.

SCREENING FOR COGNITIVE IMPAIRMENT

The forensic psychologist, as previously noted, is often hired to screen for neuropsychological impairment. The first step in screening requires consideration of how sensitive the screening approach should be, often at the sacrifice of specificity, as screens that are more sensitive usually come with the risk of less specificity and, therefore, more false-positive errors. The degree of sensitivity required will depend, of course, on the risks associated with making a false-negative versus a false-positive error. When examining for impairment in a population of airline pilots or air traffic controllers, for example, it may be advisable to tolerate a higher proportion of false-positive errors rather than failing to identify persons who might truly be impaired (false-negative errors).

Some studies have shown that individual neuropsychological tests are useful for screening, such as the Trail Making Test B and the Coding (Digit Symbol) subtest of the Wechsler Adult Intelligence Scales (WAIS-III). The Processing Speed Index from the WAIS-III, which is made up of two brief tests that together take about 4 minutes to administer, is often the most sensitive measure of brain impairment. The NAB offers a screening component for each module that the clinician can use to screen for impairment without administering the entire module. Aggregate tests of mental status, such as the Mini-Mental State Examination, are generally not sufficient or sensitive enough for screening for subtle neuropsychological impairment other than cortical dementias.

Based on these considerations, recommended screening methods used by the forensic psychologist may include:

The screening modules from the NAB (recommended).

The Processing Speed Index of the WAIS-III (recommended).

Trail Making Test A/B (modest recommendation).

Mini-Mental State Examination (not recommended as a sensitive screen unless the question of dementia is raised).

NEUROPSYCHOLOGICAL TESTS AND BATTERIES

Neuropsychologists have an array of neuropsychological tests and approaches from which to select. Regardless of which battery the neuropsychologist uses, virtually all neuropsychologists now construct their own battery from a range of possible measures. This is true even for those who start with a fixed battery of tests (such as the HRNB and the NAB), as most clinicians will supplement the fixed battery with additional tests of their choosing. This is especially true in the forensic context, where most clinicians also include measures of motivation and malingering as well as instruments evaluating intelligence and personality/mood.

Currently, the HRNB and the NAB are the two most commonly used formal test batteries for forensic neuropsychological applications. Updated norms for the HRNB (Heaton, Miller, Taylor, & Grant, 2004) provide demographic adjustments for age, education, and sex, with breakdowns for African Americans and Caucasians. This represents a considerable advance from the original HRNB norms, in which an unacceptably large number of older adults were misclassified as impaired.

The NAB offers a number of unique advantages. First, the normative data have been collected on a contemporary cohort that was used for all the measures (i.e., there is a single, normative database for all the component modules of the test, an advantage no other large test battery offers). The normative data can also be broken down into a U.S. Census-matched group. Second, the NAB utilizes a module approach (attention, language, memory, spatial, and executive functions), offering the ease of administering the whole battery or only specific modules. Within each module is a screen so that the test can be utilized as a screening instrument if desired, allowing for follow-up in-depth assessment if the screen for a given module is positive. Third, the NAB provides data on the validation of the battery for groups of persons with various clinical syndromes, such as Alzheimer's disease, head injury, Attention-Deficit/Hyperactivity Disorder (ADHD), or HIV infection.

Many neuropsychologists administer a core group of standard neuropsychological tests and then add or subtract tests based on the referral question or the findings that emerge as the testing is proceeding. This not only is appropriate, but represents good clinical practice and is consistent with the prevailing practices of a large group of board certified clinical neuropsychologists (Sweet, Moberg, & Suchy, 2000).

NORMATIVE DATA

Appropriate selection of normative data is crucial for accurate interpretation of neuropsychological test results on a given individual. As has been shown, selection of norms on a post hoc basis has the potential to skew the results and interpretation of a given test (Kalechstein, van Gorp, & Rapport, 1998). For the HRNB, the recently revised norms by Heaton et al. (2004) are most appropriate; for the NAB, the norms published in the manual should be utilized. The clinician must choose whether to select the larger overall sample or a subset of this group that will match the latest census of the United States.

There are some excellent compilations of norms for neuropsychological tests. Perhaps the most useful is the second edition of the normative data authored by Mitrushina, Boone, Razani, and D'Elia (2005), which contains up-to-date norms on a wide array of neuropsychological tests. Supplementing for some tests not reviewed by Mitrushina et al. is the work by Spreen and Strauss (1998), a compendium of normative data. Several principles should guide the clinician selecting norms for neuropsychological tests:

More recently collected normative data are, in general, preferable to older normative data due to cohort effects (i.e., the Flynn effect).

As a rule, normative data with a larger N are preferable to normative data with fewer participants.

Normative data with demographic adjustments are preferable to norms without demographic breakdowns.

Normative data in which the sample most closely resembles the demographic characteristics of the evaluee are preferable.

When possible, norms should be selected on an a priori basis to avoid selection bias and skewed results.

ASSESSMENT OF NEUROPSYCHOLOGICAL DOMAINS

Whether using a published battery such as the NAB or HRNB or constructing a battery of tests made up of various published individual instruments, most neuropsychologists organize their findings (usually, but not always, reflected in a report format) into the following conceptual domains.

Motivation

Formal assessment of motivation to perform well and to expend sufficient effort on neuropsychological tests should be considered standard and customary practice in any neuropsychological evaluation in which there are direct or indirect incentives for the examinee to skew results. As this is virtually always the case in any forensic or medicolegal assessment (e.g., for monetary award, avoiding incarceration, or reducing one's sentence), thorough assessment of motivation to perform well, to feign, or to embellish should be a part of any forensic neuropsychological assessment. Individuals may feign or skew their results in either the cognitive (neuropsychological) or emotional (e.g., personality, psychiatric symptom report) domain, but not necessarily both. Therefore, "cognitive malingering" should be assessed along with "psychiatric or psychological malingering" if the evaluee is reporting symptoms in both arenas. If the examinee reports symptoms only in the cognitive arena, then the focus of motivation assessment will obviously be in the cognitive domain.

There are many tests that can potentially be used to assess cognitive malingering. First, it should be kept in mind that many examinees may have done their own due diligence (i.e., researching via the Internet instruments that may be used), and much can be learned about tests of exaggeration or malingering via the Internet (Ruiz, Drake, Glass, Marcotte, & van Gorp, 2002). Some attorneys (Youngjohn, 1995) have indicated that they consider it their ethical responsibility to coach their client on what to expect regarding assessment of motivation. Examinees can also research what is known about the neuropsychologist, evaluating him or her via the Internet or by identifying prior clinical reports the neuropsychologist has generated that may be available from open court records. Examinees may therefore know what types of tests the clinician may administer in their case. Based on this investigation, savvy examinees will know that VIP and TOMM, which they may see on answer sheets or test stimuli, stand for names of malingering tests.

The Test of Memory Malingering (TOMM; Tombaugh, 1996) has been shown to have excellent validity and discriminability in detecting persons amplifying memory complaints versus those with true memory impairment. Whereas persons with dementia or various amnestic conditions have been able to do well on the TOMM, persons who feign memory impairment often do poorly on this test (Vallabhajosula & van Gorp, 2001). The Validity Indicator Profile (VIP; Frederick, 1997) offers classifications of valid or invalid performance. If invalid, poor performance may be due to careless (inconsistent) or irrelevant (answering without regard to item content) answers or to true malingering (responding correctly or incorrectly with regard to item difficulty). Persons with genuine cognitive impairment may respond inconsistently or carelessly not because of feigning, but due to actual cognitive impairment. Therefore, profiles classified as inconsistent or careless in persons with cognitive deficits may result in false positives (Frederick, Crosby, & Wynkoop, 2000) and should be interpreted cautiously. Other useful instruments to detect exaggeration of cognitive deficits include the Computerized Assessment of Response Bias (Green & Iverson, 2001), the Word Memory Test (Green, Iverson, & Allen, 1999), and the Victoria Symptom Validity Test (Slick, Hopp, Strauss, & Spellacy, 1996).

Some studies have attempted with varying degrees of success to utilize scores from clinical neuropsychological instruments (e.g., Wechsler Memory Scale-III [WMS-III]) to differentiate exaggerated from valid responding. The advantage offered by this approach is that although savvy examinees can learn the names of specific malingering tests, it is much more difficult to know how to feign a clinical pattern of impairment on one or more clinical instruments. Examples of this approach include the weighted index of six items from the Logical Memory Delayed Recognition portion of the WMS-III to form the Rarely Missed Index (RMI; Killgore & DellaPietra, 2000). Killgore and DellaPietra reported excellent sensitivity (97%) and specificity (100%), though these data were obtained in a relatively small sample ($N = 51$ patients) and need to be cross-validated in further prospective studies. In one such attempt in a much larger clinical sample, Lange, Sullivan, and Anderson (2005) failed to find sufficient sensitivity and specificity to recommend this approach. Validation of the RMI awaits further study to determine if the initial positive results of Killgore and DellaPietra will hold or whether the cautions of Lange et al. are borne out. Regardless of the specific utility of the

RMI, this approach to detection of motivation or feigning offers promise as genuine clinical impairment is difficult to replicate in a consistent manner across a variety of measures.

A final review of the examinee's overall test performance should be made by the neuropsychologist to determine whether the actual clinical test scores make neuropsychological sense. For example, scores of 0 on measures of delayed recall of learning and memory in a person who is able to find the clinician's office on his or her own, leave for lunch and return, and provide a relevant history are noncredible manifestations of an amnesia because they do not relate to demonstrated ability. Another example of a finding that does not make neuropsychological sense is very poor performance on a computerized measure of reaction time, only to dramatically improve when the clinician informs the patient that he or she may have to be reported to the state's Department of Motor Vehicles for a driving evaluation because of such poor performance.

Intelligence

The WAIS-III (and other intelligence tests, for that matter) may be considered a neuropsychological instrument in its own right. When examining the results of IQ testing, the first question (assuming the results are deemed valid) to be asked is, "Are these findings consistent with my estimate of the evaluee's premorbid level of intellectual functioning?" as many neurologic conditions (e.g., dementia) can lower current IQ scores relative to premorbid levels. The estimate of premorbid ability is best based on actual tests of performance, most commonly a test of reading (assuming that no aphasia or serious learning disorder of reading or dementia beyond the mild stage is present). The Wechsler Test of Adult Reading (WTAR; Wechsler, 2001) offers the advantage of being conormed with the WAIS-III and provides a cross-validated estimate of premorbid IQ. The only limitation of the WTAR is its ceiling effect in persons with high levels of intelligence, which may underestimate their premorbid ability. The North American revision of the National Adult Reading Test (Blair & Spreen, 1989) also provides a useful estimate of premorbid IQ, though it was not conormed with the WAIS-III as was the WTAR. In persons with a serious reading disorder, aphasia, or dementia, scores on these tests of reading may underestimate premorbid abilities. In these circumstances, demographic variables may be utilized, as highest level of education and occupational attainment are most predictive of premorbid intellectual ability. Formulas have been developed to compute an estimated premorbid IQ (e.g., Barona, Reynolds, & Chastain, 1984) using demographic variables, though these are less reliable in persons with very high or low IQ.

The WAIS-III offers four useful indexes (index scores) of cognitive ability: Verbal Cognitive (related to verbal/language functions mediated, in part, by the left hemisphere), Perceptual/Organizational (related to right hemisphere-mediated abilities), Working Memory (attention, related to frontal and subcortical structures, including the reticular activating system), and Processing Speed (as previously noted, a sensitive indicator of brain dysfunction but not specific to any disorder or brain region per se). Considered in this light, the WAIS-III has become a neuropsychological measure in its own right.

Attention

On a practical level, adequate attention is essential for the valid assessment of other neuropsychological abilities, as deficits in attention can produce deficient performance in any arena, not because the person has a primary impairment of memory (as an example) but because of inattention in acquiring a list of words. Therefore, any interpretation of neuropsychological abilities first requires consideration of the ability of the examinee to adequately attend to tasks presented to him or her.

The WAIS-III Working Memory Index (WMI) provides an aggregate measure of attentional ability. However, persons with deficits in sustained attention (such as might be seen in cases of ADHD) or divided attention (attending to two stimuli simultaneously) may still perform normally on the WMI because the tests that contribute to this score are usually briefer measures of focused attention. Assessment of sustained vigilance and reaction time, such as through a computer-administered test of attention over many minutes (e.g., 15 or 20 minutes) or on a progressively more difficult task in which the person must sequentially add serial digits, may be necessary to document a disorder of sustained attention such as occurs in cases of ADHD. One test of divided attention often used by neuropsychologists is the Brown Peterson Distractor Technique (clinically more commonly referred to as the Auditory Consonant Trigrams; Brown, 1958).

Neurologic disorders that produce impairments in attention include a delirium or confusional state, ADHD, medication effects or substance-related intoxication, and frontal lobe dysfunction. Dramatically low scores on tasks of basic attention (digit span, working memory) are commonly seen in a delirium. Deficits on tasks of sustained or divided attention are commonly found in cases of ADHD and other mild attentional disorders such as from frontal lobe dysfunction.

Some individuals claim a lack of criminal culpability based on inattention related to ADHD. The success of these claims is modest at best. Much more frequent are requests for accommodations for either work environment or test-taking conditions (e.g., extra time on the SATs, working at home, the need for a quiet working environment) based on issues involving ADHD. In these instances, the expert considering a request for accommodations usually seeks historical documentation of attentional problems.

Language

Language abilities are important to assess not only because assessment of the dominant hemisphere (left hemisphere in most right handers) is important in determining if brain damage is present, but because language abilities are necessary for conceptual reasoning and effective verbal communication. Persons with severe aphasia, in which both comprehension and expression are impaired, may have serious difficulties communicating with their attorney, understanding the charges against them, and assisting in their own defense. In general, assessment of confrontation naming (i.e., naming of an object) is used as a sensitive screen for other impairments of language, as almost any injury to the left (dominant) hemisphere will produce a deficit in this area. After ruling out cultural, intellectual, and vision factors, low scores on such tests as the Boston Naming Test or confrontation naming portions of the NAB or other batteries may reflect dysfunction of the left hemisphere and prompt further investigation of language deficits (Lezak, Howieson, Loring, Hannay, & Fischer, 2004).

Assessment of fluency (generating words beginning with a target letter or from a semantic class, such as "animals"), comprehension, and repetition is also important in the assessment of language function. The defendant who cannot comprehend, repeat, or have lexical access to common nouns is, at the least, seriously disadvantaged in any proceeding in the legal system and, at worst, not competent to proceed because of the difficulty in communicating with his or her attorney and assisting in his or her own defense.

Frequently, neurologic damage producing either an aphasia or more discrete language dysfunction will be accompanied by a discernible lesion or abnormality found on structural brain imaging, but this is not always the case. For example, head injuries can sometimes damage the left temporal lobe, producing some impairment in naming, and some degenerative conditions (frontotemporal dementia, Alzheimer's disease) can have language impairment as the initial presenting symptom of the condition. Patients with a primary progressive aphasia usually have a normal structural brain scan but evidence progressive impairment of language function, culminating ultimately in mutism.

As noted earlier, neuropsychological tests of language function include verbal fluency (controlled oral word association test), the Boston Naming Test (Goodglass & Kaplan, 2000), the Boston Diagnostic Aphasia Examination (Goodglass & Kaplan, 1983), the Western Aphasia Battery (Kertesz, 1982), and the language module from the NAB (Stern & White, 2003).

Learning and Memory

Disorders of memory are ubiquitous in neuropsychological conditions. For this reason, thorough assessment of learning and memory is critical in any neurocognitive assessment. Conditions such as closed head injury, anoxia, various dementias, and alcohol-related cognitive impairment, including Korsakoff's syndrome, all involve primary deficits in learning and memory.

Memory is frequently assessed through administration of a memory battery, such as the WMS-III (Wechsler, 1997) or the language module of the NAB (Stern & White, 2003). The WMS-III offers the advantage of having been conormed with the WAIS-III, so a determination can be made as to whether an individual's memory scores are significantly discrepant from what would be predicted by his or her IQ score on the WAIS-III. Individual measures of learning and memory include the California Verbal Learning Test 2 (Delis, Kramer, Kaplan, & Ober, 2000), the recall of the Rey Osterrieth Complex Figure (Osterrieth, 1944; see Spreen & Strauss, 1998), and other serial list learning tests, sometimes used as stand-alone methods to assess memory or as adjunctive tests to a larger memory battery such as the WMS-III.

Memory issues are often raised in the forensic arena. In criminal cases, persons may claim not to remember certain incidents or facts. Discrete periods of amnesia, if not part of an acute intoxication, substance use, or feigning, may represent a Dissociative Amnesia (DA). Dissociative Amnesia typically involves a discrete period of amnesia with otherwise intact or nearly normal learning and memory abilities. It is sometimes said that DA involves an episode of retrograde amnesia (inability to recall some historical event, usually associated with psychological or physical trauma) but with intact or nearly normal anterograde amnesia (i.e., new learning). True cases of DA often involve poor recall of a specific period in the person's past, but nearly normal or intact performance on tests of learning and memory such as the WMS-III or California Verbal Learning Test 2.

Visuospatial Abilities

Poor performance on tasks of spatial ability can result from myriad causes, including right hemisphere disease (classically involving the parietal lobes), nonverbal learning disability, and chronic alcohol abuse. Assessment of spatial ability usually involves examination of the Perceptual Organization Index of the WAIS-III (Wechsler, 1997), the copy of the Rey Complex Figure (Osterrieth, 1944), and/or a variety of other tests, including the Benton Line Orientation Test (Benton, Sivan, & Hamsher, 1994), the NAB spatial module (Stern & White, 2003), or Raven's Progressive Matrices (Raven, 1995).

In the forensic arena, impairment of spatial abilities can potentially relate to issues involving eyewitness identification (analysis and recognition of faces), misidentification resulting in errors of judgment (e.g., misperceiving an individual holding an object such as a comb as a gun), and emotional difficulties. Persons with Nonverbal Learning Disability often have notable impairments of social function because they have difficulty perceiving facial expression, nuances of affective expression and tone, and so on.

Executive Abilities

This domain represents perhaps the most important of all the cognitive functions assessed in the forensic context, as it relates to forensic issues and neuropsychological practice. Executive abilities are the highest order cognitive abilities that are mediated by the frontal lobes. These cognitive functions include abilities in planning, strategy formation, problem solving, judgment, and inhibition of responses. Patients with frontal lobe damage are often inappropriate, are impulsive in that they act before thinking, and cannot adequately problem-solve or deal with novel situations. The case of Phineas Gage (Harlow, 1848) is illustrative of frontal lobe damage. Gage, working on the American train/rail system in the mid-1800s, had an accident in which an iron rod pierced his jaw and headed up, through, and out of his frontal lobe. Not only did Gage survive, but he remained conscious. However, he sustained a dramatic change of personality. Formerly an upstanding gentleman, Gage's personality changed and he was often inappropriate, often cursing, a dramatic change for him. In essence, he acted before he thought.

Deficits in executive function resulting from neurologic conditions may leave individuals unable to inhibit responses (relating to an irresistible impulse claim, sometimes used in insanity statutes) or unable to form clear intent prior to committing a crime or to truly appreciate the nature *and* consequences of their actions (i.e., cause and effect; see Goldstein, Morse, & Shapiro, 2003). As such, determination of specific deficits in executive functions is one of the most challenging areas of neuropsychological practice.

Psychometric assessment of constructs such as judgment and change in personality is difficult. Most tests in neuropsychology involve assessment of cognition rather than judgment and behavior. Conventional personality tests in clinical psychology were developed for and normed on patients with psychiatric illness, not neurologic disease. Perhaps even more important, clinical psychological tests of personality offer a singular snapshot in time and do not assess before-and-after changes. A few tests of this nature have been published (e.g., Ruff Neurobehavioral Inventory; Ruff, 2003), but these offer limitations as well (van Gorp & Hassenstab, 2005). Much more work needs to be done to develop solid noncognitive measures of frontal lobe changes in personality and behavior.

Another difficulty in the assessment of frontal lobe functions is that many cognitive tests are highly structured and administered in a structured, distraction-free setting, a condition very different from real life, which is unstructured with often frequent interruptions and distractions. For this reason, cognitive tests of frontal lobe functions have a much higher false-negative than false-positive rate. Performance within normal limits on these tests does not necessarily indicate that there is no frontal lobe pathology, whereas an abnormal finding on these tests is much more indicative of a problem with these structures.

Several conventional neuropsychological tests are useful to assess the cognitive deficits often present in frontal lobe or executive dysfunction. Perhaps the most well-known of frontal lobe tests is the Wisconsin Card Sorting Test (Heaton, 1981), a test of problem solving. Though persons with demonstrated frontal lobe pathology have been able to perform normally on the test (Orsini, van Gorp, & Boone, 1988), an abnormal performance is generally indicative of an impairment in problem solving. Other commonly used tests of frontal functions include the Stroop Color Interference Test (Golden, 1978), which is a verbal test of response inhibition; tests of divided attention, such as the Auditory Consonant Trigrams (Peterson & Peterson, 1959); tests of cognitive flexibility, such as the Trail Making Test B (Reitan & Wolfson, 1985); and measures of both verbal and visual fluency, including the Controlled Oral Word Association Test (Benton & Hamsher, 1989) and the Ruff Figural Fluency Test (Ruff, 1988). The executive functions module of the NAB includes tests of planning (mazes), problem solving (category test), and cognitive flexibility and offers the advantage of an aggregate "impairment score" for the module as a whole as well as impaired scores on each component of the module. Assessment of damage to the frontal lobes should also include evaluation of changes in personality or behavior following an injury to this brain region.

Motor Abilities

Most neuropsychological evaluations include assessment of fine motor abilities for each hand, using such tests as the Grooved Pegboard Test (Kløve, 1963), the Finger Tapping Test (Reitan & Wolfson, 1993), or the Purdue Pegboard Test (Tiffin, 1968). Performance of normal persons is often highly variable on these measures. For this reason, clinicians may want to administer at least two motor tests to demonstrate consistent asymmetries or motor impairment before a conclusion of impairment is reached. Additionally, if a lateralized performance is found, it is recommended that the clinician examine the rest of the cognitive profile to determine whether there are expected cognitive asymmetries as well (e.g., left hand motor impairment and spatial impairment on cognitive measures).

Personality

Conventional personality tests such as the Minnesota Multiphasic Personality Inventory 2 (MMPI-2; Butcher, Dahlstrom, Graham, Tellegen, & Kaemmer, 1989) and the Personality Assessment Inventory (Morey, 1991) must be interpreted with some caution in persons with known or suspected neurologic impairment as these tests were not normed on neurologic patients. Gass and Wald (1997) noted that some items on an MMPI-2 that reflect mental confusion will be endorsed by persons with traumatic brain injury (TBI) and do not necessarily reflect psychiatric disturbance. Though Gass and Wald have published a correction for persons with TBI on the MMPI, we do not have similar corrections for persons with epilepsy, aphasia, or frontal lobe damage. Persons with these disorders may endorse items reflective of cognitive symptoms associated with their neurologic condition rather than a psychiatric disturbance. Though personality tests are not proscribed in evaluating persons with neurologic disease, clinicians should be careful to avoid overinterpretation of profiles (e.g., elevations on Scale 8) as necessarily reflecting psychopathology when they may instead reflect symptoms involving cognitive difficulties.

INTERPRETATION OF TEST RESULTS

Interpretation must be made with as much knowledge about the evaluee as possible, with more sources of consensual information resulting in a more valid interpretation. Clinicians avoid reaching a conclusion based on a single test score, but rather examine for a *pattern* of impairment or intact abilities across numerous tests. Examination of qualitative observations is helpful to determine the reason for a failure of a test or test item, and this may help the clinician determine a pattern of difficulty or the reason for a particular problem on a group of tests. Clinicians must avoid being test bound and restricting their vision to a test score without considering the greater pattern or big picture.

APPLICATION TO CHILDREN AND ADOLESCENTS

Pediatric neuropsychology requires specialized training in brain-behavior relationships in children. Not only are specialized tests used for children and adolescents (e.g., Wechsler Intelligence Scale for Children-IV: Wechsler, 2003; MMPI-A: Butcher et al., 1992), but issues of developmental level, plasticity of the infant, and child or adolescent brain organization and reorganization after injury must be considered. Because of these issues, only persons well trained and qualified in pediatric neuropsychology should embark on these evaluations. Children are not merely smaller adults. Different tests are necessary to assess them and different principles are used to interpret their test results (see Baron, 2003).

CULTURAL FACTORS

Neuropsychologists are sometimes asked to evaluate persons who are not native speakers of English or for other reasons are nonverbal. Some individuals are English-speaking but come from different cultures. It is, of course, best for the evaluee to be examined in his or her native language by a clinician who is fully fluent and capable in that language. Tests should be interpreted only under rigorous conditions following appropriate methodology. If a translator is to be used, he or she should be a certified translator, not a family member or friend, who may have an interest in the outcome of the evaluation or who may make the evaluee self-conscious. The interpreter should not translate actual test items that require demonstrated equivalence and norms (e.g., personality questionnaire items). Cultural factors must also be taken into account in interpreting assessment results, such as verbal subtests of the WAIS-III or on personality subscales that are sensitive to cultural factors. For instance, Scale 8 (Schizophrenia) on the MMPI-2 can be artificially elevated in persons from another cultural as they appear nonconforming and atypical in thought and behavior.

CONCLUSION

Neuropsychological opinions are often requested in the forensic context as this approach offers quantification of cognitive abilities. However, specialized training is required to embark on in-depth assessment and interpretation of neuropsychological tests and functions. The clinical and forensic psychologist must be adept at knowing when it is appropriate to seek neuropsychological consultation, such as in the following cases:

- The patient is positive on a neurocognitive screening examination and the forensic psychologist believes it appropriate to follow up with a more comprehensive assessment.
- The patient has a history of significant head injury.
- The patient has a suspected or known neurologic disease such as tumor, stroke, or dementia.
- There is a suspicion of possible dementia or developing dementia versus normal aging.
- The cognitive effects of medications are to be assessed.
- There is a suspicion of learning disability or ADHD.
- The clinician observes frequent examples of inability to recall or other memory dysfunction.

The neuropsychologist and forensic psychologist can be a highly effective team in the forensic arena and offer the trier of fact much useful information. Knowing each professional's strengths and limitations is important in effective consultation to the legal system. The forensic psychologist can provide the critical bridge between forensic concepts and legal definitions with findings from the neuropsychological examination and the opinion proffered by the neuropsychologist. One professional optimally complements the other.

REFERENCES

Baron, I. S. (2003). *Neuropsychological evaluation of the child.* New York: Oxford University Press.

Barona, A., Reynolds, C. R., & Chastain, R. A. (1984). A demographically based index of premorbid intelligence for the WAIS-R. *Journal of Clinical Psychology, 52,* 885–887.

Benton, A. L., & Hamsher, K. (1989). *Multilingual aphasia examination.* Iowa City: AJA Associates.

Benton, A. L., Sivan, A. B., Hamsher, K., Varney, N. R., & Spreen, O. (1994). *Contributions to neuropsychological assessment: A clinical manual* (2nd ed.). Oxford, England: Oxford University Press.

Blair, J. R., & Spreen, O. (1989). Predicting premorbid IQ: A revision of the National Adult Reading Test. *Clinical Neuropsychologist, 3,* 129–136.

Brown, J. (1958). Some tests of the decay of immediate memory. *Quarterly Journal of Experimental Psychology, 10,* 12–21.

Butcher, J. N., Dahlstrom, W. G., Graham, J. R., Tellegen, A., & Kaemmer, B. (1989). *Manual for the restandardized Minnesota Multiphasic Personality Inventory: MMPI-2.* Minneapolis: University of Minnesota Press.

Butcher, J. N., Williams, C. L., Graham, J. R., Archer, R., Tellegen, A., Ben-Porath, Y. S., et al. (1992). *MMPI-A manual for administration, scoring, and interpretation.* Minneapolis: University of Minnesota Press.

Delis, D. C., Kramer, J. H., Kaplan, E., & Ober, B. A. (2000). *California Verbal Learning Test (CVLT-II)* (2nd ed.). San Antonio, TX: Psychological Corporation.

Frederick, R. I. (1997). *Validity Indicator Profile manual.* Minneapolis, MN: National Computer Systems.

Frederick, R. I., Crosby, R. D., & Wynkoop, T. F. (2000). Performance curve classification of invalid responding on the Validity Indicator Profile. *Archives of Clinical Neuropsychology, 15,* 281–300.

Gass, C., & Wald, H. S. (1997). MMPI-2 interpretation and closed-head trauma: Cross-validation of a correction factor. *Archives of Clinical Neuropsychology, 12,* 199–205.

Golden, C. J. (1978). *Stroop Color and Word Test: A manual for clinical and experimental uses.* Wood Dale, IL: Stoelting.

Goldstein, A. M., Morse, S. T., & Shapiro, D. L. (2003). Evaluation of criminal responsibility. In I. B. Weiner (Series Ed.) & A. M. Goldstein (Vol. Ed.), *Comprehensive handbook of psychology: Vol. 11. Forensic psychology* (pp. 381–406). Hoboken, NJ: Wiley.

Goodglass, H., & Kaplan, E. (1983). *Boston Diagnostic Aphasia Examination (BDAE).* Philadelphia: Lea and Febiger.

Goodglass, H., & Kaplan, E. (2000). *Boston Naming Test.* Philadelphia: Lippincott Williams & Williams.

Green, P., & Iverson, G. L. (2001). Validation of the Computerized Assessment of Response Bias in litigating patients with head injuries. *Clinical Neuropsychologist, 15,* 492–497.

Green, P., Iverson, G., & Allen, L. (1999). Detecting malingering in head injury litigation with the Word Memory Test. *Brain Injury, 13,* 813–819.

Hannay, H. J. (1998). Proceedings of the Houston Conference on Specialty Education and Training in Clinical Neuropsychology, September 3–7, 1997, University of Houston Hilton and Conference Center. *Archives of Clinical Neuropsychology, 13*(2), 157–249.

Harlow, J. M. (1848). Passage of an iron rod through the head. *Boston Medical and Surgical Journal, 39,* 389–393.

Heaton, R. K. (1981). *Wisconsin Card Sort Test (WCST).* Odessa, FL: Psychological Assessment Resources.

Heaton, R., Miller, W., Taylor, M. J., & Grant, I. (2004). *Revised comprehensive norms for an expanded Halstead-Reitan Battery: Demographically adjusted norms for African-Americans and Caucasians.* Odessa, FL: Psychological Assessment Resources.

Kalechstein, A., van Gorp, W. G., & Rapport, L. (1998). Variability in clinical classification of raw test scores across normative data sets. *Clinical Neuropsychologist, 12,* 339–347.

Kertesz, A. (1982). *Western Aphasia Battery.* San Antonio, TX: Psychological Corporation.

Killgore, W. D. S., & DellaPietra, L. (2000). Using the WMS-III to detect malingering: Empirical validation of the Rarely Missed Index (RMI). *Journal of Clinical and Experimental Neuropsychology, 22,* 761–771.

Kløve, H. (1963). Clinical neuropsychology. In F. M. Forster (Ed.), *The medical clinics of North America* (pp. 1647–1658). Philadelphia: Saunders.

Lange, R. T., Sullivan, K., & Anderson, D. (2005). Ecological validity of the WMS-III Rarely Missed Index in personal injury litigation. *Journal of Clinical and Experimental Neuropsychology, 27,* 412–424.

Lezak, M., Howieson, D. B., Loring, D. W., Hannay, H. J., & Fischer, J. S. (2004). *Neuropsychological assessment* (4th ed.). New York: Oxford University Press.

Mitrushina, M., Boone, K., Razani, J., & D'Elia, L. (2005). *Handbook of normative data for neuropsychological assessment* (2nd ed.). New York: Oxford University Press.

Morey, L. C. (1991). *Personality Assessment Inventory: Professional manual.* Odessa, FL: Psychological Assessment Resources.

National Academy of Neuropsychology (2001). *Definition of a neuropsychologist.* Available from http://www.nanonline.org/paio/defneuropsych.shtm.

Orsini, D., van Gorp, W., & Boone, K. (1988). *The neuropsychology casebook.* New York: Springer-Verlag.

Osterrieth, P. A. (1944). Le test de copie d'une figure complexe. *Archives de Psychologie, 30,* 206–356 [J. Corwin & F. W. Bylsma, Trans. (1993). *Clinical Neuropsychologist, 7,* 9–15].

Peterson, L. R., & Peterson, M. J. (1959). Short-term retention of individual verbal items. *Journal of Experimental Psychology, 58,* 193–198.

Raven, J. C. (1995). *Coloured Progressive Matrices Sets, A, AB, B* (Manual sections 1 & 2). Oxford, England: Oxford Psychologists Press.

Reitan, R., & Wolfson, D. (1985). *Halstead-Reitan Neuropsychological Test Battery.* Tuscon, AZ: Neuropsychology Press.

Reitan, R. M., & Wolfson, D. (1993). *Halstead-Reitan Neuropsychological Test Battery: Theory and clinical applications* (2nd ed.). Tucson, AZ: Neuropsychology Press.

Ruff, R. (1988). *Ruff Figural Fluency Test.* San Diego, CA: Neuropsychological Resources.

Ruff, R. (2003). *Ruff Neurobehavioral Inventory.* Odessa, FL: Psychological Assessment Resources.

Ruiz, M. A., Drake, E. B., Glass, A., Marcotte, D., & van Gorp, W. G. (2002). Trying to beat the system: Misuse of the Internet to assist in avoiding the detection of psychological symptom dissimulation. *Professional Psychology: Research and Practice, 33,* 294–299.

Slick, D., Hopp, G., Strauss, E., & Spellacy, F. J. (1996). Victoria Symptom Validity Test: Efficiency for detecting feigned memory impairment and relationship to neuropsychological tests and MMPI-2 validity scales. *Journal of Clinical and Experimental Neuropsychology, 18,* 911–922.

Spreen, O., & Strauss, E. (1998). *A compendium of neuropsychological tests: Administration, norms, and commentary* (2nd ed.). New York: Oxford University Press.

Stern, R., & White, T. (2003). *Neuropsychology Assessment Battery.* Odessa, FL: Psychological Assessment Resources.

Sweet, J., Moberg, P., & Suchy, Y. (2000). Ten-year follow-up survey of clinical neuropsychologists: Pt. II. Private practice and economics. *Clinical Neuropsychologist, 14,* 479–495.

Tiffin, J. (1968). *Purdue pegboard examiner's manual.* Rosemont, IL: London House.

Tombaugh, T. N. (1996). *Test of Memory Malingering (TOMM).* Toronto, Ontario, Canada: Multi-Health Systems.

Vallabhajosula, B., & van Gorp, W. G. (2001). Post-*Daubert* admissibility of scientific evidence on malingering of cognitive deficits. *Journal of the American Academy of Psychiatry and the Law, 29,* 207–215.

Van Gorp, W., & Hassenstab, J. (2005). Review of the Ruff Neurobehavioral Inventory. In R. A. Spies & B. S. Plake (Eds.), *Mental Measurements Yearbook* (16th ed, pp. 686–688). Lincoln: Buros Institute of Mental Measurements and the University of Nebraska.

Wechsler, D. (1997). *Wechsler Memory Scale manual III* (3rd ed.). San Antonio, TX: Psychological Corporation.

Wechsler, D. (2001). *Wechsler Test of Adult Reading manual (WTAR).* San Antonio, TX: Psychological Corporation.

Wechsler, D. (2003). *Wechsler Intelligence Scale for Children (WISC-IV)* (4th ed.). San Antonio, TX: Psychological Corporation.

Youngjohn, J. R. (1995). Confirmed attorney coaching prior to neuropsychological examination. *Psychological Assessment, 2,* 279–283.

PART III

Ethical Issues in Forensic Practice

CHAPTER 7

Ethics and Forensic Psychological Practice

Paul D. Lipsitt

The "Ethical Principles of Psychologists and Code of Conduct" in 1992 (American Psychological Association [APA], 1992) contained a section on "Forensic Activities," alerting psychologists to some of the unique aspects of practice at the intersection of psychology and law. The 2002 Ethics Code (APA, 2002) no longer provides a special section for forensic practice, which has now taken its place as an established branch within the field of psychology.

All psychologists who are members of the APA or who are licensed in states that have adopted the APA Code are, of course, obligated to abide by the entire Ethics Code. This chapter focuses on those sections of the Code that pertain especially to forensic practice and to the role of the forensic psychologist. In conjunction with the "Specialty Guidelines for Forensic Psychologists" (Committee on Ethical Guidelines for Forensic Psychologists, 1991), the sections of the Ethics Code selected for this chapter are intended to aid the forensic psychologist in approaching a range of circumstances in practice in the legal system. Among the issues that have special relevance in the legal arena are informed consent, confidentiality, multiple relationships, and conflicts between law and professional ethics. To effectively and competently practice as a forensic psychologist, it is imperative not only to possess the appropriate clinical skills needed to provide the service requested by judges and attorneys, but also to maintain an appropriate awareness of one's role in the legal system. This chapter is intended to aid in navigating a system based on due process and adversary procedures, while bringing to the task the professional training and skills developed in psychology.

OVERVIEW

Most established professions have a code of ethics to guide practitioners in their work. The purpose of an ethics code is to protect the rights and welfare of those served and to provide assurances that professionals are held to a standard that will engender trust in the recipients of their services. The consumer relies on the

Special thanks to Cinzia R. Lelos and Brooke K. Lipsitt for their helpful comments on an earlier draft of this chapter.

knowledge and skills of the professional who makes judgments in a highly specialized area frequently not well understood by the general public. Thus, it is imperative that the consumer believes that the professional is acting in the best interests of those being served and is not self-serving.

A common contract assumes enough knowledge on the part of the parties to make a binding agreement, often expressed as *caveat emptor,* or "Buyer beware." In a contract for goods or services, the purchaser is expected to form an independent judgment of the quality and value of the transaction. A relationship with a professional, however, is one based on trust rather than an arm's-length transaction. Similar to a lawyer-client relationship, the psychologist is under a duty to act for the benefit of another on matters within the scope of the professional relationship. This is known in the law as a "fiduciary relationship," when one person assumes control and responsibility over another or when one person has a duty to act for or give advice to another within the scope of the relationship (*Black's Law Dictionary,* 1999).

Throughout history, the professions of law and medicine have developed standards of conduct intended to regulate behavior by formulating codes of ethics. These codes provide the parameters to assure that the best interests of the client or patient will be paramount. As a more recent profession historically, psychology first developed a comparable code through the APA in 1953, even though the expertise that psychologists have to offer in the judicial system was first established in 1962 by the U.S. Supreme Court in *Jenkins v. United States.* This decision recognized that psychologists with training and experience could be qualified to offer testimony on matters of mental disease or defect. Prior to that time, such testimony had been restricted to physicians (Lipsitt, 1984).

As Fisher (2003) has observed, "Each revision of the American Psychological Association (APA) Ethics Code has been driven by the evolving roles and responsibilities of psychologists within a constantly changing sociocultural, economic, political and legal landscape" (p. 23). The 1992 APA publication of its "Ethical Principles of Psychologists and Code of Conduct" devoted one section (7) to "Forensic Activities," emphasizing issues of particular concern to the domain of practice in the legal system as a unique specialty in psychology with distinguishable practice issues. The 1992 inclusion of a specialized section on forensic activities in effect recognized forensic psychology as a unique domain of practice, although the APA did not formally recognize it as a specialty until August 2001 (see Otto & Heilbrun, 2002). However, the recognition of the need for an organizational base for the emerging specialty of forensic psychology led to the formation of the American Board of Forensic Psychology in 1978 (Kaslow, 2002).

On June 1, 2003, the current Ethics Code (APA, 2002) became operant as the ninth edition of the code, which was first published almost 50 years ago (APA, 1953). All members of the APA are obligated to adhere to its standards. The regulations governing state licensing boards in psychology are usually consistent with the APA Ethics Code, although state regulations may expand or modify ethical requirements. Although the forensic specialty section has been deleted from the revised Code, forensic psychologists will find many sections of the Ethics Code specifically relevant to their practice. The separate section on "Forensic Activities" was eliminated in the 2002 Code to alert psychologists, with or without previous training and experience in forensic psychology, to take into consideration ethical issues before assuming a forensic role. Fisher (2003) reports that "the Ethics Code Task Force (ECTF) charged with revising the 1992 Code . . . eliminate[d] the forensic section and incorporated standards relevant to court-related activities into other sections of the 2002 Ethics Code" (p. 24).

Elaboration on specifics of forensic practice are found in the "Specialty Guidelines for Forensic Psychologists" (Committee on Ethical Guidelines for Forensic Psychologists, 1991). Not intended as absolute standards of practice, the Guidelines have been endorsed by the American Board of Forensic Psychology and the American Psychology-Law Society, Division 41 of the APA. The Guidelines offer a map to follow without reaching the level of an ethical or legal requirement.

The Ethics Code (Section 2) and the Guidelines (Section III) state that psychologists will provide services only within the boundaries of their specialized knowledge, skill, experience, and education. Section 2.01(f) of the Ethics Code specifies, "When assuming forensic roles, psychologists are or become reasonably familiar with the judicial or administrative rules governing their roles." Those psychologists who are involved in a case that is before the court in the legal system but who are not forensic specialists may not be expected to be as knowledgeable about the legal system. By inserting "reasonably," the Ethics Code may be interpreted as holding a psychologist who is not qualified in the forensic area to a less strict standard than a forensic psychologist. The former may be called to the legal arena for a specific case but is not assumed to have the same level of knowledge and skill as a forensic psychologist, who is expected to understand the complexities at the intersection of psychology and law.

Prefacing the standards in the current Ethics Code is a set of "General Principles." Unlike the standards, these principles are aspirational rather than obligatory and enforceable, to inspire and guide psychologists toward the highest ideals of the profession. Some elements of the forensic section of the 1992 Code are encompassed in the General Principles. For example, Section 7.04 of the 1992 Ethics Code, "Truthfulness and Candor," is incorporated in the General Principles of the new Ethics Code as Principle C, "Integrity." References to some behaviors in the General Principles would clearly raise ethical concerns. For example, Principle B, "Fidelity and Responsibility," refers to trust and avoiding conflicts of interest that may be exploitive or harmful, and Principle C, "Integrity," emphasizes the expectation of truthfulness and honesty. Obvious prohibitions given as examples are acts of stealing, cheating, fraud, and intentional misrepresentation of fact. However, the General Principles are more general than the Ethical Standards and are not intended as obligations that would lead, in and of themselves, to the imposition of sanctions.

The aspirational intent expressed in Principle D, "that fairness and justice entitle all persons to access to and benefit from the contributions of psychology and to equal quality in the processes, procedures, and services being conducted by psychologists," is comparable to an expression of civil rights. Lawyers and judges will recognize the similarity to the concepts of due process and equal protection reflected in the Constitution. Similarly, in their role of evaluators in the legal system, forensic psychologists have a special responsibility for accuracy and fairness reflecting their respect for the dignity and rights of individuals whom they examine.

THE APPLICATION OF ETHICAL PRINCIPLES

The practitioners of forensic psychology are based in one discipline while accommodating to the requirements of another. These two professions, law and psychology, reflect values placed on the needs of both the individual and society. Whereas the legal system has the responsibility to balance individual rights with the safety of society, psychology, as a science and practice, focuses on the health and well-being of the individual. The expertise for which the forensic psychologist is valued in the legal system focuses on human behavior. The primary goal for the court is to resolve a legal issue that may or may not be harmful to one assessed by a forensic psychologist. As a treater or a caregiver, the psychologist is more closely identified with the health profession. In converging with the precepts of the law, to achieve fairness, justice, and the safety of society, the forensic psychologist diverges from the role of primarily providing psychological benefits to individuals.

The first section of the Ethics Code, "Resolving Ethical Issues," has particular relevance to forensic psychologists, recognizing the potential for conflicts between ethics and law. Section 1.02 points out the competing allegiances demanded of or pulling on the forensic psychologist in the legal system that may demand unique strategies and judgments not required in other areas of psychology practice. For example, the legal system may require consultation and negotiation with professionals from another field, such as judges and attorneys. In such a situation, the forensic psychologist must understand the ramifications of a particular case from the legal perspective and must also be aware of the risk of exposure of otherwise confidential material. Consultation with colleagues and documentation of clinical opinions and actions, advisable in any situation in which a psychologist may be unsure of a proper course, is particularly important in forensic cases. These steps will provide evidence of a thoughtful decision in the event of a future challenge to the appropriateness of the judgment made by the forensic psychologist.

Privacy and Confidentiality

Privacy implies the right of individuals to be left alone and not have their personal lives intruded on beyond their wishes. Confidentiality implies the restriction of the use of communications shared in a relationship, a key element in psychotherapy. The limits of confidentiality for the forensic psychologist are determined by the context of the task within the legal system.

Patients and clients have been protected from unauthorized disclosures in every iteration of the Code of Ethics in psychology from 1953 to the present. Confidences must not be revealed by the psychologist without the permission of the patient unless required to do so by law, or to protect the individual, or for the safety of the community.

An entire section of the 2002 Ethics Code (Section 4) is devoted to issues of privacy and confidentiality, acknowledging the uniqueness and importance of protecting the fiduciary relationship of therapist and patient. In addition, this section recognizes that "the extent and limits of confidentiality may be regulated by law."

Section 4.01 alludes to limitations on confidentiality that may be regulated by law, and it is incumbent upon all psychologists to explain those exceptions to patients and others evaluated by forensic psychologists (Section 4.02). The forensic psychologist should discuss the foreseeable uses of information produced in a court-related examination based on the client's ability to comprehend. Whether cases are referred by attorneys or are court-ordered evaluations, when the client is incapable of understanding the nature of the forensic evaluation, consultation on this issue with the legal representative is always advisable.

The limits of confidentiality of information gained during a forensic evaluation may present a conflict between lawyer-client confidentiality and that of the forensic psychologist. For example, bar associations are now debating whether lawyers are ethically bound to divulge future crimes that a client intends to commit. Usually, the information gained by the psychologist retained by a lawyer comes under lawyer-client privilege. Contrasted with a therapeutic relationship, such information might entail harm to a third party and therefore is an exception to confidentiality, obligating the psychologist to take steps to protect such a person at risk. A more clear-cut situation would be the admission of a crime during a trial competency evaluation. Such a confession would not be admissible in the evaluation report.

The legal literature and case law provide precedent protecting confidentiality and privacy of individuals. A right to privacy is not articulated directly in the U.S. Constitution, but an early recognition of its importance in American jurisprudence was highlighted in the *Harvard Law Review* in 1890 (Warren & Brandeis, 1890); it is usually referred to as the "Brandeis Brief" and succeeded in turning American law in a new direction. The *Law Review* article argued that there is an inherent right to privacy for every individual, a "quiet zone" in each person's life that the law should protect. The authors observe that the common law affords appropriate protection to "thoughts, emotions and sensations."

Twenty-four years later, Judge Benjamin Cardozo's landmark decision that a surgeon must have permission from a patient to operate recognized the right to have control of one's own body (*Schloendorff v. The Society of New York Hospital,* 1914) and was followed by more recent cases that define privacy as a right found in the Constitution (*Griswold v. Connecticut,* 1965; *Roe v. Wade,* 1973; *Bowers v. Hardwick,* 1986). In the *Griswold* case, the U.S. Supreme Court interpreted the Bill of Rights as containing specific guarantees, called "penumbras," that "create zones of privacy" (p. 484). These include the right of association (1st Amendment), the prevention of the quartering of soldiers in time of peace without the owner's consent (3rd Amendment), security against unwarranted search and seizures (4th Amendment), and the right against self-incrimination (5th Amendment). *Roe v. Wade* cites the interpretation in the *Griswold* case in finding constitutional safeguards to privacy as penumbras in the various amendments of the Bill of Rights (p. 129). A right to privacy reflected in the Brandeis Brief and Justice Cardozo's decision provide the underpinnings for confidentiality and informed consent in the practice of psychology.

Privileged communication refers to the legal rather than the ethical view of confidentiality. The privilege is a right that exists by statute that protects patients from having their confidences revealed as testimony during a legal proceeding in court or in a legislative or administrative hearing. By contrast, evaluations by forensic psychologists produced as evidence for courtroom testimony are not intended to be confidential and are not privileged communications under the law. If the defendant, for example, introduces a defense of insanity in a criminal case or claims damages for an emotional injury in a civil matter, a constructive waiver of the privilege will ensue, allowing for the revelation of past psychotherapy. The introduction of a mental state by the plaintiff or the defendant in effect triggers consent to a probative examination of all evidence relevant to a mental condition. In general, the law favors admissibility of all relevant evidence to provide those who evaluate fact, such as a judge or jury, the best chance to arrive at a proper decision in a case.

Confidentiality in the relationship between an attorney and a client has its precedent in early English common law. Not until 1996 did the U.S. Supreme Court address confidential communications between psychotherapist and patient, holding that such information was privileged from compelled disclosure in court (*Jaffee v. Redmond,* 1996). Every state had passed legislation respecting confidentiality in the psychotherapeutic relationship prior to the *Jaffee* decision. The forensic psychologist examining a party involved in a legal proceeding has more limited opportunity to protect confidentiality in the relationship with the examinee. It is important that the forensic examiner clarify this limitation with the examinee. Because the contract for services is with the attorney, the psychologist will not have complete control of the product of the evaluation.

As the primary goal is to attain the truth, courts do not wish to exclude information that is relevant, is credible, and will aid in arriving at a just decision. The privilege to withhold testimony that is confidential is an exception to the introduction of reliable evidence. However, this privilege may be nullified under certain circumstances defined by statute when the value of the evidence outweighs the privilege. For example, the mental status of a custodial parent would be subject to disclosure to assure the safety and best interest of a child.

Wigmore (1961), who is recognized in the legal profession as the preeminent authority on the rules of evidence, formulated criteria for privileged communication. His definition emphasizes why the privilege is reserved for confidential communications. Wigmore offered four points to define privilege:

1. The communications must originate in a confidence that they will not be disclosed.

2. This element of confidentiality must be essential to the full and satisfactory relationship between the parties.

3. The relationship must be one which in the opinion of the community ought to be (persistently) fostered.

4. The injury that would inure to the relation by the disclosure of the communications must be greater than the benefit thereby gained by the correct disposal of the litigation (p. 527).

In short, the right to restrict privileged communications from exposure as evidence in court belongs to the patient/client. But in cases in which the privilege is waived, either by consent of the party involved or by statutory exception to the privilege, the treating therapist or forensic examiner may not legally withhold the information that would otherwise be deemed confidential. The psychologist who defies the court under these circumstances runs the risk of contempt of court, subject to penalties including incarceration (*In re Lifschutz,* 1970). In the *Lifschutz* case, the court determined that privilege did not apply, having been constructively waived, as the plaintiff had claimed mental and emotional injury resulting from an assault. To deal with her injury, she was treated by the therapist. The *Lifschutz* decision held that the therapist was obligated to reveal evidence related to the plaintiff's claim for damages. The psychologist may not resist an order of the court to disclose, even in those situations in which the clinical judgment is that such information could be harmful to the party involved. However, steps may be taken to safeguard the privacy of the patient. When the inquiry takes place before trial, during the discovery phase of the legal proceedings, the patient or therapist may apply to the court for a protective order to limit the scope of the inquiry or to regulate the procedure of the inquiry to best preserve the rights of the patient. If the issue arises during a trial, the situation may be ameliorated or resolved by a request to meet with the judge in chambers. The forensic psychologist would then have the opportunity to describe the material under consideration with the aim of waiving the privilege only for evidence relevant to the case, allowing other confidential material to remain private. The Ethics Code, Section 4.04, "Minimizing Intrusions on Privacy," is particularly germane to the practice of forensic psychology and emphasizes that the information included in forensic evaluations by the psychologist, whether presented orally, in writing, or in consultation, will be limited to what is legally required.

The Role of the Psychologist in the Legal System

Forensic reports are tailored to the specific requirements of the legal system. The forensic expert must be apprised of the specific purpose of the examination in order to limit findings accordingly. Unlike a mental status evaluation to establish a diagnosis or for a determination of need for treatment, forensic examinations focus on a specific legal question, such as intentionality in the commission of a crime, capacity to stand trial, or the prediction of dangerousness. Fisher (2003, p. 24) offers an example of a forensic psychologist who heard a man who was being examined for a competency-for-trial determination brag about the crime. The revelation of this comment in a report or testimony would be clearly inappropriate, extending beyond the boundaries of the requirements to determine competency for trial. Section VI.G of the "Specialty Guidelines for Forensic Psychologists" (Committee on Ethical Guidelines for Forensic Psychologists 1991) reflects this position. The forensic psychologist must limit reporting of statements by the defendant in a criminal trial to those that relate to the mental condition that has been introduced in the case.

Tarasoff v. Board of Regents (1976), first addressed in California, has created an important exception to confidentiality. While in therapy in a university mental health clinic, a patient told his therapist that he planned to kill a young woman who had ended their relationship. The therapist believed that this revelation of an identified person represented a genuine threat that there was a likelihood that serious harm would be inflicted by his patient. The patient did carry out his threat, resulting in the death of this young woman. The court addressed the issue of the balance of duties of the therapist between the confidentiality of the therapeutic relationship and the safety of third parties.

Under common law, as a general rule, no duty exists to control the conduct of another. The law distinguishes between *misfeasance* and *nonfeasance.* The former is acting below an acceptable standard and the latter is not acting, even when one is in a position to spare another from harm. The law is reluctant to impose liability in the latter. Failure to help another in dire need may be immoral or even reprehensible, but the law recognizes the difficulties of setting standards for unselfish acts toward others. In recent years, courts have made inroads on this principle by expanding the lists of exceptions and in *Tarasoff* found a special exception to the rule. If, in the clinical opinion of the psychologist, the patient poses a likelihood of harm to a third party, the psychologist has a duty to take reasonable steps to protect that third party from harm. Although *Tarasoff* became legal precedent in California, psychotherapists must refer to the law in their own jurisdiction, many of which have *Tarasoff*-like laws. Some states have codified by legislation the guidelines that psychotherapists must follow. Mental health practitioners are bound by both case law and statutes in their jurisdiction.

Cohen and Swerdlik (1999) point out that the forensic psychological assessment is not intended to serve a patient "but a third party, such as a court or an attorney, and that fact (as well as its implications with respect to such issues as confidentiality) must be made clear to the assessee" (p. 500). In this connection, Section V.C of the Guidelines states "In situations where the right of the client or party to confidentiality is limited, the forensic psychologist makes every effort to maintain confidentiality with regard to any information that does not bear directly upon the legal purpose of the case" (p. 660).

In contrast to the obligation to third parties in a *Tarasoff*-like situation, the relationship of the forensic psychologist to a referring attorney will raise a different duty. The confidential relationship between lawyer and client will determine information that may be revealed during the forensic examination. If the focus of the forensic examination is to predict future dangerousness, then indications of intent to cause future harm would be included in the clinical opinion. However, the focus of an evaluation, such as one addressing an individual's competency to stand trial, would not include a revelation of a *Tarasoff* situation. As part of the lawyer's work product, the course of action should be dealt with in consultation with the defendant's attorney.

It is always prudent for the forensic psychologist to document the clinical reasoning behind the decision to follow a specific course of action. Whenever a situation arises that poses an ethical question to the psychologist, consultation with colleagues regarding their view of the issue is highly recommended. Absence of collegial recourse could be construed as an ethical violation in circumstances where it would be prudent to confirm one's clinical judgment. For example, in *White v. United States* (1986), the Court gave weight to the competence of a psychologist who obtained the opinions of others prior to deciding to release a patient who subsequently committed a violent act.

The forensic psychologist must consider the purpose of the evaluation, how it relates to the legal issue, and the potential exposure of the material in the report. The forensic psychologist must explain to the person evaluated the limits to confidentiality given the possible access to the product of the evaluation to others in addition to the client's attorney (e.g., *Commonwealth v. Lamb,* 1977). Documentation of the communication with the examinee may be critical to the acceptance of a forensic report in a court of law.

Another area of expansion of the requirement to protect others is found under statutory rules of mandated reporting. Rather than based on the relationship between therapist and patient, as in *Tarasoff,* mandated reporters include psychologists as licensed professionals who are obligated to protect certain classes in society. Psychologists must refer to the codified laws in the various states to determine the classes of persons, such as children and the elderly, who are considered vulnerable to harm and are deemed in need of special protection as a matter of public policy.

In the current Ethics Code, previous prohibitions to the release of raw test data have been relaxed. Under the 1992 Ethics Code, psychologists were obligated to restrict the release of raw test data to individuals who were qualified to use this material. Previously, only psychologists trained in assessment would have had such access. The current Ethics Code Standard 9.04(a) states that such data may be released with the authorization of the client/patient. In the legal arena, raw test data will now be more easily available to attorneys on both sides of a case. For example, when a lawyer refers a case to a forensic psychologist for an evaluation to aid the court in determining competency for trial, the specific responses of test items can be released as well as the composite evaluation and clinical interpretations of the data by the forensic psychologist who conducted the examination. One of the responsibilities of the forensic psychologist is to communicate fully to the examinee the limitations on confidentiality of the product of the exam.

Dual Relations

The Ethics Code covers a wide range of human relationships that may compromise the goals of psychotherapy by impairing a psychologist's effectiveness or objectivity (Section 3.06). For the forensic psychologist, the most common dilemma arises when a psychologist serves both as a therapist and as an evaluator for a legal procedure. An example of a dual relationship that raises a potential conflict is the case of a patient who entered psychotherapy with the intention of generating psychological testimony to be used as evidence in support of a claim in a personal injury case. Weissman and DeBow (2003) state that the "mistaken assumption is that it is permissible to serve both as a therapist and an expert in a given case" (p. 39). Referring to Greenberg and Shuman (1997), they observe that "serving both roles threatens the efficacy of psychotherapy and also threatens the accuracy of judicial determinations" (p. 39). Although dual relationships are always problematical, they are occasionally unavoidable, particularly in small communities with limited professional resources and in institutional settings. The forensic psychologist may find testimony compromised by evidence colored by the therapeutic relationship that preceded the forensic evaluation. Therapy begun after a forensic evaluation could be less problematic if the patient has not become alienated from the therapist as a result of the evaluation. Section 3.05(a) of the Ethics Code, "Multiple Relationships," instructs the forensic psychologist on boundary issues to address. Key factors in Section 3.05(a) include attention to relationships that "could reasonably be expected to impair the psychologist's objectivity, competence or effectiveness." Relationships are not unethical that "would not reasonably be expected to cause impairment or risk exploitation or harm." Section IV.D.2 of the Guidelines recognizes that there are circumstances, such as in "small forensic settings," when potential conflicts of interest may occur and both evaluation and treatment services are necessary. Under these conditions, "the forensic psychologist takes reasonable steps to minimize the potential negative effects . . . on the rights of the party, confidentiality, and the process of treatment and evaluation" (p. 659).

Fisher (2003) points out that not all multiple relationships are unethical, but "psychologists should always consider whether the particular nature of a professional relationship might lead to misperceptions regarding the encounter. If so, it may be wise to keep a record of such encounters" (p. 65). Records kept to document any situation that may raise perceptions of a conflict in the professional relationship is good practice. Documentation provides evidence that the potential problem was recognized and that the psychologist used his or her best clinical judgment after thoughtful consideration. Such practice will reduce the likelihood of any future challenge to one's professional judgment in court, in an ethics complaint, or in a malpractice lawsuit.

The forensic psychologist may become involved in a case through an attorney or though a direct referral from the court. In either case, the admissibility of testimony will be based on rules of evidence that have an impact on confidentiality and privileged communication. The forensic psychologist must understand how his or her role fits into the theory of the case and have sufficient knowledge to consult with a referring attorney in preparation for a client's evaluation. When evaluations are court ordered, for example, to safeguard the rights of defendants who may be incompetent to stand trial or lacking criminal intent, the forensic psychologist should be prepared to testify on the specific mental status issue ordered and to avoid substantive material regarding the innocence or guilt of the defendant. References to confessional information in a competency-for-trial evaluation, intended only to evaluate the individual's mental fitness to proceed, are clearly inappropriate. In addressing the mental status as to criminal responsibility, direct reference to the defendant's innocence or guilt is referred to as "the ultimate issue" and is inadmissible in most jurisdictions.

Informed Consent

Perhaps the most celebrated early case to enunciate the law of informed consent was delivered by Judge Cardozo in *Schloendorff v. The Society of New York Hospital* (1914). In the *Schloendorff* case, the patient had given permission to be anaesthetized for a diagnostic procedure but had not provided informed consent to proceed with surgery. Nevertheless, based on the diagnosis, the surgeon performed what he deemed to be appropriate surgery. Because the patient had not consented to surgery while she was under anesthesia for a diagnosis, the New York court held that the surgeon's action had fallen below an acceptable standard of care and, using the common law's legal terminology, constituted trespass against the person. Cardozo stated in his decision, "Every human being of adult years and sound mind has a right to determine what shall be done with his own body, and a surgeon who performs an operation without his patient's consent commits an assault for which he is liable in damages" (pp. 129–130).

A more recent landmark case, *Rogers v. Okin* (1979), held that involuntarily hospitalized, mentally ill patients cannot be deprived of their right to make decisions regarding medication based merely on their status. Judge Tauro held that a "basic right to be free from unwarranted government intrusion" (p. 362). The judge rejected the view of the hospital psychiatrists that "a committed mental patient is *per se* incompetent to decide whether or not to receive treatment" (p. 1360). Similarly, defendants being evaluated for competency to stand trial have the right to be warned that information they provide could be used at a later phase of the proceedings to determine dangerousness.

Under the 5th Amendment, defendants have a constitutional right not to incriminate themselves, even in court-ordered examinations. The U.S. Supreme Court held that the psychiatrist was in error in not warning the defendant during a competency-for-trial evaluation that information gained may be used in later proceedings to provide evidence of future dangerousness (*Estelle v. Smith,* 1981).

The 2002 Ethics Code is more explicit in describing information that must be included to gain informed consent than the 1992 Code, which provided detail only for therapy and research, without reference to practice within the legal system. Fisher (2003, p. 25) reports that "the 2002 Ethics Code . . . provides more specific descriptions of situations in which the requirement for informed consent may be waived," such as "when conducting the psychological activities without consent is mandated by law or governmental regulation" (Standard 3.10(a), "Informed Consent"). This expansion is particularly significant to forensic psychologists, who may be confronted with the dilemma of conducting an evaluation ordered by the court when the examinee is incapable of understanding the purpose of the evaluation. Standard 3.10(b) holds that an evaluation under a court order is not subject to informed consent, but must "provide an appropriate explanation." For example, in an evaluation of competency to stand trial, the testing for impairment that may limit the defendant's ability to participate adequately in a trial may also restrict that defendant's ability to provide informed consent. The nature of the explanation will vary depending on, among other factors, the person's developmental level, cognitive capacities, mental status, and language preferences and proficiencies. Consistent with Standard 3.10(c), the explanation will include that the client should be informed of the nature of the anticipated services, of the limits of confidentiality, and that the results of the evaluation will not be provided to the client by the psychologist. When the case has been referred to the forensic psychologist for evaluation, the report is provided only to the lawyer who has made the referral. The lawyer is in the primary relationship with the client, and the usefulness of the forensic report will be determined by the lawyer. (By contrast, the primary alliance in therapy is between the therapist and the patient.) How to proceed when questions of informed consent arise in forensic evaluations should be discussed with the defendant's attorney. Fisher further suggests that to comply with the HIPAA Notice of Privacy Act, "when working with persons who are legally incapable of giving consent, psychologists should provide the Notice of Privacy Practices to both the individual's legal guardian or personal representative and the client/patient" (p. 79).

The Guidelines (IV.E) state that forensic psychologists must inform prospective clients of the purpose of an evaluation, the nature of the procedures, the intended use of any product of their services, and the party who has employed the psychologist:

> (1) Unless court ordered, forensic psychologists obtain the informed consent of the client and (2) . . . where the client or party may not have the capacity to provide informed consent to services or the evaluation is pursuant to a court order, the forensic psychologist provides reasonable notice to the client's legal representative of the nature of the anticipated forensic services before proceeding. (p. 659)

The attorney who represents the client and has retained the forensic psychologist has the authority to instruct the psychologist to override the obligation to obtain informed consent. If the evaluation is court ordered and the client's legal representative objects, the forensic psychologist has recourse to the court for instructions as to whether the evaluation should proceed. In such circumstances, the forensic psychologist must maintain relationships with the various parties involved in the legal system, rather than attending only to the party to be examined. Limitations of testimony may be arranged through a pretrial conference in chambers with the judge and legal representatives of the parties to exclude material from therapy that is not specifically relevant to issues in the case.

Fees

Section 6.05 of the Ethics Code does not prohibit accepting goods or services in lieu of money for professional services if not clinically contraindicated or exploitive. Forensic psychologists should be especially sensitive to the likely consequences of such arrangements to the extent that boundaries may be perceived as crossed. The objectivity of the evaluation may be compromised, opening the psychologist to inferences of a dual relationship that may impact the credibility of testimony through cross-examination. In an initial consultation with the attorney for the party seeking services, the fee structure should be made clear, as delineated in the Guidelines ("Relationships," IV.A). In most cases, payment should be made to the forensic psychologist prior to submission of a final report to the court. Thus, not only is payment assured but, more important, an accusation of bias favoring one side is reduced. If, on cross-examination, the expert is asked if his or her testimony may be skewed by an anticipated fee, the response that payment has already been received will quell that concern. For similar reasons, the forensic psychologist should refuse to accept a contingency fee. To have a stake in the outcome of the case compromises the credibility of the forensic psychologist in providing testimony as an unbiased expert. Although the Ethics Code does not address the issue of contingency fees directly, this arrangement is specifically prohibited under the Guidelines (IV.B).

PRESENTATION OF EVIDENCE

The Guidelines (Section VI.F) address the issue of hearsay evidence and its exceptions, pointing out that a special ethical burden is placed on the professional to be sensitive to the admissibility of data. Traditionally, testimony that is not known personally by the witness is considered hearsay and is inadmissible as evidence. Even though such evidence will usually result in an objection by opposing counsel in court, the psychologist should make clear when data are derived from a source other than his or her own personal observation. When data from another source are incorporated into the evaluation, such as hospital records or information about a defendant from third parties, it is incumbent upon the forensic psychologist to indicate the source of these materials. In such cases, highly technical rules of evidence apply, and the judge will rule on the admissibility of such evidence. It would not be an ethical transgression to use such data, which are deemed credible to support an opinion. However, as the Guidelines suggest, hearsay data should, where possible, be corroborated, and when corroboration is not possible, reasons should be given for relying on the available data, with reservations when necessary (Section VI.F). Examples of information relevant to an evaluation include family and school background and hospital records.

Levels of proof are different in civil and criminal cases. Under the adage that it is better that nine guilty persons go free than that one innocent person be convicted, the standard of proof in criminal cases must be "beyond a reasonable doubt." In civil cases, the proof must be by a preponderance of the evidence, or 51%. However, in cases involving commitment of those with mental illness or mental defect, the Supreme Court has held (*Addington v. Texas,* 1979) that the standard is based on clear, unequivocal, and convincing evidence, thus requiring proof beyond the level required in civil cases but not reaching the strict criterion for a criminal conviction. In this case, the Court held that the preponderance standard was not sufficient proof to deprive a mentally ill person of liberty, but that "beyond a reasonable doubt" would demand an unachievable level of proof given less certainty of psychological diagnosis.

The forensic psychologist is not responsible for determining that testimony will reach a level of proof to prevail in the adversary process. The burden of proof is usually on the prosecutor in a criminal case or on the plaintiff in a civil action in order to prevail. But to prevail in a defense of not guilty by reason of insanity in the federal court, the burden falls on the defendant to prove by "clear and convincing" evidence that mental illness has prevented the accused from possessing sufficient intent to commit the crime, consistent with the legal criteria of insanity (18 U.S. Code, 1985).

THE FORENSIC PSYCHOLOGIST IN THE COURTROOM

One of the most difficult tasks for a forensic psychologist who has been retained by an attorney to conduct an evaluation is to maintain objectivity within an adversarial legal system. Whether in civil proceedings or in criminal cases, the attorney has retained the forensic psychologist to aid in providing effective advocacy for his or her client. The adversarial system obligates the attorney to prepare the case to achieve a favorable result for the client. As stated in Section VI.C of the Guidelines, the forensic psychologist maintains professional integrity by examining the issue at hand from all reasonable perspectives, actively seeking information that will differentially test plausible rival hypotheses. Familiarity with the scientific literature related to the issue may be critical, and the forensic psychologist can expect to be subjected to cross-examination by opposing counsel, who may be familiar with published research that is counter to the testimony of the expert. The forensic psychologist is expected to present credible data coupled with an opinion that appropriately interprets the data and is relevant to the issue before the court. To perform otherwise would be unethical and may result in gaining a reputation as a hired gun rather than as a credible objective witness. Although expert testimony in court is immune from charges of negligence, the psychologist may be sanctioned for unethical behavior as characterized as dishonest or incompetent.

The forensic psychologist should communicate clearly that the intention is to provide a balanced assessment based on all the data available. If relevant data are not available, for example, if all parties in a child custody matter could not be interviewed, that limitation should be noted. The Guidelines (Section VI.C) state:

> Forensic psychologists take special care to avoid undue influence upon their methods, procedures, and products, such as may emanate from the party to a legal proceeding by financial compensation or other gains. . . . The forensic psychologist maintains professional integrity by examining the issue at hand from all reasonable perspectives, actively seeking information that will differentially test plausible rival hypotheses. (p. 661)

This section focuses more specifically on the role of the forensic psychologist in legal proceedings and is stated more generally in the Ethics Code as Principle C: "Psychologists seek to promote accuracy, honesty, and truthfulness in the science, teaching, and practice of psychology."

Except for intentionally providing false testimony on the witness stand, expert opinion is also not subject to perjury or other penalties at law. Saks (1990) found that case law has held that testimony of expert witnesses is privileged and not subject to civil liability, regardless of its lack of validity or truthfulness: "A witness may say whatever he or she likes under oath and no private remedies are available to persons who may be harmed as a result" (pp. 300–301). However, ethics complaints may be brought, and a positive reputation may be severely tarnished. (See Chapter 16, for issues and cases dealing with the liability of experts' performance and testimony.) As stated in the Guidelines (VII.D), "Forensic psychologists do not . . . participate in misrepresentation of their evidence, nor do they participate in partisan attempts to avoid, deny, or subvert the presentation of evidence contrary to their own position" (p. 664).

In 1993, the Supreme Court redefined the basis for the admissibility of expert opinion in *Daubert v. Merrell Dow Pharmaceuticals,* changing the previous standard enunciated by the same Court in 1923 (*Frye v. United States,* 1923). The earlier decision admitted expert testimony when it was sufficiently established to have gained general acceptance in the field. In *Daubert* it was held that the court must determine that evidence presented by the expert is grounded in scientific method and procedure. Judges were instructed by this decision to make a preliminary assessment regarding the reliability of the scientific evidence and its relevance to the particular case. Concern that evidence based on clinical data may not meet the *Daubert* standard was allayed by a further refinement regarding admissibility in *Kumho Tire Company v. Carmichael* (1999). *Kumho* gave the trial judge broad latitude in testing an expert's reliability when the evidence is not necessarily based on scientific method, but when the expert possesses technical or other specialized knowledge. This case holds that the judge is the "gatekeeper" to determine whether technical or other specialized knowledge, such as clinical evidence, is admissible. Individuals who are not scientists may present acceptable evidence based on their training and experience, thus expanding the interpretation in the *Daubert* case, which focuses on the presence of scientific methodology. This decision provides for the admission of clinical data that have reliability and validity even if they are not based on scientific methodology. The *Kumho* case followed Rule 702 of the Federal Rules of Evidence (U.S. Code, 1985) that "a witness qualified as an expert by knowledge, skill, experience, training or education may testify thereto in the form of an opinion."

Daubert and *Kumho* highlight the importance of competence in the presentation of testimony. The forensic psychologist should be aware and knowledgeable in presenting methodology of research relevant to a case or possess appropriate training and experience to support the courtroom presentation. Standard 2 ("Competence") of the Ethics Code mandates that to effectively implement services or research, psychologists must have appropriate scientific and professional knowledge in relevant areas (Section 2.01(b)). Expanding on this issue, the Guidelines (III.B, "Competence") caution forensic psychologists providing testimony to remain within the boundaries of their competence regarding "knowledge, skill, experience, training and education."

As Brodsky and Galloway (2003) have observed, "In all court work by health professionals, the pull to affiliate with retaining attorneys can be both powerful and subtle" (p. 9). These writers point out that a tilt toward the side that has retained the forensic psychologist may be revealed in the interpretation of results. One's opinion may be skewed by many factors, but the legal structure contains features to balance this tilt and ideally reach a just and fair outcome. Such safeguards as the right to an attorney, opportunity to cross-examine, rules on the admission of evidence, and an impartial judge and jury are all intended to create the setting for a fair trial. The competent forensic psychologist has the obligation to present credible data and opinion and, when interrogated on cross-examination, to recognize and acknowledge other valid opinions that differ from the one being proffered.

Ultimate Issue Testimony

The Guidelines (VII.F) state that forensic psychologists "are aware that their own professional observations, inferences and conclusions must be distinguished from legal facts, opinions, and conclusions" (p. 665). In 1984, Congress amended the Federal Insanity Reform Act, Rule 704(b), by restricting testimony of expert witnesses, prohibiting them from introducing an opinion as to insanity in a criminal case when mental status is an element of the crime. The result of this rule is that the triers of fact, whether a judge or jury, must determine whether the facts presented by the expert meet the legal definition of insanity. (This amendment was a reaction to the experience in *The United States v. Hinckley,* 1982, trial following the attempted assassination of President Ronald Reagan.) However, under Rule 704(a), in cases in which mental status is not an element of the crime, the expert may testify to the ultimate issue. The forensic psychologist may answer the question "Was the accused suffering from a mental disease or defect?" and may explain the characteristics of the mental illness. In cases where mental illness is an element of the crime, the expert may not introduce an ultimate opinion, such as "Was the accused able to appreciate the nature and quality of his act?"

An ultimate issue opinion, for example, is the expert's testifying that the defendant could or could not appreciate the wrongfulness of his or her act. In contrast, a penultimate opinion is allowable, such as describing a defendant's belief in a delusional state that he was attacking an enemy of his country or was commanded to act by aliens from another planet.

Some commentators have taken the view that prohibiting the presentation of the ultimate opinion will not make a difference in avoiding the "battle of the experts" because varied opinions may still be presented as penultimate opinions, such as positions regarding delusional behavior or psychosis and its impact on the issue of insanity (Rogers & Ewing, 1989). An opposing view holds that preventing experts from relating the defendant's mental state directly to an opinion regarding insanity deprives the triers of fact of valuable information:

> The enactment of Rule 704(b) only confuses the law of evidence. Rule 704(b) by singling out opinion on mental state for special treatment contradicts the Rule's generally liberal approach toward expert testimony. . . . Congress underestimates jurors' power to assimilate complex psychiatric testimony. (Braswell, 1987, p. 630)

However, Slobogin (1989) observes that "most commentators, a good portion of them academics, insist on prohibition against any language in clinical testimony or reports that embraces the ultimate legal issue" (p. 259). Legalists believe that it is a leap of logic for the forensic expert to provide the relationship between concepts of mental illness and legal constructs. Other authorities on the law of evidence state that "whether Rule 704(b) will have the intended effect of substantially moderating battles of experts over mental conditions remains to be seen" (Broun et al., 1999, p. 57). Judges do provide the instruction to the jury regarding legal parameters to aid in their deliberations. Although Rule 704 is the law in the federal courts, forensic psychologists should be aware of rules and procedures governing such testimony in state courts in which they practice. The Guidelines (VII.F) are not prohibitory of presenting the ultimate opinion, suggesting only "awareness" of the distinction between clinical and legal concepts.

In the preparation of a case, the forensic psychologist must be aware that all notes, test data, and test protocols may be subject to discovery. As described by Fisher (2003), "In deposition and court testimony, psychologists are often asked when certain facts became known, and . . . in what context. Sufficiently detailed records are essential" (p. 118), as generally covered under Section 6 of the Ethics Code (see also Committee on Legal Issues, 1996).

Greenberg and Shuman (1997) describe the potential pitfalls for the psychologist providing services as a therapist and also serving as an expert witness in the same case. The court may subpoena the psychologist as a witness, and the problems arising out of this distinctively different and potentially conflicting task should be made clear to the attorneys and the judge. The therapist risks breaching implicit trust with a patient and compromising the relationship by sharing with others information that traditionally would have remained confidential between therapist and patient. The Guidelines (Section IV.D), indicate that efforts should be taken to minimize the effects of dual relationships and offer this caveat: "When it is necessary to provide both evaluation and treatment services to a party in a legal proceeding (as may be the case in a small forensic hospital setting or a small community), the forensic psychologist takes reasonable steps to minimize the potential negative effects of these circumstances on the rights of the party, confidentiality, and the process of treatment and evaluation" (p. 659).

CONFLICT BETWEEN LAW AND ETHICS

Standard 1 of the Ethics Code ("Resolving Ethical Issues") addresses potential conflicts between the rule of law and ethical standards (Section 1.02). Under this section, psychologists are instructed to "make known" a commitment to the Ethics Code in case of a conflict between law and ethics. The Code acknowledges that the demands of the law may not be consistent with the intent of the Code. Procedurally, no specific strategy or guidelines are provided for presenting such information, or to whom such information should be directed. The forensic psychologist under these circumstances should be proactive, initiating contact with the court to minimize infringement into material that should remain privileged communication and revealing only evidence that is relevant to the trial.

The forensic psychologist is expected to recognize the existence of a conflict and use good judgment in efforts to resolve differences between the rule of law and professional ethics.

The forensic psychologist must limit the boundaries of the evaluation to the theory and strategy of the case. For example, a competency-to-stand-trial evaluation would limit the evaluation to the legal criteria for competency and would address only the mental state or pathology relevant to adequately assuming the role of a defendant.

CONCLUSION

The forensic psychologist must balance ethical values as promulgated through the "Ethical Principles of Psychologists and Code of Conduct" of the APA and the requirements of the judicial system. Practicing within two systems requires a moral compass to navigate among often conflicting issues. The forensic psychologist is provided more detail in the most recent Code that relates specifically to legal issues, in addition to regulating the practice of all psychologists. Additional guidance is found in the "Specialty Guidelines for Forensic Psychologists," which provide aspirational goals rather than firm rules, while offering thoughtful and instructive approaches to negotiating the complexities encountered in the legal system.

REFERENCES

Addington v. Texas, 441 U.S. 418 (1979).

American Psychological Association. (1953). *Ethical standards of psychologists.* Washington, DC: Author.

American Psychological Association. (1992). Ethical principles of psychologists and code of conduct. *American Psychologist, 47,* 1597–1611.

American Psychological Association. (2002). Ethical principles of psychologists and code of conduct. *American Psychologist, 57,* 1060–1073.

Black's Law Dictionary (7th ed.). (1999). (B. A. Garner, Ed.). St. Paul, MN: West Group.

Bowers v. Hardwick, 478 U.S. 186 (1986).

Braswell, A. L. (1987). Resurrection of the ultimate issue rule. *Cornell Law Review, 72,* 620–640.

Brodsky, S. L., & Galloway, V. A. (2003). Ethical and professional demands for forensic mental health professionals in the post-Atkins era. *Ethics and Behavior, 13,* 3–9.

Broun, K. S., Dix, G. E., Imwinkleried, E. J., Kaye, D. H., Mosteller, R. P., & Roberts, D. F. (1999). The requirements of firsthand knowledge: The option rule—Exert testimony. In J. S. Strong (Ed.), *McCormick on evidence* (5th ed., Vol. 1, Title 2, Sect. 3, p. 57). St. Paul, MN: West Group.

Cohen, R. J., & Swerdlik, M. E. (1999). *Psychological testing and assessment.* Mountain View, CA: Mayfield.

Committee on Ethical Guidelines for Forensic Psychologists. (1991). Specialty guidelines for forensic psychologists. *Law and Human Behavior, 15,* 655–665.

Committee on Legal Issues. (1996). Strategies for private practitioners coping with subpoenas or compelled testimony for clients' records or test data.

Commonwealth v. Lamb, 311 NE2d4D; 365 Mass. 265 (1974).

Professional Psychology: Research and Practice, 27, 245–251.

Daubert v. Merrell Dow Pharmaceuticals, 113 S. Ct. 2786 (1993).

Estelle v. Smith, 451 U.S. 454 (1981).

Federal Insanity Defense Reform Act, amended 1985, 18 U.S.C. § 20 (1985).

Fisher, C. B. (2003). *Decoding the ethics code: A practical guide for psychologists.* Thousand Oaks, CA: Sage.

Frye v. United States, 293 F. 1013 (1923).

Greenberg, S. A., & Shuman, D. W. (1997). Irreconcilable conflict between therapeutic and forensic roles. *Professional Psychology: Research and Practice, 28,* 50–57.

Griswold v. Connecticut, 381 U.S. 479 (1965).

In re Lifschutz, 467 P.2d 334 (1970).

Jaffee v. Redmond, 116 S. Ct. 1923 (1996).

Jenkins v. United States, 307 F.2d 637 (1962).

Kaslow, F. W. (2002). Early history of the American Board of Forensic Psychology: A retrospective account. *Specialist, ABPP, 21*(11), 22–24.

Kumho Tire Company et al. v. Carmichael et al., 526 U.S. 137 (1999).

Lipsitt, P. D. (1984). Foreword. In D. L. Shapiro (Ed.), *Psychological evaluation and expert testimony* (pp. vii–x). New York: Wiley.

Otto, R. K., & Heilbrun, K. (2002). The practice of forensic psychology: A look toward the future in light of the past. *American Psychologist, 57,* 5–18.

Resurrection of the ultimate issue rule: Federal rule of evidence 704(b) and the insanity defense [Note]. (1987). *Cornell Law Review,* 620–640.

Roe v. Wade, 410 U.S. 113 (1973).

Rogers v. Okin, 478 F. Supp. 1342 (1979).

Rogers, R., & Ewing, C. P. (1989). Ultimate opinion proscriptions: A cosmetic fix and a plea for empiricism. *Law and Human Behavior, 13,* 357–374.

Saks, M. J. (1990). Expert witnesses, nonexpert witnesses, and nonwitness experts. *Law and Human Behavior, 14,* 291–313.

Schloendorff v. The Society of New York Hospital, 211 NY 125 (1914).

Slobogin, C. (1989). The "ultimate issue" issue. *Behavioral Sciences and the Law, 7,* 259–266.

Tarasoff v. Board of Regents, 551 P.2d 334 (1976).

United States v. Hinckley, No. 81-306, 1982 U.S. Dist. Ct.

Warren, S. D., & Brandeis, L. D. (1890). The right to privacy. *Harvard Law Review, 4,* 193–220.

Weissman, H. N., & DeBow, D. M. (2003). Ethical principles of professional competencies. In I. B. Weiner (Series Ed.) & A. M. Goldstein (Vol. Ed.), *Comprehensive handbook of psychology: Vol. 11. Forensic psychology* (pp. 33–54). Hoboken, NJ: Wiley.

White v. United States, 780 F.2d 97 (1986).

Wigmore, J. H. (1961). *Evidence in trials at common law* (Wigmore on Evidence, McNaughton Revision, Vol. 8). Boston: Little, Brown.

CHAPTER 8

Legal and Ethical Issues in Accessing and Utilizing Third-Party Information

Randy K. Otto, Christopher Slobogin, and Stuart A. Greenberg

As used in this chapter, "third-party information" (also referred to as collateral information) is best described as any information sought or obtained during the course of a forensic examination that does not come directly from the subject of the evaluation. Although recommended assessment formats for forensic evaluations vary widely, psychological, legal, and psychiatric authorities all agree that third-party information is extremely useful in the typical forensic setting (e.g., Grisso, 2003; Melton, Petrila, Poythress, & Slobogin, 1997; Simon & Gold, 2004). As the "Specialty Guidelines for Forensic Psychologists" (Committee on Ethical Guidelines for Forensic Psychologists, 1991, p. 662) advise, "Where circumstances reasonably permit, forensic psychologists seek to obtain independent and personal verification of data relied upon as part of their professional services to the court or a party to a legal proceeding."

Although the need for collateral information in forensic evaluation is well established, little has been written about the process of obtaining it and using it in court. In fact, various legal, ethical, and practical considerations can complicate that process. In this chapter, we (a) reiterate why third-party information is useful in forensic evaluation contexts; (b) analyze how evidence law might affect the type and amount of third-party information sought; (c) review various legal, ethical, and practical factors that affect the ability of the forensic psychologist to access third-party information; and (d) describe rules and practices that should govern communication with third parties once access occurs.

NEED FOR AND VALUE OF THIRD-PARTY INFORMATION

When conducting evaluations in therapeutic (as distinguished from forensic) contexts, mental health professionals rely primarily on information provided by the examinee-client. Occasionally therapists may consult other health care providers about the patient's history, but rarely is any other information sought from outside sources.

In forensic settings, in contrast, numerous other additional sources—educational and employment records, financial and tax reports, military records, and accounts and perceptions of spouses, neighbors, coworkers, and victims—are often crucial to the evaluation. Indeed, for a number of reasons, in answering legal questions about capacities and symptoms, this type of third-party information may often be even more important than information derived directly from the examinee. First, because of the significant stakes in legal proceedings, forensic examinees may be deliberately or inadvertently less than candid in their presentation (Austin, 2002; Greenberg & Shuman, 1997; Greenberg, Shuman, & Meyer, 2004; Rogers & Bender, 2003). Thus, information from third parties may be the only means of acquiring an accurate or objective depiction of legally relevant events and symptoms and may also be a powerful tool for challenging the examinee's version of events and evaluating his or her response style. Second, even the candid examinee will usually not be aware of all legally relevant information (e.g., medical reports, perceptions of eyewitnesses) and, in any event, will typically not be able to provide a completely accurate or comprehensive account of it. Third, information from third parties is necessary for administration of a number of forensically relevant instruments (e.g., Psychopathy Checklist-Revised; Hare, 1991). Finally, information from collateral sources enhances the face validity of the examination and the competence of the expert in the eyes of the legal decision maker (Heilbrun, 2001; Heilbrun, Marczyk, & DeMatteo, 2002; Heilbrun, Warren, & Picarello, 2003; Melton et al., 1997).

Mental health professionals apparently recognize as much. Research examining forensic assessment practices indicates that psychologists regularly utilize third-party information when conducting forensic evaluations, whether the context is criminal (e.g., Borum & Grisso, 1996; Christy, Douglas, Otto, & Petrila, 2004; Heilbrun & Collins, 1995; Heilbrun, Rosenfeld, Warren, & Collins, 1994; Skeem & Golding, 1998) or civil (Ackerman & Ackerman, 1997; Budd, Poindexter, Felix, & Naik-Polan, 2001; Keilin & Bloom, 1986), although some have also suggested that forensic psychologists are not doing a good enough job including such information in their evaluations (Bow & Quinnell, 2002; Christy et al., 2004; Nicholson & Norwood, 2000). Furthermore, as noted earlier, prominent authorities strongly recommend that third-party information be sought in the typical forensic evaluation.

EVIDENCE LAW GOVERNING USE OF THIRD-PARTY INFORMATION

Third-party information is clearly an essential component of a competent and thorough forensic evaluation. Before reviewing the legal and ethical rules that govern how third-party information can be obtained, the legal limitations on the use of such information must be described. Although these limitations turn out to be minimal, the principles underlying the evidentiary rules can and should shape the type and quantity of third-party information psychologists seek.

Distinctions between Lay and Expert Witnesses

The rules of evidence governing third-party information make a crucial distinction between lay and expert witnesses. When lay witnesses want to recount information from third parties, they are often barred from doing so by the rules of evidence regarding hearsay (i.e., statements by an out-of-court declarant offered for the truth of the matter asserted). For example, testimony describing what a friend or relative said about the examinee or what a document reflects about a victim is hearsay, and such testimony is often excluded on the grounds that the friend, relative, or drafter of the document is not in court to be cross-examined, and therefore cannot have his or her credibility assessed by the jury and judge.

In contrast, when the witness is qualified as an expert, hearsay rules and similar exclusionary rules are relaxed. Rule 703 of the Federal Rules of Evidence, which applies in federal court and is replicated in most state jurisdictions, states in part:

> The facts or data in the particular case upon which an expert bases an opinion or inference may be those perceived by or made known to the expert at or before the hearing. If of a type reasonably relied upon by experts in the particular field in forming opinions or inferences upon the subject, the facts or data need not be admissible in evidence in order for the opinion or inference to be admitted.

This rule explicitly allows experts to rely on hearsay and other types of normally inadmissible third-party information *if* it is "reasonably relied upon by experts in the particular field."

As applied to psychologists and other mental health professionals in forensic evaluation contexts, this language has been construed broadly. Although some courts have held otherwise (*Everett v. Town of Bristol*, 1996; *State v. Vincik*, 1987), most courts are willing to permit testimony based on virtually any third-party information, even when it is from a source whose credibility may be questionable. For example, clinical opinions based on the hearsay statements of a government agent (*United States v. Sims*, 1973, p. 149), a codefendant (*United States v. Wright*, 1986, p. 1100), and the reports of nonclinical staff (*United States v. Bramlet*, 1987, p. 856) have all been ruled admissible under Rule 703.

Some commentators have criticized these types of decisions on the grounds that they allow mental health professionals, rather than the jury, to become the judge of whether third-party accounts are trustworthy ("Hearsay Bases of Psychiatric Opinion Testimony," 1977). Courts and commentators have offered three responses to this criticism. The first is that experts can be trusted to make adequate credibility assessments of third parties because those assessments are so important to their everyday practice. As the Advisory Committee Note to Federal Rule of Evidence 703 explains, "The physician makes life-and-death decisions in reliance upon [third-party information]. His validation, expertly performed and subject to cross-examination, ought to suffice for judicial purposes." The second response is that third-party information is not actually hearsay because it is not being admitted for the truth of the matter asserted. Instead, as one court put it, "The data [are] admitted for the limited and independent purpose of enabling the jury to scrutinize the expert's reasoning" (*United States v. Wright*, 1986, p. 1100). Third, some authorities have justified experts' use of hearsay on the grounds that requiring the proponent of the evidence to bring all relevant third parties into court would be inefficient (Federal Rules of Evidence, Advisory Committee Notes, Rule 703).

None of these responses is entirely satisfactory. First, whatever may be true about physicians who make "life-or-death" decisions, mental health professionals conducting forensic evaluations seldom operate in analogous high-stakes settings, and they usually deal with information that is significantly less objective. Additionally, regardless of how a court might formally characterize an expert's descriptions of out-of-court statements, the jury is likely to consider them for their independent content, not just as a subsidiary component of, or basis for, the expert's opinion. And although producing the source of every third-party statement may prove unnecessarily burdensome, requiring the source of *decisive* third-party statements (e.g., those that incriminate a criminal defendant or suggest a parent is unfit to care for children) is unlikely to involve many witnesses, and most of those are probably closely related to one of the parties. The bottom line is that mental health professionals, including those working in forensic arenas, are not necessarily any better at evaluating the credibility of witnesses or documents than are laypeople (cf. Bonnie & Slobogin, 1980, pp. 503–508) and thus cannot be relied on to do so accurately.

The Supreme Court's new approach to the so-called "Confrontation Clause" found in the Sixth Amendment may eventually bring all courts into line with this view, at least in criminal cases. The Confrontation Clause states that a criminal accused shall have the right "to be confronted with the witnesses against him." In *Crawford v. Washington* (2004), the Supreme Court substantially modified its previous approach to the Clause by holding that in a criminal trial this language prohibits the government from introducing out-of-court statements that are "testimonial," unless the maker of the statements is unavailable and the defendant had a prior opportunity to cross-examine the declarant. The Court did not clearly define "testimony," although it did state that this concept included a declaration "made for the purpose of establishing or proving some fact" (p. 51). A New York court has since held that third-party statements solicited by a mental health professional during a forensic evaluation and relied on at trial by the state are testimonial as that word was used in *Crawford* (*People v. Goldstein,* 2005). This holding, which appears to be a correct application of *Crawford,* could have major repercussions for forensic clinicians supporting the government's position in a criminal case. If they solicit information from a third party and intend to rely on that information at trial, the government must either: (a) ensure that the third party testifies; (b) show that the third party is unavailable and that the defendant had an opportunity to cross-examine him or her at some earlier proceeding; or (c) obtain a waiver of confrontation rights.

Regardless of the ultimate outcome on this issue in the courts, forensic mental health professionals should be attentive to the underlying concerns as a matter of ethics. In particular, when interviewing third parties or reviewing records, experts should be attentive to indicia of reliability, and when presenting reports and testimony, they should justify *why they are relying on particular sources of information* (see Committee on Ethical Guidelines for Forensic Psychologists, 1991, p. 662, Principle IV.F). This admonition should be followed even when information from collateral sources is admissible under an exception to the hearsay rule (e.g., medical and psychiatric records will generally be admissible under the routine records exception; see Federal Rule of Evidence 803(6)). It is when such an exception does not apply, however, that experts should be particularly attuned to whether their reliance on the inadmissible information is "reasonable."

Providing Otherwise Inadmissible Evidence to the Jury

Assuming Rule 703 permits the introduction of an opinion based on otherwise inadmissible third-party information, a separate issue is whether the expert may describe the inadmissible information to a jury. In 2000, Rule 703 was amended to include a final sentence:

Facts or data that are otherwise inadmissible shall not be disclosed to the jury by the proponent of the opinion or inference unless the court determines that their probative value in assisting the jury to evaluate the expert's opinion *substantially* outweighs their prejudicial effect. (emphasis added)

In practice, this provision, which most state statutes do not yet include but the gist of which some state courts have endorsed (see, e.g., *Greenfield v. Commonwealth,* 1974), may preclude revelation of important third-party information by the expert examiner.

This possibility raises an ethical issue for the examiner: Should he or she testify when the basis for the expert opinion cannot be fully explained? If the inadmissible third-party information is merely corroborative, the expert can probably testify with little concern. A more challenging circumstance occurs when the inadmissible information is of independent significance and the court prohibits its introduction under Rule 703 or *Crawford* (see Committee on Ethical Guidelines for Forensic Psychologists, 1991, pp. 661–662, Principles VII.D, E, F). For example, imagine an insanity case in which the examiner is provided with a copy of the defendant's illegally seized (and inadmissible) diary, which provides considerable insight into his mental state at and around the time of the alleged offense. In this scenario, the examiner should diligently seek out admissible corroborating information. If such information is not available, but the court still insists that the inadmissible material be withheld from the jury, some examiners may choose to resist testifying, although we do not think such a course is ethically demanded given the legality of the testimony under the evidence rules.

As this example illustrates, occasionally third-party information relevant to a forensic evaluation may be inadmissible for reasons other than hearsay concerns. Information from a therapist may be privileged, a document may not be properly authenticated, or, as in the example, a diary or confession may have been illegally obtained by law enforcement officers. As is the case when the basis of testimony is hearsay, the same two issues—Can the information reasonably be relied on? and Can an opinion ethically be offered without describing it?—arise in these situations as well.

When Third-Party Information Must Be Provided to the Jury

A separate admissibility issue associated with third-party information is whether a given expert opinion *must* rely on it in order for it to be admissible. Here, the relevant federal rule is Rule 702, which provides:

If scientific, technical, or other specialized knowledge will assist the trier of fact to understand the evidence or determine a fact in issue, a witness qualified as an expert by knowledge, skill, experience, training, or education, may testify thereto in the form of an opinion or otherwise if (1) the testimony is based upon sufficient facts or data, (2) the testimony is the product of reliable principles and methods, and (3) the witness has applied the principles and methods reliably to the facts of the case.

Most states have similar rules, although few include the language after the word "otherwise," all of which was added in 2000 to reflect U.S. Supreme Court decisions in *Daubert v. Merrell Dow Pharmaceuticals* (1993) and *Kumho Tire v.*

Carmichael (1999). These two decisions construed the earlier version of Rule 702 to require that the basis of expert testimony be "reliable" (which they held should usually be assessed by considering whether the principles and methods underlying the opinion have been subjected to some means of verification, as well as any resulting error rates, peer reviews, and the extent to which the principles and methods are accepted in the relevant field). The amended Rule 702 is meant to incorporate this reliability requirement. More important for present purposes, it provides that an expert opinion must be based on "sufficient facts or data." Although this part of the rule has yet to be applied to testimony by forensic mental health professionals (at least in any reported legal opinion), in theory it could require the exclusion of testimony that does not consider third-party information, on the ground that the testimony is not based on "sufficient" facts.

Roughly half the states have chosen not to follow *Daubert,* but rather adhere to some version of the rule established in *Frye v. United States* (1923), which requires that the basis of testimony be "generally accepted" among those in the relevant field in order to be admissible (see "Post-*Daubert* Standards for Admissibility of Scientific and Other Expert Evidence in State Courts," 2001, sec. 2). In these jurisdictions, the analogous question is whether forensic mental health professionals would find acceptable an opinion that fails to consider relevant third-party data. Again, few if any cases directly address this point but, as is the case in *Daubert* jurisdictions, mental health professionals in *Frye* jurisdictions should be prepared to explain their decisions regarding seeking, using, and ignoring collateral data (cf. Committee on Ethical Guidelines for Forensic Psychologists, 1991, p. 662, Principle VII.F). Given the research showing the ubiquitous use of third-party information by forensic examiners and the consensus among authorities about its importance, any evaluator who does not access and consider such information may encounter considerable difficulty overcoming either a *Frye* or *Daubert* challenge of that investigative failure.

FACTORS AFFECTING ACCESS TO THIRD-PARTY INFORMATION

For the foregoing clinical, legal, and ethical reasons, forensic examiners must seek out third-party information in the manner most likely to assure its reliability and in a quantity sufficient to bolster any opinion that is offered. Yet little has been written about this information-gathering process, probably because, at first glance, the task appears simple. In fact, gaining access to and utilizing collateral data is complicated by several factors: the nature of the examiner's appointment, confidentiality laws, objections by opposing counsel, and objections by the third parties themselves. These factors are discussed next, and recommendations for forensic practice are presented.

The Nature of the Examiner's Appointment

The first factor that may affect the process of obtaining third-party information is the identity of the entity that retains the expert. Section VI.E of the "Specialty Guidelines for Forensic Psychologists" (Committee on Ethical Guidelines for

Forensic Psychologists, 1991) acknowledges that the nature of the psychologist's appointment affects how third-party information is accessed: "When forensic psychologists seek data from third parties, prior records, or other sources, they do so only with the prior approval of the relevant legal party or as a consequence of an order of a court to conduct the forensic evaluation" (p. 662). For purposes of this discussion, three types of examiners are differentiated: (1) *examinee-retained* examiners, retained by the attorney who represents the subject of the examination (who in criminal proceedings is usually the defendant, and in civil proceedings is usually the plaintiff); (2) *adverse party-retained* examiners, retained by the attorney representing the opponent of the examinee (which in criminal proceedings is usually the prosecution and in civil proceedings is typically the defendant); and (3) *court-appointed* examiners, who are retained by the court or are functionally equivalent to a court-appointed expert because the parties have stipulated to the examiner's involvement (as often occurs in child custody evaluations, for instance). Each type of appointment raises special considerations in connection with obtaining third-party information.

Examinee-Retained Examiners

The language of the "Specialty Guidelines for Forensic Psychologists" just quoted indicates that, in the absence of a court order, forensic psychologists should not ordinarily contact a third party without notifying the retaining party's attorney. Examiners should be most careful to abide by this guideline when retained by the examinee's attorney. In such cases, the attorney-client privilege and related ethical rules usually protect against disclosure of both the examiner's involvement in the case and the data provided to or uncovered by the examiner, unless and until the retaining attorney decides to use the expert as a witness and discloses that fact to the opposing side (e.g., American Bar Association, 1983, Rule 1.6). The attorney-client privilege might also be (inadvertently) forfeited, however, if the examiner who is retained by the examinee's attorney contacts a third party and that third party makes the contact known to the opposing side. In some jurisdictions, for example, prosecutors may call as their own witnesses experts who were originally retained by the defense but whom the defense decides not to call (see *People v. Edney,* 1976; *State v. Pawlyk,* 1990). One way the prosecution might find out about the unused defense expert is through that expert's contact with third-party witnesses or record holders in the case.

   Given these concerns, the examinee-retained examiner should always check with the examinee's attorney before contacting a third party. In many circumstances, the attorney may have no objection to such contacts. When the attorney does object, however, the forensic examiner need not necessarily abandon the evaluation. Instead, the expert can identify potentially relevant third-party information for the attorney who, in turn, can make a decision about how best to gain the information for the examiner's review. If the information is a document of any type (e.g., medical, financial, employment, school, criminal justice, or military record), the attorney can gain access via a request, authorized release, subpoena, or court order. If the desired collateral information requires an interview of a third party, the expert can submit a list of relevant questions for the attorney to follow. The limitation of such an approach, of course, is that the expert cannot develop follow-up questions or delve into additional areas of relevance that were not initially apparent, a fact that should be made clear to the attorney.

If the attorney nonetheless ends up questioning the person of interest, he or she can proceed either informally (e.g., via an interview or list of written questions) or formally (e.g., by way of a deposition or interrogatories). The use of depositions and interrogatories is the more prudent course of action, as the expert will then have available an official, sworn record of the third party's statements and will not be forced to rely on summaries and (hearsay) representations made by the (partisan) attorney.

Adverse Party-Retained Examiners

Generally, the fact that a forensic examiner has been retained by attorneys representing the government in a criminal prosecution or the defense in a civil proceeding will be known by the opposing party (the examinee) very early in the process, so the premature revelation problem that can arise for examinee-retained examiners seldom occurs with adverse party-retained evaluators. Nonetheless, prudence dictates that the latter type of examiner also follow the recommendation of the "Specialty Guidelines for Forensic Psychologists" to notify the retaining attorney before seeking collateral sources of information. Doing so allows the examiner to discuss with the attorney the third-party information that is necessary and any legal concerns that might arise in obtaining it. For example, the attorney may have suggestions about ways of memorializing the information so that a Rule 703 or *Crawford* objection is less likely at the time of trial. The attorney may also have insights into when information is considered confidential and whether legal authorization is needed to approach the third party (issues explored more fully later in the chapter). Of course, the same conversation should also take place when the examiner is examinee retained.

Court-Appointed Examiners

Perhaps the greatest latitude with respect to accessing collateral information is afforded to forensic examiners who are retained by the court. First, in contrast to experts retained by the examinee's attorney, these professionals are known to all parties, and thus premature revelation about their involvement in the case is not a concern. Second, in contrast to professionals retained by either of the parties, court-appointed examiners arguably do not need to obtain the "approval of the relevant parties" to contact other sources, because professionals retained by the court are operating under its authority, and professionals who have been selected by stipulation (a group we are including in the court appointment category) already have their approval. Third, because court-appointed examiners are extensions of the court or agreed on by both parties, they are perceived to be less affected by the biases that can influence party-retained experts. Consequently, of the three types of experts, those who are court retained have the most independence and are least likely to be challenged when seeking third-party data.

These differences do not mean that the court-appointed expert should *never* notify the parties before seeking third-party data. In some circumstances, the expert may be able to rely on the attorneys to obtain important collateral information. And, where accessing the information requires the examinee's consent or is subject to objection (see later discussion), the court-appointed examiner should notify the attorneys so that appropriate steps can be taken. In the typical case, however, the court-appointed expert can consider proceeding without reliance on or direction from the attorneys who represent the parties. For instance, when conducting a child custody evaluation, reliance on the attorneys to arrange interviews with babysitters or to obtain access to a child's school record can be time-consuming and perhaps unavailing, particularly if each attorney counts on the other to do the work. Furthermore, there is always the possibility that adversarial bias will infect information obtained in this manner.

Confidential and Privileged Information

Third-party information that is considered confidential as a matter of law imposes special requirements on psychologists who wish to obtain it in the course of a forensic evaluation. Mental health, medical, educational, and financial records are the best examples of such information. Normally, obtaining these documents requires either a court order or consent from the subject of the records (e.g., the examinee).

The law governing health records is illustrative. Under the Health Insurance Portability and Accountability Act (42 U.S.C. §§ 1320d et. seq., 1996), which governs access to all health-related information (including mental health information), either legal authorization or consent is required to obtain personal health records. Legal authorization is of two types. Legal authorization that does not require notifying the examinee can include a court order, a court-issued subpoena, a grand jury order, or an administrative order issued by an entity that has the authority to order the production of records. In contrast, other attempts to obtain health information—most prominently, a subpoena or discovery request issued by an attorney—is sufficient legal authorization only if "reasonable efforts" have been made to inform the individual of the request or a "qualified protective order" limiting further use and disclosure is obtained (see Public Welfare, 45 C.F.R. § 164.512(a) & (d), 2000). A court will usually grant legal authorization if the subject is the examinee and the records are relevant to the legal matter at hand, but the latter showing can sometimes prove burdensome. If the confidential records sought are not the examinee's or those of another party to the case, the court will be even more reluctant to grant disclosure, primarily due to privacy concerns (Melton et al., 1997, p. 180).

Thus, consent is usually a more efficient way to proceed. Consent from the examinee will presumably be readily provided to an expert who is retained by the examinee's own attorney. If, for some reason, the examinee or the examinee's attorney resists, then the evaluator should inform them that the absence of information may limit the validity of any forensic opinions offered. If resistance continues and the expert concludes that he or she cannot properly conduct the evaluation without access to the information, withdrawal from the case may be appropriate.

When the expert is retained by the court or the attorney representing the adverse party, examinee consent authorizing access to confidential information may be harder to obtain. In such cases, assuming no preexisting court order, the examiner may have to seek legal authorization through the appropriate process. If so, it is incumbent upon the expert to make clear to the attorney and the court why such information is integral to the evaluation.

Some information is not only confidential but privileged, meaning that it is not admissible in a court of law (and, therefore, is also usually not accessible even with a court order). Privilege law varies from jurisdiction to jurisdiction and according to the specific privilege involved (e.g., the attorney-client privilege versus psychotherapist-patient privilege). Generally, information that is communicated by a client to his or her attorney is absolutely privileged. However, communications to an agent of the attorney (e.g., a mental health professional retained by the attorney) or to a therapist are protected only by a qualified privilege, which can be forfeited in a number of situations. Most relevant to this chapter, such forfeiture often occurs when the litigant raises a mental state issue in a legal proceeding (e.g., in the context of an insanity defense, a child custody dispute, or personal injury litigation alleging emotional harm) and the putatively privileged information is relevant to that issue (see Melton et al., 1997, pp. 77–78). In the latter situation, the expert can assist the attorney in piercing the privilege by, once again, explaining why the information is important.

Many collateral sources are not considered confidential. For example, parents' accounts of their son's behavior prior to his alleged commission of an offense (which might be relevant to an insanity defense), a coworker's assessment of the plaintiff's work productivity and adjustment (perhaps pertinent to an employment discrimination proceeding), and babysitters' and day care workers' reports of the parents' interactions with their children (useful in a custody proceeding) all constitute nonconfidential information. Consent or special authorization is not required to gain such information. The one exception to this rule is when the source happens to be a party represented by counsel, in which case, the legal and ethical rules *forbid* contact unless the lawyer of the party consents or there is a court order (see American Bar Association, 1983, Rule 4.2). Furthermore, as explained earlier, examiners may often find it wise to confer with the relevant attorneys before making contact with any third party.

Other Objections by Counsel

There are a number of other reasons, in addition to confidentiality concerns, that might lead the examinee or adverse party to challenge access to third-party information. For example, as noted, the examinee's attorney may not want the other side to learn that an evaluation is even occurring. Or attorneys representing either party might argue that forensic evaluators do not need particular information because therapists do not ordinarily obtain it, that access to a certain source constitutes harassment or an invasion of privacy, or that the information is hearsay and cannot be relied on under Rule 703 or *Crawford*. The general response to any of these objections is the same. The examiner should make clear the distinction between therapeutic evaluation and forensic evaluation (e.g., Greenberg & Shuman, 1997) and emphasize that the latter type of evaluation *requires* access to third-party information. To bolster this point, the expert can identify the many professional authorities that cite the need for and value of information from collateral sources in the context of forensic evaluation and also point to the research documenting mental health professionals' use of and reliance on such third-party information when conducting forensic evaluations. This course of action makes clear that utilizing third-party information is within the standard of practice rather than an idiosyncratic approach on the expert's part. The examiner may also want to identify relevant law that acknowledges experts' reliance on such information (e.g., Federal Rule of Evidence 703), with the caution that mental health professionals should avoid offering legal arguments, which are best left to the attorneys.

Objections by the Third Party

Of course, resistance may also come from the third party, who is not obligated to cooperate with the examining expert in the absence of a court order. When the examiner is retained by the examinee's attorney, the third party's cooperation may be facilitated by instructing the examinee to ask the person to comply with the request. When retained by the attorney representing the adverse party or the court, the expert may need to seek the assistance of the retaining attorney, who can provide the examiner with the necessary information via a subpoena or court order. In cases in which it is necessary to subpoena the third party, the expert should again provide the attorney with a list of documents to be provided or questions to be asked so the court can make the necessary relevance assessment.

FORENSIC PRACTICE ISSUES

Assuming the examiner has obtained the authorization necessary to acquire information from a third party, several other issues may arise: (a) notification to the third party, (b) the manner of communicating with the third party, (c) the format for conducting third-party interviews, and (d) documenting and corroborating the information thereby obtained.

Notification

When seeking information from third persons (as distinguished from third-party documents or records) the expert should inform the individual of the nature of his or her involvement with the examinee and how the information obtained will be used (see Committee on Ethical Guidelines, 1991, pp. 659–660, 662, Principles IV.E.3, IV.E; American Psychological Association [APA], 2002, Section 9.03). This notification is also required by the rules governing attorney contacts with third parties, which apply to any mental health professional who is acting as an attorney's agent. Already noted is the ethical rule requiring an investigating attorney to obtain consent from the lawyer of any represented person, a procedure that presumably provides the lawyer's client with notice of the expert's role. The legal ethical rules also require investigating attorneys to provide a form of notice to *un*represented third parties they contact during the course of litigation. Under these rules, attorneys may not offer legal advice to a person who is not represented, nor mislead him or her about their role or interest in the case. Further, they are not supposed to state or imply that they are disinterested and, if the unrepresented person appears to misunderstand their role, they must make "reasonable efforts to correct the misunderstanding" (see American Bar Association, 1969, DR 7-104(A)(2); American

Bar Association, 1983, 4.3). These rules apply even to third parties who are not "adverse" to the attorney's client (Wolfram, 1986, pp. 611–618). Again, a forensic mental health professional retained by an attorney should abide by the same rules.

Perhaps even more important, the expert contacting a third party *must* reveal the nonconfidential nature of the interaction. Both the rules of evidence (see, e.g., Federal Rules of Evidence, Rule 705) and the "Specialty Guidelines for Forensic Psychologists" (Committee on Ethical Guidelines for Forensic Psychologists, 1991) make clear that the psychologist can be required to reveal any information on which he or she relied, and, of course, there is no clinician-patient privilege in third-party interview situations. The examiner should emphasize this aspect of the relationship at the outset of the contact, because many third parties do not understand this aspect of the expert's role. Indeed, it is not uncommon for psychologists interviewing third parties in forensic evaluation contexts to hear the statement "Don't tell anyone *I* said this, but . . ." or "Speaking off the record. . . . " If the collateral source insists on confidentiality, the examiner may be able to have the attorney obtain a protective order, thereby alleviating the person's concerns (see Federal Rules of Criminal Procedure, 2000, Rule 26.2(c); Federal Rules of Civil Procedure, 1979, Rule 26(c)), but this option is rarely available.

In many jurisdictions, the law regulating the practice of psychology is likely to consider contact with a third party a professional service that could require, among other things, documentation of the notification. Even in jurisdictions in which such a requirement does not apply, the prudent psychologist may choose to document the notification and its acceptance.

Manner of Communication

As in any other situation, the mental health professional who interviews third parties in the context of litigation should respect the sensitivities and integrity of the interviewee. Repeated contacts or harsh words can verge on harassment, and leading questions can shape a third party's testimony in misleading ways. Although such conduct is not legally actionable unless it involves use of force, intimidation, or deception designed to influence testimony (see Crimes and Criminal Procedure, 18 U.S.C. §§ 1505, 1512 (2005), it is proscribed by ethical principles (APA, 2002) and can negatively affect the outcome of the case. If a third party is resistant to questioning, the court or attorneys can be so informed. If the third party has difficulty communicating, ways should be found to elicit answers without suggesting them.

Format and Content of Third-Party Interviews

An outline for conducting a collateral interview, including a list of possible questions to pursue, is included in the Appendix. After appropriately notifying the third party of the nature of the interaction, the expert should determine the nature of the relationship between the informant and the subject of the examination. Then the expert can explore the information the third party has regarding relevant events or capacities. It is important to stress to the third party the value of firsthand and objective information, no matter which side it might seem to favor. The expert should also make clear that a record is being maintained of the interview, to which the examinee may have access.

Documenting Third-Party Sources

Maintaining a record of third-party contacts is essential. The "Specialty Guidelines for Forensic Psychologists" (Committee on Ethical Guidelines for Forensic Psychologists, 1991, p. 661) advise that, "with foreknowledge that their professional services will be used in an adjudicative forum, [forensic psychologists] incur a special responsibility to provide the best documentation possible under the circumstances." Thus, as is the case with examinee interviews and test data, the forensic psychologist should adequately document and maintain for review any records or information that are provided by collateral sources. Seasoned examiners know that, to facilitate review of one's work and jog one's memory, summaries of third parties' accounts are not as helpful as verbatim quotes (although summary statements can certainly be included in the record as well).

Assessing the Utility of Third-Party Information

Appropriate practice requires that mental health professionals conducting forensic examinations assess the response style of examinees and the validity of accounts offered to them. Examiners should likewise attempt to reach some conclusion regarding the validity of third-party information. Consistent with the rules of evidence discussed earlier, the "Specialty Guidelines for Forensic Psychologists" (Committee on Ethical Guidelines for Forensic Psychologists, 1991, p. 662) acknowledge that "forensic psychologists attempt to corroborate critical data that form the basis for their professional product. When using hearsay data that have not been corroborated, but are nevertheless utilized, forensic psychologists acknowledge the uncorroborated status of those data and their reasons for relying on such data." This provision encourages forensic psychologists to recognize that third-party information may not be wholly accurate due to a variety of factors, including, but not limited to, imprecise/inaccurate memory and intentional misrepresentation. As they do with forensic examinees, experts should seek multiple sources of information in an effort to reach some conclusion regarding the validity of reports offered by third parties.

Perhaps helpful in this regard is an approach described by Austin (2002) which evaluates the usefulness of third-party sources based on the type of information provided and the nature of the relationship between the informant and the parties in the litigation. The most helpful third-party observations, according to Austin's model, are those that are directly relevant to the issue at hand and that are offered by a person who is not aligned with anyone involved in the litigation. Thus, accounts that support a party but that come from a collateral source who has a significant, positive relationship with that party (e.g., the spouse of a litigant alleging sexual harassment at work) are likely to be of less value to the evaluator, as are accounts that contradict an examinee from a collateral source who has, or may be presumed to have, a significant, *negative* relationship with him or her (e.g., the best friend and colleague of a work supervisor alleged to have sexually harassed the plaintiff). In contrast, observations likely to be most helpful to the forensic examiner are those that are offered by individuals who are not aligned with any of the parties or accounts that are contrary to what might be expected given the nature and valence of the relationship between the third party and those involved in the litigation.

CONCLUSION

Mental health professionals are of most assistance to the court when providing observations that are comprehensive and opinions that are accurate. Reliance on collateral, third-party accounts is one course of action that forensic mental health professionals can take—and ordinarily *must* take—to ensure that the product they deliver is helpful. Although research indicates that mental health professionals operating as forensic experts appreciate the value of third-party information, they may not appreciate the various legal and ethical principles that govern their efforts to access and utilize this information. This chapter has described those principles, with the aim of enabling forensic evaluators to perform examinations in a way that is consistent with the law, ethics, and good clinical practice.

APPENDIX: A MODEL FOR COLLATERAL INTERVIEWS

Section I. Notifying the Collateral

- Identify role as a forensic examiner and not as a therapist, and that one's professional contact with the examinee is in the context of litigation.
- Identify attorney/party who has retained the examiner.
- Inform collateral that participation is voluntary.
- Make clear the nonconfidential nature of the interview and that the collateral should not offer anything that he or she does not want to come to the attention of others, including the subject of the examination and other parties in the case.
- Emphasize one's role as independent expert and the desire for information that might support claims of any party involved in the litigation.
- Inform the collateral that he or she could be questioned by someone else at some later date regarding what is offered to the examiner.
- Query whether the collateral has been interviewed or deposed by anyone else in connection with this case or whether he or she has provided any written statements.
- Query whether the collateral has been instructed or requested by anyone to withhold information from the expert or has been instructed in some other way regarding the interview.
- Emphasize the value and role of firsthand information.
- Query whether collateral has any questions about the interview process before proceeding.

Section II. Assessing the Nature of the Relationship with the Examinee

- Query whether collateral was aware of litigation and his or her understanding of the litigation.
- Query the collateral about when he or she first met any of the parties or attorneys in the matter.

- Query the collateral regarding his or her relationship with all relevant persons (e.g., the examinee, other parties).

Section III. Questioning Content Areas

- Focus queries on relevant psychological functioning over time.
- Focus queries on relevant historical information.
- Focus queries on specific events.

Section IV. Closure

- Query whether the collateral has withheld any information and why (e.g., the interview is not confidential, concerned about a relationship with someone, does not want the information to have an impact on the case, does not want to be involved in the legal process).
- Encourage the collateral to initiate contact at some later point in time if there is additional information that he or she may want to convey or change.
- Request to read back to the collateral the notes taken to ensure accuracy and allow elaboration.
- Ask permission from collateral to reinitiate contact if anything else arises to discuss.

REFERENCES

Ackerman, M., & Ackerman, M. (1997). Custody evaluation practice: A survey of experienced professionals (revisited). *Professional Psychology: Research and Practice, 28,* 137–145.

American Bar Association. (1969). *Model code of professional responsibility.* Washington, DC: ABA Press.

American Bar Association. (1983). *Model code of professional conduct.* Washington, DC: ABA Press.

American Psychological Association. (2002). Ethical principles of psychologists and code of conduct. *American Psychologist, 47,* 1597–1611.

Austin, W. G. (2002). Guidelines for utilizing collateral sources of information in child custody evaluations. *Family Court Review, 40,* 177–184.

Bonnie, R. J., & Slobogin, C. (1980). The role of mental health professionals in the criminal process: The case for informed speculation. *Virginia Law Review, 66,* 427–522.

Borum, R., & Grisso, T. (1996). Establishing standards for criminal forensic reports: An empirical analysis. *Bulletin of the American Academy of Psychiatry and Law, 24,* 297–317.

Bow, J., & Quinnell, F. (2002). A critical review of child custody evaluation reports. *Family Court Review, 40,* 164–176.

Budd, K., Poindexter, L. M., Felix, E. D., & Naik-Polan, A. T. (2001). Clinical assessment of parents in child protection cases: An empirical analysis. *Law and Human Behavior, 25,* 93–108.

Christy, A., Douglas, K., Otto, R. K., & Petrila, J. (2004). Juveniles evaluated incompetent to proceed: Characteristics and quality of mental health professionals' evaluations. *Professional Psychology: Research and Practice, 35,* 380–388.

Committee on Ethical Guidelines for Forensic Psychologists. (1991). Specialty guidelines for forensic psychologists. *Law and Human Behavior, 15,* 655–665.

Crawford v. Washington, 541 U.S. 36 (2004).

Crimes and Criminal Procedure, 18 U.S.C. §§ 1505, 1512 (2005).

Daubert v. Merrell Dow Pharmaceutical Co., 509 U.S. 579 (1993).

Everett v. Town of Bristol, 674 A.2d 1275 (Vt. 1996).

Federal Rules of Civil Procedure. (2000).

Federal Rules of Criminal Procedure. (1979).

Federal Rules of Evidence. (1975).

Frye v. United States, 293 F. 1013 (D.C. Cir. 1923).

Greenberg, S. A., & Shuman, D. (1997). Irreconcilable conflict between therapeutic and forensic roles. *Professional Psychology: Research and Practice, 28,* 50–57.

Greenberg, S. A., Shuman, D. W., & Meyer, R. G. (2004). Unmasking forensic diagnosis. *International Journal of Law and Psychiatry, 27,* 1–15.

Greenfield v. Commonwealth, 214 Va. 710, 204 S.E.2d 414 (1974).

Grisso, T. (Ed.). (2003). *Evaluating competencies: Forensic assessments and instruments* (2nd ed.). New York: Kluwer/Plenum Press.

Hare, R. (1991). *Manual for the psychopathy checklist-Revised.* North Tonawanda, NY: Multi-Health Systems.

Health Insurance Portability and Accountability Act, 42 U.S.C. §§ 1320d *et. seq.* (1996).

Hearsay bases of psychiatric opinion testimony: A critique of Federal Rule of Evidence, 703 [Note]. (1977). *Southern California Law Review, 51,* 129–156.

Heilbrun, K. (2001). *Principles of forensic mental health assessment.* New York: Kluwer Press.

Heilbrun, K., & Collins, S. (1995). Evaluations of trial competency and mental state at time of offense: Report characteristics. *Professional Psychology: Research and Practice, 26,* 61–67.

Heilbrun, K., Marczyk, G., & DeMatteo, D. (2002). *Forensic mental health assessment: A casebook.* New York: Oxford University Press.

Heilbrun, K., Rosenfeld, B., Warren, J., & Collins, S. (1994). The use of third-party information in forensic assessments: A two-state comparison. *Bulletin of the American Academy of Psychiatry and the Law, 22,* 399–406.

Heilbrun, K., Warren, J., & Picarello, K. (2003). Third party information in forensic assessment. In I. B. Weiner (Series Ed.) & A. M. Goldstein (Vol. Ed.), *Comprehensive handbook of psychology: Vol. 11. Forensic psychology* (pp. 69–86). Hoboken, NJ: Wiley.

Keilin, W. G., & Bloom, L. J. (1986). Child custody evaluation practices: A survey of experienced professionals. *Professional Psychology: Research and Practice, 17,* 338–346.

Kumho Tire v. Carmichael, 526 U.S. 137 (1999).

Melton, G. B., Petrila, N., Poythress, N., & Slobogin, C. (1997). *Psychological evaluations for the courts: A handbook for mental health professionals and lawyers.* New York: Plenum Press.

Nicholson, R., & Norwood, S. (2000). The quality of forensic psychological assessments, reports, and testimony: Acknowledging the gap between promise and practice. *Law and Human Behavior, 24,* 9–44.

People v. Edney, 39 NY S.2d 620, 385 NY S.2d 23, 350 N.E.2d 4000 (1976).

People v. Goldstein, 2005 WL 3477726 (N.Y.).

Post-*Daubert* standards for admissibility of scientific and other expert evidence in state courts [Annotation]. (2001). *American Law Reports, 5th ed., 90,* 453–587.

Public Welfare, 45 C.F.R. § 164.512(a) & (d) (2000).

Rogers, R., & Bender, S. D. (2003). Evaluation of malingering and deception. In I. B. Weiner (Series Ed.) & A. M. Goldstein (Vol. Ed.), *Comprehensive handbook of psychology: Vol. 11. Forensic psychology* (pp. 109–129). Hoboken, NJ: Wiley.

Simon, R. I., & Gold, L. H. (2004). *American Psychiatric Publishing textbook of forensic psychiatry.* Washington, DC: American Psychiatric Publishing.

Skeem, J., & Golding, S. (1998). Community examiners' evaluations of competence to stand trial: Common problems and suggestions for improvement. *Professional Psychology: Research and Practice, 29,* 357–367.

State v. Pawlyk, 800 P.2d 338 (1990).

State v. Vincik, 398 N.W.2d 788 (1987, Iowa).

United States v. Bramlet, 820 F.2d 851 (7th Cir. 1987).

United States v. Sims, 514 F.2d 147 (9th Cir. 1973).

United States v. Wright, 783 F.2d 1091 (D. C. Cir. 1986).

Wolfram, C. W. (1986). *Modern legal ethics.* St. Paul, MN: West Group.

PART IV

Civil Forensic Psychology

CHAPTER 9

Recent Civil Decisions: Implications for Forensic Mental Health Experts

John Petrila

The paradigmatic legal issues in forensic psychology traditionally have arisen from criminal law. In part, this is because forensic mental health practice developed as a specialty in settings in which criminal law questions such as competency to stand trial and criminal responsibility dominated. For example, regardless of jurisdiction, individuals found not guilty by reason of insanity or incompetent to proceed invariably were committed for long stays to maximum-security forensic hospitals that stood apart from the rest of the public mental health system. Also, the early scholarship that helped define forensic psychology as a specialty tended to focus on such issues (Monahan & Steadman, 1983; Roesch & Golding, 1980). The insanity defense became a preoccupation of state legislatures after John Hinckley was found not guilty by reason of insanity after shooting President Reagan, and the debate over the future of the defense was informed to some degree by a significant amount of research on the operation of the insanity defense in various states (Steadman et al., 1993). In recent years, a focus on the development of instruments to assess core criminal issues such as competency has attracted top scholars (Grisso, 1986, 2003), and the emergence of psychopathy as a dominant concern has kept attention on criminal populations.

At the same time, important civil law issues increasingly influence forensic practice. First, there has been a change in the forensic marketplace. Mental health professionals who previously would have avoided anything "forensic" in their practice have expanded their work to include cases that previously may have been considered the province of the forensic specialist (Otto & Heilbrun, 2002). Although the number of individuals who self-identify as forensic specialists may not be increasing dramatically, the number of practitioners who accept forensic cases as part of their practice appears to be growing. Second, the treatment and continuing assessment of forensic patients is no longer the exclusive province of maximum-security hospitals; like all parts of the public mental health system, the forensic system has been subject to pressures to deinstitutionalize, and so forensic patients can be found in both institutional and community settings throughout the mental health system (Petrila, 2004). Practitioners charged with providing continuing assessment and oversight to such patients may find themselves relying on civil law, for example, civil commitment when the person is nonadherent to treatment or presents a risk to self or others or an adjudication of civil incompetence if the person refuses to adhere to treatment. Third, because individuals who may present a risk to others are found in all practice spheres, legal doctrines such as the duty to warn (*Tarasoff v. Regents of University of California,* 1974, 1976) are of general concern to many practitioners, not simply the specialty forensic sector. Finally, as practice guides such as Goldstein's (2003) and others (Melton, Petrila, Poythress, & Slobogin, 1997) demonstrate simply by the topics they cover, forensic practice itself is defined more broadly than when it first emerged. Today, forensic practice embraces both the traditional criminal law issues that drove its development and civil law issues such as civil commitment, the duty to warn third parties, and the Americans with Disabilities Act (ADA).

This chapter considers significant recent developments in civil law. It begins with an overview of recent changes in civil commitment law, changes that suggest the reemergence, in at least some states, of more medically oriented commitment laws than those to which we have become accustomed. This section includes developments in the application of civil commitment law to individuals committed as sexually violent predators. The chapter then considers an important California case that may presage a broadening of the *Tarasoff* doctrine in those states that have followed *Tarasoff.* It concludes with a summary of a recent decision by a federal court of appeals in which the court applied the ADA to a state statute authorizing the use of advance directives for health care by psychiatric patients. The outcome illustrates the growing impact of the ADA on traditional legal analysis when individuals with psychiatric disabilities are involved.

DEVELOPMENTS IN CIVIL COMMITMENT

Civil commitment has long been the signature human rights issue in mental health law (Monahan et al., 2001). In the 1960s, when the civil rights era of mental health law began (Birnbaum, 1960; *Rouse v. Cameron,* 1966), medically oriented civil commitment statutes predominated. However, largely in response to constitutional challenges, nearly all states had adopted much more legalistic civil commitment statutes by the mid-1970s.

Today, there is a reemergence of the medical model of civil commitment. Both federal and state courts continue to hold to the principle that civil commitment involves a deprivation of constitutionally protected liberty. However, important recent judicial decisions have given legislatures leave to expand the reach of civil commitment statutes in ways that probably would not have survived judicial scrutiny 2 decades ago. The result has been a "remedicalization" of civil commitment statutes. The courts also have given legislatures broad discretion in using civil commitment statutes to confine individuals under sexual psychopath statutes. In doing so, the courts have refused to apply the equal protection clause to insist that such individuals be legally treated the same as other individuals who are civilly committed.

This section addresses recent developments in three areas: (1) inpatient civil commitment, (2) outpatient civil commitment, and (3) the application of civil commitment laws to sexual psychopaths. It should be emphasized that civil commitment law varies from state to state and that state courts in different jurisdictions may have sometimes conflicting views regarding the application of state constitutional principles. Therefore, the forensic mental health practitioner must be familiar with the specific laws of his or her state. Nonetheless, the developments described here appear to reflect more general attitudes in the courts regarding civil commitment laws, attitudes that diverge quite sharply from the judicial attitudes that originally reshaped civil commitment law.

A Brief Note on the History of Civil Commitment Law

In the 1960s, approximately 40 states permitted the indefinite commitment of an individual based on the certification of a single physician (Melton et al., 1997). Across the United States, individuals typically would be hospitalized in a state psychiatric hospital after civil commitment. Attorneys in public interest law firms began challenging state commitment laws based on legal principles utilized in the African American civil rights movement. Specifically, attorneys argued that indefinite civil commitment violated federal constitutional provisions prohibiting the deprivation of liberty without due process of law (U.S. Constitution, 14th Amendment). In the seminal case of *Lessard v. Schmidt* (1974), a federal district court ruled that the Wisconsin civil commitment statute violated due process both substantively and procedurally. Substantively, the court held that commitment could occur only on a finding that as a result of mental illness the person was a danger to self or others. The court also required dangerousness to be defined narrowly, holding that a person with mental illness could be civilly committed only if "there is an extreme likelihood that if the person is not confined he will do immediate harm to himself or others." The court held that the due process clause of the 14th Amendment also required a state to provide formal procedural protections to the individual prior to commitment, modeled on the protections afforded criminal defendants. These included a right to counsel, a right to trial by jury if requested, and the right to present and cross-examine witnesses. The decision in *Lessard* had a significant impact nationally; facing or anticipating similar rulings, many states revised their commitment laws to meet the criteria established by *Lessard*. As a result, by the mid-1970s, the prototypical civil commitment statute permitted a very short confinement (usually 2 to 5 days) to determine whether the individual met the standards for long-term civil commitment. Without exception, those standards required a finding of dangerousness and usually defined dangerousness narrowly (Melton et al., 1997). Academic (and sometimes judicial) debate focused on such questions as whether constitutional standards required a showing that the individual had committed an "overt act" to meet the dangerousness criterion or whether a "threat" was sufficient (Wexler, 1983) and how "imminent" the potential danger must be.

Because of both the perceived failures of deinstitutionalization and concerns regarding the prevalence of mental illness among a growing homeless population, states in the late 1970s and 1980s began moving away from a strict dangerousness model (Newell, 1989). While state laws continued to permit commitment based on suicidal acts or gestures, legislatures also began to adopt a "grave disability" standard to reach a population that more narrowly focused commitment laws ostensibly did not reach. Although the specifics of this standard varied from state to state, in general, an individual had a "grave disability" if he or she was unable to provide basic needs such as food, clothing, shelter, and medical care (Slobogin, 2003). Both federal and state courts accepted the constitutional validity of this standard, an acceptance eased by a series of decisions by the U.S. Supreme Court, which made clear that all of the procedural protections made available to criminal defendants did not have to be made available to individuals in civil commitment proceedings (*Addington v. Texas,* 1979; *Parham v. J. R.,* 1979).

In the past few years, policymakers have continued to focus on civil commitment for several reasons: changing patterns of practice (civil commitment today increasingly results in short-term hospitalization in a psychiatric unit of a general hospital rather than long-term hospitalization in a state hospital; Geller, Fisher, McDermeit, & White, 1998); continuing concerns that people with mental illness are disproportionately dangerous (Phelan & Link, 1998); and a belief that certain individuals are predictably at risk for decompensation, particularly when they are nonadherent with treatment (Torrey & Zdanowicz, 2001). The result has been the gradual reemergence of a medical model of inpatient commitment, accompanied by increased reliance on outpatient civil commitment. These developments are covered next.

Inpatient Civil Commitment

One of the most important recent developments in inpatient civil commitment law is the creation of statutory criteria that permit commitment of an individual *in anticipation of* future deterioration that *might* result in dangerousness. The evidentiary base for this finding is likely to be the person's prior history rather than specific evidence of dangerousness. As previously noted, legal challenges to medically oriented commitment laws rested on the individual's imminent dangerousness as demonstrated by specific behavior. Wisconsin provides perhaps the most explicit departure from this principle, an interesting development given that the dangerousness requirement received its earliest and most explicit endorsement in the federal district court opinion in *Lessard,* noted earlier.

The Wisconsin statute permits commitment based on traditional definitions of dangerous to others and to self, including grave disability. Where Wisconsin deviates from the norm, and perhaps presages future developments, is in what is referred to as the "fifth standard" for commitment. The statute provides for commitment when the individual

> after the advantages and disadvantages of and alternatives to accepting a particular medication or treatment have been explained to him or her and because of mental illness, evidences either incapability of expressing an understanding of the advantages and disadvantages of accepting medication or treatment and the alternatives, or substantial incapability of applying an understanding of the advantages, disadvantages, and alternatives to his or her mental illness in order to make an informed choice as to whether to accept or refuse medication or treatment; and *evidences a substantial probability, as demonstrated by both the individual's*

treatment history and his or her recent acts or omissions, that the individual needs care or treatment to prevent further disability or deterioration and a substantial probability that he or she will, if left untreated, lack services necessary for his or her health or safety and suffer severe mental, emotional or physical harm that will result in the loss of the individual's ability to function independently in the community or the loss of cognitive or volitional control over his or her thoughts or actions. The probability of suffering severe mental, emotional or physical harm is not substantial under this subdivision if reasonable provision for the individual's care or treatment is available in the community and there is a reasonable probability that the individual will avail himself or herself of these services or if the individual is appropriate for protective placement under § 55.06. Food, shelter or other care that is provided to an individual who is substantially incapable of obtaining food, shelter or other care for himself or herself by any person other than a treatment facility does not constitute reasonable provision for the individual's care or treatment in the community. The individual's status as a minor does not automatically establish a substantial probability of suffering severe mental, emotional, or physical harm. (Wisconsin Statute 51.20(1)(a)(2.e); emphasis added)

If the person meets this fairly complex standard, he or she is considered dangerous and therefore subject to commitment.

This statute was challenged on the ground that it violated due process and equal protection provisions, primarily because it did not require a finding of imminent dangerousness to self or others and "because it allowed commitment upon a finding of a substantial probability of something less than physical harm, to wit, mental or emotional harm" (*In re commitment of Dennis H.,* 2002, p. 855). However, the Wisconsin Supreme Court rejected this argument, upholding the constitutionality of the statute under both federal and state constitutions (*In re commitment of Dennis H.,* 2002).

The Wisconsin court first characterized its task as difficult. It quoted *Heller v. Doe* (1993), a U.S. Supreme Court decision that upheld the constitutionality of a Kentucky statute that imposed a higher standard of proof for the commitment of the mentally ill than was provided for the mentally retarded. The Court observed, "We deal here with issues of unusual delicacy, in an area where professional judgments regarding desirable procedures are constantly and rapidly changing" (p. 855). The Wisconsin court then went on to note that the U.S. Supreme Court had declined to impose either strict substantive or procedural requirements on states: "Accordingly, courts generally proceed with restraint in this complex, delicate, and policy-sensitive area, deferring to the procedural scheme the legislature has chosen" (p. 856).

According to the Wisconsin court, the statutory fifth standard created five separate requirements. First, the person had to be mentally ill; second, the person had to be incompetent to make treatment and medication decisions; third, the person had to show a substantial probability that he or she needed treatment to prevent further disability or deterioration; fourth, the person must show a substantial probability that if left untreated he or she would lack services necessary for health or safety; and fifth, the person must evidence a substantial probability that without treatment he or she would "suffer severe mental, emotional, or physical harm that will result in the loss of the individual's ability to function independently in the community or the loss of cognitive or volitional control over his or her thoughts or actions."

The court did not stray rhetorically from the principle that dangerousness was required as a prerequisite to commitment. Again quoting from the U.S. Supreme Court, this time from *O'Connor v. Donaldson* (1975), the Wisconsin court wrote, "Even absent a requirement of obvious physical harm such as self-injury or suicide, a person may still be 'dangerous to himself' if 'he is helpless to avoid the hazards of freedom either through his own efforts or with the aid of willing family members or friends.' " (p. 862). Furthermore,

> by requiring dangerousness to be evidenced by a person's treatment history along with his or her recent acts or omissions, the fifth standard focuses on those who have been in treatment before and yet remain at risk of severe harm, *that is,* those who are chronically mentally ill and drop out of therapy or discontinue medication, giving rise to a substantial probability of a deterioration in condition to the point of inability to function independently or control thoughts or actions. (p. 863)

According to the court, the legislature was pursuing policy goals well within the legislature's province:

> By permitting intervention before a mentally ill person's condition becomes critical, the legislature has enabled the mental health treatment community to break the cycle associated with incapacity to choose medication or treatment, restore the person to a relatively even keel, prevent serious and potentially catastrophic harm, and ultimately reduce the amount of time spent in an institutional setting. This type of "prophylactic intervention" does not violate substantive due process. (p. 863)

A concurring opinion noted that a constitutional requirement that a finding of mental illness be accompanied by imminent dangerousness assured the proper balance between the individual's liberty interests and the interests of family and others in seeing that the person obtained needed treatment. Although the concurring opinion characterized the fifth standard as "perilously close" to upsetting this balance, it concluded that the criterion passed constitutional muster as long as trial courts required substantial evidence that the statutory criteria were met and if treatment was made available to the individual.

Other states also now permit civil commitment based on a finding that the patient's past history and current condition reasonably predict significant deterioration in the absence of treatment. For example, Oregon authorizes the inpatient commitment of an individual who, within the previous 3 years, has been placed twice in a hospital or inpatient facility approved by the state mental health agency; is currently exhibiting symptoms or behaviors substantially similar to those proceeding one or more previous inpatient placements; and if untreated will to a reasonable medical probability deteriorate physically or mentally until becoming either a danger to self or others (including an inability to meet basic needs; Oregon Revised Statutes Supp. 426.005(1)(d)). Although this statute does not go as far as Wisconsin's (because Oregon ties the anticipated deterioration to the other dangerousness criteria in the statute), it is an example of a growing legislative focus on anticipated deterioration.

As the Wisconsin Supreme Court opinion upholding the fifth standard demonstrates, the courts are reluctant to uncouple mental illness and dangerousness in considering the constitutionality of civil commitment statutes. However, as the court's opinion also illustrates, the definition of dangerousness can be quite elastic. Although the fifth standard is characterized as a dangerousness standard, a mental health professional assessing whether an individual meets the criterion will be performing a comparatively straightforward clinical assessment. A prediction is required (i.e., whether there is a "substantial probability" that the individual will deteriorate in the future). However, this type of prediction is far removed from the prediction of risk required under the civil commitment statutes that have been typical in the United States since the 1970s.

Outpatient Civil Commitment

The debate regarding outpatient civil commitment reflects a similar desire on the part of policymakers to expand the reach of civil commitment statutes beyond their traditional boundaries. There are three types of outpatient commitment laws (Ridgely, Borum, & Petrila, 2001), and nearly all states have at least one type. First, individuals may be placed on conditional release upon discharge from inpatient care, usually without a judicial hearing. This was a very common practice when most people with serious mental illnesses were treated in state psychiatric facilities. It required the individual to comply with the treatment on which release was conditioned or face rehospitalization. Second, some states have amended their inpatient civil commitment laws to make outpatient treatment an alternative to inpatient care. This typically has been done by inserting a phrase such as "or outpatient treatment" whenever the commitment statute refers to inpatient treatment. The substantive and procedural standards are the same whether the court orders inpatient or outpatient care: The purpose of the language is simply to give the court an alternative to inpatient care if the person meets the standards for commitment. Third, and most important, a number of states have enacted out-patient commitment statutes with procedural and/or substantive standards that differ from inpatient commitment standards. These statutes have received the most attention because they rely on different standards and because they lie at the heart of the debate regarding the appropriate balance between individual liberty and the reach of state authority. Perhaps the best known "pure" outpatient commitment statutes are New York's and North Carolina's, the former because of the circumstances that led to passage of the statute, the latter for the amount of research that has been conducted into the impact of the law by Swartz and colleagues (Swartz & Swanson, 2004; Swartz, Swanson, Hiday, et al., 2001; Swartz, Swanson, Wagner, et al., 2001). The following discussion focuses on the New York law, also known as *Kendra's Law,* named for Kendra Webdale, a young woman pushed to her death in a subway station in 1999 by a man with a mental illness.

The New York statute permits involuntary outpatient commitment (or "assisted outpatient treatment," as used in the statute) if a court finds that several conditions exist, including the following (New York Mental Hygiene Law, Section 9.60):

• The person is 18 years of age or older.
• The person suffers from a mental illness.

- He or she is unlikely to survive safely in the community without supervision.
- He or she has a history of nonadherence with treatment that at least twice in the previous 36 months has been a significant factor in the person being hospitalized or receiving services in a forensic or correctional unit or resulted in acts, threats, or attempts at serious violent behavior to self or others within the previous 48 months.
- Because of mental illness the person is unlikely to participate voluntarily in recommended treatment.
- In view of the person's treatment history and current behavior, he or she is in need of outpatient treatment to prevent a relapse or deterioration that would be likely to result in serious harm to self or others.
- It is likely the person would benefit from outpatient treatment.

The court may order a variety of services if the individual meets these criteria, including case management services, medication, periodic blood tests, or urinalysis to determine compliance with prescribed medications, individual or group therapy, day or partial-day programming activities, educational and vocational training, alcohol or substance abuse treatment, periodic testing for the presence of alcohol or drugs, supervision of living arrangements, and any other necessary services. Since enactment of this statute, Florida has passed a similar law (Florida Statutes Annotated, 394.4655), and other states, including Michigan and New Jersey, are considering comparable legislation.

Two features of *Kendra's Law* are worth noting here. First, although the statute retains a focus on risk to self or others, it permits intervention "to prevent a relapse or deterioration" likely to result in harm. Like the fifth standard of the Wisconsin commitment statute, this changes the point at which intervention is permitted from when the person presents an imminent harm to a more speculative point in time in which deterioration or relapse is anticipated. In its findings, the New York legislature found that

> there are mentally ill persons who are capable of living in the community with the help of family, friends and mental health professionals, but who, without routine care and treatment, may relapse and become violent or suicidal, or require hospitalization. . . . Family members and caregivers often must stand by helplessly and watch their loved ones and patients decompensate. (L. 1999, c. 408)

The practical effect of this change is to dilute the focus on imminent danger that has been at the core of modern commitment statutes.

In New York, the court also may order medication. From a policy perspective, the fact that individuals with serious mental illnesses sometimes do not take prescribed medication is probably the most important reason that states have adopted outpatient commitment laws (Torrey & Zdanowicz, 2001). In fact, explanatory material prepared by the Counsel to the New York Office of Mental Health after passage of *Kendra's Law* notes that Ms. Webdale was killed by "a person who failed to take the medication prescribed for his mental illness" (Office of Counsel, 1999).

However, despite this focus on the issue of medication adherence as a rationale for enacting outpatient commitment laws, there are legal barriers to forcing individuals to take medication against their will in community settings that make enforcement of medication orders problematic. These barriers are illustrated by the decision of the New York Court of Appeals upholding *Kendra's Law* against legal challenge.

In the case *In re K. L.* (2004), an individual challenged several provisions of *Kendra's Law*. The claimant argued that permitting a 72-hour hospitalization to examine an individual who had been noncompliant with mandated outpatient treatment violated federal and state constitutional requirements against unreasonable searches and seizures. The claimant also argued that the statute violated due process because it did not require a *judicial* finding of incompetence before a court could order an individual to comply with outpatient treatment. This argument was based on an earlier decision by the New York Court of Appeals (*Rivers v. Katz,* 1986) in which the court had ruled that a judicial finding of incapacity was necessary before an individual could be medicated with psychotropic drugs over his or her refusal. However, the New York Court of Appeals rejected these arguments in considering *Kendra's Law,* stating that to require a judicial finding of incapacity would "have the effect of eviscerating the legislation, inasmuch as the statute presumes that assisted outpatients are capable of actively participating in the development of their written treatment plans, and specifically requires that they be afforded an opportunity to do so" (*In re K. L.,* 2004, p. 484). The court further noted that the claimant conceded that adoption of his viewpoint would mean that a "large number" of individuals potentially subject to the statute would become ineligible for a judicial order. In the court's view, access to treatment "may enable patients who might otherwise require involuntary hospitalization to live and work freely and productively through compliance with necessary treatment" (p. 484). The court found that *Kendra's Law* created a minimal restriction on a patient's freedom, "inasmuch as the coercive force of the order lies solely in the compulsion generally felt by law-abiding citizens to comply with court directives" (p. 485). The legislation furthered the legitimate interest of the State of New York in "warding off the longer periods of hospitalization that, as the Legislature has found, tend to accompany relapse or deterioration" (p. 487.) Of particular importance, the court also noted that *Kendra's Law* did not permit forced medication. Therefore, although a judicial finding of incapacity as required in *Rivers* would continue to be necessary to force medication, it was not necessary for *Kendra's Law* because the statute did not permit forced treatment.

This decision creates a somewhat paradoxical result. First, the New York Court of Appeals, like the Wisconsin Supreme Court, endorsed the value of early legal intervention to prophylactically prevent relapse and subsequent deterioration in the person's condition. This suggests that judicial attitudes toward civil commitment have changed significantly in the past 3 decades: The perceived value of access to treatment has risen in the eyes of at least some state high courts, compared to concerns over the deprivation of liberty that dominated judicial discourse regarding civil commitment at the height of the civil rights era. To some degree, this may reflect changes in the organization of psychiatric services in most states. In many states, individuals are no longer committed to state psychiatric hospitals, at least initially, and hospital stays are much shorter than they were when civil commitment laws were first challenged. As a result, individuals today seldom face indefinite stays in the grossly understaffed and unsafe state facilities that so influenced judicial thinking regarding civil commitment 3 decades ago. Also, as the New York Court of Appeals observes (though one may disagree with the characterization), an outpatient commitment order carries little force beyond that experienced by any citizen faced with a court order. This is not to say that liberty is no longer valued. As the court also makes clear, it is in large part because *Kendra's Law* does not permit forced treatment that the statute survived a constitutional challenge. However, this creates a paradox: It is precisely because of a perception that many individuals with long-term mental illnesses put themselves or others at risk by *not* regularly taking prescribed medication that outpatient statutes such as *Kendra's Law* are enacted. As a practical matter, a judicial decision such as *Matter of K. L.* removes this core issue from the table, or at least reserves it for more traditional due process analyses. Combined with other reported practical problems in implementing outpatient commitment statutes (e.g., the unwillingness of law enforcement to transport people who are not adhering to treatment back to a hospital for evaluation, a lack of community resources in some states that makes practitioners reluctant to use outpatient commitment statutes; see generally Ridgely et al., 2001), one might reasonably conclude that these statutes promise more than they can deliver, particularly if enacted without additional treatment resources.

SEXUAL PSYCHOPATH STATUTES: JUST ANOTHER FORM OF CIVIL COMMITMENT?

One of the most important mental health law developments in the past 15 years was the emergence of nontherapeutically oriented sexual psychopath statutes in several states. In the 1930s, many states enacted statutes that permitted indefinite confinement for treatment of those individuals labeled sexual psychopaths. However, the underlying philosophy of such statutes was generally therapeutic, based on professional optimism that sexual disorders could be treated and cured (Conroy, 2003; Group for the Advancement of Psychiatry, 1950). By the late 1970s, many states had repealed these first-generation statutes because little evidence supported the notion that a comparatively heterogeneous group of sexual offenders could be successfully treated (Group for the Advancement of Psychiatry, 1977).

Although contemporary statutes generally promise treatment, their primary aim is the indefinite detention of individuals judged to be a risk for future sexual offending. Statutes vary from state to state, but the approximately 16 statutes that currently exist typically require several common findings as a predicate to confinement (Conroy, 2003; Janus & Walbek, 2000): (a) an established history of sexual offending (typically demonstrated by a conviction for or plea to some type of sexual offense), (b) presence of an underlying mental disorder (broadly defined), which (c) places the offender at increased risk of future sexual offending (though the definition of what constitutes increased risk is not uniform across jurisdictions), and which necessitates (d) some type of commitment (some states allow for either outpatient or inpatient commitment [e.g., Washington], others allow only for inpatient commitment [e.g., Florida], and at least one state provides only for outpatient commitment [Texas]), which (e) typically lasts until the individual can demonstrate that he (or very occasionally she) no longer constitutes a future risk.

The U.S. Supreme Court upheld the constitutionality of such statutes against a number of challenges in the now well-known case of *Kansas v. Hendricks* (1997). The Court ruled that although sexually violent predator (SVP) statutes must require a finding of mental disorder as well as dangerousness, states have broad latitude in defining mental disorder and are not bound by professionally established diagnostic nomenclature in doing so. In a subsequent decision (*Kansas v. Crane,* 2002), the Court made clear, in discussing what behavioral predicate is necessary for confinement under SVP statutes, that the state need not show that the individual lacks *complete* control (or volition) over his or her conduct, but that a finding of *some* lack of control is necessary. The Court provided little definitional precision regarding the content of this requirement, observing, "Inability to control behavior will not be demonstrable with mathematical precision. It is enough to say there must be proof of serious difficulty in controlling behavior" (p. 413). The Court stated that this difficulty in behavior control

> when viewed in light of such features of the case as the nature of the psychiatric diagnosis, and the severity of the mental abnormality itself, must be sufficient to distinguish the dangerous sexual offender whose serious mental illness, abnormality, or disorder subjects him to civil commitment from the dangerous but typical recidivist convicted in an ordinary criminal case. (p. 413)

State court cases also focus on volition. For example, the California Supreme Court upheld the constitutionality of the state's sexual violent predator law in part because it requires a finding of a mental disorder that prevents the individual from controlling sexually violent behavior (*Hubbart v. Superior Court,* 1999). In 2005, the California courts extended this requirement to the state's juvenile detention statute. This law permits the indefinite civil commitment (for renewable periods of 2 years) of juveniles who otherwise would be discharged from youth authority commitments. Civil commitment is permitted when discharge "would be physically dangerous to the public because of the person's mental or physical deficiency, disorder, or abnormality" (*In re Howard N,* 2005, p. 309). The California Supreme Court upheld the constitutionality of this statute by ruling that adjudications under the law must be based on a finding that the person's mental disorder causes serious difficulty in controlling his or her behavior (*In re Howard N*). In the court's view, the absence of this requirement would render the statutory scheme unconstitutional. At the same time, the majority of state courts that have considered the issue have rejected arguments that a jury must receive a special instruction on the principle of the defendant's lack of control (see, for example, *State v. White,* 2004).

These decisions appear to insist on strict due process protections for individuals subject to SVP laws, yet courts appear to have given legislators, as well as mental health professionals, quite broad discretion in writing and applying such statutes. For example, as described in detail elsewhere (Petrila & Otto, 2001), courts have not required mental health professionals to adopt a particular approach to assessing

future risk, nor have they been particularly rigorous in scrutinizing the use of actuarial and other risk assessment tools. Rather, the courts have admitted expert opinions based on virtually any risk assessment technique. Some courts also have found
ways to distinguish legally between individuals committed under SVP statutes and
other civilly committed individuals. The fact that this distinction is drawn is important, because the constitutionality of SVP statutes rests at least in part on legislative promises to provide treatment for individuals after commitment. For
example, in its *Kansas v. Hendricks* decision (1997), the U.S. Supreme Court rejected claims that the Kansas SVP statute constituted ex post facto punishment
(i.e., punishment assessed after the individual had already been convicted and sentenced for his or her crime). The Court also rejected the claim that the statute violated the constitutional prohibition against double jeopardy, in part because

the State has represented that an individual confined under the Act is not subject to the
more restrictive conditions placed on state prisoners, but instead experiences essentially
the same conditions as any involuntarily committed patient in the state mental institution.
Because none of the parties argues that people institutionalized under the Kansas general
civil commitment statute are subject to punitive conditions, even though they may be involuntarily confined, it is difficult to conclude that persons confined under this Act are being
"punished." (p. 363)

Yet, although the U.S. Supreme Court took at face value the state's argument
that individuals committed under the SVP law were confined in circumstances similar to those encountered by individuals committed under the state's traditional
civil commitment law, the Kansas legislature itself had acknowledged that treatment was a secondary concern. In its statement of findings (also noted by the majority in *Hendricks*), the legislature stated:

A small but extremely dangerous group of sexually violent predators exist who do not have
a mental disease or defect that renders them appropriate for involuntary treatment pursuant
to the [general involuntary civil commitment statute]. . . . In contrast to persons appropriate
for civil commitment under the [general involuntary civil commitment statute], sexually violent predators generally have antisocial personality features which are unamenable to existing mental illness treatment modalities and those features render them likely to engage in
sexually violent behavior. (Kansas Statutes Annotated 59-29a01)

In short, the Kansas legislature appeared to doubt from the beginning that individuals committed under its statute were treatable. This suggests that the statutory
promise of treatment in the Kansas law ("The involuntary detention or commitment . . . shall conform to constitutional requirements for care and treatment") appears to anticipate potential equal protection claims as much as anything else.

In fact, state courts have been unsympathetic to equal protection and due process arguments on behalf of individuals committed under SVP laws. For example,
the California Supreme Court in its *Hubbart* decision rejected the claimant's argument that his treatment was inadequate. The claimant had argued that the legislature at least implicitly had assumed that individuals committed under the statute
were not amenable to treatment. He further argued that the failure to provide care

designed to cure him violated state and federal due process guarantees. The California Supreme Court cited the *Hendricks* decision for the proposition that states were not obligated to provide treatment in all circumstances in which civil commitment was used. The U.S. Supreme Court in *Hendricks* had written:

> While we have upheld state civil commitment statutes that aim both to incapacitate and to treat, we have never held that the Constitution prevents a State from civilly detaining those for whom no treatment is available, but who nevertheless pose a danger to others. A State could hardly be seen as furthering a "punitive" purpose by involuntarily confining persons afflicted with an untreatable, highly contagious disease. . . . Similarly, it would be of little value to require treatment as a precondition for civil confinement of the dangerously insane when no acceptable treatment existed. To conclude otherwise would obligate a State to release certain confined individuals who were both mentally ill and dangerous simply because they could not be successfully treated for their afflictions. (1997, p. 366)

Following this logic, the California Supreme Court held that the U.S. Supreme Court's language

> strongly suggests that there is no broad constitutional right of treatment for persons involuntarily confined as dangerous and mentally impaired, at least where "no acceptable treatment exist[s]" or where they cannot be "successfully treated for their afflictions." To the extent Hubbart suggests the contrary is true and that the sexual violent predator statute should be invalidated as a result, he is mistaken. (*Hubbart,* 1999, p. 510)

Washington state case law also distinguishes individuals committed under SVP laws from individuals committed under other provisions of the state's civil commitment statute. For example, in *In re Detention of Thorell* (2003), the Washington Supreme Court ruled that it was not necessary for the trial court conducting an initial hearing under the SVP statute to consider whether the individual could be treated in a least restrictive alternative. In earlier cases, the same court had held that equal protection required that the trial court consider this issue because civilly committed individuals had that right. However, in *Thorell,* the court held that there was a rational basis for the legislature to treat these two groups of individuals differently. First, the court cited legislative language (similar to that found in California, Kansas, and other state statutes) that said SVPs did not have a treatable mental disease or defect. Second, the legislature had stated that such individuals were much more likely than other civilly committed individuals to recidivate. Third, as a result, the legislature had concluded that the treatment needs of SVPs were much different from those of other individuals with mental illness and that their anticipated future dangerousness extended far into the future. Therefore, the court concluded that the legislature could rationally distinguish between individuals committed under the SVP statute and others, and so the equal protection argument failed.

It is worth reiterating that a judicial ruling in one state does not bind courts in another state. For the same reason, it also is often difficult to generalize from one state court decision to a more general principle. However, it is also possible to draw three tentative conclusions from these cases and others like them. First, while SVP statutes were enacted as part of state civil commitment laws; emerging case law suggests a willingness to define SVPs as a discrete class of individuals with some but not all of the rights enjoyed by other civilly committed individuals. Second, state legislative findings that people with sexual disorders are not amenable to treatment appear to be more influential with courts that have addressed these issues than statutory promises of treatment. Courts have used the latter to characterize SVP statutes as civil rather than criminal (and therefore not punitive, which would run afoul of constitutional prohibitions against ex post facto punishment and double jeopardy). However, courts also have used legislative findings that SVPs are not amenable to treatment to justify confinement that is more incapacitating than therapeutic. Third, broad judicial deference to virtually unlimited legislative discretion in defining "mental abnormality" or "mental disorder" leaves open the possibility of similar types of offender statutes in the future: One might imagine "abusive spouse" commitment laws, for example, based on legislative determinations that spouse abusers suffer from mental disorders that result in volitional problems and the risk of further abuse, thereby warranting indefinite confinement.

These SVP rulings also are consistent with the other civil commitment cases discussed previously in which both federal and state courts have increasingly deferred to legislative decision making (with some exceptions in the relationship between the U.S. Supreme Court and Congress not relevant here). As a result, the current judicial climate would appear to permit a much broader use of the state's authority to civilly commit individuals than was the case 2 decades ago. This suggests that there may be continuing efforts to expand the reach of civil commitment in the future.

DUTY TO WARN

The California Supreme Court was the first court to obligate mental health professionals to warn individuals that a patient might pose a risk to them (*Tarasoff v. Regents of the University of California,* 1974). On rehearing, the court ruled again that therapists could be liable in such situations but framed the duty more broadly as a duty to take steps to protect the third party (*Tarasoff v. Regents of the University of California,* 1976). A later ruling by the same court in *Hedlund v. Superior Court* (1983, p. 706) extended the *Tarasoff* duty beyond an identified third party "to persons in close relationship to the object of a patient's threat." The court was closely divided, with the dissent arguing that the majority opinion placed an undue reliance on the reliability of dangerousness predictions and intruded into confidentiality. In the dissent's view, this created an unrealistic burden on therapists and jeopardized the therapeutic relationship. Under *Tarasoff* and *Hedlund,* a plaintiff could establish negligence by showing that the therapist had deviated from professional norms in determining whether the patient was dangerous. This effectively created a common law claim for malpractice, in which expert testimony on the applicable professional standards would be essential.

Many states have adopted some version of the *Tarasoff* duty, either judicially or legislatively, while a number of states have rejected the doctrine. In Florida, for example, courts have ruled consistently that mental health professionals have no duty to third parties even when an outpatient has made explicit threats (*Boynton v. Burglass,* 1991). The Florida courts have provided three reasons for their stance. First, they believe that mental health professionals exercise little control over the behavior of outpatients and that, in the absence of control, it would be unreasonable to impose a duty to third parties. Second, the courts have been persuaded that risk assessment is sufficiently unsophisticated to warrant creation of a duty. Third, the Florida legislature, like other state legislatures, has enacted a statute that *permits* but does not *require* a mental health professional to breach confidentiality to protect a third party from harm (Florida Statutes Annotated 455.2415). This legislation provides a useful reminder that one of the central criticisms of *Tarasoff* was the potential impact on confidentiality as well as on the trust that most agree is at the heart of the therapeutic relationship. Indeed, the U.S. Supreme Court relied heavily on the importance of confidentiality and trust in the therapeutic relationship in creating a federal privilege for communications to psychotherapists (*Jaffee v. Redmond,* 1996). Legislation such as Florida's makes the decision to act or not a matter of the mental health professional's professional judgment. It also effectively insulates the decision from malpractice claims either that confidentiality was inappropriately breached or that the mental health professional was duty-bound to protect the third party.

After the *Tarasoff* and *Hedlund* decisions, the California legislature passed a law designed to narrow the impact of the rulings. As California law now stands, "as a general rule, a mental health professional has no duty to warn third persons about, nor any duty to predict, a patient's dangerous propensities" (*Ewing v. Northridge Hospital Medical Center,* 2004, p. 1292). However, an exception exists "where the patient has communicated an 'actual threat of violence against an identified victim' "; the legislation embodying this exception was designed to "abolish the expansive rulings of *Tarasoff* and *Hedlund . . .* that a therapist can be held liable for the mere failure to predict and warn of potential violence by his patient" (Assembly Committee on Judiciary, 1985, p. 2). The California statute states that a psychotherapist shall not be liable for failing to warn and protect a third party from a patient's threatened violent behavior "except where *the patient* has communicated to the psychotherapist a serious threat of physical violence against a reasonably identifiable victim or victims" (California Civil Code 43.92; emphasis added). Whereas *Tarasoff* created a broad duty to protect endangered third parties, the statute now provides that the psychotherapist discharges his or her duty by "making reasonable efforts to communicate the threat to the victim or victims and to a law enforcement agency" (California Civil Code 43.92). This effectively converts the therapist's duty from a duty to protect to a duty to warn. The plaintiff must prove to a jury that the therapist "actually believed or predicted" that the patient posed a serious risk of inflicting grave bodily injury on a reasonably identifiable victim (*Ewing v. Northridge Hospital Medical Center,* p. 1301).

This legislative language, on its face, significantly narrows the reach of *Tarasoff* and *Hedlund.* However, in two recent cases arising from the same set of facts (*Ewing v. Goldstein,* 2004; *Ewing v. Northridge Hospital Medical Center,* 2004), a California Court of Appeals has created a narrow but potentially significant expansion of the circumstances that trigger a therapist's duty. Although these cases have immediate implications only for California, they will undoubtedly receive scrutiny in other jurisdictions and so are worth considering here.

The facts that gave rise to the Ewing decisions may be briefly summarized. A police officer named Geno Colello had been involved romantically with Diane Williams for approximately 17 years. The relationship had ended and Williams had established a relationship with Keith Ewing (son of the plaintiffs, Cal and Janet Ewing). At dinner with his parents, Colello asked his father for his gun so he could end his own life after killing Ewing. After his father told him to not "take the coward's way out," he hit his father in the face; his father then drove his son to a hospital, where they met with Art Capilla, a social worker. Capilla found Colello to be angry and agitated and asked for protection during the clinical interview. Colello's father, also present at the interview, told Capilla that his son had hit him for the first time in his life, that he had threatened to kill Ewing, and that the father believed his son capable of carrying out the threat. During subsequent legal proceedings after Ewing's death, Capilla denied having been told about this threat, but acknowledged asking Colello whether he intended to kill Ewing. However, the case record did not record Colello's answer. Although Capilla believed Colello met statutory standards for civil commitment, he permitted Colello to voluntarily admit himself for psychiatric care because involuntary commitment would have jeopardized his status as a police officer. Colello admitted himself that evening but was discharged the next day, despite conversations between the hospital psychiatrist and David Goldstein (a marriage and family counselor who had treated Colello for approximately 4 years for work- and relationship-related issues) in which Goldstein urged that Colello be retained at least through the weekend. However, Colello was discharged and on the following day murdered Ewing and killed himself.

Ewing's parents brought suit for wrongful death (i.e., they sought monetary damages for the death of their son) on the ground of professional negligence against Goldstein, Capilla, the hospital, and attending staff. They alleged that Colello posed a foreseeable danger to their son and directly (or indirectly through the father) communicated an intention to kill their son to these various parties. Therefore, in their view, Capilla, the hospital, and Goldstein had violated their statutory duty to warn.

The trial court dismissed all of the claims. First, the court held that plaintiffs had not shown that the statute applied because there was no evidence that the *patient* had threatened Ewing. Second, the court ruled that expert testimony was required for the plaintiffs to prove liability and the Ewings had not designated an expert witness. The court of appeals ruled in two decisions (*Ewing v. Goldstein,* 2004; *Ewing v. Northridge Hospital Medical Center,* 2004) that the trial court erred on both grounds. The court recounted the legislative changes subsequent to *Tarasoff* and *Hedlund* and acknowledged that under California law, therapists no longer owed a broad duty to third parties, but the court also concluded that the Ewings' lawsuits could proceed. In the court's view:

> When the communication of a serious threat of grave bodily injury is conveyed to the psychotherapist by a *member of the patient's immediate family,* and is shared for the purpose of facilitating and furthering the patient's treatment, the fact that the family member is not a patient of psychotherapist is not material. If a therapist *actually believes* or predicts a patient poses a risk of inflicting serious physical harm upon a reasonably identifiable person,

the therapist must take steps to warn. (*Ewing v. Northridge Hospital Medical Center*, 2004, pp. 1296–1297; emphasis added; see also *Ewing v. Goldstein*, 2004)

According to the court, the "pivotal factual question" is "whether the psychotherapist actually held the belief or made the prediction." If the plaintiff could establish actual belief, then it was irrelevant that the belief or prediction was based on information derived from a member of the patient's family rather than the patient. The court also asserted that its interpretation would harmonize the therapist's duty to preserve confidentiality and the limited exception to that duty created when a patient communicated threat. The court noted that communications made by a patient's family members to a therapist had the same privilege from disclosure available to communications by the patient, and that therefore it was reasonable to apply the same statutory exception when communications by a family member caused the therapist to believe the patient posed a danger to third parties. The court stated:

> We discern no principled reason why equally important information in the form of an actual threat that a parent shares with his or her son's therapist about the risk of grave bodily injury the patient poses to another also should not be considered a "patient communication" in determining whether the therapist's duty to warn is triggered [under the statute]. (*Ewing v. Goldstein*, 2004, pp. 872–873)

In its other Ewing decision, the court ruled that a plaintiff could show a breach of duty *without* expert testimony (*Ewing v. Northridge Hospital Medical Center*, 2004). *Tarasoff* had created a common law cause of action for malpractice, which depended on expert testimony to aid a jury in determining whether a therapist had deviated from prevailing professional norms in determining whether the patient had constituted a risk and whether the therapist had taken reasonable steps to ameliorate that risk. However, under the ruling in *Ewing v. Northridge Hospital Medical Center*, breach of the limited statutory duty to warn does not require expert testimony. This is because, according to the court of appeals, it is well within a jury's knowledge to decide whether the statutory criteria were met, that is, (a) whether a psychotherapist-patient relationship existed, (b) whether the psychotherapist actually believed or predicted that the patient posed a serious risk of inflicting grave bodily injury (c) to a reasonably identifiable victim, and (d) the failure to take reasonable efforts to warn the victim and a law enforcement agency resulted in harm (*Ewing v. Northridge Hospital Medical Center*, 2004, p. 1302). The court believed that the California legislature intended to limit liability to situations involving actual belief or prediction, and "the mind-set of a therapist can be evaluated by resort to common knowledge without the aid of expert testimony" (p. 1303).

Since the *Ewing* decisions, another panel of the California Court of Appeals has dismissed a claim for damages by individuals injured during a shooting spree by a gunman, Reynoldo Rodriguez, who had been treated for mental illness (*Calderon v. Glick*, 2005). The gunman believed that he had been given human T-cell lymphotropic virus (HTLV) by his girlfriend. During several therapy sessions, his therapist asked him each time whether he intended to hurt his former girlfriend, and each time the patient denied the intention to do so. The therapist stated, "I addressed that very clearly with him and his answer was very clear to me. I looked at him and I lingered to make sure that there was no deviation in his behavior because obviously I was concerned about this issue. . . . I concluded that at that time he was not a risk" (p. 228–229). The patient eventually entered the home of his former girlfriend, killed several people, and wounded several others. He committed suicide 2 days later.

The trial court granted summary judgment (i.e., entered a verdict for the defendants without trial, on the ground that there was no triable issue of fact and that, given the facts and law of the case, the plaintiffs could not prevail under any circumstances). The court of appeals affirmed (*Calderon v. Glick*, 2005). First, the court held that the defendants owed no duty to the plaintiffs, both because it was not reasonably foreseeable that Rodriguez would cause them harm and because, "lacking clairvoyant powers, they could not predict future dangerousness" (p. 234). The patient had always denied intent to harm and, unlike in the *Ewing* cases, his family had never told his therapist that he might cause harm.

These cases are interesting for several reasons. First, they make clear that the California legislature has significantly narrowed the original *Tarasoff* duty and that a cause of action for a failure to warn a third party is now based on statute, not the *Tarasoff* holding. It is also noteworthy that the appellate court concluded that expert testimony is not necessary for a plaintiff to prove his or her case and that a jury is capable of deciding whether the therapist "actually" believed or predicted that the patient posed a threat of serious harm. However, whether the therapist *should* have concluded that the patient was a danger, but did not, is no longer a legally significant issue (though under the original *Tarasoff* ruling, that issue was germane). Second, the ruling that a communication by a family member of a threat made by the patient may give rise to a statutory duty to warn goes beyond the statutory language, which focuses on communication by the *patient*. As the *Ewing* decisions make clear, the focus in litigation is still on the therapist's actual beliefs regarding the threat posed by the patient. However, before the *Ewing* decisions, a therapist could successfully argue that because the patient had not made a threat (as was the case in *Glick*), there was no duty. Subsequent to *Ewing v. Goldstein*, communications between the family and therapist are now relevant to determining the therapist's actual belief. This suggests that a future issue may arise over whether other sources of information regarding threats made by a patient might trigger a therapist's duty. For example, assume an employer tells the therapist about a threat made by the patient at the workplace. The court in *Ewing v. Goldstein* relied for its decision in part on the privileged nature of communications made by family members to the therapist in the context of treatment, a privilege that does not extend to communications by other parties, such as employers. Therefore, one might conclude that an employer's communication to the therapist would not create a duty even though communication of the same threat by a family member would. At the same time, if the point of the statute is to force the therapist to act based on the therapist's actual belief that the patient poses a threat of serious bodily harm to others, the fact that the therapist now knows that the patient has made a threat presumably should be more important than the source of knowledge.

This raises a third and perhaps most interesting point about the evolution of the duty to warn in California. The duty now focuses on the therapist's actual belief and certain limited information (primarily knowledge that the patient has made a threat) that results in that belief. This has little to do with the myriad pieces of information that *should* inform a therapist's conclusion regarding a patient's potential violence. Our understanding of the factors associated with third-party risk has improved dramatically since the original *Tarasoff* decision. One of the major criticisms of *Tarasoff* (echoed by language in the *Ewing* and *Glick* opinions 20 years later) is that it required "clairvoyance" from the therapist. Yet, today, it is clear that mental health professionals can perform much better than chance, particularly when making short-term predictions of risk (Monahan et al., 2001). In addition, there are now a variety of tools that tie risk assessment to an empirically informed literature (for a review, see Monahan, 2003). A threat of violence certainly may be relevant to the task, but it is *a* factor, not the only factor. Today, in California, the legal duty to warn is largely divorced from this growing knowledge. Rather, it serves to put the therapist on notice that one type of communication (i.e., a direct threat), as reported by limited sources (i.e., the patient or a family member), has particular legal significance. The *Ewing* decisions broaden the potential *sources* of communication beyond the statute to include family, and therefore broaden the potential situations in which the therapist might be found liable. However, the focus is now on the therapist's actual belief, and not how the therapist reached a clinical conclusion regarding third-party risk. As a result, one can imagine a situation in which a therapist believes that a threat made by a patient should not be taken seriously, does not warn the threatened party, and is thereby insulated from liability even though the therapist ignored other risk factors that the current state of knowledge would indicate were essential to such a judgment.

APPLICATION OF THE AMERICANS WITH DISABILITIES ACT TO PSYCHIATRIC ADVANCE DIRECTIVES

Assessing whether an individual requires proxy or surrogate consent because of incapacity is a significant mental health law/forensic issue (Drogin & Barrett, 2003). Early attention to this issue focused on guardianship (Tor & Sales, 1996), yet many state legislatures have now enacted statutes permitting individuals to create advance directives. An advance directive permits a competent individual to provide direction as to his or her choices regarding treatment if the person later becomes incompetent. In recent years, there has been a growing effort to permit the creation of advance directives for psychiatric care (Swartz, Swanson, & Elbogen, 2004; for a discussion of legal and forensic mental health assessment issues related to competence to provide advance directives, see Chapter 25).

There has been comparatively little significant litigation involving advance directives. However, in 2003, the Federal Court of Appeals for the Second Circuit ruled that a Vermont statute that permitted a psychiatric advance directive to be overridden in some circumstances violated the ADA because it did not permit a similar override of physical health treatment preferences (*Hargrave v. Vermont,* 2003). Nancy Hargrave, who had a diagnosis of paranoid schizophrenia, had designated a surrogate decision maker if she became incompetent and had also prospectively declined "any and all anti-psychotic, neuroleptic, psychotropic, or psychoactive medications"

(p. 32). Vermont law permitted hospital or prison staff to seek a court order authorizing treatment of an incompetent involuntarily committed patient even when the patient had previously declared that he or she did not wish such treatment. It did not permit a court to issue an order in other circumstances, for example, when care for a physical ailment was indicated. Title II of the ADA, the basis of the lawsuit challenging the Vermont statute, provides that "no qualified individual with a disability shall, by reason of such disability, be excluded from participation in or be denied the benefits of the services, programs, or activities of a public entity, or be subjected to discrimination by such entity." The ADA has become an important source of rights for individuals with mental disabilities (Foote, 2003), though the U.S. Supreme Court has recently narrowed its reach, particularly in the context of employment litigation (Petrila, 2002).

Vermont argued before the court of appeals that involuntarily committed individuals constituted a "direct threat" that would remove them from the coverage of the ADA. However, the court rejected this argument, observing that some individuals were civilly committed for reasons other than dangerousness (note that this would be particularly true in jurisdictions adopting the more medically oriented commitment laws described earlier). The court also found that the Vermont law discriminated against individuals with mental illnesses (which are protected under the ADA) because it permitted their treatment preferences to be overturned by a court, something that the statute did not permit for the treatment of physical health conditions.

It has been suggested that *Hargrave,* if followed in other jurisdictions, could ultimately result in the creation of a class of psychiatric inpatients who cannot be treated because of advance directives that decline all forms of medication. It has also been suggested that if this happens, mental health professionals will become even more reluctant to advocate for the creation of advance directives than is already the case (Appelbaum, 2004). At the time of this writing, no other court has addressed the same issue, and so *Hargrave* stands alone as an important reminder of the continuing controversies regarding psychotropic medication and the still developing impact of the ADA.

CONCLUSION

This chapter has described a number of recent cases that reflect broader trends in civil law issues relevant to forensic mental health practice. As noted earlier, the practitioner must understand the laws of his or her own jurisdiction. This is particularly true in the civil area, where much of the relevant law is based on statutory rather than constitutional principles.

A small number of judicial decisions and legislative enactments do not necessarily reflect a national consensus on a particular issue. However, it does seem irrefutable that we are in an era of increasing interest in expanding the reach of civil commitment laws, through outpatient commitment and through more medically oriented inpatient criteria. Statutes permitting intervention *in anticipation of* future deterioration because of mental illness are a particularly noteworthy development and one that bears watching. The tendency of both state and federal courts to defer to legislative judgments in the area of civil commitment is in keeping with a more general realignment of the relationship between the judicial and legislative branches of government that has emerged in the past 2 decades. As a result, legislatures today appear to have more discretion in writing commitment laws than they have had in several decades. In addition, the turn to much more punitive criminal and juvenile justice laws that accelerated in the 1980s and 1990s manifests itself in sexual psychopath laws that promise treatment but may not deliver it. As this chapter makes clear, the courts have not been overly concerned with statutes and practices that differentiate SVPs from other civilly committed individuals, even though the legal foundation for SVP statutes rests on civil commitment law principles.

The duty to warn continues to be an interesting issue. As described here, the *Tarasoff* case has taken several turns in California. Most striking, perhaps, is the manner in which the legal duty that emerged from *Tarasoff* is now largely detached from whether the therapist assessed risk according to prevailing professional norms. Rather, analysis of whether a therapist has breached his or her duty has become a comparatively mechanistic inquiry into whether the therapist actually believed, based largely on threats recounted directly by the patient or, under *Ewing v. Goldstein*, the family, that the patient was a danger to a reasonably identifiable third party. As the law now stands, a therapist could enjoy a full defense under current California law even though he or she reached conclusions regarding risk that were basically uninformed by current knowledge regarding risk assessment.

As our definition of what constitutes forensic mental health practice continues to evolve and as more mental health professionals begin to handle forensic cases as part of a more general clinical practice, the importance of civil law is likely only to increase.

REFERENCES

Addington v. Texas, 441 U.S. 418 (1979).

Appelbaum, P. S. (2004). Psychiatric advance directives and treatment of committed patients. *Psychiatric Services, 55,* 751–752, 763.

Assembly Committee on Judiciary. (1985). Analysis of Assembly bill no. 1133 (1985 Reg. Session).

Birnbaum, M. (1960). The right to treatment. *American Bar Association Journal, 46,* 499–505.

Boynton v. Burglass, 590 So. 2d 446 (Fl. 1991).

Calderon v. Glick, 131 Cal. App. 4th 224 (Cal. 2005).

California Civil Code. 43.92.

Conroy, M. A. (2003). Evaluation of sexual predators. In I. B. Weiner (Series Ed.) & A. Goldstein (Vol. Ed.), *Comprehensive handbook of psychology: Vol. 11. Forensic psychology* (pp. 463–484). Hoboken, NJ: Wiley.

Drogin, E. Y., & Barrett, C. L. (2003). Substituted judgment: Roles for the forensic psychologist. In I. B. Weiner (Series Ed.) & A. Goldstein (Vol. Ed.), *Comprehensive handbook of psychology: Vol. 11. Forensic psychology* (pp. 301–312). Hoboken, NJ: Wiley.

Ewing v. Goldstein, 120 Cal. App. 4th 807 (2004).

Ewing v. Northridge Hospital, 120 Cal. App. 4th 1289 (Cal. 2004).

Florida Statutes Annotated 394.4655.

Foote, W. E. (2003). Forensic evaluation in Americans with Disabilities Act cases. In I. B. Weiner (Series Ed.) & A. Goldstein (Vol. Ed.), *Comprehensive handbook of psychology: Vol. 11. Forensic psychology* (pp. 279–300). Hoboken, NJ: Wiley.

Geller, J. L., Fisher, W. H., McDermeit, M., & White, C. (1998). The rights of state hospital patients: From state hospitals to their alternatives. *Administration and Policy in Mental Health, 25,* 387–401.

Goldstein, A. M. (Ed.). (2003). *Comprehensive handbook of psychology: Vol. 11. Forensic psychology.* Hoboken, NJ: Wiley.

Grisso, T. (1986). *Evaluating competencies: Forensic assessments and instruments.* New York: Kluwer Academic/Plenum Press.

Grisso, T. (2003). *Evaluating competencies: Forensic assessments and instruments* (2nd ed.). New York: Kluwer Academic/Plenum Press.

Group for the Advancement of Psychiatry. (1950). *Psychiatrically deviated sexual offenders* (GAP report 10). Washington, DC: American Psychiatric Association.

Group for the Advancement of Psychiatry. (1977). *Psychiatry and sex psychopath legislation: The 30s to the 80s (GAP report 98).* Washington, DC: American Psychiatric Association.

Hargrave v. Vermont, 340 F.3d 27 (2003).

Hedlund v. Superior Court, 669 P.2d 41 (Cal. 1983).

Heller v. Doe, 509 U.S. 312 (1993).

Hubbart v. Superior Court, 19 Cal. 4th 1138 (1999).

In re Commitment of Dennis, H., 647 N.W.2d 851 (Wis. 2002).

In re Detention of Thorell, 72 P.3d 708 (Wash. 2003).

In re Howard N., 106 P.3rd 305 (Cal. 2005).

In re K. L., 806 N.E.2d 480 (NY 2004).

Jaffee v. Redmond, 516 U.S. 1091 (1996).

Janus, E. S., & Walbek, N. H. (2000). Sex offender commitments in Minnesota: A descriptive study of second generation commitments. *Behavioral Sciences and the Law, 18,* 5–21.

Kansas v. Crane, 534 U.S. 437 (2002).

Kansas v. Hendricks, 521 U.S. 346 (1997).

Kansas Statutes Annotated 59-29a01.

L. 1999, c. 408, New York Legislature.

Lessard v. Schmidt, 349 F. Supp. 1078 (E.D. Wis. 1974).

Melton, G. B., Petrila, J., Poythress, N. G., & Slobogin, C. (1997). *Psychological evaluations for the courts: A handbook for mental health professionals and lawyers* (2nd ed.). New York: Guilford Press.

Monahan, J. (2003). Violence risk assessment. In I. B. Weiner (Series Ed.) & A. Goldstein (Vol. Ed.), *Comprehensive handbook of psychology: Vol. 11. Forensic psychology* (pp. 527–540). Hoboken, NJ: Wiley.

Monahan, J., & Steadman, H. J. (Eds.). (1983). *Mentally disordered offenders: Perspectives from law and social science.* New York: Plenum.

Monahan, J., Steadman, H., Silver, E., Appelbaum, P., Robbins, P., Mulvey, E., et al. (2001). *Rethinking risk assessment: The MacArthur Study of Mental Disorder and Violence.* New York: Oxford University Press.

Newell, L. (1989). America's homeless mentally ill: Falling through a dangerous crack. *New England Journal on Criminal and Civil Confinement, 15,* 277–299.

New York Mental Hygiene Law 9.60.

O'Connor v. Donaldson, 422 U.S. 563 (1975).

Office of Counsel for the New York State Office of Mental Health. (1999). *Summary: An explanation of Kendra's Law.* Retrieved on August 27, 2005, from http://www.omh.state.ny.us/omhweb/Kendra_web/Ksummary.htm.

Oregon Revised Statutes Supplement 426.005(1)(d).

Otto, R. K., & Heilbrun, K. (2002). The practice of forensic psychology: A look to the future in light of the past. *American Psychologist, 57,* 5–18.

Parham v. J. R., 442 U.S. 584 (1979).

Petrila, J. (2002). Law and psychiatry: The U.S. Supreme Court narrows the definition of disability under the Americans with Disabilities Act. *Psychiatric Services, 53,* 797–801.

Petrila, J. (2004). Emerging issues in forensic mental health. *Psychiatric Quarterly, 75,* 3–19.

Petrila, J., & Otto, R. K. (2001). Admissibility of expert testimony in sexually violent predator proceedings. In A. Schlank (Ed.), *The sexual predator: Legal issues, clinical issues, special populations* (p. 3–20). Kingston, NJ: Civic Research Institute.

Phelan, J. C., & Link, B. G. (1998). The growing belief that people with mental illnesses are violent: The role of the dangerousness criterion for civil commitment. *Social Psychiatry and Psychiatric Epidemiology, 33*, S7–S12.

Ridgely, M. S., Borum, R., & Petrila, J. (2001). *The effectiveness of involuntary outpatient treatment: Empirical evidence and the experiences of eight states.* Santa Monica, CA: RAND Corporation.

Rivers v. Katz, 495 N.E.2d 337 (NY 1986).

Roesch, R., & Golding, S. (1980). *Competency to stand trial.* Urbana: University of Illinois Press.

Rouse v. Cameron, 373 F.2d 451 (1966).

Slobogin, C. (2003). Rethinking legally relevant mental disorders. *Ohio Northern University Law Review, 29*, 497–530.

State v. White, 891 So.2d 502 (Fl. 2004).

Steadman, H. J., McGreevey, M. A., Morrissey, J. P., Callahan, L. A., Robbins, P. C., & Cirincione, C. (1993). *Before and after Hinckley: Evaluating insanity defense reform.* New York: Guilford Press.

Swartz, M., & Swanson, J. (2004). Reviewing the empirical data on involuntary outpatient commitment, community treatment orders and assisted outpatient treatment. *Canadian Journal of Psychiatry, 49*, 585–591.

Swartz, M., Swanson, J., & Elbogen, E. (2004). Psychiatric advance directives: Practical, legal, and ethical issues. *Journal of Forensic Psychology Practice, 4*, 97–107.

Swartz, M., Swanson, J., Hiday, V., Wagner, H., Burns, B., & Borum, R. (2001). A randomized controlled trial of outpatient commitment in North Carolina. *Psychiatric Services, 52*, 325–329.

Swartz, M., Swanson, J., Wagner, H., Burns, B., Hiday, V., & Borum, R. (2001). Can involuntary outpatient commitment reduce hospital recidivism? Findings from a randomized trial with severely mentally ill individuals. *American Journal of Psychiatry 1999, 156*, 1968–1975.

Tarasoff v. Regents of the University of California, 529 P.2d 553 (Cal. 1974).

Tarasoff v. Regents of the University of California, 551 P.2d 334 (Cal. 1976).

Tor, P. B., & Sales, B. (1996). Guardianship for incapacitated persons. In B. D. Sales & D. W. Shuman (Eds.), *Law, mental health, and mental disorder* (pp. 202–218). Pacific Grove, CA: Brooks/Cole.

Torrey, E. F., & Zdanowicz, M. (2001). Outpatient commitment: What, why, and for whom. *Psychiatric Services, 52*, 1103–1104.

Wexler, D. (1983). The structure of civil commitment: Patterns, pressures, and interactions in mental health legislation. *Law and Human Behavior, 7*, 1–18.

Wisconsin Statutes. 51.20(1)(a)(2e).

CHAPTER 10

The Role of the Psychologist in Civil Commitment

David F. Mrad and Erik Nabors

Society relies on many institutions—family, school, religion, and employment—to control its members, and it relies most heavily on two systems of control to prevent harm to the community. One, the criminal justice system, provides social control by a punitive-deterrent strategy; the other, the mental health system, uses a predictive-preventive approach (La Fond, 2000). This chapter considers the basic preventive tool of the mental health system: civil commitment. First, we focus on the development of civil commitment procedures from colonial times to the early twentieth century. Then we review the relevant general civil commitment case law from the last half of the twentieth century. Next, we discuss the case law unique to specific populations. Empirical research related to the current rules governing civil commitment is reviewed. We then describe the assessment of violence and assessment and management issues related specifically to patient self-harm. Finally, ethical issues for practitioners are addressed.

FOUNDATIONS OF CURRENT CIVIL COMMITMENT LAW

In the U.S. legal system, the authority of states to commit the mentally ill has evolved under two broad powers, *parens patriae* and the police power. In the early American colonies, the English system, in which the king acted as parens patriae, as "general guardian to all infants, idiots, and lunatics," still existed (Harvard Law Review Association, 1974, p. 1207). Following the American Revolution, state legislatures assumed the parens patriae power to protect minors. The use of parens patriae power to detain mentally ill individuals in order to rehabilitate them is traced to an 1845 decision, *In re Oakes,* by the Massachusetts Supreme Judicial Court (Harvard Law Review Association, 1974). In *Oakes,* the court established the groundwork for future courts to involuntarily commit the mentally ill for treatment and protection from harm (Perlin, 1989). The subsequent parens patriae power, strictly speaking (although not always in practice), is limited to the protection of those who are incapable of acting for their own welfare or those who are incompetent to make decisions in their own interest. This includes individuals whom many states classify as "gravely disabled."

The police power of the state, on the other hand, is the state's "inherent power to protect the public" and, as applied to civil commitment, is used to protect society's interest rather than the interest of the committed patient (Harvard Law Review Association, 1974, p. 1222). The constitutional authority of the state to exercise its police power is established in a 1905 U.S. Supreme Court decision, *Jacobson v. Commonwealth of Massachusetts.* In this holding, the Court upheld a Massachusetts law allowing city boards of health to require their citizens to be vaccinated for smallpox. This power authorized states to prevent individuals from engaging in a variety of activities harmful to themselves and others. Technically, it is this police power, rather than parens patriae, that permits states to commit individuals who are actively suicidal but not "gravely disabled" or otherwise incapable of caring for themselves.

Following *In re Oakes,* states established their own commitment laws, which afforded little in the way of due process protections to patients facing commitment. As late as 1960, the Iowa Supreme Court held that civil commitment was not such a deprivation of liberty as to implicate the 14th Amendment due process clause (Perlin, 1989). That view of civil liberties for the mentally ill, as with many other groups, was about to change drastically in the next 3 decades.

REFORMS AND FOCUS ON PATIENTS' RIGHTS

During the 1960s, a number of changes occurred in society in general, and within the legal system more specifically. These changes, which began by focusing on the rights of minorities and then on prisoners, extended to concern about the rights of the mentally disabled. The opening volleys of the battle for mental patients' rights arguably began at the interface of the criminal justice and mental health systems.

Commitments Originating in the Criminal Justice System

In 1966, the U.S. Supreme Court decided *Baxstrom v. Herold,* concerning the transfer of custody of a mentally ill inmate from the New York Department of Corrections to the Department of Mental Hygiene when his sentence expired. The Court held that the transfer was a violation of equal protection because prisoners in this circumstance were not provided a jury review of their commitment or a judicial determination that they were dangerously mentally ill, rights that were provided to other citizens who faced civil commitment.

Six years later, in *Humphrey v. Cady* (1972), the U.S. Supreme Court heard a similar equal protection claim by a Wisconsin petitioner who had been indefinitely committed under that state's Sex Crimes Act; he was not afforded a jury determination, as would have occurred under the state's Mental Health Act. Citing similarities to *Baxstrom,* the Court reversed and remanded his commitment. More important, in describing the state's civil commitment process, the Court referred to such confinement as "a massive curtailment of liberty" (p. 509), reflecting a view quite divergent from that of Iowa's Supreme Court a dozen years earlier.

The most significant of the civil commitment cases of that period, which initiated in the criminal justice system, was *Jackson v. Indiana* (1972), decided by the U.S. Supreme Court. Although the case in best known for establishing limitations on the duration of commitments for competency restoration, it established an important principle concerning civil commitment more generally. Jackson, who was mentally retarded and deaf, had been found incompetent to stand trial for charges of two robberies, each involving $5 or less. He was committed to the Department of Mental

Health under Indiana's statute until he was certified "sane" (competent to stand trial), virtually a lifelong commitment as there was no realistic hope of Jackson's ever achieving competence. In determining that the Indiana statute violated both his due process and equal protection rights, the Court set forth the following principle: "At the least, due process requires that the nature and duration of commitment bear some reasonable relation to the purpose for which the individual is committed" (p. 738). This constitutional requirement of a "reasonable relation" is frequently referred to in subsequent civil commitment case law. Perlin (1989) referred to this case as "one of the lodestars of substantive civil commitment law" (p. 79).

Liberty Interests and Due Process Reforms

These Supreme Court cases formed the background for the shift from a medical model of commitment to a legal one, but the details were painted in bold relief by a U.S. District Court decision, *Lessard v. Schmidt* (1972). Alberta Lessard was taken to a mental health center in Milwaukee by two police officers, who filled out an emergency detention order. The officers later testified before a judge, restating the allegations against her. The judge issued an order committing her for an additional 10 days and twice extended the temporary detention order for an additional 10 days. A physician at the center filed an application recommending permanent commitment, and the judge appointed two other doctors to examine her. Lessard was not informed of these proceedings. The judge appointed a guardian *ad litem,* and Lessard contacted counsel on her own. A hearing was held, and the judge committed her for an additional 30 days without any explanation other than that she was mentally ill.

A federal class action suit was filed on behalf of Lessard and all other involuntarily committed adult patients in Wisconsin, alleging several due process violations. The court concluded that civil commitment carried with it "loss of basic civil rights and loss of future opportunities" (*Lessard v. Schmidt,* 1972, p. 1090) and established a panoply of procedural rights to apply in civil commitment that closely mirrored those provided in criminal cases: (a) a 48-hour limit on emergency detention prior to a probable cause preliminary hearing; (b) a full hearing no more than 14 days later; (c) detailed advance notice of the hearing; (d) proof beyond a reasonable doubt that the detainee was mentally ill and dangerous, with the latter requiring a "recent overt act"; (e) proof that commitment was the least restrictive alternative; (f) a right to counsel; (g) a privilege against self-incrimination; and (h) exclusion of hearsay testimony.

Although *Lessard* was only a U.S. District Court decision, other courts followed the decision, as did state legislatures who revised commitment statutes in anticipation of similar challenges. In fact, Perlin (1989) referred to *Lessard* as the "high-water mark" of involuntary commitment law. Although not all of the due process procedures required in *Lessard,* such as the standard of proof and the requirement of a recent overt act, survived in subsequent cases, the requirement of dangerousness did. In fact, that requirement was highlighted in one landmark Supreme Court decision, *O'Connor v. Donaldson* (1975).

Kenneth Donaldson had been committed in 1957 to the Florida State Hospital. The commitment, by a county judge, was initiated by Donaldson's father, who thought his son suffered from delusions. He was diagnosed with Paranoid Schizophrenia and committed for "care, maintenance and treatment" for nearly 15 years.

Donaldson made frequent requests for release, but Dr. O'Connor, the superintendent of the hospital, denied them. There was no evidence that Donaldson posed a danger to anyone. During his confinement, he received only "milieu therapy," which the Court described as "enforced custodial care." Donaldson was released a few months after the superintendent retired and filed suit against the superintendent and other staff members, alleging that they "intentionally and maliciously" deprived him of his liberty. A jury awarded Donaldson compensatory and punitive damages, and the court of appeals affirmed the verdict. The court of appeals also held that committed patients had a constitutional right to individualized treatment that would give them a reasonable opportunity to be cured or improve. O'Connor appealed to the Supreme Court.

The Supreme Court held that committing a person indefinitely in simple custodial confinement could not be justified solely by a finding of mental illness, nor could a mentally ill person be confined solely to raise his or her living standards or because of public intolerance. Rather, the Court held, "A State cannot constitutionally confine without more a nondangerous individual who is capable of surviving safely in freedom by himself or with the help of willing and responsible family members or friends" (*O'Connor v. Donaldson,* 1975, p. 576).

O'Connor v. Donaldson represents perhaps the most significant U.S. Supreme Court opinion regarding substantive due process rights for individuals facing civil commitment. Perlin (1989) referred to this case (along with *Jackson v. Indiana*) as one of the "Supreme Court's early 'twin pillars' of civil commitment law" (p. 110). Melton, Petrila, Poythress, and Slobogin (1997) have pointed out that the meaning of the decision has been debated, but it at least emphasized that "the civil commitment process must answer to the Constitution" (p. 303). Parry (1994), however, noted that the Court left unresolved "what 'more' must be provided to nondangerous persons who are civilly committed" (p. 323), as well as whether there was a constitutional right to treatment.

Four years later, the Supreme Court again demonstrated its concern about the due process rights implicated in civil commitment by addressing the standard of proof required in commitment proceedings in *Addington v. Texas* (1979). Frank Addington had been temporarily committed on seven occasions with three indefinite commitments to a state hospital. In 1975, his mother sought indefinite commitment after Addington threatened her. By Texas law, he had a jury trial to determine if he was mentally ill, in need of hospitalization for his own welfare or the protection of others, and incompetent. The judge instructed the jury that a finding that Addington was in need of commitment required "clear, unequivocal and convincing evidence." (*Addington v. Texas,* 1979, p. 421) Addington objected and proposed a "beyond a reasonable doubt" standard, as in criminal cases.

An appeals court sided with Addington and reversed his commitment; however, the Texas Supreme Court reversed the appeals court decision and held that the criteria for commitment need be proven only by "a preponderance of the evidence." The U.S. Supreme Court, however, concluded that an erroneous loss of liberty was of such significance that due process required more substantial proof than preponderance of the evidence. On the other hand, the Court concluded that the consequences of an erroneous commitment were not the same as for a criminal conviction. Civil commitment was not "punitive," and it could not be concluded "that it is much better for a mentally ill person to 'go free' than for a mentally normal person to be committed" (*Addington v. Texas,* 1979, p. 429). Furthermore, psychiatric diagnoses and predictions of dangerousness were too uncertain to require proof beyond a reasonable doubt. The Court held instead that due process required proof by a middle ground: "clear and convincing evidence."

These landmark cases of the 1970s substantially changed the process of civil commitment. Prior to these decisions, civil commitment operated under a medical model justified essentially by parens patriae with little emphasis on protecting the liberty rights of the patient (Melton et al., 1997). After these cases, the procedures and commitment criteria placed greater weight on the due process rights of the committed. Civil commitment now operates under a more "legalistic model" (Melton et al., 1997), requiring not only a showing that patients are mentally ill, but also that they are dangerous or are incapable of living safely in the community. These substantive criteria must be proven in an adversarial judicial proceeding (with the patient represented by an attorney) by, at least, clear and convincing evidence.

Right to Treatment and Right to Refuse Treatment

Although the focus of this chapter is on civil commitment, two important related issues impact the treatment provided to those who have been civilly committed: the rights to treatment and to refuse treatment. Lower courts have held that committed patients have a right to treatment designed to at least improve their mental condition (*Donaldson v. O'Connor,* 1974; *Wyatt v. Aderholt,* 1974), but the U.S. Supreme Court has held only that committed patients have a right to the minimal treatment necessary to ensure their safety and minimize their restraint (*Youngberg v. Romeo,* 1982). Lower courts have held that committed patients who are competent to make treatment decisions retain a right to refuse medication (*Rennie v. Klein,* 1978; *Rivers v. Katz,* 1986; *Rogers v. Okin,*1979); the U.S. Supreme Court has not spoken to the issue. Yet, given their holdings in criminal cases (e.g., see *Riggins v. Nevada,* 1992; *United States v. Sell,* 2003), it is difficult to imagine that the Court would not uphold the right of civilly committed patients to refuse medication except in very limited circumstances. (See Chapter 11 for a full discussion of the rights of individuals to receive or refuse treatment.)

LEGAL APPLICATIONS TO SPECIFIC POPULATIONS

The rules and procedures that have developed for the involuntary civil commitment of mentally ill adults outside the criminal justice process have not been required in the commitment of all other populations.

Children and the Mentally Retarded

The U.S. Supreme Court, in *Parham v. J. R.* (1979), dealt with the question of whether children are entitled to the same due process rights and protections as adults when involuntarily hospitalized. This case involved a suit brought on behalf of two minors, J. R. and J. L., who had been admitted to Central State Hospital in Georgia at the request of the Department of Family and Student Services and parents, respectively. Both had exhibited disruptive behavior and could not be controlled by their parents or foster parents. The questions before the Court were what process was constitutionally due the minor children and whether they had a right to an adversarial hearing. The Court recognized as an important concept the family as a unit, with parents having rights and a "high duty" to make decisions in the child's best interest, and recognized the parents' (or, in the case of J. R., the state's) authority to make medical decisions for the child, even when the child disagrees. They concluded that an adversarial process would *not* be productive because it could lead to greater tension in the parent-child relationship and would needlessly take psychologists and psychiatrists away from their duties to treat children in order to participate in "time-consuming procedural minuets" (p. 605).

The Court expressed some concern about protecting the child's interests in remaining free from restraints and avoiding erroneous labeling as mentally ill, while not undercutting the parents' authority. The Court concluded that requiring a "neutral factfinder," who had the authority to refuse to admit the child, along with periodic independent reviews of continuing need for hospitalization would adequately protect the child's interests. The neutral factfinder would usually be a physician who could make an admission decision, should be independent, and needed to review all sources of information (including interviewing the child), but did not need to conduct a formal adversarial proceeding.

More recently, the U.S. Supreme Court dealt with the rights of civilly committed mentally retarded adults in *Heller v. Doe* (1993). A class action suit was brought in federal court against the State of Kentucky on behalf of mentally retarded persons who had been involuntarily committed. The suit alleged equal protection and due process 14th Amendment violations by Kentucky's commitment laws, which were different for those committed as mentally retarded and those committed as mentally ill. For *both* groups, the state had to prove the substantive criteria of their mental disability, that they presented a danger to themselves or others, and that hospitalization was the least restrictive alternative. For the mentally ill, these criteria had to be proven at the standard of beyond a reasonable doubt, but for the mentally retarded, proof only needed to be by clear and convincing evidence. Furthermore, for the mentally retarded, family members or guardians could participate as a party to the proceedings.

The Court ruled in favor of the state, agreeing that Kentucky had a rational basis for the disparity in standards of proof. The Court reasoned that there is usually documentation of mental retardation from childhood, making it an easier condition to diagnose than mental illnesses. Because mental retardation could be diagnosed more easily and was a more static condition, the Court also reasoned that determinations of dangerousness could be made more accurately. Thus, it believed that the less stringent burden of proof was appropriate and would not lead to more erroneous commitments for the mentally retarded. Additionally, the Court characterized treatments of mental illness as more intrusive, justifying the higher standard for committing the mentally ill.

The Court also concluded in *Heller* that the state had a rational basis for allowing family members and guardians to be parties only in the proceedings against the mentally retarded, reasoning that close relatives of the mentally retarded were likely to have greater knowledge of their abilities and could provide better insights to the court, again minimizing the risk of erroneous commitments. The relatives of the mentally ill were less likely to have useful observations for the court, as the onset of mental illnesses often occurred in adulthood, when individuals were no longer being cared for or supported by family. Additionally, the Court believed that "adults previously of sound mind" who were then diagnosed with mental illness may have a greater need for privacy, justifying limiting the commitment process to "the smallest group compatible with due process" (*Heller v. Doe,* 1993, p. 329).

Criminal Offenders

Some of the most significant and controversial case law in civil commitment originated with cases in the criminal justice system. *Baxstrom, Humphrey,* and *Jackson,* discussed earlier, set the stage for recognition of the liberty interests involved in civil commitment. We now turn to cases involving sentenced inmates, acquittees found not guilty by reason of insanity, and sex offenders.

The first of these cases, *Vitek v. Jones* (1980), involved a mentally ill Nebraska prisoner who was transferred for treatment against his will to a security unit of a state mental hospital. The inmate, Jones, challenged his transfer as a due process violation of the 14th Amendment because he was not provided notice, an adversarial hearing, or counsel before he was transferred. Although already incarcerated, the Court held that transfer to a mental hospital was a change in the conditions of his confinement, not within the sentence imposed on him. The Court reasoned that even incarcerated prisoners maintained a "residuum of liberty," and that transfer to a mental hospital was stigmatizing and subjected the prisoner to "mandatory behavior modification" (p. 494), for which he was entitled to some procedural protections. At the same time, the Court was sensitive to the interests and needs of the correctional institution. Because the liberty interests at stake were not the same as those of a free citizen facing civil commitment, the Court did not require a judicial hearing or representation by an attorney. Instead, the Court held that Jones's rights were adequately protected by an administrative hearing with an independent decision maker in the prison or hospital administration, with adequate notice to permit preparation. He was entitled to be present at the hearing, to present witnesses, and to confront and cross-examine witnesses for the state. He was also entitled to assistance at the administrative hearing by "a qualified and independent advisor," who did not need to be an attorney. These due process rights were similar to ones the Court had granted earlier in inmate disciplinary hearings (*Wolff v. McDonnell,* 1974) and similar to the rights it would grant 10 years later to inmates who refused treatment with psychiatric medications, in *Washington v. Harper* (1990).

Whereas the Court established the constitutional floor of due process rights for prisoners, legislatures, as always, were free to grant more rights within their jurisdictions. In 1984 (as part of the sweeping changes of the Insanity Defense Reform Act), Congress established civil commitment procedures for federal prisoners in Title 18 of the U.S. Code, §§ 4245 and 4246. Section 4245 granted sentenced federal prisoners who objected to mental health treatment a right to a judicial hearing with an attorney representing them and an independent evaluation from an examiner outside the federal prison system. Section 4246 established similar procedures for the continued civil commitment of federal prisoners at the end of their sentences or incompetent federal defendants who were deemed unrestorable. Along with these major changes in the procedures for the involuntary civil commitment of federal prisoners, the Insanity Defense Reform Act included a provision of interest to professional psychology in the implementation statute, § 4247. In specifying the qualifications to conduct examinations under these statutes, § 4247 established parity for psychologists and psychiatrists, stating that the examiner must be a licensed or certified psychiatrist or psychologist. Making psychological testimony equally admissible to psychiatric testimony (and excluding nonpsychiatric physicians) created a role for psychologists in commitment proceedings of federal offenders not always available in traditional state civil commitment hearings.

Another category of civilly committed offenders are those adjudicated not guilty by reason of insanity (NGRI). The U.S. Supreme Court rendered two important decisions regarding this group of offenders, *Jones v. United States* (1983) and *Foucha v. Louisiana* (1992). Michael Jones was found NGRI for petit larceny and was committed to St. Elizabeth's Hospital in Washington, DC, as a danger to himself and others. After more than a year of confinement, he demanded that he be released unconditionally or recommitted under usual civil commitment standards, including a trial by jury and proof of mental illness and dangerousness by clear and convincing evidence. The Court heard the case to decide whether an NGRI acquittee could be confined longer than the sentence for the underlying crime. Jones argued that continued commitment, past the time that he would have been confined if convicted, deprived him of due process protections that the Court had established in *O'Connor* and *Addington.* The Court, however, held that an NGRI finding was "sufficiently probative of mental illness and dangerousness to justify commitment" (p. 363) because it established that the defendant committed the crime and did so due to a mental illness. The Court also reasoned that a finding beyond a reasonable doubt that a person committed a criminal act "certainly indicates dangerousness" (p. 364). The Court stated that dangerousness was established even when the defendant committed only a nonviolent property crime and that it had never held that violence was a prerequisite for a constitutional commitment. The holding in this case appears to be somewhat at odds with those of *Baxstrom* and *Humphrey,* and Perlin (1989) described the impact of those two cases as having been "blunted" by *Jones.*

A decade later, the Court dealt with the continued commitment of an NGRI acquittee in *Foucha v. Louisiana* (1992). Terry Foucha was found NGRI. Four years later, when being considered for release, the examining doctors concluded that he did not suffer from a mental disease but only from an Antisocial Personality Disorder, which, they opined, was not treatable. Because of his behavior while confined, however, the doctors were unable to conclude that he would not be a "menace" to himself or others if released. Louisiana law allowed his continued confinement on the basis of dangerousness alone. Foucha appealed to the U.S. Supreme Court, arguing violations of due process and equal protection, and the Court struck down the Louisiana statute. Whereas in *Jones* it had concluded that the NGRI verdict established that the defendant was mentally ill and dangerous, in *Foucha* the Court held that he could remain confined only until he regained his sanity or was no longer dangerous. Foucha could not be held on dangerousness *alone.* (See A. M. Goldstein, Morse, & Shapiro, 2003, for a thorough discussion of issues related to insanity assessment.)

Interestingly, only a few years later, the Court appeared to change the substantive criteria necessary for indefinite civil commitment when the defendant was a sex offender, in *Kansas v. Hendricks* (1997). Kansas was one of a number of states that enacted a sexually violent predator law allowing for the indefinite civil commitment of a sex offender. Specifically, the law allowed commitment for those who were likely to engage in "predatory acts of sexual violence" due to an "abnormal mental condition" or "personality disorder." Leroy Hendricks, at the end of his prison sentence, was the first person committed under the Kansas law. At trial, he agreed that he suffered from pedophilia, had sexual desires for children, and could not control himself. After his civil commitment, he appealed to the Kansas Supreme Court on the basis of ex post facto, double jeopardy, and substantive due process claims. The court invalidated the law on the basis of the substantive due process claim, holding that civil commitment must be predicated on mental illness. Kansas appealed to the U.S. Supreme Court and Hendricks filed a cross-petition based on the ex post facto and double jeopardy claims.

In a 5 to 4 decision, the Court held that there were no ex post facto and double jeopardy violations because the commitment was not punishment. Perhaps of even greater significance, the entire Court agreed that there was no substantive due process violation because the Kansas law required not only a finding of dangerousness but proof of some additional factor, in this case "mental abnormality" or "personality disorder," which caused the individual's dangerousness to be beyond his or her control. This holding broadened the substantive criteria necessary for commitment by the use of what Melton et al. (1997) referred to as "extremely elastic" terms. La Fond (2000) warned that this decision might "transform substantive due process analysis into a requirement of adequate procedural due process and sufficient evidence" (p. 165). He further warned that, after Hendricks, there may be "no meaningful limit" to what states might construe as a sufficient mental condition for involuntary civil commitment.

Five years later, the U.S. Supreme Court clarified the meaning of the *Hendricks* decision in *Kansas v. Crane* (2002). Crane was also committed under the Sexually Violent Predator Act, but the Kansas Supreme Court reversed his commitment. In interpreting *Hendricks,* the court held that the committing court must find that the defendant cannot control his or her dangerous behavior. The U.S. Supreme Court then reversed the Kansas Supreme Court decision, holding that requiring an "absolute lack of control" would result in preventing the commitment of many dangerous and severely ill individuals. It did, however, hold that the state must prove "serious difficulty in controlling behavior" (p. 413) but it did not establish a more specific bright line. The Court believed this requirement was crucial in distinguishing those who should be civilly committed from those more properly dealt with by the criminal justice system. (See Conroy, 2003, for a thorough discussion of issues related to the assessment of sexually violent predators.)

Voluntary Patients

Although the focus of this chapter is on involuntary civil commitment, it is important to consider a voluntary commitment case, *Zinermon v. Burch* (1990), which should inform clinical practice. Darrell Burch was found disoriented and confused, wandering along a Florida highway in 1981. He signed consent forms and was voluntarily admitted to a mental health center; a few days later, he was transferred for longer term care to Florida State Hospital, where he again signed forms requesting voluntary admission. Notes by Dr. Zinermon, the admitting physician, and other staff indicated that Burch was confused, uncooperative, and believed that he was in "heaven." Burch later signed forms authorizing treatment, indicating that he gave informed consent and understood he had a right to later revoke his consent to treatment. Five months later, after improving, Burch was discharged. He later complained that he did not remember signing consent forms and filed suit in federal court against staff members of Florida State Hospital. He alleged that they had deprived him of liberty without due process and that staff knew or should have known that he was incapable of giving informed consent.

The U.S. District Court dismissed the suit on technical grounds, but the 11th Circuit reversed that decision. Zinermon appealed to the U.S. Supreme Court, which affirmed the appeals court decision. Although much of the Court's holding dealt with issues of tort law, part of its analysis focused on the risk to persons in Burch's situation. The Court reasoned that the "very nature of mental illness" made it foreseeable that some people in need of treatment would be incapable of providing informed consent to treatment or invoking their right to request discharge and yet not meet the substantive criteria for involuntary commitment. Therefore, the state, to protect the patient's due process rights, should initiate involuntary commitment proceedings, which would provide patients adequate protections of their liberty. In keeping with this decision, mental health professionals voluntarily admitting a patient to nonemergency treatment would need to assess the patient's competency to give informed consent. If the patient is incapable of giving such consent, even if he or she is assenting to treatment, the clinician needs to implement involuntary commitment procedures to assure adequate due process protections.

Outpatient Commitment

With the possible exception of sexual predator commitment statutes, the most controversial development in civil commitment in recent years has been the expansion of outpatient commitment. Outpatient commitment in the form of conditional release as a transition from inpatient commitment and as a least restrictive alternative for patients who otherwise qualify for inpatient commitment is not a new phenomenon (La Fond, 2003; Perlin, 2003; Schopp, 2003). A newer, more controversial version, sometimes referred to as "preventive commitment" (La Fond, 2003; Schopp, 2003), often modeled after the statutes of North Carolina (Perlin, 2003), has recently emerged. The North Carolina statutes allow outpatient commitment of those who can live safely in the community with assistance, but who require treatment to prevent greater disability or deterioration that would result in dangerousness, and who are incapable of making an informed decision to seek or comply with voluntary treatment. Thus, these individuals would not at the time of outpatient preventive commitment meet the substantive criteria for involuntary inpatient commitment. According to La Fond, about 20 states now permit this type of outpatient commitment, with the most well-known being *Kendra's Law* in New York State (Perlin, 2003).

A key component of this type of commitment is an involuntary medication regimen. According to both Schopp (2003) and La Fond (2003), critics have argued that this type of commitment circumvents the right (afforded committed inpatients) to refuse psychotropic medications, and does so with a population that does not even meet the criteria that warrant inpatient commitment. La Fond, however, argues that this type of commitment creates a "statutory right" to outpatient treatment. Although federal courts have not yet addressed the constitutional issues involved in such commitments, the U.S. Supreme Court did address the issue of community placement as a least restrictive alternative to institutionalization in *Olmstead v. L. C. ex rel Zimring* (1999). Although this case involved two voluntarily admitted patients, the Court held, on the basis of the Americans with Disabilities Act (ADA), that states were required to place patients in a community rather than an institutional setting when (a) the state's treatment professionals determined it was an appropriate placement, (b) the patient did not oppose the transfer, and (c) the state could reasonably accommodate the placement considering its resources and the needs of other patients. Whether this reasoning regarding the ADA will ultimately be applied to involuntary commitments remains to be seen.

CURRENT PROCEDURES FOR CIVIL COMMITMENT

We now turn to the procedures currently employed in civil commitments, procedures that generally derive from state statutes, which were often written by legislatures in response to the case law described earlier. Although states vary in their procedures and requirements, there are many commonalities resulting from the substantive and procedural due process minimum standards established by the U.S. Supreme Court. Werth (2001), Melton et al. (1997), and Parry (1994) provide excellent summaries of these procedures. As described by Melton et al., all states have at least two stages in their involuntary commitment process. The initial emergency commitment is time limited and generally has minimal procedural safeguards. Parry refers to the initial stage as "short-term commitments" and divides them into emergency commitments, when a person poses an immediate danger to self or others due to a mental disorder; commitments for observation or evaluation to provide for assessments necessary for extended commitments; and temporary commitments, which provide a bridge from emergency commitments to the procedures for extended commitments. Those who can authorize emergency commitments are usually peace officers, clinicians, or specifically designated mental health department administrative personnel. The duration of emergency commitments is typically 48 to 72 hours (Melton et al., 1997), but the duration of all types of short-term commitments ranges from 24 hours to 6 months (Parry, 1994). During the short-term commitment, the clinician must initiate procedures for extended commitments or release the patient at the end of the authorized period of time.

At the extended commitment stage, individuals are provided with a broad set of procedural rights, similar to those provided in criminal proceedings, including judicial determination in an adversarial proceeding (Melton et al., 1997). Parry (1994) tabulated and summarized the standards for extended commitment in all 50 states and the District of Columbia and found that almost all jurisdictions had commitment statutes containing at least a definition of the types of mental disorders covered and the impairments or criteria that justify commitment. The types of disorders typically had to be "severe" or "gross." Many jurisdictions specifically excluded some disorders, most commonly "mental retardation, epilepsy, developmental disabilities, drug addiction, and alcoholism" (p. 323). In summary, Parry concluded that the "typical jurisdiction" limited involuntary commitment to individuals with (a) severe or substantial mental illness, (b) which results in danger to themselves or others or grave disability, and (c) for which inpatient hospitalization is the least restrictive alternative.

More recently, Werth (2001) reviewed the commitment statutes of all 50 states and the District of Columbia, with a specific focus on the commitment criteria related to self-harm. He found that all 51 jurisdictions required mental illness and dangerousness to self (or others) to qualify for involuntary commitment. Forty-four of the jurisdictions provided at least minimal definitions of the mental illness required, and 34 had explicit descriptions of dangerousness to self. Werth also found that 43 of the jurisdictions required that the dangerousness to self be a result of the mental illness. Some jurisdictions also required that the mentally ill person be incapable of making reasonable treatment decisions. Werth considered whether involuntary commitment was required or was merely an option when a mentally ill person presented a danger of self-harm. He was able to obtain "firm data" from 26 jurisdictions, and of those, only two (Missouri and New Jersey) had statutes that mandated a clinician attempt involuntary commitment in these instances.

These studies highlight the necessity for clinicians to be knowledgeable of the specific requirements and procedures in the jurisdiction(s) of their practice. Depending on the state, forensic psychologists will find themselves involved in assessing a patient's risk to self or others, finding or ruling out less restrictive alternatives to hospitalization, seeking or authorizing emergency commitment, assessing emergency-detained patients and testifying in extended commitment hearings (although some states limit this to medical doctors), and assessing risk of committed patients to determine suitability for discharge or conditional release. Civil commitment practice requires not only the usual skills of diagnosing and treatment planning but also the more specific skills of assessing risks of danger to others or self-harm. Elaborating on all of these assessments is beyond the scope of this chapter, and in recent years the forensic literature has included numerous excellent resources on the assessment of risk to others (e.g., see Meloy, 2000; Monahan, 2003; Monahan et al., 2001). We briefly review those findings prior to a more detailed review of the assessment of self-harm.

THE VIOLENCE RISK LITERATURE

Psychologists' ability to predict violence has improved greatly in recent years. Instruments such as the Violence Risk Appraisal Guide (VRAG) and the HCR-20 have particularly helped to improve experts' ability to predict violence (G. T. Harris, Rice, & Cormier, 2002; G. T. Harris, Rice, & Quinsey, 1993; Heilbrun, Marczyk, & DeMatteo, 2002; Meloy, 2000).

Unfortunately, these instruments may not be useful in U.S. civil commitment dangerousness assessments. First, there are problems of generalizability. The VRAG and HCR-20, widely considered some of the best instruments in the field, are both normed on male Canadian criminal offenders (Douglas & Webster, 1999; G. T. Harris et al., 1993). As such, their ability to accurately predict future violence in other populations is uncertain. Second, both instruments predict violence over a multiyear period. Although this time frame is relevant for questions of correctional sentencing or capital punishment, it does not fit the civil commitment time frame of imminent harm to others.

Although not a perfect match, results from the MacArthur Study of Mental Disorder and Violence (Monahan et al., 2001) are more applicable to U.S. civil commitment proceedings. First, the MacArthur participant pool was more diverse than the VRAG and HCR-20 pools as participants came from three different regions of the United States, were White, African American, and Hispanic, and did not necessarily have a criminal record. Second, to date, the most studied outcome period has been 20 weeks since baseline, a time frame more similar to the civil commitment period of imminent risk.

Because the MacArthur study is the premier work on violence in terms of methodology and applicability to civil commitment proceedings, we focus on its findings here. The reader is cautioned, however, to consider that given the short time frame involved in civil commitment, idiographic factors may be central to a civil commitment assessment of dangerousness.

The MacArthur Study of Mental Disorder and Violence

The MacArthur study followed more than 900 individuals for up to 1 year in the community following release from one of three U.S. psychiatric institutions. A wide array of variables were measured before release, and then participants and a collateral contact were reinterviewed every 10 weeks for up to 1 year. Of primary concern in these follow-up interviews was whether the participant had engaged in violent behavior. There were two primary statistical analyses. First, a stepwise logistic regression examined the relationship between the variables measured at baseline and subsequent violence within the first 20 weeks following discharge. Second, classification tree (CT) analyses examined how different variables interact to increase or decrease risk among subjects (Monahan et al., 2001).

The stepwise logistic regression identified 18 variables that were significantly related to violence (either as risk or protective factors) within the first 20 weeks following discharge. These 18 variables were presence of psychopathy (risk); seriousness of child abuse (risk); frequency of prior arrests (risk); father's drug use (risk); threat/control-override symptoms (protective); increasing Brief Psychiatric Rating Scale (BRRS) Hostility Rating score (risk); prior loss of consciousness (risk); having been employed prior to hospitalization (protective); increasing BPRS Activation Rating score (protective); increasing Novaco Anger Scale, Behavioral Rating score (risk); involuntary admission status (risk); violent fantasies, single target focus (risk); presence of grandiose delusions (risk); increasing score on the Barratt Impulsiveness Scale, Nonplanning subscale (protective); increasing number of mental health professionals in the participant's social network (protective); a drug abuse diagnosis (risk); violent fantasies with escalating seriousness (risk); and increasing BPRS Total Score (protective). Together, these 18 variables accounted for approximately 80% of the variance in outcome (Monahan et al., 2001, pp. 94, 98).

Monahan and colleagues (2001) also used CT analysis to examine how the variables interacted with each other to affect the risk of violence. Classification tree analysis creates empirically driven classification trees that group participants together based on their risk for a given outcome depending on their values for a set of variables. The first of these analyses, which considered all variables, successfully classified 477 participants (50.8%) of subjects as either high or low risk after one iteration, and classified all remaining participants after four iterations, each of which started with any participants who had not been classified in the earlier trees (pp. 100–101).

The authors then constructed two "clinically feasible" CT models which included only variables that most clinicians would realistically be able to assess (Monahan et al., 2001, p. 108). The clinically feasible models classified 429 participants (45.6%) as either high or low risk after one iteration, and classified the remaining 510 participants after three iterations (p. 110).

The logistic regression and CT models produced similar results in terms of the number of participants classified as low or high risk, although they often classified individual participants differently, suggesting that each model was capturing a different aspect of violence. In short, perhaps there are different pathways by which people become violent, and any given model may capture only one such pathway. If this is true, then any one model will successfully predict violence only in individuals who take that pathway to violence, and not those who take a different path.

With this in mind, the MacArthur researchers next constructed 10 different CTs, each with a different initial variable and each presumably capturing a different aspect of violence. Individual participants' risk for violence was then considered in light of how they were classified in each of the 10 models. Analysis of these results suggested that use of 5 models maximized the amount of new information on violence risk to be found, making further models unnecessary (Monahan et al., 2001, p. 122).

Although the authors acknowledged that use of these five models, and the resulting calculations required to classify a given individual, was beyond the scope of the average practicing clinician, they noted that the task lends itself to computer software. With this in mind, researchers have started the process of developing a software-based assessment interview that collects all needed data for various models of violence and classifies a given individual on each of these models (Monahan et al., 2001, p. 127).

Finally, results from the MacArthur study indicated that men were more likely to be violent than women and that prior violence and criminal behavior increased risk for violence, as did the presence of violent thoughts and command hallucinations focused on violence. Other major findings were that whereas a co-occurring substance abuse or dependence diagnosis was apparently a key factor in increasing risk for violence, a diagnosis of a major mental disorder was associated with a lower risk than other disorders. In addition, delusions, even those involving violent content, were not associated with an increased risk for violence. Finally, results also indicated that risk for subsequent violence may be affected by the neighborhood in which patients are placed after hospitalization (Monahan et al., 2001; see Monahan, 2003, for a thorough discussion of issues related to violence risk assessment).

THE SUICIDE RISK LITERATURE

To date, researchers have identified several risk factors for suicide. Because an exhaustive review of these factors is beyond the scope of this chapter, we focus on those with the strongest empirical support. Before reviewing these factors, two major methodological weaknesses of the suicide prediction literature should be noted. First, there is a marked inconsistency across studies as to what constitutes a suicide (see Conwell, Duberstein, & Caine, 2002), with some studies including only purposeful, self-inflicted deaths (e.g., Kellerman et al., 1992), others including accidental deaths (e.g., Hawton, Zahl, & Weatherall, 2003), and still others using different inclusion criteria (e.g., Mann, Waternaux, Haas, & Malone, 1999; Sidley, Calam, Wells, Hughes, & Whitaker, 1999). Second, much of the literature is based on Western European samples that contain data that in some instances are several decades old (e.g., E. C. Harris & Barraclough, 1997; Hawton et al., 2003; Qin, Agerbo, & Mortensen, 2003). As such, there are important questions of generalizability and applicability of the literature to predicting suicide in a contemporary U.S. population.

Mental and Personality Disorders

In their meta-analysis, E. C. Harris and Barraclough (1997) found that of the 44 mental disorders considered, 36 were associated with a statistically significant increased risk for suicide, and five were associated with a nonstatistically significant, though still notable, increased risk. Disorders with a particularly strong association included Major Depression and substance abuse of sedatives and multiple drugs. In their respective literature reviews, Tanney (1992) and Roy (2001) also concluded that the presence of depressive symptoms was consistently and reliably associated with an increased risk for suicide. Roy added that the risk is even greater when a comorbid disorder is present. Additional research has suggested that high levels of hopelessness may be a particularly strong predictor of future suicide (see Balon, 1987; Diesrud, Roysamb, Ekeberg, & Kraft, 2001; King, Baldwin, Sinclair, Baker, et al., 2001; Kuo, Gallo, & Eaton, 2004; Mann et al., 1999; Maris, 1992a).

Research has also shown a relationship between Schizophrenia and increased risk for suicide, although the strength of the relationship may depend on the symptom profile. Allebeck and Allgulander (1990) reported that in their sample of 50,000 Swedish men, a diagnosis of Schizophrenia had the strongest association with suicide out of the several mental disorders considered. In their meta-analysis, however, E. C. Harris and Barraclough (1997) found that although Schizophrenia was a statistically significant risk factor, the relationship was not nearly as strong as with other disorders. More recent research has suggested that the particular symptom profile may influence risk for suicide. After analyzing data from a sample of individuals with Schizophrenia or other psychotic disorder, Radmonsky, Haas, Mann, and Sweeney (1999) found that patients with an affective component to their disorder were at increased risk for suicidal behavior. Roy (2001) reported that the Paranoid Schizophrenia subtype has a stronger association with suicide than forms of Schizophrenia with predominantly negative symptomatology.

Research on the relationship between substance abuse and suicide has produced inconsistent results. Some studies suggest that the presence of substance abuse increases risk for suicide; others found either no relationship or an inverse one. After reviewing the literature, Lester (1992) concluded that substance abuse is a significant risk factor for suicide and suggested that both are examples of an underlying pattern of self-destructive behavior. Allebeck and Allgulander (1990) reported that heavy consumption of alcohol was a statistically and clinically significant risk factor for suicide. E. C. Harris and Barraclough (1997) similarly found that substance abuse was a statistically and clinically significant risk factor for suicide in their meta-analysis and, in fact, was one of the strongest of the dozens of factors considered. There were, however, marked differences in risk among specific substances of abuse. For example, the difference in risk between use of sedatives (high risk) and marijuana (lower risk) was approximately 11-fold.

More recent research, however, has found a negative relationship between substance abuse and risk for suicide. Powell, Geddes, Deeks, Goldacre, and Hawton (2000) found that in their sample of English psychiatric inpatients, substance abuse was associated with a decreased risk for suicide. King Baldwin, Sinclair, Baker, et al. (2001) found similar results in their sample of more than 200 released English psychiatric patients. As these results were contrary to years of research, the authors of both studies suggested that participants in the substance abuse category may have had less severe levels of psychopathology compared to other groups, resulting in the general category of substance abuse failing to be significantly associated with suicide.

Although anxiety disorders have received relatively less attention than other disorders, research suggests that the presence of an anxiety disorder, broadly defined, increases the risk for suicide (see E. C. Harris & Barraclough, 1997). The risk may vary, however, among different types of anxiety disorders. Tanney (1992) has argued that whereas anxiety disorders with panic as a central feature pose a greater risk for suicide, other anxiety disorders such as Obsessive-Compulsive Disorder and somatoform disorders do not. Vickers and McNally (2004) found that data from the National Comorbidity Survey indicated that Panic Disorder on its own does not increase risk for lifetime suicide attempt, although it was a marker for comorbidity, which was itself associated with an increased risk. Placidi et al. (2000) have suggested that anxiety may actually serve as a protective factor for suicide if it heightens fears of death or injury.

Recent research has suggested that the presence of certain personality disorders also increases risk for suicide. Baxter and Appleby (1999) found an association between personality disorders and increased risk for suicide in their sample of almost 8,000 English participants. Foster, Gillespie, McClelland, and Patterson (1999) reported that personality disorders, particularly Antisocial, Avoidant, and Dependent, were associated with an increased risk for suicide, and that comorbid Axis I and II disorders posed a greater risk for suicide than the presence of an Axis I disorder alone. Soloff, Lynch, Kelly, Malone, and Mann (2000) reported that participants with Borderline Personality Disorder not only had a history of medically serious suicide attempts, but also had high levels of hopelessness and impulsivity, which were also associated with an increased risk for suicide. These results support Linehan's (1993) contention that individuals with Borderline Personality Disorder pose a serious risk for completed suicide. Black, Blum, Pfohl, and Hale (2004) specifically warn clinicians to not underestimate the risk of completed suicide in patients with Borderline Personality Disorder and provide a thorough review of the literature addressing risk factors in this population.

Demographic Characteristics

A large body of research indicates that relatively more men than women commit suicide, and relatively more White men commit suicide than any other group (Balon, 1987; R. B. Goldstein, Black, Nasrallah, & Winokur, 1991; Joe & Kaplan, 2001; Maris, 1992b; Myers, 1988; Qin, Agerbo, Westergard-Nielsen, Eriksson, & Mortensen, 2000; Schapira, Linsley, Linsley, Kelly, & Kay, 2001). It should be noted that although relatively more men successfully complete suicide, comparatively more women attempt it (Maris, 1992b). This difference has often been attributed to women's choice of less lethal means (McIntosh, 1992). Qin and colleagues suggest that this apparent difference in suicide rates could also be due to differences in risk factors between the sexes, or failing to control for factors such as social support, treatment contact, and substance abuse when examining sex differences.

Research has consistently shown higher rates of suicide among Whites than other racial groups (Balon, 1987; Canino & Roberts, 2001; Joe & Kaplan, 2001; Maris, 1992a). Joe and Kaplan suggest that the difference between Caucasians and African Americans may stem from the underreporting of suicide in the African American community and/or differences in risk factors between the groups. They further suggest that suicide rates among African Americans may be relatively unstable, with those who live in areas marked by significant differences in occupational and economic status with Caucasians at higher risk than African Americans who live elsewhere.

More recent research has specifically looked at African American samples to identify which risk factors are unique to African Americans as well as which factors identified in earlier work apply to African Americans. In their sample of largely poor African Americans with relatively low levels of education, Kaslow and colleagues (2004) found risk factors similar to those for the population as a whole. Willis, Coombs, Drentea, and Cockerham (2003), however, found that among their sample of African Americans, higher levels of education decreased risk, contrary to what has been reported in other groups.

Research indicates that elderly individuals are at greater risk for suicide than are others (see American Psychiatric Association, 2003; Conwell, Duberstein, & Caine, 2002). Furthermore, deaths due to indirect self-destructive behaviors such as intentionally failing to comply with medical treatment may not be counted as suicides even though they are intentionally brought about (Brown, Bongar, & Cleary, 2004; A. M. Goldstein, 1980). If so, this would suggest that the true difference in suicide rates between the elderly and other age groups is larger than that generally reported. Conwell and colleagues argue that the higher suicide rate among the elderly may be due to "diminished physical resilience and greater isolation . . . as well as their greater determination to die" (p. 195). Finally, it is worth noting that although there is a greater risk for suicide among the elderly across the population as a whole, this pattern does not hold true for African American males, who are at greatest risk for suicide in early adulthood (American Psychiatric Association, 2003).

Previous Attempts and Current Ideation

A history of self-harm and/or suicide attempt is a well-supported risk factor for future suicide (Maris, 1992a; Roy, 2001). E. C. Harris and Barraclough (1997) reported that of the approximately 50 risk factors included in their meta-analysis, a history of suicide attempt was one of the strongest. Maser et al. (2002) and Nordstrom, Asberg, Aberg-Wistedt, and Nordin (1995) found similar results in a U.S. and Swedish sample, respectively. Conner, Langley, Tomaszewski, and Conwell (2003) found that in their sample of New Zealanders, a history of nonsuicidal self-harm increased risk for future suicidal and nonsuicidal self-harm. Analysis of an English sample of more than 11,000 participants found that a history of self-harm, regardless of intent, increased risk for future suicide (Hawton et al., 2003).

The presence of current suicidal ideation is considered an important risk factor for suicide. The American Psychiatric Association's (2003) *Practice Guideline for the Assessment and Treatment of Patients with Suicidal Behaviors* stresses that suicidal ideation is not a dichotomous factor (i.e., present or absent) but, rather, can indicate various levels of increased risk in light of the frequency, duration, and specifics of the ideation.

Social Support

Research on social support has found that a lack of support can increase risk for suicide (Balon, 1987; Tanney, 1992). Allebeck and Allugander (1990) found that among their sample of 50,000 Swedes, a lack of friends was a risk factor for suicide. Qin and colleagues (2000) similarly found that retirement was a risk factor for suicide among Danish males, and being single was a risk factor for both men and women. Schapira and colleagues (2001) found similar results in an English sample in which participants who were living alone and/or were single were at higher risk for suicide than others.

The mere presence of family members does not, however, necessarily decrease risk for suicide. Nordentoft and Rubin (1993) reported that the most frequently offered reason for a suicide attempt in their study was a recent conflict with a family member, suggesting that, for some, the presence of a family may serve to increase risk. Kelly, Soloff, Lynch, Haas, and Mann (2000) found that among inpatients with a diagnosis of Major Depressive Episode, Borderline Personality Disorder, or both, low social adjustment within and beyond the family predicted attempter status. Joe and Kaplan (2001) have similarly suggested that poor family functioning may increase the risk for suicide in African Americans. Empirically derived models for suicide risk, developed by Diesrud and colleagues (2001), suggest that the experience of loneliness associated with poor social support may underlie the relationship between social support and risk.

Other Risk Factors

Higher levels of impulsivity have been linked to an increased risk for suicidal behaviors among psychiatric inpatients in general (Mann et al., 1999) and those diagnosed with Borderline Personality Disorder in particular (Brodsky, Malone, Ellis, Dulit, & Mann, 1997). Oquendo and colleagues (2000), however, found no such connection among individuals diagnosed with Bipolar I Disorder, although there was a relationship between higher levels of lifetime aggression and suicidal behavior. This second finding is consistent with research that found a connection between impulsive aggression and suicidal behaviors in different groups (adult inpatients with a wide array of diagnoses: Mann et al., 1999; mood disordered adult inpatients and their offspring: Brent et al., 2002; adult inpatients who met diagnostic criteria for depression: Brodsky et al., 2001; adult inpatients meeting criteria for Borderline Personality Disorder and Major Depressive Disorder: Soloff et al., 2000).

Given the intuitive link between poor problem-solving skills and possible suicidal behavior, the empirical literature on such a relationship is surprisingly limited. An often cited study by Schotte and Clum (1987) found deficits in problem-solving skills among inpatients identified as suicidal compared to controls. These deficits included poor confidence in their ability to solve problems as stress level increased, difficulty generating alternative solutions to problems, focusing on negative consequences to potential solutions, and poor execution of solutions. This finding is consistent with work by Malone et al. (2000), which found that greater survival and coping skills differentiated inpatients with and without a history of suicide attempt.

Being a parent has also been linked to reduced risk for suicide, although recent research suggests that the relationship is not necessarily straightforward. Qin and colleagues (2003) found that in their Dutch sample, parents of young children were at a particularly lower risk for suicide, although parents of children who had committed suicide or had a history of psychiatric hospitalization when their parents did not were at increased risk.

Although considered by many to be an important protective factor, religious beliefs have received relatively little attention in the literature. What research has been conducted suggests that increased levels of religiosity are associated with decreased risk for suicide (Kehoe & Gutheil, 1994) and that these differences are not simply due to increased social contact or support (Neeleman, Wessely, & Lewis, 1998). Others have suggested, however, that if one's religion leads to a belief that the individual has committed a grave sin, risk for suicide may actually increase (Exline, Yali, & Sanderson, 2000).

Research has also shown that contact with a mental health professional is linked to a decreased risk for suicide. For example, in two separate studies by King and colleagues (King, Baldwin, Sinclair, Baker, et al., 2001; King, Baldwin, Sinclair, & Campbell, 2001), a naturally occurring disruption in care increased the risk for suicide among both outpatients and inpatients. Given the change among inpatients, the increase in risk is likely not simply due to less monitoring, but rather an interruption in the specific treatment relationship.

Finally, research suggests that access to a firearm increases risk for suicide. One study found a relationship between access to a firearm and suicide among adults 50 years or older in the Rochester, New York, area (Conwell, Duberstein, Connor, et al., 2002). This relationship remained significant even after controlling for psychiatric illness. Among gun owners in their sample, storing the weapon loaded and unlocked was an independent predictor of suicide. Kellermann and colleagues (1992) also found an association between access to a firearm and suicide among all completed suicides in two Tennessee counties between 1987 and 1990. This relationship remained significant even after controlling for living alone, taking psychotropic medication, history of substance abuse, and having not completed high school.

ASSESSMENT AND MANAGEMENT OF RISK

For the past 20 years, researchers have maintained that the accurate prediction of suicide is extremely difficult, if not impossible (Balon, 1987; R. B. Goldstein et al., 1991; Jacobs, Brewer, & Klein-Benheim, 1999; Pokorny, 1983). The extreme difficulty, perhaps even impossibility, of accurately predicting a suicide should not, however, cause undue concern for forensic mental health professionals. Recognizing the difficulty inherent in suicide prediction, legal liability following a patient's death will rest not on the inaccuracy of the prediction, but on the process by which that prediction was made (Blinder, 2004; White, 1999).

The current consensus is that when conducting suicide assessments, forensic mental health experts should assess a wide variety of empirically linked factors but use their clinical judgment and skill to determine the weight each factor should receive for a given patient. One note of caution, however: When deciding how many factors to assess, more is not necessarily better. Although assessing areas without a strong empirical link to suicide may be relevant in some situations, assessing too many additional areas may prove problematic in two ways. First, the expert who assesses several areas without an empirical link to suicide may give the impression that he or she is unfamiliar with the literature and is simply assessing every conceivable factor. Attacks on the validity of such an assessment could, however, be minimized if the clinician is clear in the report as to the reasons for assessing the nonempirically linked areas and the bases for the decision. Second, assessing a multitude of areas will produce a significant amount of information. With every new piece of data, the chances of an expert overlooking or failing to consider the importance of relevant information increases. Should a decision on suicide risk prove inaccurate and a subsequent review of the expert's work reveal one or two important pieces of information that were overlooked, the likelihood of the clinician's being found liable increases.

Management of Risk

The empirical literature on reducing suicide risk is limited in size, hampered by methodological inconsistencies and shortcomings, and is only mildly supportive of even the seemingly best interventions (Arensman et al., 2001; Pearson, Stanley, King, & Fisher, 2001). Furthermore, given the statistical rarity of suicide and the extremely large sample sizes required to adequately assess interventions, strong support for specific methods is not likely to be realized in the near future. Recommendations for managing a suicidal patient are, therefore, broad.

In addition to basic therapeutic strategies such as developing and maintaining a strong therapeutic alliance with the patient and developing a case conceptualization and associated treatment plan, there are additional steps involved in managing suicide risk. Treating clinicians working with a suicidal patient may need to establish more contacts with important people in the patient's life than would otherwise be warranted or even appropriate. The initial assessment that leads to emergency commitment may be conducted by a treating clinician if the patient happens to be in therapy at the time. Often, however, suicide risk assessments will be conducted by a clinician in the role of an evaluating forensic expert who will establish different expectations concerning confidentiality and contact with collateral sources than those established in a therapeutic relationship. This is most commonly the case when a patient is seen in an emergency room setting or is being assessed during a short-term emergency commitment to determine whether longer term commitment should be pursued.

Documentation of all contact with the patient, all information gathered, and the reasoning supporting the expert's opinions is extremely important. Should the patient commit suicide and the clinician subsequently be sued, the documentation of the patient's case will be the most important, if not the only, evidence considered. Typically, information that is not documented does not exist as far as the legal fact finder is concerned. In addition, because a patient's risk for suicide is dynamic, ongoing assessment of risk is important to successful management. Subsequent assessments will, of course, be shorter in duration and typically less work intensive than the initial assessment, as historical information that has already been gathered need not be regathered, but assessment of dynamic risk and protective factors, including current distress, hopelessness, and social support, will continue to be essential (American Psychiatric Association, 2003; White, 1999).

Most essential is determining whether inpatient treatment is warranted, even if the patient refuses to agree to hospital admission. This decision will ultimately rest on the expert's estimation of suicide risk based on the information gathered in the assessment and an appreciation for both the empirical literature on risk for self-harm and an understanding of the patient's idiosyncratic characteristics (American Psychiatric Association, 2003).

Finally, a warning on the use of both "no-suicide contracts," in which the patient "contracts" with the health care provider to not hurt himself or herself over a given time period, and suicide risk questionnaires in an assessment. Recent work has stressed that there is no empirical support for the use of such contracts, and their value as protection against liability is equally uncertain (American Psychiatric Association, 2003). In addition, it is advised that experts avoid using a questionnaire on suicide risk either alone or as a major component of an assessment. The primary reason for not relying on such questionnaires is their poor psychometric properties. As Simon (2004) explains:

> Self-administered suicide scales tend to be overly sensitive but lack specificity. Moreover, checklists cannot encompass all the pertinent suicide risk factors for a specific patient. A checklist may not contain the patient's unique suicide risk factors. Moreover, a suicide risk factor that a patient does display may be overlooked and not checked. (p. 26)

This viewpoint is shared by the American Psychiatric Association's (2003) *Practice Guideline for the Assessment and Treatment of Patients with Suicidal Behaviors:*

> Although suicide assessment scales have been developed for research purposes, they lack the predictive validity necessary for use in routine clinical practice. Therefore, suicide assessment scales may be used as aids to suicide assessment but should not be used as predictive instruments or as substitutes for a thorough clinical evaluation. (p. 3)

Valuable Resources

As evident from the previous discussion, the suicide risk literature is plentiful at best and overwhelming and contradictory at worst. As such, individual works that guide the clinician through the evaluation and management of a client at risk for suicide are very valuable. Some examples of such work are offered.

American Psychiatric Association Practice Guideline

A particularly useful resource for the assessment of suicide risk, and intervention when necessary, is the *Practice Guideline for the Assessment and Treatment of Patients with Suicidal Behaviors* prepared by the American Psychiatric Association (2003), available on the Association's web site (www.psych.org). While the Association is careful to state that the *Practice Guideline* is not intended as a standard of care, it provides an excellent review of the assessment and prediction literature, including a list of factors to assess, specific questions that can be helpful to ask, and other suggestions for conducting a suicide risk assessment.

Once all relevant data have been collected, the *Practice Guideline* recommends that clinicians estimate risk based on their knowledge of the patient and their clinical judgment. In fact, the *Practice Guideline* argues that the final estimation of suicide risk is the "quintessential clinical judgment, since no study has identified one specific risk factor or set of risk factors as specifically predictive of suicide or other suicidal behaviors" (American Psychiatric Association, 2003, p. 12). This final estimation of risk is not a dichotomous at-risk or not-at-risk decision, but places the patient along a continuum of risk. The *Practice Guideline* describes how to translate the estimation of risk into appropriate intervention techniques, documentation of the entire assessment and treatment process, and how to limit liability.

How to Identify Suicidal People

The book *How to Identify Suicidal People* (White, 1999) is another valuable resource for assessing suicide risk. Based on the literature and the author's clinical experience, *How to Identify Suicidal People* reviews risk and protective factors and makes recommendations for how to conduct a suicide risk assessment and how to limit potential liability. The areas reviewed and recommendations offered are similar to those in the American Psychiatric Association's *Practice Guideline,* although *How to Identify Suicidal People* goes further, describing the logistics of performing a suicide risk assessment.

Specific Articles of Import

The primary legal question in any lawsuit against an expert is typically, "Did the defendant expert act in accordance with the standard of care?" As such, Peruzzi and Bongar (1999) surveyed clinicians as to what factors they believed important to assess when estimating suicide risk in depressed clients. Respondents listed almost 50 factors they regularly considered when estimating suicide risk, the most common of which included medical seriousness of previous suicide attempts, a history of previous attempts, acute suicidal ideation, and severe hopelessness. Canapary,

Bongar, and Cleary (2002) conducted a similar survey, focusing on patients with alcohol dependence, and found that many of the same factors as those identified in the Peruzzi and Bongar study were among the most often assessed areas. Brown et al. (2004) found similar results in their study of factors commonly assessed when evaluating risk in elderly clients.

ETHICAL CONSIDERATIONS

Any decision regarding civil commitment necessarily involves balancing the need to maintain confidentiality with concern for the patient's safety (American Psychological Association [APA], 2002, Ethics Code, Section 4.01, "Maintaining Confidentiality," and 4.05, "Disclosures"). When an expert recommends commitment, information is divulged about the patient in open court in support of the opinion that commitment is appropriate. Balanced with this concern is the patient's safety and well-being (Ethics Code, Section 4.05, allowing for disclosure of information to "protect the client/patient . . . from harm"). Although condoned and even required by APA's Ethics Code, it remains true that when a treating clinician recommends civil commitment, one of the central features of a strong and beneficial clinical relationship, confidentiality, will be sacrificed. Of course, evaluating forensic experts should clarify the lack of confidentiality at the initiation of the assessment.

A decision to civilly commit a patient also inherently involves choosing to relate to the patient in a paternalistic manner at the expense of the patient's autonomy. Although no particular section of the APA Ethics Code requires respect for client autonomy, Principle E of the Ethics Code, "Respect for People's Rights and Dignity," states, "Psychologists respect . . . the rights of individuals to . . . self-determination." Civil commitment, however, is a strong denial of self-determination. Bluntly stated, when a patient is civilly committed, that patient is, in effect, told, "You are incapable of running your life at this point, so the courts/hospital/doctors are going to run it for you." This may be a relatively easy decision in some situations (e.g., a patient with Paranoid Schizophrenia experiencing psychotic hallucinations and delusions who plans on killing himself before the CIA can abduct him); other situations may pose a more difficult decision (e.g., a patient with a history of Paranoid Schizophrenia who responds marginally well to medication but who wishes to die rather than become a burden to his family or a ward of the state).

Finally, the expert working with a patient at noticeable risk for self-harm must be certain to follow the empirical literature where relevant and appropriate, even if doing so provokes anxiety and concern for one's career. Ethics Code, Section 2.04, "Bases for Scientific and Professional Judgments," states, "Psychologists' work is based upon established scientific and professional knowledge of the discipline." For the sake of illustration, consider a hypothetical patient who, by every state-of-the-art evaluation, is at moderate, though not imminent, risk for suicide. When working with such a patient, some experts may be tempted to recommend commitment, even though the patient does not fall into the typical statutory language of imminent risk, in an attempt to avoid potential lawsuits and/or painstakingly close scrutiny of their work should the patient commit suicide, viewing commitment as the "safer" option to noncommitment. Ethics Code, Section 2.04, however, requires that clinicians inform their work with the available empirical literature. In a situation such as this, an empirically informed decision to not recommend commitment will likely be significantly more anxiety provoking than the seemingly safer and easier route of recommending involuntary hospitalization.

CONCLUSION

Over the past 3 decades, the criteria and procedures for civil commitment have changed substantially. Although civil commitment continues to play an important role in the protection of the mentally disabled and society as a whole, it has evolved from the more paternalistic medical model to a more legalistic one, by which patients' liberty interests are given at least as much consideration as their treatment needs. In spite of these changes, controversy remains regarding substantive due process when civil commitment is applied to sexual predators and outpatients.

Although there are many commonalities across jurisdictions, forensic mental health experts are encouraged to understand the statutes and case law of the jurisdictions in which they practice, especially legal holdings regarding qualifying mental disorders, the types and degree of impairments required for commitment, and the process of emergency commitment. Regardless of the jurisdiction, experts should be knowledgeable of the literature on empirically grounded predictions of dangerousness to self and others. Relying on that knowledge, the expert, when confronted with a situation in which commitment may be appropriate, must then balance the autonomy of the patient with the patient's safety and the safety of others.

REFERENCES

Addington v. Texas, 441 U.S. 418 (1979).

Allebeck, P., & Allgulander, C. (1990). Suicide among young men: Psychiatric illness, deviant behaviour, and substance abuse. *Acta Psychiatrica Scandinavica, 81*(6), 565–570.

American Psychiatric Association. (2003). *Practice guideline for the assessment and treatment of patients with suicidal behaviors.* Retrieved June 12, 2005, from http://www.psych.org/psych_pract /treatg/pg/prac_guide.cfm.

American Psychological Association. (2002). *Ethical principles of psychologists and code of conduct.* Retrieved June 12, 2005, from http://www.apa.org/ethics.

Arensman, E., Townsend, E., Hawton, K., Bremner, S., Feldman, E., Goldney, R., et al. (2001). Psychosocial and pharmacological treatment of patients following deliberate self-harm: The methodological issues involved in evaluating effectiveness. *Suicide and Life-Threatening Behavior, 31*(2), 169–180.

Balon, R. (1987). Suicide: Can we predict it? *Comprehensive Psychiatry, 28*(3), 236–241.

Baxstrom v. Herold, 383 U.S. 107 (1966).

Baxter, D., & Appleby, L. (1999). Case register study of suicide risk in mental disorders. *British Journal of Psychiatry, 175,* 322–326.

Black, D. W., Blum, N., Pfohl, B., & Hale, N. (2004). Suicidal behavior in borderline personality disorder: Prevalence, risk factors, prediction, and prevention. *Journal of Personality Disorders, 18*(3), 226–239.

Blinder, M. (2004). Suicide, psychiatric malpractice, and the bell curve. *Journal of the American Academy of Psychiatry and the Law, 32,* 319–323.

Brent, D. A., Oquendo, M., Birmaher, B., Greenhill, L., Kolko, D., Stanley, B., et al. (2002). Familial pathways to early-onset suicide attempt: Risk for suicidal behavior in offspring of mood-disordered suicide attempters. *Archives of General Psychiatry, 59,* 801–807.

Brodsky, B. S., Malone, K. M., Ellis, S. P., Dulit, R. A., & Mann, J. J. (1997). Characteristics of borderline personality disorder associated with suicidal behavior. *American Journal of Psychiatry, 154*(12), 1715–1719.

Brodsky, B. S., Oquendo, M., Ellis, S. P., Haas, G. L., Malone, K. M., & Mann, J. J. (2001). The relationship of childhood abuse to impulsivity and suicidal behavior in adults with major depression. *American Journal of Psychiatry, 158*(11), 1871–1877.

Brown, L. M., Bongar, B., & Cleary, K. M. (2004). A profile of psychologists' views of critical risk factors for completed suicide in older adults. *Professional Psychology: Research and Practice, 35*(1), 90–96.

Canapary, D., Bongar, B., & Cleary, K. M. (2002). Assessing risk for completed suicide in patients with alcohol dependence: Clinicians' views of critical factors. *Professional Psychology: Research and Practice, 33*(5), 464–469.

Canino, G., & Roberts, R. E. (2001). Suicidal behavior among Latino youth. *Suicide and Life-Threatening Behavior, 31*(Suppl.), 122–131.

Conner, K. R., Langley, J., Tomaszewski, K. J., & Conwell, Y. (2003). Injury hospitalization and risks for subsequent self-injury and suicide: A national study from New Zealand. *American Journal of Public Health, 93*(7), 1128–1131.

Conroy, M. (2003). Evaluations of sexual predators. In I. B. Weiner (Series Ed.) & A. M. Goldstein (Vol. Ed.), *Comprehensive handbook of psychology: Vol. 11. Forensic psychology* (pp. 463–484). Hoboken, NJ: Wiley.

Conwell, Y., Duberstein, P. R., & Caine, E. D. (2002). Risk factors for suicide in later life. *Biological Psychiatry, 52,* 193–204.

Conwell, Y., Duberstein, P. R., Connor, K., Eberly, S., Cox, C., & Caine, E. D. (2002). Access to firearms and risk for suicide in middle-aged and older adults. *American Journal of Geriatric Psychiatry, 10*(4), 407–416.

Diesrud, G., Roysamb, E., Ekeberg, O., & Kraft, P. (2001). Toward an integrative model of suicide attempt: A cognitive psychological approach. *Suicide and Life-Threatening Behavior, 31*(2), 153–168.

Donaldson v. O'Connor, 493 F.2d 507 (1974).

Douglas, K. S., & Webster, C. D. (1999). The HCR-20 violence risk assessment scheme: Concurrent validity in a sample of incarcerated offenders. *Criminal Justice and Behavior, 26,* 3–19.

Exline, J. J., Yali, A. M., & Sanderson, W. C. (2000). Guilt, discord, and alienation: The role of religious strain in depression and suicidality. *Journal of Clinical Psychology, 56*(12), 1481–1496.

Foster, T., Gillespie, K., McClelland, R., & Patterson, C. (1999). Risk factors for suicide independent of *DSM-III-R* Axis I disorder: Case-control psychological autopsy study in Northern Ireland. *British Journal of Psychiatry, 175,* 175–179.

Foucha v. Louisiana, 504 U.S. 71 (1992).

Goldstein, A. M. (1980). Indirect self-destructive behaviors in the terminally and chronically ill. In N. Farberow (Ed.), *Indirect self-destructive behavior: An exploration of suicide* (pp. 89–98). New York: McGraw-Hill.

Goldstein, A. M., Morse, S. J., & Shapiro, D. L. (2003). Evaluation of criminal responsibility. In B. Weiner (Series Ed.) & A. M. Goldstein (Vol. Ed.), *Comprehensive handbook of psychology: Vol. 11. Forensic psychology* (pp. 381–406). Hoboken, NJ: Wiley.

Goldstein, R. B., Black, D. W., Nasrallah, A., & Winokur, G. (1991). The prediction of suicide: Sensitivity, specificity, and predictive value of a multivariate model applied to suicide among 1906 patients with affective disorders. *Archives of General Psychiatry, 48,* 418–422.

Harris, E. C., & Barraclough, B. (1997). Suicide as an outcome for mental disorders: A meta-analysis. *British Journal of Psychiatry, 170,* 205–228.

Harris, G. T., Rice, M. E., & Cormier, C. A. (2002). Prospective replication of the Violence Risk Appraisal Guide in predicting violent recidivism among forensic patients. *Law and Human Behavior, 26*(4), 377–394.

Harris, G. T., Rice, M. E., & Quinsey, V. L. (1993). Violent recidivism of mentally disordered offenders: The development of a statistical prediction instrument. *Criminal Justice and Behaviour, 20*(4), 315–335.

Harvard Law Review Association. (1974). Developments in the law: Civil commitment of the mentally ill. *Harvard Law Review, 87,* 1190–1406.

Hawton, K., Zahl, D., & Weatherall, R. (2003). Suicide following deliberate self-harm: Long-term follow-up of patients who presented to a general hospital. *British Journal of Psychiatry, 182,* 537–542.

Heilbrun, K., Marczyk, G. R., & DeMatteo, D. (2002). *Forensic mental health assessment: A casebook.* New York: Oxford University Press.

Heller v. Doe, 509 U.S. 312 (1993).

Humphrey v. Cady, 405 U.S. 504 (1972).

In re Oakes, 8 Law Rep. 123 (Mass. 1845).

Jackson v. Indiana, 406 U.S. 715 (1972).

Jacobs, D. G., Brewer, M., & Klein-Benheim, M. (1999). Suicide assessment: An overview and recommended protocol. In J. G. Douglas (Ed.), *Harvard Medical School guide to suicide assessment and intervention* (pp. 3–39). San Francisco: Jossey-Bass.

Jacobson v. Commonwealth of Massachusetts, 197 U.S. 11 (1905).

Joe, S., & Kaplan, M. S. (2001). Suicide among African American men. *Suicide and Life-Threatening Behavior, 31*(Suppl.), 106–121.

Jones v. United States, 463 U.S. 354 (1983).

Kansas v. Crane, 534 U.S. 407 (2002).

Kansas v. Hendricks, 521 U.S. 346 (1997).

Kaslow, N. J., Price, A. W., Wyckoff, S., Bender Grall, M., Sherry, A., Young, S., et al. (2004). Person factors associated with suicidal behavior among African American women and men. *Cultural Diversity and Ethnic Minority Psychology, 10*(1), 5–22.

Kehoe, N. C., & Gutheil, T. G. (1994). Neglect of religious issues in scale-based assessment of suicidal patients. *Hospital and Community Psychiatry, 45*(4), 366–369.

Kellerman, A. L., Rivara, F. P., Somes, G., Reay, D. T., Francisco, J., Banton, J. G., et al. (1992). Suicide in the home in relation to gun ownership. *New England Journal of Medicine, 327*(7), 467–472.

Kelly, T. M., Soloff, P. H., Lynch, K. G., Haas, G. L., & Mann, J. J. (2000). Recent life events, social adjustment, and suicide attempts in patients with major depression and borderline personality disorder. *Journal of Personality Disorders, 14*(4), 316–326.

King, E. A., Baldwin, D. S., Sinclair, J. M. A., Baker, N. G., Campbell, M. J., & Thompson, C. (2001). The Wessex Recent In-Patient Suicide Study I: Case-control study of 234 recently discharged psychiatric patient suicides. *British Journal of Psychiatry, 178,* 531–536.

King, E. A., Baldwin, D. S., Sinclair, J. M. A., & Campbell, M. J. (2001). The Wessex Recent In-Patient Suicide Study II: Case-control study of 59 in-patient suicides. *British Journal of Psychiatry, 178,* 537–542.

Kuo, W., Gallo, J. J., & Eaton, W. W. (2004). Hopelessness, depression, substance disorder, and suicidality: A 13 year community-based study. *Social Psychiatry and Psychiatric Epidemiology, 39*(6), 497–501.

La Fond, J. (2000). The future of involuntary civil commitment in the USA after *Kansas v. Hendricks.* *Behavioral Sciences and the Law, 18,* 153–167.

La Fond, J. (2003). Outpatient commitment's next frontier: Sexual predators. *Psychology, Public Policy, and Law, 9,* 159–182.

Lessard v. Schmidt, 349 F. Supp. 1078 (1972).

Lester, D. (1992). Alcoholism and drug abuse. In R. W. Maris, A. L. Berman, J. T. Maltsberger, & R. I. Yufit (Eds.), *Assessment and prediction of suicide* (pp. 321–336). New York: Guilford Press.

Linehan, M. (1993). *Cognitive-behavioral treatment of borderline personality disorder.* New York: Guilford Press.

Malone, K. M., Oquendo, M. A., Haas, G. L., Ellis, S. P., Li, S., & Mann, J. J. (2000). Protective factors against suicidal acts in major depression: Reasons for living. *American Journal of Psychiatry, 157*(7), 1084–1088.

Mann, J. J., Waternaux, C., Haas, G. L., & Malone, K. M. (1999). Toward a clinical model of suicidal behavior in psychiatric patients. *American Journal of Psychiatry, 156*(2), 181–189.

Maris, R. W. (1992a). Overview of the study of suicide assessment and prediction. In R. W. Maris, A. L. Berman, J. T. Maltsberger, & R. I. Yufit (Eds.), *Assessment and prediction of suicide* (pp. 3–24). New York: Guilford Press.

Maris, R. W. (1992b). The relation of nonfatal suicide attempts to completed suicides. In R. W. Maris, A. L. Berman, J. T. Maltsberger, & R. I. Yufit (Eds.), *Assessment and prediction of suicide* (pp. 362–380). New York: Guilford Press.

Maser, J. D., Akiskal, H. S., Schettler, P., Scheftner, W., Mueller, T., Endicott, J., et al. (2002). Can temperament identify affectively ill patients who engage in lethal or non-lethal suicidal behavior? A 14-year prospective study. *Suicide and Life-Threatening Behavior, 32*(1), 10–30.

McIntosh, J. L. (1992). Methods of suicide. In R. W. Maris, A. L. Berman, J. T. Maltsberger, & R. I. Yufit (Eds.), *Assessment and prediction of suicide* (pp. 381–417). New York: Guilford Press.

Meloy, J. (2000). *Violence risk and threat assessment: A practical guide for mental health and criminal justice professionals.* San Diego, CA: Specialized Training Services.

Melton, G., Petrila, J., Poythress, N., & Slobogin, C. (1997). *Psychological evaluations for the courts: A handbook for mental health professionals and lawyers* (2nd ed.). New York: Guilford Press.

Monahan, J. (2003). Violence risk assessment. In I. B. Weiner (Series Ed.) & A. M. Goldstein (Vol. Ed.), *Comprehensive handbook of psychology: Vol. 11. Forensic psychology* (pp. 527–540). Hoboken, NJ: Wiley.

Monahan, J., Steadman, H., Silver, E., Appelbaum, P., Robbins, P., Mulvey, E., et al. (2001). *Rethinking risk assessment: The MacArthur study of mental disorder and violence.* New York: Oxford University Press.

Myers, E. D. (1988). Predicting repetition of deliberate self-harm: A review of the literature in the light of a current study. *Acta Psychiatrica Scandinavica, 77,* 314–319.

Neeleman, J., Wessely, S., & Lewis, G. (1998). Suicide acceptability in African and White Americans: The role of religion. *Journal of Nervous and Mental Diseases, 186*(1), 12–16.

Nordentoft, M., & Rubin, P. (1993). Mental illness and social integration among suicide attempters in Copenhagen. *Acta Psychiatrica Scandinavica, 88,* 278–285.

Nordstrom, P., Asberg, M., Aberg-Wistedt, A., & Nordin, C. (1995). Attempted suicide predicts suicide risk in mood disorders. *Acta Psychiatrica Scandinavica, 92,* 345–350.

O'Connor v. Donaldson, 422 U.S. 563 (1975).

Olmstead v. L. C. *ex rel.* Zimring, 527 U.S. 581 (1999).

Oquendo, M. A., Waternaux, C., Brodsky, B., Parsons, B., Haas, G. L., Malone, K. M., et al. (2000). Suicidal behavior in bipolar mood disorder: Clinical characteristics of attempters and nonattempters. *Journal of Affective Disorders, 59,* 107–117.

Parham v. J. R., 442 U.S. 584 (1979).

Parry, J. (1994). Involuntary civil commitment in the 1990s: A constitutional perspective. *Mental and Physical Disability Law Reporter, 18,* 320–336.

Pearson, J. L., Stanley, B. S., King, C. A., & Fisher, C. B. (2001). Intervention research with persons at high risk for suicidality: Safety and ethical considerations. *Journal of Clinical Psychiatry, 62*(Suppl. 25), 17–26.

Perlin, M. (1989). *Mental disability law: Civil and criminal* (Vol. 1). Charlottesville, NC: Michie.

Perlin, M. (2003). Therapeutic jurisprudence and outpatient commitment law: Kendra's Law as case study. *Psychology, Public Policy, and Law, 9,* 183–208.

Peruzzi, N., & Bongar, B. (1999). Assessing risk for completed suicide in patients with major depression: Psychologists' views of critical factors. *Professional Psychology: Research and Practice, 30*(6), 576–580.

Placidi, G. P. A., Oquendo, M. A., Malone, K. M., Brodksy, B., Ellis, S. P., & Mann, J. J. (2000). Anxiety in major depression: Relationship to suicide attempts. *American Journal of Psychiatry, 157*(10), 1614–1618.

Pokorny, A. D. (1983). Prediction of suicide in psychiatric patients: Report of a prospective study. *Archives of General Psychiatry, 40,* 249–257.

Powell, J., Geddes, J., Deeks, J., Goldacre, M., & Hawton, K. (2000). Suicide in psychiatric hospital inpatients: Risk factors and their predictive power. *British Journal of Psychiatry, 176,* 266–272.

Qin, P., Agerbo, E., & Mortensen, P. B. (2003). Suicide risk in relation to socioeconomic, demographic, psychiatric, and familial factors: A national register-based study of all suicides in Denmark, 1981–1997. *American Journal of Psychiatry, 160*(4), 765–772.

Qin, P., Agerbo, E., Westergard-Nielsen, N., Eriksson, T., & Mortensen, P. B. (2000). Gender differences in risk factors for suicide in Denmark. *British Journal of Psychiatry, 177,* 546–550.

Radmonsky, E. D., Haas, G. L., Mann, J. J., & Sweeney, J. A. (1999). Suicidal behavior in patients with schizophrenia and other psychotic disorders. *American Journal of Psychiatry, 156*(10), 1590–1595.

Rennie v. Klein, 462 F. Supp. 1131 (1978).

Riggins v. Nevada, 504 U.S. 127 (1992).

Rivers v. Katz, 495 N.E.2d 337 (1986).

Rogers v. Okin, 478 F. Supp. 1342 (1979).

Roy, A. (2001). Consumers of mental health services. *Suicide and Life-Threatening Behavior, 31*(Suppl.), 60–83.

Schapira, K., Linsley, K. R., Linsley, J. A., Kelly, T. P., & Kay, D. W. K. (2001). Relationship of suicide rates to social factors and availability of lethal methods. *British Journal of Psychiatry, 178,* 458–464.

Schopp, R. F. (2003). Outpatient civil commitment: A dangerous charade or a component of a comprehensive institution of civil commitment? *Psychology, Public Policy, and Law, 9,* 33–69.

Schotte, D. E., & Clum, G. A. (1987). Problem-solving skills in suicidal psychiatric patients. *Journal of Consulting and Clinical Psychology, 55*(1), 49–54.

Sidley, G. L., Calam, R., Wells, A., Hughes, T., & Whitaker, K. (1999). The prediction of parasuicide repetition in a high-risk group. *British Journal of Clinical Psychology, 38,* 375–386.

Simon, R. I. (2004). *Assessing and managing suicide risk: Guidelines for clinically based risk management.* Washington, DC: American Psychiatric Publishing.

Soloff, P. H., Lynch, K. G., Kelly, T. M., Malone, K. M., & Mann, J. J. (2000). Characteristics of suicide attempts of patients with major depressive episode and borderline personality disorder: A comparative study. *American Journal of Psychiatry, 157*(4), 601–608.

Tanney, B. L. (1992). Mental disorders, psychiatric patients, and suicide. In R. W. Maris, A. L. Berman, J. T. Maltsberger, & R. I. Yufit (Eds.), *Assessment and prediction of suicide* (pp. 277–320). New York: Guilford Press.

United States v. Sell, 539 U.S. 166 (2003).

U.S. Code. Offenders with mental disease or defect. 18 U.S.C. §§ 4241–4247 (2002).

Vickers, K., & McNally, R. J. (2004). Panic disorder and suicide attempt in the National Comorbidity Study. *Journal of Abnormal Psychology, 113*(4), 582–291.

Vitek v. Jones, 445 U.S. 480 (1980).

Washington v. Harper, 494 U.S. 210 (1990).

Werth, J. (2001). U.S. involuntary mental health commitment statutes: Requirements for persons perceived to be a potential harm to self. *Suicide and Life-Threatening Behavior, 31,* 348–357.

White, T. W. (1999). *How to identify suicidal people: A systematic approach to risk assessment.* Philadelphia: Charles Press.

Willis, L. A., Coombs, D. W., Drentea, P., & Cockerham, W. C. (2003). Uncovering the mystery: Factors of African-American suicide. *Suicide and Life-Threatening Behavior, 33*(4), 412–429.

Wolff v. McDonnell, 418 U.S. 539 (1974).

Wyatt v. Aderholt, 503 F.2d 1305 (1974).

Youngberg v. Romeo, 457 U.S. 307 (1982).

Zinermon v. Burch, 494 U.S. 113 (1990).

CHAPTER 11

Evaluating Capacity to Consent to Treatment

Jennifer Moye, Michele J. Karel, and Jorge C. Armesto

This chapter describes the legal standards, current state of research, and practice recommendations for evaluating capacity to consent to medical treatment, or "consent capacity." We focus primarily on capacity to consent to ordinary medical treatment in adults with psychiatric or neurodegenerative disorders, with an emphasis on aging populations. We do not discuss capacity issues in the context of end-of-life care, as these are addressed elsewhere in this volume (see Chapter 25).

KEY CONCEPTS

We use the term *capacity* to refer to a dichotomous (yes/no) judgment by a clinician as to whether an individual can make an autonomous treatment decision. In most health care settings, questions of consent capacity rarely proceed to adjudication, unless treatment requiring judicial authorization within the jurisdiction is involved, guardianship is being pursued, or the case is otherwise being litigated (e.g., family conflict). In this chapter, we refer to judicial determinations of consent capacity as *competency*. In reviewing the empirical literature, when we refer to *understanding, appreciation, reasoning,* and *expressing a choice,* these terms are used specifically in reference to four legal standards for decisional abilities for consent capacity, described in more detail throughout.

LEGAL BASIS

The legal basis of medical consent is found in statutory and case law subject to informed consent, surrogate health decision making, and guardianship.

Incapacity as Defined in Informed Consent Law

Informed consent for medical treatment has been defined as an autonomous action undertaken by a patient authorizing a professional to initiate a medical plan for the patient or to withdraw health care, including life-sustaining care (Berg, Appelbaum, Lidz, & Parker, 2001). Modern concepts of informed consent reflect a clinician's dual goals of promotion of patient autonomy and protection of the patient

---

We wish to thank Erica Wood, JD, for her input on the section on the legal basis of capacity to consent. Parts of this chapter were drawn from a review paper by Moye, Gurrera, Karel, Edelstein, and O'Connell (in press).

from harm. These goals represent a shift in the approach to health care related to three factors: (1) increasing technology, which resulted in the extension of life sometimes at the cost of quality of life; (2) some incidents of physician abuse, particularly in medical research; and (3) the patient rights movement of the 1960s and 1970s (Berg et al., 2001).

Informed Consent in Contrast to Simple Consent

Simple consent refers to the physician's obtaining the patient's agreement to an intervention or procedure, but without full disclosure of information about the procedure. In contrast, informed consent indicates agreement after the patient has been informed of the risks and other facts of the condition and procedure. Informed consent evolved as a legal requirement following case law in which physicians were held liable for failing to disclose the risks of procedures to patients (Grisso & P. S. Appelbaum, 1998).

Disclosure

Standards for disclosure include (a) nature of procedure or intervention, including its purpose (e.g., diagnostic versus interventional), duration, where it takes place, use of anesthesia, instruments used, bodily parts affected, and whether it is experimental; (b) risks, especially those that are material, substantial, probable, and significant, as well as the magnitude of the risk, probability, and imminence (when it will happen); (c) alternatives, including the option of no treatment; and (d) benefits, including limits to the benefits, such as that the procedure is diagnostic, not therapeutic, or that the procedure may relieve suffering only to a certain degree and not entirely (Berg et al., 2001; Wear, 1993).

Exceptions to Duty to Obtain Informed Consent

There are numerous legal exceptions to the physician's duty to obtain consent, including (a) emergencies where there is a need for action to protect against severe bodily harm, (b) when a patient freely and voluntarily waives disclosure and informed consent, (c) when a patient is undergoing court-ordered compulsory treatment, and (d) incapacity (but consent is required from another party). There is also some discussion and limited case law (Berg et al., 2001; Wear, 1993) indicating that informed consent may not be required in cases of therapeutic privilege in which disclosure of information would create a substantial adverse impact on the patient's condition.

Statutory Basis of Capacity to Consent

Surrogate Health Care Decision Making Statutes and Guardianship Statutes bear on the legal basis of consent capacity.

Incapacity as Defined in Surrogate Health Care Decision-Making Statutes

Statutes in every state provide for surrogate health care decision making for those individuals lacking the capacity to provide informed consent for treatment. Forty-seven states and the District of Columbia have living will laws allowing a person to make a written statement spelling out instructions about treatment or withholding or withdrawing treatment in the event of a terminal or end-stage condition or permanent unconsciousness. All 50 states and the District of Columbia have health care power of attorney statutes (also referred to as medical power of attorney or health care proxy) allowing an individual to appoint an agent to make health care decisions in the event of incapacity. Some state statutes, as well as the Uniform Health Care Decisions Act (National Conference of Commissioners on Uniform State Laws, 1993), have combined living wills and health care powers of attorney into a comprehensive advance directive act. In addition, more than 35 states and the District of Columbia have enacted statutes specifically authorizing default surrogate consent, generally by a hierarchy of family members. The Uniform Health Care Decisions Act also provides for default surrogates (Karp & Wood, 2003).

In all of these statutes, surrogate health care decision-making authority is triggered by a patient's lack of capacity to give informed consent for treatment. The Uniform Health Care Decisions Act defines capacity as "the ability to understand significant benefits, risks, and alternatives to proposed health care and to make and communicate a health-care decision" (National Conference of Commissioners on Uniform State Laws, 1993, § 1(3)). Various state definitions of incapacity under health care power of attorney statutes or living will statutes provide definitions of incapacity similar to the Uniform Act. For example, in Kentucky, capacity is defined as the ability to make and communicate a health care decision. In Massachusetts, capacity is defined as the ability to understand and appreciate the nature and consequences of health care decisions, including the benefits and risks of and alternatives to any proposed health care, and to reach an informed decision. In Nebraska, an incapacitated person is defined as having an inability to understand and appreciate the nature and consequences of health care decisions, including the benefits of, risks of, and alternatives to any proposed health care, or the inability to communicate in any manner an informed health care decision. Florida more succinctly defines a patient with incapacity for informed consent for health care as one who is physically or mentally unable to communicate a willful and knowing health care decision. Other states refer to the capacity standard delineated in the adult guardianship law for the state. State-by-state citations for living will and health care power of attorney statutes can be found on the American Bar Association (ABA) web site (http://www.abanet.org/aging).

Incapacity as Defined in Guardianship Statutes

Guardianship is a relationship created by state law in which a court gives one person, the guardian, the duty and power to make personal and/or property decisions for an individual determined by the court to be incapacitated. Guardians are often empowered to make medical decisions on behalf of adults who lack capacity to consent. The Uniform Guardianship and Protective Proceedings Act (National Conference of Commissioners on Uniform State Laws, 1997) defines an incapacitated individual as someone who is unable to receive and evaluate information or make or communicate decisions to such an extent that the individual lacks the ability to meet essential requirements for physical health, safety, or self-care, even with appropriate technological assistance. The 1997 model act adds an emphasis on decision making and de-emphasizes a diagnostic standard. Three states (Colorado, Minnesota, Hawaii) have statutes based on the 1997 model act; others are based on an earlier, 1982 version; still other states have incapacity standards that are particular to statutory evolution within their state.

A useful analysis of incapacity standards in state guardianship law finds that states may include one or more of the following tests or elements to define incapacity: (a) a disease or disorder, (b) cognitive or decisional impairment, (c) functional disabilities (i.e., "inability to care for self"), and (d) exceeding an essential needs threshold such that there is an unacceptable risk to the person or society (Anderer, 1990; Sabatino & Basinger, 2000). These elements are similar to a proposed general model of incapacity articulated by Grisso (2003), described in the conceptual considerations section later in the chapter. State-by-state comparison of incapacity standards for guardianship can be found on the ABA web site (http://www.abanet.org /aging/guardianship.html).

Limitations on Proxy Authority

Most states limit the authority of guardians and of health care proxies/durable powers of attorney to consent to treatment. Common limitations include the authority to make decisions concerning commitment for mental health treatment, abortion, sterilization, psychotropic medication, amputation, and electroconvulsive therapy (Richardson, 2003). Typically, these treatments require review by courts or ethics committees.

Case Law Standards for Capacity to Consent

Five standards for incapacity can be found in case law, used either individually or conjointly as a so-called compound standard (Appelbaum & Grisso, 1988; Drane, 1985; Roth, Meisel, & Lidz, 1977; Tepper & Elwork, 1984).

Expressing a Choice

Uncommunicative patients who cannot convey a treatment choice are seen to lack capacity. However, simply evidencing a choice does not, by itself, indicate capacity. Whereas some degree of vacillation or ambivalence is normal, patients must be able to convey a relatively consistent treatment choice.

Understanding

The ability to comprehend diagnostic- and treatment-related information has been recognized in many states as fundamental to capacity. Understanding includes the ability to remember and comprehend newly presented words, concepts, and phrases and to demonstrate that comprehension by paraphrasing diagnostic and treatment information.

Appreciation

The ability to relate the treatment information to one's own situation, in particular, the nature of the diagnosis and the possibility that treatment would be beneficial, is an appreciation standard of capacity (Grisso & P. S. Appelbaum, 1998a). Thus, understanding emphasizes comprehension, whereas appreciation focuses on evaluation of understood information in terms of personal relevance and beliefs. Disavowal of the diagnosis or potential treatment benefit may signify a deficit in reality testing (e.g., delusional disorder) or neurologic dysfunction (e.g., anosognosia).

Reasoning

Many states have cited the ability to state rational explanations, or to process information in a logically or rationally consistent manner, as a key element of capacity. Reasoning has been defined as the ability to evaluate treatment alternatives by integrating, analyzing, and processing information in order to compare alternatives in light of potential consequences and their likely impact on everyday life.

Rational Choice

A fifth standard encountered in some states, but considered by some commentators to be problematic, is the standard of a reasonable or rational choice. However, it is difficult, if not impossible, to provide an objective standard to the nature of the decision. In subsequent reviews of the literature, we do not discuss empirical findings concerning making a rational choice, as this has not been the subject of much study. We also do not consider empirical findings concerning evidencing a choice, because this is a threshold ability that has not been widely studied.

Consistency of Choices with Values

The four-standard model of consent capacity has advanced the field of consent capacity assessment considerably, yet this model may have diminished a focus on the role of values assessment in consent capacity determination. Various commentators have defined capacity as decisions that adhere to the patient's values, or have suggested that reasoning be operationalized not on the basis of logical consistency, but on the basis of consistency with values. The 1982 President's Commission for the Study of Ethical Problems in Medicine and Biomedical and Behavioral Research defined capacity in terms of the various cognitive standards previously described (communication, understanding, reasoning, deliberation), but also as "the possession of a set of values and goals." The commission states that a set of values and goals is foundational to the comparison of treatment alternatives.

Similar standards are recognized in language in state statutes for advance directives and guardianship that emphasize autonomy and values. More recently, the ABA's Model Rules of Professional Conduct (ABA, 2003; http://www.abanet .org/cpr/mrpc) describe factors to be balanced in the determination of capacity to include "the consistency of a decision with the known long-term commitments and values of the client (rule 1.14, comment 6)." These factors are identified in comments to the Model Rule based on recommendations from the National Conference on Ethical Issues in Representing Older Clients and, in particular, a law review article by Margulies (1994).

Berg and colleagues (2001), in a review of standards for informed consent, conclude that, from an ethical perspective, the standard of capacity that is most justifiable is one that promotes autonomy, protects welfare, and may be employed by practitioners with a minimum of bias, specifically that the "decision maker must first understand and appreciate the risks and benefits of options presented and then weigh those options to make a decision in light of her own values" (p. 105). As such, the assessment of values and the consistency of choices with values is a critical component of capacity evaluation. Such considerations may flow naturally into the forensic evaluation of the reasoning standard, as treatment risks and benefits are weighed in light of personal values. Or the values component may stand as part of the evaluator's process of capacity judgment when all sources of data (diagnosis, symptomatology, decisional abilities) are considered in light of the patient's values, attitudes, and perspectives.

CONCEPTUAL AND ETHICAL CONSIDERATIONS

How does the forensic mental health evaluator integrate standards deriving from case law, proxy consent statutes, and guardianship statutes in arriving at a useful conceptual model of capacity for clinical practice? Although evaluators are encouraged to formulate a model specific to their jurisdictional standards, an integrative model that synthesizes case and statutory models, including values, can be helpful.

An Integrative Conceptual Model for Consent Capacity

Grisso (2003) provides a starting point for such an integrative model. The five components of the Grisso model are described here vis-à-vis consent capacity. A key point is that an assessment of consent capacity does not rest on only the assessment of decisional abilities, but also the etiology and related symptoms as interpreted in context.

Causal Component

The causal component refers to the etiology or reason behind any observed decision-making difficulties. In addition to explaining *why* decision making is affected, information about the *cause* explains whether the observed deficits may be permanent or temporary. For example, consent impairments associated with Alzheimer's disease would be permanent and progressive, whereas consent impairments associated with acute confusional states or depression would be expected to improve with treatment of the underlying condition.

Functional Component

For the purposes of consent capacity, the functional component refers to decision-making abilities, as well as general cognitive abilities (memory, language, thought processes). In terms of assessment, the functional component is assessed by specific, direct questioning (using interview or standardized instruments) of key abilities relevant to consent capacity as well as more general symptomatic assessment of the presence, severity, and frequency of cognitive or psychiatric symptomatology.

Interactive Component

The interactive component recognizes that the sources of information just enumerated must be considered in view of the particulars of the situation, including the complexity of the treatment decision, the severity of risk associated with treatment outcomes, and the individual's long held values, preferences, and patterns.

Judgmental Component

The judgment component of capacity recognizes that capacity determination is a professional clinical or legal judgment wherein the various components are weighed to arrive at an outcome regarding the patient's capacity. Capacity may, in fact, be a continuous variable, with some individuals having marginally impaired decision making for some decisions, but for any specific informed consent situation a dichotomous (yes/no) decision must be rendered regarding the individual's capacity. It is not clear how clinicians or judges weigh various components, but it has been observed that a clinician's judgment may be influenced by a range of factors, including experience in the field (Clemens & Hayes, 1997), professional discipline (Marson, McInturff, Hawkins, Bartolucci, & Harrell, 1997), the weight that is given to particular cognitive deficits (Earnst, Marson, & Harrell, 2000), and competing goals and perspectives of clinicians and patients (Moye, 2000).

Dispositional Component

Any specific capacity determination will result in an outcome that may include the use of substituted judgment by a previously appointed proxy, guardian, or next of kin (for a thorough consideration of substituted judgment, see Drogin & Barrett, 2003). It is also possible that the disposition may include recommendations to treat underlying causes of incapacity or to use information-processing aids (e.g., lists, diagrams, reminders) to maximize decisional abilities in patients with marginal capacity.

Situation Specificity

The assessment of consent capacity is situation specific. That is, an individual's capacity may vary depending on the difficulty and complexity of a medical decision. An individual with neurocognitive compromise may have diminished capacity to consent to a complex medical intervention but may retain the capacity to consent to a relatively simple medical treatment. As such, consent capacity must be evaluated for each specific informed consent situation. However, in practice, particularly in activation of proxy authority, families and clinicians may find it useful to know whether an individual has the capacity to make a current treatment decision and subsequent decisions of similar complexity. Similarly, in writing guardianship orders, especially if crafting a limited order, a judge may want information relative to an individual's capacities within key decisional domains, so that the judge can articulate those decisions for which the patient retains decisional autonomy and authority.

Decisional Complexity

As a related point, it remains an unresolved question as to exactly how much information must be disclosed to the patient and how much information the patient must comprehend for adequate capacity. Although disclosure standards indicate what elements of the situation should be disclosed, how this translates to practice is unclear. Evaluators are obligated to present information in such a way as to maximize understanding in light of an individual's level of education, language ability, and medical sophistication. If simplification of information presented is acceptable, in fact necessary, at what point does simplification become a failure to disclose sufficient information? Similarly, how much information must a patient comprehend to demonstrate adequate understanding? Normative studies of consent comprehension provide some guidance (Park, Morrel, & Shifren, 1999), and interestingly reveal that healthy, unimpaired adults remember and comprehend far less information than may be assumed. Further, it remains unclear to what extent understanding forms the basis for subsequent appreciation and reasoning. If an individual cannot attend to, encode, and comprehend basic information about a treatment, to what extent can he or she be expected to appreciate its significance or reason about related risks and benefits? One study suggests that understanding, appreciation, and reasoning do not form a hierarchical model (Grisso & Appelbaum, 1995a), but such investigations are dependent on cutoff scores used for adequate comprehension.

Life span developmental studies of cognitive processing in adults indicate that implicit cognitive processing is utilized in arriving at decisions and that, as adults age, they may consider fewer pieces of information in arriving at decisions. Some have framed these findings as age-related decrements in working memory (Salthouse & Babcock, 1991); others emphasize that rapid focusing on personally salient information may be a benefit of life experience, such that individuals become more expert in decision making with more experience (Yates & Patalano, 1999). If so, assessments of understanding and subsequent appreciation and reasoning that emphasize a necessary amount of information recall or comprehension may be unfair.

In summary, there are limitations to the maxim that consent capacity is situation specific. Doctors, families, and judges may need to know an individual's decisional capacities for decisions of similar complexity. However, decisional complexity may be reduced, to a limited extent, by simplification either in the way the clinician chooses to disclose the information or in the way the patient chooses to focus on and sort key information. The limits of simplification pose two empirical questions: When does clinician simplification lead to a failure of adequate disclosure, and when does patient simplification result in inability to adequately weigh essential information?

RESEARCH REGARDING CAPACITY TO CONSENT

In recent years, empirical studies of consent capacity have increased dramatically, although the overall volume of research remains relatively small (Kim et al., 2002). These studies focus on diagnostic, cognitive, psychiatric, and demographic predictors of rated capacity, as well as the consistency of capacity ratings across methods.

Diagnostic Categories Associated with Impaired Capacity

Patients with similar diagnoses and those receiving similar levels of medical care have widely varying capacity ratings, as described in this section. Thus, consent capacity is not predicted by diagnostic status alone.

Schizophrenia

Adults with Schizophrenia have been impaired relative to controls on measures of understanding, appreciation, and reasoning in mean comparisons (Grisso & Appelbaum, 1995b). However, only 23% to 28% of patients actually were impaired on these standards using cutoff scores (Grisso & Appelbaum, 1995a; Tepper & Elwork, 1984), indicating that lower group performance was due to very poor performance in a minority of patients. Using a simplified measure of understanding for a low-risk procedure (Wong, Clare, Holland, Watson, & Gunn, 2000), mean decision-making capacity was not impaired relative to controls in 21 adults with Schizophrenia or Schizoaffective Disorder, although 10% performed within an impaired range.

Dementia

A number of studies have found that the consent capacity of individuals with dementia is reduced compared to that of healthy controls (Kim, Caine, Currier, Leibovici, & Ryan, 2001; Marson, Ingram, Cody, & Harrell, 1995; Moye, Karel, Azar, & Gurrera, 2004a; Schmand, Gouwenberg, Smit, & Jonker, 1999; Wong et al., 2000), attributable to impairments in understanding and, to a less frequent degree, to deficits in reasoning and appreciation. In a qualitative analysis, Marson and colleagues (Marson, Annis, McInturff, Bartolucci, & Harrell, 1999) noted that nonresponsive answers, along with loss of task (difficulty projecting oneself into the story) and loss of detachment (confusion over the hypothetical nature of the research-based decisional task), characterize capacity impairment in dementia.

Institutionalized or Hospitalized Patients

High rates (44% to 69%) of consent capacity impairment have been found among adults in nursing homes (Barton, Mallik, Orr, & Janofsky, 1996; Fitten, Lusky, & Hamann, 1990; Pruchno, Smyer, Rose, Hartman-Stein, & Laribee-Henderson, 1995; Royall, Cordes, & Polk, 1997). Fitten and Waite (1990) assessed consent capacity in 25 acutely hospitalized elderly patients without neurologic or psychiatric histories. Understanding was impaired in inpatients relative to community controls, indicating that at least transient capacity impairments may be present in patients who are not medically stable. Similarly, suboptimal decisional abilities despite adequate global cognitive function were observed in 60 acutely hospitalized patients, providing further support for the idea that decisional abilities may be compromised during acute medical crises (Dellasega, Frank, & Smyer, 1996).

Cognitive Predictors of Impaired Consent Capacity

Neuropsychological test performance has been found to be a significant predictor of decisional abilities in consent capacity. These relationships vary according to population, the neuropsychological battery employed, and the capacity instrument used. Understanding appears to be robustly related to neuropsychological test performance. In older patients with neurodegenerative disorders, understanding has been related to memory, executive abilities, and confrontation naming (Dymek, Atchison, Harrell, & Marson, 2001; Marson, Chatterjee, Ingram, & Harrell, 1996). In acutely hospitalized medical patients and in adults with depression and Schizophrenia, understanding was related to a linear composite of verbal functions comprising Wechsler Adult Intelligence Scales-Revised (WAIS-R) Vocabulary, Similarities, and Digit Span (Frank, Smyer, Grisso, & Appelbaum, 1999; Grisso & Appelbaum, 1995b). Appreciation was less related or not at all related to neuropsychological test performance, whereas reasoning has been associated with executive and working memory measures in older adults with neurodegenerative disorders

(Dymek et al., 2001; Marson, Cody, Ingram, & Harrell, 1995) and a linear composite of WAIS-R subtests in adults with Schizophrenia and depression (Grisso & Appelbaum, 1995b), but is unrelated to neuropsychological test performance in adults undergoing acute medical hospitalization (Frank et al., 1999).

In a number of studies, cognitive screening tests such as the Mini-Mental State Examination (MMSE) correlated with instrument-based assessments of capacity; however, the MMSE was only modestly sensitive and specific (Fitten et al., 1990; Kim & Caine, 2002). Cognitive screening has use for suggesting when further capacity evaluation is needed but is not in itself informative about specific ability deficits (Pruchno et al., 1995).

Psychiatric Predictors of Consent Capacity

The relationship of specific psychiatric symptoms and individual decisional ability deficits has not been well studied and deserves further attention. As a broad generalization, it appears that greater overall severity of clinical deficits is associated with greater decisional ability impairment. Understanding was associated with symptom severity in adults with Schizophrenia, but not in adults with depression (Grisso & Appelbaum, 1995b); psychiatric symptom severity was not correlated with reasoning in adults with Schizophrenia or depression.

Demographic Predictors of Consent Capacity

Educational level (Frank et al., 1999) and socioeconomic status (Grisso & Appelbaum, 1995b) have been associated with understanding in consent capacity. These associations are of concern, suggesting a potential source of measurement bias that may undermine the integrity of the assessment process. Consent capacity assessment should not merely reflect educational level or income.

Consistency of Capacity as Measured by Different Capacity Instruments

Overall consent capacity as measured by the Hopemont Capacity Assessment Interview (HCAI) has been associated with other measures of reasoning in long-term nursing care patients (Staats, Edelstein, & Null, 1995) and understanding in acutely hospitalized patients (Dellasega et al., 1996). The consistency of instrument-based assessment of capacity may vary depending on the decisional ability assessed. In a study comparing the assessment of four decisional abilities by three instruments (Capacity to Consent to Treatment Instrument [CCTI]; MacArthur Competency Assessment Tool for Treatment [MacCAT-T]; HCAI) with a multitrait multimethod matrix, the ability of understanding demonstrated good convergent validity (Moye, Karel, Azar, & Gurrera, 2004b), whereas evidence for the convergent validity of appreciation was poor and that for reasoning was fair.

Consistency of Consent Capacity as Assessed by Different Clinicians

Marson and colleagues (1997) found low agreement (kappa = .14) among five physicians with different specialty training who provided dichotomous capacity ratings of adults with Alzheimer's disease based on review of videotaped instrument-based assessments. Agreement improved when physicians were trained to evaluate specific legal standards (kappa = .48), but there was still considerable variability (Marson, Earnst, Jamil, Bartolucci, & Harrell, 2000). Physicians appear to vary in their weighting of different cognitive abilities in capacity assessments, emphasizing either naming, conceptualization, or memory (Earnst et al., 2000). Moreover, ratings may vary by specialty (psychiatry, neurology, and geriatrics; Marson et al., 1997).

Consistency of Consent Capacity as Assessed by Instruments versus Clinicians

Studies comparing test-based and clinician-based evaluations of capacity typically employ a cutoff score on an instrument and categorical (intact capacity/impaired capacity) clinical judgments. Fitten and Waite (1990) found poor agreement between an instrument-based assessment emphasizing recall and physician-based determinations in 25 acutely ill hospitalized elderly adults. Physician-based and instrument-based ratings disagreed in 28% of the patients, and physicians were more likely than the instrument to rate patients as having intact capacity. Similar results were found in long-term care residents (Bean, Nishisato, Rector, & Glancy, 1996; Fitten et al., 1990).

In contrast, Etchells and colleagues (1999) found higher agreement rates (83% to 95% of area under receiver operating characteristic curve) comparing an instrument-guided interview to clinician ratings in 100 adults admitted for medical or surgical interventions. Carney and colleagues (Carney, Neugroschl, Morrison, Marin, & Siu, 2001) found moderate to excellent agreement (kappa = .58 to 1.0) comparing an instrument-based assessment of capacity to a psychiatrist's judgment. In a study examining which instruments best predict clinical determinations, Pruchno and colleagues (1995) found a moderate correlation between instrument-based and clinical assessment of capacity of long-term care patients (r =.45 − .60), with MMSE and a measure of understanding best predicting clinical judgments.

Summary of the Empirical Basis of Consent Capacity Assessment

Although there is an evolving consensus regarding the decisional abilities that form the legal standard for consent capacity, a major challenge confronting researchers in this field is the lack of a clear consensus regarding the operationalization of these decisional abilities. Construct validity studies to date indicate greater consensus on the assessment of understanding associated with lexical knowledge and verbal memory, but no clear consensus on how to operationalize the concepts of reasoning and appreciation. Further, the lack of a gold standard for capacity assessment hampers the establishment of valid assessment instruments. Only a handful of studies have measured agreement between instrument-based and clinician-based ratings of capacity; these studies indicate that, despite a high overall correspondence between the two methods of assessment, a considerable proportion of patients are assessed to have capacity by physician judgment but to lack capacity by instrument assessment. Rating inconsistencies between these methods may reflect differences in reliability or validity, reliance on distinct data sources, or other, as yet unrecognized factors.

CLINICAL EVALUATION OF CAPACITY TO CONSENT

Clinical evaluation of consent capacity has been hampered by lingering problems with reliability. The introduction of instruments designed to assist clinicians in assessing capacity offer improved reliability and validity. However, a clinical opinion regarding capacity remains a professional clinical judgment integrating findings from the interview in view of the patient's decision-making style and personal values.

Problems with Current Clinical Practice

Current assessment practice typically relies on an informal process involving clinical interview, medical record review, and mental status examination (Marson, Cody, et al., 1995; Nash & Giles, 1989). In some cases, clinical practice may be quite superficial. For example, in a nursing home study, the primary factor in determining a resident's capacity to write an advance directive was orientation to person, place, and time as evaluated by the social worker, nurse, or clerical staff (Walker & Bradley, 1998). A national survey of 395 clinical practitioners found continuing confusion regarding the assessment of capacity (Ganzini, Volicer, Nelson, & Derse, 2003). Common pitfalls included confusion between clinical assessments of capacity and legal determinations of competency, the belief that actions against medical advice indicate incapacity, and the assumption that cognitive or psychiatric disorders necessarily imply incapacity.

Instruments for the Evaluation of Consent Capacity

A major empirical advance in the past 10 years has been the development of forensic assessment instruments and interview guides for evaluating capacity to consent to medical treatment. These instruments provide more structured and standardized methods of assessing capacity vis-à-vis legal standards, although many still lack basic psychometric data. Although currently available instruments show some promise, they should be used with an awareness of the limitations of each instrument and with the knowledge that a score on an instrument is not intended to supplant clinical judgment. Instruments are useful in that they provide examples of how to conceptualize and operationalize the aforementioned decisional abilities. In selecting instruments for use as resources, it seems most prudent to select tests developed for the population being assessed (i.e., Schizophrenia versus dementia). In some cases, instruments may be selected based on the appropriateness of the content (e.g., the Competency Interview Schedule [CIS] when assessing capacity to consent to electroconvulsive therapy).

Vignette-Based Instruments

An instrument with a standardized vignette is useful if the clinician believes it would be illuminating to assess a patient's decisional abilities in a treatment context separate from the one facing the patient. Also, a vignette paradigm could be necessary if there is not a specific medical decision facing the patient but, instead, the evaluator is being asked to comment more generally on likely consent capacity in a future decisional context (e.g., for the purposes of guardianship).

Capacity to Consent to Treatment Instrument

The CCTI (Marson, Cody, et al., 1995) is based on two clinical vignettes: a neoplasm condition and a cardiac condition. Vignettes are presented orally and in writing; participants are then presented questions to assess their decisional abilities in terms of understanding, appreciation, reasoning, and expression of choice. Responses are subjected to detailed scoring criteria.

Competency Interview Schedule

The CIS (Bean et al., 1996) is a 15-item interview designed to assess consent capacity for electroconvulsive therapy (ECT). Patients referred for ECT receive information about their diagnosis and treatment alternatives by the treating clinician, and the CIS is used to assess decisional abilities based on responses to the 15 items.

Decision Assessment Measure

Wong and colleagues (2000), working in England, developed the DAM, which references incapacity criteria in England and Wales (retention, understanding, reasoning, and communicating a choice). A standardized vignette regarding blood drawing is used.

Hopemont Capacity Assessment Interview

The HCAI (Edelstein, 1999) medical decision-making component consists of two clinical vignettes: treatment of an eye infection and administration of cardiopulmonary resuscitation (there are also two vignettes to assess financial capacity). The patient is introduced to general concepts of choice, risk, and benefit, followed by the two scenarios. After discussing the scenarios, patients are asked to recount factual information, explain risks and benefits, state a decision, and explain how the decision was reached.

Thinking Rationally about Treatment

The TRAT (Grisso & Appelbaum, 1993) instrument assesses eight functions relevant to decision making and problem solving: (1) information seeking (asking for additional information); (2) consequential thinking (consideration of treatment consequences); (3) comparative thinking (simultaneous processing of information about two treatments); (4) complex thinking (referencing all treatment alternatives); (5) consequence generation (ability to generate real-life consequences of the risks and discomforts described in the treatment alternatives); (6) consequence weighting (consistent rating of activity preferences); (7) transitive thinking (rating relative quantitative relationships); and (8) probabilistic thinking (rating and understanding probabilities of occurrence). These functions are assessed with a hypothetical vignette and follow-up questions. The last three functions are assessed through standardized tests unrelated to the specific vignette.

Understanding Treatment Disclosures

The UTD (Grisso & Appelbaum, 1992) instrument has three versions with three different vignettes: Schizophrenia, depression, and ischemic heart disease. Information about the disorder and its treatment is presented in either an uninterrupted or element (a paragraph at a time) disclosure format. Understanding is assessed through ratings on paraphrased recall and recognition. Of note, the TRAT and UTD are precursor instruments for the MacCAT-T, described later.

Additional Vignette Assessment Methods

A few studies do not use specifically named instruments but are based on standardized vignettes and questions that presumably could be replicated by other investigators. Research by Schmand et al. (1999) uses a vignette based on work by Sachs, Stocking, and Stern (1994) that describes physical therapy or surgery for a hip fracture. Nine questions approximate an assessment of the four decisional abilities. There is also a standardized vignette for consent to a medication research trial.

Fitten and colleagues (Fitten et al., 1990; Fitten & Waite, 1990) employ three standardized vignettes: treatment for insomnia, a procedure for diagnosis of pleural effusion, and resuscitation in the context of chronic illness. Follow-up questions address the patient's understanding of the condition, the nature and purpose of the proposed treatments and their risks and benefits, and the "quality" of the patient's reasoning process.

Structured or Semistructured Interviews

Other instruments use structured format and standard questions for assessing consent in an actual treatment situation.

Aid to Capacity Evaluation

The ACE (Etchells et al., 1999) is a semistructured assessment interview that addresses seven facets of capacity for an actual medical decision: the ability to understand (1) the medical problem, (2) the treatment, (3) the alternatives to treatment, (4) the option of refusing treatment, (5) the ability to perceive consequences of accepting treatment, and (6) of refusing treatment, and (7) the ability to make a decision not substantially based on hallucinations, delusions, or depression. These reflect legal standards in Ontario, Canada, but also correspond to U.S. legal standards. Questions in the areas 1 through 4 assess the decisional ability of understanding. Questions in areas 5 and 6 appear to tap reasoning, and in area 7 diminished appreciation based on patently false beliefs (e.g., "Do you think we are trying to harm you?").

Capacity Assessment Tool

The CAT (Carney et al., 2001) proposes to evaluate capacity based on six abilities: (1) communication, (2) understanding choices, (3) comprehension of risks and benefits, (4) insight, (5) decision/choice process, and (6) judgment. It uses a structured interview format to assess capacity to choose between two options in an actual treatment situation.

Independent Living Scales, Health and Safety Subscale (Loeb, 1996)

The ILS is an instrument designed to assess capacity for independent living, such as arises in guardianship proceedings. One subscale, the Health and Safety Subscale, assesses an individual's approach to and judgment concerning managing ongoing health and well-being. The scale does not assess consent capacity in terms of the four legal standards, but provides useful more general information regarding a person's health judgment.

MacArthur Competency Assessment Tool for Treatment

The MacCAT-T (Grisso & P. S. Appelbaum, 1998b) utilizes a semistructured interview to guide the clinician through an assessment of understanding, appreciation, reasoning, and expressing a choice. Appreciation is assessed in two sections: whether there is "any reason to doubt" the diagnosis, and whether the treatment "might be of benefit to you." Reasoning is assessed through questions considering how patients compare treatment choices and consequences and apply treatment choices to everyday situations.

Perceptions of Disorder

The POD (Appelbaum & Grisso, 1992) was developed along with the TRAT and UTD, which are precursors to the MacCAT-T. The first part, Nonacknowledgment of Disorder, presents facts of the patient's actual disorder and then asks the patient to rate agreement with those facts as applying to himself or herself. The second part, Nonacknowledgment of Treatment Potential, elicits opinions about whether treatment in general, and medication in particular, might be of some benefit. Low ratings are given when disbelief is based on grossly distorted or delusional premises.

Considerations in the Evaluation of Consent Capacity

The method by which treatment information is disclosed, and instrument performance is interpreted strongly affect the ultimate forensic judgment of capacity.

Disclosing Treatment Information

Clinicians are obligated to disclose information about the nature of the procedure, risks, benefits, and treatment alternatives. However, little is written about how information disclosure may impact the latter assessment of consent capacity. Disclosure formats that are more structured, organized, uniform, and brief serve to improve understanding of diagnostic and treatment information, as do simplified and illustrated guides (Dunn & Jeste, 2001). Not surprisingly, informed consent performance was improved when consent forms were left available for subsequent reference (Taub, Baker, Kline, & Sturr, 1987). These findings are supported by cognitive aging research finding that environmental aids (e.g., cues for the retrieval of relevant information) reduce demands on cognitive resources subserving working memory. In contrast, tasks that require effortful processing without such supports are more likely to reveal age-related impaired performance (Craik, 1994; Craik & Byrd, 1982; Craik & Jennings, 1992).

Furthermore, decisions are influenced by the manner in which risks are framed. McNeil and colleagues (McNeil, Pauker, Sox, & Tversky, 1982) showed that participants who learned that 10% of patients die from surgery and 0% die from radiation were less likely to choose surgery compared to those who were presented with information that 100% of patients immediately survive radiation and 90% immediately survive surgery. Thus, participants are most likely to choose the more positively framed outcome, despite identical outcome probabilities. This effect has been demonstrated in a wide range of populations (Kuhberger, 1998), including older adults asked to make medical decisions regarding life-threatening (Mazur & Merz, 1993) and less threatening outcomes (McKee, 2001).

Interpreting Instrument-Based Performance

Information on test-retest reliability and normal variability in test performance in healthy adults is critical for the appropriate interpretation of instrument-based assessments of capacity. Adequate short-term test-retest reliability in controls is an important measure of the instrument's ability to consistently measure a trait over time and is an essential basis of validity. However, an instrument may not demonstrate high test-retest reliability in patient groups due to fluctuating mental status in those patients, that is, valid causes of trait instability. In general, test-retest reliability is understudied. Grisso, Appelbaum, Mulvey, and Fletcher (1995) reported statistically significant 2-week test-retest reliability scores ranging from .47 to .80 for understanding and .68 for reasoning in controls, with similar findings in adults with Schizophrenia and depression, despite changing scores on the Brief Psychiatric Rating Scale and Beck Depression Inventory. Dellasega and colleagues (1996) found high 3- to 9-day test-retest correlations ($r = .64 - .75$) for understanding (UTD) and overall HCAI capacity ($r = .85$) in 60 medically hospitalized adults.

Normative data are not yet available for any of the instruments reviewed here, although information on mean performance in control samples is available for the CCTI, DAM, HCAI, MacCAT-T, POD, and TRAT. Information on race and ethnicity is provided in only two studies; little is known about the potential relationship of these characteristics to test performance.

Assessing Values Relevant to Treatment Choices

One indicator of capacity is the consistency of treatment choices with values. To date, values variables have not been well integrated into standardized decision-making capacity assessment tools. Individual differences related to cultural, religious, cohort, and personality variables can influence both the process of medical decision making and the types of decisions individuals are likely to make. Clinicians evaluating consent capacity may wish to consider the extent to which a patient is motivated to participate in an independent, rational decision-making process, as well as whether expressed treatment choices are consistent with values related to quality of life and interpersonal concerns. A number of values assessment tools can aid such evaluation (Karel, Powell, & Cantor, 2004; Pearlman, Starks, Cain, & Cole, 2005; Whitlatch, Feinberg, & Tucke, 2005), and general attention to the following health care values can be integrated into a capacity evaluation.

Preferences for Decision-Making Participation

Consent capacity assessment assumes the engagement of a patient who is interested in participating in making his or her own medical treatment decisions. This model is consistent with the bioethical emphasis on patient self-determination in the U.S. medical system. However, individuals differ in the extent to which they desire control over treatment decisions based on generational, cultural, and personality factors. Evaluators should be aware that individuals with certain decision-making styles may be relatively unmotivated to participate in, or may not perceive the relevance of, a decision-making capacity assessment.

Older cohorts were socialized during a time when patients had less active involvement in medical decision making. Therefore, older adults today may take a less active role in seeking illness-related information and be more likely to assume that family members or physicians will make medical treatment decisions for them (Beisecker, 1988; Degner & Sloan, 1992; Petrisek, Laliberte, Allen, & Mor, 1997). Moye and Karel (1999) noted this tendency in their older research subjects, some of whom seemed reluctant to participate in medical decision-making capacity discussions. This difficulty was evident in such participant responses as "I place all the decision making in the doctor's hands where it should always be, never tell him falsely of things; so a long time ago I placed myself in the hands of the doctor."

Many cultural groups, including Asian and Hispanic Americans, believe that the individual patient should not be burdened with diagnostic or prognostic information and/or that decision-making responsibility belongs to, or is shared with, the family (Blackhall, Murphy, Frank, Michel, & Azen, 1995; Hornung et al., 1998). Some individuals who score suboptimally on standardized measures of consent capacity may do so because they are less engaged or less comfortable in a process of independent medical decision making.

Individuals also differ in their interest or motivation to participate actively in medical treatment decision making based on personality style. People vary in the extent to which they believe their own actions will have an impact on important outcomes in their life, as compared to the influence of chance or powerful others, including decisions made in the realm of health outcomes. This "health locus of control" (Wallston, Wallston, & DeVellis, 1978) construct has genetic and environmental determinants (Johansson et al., 2001) and predicts many aspects of health care decision making and behaviors across diagnostic and cultural groups (Astrom & Blay, 2002; Engleman & Wild, 2003; Fowers, 1994; Wardle & Steptoe, 2003). Persons with "external health locus of control" may prefer to defer decision making to their doctors or others. In addition, for a variety of personal and interpersonal reasons, many people prefer a collaborative style of decision making wherein they consider the risks and benefits of different treatments actively with the help of loved ones, doctors, clergy, or others (Deimling, Smerglia, & Barresi, 1990; Mezey, Kluger, Maislin, & Mittelman, 1996; Puchalski et al., 2000; Singer et al., 1998).

Conceptions of Quality of Life

An important construct relevant to individual differences in medical treatment decision making is quality of life (Birren, Lubben, Rowe, & Deutschman, 1991). The extent to which individuals value preservation of life at all costs versus maintaining a certain quality of life, and what defines quality of life for different individuals, depends on deeply held values and beliefs influenced by life experience, religious/cultural background, and personality factors. Various strategies have been used to evaluate how an individual's conception of quality of life might influence medical treatment decisions. For example, patients might be asked to evaluate treatment options with respect to their impact on valued life activities or whether certain scenarios are considered states or fates "worse than death" (Ditto, Druley, Moore,

Danks, & Smucker, 1996; Lawton et al., 1999; Pearlman et al., 1993). Although an individual's sense of what would be a tolerable or intolerable quality of life may change with changing life circumstances (Lockhart, Ditto, Danks, Cooppola, & Smucker, 2001), the patient's responses to questions about valued life activities may illuminate why various treatment options were selected or rejected in the current capacity evaluation. The evaluation should determine whether the stated treatment choices are consistent with the individual's conceptions of quality of life.

It is critical to understand how salient life experiences, such as previous experience with life-threatening illness in oneself or others, or strongly held religious or cultural values can influence participation in decision-making capacity assessment. For example, African Americans are more likely to choose life-sustaining medical treatments, with less concern about quality of life than Caucasian Americans (Caralis, Davis, Wright, & Marcial, 1993; Eleazer et al., 1996; Hopp & Duffy, 2000). An individual's experiences with illness or caregiving may also influence medical treatment choices (Allen-Burge & Haley, 1997; Collopy, 1999; Karel et al., 2004). Life experience may be an especially strong predictor of decision making in older adults, who tend to focus more on interpersonal and experiential elements of problems than do younger adults (Blanchard-Fields, 1996).

Interpersonal Context

Most medical decisions are made in a social context (Rolland, 1994). Families are intimately affected—practically and emotionally—by patients' medical treatment decisions. The family's emotional, practical, and financial resources for coping with illness, caregiving, grief, and uncertainty will affect how they interact with and influence the patient (Hardwig, 1990; Rothchild, 1994). Similarly, patients are often concerned about the impact of their illness and treatment on loved ones, and older adults in particular express concern about being a burden to their families (Karel & Gatz, 1996). The impact of these interpersonal variables, including the extent to which patients may consider the well-being of others in making medical decisions, should be considered in a capacity evaluation.

A Model for Clinical Evaluation

Evaluation of consent capacity includes several steps: evaluation of the diagnosis and its symptoms, assessment of decisional abilities, exploration of values, and weighing of these factors in the context of ethical principles of beneficence and autonomy (Moye, 1999). This evaluation should be preceded by an investigation of the referral question and an effort to obtain informed consent for the evaluation from the patient.

Referral Clarification and Informed Consent

A referral to evaluate consent capacity most often occurs in two contexts: (1) an acute or long-term care medical setting where a patient with noted cognitive or psychiatric illness is refusing medical treatment (such requests for evaluations often come from attending physicians who seek clarification about the patient's capacity to consent); and (2) a hospital, long-term care, or community setting where a clinician, family member, service agency, or legal professional is seeking guardianship due to questions about a specific urgent medical decision or a series of current and anticipated medical decisions. In both situations, it is important to clarify the specifics of the case: what specific treatment issue is now at hand, the facts and nuances of the particular condition and treatments, and whether there are any other decisions for which capacity is questioned. At times, a referral for capacity evaluation represents a conflict between the patient and the provider or family. In these cases, it is useful to clarify if a capacity evaluation will resolve the conflict by granting decisional authority to one person, or if the situation would be better addressed through an intervention that mediates the conflict. On occasion, a capacity evaluation may be requested for guardianship when there are already other proxy mechanisms in place. For this reason, it is always important to clarify whether the patient has already appointed a durable power of attorney for health care, recorded other advance directives, or initiated other surrogate decision-making mechanisms.

Of course, the evaluator will want a firm sense of the history of decisional problems and the social and contextual issues: Who is the patient's family? How much are they involved? What is the quality of the relationships? Are there other sources of social support? Finally, the evaluator will need a sense of the urgency of the request and when a decision on consent capacity will need to be rendered.

Assuming the patient is communicative, the evaluator must attempt to obtain informed consent for the evaluation of capacity. The main goal is to inform the patient of the potential risks in cooperating with a capacity evaluation. The evaluator should briefly explain why she or he has been called to evaluate capacity, what is involved (interviews, tests), the purpose of the evaluation, the potential risks (the patient may lose the right to make autonomous decisions; the patient may have a guardian appointed), and the potential benefits (information gained may help in planning for the patient's treatment). The patient's reaction to each of these elements should be described in the evaluation report. Three outcomes are possible: The patient consents, the patient won't consent (refuses), or the patient can't consent or refuse (lacks the capacity to consent to the evaluation). In the last situation, some patients will comply with the evaluation but show questionable comprehension of the risks and benefits. These same decisional deficits may be affecting the patient's capacity to consent to treatment. In such cases, it is typical to note the patient's assent, detailing any areas of questionable ability to consent to the evaluation (in the absence of outright refusal). It is ethical to continue with a capacity evaluation for patients who are unable to fully consent to the evaluation as long as the evaluator has attempted to obtain informed consent and has fully disclosed the risks of the evaluation. However, a referral where there is questionable capacity to consent to a capacity evaluation does not, in itself, obviate the need to disclose the risks of the evaluation and attempt to obtain consent.

Assessment of Diagnosis

Medical, psychiatric, and neurocognitive disorders potentially impacting treatment decision making should be evaluated through examination of history and appropriate medical records, including laboratory and imaging results. Where appropriate (e.g., in cases in which an individual is not profoundly impaired), capacity assessment should include structured assessment of psychiatric symptomatology through standardized rating scales and/or neurocognitive abilities (e.g., attention, memory, executive function, language) through neuropsychological assessment. In most cases, a full neuropsychological battery is not necessary, but focused testing in areas of decisional deficit may be useful in clarifying the extent of the deficit in brain functioning.

Assessment of Decisional Abilities

In assessing decisional abilities, clinicians may utilize a capacity instrument, such as those previously described, or a clinical interview. A few suggestions for assessing decisional abilities through clinical interview follow.

It can be helpful to begin with the patient's perception of the situation by asking questions such as the following: What is your understanding of your problem/diagnosis? What is your understanding of the prognosis, or what will happen if the problem is not treated? What are the treatment options? What do they involve? How will they affect your daily life? How will each help? What do you want to do? If diagnostic and treatment information has not already been disclosed to the patient, it is more useful to first disclose the information to the patient and assess understanding and appreciation. Even in cases where the information has been disclosed, it is typically important to review this information with the patient, as some questions of capacity arise from patients' refusing treatment in the context of inadequate treatment description. Unfortunately, some obvious oversights can occur, such as the patient's being given information in English although his or her primary language is not English.

For more in-depth assessment of understanding, the method suggested by Grisso and P. S. Appelbaum (1998a) may prove useful. Disclosure is followed by questions that encourage patients to state "in their own words" their understanding of the information just provided. This approach can be augmented by providing the information in writing using a simplified, bulleted list, diminishing the memory component for the assessment of understanding, and focusing instead on comprehension. For some patients, it is useful and, in other cases, necessary to assess understanding through yes/no questions. For example, consider a patient with advanced multiple sclerosis who refuses hospital transfer, although this is at odds with a previously provided advance directive. In assessing his understanding of his condition, a series of yes/no questions was used: Does MS affect the brain? Is it a disease whose effects get worse over time? In this case, the patient answered no, although information about the condition had been disclosed to him just before the questioning. His responses to these and other yes/no questions indicated that he was unable to understand information about his condition.

In assessing appreciation, it is suggested that evaluators explore two means by which appreciation deficits may become manifest: either through disavowal of the condition and treatment benefits, or through difficulty in foresight (projecting treatment outcomes into the future). In our clinical experience, the former may be more impacted by psychiatric illness, whereas the latter may be impacted by neurodegenerative disorders affecting the frontal lobe (such as frontotemporal dementia). In assessing disavowal, a screening strategy can be useful. First, ask a neutral question, such as What do you believe is really wrong with you now? or Why is the doctor recommending the treatment? If answers suggest doubt or concern on the part of the patient, more directed questions may follow, such as Do you have doubt that the treatment will help you? or Do you believe the doctor may try to harm you? Another way that appreciation has been assessed is to ask What do you believe will happen to you without treatment? Some patients with dementia will not express disavowal based on paranoid processes but will have trouble projecting treatment benefits due to problems with foresight. In this case, it can be useful to ask What do you think will happen to you with the treatment? or What do you think your life will be like after the treatment? In our experience, some patients with dementia are acquiescent to a doctor's recommendations and profess they will be "fine," but when detailed follow-up questions are asked, they are unable to appreciate how the condition may affect them over time, or how the treatment may or may not ameliorate the problem.

In assessing reasoning, several approaches may be used. Grisso and P. S. Appelbaum (1998) recommend questions that direct the patient to explicitly compare treatment alternatives, such as Why do you think treatment x is better than treatment y? or What is it about treatment x that makes it seem better for you? Another approach is to attempt to elicit the reasons for a treatment decision by asking a question such as What are all the reasons you decided to do treatment x? or What risks and benefits did you consider in choosing treatment x? At this point in the interview, the expert may wish to consider the consistency of choices with values. For example, the evaluator could ask the patient to explain how various risks and benefits impact valued life activities, such as How would the tremors that may be caused by this medication affect your ability to do things that you enjoy? It is often useful to assess the patient's valued activities, relationships, and cultural/religious beliefs prior to the assessment of decisional abilities, as this creates a reference for in-depth questioning about the relationship of choices to stated values, preferences, and attitudes during the assessment of reasoning.

The assessment of the ability to communicate a choice is straightforward, by asking the patient to state which treatment is preferred. This may be done at both the beginning and end of the interview to evaluate the consistency of a choice.

Preferences for Decision-Making Participation

It is important to assess patients' motivation for and comfort with making their own medical treatment decisions. For example, the evaluator can ask: How do you usually make decisions about your medical care—alone or with the help of family or others? Is there anyone you would want to help you make this decision? Would you prefer that someone else make this decision for you? Who would you trust, and why? Is there anyone you would not trust to make decisions for you? After exploring the patient's level of interest to participate in medical decision making, and especially if he or she expresses discomfort about participating, it is important to ask: Is it all right to continue to guide you through your thoughts about this medical decision? If not, is there someone you would prefer I talk to?

Also, the evaluator can assess the patient's attitudes about proxy decision making. For example: If at some point you were so sick that you could not speak for yourself, who would you want to make decisions on your behalf? How do you want that person to make decisions: based on what he or she thinks you would have wanted ("substituted judgment" standard), or on whatever he or she feels is best at the time, all things being considered ("best interest" standard)?

Conceptions of Quality of Life

The assessment of values should focus on what makes life worthwhile for this particular patient and whether there are any life situations this patient would find intolerable. In addition, it is important to assess the individual's perspective on preserving life in any condition versus concern for maintaining a minimally acceptable quality of life. Here, asking about specific religious, cultural, or moral beliefs that may influence treatment decisions is important, especially regarding life-and-death medical decisions (e.g., whether to start or withdraw a life-sustaining treatment).

Regarding quality of life, it can help to ask about previous experiences with illness and medical care for the patient or others he or she knows. Experiences with pain, medical complications, loss, or related suffering—as well as positive experiences with healing, caregiving, or coping with disability—can profoundly influence current medical care decisions. It can be helpful to ask explicit questions, such as Can you imagine any circumstances in which you would rather be dead than remain alive ("fates worse than death")? It may be useful to assess what specific daily activities or abilities are most central to this patient's conception of a life worth living. For example, it can help to ask the patient how important it is to be able to communicate with loved ones, to think clearly, to move around (e.g., out of bed), to chew and swallow food, to take care of one's personal hygiene, to enjoy activities such as reading, television, and music. It can also help to ask patients what their worst fears are when they think about difficult medical decisions.

Interpersonal/Social Context

Medical treatment decisions do not occur in a social vacuum. It can be important to assess the extent to which patients may be making decisions in consideration of the interests of others or as influenced by the feelings of others. Patients may consider others' interests in valid ways consistent with their own values (e.g., concern for being an emotional or financial burden to one's spouse) or in ways subject to undue influence by others (e.g., overacquiescence to the values of others for fear of losing the relationship). Also, the current social context may greatly influence treatment decisions. For example, an elderly patient may want to risk a difficult surgery if the spouse is still alive but be ready to accept death if widowed, or a patient may want to survive for a specific event, such as the birth of a grandchild. It can be informative to ask: What thoughts do you have about how your illness or care might affect others in your life? Have other people's emotional or financial interests influenced your wishes about medical care?

Conclusion

The next step is to determine the conclusions of the assessment, both general findings and capacity-related findings, and share them with the patient, medical team, and relevant family members. In many settings, the results of a capacity assessment can provide a clinical diagnosis and treatment recommendations but should also clearly and directly answer the question of capacity, outline appropriate legal interventions, and, whenever possible, address less restrictive alternatives. Here, the clinician must balance the information at hand about the diagnosis, cognitive and psychiatric symptoms, and decisional functioning in view of interactive and contextual factors, such as the person's values, goals, preferences, and history and the situational risks. No cookbook exists for combining these factors; capacity conclusions are a professional clinical judgment. However, when the evaluator has carefully collected information regarding all the components, including standardized testing of cognition and behavior, the key elements to make such a judgment are at hand.

We find that capacity conclusions fall into three categories: (1) persons with gross and severe impairment; (2) persons with moderate impairments in some areas of function; and (3) persons with subtle or variable impairments, unique perspectives or values, or eccentric decisional styles. Detailed evaluation of a person with obvious and severe impairment, such as those who are unconscious following an accident or medical trauma, those in a persistent vegetative state, or those with advanced cases of dementia, is not appropriate. In situations in which the degree of impairment is extensive, the treating physician's documentation of the case is often sufficient to establish incapacity and frequently leads to the appointment of a surrogate decision maker with plenary powers. Assessment of individuals with moderate impairments, or who have significant impairments in some areas but not others, although not cursory, can be relatively straightforward. Following assessment of the diagnosis, functional abilities, and contextual factors, the assessment results should naturally lead to conclusions about the individual's ability to make decisions in various domains and should reveal more information about strengths and weaknesses than could be determined from a clinical diagnosis alone. Patients with subtle or variable impairments, unique values, or eccentric styles are indeed more challenging to assess. In these cases, more in-depth evaluation using capacity instruments and values interviews can help the clinician to sort through the issues of autonomy versus protection.

Dispositional Element

In some cases, the expert's job is to describe his or her capacity findings and then to leave the determination of legal capacity and appropriate actions to a judge. In other cases, the evaluator will offer recommendations for disposition. For example, the expert may conclude that a substitute decision maker is needed and recommend that a previously appointed health care proxy be activated or, if unavailable, that the hospital implement its policy of obtaining consent from the next of kin. At other times, when time allows, the evaluator will recommend that a medical decision await treatment of an underlying psychiatric or neurocognitive condition prior to pursuing medical treatment. The evaluation may also uncover decisional aids or cultural, language, or religious concerns that should be addressed as consent is obtained.

–––––––––––––––––––––––––––––––– **Illustrative Case** ––––––––––––––––––––––––––––––––

This is a summary of an evaluation for consent capacity. In the actual case, the full report provided more details on the patient's social, medical, and psychiatric history and specific test results.

This case illustrates several points: the importance of assessing individuals in their preferred language; the importance of assessing over several occasions when the patient may be delirious; the difference in abilities for simple versus complex decision making; the issue of consistency of stated values/beliefs with treatment choices; and capacity evaluation as an opportunity to make treatment recommendations.

Referral Question

Mr. R. is a 65-year-old, White Hispanic, Spanish- (preferred) and English-speaking male, residing in a nursing home. He was referred by his primary care physician, who requested an evaluation to assess patient's ability to consent to dialysis (patient is expressing reluctance/refusal). He has previously appointed his cousin Maria as his health care proxy.

Informed Consent

The patient was informed of the purpose of the evaluation (i.e., assessing his capacity to consent to dialysis), its risks and benefits, and his right not to cooperate. Mr. R. demonstrated limited but adequate understanding of the information. He understood that the purpose was "to help the doctor help me," that he did not have to participate, and that the results would be provided in a report to his doctor.

Current Diagnoses

Medical diagnoses include hepatitis B and C with associated cirrhosis and fluctuating mental status (hepatic encephalopathy), diabetes mellitus, chronic renal failure with progressively increasing creatinine, polysubstance dependence in remission, and Schizoaffective Disorder, depressed type. He has had multiple psychiatric hospitalizations with hallucinations and suicidal ideation. His medications are insulin, quetiapine 100 mg bid, 400 mg qhs, oxycodone 5 to 10 mg prn for pain, omeprazole, 20 mg po qd, salmeterol inhl, oral 1 puff bid, spironolactone BID Hold for BP 100 systolic or less; also, he takes eyedrops, a multivitamin, acetaminophen prn for pain, and stool softener prn.

Social History

Mr. R. grew up in Puerto Rico. His father is deceased; his mother, who has Schizophrenia, is alive. Most of his family is in Puerto Rico. He has limited contact with his family, except for his cousin Maria, who lives locally. He has a long history of unemployment and homelessness secondary to substance abuse and mental illness. He has never been married.

Behavioral Observations

Across the different days of testing, Mr. R. consistently exhibited depressed mood, flat affect, difficulty sustaining attention, poor eye contact, and auditory hallucinations. These symptoms appeared to be frequent, severe, and chronic in nature and reflected Mr. R.'s current baseline functioning. He was otherwise alert and oriented to person, place, and time. Mr. R. denied having suicidal or homicidal thoughts. He was able to engage in simple, meaningful conversations. He had good insight into his mental illness and mixed insight into his medical diagnoses.

Procedures

All interviews and testing were conducted in Spanish by a Spanish-speaking clinician. The evaluation was completed across 4 separate days (1 hour, 45 minutes total) to minimize the demands on the patient's attention and to provide an opportunity to observe him on different days and at different times of day.

Cognitive Abilities

On structured cognitive tests (MMSE, WAIS-III and Wechsler Memory Scale III subtests, Clock Drawing) he had moderate impairments in attention, concentration, and immediate memory, and severe impairments in delayed memory and judgment/planning (executive functions; MMSE = 18/30).

Decisional Abilities

On a structured interview of medical decision making adapted to the patient's condition, he had adequate *understanding* of his current problem: "The doctor says that my kidneys are not working because of my diabetes and I need to have dialysis, you know, when they put you on a machine to clean your blood." When asked to describe his feelings about the potential benefits of treatment (*appreciation*), he was reluctant, saying, "I am not sure that this will work for me; I don't think that a machine can clean my blood better than my body." When asked to explain why not having dialysis is better than having dialysis (*reasoning*), he stated, "I only want to have what is mine, and I don't want my blood outside my body going through a machine." When asked to describe what would happen without dialysis, he stated, "I hope that my body will heal by itself." When reminded that his doctor told him that he would die without dialysis, he said, "I want to live and I trust God will help my body heal without dialysis."

On a structured test of judgment regarding health and personal safety (Independent Living Scales [Loeb, 1996] Health and Safety subscale), he scored in the low/dependent range. He demonstrated the ability to call the police, get medical help, and handle aspects of his physical care. However, he did not show good judgment for personal safety, remembering to take his medications as prescribed, and the importance of knowing about the side effects of medications.

Values

Mr. R. said that what makes life worth living is "My mother, I do not want her to suffer and I know that she will if something happens to me." When asked whether the well-being of others influences his medical decision making, he said, "My mother told me to make sure I get better and that I listen to the doctors' recommendations." When asked who he wants involved in making medical decisions on his behalf, he said, "My cousin Maria; I can trust her to make decisions for me if I cannot do it myself." When asked for his preferences regarding resuscitation, he said, "I want to be revived; I want to live." He was unable to fully explain his reasoning other than that he just wanted to live. When asked if he had any religious beliefs that would prevent him from having dialysis, he said, "I don't, I just know that my body can heal with the help of God."

Summary

Mr. R. has ongoing hallucinations and displays considerable deficits in attention, memory, and planning. He has limited judgment in caring for his medical needs. In terms of medical decision making, he displays some understanding of his medical conditions, but his appreciation and reasoning about treatments are limited. These decisional abilities are influenced by his confusion, poor memory, concrete thinking, and psychiatric symptoms associated with Schizoaffective Disorder and chronic delirium.

Mr. R. can make simple medical decisions such as designating a family member as his health care proxy. However, complex medical decisions (i.e., receiving dialysis) will tax his ability to deliberate about the risks and benefits of treatments. Mr. R.'s expressed values are not consistent with his unwillingness to consider dialysis as a life-saving medical treatment. He reported, for example, how important it was for him to follow his mother's advice (i.e., "listen to the doctors"), and he also expressed a clear preference to be resuscitated because he wants to live. However, Mr. R. was unable to fully appreciate the consequences of not receiving dialysis and was fixated on the idea that his body will heal by itself with the help of God.

Mitigating Factors

His performance during the interview and testing was influenced by his medical conditions, pain, and fatigue, and also may be influenced by his medications, some of which could contribute to his confusion. His mental status could improve with dialysis, which could potentially improve his medical decision making.

Recommended Actions and Interventions

- If Mr. R. is alert and provided simple information in a structured manner, in Spanish, he can make very simple medical decisions. If possible, discuss situations with Mr. R. prior to his receiving sedating medications and when he is not in severe pain.
- For complex medical decisions, his health care proxy should make decisions. Mr. R. should be included in discussions.
- Regarding dialysis, his health care proxy should make the decision. However, it is not practical to force a patient to accept dialysis if he refuses. Thus, a discussion among Mr. R., his cousin, and the doctor should be encouraged that emphasizes why dialysis is being recommended and discusses means to make Mr. R. most comfortable during dialysis should his health care proxy consent and

should Mr. R. assent to the procedure. Given Mr. R.'s religious values, it may be useful to include a chaplain in this discussion. Finally, it may be helpful to encourage Mr. R. to try dialysis for a brief period of time to determine if he can tolerate it. The decision to dialyze could be reconsidered after there is more information as to how Mr. R. finds it.

- Given Mr. R.'s complex medical problems and prognosis, it is important to facilitate a discussion with family members about their understanding of his specific preferences and values regarding advanced illness interventions.

- Ongoing assessment and treatment of his psychiatric symptoms are recommended. Given Mr. R.'s ongoing hallucinations, his psychiatric treatment regimen should be reviewed.

RESEARCH PRIORITIES

The empirical foundations of consent capacity can be improved by studies that address the following aspects of capacity evaluation.

Instrument Development

Although the introduction of various forensic assessment instruments to assess consent capacity is a major advance in the field, the psychometric properties of these instruments are not well understood. Test-retest reliability is greatly understudied in both normal and patient populations. Intraindividual variability in capacity assessment-reassessment outcomes has important clinical and legal implications, as capacity is generally assumed to be relatively unchanging over short periods of time. A better understanding of the intrinsic variability in this functional domain is necessary for optimal application of current legal standards. For example, what is an appropriate time frame within which a capacity assessment should be conducted so as to be pertinent to a medical decision that has to be implemented? In addition, although most research teams can achieve good interscorer reliability with their own instruments, the interrater reliability of these instruments in the hands of practicing clinicians not involved in the research project is modest to disappointing.

Studies That Integrate Decisional Ability Assessment with Values Assessment

Many commentators describe the importance of assessing capacity as personally authentic decision making, that is, decisions that are consistent with an individual's values, preferences, and goals. The importance of values is seen in statutory language that emphasizes the need to promote an individual's autonomy and to consider the characteristic patterns and goals of the patient. More work is needed to describe and evaluate a values standard of capacity (i.e., capacity as choice consistent with values) and to also explore the impact of values on decision making. In some cases, values may act as a moderator of measured decision making, when interpersonal preferences (desire for input from others, concern for others, health locus of control, medical dissatisfaction) or decisional styles (focusing on salient aspects only) may color an individual's performance. Similarly, cohort, cultural, religious, or ethnic differences may explain some variability in obtained capacity scores, and in some cases indicate the inappropriateness of particular capacity assessment methods in certain populations.

Studies That Compare How Psychiatric and Neurocognitive Disorders Affect Decisional Abilities

At this point, it is not clear which specific cognitive or psychiatric impairments are likely to be associated with diminished decisional abilities, but the overall severity of these deficits is likely to correlated with capacity impairment. Adults with moderate dementia are likely to demonstrate the greatest problems in understanding diagnostic and treatment information, particularly in relation to memory deficits. Research confirms that diagnosis alone does not predict capacity impairment, underscoring the importance of functional assessment. More study of the impact of specific diagnoses on decisional abilities is needed. Current research is drawn from relatively small sample sizes, many of which lack control groups. Studies comparing decisional abilities across discrete diagnostic groups using the same methods are needed. When studies use different methodologies to compare different groups, it is unclear whether group differences are due to characteristics of the group or of the method. When studies use the same methodology to directly compare different groups, it eliminates the role of method variance in explaining observed differences between populations.

Studies That Compare Patient Populations to Normative Samples

Research regarding medical decision making in nonimpaired populations helps to broaden the empirical knowledge base concerning consent capacity. Informed consent and information-processing research is also relevant to improving the assessment of decisional capacity in elderly adults. This research shows that decision-making capacity evaluations aiming to optimize decisional abilities should utilize disclosure formats that are simplified and guided to enhance understanding (Dunn & Jeste, 2001; Taub et al., 1987). These may closely mimic good doctor-patient dialogues in which information is presented in a manner that maximizes patient participation, as compared to a test-like situation where a patient is required to memorize information. Capacity evaluations should not neglect to consider the impact of framing, order, and phrasing on the decision-making process. In addition, capacity evaluation should examine the age-appropriateness of and the cultural background for decision-making styles. Methods of scoring that emphasize the quantity of information recalled may penalize individuals who are lower in information seeking or who quickly sort and discard less relevant information (Johnson, 1990; Meyer, Russo, & Talbot, 1995; Streufert, Pogash, Piasecki, & Post, 1990). As another example, procedures that require rational manipulations of risks and benefits may penalize those individuals who make valid decisions in a more automatic or rule-based approach using expertise gained through life experience (Yates & Patalano, 1999).

An awareness of the subtle and complex factors that influence medical decisions in unimpaired adults has implications for how we conceptualize and craft instruments designed to improve the assessment of medical decision-making capacity in cognitively impaired patients. Unfortunately, normative studies of capacity assessment are limited. Little is known about how variables such as values, beliefs, experience, ethnicity, procedural variables, and processing styles impact capacity assessment, and what constitutes normal variability in decision-making styles as it relates to capacity.

Studies That Integrate Multiple Indexes of Validity

It is difficult to draw coherent conclusions from the empirical literature due to the heterogeneity of definitions and measures of decisional abilities that are applied to small samples using limited predictor variables. Integrated studies are needed that investigate the validity of capacity instruments and of capacity constructs themselves, through comparison of multiple methods of content and criterion validity. These studies should rigorously evaluate how decisional abilities (e.g., understanding, appreciation, reasoning, and expressing a choice) are defined and operationalized by both instruments and evaluators. We cannot assume that various conceptualizations and operationalizations are comprehensive or valid for all populations, or that because an instrument purports to measure a decisional ability, it does so. More work is especially needed to elaborate and validate the concept of appreciation. Is appreciation best thought of as insight, foresight, or judgment, and is appreciation impaired in different ways in different patient populations?

Research is needed to evaluate the relationship between decisional abilities and other variables to establish the criterion validity of instruments and, more broadly, to provide empirically grounded theoretical models of the relation between decisional abilities and various predictor and moderator variables. In considering cognitive predictors of capacity, it will be helpful to utilize broad neuropsychological batteries and multivariate approaches. Similarly, it will be useful to study the relationship between specific psychiatric impairments and individual decisional ability deficits.

Another important goal for research is to better define the relation between instrument-based and expert assessment. The ability to explain correspondence (or lack there of) between these two methods of assessment will enhance the empirical underpinnings of both. Similarly, studies that compare the correspondence of clinical judgments made by different clinicians are very much needed. A final area for criterion validity studies concerns the predictive validity of instrument-assessed capacity today with future performance when making medical decisions in real life.

Studies of Clinical Decision Making

A major advance during the 1990s was the introduction of consent capacity instruments that allowed the study of decisional abilities in various patient groups. These instruments allowed for investigations of consent capacity that began to elucidate the role of various decisional abilities and allowed for some comparison across studies. However, it is wrong to conclude that an instrument assessment of decisional abilities replicates the clinical assessment and judgment process; indeed, the developers of various instruments emphasize that such instruments are tools for clinical judgment and are not meant to supplant such judgment. Ideally, expert evaluators consider etiology, symptoms, and values along with an assessment of discrete decisional abilities and weigh these in the context of dual obligations of protection and autonomy. Study is needed to explore how clinicians integrate these various sources of data to arrive at an expert judgment. Repeatedly, those studies that examine instrument-based assessment and clinical determination find some, but not perfect, agreement. What other factors are clinicians considering, and how are they assessing and using that information? Also, given the suggestion that clinician's judgments may be influenced by disciplinary training, experience in the field, or other factors, it will be most significant to explore how and whether clinicians' own values impact their assessment of consent capacity.

REFERENCES

Allen-Burge, R., & Haley, W. E. (1997). Individual differences and surrogate medical decisions: Differing preferences for life-sustaining treatments. *Aging and Mental Health, 1,* 121–131.

American Bar Association. (2003). *Model rules of professional conduction.* Washington, DC: Author.

Anderer, S. J. (1990). *Determining competency in guardianship proceedings.* Washington, DC: American Bar Association.

Appelbaum, P. S., & Grisso, T. (1988). Assessing patients' capacities to consent to treatment. *New England Journal of Medicine, 319,* 1635–1638.

Appelbaum, P. S., & Grisso, T. (1992). *Manual for perceptions of disorder.* Worcester: University of Massachusetts Medical School.

Astrom, A. N., & Blay, D. (2002). Multidimensional Health Locus of Control scales: Applicability among Ghanaian adolescents. *East African Medical Journal, 79,* 128–133.

Barton, C. D., Mallik, H. S., Orr, W. B., & Janofsky, J. S. (1996). Clinicians' judgment of capacity of nursing home patients to give informed consent. *Psychiatric Services, 47,* 956–960.

Bean, G., Nishisato, S., Rector, N. A., & Glancy, G. (1996). The assessment of competence to make a treatment decision: An empirical approach. *Canadian Journal of Psychiatry, 41,* 85–92.

Beisecker, A. (1988). Aging and the desire for information and input in medical decisions: Patient consumerism in medical encounters. *Gerontologist, 28,* 330–335.

Berg, J. W., Appelbaum, P. S., Lidz, C. W., & Parker, L. S. (2001). *Informed consent: Legal theory and clinical practice.* New York: Oxford University Press.

Birren, J. E., Lubben, J. E., Rowe, J. C., & Deutschman, D. E. (Eds.). (1991). *The concept and measurement of quality of life in the frail elderly.* San Diego, CA: Academic Press.

Blackhall, L. J., Murphy, S. T., Frank, G., Michel, V., & Azen, S. (1995). Ethnicity and attitudes toward patient autonomy. *Journal of the American Medical Association, 274,* 820–825.

Blanchard-Fields, F. (1996). Emotion and everyday problem solving in adult development. In C. Magai & S. H. McFadden (Eds.), *Handbook of emotion, adult development, and aging* (pp. 149–165). London: Academic Press.

Caralis, P. V., Davis, B., Wright, K., & Marcial, E. (1993). The influence of ethnicity and race on attitudes towards advance directives, life-prolonging treatments, and euthanasia. *Journal of Clinical Ethics, 4,* 155–165.

Carney, M. T., Neugroschl, J., Morrison, R. S., Marin, D., & Siu, A. L. (2001). The development and piloting of a capacity assessment tool. *Journal of Clinical Ethics, 12,* 17–23.

Clemens, E., & Hayes, H. E. (1997). Assessing and balancing elderly risk, safety and autonomy: Decision making practices of elder care workers. *Home Health Care Services Quarterly, 16,* 3–20.

Collopy, B. J. (1999). The moral underpinning of the proxy-provider relationship: Issues of trust and distrust. *Journal of Law, Medicine, and Ethics, 27,* 37–45.

Craik, F. I. M. (1994). Memory changes in normal aging. *Current Directions in Psychological Science, 3,* 155–158.

Craik, F. I. M., & Byrd, M. (1982). Aging and cognitive deficits: The role of attentional resources. In F. I. M. Craik & S. Trehub (Eds.), *Aging and cognitive processes* (pp. 191–211). New York: Plenum Press.

Craik, F. I. M., & Jennings, J. M. (1992). Human memory. In F. I. M. Craik & T. A. Salthouse (Eds.), *The handbook of aging and cognition* (pp. 51–110). Hillsdale, NJ: Erlbaum.

Degner, L., & Sloan, J. (1992). Decision making during serious illness: What role do patients really want to play? *Journal of Clinical Epidemiology, 45,* 941–950.

Deimling, G. T., Smerglia, V. L., & Barresi, C. M. (1990). Health care professionals and family involvement in care-related decisions concerning older patients. *Journal of Aging and Health, 2,* 310–325.

Dellasega, C., Frank, L., & Smyer, M. (1996). Medical decision-making capacity in elderly hospitalized patients. *Journal of Ethics, Law, and Aging, 2,* 65–74.

Ditto, P. H., Druley, J. A., Moore, K. A., Danks, J. H., & Smucker, W. D. (1996). Fates worse than death: The role of valued life activities in health-state evaluations. *Health Psychology, 15,* 332–343.

Drane, J. F. (1985). The many faces of competency. *Hastings Center Report, 15,* 17–21.

Drogin, E. Y., & Barrett, C. L. (2003). Substituted judgment: Notes of one forensic psychologist. In I. B. Weiner (Series Ed.) & A. M. Goldstein (Vol. Ed.), *Comprehensive handbook of psychology: Vol. 11. Forensic psychology* (pp. 305–334). Hoboken, NJ: Wiley.

Dunn, L. B., & Jeste, D. V. (2001). Enhancing informed consent for research and treatment. *Neuropsychopharmacology, 24,* 595–607.

Dymek, M. P., Atchison, P., Harrell, L., & Marson, D. C. (2001). Competency to consent to medical treatment in cognitively impaired patients with Parkinson's disease. *Neurology, 56,* 17–24.

Earnst, K. S., Marson, D. C., & Harrell, L. E. (2000). Cognitive model of physicians' legal standard and personal judgments of competency in patients with Alzheimer's disease. *Journal of the American Geriatric Society, 48,* 919–927.

Edelstein, B. (1999). *Hopemont Capacity Assessment Interview manual and scoring guide.* Morgantown: West Virginia University.

Eleazer, G. P., Hornung, C. A., Egbert, C. B., Egbert, J. R., Eng, C., Hedgepeth, J., et al. (1996). The relationship between ethnicity and advance directives in a frail older population. *Journal of the American Geriatrics Society, 44,* 938–943.

Engleman, H. M., & Wild, M. R. (2003). Improving CPAP use by patients with the Sleep Apnoea/Hypopnoea syndrome (SAHS). *Sleep Medicine Review, 7,* 81–99.

Etchells, E., Darzins, P., Silberfeld, M., Singer, P. A., McKenny, J., Naglie, G., et al. (1999). Assessment of patients' capacity to consent to treatment. *Journal of General Internal Medicine, 14,* 27–34.

Fitten, L. J., Lusky, R., & Hamann, C. (1990). Assessing treatment decision-making capacity in elderly nursing home residents. *Journal of the American Geriatrics Society, 38,* 1097–1104.

Fitten, L. J., & Waite, M. S. (1990). Impact of medical hospitalization on treatment decision making capacity in the elderly. *Archives of Internal Medicine, 150,* 1717–1721.

Fowers, B. J. (1994). Perceived control, illness status, stress, and adjustment to cardiac illness. *Journal of Psychology, 128,* 567–576.

Frank, L., Smyer, M., Grisso, T., & Appelbaum, P. (1999). Measurement of advance directive and medical treatment decision-making capacity of older adults. *Journal of Mental Health and Aging, 5,* 257–274.

Ganzini, L., Volicer, L., Nelson, W., & Derse, A. (2003). Pitfalls in the assessment of decision-making capacity. *Psychosomatics, 44,* 237–243.

Grisso, T. (2003). *Evaluating competences* (2nd ed.). New York: Plenum Press.

Grisso, T., & Appelbaum, P. S. (1992). *Manual for understanding treatment disclosures.* Worcester: University of Massachusetts Medical School.

Grisso, T., & Appelbaum, P. S. (1993). *Manual for thinking rationally about treatment.* Worcester: University of Massachusetts Medical School.

Grisso, T., & Appelbaum, P. S. (1995a). Comparison of standards for assessing patient's capacities to make treatment decisions. *American Journal of Psychiatry, 152,* 1033–1037.

Grisso, T., & Appelbaum, P. S. (1995b). The MacArthur Treatment Competency Study III: Abilities of patients to consent to psychiatric and medical treatment. *Law and Human Behavior, 19,* 149–174.

Grisso, T., & Appelbaum, P. S. (1998a). *Assessing competence to consent to treatment.* New York: Oxford University Press.

Grisso, T., & Appelbaum, P. S. (1998b). *MacArthur Competency Assessment Tool for Treatment (MacCAT-T).* Sarasota, FL: Professional Resource Press.

Grisso, T., Appelbaum, P. S., Mulvey, E. P., & Fletcher, K. (1995). The MacArthur Treatment Competency Study II: Measures of abilities related to competence to consent to treatment. *Law and Human Behavior, 19,* 127–148.

Hardwig, J. (1990). What about the family? *Hastings Center Report, 30,* 5–10.

Hopp, F. P., & Duffy, S. A. (2000). Racial variations in end-of-life care. *Journal of the American Geriatrics Society, 48,* 658–663.

Hornung, C. A., Eleazer, G. P., Strothers, H. S., Wieland, G. D., Eng, C., McCann, R., et al. (1998). Ethnicity and decision-makers in a group of frail older people. *Journal of the American Geriatrics Society, 46,* 280–286.

Johansson, B., Grant, J. D., Plomin, R., Pedersen, N. L., Ahern, F., Berg, S., et al. (2001). Health locus of control in late life: A study of genetic and environmental influences in twins aged 80 years and older. *Health Psychology, 20,* 33–40.

Johnson, M. M. S. (1990). Age differences in decision making: A process methodology for examining strategic information processing. *Journal of Gerontology, 45,* 75–78.

Karel, M. J., & Gatz, M. (1996). Factors influencing life-sustaining treatment decisions in a community sample of families. *Psychology and Aging, 11,* 226–234.

Karel, M. J., Powell, J., & Cantor, M. (2004). Using a values discussion guide to facilitate communication in advance care planning. *Patient Education and Counseling,* 22–31.

Karp, N., & Wood, E. (2003). *Incapacitated and alone: Health care decision-making for the unbefriended elderly.* Washington, DC: American Bar Association.

Kim, S. Y. H., & Caine, E. D. (2002). Utility and limits of the Mini Mental State Examination in evaluating consent capacity in Alzheimer's disease. *Psychiatric Services, 53,* 1322–1324.

Kim, S. Y. H., Caine, E. D., Currier, G. W., Leibovici, A., & Ryan, J. M. (2001). Assessing the competence of persons with Alzheimer's disease in providing informed consent for participation in research. *American Journal of Psychiatry, 158,* 712–717.

Kim, S. Y. H., Karlawish, J. H. T., & Caine, E. D. (2002). Current state of research on decision-making competence of cognitively impaired elderly persons. *American Journal of Geriatric Psychiatry, 10,* 151–165.

Kuhberger, A. (1998). The influence of framing on risky decisions: A meta-analysis. *Organizational Behavior and Human Decision Processes, 75,* 23–55.

Lawton, M. P., Moss, M., Hoffman, C., Grant, R., Have, T. T., & Kleban, M. H. (1999). Health, valuation of life, and the wish to live. *Gerontologist, 39,* 406–416.

Lockhart, L. K., Ditto, P. H., Danks, J. H., Cooppola, K. M., & Smucker, W. D. (2001). The stability of older adults' judgments of fates better and worse than death. *Death Studies, 25,* 299–317.

Loeb, P. A. (1996). *Independent living scales.* New York: Psychological Corporation.

Margulies, P. (1994). Access, connection, and voice: A contextual approach to representing senior clients of questionable capacity. *Fordham Law Review, 62,* 1073.

Marson, D. C., Annis, S. M., McInturff, B., Bartolucci, A., & Harrell, L. E. (1999). Error behaviors associated with loss of competency in Alzheimer's disease. *Neurology, 53,* 1983–1992.

Marson, D. C., Chatterjee, A., Ingram, K. K., & Harrell, L. E. (1996). Toward a neurologic model of competency: Cognitive predictors of capacity to consent in Alzheimer's disease using three different legal standards. *Neurology, 46,* 666–672.

Marson, D. C., Cody, H. A., Ingram, K. K., & Harrell, L. E. (1995). Neuropsychological predictors of competency in Alzheimer's disease using a rational reasons legal standard. *Archives of Neurology, 52,* 955–959.

Marson, D. C., Earnst, K., Jamil, F., Bartolucci, A., & Harrell, L. E. (2000). Consistency of physicians' legal standard and personal judgments of competency in patients with Alzheimer's disease. *Journal of the American Geriatrics Society, 48,* 911–918.

Marson, D. C., Ingram, K. K., Cody, H. A., & Harrell, L. E. (1995). Assessing the competency of patients with Alzheimer's disease under different legal standards. *Archives of Neurology, 52,* 949–954.

Marson, D. C., McInturff, B., Hawkins, L., Bartolucci, A., & Harrell, L. E. (1997). Consistency of physician judgments of capacity to consent in mild Alzheimer's disease. *American Geriatrics Society, 45,* 453–457.

Mazur, D. J., & Merz, J. F. (1993). How the manner of presentation of data influences older patients in determining their treatment preferences. *Journal of the American Geriatrics Society, 41,* 223–228.

McKee, D. R. (2001). *The effects of framing on younger and older adults' medical decision making.* Unpublished doctoral dissertation, West Virginia University, Morgantown.

McNeil, B. J., Pauker, S. G., Sox, H. C., & Tversky, A. (1982). On the elicitation of preferences for alternative therapies. *New England Journal of Medicine, 305,* 1259–1262.

Meyer, B. J. F., Russo, C., & Talbot, A. (1995). Discourse comprehension and problem solving: Decisions about the treatment of breast cancer by women across the lifespan. *Psychology and Aging, 10,* 84–103.

Mezey, M., Kluger, M., Maislin, G., & Mittelman, M. (1996). Life-sustaining treatment decisions by spouses of patients with Alzheimer's disease. *Journal of the American Geriatrics Society, 44,* 144–150.

Moye, J. (1999). Assessment of competency and decision making capacity. In P. Lichtenberg (Ed.), *Handbook of assessment in clinical gerontology* (pp. 488–528). New York: Wiley.

Moye, J. (2000). Mr. Franks refuses surgery: Cognition and values in competency determination in complex cases. *Journal of Aging Studies, 14,* 385–401.

Moye, J., Gurrera, R., Karel, M. J., Edelstein, B., & O'Connell, C. (in press). Empirical advances in the assessment of the capacity to consent to medical treatment: Clinical implications and research needs. *Clinical Psychology Review.*

Moye, J., & Karel, M. (1999). Evaluating decisional capacities in older adults: Results of two clinical studies. *Advances in Medical Psychology, 10,* 71–84.

Moye, J., Karel, M. J., Azar, A. R., & Gurrera, R. J. (2004a). Capacity to consent to treatment: Empirical comparison of three instruments in older adults with and without dementia. *Gerontologist, 44,* 166–175.

Moye, J., Karel, M. J., Azar, A. R., & Gurrera, R. J. (2004b). Hopes and cautions for instrument-based evaluations of consent capacity: Results of a construct validity study of three instruments. *Ethics, Law, and Aging Review, 10,* 39–61.

Nash, D. L., & Giles, S. L. (1989, August). Assessing competency competently. *VA Practitioner,* 93–100.

National Conference of Commissioners on Uniform State Laws. (1993). *Uniform Health Care Decisions Act.* Available from http://www.law.upenn.edu/bll/ulc/fnact99/1990s/uhcda93.pdf.

National Conference of Commissioners on Uniform State Laws. (1997). *Uniform Guardianship and Protective Proceedings Act.* Available from http://www.law.upenn.edu/bll/ulc/fnact99/1990s/ugppa97.htm.

Park, D. C., Morrel, R. W., & Shifren, K. (1999). *Processing of medical information in aging patients: Cognitive and human factors perspectives.* Mahwah, NJ: Erlbaum.

Pearlman, R. A., Cain, K. C., Patrick, D. L., Appelbaum-Maizel, M., Starks, H. E., Jecker, N. S., et al. (1993). Insights pertaining to patient assessments of states worse than death. *Journal of Clinical Ethics, 4,* 33–41.

Pearlman, R. A., Starks, H., Cain, K. C., & Cole, W. G. (2005). Improvements in advance care planning in the Veterans Affairs system: Results of a multifaceted intervention. *Archives of Internal Medicine, 165,* 667–674.

Petrisek, A. C., Laliberte, L. L., Allen, S. M., & Mor, V. (1997). The treatment decision-making process: Age differences in a sample of women recently diagnosed with nonrecurrent, early-stage breast cancer. *Gerontologist, 37,* 598–608.

President's Commission for the Study of Ethical Problems in Medicine and Biomedical and Behavioral Research. (1982). *Making health care decisions (Vol. 1).* Washington, DC: U.S. Government Printing Office.

Pruchno, R. A., Smyer, M. A., Rose, M. S., Hartman-Stein, P. E., & Laribee-Henderson, D. L. (1995). Competence of long-term care residents to participate in decisions about their medical care: A brief, objective assessment. *Gerontologist, 35,* 622–629.

Puchalski, C. M., Zhong, Z., Jacobs, M. M., Fox, E., Lynn, J., Harrold, J., et al. (2000). Patients who want their family and physician to make resuscitation decisions for them: Observations from support and help. *Journal of the American Geriatrics Society, 48,* S84–S90.

Richardson, S. (2003). Health care decision-making: A guardian's authority. *Bifocal, 24,* 1–10.

Rolland, J. D. (1994). *Families, illness, and disability: An integrative treatment model.* New York: Basic Books.

Roth, L. H., Meisel, C. A., & Lidz, C. A. (1977). Tests of competency to consent to treatment. *Canadian Journal of Psychiatry, 134,* 279–284.

Rothchild, E. (1994). Family dynamics in end-of-life treatment decisions. *General Hospital Psychiatry, 16,* 251–258.

Royall, D. R., Cordes, J., & Polk, M. (1997). Executive control and the comprehension of medical information by elderly retirees. *Experimental Aging Research, 23,* 301–313.

Sabatino, C. P., & Basinger, S. L. (2000). Competency: Reforming our legal fictions. *Journal of Mental Health and Aging, 6,* 119–143.

Sachs, G. A., Stocking, C. B., & Stern, R. (1994). Ethical aspects of dementia research: Informed consent and proxy consent. *Clinical Research, 42,* 403–412.

Salthouse, T. A., & Babcock, R. L. (1991). Decomposing adult age differences in working memory. *Developmental Psychology, 27,* 763–776.

Schmand, B., Gouwenberg, B., Smit, J. H., & Jonker, C. (1999). Assessment of mental competency in community-dwelling elderly. *Alzheimer Disease and Associated Disorders, 13,* 80–87.

Singer, P. A., Martin, D. K., Lavery, J. V., Theil, E. C., Kelner, M., & Mendelssohn, D. C. (1998). Reconceptualizing advance care planning from the patient's perspective. *Archives of Internal Medicine, 158,* 879–884.

Staats, N., Edelstein, B., & Null, J. (1995, November). *Neuropsychological correlates of thinking rationally about treatment tests.* Paper presented at the meeting of the Gerontological Society of America, Los Angeles.

Streufert, S., Pogash, R., Piasecki, M., & Post, G. M. (1990). Age and management team performance. *Psychology and Aging, 5,* 551–559.

Taub, H. A., Baker, M. T., Kline, G. E., & Sturr, J. F. (1987). Comprehension of informed consent by young-old and old-old volunteers. *Experimental Aging Research, 13,* 173–178.

Tepper, A., & Elwork, A. (1984). Competency to consent to treatment as a psycholegal construct. *Law and Human Behavior, 8,* 205–223.

Walker, L., & Bradley, E. (1998). Assessment of capacity to discuss advance care planning in nursing homes. *Journal of the American Geriatrics Society, 46,* 1055–1056.

Wallston, K. A., Wallston, B. S., & DeVellis, R. (1978). Development of the Multidimensional Health Locus of Control (MHLC) scale. *Health Education Monographs, 6,* 160–170.

Wardle, J., & Steptoe, A. (2003). Socioeconomic differences in attitudes and beliefs about healthy lifestyles. *Journal of Epidemiology and Community Health, 57,* 440–443.

Wear, S. (1993). *Informed consent: Patient autonomy and physician beneficence within clinical medicine.* Boston: Kluwer Press.

Whitlatch, C. J., Feinberg, L. F., & Tucke, S. S. (2005). Measuring the values and preferences for everyday care of persons with cognitive impairment and their family caregivers. *Gerontologist, 45,* 370–380.

Wong, J. G., Clare, I. C. H., Holland, A. J., Watson, P. C., & Gunn, M. (2000). The capacity of people with a "mental disability" to make a health care decision. *Psychological Medicine, 30,* 295–306.

Yates, J. F., & Patalano, A. L. (1999). Decision making and aging. In D. C. Park, R. W. Morrell, & K. Shifren (Eds.), *Processing of medical information in aging patients: Cognition and human factors perspective* (pp. 31–54). Mahwah, NJ: Erlbaum.

CHAPTER 12

Termination of Parental Rights

Lois Oberlander Condie and Don Condie

Public policy relevant to child protective services allows the state to intervene on behalf of child victims of maltreatment, and, in the most serious cases, the law provides for termination of parental rights under specified circumstances. In termination of parental rights proceedings, the court frequently seeks the expertise of mental health professionals to assess the capacity of parents to care for and meet the needs of their children. Although parenting involves a broadly defined set of proficiencies, in termination proceedings, the court is concerned with the minimal level of parenting competence needed to adequately care for and protect children.

Each state has statutorily defined jurisdiction to strengthen and encourage family life for the protection and care of children, with the goal of ensuring the rights of children to sound physical, mental, and moral development. Statutes governing the care and protection of children contain provisions for mandatory reporting of maltreatment, and all states allow for intervention in substantiated cases of child maltreatment. States have the authority to encourage the use, by any family, of available resources to promote the safety of children. In a termination of parental rights proceeding, the state alleges that even after the provision of relevant services, the parent remains unable or unfit to care for the child. The court is concerned with the behaviors and capacities of the adult in his or her role as parent, and the harm that may, or has, come to the child. Forensic mental health professionals may be called on to provide expertise on the functioning and competence of adults in their role of parent and for expertise on the well-being of the children and their responses to maltreatment. In the case of complex blended families, often without clear familial structures and sometimes with unique cultural or community definitions of who is part of a family, forensic evaluations usually focus on more than one party. Cases are notable for the number of involved parties, the number of relevant issues within individuals and across relationship and family dynamics, and the cultural and socioeconomic features of child-rearing and family norms.

Opinions by the expert are sought to inform the legal decision maker's judgments about the suitability of an eventual return of the child to the custody of the parent and about what, if anything further, must take place for the reunification to be successful. If the judge is persuaded by the state's evidence to rule in favor of termination of parental rights, then termination results in a complete severance of all legal ties between a parent and a child and ends all parental rights. Thereafter, the child is free to be adopted without notice to or consent of the parent. Some post-termination contact may be permitted, depending on any preadjudication agreements that may have been reached.

The prevailing standard for the care and protection of children is the *best interest* standard, the underlying philosophy that shapes and sets the tone for state intervention. Upon the court's granting of a care and protection petition, a parent may temporarily lose physical custody of the child, as well as substantial legal power to make day-to-day decisions about the child. The parent retains procedural rights to notice and to be heard regarding the child, along with presumptive substantive rights to reunification services, visitation, communication, and eventual reunification. Evaluations take place as cases move through multiple steps that involve varying degrees of parent-child contact. The unique emotional connection between parents and children, whether deep or seemingly superficial in some cases, envelop cases with passion and sentiment that usually are kept at arm's length in the impartial context of the courtroom. Although objectivity among evaluators, attorneys, judges, and guardians ad litem is always important, emphasizing objectivity in one's manner and approach is particularly important in termination proceedings.

This chapter describes the role of the forensic mental health professional in care and protection matters, with emphasis on those cases that proceed to a court hearing on termination of parental rights. We begin with a review of the landscape of relevant legal standards and supporting case law. We then review relevant psychological principles and theories of parenting and child development, their application to individual cases of maltreatment, and standards of practice for forensic mental health assessment in the context of care and protection matters. The final section provides suggestions for report preparation, organization, and strategies for interpretation.

THE CHILD CARE AND PROTECTION SYSTEM

The legal framework of child protective service intervention is found in state statutes, typically modeled after federal policy initiatives. State statutes vary, but one common feature is intervention in cases of harm or risk of serious harm resulting from physical abuse, sexual abuse, and neglect of children by caregivers. The organization of legal and administrative systems for child protection also varies across states; child protective cases may be heard in either probate or juvenile court, depending on how the system is organized within a given state. When the court grants jurisdiction of a care and protection matter to the state child protective services agency, it includes the power to determine the child's placement, medical care, and educational care (R. D. Goldstein, 1999). Under conditions of serious harm or risk of harm to a child, statutes contain provisions for emergency placement outside the family home, usually for up to 3 days. The child is then returned to the parents if the matter is resolved, or the case moves to a court hearing to determine whether there is sufficient evidence of maltreatment, as defined by statutes and relevant state policies, to warrant state jurisdiction (Melton, Petrila, Poythress, & Slobogin, 1997). Evidence includes the child protective agency's investigation of facts related to the child's safety and a mechanism for subjecting investigators and their records to cross-examination. If jurisdiction is assumed, the state is granted power to place the child in foster or residential care and to control visitation between the parent and the child. Parent-child visitation cannot be barred altogether unless the state demonstrates that visitation poses a risk of harm to the child. Care and protection statutes sometimes are linked to criminal codes, so that state child protective service jurisdiction results in an automatic referral of the case to the criminal justice system. Administrative regulations specify the responsibilities of child protective service officials and procedural issues. Procedurally, there is a provision for a hearing if the parent objects to the child protective or judicial decisions (R. D. Goldstein, 1999). Forensic evaluators may be called on to provide data at hearings that support a parent's petition for modifications in service plans, if indicated by the data.

The state, via the child protective services agency, is one source of evaluation referrals for forensic psychologists. Attorneys for parents represent another source of assessment referrals. In some states, parents are provided attorneys through indigent funding mechanisms, but states are not constitutionally obligated to provide funding (Condie, 2003). Indigent funding has direct bearing on financial support for parents who seek an independent forensic evaluation. In care and protection matters, children are appointed their own counsel (Melton et al., 1997), and the child's attorney may serve as the referring party for an evaluation. Annual permanency hearings are conducted to determine the status of the case and whether continued jurisdiction is warranted, and it is in preparation for those hearings that expert consultation may be sought. Statutes provide for voluntary surrender of parental custody of children for the purpose of consenting to adoption. Child protective service officials often will attempt to negotiate a voluntary surrender before petitioning the court for termination of parental rights. Should the parent agree to a surrender, an evaluation referral might be made to assist the court in determining whether the parent is competent to enter into an agreement for a voluntary surrender of parental rights (Condie, 2003). In cases in which termination of parental rights is not granted, but a return home is premature, a referral for legal guardianship may be sought. In cases involving adolescents, provisions are made for eventual transition to independent living (Kantrowitz & Limon, 2001).

Care and protection evaluation referrals may be initiated in the early, middle, or termination phase of a case. Initial referrals are made to assist with the identification of goals for parents. Later referrals tend to focus on helping the child protective services agency to evaluate case outcomes or assisting in the determination of whether the case warrants a move by the agency to the final step of petitioning the court for termination of parental rights. Although referrals may take many forms, there are recurring evaluation requests: (a) identification of the caregiver's need for services after the court assumes jurisdiction, (b) the current risk the parent poses to the child, (c) the child's current functioning and treatment needs, (d) the impact of maltreatment on the child, (e) the caregiver's amenability to interventions, (f) the child's capacity to provide an account of the maltreatment, (g) the child's attachment to substitute caregivers, and (h) the child's readiness for adoption (Condie, 2003). The legal context for these referral questions is found in state statutes governing care and protection proceedings and statutory criteria for the termination of parental rights.

THE LEGAL BASIS OF CHILD CARE AND PROTECTION

What follows is a brief review of the broader context of constitutional law and case law. Forensic experts benefit from contextual knowledge of the strategies relied on by attorneys to provide a legal defense for parents facing possible termination of parental rights, and those used by attorneys to advocate for children who might not recognize their own safety needs.

Child Welfare and Safety

Over time, there have been fluctuations in law and public policy relevant to parental rights, family privacy, and children's safety needs. Although parental rights and child safety are not inherently opposed, the relative weight accorded to each has changed over time (Condie, 2003). Parental rights have their basis in English common law and its subsequent manifestations in U.S. law, and more recently in U.S. Supreme Court family privacy cases. Historically, parents have possessed relatively strong rights because of traditional views of children as the property of parents (R. D. Goldstein, 1999). As a counterbalance to the U.S. Supreme Court cases that protect parental rights and family autonomy, attorneys turn to cases and statutes relevant to child safety and protection as a basis for arguing that a child would be best protected if he or she were permanently removed from the family of origin and placed with substitute caregivers. Until approximately the eighteenth century, children were viewed as small adults who had no rights. Begging by children, child labor, and infanticide were not uncommon. The concept of childhood itself was hardly recognized.

Mary Ellen McCormack

The absolute nature of parental rights was eroded because of cases like that of Mary Ellen Wilson, later known as Mary Ellen McCormack (Shelman & Lazoritz, 2005). In 1864, Mary Ellen was born to Thomas and Frances Wilson. Later that same year, Thomas Wilson, Mary Ellen's biological father, was killed in the U.S. Civil War. Frances was unable to support herself and her daughter with her pension, so she took a job, placing Mary Ellen in the care of Mary Score, a private foster care provider. When Frances stopped sending her $2 per week foster care payment, Mary Ellen was turned over to the New York Department of Charities, who placed her in an institution for destitute children. On January 2, 1866, a couple unknown to Mary Ellen, Thomas and Mary McCormack, appeared before the Department of Charities, claiming that Mary Ellen was born to Thomas's mistress and then abandoned by her. Mary Ellen was turned over to the McCormack couple despite the lack of documentation of their claim. Thomas McCormack, the gentleman making the claim with his wife, died within the next 9 months. Mary McCormack, Mary Ellen's new mother, then married Francis Connolly. Over the next 6 years, neighbors became increasingly concerned about Mary Ellen, whose body was covered with bruises and cuts. The landlady observed that Mary Ellen was confined to her room in the hot summer, she was underdressed in the cold winter, she was forced to do manual labor beyond the capacity of a child, and she was more malnourished than other impoverished children in the overcrowded neighborhood (Shelman & Lazoritz, 2005).

When Mary Ellen was 9, the landlady brought her to the attention of Etta Wheeler, a social worker affiliated with a local church. Under the pretense of inquiring about a sick neighbor, Wheeler observed Mary Ellen and her living conditions. She sought help on behalf of Mary Ellen, but the New York City Police would not intervene without proof of assault because there was no law allowing intervention inside a child's home and no way to enter the home without proof that a crime had been committed. Wheeler approached numerous charitable organizations, and all agreed to help, but only by legal means. Wheeler finally approached Henry Bergh, the founder of the American Society for the Prevention of Cruelty to Animals (ASPCA), prepared with an argument that Mary Ellen, as a human, was a member of the animal kingdom and therefore entitled to the protection of the ASPCA (Shelman & Lazoritz, 2005).

Sensationalized journalistic accounts at the time left some facts unclear, but it appears likely that Bergh hired a private investigator, learned how Mary Ellen became a member of the Connolly household, and used the information to argue that the Connolly parents were not Mary Ellen's biological parents nor her lawful custodians. The argument was upheld because there was no documentation to support the claims that Thomas McCormack or Mary (McCormack) Connolly, the couple who had claimed Mary Ellen, were in any way related to Mary Ellen. Bergh offered ample evidence that Mary Ellen was in clear danger of being maimed or possibly killed, and the judge issued a warrant for Mary Ellen's appearance. A popular, but perhaps apocryphal, journalistic account cites Bergh pleading that if there was no justice for Mary Ellen as a human being, then she should at least be accorded the same rights of an animal in the street not to be abused. A journalist noted that the first chapter of children's rights was being written in the courtroom. Mary Ellen was turned over to the temporary custody of the matron of police headquarters, and the next day, five indictments were brought against Mary Connolly. The jury reached a verdict of guilty of assault and battery, and Mrs. Connolly was sentenced to 1 year of hard labor in the city penitentiary. As a result of publicity generated by this case, there was a public outcry for change in the way children were treated. The Society for the Prevention of Cruelty to Children was formed, and by 1900, there were 161 such groups in the United States.

The Best Interest Standard

A second turning point was the case of *Chapsky v. Wood* (1881), the standard-bearer for children's interests and autonomy. Although there was an historical trend away from viewing children as property in favor of honoring the bonds of affection between children and caregivers, it was not until *Chapsky v. Wood* that the legal system first formally acknowledged the *best interest* doctrine that forms the basis for current policies and procedures in care and protection matters. In *Chapsky v. Wood*, a biological father sought to reclaim custody of his child after the death of his wife, from a maternal aunt who had cared for the child since infancy. Custody of the child was awarded to the aunt after the court rendered a judgment that the psychological tie that had formed between the aunt and the child was stronger and more potent that any that sprung from the biological relatedness between the absent father and the child. In upholding the decision to leave the child in the aunt's care, the *Chapsky* court recognized the psychological ties that bind children to nonparents. The court specifically stated that children are not chattel, and the right to custody by a biological parent is not absolute. The court held that over time, the ties of biological relatedness weaken and the ties of companionship strengthen and that the prosperity and welfare of the child depended on the strength of those ties of affection. The court set the framework for modern views of attachment and family relationships as a benchmark for judging the needs and safety interests of children, and it abandoned the traditional view of children as property (Condie, 2003).

The procedures and details for bringing the best interest doctrine to fruition are found in state statutes, and the reach and limitations of the doctrine are found in case law. Cases like *McCormack* and *Chapsky* spawned the emergence of child protective legislation and mandated reporting of child maltreatment in the twentieth century.

Constitutional Protection of Family Privacy

In the twentieth century, family privacy legislation inadvertently began to serve as a counterweight to the movement for children's rights and protection by emphasizing modern limitations of state invasions into family autonomy. Family privacy stems from the general legal construct of privacy; examples include marital rights, family rights, sexual activity, abortion, and the right to die (R. D. Goldstein, 1999). To appreciate the relative weight that is accorded parental rights in care and protection proceedings, it is important to understand the constitutional basis of parental rights and autonomy.

Landmark Supreme Court Family Privacy Cases

U.S. Supreme Court cases have relied on the liberty, equal protection, and due process clauses of the 14th Amendment and on the zones of privacy that emanate from the Bill of Rights. Parental rights relevant to termination proceedings have their roots in cases involving family autonomy. Supreme Court cases involving family privacy first emerged in *Meyer v. Nebraska* (1923), when the Supreme Court struck down a state statute that prohibited teaching foreign languages in elementary school and that forbade teaching in any language other than English. The Court held that Nebraska's law violated the due process clause of the 14th Amendment. In *Pierce v. Society of Sisters* (1925), the Court voided a state statute requiring children to attend public school, a decision based on the liberty of parents to raise and educate their children. In the 1960s and 1970s, privacy cases addressed permissible family autonomy related to sexual conduct and the decision to bear children. In *Griswold v. Connecticut* (1965), the Court voided a state statute that criminalized contraceptive use and counseling. In voiding the statute, the Court held that several Bill of Rights guarantees protected the privacy interest by creating a zone of privacy, and it concluded that the right of married persons to use contraceptives fell within this zone of privacy. A later case extended family privacy reach to all persons, regardless of marital status (*Eisenstadt v. Baird,* 1972), when the Court invoked equal protection and substantive due process arguments, stating that the right of privacy is an individual right. The Court invoked the equal protection clause in *Loving v. Virginia* (1967), voiding state laws prohibiting interracial marriage. *Roe v. Wade* (1973) was based on the right to family privacy and was found to be part of the liberty guaranteed by the 14th Amendment.

Landmark Supreme Court Cases Specific to Parental Rights Termination

In *Lassiter v. Department of Social Services* (1981), the Court upheld a state's refusal to appoint publicly funded counsel for an indigent mother in a battle for reunification with her child. The Court concluded that a state was free to provide counsel to indigent parents if it so wished. In *Santosky v. Kramer* (1982), the Court held that due process required a higher standard of proof than a fair preponderance of evidence, namely, one of clear and convincing evidence, to support a state's allegations of parental unfitness before permanent removal of a child from the custody of an abusive or neglectful parent.

Parental Rights Termination Statutes

Every state has a statute that specifies the grounds for termination of parental rights. Grounds for termination typically invoke or contain definitions of maltreatment, they describe factors the court should consider before returning a child to the custody of the parent, and they specify factors relevant to the parent's involvement in and response to interventions. Because of financial incentives provided by the Adoption and Safe Families Act of 1997 for states that demonstrate progress in moving children from foster care to adoption, many statutes specify time frames within which successful rehabilitation of parents must occur. In cases with aggravated circumstances (i.e., abandonment, torture, chronic abuse, and sexual abuse), the Adoption and Safe Families Act removes the federal requirement that states must make reasonable efforts toward reunification of children with birth parents. Most states have provisions for an expedited process of early termination under conditions of severe maltreatment.

Grounds for termination typically include (a) parental incapacity to care for the child by reason of mental illness, substance abuse, or mental defect; (b) extreme disinterest in or abandonment of the child; (c) extreme or repeated abuse or neglect; (d) conviction of a crime carrying a sentence of long-term incarceration with early parole unlikely; (e) failure of the parent to improve in response to interventions; and (f) limitations on the length of time the child remains in state-sponsored placement. Consideration is given to the child's significant relationships with parents, siblings, foster parents, and potential adoptive parents. Even when parents eventually address maltreatment, whether sufficiently or insufficiently, statutes may provide latitude for termination based on the quality and strength of the child's relationship to substitute caregivers and based on the length of time the child has been in an alternative placement. Most state statutes specify an obligation for the child protection agency to offer services intended to correct the conditions that led to the parenting breach. Those services must be reasonably available on a consistent basis (Condie, 2003).

Some state statutes exclude conditions that are beyond the control of the parent, such as impoverishment, lack of availability of services, inadequate housing, low income, and inadequate medical care. Incarcerated parents present a challenge to child protective service systems because of the length of forced separation imposed by criminal justice system sanctions. Incarceration alone rarely is grounds for termination unless it is protracted, but some states specify categories of crime (e.g., murder, rape, sexual abuse of minors) that may result in termination of parental rights regardless of length of incarceration (R. D. Goldstein, 1999).

Case Law

Accepting referral questions, addressing them in evaluation reports, and preparing for court testimony takes place within the rules of admissibility of evidence. In care and protection matters, there are rules against invading the province of the jury to assess child witness credibility. The court has made a distinction between making credibility judgments about a particular witness and providing expert testimony on the unreliability of child witnesses in general. Expert testimony is inadmissible unless it assists the trier of fact, but informing the jury of principles already known is permissible if the expert provides an empirical base for the information. For example, a jury might understand that children sometimes are suggestible, but they might not be aware of or fully understand the scientific basis for that information (Sagatun, 1991). Expert testimony must be scientifically valid. Under *Daubert v. Merrell Dow Pharmaceuticals* (1993), the trial judge acts as a gatekeeper, determining whether the expert's data are admissible, reliable, and relevant. Most courts follow *Daubert* in establishing rules for the validity and reliability of scientific techniques and expert testimony. The testimony must be tied to the facts of the case so that it will sufficiently aid the jury in resolving the dispute. If research or techniques lack relevance to the legal standards of the case or touch on tangential details, the information might not meet admissibility standards (Walker, 1990).

A frequently contentious issue relevant to parental rights termination cases is the tension between research and clinical definitions of maltreatment, and definitions found in state statutes and supporting case law. The definitions of maltreatment required to support a petition for initial state jurisdiction of a case may be less rigorous than those that are relevant to termination of parental rights. Case law relevant to termination proceedings has established that parents have the latitude to engage in acts of corporal punishment, other forms of relatively coercive discipline, and atypical patterns of care that might be understood as abusive in some circles, but be viewed differently by others. Surveys show that 90% of parents have used some form of physical punishment on their children (Straus, 1983; Wauchope & Straus, 1990). Although researchers have demonstrated a link between the use of physical discipline and physical abuse, the law cannot assume that link will be made in all cases. To illustrate, for a case in which a parent whipped children as a form of discipline, attorneys for the child protective services agency must take an interest in whether the whippings caused severe harm. Although the agency likely would educate the parent about appropriate forms of discipline, the court would not support ongoing intervention if the whippings were shown in court to fall under the parental privilege to discipline, and if it was shown that they did not physically harm the child in a significant manner. More would be needed to keep the child protective services case active (e.g., *State v. Jones,* 1986). The dissonance that this creates across child protective service agencies is palpable. From a forensic evaluation standpoint, any form of coercive discipline may be relevant to some aspects of the evaluation, such as risk assessment. But from a legal perspective, arguments relevant to family autonomy and parental privilege to discipline are rather common in physical and emotional abuse cases.

Socioeconomic arguments tend to be used by attorneys for parents in neglect cases, with debate centering on whether a parent was neglectful due to a lack of resources and support or because of inappropriate parenting (e.g., *State v. Hollingsworth,* 1991). In sexual abuse cases, there often is a corresponding finding of neglect, but the strategies at hearings differ. Emphasis tends to be placed on whether the child's allegations were credible, whether a perpetrator can be identified, and whether the nonperpetrating caregiver made reasonable attempts to protect the child (Oberlander, 1995b). In the context of forensic assessment, the broad spectrum of approaches to parenting must be considered, along with cultural and socioeconomic features of cases, formal legal definitions of maltreatment, and areas of ambiguity left unspecified in formal definitions of maltreatment. Although it is not the role of the evaluator to determine whether maltreatment has taken place, the seriousness of the maltreatment in the eyes of various parties to the proceedings often is a factor of relevance.

THE THEORETICAL BASIS OF EVALUATIONS

A strong theoretical and empirical foundation serves as a conceptual framework for understanding child maltreatment, choosing appropriate assessment methods, gathering and interpreting data, and rendering opinions. This section reviews several of the most widespread theories that are used to frame methodology and interpretation in parental rights termination cases. This review is not exhaustive, and it is meant to provide only a sample of theoretical approaches to evaluations.

Biological Features of Parenting

The terms *attachment* and *bonding* have become so commonplace in termination of parental rights nomenclature that attorneys will call evaluators and state, "I need a bonding study." No amount of explanation of the theoretical differences between attachment and bonding will change the form of the request, but its underlying intent is driven by the attorney's need for a forensic evaluation that has a sound empirical basis. From a biological perspective, human parenting is evolutionarily distinct from other mammals by its intensely social nature, its extended period, and the long-term affiliation between parents and children (Rutter & O'Connor, 1999). From an evolutionary standpoint, attachment between individuals who spend extensive amounts of time with one another makes sense because it enhances survival by promoting affection, comfort, and the desire to remain together. *Attachment* describes a mutual but not symmetrical process (Ainsworth, 1989), whereas *bonding* is more specific to one person's reaction to another within an interactional and interdependent dyadic process and within a specific time frame, usually in the first months of infancy (Sperling & Berman, 1994).

Imprinting and Bonding

The term *bond* or *bonding* was coined in the 1930s in the context of ethological research on imprinting, an evolutionary process whereby a newly hatched gosling focuses on the first thing it sees and follows it around. The bond is established as the infant seeks proximity during the critical imprinting period (Small, 1998; Trevathan, 1987). After the critical period, the newborn cannot be persuaded to attach to any other object (Lorenz, 1935). For more physically dependent animals, it is the mother or other adult who establishes proximity and a bond with the infant (Trevathan, 1987). Without the opportunity for postbirth contact, mothers of premature human infants have a higher incidence of rejection of the infants (Klaus et al., 1972). In the 1960s, Harlow (1962; Harlow & Harlow, 1965) demonstrated that food and relief from physical discomfort had less to do with the development of the mother-infant bond than did attachment. In his famous study of rhesus monkeys, he found that newborn monkeys sporadically nursed from a mesh wire milk-producing mother but spent the majority of their time clinging to a terry cloth mother that provided no milk. Harlow demonstrated that the tendency to seek comfort takes precedence over the tendency to seek sustenance. When the motherless monkeys grew to adulthood, their capacity for mothering was socially inept and inadequate because they never bonded with their own mother.

Attachment

In explaining attachment, Bowlby (1956, 1969) borrowed the concepts of bonding and behavioral systems from ethology and broadened them into the realm of social interaction and caregiving by demonstrating that children became attached to parents whether or not the parents meet the child's physiological needs. The behavior system that reflects attachment consists of a variety of behaviors that might differ across populations and across the course of child development but have similar meaning and serve similar functions (Sroufe & Waters, 1977). In a caregiving behavior system, immature behaviors develop into integrated, flexible, and mature behaviors. A variety of behaviors are coordinated to achieve a specific goal and adaptive function, and goal-directed behaviors are activated and terminated by internal and environmental cues via a feedback system. Caregiving behaviors become organized and integrated over time by mental representations (George & Solomon, 1999).

Attachment is persistent, specific, and emotionally significant. It is reflected by the level of proximity to the person, level of distress at involuntary separation, emotional discomfort that is felt even when separation is voluntary, and tendency to seek security and comfort from that person. Seeking security or protection is central to the notion that attachment is primarily a child-to-adult phenomenon, but the parental response creates an interaction process (Bowlby, 1969). Caregiver sensitivity is related to a child's development of secure relationships with attachment figures (Ainsworth & Bell, 1974). Secure attachment develops when the child's security needs consistently are met with acceptance and warmth, and maladaptive attachment develops when security needs consistently are met with rejection, inconsistency, and inadequate parental control or when the parent is frightened of or frightening to the child (Ainsworth & Bell, 1974).

Child Maltreatment

Violence against offspring is so widespread that it would seem as natural as nurturing and sensitive parental behavior (Belsky, 1993). Although theorists caution against broad interpretations of comparative studies (Umberson, 1986), a fundamental premise in evolutionary explanations of maltreatment is that the interests of parents and offspring are not always synonymous (Burgess, 1994). Evolutionary theory emphasizes survival of the species and reproductive fitness, but when the provision of sensitive and nurturing care contributes nothing to or even undermines reproductive fitness, conflict is created that engenders maltreatment (Daly & Wilson, 1981). Risk of child maltreatment increases in contextual conditions, such as scarce resources, that accentuate a biological conflict of interest between parent and child (Burgess & Draper, 1989).

Attachment theory helps explain the intergenerational transmission of abuse and other propensities for child maltreatment (Green, 1998; Page, 1999), with specific emphasis on altered attachments and internal representations in early childhood (Schmidt & Eldridge, 1986) that continue into adulthood (Weinfield, Sroufe, & Egeland, 2000). Maltreated children show classic signs of attachment problems when rated for proximity, contact seeking, contact maintenance, resistance, avoidance, search, and distance interaction; the early parent-infant relationship later forms a prototype for future relationships (Morton & Browne, 1998). Attachment problems persist throughout development, although there also is evidence for the capacity of some individuals to transition to more healthy attachments with adults and with their own children (Weinfield et al., 2000). Attachment problems often covary with heightened risk of developing mental illness, and they interact to heighten the risk of child maltreatment (Jacobson & Frye, 1991). In a 7-year study of substantiated reports to child protective service agencies, Zuravin and colleagues (Zuravin, McMillen, DePanfilis, & Risley-Curtiss, 1996) found that poor attachment relationships in childhood, based on retrospective self-report data, were predictive of intergenerational transmission of abuse.

Cognitive and Socioemotional Features of Parenting

An evaluation of parenting typically involves an analysis of the parent's quality of thinking, judgment, reasoning, and capacity to follow through on child-rearing decisions. Cognitive theories focus on individual cognitive constructs that form the basis for parenting and their influence on problem solving in parenting. Socioemotional theories focus on how the interaction of cognition and emotion orients, organizes, and motivates parenting behaviors, especially during periods of arousal. Problem-solving quality influences parent-child conflict resolution (Klein, Alexander, & Parsons, 1977); it includes the ability to generate multiple possible solutions to an interpersonal problem or conflict, to foresee both immediate and long-term consequences of a response, to think through a series of specific actions needed to reach a specific goal, to recognize potential obstacles to specific actions, and to plan a sequence of behaviors within a realistic time frame (Kendall & Urbain, 1982).

Attributional Theory, Affective Organization, and Socioemotional Development

Researchers studying the influence of causal attributions on parent-child relation-ships have focused on parents' attributions for their own behavior and for the be-havior of their children. An internal locus of control is associated with parental autonomy, whereas an external locus of control is associated with parental helpless-ness. Parental attributions for children's behavior focus on appraisals of children's intentions. Parents with an attributional style that presumes personal control and a relative lack of negative intent in the child tend to experience little arousal in en-countering difficult behavior, whereas parents who presume little personal control and who interpret the child's behavior as threatening or involving negative intent tend to experience hyperarousal (Bugental, Mantyla, & Lewis, 1989). Parents be-come upset when they conclude that children understand, intend, and have control over difficult behavior (Dix & Reinhold, 1991). They experience stronger negative emotion if they conclude that they are incompetent as parents, unable to cope, or unable to control events (Bugental & Cortez, 1988). Parents who quickly turn to co-ercive interactions tend to be more physiologically and affectively aroused than those who use other methods of interaction (Frodi & Lamb, 1980).

Child Maltreatment

Cognitive and socioemotional researchers have emphasized the importance of neg-ative reactivity and attributional style (Belsky, 1993). Maltreating parents, be-cause of early learning and their own maltreatment, are particularly reactive to aversive events in their emotional arousal and in their interpretations of those events (Bugental, Blue, & Lewis, 1990). Maltreating parents report less sympathy and greater irritation and annoyance in response to the crying of infants (Frodi & Lamb, 1980). They show greater physiological reactivity to videotapes of both stressful and nonstressful mother-child interactions (Wolfe, 1985; Wolfe, McMa-hon, & Peters, 1997). Maltreating parents have a higher rate of negative interac-tions with their children than nonmaltreating parents. Compared to nonmaltreating parents, physically abusive parents show fewer positive approaches to children, such as supportiveness, instruction, joining play, talking to the child, praising the child, responding to initiations by the child, and expressing positive affection (Bousha & Twentyman, 1984). They are more likely to be controlling, interfering, or hostile (Crittenden, 1981, 1985). Studies of neglectful parents indicate that the frequency and level of negative responses to children may be high in neglectful par-ents. Neglectful mothers of infants were unresponsive, and they infrequently initi-ated interaction with or responded to their infants. With older children, neglectful parents showed low rates of social interaction (Burgess & Conger, 1978).

There is a link between parental negative interactions with children and the use of physical discipline, and a link between the use of physical discipline and physical abuse (Belsky, 1993). Parents using physical discipline attempted to control tod-dlers more often, were less likely to rely on a combination of control and guidance strategies, and experienced more escalation of negative affect during control encounters (Belsky, Woodworth, & Crnic, 1996). Physically abusive parents were more likely to rely on physical discipline and negative physical acts (i.e., pushing, hitting, grabbing, pinching) compared to nonabusive parents (Lahey, Conger, Atkeson, & Treiber, 1984). They used power tactics such as threats and disapproval more than reasoning and discussion (Trickett & Susman, 1988), and they were less likely to vary their discipline strategy or rely on nonphysical forms of discipline (Webster-Stratton, 1985). Punitiveness was heightened by stress, regardless of whether the stress was related to child misbehavior (Passman & Mulhern, 1977).

Sociological Features of Parenting

Social factors influence parental access to resources, community support, and family support. Social mores and expectations influence societal views of family structure and family life. Families that come to the attention of state authorities tend to have faced social and financial adversity.

Socioeconomic Status

Child maltreatment is by no means limited to parents of low socioeconomic status (SES), but it is not uncommon for parents who are referred for parenting evaluations to have low income, unemployment or underemployment status, and some degree of social isolation. Poverty affects health and nutrition, parental mental health, parent-child interactions, marital relationships, and home and neighborhood conditions. Impoverished children have increased rates of low birthweight and growth stunting, conditions that are associated with reduced intellectual functioning, learning disabilities, grade retention, and school dropout (Brooks-Gunn & Duncan, 1997). Impoverished parents are less likely than nonpoor parents to be emotionally and physically healthy (Adler et al., 1994). Stressful conditions such as inadequate housing and unsafe neighborhoods are associated with poverty (Brooks-Gunn, Britto, & Brady, 1999). Chronic job loss and unemployment have a greater impact than transient unemployment, but both negatively influence parenting (McAdoo, 1986; McLoyd, 1989, 1990). Low income is related to residence in neighborhoods characterized by social disorganization, low cohesion, and few resources (Sampson & Morenoff, 1997).

The finding that poverty and low income are related to child maltreatment has been replicated many times (Burgdoff, 1980; Pelton, 1978; Zuravin, 1989). Length of time on public assistance and length of time classified as an impoverished family increases the risk of maltreatment (Dubowitz, Hampton, Bithoney, & Newberger, 1987; Zuravin & Grief, 1989). Limited parental education and underemployment are linked to maltreatment (Zuravin & Grief, 1989). Contemporaneous and longitudinal studies have shown that under- and unemployment affect rates of child maltreatment, suggesting a casual, not a correlational, link (Bycer, Breed, Fluke, & Costello, 1984). Family size and amount of time between births contributes to maltreatment (Zuravin, 1991).

Parental Age and Maturity

There is an inverse relationship between maternal age and child maltreatment (Connelly & Straus, 1992), primarily because of higher rates of maltreatment among young teenage parents (Bolton & Laner, 1981; Leventhal, 1981). Less positive parental nurturing and discipline were seen in mothers who were younger, had more than one child living at home, were single, had a lower income level, and had lower levels of educational attainment (Fox, Platz, & Bentley, 1995). Teenage mothers were less likely than nonmothers to complete high school or seek vocational training (McLanahan & Teitler, 1999). Children of adolescent parents are at risk for infant mortality and morbidity, cognitive impairment, delay in emotional development, abuse and neglect, and early and pervasive school failure (Furstenberg & Brooks-Gunn, 1987). Support from the child's father enhances maternal efficacy, but it adds to life stress. Support from immediate family members has little impact on risk, perhaps because adolescents are still in the process of individuation, but younger adolescents tend to benefit from family support (Shapiro & Mangelsdorf, 1994).

Social Networks and Community Involvement

In neighborhoods matched for social class, families with lower rates of maltreatment have more extensive social networks (Garbarino & Kostelny, 1992), and parents have larger peer networks (Starr, 1982), more contact with and help from family members (Zuravin & Grief, 1989), and access to a telephone (Dubowitz et al., 1987). The buffering quality of social networks is strengthened when families remain in their neighborhood and communities for a relatively long time (Spearly & Lauderdale, 1983). Families are less prone to maltreatment when they use available resources and when they involve themselves in community activities (Polansky, Ammons, & Gaudin, 1985). Although community cohesion contributes to the strength of social support, individual qualities also play a role. Parents with lower rates of child maltreatment interpret the quality of neighborhood friendliness and helpfulness in more positive terms than do neglectful parents (Polansky et al., 1985). In a comparison of neighborhoods matched for social class, community climate had a strong relationship to rates of maltreatment. In cohesive neighborhoods, people were eager to discuss their neighborhood, describing it as a poor but decent place to live, as having strong leadership, and as having available resources and services. Less cohesive neighborhoods were described as having poor leadership, high crime, and few open and light spaces for community events (Garbarino & Kostelny, 1992). Maltreating families were more transient, moving more frequently than other families (Zuravin, 1989).

Substance Abuse and Child Maltreatment

There are biological and psychological variables associated with substance abuse, but it is best viewed as a social problem because of its impact on family and community life, school and job performance, child care, household responsibilities, and the legal system and because of the creation of physically hazardous circumstances such as driving under the influence of alcohol or drugs. Children of substance-abusing parents are at increased risk for child maltreatment (Chasnoff, 1988; Murphy et al., 1991). State child protective agency reporting records indicate that substance abuse is a factor in 20% to 90% of all reported cases, and research studies have estimated that 10% to 67% of child protective service cases involve parental substance abuse (Famularo, Kinscherff, & Fenton, 1992; Kelley, 1992; B. A. Miller, 1990; Murphy et al., 1991).

The impact of substance abuse on child maltreatment begins in the prenatal period. Mothers who use drugs delay seeking prenatal care, speak less to their newborn children, and appear awkward holding and playing with their babies (M. Black, Schuler, & Nair, 1993). Families with at least one substance-abusing parent are described as lacking cohesion, attachment, emotional expression, and shared activities (Berlin & Davis, 1989), and parental substance abuse is correlated with less effective discipline (Tarter, Blackson, Martin, Loeber, & Moss, 1993). In a study of 24 mothers of drug-exposed children (and a comparison group matched in age, race, gender, and SES), a strong association was found between maternal drug use and child maltreatment resulting in removal of the children by child protective services. Over 40% of drug-exposed children were in foster care (Kelley, 1992). In a study of mothers who were polysubstance abusers during pregnancy, with cocaine being the drug of preference, mothers made more negative statements and demonstrated more negative affect than did comparison adults matched for SES. They engaged in positive interactions, but they made more coercive and negative verbal exchanges with their children. The polysubstance abuse mothers had difficulty terminating negative exchanges. Rather than trying to change the negative pattern to a positive one, they engaged in further coercive behaviors. They began with negative affect and mildly aversive requests, and escalated to strong demands with increased negative affect (Heller, Sobel, & Tanaka-Matsumi, 1996).

CHILD DEVELOPMENT THEORY

Thorough understanding of child development theory is needed to appreciate children's capacities for verbal expression across multiple contexts, their understanding and appreciation of the legal context of care and protection matters, and their credibility as reporters of maltreatment. The burgeoning research on these topics serves as a foundation for sound assessment methodology.

Linguistic Capacity, Competence, and Credibility

Expertise in child development is essential in termination of parental rights cases because of judicial concern relevant to children's abilities to speak on their own behalf. Attorneys, judges, and child protective service representatives request evaluations to better understand the capacities of children to report maltreatment and trauma and to testify competently (Saywitz, Jaenicke, & Camparo, 1990). Cases in the legal system have addressed children's language development (*Griffin v. State,* 1988; *People v. District Court In and For Summit County,* 1990), spontaneous utterances or fresh complaints of child maltreatment (*Commonwealth v. Caracino,* 1993; *Commonwealth v. Snow,* 1991), children's memory capacity (*Commonwealth v. Corbett,* 1989; *State v. Hudnall,* 1987), children's understanding and appreciation of the difference between the truth and a lie (*Griffin v. State,* 1988), and the suggestibility of children (*People v. Brown,* 1994; *State v. Michaels,* 1994; *Tome v. United States,* 1995). Children as young as 3 years have been deemed competent and credible testimonial witnesses in court (*Macias v. State,* 1989; *People v. Draper,* 1986; *State v. Brovold,* 1991; *State v. Hussey,* 1987; *State v. Ward,* 1992; *Strickland v. State,* 1988). Cases involving the competence of child witnesses date back to *Wheeler v. United States* (1895). The *Wheeler* Court stated, "There is no precise age which determines the question of competency. This depends on the capacity and intelligence of the child, his appreciation of the difference between truth and falsehood, as well as his duty to tell the former" (p. 523).

Trial judges are given broad discretion to determine the testimonial competence of witnesses and to bar witnesses deemed not competent (*Commonwealth v. Corbett,* 1989; *Doran v. United States,* 1953). Witnesses who are deemed incompetent tend to be very young children or individuals suffering from mental disabilities (Haugaard, Reppucci, Laird, & Nauful, 1991). Nearly every state has held that a child must know the difference between the truth and a lie to testify competently, but states differ in other criteria, such as the ability to recall past events (R. D. Goldstein, 1999). Witness credibility, in contrast to competence, is determined by the willingness of a witness to offer truthful testimony or to accurately recall information. The judge has no discretion to bar testimony that is deemed not credible or not persuasive (*Western Industries v. Newcor Canada Ltd.,* 1984). Credibility is relevant only after competence has been determined, and it includes the child's understanding of the responsibility to speak the truth, the child's capacity at the time of the occurrence to perceive events accurately, the child's ability to retain an independent memory of the occurrence, the child's capacity to translate memory into words, and the child's capacity to respond to questions about the occurrence (Haugaard et al., 1991).

Children up to 7 years of age have difficulty defining "truth" and "lie" and explaining the difference between the terms (Lyon & Saywitz, 1999). Children do not have a clear conception of lying relative to adult constructs (Kalish, Weissman, & Bernstein, 2000). Children narrow their definition of lies between ages 5 and 7, dropping "swearing" or "naughty words" from their definitions of lies (Piaget, 1932/1962). A child's definition of a truthful statement might center on whether or not it results in punishment (Haugaard, 1993). At approximately age 7, children begin to consider the intention of the speaker in their definition of what constitutes a lie (Burton & Strichartz, 1991). Knowing the difference between the truth and a lie might be necessary for telling the truth, but it is not a sufficient condition for truth telling (Burton & Strichartz, 1991). In a review of studies that manipulated children's moral behavior, younger children were found to show uncompromising judgments of culpability and were unwilling to lie, even for someone who helped them gain a reward. Young adolescents made more flexible and situation-specific judgments of culpability, varying their truth-telling behavior according to the social context. Therefore, it is possible that young witnesses might be more honest than older witnesses under some circumstances (Burton, 1984). Honesty, as a personality variable, influences children's willingness to tell the truth (Burton, 1976). Research on children's testimonial competence and credibility has found no pronounced developmental trends in honesty (Melton, 1981). Lying in older children and young adolescents is reduced by group discussions or lecture on the reasons why it is wrong (Fischer, 1970) and when children are reminded of their obligation to tell the truth (Burton & Strichartz, 1991).

The Accuracy of Children's Memories

At ages 2 and 3, children have the ability to accurately describe the core features of some events (Melton et al., 1995). Two-year-old children sometimes accurately recall events that occurred 6 months earlier (Fivush & Hammond, 1989). Recall is stronger for negative events (P. J. Miller & Sperry, 1988). Young children show the ability to recall distinctive novel events and central features of repeated events (Nelson, 1986), but they are more likely than older children and adults to confuse similar events that they have experienced (McNichol, Shute, & Tucker, 1999). Children's memory capacity to report child maltreatment is complicated by delays that often occur in children's disclosures. Reporting delays typically are followed by other delays, such as the amount of time that it takes a case to reach the trial phase, continuances, and other delays endemic to the legal system (Melton et al., 1995). Existing data suggest that children's memory for novel or unusual events can be sustained for many years, especially when they are provided with reminders or repeated questions (Goodman, Hirschman, Hepps, & Rudy, 1991). Although negative memories can be forgotten (Gaensbauer, 1995), children are less likely to forget personally significant, embarrassing, emotional, or rehearsed information, especially that involving actions, than less salient information (Jones, Swift, & Johnson, 1988).

Suggestibility

Suggestibility is defined as a situational and interaction process, occurring prior to or after an event, that might or might not alter actual event memory. It may involve acquiescence to social demands or lying to please others; it might involve a more subtle process that indeed alters memory; and it can result from social or cognitive factors. Although personality variables are relevant, with some people showing greater vulnerability to suggestibility, the phenomenon of suggestibility is viewed as an interactive social process rather than an intrapsychic variable (Ceci & Bruck, 1993). Developmental variables have an influence on suggestibility. Nearly all relevant studies comparing 3-year-old children to older children or adults have found an age effect (Goodman et al., 1991; Leichtman & Ceci, 1995). Suggestibility is multiply determined by cognitive, social, motivational, and personality factors in children (Ceci & Bruck, 1993; Goodman & Reed, 1986) and by interviewer characteristics (Bruck, Ceci, & Hembrooke, 1998). Although cognitive and social factors interact with the type of information suggested, the cumulative and interactive effects are not well understood. There is no doubt that suggestibility sometimes affects children's responses in forensic evaluation interviews, but because most research on suggestibility has taken place in laboratories, the forensic evaluator must be cautious about generalizing the results of such studies to clinical populations. (For a comprehensive review of factors underlying susceptibility to suggestibility, see Ceci & Bruck, 1993.) Researchers (Saywitz & Snyder, 1996; Saywitz, Snyder, & Nathanson, 1999) have developed strategies for minimizing suggestibility in research samples of children. Although there are no existing adaptations for clinical forensic interviews, the narrative elaboration procedure provides a useful template for understanding possible ways to minimize suggestibility for children age 6 and older.

The obverse of concern about the influences of suggestibility in clinical forensic interviews of children is the possibility of disavowals or denials of true cases of child maltreatment. Nondisclosures of maltreatment occur in the context of fear, embarrassment, and confusion and because of pathological processes such as identification with the aggressor and use of dissociation and other primitive defense mechanisms (Davies, 1996; Green, 1998). Child victims of intrafamilial abuse are in a double bind as the family unit dually threatens and promotes the physical and emotional survival of the child. The pain of maltreatment becomes muted over time because chronic maltreatment becomes routine in a cruel or exploitive family system (Maddock, 1988). Factors influencing a child's reluctance to provide information about true events include emotional discomfort, fear of reprisal, threats or bribery, and prolonged seductive approaches to abuse containing elements of victim blame (Bander, Fein, & Bishop, 1982). At least some percentage of children who render true allegations later recant the allegations. Many adult survivors of sexual abuse report never making a disclosure in childhood, keeping it a secret into adulthood (Blume, 1991).

EVALUATION METHODOLOGY FOR CAREGIVERS

Evaluation methodology includes carefully selected techniques and measures that logically are connected to the referral question and that have reliability and validity consistent with the purposes of the assessment. No approach to a forensic evaluation has been empirically demonstrated to be perfectly valid or reliable (Barnum, 1997). There is little consensus, either clinically or legally, on the criteria used to determine minimal parenting competence (Melton et al., 1997). Measures that are used in the assessment of caregivers or their children might have theoretical applicability, but there is little supplementary normative data for population samples of families involved in care and protection matters. After determining the appropriateness of the referral question for forensic assessment, methodology should be individually crafted to address the referral question (Condie, 2003). Evaluators choose the best available measures and they interpret them with appropriate caution. When used with appropriate caution in the context of a multimodal assessment, measures provide meaningful information because they contribute to converging data (Wolfe, 1988). Although approaches to care and protection cases take many forms, it is common for psychologists to use some form of psychological testing in care and protection evaluations (Budd, Poindexter, Felix, & Naik-Polan, 2001).

The Clinical Interview

The comprehensiveness of the clinical interview, in terms of breadth and depth, is determined by the referral question. Some interviews address an extensive range of historic and current factors. Other interviews are highly specific to one or two areas of functioning (Ownby, 1997). A strong clinical interview balances inquiry into both positive and negative features of functioning (Schwartz, 1987).

Historical Information

In care and protection evaluation practice, it is common to ask for the parent's perspective of his or her history of involvement with the child protective service system (Crenshaw & Barnum, 2001). The interviewee's first account of the history of child protective service involvement typically lacks some or many details of the actual maltreatment (Coburn, 2000; Crenshaw & Barnum, 2001). Interviewers may ask follow-up questions or request another full account later in the interview. It is useful to point out inconsistencies, seek clarification, and provide an opportunity for the interviewee to acknowledge details that were omitted or possibly distorted. Multiple inquiries may assist in determining whether the interviewee will divulge or acknowledge relevant information concerning the allegations of child maltreatment. To avoid the risk of acquiescence, caution should be used in asking multiple questions in single interviews of adults with cognitive limitations (Sigelman, Budd, Spanhel, & Schoenrock, 1981). Other interview content depends on the nature of the inquiry. When comprehensive data are needed, usual areas of inquiry include family of origin, important adulthood relationships, current family relationships, dating and marital history, the decision process (or lack thereof) to bear children, educational and occupational history, social network, mental and physical health history, neurological history, psychosexual history, substance use or abuse history, violence history, and criminal record (Dolan & Doyle, 2000).

Substance Abuse

For a parent with a history of substance abuse and child maltreatment, interview questions should cover patterns of alcohol and drug use, the individual's history and duration of periods of sobriety, factors that potentiated and hindered sobriety, the effectiveness of past rehabilitation, the individual's level of participation in and stage of rehabilitation, motivating influences for remaining sober, options available for reducing urges to drink or use drugs, and relapse prevention plans (Bernardi, Jones, & Tennant, 1989; B. A. Miller, 1990). The rehabilitation modality has bearing on follow-up questions. For individuals enrolled in self-help groups, it is important to inquire about the nature and frequency of meetings, the steps or stages of the self-help process, use of sponsors, and the types of meetings attended. For individuals using relapse prevention, the expert should inquire about the phase of relapse prevention planning, whether the plan is committed to memory or readily available in written form, the level of detail in the plan, and the adaptability of the plan to different settings.

Risk Assessment

Risk assessment originated out of concern for the postinstitutionalization behavior of individuals with mental illness or criminal justice involvement who had prior histories of violence. Risk assessment research has maintained this focus (Monahan et al., 2000; Steadman et al., 2000). A few studies of parents involved in maltreatment have isolated comparable risk factors (Dubowitz, 1999; Hanson, 1998; Haskett, Scott, & Fann, 1995), but the degree of generalizability for specific risk factors or for cumulative risk is unknown. A related external validity problem is the type of violence studied. Researchers studying inpatient psychiatric and criminal populations tend to focus on physical violence (Monahan et al., 2000), but care and protection matters also include individuals at risk of sexual violence and neglect (Dubowitz, 1999; Hanson, 1998; Haskett et al., 1995). Studies of risk of child maltreatment have been based on small sample sizes and a small dimension of variables (Milner, Robertson, & Rogers, 1990; Murphy et al., 1991). Some wide-scope studies of risk of maltreatment are beginning to appear (Widom, 1989a, 1989b; Wolfe, 1985, 1987, 1988). When factors are identified, their relevance to specific populations of maltreating parents, such as mentally retarded parents, may be limited (Roszkowski, 1984). The weight and relevance of risk factors differ for physical violence, neglect, and sexual offending (Condie, 2003).

Advances in risk assessment research have been seen in the area of domestic violence risk, and some of this research has taken place in the context of child maltreatment investigations. Researchers have suggested that risk should be specific to the nature and targets of violent behavior, hypothesizing that domestic violence shows a different manifestation and risk configuration from other forms of violence (Dutton & Kropp, 2000). Other researchers have found that violence risk variables carry the same predictive valence regardless of the population of interest, and that variables are equally predictive in populations with and without an appreciable psychiatric disorder (Webster, Douglas, Eaves, & Hart, 1997). Static risk factors are historical factors of the caregiver that cannot be modified (e.g., documented substance abuse history, number of prior convictions of violent offenses); dynamic risk factors have the potential to change with the passage of time, with treatment interventions, or with personal motivation (Borum, Otto, & Golding, 1993). Dynamic risk factors include the caregiver's degree of acknowledgment of the problem, the intensity of relevant symptoms, and the individual's justification for the maltreatment. The potency and individual relevance of specific risk factors cannot be determined from aggregate group data. Less is known about the desistance of risk in maltreating parents compared to other populations whose risk has been studied over time (Dubowitz, 1999).

Risk of Physical Abuse

Stress, family resources, and social support are predictive of child abuse potential (Burrell, Thompson, & Sexton, 1994). Because of problems with self-report data, it is difficult to demonstrate in applied research whether personality features or behaviors, such as hostility, criticism, and threats, have predictive or discriminative validity for physical abuse (Wolfe, 1985, 1987, 1988). Jacobsen, Miller, and Kirkwood (1997) identified risk factors with at least a moderate link to risk of physical abuse: untreated major mental illness, failure to acknowledge a mental illness or the need for treatment, a history of violent temper outbursts, active drug or alcohol addiction, a childhood history of abuse, other adverse childhood events, few ties to neighbors or community agencies, violent relationships with spouses or dating partners, gross misperceptions about the child or child development, gross misperceptions about appropriate discipline strategies, unrealistic expectations of children, difficulty discerning and responding to cues from the child, insecure parent-child attachment, role reversals, scapegoating the child, extreme worry about the child's well-being, high levels of parenting stress or social isolation, and a history of violent behavior.

In a descriptive study of parents facing termination of parental rights, Schetky, Angell, Morrison, and Sack (1979) identified historical factors relevant to risk: a history of victimization by maltreatment, frequent separations or losses, frequent moves, institutionalization in childhood, poor relationships with or attachment to parents, few family or community support figures, one or more psychiatric admissions, a history of arrest and incarceration, and mental retardation. Other hypothesized risk factors for physical abuse include the deliberateness with which the individual harmed the child in the past, the extent of harm to the child, the frequency of harm to the child, patterns of allowing the perpetrator access to the child, adequacy of supervision, age and visibility of the child, the child's capacity to report on his or her own behalf, the level of fear the child expressed about the caregiver or the home environment, the presence of other adequate caregivers, and the caregiver's history of childhood maltreatment or victimization in adulthood. Also relevant are variables such as the physical health of the caregiver, cognitive appraisals of caregiver-child conflict, attributions of blame and responsibility, anger management skills, the caregiver's recognition of the problem, the caregiver's capacity to select suitable substitute caregivers, and appropriate assignment of family roles (Milner et al., 1990; Moncher, 1996; Murphy et al., 1991; Widom, 1989a, 1989b; Wolfe, 1988).

Risk of Sexual Abuse

Potent predictive factors for sexual abuse include a reduction in family boundaries and individual autonomy, cognitive distortions in identification and affiliation, hostility and aggression, and a misdirection of sexuality. Sexual abuse is not necessarily sexually motivated (Finkelhor, 1984). Sexual acts can be characterized by the degree to which the sexual element is low versus high and the degree to which the desire to punish or humiliate is low versus high. Theories to explain sexual offending against children include arrested psychological development, low self-esteem and self-efficacy, inadequacy, immaturity, shame and humiliation in childhood, identification with the aggressor, symbolic mastery over childhood trauma, conditioning from childhood sexual victimization, and socialization that values dominance and power (Groth, Hobson, & Gary, 1982). Offenders are described as timid, unassertive, awkward, poorly socially skilled, and moralistic (M. J. Goldstein, Kant, & Hartman, 1973).

Dynamic risk factors associated with sexual abuse have been described by the developers of treatment programs. Stress in combination with substance abuse contributes to disinhibition, as do victim blame and the reluctance of the legal system to prosecute and punish offenders (Armstrong, 1983). Most theories and treatment programs require offenders to acknowledge the problem and to implement various methods of self-control to prevent relapse (Abel, Rouleau, & Cunningham-Rathner, 1986; Prentky & Bird, 1997). Treatment programs focus on compulsive thoughts and urges, cognitive distortions and rationalizations, justifications and minimizations, antisocial conduct outside the sexual domain, ruminations and fantasies during masturbation, interest in deviant sexual themes, postoffense transient guilt, temporary regaining of control, and dissipation of guilt over time. They focus on assertiveness and social skills deficits, insufficient arousal to nondeviant stimuli, deficits in sexual knowledge and function, and the cyclical nature of offending (Abel et al., 1986). Recidivism is common (Studer, Clelland, Aylwin, Reddon, & Monro, 2000), and the level of violence used against children is especially high in paraphiliacs who select child victims unknown to them (DeFrancis, 1969).

Areas of inquiry relevant to sex offending risk recommended by Lane (1997) include self-initiation of disclosure, recall of details, degree of aggression or overt violence in offenses, frequency and duration of offenses, length and progression of sexual offending, offense characteristics other than sexual aggression, number of victims in relation to victim access, victim selection characteristics, preferred victim type, victim blame, appraisal of victim harm, personal responsibility for offending, precipitating factors, and degree of arousal and habituation. Additional areas of focus include other exploitive or addictive behavior, family system functioning, stability of school or employment, stability of social relationships, nonoffending sexual history, past victimization, external and internal motivation for rehabilitation, response to confrontation, treatment history and response, criminal arrests and convictions, and current access to victims (Lane, 1997). Inquiry into related factors includes substance abuse history, depression, suicidal ideation, family roles and structure, intellectual capacities, and the quality of expression and management of anger and conflict. Preliminary research outcomes have shown that dynamic risk factors have a greater relationship to sex offending recidivism than do static risk factors, even after controlling for preexisting static risk factor differences (Hanson & Harris, 2000).

Risk of Neglect

There is enormous heterogeneity among neglectful families (Gaudin & Dubowitz, 1997). Neglect commonly co-occurs with other forms of maltreatment, and it may not represent as discrete a set of risk variables as have been identified for physical and sexual abuse (Dubowitz, 1999). Neglect is associated with blunted affect, apathetic or passive-dependent parent-child interaction, nonreciprocal relationships among family members, cycling between passive and aggressive behavior, chaos and poor planning, impulsive actions in parents, and conflicted relationships between parents (Crittenden, 1988; Kadushin, 1988). Social isolation, poor social support, poor social skills, and rejection by the community may be indicative of neglect (Gaudin & Polansky, 1986). Other variables include critical statements, little positive attention, little stimulation and nurturance, unresponsiveness and limited sensitivity, speaking less, issuing more demands, expressing less acceptance (Crittenden & Bonvillian, 1984), difficulty connecting with others, apathy and futility, disorganization, hostility, and hopelessness (Gaudin & Dubowitz, 1997). There is little research on personality variables in neglectful fathers, but data suggest that children of single parents and children in family units having different fathers are vulnerable to greater paternal neglect (Dubowitz, 1999).

Malingering, Embellishments, Dissimulation, and Underreporting

In care and protection evaluations of caregivers, there usually is greater concern about dissimulation and underreporting compared to concern about malingering and embellishment. Because of the high stakes in care and protection evaluations, it is not surprising that caregivers would attempt to present themselves in a socially desirable manner (Budd & Holdsworth, 1996). A few standardized assessment measures contain validity indices for fake-good and fake-bad presentations (Butcher, Dahlstrom, Graham, Tellegen, & Kaemmer, 1989; Milner, 1986). Validity indices provide useful information about the individual's approach to the assessment, alerting the evaluator to possible distortions in responses to assessment items. Supporting theory for the use of social desirability responding measures is based on broad constructs of personality functioning, with applicability to many population samples (Merydith & Wallbrown, 1991). When there are indicators of dissimulation or social desirability responding, the motivation for responding may be due to defensiveness, deceptive practices, attempts to conceal pathology, innocuous factors such as impression management, self-deception, or repression (Becker & Cherny, 1992). The motivations of a parent should be considered, and hypotheses relevant to the parent's approach to assessment instruments should be considered in context and supported with converging data. Interpretation of validity indices should be made with caution and appropriately limited (Butcher et al., 1989; Milner, 1986).

Child Protective Service Records and Other Data

Child protective service records usually contain documentation of the allegations of child maltreatment, investigation records, and an indication of why the allegations were supported. If the records are descriptive and reliable, they can be used to gauge caregiver progress in acknowledging the frequency and severity of maltreatment, a necessary step toward meaningful intervention (Hanson & Harris, 2000). Child protective service records usually contain a service plan for the caregivers and the children (Condie, 2003). A caregiver with little recollection of the service plan is unlikely to have taken the plan seriously. Records might clarify whether the service plan included interventions relevant to the caregiver's level of cognitive functioning, and they might clarify whether potentially effective interventions were included or neglected in the service plan. They may assist the expert in determining whether interventions were relevant to the factors that led to the maltreatment. Child protective service records sometimes contain documentation of parental self-reports of child maltreatment, visitation records, parental adherence to visitation schedules, recorded observations of parental visitation of children, and observations of children's reactions to visitation commencement or termination. Records may contain information relevant to the parent-child relationship, the parent's participation in and response to interventions, and any past or pending criminal actions against the parent (Condie, 2003).

Other useful records include those documenting participation in or response to rehabilitation efforts, psychiatric treatment, prior psychological evaluations, substance abuse rehabilitation, educational history, medical treatment, criminal history, visitation center adherence to appointments, and police investigations relevant to child maltreatment (Grisso, 1986). Records may contain relevant maltreatment information that helps to frame interview and follow-up interview questions. They may include documentation of the parent's attendance and participation in treatment and the reasonableness of the caregiver's explanation for failure to attend or effectively use recommended interventions (Azar, 1992).

After obtaining appropriate releases to collect third-party information, the evaluator determines the scope of questions appropriate to each collateral contact. Possible sources of information are teachers, child care workers, foster parents, relatives, child maltreatment investigators for the state, physicians, mental health service providers, substance abuse rehabilitation providers, and caregiver-child visitation supervisors (Enfield, 1987). Treatment providers are a potentially valuable source of information when the parent's response to intervention is being examined. The evaluator should be alert to higher confidentiality standards for substance abuse treatment providers and to the possibility that not all collateral sources will be motivated to provide forthright information (Stahl, 1994; Williams, Siegel, & Pomeroy, 2000). Stahl recommends avoiding overreliance on information from close family members, friends, and relatives because of their allegiances to the parties involved in a case. To prevent the parties to the case from feeling as though their third-party sources have been disregarded, he invites them to ask their friends, family, and relatives to write letters to him, delineating relevant issues of concern. Letters yielding useful data can be followed up with telephone calls. (For a thorough discussion of the role of third-party information in forensic assessment, see Heilbrun, Warren, & Picarello, 2003.)

EVALUATING CHILDREN

Children fare best in evaluations that respect their developmental level, their perspective, and their apprehension. A child friendly setting geared toward the comfort and security of the child helps to set the child at ease. Rapport building should be paced to match the child's readiness and level of comfort.

Historical Information

The comprehensiveness of historical data obtained from children depends on the nature of the referral question and on the children's reporting capacity. Historical information relevant to young children is best gathered from other sources that supplement the child interview. Gathering historical data on the child usually requires an interview of caregivers and a review of records. When children report information, it sometimes is useful to compare their reports of historical data or maltreatment details to other reports (Poole & Lamb, 1998). Data of significant relevance to the evaluation that a child solely provides should be checked for accuracy whenever possible. An evaluator must make a decision about whether to include information of central relevance that remains uncorroborated; its inclusion would depend on the potential salience of the information for the fact finder and hearsay provisions. Appropriate caveats should be used in reports if the evaluator believes it is important to include historical data for which the child is the sole source (Saywitz & Camparo, 1998).

Relevant historical data in child interviews may include a description of family structure and relationships and changes in these across time. The child's report of the parent-child relationship and of the frequency and progression of trauma is relevant in most evaluations, but its inclusion in a forensic assessment depends on the child's reporting capacity. Information sometimes is needed that is relevant to the child's developmental milestones, educational history, mental and physical health history, substance use, and juvenile justice history (Oberlander, 1995a, 1995b). Content areas and the degree of breadth and depth of child interviews should be tailored to the referral question.

Interviewing Children about Recollections of Maltreatment

There is no foolproof method for determining a child's capacity to provide a credible report of maltreatment. It is important to minimize influences that might result in questionable data. Although it is not appropriate to make judgments about children's truthfulness, estimates of children's capacities to report and describe trauma sometimes are requested. The child's description may be used by the fact finder to determine the merits of a maltreatment case; it might reveal the child's inner world and perceptions of what took place; or it might be used as a benchmark for the child's progress in treatment relevant to coping with trauma. Heiman (1992) recommends examining children's accounts of maltreatment for the development of a context, idiosyncratic words or data, peripheral or unnecessary information, explicit details, and details that exceed the child's developmental level. Other relevant descriptive features that a child might provide are a progression of grooming for maltreatment, other engagement processes, strategies to discourage the child from reporting the maltreatment, affective responses or details that are congruent with the reported maltreatment, consistency of salient details, a varied and rich description rather than a rehearsed litany, a narrative from a child's perspective, and details of attempts to resist or avoid the maltreatment. Depending on the capacity of the child to provide an organized and coherent narrative, the details may be provided in response to specific interview questions, or they might be given in a piecemeal fashion across several evaluation sessions (Condie, 2003).

Children with Special Needs

The challenges of interviewing children with disabilities are similar to those of interviewing young children (Poole & Lamb, 1998). Intelligence, in part, determines children's capacities to describe maltreatment (Fundudis, 1989), but few studies have demonstrated how cognitive impairment impedes their reporting capacities (Westcott & Jones, 1999). The interviewer should expect difficulty with narratives, sentence structure, recall and correct sequencing of details, susceptibility to suggestion, and social desirability responding in the form of acquiescence (Sigelman et al., 1981; Westcott & Jones, 1999).

Third-Party Interviews and Records

Child interview and assessment data should be supplemented with data from third-party contacts and records. Records of relevance include documentation of the child's self-report of maltreatment (usually contained in child protective services investigation reports, but sometimes also found in medical, mental health, or police investigation records), records of the child's functioning and adaptation to placement, records of the child's relationship with caregivers and substitute caregivers, educational records, and physical and mental health records.

DATA INTEGRATION AND INTERPRETATION

The key to a relevant and thorough report is the integration and interpretation of data in light of the original referral question. Quality reports include interpretations that are made within a theoretical and developmental context, consideration of possible influences on the evaluation, appropriate caveats, a tone that is respectful of the audience of readers, and highlights of the strengths and weaknesses in the examinee's functioning. One format for organizing data interpretation is to reiterate the referral question, review the reliability and validity of the data that were gathered in the assessment process, address the referral question, entertain competing explanations or hypotheses, and offer a conclusion as to why competing hypotheses remain viable or why they were ruled out. The process should include consideration of possible influences on the evaluation process and results (e.g., social desirability responding in caregivers; suggestibility, avoidance, and embarrassment in children). A quality report is cogent, but it contains relevant descriptive information. It is useful to follow a structure in which interpretations of data are offered; for example, develop an outline of the main points, address one or two main points in each paragraph, and summarize the interpretation in a final paragraph. Main points might include (a) the caregiver's functioning; (b) the child's functioning and level of development; (c) a description of the parent-child relationship; (d) hypothesized etiological factors related to maltreatment, along with explanatory reasons for the link to maltreatment; (e) risk factors and mitigating factors for future maltreatment, with appropriate caveats concerning limitations in the predictive utility of risk matrices; and (f) amenability to treatment (Condie, 2003).

In a report on the impact of child maltreatment on the child's current functioning, the interpretation section might include descriptive data about current functioning; conclusions about diagnostic clusters of symptoms and behaviors, if relevant; a comparison of current functioning to documentation of past functioning; an analysis of the link, if any, to child maltreatment; the child's view of the caregiver; the child's attachment to substitute caregivers; and the child's prognosis. Some evaluators prefer to write with testimony in mind, so that key points and supporting data are presented in a manner that facilitates smooth and reasonably detailed testimony. Other evaluators prefer to use different organizational strategies, addressing the highlights in the report but reserving elaboration for courtroom testimony. It is important to base such judgments on personal style or experience and jurisdictional expectations. Some court jurisdictions require that evaluators adhere to a particular report structure (Condie, 2003).

Reviewing the Reliability and Validity of the Data

Opinions that are based, in part, on psychological test scores should be integrated with observations and reliable information contained in the individual's records. Records often provide data that can be used to establish baseline functioning for behaviors or constructs of concern. Multimodal assessment, using either records or other forms of assessment to bolster conclusions, can guard against measurement error due to poor reliability. Conclusions withstand challenges to reliability and validity to a greater extent when they are gleaned objectively from multiple sources (Condie, 2003). It is important to consider the cultural relevance of the data (Budd & Holdsworth, 1996), and normative data relevant to cultural status should be reported if available. Cultural context, socioeconomic concerns, and other potential influences on the meaning of the data should be considered (Dana, 1993). Appropriate caveats should be given in the absence of such data.

Describing Risk and Mediators of Risk of Child Maltreatment

Causal inferences often are a central feature of the interpretive process concerning risk and mediators of risk. A parental manifestation of a desirable trait or adequate abilities may reflect a positive attribute in one parent and dissimulation in another parent whose history, assessment data, and validity indices are inconsistent with what might be a transient manifestation of an attribute (Grisso, 1986). There are many possible causal explanations for deficiencies in parenting, including situational stress or crises, evaluation-related stress, parental ambivalence about regaining custody, lack of knowledge or information about adequate parenting, substance abuse problems, mental health problems, psychopathy or other negative character traits, maladaptive caretaking patterns, cognitive limitations, neurological impairment, and adult conduct problems or incarceration (Dyer, 1999). Factors in the literature that are linked to increased or decreased risk of child maltreatment should be considered (Monahan et al., 2000). Risk should be characterized in the context of caregiver strengths and weaknesses and within the framework of the caregiver's need to respond to the child's level of development.

Describing Amenability and Nonamenability to Treatment and Reunification

Judgments about amenability are based on what is known about the efficacy and predictive validity of various treatment methods, their applicability to child maltreatment, and their relevance in light of the individual's intellect or level of education. Other relevant factors include the individual's attendance and participation in the rehabilitation, information from rehabilitation providers, the caregiver's self-assessment of rehabilitation impact, and caregivers' ability to demonstrate or describe what they have acquired from rehabilitation (Coley, 2001; Eiden & Reifman, 1996). Amenability may depend on the availability of ongoing support, monitoring, or supervision (Mohit, 1996). Although amenability judgments ought to be based on supporting treatment outcome data, research studies may not be directly relevant to care and protection population samples. Clinical outcome research typically is based on pure clinical samples, but care and protection samples usually contain individuals with complex comorbidity of multiple mental health, health, and/or substance abuse issues (Condie, 2003). Although the treatment outcome literature has applicability to some individuals involved in care and protection actions, it frequently lacks specificity to individuals with multiple and complex diagnostic concerns or environmental complications such poor neighborhood quality and low socioeconomic status (Hipwell & Kumar, 1996; Morey, 1999). For example, much is known about expectations of treatment compliance and treatment progress in samples of substance abusers (Marlatt, Blume, & Parks, 2001), but less is known about expected treatment progress when substance abuse interacts with the stress of legal actions (Mejta & Lavin, 1996). Offering opinions about the expected duration of treatment is complicated by these factors (Condie, 2003).

Although studies lack specificity to care and protection populations, much is known about factors that facilitate measurable treatment outcome. Treatments that target specific behavioral indicators usually are more effective in the short term

(Piper & Joyce, 2001). For some mental illnesses, the duration of untreated symptoms is predictive of treatment outcome (K. Black et al., 2001). Depending on the severity of the trauma that precipitated the disorder, some approaches to treatment may prove disorganizing for the patient (McEvoy & Wilkinson, 2000). Studies that target comorbid mental illness and substance abuse in adults have indicated that addiction severity is the most potent predictor of treatment outcome, with preexisting mental illness having little relationship to substance abuse outcomes or relapse despite its prevalence as a comorbid factor (Marsden, Gossop, Stewart, Rolfe, & Farrell, 2000; McNamara, Schumacher, Milby, Wallace, & Usdan, 2001). Character pathology and associated problems are predictive of poor outcomes, with antisocial characteristics having a particularly pronounced effect on risk of relapse (Galen, Brower, Gillespie, & Zucker, 2000; Thomas, Melchert, & Banken, 1999). Polysubstance abuse, especially alcohol combined with the individual's drug of choice, is more predictive of poor treatment outcome than abuse of single substances (Heil, Badger, & Higgins, 2001). The predictive effect of addiction severity is mediated by employment (Marlatt et al., 2001). Positive outcomes in self-help treatment groups are linked to the individual's commitment to self-help practices, meeting attendance, and subjective impressions of the principles of the approach (Tonigan, Miller, & Connors, 2000).

When sexual offending is the treatment target, cognitive-behavioral approaches to sex offender treatment tend to be more effective than psychodynamic or purely behavioral approaches (Polizzi, MacKenzie, & Hickman, 1999; Wood, Grossman, & Fichtner, 2000); however, they are not optimal for individuals with high levels of self-centeredness, secrecy, minimization, and destructive influences in group treatment settings (Barker & Beech, 1993). Treatment effectiveness varies among categories of sex offending (Marques, Day, Nelson, & Miner, 1989). Overall effectiveness is difficult to measure. Most outpatient sex offender treatment outcome data are based on arrests or recidivism (Geer, Becker, Gray, & Krauss, 2001). Treatment outcome studies relevant to reducing violence risk have produced positive but mixed results (Griffin, Steadman, & Heilbrun, 1991), and their applicability to care and protection samples is not well established (see Heilbrun & Griffin, 1999, for a description of suggested methods for evaluating potential treatment effectiveness for individuals with histories of violence).

Amenability to treatment is described in the context of individual variables and embedded in theories and supporting data about expected treatment outcomes. Judgments about expected time frames for treatment should be addressed with appropriate caveats. Opinions as to whether a parent has demonstrated adequate treatment benefit should be rendered with cautionary comments about the limitations of the long-term predictive validity of treatment outcome studies (Condie, 2003).

CONCLUSION

Care and protection evaluations address complicated family dynamics, comorbid compromises to parental functioning, complex child variables, and cumulative risk factors that are understood in the aggregate but less well illustrated in individual cases. Although the safety of children is a paramount goal of our society, the system for the protection of children often is described as overburdened and as functioning with insufficient resources. Care and protection matters coming before the court benefit from mental health expertise in addressing statutorily relevant but complex questions about the safety of children, family separation and reunification, the child's attachment to substitute caregivers, and the child's experience of the care and protection system. When evaluators use appropriate caution and multimodal methods of assessment, when they integrate data in a manner that considers current and historical factors, and when they soundly embed their opinions in theories of parenting and child development, the court, children, families, and child protective service agencies benefit from their expertise.

REFERENCES

Abel, G. G., Rouleau, J. L., & Cunningham-Rathner, J. (1986). Sexually aggressive behavior. In W. Curran, L. McGarry, & S. Shah (Eds.), *Forensic psychiatry and psychology: Perspectives and standards for interdisciplinary practice* (pp. 289–313). Philadelphia: F. A. Davis.

Adler, N. E., Boyce, T., Chesney, M. A., Cohen, S., Folkman, S., Kahn, R. L., et al. (1994). Socioeconomic status and health: The challenge of the gradient. *American Psychologist, 49,* 15–24.

Ainsworth, M. D. S. (1989). Attachments beyond infancy. *American Psychologist, 44,* 709–716.

Ainsworth, M. D. S., & Bell, S. M. (1974). Mother-infant interaction and the development of competence. In K. Connolly & J. Bruner (Eds.), *The growth of competence* (pp. 97–118). New York: Academic Press.

Armstrong, I. (1983). *The home front.* New York: McGraw-Hill.

Azar, S. T. (1992). Legal issues in the assessment of family violence involving children. In R. T. Ammerman & M. Hersen (Eds.), *Assessment of family violence: A clinical and legal sourcebook* (pp. 47–70). New York: Wiley.

Bander, K. W., Fein, E., & Bishop, G. (1982). Evaluation of child sexual abuse programs. In S. M. Sgroi (Ed.), *Handbook of clinical intervention in child sexual abuse* (pp. 345–376). Lexington, MA: Lexington Books.

Barker, M., & Beech, T. (1993). Sex offender treatment programs: A critical look at the cognitive-behavioral approach. *Issues in Criminological and Legal Psychology, 19,* 37–42.

Barnum, R. (1997). A suggested framework for forensic consultation in cases of child abuse and neglect. *Journal of the American Academy of Psychiatry and Law, 25,* 581–593.

Becker, G., & Cherny, S. S. (1992). A five-factor nuclear model of socially desirable responding. *Social Behavior and Personality, 20,* 163–191.

Belsky, J. (1993). Etiology of child maltreatment: A developmental-ecological analysis. *Psychological Bulletin, 114,* 413–434.

Belsky, J., Woodworth, S., & Crnic, K. (1996). Trouble in the second year: Three questions about family interaction. *Child Development, 67,* 556–578.

Berlin, R., & Davis, R. B. (1989). Children from alcoholic families: Vulnerability. In T. F. Dugan & R. Coles (Eds.), *The child in our homes: Studies in the development of resiliency* (pp. 81–108). New York: Brunner/Mazel.

Bernardi, E., Jones, M., & Tennant, C. (1989). Quality of parenting in alcoholism and narcotic addicts. *British Journal of Psychiatry, 154,* 677–682.

Black, K., Peters, L., Rui, Q., Milliken, H., Whitehorn, D., & Kopala, L. C. (2001). Duration of untreated psychosis predicts treatment outcome in an early psychosis program. *Schizophrenia Research, 47,* 215–222.

Black, M., Schuler, M., & Nair, P. (1993). Prenatal drug exposure: Neurodevelopmental outcome and parenting environment. *Journal of Pediatric Psychology, 18,* 605–620.

Blume, E. S. (1991). *Secret survivors: Uncovering incest and its aftereffects in women.* New York: Ballantine Books.

Bolton, F., & Laner, R. (1981). Maternal maturity and maltreatment. *Journal of Family Issues, 2,* 485–508.

Borum, R., Otto, R., & Golding, S. (1993). Improving clinical judgment and decision making in forensic evaluation. *Journal of Psychiatry and Law, 21,* 35–76.

Bousha, D. M., & Twentyman, C. T. (1984). Mother-child interactional style in abuse, neglect, and control groups: Naturalistic observations in the home. *Journal of Abnormal Psychology, 93,* 106–114.

Bowlby, J. (1956). The growth of independence in the young child. *Royal Society of Health Journal, 76,* 587–591.

Bowlby, J. (1969). *Attachment and loss: Vol. 1. Attachment.* New York: Basic Books.

Brooks-Gunn, J., Britto, P. R., & Brady, C. (1999). Struggling to make ends meet: Poverty and child development. In M. E. Lamb (Ed.), *Parenting and child development in "nontraditional" families* (pp. 279–304). Mahwah, NJ: Erlbaum.

Brooks-Gunn, J., & Duncan, G. J. (1997). The effects of poverty on children. *Future of Children, 7,* 55–71.

Bruck, M., Ceci, S. J., & Hembrooke, H. (1998). Reliability and credibility of young children's reports: From research to policy and practice. *American Psychologist, 53,* 136–151.

Budd, K. S., & Holdsworth, M. J. (1996). Issues in clinical assessment of minimal parenting competence. *Journal of Clinical Child Psychology, 25,* 2–14.

Budd, K. S., Poindexter, L. M., Felix, E. D., & Naik-Polan, A. T. (2001). Clinical assessment of parents in child protection cases: An empirical analysis. *Law and Human Behavior, 25,* 93–108.

Bugental, D. B., Blue, J., & Lewis, J. (1990). Caregiver beliefs and dysphoric affect directed to difficult children. *Developmental Psychology, 26,* 631–638.

Bugental, D. B., & Cortez, V. L. (1988). Physiological reactivity to responsive and unresponsive children as moderated by perceived control. *Child Development, 59,* 686–693.

Bugental, D. B., Mantyla, S. M., & Lewis, J. (1989). Parental attributions as moderators of affective communication to children at risk for physical abuse. In D. Cicchetti & V. Carlson (Eds.), *Child maltreatment: Theory and research on the causes and consequences of child abuse and neglect* (pp. 254–279). Cambridge, England: Cambridge University Press.

Burgdoff, K. (1980). *Natural study of the incidence and severity of child abuse and neglect.* Washington, DC: U.S. Department of Health and Human Services, National Center on Child Abuse and Neglect.

Burgess, R. L. (1994). The family in a changing world: A prolegomenon to an evolutionary analysis. *Human Nature, 5,* 203–221.

Burgess, R. L., & Conger, R. D. (1978). Family interaction in abusive, neglectful, and normal families. *Child Development, 49,* 1163–1173.

Burgess, R. L., & Draper, P. (1989). The explanation of family violence: The role of biological, behavioral, and cultural selection. In L. Ohlin & M. Tonry (Eds.), *Family violence* (pp. 59–116). Chicago: University of Chicago Press.

Burrell, B., Thompson, B., & Sexton, D. (1994). Predicting child abuse potential across family types. *Child Abuse and Neglect, 18,* 1039–1049.

Burton, R. V. (1976). Honesty and dishonesty. In T. Lickona (Ed.), *Moral development and behavior: Theory, research, and social issues* (pp. 173–197). New York: Holt, Rinehart and Winston.

Burton, R. V. (1984). A paradox in theories and research in moral development. In W. M. Kurtines & J. L. Gewirtz (Eds.), *Morality, moral behavior, and moral development* (pp. 193–207). New York: Wiley.

Burton, R. V., & Strichartz, A. F. (1991). Children on the stand: The obligation to speak the truth. *Developmental and Behavioral Pediatrics, 12,* 121–128.

Butcher, J., Dahlstrom, W., Graham, J., Tellegen, A., & Kaemmer, B. (1989). *Minnesota Multiphasic Personality Inventory 2 (MMPI-2): Manual for administration and scoring.* Minneapolis: University of Minnesota Press.

Bycer, A., Breed, L. D., Fluke, J. E., & Costello, T. (1984). *Unemployment and child abuse and neglect reporting.* Denver, CO: American Humane Association.

Ceci, S. J., & Bruck, M. (1993). Suggestibility of the child witness: A historical review and synthesis. *Psychological Bulletin, 113,* 403–439.

Chapsky v. Wood, 26 Kan. 650, 42, 499n.12, 511n.32 (1881).

Chasnoff, I. J. (1988). Drug use in pregnancy: Parameters of risk. *Pediatric Clinics of North America, 35,* 1408–1412.

Coburn, W. J. (2000). The organizing forces of contemporary psychoanalysis: Reflections on nonlinear dynamic systems theory. *Psychoanalytic Psychology, 17,* 750–770.

Coley, R. L. (2001). (In)visible men: Emerging research on low-income, unmarried, and minority fathers. *American Psychologist, 56,* 743–753.

Commonwealth v. Caracino, 33 Mass. App. Ct. 787 (1993).

Commonwealth v. Corbett, 26 Mass. App. Ct. 773, 533 N.E.2d 207 (1989).

Commonwealth v. Snow, 30 Mass. App. Ct. 433 (1991).

Condie, L. (2003). *Perspective in law and psychology: Vol. 18. Parenting evaluations for the court.* New York: Kluwer-Plenum Press.

Connelly, C., & Straus, M. (1992). Mother's age and risk for physical abuse. *Child Abuse and Neglect, 16,* 709–718.

Crenshaw, W., & Barnum, D. (2001). You can't fight the system: Strategies of family justice in foster care reintegration. *Family Journal: Counseling and Therapy for Couples and Families, 9,* 29–36.

Crittenden, P. M. (1981). Abusing, neglecting, problematic, and adequate dyads: Differentiating by patterns of interaction. *Merrill-Palmer Quarterly, 27,* 1–18.

Crittenden, P. M. (1985). Maltreated infants: Vulnerability and resilience. *Journal of Child Psychology and Psychiatry, 26,* 85–96.

Crittenden, P. M. (1988). Distorted patterns of relationship in maltreating families: The role of internal representational models. *Journal of Reproductive and Infant Psychology, 6,* 183–199.

Crittenden, P. M., & Bonvillian, J. D. (1984). The relationship between maternal risk status and maternal sensitivity. *American Journal of Orthopsychiatry, 54,* 250–262.

Daly, M., & Wilson, M. (1981). Child maltreatment from a sociobiological perspective. *New Directions in Child Development: Developmental Perspectives on Child Maltreatment, 11,* 92–112.

Dana, R. H. (1993). *Multicultural assessment perspectives for professional psychology.* Boston: Allyn & Bacon.

Daubert v. Merrell Dow Pharmaceuticals, Inc., 509 U.S. 579, 113 S. Ct. 2786 (1993).

Davies, J. M. (1996). Dissociation, repression, and reality testing in the countertransference: The controversy over memory and false memory in the psychoanalytic treatment of adult survivors of childhood sexual abuse. *Psychoanalytic Dialogues, 6,* 189–218.

DeFrancis, V. (1969). *Protecting the child victim of sex crimes committed by adults.* Denver, CO: American Humane Association.

Dix, T., & Reinhold, D. P. (1991). Chronic and temporary influences on mothers' attributions for children's disobedience. *Merrill-Palmer Quarterly, 37,* 251–271.

Dolan, M., & Doyle, M. (2000). Violence risk prediction: Clinical and actuarial measures and the role of the Psychopathy Checklist. *British Journal of Psychiatry, 177,* 303–311.

Doran v. United States, 205 F.2d 717 (1953).

Dubowitz, H. (1999). The families of neglected children. In M. E. Lamb (Ed.), *Parenting and child development in "nontraditional" families* (pp. 327–345). Mahwah, NJ: Erlbaum.

Dubowitz, H., Hampton, R. L., Bithoney, W. G., & Newberger, E. H. (1987). Inflicted and noninflicted injuries: Differences in child and familial characteristics. *American Journal of Orthopsychiatry, 57,* 525–535.

Dutton, D. G., & Kropp, P. R. (2000). A review of domestic violence risk instruments. *Trauma Violence and Abuse, 1,* 171–181.

Dyer, F. J. (1999). *Psychological consultation in parental rights cases.* New York: Guilford Press.

Eiden, R. D., & Reifman, A. (1996). Effects of Brazelton demonstrations on later parenting: A meta-analysis. *Journal of Pediatric Psychology, 21,* 857–868.

Eisenstadt v. Baird, 405 U.S. 438 (1972).

Enfield, R. (1987). A model for developing the written forensic report. In P. A. Keller & S. R. Heyman (Eds.), *Innovations in clinical practice: Vol. 6. A sourcebook* (pp. 379–394). Sarasota, FL: Professional Resource Exchange.

Famularo, R., Kinscherff, R., & Fenton, T. (1992). Parental substance abuse and the nature of child maltreatment. *Child Abuse and Neglect, 16,* 475–483.

Finkelhor, D. (1984). *Child sexual abuse: New theory and research.* New York: Free Press.

Fischer, C. T. (1970). Levels of cheating under conditions of informative appeal to honesty, public affirmation of values, and threats of punishment. *Journal of Educational Research, 64,* 12–16.

Fivush, R., & Hammond, N. R. (1989). Time and again: Effects of repetition and retention interval on 2-year-olds' event recall. *Journal of Experimental Child Psychology, 47,* 259–273.

Fox, R. A., Platz, D. L., & Bentley, K. S. (1995). Maternal factors related to parenting practices, developmental expectations, and perceptions of child behavior problems. *Journal of Genetic Psychology, 156,* 431–441.

Frodi, A. M., & Lamb, M. E. (1980). Child abusers' responses to infant smiles and cries. *Child Development, 51,* 238–241.

Fundudis, T. (1989). Children's memory and the assessment of possible child sex abuse. *Journal of Child Psychology and Psychiatry and Allied Disciplines, 30,* 337–346.

Furstenberg, F., & Brooks-Gunn, J. (1987). *Adolescent mothers in later life.* New York: Cambridge University Press.

Gaensbauer, T. J. (1995). Trauma in the preverbal period: Symptoms, memories, and developmental impact. *Psychoanalytic Study of the Child, 50,* 122–149.

Galen, L. W., Brower, K. J., Gillespie, B. W., & Zucker, R. A. (2000). Sociopathy, gender, and treatment outcome among outpatient substance abusers. *Drug and Alcohol Dependence, 61,* 23–33.

Garbarino, J., & Kostelny, K. (1992). Child maltreatment as a community problem. *Child Abuse and Neglect, 16,* 455–464.

Gaudin, J. M., & Dubowitz, H. (1997). Family functioning in neglectful families: Recent research. In J. Berrick & N. Barth (Eds.), *Child welfare research review* (Vol. 2, pp. 26–28). New York: Columbia University Press.

Gaudin, J. M., & Polansky, N. A. (1986). Social distancing of the neglectful family: Sex, race, and social class influence. *Children and Youth Services Review, 8,* 1–12.

Geer, T. M., Becker, J. V., Gray, S. R., & Krauss, D. (2001). Predictors of treatment completion in a correctional sex offender treatment program. *International Journal of Offender Therapy and Comparative Criminology, 45,* 302–313.

George, C., & Solomon, J. (1999). Attachment and caregiving: The caregiving behavioral system. In J. Cassidy & P. R. Shaver (Eds.), *Handbook of attachment: Theory, research, and clinical applications* (pp. 649–670). New York: Guilford Press.

Goldstein, M. J., Kant, H. S., & Hartman, J. J. (1973). *Pornography and sexual deviance.* Los Angeles: University of California Press.

Goldstein, R. D. (1999). *Child abuse and neglect: Cases and materials.* St. Paul, MN: West.

Goodman, G. S., Hirschman, J., Hepps, D., & Rudy, L. (1991). Children's memory for stressful events. *Merrill-Palmer Quarterly, 37,* 109–158.

Goodman, G. S., & Reed, R. S. (1986). Age differences in eyewitness testimony. *Law and Human Behavior, 10,* 317–332.

Green, A. H. (1998). Factors contributing to the generational transmission of child maltreatment. *Journal of the American Academy of Child and Adolescent Psychiatry, 37,* 1334–1336.

Griffin v. State, 526 So. 2d 752 (Fla. Dist. Ct. App. 1988).

Griffin, P. A., Steadman, H. J., & Heilbrun, K. (1991). Designing conditional release systems for insanity acquittees. *Journal of Mental Health Administration, 18,* 231–241.

Grisso, T. (1986). *Evaluating competencies: Forensic assessments and instruments.* New York: Plenum Press.

Griswold v. Connecticut, 381 U.S. 479 (1965).

Groth, N. A., Hobson, W., & Gary, T. (1982). The child molester: Clinical observations. In J. Conte & D. Shore (Eds.), *Social work and child sexual abuse* (pp. 129–144). New York: Hawthorn.

Hanson, R. K. (1998). What do we know about sex offender risk assessment? *Psychology, Public Policy, and the Law, 4,* 50–72.

Hanson, R. K., & Harris, A. J. R. (2000). Where should we intervene? Dynamic predictors of sexual assault recidivism. *Criminal Justice and Behavior, 27,* 6–35.

Harlow, H. F. (1962). The development of affectional patterns in infant monkeys. In B. M. Foss (Ed.), *Determinants of infant behavior* (Vol. 1, pp. 75–88). New York: Wiley.

Harlow, H. F., & Harlow, M. K. (1965). The affectional systems. In A. M. Schrier, H. F. Harlow, & F. Stollnitz (Eds.), *Behavior of non-human primates* (Vol. 2, pp. 287–334). New York: Academic Press.

Haskett, M. E., Scott, S. S., & Fann, K. D. (1995). Child Abuse Potential Inventory and parenting behavior: Relationship with high-risk correlates. *Child Abuse and Neglect, 19,* 1483–1495.

Haugaard, J. J. (1993). Young children's classification of the corroboration of a false statement as the truth or a lie. *Law and Human Behavior, 17,* 645–659.

Haugaard, J. J., Reppucci, N. D., Laird, J., & Nauful, T. (1991). Children's definitions of the truth and their competency as witnesses in legal proceedings. *Law and Human Behavior, 15,* 253–271.

Heil, S. H., Badger, G. J., & Higgins, S. T. (2001). Alcohol dependence among cocaine-dependent outpatients: Demographics, drug use, treatment outcome and other characteristics. *Journal of Studies on Alcohol, 62,* 14–22.

Heilbrun, K., & Griffin, P. (1999). Forensic treatment: A review of programs and research. In R. Roesch, S. D. Hart, & J. R. P. Ogloff (Eds.), *Psychology and law: The state of the discipline* (pp. 242–274). New York: Kluwer Academic/Plenum Press.

Heilbrun, K., Warren, J., & Picarello, K. (2003). Third party information in forensic assessment. In I. B. Weiner (Series Ed.) & A. M. Goldstein (Vol. Ed.), *Comprehensive handbook of psychology: Vol. 11. Forensic psychology* (pp. 69–86). Hoboken, NJ: Wiley.

Heiman, M. L. (1992). Annotation: Putting the puzzle together—Validating allegations of child sexual abuse. *Journal of Child Psychology and Psychiatry, 33,* 311–329.

Heller, M. C., Sobel, M., & Tanaka-Matsumi, J. (1996). A functional analysis of verbal interactions of drug-exposed children and their mothers: The utility of sequential analysis. *Journal of Clinical Psychology, 52,* 687–697.

Hipwell, A. E., & Kumar, R. (1996). Maternal psychopathology and prediction of outcome based on mother-infant interaction ratings (BMIS). *British Journal of Psychiatry, 169,* 655–661.

Jacobsen, T., Miller, L. J., & Kirkwood, K. P. (1997). Assessing parenting competency in individuals with severe mental illness: A comprehensive service. *Journal of Mental Health Administration, 24,* 189–199.

Jacobson, S. W., & Frye, K. F. (1991). Effect of maternal social support on attachment: Experimental evidence. *Child Development, 62,* 572–582.

Jones, D. C., Swift, D. J., & Johnson, M. (1988). Nondeliberate memory for a novelty event among preschoolers. *Developmental Psychology, 24,* 641–645.

Kadushin, A. (1988). Neglect in families. In E. W. Nunnally, C. S. Chilman, & F. M. Cox (Eds.), *Mental illness, delinquency, addictions, and neglect* (pp. 147–166). Newbury Park, CA: Sage.

Kalish, C. W., Weissman, M., & Bernstein, D. (2000). Taking decisions seriously: Young children's understanding of conventional truth. *Child Development, 71,* 1289–1308.

Kantrowitz, R. M., & Limon, S. M. (2001). *2002 Massachusetts juvenile law sourcebook.* Boston: Massachusetts Continuing Legal Education.

Kelley, S. J. (1992). Parenting stress and child maltreatment in drug-exposed children. *Child Abuse and Neglect, 16,* 317–328.

Kendall, P. C., & Urbain, E. (1982). Social-cognitive approaches to therapy with children. In J. R. Lachenmeyer & M. S. Gibbs (Eds.), *Psychopathology in childhood* (pp. 298–326). New York: Gardner Press.

Klaus, M. H., Jerauld, R., Kreger, N., McAlpine, W., Steffa, M., & Kennell, J. H. (1972). Maternal attachment: Importance of the first post-partum days. *New England Journal of Medicine, 286,* 460–463.

Klein, N. C., Alexander, J. F., & Parsons, B. V. (1977). Impact of family systems intervention on recidivism and sibling delinquency: A model of primary prevention and program evaluation. *Journal of Consulting and Clinical Psychology, 45,* 469–474.

Lahey, B. B., Conger, R. D., Atkeson, B. M., & Treiber, F. A. (1984). Parenting behavior and emotional status of physically abusive mothers. *Journal of Consulting and Clinical Psychology, 52,* 1062–1071.

Lane, S. (1997). Assessment of sexually abusive youth. In G. Ryan & S. Lane (Eds.), *Juvenile sexual offending: Causes, consequences, and correction* (pp. 166–219). San Francisco: Jossey-Bass.

Lassiter v. Department of Social Services, 452 U.S. 18 (1981).

Leichtman, M., & Ceci, S. J. (1995). Effects of stereotypes and suggestions on preschoolers' reports. *Developmental Psychology, 31,* 568–578.

Leventhal, J. (1981). Risk factors to child abuse: Methodologic standards in case control studies. *Child Abuse and Neglect, 6,* 113–123.

Lorenz, K. (1935). Der Kumpan in der Umwelt des Vogels [Imprinting in the environment of the bird]. *Journal of Ornithology, 83,* 137–213.

Loving v. Virginia, 388 U.S. 1, 87 S. Ct. 1817, 18 L.Ed.2d 1010 (1967).

Lyon, T. D., & Saywitz, K. J. (1999). Young maltreated children's competence to take the oath. *Applied Developmental Science, 3,* 16–27.

Macias v. State, 776 S. W.2d 255 (Tx. App. 1989).

Maddock, J. W. (1988). Child reporting and testimony in incest cases: Comments on the construction and reconstruction of reality. *Behavioral Sciences and the Law, 6,* 201–220.

Marlatt, G. A., Blume, A. W., & Parks, G. A. (2001). Integrating harm reduction therapy and traditional substance abuse treatment. *Journal of Psychoactive Drugs, 33,* 13–21.

Marques, J. K., Day, D. M., Nelson, C., & Miner, M. H. (1989). The Sex Offender Treatment and Evaluation Project: California's relapse prevention program. In R. D. Laws (Ed.), *Relapse prevention with sex offenders* (pp. 247–267). New York: Guilford Press.

Marsden, J., Gossop, M., Stewart, D., Rolfe, A., & Farrell, M. (2000). Psychiatric symptoms among clients seeking treatment for drug dependence: Intake data from the National Treatment Outcome Research Study. *British Journal of Psychiatry, 176,* 285–289.

McAdoo, H. P. (1986). Strategies used by Black single mothers against stress. In M. Simms & J. Malveaux (Eds.), *Slipping through the cracks: The status of Black women* (pp. 153–166). New Brunswick, NJ: Transaction Books.

McEvoy, J. P., & Wilkinson, M. L. (2000). The role of insight in the treatment and outcome of bipolar disorder. *Psychiatric Annals, 30,* 496–498.

McLanahan, S., & Teitler, J. (1999). The consequences of father absence. In M. E. Lamb (Ed.), *Parenting and child development in "nontraditional" families* (pp. 83–102). Mahwah, NJ: Erlbaum.

McLoyd, V. C. (1989). Socialization and development in a changing economy: The effects of paternal job and income loss on children. *American Psychologist, 44,* 293–302.

McLoyd, V. C. (1990). The impact of economic hardship on Black families and children: Psychological distress, parenting, and socioemotional development. *Child Development, 61,* 311–346.

McNamara, C., Schumacher, J. E., Milby, J. B., Wallace, D., & Usdan, S. (2001). Prevalence of nonpsychotic mental disorders does not affect treatment outcome in a homeless cocaine-dependent sample. *American Journal of Drug and Alcohol Abuse, 27,* 91–106.

McNichol, S., Shute, R., & Tucker, A. (1999). Children's eyewitness memory for a repeated event. *Child Abuse and Neglect, 23,* 1127–1139.

Mejta, C. L., & Lavin, R. (1996). Facilitating healthy parenting among mothers with substance abuse or dependence problems: Some considerations. *Alcoholism Treatment Quarterly, 14,* 33–46.

Melton, G. B. (1981). Children's competency to testify. *Law and Human Behavior, 5,* 73–85.

Melton, G. B., Goodman, G. S., Kalichman, S. C., Levine, M., Saywitz, K. J., & Koocher, G. P. (1995). Empirical research on child maltreatment and the law. *Journal of Clinical Child Psychology, 24,* 47–77.

Melton, G. B., Petrila, J., Poythress, N. G., & Slobogin, C. (1997). *Psychological evaluation for the courts* (2nd ed.). New York: Guilford Press.

Merydith, S. P., & Wallbrown, F. H. (1991). Reconsidering response sets, test-taking attitudes, dissimulation, self-deception, and social desirability. *Psychological Reports, 69,* 891–905.

Meyer v. Nebraska, 262 U.S. 390 (1923).

Miller, B. A. (1990). The interrelationships between alcohol and drugs and family violence. *National Institute on Drug Abuse Research Monograph Series, 103,* 177–207.

Miller, P. J., & Sperry, L. L. (1988). Early talk about the past: The origins of conversational stories of personal experience. *Journal of Child Language, 15,* 293–315.

Milner, J. S. (1986). *Child Abuse Potential Inventory: Manual* (2nd ed.). Webster, NC: Psytec.

Milner, J. S., Robertson, K. R., & Rogers, D. L. (1990). Childhood history of abuse and adult child abuse potential. *Journal of Family Violence, 5,* 15–34.

Mohit, D. L. (1996). Management and care of mentally ill mothers of young children: An innovative program. *Archives of Psychiatric Nursing, 10,* 49–54.

Monahan, J., Steadman, H. J., Appelbaum, P. S., Robbins, P. C., Mulvey, E. P., Silver, E., et al. (2000). Developing a clinically useful actuarial tool for assessing violence risk. *British Journal of Psychiatry, 176,* 312–319.

Moncher, F. J. (1996). The relationship of maternal adult attachment style and risk of physical child abuse. *Journal of Interpersonal Violence, 11,* 335–350.

Morey, L. C. (1999). Personality Assessment Inventory. In M. E. Maruish (Ed.), *The use of psychological testing for treatment planning and outcome assessment* (2nd ed., pp. 1083–1121). Mahwah, NJ: Erlbaum.

Morton, N., & Browne, K. D. (1998). Theory and observation of attachment and its relation to child maltreatment: A review. *Child Abuse and Neglect, 22,* 1093–1104.

Murphy, J. M., Jellinek, M., Quinn, D., Smith, G., Poitrast, F. G., & Goshko, M. (1991). Substance abuse and serious child mistreatment: Prevalence, risk, and outcome in a court sample. *Child Abuse and Neglect, 15,* 197–211.

Nelson, K. (1986). *Event knowledge: Structure and function in development.* Hillsdale, NJ: Erlbaum.

Oberlander, L. B. (1995a). Ethical responsibilities in child custody evaluations: Implications for evaluation methodology. *Ethics and Behavior, 3,* 311–332.

Oberlander, L. B. (1995b). Psycholegal issues in child sexual abuse evaluations: A survey of forensic mental health professionals. *Child Abuse and Neglect, 19,* 473–490.

Ownby, R. L. (1997). *Psychological reports: A guide to report writing in professional psychology* (3rd ed.). New York: Wiley.

Page, T. (1999). The attachment partnership as conceptual base for exploring the impact of child maltreatment. *Child and Adolescent Social Work Journal, 16,* 419–437.

Passman, R. H., & Mulhern, R. K. (1977). Maternal punitiveness as affected by situational stress: An experimental analogue of child abuse. *Journal of Abnormal Psychology, 86,* 565–569.

Pelton, L. (1978). Child abuse and neglect: The myth of classlessness. *American Journal of Orthopsychiatry, 48,* 608–617.

People v. Brown, 8, Cal. 4th 746, 35 Cal. Rptr. 2d 407, 883 P.2d 949 (1994).

People v. District Court In and For Summit County, 791 P.2d 682, 685 (Colo. 1990).

People v. Draper, 150 Mich. App. 481, 389 N.W.2d 89 (1986).

Piaget, J. (1962). *The moral judgment of the child.* New York: Free Press. (Original work published 1932)

Pierce v. Society of Sisters, 268 U.S. 510 (1925).

Piper, W. E., & Joyce, A. S. (2001). Psychosocial treatment outcome. In W. J. Livesley (Ed.), *Handbook of personality disorders: Theory, research, and treatment* (pp. 323–343). New York: Guilford Press.

Polansky, N. A., Ammons, P. W., & Gaudin, J. M. (1985). Loneliness and isolation in child neglect. *Social Casework: Journal of Contemporary Social Work, 66,* 38–47.

Polizzi, D. M., MacKenzie, D., & Hickman, L. J. (1999). What works in adult sex offender treatment? A review of prison- and non-prison-based treatment programs. *International Journal of Offender Therapy and Comparative Criminology, 43,* 357–374.

Poole, D., & Lamb, M. (1998). *Investigative interviews of children: A guide for helping professionals.* Washington, DC: American Psychological Association.

Prentky, R., & Bird, S. (1997). *Assessing sexual abuse: A resource guide for practitioners.* Brandon, VT: Safer Society Press.

Roe v. Wade, 410 U.S. 113 (1973).

Roszkowski, M. J. (1984). Validity of the similarities ratio as a predictor of violent behavior: Data from a mentally-retarded sample. *Personality and Individual Differences, 5,* 117–118.

Rutter, M., & O'Connor, T. G. (1999). Implications of attachment theory for child care policies. In J. Cassidy & P. R. Shaver (Eds.), *Handbook of attachment: Theory, research, and clinical applications* (pp. 823–844). New York: Guilford Press.

Sagatun, I. J. (1991). Expert witnesses in child abuse cases. *Behavior Sciences and the Law, 9,* 201–215.

Sampson, R., & Morenoff, J. (1997). Ecological perspectives on the neighborhood context of urban poverty: Past and present. In J. Brooks-Gunn, G. J. Duncan, & J. L. Aber (Eds.), *Neighborhood poverty: Context and consequence for children: Vol. 2. Conceptual, methodological, and policy approaches to studying neighborhoods* (pp. 1–23). New York: Russell Sage Foundation.

Santosky v. Kramer, 455 U.S. 745 (1982).

Saywitz, K. J., & Camparo, L. (1998). Interviewing child witnesses: A developmental perspective. *Child Abuse and Neglect, 22,* 825–843.

Saywitz, K. J., Jaenicke, C., & Camparo, L. (1990). Children's knowledge of legal terminology. *Law and Human Behavior, 14,* 523–535.

Saywitz, K. J., & Snyder, L. (1996). Narrative elaboration: Test of a new procedure for interviewing children. *Journal of Consulting and Clinical Psychology, 64,* 1347–1357.

Saywitz, K. J., Snyder, L., & Nathanson, R. (1999). Facilitating the communicative competence of the child witness. *Applied Developmental Science, 3,* 58–68.

Schetky, D. H., Angell, R., Morrison, C. V., & Sack, W. H. (1979). Parents who fail: A study of 51 cases of termination of parental rights. *Journal of the American Academy of Child Psychiatry, 18,* 366–383.

Schmidt, E., & Eldridge, A. (1986). The attachment relationship and child maltreatment. *Infant Mental Health Journal, 7,* 264–273.

Schwartz, N. H. (1987). Data integration and report writing. In R. S. Dean (Ed.), *Introduction to assessing human intelligence: Issues and procedures* (pp. 289–313). Springfield, IL: Charles C. Thomas.

Shapiro, J. R., & Mangelsdorf, S. C. (1994). The determinants of parenting competence in adolescent mothers. *Journal of Youth and Adolescence, 23,* 621–641.

Shelman, E. A., & Lazoritz, S. (2005). *Mary Ellen Wilson child abuse case and the beginning of children's rights in nineteenth century America.* Jefferson, NC: McFarland.

Sigelman, C. K., Budd, E. C., Spanhel, C. L., & Schoenrock, C. J. (1981). Asking questions of retarded persons: A comparison of yes-no and either-or formats. *Applied Research in Mental Retardation, 2,* 347–357.

Small, M. F. (1998). *Our babies, ourselves: How biology and culture shape the way we parent.* New York: Anchor Books.

Spearly, J. L., & Lauderdale, M. (1983). Community characteristics and ethnicity in the prediction of child maltreatment rates. *Child Abuse and Neglect, 7,* 91–105.

Sperling, M. B., & Berman, W. H. (Eds.). (1994). *Attachment in adults: Clinical and developmental perspectives.* New York: Guilford Press.

Sroufe, L. A., & Waters, E. (1977). Attachment as an organizational construct. *Child Development, 48,* 1184–1199.

Stahl, P. M. (1994). *Conducting child custody evaluations: A comprehensive guide.* Thousand Oaks, CA: Sage.

Starr, R. H. (1982). A research-based approach to the prediction of child abuse. In R. H. Starr (Ed.), *Child abuse predictions: Policy implications* (pp. 105–134). Cambridge, MA: Ballinger.

State v. Brovold, 477 N.W.2d 775 (Minn. Ct. App. 1991).

State v. Hollingsworth, 160 Wis. 2d 883, 467 N.W.2d 555 (Wis. Ct. App. 1991).

State v. Hudnall, 293 S.C. 97, 359 S.E.2d 59 (1987).

State v. Hussey, 521 A.2d 278 (Me. 1987).

State v. Jones, 95 N.C. 588 (1986).

State v. Michaels, 136 N.J. 299, 642 A.2d, 1372 (1994).

State v. Ward, 619 N. E.2d 1119 (Ohio. App. 1992).

Steadman, H. J., Silver, E., Monahan, J., Appelbaum, P. S., Robbins, P. C., Mulvey, E., P., et al. (2000). A classification tree approach to the development of actuarial violence risk assessment tools. *Law and Human Behavior, 24,* 83–100.

Straus, M. A. (1983). Ordinary violence, child abuse, and wife beating: What do they have in common? In D. Finkelhor, R. J. Gelles, G. T. Hotaling, & M. A. Straus (Eds.), *The dark side of families* (pp. 213–234). Beverly Hills, CA: Sage.

Strickland v. State, 550 So. 2d 1042 (Ala. 1988).

Studer, L. H., Clelland, S. R., Aylwin, A. S., Reddon, J. R., & Monro, A. (2000). Rethinking risk assessment for incest offenders. *International Journal of Law and Psychiatry, 23,* 15–22.

Tarter, R. E., Blackson, T., Martin, C., Loeber, R., & Moss, H. B. (1993). Characteristics and correlates of child discipline practices in substance abuse and normal families. *American Journal on Addictions, 2,* 18–25.

Thomas, V. H., Melchert, T. P., & Banken, J. A. (1999). Substance dependence and personality disorders: Comorbidity and treatment outcome in an inpatient treatment population. *Journal of Studies on Alcohol, 60,* 271–277.

Tome v. United States, 513 U.S. 150, 115 St. Ct. 696 (1995).

Tonigan, J. S., Miller, W. R., & Connors, G. J. (2000). Project MATCH client impressions about Alcoholics Anonymous: Measurement issues and relationship to treatment outcome. *Alcoholism Treatment Quarterly, 18,* 25–41.

Trevathan, W. R. (1987). *Human birth: An evolutionary perspective.* New York: Aldine de Gruyter.

Trickett, P. K., & Susman, E. J. (1988). Parental perceptions of child-rearing practices in physically abusive and nonabusive families. *Developmental Psychology, 24,* 270–276.

Umberson, D. (1986). Sociobiology: A valid explanation of child abuse? *Social Biology, 33,* 131–137.

Walker, L. E. A. (1990). Psychological assessment of sexually abused children for legal evaluation and expert witness testimony. *Professional Psychology: Research and Practice, 21,* 344–353.

Wauchope, B., & Straus, M. A. (1990). Physical punishment and physical abuse of American children: Incidence rates by age, gender, and occupational class. In M. A. Straus & R. J. Gelles (Eds.), *Physical violence in American families: Risk factors and adaptations to violence in 8,145 families*. New Brunswick, NJ: Transaction Books.

Webster, C. D., Douglas, K. S., Eaves, D., & Hart, S. D. (1997). Assessing risk of violence to others. In C. D. Webster & M. A. Jackson (Eds.), *Impulsivity: Theory, assessment, and treatment* (pp. 251–277). New York: Guilford Press.

Webster-Stratton, C. (1985). Comparison of abusive and nonabusive families with conduct-disordered children. *American Journal of Orthopsychiatry, 55,* 59–69.

Weinfield, N. S., Sroufe, L. A., & Egeland, B. (2000). Attachment from infancy to early adulthood in a high-risk sample: Continuity, discontinuity, and their correlates. *Child Development, 71,* 695–702.

Westcott, H. L., & Jones, D. P. H. (1999). Annotation: The abuse of disabled children. *Journal of Child Psychology and Psychiatry and Allied Disciplines, 40,* 479–506.

Western Industries v. Newcor Canada Ltd., 739 F.2d 1198 (1984).

Wheeler v. United States, 159 U.S. 523 (1895).

Widom, C. S. (1989a). Child abuse, neglect, and adult behavior: Research design and findings on criminality, violence, and child abuse. *American Journal of Orthopsychiatry, 59,* 355–367.

Widom, C. S. (1989b). Does violence beget violence? A critical examination of the literature. *Psychological Bulletin, 106,* 3–28.

Williams, L. M., Siegel, J. A., & Pomeroy, J. J. (2000). Validity of women's self-reports of documented child sexual abuse. In A. A. Stone, J. S. Turkkan, C. A. Bachrach, J. A. Jobe, H. S. Kurtzman, & V. S. Cain (Eds.), *The science of self-report: Implications for research and practice* (pp. 211–226). Mahwah, NJ: Erlbaum.

Wolfe, D. A. (1985). Child-abusive parents: An empirical review and analysis. *Psychological Bulletin, 97,* 462–482.

Wolfe, D. A. (1987). *Child abuse: Implications for child development and psychopathology.* Newbury Park, CA: Sage.

Wolfe, D. A. (1988). Child abuse and neglect. In E. J. Mash & L. G. Terdal (Eds.), *Behavioral assessment of childhood disorders* (2nd ed., pp. 627–669). New York: Guilford Press.

Wolfe, D. A., McMahon, R. J., & Peters, R. D. (Eds.). (1997). *Child abuse: New directions in prevention and treatment across the lifespan.* Thousand Oaks, CA: Sage.

Wood, R. M., Grossman, L. S., & Fichtner, C. G. (2000). Psychological assessment, treatment, and outcome with sex offenders. *Behavioral Sciences and the Law, 18,* 23–41.

Zuravin, S. J. (1989). The ecology of child abuse and neglect: Review of the literature and presentation of the data. *Violence and Victims, 4,* 101–120.

Zuravin, S. J. (1991). Unplanned childbearing and family size: The relationship to child neglect and abuse. *Family Planning Perspective, 23,* 155–161.

Zuravin, S. J., & Grief, G. (1989). Normative and chlid-maltreating AFDC mothers. *Social Casework: Journal of Contemporary Social Work, 74,* 76–84.

Zuravin, S. J., McMillen, C., DePanfilis, D., & Risley-Curtiss, C. (1996). The intergenerational cycle of child maltreatment: Continuity versus discontinuity. *Journal of Interpersonal Violence, 11,* 315–334.

PART V

Criminal Forensic Psychology

CHAPTER 13

Recent Criminal Legal Decisions: Implications for Forensic Mental Health Experts

Michael L. Perlin

Several years ago, I suggested that "the Supreme Court, like the moth to the flame, remains fleetingly fascinated with all aspects of mental disability law" (Perlin, 1996b, p. 605; 1999, p. 12). The intervening years have only served to reinforce this position. Since 2001, the U.S. Supreme Court has returned twice more to questions involving the impact of mental disability law on the criminal trial process (*Atkins v. Virginia,* 2002; *Sell v. United States,* 2003), has returned on multiple occasions (e.g., *Connecticut Department of Public Safety v. Doe,* 2003; *Kansas v. Crane,* 2002; *Seling v. Young,* 2001; *Smith v. Doe,* 2003) to questions of sexually violent predator law (which, although nominally considered civil [see *Kansas v. Hendricks,* 1997], in fact are far closer to a criminal punishment model; Perlin, 1998), and has boldly restructured the rules on federal sentencing (*United States v. Booker & Fanfan,* 2005) in ways that will inevitably result in a new, future focus on mental disability issues.

This chapter focuses on *Atkins* and *Sell* and briefly discusses the other cases just cited. I consider the implications of all of these cases for forensic mental health experts.

DEATH PENALTY LAW

Few areas of criminal procedure law are as contentious as that of the death penalty. And within the universe of "death penalty cases," the subuniverse of those cases involving a defendant with mental disability is even more contentious. The Supreme Court's 2002 decision of *Atkins v. Virginia* (2002) requires forensic psychologists (and all other mental health professionals who do evaluations or testify in death penalty cases) to bring new focus to this area of the law.

The Atkins Case

Few criminal procedure decisions of the U.S. Supreme Court are analyzed as thoroughly and consistently as those involving the death penalty. There are many reasons for this, among them: Death *is* different from other penalties; the debate on the legality and morality of the penalty has not abated over the years; the cases so often involve *media circus*-type crimes; and no politician has ever lost votes by demanding strict enforcement of the criminal laws. But on a professional level, most of these decisions are exclusively (or primarily) of great interest to lawyers and to those directly involved in the legal/penal systems.

Yet, every once in a while, there is a decision that is equally important to non-lawyer professionals. Such a case is *Atkins v. Virginia* (2002). In holding that the 8th Amendment's ban on "cruel and unusual punishment" prohibits the imposition of the death penalty in cases involving persons with mental retardation, the Court immediately recalibrated the relationship between expert witnesses and the law in capital and potentially capital cases. Further, this recalibration may lead to a far broader role for experts in such cases than had ever been previously considered. It may also allow us (or force us) to refocus on many of the beneath-the-radar issues in death penalty cases that often are the true determinant of who lives and who dies, especially the quality of counsel and, specifically, counsel's ability to work with experts.

There has already been a robust first-generation literature about the *Atkins* case, mostly dealing with the doctrinal issues and with the likely impact *Atkins* will have on death penalty jurisprudence in general (e.g., Mossman, 2003; Slobogin, 2003). Little attention, however, has been paid to the potentially profound impact that *Atkins* will have on the work of expert witnesses. Forensic experts (both evaluators and those who testify in court) need to read *Atkins* carefully on multiple levels:

- As a case that establishes new standards on the question of who is eligible to die.
- As a case that focuses (perhaps *disproportionately*) on one aspect of mental functioning (the defendant's IQ) as the tie breaker in death penalty cases.
- As a case that extends the mitigation case law path beyond its prior endpoint in *Penry v. Lynaugh* (1989).
- As a case that makes new demands on lawyers, judges, and jurors.
- Finally, and most important for the purposes of this chapter, as a case that requires experts to think very hard about the preexisting bias of jurors, what I refer to regularly as *sanism* (see Perlin, 2000a), and the teleological desire of courts to reach the "morally right" result, what I refer to regularly as *pretextuality* (see Perlin, 2000a), and how these biases and attitudes must be directly confronted in their testimony.

This section presents some historical background, looking primarily at the development of the mitigation standard in death penalty cases (from *Lockett v. Ohio,* 1978, to *Eddings v. Oklahoma,* 1982, to *Penry,* 1989) and at the development of the executability standard in such cases (from *Ford v. Wainwright,* 1986, again to *Penry*). I then look at the *Atkins* case and list what I have written about elsewhere as the "pressure points" in *Atkins* that must be taken seriously in any analysis of the case and its potential impact (see Perlin, 2003a), focusing on those points that directly involve the work of expert witnesses. I define and explain sanism and pretextuality and underscore why these concepts are so important in this area of criminal procedure jurisprudence. Next, I focus on those issues in *Atkins* of particular significance to an expert witness: the ability to contextualize the meaning of IQ scores and functional abilities for fact finders; the ability to work with a lawyer (who may or may not be a death penalty specialist); the ability to rebut the jurors' inherent reliance on sanism and the judge's inherent reliance on pretextuality; and the ability to work with counsel at the postconviction stage and the possible extension of *Atkins* to persons with other mental disabilities.

The Mitigation Standard

In *Lockett v. Ohio* (1978), the Supreme Court concluded, "The Eighth and Fourteenth Amendments require that the sentencer, in all but the rarest kind of capital case, not be precluded from considering, as a mitigating factor, any aspect of a defendant's character or record . . . that defendant proffers as a basis for a sentence less than death" (p. 604; see Perlin, 1996a, pp. 210–214). Four years later, the Court expanded on its *Lockett* rule in *Eddings v. Oklahoma* (1982, p. 114), holding that the sentencing authority must consider any relevant mitigating evidence. In *Eddings,* during the sentencing hearing, the defendant presented testimony that he was the product of a broken family and the victim of child abuse (pp. 107–108). Psychological testimony also showed that Eddings was emotionally disturbed and that his mental and emotional developments were at a level below his chronological age (p. 107). Further, a psychiatrist and a sociologist testified that Eddings could be treated and rehabilitated (p. 108). Despite this testimony, the trial judge considered only Eddings's youth as a mitigating factor, which, though important, did not outweigh the aggravating factors presented by the prosecution (pp. 108–109). Reversing and remanding the sentence, the Supreme Court concluded that the sentencer must consider all mitigating evidence and then weigh this evidence against the aggravating circumstances (pp. 113–117). Thus, *Eddings*'s restatement of the *Lockett* rule requires the sentencing tribunal to "listen" to any relevant evidence proffered to mitigate in a death penalty case (p. 115 n. 10). Testimony found relevant as to Eddings's mental disorder, then, could not be ignored. Read together, *Lockett* and *Eddings* thus "require the courts to admit into evidence, and to consider, any claim raised by the defendant in mitigation" (Showalter & Bonnie, 1984, p. 161).

In *Penry v. Lynaugh* (1989), the Court's most recent pre-*Atkins* decision on this question involving a mentally disabled defendant, the Court held that evidence as to the defendant's mental retardation was relevant to his culpability and that, without such information, jurors could not express their "reasoned moral response" in determining the appropriateness of the death penalty (p. 321, quoting *Franklin v. Lynaugh,* 1988, p. 185). There, the Court found that assessment of the defendant's retardation would aid the jurors in determining whether the commission of the crime was "deliberate" (pp. 322–326). Without a special instruction as to such evidence, a juror might be unaware that an evaluation of the defendant's moral culpability could be informed by his or her handicapping condition. Also, in attempting to grapple with questions of future dangerousness or of the presence of provocation (both questions that must be considered under the Texas state sentencing scheme), jurors were required to have a "vehicle" to consider whether the defendant's background and childhood should have mitigated the penalty imposed (p. 321). Without such testimony, the jury could not appropriately express its "reasoned moral response" on the evidence in question (p. 328).

The Executability Standard

The Supreme Court's 1986 decision in *Ford v. Wainwright* brought limited doctrinal coherence to the question of whether or not an "insane" person could be executed (see Perlin, 1996a, pp. 214–215). There, a divided Court concluded that the 8th Amendment did prohibit the imposition of the death penalty on an insane prisoner (*Ford,* 1986, pp. 405–410). On this point, Justice Rehnquist dissented on behalf of himself and Chief Justice Burger (p. 431). In his view, the Florida procedures were "fully consistent with the 'common-law heritage' and current practice on which the court purport[ed] to rely" and, in their reliance on executive branch procedures, "faithful to both traditional and modern practice" (pp. 431–433). He thus rejected the majority's conclusion that the 8th Amendment created a substantive right not to be executed while insane. Writing for herself and Justice White, Justice O'Connor agreed fully with this aspect of Justice Rehnquist's two-justice dissent (p. 427).

Ford is a curious and difficult opinion, reflecting the ambiguity and ambivalence that permeate this subject matter (see Perlin, 2002, § 12-9, pp. 539–542). It is especially perplexing in light of the Court's subsequent decision in *Penry* (1989, p. 336), in which it initially rejected the argument that defendant's mental retardation barred capital punishment. Although she conceded that the execution of the "profoundly or severely retarded" might violate the 8th Amendment, Justice O'Connor suggested that such persons were unlikely to be convicted or face that penalty in light of "the protections afforded by the insanity defense today" (p. 333), an observation astonishing either in its naivete or its cynicism (Perlin, 1996a).

The Relationship of Ford *and* Penry

Some years ago, I wrote this about these two cases:

> To some extent, *Ford* and *Penry* serve as paradigms for the Court's confusion about cases involving mentally disabled criminal defendants. Justice Rehnquist's and Justice O'Connor's opinions in *Ford* and Justice O'Connor's opinion in *Penry* remain infused with the obsessive fear that defendants will raise "false" or "spurious claims" in desperate attempts to stave off execution. This fear—a doppelganger of the public's "swift and vociferous . . . outrage" over what it perceives as "abusive" insanity acquittals, thus allowing "guilty" defendants to "beat the rap"—remains the source of much of the friction in this area. (Perlin, 1996a, p. 216)

To what extent will *Atkins* put this to rest?

The Meaning of Atkins

In *Atkins* (2002, p. 316), the Court held that the execution of people with mental retardation violated the 8th Amendment's prohibition against cruel and unusual punishment, effectively overruling *Penry* on this point. The opening paragraph of Justice Stevens's majority opinion provides important signposts as to the development of the case:

> Those mentally retarded persons who meet the law's requirements for criminal responsibility should be tried and punished when they commit crimes. Because of their disabilities in areas of reasoning, judgment, and control of their impulses, however, they do not act with

the level of moral culpability that characterizes the most serious adult criminal conduct. Moreover, their impairments can jeopardize the reliability and fairness of capital proceedings against mentally retarded defendants. Presumably for these reasons, in the 13 years since we decided *Penry,* the American public, legislators, scholars, and judges have deliberated over the question whether the death penalty should ever be imposed on a mentally retarded criminal. The consensus reflected in those deliberations informs our answer to the question presented by this case: whether such executions are "cruel and unusual punishments" prohibited by the Eighth Amendment to the Federal Constitution. (p. 306)

In coming to its decision, the Court underscored its position that "it suggests that some characteristics of mental retardation undermine the strength of the procedural protections that our capital jurisprudence steadfastly guards" (*Atkins,* 2002, p. 317). Mental retardation, the Court found, involves "not only subaverage intellectual functioning, but also significant limitations in adaptive skills such as communication, self-care, and self-direction that became manifest before age 18" (p. 318). It continued in the same vein:

> Mentally retarded persons frequently know the difference between right and wrong and are competent to stand trial. Because of their impairments, however, by definition they have *diminished capacities* to understand and process information, to communicate, to abstract from mistakes and learn from experience, to engage in logical reasoning, to control impulses, and to understand the reactions of others. There is no evidence that they are more likely to engage in criminal conduct than others, but there is abundant evidence that they often act on impulse rather than pursuant to a premeditated plan, and that in group settings they are followers rather than leaders. Their deficiencies do not warrant an exemption from criminal sanctions, but they do diminish their personal culpability. (p. 318; emphasis added)

In light of these deficiencies, the Court found that its death penalty jurisprudence provided two reasons "consistent with the legislative consensus that the mentally retarded should be categorically excluded from execution" (*Atkins,* 2002, p. 318). First, there is a serious question as to whether either justification that has been recognized as a basis for the death penalty applies to mentally retarded offenders. *Gregg v. Georgia* (1976, p. 183) identified "retribution and deterrence of capital crimes by prospective offenders" as the social purposes served by the death penalty. Unless the imposition of the death penalty on a mentally retarded person "measurably contributes to one or both of these goals, it 'is nothing more than the purposeless and needless imposition of pain and suffering,' and hence an unconstitutional punishment" (*Atkins,* 2002, p. 319, quoting, in part, *Enmund v. Florida,* 1982, p. 798).

On the question of retribution, the Court reasoned that, in light of its precedents in this area (e.g., *Godfrey v. Georgia,* 1980, p. 433, vacating death sentence because petitioner's crimes did not reflect "a consciousness materially more 'depraved' than that of any person guilty of murder"):

> If the culpability of the average murderer is insufficient to justify the most extreme sanction available to the State, the lesser culpability of the mentally retarded offender surely does not merit that form of retribution. Thus, pursuant to our narrowing jurisprudence,

which seeks to ensure that only the most deserving of execution are put to death, an exclusion for the mentally retarded is appropriate. (*Atkins,* 2002, p. 319)

On the question of deterrence, the Court again looked at earlier cases for a restatement of the proposition that "capital punishment can serve as a deterrent only when murder is the result of premeditation and deliberation" (*Enmund,* 1982, p. 799) and pointed out, "Exempting the mentally retarded from that punishment will not affect the cold calculus that precedes the decision of other potential murderers," that sort of calculus being "at the opposite end of the spectrum from behavior of mentally retarded offenders" (*Atkins,* 2002, p. 320, citing, in part, *Gregg,* 1976, p. 186). Deterrence, the Court noted, is predicated on the notion that the increased severity of the punishment will inhibit criminal actors from carrying out murderous conduct.

> Yet it is the same cognitive and behavioral impairments that make these defendants less morally culpable—for example, the diminished ability to understand and process information, to learn from experience, to engage in logical reasoning, or to control impulses—that also make it less likely that they can process the information of the possibility of execution as a penalty and, as a result, control their conduct based upon that information. (*Atkins,* 2002, p. 320)

Nor will exempting persons with mental retardation from execution lessen the deterrent effect of the death penalty with respect to nonretarded offenders, the Court added. "Such individuals are unprotected by the exemption and will continue to face the threat of execution. Thus, executing the mentally retarded will not measurably further the goal of deterrence" (p. 320).

The reduced capacity of mentally retarded offenders provided an additional justification for a categorical rule making such offenders ineligible for the death penalty (*Atkins,* 2002, p. 320). The Court noted that there was an "enhanced" risk of improperly imposing the death penalty in cases involving defendants with mental retardation because of the possibility of false confessions, as well as "the lesser ability of mentally retarded defendants to make a persuasive showing of mitigation in the face of prosecutorial evidence of one or more aggravating factors" (p. 320). The Court also stressed several additional interrelated issues: the difficulties that persons with mental retardation may have in providing meaningful assistance to their counsel, their status as "typically poor witnesses," and the ways their demeanor "may create an unwarranted impression of lack of remorse for their crimes" (p. 321).

Here, the Court acknowledged an important difficulty: "Reliance on mental retardation as a mitigating factor can be a two-edged sword that may enhance the likelihood that the aggravating factor of future dangerousness will be found by the jury," raising the specter that "mentally retarded defendants in the aggregate face a special risk of wrongful execution" (*Atkins,* 2002, p. 321). It thus concluded:

> Construing and applying the Eighth Amendment in the light of our "evolving standards of decency," we therefore conclude that such punishment is excessive and that the Constitution

"places a substantive restriction on the State's power to take the life of a mentally retarded offender." (p. 321, quoting, in part, *Ford,* 1986, p. 305)

There were two dissents. Dissenting for himself, Justice Thomas, and Justice Scalia, the Chief Justice criticized that part of the majority's methodology that had relied on public opinion polls, the views of professional and religious organizations, and the status of the death penalty in other nations as part of the basis for its decision (*Atkins,* 2002, pp. 323–335). Justice Scalia also dissented (for himself, the Chief Justice, and Justice Thomas), noting immediately, "Seldom has an opinion of this court rested so obviously upon nothing but the personal views of its members" (p. 338).

On the deterrence issue, Justice Scalia concluded that "the deterrent effect of a penalty is adequately vindicated if it successfully deters many, but not all, of the target class" (*Atkins,* 2002, p. 338). Again, he rejected what he characterized as the majority's "flabby" argument that persons with mental retardation faced a "special risk" for wrongful execution (suggesting that "just plain stupid . . . inarticulate . . . or even ugly people" might face a similar risk, but that, if this were in fact so, it was not an issue that came within the ambit of the 8th Amendment; p. 352).

Finally, he expressed his "fear of faking":

> One need only read the definitions of mental retardation adopted by the American Association of Mental Retardation and the American Psychiatric Association to realize that the symptoms of this condition can readily be feigned. And . . . the capital defendant who feigns mental retardation risks nothing at all. (*Atkins,* 2002, p. 354)

"Nothing has changed," he concluded, in the nearly 300 years since Hale wrote his *Pleas of the Crown:*

> [Determination of a person's incapacity] is a matter of great difficulty, partly from the easiness of counterfeiting this disability . . . and partly from the variety of the degrees of this infirmity, whereof some are sufficient, and some are insufficient to excuse persons in capital offenses. (p. 354)

Atkins's *Pressure Points*

There are many unanswered questions in *Atkins* beyond the scope of this chapter:

- The extent to which states will adopt new prophylactic implementation procedures.
- The dangers in using a numerical IQ score as the primary cutoff factor (see Mossman, 2003).
- The difficulties in assessing mental retardation in persons who are not English speaking (compare, e.g., *Larry P. by Lucille P. v. Riles,* 1984, on the discriminatory impact of IQ tests in school placements).
- The allocation of the burden of proof in making that assessment (see Slobogin, 2003).
- The application of *Atkins* in cases of borderline mental retardation (see, e.g., *Smith v. State,* 2002, p. 477, listing defendant's "verbal IQ of 75, classified as the borderline range between mild retardation and low-average intelligence" as a "properly found" mitigating factor; decided prior to *Atkins*).

- The interplay between judge and jury in the determination of who *is* mentally retarded (no matter how that term is ultimately defined; compare *Apprendi v. New Jersey,* 2000: enhancing jury role in determination of factors increasing defendant's potential punishment; *Ring v. Arizona,* 2002: Arizona statute authorizing trial judge to determine the presence or absence of the aggravating factors in death penalty case violates the 6th Amendment right to a jury trial in capital prosecutions).

- The question of retroactivity of application.

- Costs of implementation or the means by which we restructure the ways that counsel represents persons with mental retardation so as to assure that such individuals are provided with competent counsel with competent experts to assist them (see, e.g., Martin, 2002).

In an earlier article, I discussed at some length 17 "pressure point" issues arising from the *Atkins* decision on questions of *implementation*—issues that we must take seriously if we are to understand the greater significance of the *Atkins* case (see generally, Perlin, 2003a, p. 332):

1. The capacity of lawyers to understand the concept of mental retardation.

2. The extent to which defense lawyers can explain what may appear to jurors to be a lack of remorse on the part of defendants with mental retardation.

3. The ways that failure to develop mental retardation evidence are treated in cases that construe the adequacy-of-counsel standard of *Strickland v. Washington* (1984).

4. The underlying sanism of jurors in weighing evidence about mental retardation.

5. The ability of fact finders to understand the difference between cases involving the *types* of violent crimes more likely to be committed by persons with mental retardation (nondeliberate) and the types more likely to be committed by *some* persons with severe mental illness (very deliberate and planful, but equally immune from deterrence).

6. The extent to which jurors will use retardation evidence as an aggravating, rather than mitigating, factor.

7. The capacity of jurors to empathize with persons with mental retardation.

8. The willingness of states to read *Ake v. Oklahoma* (1985)—holding that a criminal defendant who makes a threshold ex parte showing that sanity at time of offense is likely to be a "significant factor" at trial is constitutionally entitled to state-funded psychiatric expert assistance—expansively to ensure access to appropriate experts.

9. The role of experts in explaining the meanings of IQs, functional abilities, capacity for moral development, and so on in persons with mental retardation.

10. The reluctance of criminal defendants, even those facing the death penalty, to identify themselves as mentally retarded.

11. The ability of post-*Atkins* defendants to provide meaningful assistance to counsel, assuming a finding of competence to stand trial.

12. The impact of the morass created by *Godinez v. Moran* (1993), holding that the standard for pleading guilty and waiving counsel is no higher than that for standing trial.

13. The willingness of judges to enforce *Atkins.*

14. The extent to which Justice Scalia's fear-of-faking concerns will dominate post-*Atkins* jurisprudence.

15. The ability of all participants to understand the relationship between such cases and the insanity defense.

16. The attitude of prosecutors toward such cases.

17. The ability of society to accept the reality of the number of death-eligible defendants with mental retardation.

This section addresses only those issues that have a direct bearing on the forensic evaluation process.

The Significance of Sanism and Pretextuality

Sanism is an irrational prejudice of the same quality and character of other irrational prejudices that cause and are reflected in prevailing social attitudes of racism, sexism, homophobia, and ethnic bigotry. It infects both our jurisprudence and our lawyering practices. Sanism is both largely invisible and largely socially acceptable. It is based predominantly on stereotype, myth, superstition, and deindividualization and is sustained and perpetuated by our use of alleged "ordinary common sense" and heuristic reasoning in an unconscious response to events both in everyday life and in the legal process (Perlin, 1999, 2003b).

Pretextuality defines the ways courts accept, either implicitly or explicitly, testimonial dishonesty and engage similarly in dishonest (and frequently meretricious) decision making, specifically when witnesses, especially expert witnesses, show a high propensity to purposely distort their testimony to achieve desired ends. This pretextuality is poisonous; it infects all participants in the judicial system, breeds cynicism and disrespect for the law, demeans participants, and reinforces shoddy lawyering, blasé judging, and, at times, perjurious and/or corrupt testifying (Perlin, 1999, 2003b). All aspects of mental disability law are pervaded by sanism and by pretextuality, no matter whether the specific presenting topic is involuntary civil commitment law, right to refuse treatment law, the sexual rights of persons with mental disabilities, or any aspect of the criminal trial process (Perlin, 2000a).

The Relationship between Sanism and Pretextuality and Death Penalty Jurisprudence

In this environment, it is easy to see how evidence of mental illness ostensibly introduced for mitigating purposes can be construed as aggravating instead (Berkman, 1989). To a great extent, sanism in the death penalty decision-making process mirrors sanism in the context of insanity defense decision making (Perlin, 1994a). Such decision making is often irrational, rejecting empiricism, science, psychology, and philosophy, and substituting in its place myth, stereotype, bias, and distortion. It resists educational correction, demands punishment regardless of responsibility, and reifies medievalist concepts based on fixed and absolute notions of good and evil and of right and wrong.

Although the question under consideration here has not been widely studied, there is an impressive database focusing on juror behavior in insanity defense cases that is relevant here. First and foremost, the public has always demanded that mentally ill defendants comport with its visual images of "craziness" (Gilman, 1982). Yet, the lay public cannot, by using its intuitive "common sense" effectively, determine who is or is not criminally responsible by whether or not the individual "looks crazy" (*State Farm Fire & Casualty Co. v. Wicka,* 1991, p. 327).

This data must be read side by side with what is known about juror use of schemas: that they are especially confused and confusing in death penalty cases; that they play to menacing and dangerous stereotypes of mentally disabled persons; and that, when there are dissonances in these schemas, they are interpreted in ways "consistent with criminality" (Diamond, 1993, pp. 329–330; Hayman, 1990, pp. 47–48). The data also must be considered against the backdrop of ongoing judicial hostility toward mental disability-based excuses for crime and toward mental disability evidence in general (Perlin, 1994a).

As a result of these factors, application of the mitigation doctrine is revealed, in certain individual cases, to be a pretextual hoax. Consider the Florida case of *Mason v. State* (1992). Mason was convicted of murder after the trial court failed to inform the jury about his long history of mental illness, the fact that he suffered from organic brain damage, that he suffered from mental retardation, had a history of drug abuse, that he attempted suicide on four occasions during the year prior to trial, and that he had a history of suffering from depression and hallucinations (p. 780). The dissonance between the trial court's behavior in this case and Supreme Court case law suggests that doctrinal analysis and recalibration can never be a total solution to the underlying problems.

In an earlier paper, I challenged the Supreme Court's assumption that jurors can be relied on to apply the law in this area conscientiously and fairly (Perlin, 1994b). In that paper, I concluded that jurors' general distrust of mental disability evidence

> results from a combination of important factors: jurors' use of cognitive simplifying devices (heuristics) in which vivid, negative experiences overwhelm rational data (and a death penalty case is a fertile environment for such cognitive distortions) and which reify their sanist attitudes, courts' pretextuality in deciding cases involving mentally disabled criminal defendants, and courts' teleological decision-making in reviewing such cases. (pp. 241–242)

Nothing that has taken place in the 12 years since I wrote that paper has led me to change my mind. These issues must be addressed if *Atkins* is to be implemented in a meaningful and coherent manner.

Atkins *for Experts*

The expert's role in almost any case involving a defendant with a mental disability charged with a crime is significant. But in death penalty cases in which the question as to death eligibility is whether the defendant can be categorized in a way that comports with a specific disabling condition, the role of the expert is perhaps greater than in virtually any other area of the criminal law.

There are multiple roles for experts in death penalty cases involving defendants with mental retardation. An expert witness may be utilized to explain the relevance of mental retardation in either the guilt or penalty phases of trial, or both (including relevant aspects of confessions, waiver of Miranda rights, culpability, and potential future dangerousness; Keyes, 1998, p. 536). Often, a multidisciplinary team of experts is critical to the defense of capital defendants with mental retardation. One of the leading practice articles instructs that defense counsel should "*always* contact a mitigation or mental health expert to determine the existence of mental retardation and complete a social-medical history before requesting the assistance of a psychologist or psychiatrist" (Desai, 2001, p. 267) and cautions that "ordinary psychiatrists and most psychologists are not trained in areas involving mental retardation and courts frequently fail to make the distinction between these experts" (p. 268).

What are some of the factors that the expert must consider? "Speech, language and memory impairments, physical and motor disabilities, IQ examinations and other tests require a professional evaluation and assessment by various mental health experts" (Desai, 2001, p. 268). Such experts should be able to convey to the jury "the effects that mental retardation has on behavior and decision-making, explain the vulnerable and suggestible nature of a mentally retarded individual, and educate juries about the full spectrum of mental retardation, irrespective of the defendant's appearance or demeanor," and must be able to "state their findings in plain, comprehensible language and common sense terms used by the average person" (p. 268, quoting Blume & Blume, 2000, p. 67). Also, the expert must be willing and able to "consult school records, placement records, psychoeducational reports, individualized education plans, interviews with parents and teachers if possible, vocational, employment, and military records, criminal records, prison records, and probation and state agency records" (Fabian, 2003, p. 114, citing Keyes, 1998, pp. 533–535).

Most important, the post-*Atkins* expert must have the ability to contextualize the meaning of IQ scores and functional abilities for fact finders. *Atkins* endorses a definition of mental retardation that subsumes "subaverage intellectual functioning [and] significant limitations in adaptive skills such as communication, self-care, and self-direction that became manifest before age 18" (*Atkins,* 2002, p. 318). There is no question that, in assessing who is "subaverage," the defendant's IQ score will be of critical, perhaps dispositive, importance in determining death eligibility. This is inherently problematic for multiple real-life reasons.

The difference between an IQ score of 68 (and thus within the definition of mentally retarded) and a score of 72 (and thus outside that definition) is often statistically and functionally meaningless. Already, some post-*Atkins* decisions and many post-*Atkins* statutes have talismanically focused on the 70 IQ cutoff as a precise eligibility number (see Mossman, 2003, pp. 268–269, discussing *Murphy v. State,* 2002, p. 568; *State v. Lott,* 2002, p. 1014). Given the accepted and well-known error of measurement of 5% (Mossman, 2003, p. 269), the arbitrariness of using a unitary cutoff score ("Implementing Atkins," 2003, pp. 2573–2574), the subjectivity in scoring (Mossman, 2003, p. 269), the phenomenon known as the "Flynn effect" (documenting a worldwide rise in IQ scores; Flynn, 2000), and the "slipperiness" of quantifying "adaptive skills" ("Implementing Atkins," 2003, pp. 2575–2576), experts are in the untenable position of working in a legal environment that presumes a dyadic universe (retarded/not retarded) that does not exist elsewhere. Cases such as *Walters v. Johnson* (2003, p. 695) and *State v. Kelly* (2002, p. *11)—that refer to the Wechsler Adult Intelligence Scales as the gold standard of testing—inevitably make the enterprise more difficult.

The expert must understand that courts—often following the direct orders of state statute—will seek to limit their testimony to nothing more than numbers. In response, the expert must be ready to (a) explain the limitations of *any* numerical cutoff and (b) contextualize the score in light of the defendant's adaptive and functional abilities.

The Relationship between Experts and Trial Lawyers

Experts must acknowledge that they will be working with a wide range of lawyers, from the very best to the very worst. In no area of the law is this range more puzzling and more confounding than in death penalty litigation: Some defendants are represented by death penalty specialists whose entire careers are devoted to this difficult work; others are represented by the "bottom of the barrel" (Saul, 1991, p. 8), a universe whose profound ineptitude has led some scholars to conclude that the most important variable in determining which defendants are to be put to death is the quality of the defendant's trial lawyer (Bright, 1990, p. 695). Such lawyers were characterized some 30 years ago by Judge David Bazelon (1973, p. 2) as "walking violations of the Sixth Amendment." That characterization, unfortunately, has not worn thin.

Even if the defendant is fortunate enough to *not* be assigned such counsel, the expert may still find that counsel is, nonetheless, poorly informed about mental disabilities. The lawyer may not understand what mental retardation *is*. The lawyer may not know the difference between mental retardation and mental illness. The lawyer may rely solely on visual stereotypes of mental retardation (e.g., Is the defendant rocking? Drooling?; Keyes, 1998, p. 536). He or she may rely on one piece of evidence of "normal" behavior as a sufficient basis on which to reject retardation. He or she may misinterpret a defendant's obliging, confirmatory response to questions as evidence of the defendant's average (or better than average) intelligence. In the cases of defendants whose retardation falls just outside the numerical cutoff range (in those jurisdictions using such cutoffs), the lawyer may have no idea how to develop mitigation evidence based on the client's mental state (Fabian, 2003).

In *Ake v. Oklahoma* (1985, p. 83), the Supreme Court held that indigent defendants are constitutionally entitled to psychiatric assistance when they make a preliminary showing that their sanity "is [likely] to be a significant factor at trial." Courts have split on the significance of professional background in satisfying *Ake*'s command, on the question, for instance, of whether a defendant is entitled to the appointment of a psychologist. In *Jones v. State* (1988, p. 652), the defendant was not entitled under *Ake* to appointment of a psychologist, but in *Funk v. Commonwealth* (1989, pp. 371–374), the court ruled that the appointment of a clinical psychologist—certainly the appropriate professional in many cases involving defendants with mental retardation—satisfied *Ake* (Parry & Drogin, 2001). A leading criminal procedure treatise concludes, "Generally speaking, the courts have read *Ake* narrowly, and have refused to require appointment of an expert unless it is absolutely essential to the defense" (Saltzburg & Capra, 2000, p. 802). The problems here are heightened by some experts' lack of expertise. Commentators have noted how even mental disability professionals often inappropriately confuse mental retardation with mental illness (Keyes, 1998), an error that could be literally fatal, in a post-*Atkins* case.

The Burden on Expert Witnesses

The *Atkins* case was revolutionary in its determination that certain persons with mental retardation would no longer be eligible for the death penalty. Yet, the revolution embedded in the *Atkins* decision will be meaningless unless expert witnesses understand its full meaning, take seriously the demands it places on them, reflect on the pervasiveness of bias in this area, and consider seriously their need to be connected with counsel throughout the entire enterprise. (For a thorough discussion of legal, ethical, and methodological issues in death penalty case assessments, see Cunningham & Goldstein, 2003.)

MEDICATING INCOMPETENT DEFENDANTS

One of the most controversial questions in mental disability law is—and has been for decades—that of the right of a patient to refuse antipsychotic medication. The issues in such cases are exacerbated when the case involves a forensic patient, often in the context of a currently incompetent criminal defendant who seeks to refuse such medication that is being proposed by the state, at least in part, to make him or her competent to stand trial. The Supreme Court's 2003 decision in *Sell v. United States* casts new light on this area of the law and requires forensic mental health professionals to think about such cases in new ways.

Historical Background

One of the most perplexing substantive and procedural problems in the area of competency to stand trial is the question of what has been characterized as the "synthetic" or "artificial" induction of competency (*State v. Hampton,* 1969, p. 312): whether incompetent defendants can be medicated against their will to make them competent to stand trial (see Perlin, in press). The vast majority of early cases held that it *was* permissible to medicate criminal defendants to meet the threshold standards for competency to stand trial (see, e.g., *Craig v. State,* 1986; *People v. Hardesty,* 1984; *State v. Hayes,* 1978; *State v. Law,* 1978; *State v. Lover,* 1985; *State v. Stacy,* 1977). Courts variously suggested that (a) the fact that a defendant's competency arises from such medication is of "no legal consequence," as only the defendant's "condition" can be considered (*Hampton,* 1969, p. 312); (b) the use of drugs "enhanced, rather than diminished defendant's ability to engage in rational thought and assist counsel at trial" (*Hardesty,* 1984, p. 793); and (c) given the state's interest in bringing an accused to trial, the use of such drugs is thus "fundamental to a scheme of ordered liberty" (*Lover,* 1985, p. 1354, quoting *State v. Maryott,* 1971, p. 243, and quoting, in part, *Illinois v. Allen,* 1970, p. 347). As the 5th Circuit noted, the contrary argument "is akin to declaring comatose all those diabetics who, but for periodic insulin injections, would lapse into coma" (*United States v. Hayes,* 1979, p. 823; see generally Perlin, 2002, § 8A-4.2).

Such holdings acknowledged what was perceived as the clinical reality that the administration of drugs "under proper medical supervision has effectively restored many mentally ill citizens to a useful life in which they can function as normally as other citizens not so impaired" (*State v. Stacy,* 1977, pp. 557–558), and that to suggest otherwise would "constitute an atavistic repudiation of [such] advances" (*People v. Parsons,* 1975, p. 842). One major task force study concluded that, when a defendant is medically made competent, the judge and attorneys be told "(1) that the defendant is appearing under the influence of drugs, and (2) the type of drug administered to the defendant, the dosage, and the effect the drug has on the defendant's demeanor" (Group for the Advancement of Psychiatry, 1974, p. 901).

On the other hand, several cases rejected these approaches, suggesting that it would violate due process to try to convict a defendant who was rendered *incompetent,* either by overmedication (*Whitehead v. Wainwright,* 1978, pp. 899–901) or by mismedication (*Maryott,* 1971, p. 240; so that he or she failed to meet the substantive standards for competency to stand trial: *Dusky v. United States,* 1960; for a thorough discussion of the *Dusky* standard and the research and methodology employed in the assessment of competency to stand trial, see Stafford, 2003).

The *Charters* Cases and Their Aftermath

Some measure of coherence appeared to be brought to this area of the law in the late 1980s. In *United States v. Charters* (1988), the 4th Circuit, *en banc,* sharply curtailed the right to refuse antipsychotic medication of federal detainees at a time when they were incompetent to stand trial. Applying the "professional judgment" standard of *Youngberg v. Romeo* (1982), the court limited its inquiry to whether the drugging decision was made "by an appropriate professional" and allowed for "only one question" to be asked of experts in actions proceeding from medication decisions: "Was this decision reached by a process so completely out of professional bounds as to make it explicable only as an arbitrary, nonprofessional one?" (*Charters,* 1988, p. 813).

The *en banc* court vacated an earlier panel decision in the same case that had provided detainees with significantly greater procedural and substantive due process protections. The panel had premised its conclusion on arguments grounded in the right to privacy, the right to freedom of thought process, and the right to freedom from unwanted physical intrusion (*Charters,* 1987, p. 490). In rejecting the panel's reasoning, the *en banc* court "revealed its apprehensiveness about dealing with underlying social, psychodynamic, and political issues that form the overt and hidden agendas in any right-to-refuse case" (Perlin, 1990, p. 996) and "incorporated many heuristic devices in its reading of trial testimony: availability, typification, the myth of particularistic proofs and the vividness effect" (Perlin, 1993, pp. 666–667).

Until the late 1990s, *Charters* became the lodestar of this area of the law (Perlin, 2002, § 8A-4.2c, p. 55). However, decisions in 1998 by the 6th Circuit, the Illinois

Supreme Court, and the 9th Circuit stressed the significance of the impact of psychotropic medication on the competency-to-stand-trial determination and held that the strict scrutiny standard of substantive due process review applied to this question, finding that the government must prove its case by clear and convincing evidence (*Kulas v. Valdez,* 1998; *People v. Burton,* 1998; *People v. Kinkead,* 1998; *United States v. Brandon,* 1998). Each decision implicitly rejected the *Charters* methodology, and each seemed to indicate a new willingness to question the methodology used by the *en banc* 4th Circuit in *Charters.*

Subsequently, the DC Circuit held in *United States v. Weston* (2001) that the defendant could be medicated against his will in a decision that was clearly influenced by the availability of the so-called atypical antipsychotics (see Mossman, 2002). Added the court:

> Antipsychotic drugs have progressed. . . . There is a new generation of medications having better side effect profiles. See *Weston,* 134 F.Supp.2d at 134 (citing Justice Kennedy's concurrence [in *Riggins v. Nevada,* 1992], noting that "[a]dvances in the primary antipsychotic medications and adjunct therapies make such side effects less likely"); Paul A. Nidich & Jacqueline Collins, Involuntary Administration of Psychotropic Medication: A federal court Update, 11 No. 4 Health Lawyer 12, 13 (May 1999); [I]n light of the progress made in the development of new antipsychotic medications since the Supreme Court's *Riggins* decision in 1992, the courts should revisit this issue with an open mind. . . . [Because of new atypicals,] the fear of side effects should not weigh heavily in the decision whether to treat pre-trial detainees or civilly committed persons with antipsychotic medication against their will when that treatment is medically appropriate. (*Weston,* 2001, p. 886 n.7)

On the other hand, there *were* two more federal appellate cases that considered the role of atypicals. In *United States v. Gomes* (2002, p. 82), the 2nd Circuit held that, as the "heightened scrutiny standard" was appropriate for determining when nondangerous criminal defendants could be forcibly medicated with antipsychotic drugs for purpose of rendering the defendants competent, a four-part test was needed:

> We think that the government must show, and the district court must explicitly find, by clear and convincing evidence: (1) that the proposed treatment is medically appropriate, (2) that it is necessary to restore the defendant to trial competence, (3) that the defendant can be fairly tried while under the medication, and (4) that trying the defendant will serve an essential government interest.

The court stressed that the process of medicating a defendant is a "dynamic one" that can be evaluated over the course of treatment "to ascertain, with expert assistance, both its effectiveness and the nature of any side effects" (p. 82). Thus, the court of appeals admonished the district court to "closely monitor the process to ensure that the dosage is properly individualized to the defendant, that it continues to be medically appropriate, and that it does not deprive him of a fair trial or the effective assistance of counsel" (p. 82).

Of particular importance, in explaining why it adopted this standard, the *Gomes* court looked closely at "recent advances in antipsychotic medication" that "reduce our concerns that the defendant's health interests and fair trial rights cannot be adequately protected when he is involuntarily medicated to render him competent to stand trial" (*Gomes,* 2002, p. 83). After carefully considering Justice Kennedy's concurrence in *Riggins* (1992, pp. 138–145), the court "first note[d] that significant improvements have been made in antipsychotic medication in the decade since Justice Kennedy expressed his misgivings in *Riggins*" (*Gomes,* 2002, p. 83), stressing the creation of a new generation of antipsychotic drugs, largely postdating *Riggins* with a "more favorable side effect profile" (p. 83). Most of these drugs—the atypicals—"present relatively low risks of the serious side effects associated with conventional drugs such as Mellaril, the drug at issue in *Riggins*" (p. 83). On this point, the court dismissed Gomes's effort to discount the significance of the atypicals as "not convincing" (p. 83). It concluded by remanding the case for a new hearing in light of its findings.

In another case, decided less than a month prior to *Gomes,* the 8th Circuit in *United States v. Sell* (2002a) considered the same question with virtually the same results, concluding that the government could, subject to limitations, forcibly administer antipsychotic medication for the sole purpose of rendering a pretrial detainee competent to stand trial because its interest in restoring the defendant's competency for trial was paramount and as no less intrusive means of restoring defendant's competency were available. The Supreme Court then granted *certiorari* in *Sell* (2002b).

The *Sell* Case

The Supreme Court spoke on this issue in 2003 in *Sell v. United States,* holding that the federal government may involuntarily administer antipsychotic drugs to render a mentally ill defendant competent to stand trial only if the treatment is medically appropriate, substantially unlikely to have side effects that may undermine the trial's fairness, and necessary to significantly further important governmental trial-related interests (pp. 179–180).

Charles Sell, formerly a practicing dentist, was charged with several counts of mail fraud, Medicaid fraud, and money laundering in connection with submitting fictitious insurance claims to the federal government for payment. He was found incompetent to stand trial and ordered hospitalized for up to 4 months to determine whether there was "substantial probability" that he would attain competency (*Sell,* 2003, p. 173). Two months into the hospitalization, hospital staff recommended that Sell take antipsychotic medication, and Sell refused (p. 171).

After administrative proceedings authorized the hospital's involuntary administration of the medication, Sell obtained a hearing before the same magistrate who had ordered his commitment. The magistrate found that Sell was a danger to himself and others at the hospital and that "the government has shown in as strong a manner as possible, that anti-psychotic medications are the only way to render the defendant not dangerous and competent to stand trial" (*Sell,* 2003, p. 173). He then stayed his order authorizing the involuntary administration of the medication to allow Sell to file an appeal in federal district court.

The district court held that the magistrate's finding of dangerousness was "clearly erroneous," limiting this conclusion to Sell's "dangerousness *at this time* to himself and to those around him *in his institutional context*" (*Sell*, 2003, p. 174). Nevertheless, the court affirmed the magistrate's order, holding that the medication represented the "only viable hope of rendering defendant competent to stand trial" and appeared "necessary to serve the government's compelling interest in obtaining an adjudication of defendant's guilt or innocence of numerous and serious charges" (p. 174). The 8th Circuit affirmed (pp. 174–175).

The Supreme Court vacated the 8th Circuit's decision and remanded the case for further proceedings. The Court recognized that under *Washington v. Harper* (1990) and *Riggins v. Nevada* (1992), Sell had a liberty interest in avoiding the involuntary administration of antipsychotic drugs, and this interest was protected by the 5th Amendment's due process clause against all but "essential" or "overriding" state interests (*Sell*, 2003, pp. 178–179). The Court held:

> These two cases, *Harper* and *Riggins,* indicate that the Constitution permits the Government involuntarily to administer antipsychotic drugs to a mentally ill defendant facing serious criminal charges in order to render that defendant competent to stand trial, but only if the treatment is medically appropriate, is substantially unlikely to have side effects that may undermine the fairness of the trial, and, taking account of less intrusive alternatives, is necessary significantly to further important governmental trial-related interests. (p. 179)

The Court considered these factors separately. First, using italics to stress the key words, it noted: A court "must find that *important* governmental interests are at stake" (*Sell*, 2003, p. 180); bringing an individual to trial who is accused of a "serious crime" is "important" (p. 180). Second, the court must conclude that "*involuntary medication will *significantly further* those concomitant state interests" and must find that administration of the drugs is "substantially likely" to render the defendant competent to stand trial (p. 181). At the same time, the Court warned, the trial court must find that administration of the drugs is "substantially unlikely to have side effects that will interfere significantly with the defendant's ability to assist counsel in conducting a trial defense, thereby rendering the trial unfair," citing Justice Kennedy's concurrence in *Riggins* (p. 181, citing *Riggins,* 1992, pp. 142–145).

Third, the trial court must conclude that involuntary medication is "*necessary* to further those interests" and that "any alternative, less intrusive treatments are unlikely to achieve substantially the same results" (*Sell*, 2003, p. 181), citing briefs of amici American Psychological Association and American Psychiatric Association (p. 181). Finally, the trial court must conclude that "administration of the drugs is *medically appropriate, that is,* in the patient's best medical interest in light of his medical condition" (p. 181). Here, the Court made its only reference to the issue that had been the focus of much attention both in the circuit decision in *Sell* and in the circuit decisions in *United States v. Gomes* (2002): whether the availability of the new atypical antipsychotics would cause a reformulation of the Court's policies: "The specific kinds of drugs at issue may matter here as elsewhere. Different kinds of antipsychotic drugs may produce different side effects and enjoy different levels of success" (*Sell*, 2003, p. 181).

The Court emphasized that the governmental interest under this standard is the interest in rendering the defendant competent to stand trial:

A court need not consider whether to allow forced medication for that kind of purpose, if forced medication is warranted for a *different* purpose, such as the purposes set out in *Harper* related to the individual's dangerousness, or purposes related to the individual's own interests where refusal to take drugs puts his health gravely at risk. There are often strong reasons for a court to determine whether forced administration of drugs can be justified on these alternative grounds *before* turning to the trial competence question. (*Sell,* 2003, pp. 181–182)

The Court stressed that "the inquiry into whether medication is permissible, say, to render an individual nondangerous is usually more objective and manageable than the inquiry into whether medication is permissible to render a defendant competent," and closer to the court's familiar role in assessing dangerousness for the purposes of involuntary civil commitment (*Sell,* 2003, p. 182). If courts can authorize involuntary medication on alternative grounds such as dangerousness, "the need to consider authorization on trial competence grounds will likely disappear" (p. 183). If medication cannot be authorized on other grounds, then "the findings underlying such a decision will help to inform expert opinion and judicial decisionmaking in respect to a request to administer drugs for trial competence purposes" (p. 183).

Sell will likely prove to be an extraordinarily important decision for several reasons. First, it appears to elevate much of Justice Kennedy's concurring opinion in *Riggins* to majority status. Justice Kennedy's *Riggins* opinion is relied on at least four times in the course of *Sell,* suggesting that, in the 11 years after *Riggins* and before *Sell,* the majority of the Court became more comfortable with his position (increasing the burden on the government when it seeks to involuntarily medicate someone in the criminal trial process). Also, Justice Kennedy was the most critical of all the justices of the potential harms of drug side effects, and *Sell* suggests that this is now a position with which a majority of the Court is comfortable.

Second, the language that the Court uses in *Sell* in its harmonization of *Harper* and *Riggins* is significant. It italicizes many phrases: "*important* governmental interests," "*significantly further* concomitant state interests," that involuntary medication is *necessary* to further those interests, that administration of the drugs is *medically appropriate.* This added emphasis suggests that the Court wants lower courts to take these issues seriously.

Third, the Court stresses, much more clearly than it did in *Riggins,* the need to engage in a "least restrictive alternative" analysis in every such case. The words "intrusive" and "restrictive" appear in the opinion well over a dozen times, and the significance of that use of language should not be underestimated.

Fourth, it is not at all clear what impact *Sell* will have on civil cases. In its discussion, the Court makes clear, albeit in dicta, that decisional incompetence and current danger are the only two acceptable overrides in civil cases. It has been over 2 decades since the Court considered a civil right to refuse medication case (*Mills v. Rogers,* 1982), and thus the Court's endorsement of these factors in this context takes on an even more important meaning.

Fifth, *Sell* makes clear that the hearing must be a judicial hearing and *not* the bare-bones administrative hearing that the Supreme Court had countenanced in *Harper* (1990; see Appelbaum, 2003, p. 1336).

Impact of *Sell* on Expert Witnesses

It can reasonably be expected that *Sell* will have a significant impact on expert witness practice on several levels. First, it is the first time that the Supreme Court has attempted, in any way, to harmonize its decisions in *Riggins* and *Harper,* and in doing this, it may end some of the confusion that has confronted witnesses in the 15 years since *Harper* was decided. Previously, I have used the phrase "litigational side-effects" (Perlin, 1994b, p. 251; 2000b, p. 1019) to discuss the reality that, at least prior to *Sell,* the most critical question in a right-to-refuse evaluation was the defendant's precise place in the criminal justice system (Was the defendant awaiting trial? Proffering an insanity defense? Permanently incompetent to stand trial? A successful insanity acquittee? A convicted prisoner?). *Sell* may eventually minimize this confusion, thus making the work of expert witnesses marginally easier.

Second, although *Sell* did not deal directly with the "typicals versus atypicals" debate, its comment that "The specific kinds of drugs at issue may matter here as elsewhere" (2003, p. 181) will probably lead other courts to take seriously arguments as to whether the law on right to refuse treatment should depend on the type of medication used. The side effects of the "atypicals" are very different from the side effects of the "typicals" (compare Mossman, 2002, to Jackson, 2005), and, given the heavy weight the Supreme Court has put on side effects in crafting its jurisprudence in this area, some sort of recalibration here is certainly possible.

Third, questions about the "least restrictive alternative" will likely be facing expert witnesses more frequently than in past years. Although the Supreme Court returned to this methodology in 1999 in the Americans with Disabilities Act case of *Olmstead v. L. C.* (see Perlin, 2000b, 2001–2002), that decision has not had much of an impact on right-to-refuse-medication litigation. *Sell* will most likely have such an impact, and experts must familiarize themselves with this aspect of the case as well.

Finally, as I have already suggested, *Sell* increases the burden on the government when it seeks to involuntarily medicate someone in the criminal trial process. It is critical that all experts testifying in such cases understand this.

SEXUALLY VIOLENT PREDATOR ACTS

In 1997, the U.S. Supreme Court upheld Kansas's sexually violent predator law, rejecting theories premised on substantive due process and on the double jeopardy and ex post facto clauses of the Constitution (*Hendricks,* 1997). Much of the Court's decision turned on whether Hendricks's pedophilia was a "mental illness" or a "mental abnormality." On this point, the Court concluded:

> Contrary to Hendricks' assertion, the term "mental illness" is devoid of any talismanic significance. Not only do "psychiatrists disagree widely and frequently on what constitutes mental illness," but the court itself has used a variety of expressions to describe the mental condition of those properly subject to civil confinement. (p. 359, quoting *Ake v. Oklahoma,* 1985, p. 81)

Pedophilia, the Court reasoned, was classified by "the psychiatric profession" as a "serious mental disorder"; this disorder, marked by a lack of volitional control, coupled with predictions of future dangerousness, "adequately distinguishes Hendricks from other dangerous persons who are perhaps more properly dealt with exclusively through criminal proceedings" (p. 360). Hendricks's diagnosis as a pedophile, which qualified as a "mental abnormality" under the Act, thus "plainly suffice[d]" for due process purposes (p. 360; see Perlin, 1998).

Soon after *Hendricks* was decided, Shapiro (1997, p. 200) noted that the decision was implicitly premised on the Court's "assum[ption] that mental health professionals possess the expertise to predict future violent behavior and violent sexually predatory behavior," an assumption not supported in the Court's opinion or, in this context, elsewhere in the professional literature (for a similar pre-*Hendricks* analysis, see Wettstein, 1992).

Post-*Hendricks* Cases

The Supreme Court has since returned to the question of the constitutionality of sexually violent predator (SVP) acts. In *Kansas v. Crane* (2002), the Court revisited a statement from *Hendricks* that the Kansas statute requires an abnormality or disorder that makes it "difficult, if not impossible, for the person to control his dangerous behavior" (*Hendricks*, 1997, p. 358). In *Crane*, the Supreme Court held that the Constitution does not require that a state prove complete or absolute lack of control, but does preclude an SVP-based commitment without any lack-of-control determination at all. The Court required "proof of serious difficulty in controlling behavior" which, when viewed in light of the circumstances of the case, "must be sufficient to distinguish the dangerous sexual offender whose serious mental illness, abnormality, or disorder subjects him to civil commitment from the dangerous but typical recidivist convicted in an ordinary criminal trial" (*Crane,* 2002, p. 413).

In 2003, the Supreme Court issued two more decisions on the retroactive application of SVP laws. In *Smith v. Doe* (2003), the Court held that the retroactive application of the registration and notification requirements of the Alaska SVP statute did not violate the ex post facto clause. The Court concluded that the requirements were part of a civil regulatory scheme designed to protect the public from potentially dangerous sex offenders and were, therefore, not punitive in nature. On the other hand, in *Stogner v. California* (2003), the Court held that California could not revive causes of action for sex offenses against children by applying a new statute of limitations after the originally applicable statute of limitations had already expired.

In the same term, the Supreme Court also affirmed the constitutionality of the public notification provisions of the Connecticut SVP Act. In *Connecticut Department of Public Safety v. Doe* (2003), a purportedly nondangerous sex offender challenged the constitutionality of the SVP statute's requirement that the Department of Public Safety post the names, addresses, photographs, and descriptions of sex offenders on the Internet. The Court held that even if the public notification procedures implicated a liberty interest, sex offenders were not entitled to a hearing to determine whether they were currently dangerous before their inclusion in the registry. Because the notification requirement was triggered by a conviction alone, the issue of dangerousness was immaterial, and therefore a hearing on that issue was not required to satisfy due process.

Implications for Expert Witnesses

There is a robust body of legal literature questioning the basic premises of SVP laws. Janus (2004, pp. 1236–1237), one of the most important voices of this cohort, recently argued:

> [The] promises [of SVP laws are] empty window dressing. First, the "most dangerous" claim is dubious because of the limitations in our ability to predict dangerousness. The claim has been further undercut by court decisions that systematically fail to set high, consistent, and accountable standards for risk assessment. Second, the "mental disorder" limitation is untenable because it is so vague and broad that it excludes almost no one. Finally, the promise of treatment and time-limited confinement is belied by the almost nonexistent treatment graduation rates in SVP programs across the country. (See also Janus, 1997, 1998, 2003; Janus & Meehl, 1997; Janus & Prentky, 2003.)

Scholars have recently stressed the important point that neither legislators, jurors, nor police officers have scientific expertise in diagnosing, labeling, or treating sexually violent individuals (Shuman, 2003; Wells & Motley, 2001). Each of the allegations made by Janus must be considered by expert witnesses in this light. (For a discussion of research and methodology related to SVP evaluations, see Conroy, 2003.)

FEDERAL SENTENCING GUIDELINES

Writing with a coauthor over a decade ago about the federal sentencing guidelines, I argued that, although the guidelines:

> were written to eliminate, or at least to lessen, arbitrariness and caprice and to establish objective, normative standards against which convicted defendants' behavior could be assessed, . . . the cases reported so far reflect no coherent reading of the Guidelines and no real understanding of the role of mental disability, short of an exculpating insanity defense, in criminal behavior. (Perlin & Gould, 1995, pp. 431–433)

Until 2003, little changed to require a recalibration of this conclusion.

The Feeney Amendment

The passage of the Feeney Amendment in 2003 (Pub. L. No. 108-121, 117 Stat. 650, 2003) was the first important development in this area of the law in a decade. That law severely limited the circumstances under which a court could depart from the range of sentences prescribed in the guidelines. Among other restrictions, the amendment eliminated downward departures based on gambling dependence and limits departures based on aberrant behavior and physical impairment (U.S. Sentencing Guidelines §§ 5K2.20. 5K2.22, 2003). The amendment also prohibited departures based on diminished capacity in cases involving crimes against children and sexual offenses (18 U.S.C. § 3553 (b)(2) [amended 2003]; U.S. Sentencing Guidelines § 5K2.0(b) [amended 2003]). This law has been characterized as "the most drastic, and certainly the most blatantly intentional example of [congressional] disruption" (Sanderford, 2005, pp. 737–738) of the federal sentencing guidelines' schemata. It raised serious questions as to any role for disability-based downward departures in federal sentencing (see Perlin, 2004b, § 11-2.1).

Blakeley, Booker, and Fanfan

More recent developments, however, have had far greater impacts on the law of federal sentencing. In *Blakeley v. Washington* (2004), the Supreme Court struck down the Washington State sentencing guidelines as unconstitutional, applying its earlier ruling in *Apprendi v. New Jersey* (2000), to hold that a defendant's 6th Amendment right to a jury trial was violated by a sentencing scheme that allowed a judge to impose a sentence above the statutory maximum based on facts neither admitted by the defendant nor found beyond a reasonable doubt by a jury.

In its next term, a deeply divided Supreme Court then ruled in *United States v. Booker & Fanfan* (2005), that the federal sentencing guidelines were subject to jury trial requirements of the 6th Amendment, and that the 6th Amendment's requirement that the jury find certain sentencing facts was incompatible with the Federal Sentencing Act, thus requiring severance of the Act's provisions that had made guidelines mandatory.

The Meaning of Booker and Fanfan for Expert Witnesses

At present, *Booker/Fanfan* have not been construed in a mental disability case. In a thoughtful early analysis, Parry (2005), who believes that their impact on mental disability law will most likely be "limited," has observed:

> *Booker* and other recent cases—for example, *Blakeley; Apprendi; Ring*—create the impression that in sentencing matters juries are sacrosanct, or close to it. The good aspect for defendants is that they have a Sixth Amendment right to have juries decide sentencing matters. This gives defense lawyers an important constitutional card to play in defending their clients, which is particularly important when mitigating circumstances are to be presented. (p. 137)

Continuing, Parry expressed concern that "this trend . . . helps fuel the misimpression that juries are somehow better suited to assessing expert evidence related to sentencing than are judges" (p. 137), adding:

> One of the critical problems in the criminal justice system for defendants with mental and other disabilities is that jurors are not particularly competent in dealing with complex expert evidence, and like many people in society, tend to have a bias against such defendants, who tend to be stigmatized by their disabilities. . . . The notion that expert evidence regarding a person's mental status—which even in the best circumstances engenders considerable doubts in terms of its relevance and accuracy—can be made more relevant and accurate after being "weighed" by a jury is not only naive but is also incredible. (p. 137)

Parry's (2005) observations on the question of whether judges or jurors are better suited to understand mental disability evidentiary matters (on their shared sanism, see Perlin, 1994b, p. 277 [jurors]; 2004a, p. 251 n. 6 [judges]) are important, and forensic experts must consider them carefully in sentencing matters in the future. (See Chapter 14 for a thorough discussion of implications of the Court's decisions on federal sentencing guidelines on forensic practice.)

CONCLUSION

In 2002, I wrote that "the Supreme Court has remained fascinated . . . for 3 decades . . . with the full range of questions involving the intersection of the criminal trial process and mental disability law" (Perlin, 2002–2003, p. 539). This was before *Atkins* (2002), before *Sell* (2003), before the post-*Crane* (2002) sex offender cases, and before *Blakely* (2004), *Booker and Fanfan* (2005). It is certainly logical, based on past experience, for there to be more developments in the coming years. Forensic experts must familiarize themselves with these cases, with the new issues posed by the Court, and with the social dynamics of the decisions themselves. In the past, I argued that lawyers representing persons with mental disabilities must familiarize themselves with the language and data of cognitive psychology (Perlin, 1992). It is equally important, if not more so, for psychologists to familiarize themselves with the cases discussed in this chapter.

REFERENCES

Ake v. Oklahoma, 470 U.S. 68 (1985).

Appelbaum, P. (2005). Treating incompetent defendants: The Supreme Court's decision is a hard *Sell*. *Psychiatric Services, 54,* 1335–1341.

Apprendi v. New Jersey, 530 U.S. 466 (2000).

Atkins v. Virginia, 536 U.S. 304 (2002).

Bazelon, D. L. (1973). The defective assistance of counsel. *University of Cincinnati Law Review, 42,* 1–44.

Berkman, E. F. (1989). Mental illness as an aggravating circumstance in capital sentencing. *Columbia Law Review, 89,* 291–313.

Blakeley v. Washington, 124 S. Ct. 2531 (2004).

Blume, J. H., & Blume, L. P. (2000, November). Principles of developing and presenting mental health evidence in criminal cases. *Champion, 24,* 63–78.

Bright, S. (1990). Death by lottery: Procedural bar of constitutional claims in capital cases due to inadequate representation of indigent defendants. *West Virginia Law Review, 92,* 679–695.

Connecticut Department of Public Safety v. Doe, 538 U.S. 1 (2003).

Conroy, M. A. (2003). Evaluations of sexual predators. In I. B. Weiner (Series Ed.) & A. M. Goldstein (Vol. Ed.), *Comprehensive handbook of psychology: Vol. 11. Forensic psychology* (pp. 463–484). Hoboken, NJ: Wiley.

Craig v. State, 704 8S. W.2d 948 (Tex. Ct. App. 1986).

Cunningham, M. D., & Goldstein, A. M. (2003). Sentencing determinations in death penalty cases. In A. M. Goldstein (Ed.), *Forensic psychology* (Vol. 11, pp. 407–436). Hoboken, NJ: Wiley.

Desai, S. B. (2001). Effective capital representation of the mentally retarded defendant. *Washington and Lee University School of Law, Capital Defense Journal, 13,* 251–278.

Diamond, S. (1993). Instructing on death: Psychologists, juries, and judges. *American Psychologist, 48,* 423–429.

Dusky v. United States, 362 U.S. 402 (1960).

Eddings v. Oklahoma, 455 U.S. 104 (1982).

Enmund v. Florida, 458 U.S. 782 (1982).

Fabian, J. (2003). Death penalty mitigation and the role of the forensic psychologist. *Law and Psychology Review, 27,* 73–129.

Flynn, J. (2000). The hidden history of IQ and special education: Can the problems be solved? *Psychology, Public Policy, and Law, 6,* 191–199.

Ford v. Wainwright, 477 U.S. 399 (1986).

Franklin v. Lynaugh, 487 U.S. 164 (1988).

Funk v. Commonwealth, 379 S. E.2d 371 (Va. App. 1989).

Gilman, S. L. (1982). *Seeing the insane.* New York: WileyInterscience/Brunner/Mazel.

Godfrey v. Georgia, 446 U.S. 420 (1980).

Godinez v. Moran, 509 U.S. 389 (1993).

Gregg v. Georgia, 428 U.S. 153 (1976).

Group for the Advancement of Psychiatry. (1974). *Misuse of psychiatry in the criminal courts: Competency to stand trial.* Washington, DC: American Psychiatric Publishing.

Hayman, R. L., Jr. (1990). Beyond Penry: The remedial use of the mental retardation label in death penalty sentencing. *University of Missouri at Kansas City Law Review, 59,* 17–57.

Illinois v. Allen, 397 U.S. 337 (1970).

Implementing Atkins [Note]. (2003). *Harvard Law Review, 116,* 2565–2600.

Jackson, G. (2005). *Rethinking psychiatric drugs: A guide for informed consent.* Bloomington, IN: Authorhouse.

Janus, E. S. (1997). Sex offender commitments: Debunking the official narrative and revealing the rules in use. *Stanford Law and Policy Review, 8,* 71–123.

Janus, E. S. (1998). Foreshadowing the future of *Kansas v. Hendricks. Northwestern University Law Review, 92,* 1279–1311.

Janus, E. S. (2003). Minnesota's sex offender commitment program: Would an empirically-based prevention policy be more effective? *William Mitchell Law Review, 29,* 1083–1141.

Janus, E. S. (2004). Closing Pandora's box: Sexual predators and the politics of sexual violence. *Seton Hall Law Review, 34,* 1233–1260.

Janus, E. S., & Meehl, P. E. (1997). Assessing the legal standard for predictions of dangerousness in sex offender commitment proceedings. *Psychology, Public Policy, and Law, 3,* 33–70.

Janus, E. S., & Prentky, R. A. (2003). The forensic use of actuarial risk assessment with sex offenders: Accuracy, admissibility, and accountability. *American Criminal Law Review, 40,* 1443–1506.

Jones v. State, 375 S.E.2d 648 (Ga. App. 1988).

Kansas v. Crane, 534 U.S. 407 (2002).

Kansas v. Hendricks, 521 U.S. 346 (1997).

Keyes, D. W. (1998, August). Mitigating mental retardation in capital cases: Finding the "invisible" defendant. *Mental and Physical Disability Law Reporter, 22,* 529–548.

Kulas v. Valdez, 159 F.3d 453 (9th Cir. 1998), *cert. denied,* 528 U.S. 1167 (2000).

Larry P. by Lucille P. v. Riles, 793 F.2d 969 (9th Cir.1984).

Lockett v. Ohio, 438 U.S. 586 (1978).

Martin, E. (2002). Masking the evil of capital punishment. *Virginia Journal of Social Policy and the Law, 10,* 179–248.

Mason v. State, 597 So. 2d 776 (Fla. 1992).

Mills v. Rogers, 457 U.S. 291 (1982).

Mossman, D. (2002). Unbuckling the "chemical straitjacket": The legal significance of recent advances in the pharmacological treatment of psychosis. *San Diego Law Review, 39,* 1033–1196.

Mossman, D. (2003). *Atkins v. Virginia:* A psychiatric can of worms. *New Mexico Law Review, 33,* 255–310.

Murphy v. State, 54 P.3d 556 (Okla. Crim. App. 2002).

Olmstead v. L. C., 527 U.S. 581 (1999).

Parry, J. (2005, January/February). Summary U.S. Supreme Court actions. *Mental and Physical Disability Law Reporter, 29,* 137–138.

Parry, J., & Drogin, E. (2001). *Civil law handbook on psychiatric and psychological evidence and testimony.* Washington, DC: ABA Commission on Mental and Physical Disability Law.

Penry v. Lynaugh, 492 U.S. 302 (1989).

People v. Burton, 703 N.E.2d 49 (Ill. 1998), *cert. denied,* 526 U.S. 1075 (1999).

People v. Hardesty, 362 N.W.2d 787 (Mich. App. 1984).

People v. Kinkead, 695 N.E.2d 1255 (Ill. 1998).

People v. Parsons, 371 NY S. 2d 840 (Cty. Ct 1975).

Perlin, M. L. (1990). Are courts competent to decide questions of competency? Stripping the facade from *United States v. Charters. University of Kansas Law Review, 38,* 957–1001.

Perlin, M. L. (1992). Fatal assumption: A critical evaluation of the role of counsel in mental disability cases. *Law and Human Behavior, 16,* 39–55.

Perlin, M. L. (1993). Pretexts and mental disability law: The case of competency. *University of Miami Law Review, 47,* 625–690.

Perlin, M. L. (1994a). *Jurisprudence of the insanity defense.* Durham, NC: Carolina Academic Press.

Perlin, M. L. (1994b). The sanist lives of jurors in death penalty cases: The puzzling role of "mitigating" mental disability evidence. *Notre Dame Journal of Law, Ethics, and Public Policy, 8,* 239–276.

Perlin, M. L. (1996a). "The executioner's face is always well-hidden": The role of counsel and the courts in determining who dies. *New York Law School Law Review, 41,* 201–245.

Perlin, M. L. (1996b). "No direction home": The law and criminal defendants with mental disabilities. *Mental and Physical Disability Law Reporter, 20,* 605–613.

Perlin, M. L. (1998). "There's no success like failure/and failure's no success at all": Exposing the pretextuality of *Kansas v. Hendricks. Northwestern University Law Review, 92,* 1247–1284.

Perlin, M. L. (1999). "Half-wracked prejudice leaped forth": Sanism, pretextuality, and why and how mental disability law developed as it did. *Journal of Contemporary Legal Issues, 10,* 3–31.

Perlin, M. L. (2000a). *Hidden prejudice: Mental disability on trial.* Washington, DC: American Psychological Press.

Perlin, M. L. (2000b). Their promises of paradise: Will *Olmstead v. L. C.* resuscitate the constitutional least restrictive alternative principle in mental disability law? *Houston Law Review, 37,* 999–1084.

Perlin, M. L. (2001–2002). "What's good is bad, what's bad is good, you'll find out when you reach the top, you're on the bottom": Are the Americans with Disabilities Act (and *Olmstead v. L. C.*) anything more than "idiot wind"? *University of Michigan Journal of Law Reform, 35,* 235–277.

Perlin, M. L. (2002). *Mental disability law: Civil and criminal* (2nd ed., Vol. 4). Newark, NJ: Lexis Law Publishing.

Perlin, M. L. (2002–2003). "Things have changed": Looking at non-institutional mental disability law through the sanism filter. *New York Law School Law Review, 46,* 535–552.

Perlin, M. L. (2003a). "Life is in mirrors, death disappears": Giving life to Atkins. *New Mexico Law Review, 33,* 315–374.

Perlin, M. L. (2003b). "She breaks just like a little girl": Neonaticide, the insanity defense, and the irrelevance of "ordinary common sense." *William and Mary Journal of Women and the Law, 10,* 1–41.

Perlin, M. L. (2004a). "Everything's a little upside down, as a matter of fact the wheels have stopped": The fraudulence of the incompetency evaluation process. *Houston Journal of Health Law and Policy, 4,* 239–262.

Perlin, M. L. (2004b). *Mental disability law: Civil and criminal* (Cum. Supp.). Newark, NJ: Lexis Law Publishing.

Perlin, M. L. (in press). Competency to stand trial. In R. L. Sadoff & F. Dattilio (Eds.), *Crime and Mind.* Chicago: American Barr Association Press.

Perlin, M. L., & Gould, K. K. (1995). Rashomon and the criminal law: Mental disability and the Federal Sentencing Guidelines. *American Journal of Criminal Law, 22,* 431–459.

Pub. L. No. 108-21, 117 Stat. 650 (2003).

Riggins v. Nevada, 504 U.S. 127 (1992).

Ring v. Arizona, 536 U.S. 584 (2002).

Saltzburg, S. A., & Capra, D. J. (2000). *American criminal procedure* (6th ed.). St. Paul, MN: West Group.

Sanderford, O. D. (2005). The Feeney amendment, *United States v. Booker,* and new opportunities for the courts and Congress. *North Carolina Law Review, 83,* 736–791.

Saul, S. (1991, November 25). When death is the penalty: Attorneys for poor defendants often lack experience and skill. *New York Newsday, 8.*

Seling v. Young, 531 U.S. 250 (2001).

Sell v. United States, 539 U.S. 166 (2003).

Shapiro, D. L. (1997). Ethical dilemmas for the mental health professions: Issues raised by recent Supreme Court decisions. *California Western Law Review, 46,* 177–184.

Showalter, C. R., & Bonnie, R. J. (1984). Psychiatry and capital sentencing: Risks and responsibilities in a unique legal setting. *Bulletin of the American Academy of Psychiatry and Law, 12,* 159–167.

Shuman, D. W. (2003). Science, law, and mental health policy. *Ohio Northern University Law Review, 29,* 587–608.

Slobogin, C. (2003). What Atkins could mean for people with mental illness. *New Mexico Law Review, 33,* 293–325.

Smith v. Doe, 538 U.S. 84 (2003).

Smith v. State, 838 So. 2d 413 (Ala. Crim. App. 2002).

Stafford, K. P. (2003). Assessment of competence to stand trial. In I. B. Weiner (Series Ed.) & A. M. Goldstein (Vol. Ed.), *Comprehensive handbook of psychology: Vol. 11. Forensic psychology* (pp. 359–406). Hoboken, NJ: Wiley.

State v. Hampton, 218 So. 2d 311 (La. 1969).

State v. Hayes, 389 A.2d 1379 (NH 1978).

State v. Kelly, 2002 WL 31730874 (Tenn. Ct. Crim. App. 2002).

State v. Law, 244 S. E.2d 302 (S.C. 1978).

State v. Lott, 779 N.E.2d 1011 (Ohio 2002).

State v. Lover, 707 P.2d 1351 (Wash. App. 1985).

State v. Maryott, 492 P.2d 239 (Wash. App. 1971).

State v. Stacy, 556 S. W.2d 552 (Tenn. Crim. App. 1977).

State Farm Fire & Casualty Co. v. Wicka, 474 N. W.2d 324 (Minn. 1991).

Stogner v. California, 539 U.S. 607 (2003).

Strickland v. Washington, 466 U.S. 668 (1984).

United States v. Booker & Fanfan, 543 U.S. 220 (2005).

United States v. Brandon, 158 F.3d 947 (6th Cir. 1998).

United States v. Charters, 829 F.2d 479 (4th Cir. 1987), *on reh'g,* 863 F.2d 302 (4th Cir. 1988) *(en banc),* *cert. denied,* 494 U.S. 1016 (1990).

United States v. Charters, 863 F.2d 302 (4th Cir. 1988) *(en banc), cert. denied,* 494 U.S. 1016 (1990).

United States v. Gomes, 289 F.3d 71 (2d Cir. 2002), *vacated,* 539 U.S. 939 (2003), *on remand with orders to vacate,* 69 Fed. Appx. 36 (2d Cir. 2003).

United States v. Hayes, 589 F.2d 811 (5th Cir. 1979).

United States v. Sell, 282 F.3d 560 (8th Cir. 2002a), *cert. granted,* 537 U.S. 999 (2002b), *vacated and remanded,* 539 U.S. 166 (2003).

United States v. Weston, 255 F.3d 873 (D.C. Cir. 2001), *aff'g,* 134 F. Supp. 2d 115 (D.D.C. 2001), *cert. denied,* 534 U.S. 1067 (2002).

U.S. Sentencing Guidelines § 5K2.0(b) (amended 2003).

U.S. Sentencing Guidelines §§ 5K2.20, 5K2.22 (2003).

18 U.S.C. § 3553 (b)(2) (amended 2003).

Walters v. Johnson, 269 F. Supp. 2d 692 (W.D. Va. 2003).

Washington v. Harper, 494 U.S. 210 (1990).

Wells, C., & Motley, E. (2001). Reinforcing the myth of the crazed rapist: A feminist critique of recent rape legislation. *Boston University Law Review, 81,* 127–216.

Wettstein, R. (1992). A psychiatric perspective on Washington's sexually violent predators statute. *University of Puget Sound Law Review, 15,* 597–628.

Whitehead v. Wainwright, 447 F. Supp. 898 (M.D. Fla. 1978), *vacated and remanded on other grounds,* 609 F.2d 223 (5th Cir. 1980).

Youngberg v. Romeo, 457 U.S. 307 (1982).

CHAPTER 14

The Role of Forensic Mental Health Experts in Federal Sentencing Proceedings

Daniel A. Krauss and Alan M. Goldstein

For a defendant to be found guilty of a crime, whether in state or federal court, the prosecution must prove beyond a reasonable doubt all elements that, by statute or case law, define the specific illegal activity of which the defendant has been accused. To establish culpability, it must be established not only that the defendant engaged in the proscribed criminal activity (*actus reas*), but that he or she possessed the requisite mental state (*mens rea*) associated with that behavior. For example, if a defendant is charged with murder in the second degree in New York State, the district attorney must prove not only that the defendant committed the physical act that resulted in a person's death, but that at the time of the killing, the defendant committed the act either purposefully or knowingly (with an awareness and with the conscious object that the person would die), legal terms defined in penal law and elaborated on in case law.

The need to prove both the conduct and the mental state elements that define specific crimes is in part based on the recognition that, in some instances, although the result may be the same (i.e., someone is killed by a defendant), the underlying mental state that served to fuel that act may differ significantly in degree of intentionality or "evilness." Furthermore, even if the appropriate mental state is achieved by the defendant, a legitimate justification or excuse may exist for the proscribed conduct. For example, in the following four scenarios, a life has been taken, but the mens rea and/or rationale for the action is different in each illustrative case.

1. Defendant A owned a small grocery store and (soon to become) Victim B attempted to rob the store at gunpoint. After receiving the cash, Victim B fired his gun at the storeowner, missing him. The storeowner removed a gun from under the counter and fired a single shot, killing the robber instantly. Although Defendant A intentionally took a life, given this scenario, a self-defense justification may eliminate any culpability.

2. Defendant C is to inherit money from Victim D upon her death. The defendant owes a considerable sum of money to bookmakers, has been threatened by them, and formulates a plan to kill the victim. The defendant acts on that plan, waiting for the victim to arrive home, and kills her as she enters her

house. In this example, the defendant will most likely face a charge of murder. In fact, if this crime occurs in a jurisdiction that has the death penalty, Defendant C may be charged with a capital offense, because many death penalty jurisdictions consider a murder committed for financial gain more evil and blameworthy, and thus possibly deserving of the ultimate punishment of death.

3. Defendant E is a paranoid schizophrenic, actively experiencing religious and grandiose delusions and auditory hallucinations. He hears the voice of God informing him that he must take the life of his sister to ensure her place in heaven and protect her from evil forces that will soon cause her to fall from grace. Defendant E acts on these psychotic symptoms, believing that he is following God's will, and as such, he does not appreciate the wrongfulness of his action. In this case, an attorney might argue that his client's diagnosis and behavior is consistent with an insanity defense, and if this defense were successful at trial, Defendant E would be adjudicated not guilty by reason of insanity.

4. Defendant F and Victim G are involved in a minor automobile accident. Words are exchanged, the argument escalates, and both parties come to blows. During the altercation, Defendant F reaches into his pocket, pulls out a pen, and stabs Victim G in the eye. Unfortunately, for both, the pen pierces the victim's brain, he enters a coma, and days later, Victim G dies. It was never the intent of Defendant F to take the victim's life. However, if it can be established that the defendant sought to cause serious bodily injury to the victim (and that, as a result of his conduct, the victim died), in some jurisdictions, he or she may be found guilty of manslaughter, an offense carrying a lesser degree of punishment.

In all four cases, a life has been taken—someone has been killed. However, in each, the defendant's mens rea and/or justification for his or her action was different. The conduct that took a life was motivated or driven by different mental states and by different external and internal circumstances; thus, a number of defenses involving justifications (e.g., self-defense) or excuses (e.g., insanity) may be available (see Goldstein, Morse, & Shapiro, 2003, for a description of justification and excuse defenses). Again, the defendant's mens rea and/or rationale may be critical in shaping the defense and, if the defendant is found guilty, it may impact the sentence pronounced by the judge.

Why do state and federal criminal statutes address a number of different mental states and external and internal circumstances associated with the same illegal action or result? In part, it is because state and federal criminal justice systems reflect the adage "The punishment should fit the crime." Some crimes are more worthy of punishment than others; some mental states are considered to be more evil than others, even if the criminal conduct and its result are the same. As expressed by Goldstein et al. (2003), "Moral responsibility depends crucially on the mental state with which a person acts" (p. 382). For example, in some states, the type or degree of arson with which a person is charged is based on whether he or she was aware that someone *was* actually present in the structure before the fire was started, was aware that someone *may* have been present in that structure, or was aware that the building was *uninhabited* before starting the fire. A building was burned to the ground, but the defendant's culpability varies with his or her knowledge at the moment of the offense. In addition, at the time of sentencing, judges may take into account aggravating and mitigating factors that may serve to enhance or reduce the length of punishment the defendant is to receive. Such factors may not rise to the level required for a defense against the charges, but the court may consider them at the time of sentencing. For example, although a history of prior violent criminal convictions may be irrelevant to the establishment of guilt on a new charge, the court may consider prior offenses when sentencing is pronounced.

In most jurisdictions in the United States, it would not be uncommon for a forensic mental health professional to submit a report or proffer expert testimony during criminal sentencing on factors such as a defendant's mental health history, drug addiction, or emotional abuse history. Retaining attorneys would hope that such testimony would persuade the court to be more lenient in sentencing. In federal sentencing, however, such expert testimony is not ordinarily relevant (Lutjen, 1996). The federal sentencing system, which is now responsible for the nation's largest population of prisoners, differs in substantial ways from most state jurisdictions' systems, in terms of (a) the subset of crimes it most commonly sentences, (b) its longer-than-average length of prison sentences, and (c) its judges' limited discretion to deviate from prescribed sentencing ranges (Bowman, 2005). For example, 75% of federal sentencing involves drug crimes, immigration offenses, and white-collar crimes, and these crimes are committed by groups of offenders substantially dissimilar from those most commonly seen in state systems (U.S. Sentencing Commission [USSC], 2004).

Until the recent U.S. Supreme Court decisions in *United States v. Booker* (2005) and *United States v. Fanfan* (2005), the federal sentencing guidelines (hereinafter, "the guidelines") had, for most of the past 18 years, dictated and constrained the manner in which federal courts sentenced criminal defendants. (The guidelines were adopted in 1987, but based on separation of powers concerns, their constitutionality was questioned by a number of federal courts until the U.S. Supreme Court decision in *United States v. Mistretta* in 1989. As a result, the guidelines' widespread implementation did not occur until after the *Mistretta* decision.) The recent *Booker/Fanfan* decision, however, represents a dramatic change in federal sentencing practice. In fact, Justice O'Connor, in referring to the *Blakeley v. Washington* (2004) decision, which foreshadowed the holding in *Booker/Fanfan,* and in describing its import to the 9th Circuit judicial conference, suggested that the decision "looked like a number 10 earthquake" (Chorney, 2004, p. 1).

In *Booker/Fanfan,* the Court held that the guidelines were unconstitutional in their present form and that they could remain legitimate only if they were interpreted as *advisory* rather than mandatory in federal sentencing. As a consequence of this recent change, it is clear that federal courts must use the guidelines as advisory in their decisions, but it is less clear how each court will use them to make specific sentencing decisions in practice. Nevertheless, the now advisory guidelines will remain an important component of federal sentencing.

The formulaic guidelines offered little discretion for federal judges to deviate in their sentencing decisions from a sentencing grid based on the severity of the crime committed and the criminal history of the perpetrator (see Table 14.1 for the most recent version of the guidelines' sentencing table). They left little room for mental professionals to offer their expertise to federal courts. In fact, although judicial departures both upward and downward from the guidelines sentencing table were specifically allowed, such departures were legitimate only under a limited set of circumstances (USSC, 1987a). Moreover, in the past several years, the guidelines had been amended by Congress, so that (a) the crimes eligible for downward departures, (b) the types of departures that were legally recognized, and (c) the appellate standard of review for downward departures had been modified, such that the types and number of judicial departures from the guidelines would diminish (Prosecutorial Remedies and Other Tools to End the Exploitation of Children Today [PROTECT] Act, 2003; USSC, 2004). As a result, under the mechanistic and mandatory guidelines regime that existed until recently, there were few avenues for mental health professionals to offer their expertise during federal sentencing, and these avenues were narrowing over time.

This chapter first describes the development and complicated structure of the guidelines. Next, it explores the limited role for mental health professionals' expertise during the guidelines era, and it concludes by examining how the recent *Booker/Fanfan* decision may, in fact, allow for a reemergence, or at least a broadening, of mental health professional expert testimony during federal sentencing.

THE DEVELOPMENT AND STRUCTURE OF THE GUIDELINES

For the majority of the twentieth century, judges possessed almost unlimited discretion to sentence defendants. Specifically, in the federal system, judges could sentence a defendant to any period of incarceration or probation within a wide range provided by the statutory minimum and maximum for that offense, and this decision was largely unreviewable. Further, the Parole Commission had substantial discretion to release an inmate once one-third of a sentence had been served (Breyer, 1988). This nearly indeterminate sentencing structure was based on several important premises: (a) Judges were well suited to evaluate factors relevant to sentencing; (b) judges were unbiased in their decision making for similar defendants committing similar crimes; and (c) the Parole Commission was capable of determining when an offender had been significantly rehabilitated.

During the 1970s and 1980s, the rehabilitative ideal as the preeminent purpose in sentencing was replaced by crime control and just deserts philosophies such that more structured and longer sentences for criminal defendants were favored (Bowman, 2005). In addition, a confluence of research findings and public perception suggested that extreme regional, jurisdictional, defendant-based (e.g., according to the race, sex, or ethnic origin of the defendant), and judicial differences existed in sentencing for similar defendants committing similar acts. Consequently, society's faith in judges as unbiased and consistent decision makers was significantly diminished (Bowman, 2005). A series of empirical studies further substantiated this concern, finding that substantial regional differences existed in federal sentencing decisions for similar defendants committing similar criminal acts (Frankel, 1972; Patridge & Eldridge, 1974).

Table 14.1 Sentencing Table of the Federal Sentencing Guidelines (in Months of Imprisonment)

	Offense Level	Criminal History Category (Criminal History Points)					
		I (0 or 1)	II (2 or 3)	III (4, 5, 6)	IV (7, 8, 9)	V (10, 11, 12)	VI (13 or more)
	1	0–6	0–6	0–6	0–6	0–6	0–6
	2	0–6	0–6	0–6	0–6	0–6	1–7
	3	0–6	0–6	0–6	0–6	2–8	3–9
	4	0–6	0–6	0–6	2–8	4–10	6–12
Zone A	5	0–6	0–6	1–7	4–10	6–12	9–15
	6	0–6	1–7	2–8	6–12	9–15	12–18
	7	0–6	2–8	4–10	8–14	12–18	15–21
	8	0–6	4–10	6–12	10–16	15–21	18–24
Zone B	9	4–10	6–12	8–14	12–18	18–24	21–27
	10	6–12	8–14	10–16	15–21	21–27	24–30
Zone C	11	8–14	10–16	12–18	18–24	24–30	27–33
	12	10–16	12–18	15–21	21–27	27–33	30–37
Zone D	13	12–18	15–21	18–24	24–30	30–37	33–41
	14	15–21	18–24	21–27	27–33	33–41	37–46
	15	18–24	21–27	24–30	30–37	37–46	41–51
	16	21–27	24–30	27–33	33–41	41–51	46–57
	17	24–30	27–33	30–37	37–46	46–57	51–63
	18	27–33	30–37	33–41	41–51	51–63	57–71
	19	30–37	33–41	37–46	46–57	57–71	63–78
	20	33–41	37–46	41–51	51–63	63–78	70–87
	21	37–46	41–51	46–57	57–71	70–87	77–96
	22	41–51	46–57	51–63	63–78	77–96	84–105
	23	46–57	51–63	57–71	70–87	84–105	92–115
	24	51–63	57–71	63–78	77–96	92–115	100–125
	25	57–71	63–78	70–87	84–105	100–125	110–137
	26	63–78	70–87	78–97	92–115	110–137	120–150
	27	70–87	78–97	87–108	100–125	120–150	130–162
	28	78–97	87–108	97–121	110–137	130–162	140–175
	29	87–108	97–121	108–135	121–151	140–175	151–188
	30	97–121	108–135	121–151	135–168	151–188	168–210
	31	108–135	121–151	135–168	151–188	168–210	188–235
	32	121–151	135–168	151–188	168–210	188–235	210–262
	33	135–168	151–188	168–210	188–235	210–262	235–293
	34	151–188	168–210	188–235	210–262	235–293	262–327
	35	168–210	188–235	210–262	235–293	262–327	292–365
	36	188–235	210–262	235–293	262–327	292–365	324–405
	37	210–262	235–293	262–327	292–365	324–405	360–life
	38	235–293	262–327	292–365	324–405	360–life	360–life
	39	262–327	292–365	324–405	360–life	360–life	360–life
	40	292–365	324–405	360–life	360–life	360–life	360–life
	41	324–405	360–life	360–life	360–life	360–life	360–life
	42	360–life	360–life	360–life	360–life	360–life	360–life
	43	life	life	life	life	life	life

The zones indicate whether probation is available as an alternative sentence. Zone A allows for sentencing with no imprisonment, as all time can be served in probation. Zone B requires no imprisonment, but probation must include confinement. Zone C requires that at least one-half the sentence be served in prison, and Zone D requires that the complete sentence be served in prison.

The Sentencing Reform Act (SRA) of 1984 created the U.S. Sentencing Commission, an independent agency in the judicial branch of government, to combat these problems in federal sentencing. The Commission was charged with the development of guidelines for federal sentencing, maintaining a database of federal sentencing decisions, and modifying the guidelines as needed over time (USSC, 1987a). In crafting the guidelines over the next 3 years, the Commission, which was composed of seven members, more than three of whom were required to be federal judges, was required to achieve three predominant aims for the new sentencing scheme: (a) "honesty in sentencing," (b) increased uniformity in sentencing, and (c) increased proportionality in sentencing (28 U.S.C. § 994 *et seq.*, 1984). The issue of honesty in sentencing was accomplished by the elimination of the parole system for future federal defendants. Under the guidelines, federal defendants now serve the amount of time they were sentenced, absent small decreases for good conduct while imprisoned. A defendant may earn up to 54 days of good time per year while serving his or her sentence, leading the defendant, under the most favorable circumstances, to serve approximately 85% of his or her original sentence (Breyer, 1988).

To ameliorate the problems of uniformity and disparity in sentencing, the commissioners constructed a grid system, designed to remove most judicial discretion in sentencing and to create uniform sentence lengths for similar crimes committed by similar defendants. They also attempted to maintain proportionality in sentencing by creating a measure of crime severity, which dictated that severe crimes would be punished by more harsh sentences and less severe crime by less harsh punishments ("Supplementary Report," USSC, 1987b). At the same time that the Commission was formulating the guidelines, however, Congress began passing mandatory minimum penalties for certain drug crimes (see Anti-Drug Abuse Act, 1986). These mandatory minimum sentences further complicated the guidelines because the Commission set their drug penalties based on the requirements of these laws. (For a discussion of sentencing issues related to these laws, see USSC, 1991.)

Under the guidelines grid, a criminal defendant's eventual sentence is determined by a combination of the defendant's offense level (severity of offense), as measured on a 43-point vertical axis, and a criminal history score (prior criminal behavior), as measured by a six-category horizontal axis. For example, a defendant found to have an offense level of 32 and a criminal history category of II would most likely receive a sentence of 135 to 168 months. A judge generally may sentence a defendant anywhere within the range designated by these two points' intersection but may depart from this range based on some limited circumstances (described later in this chapter) and an explicit rationale. If the sentence falls within the designated range, the judge does not have to justify the prescribed sentence.

Offense Level

Before a final offense level can be determined, however, the defendant's convicted criminal conduct (or base offense level) is combined with specific offense characteristics and mitigating and aggravating factors which cause the offense level to either increase or decrease. The eventual offense level assessed by the guidelines represents a compromise between a convicted criminal conduct system and an actual/real criminal conduct scheme, as many of the offense characteristics that allow for enhanced sentences are based not only on the crime for which the defendant was convicted but also on what actually occurred during the crime (USSC, 1987a). These so-called sentencing factors need only be found to exist by a preponderance of evidence by the sentencing judge and need not be found beyond a reasonable doubt by the trier of fact at trial. For example, the initial base offense level for robbery is 20, which can be increased to additional offense levels based on specific offense characteristics, such as (a) the offender brandishing a gun during the commission of the crime (increases 5 levels); (b) whether serious bodily harm occurred during the crime (increases 4 levels); and (c) how much money was taken during the commission of the crime (greater than $10,000 increases 1 level; Ruback & Wrobelwoski, 2001). In addition, the defendant's role in the offense (i.e., a major role in the offense would lead to an increase in offense level, and a minor role would lead to a decrease), the vulnerability of the victim (i.e., crimes committed against a child or the elderly would lead to an increase in offense level), and acceptance of responsibility (i.e., the defendant's acceptance of responsibility would lead to a decrease in offense level) can lead to additional modifications.

Criminal History Category

Once a final offense level is calculated, it is combined with the defendant's criminal history category to determine a sentencing range. The criminal history category is based on the seriousness, recency, and number of prior criminal convictions of the defendant and is derived from a scale based on two recidivism instruments that have demonstrated predictive accuracy (Blumstein, 1986; USSC, 1987b). The computation of the criminal history score is determined by the following rules concerning a defendant's past criminal behavior:

(a) add 3 points for each prior sentence of imprisonment exceeding 1 year,
(b) add 2 points for each prior sentence of imprisonment exceeding 60 days not counted in (a),
(c) add 1 point for each prior sentence not counted in (a) or (b), up to a total of 4 points for this item,
(d) add 2 points if the defendant committed the instant offense while under any criminal justice sentence, including probation, parole, supervised release, imprisonment, work release or escape status, and
(e) add 2 points if the defendant committed the instant offense less than 2 years after the release from imprisonment on a sentence counted under (a) or (b) or while in imprisonment or escape status on such a sentence. If 2 points are added for item (d), add only 1 point.
(f) add 1 point for each prior sentence resulting from a conviction of a crime of violence that did not receive any points under (a), (b), or (c) above because such a sentence was considered related to another sentence resulting from a conviction of a crime of violence, up to a total of 3 points for this item (USSC, § 4A1.1, 2004; in 1991, the Commission added subsection (f) to § 4A1.1, which adds points for certain types of violent felony offenses, Hoffman & Beck, 1997).

An offender's criminal history category is determined by summing these points, and based on this summation, the offender is placed in the appropriate category. For example, an offender who receives 0 or 1 criminal history point would be placed in Criminal History Category I; a defendant who receives 2 or 3 points falls in Criminal History Category II; a defendant who receives 4, 5, or 6 points falls in Category III; a defendant who receives 7, 8, or 9 points falls in Category IV; a defendant who receives 10, 11, or 12 points falls in Category V; and a defendant who receives more than 13 points falls in Category VI. There are also complicated "decay provisions" associated with the computation of the criminal history points so that older crimes may receive fewer or no points (USSC, 1987a). There has been some limited support for the use of the criminal history score as a recidivism prediction scheme (USSC, 2004; but see Krauss, in press, for weaknesses of the criminal history score as a recidivism prediction instrument).

Derivation of Sentence Lengths under the Guidelines

The sentence lengths in the sentencing table grid were originally formulated by the Commission based on a number of factors. The Commission analyzed 10,000 previously sentenced cases and used these decisions to anchor penalties for certain crimes and to identify both the characteristics of specific offenses and aggravating and mitigating factors that had been relevant to judicial sentencing decisions in the past (USSC, 1987a). The SRA also mandated that penalties be increased for certain crimes, most notably white-collar offenses and drug trafficking crimes, and required that the grid created not include sentencing ranges in which the upper sentencing bound for a particular box in the grid was more than 25% greater than the lower bound for the same box (USSC, 1987a).

Finally, along with the creation of the USSC under the 1984 SRA and the development of the original guidelines (1984–1987), Congress passed a series of mandatory minimum laws during the development of the guidelines that specifically targeted violent offenses and drug crimes. Mandatory minimum laws are statutory provisions that specify the imposition of at least a required minimum term of imprisonment when the elements enumerated in the statute are met. The required terms of imprisonment in these penalties are sometimes referred to as sentencing "floors" because judges are prohibited, under most circumstances, from offering a sentence below the term (i.e., the floor) specified in the statute. The exact criteria necessary for the application of a mandatory minimum penalty vary from statute to statute, but the majority of such laws are triggered either by offense characteristics (e.g., the quantity of drugs involved in the offense), offender characteristics (e.g., an offender's prior convictions for the same offense), or victim characteristics (e.g., the age of the victim who was sold the drugs at issue in the offense).

Over 90% of crimes sentenced under mandatory minimum statutes have involved penalties linked to the quantity of drugs involved in a drug trafficking offense (USSC, 1991). For example, under one such law, a conviction for a drug offense involving distribution or possession with intent to distribute "500 grams or more of a mixture or substance containing cocaine" was subject to a 5-year mandatory term of imprisonment (21 U.S.C. § 841(b)(1)(B)). Because of the existence of these quantity-based drug mandatory minimum penalties, the Commission designed the original sentencing table to make all drug trafficking crimes' sentences dependent on the quantity of drugs involved in the offense and set the guidelines range for these offenses based on the mandatory minimum penalty (USSC, 1987b). As such, the guidelines set the offense level for distribution of 500 grams of cocaine at level 26, so that even an offender with no criminal history would receive a sentence in the 63- to 78-month range, consistent with the 5-year statutory mandatory minimum penalty for that quantity of drugs.

A Fifteen-Year Review of the Guidelines

A recent exhaustive review of the guidelines' operation has suggested that the guidelines have been successful in accomplishing some, but not all, of their central purposes. This 15-year review indicated that increases in the (a) severity of punishment, (b) transparency and rationality of sentencing decisions, and (c) certainty of imprisonment have all been substantially achieved by the guidelines. Federal criminal defendants are clearly punished with longer sentences (e.g., the average criminal sentence preguidelines was 25 months, and it is now almost 50 months), federal criminal defendants are more likely to be imprisoned (e.g., 69% of preguidelines sentenced defendants received sentences with at least some prison time, and 86% of defendants received such sentences in 2002), and the reasoning behind federal criminal defendants' sentences are more explicit than in the preguidelines era (e.g., specific findings are made with regard to factors that increase or decrease sentences, and these determinations are reviewable; USSC, 2004). The review also notes that regional disparity in judicial sentences for similar crimes committed by similar defendants has been significantly reduced for all crimes except robbery and immigration offenses (USSC, 2004).

However, the guidelines have been less successful in eliminating racial disparity in sentencing, and some critics have noted that these differences have increased during the guidelines operation. Yet the majority of this disparity appears to be related to legally relevant factors incorporated into the guidelines that punish certain racial groups differentially. For example, the guidelines include a 100 to 1 quantity difference in sentencing for crack and powder cocaine (i.e., trafficking 5 grams of crack cocaine is punished similarly to trafficking 500 grams of powder cocaine). Minority group members are more likely to be convicted of trafficking crack cocaine than powder cocaine, and thus receive longer sentences than other racial groups. Similarly, minority group members are more likely to be convicted of crimes that include guidelines' recognized factors that enhance their sentences, such as the use of a firearm during an offense. In the end, the 15-year review concludes that there still appears to be some limited racial and ethnic discrimination in sentencing, but that it is relatively minor once legally relevant grounds for discrimination are taken into consideration (USSC, 2004).

DEPARTURES AND FORENSIC MENTAL HEALTH EVALUATIONS

Having explained the operation, derivation, and successes and failures of the guidelines, it is now useful to explore the limited role that mental health professionals have played in evaluating the presence or absence of grounds for recognized departures.

Not Ordinarily Relevant Departures

As previously described, a judge cannot depart from the appropriate guidelines sentencing box absent an explicit rationale. The guidelines offer specific and complicated directions with regard to what are and what are not justifiable grounds for departure. These departure rationales, especially those for downward departures, have served as one of the limited avenues in which mental health professionals have been able to offer their expertise to the federal courts. Generally, the factors on which a forensic mental health professional might proffer expert testimony in a *state* sentencing proceeding are the offender's family background, mental health history, chemical dependence, and sexual or emotional abuse history. In federal court, these factors are not explicitly relevant grounds for departure under the guidelines (Lutjen, 1996). These factors can, however, be used as grounds for departure "only if such offender characteristics or circumstances are present to an exceptional degree" (§ 5K2.0). What represents an "exceptional degree" remains an area of controversy and litigation (see, e.g., Burrow & Koons-Witt, 2003, for discussion of this issue with regard to elderly status), but data from the USSC (2003) suggest that judicial departures based on these rationales are uncommon but not rare occurrences. For example, in fiscal year 2003, judicial departures for family ties and responsibilities represented 7.2%, physical condition accounted for 4.5%, and mental and emotional condition represented 1.8% of the approximately 6,000 downward departures for that time period (USSC, 2003).

The ability of judges to recognize these grounds for downward departure for certain crimes was even further constrained by the passage of the PROTECT Act of 2003 (USSC, 2004). The PROTECT Act, passed in part because it was believed judges were departing downward too frequently from the guidelines, completely eliminated these departures for certain child crimes and sexual offenses. However, because the PROTECT Act involved direct congressional modification of the guidelines, it, like the rest of the guidelines, is no longer binding following the *Booker/Fanfan* decision, a point more fully explored later in this chapter.

Explicitly Recognized Departures

In addition to departures not ordinarily relevant, the guidelines explicitly recognize a number of grounds for downward and upward departures concerning which forensic mental health professionals may offer expert testimony. Factors a judge may consider include diminished capacity (§ 5K2.13); aberrant behavior (§ 5K2.20); coercion and duress (§ 5K2.12); inadequacy of the Criminal History Category (§ 4A1.3b) for downward departures and extreme psychological injury (§ 5K2.3); and inadequacy of the Criminal History Category for upward departures (§ 4A1.3a). It should be noted that upward departures under the guidelines regime have become extremely uncommon, hovering around .7% of all cases, whereas downward departures are more common and evidence greater variability, occurring in approximately 14% to 18% of all federally sentenced cases (USSC, 2002). As a result of the infrequency of upward departures, and the unlikely possibility that mental health expertise would be relevant to the upward departures that do occur, the focus of this chapter is on forensic mental health professionals' role in downward departures.

Diminished Capacity

Of the explicitly recognized departure grounds relevant to mental health professionals, the diminished capacity departure (§ 5K2.13) is by far the most common reason cited by judges and the most likely to involve mental health professional expert testimony. This departure rationale, however, includes a restrictive definition and occurs at a low rate. For example, there were 284 departures based on this reason granted in the approximately 65,000 cases sentenced in 2002, and 272 departures based on this rationale were granted in the approximately 70,000 cases sentenced in 2003. According to the guidelines, a downward departure may be appropriate for a defendant because of diminished capacity if (a) the defendant committed the offense while suffering from a significantly reduced mental capacity, and (b) the significantly reduced mental capacity contributed substantially to the commission of the offense (§ 5K2.13, 1987). The guidelines further clarify that "significantly reduced mental capacity" means that the defendant has a significantly impaired ability to (a) understand the wrongfulness of the behavior comprising the offense or to exercise the power of reason or (b) control behavior the defendant knows is wrongful (§ 5K.13, policy statement 1987).

Additionally, the guidelines require that the departure be limited to the extent to which the mental capacity affected the commission of the offense and prohibits the use of this departure if (a) the reduced capacity was caused by intoxication, (b) the offense involved actual or threatened violence, or (c) the defendant's criminal history is substantial (USSC, 1987b).

The diminished capacity departure criteria used by the guidelines is somewhat akin to the pre-*Hinckley* federal insanity standard (the Insanity Defense Reform Act [IDRA] of 1984 abolished diminished capacity as a defense in federal court; see Goldstein et al., 2003). Under both standards, either a cognitive impairment (i.e., not knowing the difference between right and wrong as a result of a mental illness) or volitional impairment (i.e., not being able to control one's behavior as a result of a mental illness) may cause the defendant's culpability to be lessened. Yet, given that the current federal insanity standard (18 U.S.C. § 17) may excuse criminal conduct based on substantial mental health impairment of cognitive ability, the only apparent advantage of the diminished capacity departure appears to be that it allows for a proportional reduction in sentences of the mentally ill who are significantly volitionally impaired or whose cognitive impairments do not conform to the high threshold of impairment that is required under IDRA. This group of mentally ill persons is further restricted by the standard's prohibition against its use with defendants who have a significant criminal past or who have committed a crime that involved actual or threatened violence. Consequently, this departure standard's numerous restrictions and limited benefits may explain its infrequent use.

———————————————— **Illustrative Case 1** ————————————————

A Diminished Capacity Downward Departure

Bob Stevens, age 67, entered a plea of guilty to extortionate collection of credit conspiracy and extortionate collection of credit. (In all illustrative cases, identifying data have been changed to maintain confidentiality.) Because Stevens appeared to be intellectually limited and was reported to be functionally illiterate, his attorney requested a forensic psychological assessment to evaluate his judgment, reasoning, and decision-making abilities for consideration by the federal trial court judge at the time of sentencing. He was seen twice and was interviewed regarding his background, his history, and the circumstances of the offense. A battery of tests was administered, including the Wechsler Adult Intelligence Scales-III (WAIS-III), Wide Range Achievement Test-3 (WRAT-3), Symbol Digit Modalities Test, the Test of Memory Malingering, Validity Indicator Profile (Non-Verbal section), HCR-20, and the Psychopathy Checklist-Revised (PCL-R, second edition). His ex-wife and current wife were interviewed, and his school and employment records and relevant discovery related to this offense were reviewed.

According to his current and former wives, Stevens was naive and, according to his ex-wife, "not very smart when it comes to people. Anyone can talk him into anything. If you smile at him or tell him a joke, he thinks you're his best friend." Both claimed he was unable to read or write, and, according to his current wife, "I do all his paperwork." Records find that Stevens completed the eighth grade. He was held back in the third and seventh grades. According to standardized reading test results, in the seventh grade, Stevens read at the second-grade level. After dropping out of junior high school, he obtained a job as a longshoreman, until an on-the-job injury forced him to retire. He sued for damages suffered while working and received a settlement of $245,000.

When interviewed for the evaluation, Stevens provided a history consistent with his records and with the information provided by his former and current wives. He frequently asked the examiner inappropriate personal questions, and he had difficulty understanding questions put to him. He did not know the meaning of commonly used words, such as "aggression" and "relevant," and offered numerous self-deprecating comments throughout both evaluation sessions. In describing the instant offense, Stevens explained that when he received his settlement check, "I didn't know how to invest it" and deposited it in a joint checking account he had with his wife. He recalled that he walked into a local office of an investment firm for advice and sat down with a broker but could not follow what he was being told. Stevens claimed that he was given "papers to read and forms [to sign]; hell, I don't read and I threw them out. Forget about it." He claimed that he asked friends for advice about what to do with his money, and a neighbor, whom he described as a "wise guy" known to have connections to organized crime, suggested that he would help Stevens "put the money out on the street" (in effect, to be a loan shark). For 4 months, Stevens loaned small amounts of money, $1,000 to $2,000, to friends and neighbors. He then began to loan larger sums of money, "Because I got asked." There came a time when a "friend" did not make his weekly repayment on a $25,000 loan to Stevens. After a series of excuses and delays, this person flatly refused to repay his debt. However, despite this unanticipated development, Stevens continued to loan large sums of money to others, "Because they asked me to. They needed it." He explained that when others learned that "I was not with anyone" (not connected to organized crime), they, too, refused to make weekly repayments on their loans. He described his predicament to the man who initially suggested that he loan money to others, and this neighbor, known in the neighborhood as "Tommy Muscle," offered to help him with collection. Two days later, Tommy informed Stevens that one person had given him $8,000 in cash and that Stevens would "soon" be given the payment: "Take it easy, don't worry where the money is." His neighbor continued to collect money, supposedly for Stevens, but after 2 months of waiting, Stevens had received nothing. When he finally pressed Tommy, he was asked, "Do you want to screw with wise guys?" In a final encounter with Tommy, Stevens was ordered to empty his pockets. Tommy took $1,200 from him, laughed, and told Stevens, "Boy, are you a dope." Stevens explained that because he had operated as a loan shark, and because he was frightened of repercussions should he go to the police, he remained silent. Unfortunately, Tommy had been under surveillance by the FBI because of other suspected criminal activities, and they documented much of what had occurred. Stevens was arrested because of his involvement in the extortionate collection of credit.

On the WAIS-III, Stevens obtained Verbal, Performance, and Full-Scale IQs of 73, 74, and 71, respectively. Scores on the subtests were homogeneous, with deficits noted in his reasoning, judgment, and verbal abilities. Thinking was concrete, rigid, and simplistic. On the WRAT-3, Stevens was found to read and spell at the first-grade level; his arithmetic ability fell at the fourth-grade level. Because of his poor vocabulary and low reading level, no objective personality tests could be administered. Tests sensitive to malingered or exaggerated cognitive impairments found that Stevens was not attempting to malinger cognitive and intellectual deficits (his level of functioning was also consistent with information contained in the records).

It was opined that Stevens's cognitive limitations were such that he based his judgments on his limited experiences, on simplistic thinking, and on only a superficial understanding of the potential consequences of his actions. His decision-making processes did not typically include a reasoned consideration of alternatives and the ability to weigh the pros and cons of his actions. Stevens was described in the report as "highly gullible, intellectually limited, insecure with a strong need for acceptance and to please, and easily taken advantage of by others. His inability to consider his obvious lack of success as a 'shylock' corroborates his intellectual limitations and poor judgment." Stevens's attorney submitted the report and he received a downward departure at the time of sentencing, consistent with the diminished capacity factor (§ 5K2.13).

Aberrant Behavior

The guidelines recognize a downward departure rationale for criminal behavior that deviates markedly from a federal defendant's previous behavior (§ 5K2.20), and mental health expert testimony could also have bearing on this inquiry. Unfortunately, much like the diminished capacity standard, the guidelines' requirements to meet this standard are stringent, and it is not frequently found by sentencing judges (USSC, 2002, 2003). Further, even in the limited cases in which it is used, it is not clear that mental health professional expert testimony is necessary to meet its criteria.

To qualify for an aberrant behavior departure under the guidelines, the crime (a) must have been committed without significant planning, (b) must have involved limited duration, and (c) the criminal behavior must represent a "marked deviation by the defendant from an otherwise law-abiding life" (§ 5K2.20). Further, if the offense involved serious injury, the defendant discharged a firearm, the offense was a drug trafficking offense, or the defendant had any significant criminal history, then the departure is prohibited. Of the criteria necessary for this departure, only the defendant's deviation from a normal law-abiding life lends itself to mental health expert testimony. Yet the guidelines have specifically defined "law-abiding life" as a lack of criminal history, making it less likely that mental health expert testimony on a criminal defendant's good nature or personality would be informative in these decisions.

Illustrative Case 2

An Aberrant Behavior Downward Departure

John Martin, age 54, pled guilty to a violation of 18 U.S.C. § 1030, having admitted that he had accessed a protected computer system beyond his authorized authority and, in doing so, had knowingly caused the transmission of a program that would cause damage to that computer system. Based on the facts of the case, his attorney requested a forensic psychological assessment focusing on whether his client's actions were aberrant behavior under the guidelines (§ 5K2.20).

Techcom, a firm that provides consulting services to the telecommunications industry, had employed Martin for approximately 23 years. For the prior 3 years, he and three other coworkers had been assigned to a special project: developing a program for use on cellular phones that would make the transmission of the spoken word clearer than the current standard in the field. Cleartell, the cellular phone company, offered to hire the members of this group directly, and Techcom agreed to their offer. However, although all four team members were to receive the same salary as that paid by Techcom, their pension benefits with Techcom would stop just short of the time required to fully fund their full pensions if and when they accepted Cleartell's offer. For all members of the group, this would mean a significant cut in pension payments, and Martin would receive only 60% of the benefits he would have received had he worked one additional year for Techcom. Members of the group agreed to stick together and refused to sign contracts with Cleartell until their original employer guaranteed them full pensions. After 3 months of negotiations, Techcom issued an ultimatum: Either sign Cleartell's contract or be fired. For another 2 weeks, the members resisted this threat, until a member of the group signed a contract to work for Cleartell. Martin became both dejected and resentful of the position he had been placed in by his long-time employer. After thinking about it for days, according to Martin, he altered the program the group had been working on for years, inserting a bug that would destroy the rest of the program, timing it to activate in 2 months. Days after sending this program to Cleartell, Martin informed a fellow member of his team as to what he had done. She immediately contacted Techcom and alerted them to the potential problem. Unbeknown to her, after confessing to this colleague, Martin had second thoughts, removed the bug from the program, and returned it to its original state. Techcom discharged Martin and notified authorities and, after an investigation, federal charges were filed.

Martin was evaluated on three separate dates. He was questioned about his background and the circumstances of the charges to which he had pled. Psychological tests were administered, including the WAIS-III, Minnesota Multiphasic Personality Inventory-2 (MMPI-2), Personality Assessment Inventory (PAI), Millon Clinical Multiaxial Inventory-III (MCMI-III), and the Psychopathic Checklist-Revised, second edition. His wife, a former coworker, and his prior supervisor at Techcom were interviewed, and his academic, employment, and military records as well as discovery information related to this offense were reviewed. Martin's wife explained that her father-in-law had lost his job when he was age 55, was unable to obtain another position, and became increasingly depressed until his suicide 4 years later. She related her husband's concern that he would experience a similar fate and his preoccupation with a company "who only cared about the bottom line, never about those who were loyal employees for years. He was treated like a piece of furniture and they knew he and the others were shy and quiet and thought they'd get away with it." She reported that her husband would spend hours with calculations and prepared tables and graphs to estimate the amount of loss he would suffer if he were to accept Cleartell's offer. Martin's supervisor at Techcom, though somewhat reluctant to provide information, did indicate that Martin was a hard worker, honest, dependable, and "always gave 110%." A review of the records painted a similar picture—that of a man who worked hard, achieved, and made a positive impression on those who knew him. During the interviews, Martin explained, "I did all the right things to work this out." He recalled his feelings of powerlessness at Techcom's refusal to consider the financial impact their actions would have on his future and on the lives of his wife and children. He expressed his growing feelings of depression, anxiety, and outrage, seeing his financial security disappear. He explained that he used his personal laptop to change the program, that he had not disguised his identity in altering the program, that he inserted the bug with the belief that a satisfactory contract would eventually be worked out, and that when he began work at his new job with Cleartell, he would remove the bug.

Not surprisingly in light of his education and occupation, on the WAIS-III Martin obtained Verbal, Performance, and Full-Scale IQs of 139, 135, and 141, respectively. He responded to the MMPI-2 in an open, nondefensive manner, and the computer-generated interpretive report hypothesized that he would tend to "develop persistent tendencies around accumulated resentment and unrevealed anger." It also suggested that he might respond with anger "as a defensive reaction." The PAI computer-generated report suggested that Martin was likely to respond to stressful situations in a self-critical, uncertain, and indecisive manner. His self-image was described as negative, colored by feelings of self-doubt and a lack of confidence. The MCMI-III computer-generated report suggested that Martin frequently anticipates and experiences a sense of degradation and disillusionment and is quick to feel a deflated sense of self-worth, humiliation, and failure. According to the report, those with his pattern of responses are likely to withdraw and become increasingly more irritable when they feel cheated or misunderstood, rather than act out. Results suggested that Martin might engage in "fantasy solutions" and, at times, "act out momentarily and then retreat again into his fantasies or his despondency." Based on all of the data, Martin received a score of zero on the PCL-R, second edition.

A report reflecting these findings was submitted to the judge for consideration at the time of sentencing. The judge found that Martin's criminal conduct constituted aberrant behavior within the meaning of § 5K2.20 (see *United States v. Gonzales,* 2002), and a downward departure in sentencing was granted.

Coercion and Duress

A less common ground for downward departure under the guidelines than either aberrant behavior or diminished capacity, but one more likely to involve forensic mental health professional expert testimony than aberrant behavior, is coercion and duress (§ 5K2.12). Under this departure standard, a downward departure for a criminal defendant may be warranted if the defendant committed the criminal act in question because he or she was threatened with physical injury or damage to personal property and the coercion or duress was not found to rise to the level of a complete defense at the guilt/innocence phase of the trial. This definition, however, specifically prohibits financial incentives as means of coercion. With regard to this departure, a forensic mental health professional could offer expert testimony explaining how certain individuals (e.g., a defendant of young age, a defendant who is mentally ill) may be especially susceptible to coercive pressures, and could indicate how, psychologically, threats of violence may have induced the defendant to engage in criminal acts.

——————————— **Illustrative Case 3** ———————————

A Coercion and Duress Downward Departure

Tanya Warren, age 25, pled guilty to having unlawfully, intentionally, and knowingly conspired and agreed together with others to violate the narcotics laws of the United States by filling a number of forged prescriptions for hydrocodone (Vicodin) at local pharmacies. Her attorney explained that she was involved in an abusive relationship with her boyfriend, Ralph Taylor, allegedly a member of an organized crime family, and that, in his opinion, she had been coerced into filling these illegal prescriptions. Warren was referred for forensic evaluation to consider the possible role of duress and coercion (§ 5K2.12) in her involvement in this crime. She was interviewed twice, and a detailed history was taken, along with her rendition of her role in the instant offense. Tests administered to her included the WAIS-III, MMPI-2, MCMI-III, PAI, and the PCL-R. Third-party interviews were conducted with her parents, who were divorced when Warren was age 8, and her older brother. Her school records were reviewed, along with complaints she had filed with her local police department alleging physical abuse by her current boyfriend (and co-conspirator) and a former boyfriend. Discovery related to this case, including transcripts of a number of wiretapped calls made by Taylor to others about Warren's role in this crime, was reviewed as well.

According to her father, Warren began to experience difficulties when she started high school. He recalled that his daughter became depressed and immobilized and was unable to leave home for extended periods of time. In the 10th grade, his daughter had been involved in an abusive relationship prior to meeting Taylor. Her father claimed to have been present on one occasion when police arrived because of an altercation between his daughter and Taylor and, on a separate occasion, that he had driven her to the police station to file a complaint against Taylor. At that time, Warren was 23 years old. Ms. Locke, the defendant's mother, explained that she had been involved in a physically and verbally abusive relationship with her husband and that her daughter had been a frequent witness to the violence in the home. She described a prior relationship her daughter had while a student in high school, with an older man who would "push, kick, and punch her. I'd see the bruises." Her mother did not satisfactorily explain why she did not intervene in that relationship, nor in the relationship her daughter established with Taylor. Although she claimed to have been present on two occasions when Taylor allegedly assaulted her daughter, Locke explained that she herself felt threatened by him and never called the police. Philip Warren, the defendant's brother, stated that their mother was a compulsive gambler and a person who kept his sister highly dependent on her for both emotional and financial support. He described their father as "unavailable, and he just shuts down and doesn't do anything." Although he was never present when Taylor assaulted his sister, he reported seeing bruises and did hear him verbally attack his sister. He stated that on one occasion, for a period of 1 week, his sister had moved in with him "because she was scared of Ralph and wouldn't go home until she got him arrested." However, he recalled that Taylor "wore her out with his calls and she went back to him because she was being stupid or [because of] her need to be with him." Transcripts of wiretapped calls made by Taylor indicate that he was "fighting" with her. Taylor told another codefendant about his girlfriend's resistance to filling prescriptions, "She didn't go for me. She's making me wait and wait . . . she won't do it, no." He told another individual that he had advised Warren to "do that for me and stop all the problems."

During the evaluation interviews, Warren explained that after her parents' divorce, her mother "tried to keep him [Warren's father] away." Because of her mother's gambling and drinking, Warren would spend as much time as possible at friends' homes because "I hated being by myself." When she was 15 years old, Warren dated a man 4 years older than she. She claimed that she was physically and verbally abused by this man, who "kept me isolated from my friends." The relationship ended when he suddenly moved in with another woman. Warren recalled meeting Taylor at a party and claimed she was unaware of his criminal background until they had been dating for approximately 1 month. "He had kept his personal life in a box, shaded." At the start of their relationship, she "felt bad for him, I don't know why." One month after moving in together, she reported, Taylor's treatment of her suddenly changed. She described a number of instances in which he had beaten her, thrown objects at her, pushed her, and shoved her onto the bed. On another occasion, she reported that he had twisted her arms and legs. In describing her relationship with Taylor, she said, "It was walking on egg shells." Although she could not recall the exact date when she first began to fill prescriptions at Taylor's request, she claimed that when he handed her the prescriptions, she would initially refuse to fill them; she said, "We'd fight for a few days and I couldn't take it anymore—the yelling, screaming, threatening, and he had such a bad temper and it would get up there, and he'd pick up things and throw them across the room or hit me and call me names." (Warren was somewhat overweight and was sensitive about this; Taylor would call her "Miss Piggy" or "Moose"). She claimed that on approximately five occasions, she never acceded to her boyfriend's demands, explaining, "He'd take it [the prescription] back and I don't know what he did with it. We'd fight over it even when he took it back." Although Warren had called the police (documented in the records) on two occasions, she never informed them about her boyfriend's involvement in these narcotics violations, because "I was scared, not knowing what he was capable of." She explained that although Taylor had never threatened to kill her, "He was so angry, I was scared he'd accidentally kill me [during one of his assaults]."

Warren obtained Verbal and Performance IQs of 109 and 93, respectively. On the MMPI-2, MCMI-III, and PAI, she tended to minimize emotional difficulties, reflecting, in general, her concern that she might be perceived or judged in a negative light. Nonetheless, all of the test protocols were valid. The MMPI-2 results suggest that Warren is a repressed woman, lacking in confidence and with limited self-awareness. The computer-generated report suggests that she is overly sensitive to real or imagined criticism and is likely to experience episodes of agitation. Difficulties in expressing her resentments are indicated, along with marked tendencies to blame herself for whatever befalls her. Warren's strong need for approval and her need to be seen in a highly positive light are reported on the MCMI-III. She is described as a person who presents with "general naivete about psychological matters, including a possible deficit in self-knowledge . . . [and is] preoccupied with approval and frequently conforms to the social expectations of others, particularly those with a status or in authority." Her tendencies to "become socially adaptable, willingly deferential to others" are reported as well. The PAI computer-generated report described her as "warm, friendly and sympathetic," a person who goes out of her way to maintain harmony because she "is likely to be uncomfortable with interpersonal confrontation and conflict, and she would be likely to shun controversy." It was hypothesized that Warren would be quick to forgive, readily willing to give others a second chance.

Warren was aware of the illegality of her actions, stating that, on occasion, she was successful in resisting her boyfriend's requests to fill prescriptions. However, her prior history, her low self-esteem, her fear of continued physical and verbal abuse, and her need to avoid conflict played major roles in her decision to acquiesce to Taylor's demands. A report was submitted to the court, and a downward departure was granted, consistent with the guidelines' criteria related to duress and coercion (§ 5K.2.12).

Additional Departure Grounds

Beyond the explicitly recognized and not ordinarily relevant departures, the guidelines also allow for departures, both upward and downward, on the basis of factors that represent "an aggravating or mitigating circumstance of a kind, or to a degree, that was not adequately taken into consideration by the Sentencing Commission" (18 U.S.C., § 3553(b), § 5K2.0). This exception is a catch-all that allows for expert testimony and departure decisions based on any conceivable rationale not adequately addressed by the guidelines. Departures based on this standard that involve expert testimony by mental health professionals are rare (USSC, 2002, 2003).

In addition, the PROTECT Act of 2003 also limited the use of both explicitly recognized departures and the catch-all departure exception for certain child crimes and sexual offenses. As a result, the catch-all departure exception is not available in such cases, and specific provisions of the explicitly recognized departures are also prohibited in these cases. For example, the use of diminished capacity (§ 5K2.13) and aberrant behavior (§ 5K.2.20) downward departures are not available in these cases. The PROTECT Act also made one additional important contribution to guidelines departures: It lessened the deference that downward departures were shown by appellate courts (Bowman, 2005). Prior to the PROTECT Act, the U.S. Supreme Court held that judicial departures should be reviewed based on a deferential abuse of discretion standard, making it unlikely that a departure decision would be overturned on appellate review (*Koon v. United States,* 1996). The PROTECT Act created *de novo,* or fresh, review of downward departure decisions, making it easier for an appellate court to overturn a downward departure adjudication.

Taken as a whole, the guidelines and their modification by the PROTECT Act left little room for mental health practitioners to offer their expertise during federal sentencing. Beyond a restrictive diminished capacity defense, there were few opportunities for experts to offer guidance to the courts. As a result, mental health professionals were infrequent participants as experts in federal sentencing decisions. Before turning to how the recent *Booker/Fanfan* decision may increase mental health professionals' participation in federal sentencing, it is necessary to briefly review the limited grounds that exist outside the guidelines structure on which mental professionals can affect federal sentencing decisions.

Need for Treatment

Several provisions of the federal code allow for convicted federal defendants to be evaluated with regard to their need for treatment. Under these provisions, the court or an attorney may request a psychological evaluation to determine whether a federal defendant, prior to sentencing but after having been found guilty, is suffering from a mental illness and whether the mental illness is such as "to require his custody for care or treatment in a suitable facility" (18 U.S.C. § 4244). These evaluations, which may require the expert testimony of a mental health professional if the assessment is contested, are much more frequent than downward departures evaluations in the federal court system (Edward Landis III, personal communications, April 14, 2005). In the course of this evaluation, a forensic mental health expert may offer an opinion to the court concerning whether one of the federal medical center prisons would be a more appropriate environment for the convicted defendant than a standard federal prison facility.

The main issue in these evaluations is not only the severity of the mental illness from which the defendant suffers, but also how well the mentally ill defendant can adapt to prison society at a standard federal prison facility. In essence, it is a question of the fit between the mentally ill defendant's needs, the prison's treatment abilities, and the prisoner's perceived coping abilities. In these cases, if the need for treatment is recognized by the court, the defendant is placed in the appropriate care facility until the maximum term authorized by law for the offense expires or until the defendant sufficiently recovers and is no longer in need of such care (18 U.S.C. § 4244 d-e). If the latter event occurs, the defendant is returned to court and resentenced consistent with the guidelines. A similar provision, 18 U.S.C. § 4245, exists for sentenced defendants who develop or exacerbate their mental illness while serving their federal incarceration.

SHIFT FROM MANDATORY TO ADVISORY ROLE OF THE GUIDELINES

The initial intent of the guidelines, as described previously, was to ensure fairness and uniformity in federal sentencing. As such, application of the guidelines at the time of sentencing was mandatory; federal judges had no choice but to consider and impose sentences based on the rigid formula contained in the guidelines. However, in a series on landmark U.S. Supreme Court cases, a trend developed, marking the end of the *mandatory* nature of the guidelines. It resulted in the application of the guidelines as an *advisory* document, once again returning some discretionary power to federal trial judges.

Jones v. U.S.

In *Jones v. U.S.* (1999), Jones was found guilty by a jury of federal carjacking. Three different sentences could be imposed by the judge, each of which was linked to the degree of physical harm caused to the victim: (a) 15 years if there was no serious harm, (b) 25 years if the victim experienced serious bodily harm, and (c) life imprisonment if death resulted from the carjacking. The Court reasoned that if the degree of harm was an element of the crime (because it was a factor used to determine the sentence the defendant would receive), this was a fact to be determined by the jury rather than the judge. Otherwise, as the Court held, the role of the jury would be reduced "to the relative importance of low-level gatekeeper" (p. 244). This decision opened the floodgates to a range of other decisions that directly or indirectly supported the opinion that the "jury determines the 'facts' that raise a sentencing ceiling" (p. 251) and marked the beginning of the end of the mandatory nature of the guidelines.

Apprendi v. New Jersey

The State of New Jersey, by statute, permitted trial court judges to sentence defendants found guilty of specific crimes to longer prison sentences if the judge believed that the crime for which the defendant was convicted was a "hate crime." In *Apprendi v. New Jersey* (2000), the U.S. Supreme Court addressed the constitutionality of enhanced sentences based on this hate crime statute. Apprendi pled guilty to second-degree possession of a firearm for unlawful purposes and was eligible for a sentence of 5 to 10 years. At the time of sentencing, however, the judge found that the defendant had violated the state's hate crime law, ruling that Apprendi's crime was motivated by racism, and enhanced his sentence both beyond the maximum allowed for by the New Jersey statute for possession of a firearm and beyond that which he would have received based solely on the jury's verdict. Consistent with the Court's holding in *Jones* (1999), the sentence was found to be unconstitutional because, in classifying the crime as a hate crime, the judge deprived the defendant of his due process right to a trial by jury to determine *if* this element of the crime existed beyond a reasonable doubt.

Ring v. Arizona

It did not take long for petitions for relief to be submitted to the court related to death sentences imposed solely by judges without consideration by a jury. Cunningham and Goldstein (2003) describe the mechanism by which a defendant, convicted of a capital offense, may be sentenced to death. In short, evidence is presented at a separate sentencing hearing, most typically to a jury, as to the presence of mitigating and aggravating factors that are to be weighed or balanced to determine whether or not the defendant deserves the death penalty. In some states, although a jury may determine if a defendant is guilty of a capital crime, the decision as to a sentence of life versus death is left entirely to the trial judge, who conducts a separate sentencing hearing. In still other states, the jury makes a "recommendation" to the judge, who, by statute, can accept or override the jury's decision.

In *Ring v. Arizona* (2002), the U.S. Supreme Court held that a jury, not a trial judge, has the responsibility (if recommendation for the death penalty is made by the prosecutor) "to determine the presence or absence of aggravating factors required by Arizona law for imposition of the death penalty" (p. 588). As such, if a determination is made for a finding of death—a sentence greater than that authorized for the crime of murder—then the jury's decision, "contingent on the finding of a fact, that fact—no matter how the State labels it—must be found by a jury beyond a reasonable doubt" (p. 602). The *Ring* decision clearly indicated that juries, and not the trial judge, must make the recommendation of whether death is an appropriate punishment. Subsequent decisions have not yet determined, however, whether a jury's *recommendation* of death to a judge represents a violation of the *Apprendi* principle.

Blakeley v. Washington

In 2004, the Court considered the case of *Blakeley v. Washington*. The defendant had pled guilty to a charge of kidnapping, punishable by no more than 10 years imprisonment. Washington's law provides a sentence for this crime of 49 to 53 months, unless the trial judge finds that aggravating facts exist. At sentencing, the judge sentenced Blakeley to a 90-month term, finding that the defendant, at the time of the crime, had acted with "deliberate cruelty." Consistent with precedent established in prior cases, the U.S. Supreme Court held that unless a jury finds by the beyond a reasonable doubt standard or a defendant admits these aggravating facts exist, consideration of any factors that would result in a sentence above that indicated for a specific crime by a lower evidentiary standard represents a violation of the defendant's rights.

United States v. Booker and *United States v. Fanfan*

These earlier cases set the stage and provided the legal context for two cases decided by the Court in 2005, *United States v. Booker* and *United States v. Fanfan,* involving the guidelines. In *Booker,* the defendant was found guilty by jury verdict of possession of over 92 grams of crack cocaine, a crime carrying with it a sentence of 210 to 262 months in prison. However, at the time of sentencing, the judge found by a preponderance of the evidence that Booker had been in possession of considerably more cocaine, 566 grams of crack, evidence not considered by the jury. In following the guidelines, the judge sentenced Booker to a sentence 10 years longer than that authorized by the jury's verdict. Majority opinions were written, in part, by Justices Stevens and Breyer. In the main, the Stevens majority opinion addressed the constitutionality of the enhanced sentence, and the Breyer opinion focused on the remedies required in altering the applicability of the guidelines. Citing *Blakeley v. Washington* (2004), Justice Stevens wrote that Booker's sentence violated the 6th Amendment and instructed the district court to sentence Booker within the range supported by the jury's verdict (or to conduct a separate sentencing hearing before a jury). The phrase "shall impose a sentence of the kind, and within the range" established by the guidelines made them mandatory, and, as such, Booker was deprived of his due process right to a trial by jury to establish this sentence-enhancing factor.

In *United States v. Fanfan,* the defendant was convicted of conspiracy to distribute and possession with intent to distribute at least 500 grams of cocaine. Based solely on the jury verdict, Fanfan was to receive a sentence in the range of 5 to 6 years. At sentencing, however, the judge, relying on evidence not heard by the jury, found that the defendant was responsible for 2.5 kilograms of cocaine powder and was an organizer, leader, manager, or supervisor of the criminal activity for which he was convicted. By a preponderance of the evidence, consistent with the guidelines, Fanfan was to receive an enhanced sentence of 15 to 16 years. Citing, among other reasons, the Court's decision in *Blakeley* (2004), the judge indicated that the mandatory guidelines could not be followed, and imposed the sentence based solely on the jury's verdict. The government appealed this decision to both the 1st Circuit Court of Appeals and the U.S. Supreme Court, and the Supreme Court granted the petition for appeal.

In a combined decision, the Court again affirmed that enhanced sentences, not based on evidence to support by a jury's findings beyond a reasonable doubt, were a violation of the 6th Amendment. The Court determined that the guidelines are "inapplicable . . . such that the sentencing court *must* exercise its discretion to sentence the defendant within the maximum and minimum set by the statute for the offense of conviction" (p. 756; emphasis added). Justice Breyer, however, writing for a majority of the Court, concluded that although the guidelines were no longer mandated, they should serve as an advisory document for the sentencing judge. As an advisory document, the guidelines would continue to maintain "a strong connection between the sentence imposed and the offender's real conduct—a connection important to the increased uniformity of sentencing the Congress intended its Guidelines system to achieve" (p. 757).

FUTURE DIRECTIONS FOR FORENSIC MENTAL HEALTH EXPERTS IN FEDERAL SENTENCING

As just described, the U.S. Supreme Court in *Booker/Fanfan* held that the guidelines are now advisory for federal sentencing. The full repercussions of this decision in practice and in specific sentencing decisions are far from being determined, but the Court's decision appears to leave some optimism for a broadening of the use of forensic mental health experts in federal sentencing decisions. As noted throughout this chapter, the guidelines served to severely curtail the discretion of judges, and with that constraint, also inhibited the ability of forensic mental health professionals to offer their expertise to the federal courts.

Forensic Practice

By finding the guidelines advisory rather than mandatory, the Court has, in some sense, lifted the prohibitions placed on judicial discretion in sentencing. In particular, as judges are no longer required to follow the guidelines, they may use forensic mental health experts' reports and testimony to deviate from what the guidelines would suggest for a specific federal offender and crime. For example, whereas the guidelines prohibited diminished capacity downward departures for certain childhood offenses and sexual crimes, in an advisory guidelines system expert testimony by a forensic mental health expert on this topic may be allowable. In essence, the advisory nature of the guidelines may mean greater discretion for judges to consider mental health professionals' expertise in their sentencing decisions.

It is not clear at this point whether such optimism is justified for federal sentencing in an advisory guidelines regime. Much will depend on what standards federal courts adopt to review the sentencing decisions of lower federal courts and how different courts use the advisory guidelines in actual practice, and this is presently an area of considerable confusion and debate (Bowman, 2005). Justice Breyer, in his decision in *Booker/Fanfan,* appeared to suggest that "reasonableness" would be the appropriate standard for appellate review in sentencing decisions. This deferential standard would allow federal trial courts considerable discretion in making their sentencing decisions and would likely allow for greater participation of forensic mental health expert testimony on relevant sentencing concerns. It is important to remember, even under this deferential standard, that guidelines sentencing has been mandated for almost 2 decades and that normative and jurisprudential changes may have to occur before the guidelines become genuinely advisory. Additionally, courts could legally determine that deviations from or use of information prohibited by the guidelines, such as the not ordinarily relevant factors described previously, is unreasonable. If this were to occur, there would be little difference between the current federal sentencing regime and the role it allows mental health professionals, and the very restrictive scheme that existed under the guidelines. Future legal decisions and judicial practice will hold the answers to these questions.

It is of interest that lawmakers have responded to the *Booker/Fanfan* decision by proposing new legislation that would mandate minimum sentences for crimes committed under specific conditions. For example, the *New York Times* (Kirkpatrick, 2005, p. A14) reports that the House was expected to approve a bill that would increase federal sentences for crimes committed by street gangs, changing "the definition of a criminal street gang to three people who have committed at least two crimes together, at least one of them violent, from five [people]." Other pending legislation includes bills that would provide for increased sentences for federal drug offenses and for crimes committed in courthouses. Attorney General Alberto Gonzales, who is highly critical of the impact of *Booker/Fanfan,* is quoted as stating:

> More and more frequently, judges are exercising their discretion to impose sentences that depart from the carefully considered ranges developed by the U.S. Sentencing Commission. In the process, we risk losing a sentencing system that requires serious sentences for serious offenders and helps prevent disparate sentences for equally serious crimes. (Lichtblau, 2005, p. A15)

Lichtblau states that a U.S. Justice Department official reported that, since the *Booker/Fanfan* decision, downward departures in sentencing approved by judges increased 12.7% from the approval rate of 7.5% in 2003.

Forensic Research

In their decisions in *Booker* and *Fanfan,* the Court recognized that Congress could create through legislation a new federal sentencing system, consistent with the letter and spirit of these cases. Robbennolt and Studebaker (2005) indicate that this "invitation for legislation raises interesting questions about how sentencing decisions are made, the roles of judges and juries in sentencing and what guidance is used to structure these decisions" (p. 69). (See Chapter 26 for a review of research addressing sentencing decision making by judges.) They suggest a number of research questions that relate to these court decisions and their implications. Among the areas of future research for forensic psychologists they list are (a) the ways sentencing formulas are affected by extralegal factors such as race, (b) the ways sentencing decisions made by judges differ from those of juries, (c) the potential effects of a jury determining both guilt and the sentence, and (d) the impact these cases have on plea bargaining negotiations. Robbennolt and Studebaker conclude, "Answers to these and other questions can play a vital role in the crafting of sentencing policy" (p. 69).

CONCLUSION

The role of forensic mental health practitioners' expertise in federal sentencing proceedings remains unclear. Under the mandatory and stringent guidelines regime that constrained the behavior and discretion of federal judges, there were limited rationales (i.e., diminished capacity, aberrant behavior, and coercion and duress) and severe restrictions placed on sentencing issues commonly addressed by mental health practitioners. Although mental health professionals had been called on to offer their expertise in these limited cases, this was an uncommon occurrence in the majority of federal sentencing decisions.

The U.S. Supreme Court's recent decision in *Booker/Fanfan,* finding the guidelines advisory, has potentially opened the door to greater mental health practitioner research and direct participation in federal sentencing decision making. The now advisory guidelines have returned a substantial measure of discretion to federal judges to call on mental health practitioner expertise as they see fit. Future legal decisions will be needed to clarify the extent of discretionary power afforded to federal judges and the size of the role mental health practitioners will play in a new era of federal sentencing.

REFERENCES

Anti-Drug Abuse Act of 1986, Pub. L. 99-570, 100 Stat. 3207 (1986).

Apprendi v. New Jersey, 530 U.S. 466 (2000).

Blakeley v. Washington, 124 S. Ct. 2531 (S. Ct. 2004).

Blumstein, A. (1986). *Criminal careers and "career criminals"* (Vols. 1 & 2). Washington, DC: National Academy Press.

Bowman, F. (2005). The failure of the federal sentencing guidelines: A structural analysis. *Columbia Law Review, 105,* 1315–1350.

Breyer, S. (1988). The federal sentencing guidelines and the key compromises upon which they rest. *Hofstra Law Review, 1,* 17–34.

Burrow, J., & Koons-Witt, B. (2003). Elderly status, extraordinary physical impairments, and intercircuit variation under the federal sentencing guidelines. *Elder Law Journal, 11,* 273–328.

Chorney, J. (2004). O'Connor to judges: Explain yourselves. *Recorder, 1.* Available from http://www.law .com/jsp/article.jsp?id=1090180161284.

Cunningham, M. D., & Goldstein, A. M. (2003). Sentencing determinations in death penalty cases. In I. B. Weiner (Series Ed.) & A. M. Goldstein (Vol. Ed.), *Comprehensive handbook of psychology: Vol. 11. Forensic psychology* (pp. 407–436). Hoboken, NJ: Wiley.

Frankel, J. (1972). Lawlessness in sentencing. *University of Cincinnati Law Review, 41,* 1–61.

Goldstein, A. M., Morse, S. J., & Shapiro, D. L. (2003). Evaluation of criminal responsibility. In I. B. Weiner (Series Ed.) & A. M. Goldstein (Vol. Ed.), *Comprehensive handbook of psychology: Vol. 11. Forensic psychology* (pp. 381–406). Hoboken, NJ: Wiley.

Hoffman, P., & Beck, J. (1997). The origins of the federal Criminal History Score. *Federal Sentencing Reporter, 9,* 192–197.

Insanity Defense Reform Act. (1984). Pub. L. 98-473, 18 U.S.C. §§ 401–406.

Jones v. U.S., 526 U.S. 277 (1999).

Kirkpatrick, D. D. (2005, May 11). Congress rekindles battle on mandatory sentences. *New York Times,* A14.

Koon v. United States, 518 U.S. 81 (S. Ct. 1996).

Krauss, D. (in press). Evaluating science outside the trial box: Applying *Daubert* to the federal sentencing guidelines' Criminal History Score. *International Journal of Law and Psychiatry.*

Lichtblau, E. (2005, June 22). Gonzales is seeking to stem light sentences. *New York Times,* A15.

Lutjen, K. (1996). Culpability and sentencing under the mandatory minimums and the federal sentencing guidelines: The punishment no longer fits the criminal. *Notre Dame Journal of Law and Ethics, 10,* 389–432.

Patridge, A., & Eldridge, W. (1974). *Second Circuit Sentencing Study: A report to judges.* Washington DC: Federal Judicial Center.

Prosecutorial Remedies and Other Tools to End the Exploitation of Children Today Act of 2003, Pub. L. No. 108-21, 117 Stat. 650 (April 30, 2003).

Ring v. Arizona, 536 U.S. 584 (2002).

Robbennolt, J. K., & Studebaker, C. A. (2005, March). Court rules on validity of sentencing guidelines. *Monitor on Psychology, 36,* 69–70.

Ruback, R., & Wroblewoski, J. (2001). Federal sentencing guidelines: Psychological and policy reasons for simplification. *Psychology, Public Policy, and Law, 7,* 739–775.

United States v. Booker, 125 S. Ct. 738 (2005).

United States v. Fanfan, 125 S. Ct. 738 (2005).

United States v. Gonzales, 281 F.3d 38 (2002).

United States. v. Mistretta, 488 U.S. 361 (S. Ct. 1989).

U.S. Code, Chapter 28, § 994 *et seq.* (1984).

U.S. Code, Chapter 21, § 841b(1)B (1986).

U.S. Code, Chapter 18, §§ 4244–4245 (2001).

U.S. Sentencing Commission. (1987a). *Federal sentencing guidelines manual.* Washington, DC: Westlaw.

U.S. Sentencing Commission. (1987b). *Supplementary report on the initial sentencing guidelines and policy statements.* Washington, DC: U.S. Sentencing Commission.

U.S. Sentencing Commission. (1991). *Mandatory minimum penalties in the federal criminal justice system.* Special Report to Congress. Washington, DC: U.S. Sentencing Commission.

U.S. Sentencing Commission. (2002). *2002 sourcebook of federal sentencing statistics.* Available from http://www.ussc.gov/ANNRPT/2002/SBTOC02.htm.

U.S. Sentencing Commission. (2003). *2003 sourcebook of federal sentencing statistics.* Available from http://www.ussc.gov/ANNRPT/2003/SBTOC03.htm.

U.S. Sentencing Commission. (2004). Fifteen years of guidelines sentencing: An assessment of how well the federal criminal justice system is achieving the goals of sentencing reform. Available from http://www.ussc.gov/15_year/15year.htm.

CHAPTER 15

Postconviction Assessment

Eric Y. Drogin

Postconviction assessment addresses the full range of issues regarding persons who have been found guilty of, or who have pled guilty to, state or federal criminal charges. A defendant may have been subjected to flawed pretrial examinations or may not have been examined at all. Trial counsel may have ignored important reports, testimony, or symptoms, may have failed to get such evidence before a jury, or may have failed to seek the jury instructions necessary to provide the context for an acquittal or a lesser sentence. The trial judge may have failed to appreciate the legal relevance of a defendant's mental condition or may have denied trial counsel or the prosecutor the funding necessary to obtain competent forensic expertise. Now that the trial is over (or a plea bargain has been struck), sentence has been handed down, time is being served (or an execution is pending), and an aggrieved defendant has made allegations of error, how shall the legal system determine the role forensic psychological evidence should have played in the past, and what role such evidence should play in the future?

Although postconviction assessment is increasingly utilized by defending and prosecuting attorneys alike, and although it may substantially influence the course of subsequent legal proceedings, it has been virtually ignored in the forensic psychological literature. The few scientific articles addressing this topic tend to focus on prerelease functions of sexual offender risk assessment (Conroy, 2003; Kokish, 2003; Kokish, Levenson, & Blasingame, 2005), a mode of evaluation typically more reliant on actuarial than clinical examination methods (Drogin, 2000b). Similarly, although the past few decades have witnessed a steady stream of law review articles on postconviction matters, the mental health component of this topic has been surprisingly underrepresented.

This chapter provides an overview of the legal background, scope of inquiry, ethical considerations, and specialized applications of postconviction assessment, for forensic mental health experts wishing to establish and enhance their expertise in this expanding area of forensic practice. Rather than fostering a professional culture in which colleagues will be encouraged to second-guess the jury's conclusions (Bodenhausen, 1990) and gratuitously criticize each other's clinical contributions to the detriment of the legal system, it is contended that the increased participation of psychologists in postconviction proceedings will provide an incentive for more ethically informed and methodologically sound pretrial forensic services while continuing to serve the interests of justice.

LEGAL BACKGROUND

Postconviction relief is not lightly granted. The annual cost of prosecuting state and local criminal cases was recently estimated at $19 billion (D. A. Anderson, 1999), and even minor offenses can trigger a seemingly endless procession of investigations, evaluations, status conferences, evidentiary hearings, and rescheduled trial dates, persisting in some cases over the course of several years (Carrington, 1969; Kerekes, 1994). Considerable deference is accorded the decisions of trial judges and juries (Whitmore, 2005), and the evidentiary and procedural bar for overturning a conviction is set correspondingly high (Levy & Pujol, 2000).

Article I of the U.S. Constitution extends to federal prisoners the "privilege of the writ of *habeas corpus,*" which "for many prisoners . . . stands as the last opportunity to challenge the constitutionality of their convictions or sentences" (Blume & Voisin, 1996, p. 272). This remedy applies to such constitutionally based allegations as "ineffective assistance of counsel claims, prosecutorial and police misconduct claims, and claims based on watershed interpretations of the substantive law" (Newton, 2005, p. 17). Such writs could once be filed at any time subsequent to conviction (Hack, 2003):

> In 1996, however, after several years of debate about the abuses and delays of the federal appeals process, and spurred into action by the Oklahoma City bombing, Congress passed the Antiterrorism and Effective Death Penalty Act (AEDPA). Among other things, AEDPA [provided] for a 1-year statute of limitations for those seeking postconviction relief from their federal conviction or sentence. (Iandiorio, 2004, p. 1141)

In *Dodd v. U.S.* (2005), the U.S. Supreme Court recently specified that in determining the parameters of the AEDPA statute of limitations, "the applicant has 1 year from the date on which the right he asserts was initially recognized by this Court" (p. 2482). The Court further stated, in *Mayle v. Felix* (2005), that this statute of limitations cannot be circumvented by amending a previously filed habeas corpus petition to reflect a new ground for relief when the time and the type of the facts asserted are different from the ones set forth in the original pleading.

"State postconviction remedies . . . are the counterparts to [federal] *habeas corpus* statutes [and] they exist because of, and are modeled on or interpreted in light of, the federal statutes that allow relief to those in custody in violation of the Constitution of the United States" (Robertson, 1992, p. 333). Criminal defendants, convicted in state court proceedings, thus "have the opportunity to file two types of *habeas corpus* actions—the first in the state court system and a subsequent action in the federal court system" (Newton, 2005, p. 16). In state court habeas corpus proceedings, time limits are a significant factor as well (Harris, Nieves, & Place, 2003; McCloud, 2002), varying in length from jurisdiction to jurisdiction (Bartle, 2002). Successful writs may ultimately result in exoneration (Rowe, 2002) or perhaps a deal consisting of a lesser sentence, conviction of a lesser charge, or both, in light of the desire of both sides to avoid the ever-increasing procedural burdens of postconviction practice (Steiker, 1998).

The seminal U.S. Supreme Court case of *Gideon v. Wainwright* (1963) confirmed the right of criminal defendants to legal representation at trial, although the

Court later maintained that defendants seeking state postconviction relief possess no constitutional right to counsel beyond the first tier of appellate review (*Ross v. Moffitt,* 1974). "Although the Court has not directly addressed whether the Constitution requires counsel on federal *habeas* review, the Court's reasoning in the state postconviction cases suggests the same rule would apply in the federal postconviction context as well" (McConville, 2003, p. 34). In the recent case of *Halbert v. Michigan* (2005), the Court determined that conviction on the basis of a plea does not deprive defendants of their right to counsel during first-tier state court appeals. As indigent funding for representation in postconviction proceedings is guaranteed by statute in some states and not in others, this disparity and its consequences have sparked considerable debate among constitutional scholars and social scientists alike (Cunningham & Vigen, 1999; Givelber, 1999; Hammel, 2003; Howard, 1996; Parry, 1986; Place, 1996; Richardson-Stewart, 2003; Rosichan, 2004; Rundlet, 1999; Saylor, 1998; C. Smith & Starns, 1999; Snyder, 1998).

The Court did establish in *McCann v. Richardson* (1970) that, when afforded, "the right to counsel is the right to the *effective* assistance of counsel" (p. 771, emphasis added). In *Strickland v. Washington* (1984), the Court promulgated a two-pronged standard for determining when a trial attorney's services have failed to qualify as "effective":

> First, the defendant must show that counsel's performance was deficient. This requires showing that counsel made errors so serious that counsel was not functioning as the "counsel" guaranteed the defendant by the Sixth Amendment. Second, the defendant must show that the deficient performance prejudiced the defense. This requires showing that counsel's errors were so serious as to deprive the defendant of a fair trial, a trial whose result is reliable. (p. 687)

Concerning the "performance" prong of this test, the Court observed in *Strickland* (1984) that whereas "strategic choices made after thorough investigation of law and facts relevant to plausible options are virtually unchallengeable," a trial attorney's "strategic choices made after less than complete investigation are reasonable precisely to the extent that reasonable professional judgments support the limitations on investigation." In this regard, the Court concluded that "counsel has a duty to make reasonable investigations or to make a reasonable decision that makes particular investigations unnecessary" (p. 691).

The Court in *Strickland* (1984) further indicated that, to invoke the "prejudice" prong of this test, a "reasonable probability" must exist that, had such "reasonable investigations" been made, "the factfinder would have had a reasonable doubt respecting guilt," or that "the sentencer—including an appellate court, to the extent it independently reweighs the evidence—would have concluded that the balance of aggravating and mitigating circumstances did not warrant death" (p. 695). Although forged in a capital litigation context, the *Strickland* test has since regularly been utilized in all manner of criminal proceedings (Gable & Green, 2004).

Applying this standard in a forensic psychological evidentiary context, the inquiry becomes: Did the defense team conduct a "thorough" investigation into "relevant" mental health-related information? If not, did they conduct an investigation that was "reasonable," pursuant to a choice supported by "reasonable professional judgments"? Would performing such an investigation have led the jury to harbor a "reasonable doubt" concerning guilt? Would performing such an investigation have led to a more desirable result during the sentencing phase of a trial?

"Regarding mental health evidence in particular, the practical standard for what sort of investigation is 'reasonable' has evolved considerably in the last 2 decades" (Drogin, 2004, p. 496). In *Ake v. Oklahoma* (1985), just 1 year after rendering its decision in *Strickland,* the Court maintained that trial counsel need not attempt to make sense of mental health evidence on his or her own:

> Without the assistance of a psychiatrist to conduct a professional examination on issues relevant to the defense, to help determine whether the insanity defense is viable, to present testimony, and to assist in preparing the cross-examination of a State's psychiatric witnesses, the risk of an inaccurate resolution of sanity issues is extremely high. With such assistance, the defendant is fairly able to present at least enough information to the jury, in a meaningful manner, as to permit it to make a sensible determination. (p. 82)

Although *Ake,* like *Strickland,* was determined on the basis of a capital murder case, some state courts (such as those in Kentucky, Tennessee, Texas, and Virginia) and legislatures (such as those in Colorado and Florida) have seen fit to extend this guarantee specifically to noncapital matters as well to "ensure a fair, consistent application of the *Ake* rule and further the constitutional principles on which the decision was based" (McGraw, 2001, p. 972). For example, in *Binion v. Commonwealth* (1995), the Supreme Court of Kentucky declared that even in trials in which the death penalty is not at issue,

> there must be an appointment of a psychiatrist to provide assistance to the accused to help evaluate the strength of his defense, to offer his own expert diagnosis at trial, and to identify weaknesses in the prosecution's case by testifying and/or preparing counsel to cross-examine opposing experts. (p. 386)

The U.S. Supreme Court revisited the issue of "reasonable investigations" in the case of *Wiggins v. Smith* (2003), when it held that the defense team's investigation into the defendant's background "did not reflect reasonable professional judgment," given the nature of "evidence counsel uncovered in the social services records—evidence that would have led a reasonably competent attorney to investigate further." The Court stated that "counsel were not in a position to make a reasonable strategic choice as to whether to focus on Wiggins' direct responsibility, the sordid details of his life history, or both, because the investigation supporting their choice was unreasonable," and concluded that "the mitigating evidence counsel failed to discover and present" was so "powerful" that had the jury been allowed to "place his excruciating life history on the mitigating side of the scale, there is a reasonable probability that at least one juror would have struck a different balance" (pp. 534–537).

Reflecting this reasoning, the 9th Circuit Court of Appeals recently ruled in *Stankewitz v. Woodford* (2004) that trial counsel's failure to "take [certain] steps to look into Stankewitz's life history, despite tantalizing indications in the record," fell short of a "duty to investigate what evidence potentially could have been presented" (pp. 719–722). Although the defendant in *Wiggins* had lacked "a record of violent conduct that could have been introduced by the State" (p. 513), the 9th Circuit emphasized in *Stankewitz* that "the presentation of mitigating evidence is vital even where, as here, the aggravating evidence is powerful" (p. 714).

Most recently, the U.S. Supreme Court held in *Rompilla v. Beard* (2005) that despite the state's argument that "defense counsel's efforts to find mitigating evidence by other means" excused his failure to review prior conviction records, "it flouts prudence to deny that a defense lawyer should try to look at a file he knows the prosecution will cull for aggravating evidence" (p. 2467). The Court further noted:

> When new counsel entered the case to raise Rompilla's postconviction claims . . . they identified a number of likely avenues the trial lawyers could fruitfully have followed in building a mitigation case. School records are one example, which trial counsel never examined in spite of the professed unfamiliarity of the several family members with Rompilla's childhood, and despite counsel's knowledge that Rompilla left school after the ninth grade. Other examples are Rompilla's juvenile and adult incarcerations, which counsel did not consult, although they were aware of their client's criminal record. And while counsel knew from police reports provided in pretrial discovery that Rompilla had been drinking heavily at the time of his offense, and although one of the mental health experts reported that Rompilla's troubles with alcohol merited further investigation, counsel did not look for evidence of a history of dependence on alcohol that might have extenuating significance. (p. 2463)

This progression of federal cases, with growing reflection in state-level decisions and statutes (Di Giulio, 1999; McGraw, 2001), begs the following question: Apart from analyzing the aspersions cast by appellate judges upon a review of records going back a decade or more, how is trial counsel to determine what is indeed "reasonable" when it comes to the investigation of forensic mental health evidence?

LEGAL PRACTICE STANDARDS

Predictably, postconviction legal practice emerges from the juxtaposition of two sharply defined and innately opposed perspectives. From a prosecutorial point of view, Kreeger and Weiss (2004) have observed:

> It's a great feeling for a prosecutor to know that another dangerous criminal has been removed from the street, and even better to know that the conviction will stick. [After a conviction], a prosecutor may fear that opposing counsel's performance will be characterized, mistakenly or inaccurately, as "ineffective assistance." Even worse is a fear that an unclear record will not expose the defendant's self-serving misrepresentation of his attorney's work. What can the prosecutor do to prevent such mischaracterization? The shortest answer is to create a comprehensive record that clearly reflects the facts, the available defenses, the subsequent strategies and both attorneys' pretrial and trial conduct. (p. 18)

The defense point of view is expressed differently, in terms of both emphasis and tone. As Mogin (2003) has maintained:

> In the past 3 decades, the courts and Congress have erected significant new barriers in the path of a citizen who seeks to show that he was wrongfully convicted of a crime. They have

drastically curtailed federal *habeas corpus* review of state convictions . . . and the courts have greatly expanded the range of constitutional violations that can be found "harmless." One remedy, however, has remained largely intact—the motion for new trial based on newly discovered evidence. Maybe it's because such motions are seldom granted. Whatever the reason, be thankful for small favors. (p. 26)

In the decade following *Ake,* and in reflection of the tensions and practical considerations that this case and successive appellate decisions engendered (Goldberg & Siegel, 2002; Medwed, 2004; Siegel, 1999), a series of standards and guidelines were promulgated to address the specific requirements for counsel practicing in the postconviction arena.

American Bar Association Criminal Justice Mental Health Standards

In 1989, the American Bar Association (ABA) Criminal Justice Standards Committee published its *ABA Criminal Justice Mental Health Standards,* specifying that "the prosecution should promptly provide to the defense all written reports prepared by mental health and mental health professionals for the prosecution," and "the defense should promptly provide to the prosecution all written reports prepared by any mental health or mental retardation professional whom defendant intends to call as an expert witness on defendant's mental condition at the time of the alleged crime" (§ 7-3.8(b)).

Under the best of circumstances, obtaining such discovery information can be a complex and labor-intensive exercise for prosecutors and defenders alike (Davis, 1997; Hannah, 1994); however,

> denying forensic psychologists who are asked to assist our legal system the necessary information upon which to form their opinions encourages them to ignore their own scientific realities. . . . Our legal system cannot continue to seek the assistance of these experts and deny them and their patients the tools necessary for them to be accurate in their opinions. (Russell, 1996, p. 233)

The failure of trial attorneys to at least seek necessary consultation on such materials, when eventually (and in many cases, inevitably) obtained, may raise the specter of malpractice (Hoffman, 2000) and can hardly, in light of these Standards, be seen as reasonable.

American Bar Association Guidelines for the Appointment and Performance of Defense Counsel in Death Penalty Cases

Also in 1989, the ABA published *Guidelines for the Appointment and Performance of Defense Counsel in Death Penalty Cases,* and subsequently revised them 14 years later (ABA, 2003). The most recent version of these Guidelines were subsequently cited, with favor, by the U.S. Supreme Court as constituting "well-defined norms" for investigations into mitigating evidence (*Wiggins,* 2003, p. 524).

These Guidelines describe a requisite series of steps that clearly implicate forensic mental health input. For example, it is recommended that the defense team include "at least one member qualified by training and experience to screen individuals for the presence of mental or psychological impairments" (ABA, 2003,

p. 1000) and that the defense team also pursue "necessary releases for confidential records relating to any of the relevant histories," which may include "medical records" and "alcohol and drug abuse assessment or treatment records" (p. 1025) a measure seen as particularly important due to the following reasoning:

> Even if the institution that responded to the client was not grossly abusive or neglectful, it may have been incompetent in a number of ways. For example, IQ testing or other psychological evaluations may have been performed by untrained personnel or using inappropriate instruments—flaws that might not appear on the face of the institutional records. (pp. 1025–1026)

The 6th Circuit Court of Appeals recently opined that these Guidelines added "clarity, detail and content" to contemporary applications of the *Strickland* standard by providing "a codification of longstanding, common-sense principles of representation understood by diligent, competent counsel in death penalty cases" (*Hamblin v. Mitchell,* 2003, pp. 486–487). Based on the nature of their initial reception, these Guidelines will likely have a substantial impact on the activities of both lawyers and judges in capital and other postconviction proceedings for years to come (Freedman, 2003).

Performance Guidelines for Criminal Defense Representation

In 1995, the National Legal Aid and Defender Association (NLADA) published *Performance Guidelines for Criminal Defense Representation.* These Performance Guidelines sought to establish "the paramount obligation of criminal defense counsel . . . to provide zealous and quality representation to their clients at all stages of the criminal process" (§ 1.1), and included, among the standards for this representation, a responsibility to "obtain copies of any relevant documents which are available," including "mental health" and "educational" records (§ 2.2). Defense attorneys adhering to these Performance Guidelines are further encouraged to seek "all results or reports of relevant . . . mental examinations, and of scientific tests" (§ 4.2), and to "secure the assistance of experts where it is necessary or appropriate" (§ 4.1).

These Performance Guidelines have garnered favorable references in various federal appellate and trial decisions (*Mojica v. Reno,* 1997; *St. Cyr v. INS,* 2000), and they continue to appear in scholarly and practice-oriented articles addressing the appropriate standards for criminal defense representation (Bernhard, 2002; Monahan & Clark, 1997; Welch, 2004).

SCOPE AND SOURCES OF POSTCONVICTION INQUIRY

Drogin and Barrett (1996b) have opined:

> The difference between the administration of a prescribed series of tests, and the ability to knit results from all sources of data into a responsive, compelling, and ultimately convincing whole before the trier of fact, is the difference between the clinical psychologist who performs an *examination* and the forensic psychologist who conducts an *evaluation.* (p. 14)

Melton, Petrila, Poythress, and Slobogin (1997) have also emphasized the crucial distinction between what they termed "therapeutic assessment" and "forensic assessment," and Heilbrun (2001) has identified 29 foundational principles of forensic mental health assessment, detailing their practical applications to such subspecialties as neuropsychological assessment (Heilbrun et al., 2003) and sexual offender risk assessment (Heilbrun, 2003; Chapter 2). The accessibility as well as prominence of these recommendations in the scientific literature has recently been enhanced by the provision of detailed case examples (Heilbrun, Marczyk, & DeMatteo, 2002; see Heilbrun, Warren, & Picarello, 2003, for a description of the use of third-party information in forensic assessment).

Concerning the discipline of forensic psychiatry, Wettstein (2004) has encouraged psychiatrists to review "previous psychiatric evaluations and treatment, previous psychological testing, medical hospital and office records, academic records, occupational evaluations and employment documents, Social Security disability records, military records, discovery regarding the legal case, and diaries and journals written by the evaluee," with sensitivity to the fact that "attorneys have been known to selectively provide information to their own expert witnesses, either inadvertently or with the intent of manipulating the evaluator" (p. 144). In the most recent edition of their influential *Clinical Handbook of Psychiatry and the Law*, Gutheil and Appelbaum (2000) maintain that "statements of victims, bystanders, arresting officers, and family members must be obtained because the heart of the forensic evaluation is its transcendence of the examinee's unsupported self-report" (p. 294). Reid (2003) has found therapeutic and forensic psychiatric assessment modalities so distinct that he has gone so far as to postulate simply that "nonforensic clinicians should decline forensic referrals" (p. 163).

While acknowledging that "there is no solitary, bottom-line reference which definitively and comprehensively states the necessary components of a competent forensic psychological evaluation and/or report," Drogin and Barrett (1996a) have asserted that "the confluence of data from various sources such as examination, review, interview, research and consultation . . . informs the scientific basis for an expert opinion" (pp. 15–16). Components of each of these data sources are analyzed next in terms of their relevance to postconviction assessment.

Examination

The forensic psychological examination in postconviction assessment consists of three basic components: interview, observation, and—based upon the capabilities of the examinee—psychological testing.

Interview

Notwithstanding the unique insights and critical objectivity afforded by the use of standardized psychological testing, a properly conducted clinical interview is an indispensable component of a competent forensic evaluation (Collins, Lincoln, & Frank, 2002; Kebbell, Milne, & Wagstaff, 1999; Orbach, Hershkowitz, Lamb, Esplin, & Horowitz, 2000). Patience is assuredly a virtue in the context of the postconviction interview, as the examinee has likely been through multiple interviews in the past and may be visibly frustrated and somewhat wary regarding the interviewing process. What information has this person attempted to convey on numerous occasions, only to be diverted into structured or patterned methods of discourse that have failed to identify key aspects of mitigating, exculpatory, or inculpatory evidence (Barnett, Brodsky, & Davis, 2004; Chamberlain, 2004)? Interview at the postconviction phase should focus on what the examinee recalls about the length, nature, tone, and content of prior interviews. Did prior interviewers make a substantial investment of time in their examinations? Did they take a personal history (Fogelson, Nuechterlein, Asarnow, Payne, & Subotnik, 2004; Mason, 2004)? Did they delve into (or stray from) issues germane to the referral question that was provided by a judge or by trial counsel?

Observation

The apparent physical condition and observed nonverbal behaviors of forensic examinees will, in some instances, provide data every bit as relevant to a valid assessment as oral statements and performance on psychological test measures (Pell, 2002; Vrij, Evans, Akehurst, & Mann, 2004). Gait, tremor, eye contact, mode of dress, and other presentation variables have long been recognized as collateral observations to the mental status examination, which remains a standard component of psychiatric and psychological evaluations (Birndorf & Kaye, 2002; Serby, 2003). Postconviction evaluators should determine the extent to which the reports and testimony of other clinicians reflect due attention to observed phenomena. Observation of another kind occurs when, rather than confining the analysis of others' work to written records of prior clinical and courtroom activities, the postconviction evaluator undertakes to view and even to record others' actual examinations. The propriety of such a third-party presence and its alleged effects on examination outcomes have been continuously debated, without resulting in outright proscription or clearly defined negative impact (American Academy of Clinical Neuropsychology, 2001; Binder & Johnson-Greene, 1995; McCaffrey, Fisher, Gold, & Lynch, 1996; McSweeny et al., 1998; National Academy of Neuropsychology Policy and Planning Committee, 2000). Those seeking to sit in on another mental health professional's forensic evaluation may require the support of a court order, the permission of all parties, or both.

Psychological Testing

"Psychological testing may be crucial in linking an individual's mental condition to the functional abilities required by the legal standard in question" (Parry & Drogin, 2000, p. 34). Tests administered in a postconviction context, in which the choice, administration, and interpretation of previously utilized measures are already likely to have been the focus of substantial scrutiny, should possess, to the extent feasible, sound and demonstrable psychometric properties suited to the rigors of a potential challenge to admissibility (Heilbrun, 1992; Medoff, 2003; Mossman, 2003). The scientific literature occasionally reflects intraprofessional controversy over the forensic attributes and applicability of specific assessment measures, for example, the Millon Clinical Multiaxial Inventory (Dyer & McCann,

2000; McCann, 2002; R. Rogers, Salekin, & Sewell, 1999; Schutte, 2001) and, most recently, various measures utilized to gauge an arrestee's competency to confess to alleged criminal activity (Grisso, 2004; R. Rogers, Jordan, & Harrison, 2004). The use of psychological testing may be especially pertinent to death row examinations, where surveys have suggested that severe mental illness and neuropsychological impairment are significantly overrepresented in the capital defendant population (Drogin & Monahan, 2001; Lewis et al., 1988; Lewis, Pincus, Feldman, Jackson, & Bard, 1986).

Review of Records

Postconviction assessment includes the review of a range of potential sources, including prior legal records, school records, treatment records, military records, forensic records, discovery, and work product.

Prior Legal Records

In addition to reviewing all pertinent pretrial and other trial-related legal records during postconviction, the forensic evaluator should determine the extent to which such records were examined by counsel or by a retained mental health expert prior to or during the sentencing phase. This sort of review is not restricted simply to records stemming from the matter currently under consideration. What useful information is contained in records now maintained by courts or by previously retained criminal defense attorneys? Did prior counsel obtain, or attempt to obtain, trial competency, criminal responsibility, or diminished capacity evaluations in response to the defendant's prior charges? If the defendant was the subject of a custody dispute or was a party to a custody dispute concerning his or her own children, what privately commissioned or court-mandated evaluations were performed in that context? The often starkly adversarial nature of such cases (Schepard, 2005) and the court's need to ensure deference to the best interests of the child (Artis, 2004; Leek, Liebert, & Filipelli, 1999) may have resulted in highly detailed and far-ranging mental health evaluations of defendants and victims alike, the results of which may be admissible in postconviction proceedings.

School Records

Not only should school records, if sufficiently preserved, contain academic grades, program placement reviews, and disciplinary files, they are also likely to include reports of counseling sessions, cognitive testing, and even personality assessment (Culross & Nelson, 1997). Although test user qualifications (Turner, DeMers, Fox, & Reed, 2001), supervision requirements (Fischetti & Crespi, 1999), standards for documentation (Merlone, 2005) and adherence to professional ethical guidelines (Knauss, 2001) remain highly variable in educational settings, and although in some situations the lack of even basic legibility can be a problem, school records have distinct advantages in terms of both admissibility (Ford & Nembach, 1992) and objectivity, unless it is the school system itself that may be criminalizing the child's behavior, in flight from a presumed duty to provide federally mandated services (Altshuler & Kopels, 2003; Summers & Semrud-Clikeman, 2001). When it comes to the assessment of malingering, school records may be especially relevant, as the trier of fact is asked to consider just how likely it is that the criminal defendant has been faking a documented disorder, not just recently, but since early childhood (Drogin, 2001).

Treatment Records

Treatment records are created for substantially different purposes and with a substantially different clinical mind-set than are forensic evaluation records, which is one reason some experts have argued that treating and forensic assessment roles, be they simultaneous or consecutive, are incompatible (Greenberg & Shuman, 1997; Shuman, Greenberg, Heilbrun, & Foote, 1998). Although the criminal defendant's psychotherapist is likely to function in some ways as his or her advocate (Sweetwood & Sweetwood, 2001; Tannous, 2000; Wolff & Schlesinger, 2002), this does not, of course, obviate the utility of treatment records as an important source of clinical data, particularly when such records were not developed in contemplation of litigation. A thorough search for treatment records is likely to uncover mental health professionals who, though prevented for the earlier stated reasons from rendering forensic opinions, may nonetheless be featured as informative and persuasive fact witnesses (Dwyer, 2000) concerning the criminal defendant's condition and prognoses during a specified period of time.

Military Records

Military records are among the most difficult to obtain, due to the bureaucratic hurdles that must be overcome by those requesting them and also because "trial and defense counsel accustomed to obtaining information about the accused and witnesses in criminal justice actions from military personnel records jackets will have that ability curtailed as documents are removed" in accordance with cost-cutting and streamlining directives (Garcia, 1995, p. 38). Despite barriers to their availability, military records should invariably be sought when they contemporaneously address mental conditions of relevance to pretrial or postconviction mental status, for example, in cases in which combat-related Posttraumatic Stress Disorder has been alleged (Berthier, Posada, & Puentes, 2001; Mozley, Miller, Weathers, Beckham, & Feldman, 2005). In some cases, military records may be relevant due to a criminal defendant's having been rejected as unfit or marginally fit for duty, either at the time of induction or during the course of military service (Rona, Hyams, & Wessely, 2005).

Forensic Records

The records generated by other forensic examiners are important not only to the extent that they lend themselves to the confirmation or disconfirmation of one's own hypotheses, but also because it is necessary to maintain a sense of substance and boundaries of the broader legal debate into which one's own testimony and reports will be injected. To what extent did the timing of prior forensic psychological assessments lead to unintended and unidentified "practice effects" (Benedict & Zgaljardic, 1998; Bors & Vigneau, 2001; Collie, Maruff, Darby, & McStephen, 2003; Lemay, Bédard, Rouleau, & Tremblay, 2004; Zgaljardic & Benedict, 2001) as a result of the serial administration of cognitive test measures? To what extent did errors in prior test scoring (Allard & Faust, 2000; Charter, Walden, & Padilla, 2000;

Simons, Goddard, & Patton, 2002) result in faulty pretrial forensic conclusions, in turn resulting in challengeable legal rulings? Postconviction counsel should recognize the value in identifying errors by both prosecution and defense experts, as reliance on flawed (and thus unreliable) data by either side may be relevant to the issue of whether a new trial or other relief should be granted (Gilleran-Johnson & Kristopek, 2001).

Discovery

Forensic evaluators may question the value of sifting through several hundreds, perhaps even thousands of pages of pretrial discovery material. The advantages of such admittedly laborious attention to detail, however, are easy to understand when one considers the confluence of several factors: (a) a fuller understanding of the overall nature of the case at issue; (b) the ability to represent in reports, on the witness stand, and in depositions that one reviewed the entire file and not merely those portions identified by counsel as relevant; (c) the opportunity to discover some hitherto unidentified information directly pertinent to the determination of a criminal defendant's mental health status; and (d) the identification of potential witnesses for further interview and investigation. As Roberts (2004) notes, "A defendant might: not know who the witnesses are or where to find them; distrust her lawyer; be incarcerated (and thus unable to lead the attorney to witnesses whose names she does not know); have poor recollection; or suffer from mental health problems" (p. 1139). Whether working for the prosecution or for the defense, the forensic evaluator performs a valuable service, not only by scanning such information, but also, by virtue of his or her availability, constructively prompting counsel to develop it for review.

Work Product

Chief among the concerns related to the psychologist's review of pretrial or postconviction work product—definable as "materials prepared by an attorney in anticipation of trial" (Rothenberg, 1999, p. 825)—is the possibility that reliance by an expert on this material may serve to impair the privilege that prevents its disclosure. Criminal courts are unlikely to call for the revelation of communications between lawyers and their testifying expert witnesses or consultants, absent some showing of "bad faith" (Jebo, 2003) or overtly fraudulent activity; less certain is the extent to which protection will be afforded those documents (e.g., the report of a private investigator retained by counsel) on which the examining expert has admittedly relied in reaching a forensic conclusion. When conducting postconviction assessments, forensic mental health evaluators should reach a preliminary understanding with counsel concerning the potential ramifications of reviewing materials not found in the traditionally construed discovery file. Sometimes, of course, it is actually the most clearly definable of work product documents that an attorney wishes the examiner to review, such as when it is trial counsel's own internal memoranda that memorialize the reasoning behind questionable decisions to seek (or not to seek) a pretrial mental health evaluation, despite the presence of evidence clearly (with hindsight) dictating a contrary approach.

Interviews of Others

Postconviction assessment is likely to involve interviews that range beyond the individual seeking relief to include a host of other persons, including teachers, family, friends, police, jailers, and witnesses.

Teachers

Teachers often serve as virtual surrogate parents for criminal defendants, particularly for those whose abuse histories may play a crucial role in the development of evidence at the postconviction level (Hughes, Cavell, & Willson, 2001; Muller, 2001). The fact that a child made such an impression on a teacher that he or she is able to recall that child with clarity, even decades later, may lend particular weight to testimony from that source during the sentencing phase of a criminal trial. Teacher recollections may also be the most important source—indeed, the only source—of information concerning a criminal defendant's academic struggles and achievements in those situations in which school records are not accessible (Stake, 2002).

Family

Families are a rich source of interview data regarding the criminal defendant over the course of his or her entire life. Developmental milestones, childhood injuries and diseases, sibling relationships, family histories for both genetically and environmentally influenced medical and psychological conditions may all be accessible via family interview with a breadth and depth unattainable in any other context (Wackerbarth, Streams, & Smith, 2002). Family members often maintain diaries that may serve as a particularly compelling form of evidence concerning mitigation or mental health defenses, and may be encouraged to use diary methods as a tool to develop retrospective insight into additional relevant issues (Laurenceau & Bolger, 2005).

Friends

A criminal defendant's adolescent and adult peer relationships can lend insight into his or her inclinations, preferences, emotional needs, and stated desires during periods other than the date on which a crime is alleged to have occurred (Burk & Laursen, 2005; Oswald, Clark, & Kelly, 2004), offering a fuller picture than that afforded by crime scene witness statements. The enlistment of friends will often provide incentive and opportunity for a criminal defendant to recall and share details and perspectives that might otherwise be absent from the pool of potentially mitigating information. Psychobiographical information of this nature may prove particularly important at each level of criminal proceedings (Connell, 2003).

Police

The arresting or interrogating police officer is often a highly experienced observer of human behavior, and though subject like others to the interfering effects of stress on recall (Stanny & Johnson, 2000), he or she may be responsible for the most critical and detailed documentation of a criminal defendant's statements and behaviors on the date in question. To what extent has this information been reviewed by the examining forensic expert during either pretrial or postconviction proceedings? In addition, police officer recollections may extend well beyond those data preserved in the police reports and interview transcripts found in standard discovery materials, although issues of confirmatory bias must naturally be taken into account when assessing the validity of subsequently obtained statements (M. F. Davies, 2003).

Jailers

Once the arresting or interrogating police officer has performed his or her duties, a criminal defendant's closest and most meaningful personal contacts, for months or even years before or after a trial, may be with jail or prison personnel: the persons responsible for feeding, clothing, disciplining, and medicating inmates and, in some cases, keeping them alive (Blaauw, Arensman, Kraaij, Winkel, & Bout, 2002; Blaauw, Kerkhof, & Hayes, 2005; Cox, 2003; Daigle, 2004). Correctional employees often maintain detailed records regarding symptoms of chronic mental illness, whether the purpose of this documentation is to evade long-term responsibility for psychotic or otherwise problematic inmates (Lamberg, 2004), to comply with externally imposed detection standards (McLearen & Ryba, 2003), or to gauge the need for community treatment services upon release (McCoy, Roberts, Hanrahan, Clay, & Luchins, 2004). Such materials may not make their way into a criminal defendant's discovery file without a specific request from counsel. In addition to records, the individual reminiscences of jail personnel can amount to highly persuasive evidence regarding mental disability, particularly as these individuals are not automatically identified with one side of the criminal justice system as opposed to the other (American Association for Correctional Psychology, 2000).

Witnesses

The process of investigating and supplementing witness statements is complicated by the need to avoid any inference that such contacts amount to intimidation (P. Rogers, 2003; Studnicki & Apol, 2002). Although obtaining additional comments that illuminate and expand on previous (or future) testimony may uncover new evidence (Jaworsky, 2003), it may also run the risk of eliciting inconsistent statements that may complicate or even nullify the participation of a lay witness during postconviction proceedings (Saltzburg, 2004). Although the role of the forensic examiner is one of studied neutrality (Gutheil & Simon, 2004), permission should be sought from counsel or the courts before undertaking to question witnesses, particularly those who may still have an active role to play in the case at hand. Once access has been secured, it is clear that those actually witnessing the events in question may possess critically important recollections and insight into a criminal defendant's state of mind at a given point in time, mediated by the circumstances of observation, the passage of time, and other factors (G. Davies & Alonso-Quecuty, 1997; Granhag, 1997; Schreiber & Parker, 2004).

Research

Supplemental research in postconviction assessment will frequently include a review of statutes, case law, rules, regulations, texts, articles, and ethical codes.

Statutes

Not only will the postconviction evaluator want to possess a thorough understanding of the statutory scheme defining the legal issues relevant to the case at hand, but he or she will also want to determine the extent to which prior examiners cited such statutes, interpreted them correctly, and applied clinical and forensic findings to them appropriately. It may be that a statute on which a prior examiner relied has now been superseded, opening up old data to new interpretations. Cases that were once determined on the basis of state statutes may now have become federal, or vice versa. Statutes pertaining to a specific criminal charge may no longer be relevant now that a different criminal charge, with a different requirement mental state (Barrat & Felthous, 2003; Carson & Felthous, 2003; Merikangas, 2004), perhaps a "lesser included offense," that counsel now argues was erroneously removed from the jury's consideration, is the focus of postconviction inquiry.

Case Law

The postconviction evaluator's concerns regarding case law are similar to those regarding statutory law, but with two additional elements. The first of these is a need to become familiar with published and unpublished cases pertaining to the current examinee, both at the trial level and as a result of any appeals that have been taken and decided in the interim. The second of these is a need to become familiar with published and unpublished cases pertaining to the current examiner, as well as to other examiners whose prior work may become the focus of postconviction proceedings. Both counsel and the postconviction evaluator need to be aware of the extent to which (a) reputations, (b) previously endorsed or rejected mental health theories from particular sources, and (c) particular judges' stated perspectives and attitudes (Aruguete & Robinson, 2004; Slovenko, 2002; Wild et al., 2001) may influence the future course of the legal matters under review. This confluence of circumstances may inspire counsel to hire a different examiner, based on considerations that, for the benefit of both of these professionals, should surface sooner rather than later.

Rules and Regulations

Statutes and case law provide foundational legal guidance, but the devil often resides in the details of state, local, and particular rules and regulations. These are often comparatively inaccessible to experts who lack access to proprietary legal search engines or local contacts. As such, counsel should be contacted early in the course of postconviction proceedings to identify and procure the necessary materials. Rules and regulations play a central role, for example, in qualifying the postconviction expert to evaluate or testify at all. Drogin (1999) provided the following guidance to counsel seeking forensic mental health assistance at all levels of criminal proceedings:

(1) Review the statutory and regulatory language for your particular state before dispatching your expert to perform an evaluation. These rules change frequently, are open to variable interpretation, and may contain "exceptions within exceptions" relevant to the particular psychologist you have employed.

(2) Consult with your state's psychology board before assuming that you have understood the language you have reviewed. The board—made up of volunteer psychologists, not attorneys—may have a different interpretation of the law than you do. This interpretation is important since the board makes any decisions regarding, for example, the temporary admission of your expert to practice.

(3) Ask if the board adheres to any internal rules in processing such cases, which may or may not be committed to writing. The present author, when obtaining licensure and certification in other states, has encountered customary, often unrecorded board practices, which can make this process infinitely less complicated. (pp. 769–770)

Postconviction expertise is increasingly likely to be sought across state lines, as the local pool of experts may be depleted due to conflicts of interest and as forensic practice becomes increasingly specialized. Related mobility issues have received correspondingly greater attention in the forensic practice literature in recent years (Shuman, Cunningham, Connell, & Reid, 2003; Simon & Shuman, 1999; Tucillo, DeFilippis, Denney, & Dsurney, 2002).

Texts and Articles

The extent to which forensic evaluators cite textual authority for their written assertions is highly variable and remains essentially a matter of report-writing style, as long as they are willing and able to conjure up such sources when asked to do so during depositions or on direct and cross-examination. Postconviction evaluators will naturally want to ensure that their own scientific references are as contemporary and well-supported as possible and should be willing to seek out and review copies of any materials on which prior examiners have stated reliance. Are such references research-based, relevant, up-to-date, case-specific, accurately cited, faithfully interpreted, and correctly applied? The peer-reviewed status of texts and articles will often become a factor during challenges to admissibility (Cooperstein, 1998; Johnson-Greene & Bechtold, 2002).

Ethical Codes

Not only must the forensic contributions of postconviction and prior examiners pass clinical muster, they must also comport with relevant ethical codes and guidelines of their respective professions (Brodsky & Galloway, 2003; Reid, 2002; Wettstein, 2004). This form of forensic work requires access not only to current iterations of these sources, but to prior versions as well, as the mental health assessments being reviewed may span decades and the applicable ethical standard will be the one in effect at the time that preceding services were performed and their results conveyed. The expert may find it appropriate to recommend to counsel that a consultant be retained to determine whether specific individuals ran afoul of ethics committees or licensing boards (Peterson, 2001; Schoenfeld, Hatch, & Gonzalez, 2001; Williams, 2001) at some relevant juncture in the past. It is also advisable to offer a full and detailed description to counsel of the postconviction evaluator's own negative history in this regard, as such information will be infinitely more damaging when it surfaces in the context of depositions or during a hearing or trial.

Consultation

Postconviction assessment will often extend beyond one's own direct inquiries and research, to include consultation with attorneys, investigators, and other colleagues.

Attorneys

> Functioning within a system inured to spending hundreds of dollars an hour on specialized mental health expertise, many criminal defense attorneys adopt a deferential, even disingenuous manner when compelled to comment on the behavior of their own clients: "What do I know? I'm not a psychologist!" For expert witnesses to wish they had a dollar for every time they heard this would be to ignore the fact that, of course, they already do. Many dollars. . . . What is frequently overlooked in such cases is that the defense team already has considerable expertise at its disposal. Attorneys, investigators, and other staff persons have their own varied life experiences on which to draw. In addition, in a somewhat different way from their mental health colleagues, they are themselves students (and, in the courtroom, teachers) of human nature, whose stock in trade already consists of identifying, explaining, and normalizing the behavior of persons from every walk of life. (Drogin, 2000a, p. 27)

Trial or postconviction counsel may go out of his or her way to avoid somehow biasing the forensic expert, yet psychologists should accept the attorney's advocacy role for what it is, rely on their own abilities to separate factual disclosure from legal argument, and take advantage of the opportunity to learn (a) counsel's theory of the case, (b) what other theories have been posited and arguably discredited, and (c) what information counsel possesses about the examinee that has not surfaced during the investigation of other sources. Counsel will also be an important source of guidance concerning a local court's perspective on various theories of mental health defenses and mitigation. This will not, of course, color the expert's clinical and forensic findings, but he or she will often find it useful to know which notions may require additional research support and practical explanation in a given forum.

Investigators

As noted earlier, consultation with investigators may raise certain work product privilege issues; however, once such considerations have been addressed to the satisfaction of all parties, experts often find that the investigators are a rich source of data concerning examinees and about the identities, backgrounds, statements, opinions, and attitudes of witnesses, friends, and family members (Schroeder, 2003). Interviewees may have disclosed information to an investigator retained by counsel that they would be reluctant or unwilling to share with a mental health professional. At times, the intercession of a trusted investigator may be necessary to facilitate contact by a psychologist. Interviewees may also have forgotten, or recently failed to recall, information disclosed during an investigation that occurred months or years earlier (M. C. Anderson & Bell, 2001; Tekcan & Akturk, 2001).

Colleagues

Peer, case, or collegial consultation is an established and often necessary exercise in support of the provision of accurate and up-to-date clinical and forensic services

(Markus et al., 2003; Powell, 1996). Professional colleagues may have had recent experience with similar cases, in similar venues, with similar types of examinees. They may have recently reviewed the scientific literature on obscure forensic topics, weeding out studies that are poorly conveyed or lacking support. They may have access to newer or more specialized clinical and forensic assessment instruments, as well as familiarity with alternative scales and scoring systems optimally suited to the legal issues at hand (Lally, 2003). They may also have had direct prior treatment or assessment contact with examinees, witnesses, friends, and family members (raising ethical issues of confidentiality and privilege addressed in the next section of this chapter), or they may know or have knowledge of the mental health professionals who have provided services to such persons. Consultation with professional colleagues should not be confused with enlisting them as coevaluators or as psychometrists, and postconviction counsel should be apprised when the nature of consultation begins to resemble collaboration.

ETHICAL CONSIDERATIONS IN POSTCONVICTION ASSESSMENT

Similar to other modes of forensic psychological service provision, postconviction assessment involves careful attention to ethical considerations that attach to peer consultation, partisanship, obtaining data, and reporting obligations.

Peer Consultation

The peer consultation function just described is governed by ethical provisions that speak directly to this activity. Standard 4.01 ("Maintaining Confidentiality") of the *Ethical Principles of Psychologists and Code of Conduct* (American Psychological Association [APA], 2002) states that psychologists have a "primary obligation . . . to protect confidential information" (p. 1066). Principle B ("Fidelity and Responsibility") acknowledges that psychologists "consult with, refer to, or cooperate with other professionals to the extent needed to serve the best interests of those with whom they work" (p. 1062), and Standard 4.05 ("Disclosures") allows for some potential latitude regarding confidentiality when seeking to "obtain appropriate professional consultations" (p. 1066). However, Standard 4.06 ("Consultations") specifies:

> When consulting with colleagues, (1) psychologists do not disclose confidential information that reasonably could lead to the identification of a client/patient, research participant, or other person or organization with whom they have a confidential relationship unless they have obtained the prior consent of the person or organization or the disclosure cannot be avoided, and (2) they disclose information only to the extent necessary to achieve the purposes of the consultation. (p. 1066)

Therefore, the transfer of test protocols for rescoring, provision of hypothetical demographic and offense details, and conveyance of other relevant information must be achieved in a manner that does not serve to expose the examinee's identity. In cases of sufficient notoriety, this will likely require seeking peer consultation from colleagues in another jurisdiction.

Partisanship

It is an inescapable aspect of postconviction practice that one is hired by counsel with the achievement of a particular legal result in mind and that, as described repeatedly earlier, one will encounter others' clinical and forensic work with an obligation to offer criticism where appropriate. It is also true, however, that one has an obligation to refrain from unwarranted criticism and to acknowledge competency when appropriate, irrespective of whether counsel decides to bring the results of this determination into the adversarial forum and irrespective of whatever pleading or inducements counsel may see fit to offer. According to Principle A ("Beneficence and Nonmaleficence") of the Ethical Principles, psychologists "are alert to and guard against . . . factors that might lead to misuse of their influence" (APA, 2002, p. 1062).

The "Specialty Guidelines for Forensic Psychologists" (Committee on Ethical Guidelines for Forensic Psychologists, 1991) address partisanship-related issues in a number of instances. According to Guideline VI ("Methods and Procedures"), "The forensic psychologist maintains professional integrity by examining the issue at hand from all reasonable perspectives, actively seeking information that will differentially test rival hypotheses" (p. 661). According to Guideline VII ("Public and Professional Communications"), "When evaluating or commenting upon the professional work product or qualifications of another expert or party to a legal proceeding, forensic psychologists represent their professional disagreements with reference to a fair and accurate evaluation of the data, theories, standards, and opinions of the other expert or party"; furthermore, "forensic psychologists do not, by either commission or omission, participate in a misrepresentation of their evidence, nor do they participate in partisan attempts to avoid, deny, or subvert the presentation of evidence contrary to their own position" (p. 664).

Therefore, though it may be appropriate for the postconviction evaluator to develop and proffer opinions distinctly critical of others' professional performance, such opinions must be objectively derived as well as fairly represented. This ethical obligation should be explained to counsel at the point of retention. This disclosure may help avoid misunderstandings that may emanate, at least in part, from the attorney's prior experiences and expectations in procuring second-look evaluations conducted by members of other health professions.

Obtaining Data

The most recent version of the APA's (2002) Ethical Principles represents a significant departure from earlier incarnations in the distinction it now draws between "test data" (Standard 9.04, "Release of Test Data") and "test materials" (Standard 9.11, "Maintaining Test Security"). The result is that, according to Standard 9.04, "pursuant to a client/patient release, psychologists provide test data to the client/patient or other persons identified in the release" (p. 1071). One result of this change may be that counsel need no longer (a) disclose the retention of a potentially testifying postconviction evaluator in order to "ask the court to allow delivery of secure material only to psychologists or other professionals who are bound by the same duty to protect them" (APA, 1999, p. 1078) or (b) risk what counsel may see as premature disclosure of mental health information to the judge by agreeing that

the data in question be sent to "another appropriately qualified psychologist designated by the court" (Committee on Legal Issues, 1996, p. 247). Irrespective of the
possibility that copyrighted or otherwise proprietary testing documents may have
been directed to the postconviction expert through counsel's hands, an obligation
still remains pursuant to Standard 9.11 to "make reasonable efforts to maintain the
integrity and security of test materials and other assessment techniques consistent
with law and contractual obligations" (APA, 2002, p. 1072).

Reporting Obligations

The review function of postconviction assessment will frequently turn up collegial
shortcomings that range from clearly inadvertent typographical errors to outright
fraud. Discoveries occupying the latter end of the spectrum would appear to trigger
some manner of reporting obligation, the nature and scope of which remain unclear.
According to Standard 1.05 ("Reporting Ethical Violations") of the Ethical Principles, the guidance offered for proceeding under circumstances that involve "substantial harm" or that are otherwise "not appropriate for informal resolution" does
not apply "when psychologists have been retained to review the work of another
psychologist whose professional conduct is in question" (APA, 2002, p. 1063). Determining just when and in what context this question arose will be critical to fashioning the appropriate intervention, or lack thereof.

Brodsky and McKinzey (2002) framed the broader issue as follows:

> But what to do when a clinical or forensic colleague seems to need correction? Consider
> this real example: After reviewing another's work, a psychologist discovered that the other
> psychologist was apparently falsely claiming a modestly important credential. When the
> issue was raised with colleagues, a debate followed about the proper action to take. Notify-
> ing the appropriate licensing board seemed draconian. Filing an ethical complaint was dis-
> missed as excessive given that other credentials related to the work were in order. Besides,
> the ethical code mandates that the apparently offending psychologist be personally con-
> fronted first. The manner such a confrontation could take was also debated, but no method
> met with wide approval. (p. 307)

Child custody and personal injury evaluators have long been accustomed to aggrieved parties proceeding against them *in terrorem,* in the very midst of legal proceedings, with threats or actual filings of ethics committee and licensing board
complaints (Glassman, 1998; Kirkland & Kirkland, 2001; Sweet, 2003). No clear
track record exists for such behavior in the criminal practice arena. The restrained
approach espoused by Brodsky and McKinzey (2002) appears prudent, at least
for the duration of postconviction proceedings, so that the court is not distracted
from the clinical and forensic contributions of the mental health professionals involved to the detriment of the legal process and the parties thereto. Even without the
specter of conflicts of interest, psychologists in some jurisdictions are likely to receive conflicting guidance from statutes, regulations, and ethical codes haphazardly
incorporated by reference (Drogin & Howard, 2001; for a review of other ethical issues and conflicts inherent in the practice of forensic psychology, see Chapter 7).

SPECIALIZED APPLICATIONS

Postconviction assessment may address several distinct issues within criminal proceedings, including criminal responsibility, competency to stand trial, prison programming, parole board review, release of insanity acquittees, competency to
confess, and competency to be executed.

Criminal Responsibility

The evaluation of criminal responsibility during any phase of legal proceedings is
complicated by the passage of time between the defendant's relevant alleged behavior and the point at which an examination has been authorized, scheduled, and then
performed (Giorgi-Guarnieri et al., 2002). For the postconviction evaluator, of
course, this task becomes even more complicated, given the additional time that has
passed since trial, conviction, sentencing, incarceration, and appeal. One advantage
is the likelihood of obtaining institutional records (Carter, 1998; Lamb & Weinberger, 1998) that, if nothing else, reflect a symptom course that either does or does
not support the existence of certain forms of chronic mental illness. Even when
such records are minimally illuminating or unavailable, the postconviction evaluator is presented with the chance to observe whether a qualifying mental condition,
if arguably present at the relevant time in the past, is manifesting itself in a fashion
appropriate to the evaluee's current age and developmental status (Friedman et al.,
2001; Kurtz, 2005).

Competency to Stand Trial

Retrospective postconviction assessments of trial competency are subject to the
same temporal hurdles that complicate evaluations of criminal responsibility at any
point during litigation. As the U.S. Supreme Court commented in *Drope v. Missouri*
(1975), when directing a remand some 6 years after trial:

> The question remains whether petitioner's due process rights would be adequately protected
> by remanding the case now for a psychiatric examination aimed at establishing whether pe-
> titioner was in fact competent to stand trial in 1969. Given the inherent difficulties of such
> an [attenuated] determination under the most favorable circumstances, we cannot conclude
> that such a procedure would be adequate here. The State is free to retry petitioner, assum-
> ing, of course, that at the time of such trial he is competent to be tried. (p. 183)

Postconviction evaluators cannot always count on the courts to recognize the
practical obstacles to determining whether a criminal defendant was competent to
stand trial at a particular point in the past. Invaluable under such circumstances, in
deference to the privilege-related concerns raised by such potential evidence,
would be access to writings generated by the defendant prior to or during trial and
notes taken by counsel concerning the defendant's statements and behavior during
that same period, in addition to trial transcripts, trial audiotapes and videotapes,
and the sworn affidavits of persons actually present and interacting with or observing the defendant during the trial period.

Prison Programming

In the case of *Pennsylvania Department of Corrections v. Yeskey* (1998), the U.S. Supreme Court held that a criminal defendant, who was denied access on the basis of his treatable medical condition to a prison "boot camp" program, the successful completion of which would have ensured his early release, had thus been subjected to undue discrimination in violation of the Americans with Disabilities Act (1990). Apart from the impact that *Yeskey* and its state progeny have had on traditional sentencing evaluations (Cockram, 2005; Metzner, 1998), there exists a postconviction context for such considerations. It may be that a criminal defendant, deemed to have been noncompliant with sexual offender, anger management, or other prison programs, is found instead to have been incapable of valid participation due to (a) poor reading ability, (b) deficient oral vocabulary, or (c) a psychiatric condition that interfered substantially with the ability to work effectively with group peers or program staff. The postconviction evaluator investigating such issues will benefit, when such data are available, from a review of curricula and course materials, as well as the opportunity to gauge a particular defendant's potential to achieve relevant and requisite mastery in the prison environment.

Parole Board Review

Parole is not a right under constitutional law (Palmer, 1999, § 9.2), thus obviating the need for funding of postconviction assessments informing parole eligibility. However, mental health professionals are often drawn into such proceedings, particularly in cases in which private compensation is made available. It is clear that forensic mental health experts have much to offer concerning the parole board's deliberations (Cassel, 2003), which so often focus on substance abuse relapse (Zanis et al., 2003), sexual offense relapse (McGrath, Cumming, & Holt, 2002), amenability to supervision (Seiter & West, 2003), availability and efficacy of family support (Gavazzi, Yarcheck, Rhine, & Partridge, 2003), societal reintegration (Jones, 2004), and, of course, standard notions of risk and dangerousness (Gagliardi, Lovell, Peterson, & Jemelka, 2004; Tidmarsh, 1997).

The postconviction assessment standing the greatest chance of constituting an effective contribution to parole board proceedings is one that results from a thorough review of those materials that the board itself is likely to have examined, including institutional disciplinary and treatment records, prerelease reports, and, in some cases, pretrial discovery documents and trial transcripts. Furthermore, the postconviction evaluator would do well to discern and anticipate those issues that a particular board has previously found relevant to determining the suitability of persons (who, ideally, were convicted of similar crimes) for release. If an inmate has been rejected for parole on a prior occasion, reviewing the stated reasons for that rejection may be of value in assessing the petitioner's relevant progress during a period of additional confinement.

Release of Insanity Acquittees

The forensic literature is rife with articles addressing the treatment (Heilbrun, Lawson, Spier, & Libby, 1994; Young, Frierson, Dwyer, & Shah, 2002) and disposition (Nwokike, 2005; Patterson & Wise, 1998) of insanity acquittees. The practical difference between postconviction assessments conducted in this context, as opposed to that of parole board reviews, is twofold. First, there is a greater likelihood of adequate funding, given the state's constitutionally mandated burden of proving, on the basis of clear and convincing evidence, that ongoing dangerousness is present and constitutes a ground for an insanity acquittee's continued confinement (Appelbaum, 1993; *Foucha v. Louisiana,* 1992). Second, the potential release of insanity acquittees will typically be addressed in a more traditional courtroom setting, with the predictability afforded by the presence of usual procedural safeguards. Although a fact finder's (and the community's) perceptions are likely to be colored by the criminal nature of the conduct that precipitated the evaluee's commitment in the first place (Miller, 2002), the general process of evaluation will be substantially similar to that involved in the civil commitment process (as described in Chapter 10).

Competency to Confess

According to Oberlander, Goldstein, and Goldstein (2003):

> A confession serves as a strong source of evidence against a defendant in a criminal trial. Once offered into evidence, it is extremely difficult for defense counsel to overcome the impact a defendant's inculpatory statements might have on a judge or jury. If left unchallenged, the defendant's confession is highly influential on the trial's outcome. In many cases, a confession serves as the single most influential factor in leading the trier of fact to reject the attorney's defense strategy and render a verdict of guilty. Sometimes, impairments in the defendant's functioning compromise the defendant's abilities relevant to the confession process. (p. 335)

Postconviction evaluators sometimes determine that pretrial efforts to determine confession competency (a) were not conducted, (b) lacked the application of standardized psychological testing, (c) were not geared specifically to the text of the written form or verbal inquiry used to elicit a confession, (d) were not geared specifically to the wording of the statement in question, or (e) were not supplemented by a review of existing and available audio- or videotaped evidence (Brinded, 1998; Kassin, 2005; Lassiter, Munhall, Geers, Weiland, & Handley, 2001). Probing such issues at the postconviction stage, evaluators will need to determine not only whether certain clinical forensic assessment was performed, but also the extent to which the examinee's exposure to that process and to the criminal justice system, in general, may have affected his or her competency during the intervening period.

Competency to Be Executed

In *Ford v. Wainwright* (1986), the U.S. Supreme Court held that "the Eighth Amendment prohibits the State from inflicting the penalty of death upon a prisoner who is insane" (p. 409) and defined a person so afflicted as "one whose mental illness prevents him from comprehending the reasons for the penalty or its implications" (p. 417). The Court later held in *Atkins v. Virginia* (2002) that "the large number of States prohibiting the execution of mentally retarded persons (and the complete absence of legislation reinstating such executions) provides powerful evidence that today society views mentally retarded offenders as categorically less culpable than the average criminal" (p. 304), further maintaining that "the reduced capacity of mentally retarded offenders provides a second justification for a categorical rule making such offenders ineligible for the death penalty" (p. 320).

In such cases, the postconviction evaluator is unhampered by many of the temporal considerations that complicate other forms of assessment performed subsequent to the rendering of sentence. The review of others' prior contributions may still be a factor in the relevant exploration of etiology (Ackerson, Brodsky, & Zapf, 2005; S. D. Smith & Morris, 2005), but what matters most in determining competency to be executed is how the evaluee is functioning currently or will be functioning in the foreseeable future.

Concerning evaluations of competency to be executed in light of *Ford* criteria, Zapf, Boccaccini, and Brodsky (2002) have developed the Interview Checklist for Evaluations of Competency for Execution, with annotations concerning "specific areas of inquiry," including "understanding of the reasons for punishment," "understanding of the punishment," "ability to appreciate and reason in addition to simple factual understanding," and "ability to assist attorney" (pp. 117–120). Given the likelihood that current or potential effects of psychotropic medication may play a role in these cases (Zonana, 2003), the postconviction evaluator may wish to procure psychiatric consultation where indicated.

Specific evaluation standards have been slower to emerge in response to the need for protocols addressing *Atkins* execution competency criteria (Watt & MacLean, 2003), given the recency of that decision and the fact that clinical and state statutory definitions of mental retardation may vary significantly (Bonnie, 2004; Scott & Gerbasi, 2003). A competent postconviction assessment of this nature will proceed in consideration of every definition of mental retardation that counsel and the evaluator have determined is likely to be considered.

CONCLUSION

Postconviction assessment provides forensic psychologists with an opportunity to enhance the validity and effectiveness of the entire spectrum of pretrial, trial, and appellate mental health interventions, while supporting the criminal justice system's attempt to identify systemic failures that may merit the revisitation of such critical issues as culpability, competency, and disposition. Such services may be solicited and applied with equal legitimacy and effectiveness by prosecutors and defense counsel alike. All parties benefit when the products of forensic assessment are subjected to an objective, honest, and searching review.

REFERENCES

Ackerson, K. S., Brodsky, S. L., & Zapf, P. A. (2005). Judges' and psychologists' assessments of legal and clinical factors in competence for execution. *Psychology, Public Policy, and Law, 11,* 164–193.

Ake v. Oklahoma, 470 U.S. 68 (1985).

Allard, G., & Faust, D. (2000). Errors in scoring objective personality tests. *Assessment, 7,* 119–129.

Altshuler, S. J., & Kopels, S. (2003). Advocating in schools for children with disabilities: What's new with IDEA? *Social Work, 48,* 320–329.

American Academy of Clinical Neuropsychology. (2001). Policy statement on the presence of third party observers in neuropsychological assessments. *Clinical Neuropsychologist, 14,* 433–439.

American Association for Correctional Psychology. (2000). Standards for psychology services in jails, prisons, correctional facilities, and agencies. *Criminal Justice and Behavior, 27,* 433–494.

American Bar Association. (1989). *ABA guidelines for the appointment and performance of defense counsel in death penalty cases.* Washington, DC: Author.

American Bar Association. (2003). ABA guidelines for the appointment and performance of counsel in death penalty cases (revised edition). *Hofstra Law Review, 31,* 913–1090.

American Bar Association Criminal Justice Standards Committee. (1989). *ABA criminal justice mental health standards.* Washington, DC: American Bar Association.

American Psychological Association. (1999). Test security: Protecting the integrity of tests. *American Psychologist, 54,* 1078.

American Psychological Association. (2002). Ethical principles of psychologists and code of conduct. *American Psychologist, 57,* 1060–1073.

Americans with Disabilties Act, 42 U.S.C. § 12101 *et seq.* (1990).

Anderson, D. A. (1999). The aggregate burden of crime. *Journal of Law and Economics, 42,* 611–630.

Anderson, M. C., & Bell, T. (2001). Forgetting our facts: The role of inhibitory processes in the loss of propositional knowledge. *Journal of Experimental Psychology: General, 130,* 544–570.

Appelbaum, P. S. (1993). *Foucha v. Louisiana:* When must the state release insanity acquittees? *Hospital and Community Psychiatry, 44,* 9–10.

Artis, J. E. (2004). Judging the best interests of the child: Judges' accounts of the tender years doctrine. *Law and Society Review, 38,* 769–806.

Aruguete, M. S., & Robinson, R. L. (2004). Attitudes toward sentencing guidelines and simulated sentencing among Missouri circuit court judges. *American Journal of Criminal Justice, 28,* 201–213.

Atkins v. Virginia, 536 U.S. 304 (2002).

Barnett, M. E., Brodsky, S. L., & Davis, C. M. (2004). When mitigation evidence makes a difference: Effects of psychological mitigating evidence on sentencing decisions in capital trials. *Behavioral Sciences and the Law, 22,* 751–770.

Barrat, E. S., & Felthous, A. R. (2003). Impulsive versus premeditated aggression: Implications for mens rea decisions. *Behavioral Sciences and the Law, 21,* 619–630.

Bartle, H. (2002). One bite at the apple: The effect of recharacterization on post-conviction relief under 28 U.S.C. § 2255. *Temple Law Review, 75,* 613–633.

Benedict, R. H., & Zgaljardic, D. J. (1998). Practice effects during repeated administrations of memory tests with and without alternative forms. *Journal of Clinical and Experimental Neuropsychology, 20,* 339–352.

Bernhard, A. (2002). Take courage: What the courts can do to improve the delivery of criminal defense services. *University of Pittsburgh Law Review, 63,* 293–346.

Berthier, M. L., Posada, A., & Puentes, C. (2001). Dissociative flashbacks after right frontal injury in a Vietnam veteran with combat-related posttraumatic stress disorder. *Journal of Neuropsychiatry and Clinical Neurosciences, 13,* 101–105.

Binder, L., & Johnson-Greene, D. (1995). Observer effects on neuropsychological performance: A case report. *Clinical Neuropsychologist, 9,* 74–78.

Binion v. Commonwealth, 891 S.W.2d 383 (Ky. 1995).

Birndorf, C. A., & Kaye, M. E. (2002). Teaching the mental status examination to medical students by using a standardized patient in a large group setting. *Academic Psychiatry, 26,* 180–183.

Blaauw, E., Arensman, E., Kraaij, V., Winkel, F. W., & Bout, R. (2002). Traumatic life events and suicide risk among jail inmates: The influence of types of events, time period and significant others. *Journal of Traumatic Stress, 15,* 9–16.

Blaauw, E., Kerkhof, J. F., & Hayes, L. M. (2005). Demographic, criminal, and psychiatric factors related to inmate suicide. *Suicide and Life-Threatening Behavior, 35,* 63–75.

Blume, J. H., & Voisin, D. P. (1996). An introduction to federal habeas corpus practice and procedure. *South Carolina Law Review, 47,* 271–304.

Bodenhausen, G. V. (1990). Second-guessing the jury: Stereotypic and hindsight biases in perceptions of court cases. *Journal of Applied Social Psychology, 20,* 1112–1121.

Bonnie, R. J. (2004). The American Psychiatric Association's resource document on mental retardation and capital sentencing: Implementing *Atkins v. Virginia. Journal of the American Academy of Psychiatry and the Law, 32,* 304–308.

Bors, D. A., & Vigneau, F. (2001). The effect of practice on Raven's Advanced Progressive Matrices. *Learning and Individual Differences, 13,* 291–312.

Brinded, P. M. (1998). A case of acquittal following confession in a police videotaped interview. *Psychiatry, Psychology, and Law, 5,* 133–138.

Brodsky, S. L., & Galloway, V. A. (2003). Ethical and professional demands for forensic mental health professionals in the post-Atkins era. *Ethics and Behavior, 13,* 3–9.

Brodsky, S. L., & McKinzey, R. K. (2002). The ethical confrontation of the unethical forensic colleague. *Professional Psychology: Research and Practice, 33,* 307–309.

Burk, W. J., & Laursen, B. (2005). Adolescent perceptions of friendship and their associations with individual adjustment. *International Journal of Behavioral Development, 29,* 156–164.

Carrington, P. D. (1969). Crowded dockets and the courts of appeals: The threat to the function of review and the national law. *Harvard Law Review, 82,* 542–617.

Carson, D. C., & Felthous, A. R. (2003). Introduction to this issue: Mens rea. *Behavioral Sciences and the Law, 21,* 559–562.

Carter, J. H. (1998). Treating the severely mentally ill in prisons and jails. *Forensic Examiner, 7,* 28–29.

Cassel, R. N. (2003). First, second, and third force psychology serve as the only scientific means for determining parole readiness and prison reform. *Journal of Instructional Psychology, 30,* 144–155.

Chamberlain, J. R. (2004). The use of a psychiatric expert who might offer both damaging and mitigating testimony does not constitute ineffective assistance of counsel. *Journal of the American Academy of Psychiatry and the Law, 32,* 329–331.

Charter, R. A., Walden, D. K., & Padilla, S. P. (2000). Too many clerical scoring errors. *Journal of Clinical Psychology, 56,* 571–574.

Cockram, J. (2005). Justice or differential treatment? Sentencing of offenders with an intellectual disability. *Journal of Intellectual and Developmental Disability, 30,* 3–13.

Collie, A., Maruff, P., Darby, D. G., & McStephen, M. (2003). The effects of practice on the cognitive test performance of neurologically normal individuals assessed at brief test-retest intervals. *Journal of the International Neuropsychological Society, 9,* 419–428.

Collins, R., Lincoln, R., & Frank, M. G. (2002). The effect of rapport in forensic interviewing. *Psychiatry, Psychology, and Law, 9,* 69–78.

Committee on Ethical Guidelines for Forensic Psychologists. (1991). Specialty guidelines for forensic psychologists. *Law and Human Behavior, 15,* 655–665.

Committee on Legal Issues. (1996). Strategies for private practitioners coping with subpoenas or compelled testimony for client records or test data. *Professional Psychology: Research and Practice, 27,* 245–251.

Connell, M. A. (2003). A psychobiographical approach to the evaluation for sentence mitigation. *Journal of Psychiatry and Law, 31,* 319–354.

Conroy, M. A. (2003). Evaluation of sexual predators. In I. B. Weiner (Series Ed.) & A. M. Goldstein (Vol. Ed.), *Comprehensive handbook of psychology: Vol. 11. Forensic psychology* (pp. 463–484). Hoboken, NJ: Wiley.

Cooperstein, M. A. (1998, July/August). Peer review process: Guidelines for clinical and forensic psychological reviews. *Forensic Examiner,* 17–22.

Cox, G. (2003). Screening inmates for suicide using static risk factors. *Behavior Therapist, 26,* 212–214.

Culross, R. R., & Nelson, S. (1997). Training in personality assessment in specialist-level school psychology programs. *Psychological Reports, 81,* 119–124.

Cunningham, M. D., & Vigen, M. P. (1999). Without appointed counsel in capital postconviction proceedings: The self-representation competency of Mississippi death row inmates. *Criminal Justice and Behavior, 26,* 293–321.

Daigle, M. (2004). MMPI inmate profiles: Suicide completers, suicide attempters, and non-suicidal controls. *Behavioral Sciences and the Law, 22,* 833–842.

Davies, G., & Alonso-Quecuty, M. (1997). Cultural factors in the recall of a witnessed event. *Memory, 5*, 601–614.

Davies, M. F. (2003). Confirmatory bias in the evaluation of personality descriptions: Positive test strategies and output interference. *Journal of Personality and Social Psychology, 85*, 736–744.

Davis, L. S. (1997). Discovery in criminal cases: Obtaining evidence and information necessary for an effective defense. *Alabama Lawyer, 58*, 352–355.

Di Giulio, L. S. (1999). Dying for the right to effective assistance of counsel in state post-conviction proceedings: State statutes and due process in capital cases. *Boston University Public Interest Law Journal, 9*, 109–131.

Dodd v. U.S., 125 S. Ct. 2478 (2005).

Drogin, E. Y. (1999). Prophets in another land: Utilizing psychological expertise from foreign jurisdictions. *Mental and Physical Disability Law Reporter, 23*, 767–771.

Drogin, E. Y. (2000a). Breaking through: Communicating and collaborating with the mentally ill defendant. *Advocate, 22*, 27–34.

Drogin, E. Y. (2000b). In search of psychology: A jurisprudent therapy perspective on sexual offender risk assessment. *Advocate, 22*, 17–19.

Drogin, E. Y. (2001). "When I said I was lying, I might have been lying": The phenomenon of psychological malingering. *Mental and Physical Disability Law Reporter, 25*, 711–715.

Drogin, E. Y. (2004). Counsel's "reasonable investigation" of mental health evidence in capital litigation: Implications for post-conviction proceedings. *Mental and Physical Disability Law Reporter, 28*, 496–500.

Drogin, E. Y., & Barrett, C. L. (1996a). "But doctor, isn't that just your opinion?" Contributing to the decision-making process of the forensic psychologist as expert witness. *Advocate, 18*, 14–20.

Drogin, E. Y., & Barrett, C. L. (1996b). Forensic mental health assessment: Moving from examination to evaluation. *Advocate, 18*, 129–133.

Drogin, E. Y., & Howard, M. E. (2001). Jurisprudent therapy: Deriving optimal assistance from psychological science, practice, and roles. *Vermont Bar Journal, 27*(31), 34–38.

Drogin, E. Y., & Monahan, E. C. (2001). Acknowledging the prevalence of severe mental illness on death row. *Advocate, 23*, 56–57.

Drope v. Missouri, 420 U.S. 162 (1975).

Dwyer, C. W. (2000). Treating physicians: Fact witnesses or retained expert witnesses in disguise? *Drake Law Review, 48*, 719–740.

Dyer, F. J., & McCann, J. T. (2000). The Millon clinical inventories, research critical of their forensic application and *Daubert* criteria. *Law and Human Behavior, 24*, 487–497.

Fischetti, B. A., & Crespi, T. D. (1999). Clinical supervision for school psychologists: National practices, trends and future implications. *School Psychology International, 20*, 278–288.

Fogelson, D. L., Nuechterlein, K. H., Asarnow, R. F., Payne, D. L., & Subotnik, K. L. (2004). Validity of the family history method for diagnosing schizophrenia, schizophrenia-related psychoses, and schizophrenia-spectrum personality disorders in first-degree relatives of schizophrenia probands. *Schizophrenia Research, 68*, 309–317.

Ford v. Wainwright, 477 U.S. 399 (1986).

Ford, M. A., & Nembach, P. A. (1992). The victim's right to privacy: Imperfect protection from the criminal justice system. *Saint John's Journal of Legal Commentary, 8*, 203–223.

Foucha v. Louisiana, 504 U.S. 71 (1992).

Freedman, E. M. (2003). The revised ABA guidelines and the duties of lawyers and judges in capital post-conviction proceedings. *Journal of Appellate Practice and Process, 5*, 325–346.

Friedman, J. I., Harvey, P., Coleman, T., Moriarty, P., Bowie, C., Parella, M., et al. (2001). Six-year follow-up study of cognitive and functional status across the lifespan in schizophrenia: A comparison of Alzheimer's disease and normal aging. *American Journal of Psychiatry, 158*, 1441–1448.

Gable, E., & Green, T. (2004). *Wiggins v. Smith:* The ineffective assistance of counsel standard applied 20 years after Strickland. *Georgetown Journal of Legal Ethics, 17*, 755–771.

Gagliardi, G. J., Lovell, D., Peterson, P. D., & Jemelka, R. (2004). Forecasting recidivism in mentally ill offenders released from prison. *Law and Human Behavior, 28*, 133–155.

Garcia, M. (1995, November). Elimination of the military personnel records jacket. *Army Lawyer*, 36–38.

Gavazzi, S. M., Yarcheck, C. M., Rhine, E. E., & Partridge, C. R. (2003). Building bridges between the parole officer and the families of serious juvenile offenders: A preliminary report on a family-based parole program. *International Journal of Offender Therapy and Comparative Criminology, 47,* 291–308.

Gideon v. Wainwright, 872 U.S. 335 (1963).

Gilleran-Johnson, B., & Kristopek, G. A. (2001). Post-conviction challenges to the death penalty: Mental health records and the Fifth Amendment. *Loyola University Chicago Law Journal, 32,* 425–450.

Giorgi-Guarnieri, D., Janofsky, J., Keram, E., Lawsky, S., Merideth, P., Mossman, D., et al. (2002). AAPL practice guideline for forensic psychiatric evaluation of defendants raising the insanity defense. *Journal of the American Academy of Psychiatry and the Law, 30,* S3–S40.

Givelber, D. (1999). The right to counsel in collateral, post-conviction proceedings. *Maryland Law Review, 58,* 1393–1416.

Glassman, J. B. (1998). Preventing and managing board complaints: The downside risk of custody evaluation. *Professional Psychology: Research and Practice, 29,* 121–124.

Goldberg, J. A., & Siegel, D. M. (2002). The ethical obligations of prosecutors in cases involving post-conviction claims of innocence. *California Western Law Review, 38,* 389–412.

Granhag, P. A. (1997). Realism in eyewitness confidence as a function of type of event witnessed and repeated recall. *Journal of Applied Psychology, 82,* 599–613.

Greenberg, S. A., & Shuman, D. W. (1997). Irreconcilable conflict between therapeutic and forensic roles. *Professional Psychology: Research and Practice, 28,* 50–57.

Grisso, T. (2004). Reply to "A critical review of published competency-to-confess measures." *Law and Human Behavior, 28,* 719–724.

Gutheil, T. G., & Appelbaum, P. S. (2000). *Clinical handbook of psychiatry and the law* (3rd ed.). Philadelphia: Lippincott, Williams & Wilkins.

Gutheil, T. G., & Simon, R. I. (2004). Avoiding bias in expert testimony. *Psychiatric Annals, 34,* 260–270.

Hack, P. (2003). The roads less traveled: Post-conviction relief alternatives and the Antiterrorism and Effective Death Penalty Act of 1996. *American Journal of Criminal Law, 30,* 171–223.

Halbert v. Michigan, 125 S. Ct. 2582 (2005).

Hamblin v. Mitchell, 354 F.3d 482 (6th Cir. 2003).

Hammel, A. (2003). Effective performance guarantees for capital state post-conviction counsel: Cutting the Gordian knot. *Journal of Appellate Practice and Process, 5,* 347–408.

Hannah, J. A. (1994). Pre-trial proceedings: Provide for discovery and inspection of evidence by the prosecution and defendants in criminal cases. *Georgia State University Law Review, 11,* 137–156.

Harris, D. J., Nieves, K., & Place, T. M. (2003). Dispatch and delay: Post-conviction relief act litigation in non-capital cases. *Duquesne Law Review, 41,* 467–494.

Heilbrun, K. (1992). The role of psychological testing in forensic assessment. *Law and Human Behavior, 16,* 252–272.

Heilbrun, K. (2001). *Principles of forensic mental health assessment.* New York: Kluwer Academic/Plenum Press.

Heilbrun, K. (2003). Principles of forensic mental health assessment: Implications for the forensic assessment of sexual offenders. In R. A. Prentky, E. Janus, & M. E. Seto (Eds.), *Sexually coercive behavior: Understanding and management* (pp. 1–18). New York: Annals of the New Academy of Sciences, 989.

Heilbrun, K., Lawson, K., Spier, S., & Libby, J. (1994). Community placement for insanity acquittees: A preliminary study of residential programs and person-situation fit. *Bulletin of the American Academy of Psychiatry and the Law, 22,* 551–560.

Heilbrun, K., Marczyk, G., & DeMatteo, D. (2002). *Forensic health assessment: A casebook.* New York: Oxford University Press.

Heilbrun, K., Marczyk, G. R., DeMatteo, D., Zillmer, E. A., Harris, J., & Jennings, T. (2003). Principles of forensic mental health assessment: Implications for neuropsychological assessment in forensic contexts. *Assessment, 10,* 329–343.

Heilbrun, K., Warren, J., & Picarello, K. (2003). Use of third party information in forensic assessment. In I. B. Weiner (Series Ed.) & A. M. Goldstein (Vol. Ed.), *Comprehensive handbook of psychology: Vol. 11. Forensic psychology* (pp. 69–86). Hoboken, NJ: Wiley.

Hoffman, R. J. (2000). Legal malpractice in the criminal context: Is postconviction relief required? *Florida Bar Journal, 74,* 66–68.

Howard, R. C. (1996). The defunding of the post-conviction defense organizations as a denial of the right to counsel. *West Virginia Law Review, 98,* 863–921.

Hughes, J. N., Cavell, T. A., & Willson, V. (2001). Further support for the developmental significance of the quality of the teacher-student relationship. *Journal of School Psychology, 39,* 289–301.

Iandiorio, T. J. (2004). Federal postconviction relief and 28 U.S.C. § 2255(4): Are state court decisions "facts"? *University of Chicago Law Review, 71,* 1141–1172.

Jaworsky, T. E. (2003). A defendant's right to exculpatory evidence: Does the constitutional duty to disclose exculpatory evidence extend to new evidence discovered post-conviction? *St. Thomas Law Review, 15,* 245–264.

Jebo, J. R. (2003). Overcoming attorney-client privilege and work product protection in bad-faith cases. *Defense Counsel Journal, 70,* 261–271.

Johnson-Greene, D., & Bechtold, K. T. (2002). Ethical considerations for peer review in forensic neuropsychology. *Clinical Neuropsychologist, 16,* 97–104.

Jones, R. S. (2004). When prisoners come home: Parole and prisoner reentry. *Howard Journal of Criminal Justice, 43,* 450–452.

Kassin, S. M. (2005). On the psychology of confessions: Does innocence put innocents at risk? *American Psychologist, 60,* 215–228.

Kebbell, M. R., Milne, R., & Wagstaff, G. F. (1999). The cognitive interview: A survey of its forensic effectiveness. *Psychology, Crime, and Law, 5,* 101–115.

Kerekes, R. J. (1994). The crisis of congested courts. *Seton Hall Legislative Journal, 18,* 489–551.

Kirkland, K., & Kirkland, K. L. (2001). Frequency of child custody evaluation complaints and related disciplinary action: A survey of the Association of State and Provincial Psychology Boards. *Professional Psychology: Research and Practice, 32,* 171–174.

Knauss, L. K. (2001). Ethical issues in psychological assessment in school settings. *Journal of Personality Assessment, 77,* 231–241.

Kokish, R. (2003). The current role of post-conviction sex offender polygraph testing in sex offender treatment. *Journal of Child Sexual Abuse, 12,* 175–194.

Kokish, R., Levenson, J. S., & Blasingame, G. D. (2005). Post-conviction sex offender polygraph examination: Client-reported perceptions of utility and accuracy. *Sexual Abuse: Journal of Research and Treatment, 17,* 211–221.

Kreeger, L., & Weiss, D. (2004, March/April). Preparing for post-conviction challenges. *Prosecutor,* 18–21.

Kurtz, M. M. (2005). Neurocognitive impairment across the lifespan in schizophrenia: An update. *Schizophrenia Research, 74,* 15–26.

Lally, S. J. (2003). What tests are acceptable for use in forensic evaluations? A survey of experts. *Professional Psychology: Research and Practice, 34,* 491–498.

Lamb, H. R., & Weinberger, L. E. (1998). Persons with severe mental illness in jails and prisons: A review. *Psychiatric Services, 49,* 483–492.

Lamberg, L. (2004). Efforts grow to keep mentally ill out of jails. *Journal of the American Medical Association, 292,* 555–556.

Lassiter, G. D., Munhall, P. J., Geers, A. L., Weiland, P. E., & Handley, I. M. (2001). Accountability and the camera perspective bias in videotaped confessions. *Analyses of Social Issues and Public Policy, 1,* 53–70.

Laurenceau, J., & Bolger, N. (2005). Using diary methods to study marital and family processes. *Journal of Family Psychology, 19,* 86–97.

Leek, F., Liebert, D., & Filipelli, J. (1999). In pursuit of meeting the best interest of the child: A phase related intervention model. *American Journal of Forensic Psychology, 17,* 29–48.

Lemay, S., Bédard, M., Rouleau, I., & Tremblay, P. G. (2004). Practice effect and test-retest reliability of attentional and executive tests in middle-aged to elderly subjects. *Clinical Neuropsychologist, 18,* 284–302.

Levy, A. R., & Pujol, P. (2000, August). Challenges for cause: How to preserve error for appeal when the judge denies your motion. *Houston Lawyer,* 24–26.

Lewis, D. O., Pincus, J., Bard, B., Richardson, E., Prichep, L., Feldman, M. et al. (1988). Neuropsychiatric, psychoeducational, and family characteristics of 14 juveniles condemned to death in the United States. *American Journal of Psychiatry, 145,* 584–589.

Lewis, D. O., Pincus, J. H., Feldman, M. A., Jackson, L. J., & Bard, B. (1986). Psychiatric, neurological, and psychoeducational characteristics of 15 death row inmates in the United States. *American Journal of Psychiatry, 143,* 838–845.

Markus, H. E., Cross, W. F., Halewski, P. G., Quallo, H., Smith, S., Sullivan, M., et al. (2003). Primary process and peer consultation: An experiential model to work through countertransference. *International Journal of Group Psychotherapy, 53,* 19–37.

Mason, J. (2004). Personal narratives, relational selves: Residential histories in the living and telling. *Sociological Review, 52,* 162–179.

Mayle v. Felix, 125 S. Ct. 2562 (2005).

McCaffrey, R. J., Fisher, J. M., Gold, B. A., & Lynch, J. K. (1996). Presence of third parties during neuropsychological evaluations: Who is evaluating whom? *Clinical Neuropsychologist, 10,* 435–449.

McCann v. Richardson, 397 U.S. 759 (1970).

McCann, J. T. (2002). Guidelines for forensic application of the MCMI-III. *Journal of Forensic Psychology Practice, 2,* 55–70.

McCloud, S. G. (2002, December). To limit post-conviction petitions, repeal the time limits. *Champion,* 36–37.

McConville, C. R. (2003). The right to effective assistance of capital post-conviction counsel: Constitutional implications of statutory grants of capital counsel. *Wisconsin Law Review,* 31–113.

McCoy, M. L., Roberts, D. L., Hanrahan, P., Clay, R., & Luchins, D. J. (2004). Jail linkage assertive community treatment services for individuals with mental illness. *Psychiatric Rehabilitation Journal, 27,* 243–250.

McGrath, R. J., Cumming, G., & Holt, J. (2002). Collaboration among sex offender treatment providers and probation and parole officers: The beliefs and behaviors of treatment providers. *Sexual Abuse: Journal of Research and Treatment, 14,* 49–65.

McGraw, A. J. (2001). Life but not liberty? An assessment of noncapital indigent defendants' rights to expert assistance under the *Ake v. Oklahoma* doctrine. *Washington University Law Quarterly, 79,* 951–972.

McLearen, A. M., & Ryba, N. L. (2003). Identifying severely mentally ill inmates: Can small jails comply with detection standards? *Journal of Offender Rehabilitation, 37,* 25–40.

McSweeny, A. J., Becker, B. C., Naugle, R. I., Snow, W. G., Binder, L. M., & Thompson, L. L. (1998). Ethical issues related to the presence of third party observers in clinical neuropsychological evaluations. *Clinical Neuropsychologist, 12,* 552–559.

Medoff, D. (2003). The scientific basis of psychological testing: Considerations following *Daubert, Kumho,* and *Joiner. Family Court Review, 41,* 199–213.

Medwed, D. S. (2004). The zeal deal: Prosecutorial resistance to post-conviction claims of innocence. *Boston University Law Review, 84,* 125–183.

Melton, G. B., Petrila, J., Poythress, N. G., & Slobogin, C. (1997). *Psychological evaluations for the courts: A handbook for mental health professionals and lawyers* (2nd ed.). New York: Guilford Press.

Merikangas, J. (2004). Commentary: Alcoholic blackout—Does it remove mens rea? *Journal of the American Academy of Psychiatry and the Law, 32,* 375–377.

Merlone, L. (2005). Record keeping and the school counselor. *Professional School Counseling, 8,* 372–376.

Metzner, J. L. (1998). *Pennsylvania Department of Corrections et al. v. Ronald R. Yeskey:* Prisons and the Americans with Disabilities Act of 1990. *Journal of the American Academy of Psychiatry and the Law, 26,* 665–668.

Miller, R. D. (2002). Automatic commitment of insanity acquittees: Keeping up with the Joneses? *Journal of Psychiatry and Law, 30,* 59–96.

Mogin, P. (2003, September/October). Using new evidence of a constitutional violation to get a new trial. *Champion,* 26–28.

Mojica v. Reno, 970 F. Supp. 130 (E.D.N.Y. 1997).

Monahan, E. C., & Clark, J. J. (1997, May). Funds for defense expertise: What national benchmarks require. *Champion,* 12–13, 51–54.

Mossman, D. (2003). *Daubert,* cognitive malingering, and test accuracy. *Law and Human Behavior, 27,* 229–249.

Mozley, S. L., Miller, M. W., Weathers, F. W., Beckham, J. C., & Feldman, M. E. (2005). Personality Assessment Inventory (PAI) profiles of male veterans with combat-related posttraumatic stress disorder. *Journal of Psychopathology and Behavioral Assessment, 27,* 179–189.

Muller, C. (2001). The role of caring in the teacher-student relationship for at-risk students. *Sociological Inquiry, 71,* 241–255.

National Academy of Neuropsychology Policy and Planning Committee. (2000). Presence of third party observers during neuropsychological testing: Official statement of the National Academy of Neuropsychology. *Archives of Clinical Neuropsychology, 15,* 379–380.

National Legal Aid and Defender Association. (1995). *Performance guidelines for criminal defense representation.* Washington, DC: Author.

Newton, B. E. (2005, June). A primer on post-conviction habeas corpus review. *Champion,* 16–22.

Nwokike, J. (2005). Federal insanity acquittees. *Journal of the American Academy of Psychiatry and the Law, 33,* 126–128.

Oberlander, L. B., Goldstein, N. E., & Goldstein, A. M. (2003). Competency to confess. In I. B. Weiner (Series Ed.) & A. M. Goldstein (Vol. Ed.), *Comprehensive handbook of psychology: Vol. 11. Forensic psychology* (pp. 335–357). Hoboken, NJ: Wiley.

Orbach, Y., Hershkowitz, I., Lamb, M. E., Esplin, P. W., & Horowitz, D. (2000). Assessing the value of structured protocols for forensic interviews of alleged child abuse victims. *Child Abuse and Neglect, 24,* 733–752.

Oswald, D. L., Clark, E. M., & Kelly, C. M. (2004). Friendship maintenance: An analysis of individual and dyad behaviors. *Journal of Social and Clinical Psychology, 23,* 413–441.

Palmer, J. W. (1999). *Constitutional rights of prisoners* (6th ed.). Cincinnati, OH: Anderson.

Parry, J. (1986). Postconviction procedures considered. *Mental and Physical Disability Law Reporter, 10,* 20–21.

Parry, J., & Drogin, E. Y. (2000). *Criminal law handbook on psychiatric and psychological evidence and testimony.* Washington, DC: American Bar Association.

Patterson, R. F., & Wise, B. F. (1998). The development of internal forensic review boards in the management of hospitalized insanity acquittees. *Journal of the American Academy of Psychiatry and the Law, 33,* 661–664.

Pell, M. D. (2002). Evaluation of nonverbal emotion in face and voice: Some preliminary findings on a new battery of tests. *Brain and Cognition, 48,* 499–504.

Pennsylvania Department of Corrections v. Yeskey, 524 U.S. 206 (1998).

Peterson, M. B. (2001). Recognizing concerns about how some licensing boards are treating psychologists. *Professional Psychology: Research and Practice, 32,* 339–340.

Place, T. M. (1996). Ineffective assistance of counsel under the Pennsylvania Post-conviction Relief Act. *Temple Law Review, 69,* 1389–1412.

Powell, D. (1996). A peer consultation model for clinical supervision. *Clinical Supervisor, 14,* 163–169.

Reid, W. H. (2002). Ethics and forensic work. *Journal of Psychiatric Practice, 8,* 380–385.

Reid, W. H. (2003). Why nonforensic clinicians should decline forensic referrals. *Journal of Psychiatric Practice, 9,* 163–166.

Richardson-Stewart, J. B. (2003). One full bite at the apple: Defining competent counsel in Texas capital post-conviction review. *Texas Wesleyan Law Review, 9,* 221–254.

Roberts, J. (2004). Too little, too late: Ineffective assistance of counsel, the duty to investigate, and pretrial discovery in criminal cases. *Fordham Urban Law Journal, 31,* 1097–1155.

Robertson, H. (1992). The needle in the haystack: Towards a new state postconviction remedy. *DePaul Law Review, 41,* 333–358.

Rogers, P. (2003). Client and witness: The provision of therapy for vulnerable or intimidated adult witnesses prior to a criminal trial. *Journal of Psychiatric and Mental Health Nursing, 10,* 372–374.

Rogers, R., Jordan, M. J., & Harrison, K. S. (2004). A critical review of published competency-to-confess measures. *Law and Human Behavior, 28,* 707–718.

Rogers, R., Salekin, R. T., & Sewell, K. W. (1999). Validation of the Millon Clinical Multiaxial Inventory for Axis II disorders: Does it meet the *Daubert* standard? *Law and Human Behavior, 23,* 425–443.

Rompilla v. Beard, 125 S. Ct. 2456 (2005).

Rona, R. J., Hyams, K. C., & Wessely, S. (2005). Screening for psychological illness in military personnel. *Journal of the American Medical Association, 293,* 1257–1260.

Rosichan, M. K. (2004). A meaningless ritual? The due process mandate for the provision of competent counsel in Arkansas capital post-conviction proceedings. *University of San Francisco Law Review, 38,* 749–780.

Ross v. Moffitt, 417 U.S. 600 (1974).

Rothenberg, K. L. (1999). Evidence: Attorney-client privilege and work product doctrine. *Denver University Law Review, 76,* 825–844.

Rowe, M. A. (2002). Exoneration by post-conviction relief. *Journal of Legal Advocacy and Practice, 4,* 268–273.

Rundlet, A. (1999). Opting for death: State responses to the AEDPA's opt-in provisions and the need for a right to post-conviction counsel. *University of Pennsylvania Journal of Constitutional Law, 1,* 661–718.

Russell, J. R. (1996). Criminal discovery and psychological defenses in West Virginia: "Squeezing a lemon" or "kicking a dog." *West Virginia Law Review, 99,* 207–233.

Saltzburg, S. A. (2004, Fall). Prior inconsistent statements and collateral matters. *Criminal Justice,* 45–47.

Saylor, T. G. (1998). Post-conviction relief in Pennsylvania. *Pennsylvania Bar Association Quarterly, 69,* 1–6.

Schepard, A. (2005). Mental health evaluation in child custody disputes. *Family Court Review, 43,* 187–190.

Schoenfeld, L. S., Hatch, J. P., & Gonzalez, J. M. (2001). Responses of psychologists to complaints filed against them with a state licensing board. *Professional Psychology: Research and Practice, 32,* 491–495.

Schreiber, N., & Parker, J. F. (2004). Inviting witnesses to speculate: Effects on age and interaction on children's recall. *Journal of Experimental Child Psychology, 89,* 31–52.

Schroeder, J. (2003). Forging a new practice area: Social work's role in death penalty mitigation investigations. *Families in Society, 84,* 423–432.

Schutte, J. W. (2001). Using the MCMI-III in forensic evaluations. *American Journal of Forensic Psychology, 19,* 5–20.

Scott, C. L., & Gerbasi, J. B. (2003). *Atkins v. Virginia:* Execution of mentally retarded defendants revisited. *Journal of the American Academy of Psychiatry and the Law, 31,* 101–105.

Seiter, R. P., & West, A. D. (2003). Supervision styles in probation and parole: An analysis of activities. *Journal of Offender Rehabilitation, 38,* 57–75.

Serby, M. (2003). Psychiatric resident conceptualizations of mood and affect within the mental status examination. *American Journal of Psychiatry, 160,* 1527–1529.

Shuman, D. W., Cunningham, M. D., Connell, M. A., & Reid, W. H. (2003). Interstate forensic psychology consultations: A call for reform and proposal of a model rule. *Professional Psychology: Research and Practice, 34,* 233–239.

Shuman, D. W., Greenberg, S., Heilbrun, K., & Foote, W. E. (1998). An immodest proposal: Should treating mental health professionals be barred from testifying about their patients? *Behavioral Sciences and the Law, 16,* 509–523.

Siegel, D. M. (1999). My reputation or your liberty (or your life): The ethical obligations of criminal defense counsel in postconviction proceedings. *Journal of the Legal Profession, 23,* 85–95.

Simon, R. I., & Shuman, D. W. (1999). Conducting forensic examinations on the road: Are you practicing your profession without a license? *Journal of the American Academy of Psychiatry and the Law, 27,* 75–82.

Simons, R., Goddard, P., & Patton, W. (2002). Hand-scoring error rates in psychological testing. *Assessment, 9,* 292–300.

Slovenko, R. (2002). Commentary: Tragicomedy in trials and appellate opinions. *Journal of Psychiatry and Law, 30,* 299–303.

Smith, C., & Starns, R. (1999). Folly by fiat: Pretending that death row inmates can represent themselves in state capital post-conviction proceedings. *Loyola Law Review, 45,* 55–119.

Smith, S. D., & Morris, C. A. (2005). Planning studies of etiology. *Applied Psycholinguistics, 26,* 97–110.

Snyder, B. (1998). Disparate impact on death row: M.L.B. and the indigent's right to counsel at capital state postconviction proceedings. *Yale Law Journal, 107,* 2211–2247.

St. Cyr v. INS, 229 F.3d 406 (2nd Cir. 2000).

Stake, R. E. (2002). Teachers conceptualizing student achievement. *Teachers and Teaching: Theory and Practice, 8,* 303–312.

Stankewitz v. Woodford, 365 F.3d 706 (9th Cir. 2004).

Stanny, C. J., & Johnson, T. C. (2000). Effects of stress induced by a simulated shooting on recall by police and citizen witnesses. *American Journal of Psychology, 113,* 359–386.

Steiker, J. (1998). Restructuring post-conviction review of federal constitutional claims raised by state prisoners: Confronting the new face of excessive proceduralism. *University of Chicago Legal Forum,* 315–347.

Strickland v. Washington, 466 U.S. 668 (1984).

Studnicki, S. M., & Apol, J. P. (2002). Witness detention and intimidation: The history and future of material witness law. *Saint John's Law Review, 76,* 483–533.

Summers, A. P., & Semrud-Clikeman, M. (2001). Implementation of the IDEA by school psychologists: An exploratory study using the theory of street-level bureaucracy. *School Psychology Quarterly, 15,* 255–278.

Sweet, J. (2003). Official position of the American Academy of Clinical Neuropsychology on ethical complaints made against clinical neuropsychologists during adversarial proceedings. *Clinical Neuropsychologist, 17,* 443–445.

Sweetwood, L. A., & Sweetwood, H. M. (2001). Psychologist as advocate for elders in determination of competency and long-term care placement. *Clinical Gerontologist, 23,* 117–126.

Tannous, C. (2000). Therapists as advocates for their clients with disabilities: A conflict of roles? *Australian Occupational Therapy Journal, 47,* 41–46.

Tekcan, A. I., & Akturk, M. (2001). Are you sure you forgot? Feeling of knowing in directed forgetting. *Journal of Experimental Psychology: Learning, Memory, and Cognition, 27,* 1487–1490.

Tidmarsh, D. (1997). Risk assessment among prisoners: A view from a parole board member. *International Review of Psychiatry, 9,* 273–281.

Tucillo, J. A., DeFilippis, N. A., Denney, R. L., & Dsurney, J. (2002). Licensure requirements for interjurisdictional forensic evaluations. *Professional Psychology: Research and Practice, 33,* 377–383.

Turner, S. M., DeMers, S. T., Fox, H. R., & Reed, G. (2001). APA's guidelines for test user qualifications: An executive summary. *American Psychologist, 56,* 1099–1113.

Vrij, A., Evans, H., Akehurst, L., & Mann, S. (2004). Rapid judgments in assessing verbal and nonverbal cues: Their potential for deception researchers and lie detection. *Applied Cognitive Psychology, 18,* 283–296.

Wackerbarth, S. B., Streams, M. E., & Smith, M. K. (2002). Capturing the insights of family caregivers. *Qualitative Health Research, 12,* 1141–1154.

Watt, M. J., & MacLean, W. E. (2003). Competency to be sentenced and executed. *Ethics and Behavior, 13,* 35–41.

Welch, J. (2004). Defending against deportation: Equipping public defenders to represent noncitizens effectively. *California Law Review, 93,* 541–583.

Wettstein, R. M. (2004). The forensic examination and report. In R. I. Simon & L. H. Gold (Eds.), *Textbook of forensic psychiatry* (pp. 139–164). Washington, DC: American Psychiatric Publishing.

Whitmore, L. (2005, June). Abuse of discretion: Misunderstanding the deference accorded trial court rulings. *Florida Bar Journal,* 83–87.

Wiggins v. Smith, 539 U.S. 510 (2003).

Wild, T. C., Newton-Taylor, B., Ogborne, A. C., Mann, R., Erickson, P., & Macdonald, S. (2001). Attitudes toward compulsory substance abuse treatment: A comparison of the public, counselors, probationers and judges' views. *Drugs: Education, Prevention, and Policy, 8,* 33–45.

Williams, M. H. (2001). The question of psychologists' maltreatment by state licensing boards: Overcoming denial and seeking remedies. *Professional Psychology: Research and Practice, 32,* 341–344.

Wolff, N., & Schlesinger, M. (2002). Clinicians as advocates: An exploratory study of responses to managed care by mental health professionals. *Journal of Behavioral Health Sciences and Research, 29,* 274–287.

Young, S. A., Frierson, R. L., Dwyer, G., & Shah, A. (2002). Commitment versus confinement: Therapeutic passes in the management of insanity acquittees. *Journal of the American Academy of Psychiatry and the Law, 30,* 563–567.

Zanis, D. A., Mulvaney, F., Coviello, D., Alterman, A. I., Savitz, B., & Thompson, W. (2003). The effectiveness of early parole to substance treatment facilities on 24-month criminal recidivism. *Journal of Drug Issues, 33,* 223–236.

Zapf, P. A., Boccaccini, M. T., & Brodsky, S. L. (2002). Assessment of competency for execution: Professional guidelines and an evaluation checklist. *Behavioral Sciences and the Law, 21,* 103–120.

Zgaljardic, D. J., & Benedict, R. H. (2001). Evaluation of practice effects in language and spatial processing test performance. *Applied Neuropsychology, 8,* 218–223.

Zonana, H. V. (2003). Competency to be executed and forced medication: *Singleton v. Norris. Journal of the American Academy of Psychiatry and the Law, 31,* 372–376.

PART VI

Forensic Mental Health Experts in the Courtroom

CHAPTER 16

Expert Witness Testimony: Law, Ethics, and Practice

Steven C. Bank and Ira K. Packer

The judicial system of the United States rests on the belief that justice is served through the fair and open combat of ideas in a court of law. Adhering to the highest clinical, legal, and ethical standards will position mental health professionals who participate in the adversary process as expert witnesses to provide courts with ethical and effective testimony. Expert witnesses who understand the dynamics and spirit of courtroom communication will be best prepared to protect the integrity of their testimony.

Psychologists who serve as expert witnesses need to be cognizant of the significant differences between the standards and ethics that govern their professional practice and legal rules and ethics (Anderten, Staulcup, & Grisso, 1980; Fitch, Petrella, & Wallace, 1987). One of the most salient differences relates to presenting data. Psychologists who venture into the courtroom are required to present all relevant data, even when those data are not consistent with their conclusions. The "Specialty Guidelines for Forensic Psychologists" (Committee on Ethical Guidelines, 1991, Section VII.D) state, "Forensic psychologists do not, by either commission or omission, participate in a misrepresentation of their evidence, nor do they participate in partisan attempts to avoid, deny, or subvert the presentation of evidence contrary to their own position." By contrast, attorneys are not so constrained; indeed, the adversarial system is based on each side making its most persuasive argument, often by marshaling only the data consistent with their position. Furthermore, witnesses can only answer questions posed by the attorneys; therefore, even if the expert would like to present the opposing data, he or she may not be given the opportunity to do so.

Psychologists may thus find themselves in a situation in which their approach to testifying, based on professional ethics and standards, is in conflict with the preferences of the attorney retaining them. However, similar to the laws of physics, for each expert witness who testifies, the other side has an "equal and opposite expert." Consequently, even if the attorney would like to suppress certain data, it is likely that this information will be introduced by the other side's expert. In most cases, it is not good strategy for attorneys to allow this information to be introduced by the opposition without first allowing their expert to discuss (and rebut) those points. It is usually more effective for attorneys to have their witness steal the thunder of the other side by introducing and accounting for contradictory data during direct examination. Therefore, the ethical standards of psychologists and the strategic interests of attorneys often coincide, creating a situation in which adherence to ethical standards by psychologists is also an effective strategy for the attorney (Slovenko, 1987).

THE HISTORICAL EVOLUTION OF THE ADVERSARY PROCESS AND EXPERT WITNESS TESTIMONY

People have always argued. Laws provide formal procedures for settling disputes so that societies maintain order. All disputes have opposing or adversary positions. That is why the spirit and rules for Anglo-American courtrooms are collectively known as the "adversary process" (Kempin, 1973). This process is based on the belief that each adversary is best able to advocate for his or her side of a case. The judge or jury is then asked to decide which lawyer's argument is more convincing. Mental health professionals who assume the role of expert witness become part of this adversarial process.

Trial by Ordeal

Trial by battle and trial by ordeal predated civilized legal proceedings. Twelfth-century English law allowed wealthy landowners to settle disputes by substituting a "champion" (a person who fights in an armed conflict in the place of another) to do judicial combat for them (Holdsworth, 1956). Twenty-first-century law allows attorneys to champion the cause of their clients.

Medieval trial by ordeal was an appeal to divine intervention to determine guilt or innocence (Landsman, 1995). These proceedings were often held during church rituals at the high moment of the Mass. The Saxons developed several ordeals. The ordeal of the "hot iron" had the accused carry a red-hot iron in his hand for a specified distance. The accused was considered to be innocent if, after a set period of time, he had no marks on his hands. The "cursed morsel" had the accused swallow a piece of dry bread with a feather baked into it. The accused was considered to be innocent if he did not choke. However, in the early thirteenth century, the Church of England forbade priests to participate in the highly subjective trial by ordeal. Consequently, the chief procedure for resolving criminal cases in England, appealing to the supernatural, was eliminated. A new legal process was needed.

Jurors as Witnesses

The English were uncomfortable with allowing one person, a judge, to decide cases because it was believed that this person would be replacing the voice of God. Consequently, the responsibility became shared by villagers who had some knowledge of the alleged offense or offender. The villagers and judge (and God) could then resolve criminal cases. During this time, jurors could be both witnesses to the alleged offense and also the body that determined guilt or innocence. Even those who accused the defendant of a crime could sit on the jury. Consequently, most defendants were not eager to undergo trial by jury.

Approximately 300 years later, our contemporary distinction between jurors and witnesses was formalized. Whereas jurors were originally required to know all they could about a case, now they were to enter the courtroom *tabula rasa*— as clean slates. Evidence, witness testimony, and attorney arguments would fill those slates.

Credibility of Witnesses to Testify

The integrity of trial by jury relies on the credibility of witnesses. Witnesses, being human, are not always truthful or accurate. For justice to be served, there must be a way to gauge the veracity of those whom the judge has allowed to testify. Cross-examination is the essence of the adversary process.

Witnesses can usually be compelled to answer almost any relevant question. The only constitutional exception is the 5th Amendment, the right against self-incrimination. However, certain witnesses, in certain circumstances, can withhold information acquired during confidential or privileged relationships (e.g., therapist-patient privilege, spousal privilege, and clergy-penitent privilege).

Witnesses with Special Knowledge

The first documented appearance of an expert witness on the legal landscape appeared in 1311 and concerned medical testimony (Eigen & Andoll, 1986). The court would then decide what weight to give the testimony. Courts in the Middle Ages also selected jury members who had special knowledge or experience about the issue before the court. Thus, courts during that time period utilized juror expertise and witness expertise. In our current legal system, witness expertise is currently used because citizens can no longer serve in the dual role of juror and witness. Medical and mental health testimony was common by the mid-nineteenth century (Smith, 1989).

Today, expert witnesses are either retained by one of the parties or court appointed. Witnesses should be aware that their status as court-appointed experts does not necessarily protect them from aggressive cross-examination. Although they were appointed at the behest of the court, by the time they testify, they will likely have formed an opinion that is consistent with the position of one of the parties and opposed by the other.

Testimony: Fact versus Opinion

The lay or nonexpert witness is generally restricted to testify about facts (what he or she has directly experienced or observed). The expert witness, because of specialized knowledge, can testify to questions of fact and to questions of opinion and can offer the court opinions and conclusions (Federal Rules of Evidence, Rule 702).

Experts providing opinions are assisting the trier of fact, but expert opinions do not establish case "facts." Whereas a lay witness can testify to observing someone "discussing tax law with his beagle," only the expert witness can offer opinions or conclusions as to whether the individual was mentally ill at the time. And just as it was during medieval times, only the judge or jury can decide the weight and credibility of expert testimony.

TESTIFYING

Appropriate knowledge of clinical, legal, ethical, and practice issues will best prepare experts for court. Testimony can usually be made most effective by pretrial consultation between the attorney and the expert witness. The goal of preparation is for the expert and attorney to work together to provide the court with ethical and meaningful testimony. Because the attorney's behavior will impact the expert's credibility, experts should take the time, before appearing in court, to educate the attorney conducting direct examination on the case's psycholegal issues. The expert and the attorney should also agree on appropriate lines of questioning and discuss the attorney's courtroom style (e.g., whether the attorney will ask open-ended or highly focused questions).

Experts routinely testify about the following: diagnosis, etiology, treatment, prognosis, research, and psychological testing. The psychologist needs to be able to demonstrate that all psychological tests that have been administered have been developed for, or can be reasonably applied to, the legal issue before the court. Psychological tests used for forensic purposes require a high standard of reliability and validity, including ensuring that they have been validated on the relevant population, that they have been administered properly, and that they have been scored accurately.

Legally, experts should develop a fundamental understanding of relevant legal issues, terms, laws, criteria, procedures, and competing case theories. Always explain how clinical data apply or do not apply to the legal issue being litigated. Facts should be distinguished from inferences.

Ethically, expert witnesses need to familiarize themselves with the ethics and practice issues associated with forensic work by thoroughly reviewing the American Psychological Association's (APA, 2002) "Ethical Principles of Psychologists and Code of Conduct" and the Specialty Guidelines (Committee on Ethical Guidelines, 1991). They should understand that the APA Ethical Principles are aspirational but that the Standards are enforceable; the Specialty Guidelines are aspirational but not enforceable. (For a thorough discussion of ethics issues in forensic psychology, see Bersoff, 2003; Weissman & Debow, 2003; and Chapter 7.)

Sometimes there are not clear delineations between ethics and practice issues. Participation in death penalty cases is not unethical; deciding whether or not to partake in such proceedings is a practice issue (Cunningham & Goldstein, 2003). However, if a psychologist participates in a death penalty case and then realizes that his or her objectivity is being compromised by moral concerns about the death penalty, it then becomes an ethics issue.

Experts must be vigilant about not allowing an attorney to determine how a case is handled. Attorneys do not decide which tests to administer, whom to interview, or which records to review. The forensic specialist needs to use the most appropriate methodology depending on the psycholegal issue and case specifics. It is reasonable to listen to an attorney's suggestions and to adopt them if they are needed for the foundation of an opinion rather than solely for advocacy purposes.

Prepare for each phase of a legal proceeding by predicting the issues and questions that may be posed. Legal proceedings, such as a trial, progress according to a prearranged chronology:

- Deposition (pretrial).
- Direct examination voir dire.
- Cross-examination voir dire.
- Direct examination.
- Cross-examination.
- Redirect examination.
- Re-cross-examination.

It is essential for experts to have command of all case facts and the content of their reports. Prior to the trial, the expert should consult with the retaining attorney to prepare for every phase of the proceeding. This also provides the expert with an opportunity to assess the attorney's personality, skills, and potential willingness to listen to suggestions. It allows experts to determine how much assistance the attorney might offer if they encounter a difficult or unfair cross-examination. It is advisable to ask the retaining attorney about the courtroom style (e.g., businesslike or flamboyant) of the opposing counsel and judge and the educational level of the jury. During pretrial preparation, the expert and the attorney should come to a mutual understanding of the boundaries of expertise, testimony, and opinions to be offered.

Taking a copy of the expert's report or documents to the stand is appropriate if they will likely be referred to during testimony and if it reduces stress. However, the expert should be aware that whatever is taken to the stand can be scrutinized by the opposing counsel. Prior to testimony, the expert should discuss with the retaining lawyer whether there is a sequestration order (e.g., when the judge specifically bars the expert from observing other testimony in the case). Additionally, even if the expert is not sequestered, the advantages and disadvantages of being in the courtroom and observing other witnesses should be considered. Observing lay and expert witnesses may provide additional information to the expert and aid in preparation for testimony. However, maintaining a presence in the courtroom may suggest overinvestment and lack of impartiality. The psychologist should bring at least three copies of his or her resume to court (one for each attorney and one for the court record).

THE EXPERT'S ROLE

Expert witnesses must, by definition, assume the roles of *expert* and *witness*. The two roles consequently create two responsibilities for expert witnesses. First, experts are obliged to be knowledgeable in their chosen area of specialization. Second, witnesses have an ethical responsibility to "become reasonably familiar with the judicial or administrative rules governing their roles" (APA, 2002, 2.01(f)). Psychologists are generally allowed to testify as expert witnesses if they have relevant specialized knowledge that "will assist the trier of fact to understand the evidence or to determine a fact in issue" (Federal Rules of Evidence, Rule 702). Less clear is the role experts should adopt to disseminate their specialized knowledge. Is the proper role for the expert serving as a witness to be that of educator, advocate, advisor, or some combination (Saks, 1990)? The debate will likely continue as long as there are experts and lawyers. (For a thorough description of expert witness roles and legal issues related to expert testimony, see Ewing, 2003.)

There is general acceptance of the position that experts should be persuasive advocates for their *opinions,* not for the party retaining them. Although opinions can never be absolutely objective (clinicians have personal histories, emotions, and theoretical leanings), the expert must attempt to achieve as much objectivity as possible. Experts viewing themselves as advocates for the party retaining them have chosen to become partisan and may have greater difficulty being credible.

Aside from trying to achieve objectivity, psychologists serving as expert witnesses have an ethical obligation (APA, 2002, 1.01) and professional responsibility (Committee on Ethical Guidelines, 1991, VII.A.1) to ensure that their testimony, a product of their scientific and professional judgment, is not misrepresented or misused. Attorneys, whether on direct or cross-examination, may "reinterpret" testimony to their advantage. Although psychologists may not be able to control an attorney's behavior, they have an obligation to resist attempts to misrepresent data or mislead the trier of fact.

Psychologists should be careful to remain in the role of expert witness rather than trial consultant. It is appropriate to discuss the psychologist's report, upcoming testimony, and the reports and testimony of other experts with the referring attorney. However, it is not good practice to offer opinions on other facets of the trial, such as how a litigant should be dressed or how lay witnesses should be questioned. Experts who assume dual roles for an individual case by serving as both expert witness and trial consultant, risk their objectivity. Credibility can also be compromised, as the opposing counsel may question experts on issues they discussed with the retaining attorney during pretrial conferences.

For experts to maintain the integrity of their opinions, they must not only admit to legitimate shortcomings, but also defend their opinions against nonsubstantive attacks. By embracing their dual roles of expert and witness, and by understanding the adversary process and courtroom communication, experts can preserve their dignity, their profession's credibility, and the probity of their testimony.

THE COURTROOM COMMUNICATIONS MODEL

To be of value to the judge or jury, the expert witness must be an effective courtroom communicator. There is an abundance of literature, research based and anecdotal, offering advice to experts on testifying (e.g., Bank & Poythress, 1982; Brodsky, 1999) and providing attorneys with strategies for cross-examination (e.g., Ziskin & Faust, 1995). The Courtroom Communications Model (Bank, 2001) identifies persuasive processes to help expert witnesses become skilled courtroom communicators by applying theory and research from social psychology to courtroom dynamics (Melton, Petrila, Poythress, & Slobogin, 1997; Saks & Hastie, 1978).

Courts of law resolve cases by considering evidence, fact, and expert witness testimony and by listening to attorneys present biased arguments in the most persuasive fashion possible. Many judges and jurors understandably want to be persuaded by expert testimony because they can then attribute their verdict to the expert's opinions. Experts reduce a juror's "verdict stress" by allowing the trier of fact to think, "I made my decision based on the expert's testimony." How influential a particular expert witness may be will vary.

The expert's impact on jurors may, at times, depend more on elements of persuasion than on the validity of his or her analyses. Unfortunately, even testimony of questionable validity may be persuasive if presented forcefully (Naftulin, Ware, & Donnelly, 1973). Conversely, eminently sound testimony may fall on deaf ears. Experts, however, should never utilize persuasive techniques at the expense of honesty. Expert witnesses must, with equal candor, advocate for their opinion and admit any theoretical, research, or methodological weaknesses in their case (Bonnie & Slobogin, 1980).

The expert who is an effective communicator is best able to convey his or her opinion accurately and thus prevent testimony from being distorted during direct examination, cross-examination, and, to a lesser extent, closing arguments. Regardless of the legal issue before the court, the process of testifying persuasively and ethically remains the same. All verbal exchanges in a courtroom can be explained by a three-component communications model: the *speaker,* the *message,* and the *audience.* For our purposes, the speaker is the expert witness, the message is the testimony, and the audience is the judge and/or jury. The Courtroom Communications Model is described next.

The Speaker: Source Credibility

The expert must be perceived as a credible source of information for weight to be given to his or her testimony. The concept of credibility comprises three dimensions: expertise, trustworthiness, and presentational style.

Expertise

Witnesses must present credentials attesting to their expertise for the specific forensic issue of concern to the court before the trial judge will qualify a witness as an expert. This includes reviewing academic background, professional training, experience, and other indexes of competence.

Attorneys typically elicit such information from experts chronologically. Perhaps a more effective recitation of qualifications is achieved by presenting credentials categorically. This approach provides the judge and jury with a commonsense conceptual framework for defining an expert. The categorical credentialing process has three phases:

1. The attorney conducting direct voir dire conveys to the jury that to be considered a mental health expert, the witness must document academic training, experience, and familiarity with current advances in the expert's specialization.

2. The witness then meets the three stated requirements to be considered an expert by satisfactorily answering the attorney's categorical questions regarding credentials.

3. The judge, acknowledging the psychologist's qualifications, allows the witness to testify as an expert.

Trustworthiness

Once the judge declares someone an expert, the trustworthiness factor of credibility becomes critical to how the witness's testimony will be received. Doubts concerning the expert's trustworthiness stem from factors such as the expert's being retained and paid by the attorney (a "hired gun"), always testifying for one side, and presenting statements that are inconsistent with those made in prior trials.

Research demonstrates that testimony from an unbiased source of high expertise can be given more weight than biased sources with the same perceived expertise (Birnbaum & Stegner, 1979). Unfortunately, even the most objective and honest witness may not be accurately perceived.

Experts are likely to be seen as less trustworthy when they alter their demeanor, from the cooperative witness responding to direct examination to the hostile witness coping with cross-examination. Due to anxiety and/or cautiousness, experts typically become more hesitant while responding during cross-examination. This hesitation can lead judges or jurors to believe that the expert is trying to be deceptive (Conley, O'Barr, & Lind, 1978).

Experts can avoid contributing to this misperception by presenting the same demeanor while testifying under direct and cross-examination. Specifically, if the expert allows for a short latency of response during direct examination (even though the question could be answered immediately), the expert can then take the same pause while responding under cross-examination without appearing to be more hesitant. Under direct examination, experts do not want to be misperceived as a "yeah sayer" for the party retaining them. Experts can increase their credibility along the trustworthiness dimension by acknowledging legitimate weak points in their evaluation procedures, data, or case theory during direct examination. When experts provide opinion testimony, they should state, when appropriate, "I don't know" and "I do not have an opinion on what you asked."

Expert witnesses should always be alert to potential ethical pitfalls associated with the expertise and trustworthiness dimensions of source credibility. Regarding expertise, the attorney conducting direct examination may attempt to induce the expert to make exaggerated claims of his or her knowledge or to offer unwarranted criticism of an opposing expert's competence. With reference to trustworthiness, the expert may be encouraged to understate or omit references to procedures or theories that may undermine the retaining attorney's case. Expert witnesses are, of course, sworn to tell the whole truth, regardless of how it affects either side.

Presentational Style

This is the most elusive of the three dimensions of credibility. In general, the person testifying must have the demeanor of an expert in order to convince the judge and jury that he or she *is* expert. Experts should dress appropriately, speak clearly and loudly enough for everyone to hear, and avoid appearing defensive even when the cross-examining attorney unloads with both barrels. Understanding that the attorney conducting cross-examination is ethically bound to present the best case for his or her client may help to minimize feeling personally attacked.

Experts are often advised to avoid the use of technical jargon when testifying. This is not necessarily sound advice because experts who avoid all jargon may not meet the judge's or jury's expectations of how an expert should testify. It is often appropriate to employ some technical terms and concepts as long as they are used sparingly and then explained in terms that are understandable to jurors.

The Message: Presenting Effective Testimony

The second component of the Courtroom Communications Model is the expert's message, the testimony. Even the most brilliant case analysis may be afforded little weight if the expert cannot present his or her opinions clearly and convincingly.

Emotional and Logical Appeals

There are two types of persuasive appeal: logical and emotional. Logical appeals invite the trier of fact to reason along with the expert, either inductively or deductively. Emotional appeals utilize affectively laden language in an attempt to evoke emotions such as anger, sympathy, or fear, which may facilitate attitude change.

The judicial system acknowledges that jurors have two roles: They are triers of fact and the conscience of the community. Logical appeals are aimed at jurors in their role as trier of fact. Emotional appeals strike a chord with jurors who sometimes function as the conscience of the community. When jurors' emotions and/or moral values lead them to ignore the letter of the law, they are applying the controversial doctrine of jury nullification (Noah, 2001). Jury nullification occurs when jurors intentionally disregard the law and evidence because they are concerned with issues such as sentences being too harsh, the government acting improperly, or racism (Brooks, 2004). Jurors do not have a legal right to ignore the law, but they do have the power to do so. The controversy is whether jurors should knowingly disregard the law if they believe following the law would lead to an unjust or inequitable verdict (Horowitz, 1985).

Legal scholars continue to debate the appropriateness and social value of jurors allowing their emotions or morals to lead them to a verdict that is not bound by a strict application of law (Brown, 1997). Experts, however, are ideally envisioned as objective professionals. If an expert appears too emotionally involved, the judge and jury may think the expert has lost objectivity and therefore give less weight to his or her testimony. For reasons of credibility and ethics, experts should focus on logic, leaving the extralegal factors of emotions and theatrics to attorneys.

The Use of Counterarguments

Perhaps the only constant in court is knowing that one of the two attorneys is going to challenge the expert's case analysis with a rival theory. The expert can mitigate the negative effects of cross-examination by utilizing the following strategy during direct examination. Experts should:

- Make a strong appeal for their opinion.
- Identify and explain rival opinions.
- Discount rival opinions by pointing out their weaknesses.
- Conclude testimony on a strong note by reiterating the validity of their opinion.

This strategy is akin to the medical model's approach to disease prevention because the expert "inoculates" the judge and jury against rival opinions that will be raised by the opposing side, either through a rebuttal expert witness or cross-examination.

The Audience: Factors Affecting Receptivity to Testimony

The third element of the Courtroom Communications Model concerns the audience's receptivity to testimony. Although experts participate in civil litigation more frequently than criminal trials (Gross, 1991), research has, appropriately, focused on juror reaction to both civil and criminal expert testimony. The intrinsic paradox for jurors (and the legal system) is how jurors evaluate the credibility of expert testimony when they lack the knowledge to do so. As discussed later in the chapter, both jury simulation studies and research with actual jurors reveal that factors such as the complexity of testimony, the type of expert, and the quality of expert testimony can affect the impact of expert testimony on jurors.

Ivković and Hans (2003) analyzed transcripts of semistructured interviews to determine factors that actual jurors from civil trials consider when assessing experts and their testimony. They state, "Contrary to the frequent criticism that jurors primarily evaluate expert evidence in terms of its subjective characteristics, the results of our study indicate that jurors consider both the messenger and the message in the course of evaluating the expert's credibility" (p. 441). Specifically, the jurors considered the messengers' credentials, motives, and general impressions, as well as the presentational style and content of the message. Jurors expressed worry or disdain when opposing attorneys raised issues about experts who testify frequently for financial compensation. In addition to the message and messenger, Vidmar (1995) found that when jurors in medical malpractice cases determine the credibility of experts they also consider the courtroom's context and the adversarial pressures placed on experts.

In their simulation, Cooper, Bennett, and Sukel (1996) varied the credentials of experts and the complexity of their testimony. They concluded that only when testimony was highly complex and difficult to understand were mock jurors more persuaded by a well-credentialed expert than an expert with lesser credentials. They hypothesized that this interactive effect resulted from jurors shifting from central processing (evaluating the validity of the testimony itself) to peripheral processing (using subjective characteristics such as the expert's credentials) to determine the credibility of testimony.

Shuman, Whitaker, and Champagne (1994) surveyed jurors and determined that the expert's specialty and occupation did not significantly impact how jurors evaluated credibility. However, the expert's qualifications, quality of reasoning, and lack of bias and who retained the expert did contribute to how jurors perceived experts. Shuman, Champagne, and Whitaker (1996) raise the possibility that jurors may be less influenced by a psychologist (because they may think they do not need assistance to judge human behavior) than by other types of experts (e.g., economist, brain surgeon). Interestingly, Ivković and Hans (2003) observed that jurors are in substantial agreement with what scientists and lawyers (Chesler, Sanders, & Kalmuss, 1988) view as the characteristics of credible experts (e.g., has good credentials, is a clear communicator, avoids being adversarial).

Credibility factors will, of course, vary in significance depending on the particulars of each case. There may also be cases where the facts are so emotionally overwhelming that the potential influence of expert testimony may be significantly undermined (e.g., a mentally ill defendant who slaughtered his entire family may be found guilty—due to jury nullification—even though the evidence and expert testimony indicate that he met statutory criteria for legal insanity).

In addition to the particulars of a case, jury composition may also affect the effectiveness of experts. Most juries are composed of a mix of people with different educational backgrounds, values, and established views on life. Juries are best thought of as a collective of individuals rather than a homogeneous group with shared life experiences and values (Bettinghaus, 1973). To maximize the impact of testimony on a jury, experts must customize their presentational style so that their testimony can be best understood by their audience, the jurors.

Consequently, the most effective strategy for reaching the maximum number of jurors is to state opinions in a variety of ways. Wrapping the same content in different verbal packages will likely increase the number of jurors the expert will educate. For example, at various points during testimony, the expert can explain that someone diagnosed with Schizophrenia has a mental illness, is psychotic, is not in touch with reality, has hallucinations, hears voices, is chemically imbalanced, and is not a "split personality."

Experts can effectively utilize voice inflection and eye contact to help maintain the jury's attention. Expert witnesses should not presume that the judge or jury can accurately assess which aspects of their testimony are most critical to their formulation of the case. It is helpful to identify any important information or formulations for the court. Simply state, "The hospital records documenting Mr. Smith's behavior one hour after the crime were critical to my opinion that he meets the statutory criteria for legal insanity." An expert's unspoken thoughts are not testimony and never become part of the court record.

STRATEGIES TO DISCREDIT EXPERT WITNESS TESTIMONY

The same social psychological principles that affect the credibility of testimony underlie attempts by the opposing attorney to undermine the witness's credibility. Strategies to discredit expert witness testimony, which can negatively impact the expert's presentational style, can be characterized in a variety of ways:

- Demonstrating that the witness does not possess the specific expertise needed for the case.
- Arguing that the methodology used to collect and analyze data is faulty.
- Claiming that the witness made errors in statements of fact.
- Noting that the witness made prior statements inconsistent with his or her current courtroom testimony.
- Portraying the witness as biased (i.e., undermining the trustworthiness dimension of credibility).
- Attacking the general character of the witness.

Witness Lacks Specific Expertise

This approach is often used in voir dire but can be employed during cross-examination as well. The attorney may question the witness's relevant expertise (e.g., "Have you ever been qualified as an expert in a child custody case?") or specialized training (e.g., "Did you ever take courses in the area of violence risk assessment?"). In preparing to testify, psychologists should anticipate these questions and be ready to present their qualifications in a clear, confident manner, readily acknowledging any lack of knowledge or training that is relevant to the issue at hand. Experts should appreciate that sometimes these questions are not designed to disqualify the witness, but rather to diminish credibility along the expertise dimension. It is therefore important to present credentials in a nondefensive manner and be aware that having limited previous courtroom experience is not necessarily a significant negative factor (because the witness would not then be perceived as a long-time "professional witness"). Furthermore, when attempting to demonstrate expertise, psychologists should not minimize their general clinical background; the extensive education and training required to become a licensed psychologist form the bedrock on which forensic expertise is based.

Faulty Methodology

The cross-examining attorney may attempt to question why the witness did not use the same methodology employed by the opposing expert (e.g., questioning why the witness did not administer the same tests). The attorney may also question the reliability and validity of any psychological opinions on the matter before the court. For example, in cases involving violence risk assessment, the attorney may argue that there is no acceptable scientific basis for any mental health professional to predict whether a particular individual is likely to be violent in the future. Expert witnesses should be prepared for this line of questioning and be able to explain the rationale for their methodology and conclusions. In the case of violence risk assessment, the expert could cite recent literature that demonstrates that clinicians' risk assessments are significantly more accurate than chance (e.g., Borum, 1996; Lidz, Mulvey, & Gardner, 1993; Monahan, 2003; Monahan et al., 2001; Otto, 1992).

If a test has been administered, the witness should be prepared to respond to questions about whether it meets standards for admissibility. Some states continue to follow the standard of *Frye v. United States* (1923), which established that methodology must be based on scientific theories and methodologies that have "gained general acceptance in the particular field in which it belongs" (p. 1014). Others follow the federal standard elaborated in *Daubert v. Merrell Dow Pharmaceuticals* (1993), which established four criteria for the court to weigh when considering whether to admit specialized or expert testimony:

- Whether the methodology can be, or has been, tested (and could be proven false).
- Whether the proposed method or procedure has been subject to peer review or publication.
- Whether it has a known or potential error rate (and whether that rate is acceptable).
- Whether it is generally accepted in the relevant scientific community (similar to the *Frye* standard).

Psychologists should be able to provide testimony relevant to these factors, particularly if they are using newer tests and methodologies or applying tests developed in one context to a different situation. Psychologists should also know whether the instrument used has been validated for the target population it is being applied to, including consideration of racial, ethnic, and gender differences.

Errors in Fact

The attorney may attempt to demonstrate that the psychologist obtained inaccurate factual data (e.g., that the expert's opinion about the extent of substance abuse was based solely on the report of the party interviewed and was not substantiated by third-party sources). Psychologists need to be specific about data sources and also be prepared to clarify whether any factual discrepancies are significant regarding formulating an opinion. Attorneys sometimes knowingly attack the expert's use of an insignificant datum that is not relevant to the opinion in order to undermine the expert's presentational style, particularly when an attorney has already unsuccessfully attempted to attack the witness's expertise and trustworthiness (e.g., if an expert miscalculated and testified that a defendant was 78 years old when he was actually 77). By making the expert appear uncertain, the attorney hopes that jurors will begin thinking that the expert is not so sure about his or her "alleged" expertise.

Prior Inconsistent Statements

Due to advances in technology and Internet capacity, attorneys may have access to the witness's professional publications and prior testimony. It is not possible for witnesses to review all such material in preparation for each court appearance. Experts who have staked out a particular position on a controversial issue should be prepared to explain why these prior statements are either not relevant or not inconsistent with the extant case. The one area that always should be reviewed prior to taking the stand is deposition testimony for the current case. Experts should peruse the transcript of their deposition and be ready to explain any discrepancies between deposition testimony and courtroom testimony. The psychologist may explain, for example, that statements quoted from the deposition were taken out of context. If, however, the expert does change a prior opinion or statement in response to new information, the expert should readily acknowledge this.

Witness Bias

A common cross-examination strategy is to portray the witness as having a sustained bias, based on prior testimony and/or publication record. An attorney may point out that the expert typically testifies only for the prosecution. Psychologists can respond by explaining their pattern of testimony (e.g., the base rates in their jurisdiction show that only 7% of criminal defendants evaluated are adjudicated not guilty by reason of insanity). It is also important to distinguish between the percentage of times an expert recommends that a defendant be found criminally responsible and the percentage of times the expert is called to testify for the prosecutor or defense attorney. (A more detailed examination of this issue is provided under sample cross-examination questions later in the chapter.) Attorneys who purposely blur this distinction could make an expert appear biased when, in fact, the expert's work does not justify this insinuation.

Attorneys may also claim that the witness is a hired gun, paid to find whatever the retaining lawyer wants to be entered into the record. Expert witnesses should explain that they are being paid for *time* spent on evaluating the party, preparing a report, and testifying, as opposed to being paid for their *opinion*. Being paid in advance of preparing the written report often undermines this allegation.

Witness's Character

Although rarely used, this issue raises anxiety that the witness's personal life will be discussed in court. In one case involving a court-appointed counselor (following a divorce proceeding), the appellate court ruled that the counselor's own mental health records should be produced (*Cheatham v. Rogers,* 1992). However, provided that the questions are not clearly relevant to the case, experts will likely be supported (by the judge sustaining an objection from the attorney who has retained the witness) in not answering questions about their personal lives. When experts anticipate that aspects of their personal life might be raised during a trial, they should be prepared to respond appropriately. Ideally, in such situations experts should consider at the outset whether to accept a particular case.

VOIR DIRE

Voir dire, meaning "to speak the truth," is an examination by both attorneys that provides the judge with preliminary testimony to determine whether the witness will be allowed to present substantive testimony as an expert on a specific topic. Direct voir dire is conducted by the attorney who called the witness. Cross-voir dire involves questioning by opposing counsel. The judge may also question the witness during this phase of testimony.

In some jurisdictions, at the conclusion of voir dire the judge rules on the witness's qualifications and establishes the limitations of testimony for the trial or hearing. From an impression management viewpoint, voir dire is critical to establishing credibility because it is the witness's first impression on the trier of fact. Regarding testimony by experts, Federal Rule 702 (and similar rules in most states) reads, "[A] witness qualified as an expert by knowledge, skill, experience, training, or education, may testify thereto in the form of an opinion or otherwise." Interestingly, formal education and advanced degrees are not necessary for a witness to be qualified as an expert; Federal Rule 702, and similar rules in most jurisdictions, allow the trial judge discretion.

Voir dire is conducted before the judge whether the legal proceeding is a hearing, bench trial, or jury trial. During voir dire, questioning focuses on whether, based on credentials, the witness has the specific expertise needed to address the disputed issues for the case before the court. Consequently, the witness may be examined about education, training, profession, occupation, experience, publications, and board certification and whether that background constitutes expertise germane to the litigation issues. (For a discussion of board certification in forensic psychology, see Packer & Borum, 2003.) The witness will not offer opinions regarding contested issues for the extant case until after voir dire, providing the judge accepts the witness as an expert.

When an expert has exceptional credentials, opposing counsel may try to stipulate to them to prevent the jury from being overly impressed by the opposing expert. This strategy rarely works because the counsel retaining the witness wants the judge and/or jury to hear the witness's credentials so they *can* be impressed.

Therefore, voir dire not only determines whether a witness will be allowed to testify as an expert, but also allows each attorney the opportunity to influence the trier of fact's perceptions about a witness's credibility. Although voir dire purports to address the expertise dimension of credibility, effective attorneys also try to spin perceptions about the witness's trustworthiness and presentational style.

It is essential to demonstrate during voir dire that the witness has the *relevant* expertise needed to address the *specific* case issues. There is no such thing as a generic expert. A clinician with in-depth knowledge, skill, experience, training, and education pertaining only to child psychotherapy is not an appropriate expert for an insanity defense case involving an adult. The expert's specialized knowledge is the key that the court hopes will unlock the litigation's disputed issues. The better the key fits, the more likely the judge will qualify the witness as an expert. It is unethical for mental health professionals to become involved in cases for which they do not have the appropriate expertise.

As with any phase of a legal proceeding, preparation is key. For reasons of ethics and credibility, voir dire should address specific strengths and weaknesses in the witness's credentials. If relevant weaknesses are not addressed by the attorney calling the witness, they most likely will be dealt with on cross-voir dire.

There are also parallels between rebuttal *witnesses* and rebuttal *professions.* Therefore, if a psychologist and a psychiatrist are opposing experts, voir dire can speak to the specific strengths and weaknesses of each profession's ability to assist the trier of fact (e.g., psychologists administer psychological tests and psychiatrists administer psychotropic medication). When experts are of the same profession, both attorneys will typically avoid emphasizing any weaknesses in their expert's discipline.

Mental health professionals have an ethical and legal obligation not to exaggerate credentials or misrepresent any involvement they have with the case. Similarly, experts are obligated to correct an attorney who misrepresents their qualifications or methods. Most attorneys will not pressure experts into misrepresentation for reasons of law, ethics, and credibility. It should also be noted that how well voir dire is orchestrated is typically less important for bench trials as judges are sensitized to the ways of attorneys and experts.

As mentioned in the expertise section of the Courtroom Communications Model described earlier, an effective method during direct voir dire is to use the jury-friendly approach of presenting credentials categorically. The attorney conducting direct voir dire attempts to provide a conceptual framework for the jurors to acknowledge the witness as an expert. The attorney will accomplish this by demonstrating that the expert has significant training, experience, and current familiarity with his or her field. The opposing attorney may seek to minimize the accomplishments of the expert, raise issues about the extent of expertise and its relevance to the case at hand, or suggest that the expert is biased.

Some examples of questions to anticipate during direct and cross-voir dire are provided next. For simplicity, the questions are based on a hypothetical case in which a witness is testifying in a personal injury lawsuit in which the plaintiff claims to suffer from Posttraumatic Stress Disorder.

Representative Direct Examination Voir Dire Questions

Could you describe to the court your training and education in psychology?

Could you detail any specialized training you received in the area of Posttraumatic Stress Disorder?

How many times have you evaluated parties involved in personal injury lawsuits?

How do you keep up to date with new research and developments in your field?

How many times have you been qualified as an expert in personal injury lawsuits?

Cross-Examination–Voir Dire Questions

Are you board certified? Note: If the expert answers yes, the attorney may ask: By which board? What were the requirements to obtain this board certification? If the expert answers no, the attorney may ask: Why have you not attained board certification?

Do you have a medical degree?

Isn't it true, then, that you cannot prescribe medications?

Isn't it true that you have testified many more times for plaintiffs than for defendants?

How much are you being paid for your opinion today?

Analysis

Experts should present their education, training, and experience in a coherent manner, emphasizing those elements most germane to the case's forensic issues. It is important for expert witnesses not to be defensive; rather, psychologists should be confident and clear about the thoroughness of their clinical and forensic background, allowing them to provide expertise beyond the ken of the typical juror or judge. It is helpful to prepare for questions that differentiate psychological training from that of physicians. The essential point is to elucidate the relevant special expertise of psychologists (e.g., psychological testing).

In terms of questions concerning board certification, psychologists should be careful about claiming diplomate status granted by organizations other than the American Board of Professional Psychology (ABPP; e.g., Hansen, 2000). Attorneys are becoming increasingly sophisticated about the issue of "vanity boards" and, if diplomate status has not been awarded by ABPP (which is the only board certification in forensic psychology included by APA in its directory), the psychologist's credibility may be undermined by focused cross-examination (Dattilio, Sadoff, & Gutheil, 2003; Golding, 1999; Packer & Borum, 2003). Unlike in the field of medicine, ABPP has determined that it is not appropriate in psychology to claim to be board eligible.

In terms of payment for services provided, most experts receive professional fees that are substantial compared to the income of an average juror. The opposing attorney may want to emphasize this point to undermine trustworthiness. It is important to respond matter-of-factly to such questions (as opposed to cavalier responses, such as "I'm being paid substantially less than you are, counselor"). Experts should be clear that they are being paid for their time and professional work, not for their opinions per se, and that their fees are consistent with those charged by other experts with similar credentials and experience.

As noted earlier, attorneys may attempt to undermine the psychologist's credibility by pointing out that the psychologist has testified more often for one side than another (e.g., for plaintiffs in personal injury cases or for defendants in criminal cases). If you have been retained on numerous occasions but did not testify because your opinion did not conform to the position of the attorney who hired you, it is essential to include this information to rebut the presumption of bias inherent in this question. Psychologists who keep records pertaining to this issue are better able to accurately respond to such questions.

At the conclusion of voir dire, depending on the jurisdiction, the attorney calling the witness may ask the judge to qualify the witness as an expert. Should the witness be accepted as an expert, direct examination follows by focusing on the case's substantive disputed issues. The expert witness can now provide opinions based on facts and inferences, unless the judge has imposed limits (which can vary greatly). In other jurisdictions, the judge will not formally qualify the witness as an expert at the conclusion of voir dire, and the cross-examining attorney may subsequently object once the witness offers an opinion. At that point, the judge will rule on whether the witness is qualified to provide expert testimony.

Limits for specific issues might restrict the expert to describing rather than offering conclusions. The judge could also instruct the jury to consider the limitations of the expert's qualifications or the evaluative methods used by the expert when deciding what weight, if any, to assign to the testimony. Additionally, the expert may not be allowed to testify on certain issues (e.g., childhood disorders or neuropsychological testing).

Voir dire does not generally produce surprises for either attorneys or expert witnesses, provided that all parties are prepared. Voir dire also serves as a time for the witness to become comfortable with the courtroom setting and with the attorneys, judge, and jury. The next phase for the expert witness is direct examination on the forensic issues relevant to the court.

DIRECT EXAMINATION

Direct examination begins after voir dire. The attorney calling the expert asks questions that allow the witness to inform the trier of fact about the expert's conception of the case. Direct examination may be elicited in a fragmented format (the expert is asked to respond to highly focused questions that often elicit only brief responses) or in a more open-ended style (the expert is allowed to provide a more elaborate explanation). In some circumstances, the attorney may be permitted by the judge to elicit testimony as a narrative (the expert witness is allowed to provide a lengthier, free-flowing recitation). Regardless of the interrogatory style used by the attorney, a goal of direct examination is to convince the trier of fact that the expert is knowledgeable and trustworthy. Direct examination may be interrupted by opposing counsel's objections, which will be sustained or overruled by the judge.

Direct examination should allow the expert to address those issues that may be brought forth on cross-examination. For reasons both of ethics and credibility, any weaknesses in the expert's evaluative procedures or conceptions should be explained on direct examination. Experts should also avoid being depicted as lie detectors; that is, they should not attest to the truthfulness of parties who were examined. Additionally, it is often best to refrain from ad hominen attacks on the credibility of opposing experts, although it is acceptable to critique their methodology (e.g., explaining why a test administered in a nonstandardized format is invalid) and opinions (e.g., explaining the basis for disagreeing with the opposing expert's opinion). To demonstrate expertise and trustworthiness, the witness can explain that rival hypotheses about the case were considered and deemed not valid, stating the reasons why this is the case.

Before testifying, experts and attorneys need to decide whether to present the bottom-line opinion at the start or end of the direct examination. Some prefer stating the opinion at the start of direct examination to make it clear where the testimony will lead. Others prefer to build a foundation for the opinion before placing it on the record. The judge and jury, of course, have a general idea of what the expert's opinion will be simply by observing who has called the expert to testify. Exactly when experts state their opinions is a matter of preference and style, rather than of ethical or legal concern, as long as the basis for the opinion is provided.

Because the rules in all jurisdictions governing expert testimony include exceptions to hearsay testimony, experts may form opinions based on statements and information generated by others. However, not all such sources of information may be allowed as evidence. Usually, only statements or information typically relied on by experts, and that would be admissible if entered directly, will be accepted (Federal Rules of Evidence, Rule 703). Examples of such exceptions to the hearsay rule include review of medical records and obtaining collateral information from third parties that are used to establish a forensic judgment (as opposed to a factual determination). The specific rules regarding this issue vary across jurisdictions, and it is not the expert witness's responsibility to determine whether certain data sources will be found admissible by the court; this is a legal issue that will be argued by the attorneys and ultimately decided by the judge. However, it behooves experts to be reasonably familiar with the rules of admissibility in their jurisdictions to guide them in obtaining admissible data. It is also advisable, when in doubt, to consult with the retaining attorney prior to relying on information that may not be admissible.

There is an ongoing debate in the mental health profession about the appropriate limits of expert witness testimony. Some argue that experts should never provide ultimate issue testimony (i.e., experts should not give an opinion about an ultimate legal issue, such as whether a father or mother should be given custody or whether a defendant was insane at the time of the crime). Proponents of this view (e.g., Tillbrook,

Mumley, & Grisso, 2003) argue that offering opinions on ultimate issues exceeds the clinical expertise of the witness and invades the province of the trier of fact. By contrast, Rogers and Ewing (2003) argue that failure to provide an opinion on the ultimate issue leads to confusion for the trier of fact as well as artifice (i.e., the expert uses language that is equivalent to the ultimate issue). It is worth noting that the Specialty Guidelines do not prohibit ultimate issue testimony but do caution that "professional observations, inferences, and conclusions must be distinguished from legal facts, opinions, and conclusions. Forensic psychologists are prepared to explain the relationship between their expert testimony and the legal issues and facts of an instant case" (Committee on Ethical Guidelines, 1991, Section VII.F). (Further discussion on this issue is found in Chapter 7.)

Representative Questions, Answers, and Analysis

This section offers examples of direct examination questions, answers, and analysis for the personal injury case used in the voir dire section. For parsimony, not every question is answered or analyzed. Also, this sample transcript does not reflect the typical order of questions asked but does represent customary areas of inquiry.

Q: Doctor, how did you inform the plaintiff of your role and the limits of confidentiality?

A: At the outset of the first interview, I informed the plaintiff about my role, the purpose of the evaluation, and with whom the information would be shared. I asked the plaintiff to paraphrase the explanation and determined that he understood all of the information. I also then had the plaintiff read and sign a written explanation.

Analysis: It is good practice to include a written consent form, although it is not advisable to rely only on such a form because a signature by the party does not necessarily signify full comprehension. The expert in this case provided, in both oral and written form, an explanation of the evaluation's purpose and the limits of confidentiality and asked the plaintiff to paraphrase this explanation in his own words. Evaluators should document this assessment of the party's comprehension (Shapiro, 1991).

Q: Can you describe the procedures you employed in evaluating Mr. Jones?

A: I conducted two forensic interviews of Mr. Jones, obtained collateral information from his wife, reviewed previous employment records, and reviewed progress notes from his treating psychiatrist. In addition, I administered the MMPI-2, the WAIS-III, and the SIRS.

Analysis: The witness provided a comprehensive list of evaluative procedures used. However, the expert should explain that an MMPI-2 and a WAIS-III are psychological tests and that the SIRS is a forensic assessment instrument designed to assess malingering or exaggeration. In addition, the expert should provide the full names of the tests and instruments (Minnesota Multiphasic Personality Inventory-2, Wechsler Adult Intelligence Scale-III, Structured Interview of Reported Symptoms), always noting that the trier of fact should not be presumed to be knowledgeable about psychological jargon, concepts, and tests. If the full test names are not stated, the testimony will be less meaningful. Additionally, the purpose and uses of the tests should be explained.

Q: Based on your interviews, did you consider Mr. Jones to be truthful?

A: Although assessing the truthfulness of a plaintiff is beyond the scope of a mental health professional, I can note that the information he provided was internally consistent and was corroborated by other sources of information. Furthermore, based on both the MMPI-2 and the SIRS that I administered and interpreted, his responses indicated that he was not attempting to either exaggerate or minimize his symptoms.

Analysis: The witness appropriately reframed the question, thus avoiding overstepping the boundaries of clinical/forensic expertise by commenting on truthfulness. The witness's response was limited to the clinical data relevant to the issue. Furthermore, by not endorsing what the retaining attorney asked, the witness enhanced his trustworthiness by demonstrating independence from the attorney.

Q: Did you arrive at a diagnosis of the plaintiff?

A: Yes.

Q: And what was that diagnosis?

A: Posttraumatic Stress Disorder.

Q: Can you explain what Posttraumatic Stress Disorder is?

A: In my opinion, Mr. Jones is diagnosed with Posttraumatic Stress Disorder, which, in his case, is marked most prominently by intrusive thoughts, recurrent nightmares, attempts to avoid situations that are similar to that of the original trauma, and a startle reaction whenever he hears a train whistle.

Analysis: The expert listened carefully and answered the yes/no question about diagnosis directly, waiting for the attorney to ask for more detail. The expert then provided specific symptoms, consistent with the *Diagnostic and Statistical Manual of Mental Disorders,* fourth edition text revision (American Psychiatric Association, 2000), in a clear presentational style, thereby enhancing credibility on the expertise dimension.

Q: In your opinion, was the accident the proximate cause of the plaintiff's injuries?

A: In my opinion, the plaintiff was functioning without significant impairment until he experienced the accident. Following the accident, his functioning deteriorated, as evidenced by an inability to work and a withdrawal from social interactions with others. I considered alternative explanations but can find no other reasonable explanation for his impairment.

Analysis: In response to this question, the witness avoided using legal terminology ("proximate cause") and explained the opinion clearly, using clinical data, and related it to the legal criteria. Furthermore, the response demonstrated that the expert considered alternative hypotheses and explanations, which could elevate the expert's trustworthiness.

CROSS-EXAMINATION

Cross-examination follows direct examination and is conducted by the opposing counsel. Depending on the jurisdiction, judges either allow or restrict questioning on cross-examination to the scope of direct examination. The cross-examining attorney will typically use variations of the strategies described earlier in this chapter to discredit the witness's credibility across the dimensions of expertise, trustworthiness, and presentational style. Cross-examination is best diffused when weak points have been raised on direct examination and the expert has been informed in advance of the style of the opposing attorney. The expert should also be aware that judges occasionally question experts, although most are careful to not undermine what an attorney is attempting to accomplish.

Cross-examination allows the opposing attorney an opportunity to challenge the credibility of the expert testimony. During cross-examination, attorneys will attempt to paint experts in the most negative light possible. Court rules facilitate these efforts by allowing attorneys to ask leading questions (e.g., "You didn't speak to Mr. Jones's ex-wife, did you, Doctor?") on cross-examination. The lawyer may claim that much of what the so-called expert did was "not good enough," and that whatever the expert did not do, or neglected to ask the plaintiff, was essential.

When thinking about cross-examination, the word "stress" (or "flight") may come to mind. Experts should not take a vigorous cross-examination personally. It is the attorney's professional responsibility to attempt to discredit the opposing witness, even if the techniques may seem to the expert unfair or unwarranted. Being aware of the strategies that attorneys employ will help the expert maintain composure and avoid the perception of being defensive or argumentative.

Representative Questions, Answers, and Analysis

This section presents examples of cross-examination questions, answers, and analysis for the personal injury case used in the voir dire and direct examination sections. As in the previous sections, this sample transcript does not reflect the typical order of questioning but does represent customary areas of inquiry.

Q: Ms. Smith, how much time did you spend interviewing the plaintiff, Mr. Jones?

A: First, I'd like to clarify that I have a PhD in psychology and my proper title is Dr. Smith. I spent a total of five hours interviewing Mr. Jones.

Analysis: If the attorney continually refers to a psychologist as "Mr." or "Ms.," it is acceptable practice to calmly correct the attorney once. If the attorney persists, it is best not to continue arguing this point, as this will detract from the substantive issues and portray the psychologist as ego involved. Furthermore, if this tactic continues to be used by the attorney, it will likely be perceived by the judge and/or jury as inappropriate.

Q: If I understood you correctly, on direct examination you testified that the plaintiff may have misrepresented elements of his account of the accident.

A: Actually, what I stated was that the issue of truthfulness is not one that I, or any mental health professional, can testify to. However, all of the data available to me indicated that the plaintiff's responses were consistent and that his responses on psychological testing did not indicate a deliberate attempt to misrepresent his mental condition.

Analysis: The cross-examining attorney attempted to distort the psychologist's direct testimony. However, the psychologist's response demonstrated careful attention to the question and an accurate characterization of the direct examination testimony. It is critical to listen carefully to questions and not be lulled by an attorney's cadence or matter-of-fact tone.

Q: You testified that the only tests you administered to the plaintiff were the MMPI-2, the WAIS-III, and the SIRS. If you had more time, would you have administered more tests that could have disproved the accuracy of your diagnosis and conclusions?

A: I chose the tests to administer based on the particular issues that were raised by the plaintiff's history and clinical presentation. I was under no time constraints and, had I felt that additional tests would have been useful, I would have administered them as well. However, it was my professional opinion as a psychologist that the tests I administered were sufficient to allow me to address the relevant forensic issues in this case.

Analysis: The concept of "more is always better" can be misleading. It is not considered good practice to administer tests that do not help elucidate the psycholegal issues under consideration. Only tests that are relevant to the particular issue (i.e., by helping to clarify a diagnosis, establishing validity or response bias, or assessing functional capacity relevant to the legal matter) and that are valid for the population should be used (Heilbrun, 1992; see also Chapter 2).

Q: How many times have you testified in personal injury cases?

A: I have testified approximately twenty times in such cases.

Q: In how many of those cases did you testify for the plaintiff?

A: I have testified fourteen times for plaintiffs.

Q: So, if my math is right, in 70% of the cases in which you have testified, you offered an opinion favorable to the plaintiff. Isn't this because you have a bias toward the plaintiff side in such cases?

A: That is not the case. I have been retained by plaintiffs' attorneys in many more cases—I would estimate about thirty times in all—and in many of these cases I formed an opinion that was not favorable to the plaintiff's side, so they chose not to call me to testify.

Analysis: Although questioning designed to undermine the expert's trustworthiness by implying a systematic bias toward one side often occurs during voir dire, it is also sometimes used during cross-examination. The expert parried this question by pointing out that she had frequently formed opinions contrary to the plaintiff's position and that she was therefore not called to testify. This information bolsters trustworthiness because the expert attested to a track record of independence from the side retaining her.

Experts who consistently provide expert testimony for only one side (e.g., fathers in child custody cases) need to carefully consider the reasons for this pattern. For example, the psychologist may have developed a theory or published in an area that is relevant to a specific issue and therefore is more likely to be retained by a particular side. However, if the unbalanced pattern is due to the psychologist's personal value system, the Specialty Guidelines (Committee on Ethical Guidelines, 1991, III.E) specifically caution psychologists about involvement in cases in which personal beliefs or moral values "may interfere with their ability to practice competently."

After cross-examination, the retaining attorney may choose to follow up with redirect examination; the cross-examining attorney may then respond with re-cross-examination. The conclusion of testimony does not mean that the judge and jury stop assessing credibility. Even after testimony is completed, the manner in which the expert acts in the courtroom will impact credibility. Experts who voluntarily become part of the gallery after their testimony is completed, or sit by an attorney, risk being perceived as biased or identified as part of the legal team retaining them. This may damage the credibility of the expert along the trustworthiness dimension and undermine the expert's being perceived as an objective witness whose job is to assist the trier of fact, rather than as an advocate for the retaining attorney. Experts should also be aware that jurors may observe them outside the courtroom, such as in the corridor or in the cafeteria.

CONCLUSION

Legal systems have utilized expert witnesses for approximately 700 years. Experts have testified on everything from bloodletting to DNA analysis. The twenty-first century will witness experts testifying about issues we cannot presently envision. The rules governing expert testimony and the substance of expert testimony are works in progress because human nature and science are ever changing. What will not change is the need for assistance on topics beyond the knowledge of jurors and courts. As technology progresses, the disparity between lay and expert knowledge widens, and the need for expert witnesses increases.

Experts must always strive to formulate inferences as objectively as possible. It is incumbent on experts to prevent misuse or misrepresentation of their work. To accomplish this, it is appropriate for experts to persuasively advocate for their positions. To be persuasive, experts must appear credible. Expertise, trustworthiness, and presentational style synergistically blend to determine the expert's credibility. When called to court, the expert should leave his or her ego at home. Do not become arrogant during direct examination or defensive on cross-examination. Understand that attorneys, not experts, win and lose cases. Experts must remain within the boundaries of their competence and thoroughly prepare for clinical issues, ethical concerns, and legal matters relevant to each phase of the trial.

The clinical content and legal process associated with expert witness testimony will constantly evolve even though the goal of providing courts with specialized knowledge will remain immutable. Experts should participate in every case as if it will be appealed and the proffered testimony will be responsible for a change in law or court rules. The credibility of expert testimony depends on the credibility of everything done before testifying, such as reviewing relevant case law and scientific literature, accurately explaining the purpose of the interview and limitations of confidentiality, selecting an appropriate assessment methodology, and interpreting data properly. The credibility of our legal system depends on the credibility of its witnesses.

REFERENCES

American Psychiatric Association. (2000). *Diagnostic and statistical manual of mental disorders* (4th ed., text rev.). Washington, DC: Author.

American Psychological Association. (2002). Ethical principles of psychologists and code of conduct. *American Psychologist, 57,* 1060–1073.

Anderten, P., Staulcup, V., & Grisso, T. (1980). On being ethical in legal places. *Professional Psychology, 11,* 764–773.

Bank, S. (2001). From mental health professional to expert witness: Testifying in court. *New Directions for Mental Health Services, 91,* 57–66.

Bank, S., & Poythress, N. (1982). Elements of persuasion in expert testimony. *Journal of Psychiatry and Law, 10,* 173–204.

Bersoff, D. N. (2003). *Ethical conflicts in psychology* (3rd ed.). Washington, DC: American Psychological Association.

Bettinghaus, E. (1973). *Persuasive communication* (2nd ed.). New York: Holt, Rinehart and Winston.

Birnbaum, M., & Stegner, S. (1979). Source credibility in social judgment: Bias, expertise, and the judge's point of view. *Journal of Personality and Social Psychology, 37,* 48–74.

Bonnie, R., & Slobogin, C. (1980). The role of mental health professionals in the criminal process: The case for "informed speculation." *Virginia Law Review, 66,* 427–522.

Borum, R. (1996). Improving the clinical practice of violence risk assessment: Technology, guidelines, and training. *American Psychologist, 51,* 945–956.

Brodsky, S. L. (1999). *The expert expert witness: More maxims and guidelines for testifying in court.* Washington, DC: American Psychological Association.

Brooks, T. (2004). A defense of jury nullification. *Res Publica, 10,* 401–423.

Brown, D. K. (1997). Jury nullification within the rule of law. *Minnesota Law Review, 81,* 1149–1200.

Cheatham v. Rogers, 824 S.W.2d 231 (1992).

Chesler, M. A., Sanders, J., & Kalmuss, D. S. (1988). *Social science in court: Mobilizing experts in the school desegregation cases.* Madison: University of Wisconsin Press.

Committee on Ethical Guidelines. (1991). Specialty guidelines for forensic psychologists. *Law and Human Behavior, 15,* 655–665.

Conley, J., O'Barr, W., & Lind, E. (1978). The power of language: Presentational style in the courtroom. *Duke Law Journal, 6,* 1375–1399.

Cooper, J., Bennett, E. A., & Sukel, H. L. (1996). Complex scientific testimony: How do jurors make decisions? *Law and Human Behavior, 20,* 379–394.

Cunningham, M. D., & Goldstein, A. M. (2003). Sentencing determinations in death penalty cases. In I. B. Weiner (Series Ed.) & A. M. Goldstein (Vol. Ed.), *Comprehensive handbook of psychology: Vol. 11. Forensic psychology* (pp. 407–436). Hoboken, NJ: Wiley.

Dattilio, F. M., Sadoff, R. L., & Gutheil, T. G. (2003). Board certification in forensic psychiatry and psychology: Separating the chaff from the wheat. *Journal of Psychiatry and Law, 31,* 5–19.

Daubert v. Merrell Dow Pharmaceuticals, Inc., 509 U.S. 579 (1993).

Eigen, J., & Andoll, G. (1986). From mad-doctor to forensic witness: The evolution of early English court psychiatry. *International Journal of Law and Psychiatry, 9,* 159–169.

Ewing, C. P. (2003). Expert testimony: Law and practice. In I. B. Weiner (Series Ed.) & A. M. Goldstein (Vol. Ed.), *Comprehensive handbook of psychology: Vol. 11. Forensic psychology* (pp. 55–66). Hoboken, NJ: Wiley.

Federal Rules of Evidence, Rule 702.

Federal Rules of Evidence, Rule 703.

Fitch, L., Petrella, R., & Wallace, J. (1987). Legal ethics and the use of mental health experts in criminal cases. *Behavioral Sciences and the Law, 5*(2), 105–117.

Frye v. United States, 293 F. 1013 (1923).

Golding, S. L. (1999, August). *The* voir dire *of forensic experts: Issues of qualification and training.* Presented at American Psychological Association Annual Convention, Boston.

Gross, S. (1991). Expert evidence. *Wisconsin Law Review,* 1113–1232.

Hansen, M. (2000). Expertise to go. *ABA Journal, 86,* 44–52.

Heilbrun, K. (1992). The role of psychological testing in forensic assessment. *Law and Human Behavior, 16,* 257–272.

Holdsworth, W. (1956). *A history of the English law.* London: Methuen.

Horowitz, I. A. (1985). The effect of jury nullification instruction on verdicts and jury functioning in criminal trials. *Law and Human Behavior, 9,* 25–36.

Ivković, S. K., & Hans, V. P. (2003). Jurors' evaluations of expert testimony: Judging the messenger and the message. *Law and Social Inquiry, 28,* 441–482.

Kempin, F. (1973). *Historical introduction to Anglo-American law* (2nd ed.). St. Paul, MN: West.

Landsman, S. (1995). Of witches, madmen, and products liability: An historical survey of the use of expert testimony. *Behavioral Sciences and the Law, 13,* 131–157.

Lidz, C. W., Mulvey, E. P., & Gardner, W. (1993). The accuracy of predictions of violence to others. *Journal of the American Medical Association, 269,* 1007–1011.

Melton, G., Petrila, J., Poythress, N., & Slobogin, C. (1997). *Psychological evaluations for the courts* (2nd ed.). New York: Guilford Press.

Monahan, J. (2003). Violence risk assessment. In I. B. Weiner (Series Ed.) & A. M. Goldstein (Vol. Ed.), *Comprehensive handbook of psychology: Vol. 11. Forensic psychology* (pp. 527–540). Hoboken, NJ: Wiley.

Monahan, J., Steadman, H. J., Silver, E., Appelbaum, P. S., Robbins, P. C., Mulvey, E. P., et al. (2001). *Rethinking risk assessment: MacArthur study of mental disorder and violence.* New York: Oxford University Press.

Naftulin, D., Ware, J., & Donnelly, F. (1973). The Doctor Fox lecture: A paradigm of educational seduction. *Journal of Medical Education, 48,* 630–635.

Noah, L. (2001). Civil jury nullification. *Iowa Law Review, 88,* 1601–1658.

Otto, R. (1992). Prediction of dangerous behavior: A review and analysis of "second-generation" research. *Forensic Reports, 5,* 103–133.

Packer, I. K., & Borum, R. (2003). Forensic training and practice. In I. B. Weiner (Series Ed.) & A. M. Goldstein (Vol. Ed.), *Comprehensive handbook of psychology: Vol. 11. Forensic psychology* (pp. 21–32). Hoboken, NJ: Wiley.

Rogers, R., & Ewing, C. P. (2003). The prohibition of ultimate opinions: A misguided enterprise. *Journal of Forensic Psychology Practice, 3,* 65–75.

Saks, M. (1990). Expert witnesses, nonexpert witnesses, and nonwitness experts. *Law and Human Behavior, 14,* 291–313.

Saks, M., & Hastie, R. (1978). *Social psychology in court.* New York: Van Nostrand.

Shapiro, D. (1991). Informed consent in forensic evaluations. *Psychotherapy in Private Practice, 9,* 145–154.

Shuman, D. W., Champagne, A., & Whitaker, E. (1996). Juror assessments of the believability of expert witnesses: A literature review. *Jurimetrics Journal, 36,* 371–382.

Shuman, D. W., Whitaker, E., & Champagne, A. (1994). An empirical examination of the use of expert witnesses in the courts: Pt. 2. A three city study. *Jurimetrics Journal, 34,* 193–208.

Slovenko, R. (1987). The lawyer and the forensic expert: Boundaries of ethical practice. *Behavioral Sciences and the Law, 5,* 119–147.

Smith, S. (1989). Mental health expert witnesses: Of science and crystal balls. *Behavioral Sciences and the Law, 7,* 145–180.

Tillbrook, C., Mumley, D., & Grisso, T. (2003). Avoiding expert opinions on the ultimate legal question: The case for integrity. *Journal of Forensic Psychology Practice, 3,* 77–87.

Vidmar, N. (1995). *Medical malpractice and the American jury: Confronting the myths about jury incompetence, deep pockets, and outrageous damage awards.* Ann Arbor: University of Michigan Press.

Weissman, H. N., & DeBow, D. M. (2003). Ethical principles and professional competencies. In I. B. Weiner (Series Ed.) & A. M. Goldstein (Vol. Ed.), *Comprehensive handbook of psychology: Vol. 11. Forensic psychology* (pp. 33–53). Hoboken, NJ: Wiley.

Ziskin, J., & Faust, D. (1995). *Coping with psychiatric and psychological testimony* (5th ed.). Los Angeles: Law and Psychology Press.

CHAPTER 17

Lessons for Forensic Practice Drawn from the Law of Malpractice

Stuart A. Greenberg, Daniel W. Shuman, Stephen R. Feldman, Collin Middleton, and Charles Patrick Ewing

Greenberg and Shuman (1997) identified 10 principal differences in therapeutic and forensic roles and addressed the problems of these conflicting roles in the context of an individual forensic case. This chapter focuses on an 11th difference between the roles, namely, the difference in the ways forensic examiners and therapists are at risk for malpractice claims. Because one of the goals of this chapter is to provide a concise review of the law of expert witness tort liability for malpractice, we begin with a discussion of the law of expert witness malpractice and its grounding in the principles of tort law, as well as those malpractice risks that are substantially greater in forensic practice than in the practice of psychotherapy. But our goal is not merely descriptive. Rather, we seek to examine the differences in the tensions that exist for therapists and forensic mental health professionals to provide recommendations for how to be a better expert, not just how to avoid being sued successfully.

The law of malpractice, legally conceptualized, is about tort claims and defenses. Accordingly, this chapter does not address professional sanctions and licensure issues, although many of the same normative concerns exist. The approach we take, however, unlike many authors on professional malpractice, is not fear driven. Although the risk of malpractice exposure does exit, it remains small. Nonetheless, addressing that risk is consistent with increasing an expert's efficacy.

THE LAW OF EXPERT WITNESS MALPRACTICE

The risk that a testifying mental health professional may be successfully sued for malpractice as an expert, though not great, has nonetheless increased beyond the level of insignificance that once existed:

> Not long ago expert witnesses were considered to be friends of the court, people whose willingness to take time out of their busy professional lives and participate in the judicial process entitled them to absolute immunity from civil liability for anything they said on the witness stand. . . . Lawsuits against so-called friendly experts, while still relatively rare, are multiplying. And those efforts have been meeting with increasing success. (Hansen, 2000, p. 17)

There are several potential explanations for this changing landscape: (a) economic pressures to recoup litigation losses, (b) a decrease in the valuation of long-term alliances, and (c) an increase in untrained experts seeking to supplement falling incomes with expert testimony (Shuman & Greenberg, 2003). Whatever the reason, there is a modest but demonstrable increase in such claims.

In the past, the risk of successful malpractice litigation against expert witnesses was lessened by the doctrine of immunity, which, when applicable, bars claims that would otherwise be valid. Immunity is recognized by courts and legislatures to further certain social policies (e.g., encouraging helpful expert testimony) regarded as more important than compensating an individual for harm caused by the immunized conduct. Some courts and commentators conclude that the absence of any risk of civil liability will best encourage the unfettered participation of potential witnesses in providing helpful testimony; others conclude that the threat of civil liability will provide the optimal incentive for their most careful and well-considered participation (Hanson, 1996).

Competing policy considerations, not concerns for the welfare of expert witnesses, drive this debate. From one perspective, immunity insulates experts from partisan pressures imposed by parties and their advocates, leaving them free to speak the truth without fear of retaliation. From another perspective, accountability encourages responsible and trustworthy performance and discourages negligent, unreliable, and irresponsible testimony. Immunity is not conferred for the benefit of any individual but for society and its institutions. The central question is which policy will result in the court's being able to benefit from the most reliable, helpful, and trustworthy testimony? Trials, after all, seek to ascertain the truth of the facts in dispute.

THE CASE FOR WITNESS IMMUNITY

Those who argue in favor of witness immunity as an incentive for frank and forthright witness participation reject the argument that tort liability provides a useful incentive for witnesses. Noting that there remains both the threat of criminal prosecution for perjured testimony and the powerful tool of cross-examination, they argue that the further risk of civil liability is both unnecessary and redundant:

> If witnesses are concerned about being sued by clients, they will be unwilling to participate or may shade their responses in ways they anticipate will minimize their liability. Protecting witness from liability will prevent witnesses from adopting extreme positions favorable to their clients merely to avoid litigation by dissatisfied clients. Arguably, the present legal system format already adequately achieves justice without holding witnesses liable. All expert witnesses are subject to cross examination, and the threat of perjury adequately protects the legal system from erroneous witness statements. (Hanson, 1996, pp. 508–509)

This argument is applied with equal force to the immunity of expert witnesses:

> In sum, the fact that an expert witness is retained by a party has no bearing on the underlying rationale of witness immunity. That basic rationale—ensuring objective, reliable testimony—dictates in favor of immunity for experts. As a policy matter, the economics of

Table 17.1   The Rationale for Immunity

Candor: Immunity encourages frank testimony and withdraws pressures to avoid subsequent lawsuits; without immunity, objectivity would be threatened.

Judicial efficiency: Immunity prevents the endless proliferation of lawsuits.

Availability of expertise: A wide cross-section of impartial experts would be available; liability would discourage occasional experts because of costs and risks.

Facilitates crucial functions of the trier of fact: Expert immunity aids the trier of fact in, for example, malpractice determinations that require expert testimony as to the standard of care and mental illness determinations.

Being retained is conceptually irrelevant: An expert witness being retained by a party has no bearing on the underlying rationale of witness immunity.

> expert testimony generally also favor immunity as a means of ensuring that a wide cross section of impartial experts are not deterred from testifying by the threat of liability. (*Bruce v. Byrne-Stevens,* 1989, p. 670)

In an adversary-based legal system, controversy, if not open conflict, between litigants is common, and the courts, counsel, and expert witnesses all may be blamed by litigants for their losses. Were the law to allow for the filing of subsequent lawsuits against expert witnesses, nonprevailing litigants would be provided the opportunity to endlessly relitigate the underlying conflicts. To prevent this potential cycle of relitigation, most jurisdictions grant expert witnesses immunity from such civil liability. The principal arguments for witness immunity are summarized in Table 17.1.

THE CASE AGAINST WITNESS IMMUNITY

Those who argue against immunity for expert witnesses maintain that the risk of civil liability provides a powerful incentive for witnesses to testify truthfully and honestly. "The main arguments against witness immunity for expert witnesses center on the basic premise that the threat of liability will encourage experts to be more careful and more accurate in their testimony" (Hanson, 1996, p. 509). In particular, as applied to expert witnesses, opponents of immunity conceptualize the relationship between litigant and expert as being no different from any other professional-client relationship for which a breach of the standard of care may give rise to a claim of liability. Noting that the duty is to the client who has retained the expert, those who argue against immunity for expert witnesses maintain:

> We . . . do not believe that the threat of liability will encourage experts to take extreme and ridiculous positions in favor of their clients in order to avoid a suit by them. Rather, imposing liability would encourage experts to be careful and accurate. They are liable if they perform their service negligently. Certainly these professional individuals are subject to liability in any of their other work if they fail to comply with the degree of care, skill and

Table 17.2   The Rationale against Immunity

Accountability: Risk of liability would encourage experts to be careful and accurate.

Voluntary participation: With rare exception, experts cannot be compelled to testify.

Fee for services: Experts are retained and compensated for the attendant risks.

Advocacy: Experts function as professionals selling their expert services rather than as unbiased court servants.

Client protection: The fact that this service may be related to litigation should not bar their clients from protection against negligent service.

proficiency commonly exercised by ordinarily skillful, careful and prudent professionals and if their failure to do so causes injury to their client. The fact that this particular service may be related to litigation should not bar their clients this protection. . . . There is no reason to believe that professionals will abandon the area of litigation support merely because they will be held to the same standard of care applicable to their other areas of practice. (*Murphy v. Mathews*, 1992, p. 680)

The main arguments against immunity are summarized in Table 17.2. In essence, they reason that, no more or less than any other member of society, experts owe an obligation to others to act reasonably, avoiding both intentional and negligent harm, and that, like other members of society, experts should be bound to meet their professional obligations in and out of the courtroom.

DECISIONS RECOGNIZING WITNESS IMMUNITY

As a general rule, courts grant lay and expert witnesses immunity for defamation claims based on the witnesses' pretrial or trial testimony (*Bird v. W. C. W.,* 1994): "A witness is absolutely privileged to publish defamatory matter concerning another in communications preliminary to a proposed judicial proceeding or as a part of a judicial proceeding in which he is testifying, if it has some relation to the proceeding" (American Law Institute, 1981, 588). There is general agreement that this grant of immunity for defamation claims does not include criminal or disciplinary proceedings. This consensus about immunity, however, breaks down in the consideration of its scope. Should the grant of immunity include claims based in theories other than defamation?

Bruce v. Byrne-Stevens (1989), recognizing absolute immunity for experts, represents one of the broadest grants of immunity. Refusing to limit this grant of immunity to defamation claims or appointed experts, the court reasoned:

In sum, the fact that an expert witness is retained by a party has no bearing on the underlying rationale of witness immunity. That basic rationale—ensuring objective, reliable testimony—dictates in favor of immunity for experts. As a policy matter, the economics of expert testimony generally also favor immunity as a means of ensuring that a wide cross section of impartial experts are not deterred from testifying by the threat of liability. (p. 670)

Construed most broadly by other courts, this grant of immunity includes not only conduct on the witness stand but conduct in preparation for testimony, even when that occurred prior to the filing of the instant action:

> Petitioner also argues that he is entitled to judicial witness immunity for his . . . appraisals . . . which were prepared prior to the filing of the underlying eminent domain proceeding. . . . Experts' preliminary reports must be entitled to immunity because: if this were not so, every expert who acts as a consultant for a client with reference to proposed or actual litigation, and thereafter appears as an expert witness, would be liable to suit at the hands of his client's adversary on the theory that while the expert's testimony was privileged, his preliminary conferences with and reports to his client were not. (*Darragh v. Superior Court,* 1995, p. 1218)

Rejecting the use of a fraud claim as an exception to this grant of immunity, the Texas courts have held that even a claim of perjury by the witness does not defeat a claim of immunity: "Any communication, even perjured testimony, made in the course of a judicial proceeding, cannot serve as the basis for a suit in tort" (*Laub v. Pesikoff,* 1998, p. 689).

Another aspect of immunity relates to an expert's attempt to respond ethically to a difficult situation by changing his or her testimony in light of newly discovered information. Those courts that have taken a broad approach to immunity have included this conduct within its scope: "To allow a party to litigation to contract with an expert witness and thereby obligate the witness to testify only in a manner favorable to the party, on threat of civil liability, would be contrary to public policy" (*Panitz v. Behrend,* 1993, pp. 656–666) and "Contractual arrangements to appear at a trial between an expert witness and a litigant will be enforced as will contractual arrangements between such parties for reasonable compensation; but under no circumstances will an agreement to give favorable testimony be sanctioned by the courts" (*Griffith v. Harris,* 1962, p. 136).

EXCEPTIONS TO WITNESS IMMUNITY

Not all courts, however, have recognized the same level of immunity. One important category of cases that some jurisdictions have excluded from grants of absolute immunity is litigation support services. Litigation support services play a fundamentally different role from that of ordinary lay or expert witnesses. Unlike the ordinary witness who provides relevant evidence to the fact finder, litigation support services are retained to assist in advocating for a party (see Chapter 18). Thus, courts have been more willing to treat liability claims against these services in the same way that they treat claims for attorney malpractice:

> Witness immunity is an exception to the general rules of liability. It should not be extended unless its underlying policies require it be so. . . . This narrow restriction is consistent with the historical development of immunity. While witness immunity might properly be expanded in other circumstances, we do not believe that immunity was meant to or should apply to bar a suit against a privately retained professional who negligently provides litigation support services. (*Murphy v. Mathews,* 1992, p. 680)

Other types of claims that some courts have excepted from the grant of immunity involve conduct that directly frustrates the truth-finding process, such as spoliation of evidence. Spoliation occurs when original documents in the custody of the expert are destroyed, either accidentally or purposefully. Although the majority of jurisdictions do not recognize a claim against a witness for spoliation of evidence, usually because there is no legal duty to maintain the records (*Black Radio Network, Inc. v. NYNEX Corp.,* 1999), a number of state courts have recognized a claim against a witness for spoliation of evidence that is not barred by grants of witness immunity (*Holmes v. Amerex Rent-A-Car,* 1999; *Ingham v. U.S.,* 1999; *Smith v. Howard Johnson Co.,* 1993).

Some courts have also left open the possibility of claims that would exist independent of the witness's testimony. For example, another potential claim that has been recognized as an exception to a less than absolute grant of witness immunity is a claim for negligent diagnosis. In *James v. Brown* (1982), the subject of a civil commitment proceeding subsequently brought an action for defamation against the physician whose diagnosis served as the basis for her commitment. The Texas courts rejected the defamation claim on immunity grounds but left open the possibility of a claim for negligent diagnosis: "While the doctors' communications to the court of their diagnoses of Mrs. James' mental condition, regardless of how negligently made, cannot serve as the basis for a defamation action, the diagnoses themselves may be actionable on other grounds" (pp. 917–918; see also *Awai v. Kotin and Boeding,* 1993).

Reflecting this same theme of limiting grants of immunity to conduct that bears directly on the presentation of testimony, another limitation that some courts recognize is that immunity will encompass *only* the expert's behavior on the witness stand, not the expert's extrajudicial conduct. So, for example, in some jurisdictions, the grant of immunity applies only to conduct that occurred after the initiation of litigation (*Twelker v. Shannon & Wilson,* 1977, p. 1134).

Finally, reflecting one of the broadest immunities for experts are those decisions that have held that serving as a court-appointed expert provides the expert quasi-judicial immunity, the same immunity granted a judge when deciding the matter before the court. The role of the court-appointed expert is intended only to benefit the fact finder and not the parties (*Lythgoe v. Guinn,* 1994). Indeed, one reason that experts prefer to serve as court-appointed rather than as retained experts rests on an assumption regarding immunity for such services (Champagne, Easterling, Shuman, Tomkins, & Whitaker, 2001). Yet, a small number of jurisdictions have concluded that "court-appointment is not a talisman for immunity" (*Levine v. Wiss,* 1984, p. 402).

WHEN WITNESS IMMUNITY IS NOT RECOGNIZED

Most successful recent civil claims against experts have been grounded in negligence. Negligence is the breach of a duty, proximately causing harm. Thus, the first question to be addressed in a negligence claim against an expert not barred by immunity is whether the expert owes a duty to the party bringing the claim to avoid the harm caused. The question of duty breaks down further into the question of the duty owed by the expert to the party who retained the expert and the question of the duty owed by the expert to persons other than the party who retained the expert.

Duty

Parties retain experts who may both consult and testify, depending on the helpfulness of the opinions they eventually form, or who may only consult with the party but not testify at trial. Much of the upsurge in recent claims against experts has been against friendly experts (i.e., claims by the parties who retained the experts) who have provided consultation or testimony. In the case of retained consulting experts, courts have had no difficulty recognizing that the expert owes a duty to the party who retained the expert to perform according to the standard of a reasonable member of the relevant profession. Thus, in *Hart v. Browne* (1980), the California Court of Appeals found that a physician consultant could be found liable for negligently advising an attorney as to the viability of a medical malpractice suit. The consultant's negligent opinion had been that the conduct of an orthopedic surgeon who amputated the attorney's client's leg did not fall below the standard of care. This allegedly incorrect opinion resulted in the failure by the amputee to institute a lawsuit against the orthopedic surgeon in a timely manner.

Although there is slightly less unanimity in the category of experts who are retained to testify, as opposed to consult, most courts have had little trouble finding that such experts owe a duty to the parties who retained them to render services at the level of reasonable professional competence (*Mattco Forge v. Arthur Young & Co.,* 1997; *Murphy v. Mathews,* 1992).

More recently, for example, in *Pollock v. Panjabi* (2000), a plaintiff retained experts to testify on his behalf in a lawsuit filed against the police. When the trial court excluded the expert testimony on the ground that it was based, in part, on improperly conducted analyses, the plaintiff sued the experts. In affirming the plaintiff's right to sue the experts, the court held that:

> [The] policy reasons undergirding the absolute privilege accorded witnesses are not implicated here. This is not a case in which the right of a witness to speak freely, in or out of court, is involved. While conduct, objects and experiments may have communicative aspects . . . the plaintiffs do not complain about what [the defendants] said or communicated. Rather, the plaintiffs complain of the defendants' failure to perform work, as agreed upon, according to scientific principles as to which there are no competing schools of thought. This is a case where the defendants performed an experiment that turned out to support the thesis of an opposing party. . . . There must be a nexus between the immunity, the fact-finding function of the court and the interest in having witnesses speak freely. That nexus is not implicated by the allegations of the plaintiffs' complaint. (p. 188)

The more difficult duty question occurs when someone other than the party who retained the expert institutes a tort claim against the expert, alleging that the expert's negligence injured that third party. Typical of this claim is the case of the expert retained by one parent who testifies that the other parent sexually abused their child. The duty question here is reminiscent of that posed in *Tarasoff v. Board of*

Regents of the University of California (1976). Does a mental health professional owe a duty to anyone other than the person who retained the professional?

One line of cases holds that the professional retained as a witness does not owe a duty to anyone but the party who retained the expert:

> In this case, a psychologist, Esther Bird, examined a child for signs of sexual abuse . . . [and] concluded that the child had been sexually abused and that the natural father, W. C. W., was the abuser. The psychologist then signed an affidavit reporting these conclusions. The affidavit was filed by the child's mother, B. W., in the family court in an effort to modify child custody and visitation orders. All matters, criminal and civil, predicated upon the assertion that the natural father was a child abuser were eventually dropped. The natural father then sued the psychologist and her employer. . . . The question presented is whether the psychologist owed a professional duty of care to the natural father to not negligently misdiagnose the condition of the child. In defense, the psychologist asserts there is no professional duty running to third parties as a matter of law, and regardless, the affidavit asserting the natural father to be the abuser of the child was used as a part of the court litigation process, and consequently, the statement was privileged as a matter of law. . . . We hold that as a matter of law there is no professional duty running from a psychologist to a third party to not negligently misdiagnose a condition of a patient. (*Bird v. W. C. W.,* 1994, p. 768)

Most of the reported decisions on third-party claims come from relatives of patients accused of sexual abuse by the patient as the result of the alleged negligence of the therapist. Although most courts have limited claims in this setting to the party who sought the services of the mental health professional (*Bird v. W. C. W.,* 1994), other courts have been willing to permit claims by third parties who might foreseeably suffer harm from negligent services rendered to the patient (*Tuman v. Genesis Associates,* 1996).

A different conceptual framework is used to address the duty question when a claim is made against a court-appointed expert. The court-appointed expert's obligation is not to provide assistance to the parties but, rather, to provide independent assistance to the court. Consequently, most courts do not recognize a duty, enforceable in a tort claim, owed by the court-appointed expert to a party. Nonetheless, some courts have found that an investigator not retained by the parties may nonetheless owe a legal duty to the parties to avoid negligent injury in performing his or her professional duties. For example, in *Tyner v. Department of Social & Health Servs., Child Protective Servs.* (2000, p. 1155), the Washington Supreme Court held that "CPS owes a duty of care to a child's parents, even those suspected of abusing their own children, when investigating allegations of child abuse."

Breach

If it is determined that a duty exists, the standard of care for measuring a breach of that duty must be determined. In general, the law utilizes the reasonable person standard to express the obligation we owe toward one another. In the case of professional conduct, this standard translates into a reasonable professional acting under similar circumstances. This same approach to measuring the conduct of a professional applies to mental health professionals, whether their negligence is alleged in the context of a therapeutic or forensic relationship:

[A] professional owes to his or her client a duty of care commensurate with the degree of care, skill and proficiency commonly exercised by ordinarily skillful, careful and prudent professionals. When the degree of care provided does not meet this standard, a cause of action for damages may be stated. (*Murphy v. Mathews,* 1992, p. 674)

The reasonable person standard says everything and, at the same time, nothing to the professional. What does it mean to be reasonable? How is reasonableness to be judged? The cases provide some guidance. For example, they explain that the reasonable expert is an experienced expert. Inexperience does not excuse error; tort law does not countenance learning on the job (*Mattco Forge v. Arthur Young & Co.,* 1997).

Professional codes and guidelines provide courts a guide to what professionals judge as necessary (although not necessarily what courts should regard as sufficient) professional behavior in circumstances addressed by those norms (Shuman & Greenberg, 1998). When the expert is the object of a complaint, relevant professional codes and guidelines for practice provide a template against which the reasonableness of the expert's testimony behavior can be measured. For example, for psychologists, these codes and guidelines take the form of the American Psychological Association's (2002), "Ethical Principles of Psychologists" and the "Specialty Guidelines for Forensic Psychologists" jointly promulgated by the American Psychology-Law Society and the American Academy of Forensic Psychology (Committee on Ethical Guidelines for Forensic Psychologists, 1991). For psychiatrists, such codes and guidelines are spelled out in the American Psychiatric Association's (2001) "Principles of Medical Ethics with Annotations Especially Applicable to Psychiatry" and the "Ethical Guidelines for the Practice of Forensic Psychiatry," developed by the American Academy of Psychiatry and the Law (1995).

Causation and Harm

To constitute actionable negligence, the breach of the duty must have actually caused harm to the person seeking recovery. Tort cases frequently address this issue by stating that there is "no negligence in the air." By this they mean that substandard conduct (e.g., DWI) that does not cause harm (e.g., no accident occurs) may be the subject of criminal prosecution or moral condemnation, but it does not constitute a tort. In the context of negligence claims against experts, this requirement typically demands that the plaintiff seeking recovery for negligence must demonstrate that, "but for" the negligence of the expert, the plaintiff would have prevailed in the primary action. Therefore, if the plaintiff would, nonetheless, have lost or fared no better even if the expert testimony met professional norms, this causal requirement is not met.

This "case within a case requirement" presents interesting variations in this context, one of which is illustrated by *Mattco Forge v. Arthur Young & Co.* (1997). Mattco Forge retained the accounting services of Arthur Young & Co. to establish its damages in its civil rights claim against General Electric, alleging that its elimination as an approved subcontractor was racially motivated. After finding that some of the original records needed to compute damages were missing, Arthur Young reconstructed those records but failed to identify them as reconstructions. Mattco Forge then supplied these records to General Electric. After General Electric brought these records to the attention of the trial judge, he refused to permit any of these records to be used to support Mattco Forge's damage claim. In addition, the trial court ruled that

> due to the intimate involvement of the accounting firm of Arthur Young in the production of [Mattco's] evidence concerning damages, Arthur Young is prohibited from involvement in any future production of evidence concerning [Mattco's] damages in this action, and no work papers, files, or any other materials produced by Arthur Young in the past to calculate [Mattco's] damages shall be used in any future production of evidence on that subject. . . . For the purpose of compensating [GE] for the litigation costs they have borne due to [Mattco's] misconduct, [GE] will submit to the Court an accounting of its attorneys' fees, costs and expenses relating to the production of evidence concerning [Mattco's] damages in this action. (p. 829)

Mattco was forced to dismiss its civil rights claim.

Mattco Forge brought an accounting malpractice claim against Arthur Young, for which it was ultimately awarded $42 million at trial. Arthur Young & Co. argued, unsuccessfully at trial, that Mattco Forge should be required to prove that it would ultimately have prevailed in the underlying claim against General Electric "but for" Arthur Young's negligence. Ultimately, the court of appeals agreed with Arthur Young that the trial within a trial requirement applied to their expert malpractice claim and reversed the trial court's damage award: "In order to prevail against Arthur Young in this action, Mattco has the burden to establish that had Arthur Young properly handled the underlying case, Mattco would have prevailed against GE" (1997, p. 837).

These are the basic principles that govern expert witness malpractice liability. But there is more for an expert to learn from this body of law than how to avoid being successfully sued. Properly understood, the lessons to be learned also teach how to be a better expert.

IRRECONCILABLE CONFLICTS BETWEEN THERAPEUTIC AND FORENSIC ROLES AND THE LAW OF MALPRACTICE

In addition to the 10 fundamental differences in therapeutic and forensic roles described by Greenberg and Shuman (1997), we now add an 11th difference. When each type of practitioner is testifying as a witness in court, therapeutic practitioners do not typically face the same risks of malpractice litigation as do forensic practitioners. We note this enhanced risk not to increase forensic practitioners' anxiety. Rather, by understanding these differences, forensic experts can not only reduce their risk of successful malpractice claims, but they also can increase the efficacy of their performance as experts. Our conclusion about this enhanced risk of malpractice claims for forensic experts, and the lessons it offers for forensic practice, are best grasped by understanding the ways the risks for each group differ:

- *To whom is the professional obligated?* In the therapeutic realm, in most cases, the therapist's duty is owed exclusively to the patient. In the forensic realm, the examiner ordinarily serves multiple masters: the judge and jury, the party, and the retaining lawyer. For therapists, the question of who is owed a professional obligation is typically clear and devoid of inherent conflicts: It is the patient. Not so in the case of the forensic examiner, whose candor with the judge and jury, for example, may undermine the legal claim or defense of the party on whose behalf the examiner was retained. The necessity to balance these competing forensic obligations, and the skills they must master to perform their role competently, adds to the malpractice risks that forensic mental health professionals face. The impartial advocacy necessary to avoid malpractice and properly balance these forensic obligations also increases forensic credibility (Shuman & Greenberg, 2003).

- *The patient/litigant's incentive to present accurately.* The incentives that exist for patients to present accurately in the therapeutic realm are (a) the patient's own therapeutic best interest and (b) the regard with which the patient wishes to be held by the therapist. In contrast, in the forensic realm, the patient/litigant's best interest may be served by distorting the presentation of his or her own trustworthiness, distress, impairment, and pathology (Greenberg, Shuman, & Meyer, 2004, 2005). The task of the forensic examiner is made more difficult as the result of this difference in incentives, and concomitantly, the risk of error leading a disgruntled party to bring suit against an expert is enhanced. Recognizing and addressing the patient/litigant's incentive to present accurately not only reduces the commission of malpractice by the expert, it also enhances the expert's forensic credibility.

- *The availability of validated instruments.* The clinician has a wide battery of well-validated instruments and techniques, but relatively few well-validated forensic assessment instruments exist for use by the forensic practitioner. Consequently, the forensic examiner is frequently left without an independent trustworthy measure for accurately judging legally relevant behavior. There is a paucity of tests that are directly relevant to a specific legal standard and that directly assess the functional capacities of the examinee. A number of forensic instruments have been published and promulgated for use in forensic evaluations after only preliminary research and development (Otto, Edens, & Barcus, 2000). Many clinical measures are the product of careful development, benefit from a considerable research base, and have been well validated. However, they typically assess constructs (e.g., intelligence, depression, academic abilities, anxiety level) that are considerably removed from the specific question before the legal decision maker (Heilbrun, Marczyk, & DeMatteo, 2002). This forces the forensic examiner to use clinical measures and assessment techniques that were developed for assessment, diagnosis, and treatment planning with clinical populations in therapeutic contexts. Ironically, the peculiar circumstance in which psychologists conducting forensic evaluations find themselves is that the best-validated assessment instruments are often those that are least relevant to the legal issue(s) (Rogers, 1997). As such, they require the examiner to exercise a greater level of inference to move from the construct assessed to the issue before the court (Greenberg, Otto, & Long, 2004; Otto et al., 2000), which in turn increases the opportunity for assessment error and opens the examiner to associated malpractice complaints. Mastering the appropriate use and limitations of these instruments is also essential to reduce the risk of expert witness malpractice and, concomitantly, to increase forensic competence.

- *The existence of shared goals.* In the therapeutic realm, all those who have a role to play in the patient's care (patient, therapist, family, friends) share the same goal: the improvement of the patient's mental health. These parties are natural allies of the therapist. In the forensic realm, the participants have different and often inconsistent goals that constrain their agreement with any other expert's conclusion. For example, a defense expert's conclusion that the defendant's mental state at the time of the crime meets the requirements of an insanity defense may advance the defendant's therapeutic interests but frustrate the prosecution or the victim's desire for retribution. To have their goals prevail, opposing parties are typically motivated to find fault with the opinions of the opposing expert, exposing errors that would have gone unnoticed or would have been addressed constructively in therapy. Recognizing and explicitly addressing this discordance is essential to reduce the risk of malpractice by the expert and for an expert's effective pretrial preparation and in court testimony.

- *The temporal framework.* Most mistakes and misperceptions in therapy are self-correcting. Over the course of therapy, incorrect diagnoses or treatment plans are generally discovered and corrected with minimal harm to the patient because therapy is an evolving process. Legal decision making, governed by rules of preclusion (i.e., collateral estoppel, *res judicata*), allow the parties a fair day in court. Because of the artificial time constraints imposed by these rules of preclusion as well as rules designed to manage cases efficiently, forensic evaluations are inherently more demanding to conduct than therapeutic evaluations. Errors in forensic evaluations are also potentially more harmful because there is rarely a timely opportunity to correct them. Thus, they are more likely to result in a disgruntled litigant seeking redress by way of a tort claim.

PRACTICE IMPLICATIONS

The risk of malpractice created by these five differences in therapeutic and forensic roles can be reduced, and an expert's performance enhanced, by adequately informing the examinee about these differences. No matter how sophisticated parties may be, they are likely to expect psychologist experts to behave like helping professionals, as advocates, when, in fact, they are retained to perform a forensic function. The public and many legal representatives may assume incorrectly that the sole responsibility of the forensic mental health professional is to provide partisan advocacy (Shuman & Greenberg, 2003).

The institution of malpractice litigation is not only about mistakes. Anger, surprise, and disappointed expectations play a critical role as well. "The anatomy of a claim is best expressed by the equation: Negligence + Injury + Anger = Claim" (Doctors' Company, 2005). Thus, although the forensic expert's doing the right thing is essential, the expert's making sure that the party knows the right thing to expect is also critically important. It is not only about what the expert does, it is also about how it is done and about whether what was done is what was expected.

Using the expert witness malpractice literature described in this chapter as a guide, experts may be able to reduce the elements of anger, surprise, and disappointment by discussing with examinees and their attorneys what they may anticipate as they conduct forensic assessments, submit reports, and testify in court. From the *examiner's* perspective, the goal is to enhance performance as an expert by reinforcing a role orientation that correlatively reduces the risk of malpractice. From the *examinee's* perspective, the goal is to increase understanding of the role that the expert witness will play in order to avoid the anger or surprise that may enhance the willingness to bring suit for malpractice.

As suggested by the five differences in malpractice risks described here, and making no pretense that these ideas are exhaustive, it may be helpful in reducing the risk of a malpractice claim for the expert to go beyond providing a written forensic office policy and to additionally discuss with the examinee and/or attorney, topics such as the following:

- Forensic examination is not treatment and is not intended to be therapeutic to the examinee.
- Information received from or discussed by an examinee is not confidential or privileged and may be shared with the opposing party.
- The examiner may talk to relevant collaterals, especially those offered by opposing counsel, without a clinical release of information from the examinee.
- Forensic examination records are not health care information. Forensic examination records and reports may be obtained only through a retaining attorney request or a subpoena, and not through a release of information.
- Records and reports may contain errors, and the examinee or counsel may provide corrections to any substantial factual error that the examiner may have made.
- There are no reliable and valid forensic assessment instruments that by themselves will directly resolve particular legal claims or defenses.
- Mental health experts cannot reliably determine and will not testify as to whether a specific event, such as sexual abuse or sexual harassment, actually occurred.
- An examiner's credibility in court may be severely compromised by lack of candor by an examinee.
- It is not the examiner's task to be partisan or to omit information from reports or testimony that may not be helpful to the examinee's or the retaining attorney's case.
- At least some of the opinions formed by the expert are likely to be unhelpful to the examinee's claim or defense.

- The examiner's task is to test plausible rival hypotheses.

- No opinion will be offered unless adequately supported by the results of the examination.

- Even while in the process of testifying, the expert may change an opinion if offered persuasive new information while on the stand.

- Any testimony based on problem-focused personality testing is likely to provide a disproportionately negative view of the examinee's emotions, behaviors, cognitions, and character.

- The expert will attempt to provide services in a manner that is consistent with the "Specialty Guidelines for Forensic Psychologists," a copy of which will be provided on request to the examinee and counsel.

- The expert should ensure that written forms, policies, and releases have been provided and read, the examination process for this matter's type of forensic examination was described, and all of the examinee's questions were adequately answered.

This list of topics is not exhaustive. Any such list should be modified to reflect the type of forensic matter under consideration, the examiner's practices, and the forensic mental health professional's ethics and judgment regarding what is best forensic practice.

Discussion of these issues is part of a process intended to encourage questions about the forensic process and to establish a realistic forensic rapport with the examiner rather than a therapeutic alliance. It is intended to yield an informed expectation for an objective and impartial examination rather than what might otherwise be anticipated as the helping professional's intent to assist the examinee's claim or defense. Such dissuasion could not be more critical both to providing an objective examination and in helping to reduce a disgruntled examinee's inclination to file a malpractice action because the examinee did not appreciate or anticipate the examination's potentially critical or unhelpful outcome. Further, should a malpractice claim by an attorney or the examinee include a cause of action for lack of adequate informed consent, forensic forms and policies, combined with a record of having adequately discussed these issues, may go a long way in assisting in the examiner's defense of that claim.

CONCLUSION

Experts are often needed to assist the fact finder to navigate the maze of information presented for resolution. Fact finders often look to experts as a source of reliable, independent assistance. Indeed, a poll conducted by the *National Law Journal* and Lexis/Nexis found that paid experts were thought believable by 89% of those jurors interviewed (Cheever & Naimen, 1993).

It is small wonder, then, that out of the thousands of experts testifying in the courtrooms across the United States on any given day, few are sued. This may be because most experts maintain their objectivity and form only those opinions for court that they would form for peer-reviewed publications. Or it may be because of an uneasy truce that can be undone at a moment's notice.

There will always be disappointed parties to a lawsuit in which an expert testifies. This is a technical world, and it is a litigious one. Disappointed parties may sue their experts. We have examined how those suits fare in the courts, as contrasted to malpractice claims against therapists, and have sought to convey that the risk of a lawsuit is present but manageable. Indeed, managing that risk is not in conflict with one's role as an expert. Properly understood, efficacy as an expert is advanced by the same strategies that reduce an expert's risk of malpractice liability.

REFERENCES

American Academy of Psychiatry and the Law. (1995). *Ethical guidelines for the practice of forensic psychiatry.* Available from http://appl.org/pdf/ethicsgdlns.pdf.

American Law Institute, Restatement (Second) of Torts 588 (1981).

American Psychiatric Association. (2001). *Principles of medical ethics with annotations especially applicable to psychiatry.* Available from http://www.psych.org/psych_pract/ethics/ppaethics.cfm.

American Psychological Association. (2002). *Ethical principles of psychologists and code of conduct.* Available from www.apa.org/ethics/code2002.html.

Awai v. Kotin and Boeding, 872 P.2d 1332 (1993).

Bird v. W. C. W., 868 S.W.2d 767 (Tex. 1994).

Black Radio Network, Inc. v. NYNEX Corp., 44 F. Supp. 2d 565 (S.D.N.Y. 1999).

Bruce v. Byrne-Stevens, 776 P.2d 666 (Wash. 1989).

Champagne, A., Easterling, D., Shuman, D., Tomkins, A., & Whitaker, E. (2001). Are court-appointed experts the solution to the problems of expert testimony? *Judicature, 84,* 178–183.

Cheever, J. M., & Naimen, J. (1993, February). The view from the jury box. *National Law Journal.*

Committee on Ethical Guidelines for Forensic Psychologists. (1991). Specialty guidelines for forensic psychologists. *Law and Human Behavior, 15,* 655–665.

Darragh v. Superior Court, 183 Ariz. 79, 900 P.2d 1218 (1995).

Doctors' Company. (2005). *Risk management sourcebook pathology: A report of claims review panels.* Available from http://www.thedoctors.com/risk/specialty/pathology/J3236.asp.

Greenberg, S., Otto, R., & Long, A. (2004). The utility of psychological testing in assessing emotional damages in personal injury litigation. *Assessment, 10,* 4.

Greenberg, S., & Shuman, D. (1997). Irreconcilable conflict between therapeutic and forensic roles. *Professional Psychology: Research and Practice, 28,* 50–57.

Greenberg, S. A., Shuman, D. W., & Meyer, R. G. (2004). Unmasking forensic diagnosis. *International Journal of Law and Psychiatry, 27,* pp. 1–15.

Greenberg, S. A., Shuman, D. W., & Meyer, R. G. (2005). Forensic psychiatric diagnosis unmasked. Adapted and reprinted by invitation in Judicature. *Journal of the American Judicature Society* with permission of *International Journal of Law and Psychiatry.*

Griffith v. Harris, 116 N.W.2d 133 (Wis. 1962).

Hansen, M. (2000). Experts are liable, too: Client suits against "friendly experts" multiplying, succeeding. *American Bar Association Journal, 86,* 17.

Hanson, R. K. (1996). Witness immunity under attack: Disarming hired guns. *Wake Forest Law Review, 31,* 497–511.

Hart v. Browne, 163 Cal. Rptr. 356 (Cal. App. 1980).

Heilbrun, K., Marczyk, G., & DeMatteo, D. (2002). *Forensic mental health assessment.* New York: Oxford University Press.

Holmes v. Amerex Rent-A-Car, 180 F.3d 294 (D.C. Cir. 1999).

Ingham v. U.S., 167 F.3d 1240 (9th Cir. 1999).

James v. Brown, 637 S.W.2d 686 (Tex. 1982).

Laub v. Pesikoff, 979 S.W.2d 686 (Tex. Civ. App. 1998).

Levine v. Wiss, 478 A.2d 397 (NJ 1984).

Lythgoe v. Guinn, 884 P.2d 1085 (Alaska 1994).

Mattco Forge v. Arthur Young & Co., 52 Ca. App. 4th 820 (Cal. App. 2d 1997) *rev. denied*, 1997; 60 Cal. Rptr. 2d 780.

Murphy v. Mathews, 841 S.W.2d 671 (Mo. 1992).

Otto, R., Edens, J., & Barcus, E. (2000). The use of psychological testing in child custody evaluations. *Family and Conciliation Courts Review, 38,* 312–340.

Panitz v. Behrend, 632 A.2d 562 (Pa. Super. 1993).

Pollock v. Panjabi, 781 A.2d 518 (Conn. Super. 2000).

Rogers, R. (Ed.). (1997). *Clinical assessment of malingering and deception* (2nd ed.). New York: Guilford Press.

Shuman, D., & Greenberg, S. (1998). The role of ethical norms in the admissability of expert testimony. *Judges' Journal: A Quarterly of the Judicial Division of the American Bar Association, 37*(1), 4–43.

Shuman, D., & Greenberg, S. (2003). Expert witnesses, the adversary system, and the voice of reason: Reconciling impartiality and advocacy. *Professional Psychology: Research and Practice, 34,* 219–224.

Smith v. Howard Johnson Co., 615 N. E.2d 1037 (Ohio 1993).

Tarasoff v. Board of Regents of the University of California, 551 P.2d 334 (Cal. 1976).

Tuman v. Genesis Associates, 935 F. Supp. 1375 (E.D. Pa. 1996).

Twelker v. Shannon & Wilson, 564 P.2d 1131 (Wash. 1977).

Tyner v. Department of Social & Health Servs., Child Protective Servs., 1 P.3d 1148 (Wash. 2000).

PART VII

Forensic Psychological Consultation

CHAPTER 18

Off the Witness Stand: The Forensic
Psychologist as Consultant

Eric Y. Drogin and Curtis L. Barrett

Harvard professor Hugo Münsterberg "is generally credited with founding the field of forensic psychology" (Goldstein, 2003, p. 6), primarily on the strength of his textbook *On the Witness Stand* (1908), which highlighted many issues that resonate to this day, including eyewitness identification, crime prevention, and the application of psychological principles to judicial procedures (Vaccaro & Hogan, 2004). The last of these notions is most prominently pursued in the contemporary literature by advocates of Therapeutic Jurisprudence, "an innovative, interdisciplinary field that brings together law and the social sciences by studying the role of law as a therapeutic agent" (Daicoff & Wexler, 2003, p. 561). Put another way, "Therapeutic Jurisprudence [examines] the extent to which substantive rules, legal procedures, and the roles of lawyers and judges produce therapeutic or antitherapeutic consequences" (Wexler & Winick, 1991, p. ix).

Encouraging the law to adopt perspectives consistent with the goals and beliefs of mental health professionals represents, of course, only one side of the discourse between these two disciplines. The Therapeutic Jurisprudence model can also be inverted to accommodate a Jurisprudent Psychology perspective, in which mental health professionals are encouraged to apply their clinical and research efforts in a fashion consistent with the goals and beliefs of the legal system so that multidisciplinary efforts "can pinpoint desirable developments in the concision and utilization of mental health science, practice and roles in the service of justice for litigants and the broader public" (Drogin, 2000c, p. 284). Along these lines, Wexler (1990) opined that "if mental health information, a subset of the behavioral sciences, is looked to by the law with a healthy skepticism, we ought to be able to profit from some of that information without having the law succumb to passing psychological fads" (p. 4).

One practical vehicle for simultaneously monitoring and improving the quality of social scientific contributions to the legal system, while indulging the law's healthy skepticism even as we enable it to profit from the more positive aspects of legitimate expertise, is forensic psychological consultation:

> Forensic psychological evidence—involving the application of mental health principles to the resolution of legal issues—is a prominent factor in civil and criminal trial practice.

> This phenomenon reflects the increasing sophistication (or at least specificity) of assessment instruments, as well as the attorney's need to keep pace with evolving standards for the quantification of damages and assertion of defenses and mitigation. There has also been a dramatic proliferation of "experts" themselves, largely due to the established popularity of forensic graduate programs and the withering effects of managed care on the traditional psychotherapeutic foundation of clinical practice. How then is the contemporary trial lawyer to identify, retain, and utilize a forensic psychological examiner, while ascertaining the strengths and weaknesses of experts employed by opposing counsel? (Drogin, 2001d, p. 17)

When supported by requisite training and experience (Leonard, 1999) and when appropriately focused on the specific needs of an identified class of litigators (Ardichvili, 2000), the contributions of forensic psychological consultants "are increasingly recognized as a vital adjunct to legal and scientific practice" (Drogin, 2000e, p. 5). In this chapter, we seek to place forensic psychological consultation in its appropriate social scientific context, review key legal and ethical considerations for pursuing its practice, and explore its specialized applications.

THE NATURE OF PSYCHOLOGICAL CONSULTATION

In our experience, forensic psychologists often view consultation as little more than a streamlined or segmented approach to their familiar, customary activities: for example, performing an evaluation without having to testify, reviewing a report without having to compose one, or locating a specialized expert without having to be one. Adopting this perspective, senior practitioners, after years of laboring to prove each point the hard way, may view themselves as finally "getting paid for what I know, instead of getting paid for what I do." In fact, psychological consultation is not merely the selective application of isolated components of traditional service; rather, it is a complex, dynamic, and free-standing discipline with a distinct history, research base, and methodology.

Clinical consultation in medical settings "began as early as the thirteenth century, and was widely practiced by the middle of the nineteenth century" (Brown, Pryzwansky, & Schulte, 1998, p. 2). Entrenched as a traditional procedure from the inception of American medicine (Alderfer, 1998), clinical consultation also played a consistent role in the rise of American psychiatry in the early 1900s (R. S. Friedman & Molay, 1994). As psychiatry's focus extended beyond reactive cures to prevention and skills development, the Adlerian notion that "behavior is goal oriented" inspired a new breed of psychiatric consultants to "disclose the essence of individuals' goals to guide them in their work" (Brown, Pryzwansky, & Schulte, 2005, p. 84). The influence of psychiatry soon provided a context for the recognition and inclusion of other mental health-related disciplines as well, and "consulting psychology emerged [during] the 1910s, as more and more applied psychologists appeared in industry, education, and other organizations" (Weigel, 1998, p. 11).

In 1920, the American Psychological Association (APA) directed the prototype of its Division of Consulting Psychology (DCP), the Standing Committee on Certification of Consulting Psychologists, to "specify the competencies and knowledge bases associated with consulting psychology and to assure that division members had the prerequisites for recognition as consulting psychologists" (O'Roark, 1999, p. 219); however, once this was accomplished, "the selectors of expert psychologists found that most persons doing clinical work at that time did not meet the high standards set for division membership," and APA eventually abandoned the DCP in 1927 (p. 219). In the wake of a mandate to "explore ways of organizing psychology, including psychological services, for the national welfare during World War II" (Benjamin, 1997, p. 728), the DCP was reinstituted as "one of the charter divisions of the reorganized [APA] in 1946" (Weigel, 1998, p. 3). Today, the Society of Consulting Psychology (SCP) boasts more than 1,000 members (Chamberlin, 2004).

When compared to the well-established and frequently researched specialty of jury selection (Kovera, Dickinson, & Cutler, 2003), the other consulting contributions of forensic psychologists, whether styled as courtroom consultation (Nietzel & Dillehay, 1986), trial consultation (Boccaccini & Brodsky, 2002; Lecci, Snowden, & Morris, 2004; Posey & Wrightsman, 2005; Strier, 1999), litigation support (H. J. Friedman & Klee, 2001), or forensic consultation (Drogin, 2000f, 2001d), have received minimal emphasis in the professional literature of either law or psychology. To some extent, this may reflect widely held suspicions that have been identified by Stolle, Robbenolt, and Weiner (1996):

> Throughout the history of scientific trial consulting, many commentators—both lawyers and social scientists—have expressed skepticism regarding the ability of psychologist consultants to be of any real assistance in winning cases. Those skeptics from the legal community typically argue that trial preparation, including jury selection, is an art not a science, and that the instincts of a seasoned trial lawyer are superior to any social scientific approach. In contrast, skeptics from the social science community have typically argued that social scientific approaches are probably no worse than reliance on lawyers' instincts but that any benefits of social scientific approaches may not outweigh the costs. (p. 143)

Agreeing that "credibility is of prime concern to consultants" (Glasser, 2002, p. 29), Glasser noted that "technical competencies of the consultant are often presumed or taken for granted on the basis of such proxies as years of experience or affiliation with a reputable firm," because "professional codes and certifications have yet to be developed" and because "accepted indicators of competency" are still lacking (p. 40). According to a survey conducted by Blanton (2000), consultants, like psychotherapists, have tended to make relatively little use of empirical research in their practice, at least in part because "we need more groundwork to operationalize our concepts and theories" (p. 240). Such phenomena appear, however, to reflect not a paucity of applicable research and marketable skills, but the lack of an optimally integrated and popularized professional identity.

In 2003, 4 years of administrative research and development culminated in the establishment of an American Board of Organizational and Business Consulting (ABOBC) as a specialty board of the American Board of Professional Psychology (ABPP; Amberg, 2004). An ABPP specialty "is a defined area in the practice of psychology that connotes special competency acquired through an organized sequence of formal education, training, and experience," and certification is granted on the basis of "an examination designed to assess the competencies required to provide quality services in that specialty" (Amberg, 2002, p. 13). With the exception of one credential pertaining to hypnosis, "it is noteworthy that the ABPP diplomate is the only one recognized by APA in terms of allowing this designation to be included as part of a member's credentials in the APA directory" (Packer & Borum, 2003, p. 29). Although the ABOBC maintains "a licensed practitioner orientation" (Bent, 2004), "nonlicensed applicants may apply for an exception from this requirement if they practice in a state or province in which this specialty is excluded from the definition of the practice of psychology" (Amberg, 2002, p. 14).

Some have argued that licensure for forensic psychological consultants should become a legislative priority, irrespective of whether a particular jurisdiction's statutory scheme includes the term "consultation" in its description of regulated psychological services. Licensure proponents warn that the lack of defined standards for education, training, and ethical conduct may lead to dire and unforeseen consequences to litigants (Strier, 2001). Those who assert that licensure is unnecessary point to the established professional status of those persons providing the bulk of forensic consultation (in particular, psychologists), while suggesting at the same time that the impact of such services, be it positive or negative, has been overstated (Moran, 2001). The SCP's own position is that "psychologists who limit their practice to consulting for businesses and organizations should be allowed to do so in another state for 'a reasonable period of time,' such as 60 days, without having to obtain a license in that state" (Chamberlin, 2004, p. 88). Psychologists seeking to provide consultation in a novel jurisdiction should take special care to determine whether their contemplated duties run afoul of "rules for utilizing out-of-state forensic assistance," proper adherence to which may require them to procure legal representation (Drogin, 1999a, p. 770).

Although the licensure woes of testifying experts will likely capture counsel's interest when raising the specter of inadmissibility of behavioral scientific evidence (Simon & Shuman, 1999), busy attorneys can afford little if any attention to the jurisdictional concerns of the nontestifying forensic psychological consultant. In the current litigation environment, counsel's uppermost concern is not consultant exposure, but consultant overhead. Spiraling consultation fees for experts in every professional discipline have compelled lawyers to take affirmative steps to contain costs (Hansen, 2005; Tripoli, 1998). Given a growing recognition that "one of the best ways to limit consulting costs is to team with your consultant and stay involved" (Bortolus, 2000, p. 41), forensic psychological consultants can expect fiscal scrutiny not only at the point of retention, but over the course of their entire involvement in the legal case at hand.

The financial imperatives of the modern litigation support marketplace add more pressure than ever before for forensic psychological consultants to enter into some manner of formal agreement with the courts, attorneys, or other parties seeking to retain their services. Based on a sequence of considerations originally proposed by McGonagle (1981), Brown et al. (2005, pp. 304–305) have identified the following core components of the psychological consultant's contract:

(a) statement of the terms of the agreement, including identification of the beginning and end dates of consultation;
(b) description of the precise nature of the consultant's activities during the period of consultation;

(c) specification of consulting fees and parameters for the reimbursement of related expenses;

(d) clarification of work facilities to be provided, such as offices, secretaries, and equipment;

(e) identification of the content and boundaries of consultation reports and work product;

(f) establishment of the consultant as an independent contractor;

(g) provision for termination of the contract, either for cause or with an agreed-upon notice period;

(h) confirmation that information gained over the course of consultation shall remain confidential; and,

(i) delineation of details of the assignability, arbitration, integration, and closure of the contract.

LEGAL AND ETHICAL CONSIDERATIONS

In *Ake v. Oklahoma* (1985), the U.S. Supreme Court addressed the role of forensic consultation in criminal cases in the following fashion:

> By organizing a defendant's mental history, examination results and behavior, and other information, interpreting it in light of their expertise, and then laying out their investigative and analytic process to the jury, the psychiatrists for each party enable the jury to make its most accurate determination of the truth on the issue before them. It is for this reason that States rely on psychiatrists as examiners, consultants, and witnesses, and that private individuals do as well, when they can afford to do so. In so saying, we neither approve nor disapprove the widespread reliance on psychiatrists but instead recognize the unfairness of a contrary holding in light of the evolving practice. (pp. 81–82)

Based on this reasoning, the Court then made it clear that the defined scope of this requisite assistance extends well beyond the mere provision of another forensic mental health evaluation, of a sort that would be distinguishable only in the sense that it was commissioned by the defense instead of the prosecution:

> The foregoing leads inexorably to the conclusion that, without the assistance of a psychiatrist to conduct a professional examination on issues relevant to the defense, to help determine whether the insanity defense is viable, to present testimony, and to assist in preparing the cross-examination of a State's psychiatric witnesses, the risk of an inaccurate resolution of sanity issues is extremely high. With such assistance, the defendant is fairly able to present at least enough information to the jury, in a meaningful manner, as to permit it to make a sensible determination. (p. 82)

Ake thus laid the groundwork for the role of the forensic psychological consultant as an active, affiliated member of the defense or prosecution team, who not only seeks to develop the mental health "theory of the case" (Bocchino & Solomon, 2000; Pozner & Dodd, 2004) in a fashion approved by retaining counsel, but who also participates affirmatively in probing the weakness of the opposition's arguments, methods, and expert personnel. Given the potentially adversarial cast that distinguishes some activities of the consultant from those of the testifying witness, a separation of roles must be observed:

Attorneys frequently wonder why the same mental health professional cannot assume both "witness" and "consultant" duties in the same proceedings. After all, they reason, the expert is a member of the legal team, and has been hired to espouse a particular point of view. Is it not disingenuous to suggest that, having professed an opinion and "chosen sides" in a case, the psychologist must hold back at some poorly defined point from offering the full benefit of his or her "knowledge, skill, experience, training, or education"?

The reason why consultants should not serve as both a witness and a consultant is bound up in the way an expert arrives at and then conveys a competent, supportable, and convincing opinion. This opinion must be the product of a two-stage process. The first stage requires the witness to approach the case with a *tabula rasa* or "blank slate" perspective, as free as possible of bias or preconception. An evaluation is then performed, resulting in a forensic conclusion. At the second stage, the expert is free to serve in an advocacy role. This "advocacy" is not for a client or for a legal conclusion. Rather, it occurs for the expert's own opinion, which would not be sought on direct examination if it did not serve the client's interests. (Drogin, 2001d, p. 17)

Lawyers and experts occasionally seek to determine whether it is permissible to migrate from one role to another in the course of legal proceedings, for example, to become a consultant in the event that one's anticipated trial testimony is seen as unhelpful, or even harmful, to the party represented by retaining counsel. Brodsky (1999) has insisted that for psychologists, such a transformation is "a one-way street" that "works only to change their role from evaluating expert to trial consultant," as "once committed to an advocacy role, the alliance with the attorneys includes a commitment to help win the case" (p. 134).

Four years after *Ake,* the American Bar Association Criminal Justice Standards Committee (1989) published its *ABA Criminal Justice Mental Health Standards.* Seeking to convey the proper distinctions between the various "roles of mental health and mental retardation professionals in the criminal process," these Standards asserted that those serving in "evaluative roles" bore "an obligation to make a thorough assessment based on sound evaluative methods and to reach an objective opinion on each specific matter referred for evaluation" (§ 7-1.1(b)). By contrast:

Consultative Role: When providing consultation and advice to the prosecution or defense on the preparation or conduct of the case, the mental health or mental retardation professional has the same obligations and immunities as any member of the prosecution or defense team. Nevertheless, the prosecutor and defense counsel should respect the professional's ethical and professional standards. Any attempt to compromise the professional's standards would constitute unprofessional conduct. (§ 7-1.1(c))

These statements of ethical concern mirror multiple provisions of the "Specialty Guidelines for Forensic Psychologists" (Committee on Ethical Guidelines for Forensic Psychologists, 1991). According to Guideline III ("Competence"), when aspects of the professional relations with counsel may threaten the integrity of their participation, "forensic psychologists are obligated to decline participation or to limit their assistance in a manner consistent with professional obligations" (p. 658). Guideline VI ("Methods and Procedures") directs forensic psychologists to "take special care to avoid undue influence upon their methods, procedures, and products, such as might emanate from the party to a legal proceeding by financial compensation or other gains" (p. 661). The potentially quasi-adversarial review aspect of the consultant's participation is addressed by Guideline VII, by which, "when evaluating or commenting upon the professional work product of another expert or party to a legal proceeding, forensic psychologists represent their professional disagreements with reference to a fair and accurate evaluation of the data, theories, standards, and opinions of the other expert or party" (p. 664).

Concerning those matters to be addressed "during the initial consultation with the legal representative of the party seeking services," forensic psychologists are charged by Guideline IV ("Relationships") with reviewing a number of key issues, including "the fee structure for anticipated professional services," "prior and current professional activities, obligations, and relationships that might produce a conflict of interests," "their areas of competence and the limits of their competence," and "the known scientific bases and limitations of the methods and procedures that they employ and their qualifications to employ such methods and procedures" (Committee on Ethical Guidelines for Forensic Psychologists, 1991, p. 658).

The APA's (2002) "Ethical Principles of Psychologists and Code of Conduct" mandates in Standard 4.06 ("Consultations") that information obtained in this context be disclosed "only to the extent necessary to achieve the purposes of the consultation" (p. 1066). Similar to the initial contact requirements described in the "Specialty Guidelines for Forensic Psychologists," when it comes to defining the parameters of the consultant's involvement at the inception of the professional relationship for the edification and benefit of all parties, Standard 3.07 ("Third-Party Requests for Services") asserts:

> When psychologists agree to provide services to a person or entity at the request of a third party, psychologists attempt to clarify at the outset of the service the nature of the relationship with all individuals or organizations involved. This clarification includes the role of the psychologist (e.g., therapist, consultant, diagnostician, or expert witness), an identification of who is the client, the probable uses of the services provided or the information obtained, and the fact that there may be limits to confidentiality. (p. 1065)

Not only do such guidelines and standards serve to protect the forensic psychological consultant; they also inform counsel where the boundaries lie when he or she seeks to protect the client from compelled, premature, or inadvertent discovery of the consultant's work product. The potential for damage is significant in both criminal and civil cases, but the procedural rules in each context are quite different, and they call on attorneys and forensic psychological consultants to pay attention to varying aspects of the designation, timing, and documentation of each of the professional services rendered.

In the criminal law context, if a defendant requests disclosure of the prosecution's mental health evidence in federal cases (or in state cases bound by similar rules), then prosecutors may have the opportunity to review mental health evidence developed by the defendants, as long as "the defendant intends to use the item in the defendant's case-in-chief at trial, or intends to call the witness who prepared the report and the report relates to the witness' testimony" (*Fed. R. Crim. P.* 16(b)(1)(B)(ii)). Properly styling and limiting the forensic psychological consultant's role from the outset should cure the prospect of his or her being characterized by prosecutors as a witness. But what of those situations in which defense counsel, having originally intended to ask the forensic psychologist to testify in court, decides later that this would not be in the defendant's interest, and intends from that point to utilize the forensic psychologist as a consultant only? Most jurisdictions adhere to the reasoning expressed in *U.S. ex rel. Edney v. Smith* (1976), espousing a negative view of what might be characterized as "expert shopping," and a minority of jurisdictions identify instead with the perspective expressed in *U.S. v. Alvarez* (1975,), that defense counsel should be free to chose the most appropriate means of presenting a case "without the inhibition of creating a potential government witness" (p. 1047).

In civil litigation, counsel is steered in federal cases (or in state cases bound by similar rules) toward early decision making by the pretrial disclosure requirements that he or she reveal "the name and, if not previously provided, the address and telephone number of each witness, separately identifying those who the party expects to be present and those whom the party may call if the need arises" (*Fed. R. Civ. P.* 26(a)(3)(A)). Additionally, "a party may depose any person who has been identified as an expert whose opinions may be presented at trial" (*Fed. R. Civ. P.* 26(b)(4)). Most ominously, a showing of "substantial need" may suffice in some cases for the disclosure of materials "prepared in anticipation of litigation" by a range of individuals, including "the other party's . . . consultant" (*Fed. R. Civ. P.* 26(b)(3)). Noting that "disputes arising from one party's attempt to get its hands on trial consultant material of an adversary seem to occur with increasing frequency" (Davis & Beisecker, 1994, p. 582), Davis and Beisecker have cautioned civil litigators to observe a number of precautions in this regard, including the following:

(a) trial consultants should be retained by a written agreement with counsel, not with the party to the litigation;

(b) the retainer should contain an explicit confidentiality provision under which the consultant agrees to share the work product only with counsel and her designee;

(c) to the extent possible, counsel should be present during all research or witness preparation sessions with the trial consultant;

(d) separate engagements should be entered for research projects likely to generate work product that will be placed "in issue" and projects designed to be used in confidence for trial preparation;

(e) unless absolutely necessary, do not use trial consultants to prepare witnesses who are neither clients nor retained experts; and

(f) the trial consultant should explicitly agree and understand that any relevant facts about the dispute uncovered in the research process must be shared with trial counsel. (p. 635)

Ratcliff (2002) has encouraged attorneys in civil cases to "consider making a motion to preclude discussion about non-testifying experts by the other side," although "jurors, who have become increasingly sophisticated, seem to expect the participation of [consultants] in important cases" (p. 39). The significance of such advice is underscored by the observation of Myers and Arena (2001) that "many attorneys would prefer to contract out many of their trial duties," with the result that "they tend to ignore their true target—the jury" (p. 386). Stolle et al. (1996) investigated the impressions of both civil and criminal mock juries and found that "in terms of procedural fairness, the presence of a trial consultant for the defense had no effect on the perceived fairness of the procedures utilized when the prosecution or plaintiff had a consultant," yet it also appeared that "when the prosecution or plaintiff did not have a consultant, the procedures were thought to be more fair when the defense also did not have a consultant than when the defense alone had a consultant" (p. 161).

Apart from issues of discoverability, ethics, and juror attitudes, Wilkins (2004) has identified a number of practical considerations for the separation of consultant and expert roles in medical malpractice and other personal injury claims, citing reasons that are, arguably, applicable to criminal cases as well:

> Why not use the eventual testifying expert to do the review? Being able to identify what kind of expert will eventually be needed is unrealistic. Testifying often requires specialists whose rates for such an initial review are prohibitive, even in this high-stakes game. It is difficult to assess availability of the testifying expert when the time from initial review until trial can be years. What's more, many specialist reviewers focus only on their own backyard. . . . Other specialist reviewers may tend to justify the actions of their specialty group peers and place the blame on other specialists in other fields. Only later, when experts in these other fields are hired to review, at an additional expense, is misdirection suspected. (p. 43)

Uniting each of these considerations is the critical obligation and pressing need to reach a working understanding about the roles, rights, and risks of all parties as soon as feasible. When the mutual expectations of trial attorneys and forensic psychological consultants are clearly stated, it is far more likely that those expectations can be realized to the satisfaction of all concerned. Should certain options prove unavailable, certain barriers prove insurmountable, or certain risks prove unavoidable, both counsel and consultants are infinitely better served by reaching this conclusion at the inception of a professional relationship, rather than at its premature and stressful termination.

SPECIALIZED APPLICATIONS

The role of the forensic psychologist as consultant is played out in a myriad of civil and criminal law contexts, including case analysis and development; report and file review; identifying and retaining the expert witness; assisting in the development of direct and cross-examination; and preparing the witness for trial.

Case Analysis and Development

Retaining a forensic psychological consultant for the limited purpose of addressing another expert's adverse work product, or solely in response to the surfacing of a previously defined social scientific issue, may be precisely what the litigation team requires in some cases. In other cases, however, it may rob the client of an opportunity to benefit from that consultant's input during the crucial, formative stages of case analysis and development. The unique training and experience of the forensic psychologist (Bersoff et al., 1997; Melton, Huss, & Tomkins, 1999; Packer & Borum, 2003) can prove an invaluable factor in grappling with the initial rigors of complex litigation, as a slew of rudimentary, experimental theories of the case are quickly designed, quickly analyzed, and, for the most part, just as quickly discarded in the search for a winning strategy.

The most popular modality for such work, at least if the profusion of agency training seminars incorporating the topic is to be believed, is the process of "brainstorming" (Dugosh & Paulus, 2005). In its most basic form, brainstorming consists of a group of persons contributing as many ideas as possible, with the only qualification for such ideas being that they bear some demonstrable relationship to the case at hand. More evolved brainstorming models, however, incorporate complex strategies for individual and group goal setting (Chaffin, 1985; Larey & Paulus, 1995). Variations have included "brainsketching," whereby participants literally draw their ideas on large pieces of paper attached to the walls (van der Lugt, 2002), and "brainwriting," whereby ideas are written on sheets of paper and passed around the room using existing concepts as stimuli (Paulus & Yang, 2000).

One brainstorming technique with particular applicability to forensic psychological consultation involves the use of "generators": basic visual models used to plot every conceivable connection between different parties, locations, or other factors in a particular case. Once all of the interactions have been examined, the generator is then "rewired" by the gradual introduction of additional factors (Drogin, 1997). Although earlier studies tended to downplay the measurable productivity of face-to-face and other interactive processes, more recent research has identified promising results with the proper uniformity of modeling and training (Faure, 2004; Kramer, Fleming, & Mannis, 2001).

Brainstorming can also be facilitated, either in group settings or on an individual basis, by employing a nine-celled diagram that "portrays the foci of a Jurisprudent Psychology—formerly Jurisprudent Therapy—based inquiry in a considerably more accessible fashion" (Drogin, 2004, p. 48; see Table 18.1). By this device, multiple aspects of the same forensic issue can be analyzed in terms of their positive, neutral, or negative potential effects on the case at hand. For example, the forensic psychological consultant might conclude from a defense perspective that the mental health science of risk assessment has been suitably established from a demographic research perspective, thus offering a potentially positive (jurisprudent) effect; he or she may also conclude that mental health practice, as represented by clinical and actuarial instruments employed in cases of individual testing, lack sufficient predictive utility for reliance in a legal context, thus offering a potentially negative (antijurisprudent) result. Regarding mental health roles, the forensic psychological consultant might conclude that existing ethical and practice guidelines serve to raise cautions but also to enable practice with ultimately inadequate measures, thus offering a potentially neutral result.

Table 18.1   Jurisprudent Psychology Analytical Model

	Mental Health		
	Science	Practice	Roles
Positive (Jurisprudent)			
Neutral			
Negative (Antijurisprudent)			

Jurisprudent Psychology analyses have been employed to address such diverse forensic psychological topics as intellectual assessment in capital murder cases (Drogin, 1999c), child advocacy (Grover, 2002), malingering (Drogin, 2002b), waiver of *Miranda* rights (Fulero & Everington, 2004), federal sentencing (Drogin, 2001b; Drogin & Howard, 2001), ineffective assistance of counsel (Drogin, 2002a), testamentary capacity and undue influence (Marson, Huthwaite, & Hebert, 2004), sex offender risk assessment and treatment (Drogin, 2000e; Drogin, 1999b; Glaser, 2003), standards of professional conduct (Drogin & Barrett, 2000), competency to stand trial (Drogin, 2004), restorative justice and mediation (Drogin, Howard, & Williams, 2003), and personal injury litigation (Drogin, 2000b). A structured and structural review of each basic category of forensic mental health involvement in a legal issue serves not only to generate ideas to alter or supplement retaining counsel's theory of the case, but also to provide a mutual understanding of cross-disciplinary perspectives on issues germane to psychology as well as the law (Drogin, 2000d).

Report and File Review

> The report and the clinician who writes it will, or at least should, receive close scrutiny during adversary negotiations or proceedings. A well-written report may obviate courtroom testimony. A poorly written report may become, in the hands of a skillful lawyer, an instrument to discredit and embarrass its author. (Melton, Petrila, Poythress, & Slobogin, 1997, p. 523)

The psychological literature abounds with advice when it comes to the writing of psychological and psychiatric reports in forensic and other contexts (Babitsky & Mangraviti, 2002; Bugental, 1995; Donders, 2001a, 2001b; Hoffman, 1986; Karson, 2005; Meyers, 1985). However, such advice is unlikely to be established in court as authoritative, and forensic psychological consultants have learned (sometimes in frustration, and sometimes with relief) that the various ethics codes and specialty guidelines, while emphasizing such issues as confidentiality and data preservation, afford comparatively little attention to the specifics of report content and structure.

This is not to suggest that clinical and forensic reports do not merit a thorough and detailed review whenever they surface in a criminal or civil case. On the contrary, it is difficult to imagine how such an important source of direct and cross-examination inquiry could be ignored or afforded merely an offhand reading. Do the test results in the report comport with the data the consultant has obtained and rescored? Are assertions in the report concerning the underlying scientific literature consistent with the consultant's understanding and with assertions the report's author has made in other reports and on the witness stand? Does the report claim to represent a unanimous perspective on the part of its author and other multidisciplinary team members, whose individual reports or memoranda may or may not be attached? Does the report bear more than one signature, suggesting the possibility that a graduate trainee performed some or all of the testing and interviews informing reported results, with the additional possibility that the testifying clinician never actually examined or even met with the examinee?

In criminal cases, state statutes often provide specific guidance as to issues that a criminal responsibility, trial competency, or other forensic report must address, for example, the defendant's potential for restoration of competency (Hubbard,

Zapf, & Ronan, 2003; Miller, 2003; Stafford, 2003) or a direct statement as to the presence or absence of an insanity defense, irrespective of the clinician's reservations about addressing the "ultimate issue" (Drogin, 2000b, 2001b; Ewing, 2003; Fulero & Finkel, 1991; Slobogin, 1989). If the testifying clinician was (or assumed that he or she was) compelled to provide Health Insurance Portability and Accountability Act (HIPAA) or other statutorily mandated confidentiality warnings, the consultant may attempt to gauge the potential impact of the fashion in which these were conveyed or the potential legal and ethical ramifications of any failure to make such disclosures (Connell & Koocher, 2003; Drogin, 2001a).

Specific to civil practice, *Fed. R. Civ. P.* 26(a)(2)(B) mandates that reports in federal cases (or in state cases bound by similar rules) must include the following components:

(a) a complete statement of all opinions to be expressed;

(b) the basis and reasons for the opinions;

(c) the data or other information considered;

(d) any exhibits to be used in summary of the opinions;

(e) any exhibits to be used as support for the opinions;

(f) the qualifications of the witness;

(g) the compensation to be paid for the study and testimony; and,

(h) a listing of any other cases in which the witness has testified as an expert at trial or by deposition within the preceding 4 years.

The forensic psychological consultant, sufficiently armed with notes and data from the evaluation in question, is in a position not only to identify the presence or absence of such components, but also to determine how relevant issues could or should have been addressed and, under some circumstances, why they may not have been addressed. For example, failure to include reference to the testifying expert's participation in a prior case may be relevant to more than a lapse of compliance with federal standards. The listing of "compensation to be paid" sometimes leads to the opportunity for a review of the testifying expert's actual bill, which may yield important insight into such practices as outsourcing of evaluative functions, minimal time spent on review of records, and overcharging for travel.

In many cases, the review of ancillary documents serves a broader purpose than merely offering the opportunity to support or diminish the impact of the testifying clinician's report. File review as a discrete function is particularly relevant to civil cases, not only in assisting counsel to prevail during litigation, but also as a method for evaluating likely benefits and potential damages when legal action has yet to be threatened or even contemplated. Hadjistavropoulos and Bieling (2001) have identified the following factors for reviewing files in the potential adjudication of mental health and chronic disability claims:

(a) Has a determination of impairment been made by a specialist? Determinations of specialists may sometimes be given more weight than determinations made by a general practitioner.

(b) Are detailed descriptions of symptoms and their severity and frequency available? The mere presence of symptoms does not imply disability.

(c) Are prescribed or otherwise recommended treatments intensive and thoroughgoing? A person who needs to see a treatment provider once every 4 months may be more likely to function independently than someone who needs to see a treatment provider weekly.

(d) Are there descriptions of and a discussion of the patient's subjective complaints in chart notes? Severe complaints are more likely to be the focus of many clinical sessions than are less severe ones.

(e) Has a general practitioner made a referral to a medical specialist or psychologist? Such a referral may be taken to suggest that the general practitioner regarded the claimant's condition to be of sufficient severity or complexity to warrant specialized treatment by a highly skilled practitioner.

(f) Are there comorbid conditions (e.g., substance abuse) that may affect impairment or disability? There is increasing focus on the issue of diagnostic specificity and comorbidity, especially when functioning and symptoms are chronic or have not responded to standard therapeutic modalities.

(g) Is corroborating information available from significant others? Such information can often be found in some medical-psychological reports and may serve to support the validity of the claimant's complaints.

(h) Has hospitalization occurred? In most instances, hospitalization implies a severe problem.

(i) What is the nature of the job? The specific characteristics of the claimant's occupation need to be taken into account because many patients have symptoms that would cause significant problems in some but not all occupations. (pp. 56–57)

File review gains particular importance when it becomes the only data-oriented mode of investigation available to the forensic psychological consultant. In some cases, for example, a "psychological autopsy" is commissioned, typically when a malpractice action is based on patient suicide or institutional neglect, or when the next of kin is seeking to assert damages for pain and suffering in the aftermath of a catastrophic accident (Annon, 1995; Cavanagh, Carson, Sharpe, & Lawrie, 2003; Drogin & Barrett, 2003; Hawton, Houston, Malmberg, & Simkin, 2003; Isometsa, 2001; Selkin, 1994; Shneidman, 1994; Young, 1992). The advent of the electronic medical record, electronic mail communication of patient information, and other forms of "digital evidence" (Drogin, 2000b, 2000c; Lange & Nimsger, 2004) will often require the development of substantial computer technical skill as well as clinical insight.

Identifying and Retaining the Expert Witness

The level at which the forensic psychological consultant can begin assisting in the identification and retention of expert witnesses depends on counsel's own combination of experience and educability. On the one hand, is the attorney even aware that a mental health expert is required or may be useful for the case in question, and if so, does he or she have a sense of even the basic differences among the various mental health professions? On the other hand, is the attorney willing and able to devote the time and resources necessary to learn and apply relevant distinctions, and is the attorney sufficiently conversant with his or her own profession to make the most of this newly acquired knowledge?

To play a fully comprehensive and effective supporting role, the forensic psychological consultant will need to obtain a detailed overview of the current or contemplated litigation with which the sought-after expert witness will become involved. It is not enough to claim to be able to put counsel in touch with "the best psychiatrist in Cleveland"; rather, the consultant must begin, from the outset, to hone his or her expert short list or begin to develop a wish list of attributes for an expert as yet unidentified based on the unique requirements of the individual case. Attorneys should be queried about the background, parties, venue, theories, records, lawyers, judges, and other experts involved in the current matter, with the same breadth and depth as if consultants were planning on serving as the expert witness themselves.

As all of this is occurring, the forensic psychological consultant with a clinical orientation will begin to speculate about the sort of expert witness whose personality and work style will most effectively mesh with those of counsel. Does the attorney seem prepared, focused, patient, insightful, and sensitive, or do some or all of these qualities appear to be lacking? To what extent would he or she be able to tolerate (or to hold his or her ground with) certain experts known to the consultant, or a certain type of expert? Daicoff (2004) has recently provided an extensive overview of lawyer personality styles, and studies of the personality styles of mental health professionals have long been a staple component of the professional psychotherapeutic literature (Hersoug, 2004; Macran, Stiles, & Smith, 1999; Smith, 2003). The consultant may also have the opportunity to gauge counsel's ability to interact effectively with the client (Drogin, 2000a), leading to the generation of further hypotheses regarding the attorney-expert relationship.

In some cases, retaining counsel will already have an expert, a list of experts, or a type of expert in mind and will request that the forensic psychological consultant assist in narrowing the available options. The consultant should be well versed in the range of available credentialing bodies and their actual and alleged strengths and weaknesses. Does the organization in question require a rigorous review of credentials, a written qualifying examination, submission of acceptable redacted samples of professional practice, and a peer-conducted oral examination, or is it instead a "vanity board" for which membership requires little more than the submission of a fee (Dattilio & Sadoff, 2002; Heilbrun & Otto, 2003; Otto & Heilbrun, 2002)? Given the opportunity to review the curricula vitae of individual expert witnesses, and to interview these persons with or on behalf of counsel, the consultant can probe for the possibility that they represent one or more broad (and colloquially styled) categories of "problem experts," with the following advice to attorneys who may encounter them:

(a) *The Fraud:* Some experts have testified in court with falsified experience, publications, even academic degrees and licenses. Perform a thorough background check on your experts. Look up some of their publications. Call their state boards of licensure: Are these professionals in good standing?

(b) *The Hired Gun:* Beware the experts who see things your way regardless of the facts. You and your clients cannot afford to go into the courtroom with people who are not going to tell the truth, the whole truth, and nothing but the truth. Are the expert's explanations of the case plausible? Are (his or her) opinions literally too good to be true?

(c) *The Mystic:* We read more and more these days about "junk science" in the courtroom. Some experts are so caught up in the "spirit" of their work that attention to the research and training fundamentals may suffer. Are your experts' opinions supported by the scientific literature and by the consensus of respected colleagues?

(d) *The Savior:* Are these experts' political or moral agendas clouding their judgment? Do they have a tendency to see every case the same way? Ask your experts for some sample "work product" from other cases. Investigate to see how they testified in other cases. Consult with resources that monitor expert testimony in your area.

(e) *The Prospector:* Beware the experts who want to talk about the fee and nothing else before accepting a case. Check to discover if the proposed compensation is reasonable based upon your experts' specialties, region, and experience.

(f) *The Sheriff:* Do your experts have a "law and order" orientation? Even some experts who work frequently for the defense may exhibit presumptions of guilt and a deterministic perspective. How concerned do your experts appear to be about your clients "returning to the street"? Does your expert usually testify for the prosecution, or exclusively in civil matters?

(g) *The Know-It-All:* Beware experts who are the world's foremost authorities on every topic, inside or outside of their own disciplines. Is there apparent resistance to thinking creatively in individual cases? Sometimes knowing it all is the symptom of a closed mind; as an attorney, you know that every litigant is a unique individual and that every case is different.

(h) *The Sandbagger:* Are these experts just making it up as they go along? Are their findings based on recognized scientific principles or on "hunches"? Run some of your experts' reasoning past other scientists functioning as paid or *pro bono* consultants. Where did your experts obtain their training and experience in this area?

(i) *The Rookie:* Some experts are bright, well-intentioned, and utterly lacking in experience. How many cases have they evaluated in the forensic arena? How many cases with this type of litigant? How many times did these cases result in courtroom testimony? Have your colleagues ever heard of your experts? Who supervised them?

(j) *The Lawyer:* There will always be those experts who come to believe, with forensic experience, that their expertise extends beyond their own training into the law. Some may actually be lawyers in their own right. It does not matter; *you* are the attorney handling this case. That does not mean that some experts would not give you helpful legal suggestions, but be sure to keep these roles straight in everyone's mind.

(k) *The Technician:* Some experts are highly effective in conveying their ideas to other scientists, but may leave you scratching your head. The sheer density of their data and arguments is overwhelming. Think how this will go over with the jury. This does not mean your experts are smarter than you are: they are just speaking another language. Ask for a translation, and listen closely to see if they can actually provide one.

(l) *The Waffler:* "He's telling the truth . . . *as far as I can tell.* She's definitely competent to stand trial . . . *unless there's something else going on.* Is he criminally responsible? *That depends on how you look at it.*" Some experts are notorious for altering their opinions whenever they receive a report written by an "opposing" expert; others will do it on the witness stand. How many times have you found yourself telling some experts, "I just want to know what we're dealing with here"?

(m) *The Egoist:* These experts know they are the best the field has to offer. Sometimes they exhibit extraordinary patience in waiting for you to figure it out, too. Experts who are narcissistically enmeshed with their work are "easy pickings" for the experienced cross-examiner, and may be uncomprehending or resistant to your efforts to insulate them on direct or to rehabilitate them on re-direct. Hint: Casually inquire about how any minor errors in assessment might be handled prior to report-writing, and listen carefully. Only repeat this question once . . . then change the subject.

(n) *The Muddler:* These experts may be the greatest scientists in the world. No one will ever know. You can tell them apart from the Technician only because the Technician cannot understand them either. *Nobody* understands these people. Are they really the Mystic or the Sandbagger in disguise? You do not have time to find out. There is a trial coming up, and you need to find another expert.

(o) *The MIA:* Experts whose reports and testimony make judges and juries weep with sympathy or fear are useless when they file reports after the deadline and show up late for court . . . or not at all. *It happens.* Hint: Ask for little things like letters, articles, and the like, and watch to see when these arrive. (Drogin, 2001c, pp. 143–146)

When the forensic psychological consultant has identified (or confirmed the utility of) an expert witness, it is just as important for that witness and counsel to enter into a mutual contract as it is for the consultant to do so. Shuman (1997, § 6.12) has identified key components of the "expert psychiatrist or psychologist assistance agreement," addressing:

(a) phases of the case in which assistance will be rendered;

(b) methods and procedures for evaluations and/or reports;

(c) anticipated location of testimony and parameters of preparation;

(d) compensation, in terms of fee caps and hourly rates;

(e) retainers and timing of subsequent payments;

(f) guarantees (if any) of payment of the expert's compensation by the client;

(g) recognition of confidentiality and forms of waiver;

(h) notification to the attorney of the expert's progress with various phases of assistance; and,

(i) bases for termination of the service contract.

Involved parties may consider adding to this list a clause reflecting any ongoing role of the consultant, particularly concerning such issues as review of work product, observation of examinations, or assistance in the selection of interview protocols and assessment instruments. The forensic psychological consultant can often provide invaluable assistance in translating and contextualizing the professional and ethical concerns of both the attorney and the expert witness as the contract is negotiated.

Assisting in the Development of Direct and Cross-Examination

A good narrative has the total package: essential information, how it made a difference, the interrelated nature of the character of the defendant or plaintiff with respect to the key events, and a lucid style of presenting. . . . As you describe the nature of the person you have evaluated, explain in a way that helps along the understanding of what happened at the central event, how the person reacted, and why. (Brodsky, 2004, p. 26)

The influence of narrative theory is well established in the fields of both law (Amsterdam & Bruner, 2000; Bruner, 2002) and psychology (Bruner, 1990; Herman, 2001). People communicate and learn by telling stories. Patients find meaning in the context of the events of a life lived in an unbroken procession of days, weeks, months, and years. The courtroom perceptions of jurors are substantially impacted by exposure to thousands of hours of filmed entertainment, often with explicitly legal themes (Clover, 1998; Graham, 1991). On direct examination, the storytelling skills of the mental health professional must, in most cases, be poured into a specific mold: that of a seeming (but not actual) conversation between the expert witness and the attorney (Small, 2004), with the latter responsible not only for knowing the tale as well as its narrator (Gray, 1997; Tate & Parker, 1999), but also for anticipating how malicious interruptions and demands for retelling will be employed in an attempt to pervert its meaning (Gutheil, 1998a). The salient contribution of the forensic psychological consultant to the development of cross-examination is to serve as a combination of translator and tour guide. What intended and unintended meaning and effect might the same words have for those speaking the distinctly different languages of psychology and the law? Where might following the path of certain psychotherapeutic and assessment notions lead, and what traps must be avoided on the return journey?

The forensic psychological consultant often will encourage the expert witness to style his or her own report in a fashion that lays out a compelling tale of a competently performed mental health assessment, both for its narrative value and as an easily referenced aid for effective delivery of critical information on direct examination, despite the inevitable interruptions and calls for repetition. Of course, such a story must be supported by available data and must not represent an attempt to oversimplify or camouflage an opinion. "The direct examination should optimally have a theme or 'story' to permit understanding by lay audiences" (Gutheil & Simon, 2002, p. 28). An audience of jurors is quite likely to forgive being subjected to some unavoidable social scientific jargon, in return for the opportunity to accompany the testifying witness on a vicarious journey through a day in the life of a forensic evaluator. There is, of course, a corresponding danger of smugness and self-absorption when assuming the combined statuses of healer, truth teller, and even entertainer. Brodsky (1991) cautions against adoption of the "star-witness fantasy" and cautions that "a witness' self-centeredness about the importance of personal testimony can serve as blinders that interfere with clarity, self-assurance, and nondefensiveness" (p. 181).

> What shall be our first mode of attack? Shall we adopt the fatal method of those we see around us daily in the courts, and proceed to take the witness over the same story that he has already given our adversary, in the absurd hope that he is going to change it in the repetition, and not retell it with double effect upon the jury? Or shall we rather avoid carefully his original story, except insofar as is necessary to refer to it in order to point out its weak spots? (Wellman, 1936, p. 39)

When assisting in the development of cross-examination, the forensic psychological consultant not only informs counsel of the full range of affirmative errors allegedly committed by the adverse expert mental health witness, but also participates in the cataloguing of sins of omission:

> In both civil and criminal cases, the best method of cross-examination of the opposing expert is not to discuss the things the expert has done, but the things he has not done. First show the importance of the things to be questioned on, and then show that they were not done. By doing so, the lawyer may cast doubt on the credibility of the expert's ultimate

judgment and conclusions. By placing the things not done into groups, the lawyer can more persuasively argue them to the jury. (Pozner & Dodd, 2004, § 25.15)

This vital function cannot be supplied for counsel by the consultant whose sole talent is the identification and characterization of scoring errors, superseded test measures, and poorly drafted reports (Babitsky & Mangraviti, 1997, 2003; Campbell & Lorandos, 2001). To educate the attorney concerning what should have been done, it follows that counsel must *know* what should have been done. Judges and juries alike will soon tire of the cross-examination strategy and underlying case theory that seek only to undermine credibility and impugn integrity (Imwinkelried, 2004). It is axiomatic that two sides can play this game. A way must be found to convey both the spirit and the technique of the competent mental health professional and to encourage the fact finder to mourn that individual's absence from the field at that crucial juncture when injury occurred or when the opportunity to diagnose or heal effectively was irreparably lost.

Preparing the Witness for Trial

Witness preparation, though sometimes misunderstood and consequently misapplied, is nonetheless a scientifically proven means of amplifying confidence while at the same time reducing nervousness and any accompanying testimonial errors and omissions (Boccaccini, 2002; Boccaccini, Gordon, & Brodsky, 2003). Small (2004) has identified several basic pointers for prospective witnesses, exhorting them, among other things, to "take your time," "always remember you are making a record," "tell the truth," "be relentlessly polite," "don't answer a question you don't understand," "if you don't remember, say so," "don't guess," and "keep it simple" (pp. 37–82). There is little in our own contemporary observations of courtroom testimony to suggest that such advice should not be proffered at least as vigorously to mental health experts as it is to the greenest of lay witnesses. Additionally, of course, the forensic psychological consultant will want to develop a case-specific checklist of attributes and exercises for the testifying expert, including some combination of the following components:

(a) *Relevant:* Is the anticipated testimony of actual value for the client's case, or does it subtly undermine the case?

(b) *Admissible:* Do experts understand the evidentiary rules, case law, and statutes as applied in their jurisdiction, and have they considered how their conclusions meet this standard?

(c) *Pertinent:* Is the anticipated testimony pertinent to matters really at issue in this case, or is it instead inflammatory, harassing, or speculative?

(d) *Consistent:* Do proffered diagnoses comport with the relevant diagnostic criteria?

(e) *Ethical:* Are all aspects of the conduct of the examination, reporting, characterizations, conclusions, and recommendations consistent with the ethical code relevant to the expert's particular profession?

(f) *Accurate:* Have the professional report and supportive test data been scanned for typographical errors, mathematical accuracy, and potentially misleading language?

(g) *Authoritative:* Have experts satisfactorily documented relevant degrees, credentials, and experience, with the type of supporting documentation that underscores the appropriateness of these particular professionals addressing the forensic issues at hand?

(h) *Supported:* Are experts prepared to provide copies of, and to cite at trial, research and other literature supportive of their methodology and positions?

(i) *Comfortable:* Are experts aware of and comfortable with the ramifications of stating their opinions, in light of the potential reactions of various professional and public interest communities?

(j) *Oriented:* Do experts fully understand where they are to be, when they are to testify, how early they are to arrive, where they are to park, in what order the case is expected to proceed, and for how long the case is expected to continue? (Drogin, 2000b, pp. 308–309)

More generally, Gutheil (1998b, pp. 56–58) has identified the "Six Ps of Trial Preparation": "preparation," "planning," "practice," "pretrial conference," "[avoiding] pitfalls," and "presentation." The forensic psychological consultant can assist counsel in running pretrial direct and cross-examination drills (Blau, 1998), in addition to reviewing written drafts or outlines of more elaborate anticipated responses. Perhaps unnoticed among all of these technical, even mechanical, considerations is the simple ingredient of shared experience and companionship. For the expert witness to run the gauntlet of pretrial preparation in the company of a like-minded colleague adds a compelling dimension of mutuality, respect, and even enjoyment to the process.

CONCLUSION

Almost a century after Hugo Münsterberg's (1908) *On the Witness Stand,* forensic psychologists have extended their influence to the full range of civil and criminal proceedings, offering testimony that draws on every research and practice aspect of contemporary mental health science. Driven in equal measure by the expressed needs of the legal system and their own desire to enhance the profile and integrity of their parent discipline, forensic psychological consultants are now venturing off the witness stand in ever increasing numbers. It cannot be overemphasized that one should not serve simultaneously as both a testifying witness and a consultant in the course of the same legal matter, and we are confident that as forensic psychological consultation becomes more popular with attorneys and psychologists alike, such role-specific ethical issues will be addressed in the professional literature with increasing specificity. We hope that in the future more of our colleagues will be encouraged to engage in this fascinating and vital mode of service, both inspired by the contributions it can offer and mindful of the responsibility it entails.

REFERENCES

Ake v. Oklahoma, 470 U.S. 68 (1985).

Alderfer, C. P. (1998). Group psychological consulting to organizations: A perspective on history. *Consulting Psychology Journal: Practice and Research, 50,* 67–77.

Amberg, W. F. (2002). ABPP recognizes the American Board of Organizational and Business Consulting Psychology. *Consulting Psychology Journal: Practice and Research, 54,* 13–14.

Amberg, W. F. (2004, Winter). The American Board of Organizational and Business Consulting Psychology becomes the 13th ABPP affiliated specialty board. *ABPP Specialist, 54,* 6.

American Bar Association Criminal Justice Standards Committee. (1989). *ABA Criminal Justice Mental Health Standards.* Washington, DC: American Bar Association.

American Psychological Association. (2002). Ethical principles of psychologists and code of conduct. *American Psychologist, 57,* 1060–1073.

Amsterdam, A. G., & Bruner, J. (2000). *Minding the law.* Cambridge, MA: Harvard University Press.

Annon, J. S. (1995). The psychological autopsy. *American Journal of Forensic Psychology, 13,* 39–48.

Ardichvili, A. (2000). Critical dilemmas for the independent consultant. *Consulting Psychology Journal: Practice and Research, 52,* 133–141.

Babitsky, S., & Mangraviti, J. J. (1997). *How to excel during cross-examination.* Falmouth, MA: SEAK.

Babitsky, S., & Mangraviti, J. J. (2002). *Writing and defending your expert report: The step-by-step guide with models.* Falmouth, MA: SEAK.

Babitsky, S., & Mangraviti, J. J. (2003). *Cross-examination: The comprehensive guide for experts.* Falmouth, MA: SEAK.

Benjamin, L. T. (1997). The origin of the psychological species: History of the beginnings of American Psychological Association divisions. *American Psychologist, 52,* 725–732.

Bent, R. J. (2004, Winter). Perspectives. *ABPP Specialist, 3,* 22.

Bersoff, D. N., Goodman-Delahunty, J., Grisso, T., Hans, V., Poythress, N., & Roesch, R. (1997). Training in law and psychology: Models from the Villanova conference. *American Psychologist, 52,* 1301–1310.

Blanton, J. (2000). Why consultants don't apply psychological research. *Consulting Psychology Journal: Practice and Research, 52,* 235–247.

Blau, T. H. (1998). *The psychologist as expert witness* (2nd ed.). New York: Wiley.

Boccaccini, M. T. (2002). What do we really know about witness preparation? *Behavioral Sciences and the Law, 20,* 161–189.

Boccaccini, M. T., & Brodsky, S. L. (2002). Believability of expert and lay witnesses: Implications for trial consultation. *Professional Psychology: Research and Practice, 33,* 384–388.

Boccaccini, M. T., Gordon, T., & Brodsky, S. L. (2003). Effects of witness preparation on witness confidence and nervousness. *Journal of Forensic Psychology Practice, 3,* 39–51.

Bocchino, A. J., & Solomon, S. H. (2000). What juries want to hear: Methods for developing persuasive case theory. *Tennessee Law Review, 67,* 543–567.

Bortolus, D. (2000, November/December). The ABC's of using consultants. *Paytech,* 32–42.

Brodsky, S. L. (1991). *Testifying in court: Guidelines and maxims for the expert witness.* Washington, DC: American Psychological Association.

Brodsky, S. L. (1999). *The expert expert witness: More maxims and guidelines for testifying in court.* Washington, DC: American Psychological Association.

Brodsky, S. L. (2004). *Coping with cross-examination and other pathways to effective testimony.* Washington, DC: American Psychological Association.

Brown, D., Pryzwansky, W. B., & Schulte, A. C. (1998). *Psychological consultation: Introduction to theory and practice* (4th ed.). Boston: Allyn & Bacon.

Brown, D., Pryzwansky, W. B., & Schulte, A. C. (2005). *Psychological consultation and collaboration: Introduction to theory and practice* (6th ed.). Boston: Allyn & Bacon.

Bruner, J. (1990). *Acts of meaning.* Cambridge, MA: Harvard University Press.

Bruner, J. (2002). *Making stories: Law, literature, life.* New York: Farrar, Straus and Giroux.

Bugental, J. F. (1995). Context and meaning in writing case reports. *Journal of Humanistic Psychology, 35,* 99–102.

Campbell, T., & Lorandos, D. (2001). *Cross examining experts in the behavioral sciences.* St. Paul, MN: West.

Cavanagh, J. T., Carson, A. J., Sharpe, M., & Lawrie, S. M. (2003). Psychological autopsy studies of suicide: A systematic review. *Psychological Medicine, 33,* 395–405.

Chaffin, K. (1985). The difference an idea makes: The art of brainstorming. *Activities, Adaptation and Aging, 6,* 25–30.

Chamberlin, J. (2004, September). Consulting across state lines. *Monitor on Psychology,* 18.

Clover, C. J. (1998). Movie juries. *DePaul Law Review, 48,* 389–405.

Committee on Ethical Guidelines for Forensic Psychologists. (1991). Specialty guidelines for forensic psychologists. *Law and Human Behavior, 15,* 655–665.

Connell, M., & Koocher, G. P. (2003, Spring/Summer). Expert opinion: HIPAA and forensic practice. *American Psychology-Law Society News,* 16–19.

Daicoff, S. (2004). *Lawyer, know thyself: A psychological analysis of personality strengths and weaknesses.* Washington, DC: American Psychological Association.

Daicoff, S., & Wexler, D. B. (2003). Therapeutic jurisprudence. In I. B. Weiner (Series Ed.) & A. M. Goldstein (Vol. Ed.), *Comprehensive handbook of psychology: Vol. 11. Forensic psychology* (pp. 561–580). Hoboken, NJ: Wiley.

Dattilio, F. M., & Sadoff, R. L. (2002). *Mental health experts: Roles and qualifications for court.* Mechanicsburg, PA: Pennsylvania Bar Institute.

Davis, S. D., & Beisecker, T. D. (1994). Discovering trial consultant work product: A new way to borrow an adversary's wits? *American Journal of Trial Advocacy, 17,* 581–636.

Donders, J. (2001a). A survey of report writing by neuropsychologists, I: General characteristics and content. *Clinical Neuropsychologist, 15,* 137–149.

Donders, J. (2001b). A survey of report writing by neuropsychologists, II: Test data, report format, and document length. *Clinical Neuropsychologist, 15,* 150–161.

Drogin, E. Y. (1997). The use of "generators" in brainstorming: An interactive-environmental approach to case conceptualization. *Advocate, 19,* 36–38.

Drogin, E. Y. (1999a). Prophets in another land: Utilizing psychological expertise from foreign jurisdictions. *Mental and Physical Disability Law Reporter, 23,* 767–771.

Drogin, E. Y. (1999b, December). Sexual offender risk assessment and scientific evidence: A jurisprudent therapy perspective. *Bulletin of Law, Science and Technology,* 3–4.

Drogin, E. Y. (1999c). "WAIS" not, want not? A jurisprudent therapy approach to innovations in forensic assessment of intellectual functioning. *Advocate, 21,* 4–5.

Drogin, E. Y. (2000a). Breaking through: Communicating and collaborating with the mentally ill defendant. *Advocate, 22,* 27–34.

Drogin, E. Y. (2000b). Evidence and expert mental health witnesses: A jurisprudent therapy perspective. In E. Pierson (Ed.), *New developments in personal injury litigation* (pp. 295–333). New York: Aspen.

Drogin, E. Y. (2000c). Evidence and expert mental health witnesses in family law cases: A jurisprudent therapy perspective. In E. Pierson (Ed.), *2000 Wiley family law update* (pp. 281–313). New York: Aspen.

Drogin, E. Y. (2000d). From therapeutic jurisprudence . . . to jurisprudent therapy. *Behavioral Sciences and the Law, 18,* 489–498.

Drogin, E. Y. (2000e). In search of psychology: A jurisprudent therapy perspective on sexual offender risk assessment. *Advocate, 22,* 17–19.

Drogin, E. Y. (2000f, May). Jurisprudent therapy and the role of the forensic trial consultant. *Bulletin of Law, Science, and Technology,* 5–6.

Drogin, E. Y. (2001a). HIPAA: Psychotherapy's "elephant in the living room." *Networker, 13,* 6–7.

Drogin, E. Y. (2001b, June). Jurisprudent therapy and the role of mental health science in federal sentencing. *Bulletin of Law, Science and Technology,* 9–10.

Drogin, E. Y. (2001c). Jurisprudent therapy, scientific evidence, and the role of the forensic psychologist. *Scientific Evidence Review, 5,* 129–154.

Drogin, E. Y. (2001d). Utilizing forensic psychological consultation: A jurisprudent therapy analysis. *Mental and Physical Disability Law Reporter, 25,* 17–22.

Drogin, E. Y. (2002a, July). Jurisprudent therapy, ineffective assistance, and social scientific evidence. *Bulletin of Law, Science and Technology,* 8.

Drogin, E. Y. (2002b, January). Malingering and behavioral science: A jurisprudent therapy perspective. *Bulletin of Law, Science and Technology,* 8–9.

Drogin, E. Y. (2004). Jurisprudent therapy and competency. *Law and Psychology Review, 28,* 41–51.

Drogin, E. Y., & Barrett, C. L. (2000, Spring). The influence of a jurisprudent therapy perspective on standards of professional conduct. *Kentucky Psychologist, 6,* 9.

Drogin, E. Y., & Barrett, C. L. (2003). Substituted judgment: Roles for the forensic psychologist. In I. B. Weiner (Series Ed.) & A. M. Goldstein (Vol. Ed.), *Comprehensive handbook of psychology: Vol. 11. Forensic psychology* (pp. 301–312). Hoboken, NJ: Wiley.

Drogin, E. Y., & Howard, M. E. (2001). Jurisprudent therapy: Deriving optimal assistance from psychological science, practice, and roles. *Vermont Bar Journal, 27*(31), 34–38.

Drogin, E. Y., Howard, M. E., & Williams, J. R. (2003). Restorative justice: The influence of psychology from a jurisprudent therapy perspective. In D. Carson & R. Bull (Eds.), *Handbook of psychology in legal contexts* (2nd ed., pp. 423–448). London: Wiley.

Dugosh, K. L., & Paulus, P. B. (2005). Cognitive and social comparison processes in brainstorming. *Journal of Experimental Social Psychology, 41*, 313–320.

Ewing, C. P. (2003). Expert testimony: Law and practice. In I. B. Weiner (Series Ed.) & A. M. Goldstein (Vol. Ed.), *Comprehensive handbook of psychology: Vol. 11. Forensic psychology* (pp. 55–66). Hoboken, NJ: Wiley.

Faure, C. (2004). Beyond brainstorming: Effects of different group procedures on selection of ideas and satisfaction with the process. *Journal of Creative Behavior, 38*, 13–34.

Fed. R. Civ. P. 26(a)(2)(B).

Fed. R. Civ. P. 26(a)(3)(A).

Fed. R. Civ. P. 26(b)(3).

Fed. R. Civ. P. 26(b)(4).

Fed. R. Crim. P. 16(b)(1)(B)(ii)).

Friedman, H. J., & Klee, C. H. (2001). The roles of expert and ligitation support consultants in medical-legal claims. *Neurorehabilitation, 16*, 123–130.

Friedman, R. S., & Molay, F. (1994). A history of psychiatric consultation in America. *Psychiatric Clinics of North America, 17*, 667–681.

Fulero, S. M., & Everington, C. (2004). Assessing the capacity of persons with mental retardation to waive Miranda rights: A jurisprudent therapy perspective. *Law and Psychology Review, 28*, 53–69.

Fulero, S. M., & Finkel, N. J. (1991). Barring ultimate issues testimony: An "insane" rule? *Law and Human Behavior, 15*, 495–507.

Glaser, B. (2003). Therapeutic jurisprudence: An ethical paradigm for therapists in sex offender treatment programs. *Western Criminology Review, 4*, 143–154.

Glasser, J. K. (2002). Factors related to consultant credibility. *Consulting Psychology Journal: Practice and Research, 54*, 28–42.

Goldstein, A. M. (2003). Overview of forensic psychology. In I. B. Weiner (Series Ed.) & A. M. Goldstein (Vol. Ed.), *Comprehensive handbook of psychology: Vol. 11. Forensic psychology* (pp. 3–20). Hoboken, NJ: Wiley.

Graham, F. (1991). The impact of television on the jury system: Ancient myths and modern realism. *American University Law Review, 40*, 623–629.

Gray, L. N. (1997, January). Direct, cross and redirect examination. *New York State Bar Journal*, 46–52.

Grover, S. C. (2002). The psychologist as child advocate. *University of Cincinnati Law Review, 71*, 43–70.

Gutheil, T. G. (1998a). *The psychiatrist as expert witness*. Washington, DC: American Psychiatric Publishing.

Gutheil, T. G. (1998b). *The psychiatrist in court: A survival guide*. Washington, DC: American Psychiatric Publishing.

Gutheil, T. G., & Simon, R. I. (2002). *Mastering psychiatric practice: Advanced strategies for the expert witness*. Washington, DC: American Psychiatric Publishing.

Hadjistavropoulos, T., & Bieling, P. (2001). File review consultation in the adjudication of mental health and chronic pain disability claims. *Consulting Psychology Journal: Practice and Research, 53*, 52–63.

Hansen, M. (2005, August). Everyday heroes: Nonprofessional experts rank high on jury credibility at lower cost to lawyers. *ABA Journal*, 23.

Hawton, K., Houston, K., Malmberg, A., & Simkin, S. (2003). Psychological autopsy interviews in suicide research: The reactions of informants. *Archives of Suicide Research, 7*, 73–82.

Heilbrun, K. S., & Otto, R. K. (2003). Forensic psychology and board certification. *American Psychologist, 58*, 80.

Herman, D. (2001). Narrative theory and the cognitive sciences. *Narrative Inquiry, 11*, 1–34.

Hersoug, A. G. (2004). Assessment of therapists' and patients' personality: Relationship to therapeutic technique and outcome in brief dynamic psychotherapy. *Journal of Personality Assessment, 83*, 191–200.

Hoffman, B. F. (1986). How to write a psychiatric report for litigation following a personal injury. *American Journal of Psychiatry, 143*, 164–169.

Hubbard, K. L., Zapf, P. A., & Ronan, K. A. (2003). Competency restoration: An examination of the differences between defendants predicted restorable and not restorable to competency. *Law and Human Behavior, 27,* 127–139.

Imwinkelried, E. J. (2004). *The methods of attacking scientific evidence* (4th ed.). Newark, NJ: Matthew Bender.

Isometsa, E. T. (2001). Psychological autopsy studies: A review. *European Psychiatry, 16,* 379–385.

Karson, M. (2005). Ten things I learned about report writing in law school (and the eighth grade). *Clinical Psychologist, 58,* 4–11.

Kovera, M. B., Dickinson, J. J., & Cutler, B. L. (2003). Voir dire and jury selection. In I. B. Weiner (Series Ed.) & A. M. Goldstein (Vol. Ed.), *Comprehensive handbook of psychology: Vol. 11. Forensic psychology* (pp. 161–175). Hoboken, NJ: Wiley.

Kramer, T. J., Fleming, G. P., & Mannis, S. M. (2001). Improving face-to-face brainstorming through modeling and facilitation. *Small Group Research, 32,* 533–557.

Lange, M. C., & Nimsger, K. M. (2004). *Electronic evidence and discovery: What every lawyer needs to know.* Washington, DC: American Bar Association.

Larey, T. S., & Paulus, P. B. (1995). Social comparison goal setting in brainstorming groups. *Journal of Applied Social Psychology, 26,* 1579–1596.

Lecci, L., Snowden, J., & Morris, D. (2004). Using social science research to inform and evaluate the contributions of trial consultants in the voir dire. *Journal of Forensic Psychology Practice, 4,* 67–78.

Leonard, H. S. (1999). Becoming a consultant: The real stories. *Consulting Psychology Journal: Practice and Research, 51,* 3–13.

Macran, S., Stiles, W. B., & Smith, J. A. (1999). How does personal therapy affect therapists' practice? *Journal of Counseling Psychology, 46,* 419–431.

Marson, D. C., Huthwaite, J. S., & Hebert, K. (2004). Testamentary capacity and undue influence in the elderly: A jurisprudent therapy perspective. *Law and Psychology Review, 28,* 71–96.

McGonagle, J. J. (1981). *Managing the consultant.* Radnor, PA: Chilton Book.

Melton, G. B., Huss, M. T., & Tomkins, A. J. (1999). Training in forensic psychology and the law. In A. K. Hess & I. B. Weiner (Eds.), *Handbook of forensic psychology* (pp. 24–47). New York: Wiley.

Melton, G. B., Petrila, J., Poythress, N. G., & Slobogin, C. (1997). *Psychological evaluations for the courts: A handbook for mental health professionals and lawyers* (2nd ed.). New York: Guilford Press.

Meyers, C. J. (1985). An alternative approach to writing forensic mental health reports. *Journal of Psychiatry and Law, 13,* 397–418.

Miller, R. D. (2003). Hospitalization of criminal defendants for evaluation of competence to stand trial or for restoration of competence: Clinical and legal issues. *Behavioral Sciences and the Law, 21,* 369–391.

Moran, G. (2001). Trial consultation: Why licensure is not necessary. *Journal of Forensic Psychology Practice, 1,* 77–85.

Münsterberg, H. (1908). *On the witness stand.* New York: Doubleday.

Myers, B., & Arena, M. P. (2001). Trial consultation: A new direction in applied psychology. *Professional Psychology: Research and Practice, 32,* 386–391.

Nietzel, M. T., & Dillehay, R. C. (1986). *Psychological consultation in the courtroom.* New York: Pergamon Press.

O'Roark, A. M. (1999). A history of Division 13 initiatives on education and training in consulting psychology. *Consulting Psychology Journal: Practice and Research, 51,* 218–225.

Otto, R. K., & Heilbrun, K. S. (2002). The practice of forensic psychology: A look toward the future in light of the past. *American Psychologist, 57,* 5–18.

Packer, I. K., & Borum, R. (2003). Forensic training and practice. In I. B. Weiner (Series Ed.) & A. M. Goldstein (Vol. Ed.), *Comprehensive handbook of psychology: Vol. 11. Forensic psychology* (pp. 21–32). Hoboken, NJ: Wiley.

Paulus, P. B., & Yang, H. (2000). Idea generation in group: A basis for creativity in organizations. *Organizational Behavior and Human Decision Processes, 82,* 76–87.

Posey, A. J., & Wrightsman, L. S. (2005). *Trial consulting.* New York: Oxford University Press.

Pozner, L. S., & Dodd, R. J. (2004). *Cross-examination: Science and techniques* (2nd ed.). Newark, NJ: Matthew Bender.

Ratcliff, D. G. (2002). Using trial consultants: What practitioners need to know. *Journal of Legal Advocacy and Practice, 4,* 32–52.

Selkin, J. (1994). Psychological autopsy: Scientific psychohistory or clinical intuition? *American Psychologist, 49,* 74–75.

Shneidman, E. S. (1994). The psychological autopsy. *American Psychologist, 4,* 75–76.

Shuman, D. (1997). *Psychiatric and psychological evidence* (2nd ed.). Colorado Springs, CO: Shepard's/McGraw-Hill.

Simon, R. I., & Shuman, D. W. (1999). Conducting forensic examinations on the road: Are you practicing your profession without a license? *Journal of the American Academy of Psychiatry and the Law, 27,* 75–82.

Slobogin, C. (1989). The "ultimate issue" issue. *Behavioral Sciences and the Law, 7,* 259–266.

Small, D. I. (2004). *Preparing witnesses: A practical guide for lawyers and their clients* (2nd ed.). Washington, DC: American Bar Association.

Smith, W. L. (2003). *The person of the therapist.* Jefferson, NC: McFarland.

Stafford, K. P. (2003). Assessment of competence to stand trial. In I. B. Weiner (Series Ed.) & A. M. Goldstein (Vol. Ed.), *Comprehensive handbook of psychology: Vol. 11. Forensic psychology* (pp. 359–380). Hoboken, NJ: Wiley.

Stolle, D. P., Robbennolt, J. K., & Weiner, R. L. (1996). The perceived fairness of the psychologist trial consultant: An empirical investigation. *Law and Psychology Review, 20,* 139–177.

Strier, F. (1999). Whither trial consulting? Issues and projections. *Law and Human Behavior, 23,* 93–115.

Strier, F. (2001). Why trial consultants should be licensed. *Journal of Forensic Psychology Practice, 1,* 69–76.

Tate, D. M., & Parker, R. S. (1999, Spring). The art of direct. *Family Advocate,* 8–11.

Tripoli, L. (1998, January). Beyond the Ouija board: Litigators take shewd, selective approach in using diverse trial consultants. *Inside Litigation,* 1–10.

U.S. ex rel. Edney v. Smith, 425 F. Supp. 1038 (E.D.N.Y. 1976).

U.S. v. Alvarez, 519 F.2d 1036 (3d Cir. 1975).

Vaccaro, T. P., & Hogan, J. D. (2004, May/June). The origins of forensic psychology in America: Hugo Münsterberg on the witness stand. *NYS Psychologist,* 14–17.

van der Lugt, R. (2002). Brainsketching and how it differs from brainstorming. *Creativity and Innovation Management, 11,* 43–54.

Weigel, R. G. (1998). Scale of dragon, toe of frog, and the compleat consultant. *Consulting Psychology Journal: Practice and Research, 50,* 3–16.

Wellman, F. L. (1936). *The art of cross-examination* (4th ed.). New York: Collier.

Wexler, D. B. (1990). *The law as a therapeutic agent.* Durham, NC: Carolina Academic Press.

Wexler, D. B., & Winick, B. H. (1991). *Essays in therapeutic jurisprudence.* Durham, NC: Carolina Academic Press.

Wilkins, S. (2004, July/August). Early review by medical experts offers opportunity to develop theory of the case more efficiently. *New York State Bar Journal,* 42–45.

Young, T. J. (1992). Procedures and problems in conducting a psychological autopsy. *International Journal of Offender Therapy and Comparative Criminology, 36,* 43–52.

CHAPTER 19

The Disability Psychological Independent Medical Evaluation: Case Law, Ethical Issues, and Procedures

David A. Vore

A relatively recent area of focus for forensic psychology has been development of services to the insurance industry. Although the services provided are varied, the most common role for the forensic psychologist involves provision of psychological independent medical evaluations (psychological IMEs) at the request of an insurance carrier associated with management of ongoing disability claims. At first glance, functioning in this role would seem to simply encompass provision of psychological assessment procedures involving clinical skills possessed by any well-trained clinical psychologist. However, as is the case in all forensic areas, effective functioning in this capacity requires knowledge and skills that go beyond basic clinical capabilities.

In many ways, the disability psychological IME area is similar to the personal injury specialty area in terms of knowledge, skills, techniques, and approach utilized by the evaluator (identified in the insurance industry as the provider or examiner). A basic difference, however, is the lack of proximate causation as an issue to be addressed by the examiner. Although it may be necessary and appropriate to explore the circumstances that precipitated claimed psychological dysfunction, the opinion presented in the report to the referral source (hereafter referred to as the carrier) should not address proximate causation. This issue is neither a standard to be assessed in this evaluation context nor a relevant area of concern regarding the claim management process for the carrier.

Effective functioning as a psychological IME provider does involve many of the specialized skills common to any area of forensic psychology. As described by Grisso (2003), forensic evaluation must be focused on assessment of competencies relevant to the issue to be addressed by the evaluator. In the psychological IME evaluation, this focus becomes the competency of the examinee, the insured, to function in an employment capacity. The evaluation, in this context, should consist of a well-focused and detailed assessment of functional capacity of the insured relevant to the return to work issue, regarding either his or her own occupation or in any occupation. (The distinction between *own* occupation and *any* occupation is a contractual issue that is considered in more detail later in this chapter.) Further, the psychological IME provider should possess a clear understanding of case law and forensic issues relevant to the referral question(s). It is also essential that the provider communicate data obtained during the evaluation process and offer an opinion regarding the referral questions in a manner that is clear, well focused, and helpful in this arena to the carrier and claim analyst regarding the decision-making process in claim management. Finally, the provider must demonstrate the ability to communicate effectively in a litigation setting should the case proceed to court.

The focus of this chapter is on clarification of the definition of disability through review of relevant case law, discussion of potential pitfalls for the provider in establishing and maintaining a neutral position in the process, consideration of selected ethical issues pertinent to the role of psychological IME provider, and a brief discussion of important procedural issues related to the provision of a thorough evaluation and preparation of an effective report.

DEFINITION OF TERMS

The language used in the disability insurance industry is specific to contractual issues related to the policies issued by the carriers. It is important that the psychological IME provider clearly understand the terms and concepts used in the contracts issued. Absent such understanding, the opinion presented in the report regarding the evaluation completed may be irrelevant to the issues at hand and, therefore, of limited or no use to the carrier in the claim management process. The following terms are basic to the disability policy industry.

Disability Income (DI) is a term used to refer to policies issued to individuals that are designed to provide coverage for loss of income due to accident or illness. These policies, taken out by an individual, are not part of a group coverage program. They are paid for either by the individual or, in some cases, by a corporation. If paid by the individual, the benefit provided is not subject to either federal or state taxation. These policies often provide large monthly benefits and include increases that may be tied to cost of living or other indexes. Coverage provided by DI policies typically allows benefits until either age 65 or for lifetime, although this may vary according to specific policy language. An individual may purchase more than one DI policy either from the same carrier or from multiple carriers. In some cases, a carrier may not be aware of policy coverage owned by an individual from another company. Because of these factors, an individual may receive higher income from DI policy benefits than he or she received in salary when working.

Short Term Disability/Long Term Disability (STD/LTD) are terms used in the context of group policies that may provide coverage to an individual. These policies are purchased by an employer for a classified group and provide somewhat different benefits from the DI policies. Short Term Disability policies generally provide coverage for a period of 1 to 6 months, after which the individual moves into LTD coverage as appropriate and necessary. Typically, LTD coverage for psychological/psychiatric claims allows benefits for a maximum of 2 years at a level of approximately 60% to 70% of the preclaim salary level of the individual. The structure and language of the STD/LTD policies result in considerably less exposure for the carrier regarding total financial liability.

Partial Disability/Total Disability (PD/TD) are contractual terms in disability policies that define the conditions covered by the carrier. Partial Disability is defined as the inability of the insured to carry out some or most of the substantial and material duties of his or her occupation due to illness or injury. Total Disability refers to the inability of the insured to carry out any or all of the substantial and material duties of his or her occupation as a function of illness or injury. Coverage for PD is often limited to a period of 6 months, whereas TD coverage may extend to age 65 or for the lifetime of the insured.

Own occupation/any occupation are terms used in policies to define the range of employment activities covered for the insured. A policy including own occupation language provides coverage to the insured for any impairment that interferes with the ability to engage in the substantial and material duties of his or her own occupation regardless of whether the insured is able to engage in a different occupation. Thus, for example, a neurosurgeon claiming own occupation disability may be entitled to total disability benefits even though he or she is capable of effectively functioning on a full-time basis as a family practitioner, a professor in a medical school setting, or a computer expert. Any occupation language means the insured is entitled to benefits only if he or she is incapable of functioning in any occupation that would allow continuation of the pre-claim lifestyle. The neurosurgeon, therefore, would not necessarily be able to claim total disability if he or she were earning substantial income from a new occupation.

Date of onset/date of issue refer to the date of the beginning of the claimed disability and the date of issue of the policy providing the claimed coverage. Most policies specify a waiting period between the date of purchase and the date on which a claim can be filed. These terms may become relevant in assessment of a claim when the initiation of the claim occurs immediately after conclusion of the waiting period following purchase of the policy.

CHARACTERISTICS OF AN EFFECTIVE PSYCHOLOGICAL INDEPENDENT MEDICAL EVALUATION

Conducting an effective psychological IME requires the provider to address the same basic issues relevant to competent evaluation in any forensic area. The factors essential to effective evaluation in any forensic context have been addressed in detail and considerable depth by Heilbrun (2001) and in Chapter 2. The issues discussed by Heilbrun as pertinent to any forensic setting clearly apply to the psychological IME area. It is strongly recommended that the psychological IME provider be familiar with the points and issues addressed in these publications. Issues specific to the psychological IME are addressed next.

Structure of the Evaluation

Although it may seem obvious, it is essential that the psychological IME provider conduct a detailed and thorough assessment. The interview conducted with the insured should be of at least 2 to 3 hours' duration and should cover history in detail, including personal/social information, educational history, occupational history, information regarding physical and psychological problems and treatment, history regarding substance abuse, and any other areas relevant to the referral issues.

The evaluation process should include a formal mental status examination of the insured to document presentation and general functional status at the time of the assessment. The mental status examination should provide data in a number of specific areas, including presentation of the insured; communication style; and skills, mood and affect (including discussion of possible suicidal or homicidal ideation), thought processes, thought disorder, and anxiety features. General cognitive functioning should be formally documented in cases in which full intellectual testing will not be administered. During the interview process, the mental status examination should be conducted in a structured manner and documented as such.

As part of the referral process, it is appropriate to expect the carrier to provide a list of questions to be addressed by the psychological IME process. The evaluation should be structured by the provider to obtain data regarding the specific questions presented by the carrier to allow direct response to those issues in formulation of the report.

Focus on Impairments

A common pitfall reflected in opinions offered by psychological IME providers is structuring of the opinion to address the issue of disability in the insured. It is essential for the psychological IME provider to remember that the question of disability is strictly a contractual issue and, as such, is beyond the expertise of the examiner. The opinion offered in the report regarding the assessment completed with the insured should be focused strictly on identification of specific deficits, if any, that would impair his or her ability to function either from the own occupation or any occupation perspective as defined by the policy language. The issue of deficits should be addressed from the perspective of the cognitive and/or emotional capacities of the insured as appropriate to the referral questions provided by the carrier. In almost all cases, the carrier does *not* want an opinion from the examiner regarding disability of the insured. Determination of disability as related to the assessed functional capacity of the insured derives from contractual language and limits present in the policy purchased by the insured. This decision is the province of the carrier and, if necessary, the courts. The appropriate focus of the psychological IME, therefore, is on assessment of the functional capacity of the insured and identification of specific impairments that may be relevant to occupational functioning.

Given the focus of the psychological IME on functional capacity of the insured related to required occupational capabilities, it is important that the provider have a clear understanding of the demands and requirements inherent in the occupation of the insured (assuming own occupation coverage) to provide an opinion. A description of the occupation of the insured should be expected from the carrier as part of the referral process. It is also appropriate for the examiner to spend time during the interview with the insured discussing occupational requirements and what related specific areas or skills the insured claims are impaired.

The Importance of Data

As indicated, the primary need of the carrier when requesting a psychological IME is provision of an opinion from the provider regarding identification of specific impairments in the insured related to his or her functional capacity from either the own occupation or any occupation perspective. It is essential that the opinion reached by the provider be based on objective data to the greatest extent possible. The opinion should be presented in a manner that is clearly connected to and derived from data obtained during the evaluation process. Communication of the opinion is best formulated by citing data obtained from various sources, with subsequent presentation of conclusions clearly related to those data. The reader of the report should be able to follow the line of reasoning utilized by the provider in reaching the conclusions presented. It is important to remember that the carrier is seeking information from the provider on which to base decisions, not opinions regarding the ultimate issue of disability.

The most important focus of the evaluation for the provider, therefore, is generation of objective data to the greatest extent possible. Although the degree of objectivity of specific data is always an issue that may be addressed in depositions or in courtroom testimony, the goal of the provider must be to obtain a database that is maximally defensible by minimizing the influence of subjective sources of information. This is not to imply that clinical opinion is inappropriate in the psychological IME report. However, clinical conclusions and opinion should be tied to the most objective data available to the provider.

Given the importance of objective data in the psychological IME process, various data sources should be rank ordered in terms of their subjective/objective value. It is important to remember that objectivity of data sources is a continuum and not an absolute issue. Once clinical interpretation occurs, any data source involves some degree of subjectivity on the part of the provider.

The basis of opinions reached by the provider should go beyond self-report statements communicated by the insured during the examination process. In fact, the self-report statements from the insured are, most likely, the least objective data source available to the provider. Information obtained from collateral sources such as spouse, employer, relatives, or friends is the next level of data on the continuum of objectivity. Although this information is important to obtain, it must be weighted regarding the potential bias of the individual providing it when utilized by the psychological IME provider in formulating an opinion. Collateral information obtained from a primary treatment provider may represent a more objective data source than information obtained from relatives. However, the potential for bias in this data source must also be assessed by the provider. Although observation of presentation of the insured during the evaluation process is a source of information that may be more heavily weighted by the provider in the development of an opinion, it is essential that the provider be sensitive to possible bias in his or her own perceptions when utilizing this data source. For example, hostility from the insured during the evaluation process may produce a more negative and/or critical opinion from the provider than would have been the case had the insured been cooperative and open during the examination. Finally, the most objective information source available to the provider is data obtained from administration of psychological tests during the evaluation process. In determining the battery of tests to be administered, the provider should assess the degree of objectivity inherent in the various instruments considered. It is important to avoid limiting tests utilized to a single format such as self-report instruments that do not include established norms for interpretation and that do not involve some type of validity index.

The psychological IME provider is in a unique position regarding the ability to provide objective data to the carrier for use in the claim management process. No other profession has access to the vast array of test instruments available to the psychologist to utilize in development of a database on which decisions can be made. It is therefore important for the provider to use this area of specialized expertise to the extent appropriate when conducting evaluations and generating opinions in the psychological IME arena.

Assessment of Response Style

Consistent with any forensic evaluation setting, the psychological IME should address the issue of response style brought by the insured to the assessment process. The question of effort, response style, and validity of data obtained should be a focus of the evaluation regardless of whether these questions have been directly raised by the carrier in the referral to the provider.

A number of possible presentations regarding response style have been identified in the literature (Rogers, 1984, 1997; Rogers & Bender, 2003). These possible presentations include (a) *malingering* (the deliberate fabrication or gross exaggeration of symptoms to achieve an external goal), (b) *defensiveness* (deliberate denial or extreme minimization of symptoms to achieve an external goal), (c) *irrelevant responding* (disengagement from the evaluation process evidenced typically by inconsistent responding unrelated to content of the evaluation technique utilized), (d) *feigning* (deliberate fabrication or extreme exaggeration of symptoms without any assumption regarding the goal of this behavior), (e) *suboptimal effort* (lack of maximum performance on tasks administered that may reflect fatigue or frustration or a comorbid factor such as depression accompanying a physical condition), and (f) *dissimulation* (inaccurate presentation of symptoms that cannot be categorized as one of the behaviors previously defined). A full discussion of these categories can be found in Rogers and Bender (2003).

Rogers and Reinhardt (1998) have taken the position that secondary gain, development and presentation of symptoms as an unintentional response to internal (dynamic) and external (situational) forces, is a concept that should be avoided in forensic evaluations. The position of Rogers and Reinhardt is that secondary gain is relevant only in a clinical context. It is the opinion of this author, however, that secondary gain is a concept that may be relevant to the psychological IME context. As such, it should be addressed as appropriate in discussion of evaluation results and presentation of an opinion by the provider.

Heilbrun, Warren, and Picarello (2003) describe uncooperativeness as an additional response style that may impact forensic evaluations. This factor may be relevant to the psychological IME and may be manifested by the insured during the evaluation process as a refusal to respond or provision of minimal responses to assessment questions. When present in the evaluation process, it may become a severely limiting factor regarding data obtained directly from the insured for use in the development of an opinion by the provider. As indicated by Heilbrun et al., third-party data, such as collateral interview information and record review, are important variables for use as a counterbalance to lack of information provided by the insured in such situations.

Still another potential response bias factor may affect the psychological IME process. It is possible that the insured may approach the evaluation with the goal of providing information to the examiner that supports the claim of disability being presented to the carrier. The presentation of the insured may not reflect *intentional* misrepresentation or embellishment of symptoms and level of impairment. To the contrary, the insured may make a strong effort to respond honestly and openly to the evaluation process but, in the course of doing so, overrepresent or embellish symptoms as a way of clearly documenting and supporting his or her claim of disability.

An effective and thorough psychological IME must include assessment of potential response bias in the approach of the insured to the evaluation process. Several factors should be taken into account in dealing with this issue. First, the provider must remember the importance of multiple data sources as the basis for conclusions and opinions. Second, use of collateral data obtained from interviews with appropriate information sources, review of records, and so on is an essential component of the psychological IME process. Third, the provider should remember, as described by Otto (2001), that the presence of response bias, even involving malingering, does not, by itself, necessarily preclude possible coexisting symptoms of psychological or mental dysfunction. This point has been extended by DeClue (2002), who has stated that feigning, as assessed by various tests available at the present time, does not necessarily equate to an impression of malingering. DeClue clearly indicates that an opinion regarding malingering by an examinee must be based on data that go beyond test results as none of the instruments presently available actually directly measure this dimension. Once again, this position supports the importance of obtaining and utilizing multiple data sources in the psychological IME process, including record review and interviews with collateral sources of information such as spouse, employer, and primary treatment provider.

CASE LAW RELEVANT TO THE PSYCHOLOGICAL INDEPENDENT MEDICAL EVALUATION

In accepting a psychological IME referral, the provider must be aware that the case may result in litigation. In the event that litigation occurs, the report and opinion of the provider will be subject to the same type of scrutiny and eventual cross-examination as may occur in the personal injury arena. The issues addressed in this section are relevant in a disability cause of action litigation situation. Although the report prepared by the psychological IME examiner may never directly address the issues of case law presented in this section, an understanding of the case law is important from two perspectives. First, preparation of a report that reflects a clear understanding of the legal issues may be a major factor in obviating the necessity of litigation. Second, in the event that litigation does occur, it is critical during the process of evaluation and report preparation that the psychological IME examiner have a thorough understanding of the issues that he or she may be asked to address during provision of either deposition or court testimony.

The case law relevant to the issue of determination of psychological/psychiatric disability is broad and rich in content. Consequently, detailed, in-depth coverage of this literature in the present chapter is impractical. This section therefore focuses on discussion of relevant case law as it pertains to definition of disability, the presence of substance abuse as a basis for a disability claim, relapse potential issues, and liability issues pertaining to the psychological IME provider regarding the question of independence.

Definition of Disability

In a general sense, disability policies are written to provide coverage only for factual disabilities, contractually defined as impairment in the insured due to illness or injury of sufficient severity to prevent the individual from effectively engaging in the material and substantial duties of his or her own occupation (own occupation coverage) or from effectively engaging in any occupation (any occupation coverage). Through the process of litigation pertaining to disability claims, over the years case law has developed defining claims pertaining to *factual* disabilities as distinct from those presenting what are referred to as either *social* disabilities or *legal* disabilities. Although these disability categories may at times overlap, the courts have attempted to separate claims filed as factual disability but actually reflecting social disability or legal disability from those claims representing true factual disability.

Factual Disability

As defined previously, determination of a factual disability means that the claim of an insured is determined to meet the criteria for disability as stated in contractual language (i.e., due to injury or illness, the insured is unable to carry out the substantial and material duties of his or her own occupation or any occupation, as defined by language in the policy issued).

Social Disability

The issue of social disability was clearly delineated by the Appellate Court of New York in *Gates v. Prudential Insurance Co. of America* (1934). Gates, a dairy farmer, purchased a disability policy that contained any occupation coverage language. Subsequently, the New York State commissioner of health declared that Gates was a typhoid carrier, although he manifested no active symptoms of the disease. Due to the decision made by the commissioner, Gates was quarantined from any connection with the production or sale of milk, barred from his own farm, and forced to find a different place to live. Gates's claim for benefits was denied by the carrier, resulting in litigation. The trial court dismissed the case due to insufficient facts for a cause of action. This decision was subsequently upheld by the appellate court, which stated that Gates manifested no physical disability and was prevented from working only by the edict of the state for the good of the public. Consequently, the court defined Gates's status as reflecting a disability that was social in nature rather than physical, a necessary condition for disability as defined in the covering policy.

A more recent case reflecting similar reasoning on the part of the court is seen in *Dang v. Northwestern Mutual Life Insurance Co.* (1997). This case involved a physician who purchased a disability policy providing own occupation coverage, listing his occupation as general surgeon. After being diagnosed positive for hepatitis B, Dang, who was a surgery resident, transferred to a radiology residency program and claimed disability as a general surgeon. Litigation was initiated by Dang following denial of his claim by the carrier. The decision rendered by the court presented the reasoning that the term "disabled/disability" means loss of physical or mental ability. In this case, Dang was viewed as demonstrating no loss in either area affecting his ability to perform as a surgeon. Consequently, the court held that Dang was not disabled as defined by the language of his policy.

The decisions rendered by the court in both *Gates* and *Dang* underscore the point made previously that the question of disability relates specifically to language present in the policy purchased by the insured.

Legal Disability

The term legal disability is generally applied to claims presented by an insured who is a professional and whose license has been suspended or revoked or who is unable to practice because of incarceration. In *Goomar v. Centennial Life Ins. Co.* (1994, with Appellate Court affirmation in 1996) the court held that a physician who claimed that visions of astral beings caused him to molest four female patients was not due benefits because his inability to practice was secondary to license revocation rather than to disability as defined in his policy. A related decision rendered by the Vermont Supreme Court held that an optometrist charged with lewd and lascivious conduct with a minor who engaged in a plea bargain requiring him to sell his practice, surrender his license, and be imprisoned was not disabled as he claimed due to pedophilia (*Mass. Mutual Life Ins. Co. v. Ouellette,* 1992). The reasoning expressed by the court in reaching this opinion was that the insured was not disabled as defined in his policy language because he was physically and mentally able to perform all the duties of optometry until the time of the loss of his license and incarceration. In this opinion, the court also stated that intentional criminal acts should not lead to liability on the part of insurance carriers.

The time frame in which an insured discontinues his or her practice related to when the claim for disability is filed has been viewed as a critical issue by the courts. In *Allmerica Financial Life Ins. & Annuity Co. v. Llewellyn* (1996), the Oregon Appellate Court held that a chiropractor prosecuted for fraudulent billing practices was not entitled to disability benefits because he did not close his office until the day after his license was revoked. The court concluded that, because he was not practicing on the date he indicated as the onset of his disability, his regular occupation (own occupation policy) could not be listed as chiropractor as of the claimed date of disability. A Georgia court reached a similar decision in *Suarez v. Mass. Mutual Life Ins. Co. 5* (2000). The court in *Suarez* held that a disability claim filed by a physician whose license was suspended by the State Board of Medical Examiners due to criminal behavior was not entitled to disability benefits because the "legal disability" (suspension of license) preceded the claimed factual disability by 1 day. The court reasoned, therefore, that medicine was no longer the regular occupation of the insured on the date he claimed disability began.

A California decision (*Wright v. Paul Revere Life Ins. Co.,* 2003) closely mirrored the decision stated in *Suarez.* In this case, an attorney was indicted and arrested for felony tax evasion. The attorney subsequently filed a claim for disability benefits based on an alleged physical disability. The carrier denied the claim, resulting in litigation initiated by the insured. The carrier filed a motion for summary judgment based on its allegation of breach of contract and a bad faith claim. The court granted the petition for summary judgment based on several reasons that included [the reasons listed are part of the total reasoning stated by the court]:

- The policy of the insured had lapsed due to nonpayment of premiums.
- The claim was based on a legal disability rather than on a factual disability.
- Proof of loss was not filed by the insured on a timely basis determined by contractual language.

In developing this opinion, the court reasoned that:

- California insurance law indicates that carriers provide coverage for factual disabilities due to sickness or injury, not legal disabilities.
- The indictment and arrest of the insured led to suspension of his license to practice law in the State of California prior to the date of onset of his claimed physical disability. Therefore, the reason he discontinued working was due to the legal prohibition from his practice of law and not due to sickness or injury.
- In the perception of the court, there was no doubt that the insured was physically capable of practicing law if he were legally able to do so.

A slightly different perspective was evident in a decision rendered in *Damascus v. Provident Life and Accident Ins. Co.* (1996). In this decision, the court granted summary judgment to the insurance carrier on the basis that the insured discontinued his practice as a dentist following revocation of his license due to gross negligence and unprofessional conduct, not because of injury or illness. The district court determined that the claim filed by Damascus did not meet the contractual conditions of his policy and was, therefore, a legal disability. This case was subsequently heard by the U.S. Court of Appeals, 9th Circuit (1999), resulting in a decision to reverse and remand the ruling of the district court on the basis that questions of material fact were evident regarding the underlying cause of the insured's negligent acts leading to the revocation of his license. In rendering this decision, the court appears to present the position that a question of fact exists regarding whether the license revocation of Damascus was, at least in part, a function of impairment due to mental illness, in spite of the fact that he continued practicing until his license was revoked. Thus, in this case, the court seems to take the position that a factual disability may be concurrent with a legal disability, with the result that a question of fact is evident concerning eligibility of the insured for disability benefits. Assuming the existence of a question of fact, then, the matter should be heard by the trier of fact for ultimate resolution.

Although not always the case, in general, case law pertaining to legal disability suggests that courts seem to find for the insured if he or she discontinued practice prior to license revocation. However, the appellate court decision in *Damascus* (1999) indicates a willingness on the part of the court to consider factual disability and legal disability issues as concurrent in some situations.

Any Occupation Coverage

Policies that provide coverage for any occupation are generally interpreted to mean that benefits are available to the insured only if the individual is unable to function in any type of employment setting, including nonprofessional employment. On the face of it, this would mean that, for example, a physician could receive benefits only if he or she were unable to function even at any nonprofessional level, including as a cashier or bagger at a supermarket. Case law pertaining to this issue is rather limited but is represented by the two following decisions.

In *Mutual Life Ins. Co. v. Frost* (1947), a physician claimed disability due to having suffered depression and a "mental breakdown" secondary to lawsuits and criticism related to his diagnosis as a "constitutional psychopathic personality." The physician owned a disability policy that included any occupation language. In spite of this fact, however, the court found for the insured, stating that, even if he were able to sell pencils on a street corner or serve as a gateman at a railroad crossing, this would not preclude benefits because there was nothing to show that he could earn a livelihood in any way comparable to his former earnings.

A similar decision was rendered by the Supreme Court of Oklahoma in *Continental Casualty v. York* (1965). In this case, a physician suffered a stroke resulting in clear cognitive dysfunction involving attention/concentration skills, memory functioning, and organizational capabilities. Although the insured was unable to function as a physician, he retained the ability to work in other occupational settings. A trial court (jury decision) found for the insured. This decision was affirmed by the Supreme Court of Oklahoma, which stated that it was not necessary for the insured to demonstrate a "state of absolute helplessness" to be eligible for benefits. Rather, the court opined that it was necessary for the insured to show only that he was unable to engage in substantially all of the material acts necessary to function in his own business or occupation in the customary and usual manner.

In general, case law existing in other states closely follows the reasoning presented in *Frost* and *York*. That is, the real issue regarding eligibility for disability benefits involving any occupation coverage is whether the individual is capable of engaging in any occupation that would provide a standard of living equal to the preclaim standard of living enjoyed by the insured.

General Occupation versus Specific Job

In situations in which an insured has policy language that provides coverage for inability to function in his or her own occupation, the issue may become whether the individual is unable to function in his or her specific job environment rather than in the general occupational setting. In general, it appears that the term "regular occupation" refers to a *category* of employment rather than to a *specific position* within that category.

This position is clearly reflected in *Tackman v. UNUM Life Ins. Co. of America No. 2* (1994). In this decision, the U.S. District Court for the Western District of Michigan denied summary judgment to the insured because, although he could not continue functioning as an accountant in the hostile work environment of his own specific employment setting, it was evident that he could perform all of the material and substantial duties of his occupation in a different work environment.

Therefore, the court opined that the insured did not meet the policy definition of being totally disabled from his own occupation.

It follows from *Tackman v. UNUM* that it is extremely important for the psychological IME examiner to obtain a detailed description of the general occupation of the insured (examinee). In addition, information should be gathered regarding the specific position the insured occupied and the employment setting in which he or she functioned.

Substance Abuse as a Basis for Disability

In case law regarding disability claims secondary to history of substance abuse, the primary issue addressed by the court appears to be the question of whether substance abuse can serve as the basis of a disability claim, independent of the presence of other problems. Case law in this area is somewhat limited, and considerable variability is evident among jurisdictions. The general line of reasoning demonstrated by the court regarding this issue is reflected in the following three cases.

Gaines v. Sun Life Assurance Co. of Canada (1943) is a Michigan Supreme Court case in which a physician with a well-established practice until he developed severe alcoholism was granted total disability by a trial court due to his history of alcoholism and drug use. The decision was appealed by the carrier and ultimately was heard by the Michigan Supreme Court, which reversed the decision, reasoning that the claimant was not continuously inebriated during the years prior to his claim and therefore was capable of functioning at some times. Consequently, the court determined that the insured was not disabled and made the statement that alcoholism by itself was not an adequate basis for a claim for disability.

In contrast, in 1977 the U.S. Court of Appeals in Missouri ruled in *Adams v. Weinberger* that chronic, severe alcoholism could be considered the basis for a disability claim. In this decision, the court opined that the focus in such cases should be on whether the claimant was addicted to alcohol and, as a consequence, demonstrated loss of voluntary ability to control its use.

Finally, in *O'Connor v. Sullivan* (1991), the Illinois Court of Appeals reversed and remanded a decision by the lower court on several grounds that included the opinion that alcoholism could be viewed as an adequate basis for a claim of total disability if the individual is unable to control drinking behavior and is unable to do even "light physical work" unless the drinking behavior is controlled.

In general, based on these decisions, it appears that, at the present time, the court is likely to take the position that, in cases in which substance abuse is an *active* process, the substance abuse, in and of itself, may be the basis for a disability claim. As indicated previously, however, some variability is evident among jurisdictions regarding this position.

Relapse Potential as the Basis for Disability Claims

As indicated in the preceding section, in general, it appears that at the present time, the court leans toward acceptance of substance abuse as a basis for a disability claim if it is an active process. However, it is not unusual for individuals to continue to claim disability as a function of a history of substance abuse, even after successfully completing treatment and remaining substance free for an extended period of time. The basis for such claims is typically concern regarding the potential for relapse if the individual returns to the work setting. This position is a particular issue in claims presented by physicians. The following reviews the position of the court regarding these types of claims.

When dealing with risk of relapse pertaining to a clearly identified and well-defined physical problem such as heart attack, the court appears to take the position that, where the physical condition continues to be evident, it is sufficient basis for a claim of disability (*Mass. Casualty Ins. Co. v. Rief,* 1962). However, when the issue of risk of relapse is focused within the area of substance abuse, the direction of the court is less clear.

A common presenting problem regarding substance abuse in physicians involves addiction to fentanyl, an opioid readily available in most medical settings. In *Sutherland v. Paul Revere Ins. Co.* (1996), a trial court granted summary judgment for the defendant (the insurance carrier) based on the opinion that the insured had not been addicted to fentanyl or any other drug for an extended period of time. Consequently, the court opined that facts available for review indicated that the insured was mentally and physically capable of performing the duties of his own occupation as an anesthesiologist. In reversing and remanding this decision, an appellate court in 1997 stated the opinion that the issue of the ability of the insured to return to work at his own occupation was a question of material fact to be resolved by the trier of fact.

Another decision involving an anesthesiologist (*Levitt v. UNUM Life Ins. Co. of America,* 1994), reflects the opinion of the court that the burden of proof was on the insured to demonstrate by a preponderance of evidence that he was totally disabled even though he had successfully completed a course of treatment, had been drug free for an extended period of time, and had received reinstatement of both his license to practice medicine and his Drug Enforcement Administration license. Based on these facts, the opinion of the court was that the insured was not totally disabled. In reaching this decision, the court stated that, although relapse was a possibility, this possibility did not make the carrier obliged to pay benefits because the language in the policy clearly stated that the carrier was responsible to pay for "present injury or illness." The court further stated that the choice to not risk relapse, although probably a positive decision, did not equate to disability as contractually defined. This decision is consistent with the position taken by other courts regarding the need to define disability as determined by the contractual language contained in the policy obtained by the insured.

In *Hinchman v. General American Insurance Co.* (1998), an obstetrician-gynecologist with a history of polysubstance addiction involving use of alcohol and amphetamines over a period of 20 years was able to return to work on a part-time basis and perform gynecological consultations following a period of successful treatment. The opinion of the physician himself was that he was competent to perform all duties of his own occupation. However, he did not return to work on a full-time schedule due to the advice of his addiction counselors. After paying benefits for a period of time, the carrier determined that the recovery of the insured was sufficient to allow him to return to work at his own occupation on a full-time basis and denied further benefits. During the subsequent litigation process, cross motions were filed for summary judgment by both parties. In hearing this case, the court rejected the *Levitt* decision (1994), stating that the issue was "whether Dr. Hinchman's risk of relapse into active chemical dependency is itself a disability covered under the policy" (*Hinchman,* 1998, p. 14). The court then held that this issue was a question of fact that could be resolved by the trier of fact. In denying motions for summary judgment from both parties, the court stated that the insured was entitled to benefits "while he is at risk of relapse into chemical dependency if he is unable to return to practicing obstetrics without hazarding his health or risking his life" (p. 14). The court also indicated in this decision that a factual issue existed regarding "the existence and severity of the risk of relapse" (p. 14).

A second case involved an anesthesiologist with an extended period of recovery from opioid dependence. The claimant sought total disability benefits on the advice of his treatment providers that he not return to the practice of anesthesiology due to risk of relapse (*Holzer v. MBL Life Assurance Corp.,* 1999). This case extends the line of reasoning stated in *Hinchman.* The application for disability benefits was denied by the carrier as a legal, rather than factual, disability claim based on the perception that the inability of the insured to return to the practice of anesthesiology was a function of lack of licensure rather than disability, as contractually defined. In hearing this case, the court found that factual issues existed regarding problems and risks presented in the operating room to patients if the insured returned to work, and potential harm to the insured if he returned to work and relapsed. This finding by the court extended the concern regarding potential harm to the insured stated in the *Hinchman* decision to include concern regarding potential harm to patients. Significantly, however, the court also stated that assessment of these risks was a problem that could be resolved by the trier of fact utilizing the fact-finding process. In this decision, the court opined that there was "no inherent reason why addicts, including anesthesiologists, cannot recover and resume their occupation" (p. 17). The court expanded on this statement to indicate that the issue of whether the insured had reached a point where he could reengage in his occupation as an anesthesiologist without resuming drug abuse was a triable issue, once again resolvable through the fact-finding process.

The *Holzer* line of reasoning was supported in a decision issued by the court in *Kupshik v. John Hancock Mutual Life Insurance Co., 1* (2000). The opinion stated by the court in this case was that the level of risk faced by an insured (an anesthesiologist addicted to fentanyl, other narcotic drugs, and alcohol) regarding his ability to return to work at his own occupation was a question of material fact resolvable by the trier of fact.

In contrast to the line of reasoning discussed in these cases, a federal court decision in 1999 (*Laucks v. Provident Cos.*) stated that an anesthesiologist with a history of polysubstance abuse who had been substance free for a period of 5 years and had returned to work as a physician, but not in anesthesiology, was not entitled to disability benefits. The decision rendered by the court reflected the following points:

- The court rejected the position that, because of his addiction history, the insured had no control over his ability to refrain from substance use. This opinion of the court was based on the fact that the insured had been substance free for 5 years, leading to the conclusion that the urges must be controllable.

- The position that the insured would *necessarily* relapse if he returned to work in the operating room was rejected by the court, stating that, if that premise were true, the course of treatment advocated by addictionologists is ineffective. The court further indicated that the purpose of treatment is to reinforce the will and ability of an individual to abstain from substance use. The court then indicated that, although the disease of addiction is a permanent one, the promise of a treatment regimen is that *use* is not permanent and, in the case of effective treatment, becomes a matter of choice.
- No evidence of current cognitive or motor skill deficits was offered by the insured.

The court concluded that, although cases may exist in which addicted and/or recovering anesthesiologists may never be able to return to the operating room and are therefore disabled within policy language, in this case, the insured was not one of them. Thus, the court appears to be stating that each case of this type must be reviewed and decided individually.

In summary, the following conclusions can be drawn from the risk of relapse case law just reviewed:

- In general, the courts appear to accept that, in some cases, risk of relapse does equate to disability. However, the conditions underlying this perspective are rather unclear.
- The position taken by the insurance carriers is that a *present* impairment regarding the ability to work must be evident in an insured to support a decision of disability. This position sometimes prevails in the legal arena.
- Although the courts seem to have moved to a position that it is a question of material fact resolvable by the trier of fact, no consistent guidelines have been provided regarding how eminent the risk of relapse must be to equate to disability. For example, no "bright line" test has been established regarding the length of time of successful remission that is necessary to support a conclusion of denial of disability benefits.
- The substance abuse treatment provider for the insured is often used by the court to determine the issue of disability. This position on the part of the court is often problematic due to the clinical focus of the treating professional, in contrast to the forensic and contractual focus characteristic of the psychological IME provider. This distinction is dealt with in more detail later in this chapter.
- In general, resolution of the risk of relapse issue seems to turn on the question of choice as the crucial factor. However, determination of the distinction between choice and actual risk of relapse continues to be a confusing and unresolved issue.

Implications of Disability Case Law for the Psychological IME

The information presented in this section underscores the importance of the following points for consideration by the provider in conducting a psychological IME:

- It is critical to understand the issues and precedents evident in court decisions regarding relevant case law.

- Exploration of the role of choice by the insured should be a focus of the evaluation process.

- Other factors or reasons for the insured not returning to work should be examined in detail during the psychological IME process.

- The importance of obtaining and incorporating collateral information into the formulation of an opinion becomes obvious. In particular, review of detailed treatment records, direct contact with treatment providers, and, in referrals involving substance abuse issues, review of the relapse history of the insured are critical in the evaluation process.

- When dealing with referrals involving remission of substance abuse of any type, assessment of the time factor regarding history of relapse or sustained remission is crucial. Although no bright line has been established by the court in this regard, it is likely that, in the litigation process, a remission period of 4 to 6 months will probably not be viewed as a sufficient basis for denial of benefits.

- The issue of dual diagnosis should always be considered in substance abuse referrals.

- The question of potential risk to other individuals should always be addressed when relevant to evaluation of medical personnel, therapists, attorneys, and other professionals who provide service to the public.

CASE LAW REGARDING EXAMINER INDEPENDENCE (AND POTENTIAL LIABILITY)

When accepting referrals for psychological IMEs, the provider must maintain awareness that the assessment process falls within the general area of forensic psychology and, as such, may result in exposure to the legal arena. It is therefore prudent to be cognizant of issues that may bear on potential liability exposure or that may impact the admissibility in the legal process of the opinion formulated from the evaluation.

A recent case that has relevance to the perception of the provider as an independent entity by the court is *Hangarter v. The Paul Revere Life Insurance Co., et al.* (2002). The insured, a chiropractor, filed a claim for disability secondary to physical impairment. Following an IME by a physician, the carrier denied the claim, resulting in the insured's filing a legal action in the State of California. In February 2002, a jury found for the insured and assessed damages against the carrier in the amount of $7.67 million, including $5 million in punitive damages based on a decision of bad faith on the part of the carrier (*Hangarter v. Paul Revere Life Insurance Co.*, 2002). The jury verdict was appealed, resulting in a decision from a magistrate later in 2002 that addressed numerous issues, several of which have clear relevance to the provision of IMEs, including psychological IMEs. Specifically, the various issues addressed by the court included the following:

- The physician selected for the IME process was challenged by the insured on the basis of the record of his previous reports regarding IMEs conducted. The court took note of the fact that the provider had concluded that 13 out of 13 examinees were not disabled.

- The IME provider conducted his evaluation without having the claimant's description of her work, information that she had provided to the carrier when she filed her claim.

- The opinion of the IME provider was biased by the language in the referral letter from the carrier in which an in-house physician gave his opinion regarding interpretation of diagnostic tests that had been administered to the insured. This physician advised that the insured would probably improve with conservative treatment. The court saw this as the carrier's providing instruction to the examiner, potentially biasing any opinion he might reach.

- The IME examiner was not provided instruction regarding the appropriate definitions of disability by the carrier.

- There was some suggestion that the IME examiner was not provided with all relevant medical records for review, some of which were reported to have been destroyed by the carrier.

The opinion of the magistrate upholding the decision of the trier of fact in the jury trial was subsequently affirmed in part by the U.S. Court of Appeals for the 9th Circuit of California (*Hangarter v. Provident Life and Accident Insurance Co., et al.,* 2004).

Another recent decision, *Williams v. Hormel Foods Corp. and Zurich American Insurance Co.* (2003), also has clear implications for the psychological IME provider. In this decision from the Appellate Court of Oklahoma, the testimony and opinion of an IME provider was excluded after the provider was given a videotape for review prior to conducting the examination of the insured. The videotape showed the insured engaged in various physical activities. A second tape provided for review demonstrated the light duty assignment the insured claimed to be unable to perform. This decision was based on the requirement in the State of Oklahoma that videotapes are appropriate for review by the examiner only if approved by order of the court prior to submission to the provider. In cases in which all parties did not agree to the tape review process by the examiner as part of the IME examination, a pretrial hearing was necessary prior to presentation of such evidence to the provider. Based on these two factors, the appellate court determined that the trial court erred as a matter of law in admitting the IME report.

The opinions reached by the court in both *Hangarter* and *Williams* have the following clear implications for the psychological IME provider:

- Do not accept referrals that include inappropriate information, opinions, or language in the referral letter from the carrier.

- Understand the definitions of disability and address the issue of impairment based on those definitions.

- Insist on receiving a detailed description from the carrier of the insured's job or occupation. If possible, obtain a job/occupation description from the employer of the insured. If no information is provided or available in this regard, obtain a detailed job/occupation description directly from the insured during the interview process. In general, it is good practice to discuss the job/occupation description directly with the insured even if other information has been made available for review.

- Always request all relevant medical records from the carrier and document having done so.
- Be careful about reviewing videotapes or other sources of information provided by the carrier as part of the evaluation process unless it is clear they are admissible. In situations in which the referral is strictly from the carrier and no litigation is in effect, admissibility is not an issue. However, be aware that, should the situation become litigious, an issue may be raised regarding use of such data sources as part of the IME process and opinion formulation.

ETHICAL ISSUES RELATED TO THE ROLE OF THE INDEPENDENT MEDICAL EVALUATION EXAMINER

As is the case with any professional activity, individuals offering services as psychological IME examiners are bound by the "Ethical Principals of Psychologists and Code of Conduct" (American Psychological Association, 2002) and should generally adhere to the "Specialty Guidelines for Forensic Psychologists" (Committee on Ethical Guidelines for Forensic Psychologists, 1991). The psychological IME provider should be very familiar with the areas in these two documents that specifically apply to the role of the psychological IME examiner. A detailed discussion of ethical issues related to the practice of forensic psychology can be found in Weissman and Debow (2003) and Chapter 7. Space limitations do not allow for in-depth discussion of these issues in the present chapter; however, a brief discussion of selected topics follows. The psychologist offering psychological IME services should be alert to these and other areas and issues that may be pertinent to functioning in this arena.

Dual Role Issues

Greenberg and Shuman (1997) and Goldstein (2003) succinctly addressed the differences between the therapeutic and forensic roles that should serve as guidelines for individuals engaging in these two functions. The distinctions labeled by these authors can be generalized to the specific role of the psychological IME provider and have clear applicability in the psychological IME arena, as summarized in Table 19.1.

Because of the distinctions between the therapeutic and IME provider roles presented in Table 19.1, the importance of avoidance of a dual role conflict for the psychological IME provider is obvious. However, in general, dual role conflicts are not typically a problem for the psychological IME examiner as referral is always specific to the issue of evaluation and development of an opinion regarding the question of impairment in the insured related to the return-to-work issue. However, it is important that the psychological IME examiner have no history of previous contact with the examinee in other roles. Further, it is important to remember that the pro-

Table 19.1   Differences between Therapeutic and IME Roles

Issue	Therapy Role	IME Role
Identification of the client	Individual is the client.	Carrier is the client.
Nature of relationship	Supportive, accepting, and empathic to establish treatment.	Neutral and objective.
Sources of information	Primarily client report, generally accepted.	Individual's report, collateral sources, generally questioned.
Focus of inquiry	Client-structured, relatively loose, flexible.	Expert-structured, generally well defined.
Goal of relationship	Helping relationship, with therapeutic alliance.	Evaluation to obtain information on which to base an opinion.
Client agenda/agenda of the individual	Assume wellness or recovery agenda.	Disability agenda.
Competency of the provider	Competent in therapy techniques to assess and treat presenting impairments.	Competent in evaluation techniques relevant to the disability issues.

Source: "Irreconcilable Conflict between Therapeutic and Forensic Roles," by S. Greenberg and D. Shuman, 1997, *Journal of Professional Psychology: Research and Practice, 28*(1), pp. 50–57. Reprinted with permission.

cess of case management is of an ongoing nature. What, if any, follow-up may be requested from the provider in the future is never clear at the time of initial evaluation. It is not unusual for reevaluation to be requested sometimes several years after the initial assessment and often from the same provider. Consequently, the psychological IME examiner should always avoid agreeing to provide other services to the insured at a later date.

Identification of the Client

As indicated in Table 19.1, the client in the psychological IME process is the carrier making the referral, not the individual being evaluated. This distinction becomes important regarding the question of who has the authority to release records generated from the psychological IME procedure. In most cases, the carrier will take the position that the evaluation record and the report are its work product. At present, to the knowledge of this author, no case law specific to this issue exists. It is reasonable to assume that the position of the carrier on this question will certainly be challenged at some time in the future by a plaintiff's attorney. Until case law on the matter is established, although debate continues on this issue, it is recommended that the records be viewed as belonging to the carrier in this context, not to the examinee. Consequently, any request for release of records should be referred to the carrier by the provider for direction regarding response. Regardless of the position taken by the provider on this issue, there is no question that the report is discoverable in a litigation situation. Further, although the position may be taken by the carrier that the notes formulated by the provider during the psychological IME process are a work product belonging to the carrier, in general, consistent with the personal injury arena, this material as well as raw test data will be discoverable should litigation occur. It should be noted that, in general, it appears that the Health Insurance Portability and Accountability Act (HIPAA) standards are not applicable to the psychological IME setting because the evaluation process does not involve any type of patient relationship between the examinee and the provider.

It is important that the examinee clearly understand that the provider is not employed by the referral source (the carrier) but will respond within the carrier's guidelines to any request for records or other types of communication from any other party.

Informed Consent

Prior to engaging in any assessment activity, the examinee should be clearly informed of the role of the psychological IME provider. Specifically, the insured should be informed (a) of the fact that the provider is not an employee of the insurance carrier and is functioning in an independent status, (b) of the reason for and format of the independent evaluation, (c) that a report will be prepared and provided only to the referral source, and (d) that the report and other information will be available to other parties only with authorization of the insurance carrier. In addition, the insured should be informed that he or she has the right to respond or not to questions presented during the evaluation process. However, the insured should also clearly understand that, should he or she choose not to respond to specific questions or tests administered, that fact will be included in the report prepared by the provider.

After reviewing this information, the insured should be asked to sign the appropriate informed consent forms and, as appropriate, release of information forms, allowing the examiner to provide the report and any other information requested to the referring carrier. It is important to include in the materials reviewed and signed by the insured, forms authorizing the examiner to contact collateral sources of information and permitting those collateral information sources to provide information to the examiner. It is generally helpful to discuss with the insured the reason for making collateral contacts as part of the psychological IME process and the impact the absence of such data may have on the opinions formulated. The insured should be informed that he or she has the right to refuse permission for the examiner to make collateral contacts but, once again, that this information will be included in the report prepared for the referring carrier. In the event the insured refuses permission for collateral contacts, the examiner should not make the contacts but should document in the report the reason such information was not pursued.

Practice within the Boundaries of Your Areas of Expertise

Although it may seem an obvious statement, possession of a degree and a license does not make an individual expert in *all* areas of psychology. Consequently, it is important that examiners not attempt to provide services outside their own specific areas of expertise. If the referral questions clearly indicate the need for neuropsychological assessment, the evaluation should not be accepted if the examiner is not trained and an expert in this area of psychology. The same limitation applies to all other areas of psychology as well (i.e., do not accept an evaluation involving possible Posttraumatic Stress Disorder issues without experience in dealing with this specific diagnosis, good knowledge of the literature in the area).

Given this caution, it is essential for the provider to clarify the specific questions and potential issues related to the insured in any psychological IME referral situation. If the information initially provided by the carrier is not sufficient in this regard, the examiner should ask for clarification before accepting the referral.

CONCLUSION

In providing competent, professional psychological IMEs, forensic psychologists can make a significant contribution to the decision-making process of insurance carriers regarding claims of psychological/psychiatric disability. To do so, however, requires that the provider utilizes knowledge and skills beyond basic clinical capabilities and maintains a forensic, as opposed to a clinical, focus during the assessment process. Consistent with other areas of forensic psychology, effective and competent functioning in the provision of psychological IMEs requires:

- Clear understanding of the relevant psycholegal issues.
- Application of evaluation methods and techniques appropriate to the questions and issues to be addressed.
- Awareness of and adherence to ethical standards, including, but not limited to, maximizing objectivity, informed consent, and formulation of data-based opinions.
- Application of current knowledge base, including relevant research data.
- Provision of evaluations only within areas of demonstrated expertise.

Maintaining awareness of the points and issues presented in this chapter will enable the psychological IME provider to conduct evaluations and produce reports and opinions that are maximally useful to the referring insurance carrier.

REFERENCES

Adams v. Weingberger, 548 F.2d 239 (1977).

Allmerica Financial Life Ins. & Annuity Co. v. Llewellyn, 139 F.3d 664 (1996).

American Psychological Association. (2002). Ethical principals of psychologists and code of conduct. *American Psychologist, 57,* 1060–1073.

Committee on Ethical Guidelines for Forensic Psychologists. (1991). Speciality guidelines for forensic psychologists. *Law and Human Behavior, 15,* 655–665.

Continental Casualty v. York, 402 P. 2d 878 (Okla. 1965).

Damascus v. Provident Life and Accident Ins. Co., 933 F. Supp. 885 (1996).

Damascus v. Provident Life and Accident Ins. Co., 168 F. 3rd 498 (9th Cir. 1999).

Dang v. Northwestern Mutual Life Ins. Co., 960 F. Supp. 215 (D. Neb. 1997).

DeClue, G. (2002). Feigning (does not equal) malingering: A case study. *Behavioral Sciences and the Law, 20,* 717–726.

Gaines v. Sun Life Assurance Co. of Canada, 306 Mich. 192, 196 (1943).

Gates v. Prudential Ins. Co. of America, 270 N.Y.S. 282 (4th Dept. 1934).

Goldstein, A. (2003). Overview of forensic psychology. In I. B. Weiner (Series Ed.) & A. M. Goldstein (Vol. Ed.), *Comprehensive handbook of psychology: Vol. 11. Forensic psychology* (pp. 3–20). Hoboken, NJ: Wiley.

Goomar v. Centennial Life Ins. Co., 855 F. Supp. 319 (U.S. Dist. Cal. 1994).

Greenberg, S. A., & Shuman, D. (1997). Irreconcilable conflict between therapeutic and forensic roles. *Journal of Professional Psychology: Research and Practice, 28*(1), 50–57.

Grisso, T. (2003). *Evaluating competencies: Forensic assessments and instruments* (2nd ed.). New York: Kluwer Academic/Plenum Press.

Hangarter v. Paul Revere Life Insurance Co., 236 F. Supp. 2d 1096 (2002).

Hangarter v. The Paul Revere Life Insurance Co., et al., C99-5286 J.L., N.D. CA. (June 5, 2002).

Hangarter v. Provident Life and Accident Insurance Co. & The Paul Revere Life Insurance Co.; UNUM Provident Corp., 373 F.3rd 998 (2004); U.S. App. LEXIS 12841 (2004).

Heilbrun, K. (2001). *Principles of forensic mental health assessment.* New York: Kluwer Academic/Plenum Press.

Heilbrun, K., Warren, J., & Picarello, K. (2003). Third party information in forensic assessment. In I. B. Weiner (Series Ed.) & A. M. Goldstein (Vol. Ed.), *Comprehensive handbook of psychology: Vol. 11. Forensic psychology* (pp. 69–86). Hoboken, NJ: Wiley.

Hinchman v. General American Insurance Co., IP-96-0578-C-B/S (J.D. In., 1998).

Holzer v. MBL Life Assurance Corp., 1999 U.S. Dist. LEXIS 13094, 1999 W.L. 649004 (S.D.N.Y.).

Kupshik v. John Hancock Mutual Life Insurance Co., 1, 98-CV-3-CAM (M.D. Ga., 2000).

Laucks v. Provident Cos., 97-CV-1507, 1999 W.L. 33320463 (M.D. PA).

Levitt v. UNUM Life Ins. Co. of America, No. P.J.M. 93-2434 (Md. June 21, 1994).

Mass. Casualty Ins. Co. v. Rief, 227 Md. 324, 176 A.2d 777 (1962).

Mass. Mutual Life Ins. Co. v. Ouellette, 617 A.2d 132 (Vt. 1992).

Mutual Life Ins. Co. v. Frost, 164 F.2d 542 (1st Cir. 1947).

O'Connor v. Sullivan, 938 F.2d 70 (1991).

Otto, R. K. (2001, February). *Assessing malingering and deception.* Paper presented at the meeting of the American Academy of Forensic Psychology Workshop, San Antonio, TX.

Rogers, R. (1984). Towards an empirical model of malingering and deception. *Behavioral Sciences and the Law, 2,* 93–112.

Rogers, R. (Ed.). (1997). *Clinical assessment of malingering and deception* (2nd ed.). New York: Guilford Press.

Rogers, R., & Bender, S. (2003). Evaluation of malingering and deception. In I. B. Weiner (Series Ed.) & A. M. Goldstein (Vol. Ed.), *Comprehensive handbook of psychology: Vol. 11. Forensic psychology* (pp. 109–129). Hoboken, NJ: Wiley.

Rogers, R., & Reinhardt, V. (1998). Conceptualization and assessment of secondary gain. In G. P. Koocher, J. C. Norcross, & S. S. Hill III. (Eds.), Psychologist's desk reference (pp. 57–62). New York: Oxford University Press.

Suarez v. Mass. Mutual Life Ins. Co. 5, 98-CV-177-3 (M.D. Ga., March 13, 2000).

Sutherland v. Paul Revere Life Ins. Co., 95-MR-58 Cir. Ct. of 8th Judicial Circuit, Adams Co., Ill. (December 16, 1996).

Sutherland v. Paul Revere Life Ins. Co., revd. & rem. 711 N.E.2d 833 (Table, June 30, 1997).

Tackman v. UNUM Life Ins. Co. of America No. 2, 94-CV-79 (W.D. Mich. August 11, 1994).

Weissman, H. N., & Debow, D. M. (2003). Ethical principals and professional competencies. In I. B. Weiner (Series Ed.) & A. M. Goldstein (Vol. Ed.), *Comprehensive handbook of psychology: Vol. 11. Forensic psychology* (pp. 33–53). Hoboken, NJ: Wiley.

Williams v. Hormel Foods Corp. and Zurich American Insurance Co., 67 P.3rd 375 (2003); OK CIV APP 37 (2003); Okla. CIV APP LEXIS 14.

Wright v. Paul Revere Life Ins. Co., 294 F. Supp. 2d 1104 (C.D. Cal. 2003).

CHAPTER 20

Workplace Violence: Advances in Consultation and Assessment

Harley V. Stock

FORENSIC PSYCHOLOGICAL BUSINESS CONSULTATION

Who should conduct workplace violence threat assessments? Clinical psychologists treat patients. Industrial/organizational psychologists treat companies. Forensic psychologists evaluate the clinical psychologist's patient who is threatening the industrial/organizational psychologists' company. The forensic psychologist, by virtue of training and experience, is uniquely positioned to evaluate threats that emanate from the workplace (Packer & Borum, 2003).

An organization is an open system (von Bertalanffy, 1950). Such a system is dynamic and attempts to maintain equilibrium among the individual business unit requirements, overall company functioning, and the outside world the company interacts with (Levinson, 2002). A threat of violence can destabilize some or all of the system and cause significant disruption to business continuity. The forensic psychologist conducting a workplace violence threat assessment must be sensitive about and have the ability to evaluate how the organizational culture and the individual employees are contributing to the threatening event. The organization has as much of a personality as does the subject of the evaluation. Without this understanding, the forensic psychologist conducting a workplace threat assessment may encounter significant resistance from the organization to enact a risk management strategy, which is the ultimate outcome of the forensic process. For every forensic risk management suggestion involving an employee, there may be an opposite, and not equal, reaction by the organization.

BUSINESS PREPARATION AND RESPONSE FOR A WORKPLACE VIOLENCE EVENT

It is cheaper and safer to prepare a workplace to prevent potential disaster than to respond after a disaster has occurred. The following practices identify methodology to evaluate and react to individual and environmental workplace violence risk factors.

Preemployment Screening

A number of methods (psychological testing) and techniques (behavioral interviewing) exist that can, to some extent, identify behaviors and experiences that might suggest further inquiry prior to hiring an employee. The forensic psychologist must be familiar with the legal and ethical issues associated with preemployment screening. For example, certain questions on the Minnesota Multiphasic Personality Inventory 2 may be considered medical, and for legal reasons, this test may have to be administered after a conditional job offer is tendered (Klimoski & Palmer, 1994).

Background Investigation

Information on past criminal activity and financial and employment history may be investigated by a third-party security consulting firm. Multiple safeguards about disclosure of such information must be in place.

Workplace Risk Audit

This process involves evaluation of any policy, procedure, or physical barrier that contributes to the reduction of risk. Companies should have a workplace violence policy that clearly describes the commitment to a safe workplace, employees' roles and responsibilities, and remediation (reporting mechanism and responses) available. Definitions of unacceptable behavior are described, along with possible administrative remediations. A security risk audit may include an employee survey about security concerns and examination of current protective practices (liaison with local law enforcement, evacuation plans, and assessment of protective barriers such as access control).

Threat Assessment

This function can range from establishing an internal threat management team, consisting of representatives from human resources, legal, security, and occupational health, to contracting out the assessment process to a forensic psychologist. It is wiser for the business to establish this process prior to the threatening event. If not, the company will have a crisis within a crisis.

Damage Control

If an event occurs that has the potential to significantly disrupt business continuity, a critical incident stress management plan should be available (Paton & Smith, 1995). This plan addresses the stages of corporate response (i.e., precrisis, crisis phase, resolution phase, postcrisis phase) and individual response to a crisis (i.e., anxiety, denial, anger, grief, resolution).

INCIDENCE OF WORKPLACE VIOLENCE

The issue of workplace violence has received so much attention that, at least for one setting, the U.S. Postal Service (USPS), the term "going postal" has become part of everyday usage. However, this is not a fair representation of the true incidence of workplace violence within the USPS.

Over a 14-year period (1986 to 1999), there were 29 workplace homicide events resulting in 54 deaths at various postal facilities. In 15 of those episodes, a postal employee was the perpetrator (Lopez, 2005). The expected national base rate during that period of time was 1 workplace homicide per 150,000 employees/year. Given the number of USPS employees (approximately 770,000), the actual number of workplace homicides (54) in the USPS was 25% lower over that time period than the expected homicide rate of 72. Thus, such a characterization of Postal Service employees as more dangerous than employees of other occupations is a myth (USPS, 2000). As another example, discharged psychiatric patients are not the prototypical violent offender in the workplace. Approximately 0.6% committed a violent act in the workplace within 1 year of discharge (Monahan et al., 2001). This illustrates the importance for the forensic psychologist to understand base rates, or how often an event happens in a specific population.

The occurrence of a targeted homicide in the workplace, in which the nexus is an established interpersonal workplace relationship between the perpetrator and the victim, is greatly exaggerated in the press and professional publications. Often referred to as an "epidemic," an "explosion" of violence, or "a recurrent national nightmare" (S. A. Baron, 1993; Labig, 1995; Mantell, 1994), a closer analysis of the data suggests the opposite trend. Of 4,154 occupational homicides between 1997 and 2002, 80% (3,310) took place during the commission of a crime in which the victim and perpetrator had no workplace-oriented relationship prior to the event, and therefore it was not a targeted workplace homicide (Bureau of Labor Statistics, 2002).

There are two official, government-sponsored surveillance systems for workplace homicide: the Bureau of Labor Statistics (2002) national *Census of Fatal Occupational Injuries,* which gathers data from death certificates, open information sources such as newspapers, and reports from regulatory agencies, and the National Institute for Occupational Safety and Health (NIOSH), which supports the National Traumatic Occupational Fatalities system and gathers information from death certificates. The calculated base rate of workplace violence homicides for 2003 is approximately 1 per 218,000 employees annually. Over a 10-year period (1994 to 2003), the overall occupational incidents of homicide decreased from 1,080 to 631, a decline of approximately 42% (Bureau of Labor Statistics, 2003).

The vast majority of victims were workers in retail and personal services, such as cashiers, clerical personnel, and taxi drivers. These attacks are generally opportunistic and may involve venues in which protective measures (i.e., bullet-resistant glass, immediate door-locking mechanisms) are considered an expensive luxury (NIOSH, 1996). Forensic psychologists are generally not consulted about specific threat assessment in these cases as the homicidal events are usually spontaneous. However, forensic psychologists can play a role in preincident planning by helping a business become aware of situational specificity of aggression, preattack verbal and nonverbal perpetrator communication, and victim behavioral responses that can lead to increased safety.

As was the trend with workplace homicides, the overall violent victimization rate dropped precipitously from 55 to 33 per 1,000 employees between 1993 and 1999 (Bureau of Justice Statistics, 2001). In the most robust study done to date, it is estimated that approximately 6 million workers were threatened yearly in the workplace (Northwestern National Life, 1993). There are an estimated 1,700,000 "violent victimizations" yearly in the workplace. Compared to being killed in the workplace, a worker is 150 times more likely to be sexually assaulted and 1,600 times more likely to be the victim of a simple assault (U.S. Department of Justice, 2004). This data may be inaccurate due to reporting mechanisms available and the hesitancy of victims of workplace violence to acknowledge these episodes.

In general, workplace offenders were not known to their victims in over half of the assaults. However, teachers and mental health workers knew about two-thirds of their assailants. Men (49.6%) were more likely than women (40.2%) to report a workplace crime to the police. When the crime was rape or other sexual assault in the workplace, it was reported 24% of the time, compared to 71% of robberies being reported. The occupational field reporting highest workplace violence was law enforcement (74.8%), and the lowest was mental health (22.9%; Bureau of Justice Statistics, 2001).

In summary, out of about 600 to 800 annual workplace homicides, approximately 160 to 200 homicides occurred in which a personal relationship was established prior to the event (i.e., work associate; a relative, such as husband or wife; or other acquaintance, such as current or past boyfriend/girlfriend). Men were almost four times as likely to be killed by a work associate and women were almost twice as likely to be killed by an intimate partner or other personal acquaintance (Bureau of Labor Statistics, 2003). The implications for domestic violence spilling over into the workplace are addressed later in this chapter.

CONSEQUENCES OF WORKPLACE VIOLENCE

Eleven percent of employees in the Northwestern National Life (1993) survey indicated that they considered bringing Mace to work, and approximately 4% thought about bringing a gun to the job. Of those attacked at work within the year prior to the survey, 40% contemplated bringing Mace to work, and about 20% thought about bringing in a gun. The hidden and tangible costs of a workplace violence event can be substantial. Individuals who are victims of violence are likely to miss more days of work, have higher workers' compensation complaints, change jobs more frequently, make more medical claims, suffer higher rates of burnout, and generally be more dissatisfied than other workers (Budd, Arvey, & Lawless, 1996). American businesses lose over $4 billion a year in productivity and business disruption due to violence (Albrecht, 1997). However, Castillo (1995) indicated, research about nonfatal violence may not always be accurate.

DEFINITION OF WORKPLACE VIOLENCE/AGGRESSION

Over the past 30 years, aggression in the workplace has been labeled work harassment (Brodsky, 1976), unreliable workplace behavior (Hogan & Hogan, 1989), workplace violence (Kinney & Johnson, 1993), and counterproductive work behavior (Fox & Spector, 1999). A general definition of violence is "the actual, attempted, or threatened physical harm to another person that is deliberate and nonconsensual" (Webster, Douglas, Eaves, & Hart, 1997, p. 13). Reiss and Roth (1993) take a parsimonious route by defining violence as an action by a perpetrator that creates a fear in, attempts to harm, or does harm the victim. National Institute for Occupational Safety and Health (NIOSH) defines workplace violence as "all violent acts, including physical assaults and threats of assault, directed toward persons at work or on duty" (Jenkins, 1996, p. 6). Although Webster et al. (1997) note that dangerousness is viewed as a trait and violence as an event, the author of this chapter believes that violence is the outcome of putting a potentially violent person in a specific set of circumstances.

Workplace violence is a special type of violence and thus deserves a unique definition. The following definition of workplace violence is suggested: an intentional act committed by an individual or group for the purpose of (or resulting in) psychologically and/or physically affecting an organization or persons associated with an organization. This definition encompasses the following dimensions: (a) intentional act—the initiating event is a reflection of a purposeful series of behaviors; (b) individual or group—the perpetrator(s) may be acting individually or may represent an ideological position, such as a terrorists; (c) purpose of (or results in)—the behavior may have an intended course or may cause an outcome that; (d) psychologically and/or physically effects—violence can both psychologically destabilize and physically harm the intended target (most events of workplace violence are more likely to psychologically, rather than physically, impact the target); and (e) an organization or persons associated with an organization—a business's capacity for continuation can be significantly disrupted, for example, by an attack on its computer system. In that instance, no individual employee would be hurt, but all employees might suffer the repercussions of such an attack. This part of the definition also recognizes the self-injurious (suicidal) behaviors by the perpetrator, that the location of the threatening event does not have to physically be at the workplace, and that unintended targets need to be considered (Stock, 2002).

CAUSES OF WORKPLACE VIOLENCE/AGGRESSION

There is some semantic splitting between the concepts of *aggression,* such as any attempt to harm (Tedeschi & Felson, 1994), and *violence* (direct, impactful, and physical behavior; Neuman & Baron, 1998). For our purposes, workplace violence is at the far end of the workplace aggression continuum (see Table 20.1).

Forensic psychologists are most often called to consult with business or government agencies on issues of workplace violence when the content of the threat is death or significant disruption of business activity. Although aggression in the workplace has been described as a continuum in Table 20.1, forensic psychological evaluations will generally be in the high-risk (7 to 10) range.

R. A. Baron and Richardson (1994) suggest that the root causes of workplace violence can be segregated into five distinct categories: (1) physical aspects of the workplace (e.g., ambient temperature, auditory overloading, close physical proximity to others); (2) social impact (e.g., group and societal expectations as to appropriate and inappropriate workplace behavior, coupled with individual expectations and interactions); (3) biological causes (e.g., hormonal influences, specific arousal [limbic] pathways, physical/neurological disorders, level of consciousness as mediated by psychoactive substances); (4) cognitive distortions (e.g., misinterpretation of events, linked associations between the current disruptive event and past similar

Table 20.1   Aggression in the Workplace

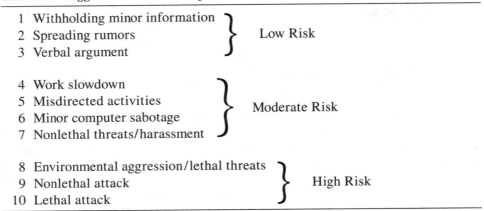

1	Withholding minor information	} Low Risk
2	Spreading rumors	
3	Verbal argument	
4	Work slowdown	} Moderate Risk
5	Misdirected activities	
6	Minor computer sabotage	
7	Nonlethal threats/harassment	
8	Environmental aggression/lethal threats	} High Risk
9	Nonlethal attack	
10	Lethal attack	

behaviors); and (5) individual personality contributions (i.e., specific personality characteristics of the aggressor).

James (1998) has identified six unique justification mechanisms that give the perpetrator an "excuse" for aggression:

1. *Hostile attribution bias:* The employee believes actions by coworkers, even those behaviors others might see as positive, are intended to hurt the employee. For example, by making the employee a project manager of a difficult endeavor, the supervisor is intentionally setting the employee up to fail. Other employees would view the same assignment as a positive challenge.

2. *Retribution bias:* Aggression is legitimized as the vehicle to regain respect or get even. Maintenance of the relationship is secondary to vindication and revenge.

3. *Derogation of target bias:* The flaws of the target are amplified and positive attributes are devalued.

4. *Victimization by powerful others bias:* Themes of exploitation and perceived injustice attributed to the target cast the perpetrator in the role of victim.

5. *Potency bias:* Being perceived by others as strong, assertive (aggressive), or fearless is enhanced by acting against those in a position of authority/strength. Conversely, any indication of weakness by the perpetrator is seen to invite aggression from the target.

6. *Social discounting bias:* Using "socially unorthodox" or antisocial ideas to justify aggression, the perpetrator will significantly embrace nontraditional values and unconventional beliefs.

LEGAL AND ETHICAL ISSUES

Forensic psychologists must be familiar with the special legal constructs, legislative requirements, and ethical constraints for the area in which they practice. Because of the unique nature of forensic consultation to the workplace, the forensic psychologist may be exposed to liabilities and issues not previously encountered. This section describes key legislative, legal, and ethical workplace-related concerns.

Legislative Issues

The U.S. Department of Labor's Occupational Safety and Health Administration (OSHA) was initially concerned about deficits in workplace environmental safety that could lead to physical injury. The OSHA general duty clause indicates that an employer "shall furnish to each of his employees employment and a place of employment which are free from recognized hazards that are causing or are likely to cause death or serious physical harm to his employees" (Occupational Safety and Health Act, 1979). In 1992, OSHA extended the general duty clause to include recognized hazards from violence. Some states, such as California, have adopted language similar to that in the OSHA general duty guideline (California Occupational Safety and Health Act, 1973). The federal OSHA subsequently recognized that specific environments, such as retail establishments that are open at night and hospitals and health care/social services settings are at increased risk for violence. OSHA (U.S. Department of Labor, 1996) eventually promulgated volunteer guidelines for these types of locations. OSHA also issued an advisory statement requiring those types of businesses to implement specific record keeping, risk analysis processes, and training. Some states (Alaska, 2003; Washington Industrial Safety and Health Services Agency, 1997) have enacted legislation concerning workplace violence that is not limited to certain types of businesses. Canada (Canadian Province of Quebec, Labour Standards Act, 2004) enacted North America's first legislation on antibullying in the workplace. "Vexatious" workplace behavior in Canada includes repetitive, hostile, or unwanted actions that are damaging to the victim's psychological integrity or personal dignity and are harmful to the work environment.

In general, to prove a violation of the OSHA general duty guideline, it must be established that

> (1) a condition or activity in the employer's workplace presented a hazard to employees, (2) the cited employer or employer's industry recognized the hazard, (3) the hazard was likely to cause death or serious physical harm, and (4) the feasible means existed to eliminate or materially reduce the hazard. (Biles, 2004, p. 3)

Legal Theories

Legal theories, which are bolstered by judicial decisions, illuminate the minefield that companies try to maneuver. Forensic psychologists conducting workplace threat assessments may find their behavior being examined under the following legal constructs.

Negligent Action

The basic elements of a negligence action are:

- *Duty:* Did the company, or with due diligence, could the company have known about the individual's propensity for violence?
- *Breach of duty:* Once put on notice about the potential risk of harm, what did the company do to mitigate that risk?

- *Causation:* Was there a direct nexus between what the company knew, or should have known, about the potential risk and a subsequent incident?

- *Damages:* The nature (physical/psychological), type (punitive), and financial award are determined in this step.

Several different types of negligent action may directly or indirectly involve the forensic psychologist:

- *Respondent superior:* An employer is acting through the facility of an employee or agent, and if an on-the-job civil liability is incurred due to some fault of the employee/agent, the employer must accept responsibility. This concept establishes a "special relationship" between an employer and employee. For example, if coworker A threatens to kill supervisor B at her home, the employer cannot abdicate its responsibility to protect the supervisor solely because the murder will not take place on company property.

- *Negligent hiring:* The majority of negligent hiring actions focus on failure to do background screening that would have revealed a record of violence (*Grove v. Rainbow International Carpet Dyeing and Cleaning Company,* 1994), but preemployment psychological screening, particularly in a law enforcement environment, may expose the forensic psychologist to examination of the selection procedures used (see Borum, Super, & Rand, 2003, for a discussion of screening for high-risk occupations).

- *Negligent security:* Based on the information available concerning a foreseeable risk of violence, did the workplace establish sufficient physical or environmental barriers to prevent or mitigate against the violent act? (*Saelzler v. Advanced Group 400,* 2001). On the surface, this issue would appear to be clearly, and only, within the purview of the security consultant. However, depending on the type of risk assessment, a question such as "What is the likelihood the subject will approach the target within the next 12 hours?" or "Should we put this person under surveillance to make sure he or she does not approach the target?" may be asked of the forensic psychologist.

- *Negligent retention:* This occurs when the employer knows an employee has a propensity toward violence but permits the employee to retain employment despite this knowledge (*Natasha Saine v. Comcast Cablevision of Arkansas, Inc.,* 2003).

- *Negligent supervision:* The company assumes liability for its management team members or agents when a management person fails to properly supervise an employee who, ultimately, inflicts harm on other coworkers (*Simmons v. U.S.,* 1986). A forensic psychologist may be asked to evaluate whether a supervisor is creating a toxic work environment that could foster organizationally disruptive behaviors in his or her subordinates. A toxic work environment is characterized by authoritarian management style, unpredictable discipline patterns, and employee devaluation.

- *Negligent training:* Companies that fail to train employees about specific issues, such as workplace risk assessment, or offer improper training may be liable. It would not be recommended for a forensic psychologist to offer a company training on workplace violence risk assessment that is only brief or superficial. Such training may lead the employer to the false belief that it can assess risk of violence in the workplace, resulting in inappropriate decisions with unfortunate outcomes.

Other civil claims arising out of a workplace risk assessment include intentional or negligent infliction of emotional distress on the victim or wrongful death of the victim. The subject of the risk assessment may also file claims of defamation of character, invasion of privacy, wrongful discharge, discrimination, and being a qualified individual under the Americans with Disabilities Act (ADA).

Forensic psychologists conducting risk/threat assessments should be familiar with the three main components of the Title I (Employment section) of ADA:

1. *Disability:* (a) a "physical or mental impairment" that "substantially limits" one or more of the "major life activities" of an individual, (b) a "record" of such an impairment, or (c) "being regarded" as having an impairment.

2. *The need for reasonable accommodation:* Employers must attempt to make "reasonable accommodations" for the identified mental or physical impairment of otherwise "qualified individuals with disabilities" unless it can be demonstrated that the accommodation would impose an "undue hardship" such as significant costs or other difficulty on the employer. A "reasonable accommodation," for example, may include physical modification of existing facilities or job restructuring. However, it is essential for the forensic psychologist to understand that, even if an employee is suffering from a major mental illness, an employer is not obligated to offer a reasonable accommodation *if* the employee represents a "direct threat" to self or others. Evidentiary factors for a "direct threat" include (a) the duration of the risk, (b) the nature and severity of the potential harm, (c) the likelihood the potential harm will occur, and (d) the imminence of the potential harm. A risk of a direct threat is significant if there is "a high probability of substantiated harm; a speculative or remote risk is insufficient" (ADA, 29 C.F.R., 1990).

3. *Discrimination:* The purpose of the ADA is to describe a "clear and comprehensive national mandate for the elimination of discrimination against individuals with disabilities" through enforceable standards (ADA, § 2, 1990). Discrimination of disabled individuals is barred in job application procedures, job advancement, discharge, compensation, job training, and "other terms, condition or privilege of employment" (ADA, § 102(a), 42 U.S.C., § 12101, 1990).

The Health Insurance Portability and Accountability Act (HIPAA, 1996) has not yet been subjected to judicial opinion regarding the relationship between a forensic psychologist in the course of conducting a risk assessment and the employee, or subject of that assessment. Connell and Koocher (2003) offer cogent arguments why the forensic practitioner needs to be HIPAA compliant: (a) Diagnosis in a forensic examination may be considered "health care," and those who perform the evaluation are "covered entities"; and (b) the forensic examiner may receive health care information from another provider. This information must be handled in a secure way. Connell and Koocher make equally persuasive arguments why the type of evaluations typically done by forensic psychologists do not fall under HIPAA requirements: (a) Forensic evaluations are not health care because there is no intent to treat the subject of the evaluation, and (b) the evaluation is undertaken to answer a psychological question and forensic evaluation services are not recognized for third-party insurance payment. They offer the caveat, "Each practitioner must engage in a careful analysis of their own practice activities that might qualify as 'health care' services" (p. 16).

Ethical Issues

The forensic psychologist must be familiar with and adhere to the "Ethical Principles of Psychologists and Code of Conduct" of the American Psychological Association (APA, 2002). Not having membership in the APA does not excuse a psychologist from behavior comporting to the generally acceptable ethical principles of the profession.

The following sections of the "Ethical Principles of Psychologists and Code of Conduct" (APA, 2002) should be carefully reviewed and followed when conducting a workplace threat assessment: 2.01 (Boundaries of Competence); 2.04 (Basics for Scientific and Professional Judgments); 3.05 (Multiple Relationships); 3.07 (Third-Party Requests for Services); 3.10 (Informed Consent); 4.02 (Discussing the Limits of Confidentiality); 4.04 (Minimizing Intrusions on Privacy); 6.01 (Documentation of Professional and Scientific Work and Maintenance of Records); 6.04 (Fees and Financial Arrangements); 9.01 (Bases for Assessment); 9.02 (Use of Assessments); 9.03 (Informed Consent in Assessments); 9.04 (Release of Test Data); 9.06 (Interpreting Assessment Results); 9.08 (Obsolete Tests and Outdated Test Results); 9.09 (Test Scoring and Interpretation Services); 9.10 (Explaining Assessment Results).

If a psychologist claims special status, such as being a forensic psychologist, there is an obligation to follow the "Specialty Guidelines for Forensic Psychologists" (Committee on Ethical Guidelines for Forensic Psychologists, 1991).

HISTORY OF RISK ASSESSMENT PRACTICES

The concept of risk assessment is not novel to forensic psychology. Risk assessment methods have been applied to unexploded bombs (Macdonald, Knopman, Lockwood, Cecchine, & Willis, 2004), environmental damage (Goklany, 2001), and various health risks (Bailar, Needleman, Berney, & McGinnis, 1993).

Monahan (1981) initially tattooed into the literature clinicians' inability to accurately assess the relationship between violence and mental illness by noting that psychologists and psychiatrists were correct in only one out of three predictions concerning future violence in a known population of violent, mentally ill individuals.

Although mental health clinicians initially argued among themselves about the inability to predict dangerousness, the U.S. Supreme Court believed that it was both necessary and possible for clinicians to comment about future violence under certain circumstances. In *Barefoot v. Estelle* (1983, p. 8), Justice White, perhaps somewhat naively, noted that the probability to predict that a "particular criminal will commit other crimes in the future and so represent a danger to the community" was not that difficult a task because "if it is not impossible for even a lay person sensibly to arrive at that conclusion," then psychiatrists should certainly be qualified. In legal challenges to violence risk assessment outcome, such as sex offender recidivism (*Kansas v. Hendricks,* 1997), the Court indicated that a risk assessment process was an acceptable procedure to assist the trier of fact in deciding whether a sex offender should be civilly committed to a mental hospital after serving a prison sentence.

Today, most clinicians are familiar with the *Tarasoff* decision (*Tarasoff v. Regents of the University of California,* 1976) in terms of duty to warn or protect an identifiable target from aggression by a patient. This decision emphasized that psychotherapists were required to follow the standards of the profession when assessing the likelihood of future violence. Justice Mosk, in a separate opinion for the case, asked, "What standards?" Amazingly, the courts today have the same view of risk assessment. In another California case that will likely extend the impact of *Tarasoff,* the Court noted that predicting a patient's dangerous propensities according to the standards of the profession presents four serious problems: (1) "It is almost universally agreed among mental health professionals themselves, that therapists are poor predictors of future violent behavior"; (2) fear of liability will cause therapists to overpredict "dangerousness"; (3) a duty to warn requirement may obfuscate clinical treatment; and (4) such expectations of prediction "holds psychotherapists to an ill-defined community standard" (*Ewing v. Northridge Hospital Medical Center,* 2004, p. 11).

Monahan's (1988) negative initial assessment about violence prediction capabilities was attenuated by his positive suggestions concerning the potential use of historical, individual, contextual, and clinical variables in risk assessment. These early insights formed the basis for the subsequent generations of risk assessment development. It is now recognized that the question of violence prediction is not generic. One model of risk assessment will not fit all possible circumstances that the forensic psychologist is called on to evaluate. This is particularly true with targeted threat assessment in the workplace.

CURRENT RISK ASSESSMENT PRACTICES AND ISSUES

There is currently debate in the forensic risk assessment arena regarding the appropriate application of actuarial versus forensic clinical risk assessment procedures. This is not an easy dichotomy to dissect.

Historically, Meehl (1954) clearly differentiated between clinical (i.e., a hypothesis about individual behavior) and actuarial (i.e., a systemized combining of information, resulting in a probability statement) methods. He supported actuarial assessment when possible. Contemporary researchers (e.g., Litwack, 2001) suggest that actuarial methods are defined by fixed and specific decision rules. For example, Monahan et al. (2001) used CHAID (Chi-squared Automatic Interaction Detector) to construct a classification tree model for risk.

Based on a review of the divergent forensic literature on actuarial versus forensic clinical risk evaluation, the following definition outlines the essential minimum components for a forensic actuarial risk assessment: (a) identification of static (fixed or unchangeable; e.g., age, past history of sexual abuse) and/or dynamic (contemporary and changeable; e.g., escalating violent fantasies) predictor variables; (b) by empirical method, theoretical formulation, or clinical observation; (c) that in optimal combination with each other produces a score; (d) that at a statistically significant level can segregate the person being evaluated into a discrete risk class membership (i.e., high, moderate, low) with both sensitivity (true positives) and specificity (true negatives); (e) on the specific dependent variable being assessed (e.g., general violence, risk of recidivism, sexual offending, workplace violence); and (f) over an identified time period.

What constitutes "clinical judgment" is not well understood. Grove and Meehl (1996) suggest that clinicians use idiosyncratic, not well-conceived, uninformed methods to formulate predictions of violence. Notwithstanding this position, other research (Menzies & Webster, 1995) reveals that clinicians have a better than chance ability to predict violence. Borum, Otto, and Golding (1993) have identified specific areas that affect clinical decision making (i.e., limitations in complex configural analysis, underutilization of base rates, confirmatory bias), but note that such decisions are not as flawed as the literature might indicate. At the other extreme, Quinsey, Harris, Rice, and Cormier (1998) believe that any form of clinical assessment of violence should be halted in favor of using solely an actuarial process. What separates true actuarial measures from clinical judgment is that statistical (mathematical) methods are consistently utilized to reach an opinion in actuarial assessment. For example, the use of receiver operating characteristics can compensate for Type I and Type II errors and adjust for alternating base rates and selection ratios in calculating an effect size.

As Monahan et al. (2001) noted after the completion of the MacArthur Study of Mental Disorder and Violence, actuarial instruments

> are best viewed as "tools" for clinical assessment (cf. Grisso & Appelbaum, 1998)—tools that support, rather than replace, the exercise of clinical judgment. This reliance on clinical judgment—aided by an empirical understanding of risk factors for violence and their interactions—reflects, and in our view should reflect, the standard of care at this juncture in the field's development. (p. 134)

Depending on the source, violence risk assessment is in its fifth (Hall, 2001), sixth (Douglas & Kropp, 2002), or seventh generation (Banks et al., 2004). The maturing of the field is characterized by the application of more refined statistical (actuarial) analysis comingling with increasingly informed forensic clinical judgment, including the reliance on multiple sources of data (see Table 20.2). The blossoming of the risk assessment field has seen outcome predictions undergo a metamorphosis from such statements as "My best guess is . . ." (unstructured clinical opinion) to "Based on a combination of multiple risk factors from these identifiable risk models, Mr. X has Y probability of committing X offense in Z time frame" (actuarial/informed forensic opinion).

Until this risk assessment issue (forensic, forensic in combination with actuarial, or purely actuarial) is settled by a court, Duggan's Law may apply: "To every PhD, there is an opposite PhD" (Dixon, 1978, p. 132).

Table 20.2 Evolution of Forensic/Actuarial Risk Assessment

	Generation	Process	Strength	Weakness	Outcome Prediction
I.	Unstructured clinical opinion	Idiosyncratic; based on knowledge and experience of examiner.	Person- and context-specific risk management strategies.	Lacks validity, reliability, and accountability.	Varies from "best guess" to precision prediction.
II.	Structured clinical opinion	Structured, but not research-driven, interview to collect data.	More uniform approach.	No rules for combination of data into prediction.	Some consistent basis for finding.
III.	Empirically guided evaluation or structured professional judgment	Assessment based on empirically derived behavior related to violence, including history, opportunity factors, and triggering stimuli.	Can be used by nonclinicians; sets minimum set of risk factors.	No restriction for inclusion, weighting, or combining risk factors.	Subject of evaluation is more or less like offender group.
IV.	Anamestic approach	Detailed examination of history of violence and threatening behavior.	Identifies unique "patterns" of violence to aid risk management.	No research; individual behavioral chains may not be predictable.	Specifically tailored to individual.
V.	Actuarial risk assessment	Comparison of individual to norm-based reference group on statistically determined risk factors.	Transparent decision process provides a precise, probabilistic estimate of the likelihood of future violence.	Generalizability; exclusion of important risk factors with low base rates; rigid interpretation.	Discrete classification of likelihood of violence.
VI.	Actuarial-forensic risk assessment	Actuarial risk factors and empirically based method are clinically modified by the unique contextual circumstances of the evaluation.	Semitransparent; can explain how certain risk factors more or less contribute to prediction.	Idiosyncratic interpretation.	Modifies actuarial prediction to individual case.
VII.	Multimodel actuarial risk assessment	Combines prediction variables of different risk assessment models into an iterative classification tree.	Superior prediction ability compared to each constituent model used individually.	Not enough research to date.	More discrete classification.

Risk Assessment Instruments

There are several current structured risk assessment guides that have utility for the forensic psychologist, depending on the population membership of the subject being evaluated: the Violence Risk Appraisal Guide (VRAG; Quinsey et al., 1998); the HCR-20 (Historical, Clinical, Risk Management), developed by Webster et al. (1997); the Sex Offender Risk Appraisal Guide (SORAG; Harris et al., 2003); the Spousal Assault Risk Assessment (SARA) Guide (Kropp, Hart, Webster, & Eaves, 1999); and the Structured Assessment of Violence Risk in Youth (SAVRY; Borum, Bartell, & Forth, 2000).

There are no purely actuarial risk assessment instruments currently available for assessing workplace violence, but strides have been made in this area. For example, this author (Stock, 1997) developed the Behavioral Risk Assessment System (BRASS), a proprietary workplace risk analysis instrument with 23 categories of behaviorally anchored risk-related activities (i.e., target compliance, volatility, perceived injustice) that were derived from the literature on violence in general and workplace violence in particular. Hall (2001) has proposed a Workplace Violence Risk Assessment Checklist that has 60 items divided into four categories: (1) historical and demographic; (2) recent events (e.g., acquires firearms or related lethal equipment or weapons); (3) work attitude and traits (e.g., sense of identity wrapped up in the job; tends to have poor assertiveness skills); and (4) organizational deficiencies (e.g., the organization uses intrusive methods to monitor employees, especially electronic monitoring; performance standards do not have built-in employee input).

By bifurcating how an organization's corporate culture might enhance the risk for workplace violence versus the risk factors that focus on an individual employee, Webster, Bloom, and Eisen (2003) have developed two complementary risk instruments. The Workplace Risk Assessment (WRA-20) samples five domains of an organization's structure that, left unchecked, may support the eruption of a violent event: (1) status (e.g., grievances/human rights complaints); (2) prevention (e.g., employee assistance program); (3) communication (e.g., reporting/disclosing events); (4) responsiveness (e.g., termination process); and (5) environment (e.g., management style). The Employee Risk Assessment (ERA-20) samples four domains: (1) historical (e.g., history of suicide attempts); (2) clinical (e.g., substance abuse); (3) attitudinal (e.g., disgruntled); and (4) situational (e.g., laid off, fired, demoted, missed promotion). Webster et al. warn about the "provisional, untested nature" (p. 5) and lack of norms for the WRA-20 and the ERA-20.

None of these instruments should be considered to have sufficiently researched psychometric properties to be considered a test. In general, the most efficacious use of these instruments is as a guide to ensure that all domains of the specific risk referral question are being evaluated and that any actuarial risk information available is factored into the risk or threat question being addressed.

A NEW MODEL FOR WORKPLACE VIOLENCE ASSESSMENT

People who threaten violence in the workplace are different from those who threaten in other environments. For example, Monahan et al. (2001) describe it as a "rare" risk factor when hospitalized psychiatric patients admit to making a threat; because "most minimally rational people who do not want to be in a hospital can consciously suppress the verbalization of such intentions while they are being evaluated, direct threats are presumably rare and for that reason will not emerge as items on an actuarial instrument" (p. 133). Yet, in an unpublished sample of 100 cases of risk assessment in the workplace by this author, in which a threat to kill was alleged to have been uttered by the subject of the evaluation, approximately 85% of the examinees acknowledged making such a threat to kill. Another significant difference between traditional and workplace risk assessment is the triggering event that propels the request for a forensic psychological threat analysis. For example, in an unpublished sample by this author of 250 cases of threats of violence in the workplace, 76% involved specific threats to kill an identifiable target(s), 12% threatened to commit suicide, 8% involved a threat to engage in a behavior that would cause significant business disruption (e.g., attacks on the critical infrastructure of the business such as computer data storage), and only 4% consisted of specific threats that were likely to have less than lethal consequences (e.g., break someone's leg). Thus, the forensic psychologist engaging in workplace risk assessment is likely to be asked to evaluate the potential for lethal outcome, as opposed to general acts of violence. In 100% of cases described previously, some type of threatening communication (face-to-face, third party, e-mail) occurred prior to the forensic psychological assessment. Given the very low base rate of interpersonally targeted workplace homicide, in the majority of the cases of threatening communication a prediction of nonlethal behavior will be correct, even without any data. However, the wrong prediction in those few cases of true positives for lethal behavior will be catastrophic to everyone involved (the victim, the victim's family, coworkers, the reputation of the workplace, and the forensic psychologist). The forensic workplace violence threat assessment process needs to be able to optimally distinguish between those people who threaten and those who actually pose a threat.

All current risk assessment instruments (e.g., VRAG, SORAG, SARA, HCR-20, WRA, BRASS) utilize HOT (history, opportunity, triggering stimuli) risk variables interacting with individual characteristics that support violence (Hall, 2001). A nonexhaustive list may include (a) history of violence, child abuse, violent parent(s); (b) opportunity factors—purchase/access to a weapon, noncompliance with use of psychotropic medication, release into an environment that supports violence; and (c) triggering stimuli—drug/alcohol use, changes in relationships.

However, little attention in the risk assessment literature has been paid to contributing behaviors of the target, or potential victim. This author (Stock, 2000) proposes a model of four separate, but potentially overlapping, interactive domains to be considered when performing a workplace risk assessment process. These domains can be sampled using actuarial assessment tools and forensic clinical judgment. Each area is discussed next and some (but not all) contributing risk variables are described. HOT issues are contained in each domain (see Figure 20.1).

I. *Employee/subject.* This factor focuses on the individual who has allegedly uttered the threat. It may be a current or past employee, vendor, customer, patient, or significant other to the target. Examples of this domain include

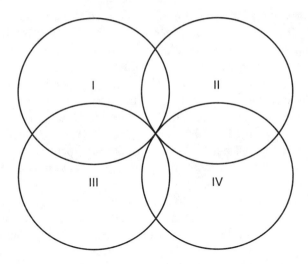

I = Employee/Subject
II = Extra Work-Related Variables
III = Work-Related Variables
IV = Target/Victim Behavior

Figure 20.1   General configural analysis.

current and past mental state, motivation and means to carry out the attack, current and past psychoactive substance use, hostile attribution bias, sense of perceived injustice, volitional controls, and likelihood of behavioral compliance with recommendations.

II. *Extra work-related variables.* These factors include situations or events that are occurring in the subject's life outside of the workplace but may be contributing to, or mitigating against, violence in the workplace. For example, health issues for self or important others, financial obligations, disruptive interpersonal interactions, social status, and support system availability may be referent conditions.

III. *Work-related variables.* These factors include workplace activities, supervisory behaviors, environmental conditions, corporate culture, and coworker relationships.

IV. *Target/victim behavior.* The target is the identified (or could be identified) focus of the threat. The target may be an individual, group of individuals, or the entire business entity. Target assessment includes reasons for target selection, likely target compliance with protective measures, psychological status of target, and relationship to the subject making the threat.

This model may serve to assist the forensic examiner in the risk abatement process. To illustrate the use of this model, consider that employee A has threatened to kill employee B. Category I analysis indicates that A currently drinks eight beers a day, is currently in treatment with a psychiatrist and is on psychotropic medication,

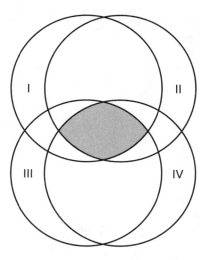

I = Employee/Subject
II = Extra Work-Related Variables
III = Work-Related Variables
IV = Target/Victim Behavior

Figure 20.2   Case-specific overlap.

believes B has treated him unfairly, and blames B for his work problems. Category II analysis finds that Employee A's father is terminally ill, causing him significant stress; the employee is filing for bankruptcy; and his wife has recently informed him that she wants a divorce. Category III analysis reveals that the employee works in a physically uncomfortable environment; his coworkers do not like him; his company is contemplating disciplinary action against him; and the corporate culture supports, by ignoring, incidents of teasing and bullying. Category IV analysis suggests that the target of the threat, Employee B, teases Employee A mercilessly. Even after human resources intervention, B continues to make inappropriate remarks to the subject. Conceptually, this case presents with significant overlap in all domains (see Figure 20.2).

To enhance the risk mitigation strategies, the company, in consultation with the forensic psychologist, decides to relocate Employee B to another plant site. This is enough to disrupt the violent event by removing the target, even though categories I through III continue to indicate contributing risk factors (see Figure 20.3).

The purpose of this model is to analyze the overlap of the four contributing behavioral areas of concern and identify those unique risk variables that can be manipulated, in a specific sequence, to reduce the risk to the identified target(s). This model suggests that not all issues need to be addressed equally. Those variables, in this case, target behavior that can be identified and changed, may be sufficient to significantly reduce the risk. As the domain overlap increases, more complicated risk reduction strategies will be in order.

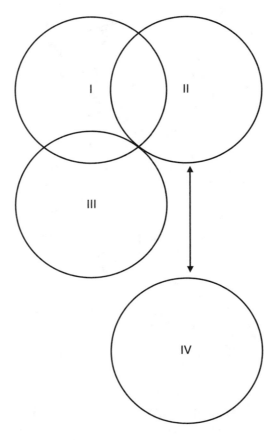

I = Employee/Subject
II = Extra Work-Related Variables
III = Work-Related Variables
IV = Target/Victim Behavior

Figure 20.3   Case-specific risk strategy.

ISSUES IN CONDUCTING A WORKPLACE TARGETED THREAT ASSESSMENT

Four general classifications of workplace aggressors have been identified:

Type I: The aggressive act is generally committed during the commission of a crime. The perpetrator has not specifically targeted the victim based on prior work-related interpersonal friction. These crimes are opportunistic and often spontaneous. (The forensic psychologist will not be called on to do a targeted violence threat assessment on the Type I perpetrator.) Prevention for this type of violence is enhanced security measures.

Type II: The perpetrator is a customer, client, resident (e.g., pupil, inmate, patient), or other recipient of services provided by the victim employee's organization.

Type III: The perpetrator has a specific current or historical employment relationship to the workplace (e.g., ex-employees, vendors, or current employees).

Type IV: The perpetrator may or may not be an employee, but the motivation for the threat is extrawork related (e.g., domestic violence). In this classification, the interpersonal tension between the perpetrator and the victim migrates from outside of the workplace (Injury Prevention Center, 2001).

Risk assessment and targeted violence threat assessment are two distinct, but sometimes overlapping processes. Reddy et al. (2001) define targeted violence as occurring "where both the perpetrator and target(s) are identified or identifiable prior to the incident" (p. 157). Some risk assessments (e.g., domestic violence) may have an identifiable target, but most risk assessments do not (e.g., Is a patient ready for discharge into the general community? Is the inmate ready for release into the general population of the prison? Does the sexual offender pose a general risk for recidivism?). The distinctions between general risk assessment and workplace targeted threat assessment are described in Table 20.3.

Table 20.3   Risk versus Threat (Targeted Violence) Assessment

Risk Assessment	Threat Assessment
Goal is to predict future behavior. Person may already be in custody or involved in some type of difficulty.	Goal is to prevent harm to targeted person; subject not likely in custody; legal control may not be possible when threat is issued.
↓	↓
Before an action is taken (release, probation), a risk assessment is initiated: Situation is static. Base rate usually available.	Some action may be taken before assessment is completed: Situation is dynamic.
↓	↓
No identifiable, specific victim.	Usually a specific target/asset identified.
↓	↓
Assessment is comparison to a known reference group (base rate).	Assessment may not have comparison to a reference group (base rate).
↓	↓
Protective options/inhibitors are already in place.	Protective options/situation management is fluid.
↓	↓
Decision is yes/no if high risk. Don't engage in questioned event (release/probation).	If credible threat, decisions depend on rapidity of activity toward target and available options to reduce harm.

Depending on the workplace environment of the target, the lack of a direct threat to the target does not decrease risk. For example, a U.S. Secret Service study found that in the past 50 years, 43 people have attempted attacks on public figures in the United States. None of them directly threatened the intended victim (Fein & Vossekuil, 1999). The targeted threat assessment approach has three guiding principles: (1) "Targeted violence is the result of an understandable and often discernable process of thinking and behavior"; (2) "violence stems from an interaction among the potential attacker, past stressful events, a current situation, and the target"; and (3) identification of the subject's "attack-related behaviors" is possible (Borum, Fein, Vossekuil, & Berglund, 1999, p. 329).

Given these rather broad contours of the threat assessment process, how does the forensic psychologist conduct a targeted workplace threat evaluation? In general, one answer is: cautiously and prudently. The following are basic issues to be considered in conducting a forensic threat assessment:

Preevaluation Issues

• What is the specific purpose of the threat assessment, and am I qualified to conduct such an evaluation? For example, a fitness-for-duty evaluation of a police officer (Borum et al., 2003) is a different process, in terms of legal, ethical, and risk factors, from evaluating an employee who has threatened to kill a coworker. Due to the current state of the art of workplace violence targeted threat assessment, the forensic psychologist must be up-to-date on those risk variables that empirically demonstrate some predictive utility, but should also use forensic/clinical acumen acquired performing similar types of evaluations. Supervision by a qualified forensic psychologist is often helpful.

• What is the relationship between the evaluator and the subject of the evaluation? In general, it is considered unethical for a forensic psychologist to both evaluate the potential perpetrator of workplace violence and treat the same individual as a patient. However, this does not mean that a treating clinician, with proper authorization, cannot provide data that may inform the risk abatement process.

• What type of notification of informed consent must be provided? Neither the "Ethical Principles of Psychologists and Code of Conduct" (APA, 2002) nor the "Specialty Guidelines for Forensic Psychologists" (Committee on Ethical Guidelines for Forensic Psychologists, 1991) specifically address informed consent in the context of a workplace violence threat assessment process, but general guidelines can be inferred and documented in the consent form:

—If the subject is being mandated to participate, this should be clearly stated.

—Under most circumstances, there is no psychologist-patient relationship; the person is undergoing a forensic threat assessment, not psychotherapy. Although the forensic psychologist will have a professional relationship to the examinee, confidentiality does not exist.

—There is no privilege (control) of the evaluation records by the subject of the evaluation. The client is the company making the referral. A report may be generated or information discussed with the referring company. The forensic psychologist, of course, should use discretion about disclosing information. It is important to be familiar with applicable state and federal statutes concerning what kind of, and under what circumstances, information can be released, even with a signed consent form.

—All possible outcomes of the risk assessment should be disclosed. For example, in a fitness-for-duty threat assessment these would include (a) fit for duty without restrictions, (b) fit for duty with mandatory counseling, (c) temporarily unfit for duty with mandatory counseling, or (d) permanently unfit for duty.

By informing subjects of the possible outcomes, they can determine if they want to participate in the evaluation. If they elect not to participate, consequences of the refusal (possible job termination) should be discussed. The minimum acceptable forensic practice in a face-to-face risk/threat assessment is written informed consent. Such notification should be carefully documented. Verbal informed consent is acceptable for those occasions when a remote threat assessment (e.g., by telephone) may be necessary.

• Who has access to the results of the evaluation? Although privilege is waived during most forensic risk assessments, the subject of the evaluation may be entitled to a summary of the examiner's findings. This feedback may be verbal or written at the forensic psychologist's discretion.

• If psychological tests will be utilized, can the examiner demonstrate the utility of the test to the assessment question being asked? There is great debate in the forensic arena about the use of projective tests, such as the Rorschach (Gacono, Evans, & Viglione, 2002; Wood, Nezworski, Stejskal, & McKinzey, 2001; Chapter 5). The justification for use of projective techniques in workplace risk assessment should be carefully considered. There are specific tests (e.g., Hilson Safety/Security Risk Inventory [HSRI]; Inwald, 1995), that, although not normed on workplace violence perpetrators, include germane questions related to violent or "risky" behavior. For example, the HSRI has scales that measure "lack of anger control," "risk taking patterns," and "lack of work ethic." Inwald, the test developer, indicates there is "an inverse relationship between lack of social judgment and work history to engaging in anti-social behaviors and risk taking patterns" (R. Inwald, personal communication, May 2005).

• Who does the evaluator question and in what order? It depends on the nature of the threat. For example, if an employee calls from home indicating that she will bring a bomb to work in 4 hours, it is probably more prudent to direct the initial risk assessment questions to her, as opposed to gathering a group of her coworkers to interview. Collateral sources are often helpful to inform the unfolding events.

THE WORKPLACE TARGETED THREAT ASSESSMENT PROCESS

One model for assessing targeted violence in the workplace is based on the threat assessment protocol developed by the United States Secret Service. This procedure is defined as "a set of operational activities that combine the use of an investigative process and information gathering strategies with target-violence relevant questions" (Reddy et al., 2001, p. 168). This definition may seem similar to other risk assessment strategies, yet there are significant differences in its theoretical underpinnings. Empirically guided or actuarial systems are inductively based (Turvey, 1999), using risk factors derived from a known population to classify the examinee into a discrete risk category and then derive an intervention strategy. The Secret Service threat assessment approach is deductive, based on a series of 10 research-based questions (Fein & Vossekuil, 1998).

Three core principals form the bulwark. First, targeted violence is predicated on the thinking processes and preattack behaviors of the subject that are identifiable. For example, weapon selection, method of attack, purpose of attack, and psychological factors should be considered. Second, targeted violence occurs because of a specific interaction between the perpetrator and the target, mediated by current and past situational (stressful) contextual experiences. Third, specific factors about the target, including environmental vulnerability and the subject's information-gathering processes about the target's behaviors and lifestyle, are considered.

This process focuses on information gathered about each unique case to generate inferences (as opposed to relying on risk factors) to determine if the individual subject is on a pathway of aggression toward an identified, or identifiable, target. Multiple collateral sources of data are explored. The rate of this acceleration toward the target is captured in the acronym ACTION (Borum & Reddy, 2001):

> *Attitudes that support or facilitate violence:* Does the subject believe that violence is a justifiable solution? What provocation is necessary to engage in the violent act? Will this violent act support the ultimate goal of the subject?
>
> *Capacity:* What are the subject's physical and intellectual abilities to carry out the threat? Does he or she have the means (e.g., access to weapons) and opportunity (e.g., proximity) to carry out the attack?
>
> *Thresholds crossed:* Has the subject engaged in illegal behaviors (e.g., stalking) to further the plan for violence? Does the subject care about going to jail?
>
> *Intent:* Many people threaten, but few carry out the threat. The key question is whether the person has psychologically shifted from rumination about an attack to action toward the target.
>
> *Others' reactions:* Some social support systems (e.g., terrorist groups) encourage violence. Other support systems (e.g., family, influential coworkers) may discourage or interfere with the aggressive act. Interpersonal insensitivity, as reflected in lack of interest in other people's opinions to mitigate violence, may put the subject at increased risk.
>
> *Noncompliance:* How likely is the subject to be compliant with work recommendations (i.e., avoid the target) and treatment recommendations? Does the subject evidence sufficient insight about his or her own contribution to the current situation?

Intervention strategies are then devised to disrupt the pathway to violence. By attempting to distinguish between the issuance of a threat and the intent to implement the content of the threat, the emphasis is placed on risk mitigation, as opposed to solely risk prediction. Following are the 10 key questions identified in the Secret Service study (Fein & Vossekuil, 1998), along with comments by this chapter's author on their application specifically to workplace targeted threat assessment.

Question 1

What motivated the subject to make statements or take action that caused him or her to come to attention? People do not necessarily threaten before they take an aggressive action. Therefore, the forensic psychologist should inquire about why this event is now taking place. In the workplace, such motivations may include (a) disruption of normal business routine, (b) informing the workplace of a potential problem, (c) intimidating the target, or (d) calling attention to self to prevent homicide/suicide. In this author's experience, a sense of "perceived injustice" frequently permeates workplace threats. This may be overlooked by forensic psychologists, perhaps because of a lack of familiarity with the organizational retaliatory behavior (ORB) literature. Skarlicki and Folger (1997) define ORB as specific disruptive behaviors by an employee who feels he or she was treated unfairly by the employer. Perceived injustice has its grounding in equity theory (Homans, 1961), which evaluates the income-output expectation ratio between two employees or an employee and an organization. *Distributive injustice* occurs when an employee perceives that he or she has not received a fair share of the bounty a company has to distribute, such as time off, a bonus recognition for a task, or a pay increase (Greenberg, 1990). A sense of *procedural injustice* occurs when the employee believes that the organization's policies and procedures are being enacted in an inconsistent, biased, or unethical way (Cropanzano & Folger, 1989). An employee may perceive *interactional (or interpersonal) injustice* by a supervisor's lack of respect, not providing adequate information about decisions, or acting in an interpersonally insensitive manner. A perception of unjust treatment in the workplace may lead to retaliatory behavior in an attempt to reestablish psychological equilibrium. Such acts generally do not include significant physical aggression (Skarlicki & Folger, 1997).

Although retaliation is certainly important to understand motivation, this author's experience suggests, and recent literature supports, that the difference between those who threaten and those who pose a realistic threat is the presence of the need for revenge (Bies & Tripp, 2005). Aquino, Tripp, and Bies (2001) define revenge as an action by an employee in the face of perceived injustice that serves to injure or punish the wrongdoer. Retaliation consists of a set of less than lethal behaviors. Revenge is the motive for interpersonal aggression. A workplace targeted threat assessment is incomplete without inquiry into perceived injustices and motivation for revenge.

Question 2

What has the subject communicated to anyone concerning his or her intentions? There are three kinds of threats:

1. *Direct threat:* The specific target, specific perpetrator, and specific outcome are clearly identifiable. Significant linguistic analysis is not necessary to understand the content of a direct threat.
2. *Conditional threat:* The unique conditions that must be present for the aggressive act to happen are described (e.g., "If you don't bring my tools back tomorrow by 8 A.M., then I'm going to punch you in the head"). A conditional threat may allow a quick de-escalation of potential aggression by satisfying the "if" part of the threat; in this case, return of the tools. However, this is not

to suggest that conditional threats are any less serious than direct threats, but this type of threat may allow for rapid mitigation strategies to be enacted.

3. *Veiled threat:* The receiver of this communication generally responds by experiencing a physiological sensation of uneasiness but cannot pinpoint the exact threat content. There is a lack of specificity of outcome and motivation for action in this type of threat, such as a statement by an employee to a supervisor: "Tomorrow you'll be sorry." Typically, threats will be delivered to one or more audiences: (a) the target, (b) coworker(s), (c) a supervisor, (d) a family member, or (e) organizational representatives (e.g., human resources, security, or occupational health). The threat delivery system may be verbal, written, or even a videotape. Special attention should be paid to the subject's report of impending loss of volitional control.

Question 3

Has the subject shown an interest in targeted violence, perpetrators of targeted violence, weapons, extremist groups, or murder? Some individuals who threaten in the workplace evidence identification with the aggressor. They may verbalize, "I understand why the person at another company killed his supervisor. I'm in the same spot he was in." Weapon inquiry should not only focus on access to weapons, but, more important, whether the subject envisions the weapon as a "power equalizer" against the target. Inquiries about contemporary weapon proficiency practice, special weapon training, and type of weapon availability is appropriate. Too frequently, a weapon is interpreted to be a handgun, rifle, or shotgun. Also inquire about explosives, biological and chemical agents, and exotic weapons such as compound hunting bows and martial arts devices. Membership or interest in extremist groups that espouse violence should be evaluated.

Question 4

Has the subject engaged in attack-related behavior, including any menacing, harassing, and/or stalking type behavior? Attack-related behaviors include gathering intelligence on the victim's habits and lifestyle, analysis of security protective barriers and procedures in the workplace, and approaching the victim in novel or unusual ways. Stalking is described as multiple approach behaviors toward a target that cause the target to fear for his or her safety (Meloy & Gothard, 1995). Meloy, Davis, and Lovette (2001) identified three risk factors of violent stalkers that differentiate them from nonviolent stalkers: (1) history of sexual intimacy with the victim, (2) lack of Axis I major mental disorder, and (3) an explicit threat.

Domestic violence, which may or may not include stalking, clearly affects the workplace. In a 1997 national survey, 74% of domestic violence victims reported being harassed at work by their abuser (Wells, 2004). Triggering behaviors by the victim should be examined. For example, Walker and Meloy (1998) noted that a woman is at highest risk for spousal homicide after a separation has been initiated. A significant finding by Rosenfeld and Harmon (2002, p. 672) in a study of "stalking and obsessional harassment" was that "criminal history and previous violence was unrelated to violence in the course of stalking and harassment cases" based on access to official arrest records. This finding is in stark contrast to other, similar research (Mullen, Pathé, Purcell, & Stuart, 1999) and suggests that in special circumstances such as harassment and stalking, the reliance on the dictum of past behavior predicting future behavior needs to be judiciously applied.

Question 5

Does the subject have a history of mental illness involving command hallucinations, delusional ideas, feelings of persecution, and so on, with indications that the subject has acted on those beliefs? The true base rate for mental disorder for those who threaten or carry out threats in the workplace is largely unknown. Feldman and Johnson (1996) studied 252 incidents of workplace violence. They gathered information from news accounts and personally conducted consultations. The most frequent diagnosis for the perpetrator was Antisocial Personality Disorder (20.71%), followed by depression (18.93%), substance abuse disorders (13.93%), and psychotic disorders (10.36%). A human resource publication (*IOMA,* 2005) cites a reconstructive study using media sources that found a mental health history of 13.4% in perpetrators of workplace violence.

Clinical common sense has suggested that the presence of a major mental illness greatly enhances the probability of violence due to lack of volitional control. Some research (Binder & McNiel, 1988) suggests that because of hyperarousability and other dyscontrol symptoms, individuals in the manic phase of a Bipolar Type Disorder are at a higher risk for acting out inappropriately. Monahan et al. (2001) found that in discharged psychiatric patients, the 1-year prevalence rate for violence was almost twice as high for those diagnosed with depression (28.5%) versus a diagnosis of Schizophrenia (14.8%). Patients diagnosed with Bipolar Disorder were in the middle (22%). However, a multiplier (two to three times) for violence across all three groups was the concomitant use of alcohol or drugs. The highest group at risk for violence was diagnosed with a personality or adjustment disorder and substance abuse.

The key forensic risk factors for those with a mental disorder are (a) substance use in combination with diminished behavioral control, (b) medication/treatment noncompliance, and (c) the presence of violent thoughts (Monahan et al., 2001). Grisso, Davis, Vesselinov, Appelbaum, and Monahan (2000) devised a useful tool, the Schedule of Imagined Violence, to systematically evaluate violent cognitions in a structural way by inquiring about presence of violent thoughts; recency, frequency, chronicity of violent thoughts; type of harm planned; target selection; change in seriousness of harm; and proximity to the target.

Threat/control override delusions should be asked about. These are a special kind of delusion that require a focused investigation. The astute forensic examiner will ask the subject: "Is someone trying to harm you?" "What is the motivation to harm you?" and "Do external forces have the ability to control your actions or thoughts?" Command hallucinations are another symptom calling for special attention. Approximately 39% to 89% of psychotic individuals who experience command hallucinations, including commands to commit violence, comply (Hersh & Borum, 1998). The forensic examiner should inquire about the identity of the voice, the frequency and context of past compliance with a specific command, current ability to resist the command, the presence of a delusional belief that supports the command, and if there is a specific command for violence.

Question 6

How organized is the subject? Is he or she capable of developing and carrying out a plan? FBI studies of serial killers have proposed an "organized" versus "disorganized" scheme (O'Toole, 1999). Even a very disorganized perpetrator is capable of carrying out a fatal attack. The forensic examiner should evaluate current cognitive abilities, focusing on the capacity to (a) concentrate on tasks, (b) link together various sources of data, (c) acquire a weapon, (d) move toward the target in a logical and perhaps undetected way, and (e) defeat security/protective barriers. By adopting the perpetrator's model of the world, the forensic psychologist should also evaluate what mitigating/aggravating factors about the attack can be envisioned.

Question 7

Has the subject experienced a recent loss and/or loss of status, and has this led to feelings of desperation and despair? Losses, real or imagined, can be pathways to impaired function. For example, Price, Choi, and Vinokur (2002) noted that an activating event such as job loss, perceived as a reduction in personal control, may be expressed as a mental health issue. The nature of the loss, ranging from the death of a pet (Sharkin & Knox, 2003) to deficits in physical ability (Rothermund & Brandstädter, 2003) and loss of a job, may not correlate with the perceived psychological value of the loss. Areas of inquiry should focus on loss of relationships, environmental/material possessions, and perceived status changes. After identifying the area(s) of loss, it is advisable to examine the relationship between perception of the loss, the psychological impact of the loss, and subsequent action regulation control. An inverse relationship exists between despair and resilience such that the more desperate the person becomes and the higher the attribution bias of cause of despair to the target, the higher the risk.

The study of resilience is relatively new (Bonanno, 2004), but application to forensic risk assessment is apparent. The core question is how sufficient is the perpetrator's ability to maintain psychological equilibrium following a significant loss. Analysis should be on the personality trait of "hardiness," which has three components: (1) finding a purpose in life, (2) the capacity to evaluate and influence the outcome of current precipitating events, and (3) the belief that one can benefit from both positive and negative life experiences (Kobasa, Maddi, & Kahn, 1982).

If an individual threatens to commit suicide, and the attribution for the suicidal ideation is attached to the workplace, he or she is at higher risk for committing homicide in the workplace (Burgess, Burgess, & Douglas, 1994). That is, employees who say "This place is driving me crazy and I'm going to kill myself here at work" have less inhibition for lethal attack on their tormentors because they have decided to end their own life.

Over a 10-year period (1992 to 2001), 2,170 workers committed suicide in the workplace, about 3.5% of all workplace fatalities. At work, an individual is at higher risk from homicide than suicide. Away from work, the opposite is true. Ninety-four percent of work-related suicides were men. Relative risk indicators that increase risk for suicide in the workplace are sex (male), race (Caucasian), age (55 and older), and being self-employed. Among all occupations, police officers had the highest relative risk (Pegula, 2004).

Question 8

Corroboration. What is the subject saying, and is it consistent with his or her actions? As noted previously, most subjects who threaten to kill in the workplace admit to the threat. This author's experience suggests that the main motivation for threatening is to call attention to perceived grievances in the workplace. Secondarily, these subjects want some intervention to disrupt their plan, without the perception that they cannot control their own behavior. Although the subject may acknowledge making the threat, he or she may tend to dissimulate about culpability in the events leading up to the threat by saying, "Yes, I said I would blow the place up, but I was just kidding. I was a little mad, but anybody in my place would be and I didn't say I would bring in dynamite and attach it to the main generator of the plant." Therefore, multiple collateral sources of information (e.g., coworkers, supervisors, and employment records) are important. The ability to assess credibility of received information is a critical skill for a forensic psychologist. Familiarity with the literature on the detection of behavioral deception (Frank & Ekman, 2004) is advisable.

Question 9

Is there concern among those who know the subject that he or she might take action based on inappropriate ideas? The potential of imminent behavioral dysregulation should be addressed. The pioneering work by Dollard, Doob, Miller, Mowrer, and Sears (1939) on the relationship between frustration and aggression is highly relevant. Specific attention should focus on environmental conditions that lead to frustration, the emotional response (such as anger to the workplace event), and the cognitive appraisal systems engaged in response to the provocation of aggression (Fox & Spector, 1999).

Question 10

What factors in the subject's life and/or environment might increase/decrease the likelihood of the subject's attempting to attack a target? Destabilizing environmental factors include access to and use of psychoactive substances. Protective (or mitigating) factors are important to assess (Swanson et al., 1997). Target availability is a key factor. A protective strategy of relocating the target does not diminish the impact of the perpetrator's psychiatric disorder but still significantly decreases risk. On the other hand, increasing the perpetrator's social support system, decreasing workplace expectancies, assessing financial stability, and enhancing treatment compliance through a workplace behavioral contract are perpetrator-centered risk mitigation strategies.

Table 20.4   The Workplace Targeted Threat Assessment Process

I. Understanding the nature of the threat	A. What is the threat? B. What is the likelihood of imminence of threat action? C. Is a forensic threat assessment needed?

II. Conducting a forensic threat assessment	A. Document everything.
	B. Review personnel file (of subject and target) and other data sources.
	C. Interview the subject(s).
	D. Interview the target(s).
	E. Interview the collateral sources.
	   1. Supervisor
	   2. Coworkers
	   3. Spouse/significant other
	   4. Past employer(s)
	F. Consider doing a background investigation.
	G. Use a structured risk assessment method.

III. Risk management	A. Protect the target.
	B. Protect property.
	C. Consider contacting law enforcement/criminal prosecution.
	D. Consider contacting emergency mental health provider.
	E. Consider a restraining order.
	F. Develop a specific plan based on the risk assessment to modify/control:
	   1. Subject behavior
	   2. Work-related variables
	   3. Extrawork-related variables
	   4. Target behavior
	G. If the subject is going to be terminated, evaluate if this is a high-risk termination.

The forensic examiner should evaluate not only current protective or destabilizing factors, but also forecast "what if" scenarios so that a proactive, rather than a reactive, risk abatement plan can be implemented. Workplace targeted violence assessment should be conducted in a logical and coherent way (see Table 20.4).

RISK COMMUNICATION

How information about the risk assessment outcome is conveyed greatly influences the utility of that information. In an attempt to explain communication errors, Karelitz and Budescu (2004) noted that when "probabilities" are not clearly explained, errors in communication occur. Such miscommunication between the sender and the receiver of the information can have disastrous results. Most communicators of risk information want to express a clinical opinion ("I don't think he is at risk for being violent"), whereas the receiver wants to get precise, numerical information ("There is a 60% probability he will be violent"; Wallsten, Budescu, Zwick, & Kemp, 1993).

Heilbrun, O'Neill, Strohman, Bowman, and Philipson (2000) identified six strategies for conveying risk information:

> (1) The probability that Mr. X will commit a violent act towards others over the next Y months is X. (2) Mr. X, a Y year old male with a certain status (e.g., 'a 45 year old male with a violence history, no substance abuse problem, and not psychopathic'). (3) Mr. X's risk of committing a violent act towards others is (high versus moderate versus low). (4) Mr. X's risk of committing a violent act towards others is dependent upon (identified risk factors); to reduce risk (specify interventions to address each risk factor). (5) Mr. X is (dangerous versus not dangerous). (6) Mr. X is (%) likely to commit a violent act towards others. (p. 142)

The purpose of evaluating an individual in the workplace who has threatened harm is not to issue a general statement as to whether the person is dangerous or not. This author believes that the best model for communicating risk assessment information is to indicate the risk posed by a particular individual (a) with identified risk factors, (b) engaging in a specific set of behaviors, (c) under described circumstances, (d) toward an identified target, (e) within a circumscribed time frame, and (f) given the information currently available.

RISK MANAGEMENT: THE FINAL STEP

> The gods today stand friendly, that we may, Lovers in peace, lead on our days to age! But since the affairs of men rest still incertain, Let's reason with the worst that may befall.
> —William Shakespeare, *Julius Caesar,* Act 5, Scene 1

As Shakespeare noted: Expect the best and plan for the worst. The goal of the workplace risk management process is to immediately assess, control, reduce, and ultimately prevent the act of targeted violence. It is not primarily to psychotherapeutically intervene with the perpetrator to assist in developing insight into the underlying dynamics that drive the threatening behavior, although this may certainly be a secondary outcome.

Risk management strategies have been applied to the determination of insurance rates (Theil, 2001), risky behavior and outcomes (Warneryd, 1996), and terrorist attacks (Fleming, 1998). Across all venues, the basic risk management process has five components:

> (1) Identification and evaluation of exposure loss; (2) Development of cost efficient and effective alternative tools and techniques to effectively avoid, retain, transfer and/or control these exposures; (3) Selection of desirable alternatives within applicable budgetary constraints; (4) Implementation and administration of the chosen alternative(s) with (5) dynamic monitoring and feedback systems to better assure long-term effectiveness and efficiency of the ongoing effort. (Ferguson & Theil, 2003, p. 1)

Current forensic risk management approaches generally suggest identification of specific risk variables and subsequent integration of these into a strategy to promote risk reduction (Webster, Douglas, Belfage, & Link, 2000). Kraemer et al. (1997) suggest that a risk assessment process is separate from the generation of risk reduction strategies. Others (Douglas, Webster, Hart, Eaves, & Ogloff, 2001) have linked risk management and treatment strategies to specific risk assessment instruments, such as the HCR-20. Monahan et al. (2001) disagree with an integrated risk assessment approach and instead opine that it should be a bifurcated process. Calling risk reduction a "crucial issue," they suggested it is "best addressed on its own merits, separate from the issue of risk assessment" (p. 139). Monahan and Appelbaum (2000) do acknowledge that there may be "clues" from the risk assessment process (e.g., substance abuse, anger, and violent fantasies) that may inform risk management efforts, but they argue that in general violence assessment, there are too many risk variables to isolate those "causal" factors unique to the individual. Most risk management strategies in violence prevention have focused on "treatable" factors that reside within the subject of evaluation (i.e., psychological issues), with the assumption that these risk variables can be manipulated and such manipulation will lower the risk of violence.

However, this author believes that effective risk management involves the ability to transform risk data into actionable information in a dynamic environment. Therefore, multiple systems external to the subject of the evaluation (e.g., work environment, support system, target compliance) should also be examined for their sensitivity to manipulation and their subsequent impact on the deceleration of the pathway to aggression. Additionally, it is imperative to factor into the risk management strategy the likely probability of implementation for each mitigation strategy. Without such consideration, a sophisticated plan on paper could translate into a real-world disaster. For example, it is determined after a risk assessment that an employee who is significantly depressed and is threatening to hurt a coworker should be referred to a psychiatrist for psychopharmacology evaluation. The employee does not meet the criteria for involuntary hospital commitment. The company is in a remote location and the next available appointment with a psychiatrist is in 6 weeks. The employee indicated that he will keep the appointment but will not take the medication. Because the probability of medication compliance is low, other protective measures (e.g., additional security at the plant) might be in order. This real-world probability assessment should form the core of the risk management process and take place prior to the final risk mitigation presentation to the company.

A complete risk assessment process includes (a) identifying the perpetrator(s); (b) identifying the target(s); (c) quantifying the financial and psychological loss value of the target, should it occur; (d) analyzing the threat content, including the capability and intent of the perpetrator; (e) analyzing environmental vulnerabilities that can be exploited by the perpetrator to gain an advantage over risk mitigation strategies, and then identifying specific countermeasures (e.g., if the target of the threat always takes the same route home, a countermeasure would be to have her take a different route each day); and (f) assessing the cost/benefit of proposed countermeasures. The focus is on protecting the target and controlling the subject. Trade-offs between cost and benefit are evaluated. For example, putting a subject

Table 20.5   Item Risk Scoring

Risk Score	1–3	4–6	7–9
Risk level	Low to moderately low	Moderately low to moderately high	Moderately high to very high

under surveillance is very costly but may have high protection benefits if the subject is stalking the target.

Workplace Risk Exposure Formula

Given the paucity of workplace risk management strategies in the forensic literature, this author postulates a formula to calculate risk exposure level. This formula does not predict, as a final outcome, the actual risk level presented by the subject. That is only one part of the calculus. The purpose of the Workplace Risk Exposure Formula (WREF) is to assist the company in recognizing the liability/risk exposure level of the specific case and what steps need to be taken to manage such exposure.

$$R = VLT + 2(IRL) + NPI + NPC$$

where R = Overall risk level. VLT = The value of the loss/impact of loss of the target. IRL = Identified risk level of the subject's currently carrying out the threat to the target based on a risk assessment evaluation (this assessment can be based on actuarial, forensic/actuarial, or forensic risk data). NPI = Negative probability of implementation of risk management strategies. This also includes target compliance. The higher the negative probability (decreased likelihood of implementation), the higher the risk. For example, a risk mitigation strategy is to enroll the subject in a drug treatment program, but he refuses. The probability of compliance is therefore low (i.e., negative probability of noncompliance is high, and continued drug use increases the chances of behavioral dysregulation). NPC = Negative probability of countermeasures/protective options being implemented. The fewer the suggested resources for protective functions that are available or utilized, the higher the risk to the target.

By using a 1 to 9 scale, each item can be assigned a risk weight (see Table 20.5).

After calculating the formula of R = VLT + 2(IRL) + NPI + NPC, a total risk exposure level is suggested (see Table 20.6). The formula emphasizes that the

Table 20.6   Risk Exposure Level

Risk Score	5–15	16–30	31–45
Risk level	Low to moderately low	Moderately low to moderately high	Moderately high to very high

identified risk level of the subject (IRL) is of paramount concern and is given a weighting of twice the other categories.

Following are three different examples using the WREF.

——————————————— **Illustrative Cases** ———————————————

Case 1

Employee A (subject) said she recently purchased a gun and wants to kill her supervisor (target) because of the way she has been treated at work. Using a targeted workplace threat assessment process, it has been determined that the subject is currently using amphetamines, recently dropped out of therapy, is going through a divorce, blames her supervisor for her not receiving a promotion, and has followed her supervisor home to see where he lives. Risk mitigation strategies include getting her into a drug treatment program, transferring her to another work location, putting her under surveillance, and getting a forensic fitness-for-duty evaluation. Countermeasures/protective options include providing protection at the supervisor's home, notifying law enforcement of the threat, and encouraging the supervisor to take out a restraining order. The supervisor will not take out a restraining order and does not want personal protection because he does not consider her to be "serious" about her threat.

Using the WREF, VLT = The threat content is homicide and the value (loss of life) is 9 (very high); IRL = Identified risk level of the perpetrator is 8 (high); NPI = Negative probability of implementation of risk strategies is 7 (moderately high); and NPC = Negative probability of enacting countermeasures/protective options is 9 (very high), where low to moderately low probability = 1 to 3, moderately low to moderately high probability = 4 to 6, and moderately high to very high probability = 7 to 9. Therefore, in this case:

$$R = VLT\ (9) + 2(IRL)(2 \times 8) + NPI(7) + NPC(9) = 41$$

This would be considered a high-risk exposure case (see Table 20.6). This score would call for reevaluation of what other protective measures must be implemented to protect the target until the subject can be physically or psychologically stabilized.

Case 2

Employee A (subject) reported that she recently purchased a gun and wants to kill her supervisor (target) because of the way she has been treated at work. Employee A stated, and it has been confirmed, that her husband has taken control of the gun and removed it from the house to a place where the employee cannot gain access to it. She acknowledges using amphetamines and recently dropped out of therapy but is now willing to immediately commit herself to a substance abuse treatment program. She is under surveillance by the company, and it has been determined she has checked herself into a treatment program. At the company's request, she has signed a release of information form so her progress in treatment can be monitored. The manager has agreed to take out a restraining order, if that is recommended.

Using the WREF, this would be considered a moderate risk case: the VLT = Loss of life as a value is rated 9 (very high); IRL = Identified risk level of the subject currently carrying out the threat is 3 (moderately low); NPI = It would not be difficult to implement risk mitigation strategies, and thus is rated a 3 (moderately low); and, NPC = Countermeasures/protective options can and will be easily put in place and is rated a 2 (low). In this example:

$$R = VLT\ (9) + 2(IRL)\ (2 \times 3) + NPI(3) + NPC(2) = 20$$

In this case, even though the value of loss of the target (homicide) is high, other factors mitigate against the lethal act currently taking place. This does not mean the risk management function is complete. For example, when the employee is released from the substance abuse treatment facility, a new risk management exposure calculation should be conducted.

Case 3

Employee A is late with an assignment and, as a result, a project may have to be put on hold. He blames the breakdown of the copy machine for his predicament. He threatens to destroy the copy machine if it does not work immediately. So far, he has banged on it several times with his fist, damaging a control knob. This has caused his coworkers to become concerned about his psychological stability.

Notice that there can theoretically be a moderate exposure risk evaluation outcome with a low-value target. In this example, the copy machine (VLT) that the subject has threatened to destroy has a value as a target (to the company) of 2 (low); IRL = The subject is at high risk (8) to destroy the machine; NPI = He states that he will not obey a direct order to stay away from the copy machine and scores an 8 (high); and, because some security measures could be implemented if the company chooses, the NPC is scored 3 (moderately low). Using the WREF:

$$R = VLT(2) + 2(IRL)\ (2 \times 8) + NPI(8) + NPC(3) = 29$$

The company does not want to move or protect the copy machine. Because the value of the target is low and the cost of implementing protective measures is moderately low, the company decided that if the employee damages the machine after being warned, he will be terminated. A company may decide based on a moderate risk exposure outcome, not to put all available resources toward a low-value target (e.g., a copying machine).

The WREF is an initial attempt to quantify the risk management process by identifying the level of risk to a specific target under specific parameters of the perpetrator's behavior, given the likely implementation of mitigation strategies in combination with available security resources allocation. This formula is dynamic and can account for the fluid changes often seen when trying to implement a risk management process. Cutoff scores are somewhat arbitrary and are based on this author's experience. The WREF is appropriately used to help guide the risk mitigation strategy decision making, but it should not replace clinical acumen or common sense. It has no psychometric properties of a test. See Figure 20.4 for a description of the complete Workplace Targeted Risk Abatement model.

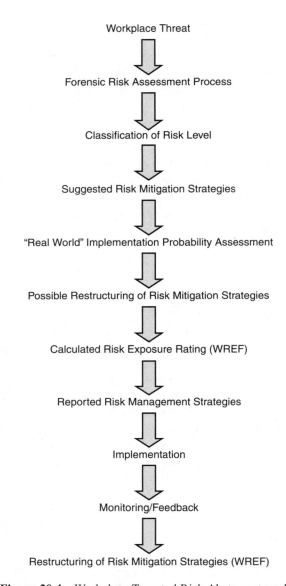

Figure 20.4   Workplace Targeted Risk Abatement model.

CONCLUSION

Forensic psychologists should embrace the opportunity to conduct workplace threat assessments. However, it is imperative that those agreeing to accept such referrals understand that these types of evaluations are significantly different from other, more traditional risk assessments. The forensic psychologist must be familiar with specific workplace-related risk factors, legal and ethical issues, and specialized evaluation techniques. Risk mitigation strategies should have real-world applications and be dynamic in relationship to the perpetrator's behavior, target compliance, and workplace ability to respond.

REFERENCES

Alaska. (2003). Chapter 85, SLA03 (House Bill 214).

Albrecht, S. (1997). *Fear and violence on the job: Prevention solutions for the dangerous workplace.* Durham, NC: Carolina Academic Press.

American Psychological Association. (2002). Ethical principles of psychologists and code of conduct. *American Psychologist, 57,* 1060–1073.

Americans with Disabilities Act, 29 C.F.R. § 1630.2(r) (1990).

Americans with Disabilities Act, 42 U.S.C. § 12101 (1990).

Americans with Disabilities Act, §§ 2(b)(1) and (2) (1990).

Aquino, K., Tripp, T. M., & Bies, R. J. (2001). How employees respond to personal offense: The effects of blame attribution, victim status, and offender status on revenge and reconciliation in the workplace. *Journal of Applied Psychology, 86,* 52–59.

Bailar, J. C., Needleman, J., Berney, B. L., & McGinnis, J. M. (Eds.). (1993). *Assessing risks to health: Methodological approaches.* Westport, CT: Auburn House.

Banks, S., Robbins, P. C., Silver, E., Vesselinov, R., Steadman, H. J., Monahan, J., et al. (2004). A multiple-models approach to violence risk assessment among people with mental disorder. *Criminal Justice and Behavior, 31,* 324–340.

Barefoot v. Estelle, 463 U.S. 880, 887, 103 S. Ct. 3383, 77 L.Ed.2d 1090 (1983).

Baron, R. A., & Richardson, D. R. (1994). *Human aggression* (2nd ed.). New York: Plenum Press.

Baron, S. A. (1993). *Violence in the workplace: A prevention and management guide for businesses.* Venture, CA: Pathfinders.

Bies, R. J., & Tripp, T. M. (2005). The study of revenge in the workplace: Conceptual, ideological, and empirical issues. In S. Fox & P. E. Spector (Eds.), *Counterproductive work behavior: Investigations of actors and targets* (pp. 65–81). Washington, DC: American Psychological Association.

Biles, P. D. (2004). OSHA issues workplace violence citation. *Workplace Violence Prevention Reporter, 10*(10), 3.

Binder, R. L., & McNiel, D. E. (1988). Effects of diagnosis and context on dangerousness. *American Journal of Psychiatry, 145,* 728–732.

Bonanno, G. A. (2004). Loss, trauma, and human resilience: Have we underestimated the human capacity to thrive after extremely aversive events? *American Psychologist, 59,* 20–28.

Borum, R., Bartell, P., & Forth, A. (2000). *Structured Assessment for Violence Risk in Youth (SAVRY)* (Version 1 consultation ed.). University of South Florida.

Borum, R., Fein, R., Vossekuil, B., & Berglund, J. (1999). Threat assessment: Defining an approach for evaluating risk of targeted violence. *Behavioral Sciences and the Law, 17,* 323–337.

Borum, R., Otto, R., & Golding, S. (1993). Improving clinical judgment and decision making in forensic evaluation. *Journal of Psychiatry and Law, 21,* 35–76.

Borum, R., & Reddy, M. (2001). Assessing violence risk in Tarasoff situations: A fact-based model of inquiry. *Behavioral Sciences and the Law, 19,* 375–385.

Borum, R., Super, J., & Rand, M. (2003). Forensic assessment for high-risk occupations. In I. B. Weiner (Series Ed.) & A. M. Goldstein (Vol. Ed.), *Comprehensive handbook of psychology: Vol. 11. Forensic psychology* (pp. 133–148). Hoboken, NJ: Wiley.

Brodsky, C. M. (1976). *The harassed worker.* Lexington, MA: Lexington Books.

Budd, J. W., Arvey, R. D., & Lawless, P. (1996). Correlates and consequence of workplace violence. *Journal of Occupational Health Psychology, 1,* 197–210.

Bureau of Justice Statistics. (2001). *Special report: Violence in the workplace, 1993–1999.* Washington, DC: U.S. Department of Justice.

Bureau of Labor Statistics. (2002). *Census of fatal occupational injuries.* Retrieved January 2005, from http://data.bls.gov/PDQ/servlet/SurveyOutputServlet.

Bureau of Labor Statistics. (2003). *Census of fatal occupational injuries.* Retrieved March 20, 2005, from http://data.bls.gov/PDQ/servlet/SurveyOutputServlet.

Burgess, A. W., Burgess, A. G., & Douglas, J. E. (1994). Examining violence in the workplace. *Journal of Psychosocial Nursing, 32,* 14.

California Occupational Safety and Health Act, Cal Lab Code § 6400 (1973).

Canadian Province of Quebec, Labour Standards Act (§ 81.18, June 1, 2004).

Castillo, D. N. (1995, July). Nonfatal violence in the workplace: Directions for future research. In C. R. Block & R. Block (Eds.), *Trends, risks, and interventions in lethal violence: Proceedings of the third annual spring symposium of the Homicide Research Working Group* (pp. 225–235). Washington, DC: U.S. Department of Justice.

Committee on Ethical Guidelines for Forensic Psychologists. (1991). Specialty guidelines for forensic psychologists. *Law and Human Behavior, 15,* 655–665.

Connell, M., & Koocher, G. P. (2003). Expert opinion: HIPAA and forensic practice. *American Psychology-Law Society News, 13,* 16–19.

Cropanzano, R., & Folger, R. (1989). Referent cognitions and task decision autonomy: Beyond equity theory. *Journal of Applied Psychology, 74,* 293–299.

Dixon, P. (1978). *Official rules.* New York: Delacorte Press.

Dollard, J., Doob, L. W., Miller, N. E., Mowrer, O. H., & Sears, R. R. (1939). *Frustration and aggression.* New Haven, CT: Yale University Press.

Douglas, K. S., & Kropp, P. R. (2002). A prevention-based paradigm for violence risk assessment: Clinical and research applications. *Criminal Justice and Behavior, 29,* 617–658.

Douglas, K. S., Webster, C. P., Hart, S. D., Eaves, D., & Ogloff, J. R. P. (2001). *HCR-20 violence risk management companion guide.* Burnaby, British Columbia, Canada: Simon Fraser University.

Ewing v. Northridge Hospital Medical Center, 120 CAL. App. 4th 1289, Cal. Rptr. 3d. (2004).

Fein, R. A., & Vossekuil, B. (1998). *Protective intelligence and threat assessment investigations: A guide for state and local law enforcement officials* (NIJ/OJP/DOJ publication, N.O. NCJ 170612). Washington, DC: US Department of Justice.

Fein, R. A., & Vossekuil, B. (1999). Assassination in the United States: An operational study of recent assassins, attackers, and near-lethal approaches. *Journal of Forensic Sciences, 50,* 321–333.

Feldman, T. B., & Johnson, P. W. (1996). Workplace violence: A new form of lethal aggression. In H. V. Hall (Ed.), *Lethal violence 2000: A sourcebook on fatal domestic, acquaintance, and stranger aggression* (pp. 311–338). Kamuela, HI: Pacific Institute for the Study of Conflict and Aggression.

Ferguson, W. L., & Theil, M. (2003). Risk management as a process: An international perspective. *Review of Business, 24,* 30–38.

Fleming, D. S. (1998). Assessing organizational vulnerability to acts of terrorism. *SAM Advanced Management Journal, 64,* 27–34.

Fox, S., & Spector, P. E. (1999). A model of work frustration: Aggression. *Journal of Organizational Behavior, 20,* 915–931.

Frank, M. G., & Ekman, P. (2004). Appearing truthful generalizes across different deception situations. *Journal of Personality and Social Psychology, 86,* 486–495.

Gacono, C. B., Evans, F. B., III, & Viglione, D. J. (2002). The Rorschach in forensic practice. *Journal of Forensic Psychology, 2,* 33–53.

Goklany, I. M. (2001). *The precautionary principle: A critical appraisal of environment risk assessment.* Washington, DC: Cato Institute.

Greenberg, J. (1990). Employee theft as a reaction to underpayment inequity: The hidden cost of pay cuts. *Journal of Applied Psychology, 75,* 561–568.

Grisso, T., & Appelbaum, P. (1998). *Assessing competence to consent to treatment: A guide for physicians and other health professionals.* New York: Oxford University Press.

Grisso, T., Davis, J., Vesselinov, R., Appelbaum, P. S., & Monahan, J. (2000, June). Violent thoughts and violent behavior following hospitalization for mental disorder. *Journal of Consulting and Clinical Psychology, 68,* 388–398.

Grove v. Rainbow International Carpet Dyeing and Cleaning Co., No. 91-3616-CA-J, Florida (1994).

Grove, W. M., & Meehl, P. E. (1996). Comparative efficiency in informal (subjective, impressionistic) and formal (mechanical, algorithmic) prediction procedures: The clinical-statistical controversy. *Psychology, Public Policy, and Law, 2,* 293–323.

Hall, H. V. (2001). Violence prediction and risk analysis: Empirical advances and guidelines. *Journal of Threat Assessment, 1,* 1–39.

Harris, G. T., Rice, M. E., Quinsey, V. L., Lalumiere, M. L., Boer, D., & Lang, C. (2003, September). A multisite comparison of actuarial risk instruments for sex offenders. *Psychological Assessment, 15,* 413–425.

Heilbrun, K., O'Neill, M. L., Strohman, L. K., Bowman, Q., & Philipson, J. (2000). Expert approaches to communicating violence risk. *Law and Human Behavior, 24,* 137–148.

Hersh, K., & Borum, R. (1998). Command hallucinations, compliance, and risk assessment. *Journal of the American Academy of Psychiatry and Law, 26,* 353–359.

Hogan, J., & Hogan, R. (1989). How to measure employee reliability. *Journal of Applied Psychology, 74,* 273–279.

Homans, G. C. (1961). *Social behavior: Its elementary forms.* New York: Harcourt, Brace and World.

Injury Prevention Center. (2001). *Workplace violence: A report to the nation.* Iowa City: University of Iowa Press.

Inwald, R. (1995). *Hilson Safety/Security Risk Inventory.* Kew Gardens, NY: Hilson Research.

IOMA. (2005, April). How to predict and prevent workplace violence. (2005, April). *HR Focus.* Retrieved April 20, 2005, from http://www.ioma.com.

James, L. R. (1998). *Organizational research methods.* Thousand Oaks, CA: Sage.

Jenkins, E. L. (1996). *Violence in the workplace: Risk factors and prevention strategies* (DHHS [NIOSH] Publication No. 96-100). Washington, DC: U.S. Government Printing Office.

Kansas v. Hendricks, 521 U.S. 346 (1997).

Karelitz, T. M., & Budescu, D. V. (2004). You say "probable" and I say "likely": Improving interpersonal communication with verbal probability phases. *Journal of Experimental Psychology: Applied, 10,* 25–41.

Kinney, J. A., & Johnson, D. L. (1993). *Breaking point: The workplace violence epidemic and what to do about it.* Chicago: National Safe Workplace Institute.

Klimoski, R., & Palmer, S. N. (1994). The ADA and the hiring process in organizations. In S. M. Bruyere & J. O'Keeffe (Eds.), *Implications of the Americans with Disabilities Act for psychology* (p. 56). New York: Springer.

Kobasa, S. C., Maddi, S. R., & Kahn, S. (1982). Hardiness and health: A prospective study. *Journal of Personality and Social Psychology, 42,* 168–177.

Kraemer, H., Kazdin, A., Offord, D., Kessler, R., Jensen, P., & Kripfer, D. (1997). Coming to terms with the terms of risk. *Archives of General Psychiatry, 54,* 337.

Kropp, P., Hart, S., Webster, C., & Eaves, D. (1999). *Spousal Assault Risk Assessment Guide user's manual.* Toronto, Ontario, Canada: Multi-Health Systems.

Labig, C. E. (1995). *Preventing violence in the workplace.* New York: American Management Association.

Levinson, H. (2002). *Organizational assessment.* Washington, DC: American Psychological Association.

Litwack, T. R. (2001). Actuarial versus clinical assessments of dangerousness. *Psychology, Public Policy, and Law, 7,* 409–443.

Lopez, R. D. (2005, January). *Managing violence in the workplace: Looking at the past, present, and future.* Paper presented at the U.S. Postal Inspection Service meeting on Workplace Violence Prevention and Investigations Training, Tampa, FL.

Macdonald, J., Knopman, D., Lockwood, J. R., Cecchine, G., & Willis, H. (2004). *Unexploded ordnance: A critical review of risk assessment methods.* Santa Monica, CA: RAND.

Mantell, M. (1994). *Ticking bombs: Defusing violence in the workplace.* New York: Richard D. Irwin.

Meehl, P. E. (1954). *Clinical versus statistical prediction: A theoretical analysis and a review of the evidence.* Minneapolis: University of Minnesota Press.

Meloy, J. R., Davis, B., & Lovette, J. (2001). Risk factors for violence among stalkers. *Journal of Threat Assessment, 1,* 3–16.

Meloy, J. R., & Gothard, S. (1995). A demographic and clinical comparison of obsessional followers and offenders with mental disorders. *American Journal of Psychiatry, 152,* 258–263.

Menzies, R., & Webster, C. D. (1995). Construction and validation of risk assessments in a 6-year follow-up of forensic patients: A tridimensional analysis. *Journal of Consulting and Clinical Psychology, 63,* 766–778.

Monahan, J. (1981). *The clinical prediction of violent behavior.* Washington, DC: U.S. Government Printing Office.

Monahan, J. (1988). Risk assessment of violence among the mentally disordered: Generating useful knowledge. *International Journal of Law and Psychiatry, 11,* 249–257.

Monahan, J., & Appelbaum, P. (2000). Reducing violence risk: Diagnostically based clues from the MacArthur Violence Risk Assessment Study. In S. Hodgins (Ed.), *Effective prevention of crime and violence among the mentally ill* (pp. 19–34). Dordrecht, The Netherlands: Kluwer Academic.

Monahan, J., Steadman, J. H., Silver, E., Appelbaum, P. S., Robbins, P. C., Mulvey, E. P., et al. (2001). *Rethinking risk assessment: The MacArthur Study of Mental Disorder and Violence.* New York: Oxford University Press.

Mullen, P. E., Pathé, M., Purcell, R., & Stuart, G. W. (1999). Study of stalkers. *American Journal of Psychiatry, 156,* 1244–1249.

Natasha Saive v. Comcast Cablevision of Arkansas, Inc., LEXIS 554, 20 IER CASES (BNA) 941 (Ark. 2003).

National Institute for Occupational Safety and Health. (1996). Violence in the workplace: Risk factors and prevention strategies. *Current Intelligence Bulletin, 57,* 14. Washington, DC: Department of Health and Human Services.

Neuman, J. H., & Baron, R. A. (1998). Workplace violence and workplace aggression: Evidence concerning specific forms, potential causes, and preferred targets. *Journal of Management, 24,* 391–419.

Northwestern National Life, Employee Benefits Division. (1993). *Fear and violence in the workplace: A survey documenting the experience of American workers.* Minneapolis, MN: Northwestern National Life.

Occupational Safety and Health Act, Sec. 5(A)(11), 29 U.S.C. § 654(a)(1) (1979).

O'Toole, M. E. (1999). Criminal profiling: The FBI uses criminal investigative analysis to solve crimes. *Corrections Today, 61,* 44–49.

Packer, I. K., & Borum, R. (2003). Forensic training and practice. In I. B. Weiner (Series Ed.) & A. M. Goldstein (Vol. Ed.), *Comprehensive handbook of psychology: Vol. 11. Forensic psychology* (pp. 21–32). Hoboken, NJ: Wiley.

Paton, D., & Smith, L. M. (1995). Work-related psychological trauma: A review of methodological and assessment issues. *Australian Psychologist, 30,* 200–209.

Pegula, S. M. (2004, January 28). *An analysis of workplace suicides, 1992–2001.* Washington, DC: Bureau of Labor Statistics. Available from http://www.bls.gov/opub/cwc/content/sh20040126ar01p1.stm.

Price, R. H., Choi, J. N., & Vinokur, A. D. (2002). Links in the chain of adversity following job loss: How financial strain and loss of personal control lead to depression, impaired functioning, and poor health. *Journal of Occupational Health Psychology, 7,* 302–312.

Quinsey, V. L., Harris, G. T., Rice, M. E., & Cormier, C. A. (1998). *Violent offenders: Appraising and managing risk.* Washington, DC: American Psychological Association.

Reddy, M., Borum, R., Berglund, J., Vossekuil, B., Fein, R., & Modzeleski, W. (2001). Evaluating risk for targeted violence in schools: Comparing risk assessment, threat assessment and other approaches. *Psychology in the Schools, 38,* 157–171.

Reiss, A. J., Jr. & Roth, J. A. (Eds.). (1993). *Understanding and preventing violence: Vol. 3. Social influences.* Washington, DC: National Academy Press.

Rosenfeld, B., & Harmon, R. (2002). Factors associated with violence in stalking and obsessional harassment cases. *Criminal Justice and Behavior, 29,* 671–691.

Rothermund, K., & Brandstädter, J. (2003). Coping with deficits and losses in later life: From compensatory action to accommodation. *Psychology and Aging, 18,* 896–905.

Saelzler v. Advanced Group 400, 25 Cal. 4th 763 (2001).

Sharkin, B. S., & Knox, D. (2003). Pet loss: Issues and implications for the psychologist. *Professional Psychology: Research and Practice, 34,* 414–421.

Simmons v. U.S., 805 F.2d 1363. (9th Cir. 1986).

Skarlicki, D. P., & Folger, R. (1997). Retaliation in the workplace: The roles of distributive, procedural, and interactional justice. *Journal of Applied Psychology, 82,* 434–443.

Stock, H. V. (1997). *Behavioral risk assessment system: Proprietary instrument.* Plantation, FL.

Stock, H. V. (2000, August). *Pathological organizational affective attachment: Why some people threaten to kill in the workplace.* Paper presented at the annual convention of the American Psychological Association, Presidential Miniconvention on Law, Psychology, and Violence in the Workplace, Washington, DC.

Stock, H. V. (2002, April). *Executive overview: Law enforcement's response to workplace violence: A new role.* Paper presented at a meeting of the National Center for the Analysis of Violent Crime, FBI Academy, Quantico, VA.

Swanson, J. W., Estroff, S., Swartz, M. S., Borum, R., Lachicotte, W. W., Zimmer, C., et al. (1997). Violence and severe mental disorder in clinical and community populations: The effects of psychotic symptoms, comorbidity and lack of treatment. *Psychiatry: Interpersonal and Biological Processes, 60,* 1–22.

Tarasoff v. Regents of the University of California, 13 Cal. 3d 177, 529 P.2d 533 (1974), VACATED, 17 Cal. 3d 425, 551 P.2d 334 (1976).

Tedeschi, J. T., & Felson, R. B. (1994). *Violence, aggression and coercive actions.* Washington, DC: American Psychological Association.

Theil, M. (2001). Demographic variables and the appraisal of insurance: The case of assistance products. *Journal of Risk Management and Insurance, 6,* 16–28.

Turvey, B. E. (1999). The deductive method of criminal profiling. In B. Turvey (Ed.) *Criminal profiling: An introduction to behavioral evidence analysis* (pp. 25–32). San Diego, CA: Academic Press.

U.S. Department of Health and Human Services (1996, August 21). *Public law 1104-191: Health Insurance Portability and Accountability Act of 1996.* Retrieved May 20, 2005, from http://aspe.hhs.gov /admnsimp/pl1104191.jtm.

U.S. Department of Justice, Federal Bureau of Investigation, National Center for the Analysis of Violent Crime. (2004). *Workplace violence: Issues in response.* Quantico, VA: FBI Academy.

U.S. Department of Labor, Occupational Safety and Health Administration. (1996). *Guidelines for preventing workplace violence for health care and social service workers.* Washington, DC: Author.

U.S. Postal Service. (2000). *Annual report: Report of the United States Postal Commission on a safe and secure workplace.* Washington, DC: U.S. Government Printing Office.

von Bertalanffy, L. (1950). An outline of general systems theory. *British Journal of Philosophical Science, 1,* 134–163.

Walker, L. E., & Meloy, J. R. (1998). Stalking and domestic violence. In J. R. Meloy (Ed.), *The psychology of stalking: Clinical and forensic perspectives* (pp. 139–161). San Diego, CA: Academic Press.

Wallsten, T. S., Budescu, D. V., Zwick, R., & Kemp, S. M. (1993, March). Preferences and reasons for communicating probabilistic information in verbal or numerical terms. *Bulletin of the Psychonomic Society, 31,* 135–138.

Warneryd, K. E. (1996). Risk attitudes and risky behaviour. *Journal of Economic Psychology, 17,* 749–770.

Washington Industrial Safety and Health Services Agency. (1997, January 14). *Regional Directive 5.05.*

Webster, C. D., Bloom, H., & Eisen, R. S. (2003). Toward the scientific and professional assessment of violence potential in the workplace. *Journal of Threat Assessment, 2,* 1–15.

Webster, C. D., Douglas, K. S., Belfage, H., & Link, B. G. (2000). Capturing change: An approach to managing violence and improving mental health. In S. Hodgins (Ed.), *Violence among the mentally ill: Effective treatments and management strategies* (pp. 119–144). Dordrecht, The Netherlands: Kluwer Academic.

Webster, C. D., Douglas, K. S., Eaves, D., & Hart, S. D. (1997). *HCR-20: Assessing risk for violence* (Version 2). Burnaby, British Columbia, Canada: Simon Fraser University.

Wells, K. (2004, November). *Domestic violence in the workplace.* Paper presented at Partnering in Workplace Violence Prevention: Translating Research to Practice Conference, National Institute for Occupational Safety and Health, Baltimore.

Wood, J. M., Nezworski, M. T., Stejskal, W. J., & McKinzey, R. K. (2001). Problems of the comprehensive system for the Rorschach in forensic settings: Recent developments. *Journal of Forensic Practice, 1,* 89–103.

PART VIII

Special Populations

CHAPTER 21

Developmental Considerations for Forensic Assessment in Delinquency Cases

Randy Borum and Thomas Grisso

In 1899, a separate system of justice for juveniles was conceived and implemented based on the largely uncontroversial proposition that children and adolescents differ from adults in ways that can affect their participation in legal proceedings, culpability, and potential for rehabilitation (Grisso & Schwartz, 2000). Those differences were assumed to arise from developmental capacities. More than 100 years later, the empirical evidence for those differences is stronger than ever. Yet, the notion that juvenile justice should take into account youths' developmental differences from adults fell out of public favor in recent years, having been replaced by a perspective that youths' transgressions should be met with punishment, as they are with adults, rather than rehabilitation. The reasons for this transformation are myriad. We discuss them briefly here, although the main purpose of this chapter is to demonstrate that developmental considerations are essential for assessing and understanding psycholegal capacities in delinquency cases and to provide some practical guidance for forensic evaluators to conduct a more developmentally informed forensic psychological assessment (Grisso, 2003).

THE RISE AND FALL OF DEVELOPMENT IN JUVENILE JUSTICE

How did such a broad and pervasive shift occur in the balance of rehabilitation and punishment in the juvenile justice system? The reasons were ideological and political, not based on a weighing of the developmental evidence as it might inform legal policy (Grisso, 1996).

An unfortunate polemic has evolved that obscures the more complex realities of human behavior (Clausel & Bonnie, 2000). At one extreme were the "hard-liners," who believed that attempts to treat juveniles did not work and that reliance on rehabilitation was contrary to the fundamental principles of jurisprudence and social control. Their viewpoint was fueled by fear in the midst of what is now known to have been a temporary increase in juvenile homicide in the late 1980s and early 1990s (U.S. Department of Health and Human Services, 2001). They believed that "adult crimes" should be met with "adult time." In their scheme of justice, the historical focus on rehabilitation in juvenile justice had contributed to an increase in juvenile offending—particularly violent crime—and sent an inappropriate message to young people that their misdeeds and bad choices were not their fault and did not have serious consequences. As the decade of the 1990s closed, another position arose that, at its extreme, seemed to hold that no youth's bad deed should go untreated. Notions of punishment and accountability had no place in this plan, which saw delinquency as a signal to treat damaged and misguided youths whose unfortunate life circumstances had ushered them into contact with the legal system.

Both extremes tend to be guided more by ideological and philosophical assumptions than by established theory and empirical evidence. Although there are gaps in the base of scientific knowledge about childhood and adolescent development, there is now much that can guide a more rational policy of juvenile justice. In this chapter, however, our focus is on the use of that body of theory and empirical evidence to assist the forensic mental health professional in conducting a more developmentally informed assessment in delinquency cases. By applying those principles, the evaluator can help bridge the gap between developmental science and juvenile justice policy.

WHAT IS A DEVELOPMENTAL PERSPECTIVE?

Developmental psychopathology is a relatively new conceptual approach (Cicchetti, 1984, 1990). It offers a useful framework not only for scholars and researchers, but also for forensic clinicians and applied psychologists. Wenar and Kerig (2000) define developmental psychopathology as "the study of the developmental processes [and pathways] that contribute to the formation of [risk factors], or resistance to [protective factors], psychopathology" (p. 19). The metaphor of the pathway is a central concept in this model of development. This perspective does not view behaviors as distinctly normal or abnormal, each with its own unique pathogenesis. Psychopathology and behavioral deviances are assumed to be the product of excesses or deficits in certain abilities, traits, or behaviors that are otherwise not uncommon. That which is unusual or abnormal is still connected to a common developmental process. Disorders are regarded as deviations in the process, not as a separate problem in the way that one might view a malignant tumor. Accordingly, this model allows for an integrated study of normal and abnormal development.

Describing a few basic terms and concepts will help to introduce the developmental psychopathology framework, particularly as it might be applied to understanding and assessing psycholegal capacities. First, developmental psychopathology takes a decidedly holistic perspective on human behavior, grounded in what is called the *organizational perspective*. Accordingly, humans (adults *and* juveniles) are viewed as an "integrated and dynamic system in which all domains of development—the cognitive, social, emotional, and biological—are in continual interaction with one another" (Wenar & Kerig, 2000, p. 19). The traditional "nature versus nurture" dichotomy of human development is outdated and inconsistent with the current state of research in the field. The organizational perspective accounts for the fact that biological, psychological, and social factors all affect development and behavior and that often these elements will also affect each other (Cicchetti & Toth, 1998).

In this model, progressions in a developmental process are also cumulative, so that the resolution of each task builds on the foundations laid by the preceding ones.

In essence, "psychological growth is a process of increasing complexity and organization, such that new structures emerge out of those that have come before" (Wenar & Kerig, 2000, p. 19). This is referred to as the *hierarchical principle*. For example, if one is using Erickson's (1963) psychosocial stage model to understand how a particular adolescent is coping with his or her crisis of identity, then it would be probative to examine how the prior stage crises, such as trust versus mistrust, have been resolved because they cumulatively form the psychosocial foundation for the present struggle.

Finally, as we noted, developmental psychopathologists characterize development as a series of *pathways*. With that perspective in mind, it is important for evaluators to appreciate that any given path may lead to different destinations; conversely, the same destination can be reached by different paths. These maxims are reflected in this framework (as they are in other physical sciences, such as biology) in the concepts of *multifinality* and *equifinality,* respectively. Simply stated, equifinality is the idea that "a number of different pathways may lead to the same outcome" (Wenar & Kerig, 2000, p. 23). Multifinality reflects the reality that "a particular risk may have different developmental implications, depending on such contextual and intraindividual factors as the child's environment and his or her particular competencies and capacities" (p. 23).

THE UTILITY OF DEVELOPMENTAL CONCEPTS FOR UNDERSTANDING YOUTHS' ILLEGAL BEHAVIORS

Children and adolescents are in a constant state of change. So are adults, of course, but children's and adolescents' capacities and characteristics change more rapidly within a given span of time. This fluid developmental status is a key part of what sets them apart from adults (Borum & Verhaagen, in press; Griffin & Torbet, 2002; Grisso, 1998; McCord, Widom, & Crowell, 2001; Rosado, 2000). There are at least three critical domains in which humans develop: physical, cognitive, and psychosocial (also referred to as social/emotional). In each of them, changes tend to evolve and develop gradually, rather than appearing as a sudden or discrete shift.

Assessing developmental maturation in legally relevant domains is a critical part of any juvenile forensic mental health assessment. Grisso (2005) has aptly noted that developmental maturity should not, however, be regarded as a dichotomous, monolithic construct. He recommends that clinicians think of "immaturity" as a concept that:

- Refers to incomplete development (having not reached one's adult level of maturation) or delayed development (in relation to one's age peers).
- Describes specific abilities or characteristics, not an overall condition of the youth.
- Depends on actual functioning, not simply on age.
- Can be expressed in degrees and in relation to one's peers. (p. 18)

In addition, when assessing the developmental level (or current pathway) of any child or adolescent, clinicians should keep in mind the following overarching principles of human development:

- The range of what is considered "normal" for attaining certain milestones in each domain varies widely between children and can be substantially affected by environmental factors. The reality of human development is that there is great variability in the age and rate at which different cognitive, social, or emotional capacities develop (Grisso, 2004; Steinberg & Cauffman, 1996, 1999). Although developmental psychology textbooks and other reference sources may publish charts that display a "typical" or "average" progression, those normative estimates often are based on Caucasian, middle-class children. Minority youth living in poverty, however, are the population most disproportionately represented in the justice system. Research has demonstrated that economic disadvantage may delay or inhibit certain developmental capacities, so the "average" trajectory of less privileged youth may be expected to differ (Grisso, 1998, 2004).

- The rate of progress or trajectory for any given domain is not necessarily the same as for another. It may be tempting to assume that "on level" or advanced abilities in one domain (or even in a particular capacity within a domain) indicates a similar level of attainment in other abilities or domains. For example, a child with an above-average IQ score might be expected to have above-average social skills. This type of assumption is one of the greatest potential sources of error in developmental assessments. Relevant capacities should be assessed directly, not simply inferred from other characteristics.

- Developmental progress does not always move forward. It is quite common to see "spurts" (periods of rapid advance), "delays" (periods when advances are not occurring at the expected rate), and "regressions" (periods when developmental progress is lost or returns to an earlier state) in different areas of development (Grisso, 1998). It is also not uncommon for certain capacities to be evident in one context or circumstance, but not in others.

We also suggest that a developmentally informed assessment, particularly one that involves psychosocial capacities, must begin with adequate consideration and understanding of the key issues that are likely to be relevant for the examinee's current stage of development. The major developmental task(s) attendant to the present (and preceding stages) have been referred to as "stage-salient issues" (Cicchetti, Toth, Bush, & Gillespie, 1988). The ways a young person navigates and resolves each developmental task will influence his or her future adaptation. Although prior developmental experiences may predispose, push, shape, or constrain future adaptations in certain ways, past experiences do not absolutely *determine* the nature or direction of future growth.

As noted previously, it is convenient to consider youths' development as involving change represented by three domains: biological, cognitive, and psychosocial. We proceed with a concise review of research relevant to developmental assessment considerations in each of these domains.

Biological Development

A young person's physical development may affect psycholegal capacities primarily in two ways: first, by the actual maturation of brain structures and functions, and second, by the effects of hormones and brain chemicals on thinking, mood, and behavior. Arguably, the first of these, the effects of brain development, has as much or more to do with cognitive as biological development. Therefore, we address the issue of structural brain development in the next section. At this juncture, we focus on physical/biological development.

Perhaps the most significant *physical* changes affecting young people occur during puberty. Not only does the body endure a serious overhaul, but those changes also affect the way the young person thinks, feels, and behaves toward self and others. These effects may, in turn, impact on actions and decisions that have legal relevance.

Both before and during puberty, it is generally observed that personality functioning is less stable and less consistent in juveniles than in adults. That is, one is more likely to see a greater range of variability in styles and behaviors across different contexts. This variability may be magnified during pubertal changes (Beaver & Wright, 2005).

Some of the instability is due to surges and changes in one's hormones, particularly the effects of testosterone (an androgen) in boys and estradiol (an estrogen) in girls, which can increase feelings of irritability or aggressiveness. But they are only part of the constellation of changes that can affect adolescents' behavior. Accommodating major changes in one's body is inherently stressful. Adolescents, however, are normatively more vulnerable and reactive to stresses than are adults. Moreover, those changes are affecting their self-image and perceptions of how they are viewed by others precisely at the time in their lives when they are *most* self-focused and *most* self-conscious about others' judgments. It is difficult to imagine how the stress of those changes could not have significant effects on one's behavior. Indeed, the moodiness of the teen years is not merely a cliché, but is a biologically based reality of human development. Adolescents do indeed "experience emotional states that are more extreme, more variable, and less predictable than those experienced by children or adults" (Steinberg & Cauffman, 1996, p. 261).

Cognitive Development

Cognitive development describes the maturational process of a person's mental and intellectual functions. It recognizes that abilities such as memory, information processing, and reasoning are not fully developed at birth, and it accounts for how these abilities are acquired over time. Piaget's (1953) theory of cognitive development has had one of the strongest and most lasting impacts on the field. Although subsequent researchers have criticized the tasks and methodology he used to develop the ideas (particularly the failure to consider cultural factors), many of the basic concepts have stood the test of time.

We do not provide here a detailed account of Piagetian theory, but a few of the basic ideas are worthy of reflection. First, Piaget saw cognition (and its development) as an active process in which an individual attempts to organize and make sense of the world. Advances in development were a product not solely (or even mainly) of acquiring new knowledge or facts, but rather of gaining new ways of understanding.

In infancy, he believed we learn about our environment mainly by the hands-on experience of seeing, hearing, and touching. Very little happens internally (mentally) or symbolically. In early childhood, a young person begins to develop an ability to represent an idea, often through images or drawing, that is not in his immediate experience. This is the beginning of symbolic representation and thought. In later childhood (approximately ages 7 to 11), a remarkable development occurs as children become able to perform tasks in their head, what Piaget refers to as an "operation." What is important is that this represents a change in one's way of thinking and reasoning toward the use of and reliance on basic logic. By early adolescence (approximately ages 11 to 15), the capacity to perform internal operations does not require a specific stimulus or example; the thought process can be more abstract or hypothetical (including what *might* happen in the future). Piaget did not claim that all youths reached the "operations" stage at any specific age, but rather that for most youths, the capacity began to appear in the early adolescent years, then proceeded to grow and mature across adolescence until it reached the level of functioning that would be characteristic for that individual.

Now, with that basic framework in mind, imagine a young person deciding whether to engage in a particular behavior—perhaps whether or not to steal an item or whether or not to accept a particular plea agreement. What are the mental functions needed to make a reasonable decision? One should be able to think through the range of possible outcomes or consequences. One should be able to assess the relative likelihood of those outcomes or consequences. One should be able to assess the incentives and constraints on the behavior, both in terms of external responses and self-responses, both in the short term and long term. Would a 10-year-old and a 20-year-old each be equally likely to have the capacity to navigate those questions? Research suggests that on average, they would not.

Some of the higher-level cognitive functions, such as reasoning and problem solving, are strongly linked to brain development. In fact, the part of the brain most responsible for many complex cognitive abilities (and incidentally for inhibiting risky impulses and choices) is the last area of the brain to fully develop (Casey, Giedd, & Thomas, 2000; Spear, 2000). Moreover, cortical and subcortical structures, including the amygdala and other structures in the limbic region, responsible for emotion are more active in children and adolescents than in adults. Yet, current evidence in cognitive neuroscience suggests that areas of the frontal cortex, which govern behavioral inhibition, planning, and emotional regulation, are less active in children and adolescents than in adults, and these structures continue to develop even into early adulthood (e.g., early 20s; Giedd et al., 1999; Sowell et al., 2003; Sowell, Thompson, Holmes, Jernigan, & Toga, 1999). Essentially, then, the nature of brain development is such that young people have much greater activity than adults in the emotional and reactive brain regions and much less activity and maturation in the planning and inhibitory areas. Accessible reviews of this research can be found in Strauch (2003) as it applies to adolescents in general and in Beckman (2004) as it applies to issues of delinquency.

Psychosocial Development

Psychosocial development is perhaps the most central and least studied domain likely to affect a juvenile's psycholegal capacities. In criminal and juvenile justice matters, the law is often interested in a juvenile's degree of "sophistication" or "maturity" to inform decisions about culpability and disposition (see *Kent v.*

United States, 1966). Translating legal concepts into clinical ones, what the law has in mind is what psychologists might refer to as psychosocial maturity (Grisso, 1998; Steinberg & Schwartz, 2000). Historically, the most fundamental problem in this area as it relates to forensic assessment has been the absence of a clearly articulated model, or even a definition, of psychosocial maturity.

Scott, Reppucci, and Woolard (1995) and Cauffman and Steinberg (2000a, 2000b; Steinberg & Cauffman, 1996) have made some of the most important advances on this front. Using Cauffman and Steinberg's (2000a) conceptualization, psychosocial maturity is "the complexity and sophistication of the process of individual decision-making as it is affected by a range of cognitive, emotional, and social factors" (p. 743). Specifically, they outline three developmental capacities that combine to shape that decision-making process. The first is *responsibility,* the ability to be self-reliant and unaffected by external pressure or influence in making decisions. The second is *perspective.* This has two components: (1) temporal (i.e., the ability to see and consider both short and long-term implications of a decision), and (2) interpersonal (i.e., the ability to take another's perspective and understand a different point of view). The third developmental capacity is *temperance,* the ability to exercise self-restraint and to control one's impulses.

Research on responsibility shows that by late adolescence, most young people are capable of being largely independent and self-reliant in decision making (Cauffman & Steinberg, 2000b). Significant decisions can be made without consultation from parents or peers. Self-reliance increases as the teenager progresses through adolescence, whereas parental influence declines as the individual gets older. Peer *pressure* steadily increases from late childhood through adolescence. However, peer *influence,* which begins to increase in early adolescence, peaks around the age of 14, then gradually declines in the later high school years.

Perspective taking, as we have noted, has both temporal and interpersonal (role perspective) facets. It is a developmental task that progressively improves over the course of adolescence for most individuals. Bad decisions result not only from youths' failures to conduct sophisticated, adultlike cost-benefit analyses, but also from fundamental differences in the "subjective values that they attach to various perceived consequences in the process of making choices" (Halpern-Felsher & Cauffman, 2001, p. 268). Specifically, before adulthood, greater weight is given to acquiring potential gains than to avoiding potential losses, and to short-term rather than long-term (future) consequences.

Finally, with regard to temperance, current research indicates that an adolescent's degree of self-restraint and impulse control changes as he or she ages. This is consistent with evidence in neuroscience that the frontal lobes are still maturing and, accordingly, that "response inhibition, emotional regulation, planning and organization continue to develop between adolescence and young adulthood" (Sowell et al., 1999, pp. 859–860). Children tend to be relatively stable in their overall impulse control from the time they are school-age until about the age of 16. Around that time, the research suggests that adolescents actually become more impulsive and engage in more sensation-seeking and risk-taking behaviors (through about age 19; Steinberg & Cauffman, 1996). In this regard, older adolescents are actually less temperate and typically exercise less control over their impulses.

APPLYING DEVELOPMENTAL CONCEPTS TO QUESTIONS OF YOUTHS' LEGAL CAPACITIES AND CULPABILITY

Current empirical evidence about the ways that children and adolescents think, feel, and behave suggest that the early twentieth-century notion that delinquent youths should be treated differently by the legal system has merit. We cannot review and critique here the entire spectrum of research that exists on developmental and age-related differences in legally relevant capacities. We do, however, highlight some of the most significant and robust empirical findings to emerge from this literature, focusing first on capacities related to participation in an adjudicative process and on making decisions about legal participation, then on capacities and deficits associated with criminal culpability.

Adjudicative Competence

The law has long recognized that a person accused of a crime must be competent to participate in the legal process before being placed in jeopardy of legal sanctions. The basic standard for competence tends to be fairly consistent across jurisdictions. Most draw from the U.S. Supreme Court case of *Dusky v. U.S.* (1960, pp. 402, 403), which declared that the "test must be whether he has sufficient present ability to consult with his lawyer with a reasonable degree of rational understanding—and whether he has a rational as well as factual understanding of the proceedings against him."

Historically, findings of impairment or incapacity in an accused's ability to understand and assist have been limited to those *caused by* some mental disorder (i.e., mental illness or mental retardation). The distinguishable issue with juveniles, however, is that many may not possess a reasonable ability to understand and assist, but the cause is developmental immaturity rather than mental illness.

Developmental incompetence has become an issue because of two relatively recent changes in the law. The first is a trend in state laws during the 1990s that resulted in juveniles accused of certain crimes being tried in adult court (rather than being adjudicated in juvenile court; Tanenhaus, 2000), bringing younger adolescents into criminal court. There was little historical or legal precedent regarding how to address the issue of immature youths' capacities to participate in their criminal trials. The second legal change has been the recent recognition by state appellate courts that youths must be competent to stand trial in juvenile court (Bonnie & Grisso, 2000; Grisso, 2005). Here, too, there was little precedent, as the concept of competence to stand trial was rarely applied in juvenile courts before the 1990s (Grisso, Miller, & Sales, 1987).

A few states have modified their laws to specifically account for developmental immaturity as a possible predicate (but not sufficient) condition for incompetence (Redding & Frost, 2002; Scott & Grisso, 2005). Most have handled the issue more informally. For example, in a recent survey of juvenile court clinical services nationwide, about two-thirds reported findings of incompetence due to immaturity, and about one-fifth said that immaturity was the most frequent reason for findings of incompetence to stand trial in their juvenile courts (Grisso & Quinlan, 2005). This suggests that many juvenile courts recognize the relevance of immaturity for questions of adjudicative competence, even though their legislators have not yet provided them specific guidance regarding its application.

Research suggests that juveniles are less likely than adults to be knowledgeable about legal processes, less likely to trust and assist their counsel, and more likely to have poorly developed cognitive and reasoning abilities. There is clearly no specific age at which a child's abilities magically and abruptly transform to be like those of adults. The current research suggests, however, that youths who are age 15 and younger are much more likely than young adults (18 to 24) to have serious impairments in their ability to understand and participate in the trial process. In a large-scale national study of juveniles' competence abilities (Grisso et al., 2003), on average, the 16- and 17-year-old juveniles had abilities similar to those of young adult defendants. Not surprisingly, younger juveniles are at the greatest risk. Nearly one-third of those age 11 to 13 had deficits in those abilities that paralleled those of mentally ill, "incompetent" adults. The same is true for one in five juveniles age 14 or 15. These results held up across groups defined by sex, ethnicity, and socioeconomic status, and they were found among youths and adults in the justice system and in the community. Grisso (1981) noted a similar age-related difference when comparing youths' and adults' abilities to comprehend *Miranda* warnings, noting that "understanding . . . was significantly poorer among juveniles who were 14 years of age or younger than among 15–16-year-old juveniles or adult offenders" (p. 192).

Intellectual capacity also appears to be an important factor in legally relevant capacities and decision making. In Grisso's (1981) study of *Miranda* comprehension, deficits in understanding were particularly pronounced in youth of all ages who had low IQ scores. Similarly, in the study of youths' adjudicative competence (Grisso et al., 2003), intellectual abilities were strongly related to performance on the competence measures. Juveniles of below-average intelligence were more likely than juveniles of average intelligence to be impaired in abilities relevant for competence to stand trial. This effect was particularly pronounced in younger adolescents. Among the youngest participants, about one-half of those who had IQ scores of 70 or lower were as impaired as seriously mentally ill adults whom forensic clinicians considered incompetent to stand trial.

Additional findings in the same study suggested that adolescents are more likely than young adults to make choices that reflect a propensity to comply with authority figures, such as confessing to the police rather than remaining silent or accepting a prosecutor's offer of a plea agreement. In addition, when being interrogated by the police, consulting with an attorney, or evaluating a plea agreement, younger adolescents are less likely, or perhaps less able, than others to recognize the risks inherent in the various choices they face or to consider the long-term, and not merely the immediate, consequences of their legal decisions. As is the case with capacities relevant for competence to stand trial, these patterns of age differences in legal decision making generally do not vary with sex, ethnicity, or socioeconomic status.

Culpability

In March 2005, the U.S. Supreme Court determined that "evolving standards of decency" rendered the death penalty an unconstitutional (*"cruel and unusual,"* 8th Amendment) punishment for any offense committed by a person under the age of 18 (*Roper v. Simmons*). The Court already had made that determination about offenders who were 15 and younger (*Stanford v. Kentucky*, 1989), so the focus really was on 16- and 17-year-old youth. The Court's majority clearly recognized that adolescents, at least those under age 18, were less mature psychosocially and neurologically than adults in ways that substantially affected their culpability or criminal blameworthiness. The dissenting opinions did not focus primarily on that premise. Rather, they argued that because science could not show that *every* adolescent did not possess more adultlike capacities, the ban would inappropriately usurp the authority of the states to set that punishment and then, using judicial discretion, to decide which youths did and did not deserve death (i.e., which were more or less mature). We raise the issue here because it highlights a critical distinction for evaluators between the developmental capacities of adolescents *in general* and those possessed by *a given individual.*

As a result of the *Simmons* case, the death penalty is off the table as a possible penalty for juveniles. Nevertheless, clinical assessments involving issues of culpability are still requested for purposes of disposition and sentencing. In addition, questions of culpability often are implied in the maturity criteria used to decide judicial transfer of youths for trial from juvenile to adult criminal court. These assessments are often ambiguous and require the evaluating forensic mental health expert to keep prominently in mind whether assessment and characterization of a youth's capacities are being made in *comparative* terms (i.e., relative to same-age youth) or *absolute* terms (i.e., relative to some set objective or normative/legal standard).

The reality is that juveniles across the socioeconomic spectrum very frequently engage in delinquency and criminal infractions. Rates of antisocial and transgressive behavior are higher during adolescence than in any other developmental period throughout the life course. This general age-related trend seems to hold across cultures and for both males and females (Hirschi & Gottfredson, 1983). There is a substantial increase in illegal activities between ages 7 and 17, and a corresponding decrease between ages 17 and 30 (Moffitt, 1993). In fact, rates of delinquent behavior during adolescence, especially when it is measured by youths' self-report rather than delinquency that is officially detected or results in arrest, are so high as to be statistically normative (Elliott, Ageton, Huizinga, Knowles, & Cantor, 1983; Hirschi, 1969; Moffitt, Lynam, & Silva, 1994). Yet, even among young people who engage in serious violent behavior during adolescence, nearly 80% will naturally desist from that behavior and not continue past age 21 (Kosterman, Graham, Hawkins, Catalano, & Herrenkohl, 2001; U.S. Department of Health and Human Services, 2001). Clearly, there is something about adolescence that offers a greater predisposition toward antisocial behavior than normatively exists in adulthood (Steinberg & Scott, 2000).

What can a developmental perspective offer regarding the question of the culpability of young people in general, and regarding guidance for experts who are appraising the culpability of individual youths? We offer some key concepts that may be of help, as well as a brief summary of developmental research findings regarding these concepts.

If one were to deconstruct the process of criminal decision making and actions among adolescents, a few core processes seem to emerge: (a) the ability to appraise risks and consequences, (b) the ability to inhibit impulses or control behavior, (c) the ability to resist peer pressure, and (d) the ability to experience victim empathy and to have that affective experience inhibit interpersonal transgression. These correspond fairly well to Cauffman and Steinberg's (2000a) elements of psychosocial maturity: responsibility, temperance, and perspective (reviewed earlier). It is fair to state that capacities among children and adolescents in each of these domains are less well developed, on average, than they are in adults. We elaborate on a couple of specific dimensions here.

Appraising Risks

Adolescents are known to take more risks and greater risks than is typical for adults. Teens are overrepresented in trends for nearly every kind of recorded reckless behavior (Arnett, 1992), and there seem to be multiple reasons for this. As we noted, the prefrontal cortex, the part of the brain responsible for planning, organizing, inhibiting, and anticipating consequences, is still structurally developing at this stage. Peer influences can also facilitate unwise decisions. But reaching across these explanations is the fact that adolescents tend not to have the cognitive capacity to reasonably anticipate future consequences in the way that most adults do. Moreover, their value schemes in any cost-benefit calculus tend to be different and less temperate than those of most adults. They ascribe greater value to fun and peer approval (as benefits), while underanticipating and undervaluing the potential costs of risk action (Steinberg, 2002). To summarize, in assessing potential risks, adolescents, in comparison to adults, tend not to be able to foresee as many possible outcomes, tend to underestimate the probability of negative outcomes (costs), and tend to overestimate the benefit value of fun, spontaneity, and others' approval (Furby & Beyth-Marom, 1992; Nurmi, 1991).

Controlling Impulses

Impulsiveness, as noted, tends to show an increase around the age of 16. There is no clear empirically based answer as to why this occurs. There is no evidence that the brain's inhibition and control mechanisms typically regress at this age. In fact, although they are not yet *fully* developed, those capacities should be *more* active and influential than in the younger years. Psychosocially, one important change that occurs around age 16, at least among American youth, is acquiring driving privileges. The ability to drive gives a young person more mobility, which provides easier access to conditions of reduced parental (and other adult) monitoring and supervision and to new choices and challenges and peer contacts. Perhaps what causes the spike in impulsivity is the sudden onset of new demands on their capacity that, at least temporarily, do not fit well with the more complex and potentially risky situations in and about which they now have to make decisions. Interestingly, however, in one of the largest studies of psychosocial abilities in adolescent decision making, Cauffman and Steinberg (2000a) found that some of the greatest developmental advances in youths' abilities to generate and evaluate alternative courses of action occurred in *later* adolescence, between the ages of 16 and 19. Adolescent decisions do tend to be more impulsive, less reflective, and, consequently, less stable and consistent than those of adults.

Resisting Peer Pressure

Earlier we indicated that most young people will engage in delinquent and antisocial behavior during adolescence but naturally desist by adulthood. One of the leading explanations for this age-limited surge relates to the power of peer influence. Peer influence is widely regarded as one of the most profound causes or risk factors for antisocial behavior among adolescents (Haynie, 2002). This is not so much true during childhood or during adulthood, but during the teen years, when the perceived value of social/peer approval is at its peak. Peer delinquency/influence essentially operates as a gateway factor for delinquency. That is, most initial forays into delinquency are facilitated by peers, and most intervention or disruption will need to address the element of peer influence to be effective (U.S. Department of Health and Human Services, 2001). Research data show that both peer influence *and* crime rates drop significantly after an individual reaches adulthood (Giordano, Cernkovich, & Holland, 2003).

Victim Perspective

One factor that may operate to inhibit delinquent impulses is empathic feelings toward the potential victim (Bjoerkqvist & Oesterman, 2000; Endresen & Olweus, 2001; Guerra & Slaby, 1990; Miller & Eisenberg, 1988). Empathy is defined as the identification, understanding, and sharing of another person's thoughts, feelings, and intentions (Eisenberg & Strayer, 1987). The emotional response, however, requires a cognitive capacity to shift perspective, that is, to understand how another person could view a situation differently, make different interpretations, and reach different conclusions, as well as the ability to reason abstractly and analyze hypotheticals. The question "How would you feel if that happened to you?" requires a person to reason and anticipate responses to a hypothetical set of facts. Empathy, then, is an emotional response that has certain cognitive requirements. The cognitive ability to shift perspective is often not fully developed during the teen years (Cauffman & Steinberg, 2000a).

In summary, developmental theory and empirical research have advanced to a degree that they provide forensic mental health experts with some guidance for assessing youths' legal capacities and culpability. As previously noted, however, the law itself is in a state of transition with regard to those legal issues pertaining to juveniles. Experts who assess youths with a developmental perspective may find that they are also influencing courts to think in ways that are new and, one hopes, helpful in shaping a developmentally sensitive system of juvenil justice.

CONCLUSION: THE VALUES AND LIMITS OF A DEVELOPMENTAL PERSPECTIVE

The recent increase in interest in the application of developmental theory and research to forensic issues in delinquency cases is clearly evident in literature of the past 10 years (for summaries, see Fagan & Zimring, 2000; Grisso, 2004, 2005; Grisso & Schwartz, 2000). What is the potential for this perspective, and what is needed to reach that potential? How does it advance the efforts of forensic assessment of youths in delinquency cases? We conclude with some observations about the potential value of a developmental perspective for law and policy, research and practice.

Law and Policy

We began by describing two ideological viewpoints. At their extreme, one argues that youths' illegal behavior should be approached as it is with adults. The other contends that delinquent youths are merely misguided and simply require treatment and rehabilitation.

Current developmental theory and research does not support either of these extreme positions. There is certainly evidence that adolescents' capacities are not like those of adults, and the differences are sufficient to warrant a separate system of justice for delinquent youths that offers the potential for different responses to their transgressions. On the other hand, nothing in the current empirical research on development suggests that youths should not be held responsible for their illegal behaviors or that punishment should be completely replaced with treatment. Moreover, developmental concepts and research recognize that (a) at least some older adolescent age groups do not differ from adults on average in their capacities to participate in their trials, and (b) variability among adolescents at any particular age creates exceptions in individual cases to age norms for capacities related to legal questions.

What a developmental perspective does support is juvenile justice policy that allows for greater flexibility and discretion in the adjudicative process, so that courts' decisions are based, in part, on an individualized developmental and forensic mental health assessment of the youth in question. This is challenging, because the risk of discretion and individualized judgments about youths has the potential for unequal application of the law on the basis of judicial bias or inadequate information about youths as individuals. A developmental perspective cannot solve that problem. But the research that it is generating argues against the alternative: a set of juvenile laws that treats all youths alike on the basis of their offense, regardless of their age or stage of development, and often treats them as though they were already adults. The implications of a developmental perspective's support for discretion in the adjudicative process has clear implications for forensic experts who perform evaluations in delinquency cases. In such a system, their assessments may be among the most important information with which courts make decisions that are responsive to youths' developmental and clinical differences. The quality of their data, therefore, becomes central to the administration of juvenile justice.

Research

Recent advances in developmental research related to youths' offending and their capacities in legal proceedings have begun to provide forensic examiners with an empirical foundation for applying a developmental perspective in their delinquency evaluations. Nevertheless, the job is quite incomplete. This is not only a matter of needing more research on the forensic application of developmental principles. While researchers are studying how youths make decisions *in specific legally relevant situations* (e.g., trials, crime scenes), they are finding that *basic* developmental research has provided only a very incomplete picture of adolescents' decision making *in general.* In this sense, applying a developmental perspective to study youths' legally relevant capacities runs some risks, much as if one decided to build the walls of a house before the foundation is complete.

Similarly, research has identified the prefrontal cortex, responsible for planning and affect modulation, as still developing through adolescence. But as yet there are no empirical studies that demonstrate that this translates into the *behaviors* that trouble us when we consider differences between youths' and adults' judgment and decision making. We do not have research that demonstrates that "immature prefrontal lobes" increase the risk of poor judgment in real situations. Experts may properly make this inference in their assessments of youths, but they must recognize that until there is empirical evidence of this type, their own conclusions are, indeed, inferences.

Forensic examiners in delinquency cases are also in need of research that translates developmental concepts into assessment tools that will provide data representing those concepts. For example, we have described the importance of attending to youths' level of psychosocial development, such as their way of perceiving risks and their degree of influence by peers. Yet, research has not yet provided forensic experts with reliable assessment tools for routine forensic use to identify individual youths' levels of development on these important dimensions. Moreover, specialized forensic assessment tools to relate those characteristics to youths' capacities in legally relevant situations are unlikely to be available for several years. Experts are not unable to estimate youths' psychosocial development; certain clinical assessment tools and careful interviewing provide some guidance. But a sound empirical basis for their descriptions of youths' psychosocial capacities related to their delinquency depends on research to create the instruments specifically designed for that purpose.

Practice

Forensic mental health experts who adopt a developmental perspective for their evaluations of delinquent youths are faced with a considerable challenge. The law, as yet, provides little guidance for them, because courts and legislators are only now deciding how to use developmental concepts to respond to issues in juvenile justice. Research has provided experts promising evidence for the validity of developmental concepts as they apply to forensic questions, but this process has only begun and does not offer clinicians the firm basis, in theory and measurement, that they would wish.

In these circumstances, the value of a developmental perspective for forensic examiners in delinquency cases rests substantially on its conceptual guidance. As we have shown, a developmental perspective offers models and concepts that can direct the expert's data gathering and interpretive process. Taking the concept of maturation seriously focuses the expert on types of data that are less often obtained in adult forensic evaluations or in the diagnosis of children's psychiatric disorders. What we know about the relation of those data to youths' misbehaviors then provides an additional perspective when interpreting for courts the relevance of youths' capacities for their delinquency and the potential for meaningful legal response to their transgressions.

If this is to happen, however, experts who conduct forensic examinations in delinquency cases must have an unusual combination of knowledge, experience, and skill that makes them different from general child clinical experts as well as general forensic experts. The base of required knowledge includes scientific and professional information about child/adolescent psychology and development, developmental psychopathology, developmental criminology, and treatment outcomes research. At the same time, it requires specialized knowledge regarding the application of developmental findings to forensic questions and about research that links child development to psycholegal capacities.

Experts who perform forensic mental health examinations of juveniles must also be skilled in assessment methods for children and adolescents, including how to conduct interviews and interpret responses and how to select and utilize appropriate tests and tools to evaluate intellectual abilities, personality, and developmental status. Understanding and diagnosing mental disorders in children and adolescents requires different methods and often uses different diagnostic categories than the diagnosis of adults' disorders. Applying diagnostic criteria to young people can also be quite complex. Because juveniles are moving targets, their disorders may take different forms as they mature and are less stable across developmental stages than in the case of adults.

As the field of forensic assessment of juveniles matures, there must be greater attention to the fact that examiners in delinquency cases should be specialized in both sets of skills and knowledge: child developmental and clinical expertise, and forensic expertise. Rigid adherence to such criteria at the moment would create serious dilemmas for juvenile courts, because clinicians with this combined specialization are not plentiful. There are very few places in the country that provide training for psychologists, psychiatrists, or social workers to perform as child clinical and forensic examiners.

Synergy

Finally, we would note that the future value of a developmental perspective that we have described for policy, research, and practice depends on interactions among these areas of professional activity. Policy and law are not likely to be able to fully use a developmental perspective until research provides more complete guidance and until clinicians teach lawyers and judges about the use of developmental guidance when they offer their assessments to the courts. Research will advance to the extent that juvenile forensic practitioners provide researchers with the questions that need to be answered. And practitioners need the encouragement of both their providers (researchers who create their empirical foundation) and their consumers (courts whom they serve). There is evidence that this synergy is beginning to function. If it continues, then a developmental perspective in juvenile justice may have an opportunity to offer a theoretical and empirical perspective that can moderate the polar extremes that historically have dominated juvenile justice.

REFERENCES

Arnett, J. (1992). Reckless behavior in adolescence: A developmental perspective. *Developmental Review, 12,* 339–373.

Beaver, K., & Wright, J. (2005). Biosocial development and delinquent involvement. *Youth Violence and Juvenile Justice, 3,* 168–192.

Beckman, M. (2004). Crime, culpability and the adolescent brain. *Science, 305*(30), 599.

Bjoerkqvist, K., & Oesterman, K. (2000). Social intelligence: Empathy = aggression? *Aggression and Violent Behavior, 5,* 191–200.

Bonnie, R., & Grisso, T. (2000). Adjudicative competence and youthful offenders. In T. Grisso & R. G. Schwartz (Eds.), *Youth on trial: A developmental perspective in juvenile justice* (pp. 73–103). Chicago: University of Chicago Press.

Borum, R., & Verhaagen, D. (in press). *A practical guide to assessing and managing violence risk in juveniles.* New York: Guilford Press.

Casey, B. J., Giedd, J. N., & Thomas, K. M. (2000). Structural and functional brain development and its relation to cognitive development. *Biological Psychology, 54,* 241–257.

Cauffman, E., & Steinberg, L. (1996). The cognitive and affective influences on adolescent decision-making. *Temple Law Review, 68,* 1763–1789.

Cauffman, E., & Steinberg, L. (2000a). (Im)maturity of judgment in adolescence: Why adolescents may be less culpable than adults. *Behavioral Sciences and the Law, 18,* 1–21.

Cauffman, E., & Steinberg, L. (2000b). Researching adolescents' judgment and culpability. In T. Grisso & R. G. Schwartz (Eds.), *Youth on trial: A developmental perspective in juvenile justice* (pp. 325–343). Chicago: University of Chicago Press.

Cicchetti, D. (1984). The emergence of developmental psychopathology. *Child Development, 55,* 1–7.

Cicchetti, D. (1990). An historical perspective on the discipline of developmental psychopathology. In J. Rolf, A. Master, D. Cicchetti, K. Nuechterlien, & S. Wintraub (Eds.), *Risk and protective factors in the development of psychopathology* (pp. 2–28). New York: Cambridge University Press.

Cicchetti, D., & Toth, S. L. (1998). The development of depression in children and adolescents. *American Psychologist, 53,* 221–241.

Cicchetti, D., Toth, S., Bush, M., & Gillespie, J. (1988). Stage-salient issues: A transactional model of intervention. *New Directions in Child Development, 39,* 123–145.

Clausel, L. E. F., & Bonnie, R. J. (2000). Juvenile justice on appeal. In J. Fagan & F. E. Zimring (Eds.), *The changing borders of juvenile justice: Transfer of adolescents to the criminal court* (pp. 181–206). Chicago: University of Chicago Press.

Dusky v. U.S., 362 U.S. 402 (1960).

Eisenberg, N., & Strayer, J. (1987). Critical issues in the study of empathy. In N. Eisenberg & J. Strayer (Eds.), *Empathy and its development* (pp. 3–16). Cambridge, England: Cambridge University Press.

Elliott, D., Ageton, S., Huizinga, D., Knowles, B., & Canter, R. (1983). *The prevalence and incidence of delinquent behavior: 1976–1980* (The National Youth Survey Report No. 26). Boulder, CO: Behavioral Research Institute.

Endresen, I. M., & Olweus, D. (2001). Self-reported empathy in Norwegian adolescents: Sex differences, age trends, and relationship to bullying. In A. C. Bohart & D. J. Stipek (Eds.), *Constructive and destructive behavior: Implications for family, school, and society* (pp. 147–165). Washington, DC: American Psychological Association.

Erickson, E. H. (1963). *Childhood and society.* New York: Norton.

Fagan, J., & Zimring, F. (Eds.). (2000). *The changing borders of juvenile justice: Transfer of adolescents to the criminal court.* Chicago: University of Chicago Press.

Furby, F., & Beyth-Marom, R. (1992). Risk taking in adolescence: A decision-making perspective. *Developmental Review, 12,* 1–44.

Giedd, J. N., Blumenthal, J., Jeffries, N. O., Castellanos, F. X., Liu, H., Zijdenbos, A., et al. (1999). Brain development during childhood and adolescence: A longitudinal MRI study. *Nature Neuroscience, 2,* 861–863.

Giordano, P., Cernkovich, S., & Holland, D. (2003). Changes in friendship relations over the life course: Implications for desistance from crime. *Criminology, 41,* 293–325.

Griffin, P., & Torbet, P. (2002). *Desktop guide to good juvenile probation practice.* National Center for Juvenile Justice, Pittsburgh, PA [producer]. Washington, DC: Office of Juvenile Justice and Delinquency Prevention.

Grisso, T. (1981). *Juveniles' waiver of rights: Legal and psychological competence.* New York: Plenum.

Grisso, T. (1996). Society's retributive response to juvenile violence: A developmental perspective. *Law and Human Behavior, 20,* 229–247.

Grisso, T. (1998). *Forensic evaluation of juveniles.* Sarasota, FL: Professional Resource Press.

Grisso, T. (2003). Forensic evaluations in delinquency cases. In I. B. Weiner (Series Ed.) & A. M. Goldstein (Vol. Ed.), *Comprehensive handbook of psychology: Vol. 11. Forensic psychology* (pp. 315–344). Hoboken, NJ: Wiley.

Grisso, T. (2004). *Double jeopardy: Adolescent offenders with mental disorders.* Chicago: University of Chicago Press.

Grisso, T. (2005). *Evaluating juveniles' adjudicative competence: A guide for clinical practice.* Sarasota, FL: Professional Resource Press.

Grisso, T., Miller, M., & Sales, B. (1987). Competency to stand trial in juvenile court. *International Journal of Law and Psychiatry, 10,* 1–10.

Grisso, T., & Quinlan, J. (2005). *A national survey of juvenile court clinical services.* Worcester: University of Massachusetts Medical School.

Grisso, T., & Schwartz, R. (Eds.). (2000). *Youth on trial.* Chicago: University of Chicago Press.

Grisso, T., Steinberg, L., Woolard, J., Cauffman, E., Scott, E., Graham, S., et al. (2003). Juveniles' competence to stand trial: A comparison of adolescents' and adults' capacities as trial defendants. *Law and Human Behavior, 27,* 333–363.

Guerra, N. G., & Slaby, R. G. (1990). Cognitive mediators of aggression in adolescent offenders: Pt. 2. Intervention. *Developmental Psychology, 26,* 106–124.

Halpern-Felsher, B., & Cauffman, E. (2001). Costs and benefits of a decision: Decision-making competence in adolescents and adults. *Journal of Applied Developmental Psychology, 22,* 257–273.

Haynie, D. (2002). Friendship networks and delinquency: The relative nature of peer delinquency. *Journal of Quantitative Criminology, 18,* 99–127.

Hirschi, T. (1969). *Causes of delinquency.* Berkeley: University of California Press.

Hirschi, T., & Gottfredson, M. (1983). Age and the explanation of crime. *American Journal of Sociology, 89,* 552–584.

Kent v. United States, 383 U.S. 541 (1966).

Kosterman, R., Graham, J. W., Hawkins, J. D., Catalano, R. F., & Herrenkohl, T. I. (2001). Childhood risk factors for persistence of violence in the transition to adulthood: A social development perspective. *Violence and Victims, 16,* 355–369.

McCord, J., Widom, C. S., & Crowell, N. A. (Eds.). (2001). *Juvenile crime, juvenile justice.* Washington, DC: National Academy Press.

Miller, P. A., & Eisenberg, N. (1988). The relation of empathy to aggressive and externalizing/antisocial behavior. *Psychological Bulletin, 103,* 324–344.

Moffitt, T. (1993). "Life course persistent" and "adolescence limited" antisocial behavior: A developmental taxonomy. *Psychological Review, 100,* 674–701.

Moffitt, T., Lynam, D., & Silva, P. (1994). Neuropsychological tests predict male delinquency. *Criminology, 32,* 101–124.

Nurmi, J. (1991). How do adolescents see their future? A review of the development of future orientation and planning. *Developmental Review, 11,* 1–59.

Piaget, J. (1953). *The origins of intelligence in children.* London: Routledge & Kegan Paul.

Redding, R., & Frost, J. (2002). Adjudicative competence in the modern juvenile court. *Virginia Journal of Social Policy and Law, 9,* 353–410.

Roper v. Simmons, 543 U.S. 551 (2005).

Rosado, L. (Ed.). (2000). *Kids are different: How knowledge of adolescent development theory can aid decision-making in court.* Washington, DC: American Bar Association Juvenile Justice Center.

Scott, E., & Grisso, T. (2005). Developmental incompetence, due process, and juvenile justice policy. *North Carolina Law Review, 83,* 101–147.

Scott, E., Reppucci, N., & Woolard, J. (1995). Evaluating adolescent decisionmaking in legal contexts. *Law and Human Behavior, 19,* 221–244.

Sowell, E. R., Peterson, B. S., Thompson, P. M., Welcome, S. E., Henkenius, A. L., & Toga, A. W. (2003). Mapping cortical change across the human life span. *Nature Neuroscience, 6,* 309–315.

Sowell, E. R., Thompson, P. M., Holmes, C. J., Jernigan, T. L., & Toga, A. W. (1999). In vivo evidence for post-adolescent brain maturation in frontal and striatal regions. *Nature Neuroscience, 2,* 859–861.

Spear, L. P. (2000). The adolescent brain and age-related behavioral manifestations. *Neuroscience and Biobehavioral Reviews, 24,* 417–463.

Stanford v. Kentucky, 492 U.S. 361 (1989).

Steinberg, L. (2002). *Adolescence* (6th ed.). New York: McGraw-Hill.

Steinberg, L., & Cauffman, E. (1996). Maturity of judgment in adolescence: Psychosocial factors in adolescent decision making. *Law and Human Behavior, 20,* 249–272.

Steinberg, L., & Cauffman, E. (1999, December). A developmental perspective on serious juvenile crime: When should juveniles be treated as adults? *Federal Probation,* 52–57.

Steinberg, L., & Schwartz, R. (2000). Developmental psychology goes to court. In T. Grisso & R. Schwartz (Eds.), *Youth on trial* (pp. 9–31). Chicago: University of Chicago Press.

Steinberg, L., & Scott, E. (2000). Less guilty by reason of adolescence: Developmental immaturity, diminished responsibility, and the juvenile death penalty. *American Psychologist, 58,* 1009–1015.

Strauch, B. (2003). *The primal teen: What the new discoveries about the teenage brain tell us about our kids.* New York: Random House.

Tanenhaus, D. S. (2000). The evolution of transfer out of the juvenile court. In J. Fagan & F. E. Zimring (Eds.), *The changing borders of juvenile justice: Transfer of adolescents to the criminal court* (pp. 13–43). Chicago: University of Chicago Press.

U.S. Department of Health and Human Services. (2001). *Youth violence: A report of the surgeon general.* Rockville, MD: Author.

Wenar, C., & Kerig, P. (2000). *Developmental psychopathology: From infancy through adolescence.* Boston: McGraw-Hill.

CHAPTER 22

Psychological Evaluation and Testimony in Cases of Clergy and Teacher Sex Abuse

William E. Foote

Psychologists hired to consult or testify in lawsuits involving allegations of sexual misconduct by clergy and teachers enter into cases that are often complex. In some, legal issues such as vicarious liability or statute of limitations guide the psychological inquiry. In others, determining the impact of abuse that occurred 20 to 50 years before the evaluation poses significant hurdles in assessing both psychological and legal causation. Other cases put forensic mental health professionals in the role of determining the veracity of the complaint. All of these issues occur in an emotionally charged legal atmosphere in which politically active survivors vie with institutional authorities to set the public and legal agenda.

This chapter provides the reader with an introduction to the legal and psychological issues encountered in cases in which teachers and members of the clergy are accused of sexually abusing someone under their care. It begins with a general overview of the scope of the issue. Next is a discussion of the legal issues that arise in these cases. The chapter then examines emotional reactions of individuals who were sexually abused as children, with particular emphasis on what happens to those who were abused by teachers or clergy. The next section considers factors that place potential victims at risk as targets of sex offenses by these caretakers. The last section focuses on discerning damages in these cases.

THE SCOPE OF THE PROBLEM

In the 2 decades between 1985 and 2005, the public increasingly became aware of what appeared to be a broad societal problem: Individuals who were trusted because of their role or position, including clergy, teachers, and psychotherapists, were sexually abusing those placed in their care. This awareness came on the heels of a number of high-profile child care and nursery school sexual abuse cases (e.g., Smith, Runyan, & Fredrickson, 1994), an increasing sensitivity to the vulnerability of children to the abuse by caretakers (Finkelhor, 1979), and spreading concern about psychotherapist sexual misconduct (e.g., Bisbing, Jorgenson, & Sutherland, 1995; Schoener, Millgrom, Gonsiorek, Luepker, & Conroe, 1990).

Priest Sexual Misconduct

In 1985, a journalist published a detailed account of how the Roman Catholic Church had dealt with and, he alleged, covered up allegations of sexual abuse against a priest, Fr. Gilbert Gauthe, in Louisiana (Barry, 1985). Accounts of similar charges in Catholic and other religiously affiliated institutions in Canada soon followed (e.g., Harris, 1990). Next, the case of Fr. James Porter surfaced. He was criminally charged with sex abuse in 1987, but the case did not reach the public until 1993, after a number of similar cases emerged in various dioceses around the United States and Canada (Rossetti, 1996). Not until early in the new millennium did the Catholic Church and other denominations finally confront a major issue that challenged not only the church's credibility and authority, but made the church vulnerable to the impact of lawsuit settlements and awards that drew on church coffers (U.S. Conference of Bishops, 2004).

A large study conducted by John Jay College of Criminal Justice and sponsored by the U.S. Conference of Catholic Bishops (2004) estimated that since 1950, 110 of the 140 religious communities responding to the survey had at least one allegation of sexual misconduct against a priest who was a member of that congregation. When the data were aggregated across the United States, between 3% and 7% of the ordained priests serving the church had been accused of sexual abuse, and some 2.7% of priests in religious communities had similar allegations (U.S. Conference of Catholic Bishops, 2004). These figures were remarkably consistent and robust across geographic areas. The study estimates that between 1950 and 2002, these priests sexually abused a total of 10,505 victims (8,499 males and 2,004 females). However, the study did not provide the total number of children exposed to priests during the 52-year period, which precluded a determination of the incidence of this abuse.

Educator Sexual Misconduct

Sexual misconduct by teachers and other educational personnel has had a somewhat different history and may be even more widespread. In this case, it is not one or several religious organizations that have had charges against their employees, but educators, school boards, and school districts scattered around North America. Until recently, the breadth and nature of this phenomenon has been difficult to grasp. However, several studies have looked at sexual misconduct by teachers and other school personnel (American Association of University Women, 1993, 2001; Cameron et al., 1986; Corbett, Gentry, & Pearson, 1993; Shakeshaft, 2003; N. D. Stein, Marshall, & Tropp, 1993; U.S. Department of Education, 2004). Unfortunately, as Shakeshaft noted, the emphasis for much of this research has been on sexual harassment and abuse perpetrated by other children, not by educators. Reading this research gives one a sense that educators are no more eager to examine the misconduct of their employees than are church authorities.

Of these studies, the 1993 and 2001 studies by the American Association of University Women are the most comprehensive, tapping the experiences of 1,632 and 2,064 students in the 8th through 12th grades. Some 6.7% of students reported sexual misconduct involving contact; 8.7% reported conduct not involving contact. Because a number of children experienced both contact and noncontact abuse, a total of 9.7% reported some sort of misconduct.

In fact, as these data suggest, many more children may be the target of educators than of clergy. This difference is most likely a matter of access: Virtually all children go to school, but a smaller proportion attend church or parochial schools. On the other hand, it may be that a higher proportion of children who go to churches and parochial schools may be abused. Absent accurate prevalence figures in the clergy data, no accurate comparisons may be made.

Trends in Data

The data also indicate changes in the incidence of clergy and teacher sexual abuse over the past 50 years. It has been a general observation that reports of child sexual abuse have been generally decreasing since the late 1980s and early 1990s (U.S. Conference of Bishops, 2004; Minnesota Department of Children, Families, & Learning, 2001; Rennison, 2001). The pattern of clergy sexual abuse indicates that the peak years for allegations of sexual abuse were in the early 1980s. The data from the two studies of sexual misconduct by teachers indicate that the incidence of misconduct dropped from 44% to 38% in the 8-year interval between the 1993 and 2001 studies.

Some commentators (Jones & Finkelhor, 2001; U.S. Conference of Catholic Bishops, 2004) suggest three reasons for the general decline in sexual abuse in the United States. First, real rates of child sexual abuse may be dropping due to the increased attention and funding directed toward child abuse prevention. These drops parallel drops in teen pregnancy, child physical abuse, and rape. Second, professionals and agencies who report child sexual abuse may be reporting fewer cases. In the worst light, this reduced reporting may relate to a backlash against reporting based on concerns about false reports. In the most favorable light, child protection professionals may be more effective in distinguishing true from false allegations of abuse. Third, fewer cases may be substantiated on investigation.

Most living survivors of clergy abuse were abused in the 1970s and 1980s. Given that most victims are abused between the ages of 8 and 14, these survivors are now in their 30s and 40s. The practical implication is that their abuse experiences occurred 20 to 30 years ago, which becomes important when considering the legal context of clergy and teacher sexual abuse cases and attempts to determine damages.

LEGAL BACKGROUND AND ISSUES

This section[1] focuses on legal issues raised in the context of litigation against school personnel, clergy, and their employers. Those issues fall into three broad categories: the legal basis for liability of the parent religious organization, private company, or governmental entity; defenses raised by these entities; and the repressed memories controversy.

Liability of Parent Organizations

As a general matter, sex offenders are legally responsible for their acts. That is, they face criminal sanctions for sex offenses and may face civil actions that make

---

[1] The author expresses his appreciation to Linda Jorgenson and Stephen Rubino for their assistance in preparing this section.

them liable for pecuniary damages based on the harm they caused their victims. However, in many cases, the offender's ability to compensate the alleged victim is very limited, and the compensation available to the victim, even one who prevails, may be inadequate. Therefore, it is not surprising that alleged victims of sexual abuse by teachers and clergy usually also sue the employer of the alleged offender. This occurs for two reasons. First, the plaintiff may seek to change the institutional practices that allowed the abuse to occur in the first place. For example, in one California case, the settlement of a single plaintiff's lawsuit resulted in the Diocese of Orange County changing its procedures for dealing with priests who were accused of abusing children (Los Angeles Archdiocese, 2001). Second, the parent organization may have sufficient assets to appropriately compensate a person who was abused as a child.

Tort Theories of Negligence

A number of fundamental tort principles govern the vicarious liability of parent organizations. Torts are legal wrongs that typically have remedies in civil court. Employers become liable for their employees' (or, if guilty, *tortfeasors'*) actions based on what the employer did or did not do in relation to that employee.

Liability begins at the time of hiring. One legal commentator noted, "The employer has a duty to exercise reasonable care in hiring individuals who, because of the nature of the employment, may pose a threat of injury to members of the public" (Shields, 2004, p. 3). This is essentially a case of direct negligence. The defendants did not do something that they had a legal duty to do. In an ecclesiastical setting, ordination is similar to hiring. Although the clergy member may have been hired at an earlier time, the rite of ordination confers full powers and obligations on clergy.

Negligent hiring is based on three elements (McKee, 2003): (1) The tortfeasor is an employee or agent of the defendant employer; (2) the employer knew or should have known of the employee's unfitness at the time the employee was hired; and (3) after the tortfeasor was negligently hired, and was incompetent, unfit, or dangerous in some way, the employee's actions caused the plaintiff's injuries.

The employer has a legal duty to exercise reasonable care in hiring an employee, including conducting a reasonable investigation into the employee's past work experience, qualifications, and character. When the employee is in a position of special trust or responsibility, or when the employee will have access to individuals who are especially vulnerable, this duty may be increased, and the employer may be expected to go beyond the usual job application and references and launch an independent and more thorough inquiry. For example, in the case of *Evan F. v. Hughson United Methodist Church* (1992), the court ruled in favor of a parishioner who sued on the basis of sexual misconduct by the pastor. The ruling turned on whether the church had a reason to believe that a pastor was unfit and whether it failed to use reasonable care in investigating him.

Legal theories of tort liability for negligent retention are similar to those for negligent hiring. Some time after the employee was hired, the employer knew or should have known that the employee had problems that indicated unfitness, but failed to take action by investigating, reassigning, or discharging the employee. In this case, the employer must have notice of or knowledge of the employee's unfitness. For example, in the case of *Doe v. Redeemer Lutheran Church* (1995), a member who had been abused by a minister sued the church council for negligent retention. The council had taken no steps to address the problem even after it had received reports that the minister had been kissing a child and after it was informed that a child had quit confirmation class after she saw the minister masturbating.

In many cases, the employer has a duty to properly supervise employees and may be held liable if the supervision is negligent or reckless. For example, in a school situation, the employer may be held liable if the employer fails to listen to and react to reports from students, teachers, or parents about inappropriate behavior or to look for and react to "danger signs, clues of misconduct and indicia of abuse" (McKee, 2003, p. 22.) In a similar action, negligent training may be part of a claim when there are allegations that an employer's failure to train the employee was the proximate cause of the plaintiff's injuries.

Respondeat Superior

"Under the doctrine of respondeat superior, an employer is liable for an employee's wrongful or negligent act committed within the scope of employment" (Bisbing et al., 1995, p. 184). As compared to tort liability, respondeat superior does not require that the employer have notice that the employee is prone to committing bad acts. Rather, several elements must be present: (a) There must be an employer-employee relationship in which the employer exerts some control over the methods and means by which the work gets done; (b) the employee must be acting within the scope of his or her employment; and (c) these are acts that are closely connected or incidental to the work the employee is hired to do. The employer need not approve of the employee's specific tasks as long as those tasks are directed toward accomplishing the employer's goals. A more recent legal theory applying to the scope of employment question is the theory of "job-created authority" (Bisbing et al., 1995). This applies to situations in which the employee has been given authority by the employer and misuses that authority against a plaintiff. Although this has been applied successfully in lawsuits against police officers, courts have been reluctant to apply it to teacher cases (c.f. *John R. v. Oakland Unified School District,* 1989) or to priests (c.f. *Destefano v. Grabrian,* 1988).

Institutional Breach of Fiduciary Duty

Some professionals are given such status that they are seen as *fiduciaries.* That is, they are expected to act primarily in the interests of the person with whom they have a professional relationship or the person who is in their care. Some professionals, such as lawyers and legal guardians, are fiduciaries in the law and may face legal sanctions if they fail to place the welfare of their clients in the foremost position. Others, such as psychotherapists, have been determined to have fiduciary responsibilities in relation to their patients (*Roy v. Hartogs,* 1975). In some cases, courts have held that the parent organization has fiduciary duties, giving rise to the cause of institutional breach of fiduciary duty (Anderson, Noaker, & Finnegan, 2004; Bisbing et al., 1995; Shields, 2004). For example, in *F. G. v. McDonell* (1997), the New Jersey Supreme Court ruled that the offending pastoral counselor had a fiduciary duty toward his parishioner victim. In *Destefano v. Grabrian* (1988), the Colorado court held that a pastor had a fiduciary relationship with the parishioner. This finding, however, has not been uniform. In *Moses v. Diocese of Colorado* (1993), the court ruled that "the clergy-parishioner relationship is not necessarily a fiduciary relationship, though it does involve the type of interaction that creates trust and reliance" (Bisbing et al., 1995, p. 250).

Defenses

Defendants in clergy and teacher sex abuse litigation have used a number of legal theories in their defense. Four of these have been used with varying success across jurisdictions: 1st Amendment protections, charitable immunity, sovereign immunity, and the statute of limitations. A defendant may use more than one of these defenses in a single case.

1st Amendment Protections

The 1st Amendment free exercise and establishment clauses have protected religious institutions from lawsuits. Religious organizations have contended that their hiring, retention, and supervision practices were constitutionally protected and that the state would be interfering with their religious practices if the court allowed the church to be sued for negligence in these acts. For example, in *Ayon v. Gourley* (1999), the free exercise and establishment clauses protected a Roman Catholic archdiocese from a lawsuit filed by a plaintiff who was allegedly sexually abused by a priest. The church contended that it must be able to choose its priests without interference by the government. The court ruled that the lawsuit would result in excessive entanglement with, and inquiry into, church policy and doctrine. However, in a Florida case, *Malicki v. Doe* (2002), the court ruled that as long as the purpose of the state law was neutral regarding the religious beliefs of the church, claims were not barred under the 1st Amendment.

Charitable Immunity

The legal principle of charitable immunity protects churches and other eleemosynary organizations from lawsuits that could interfere with the group's positive efforts on behalf of the community. Historically, the principle has barred lawsuits against religious organizations (Conder, 2004). However, in recent years, charitable immunity has frequently been rejected as a defense (Shields, 2004).

Sovereign Immunity

This judicial doctrine precludes filing suit against the government without its consent. Statutes, usually referred to as *tort claim acts,* specify procedures that must be followed to file tort claims against the state (McKee, 2003). For the states, sovereign immunity was granted by the 11th Amendment to the U.S. Constitution, which states:

> The judicial power of the United States shall not be construed to extend to any suit in law or equity, commenced or prosecuted against one of the United States by citizens of another state, or by citizens or subjects of any foreign state.

Although there are still certain situations where some states apply the principle, in practical terms, sovereign immunity has been eroded by tort claim laws and civil rights statutes. For civil rights actions, section 1983 of the Civil Rights Act of 1871 allows the state government to be sued but requires proof that the plaintiff was deprived of a constitutionally guaranteed right by a defendant acting under the color of state law. In lawsuits filed under section 1983, the plaintiff cannot assert vicarious liability under respondeat superior. In addition, the standard for liability is one of "gross negligence or reckless disregard," which are both high legal standards (Bisbing et al., 1995).

In these cases, the state has an affirmative duty to protect. That is, the state, when it has a person under its control and care, assumes an affirmative duty (arising from the 14th Amendment's due process clause) to protect the "life, liberty and property of persons within its borders against the actions of private actors" (*Walton v. Alexander,* 1994, pp. 1354–1355). Sovereign immunity may be overcome when the plaintiff demonstrates that the state failed to, for example, protect a child from a teacher who was a known pedophile.

In addition, the plaintiff may claim that the state entity demonstrated a practice, custom, or policy of deliberate or reckless indifference (Bisbing et al., 1995). This, too, is based on constitutional guarantees, and the plaintiff must prove that "the defendant's policy, practice, or custom played an affirmative role in bringing about the sexual abuse and that the defendant acted with the deliberate indifference to that abuse" (*Black by Black v. Indiana Area School District,* 1993, p. 707). This cause of action arises in cases in which the authorities actually knew about the abuse but hid it and did not act on it.

Statutes of Limitations

State and federal statutes subject all causes of action to time limitations, specifying the time period between when a cause of action accrues and when the plaintiff must file suit against the offending person or organization. Once the time limit has run, no action, no matter how meritorious, may be filed. These statutes are based on principles of practicality and fairness; over time, people forget, documents and other physical evidence disappear. In addition, defendants must be able to set aside resources to defend themselves against lawsuits and pay awards to prevailing plaintiffs. If the organization's liability is temporally limitless, planning becomes difficult. These concerns, however, must be balanced with the plaintiff's right to have his or her day in court.

At first blush, it would seem that determining when a cause of action accrues would be easy. In a case in which a tort occurs in a discrete, public event like an auto accident, specifying the date when the clock starts is usually not a problem. However, in sexual abuse cases, accrual may not be so easily determined. For example, what happens if there is a time lag between when the act occurs and when the injury happens, as in cases in which a surgeon leaves a sponge in a patient's abdomen that does not cause an abscess until weeks later? What happens if there is a lag between when the injury occurs and when the plaintiff becomes aware that there has been an injury? In sexual abuse cases, these exceptions occur often because the psychological harm caused by the abuse may impair the victim's ability to identify the conduct as abusive and, at the same time, may prevent the plaintiff from connecting the abusive conduct with the harm suffered (Anderson et al., 2004; Doyle, 2003). In some cases, the harm itself (e.g., severe depression, agoraphobia) may also prevent the plaintiff from exercising legal remedies. In these situations, the statute may have run long before the plaintiff recognizes the injury or its cause.

To deal with this problem, some jurisdictions have adopted an exception to the statute of limitations, the *discovery rule.* By this rule, the cause of action does not accrue, and the statute of limitations does not begin to run, until the plaintiff discovers or, in the exercise of due diligence, should have discovered that he or she had been harmed as the result of the defendant's conduct. The discovery rule preserves the idea of accrual (i.e., that there has to be a time when the clock starts) but recognizes that the cause of action accrues when *in fact* the plaintiff could reasonably sue. The discovery rule has been adopted by a majority of states through statute or case law. Depending on jurisdiction, the cause of action accrues at one of four points: (1) when the defendant breaches his or her duty; (2) when the plaintiff suffers harm; (3) when the plaintiff becomes aware of his or her injury; or (4) when the plaintiff discovers the causal relationship between the harm and the misconduct (Bisbing et al., 1995).

When the discovery rule is invoked, issues of reasonableness and due diligence may be the focus of inquiry. "The fact that this individual plaintiff may have lacked knowledge of his or her injury is 'irrelevant,' the statute is tolled only if a reasonable person in the plaintiff's position would have been unaware of salient facts" (*A. McD. v. John Nathaniel Rosen, MD,* 1993, p. 128). Other jurisdictions have applied the rule more conservatively, as in *Hickey v. Askren* (1991), in which the court demanded that the plaintiff had to be "completely unaware of any harm caused her by the [defendant doctor's] alleged negligent treatment of her and the sexual contact between them" (p. 228).

Statutes of limitations are usually tolled during the period of the plaintiff's minority or insanity, and in some jurisdictions, during imprisonment. It is usually necessary that the disability be present at the time the cause of action accrues. However, it gets more complicated when the disability is not so obvious. One state, Texas, has dealt with the issue statutorily (Texas Civil Practice and Remedies Code, 81.009):

> If a patient or former patient entitled to file an action under this chapter is unable to bring the action because of the effects of the sexual exploitation, continued emotional dependence on the mental health services provider, or threats, instructions, or statements by the mental health services provider, the deadline for filing an action under this chapter is tolled during that period, except that the deadline may not be tolled for more than 15 years.

Equitable Remedies

Two remedies in equity may be sought to toll the statute of limitations. Both of these are based on the conduct of the defendant. The first, *fraudulent concealment,* was established in the nineteenth century in the landmark case of *Bailey v. Glover* (1874), which determined three elements necessary to toll the statute of limitations: (1) The defendant wrongfully concealed the conduct that constitutes the cause of action; (2) the defendant's concealment prevented the plaintiff from discovering the cause of action; and (3) the plaintiff exercised due diligence in attempting to discover the cause of action. Fraudulent concealment is pled in some clergy and teacher sex abuse cases in which the defendant pedophile has convinced the plaintiff child that the sex is "part of what you have to learn in school" or "what God wants you to know."

Equitable estoppel is a form of estoppel defined as when the "party is prevented by his own acts from claiming a right to detriment of other party who was entitled to rely on such conduct and has acted accordingly" (H. C. Black, 1991, p. 383). To successfully exercise this remedy, the plaintiff must establish that the defendant "wrongfully induced [the plaintiff] to postpone bringing a suit or [has] fraudulently concealed a cause of action unknown to the plaintiff" (*Anonymous v. Anonymous*, 1992, p. 722). Equitable estoppel is argued in clergy cases in which the plaintiff or plaintiff's parents went to a church authority, such as a bishop or cardinal, and reported the abuse. The authority then told the family that they should not do anything else, because the church will take care of it, and, as a result, the family failed to timely file suit.

Repressed Memories

This Pandora's box of legal and psychological controversy was opened largely in response to statutes of limitations in civil actions. The fundamental notion is that the plaintiff had repressed or forgotten the sexual abuse, but later remembered it and was able to file suit only after the statute of limitations had run. This seemingly unresolvable scientific controversy, sometimes referred to as *delayed recall*, is far too complex and extensive to cover in this chapter. It has provoked thick tomes and prolific research to support both sides of the argument (e.g., Bornstein & Muller, 2001; D. Brown, Schleflin, & Hammond, 1998; Cannell, Hudson, & Pope, 2001; Gordon, 1998; Leavitt, 2001; Loftus, 1996; Loftus & Bernstein, 2005; Loftus & Polage, 1999; Meiser-Stedman, 2005; Ornstein, Ceci, & Loftus, 1998; Partlett & Nurcombe, 1998).

RESEARCH ON ADULTS SEXUALLY ABUSED AS CHILDREN

A review of the child sexual abuse literature reveals that child sexual abuse is a relatively frequent occurrence in the lives of women and men. Using the criterion that the sexual abuse involved contact between the perpetrator and victim, the prevalence rates vary from 2.8% to 17.3% for males (Fromuth & Burkhart, 1987; Urquiza & Capra, 1990) and from 6.8% to 28.1% for women (Finkelhor, Hotaling, Lewis, & Smith, 1990; J. A. Stein, Golding, Siegel, Burnam, & Sorenson, 1988). Broader definitions of child sexual abuse result in higher prevalence rates. For males, the inclusion of noncontact acts raises the range to 23% to 36.9%; for females, the rates climb to 19% to 53% (Finkelhor, 1979; Metcalfe, Oppenheimer, Dignon, & Palmer, 1990).

Several large review studies indicate that people with a history of child sexual abuse experience a range of abusive events (Beitchman et al., 1992; Dhaliwal,

Gauzas, Antonowicz, & Ross, 1996; Jumper, 1995; Paolucci, Genuis, & Violato, 2001; Polusny & Follette, 1995). Children who experience child sexual abuse are most likely to be boys between the ages of 7 and 11 and girls between the ages of 7 and 14. For both males and females, the average duration of abuse ranged from 2 to 6 years. Up to half of child sexual abuse victims experienced sexual intercourse, with equal numbers reporting oral intercourse. Fondling is a more frequent event, reported by as many as 92% of those with a history of child sexual abuse (Hunter, 1991; Kendall-Tackett & Simon, 1992). Most studies indicate that about half of the people with a history of child sexual abuse have experienced more than one abusive incident. Males are more likely to be perpetrators for both male and female victims. However, in some samples, the majority of boys were abused by females (Fritz, Stoll, & Wagner, 1981; Fromuth & Burkhart, 1989; Seidner & Calhoun, 1984). Between one-tenth and one-half of child sexual abuse victims were abused by family members (Dhaliwal et al., 1996; Paolucci et al., 2001).

Impact of Sexual Abuse on Adult Survivors

Many children who experience sexual abuse will face the long-term consequences of that abuse. These consequences have been studied in a series of meta-analyses (Beitchman et al., 1992; Dhaliwal, Gauzas, Antonowicz, & Ross, 1995; Jumper, 1995; Neumann, Houskamp, Pollock, & Briere, 1996; Paolucci et al., 2001; Polusny & Follette, 1995; Rind & Tromovitch, 1997). In general, people with a history of child sexual abuse are less well adjusted than those who were not abused. A number of studies have determined that a disproportionate number of people with a history of child sexual abuse are patients in psychological, psychiatric, and substance abuse treatment (G. R. Brown & Anderson, 1991; Jacobson & Herald, 1990; Paris, Zweig-Frank, & Guzder, 1994; Roesler & McKenzie, 1994; Rohsenow, Corbett, & Devine, 1988).

Child sexual abuse has also been implicated as an element of histories of people suffering from physical illnesses (Golding, Cooper, & George, 1997; Sachs-Ericsson, Blazer, Plant, & Arnow, 2005; Wurtele, Kaplan, & Keairnes, 1990). For example, Wurtele et al. found that those with a history of child sexual abuse were overrepresented in samples of female pain patients. In their sample of 135 chronic pain patients, 39% of the women and 7% of the men reported a history of child sexual abuse. A recent study that separated the impact of physical abuse from that of sexual abuse (Sachs-Ericsson et al., 2005) found that sexual abuse added to the probability that one would experience a wide range of medical problems.

Research in both community and patient samples indicates that people with a history of sexual abuse as children have an increased risk for a diagnosis of depression (Briere, Evans, Runtz, & Wall, 1988; Levitan et al., 1998; Polusny & Follette, 1995). For example, in a meta-analysis of studies on the impact of child sexual abuse, one group of researchers (Paolucci et al., 2001) determined that people with child sexual abuse histories are at a 21% increased risk for depression, a finding that was generally reproduced in other research. Suicidal ideation and behavior have also been observed more frequently in populations who have experienced sexual abuse as children. One meta-analysis (Paolucci et al., 2001) found an additional 20% factor among child sexual abuse samples for suicidal ideation and behavior. In general, the number of suicide attempts in a child sexual abuse patient population is about twice that of similar self-destructive acts in patients who were not sexually abused as children (Briere et al., 1988; Briere & Zaidi, 1989). The incidence of suicidal ideation is similarly elevated for those with a history of child sexual abuse (Saunders, Villeponteaux, Lipovsky, & Kilpatrick, 1992).

Anxiety disorders in general appear to be common consequences of child sexual abuse. The general level of anxiety reported by people with a history of child sexual abuse appears to be higher than that of persons not sexually abused as children (Briere & Runtz, 1988a; Polusny & Follette, 1995; M. B. Stein et al., 1996). Social phobia, panic disorders, and agoraphobia appear to be specially implicated as sequelae of child sexual abuse. Posttraumatic Stress Disorder (PTSD) is a syndrome commonly seen in people with child sexual abuse histories (G. R. Brown & Anderson, 1991; Pribor & Dinwiddie, 1992; Roesler & McKenzie, 1994). Some (e.g., Finkelhor, 1990) argue that PTSD is not a good model for child sexual abuse because the trauma is often repeated over a long time, as opposed to occurring in an acute episode. Others note that although the full PTSD syndrome is not always present, the survivor may experience specific clusters of symptoms. For example, Kilpatrick et al. (1989) noted that in a sample of victims of sexual assaults, the prevalence of symptoms related to PTSD was 41% for reexperiencing, 28% for avoidance, and 38% for the arousal symptom clusters.

Women who experienced sexual abuse as children are at significantly higher risk for substance abuse problems, a finding especially in research conducted in treatment settings (Polusny & Follette, 1995; Rohsenow et al., 1988). Research on men reveals a mixed picture. One community study (Polusny & Follette, 1995) found the rate of substance abuse disorders among sexually abused men was 44.9%, as compared to 7.8% among men who had not been abused. In contrast, Dhaliwal et al. (1996) observed higher rates of substance abuse in men without a history of sexual abuse than in men with that background (see G. R. Brown & Anderson, 1991).

Patterns of emotional reactions to child sexual abuse, especially long-term abuse, may resemble symptoms of a personality disorder. For example, Paris et al. (1994) determined that 47.5% of men with a Borderline Personality Disorder diagnosis had a history of child sexual abuse, although only 25% of those with other personality disorders reported child sexual abuse. In this case, the nature of the child sexual abuse had a significant impact on the personality disorder diagnosis. Those men who had experienced anal penetration or physical force had a much higher probability of the Borderline Personality Disorder diagnosis. The findings of these two studies have been widely replicated (e.g., Silk, Lee, Hill, & Lohr, 1995; Weaver & Clum, 1993). However, although child sexual abuse may be a sufficient cause of Borderline Personality Disorder, it is not a necessary one. About one-half to one-third of patients diagnosed with Borderline Personality Disorder did *not* experience child sexual abuse (Silk et al., 1995).

People who are sexually abused as children are significantly more likely to be victimized again later in life, a phenomenon referred to as *revictimization* (Arata, 2000; Grauerholz, 2000; Hamilton, 1989; Humphrey & White, 2000; Maker, Kemmelmeier, & Peterson, 2001; Romano & De Luca, 2001). The incidence of subsequent rape, domestic violence, and other crimes of violence is much higher in child sexual abuse populations than in those who were not abused. Some researchers suggest that this association is related to the occurrence of PTSD symptoms in child sexual abuse survivors (Briere & Runtz, 1983; Dansky & Kilpatrick, 1997). If the later assault or abuse context is similar to the original child sexual abuse events, the person may experience dissociation or PTSD symptoms that interfere with effective defense or escape (Briere & Runtz, 1988b; Sandberg, Matorin, & Lynn, 1994; Wilson, Calhoun, & Bernat, 1999).

Because of the nature of child sexual abuse and when it occurs in the child's developmental cycle, it is likely that sexual abuse would adversely affect the victim's later sexual adjustment. Beitchman et al. (1992) found that sexual functioning was most disturbed in women who were abused by their fathers and who suffered sexual penetration. For men, problems with increased sexual aggressivity, lower sexual self-esteem, avoidance of sexual activities, and specific sexual dysfunction are common (Dhaliwal et al., 1996). Paolucci et al. (2001) found a 14-fold increase in sexual promiscuity in child sexual abuse samples.

Research indicates that a higher proportion of child sexual abuse victims report later homosexual activity (Beitchman et al., 1992; Finkelhor, 1984; Runtz & Briere, 1986; Simari & Baskin, 1982). For women, this association occurs mostly in clinical samples and represents a marginally higher level of lesbian orientation among child sexual abuse survivors compared to nonvictims. Although being prone to developing a homosexual orientation may make a child a more likely target of a pedophile (see later discussion), for men not so oriented, being the victim of a same-sex offender may produce beliefs that one is attracted to same-sex partners. Coping with these feelings is played out in hypermasculine activities such as interpersonal violence, in the numbing effect of substance abuse, and in disturbed homosexual and heterosexual intimate relationships (Dimock, 1988; but see Sarwer, Crawford, & Durlak, 1997). In addition, same-sex victims may adopt a markedly homophobic attitude (Gerber, 1990).

Some research has been directed to the impact of child sexual abuse on work behavior. A study of patients in Vermont (Little & Hamby, 1999) found that both men and women child sexual abuse survivors listed work dysfunction as a major problem area.

A study of Roman Catholics (Rossetti, 1995) found that *any* experience of sexual abuse reduced victims' trust in religious institutions and relationship to God. Damage to spiritual life was even greater for victims of clergy sexual abuse.

Exceptions to the Rule

Not all victims of sexual abuse experience significant psychological sequelae of those experiences (Finkelhor, 1990). For example, in a review of the literature on child victims of sexual abuse, researchers found that, among children who were sexually abused, no single or even multisymptom patterns emerged (Kendall-Tackett, Williams, & Finkelhor, 1993; see Kuenhle, 2003). Although more than half the children reported some PTSD symptoms, sexualized behavior was also quite common (35% promiscuity, 28% inappropriate sexual behavior), and depressive symptoms were common, with 28% of their sample reporting feeling depressed, 22% withdrawn, and 12% suicidal. For children, anxiety symptoms tend to abate over time, whereas externalizing behaviors such as aggressiveness and sexual symptoms tend to worsen. Within the 1st year and a half after disclosure, 50% to 66% of all children became less symptomatic, and 10% to 24% became more so. The surprising finding of this study was that between 21% and 49% of sexually abused children were *asymptomatic*. The researchers opined that this large group of apparently well survivors may be accounted for in several ways: (a) The measures used may have lacked sufficient sensitivity to measure the more subtle reactions to child sexual abuse; (b) these children may have had delayed symptoms, which might later emerge under stress or particular life events; and (c) the asymptomatic group may have been children who were more resilient or had more social support and, as a result, were less affected by the stresses associated with child sexual abuse.

Research Focusing on Victims of Clergy and Teacher Abuse

The one large-scale study of clergy abuse (U.S. Conference of Catholic Bishops, 2004) indicated that the victims of Roman Catholic clergy have certain characteristics. The vast majority (80.9%) were male. Most were between the ages of 9 and 16 when the abuse occurred. Table 22.1 illustrates the age distribution of the Catholic clergy victims.

Although many child victims were in the usual age group for child abuse victims, between 8 and 12, a large proportion were teenagers, suggesting that the perpetrators of this abuse would be, in many cases, described as ephibophiles or

Table 22.1   Victim's Age at First Instance of Abuse

Age (Years)	Count	Total (%)
1	4	0.0
2	11	0.1
3	22	0.2
4	41	0.5
5	82	1.0
6	158	1.8
7	220	2.5
8	369	4.1
9	362	4.0
10	752	8.4
11	895	10.0
12	1,323	14.7
13	1,141	12.8
14	1,188	13.2
15	1,042	11.6
16	769	8.6
17	577	6.5
Total	8,956	100

Adapted from *The Nature and Scope of Sexual Abuse of Minors by Catholic Priests and Deacons in the United States 1950–2002* (p. 70), by the U.S. Conference of Catholic Bishops, 2004, Washington, DC: Author. Copyright U.S. Conference of Catholic Bishops. Adapted with permission.

Table 22.2   Alleged Acts of Abuse, by Sex

Behavior Alleged	Sex		Combined Totals
	Males	Females	
Verbal (sexual talk)	11.5	12.0	11.6
Shown pornography	2.9	0.5	2.4
Shown pornography videos	1.8	0.3	1.6
Touch over cleric's clothes	9.1	9.2	9.2
Touch over victim's clothes	37.2	38.6	37.4
Touch under victim's clothes	42.6	39.2	42.0
Cleric disrobed	12.3	9.9	11.8
Victim disrobed	14.4	16.9	14.9
Photos of victim	2.2	1.8	2.1
Sexual games	1.2	0.4	1.1
Hugging and kissing	4.2	9.8	5.3
Masturbation	8.6	4.0	7.7
Mutual masturbation	13.6	1.6	11.4
Cleric performed oral sex	15.4	15.9	15.4
Victim performed oral sex	10.4	6.4	9.6
Manual penetration	2.5	10.9	4.1
Penetration with object	0.8	1.5	0.9
Penile penetration	12.9	11.9	12.7
Group or coerced sex	0.6	0.2	0.5
Unspecified sex act	12.2	11.4	12.1
Other	6.4	4.9	6.1

Adapted from *The Nature and Scope of Sexual Abuse of Minors by Catholic Priests and Deacons in the United States 1950–2002* (p. 73), by the U.S. Conference of Catholic Bishops, 2004, Washington, DC: Author. Copyright U.S. Conference of Catholic Bishops. Adapted with permission.

hebophiles, those who show a preference for having sex with teens. This same study yielded a description of the various acts perpetrated on victims by clergy offenders. Table 22.2 shows the range of those experiences. Fondling offenses appear to be the most common, with oral sex and penile penetration occurring somewhat less often.

Research Comparing Reactions of Fiduciary Abuse Victims

One group of researchers (Disch & Avery, 2001) examined survivors of sexual abuse by medical professionals, mental health professionals, and clergy. Many survivors developed abuse-related problems. Most reported emotional turmoil following abuse, and two-thirds reported strong emotions that were difficult to handle. All reported significant intrusion and avoidance symptoms, and panic attacks and nightmares were common. Two-thirds reported a decreased ability to work, which most related to symptoms of depression. Of the sample, one-quarter had been hospitalized for emotional troubles, and many experienced increased suicide risk.

Interpersonal connections of many of the survivors were disrupted by the abuse. Some 70% of survivors report feeling isolated from others by the experience, and only 50% of respondents were in committed relationships. This disruption may have occurred because of damage to the survivor's ability to trust, as 83% reported impaired trust in others, and 70% had difficulty forming close relationships. Sexual relationships were often disrupted, and 90% reported guilt, shame, and humiliation about what happened. Emotional dyscontrol evident in rage reactions were common in later reactions to abuse. Many (80%) blamed themselves for what happened, which significantly reduced their self-esteem.

Survivors of clergy abuse particularly have disruption of their spirituality and relationship with God. A substantial portion of survivors had plans to become clergy themselves, and that plan was adversely affected by abuse. Very few stayed in the church in which they were abused. Many have no church affiliation at all, and others go to a very different setting. Protestant fundamentalist sects seem to be popular, especially those denominations without a church hierarchy.

Given the fact that statutes of limitation often apply to these cases, a number of survivors reported a delayed recognition of abuse. Of the sample, 85% reported that they had been through a period when they did not understand how the abuse had affected them. This may have been related to a finding that at some point during or after the abuse, 84% felt ambivalent and confused about the perpetrator, and many still felt this way. Of the survivors, 85% reported still unresolved issues in relation to the abuse. In spite of this confusion, 80% reported the abuse to someone, usually a significant other.

Research with Clergy Abuse Victims

In one small study with a litigation sample, Mart (2004) provided data on 25 cases. Although the author did not subject his data to statistical analysis because of the small sample size, it appeared that many of these clergy victims had problems with avoidant symptoms, which caused them to stay away from other people, especially people in groups. They appeared shy and hesitant in their interviews. The data did not indicate whether the avoidant characteristics were a result of the abuse, or whether these characteristics predated the abuse and were, in fact, a risk factor for the child becoming a target of a potential clergy sex offender.

Research with Educator Misconduct Victims

The data reported by the U.S. Department of Education (2004) provide some insight about the emotional reactions of children who were sexually abused by teachers and other education professionals. A uniform finding was that more girls than boys were targets of sexual misconduct by educators. Two studies yielded the largest proportion of female victims, about 77% of those abused by educational personnel (Corbett et al., 1993; Hendrie & Drummond, 1998). The balance of the studies showed less of a skew in the sex distribution, with the American Association of University Women (2001) study finding that girls were 56% of educator abuse victims. This same study is the source of most of what is currently known about the reactions of children to sexual misconduct by educational personnel. For many of these targets of abuse, the impact was directly on their academic achievement. About 36% did not want to go to school, 29% stayed home from school or cut a class, and 43% attempted to avoid the teacher. Attention and concentration were often casualties of teacher abuse. Affected children reported that they had trouble paying attention (31%) and found it hard to study (29%). Over 33% did not want to talk in class. For many, the context of the school itself became aversive. Some students thought about changing schools (19%), and a smaller proportion (6%) actually did transfer to a different school. School performance deteriorated for many students. About 25% admitted that they had received a lower grade on a test or assignment, had received a lower grade in a class, or felt that it was likely that they would receive a lower grade. About the same proportion got into trouble with school authorities because of their behavior. The abuse also affected basic aspects of health and well-being. Over 25% of the targets of sexual misconduct reported sleeping and appetite loss. Over 50% of these children felt embarrassed, and 39% reported feeling self-conscious. About the same proportion (37%) reported feeling less sure and self-confident. Many (36%) felt afraid or scared, and others (29%) developed confusion about their identity. As noted previously, it is not uncommon for male victims of male offenders to experience this confusion. About 29% had doubts that they could ever have a happy romantic relationship.

STYLES OF OFFENDING

Based on my work with survivors of clergy and teacher sexual abuse and on the experiences reported by other mental health professionals (e.g., Doyle, 2003; Gonsiorek, 1999), it is clear that teacher and clergy sex offenders engage in specific patterns of behavior in relation to their victims. An understanding of these patterns can assist the forensic professional in interviewing alleged victims by providing reference points for determining credibility and severity of emotional reactions. For some offenders, these patterns are repetitive and may reflect a particular paraphilia or may be responsive to constraints of the environment in which they abuse children. For others, the pattern may change frequently or may evolve over time. A number of these patterns may be evident in the behavior of the same offender over time and are not mutually exclusive, and they may be used with the same child. Other patterns characterize most, if not all, of an offender's sexual assaults.

Gradual seduction: Some offenders spend months or even years grooming the child to be a victim. For example, the teacher or clergy may involve the child in church or school duties or relieve the child of onerous tasks such as sweeping or homework. The offender may take the child on trips, which has the dual effect of seducing the child and isolating the child so the offense may be facilitated. Some offenders go to great lengths to ingratiate themselves with the child's family. Once trust is built, getting the child alone is facilitated. From the accounts of victims, it is evident that the initial behavior of the offender may be ambiguous, such as touching the child's genitals while helping the child don liturgical garments. As the seduction proceeds, the offender involves the child in activities that remove the child from the observation and control of other adults. For example, the offender may take the child from the school or church to restaurants, gyms, or wilderness areas. The offender may increasingly talk about the deep affection that has developed in relation to the child. In some cases, the seduction is so well done that the victim may not realize until some later time that what happened was, in fact, sexual abuse.

Posing as education: Some offenders disguise their actions toward the child as a form of educational exercise, often perverse sex education. For example, one offender told a number of victims, "I have to teach you so you will understand how to have sex with women when you grow up." In some cases, teachers and clergy may accompany these messages to boys with misogynistic lectures about how "girls are no good."

The power play: The clergy or teacher may use the authority of his or her position to demand that the child does what is asked. This often occurs in the context of punishment for real or fabricated offenses. For example, the child may be told, "Go to the janitor's office, and I will punish you for what you did." Once there, the offender may fondle or otherwise molest the child. In some cases, the child may not report the abuse because of relief about not getting a spanking.

Creating or taking advantage of an opportunity: Because teachers and clergy have access to a broad range of legitimate contact with children, their opportunities to offend are increased. For example, if the child is already in a state of undress for legitimate reasons, such as a shower, bedtime, or changing clothes, the teacher or clergy may use this occasion to instigate touching.

Hiding in plain sight: Because of the fiduciary nature of the work of teachers and clergy, they are sometimes assumed to be doing the right thing even when molesting children. In one case, the offending priest fondled children while standing behind them in the school yard and was never reported by the nuns and teachers who were also present. In another case, a teacher would call boys to the front of the room and fondle their penises in front of the whole class. This went on for 15 years until someone finally complained (U.S. Department of Education, 2004).

Rape: This extreme form of abuse may be the culmination of grooming and seduction or may be the offender's style of offending. In most cases, rape is predicated on getting the child alone. After the rape, the offender may use intimidation as a basis for silence.

Offender-Controlled Variables That Place Children at Risk for Abuse

When dealing with individuals who claim abuse as children by teachers or clergy, some patterns become evident. Even the most active pedophiles do not offend against all possible victims at all times. Rather, they often select victims on the basis of specific factors. A potential offender is alert for three factors in relation to his victims: access, acquiescence, and silence. Each may be accomplished in different ways, depending on the offender's work situation, the child, and the offender's preferences.

Access

The offender needs to get the child alone, away from the eyes and supervision of parents or other caretakers (Finkelhor, 1984). Gaining access may center on the locations in which the offender interacts with potential victims. For example, a priest may use a robing room as place of initial contact, and teachers may use shower rooms or coat closets. Some offenders use work-related situations to gain access.

For example, one priest engaged a child in "private Bible study" where fondling took place. An offending teacher took children to a closet for "punishment" after trivial classroom infractions. Other offenders create relationships as part of a grooming or seduction process. For example, many offending priests were effectively "members of the family" for the child victim, invited to dinner and to other family activities (Doyle, 2003). One teacher was close to family members and offered to babysit for the child victim (Foote, 2002).

In some cases, children are at risk because of a lack of clear boundaries about where the professional should be at a given time. For example, for most teachers, the classroom and other clearly educational functions are contexts in which the offender would have legitimate access to children. In contrast, a priest may be involved not only in personal or family crises such as illness and death, but potentially in every daily activity. This lack of clear limits clouds the ability of a victim and family to recognize boundary violations.

Acquiescence

The offender needs the child to submit to his or her demands. For most offenders, the authority relationship and the standing of the offender in the community assure acquiescence. For clergy, the priest, pastor, or nun may be assumed to be "close to God." A teacher in a remote native community may be the first trained educator that the community ever had (Foote, 2002). Some children are trained to be obedient to those in authority, especially clergy. For example, in many traditional Catholic homes, the priest's authority is virtually unquestioned.

For some offenders, it is necessary to develop a cover story. For example, more than one priest has told his child victim that the sex act is "something that God wants us to do." Some offenders may use more blatant bribery or favors to ensure the child's acquiescence. For example, one clergy offender set up a boys' club house at the rectory and provided X-rated movies, drugs, and alcohol to his victims. Some teachers provided food or favored treatment in class in exchange for the child's passivity. Some offenders may resort to intimidation. One priest of great physical stature threatened to strike children who did not submit. Some offenders use drugs and alcohol to make the child pliable. One schoolteacher slipped the children barbiturates in their orange juice, then molested them while they were asleep.

Some offenders will use the pattern of the "myth of complicity": They convince the child that the molestation is what the child wants because it may feel good (Gerber, 1990). Because boys may be more easily sexually aroused than girls, the boy may experience the molestation as pleasurable (Fritz et al., 1981; Mendel, 1995). The offender is then able to use the child's sexual arousal to convince him that he wanted it to happen.

As will be discussed later, some children are chosen as potential victims because of an impoverished or chaotic home life. For these children, the provision of affection may ensure acquiescence. One clergy abuse victim said, "It was the best relationship I have ever had." One teacher provided a number of boys with affection, along with food and privileges. These children, all of whom had no affection at home, maintained relationships with the offender that spanned several years.

Silence

Research indicates that many or most child sexual abuse victims tell no one about their abuse (Briere & Elliott, 1994; Mendel, 1995), sometimes even when questioned (Lawson & Chaffin, 1992). Males are especially reluctant to report, perhaps because of shame associated with the abuse (Hunter, 1991; Mendel, 1995). Some offenders ensure silence by way of threats, intimidation, and physical abuse. One group of researchers (Langevin, Curnoe, & Bain, 2000) found that victims who were not physically abused were likely to report within 1 year, whereas those who were physically abused reported only after 7 years. Some offenders convince the child not to report because of the adverse impact the disclosure would have on the community. In this context, a priest offender told the child that disclosure would "undermine God's work." A teacher in a remote Arctic community asked the victim, "Who will replace me as teacher?" Some clergy offenders misuse the principle of priest-penitent confidentiality. For example, one priest told the child, "You know that everything that happens between a priest and a parishioner is confidential, don't you?"

Sometimes, children have no idea whom to tell about the abuse. In one clergy case, a child who disclosed the abuse to the mother superior who ran the school that employed the molesting priest was severely punished for "lying about the good father." In another case, a child molested by the teacher believed that if he disclosed the abuse, the principal would side with the teacher. Accordingly, some children do not disclose for fear they will not be believed. A number of clergy and teacher victims were punished by their parents when they reported the abuse. Some children do not report because they fear ostracism by their religious community. For example, one girl who reported that the priest fondled her was publicly humiliated by nuns in the school.

Sometimes the child's own inhibitions prevent disclosure. Shame is a powerful silencer because the child believes that the real offender is himself or herself (Harper & Arias, 2004). The child may think, "It was my fault, so who would I report it to?" This shame is abetted by the silence strategy of the myth of complicity (Gerber, 1990). Because the child experiences pleasure as part of the abuse process, the child assumes that he or she wanted the abuse to happen. Perhaps aware of this tendency, offenders may say, "How can I stop myself, when you are so beautiful?"

A variation on this theme is the notion of "traumatic bonding" as it is applied to sexual abuse (Doyle, 2003; Dutton & Painter, 1993a, 1993b). In this theory, the trauma of the abuse connects the victim to the abuser. This principle is based on two elements: (1) The abuse does not happen all the time, and (2) abusive experiences are mixed with positive experiences.

Family Factors That Place Children at Risk for Abuse

The nature of the child's family and the child's place in that family may make the child more vulnerable to abuse. It has long been noted that children raised in homes where there is domestic violence, substance abuse, and child abuse are more vulnerable to sexual abuse (D. A. Black, Heyman, & Slep, 2001; Rowland, Zabin, &

Emerson, 2000). However, in cases of clergy and teacher sexual abuse, the child from a nondysfunctional home may be at equal or greater risk than the child from more chaotic circumstances (Doyle, 2003).

Positive Family Factors That Facilitate Abuse

These factors reside in the families of potential victims in which devotion to the church is a strong family value. In these homes, the parents are honored when the clergy member expresses a desire to be with the family or child. This may translate into conversations about the peripubescent boy being prepared for a vocation in the priesthood. Because the clergy member may be likened to a family member, and because of the lack of clear boundaries, the child may be at special risk. Also, these families often teach the importance of the clergy's authority. In these "good homes," the factor of "religious duress" (Doyle, 2003) may play a role. This theory, created by an expert in canon law, posits that the combination of the priest's role in relation to the family and the power and authority conferred on the priest by the church makes his demands on the child impossible to resist.

Negative Family Factors That Facilitate Abuse

Researchers have determined that some family factors may place children at risk for abuse (Finkelhor, 1984). One of the "preconditions" for child sexual abuse may be defined as "factors predisposing to overcoming external inhibitors" (p. 57), conditions that are common in the homes of children abused by teachers and clergy. For example, in many of these homes, fathers are absent, which may cause the child to seek another adult male figure with whom to bond (Mendel, 1995). The mother may be mentally or physically ill, be overcome by substance abuse, or lack bonding with the child, which would neutralize her as a protective factor for the child. Some children may be alienated from their peer group because of a recent move into the neighborhood or a cultural or linguistic difference that causes the child to have difficulty integrating with a peer group. Boys who are gay or pregay may be at special risk (Gonsiorek, 1994) because of the attendant alienation, and also because their appearance and behavior may make them more attractive to offenders. Pedophiles may assume that these boys would be less likely to report the abuse. Some children are at risk because of mental retardation or psychopathology. These conditions would render them less likely to resist or report the abuse.

DAMAGES

Damages typically relate to a finite range of harms that may be addressed through the legal process. Based on the studies reviewed in this chapter, it is clear that the sexual abuse of a minor may cause pain and suffering to the plaintiff. In addition, for victims of clergy abuse, loss of religious life or loss of faith may be a component of the betrayal by one who is responsible for developing and nurturing that faith. If the victim's sexual functioning is impaired, the plaintiff's spouse may file a claim for loss of consortium. In some jurisdictions, a similar claim for loss of love and guidance may be filed by the victim's children. Because the sexual abuse occurs during the years when the child is of school age, and may even take place in school, it is not unusual for the child to develop educational impairments that translate into economic damages. This economic loss, because it occurs at the beginning of the person's work life, may be the largest dollar component of the damages awarded in these cases. Future medical care may also be a significant line item, especially if the plaintiff has developed serious suicidal problems or has a substance abuse disorder attributable to the sexual abuse. Frequent hospitalizations and weekly counseling or psychotherapy can be large economic line items.

Legal Basis

For the court to allow the jury to consider these damages, the plaintiff must prove that there is a causal nexus between the sexual abuse and the harms claimed by the plaintiff. Legal causation may be conceptualized as a line running from the events in question to specific damages claimed by the plaintiff. *Proximate cause* is defined as "that which, in a natural and continuous sequence, unbroken by any efficient intervening cause, produces injury, and without which the result would not have occurred" (H. C. Black, 1991, p. 883). The plaintiff need not prove that the events are the only basis for the injury, as other causes may contribute to the final occurrence of the symptoms or problems. Rather, the plaintiff often must prove that "but for" the events in question, the harms would not have ensued. This "but for" or "sine qua non" test (Bisbing et al., 1995) means that psychological experts working in these cases must determine the contribution made by the sexual abuse experiences as separate from other unfortunate events that may have befallen the plaintiff.

As noted previously, many children who are subject to fiduciary abuse are already stressed by neglectful or abusive homes (Merrill, Thomsen, Sinclair, Gold, & Milner, 2001). These same children may be going through other trauma at the same time the abuse is occurring, such as ongoing physical abuse. A large body of research indicates that those who were sexually abused as children are subject to a host of subsequent stressors, including other sexual assaults and domestic violence (Hamilton, 1989; Humphrey & White, 2000; Maker et al., 2001). These events may not be directly attributable to the tortious events but may cause symptoms similar to the sequelae of the abuse. The job of determining proximate cause is a difficult one in many of these cases and is compounded by the retrospective nature of the examination (see Simon & Shuman, 2003).

In most cases, when the mental health expert is evaluating the adult who was abused as a child, several decades have passed since the abuse occurred. This means that the plaintiff's memory and the memory of collaterals and other witnesses may have faded or be subject to error (DePrince, Allard, Oh, & Freyd, 2004; Lees-Haley et al., 1997; Martelli, Zasler, Bender, & Nicholson, 2004). Documents such as treatment records and school transcripts may have been destroyed. Symptoms may have changed from acute to chronic. Deficits caused by the abuse in the middle of a developmental sequence may result in significant later alteration of behavioral patterns so that they mimic personality disorders (Herman, 1992).

Assessing the Scale of the Trauma

What follows are some guiding thoughts about how to approach the problem of explicating probable cause. This section considers predictors of severity of response. That is, the expert may develop expectations about the severity of symptoms based on well-researched variables. Some metrics for determining damages are proffered. Examining what happened (and, in some cases, what did not occur) to the child can help the expert to determine damages by providing a scale of the trauma. In general, the more severe the trauma, the more severe the reaction (Greene & Kaltman, 1995). These variables interact with two other variables, social support and coping strategies, to determine how the sexual abuse affected the plaintiff's adult functioning.

Aspects of the Abusive Relationship Itself

Research indicates that perpetrators who fill the role of a parent, as in cases of incest, are more likely to produce lasting harm in victims than those who are strangers (Finkelhor, 1979; Ketring & Feinaur, 1999). One group of researchers noted, "The weight of the evidence indicated that a perpetrator who was close to the victim caused more serious effects than one who was less close" (Kendall-Tackett et al., 1993, p. 170). As previously described, in some families, the offending priest or teacher has been accepted into the family as a special member. In these cases, one might expect the impact of the abuse to be greater than in cases in which the offender was, for example, a substitute teacher. In homes in which there is significant family dysfunction, abuse by a nonfamily member who appears supportive may be more harmful than abuse by a family member who is not trusted (Ketring & Feinaur, 1999). This has shown to be especially true in cases of sexual abuse of athletes by coaches (Brackenridge, 2001).

The duration of the abuse has generally been demonstrated to correlate highly with the severity of symptoms (Beitchman et al., 1992; Conte & Schuerman; 1987; Kendall-Tackett et al., 1993). This variable may be confounded with the severity of the abuse because the offender who abuses a child over a longer duration may have an opportunity to engage in more separate and severe acts of sexual abuse.

Aspects of the Specific Acts

The specific things that an offender does to a victim may be important in determining the severity of emotional response. If the sexual assault is accomplished with the use of force, it is typically more damaging than if it is done without force (Finkelhor, 1979; Merrill et al., 2001). Although some (e.g., Finkelhor, 1979) have argued that force may be the most important variable, other research suggests this variable may be superseded by other severity variables (e.g., Jumper, 1995).

The extent of penetration of the child by the offender has been shown to be a potent variable. Although this variable may be confounded with force, as in cases of forcible rape, even with seductive offenders, the degree of entry into the victim's body has been shown to correlate with the degree of psychological harm (Beitchman et al., 1992; Mullen, Romans-Clarkson, Walton, & Herbison, 1988; Russell, 1986; Sedney & Brooks, 1984). In general, rape or sodomy is more harmful than fellatio or cunnilingus, which is more harmful than fondling with penetration, which is more harmful than fondling without penetration (Beitchman et al., 1992; Foote, 2002).

The frequency of sexual contacts, the duration of the abusive relationship, and the duration of the abuse in the context of that relationship also correlate with severity of response (Beitchman et al., 1992; Merrill et al., 2001). Unfortunately, these results are not always uniform because of confounding with other variables. For example, the research on duration has often been conducted with incest victims, who tend to have longer term relationships with offenders. As previously discussed, a special relationship to the offender may add to this impact. Going against this trend is the fact that rape, which is by definition forcible, and often quite violent, may occur on only one instance but have a significant impact (Mullen et al., 1988). One team of reviewers conclude:

> The available evidence suggests that solitary violent sexual assaults are associated with high levels of psychopathological symptoms, but that, controlling for these effects of force or threat of force, abuse of long duration is also associated with trauma or lasting harm. (Beitchman et al., 1992)

The age of the victim, which places the abuse at a particular point in the child's developmental sequence, is a variable that has been studied in a number of settings. Data on this variable are not uniform. Some studies (Conte & Schuerman, 1987; Finkelhor, 1979; Kendall-Tackett et al., 1993; Russell, 1986) indicate that younger children experience a greater impact of abuse. Confounding this finding is that many of those children are incest victims. Other work (Sedney & Brooks, 1984) found that postpubescent children suffered more lasting harm. Confounding this finding is that older children tend to experience penetration more often than do younger ones. For the expert, the age of the child must be evaluated in light of other variables.

All of these variables may be subsumed under the general category of "severity" (Merrill et al., 2001). These studies indicate that, in general, severity of the abuse and seriousness of the emotional response are positively related. However, several variables have been shown to mediate the impact of the severity of the abuse.

Mediating Variables

Although variables such as the age of the victim and the duration and severity of the abuse are powerful predictors of the severity of the plaintiff's response, they do not exist in a vacuum. The child lives in a social environment and has personal resources that predispose that child to react to stressors with a particular range of coping strategies. These may intervene between the stressor and the individual's response, modifying the final pattern of reaction.

Parental Support

As discussed previously, whether a child becomes a victim of abuse may depend on the quality of the child's home life. That variable has also been shown to be critical in determining the impact of abuse on the child (Boney-McCoy & Finkelhor, 1995; Kendall-Tackett et al., 1993; Neumann et al., 1996). For children who were abused by authority figures, it may be especially difficult for the child to receive support because parents may refuse to believe the child or may blame the child for the abuse (Barker-Collo, 2001; Conte & Schuerman, 1987). Some (Rind, Bauserman, & Tromovitch, 1998) have argued that the impact of child sexual abuse may be entirely accounted for by variables related to the child's home life. Other researchers (e.g., Runtz & Schallow, 1997) contend that the impact of child sexual abuse on adult functioning can be accounted for by the degree of social support the child received and the way the child coped with the abuse. However, recent commentators (e.g., Merrill et al., 2001) posit that parental support is just one of a host of variables determining psychological outcome and must be placed in context. In general, the more parents or significant others in the family and community provide support for the child in the aftermath of the abuse, the more positive the outcome.

Victim's Attributional Style and Methods of Coping with Abuse

A number of researchers have noted that how a child copes with abuse can have an important impact on long-term outcome (Conte & Schuerman, 1987; Merrill et al., 2001; Runtz & Schallow, 1997; Whiffin & McIntosh, 2005). These studies indicate that the abused child may cope with the abuse in three ways: (1) The child attempts to deal with the trauma in constructive ways, such as seeking support from others and cognitive reframing; (2) the child adopts an avoidant style, characterized by attempts to repress or deny thoughts or feelings associated with the abuse; or (3) the child engages in destructive coping characterized by acting-out or escapist methods, such as drinking or drug use. Research (e.g., Merrill et al., 2001; Runtz & Schallow, 1997) indicates that if the child adopts an avoidant or destructive coping strategy, long-term outcome is poorer than for those who choose constructive means. The degree of parental support may determine which course children take (Merrill et al., 2001). Children who have strong parental support are more likely to use constructive coping and are less likely to have serious symptoms following abuse. The severity of the abuse also guides these choices. Children who are recipients of more severe abuse are more likely to choose avoidant or self-destructive coping styles, so these variables act in a cumulative fashion to produce more negative outcomes.

METHODS FOR DETERMINING DAMAGES

The determination of damages in clergy and teacher sex abuse cases poses challenges to the forensic practitioner. In order to determine what the alleged abuse has done to the now-adult plaintiff, the forensic practitioner must first rule out malingering as a basis for the data gathered in the evaluation. If the data is reliable, then the professional may use a number of anchor points that provide a basis for comparison between the currently observed condition of the plaintiff, and the status of that person prior to the onset of the alleged abuse. This section examines a number of possible bases for these comparisons.

Malingering and Symptom Exaggeration

As in all forensic evaluations, the psychologist must be aware of the possibility that the plaintiff may be malingering symptoms or exaggerating valid symptoms (e.g.,

Elhai et al., 2004; Guriel & Fremouw, 2003; Meyers & Volbrecht, 2003; Rogers, 1997; Rogers & Bender, 2003; Rosen, 2004; Slovenko, 2004; Sullivan & Richer, 2002; Ustad & Rogers, 1996). Although the assessment of malingering in forensic evaluations is beyond the scope of this chapter, it is important to note that individuals who are sexually abused as children may attribute symptoms to sexual abuse that do not originate at that source. This false attribution may be a result of malingering, but may also have a more benign explanation. For example, it may be psychologically more palatable to blame a single incident of fondling for a lifetime history of alcohol abuse than to recognize that the addiction may have more complex roots. Teasing out the symptoms that are a result of the teacher or clergy sexual abuse is always an imperfect task. In some cases, emotional reactions are multiply determined and crafted by a chain of trauma that results in a maladaptive complex of reactions.

The following are some strategies for sorting out these origins. In addition to looking at the scale of the trauma and mediating variables, the expert in clergy and teacher sex abuse cases may also use other measures to assess the severity of damages for each individual plaintiff. These metrics are not so much a product of research as those listed earlier, but are practical means designed to assist the evaluator to gather real-world data that can often have a larger influence on a jury or judge than more esoteric research.

Family-Community Comparisons

A beginning point for determining the impact of abuse on a child is to examine the outcome for nonabused siblings. In contexts in which the child is raised in an especially kind and supportive home, or in a home in which abuse and neglect are the rule, a comparison with siblings may be helpful. This is, of course, an imperfect comparison because the correlation between behavioral outcomes of nontwin siblings are moderate (Farmer et al., 2000; O'Connor, McGuire, Reiss, Hetherington, & Plomin, 1998).

Pre-Post Comparisons

In most tort or civil rights cases, the psychologist may attempt to determine the condition of the plaintiff before the incident and compare it to the condition afterward (Foote & Goodman-Delahunty, 2005; Goodman-Delahunty & Foote, 1995). In clergy and teacher cases, this comparison is more difficult, in part because of the retrospective nature of the inquiry and because the symptoms that the abuse engendered may distort the developmental sequence. A complicating factor as well is the issue of comorbidity. That is, some emotional disorders, such as depression and substance abuse, tend to be associated with posttraumatic symptoms but are not per se posttraumatic reactions (Acierno, Kilpatrick, & Resnick, 1999). Nevertheless, a number of methods, usually based on gathering additional information, may assist in making these comparisons.

Cognitive and School Functioning

Because clergy and teacher sex abuse occur while the child is of school age, it is always appropriate for the evaluator to review available school records. In some children, a clear before-and-after effect is apparent. Impairments of attention and concentration often directly interfere with learning. Indirectly, shame and social alienation may interfere with peer relationships, thus reducing school functioning. Increased disciplinary incidents, suspensions, and truancy may be an outcome of hostility against authority figures who abuse. Substance abuse may interfere with attendance and with focus on class work.

Collateral Interviews

Conversations with parents, siblings, family friends, and others who knew the child at the time of the abuse may provide valuable insight about behavioral changes (Heilbrun, Rosenfeld, Warren, & Collins, 1994). In cases in which the child adopted an acting-out strategy for coping with the abuse, the plaintiff's ability to recount changes in his or her behavior may be limited. In many cases, those who cared about the child at the time may have noticed significant changes in the child's behavior, even if they were unaware of the abuse at the time. Friends can also be a good source of information and may note that their peer became more withdrawn or started abusing drugs or alcohol in a significant way after the abuse.

Mental Health Records

Some children become so impaired following sexual abuse experiences that they require assistance from mental health professionals. However, these children may not use the occasion of treatment to report the abuse (Dimock, 1988). In cases in which the child is rendered vulnerable to abuse by a disrupted family situation or preexisting behavioral problems, the records may provide an effective anchor point for determining the extent of damage caused by the teacher's or clergy's actions.

Changes Directly Related to the Acts of the Perpetrator

In some cases, the offender engages in behavior with the child that later affects specific symptoms the child exhibits. For example, some offenders provide children with alcohol as a means of seduction. For those children, later problems with alcohol may be related to this early introduction of alcohol abuse by an authority figure and the pairing of the substance abuse with the sexual abuse. In other cases, the offender may engage in specific sexual acts with the child that the adult may recapitulate. For example, in one case, a plaintiff was repeatedly sodomized by a priest in the stairway leading up to the steeple of a church. Thereafter, the victim was compulsively attracted to anonymous sex in stairways.

Presence of Posttraumatic Symptoms

Although some have argued that PTSD is not a good model for reactions to child sexual abuse (Finkelhor, 1990), the plaintiff's posttraumatic symptoms may directly relate to the abusive incidents. For example, a teacher's victim may have nightmares about being sodomized on the floor of the bathroom, or a priest's victim may have intrusive recollections of being raped on the altar of the church. For many clergy victims, the disruption of religious life may be based on avoidance of entering the church building, which is associated, through its symbology (the crucifix, stations of the cross, vestments of the clergy), with the abusive incidents.

Comorbid symptoms may also be traceable to trauma. For example, a plaintiff may have depressive reactions that coincide with the anniversary of the first abuse incident or the marriage of a sibling in the same church in which the abuse occurred. Anger and violent behavior may be triggered by reminders of the abuse or triggered by underlying emotion, such as shame. Substance abuse may be reactive to situations reminding the person of the abuse.

Determining Vocational Impact of Abuse

If mental disorders flow from teacher or clergy abuse, then one of the classes of monetary awards available to the plaintiff is lost future wages. Although mental health experts do not necessarily have expertise in vocational evaluation or economics, it is often helpful for the expert's opinion to be used by a vocational expert or economist as a basis for lost future wages computations. If the expert is able to express symptoms and behavioral deficits in vocational terms, it can assist the vocational expert to develop reports and testimony. Several aspects of damages may relate directly to teacher or clergy abuse.

Loss of Educational Attainment

If the abuse occurred at school, the plaintiff may have dropped out of school to avoid stimuli associated with the abuse. Economists recognize that the value of future wages is directly correlated with educational level. Even the loss of 1 year of education can result in significant lifetime damages.

Impairments in Skills Related to Vocational Functioning

For those plaintiffs who cope with acting-out or avoidant strategies, the abuse may result in an impairment of the adult's ability to relate effectively to superiors or coworkers. This may be evident in chronic problems with anger, which result in on-the-job blow-ups and unpredictability. For some, avoiding others may be necessary to cope. This avoidant style may interfere with the plaintiff's ability to collaborate with others and to assume leadership roles, reducing vocational attainment. Cognitive impairment caused by anxiety or depression may interfere with education, training, or job performance. Affective disorders may interfere with motivation to pursue new tasks or take on new responsibilities. Substance abuse may interfere with attendance and job functioning. For some plaintiffs, acting-out behavior may have landed them in jail for sentences associated with domestic violence or other crimes. It does not take an economist to determine that if one is in jail, salaries are reduced. Even if these problems do not rise to that level, the authority problems seen in some plaintiffs may translate into frequent difficulties with supervisors and frequent job changes.

CONCLUSION

This chapter has focused on how mental health experts may use information that is known about child sexual abuse, and more specifically abuse by teachers and clergy, to provide effective consultation and testimony in litigation related to these events. The retrospective nature of these evaluations and the complexity of any plaintiff's life make these evaluations difficult. However, a careful and unbiased evaluation may answer questions posed by the referral source and by others involved in the litigation.

These cases may require special care on the part of the examiner to avoid retraumatizing the plaintiff (Gutheil, Bursztajn, Brodsky, & Strasburger, 2000; Haller, 2002; Wenzel, 2002). Even experts retained by defendants in these cases should conduct the evaluation in such a way as to decrease the degree of trauma to the person being examined. Allowing time for the individual to cool down after discussions of traumatic events, allowing friends or family members to wait in nearby rooms, and encouraging the plaintiff to schedule a session with a therapist right after the evaluation may all lessen the impact of the necessary discussion of these traumatic events.

In the same way, experts conducting these evaluations should be aware of the potential for vicarious traumatization. The range and depravity of what offenders do to victims sometimes staggers the imagination of even seasoned professionals. If the forensic mental health professional is asked to evaluate a large number of plaintiffs in a single case or a sequence of cases, care should be taken to decompress and to seek renewed personal balance to counteract the negative impact of the emotional distress of the plaintiffs.

Working within the legal system, the examining expert may help courts decide cases more fairly. Accurate information about the nature, extent, and origin of the plaintiff's problems can assist the judge and jury to arrive at verdicts that are just for both the institutions and the individuals who are defendants and the men and women who are the plaintiffs.

REFERENCES

A. McD. v. John Nathaniel Rosen, MD, 621 A.2d 128 (Pa. 1993).

Acierno, R., Kilpatrick, D. G., & Resnick, H. S. (1999). Posttraumatic stress disorder in adults relative to criminal victimization: Prevalence, risk factors, and comorbidity. In P. A. Saigh, J. D. Bremer, & J. D. Bremner (Eds.), *Posttraumatic stress disorder: A comprehensive text* (pp. 44–68). Boston: Allyn & Bacon.

American Association of University Women. (1993). *Hostile hallways: Bullying, teasing and sexual harassment in school.* Washington, DC: Author.

American Association of University Women. (2001). *Hostile hallways: Bullying, teasing and sexual harassment in school.* Washington, DC: Author.

Anderson, J. R., Noaker, P. W., & Finnegan, M. G. (2004). When clergy fail their flock: Litigating the clergy sexual abuse case. *American Jurisprudence, 91,* 151–204.

Anonymous v. Anonymous, 584 N.Y. S.2d 713 (1992).

Arata, C. M. (2000). From child victim to adult victim: A model for predicting sexual revictimization. *Child Maltreatment: Journal of the American Professional Society on the Abuse of Children, 5*(1), 28–38.

Ayon v. Gourley, 185 F.3d 873: 10CIR (1999).

Bailey v. Glover, 88 U.S. 342 (1874).

Barker-Collo, S. L. (2001). Adult reports of child and adult attributions of blame for childhood sexual abuse: Predicting adult adjustment and suicidal behaviors in females. *Child Abuse and Neglect, 25*(10), 1329–1341.

Barry, J. (1985). Pedophile priest: Study in inept church response. *National Catholic Reporter,* 19–21.

Beitchman, J. H., Zucker, K. J., Hood, J. E., daCosta, G. A., Akman, D., & Cassavia, E. (1992). A review of the long-term effects of child sexual abuse. *Child Abuse and Neglect, 16*(1), 101–118.

Bisbing, S. B., Jorgenson, L. M., & Sutherland, P. K. (1995). *Sexual abuse by professionals: A legal guide.* Charlottesville, VA: Michie.

Black by Black v. Indiana Area School District, 985 F.2d, 707, 3d Cir. (1993).

Black, D. A., Heyman, R. E., & Slep, A. M. S. (2001). Risk factors for child sexual abuse. *Aggression and Violent Behavior, 6*(2/3), 203–229.

Black, H. C. (1991). *Black's law dictionary* (6th ed., abridged). St. Paul, MN: West.

Boney-McCoy, S., & Finkelhor, D. (1995). Psychosocial sequelae of violent victimization in a national youth sample. *Journal of Consulting and Clinical Psychology, 63*(5), 726–736.

Bornstein, B. H., & Muller, S. L. (2001). The credibility of recovered memory testimony: Exploring the effects of alleged victim and perpetrator gender. *Child Abuse and Neglect, 25*(11), 1415–1426.

Brackenridge, C. H. (2001). *Spoilsports: Understanding and preventing sexual exploitation in sport.* London: Routledge.

Briere, J., Evans, J., Runtz, M., & Wall, T. (1988). Symptomology in men who were molested as children: A comparison study. *American Journal of Orthopsychiatry, 58*(3), 457–461.

Briere, J., & Elliott, D. M. (1994). Immediate and long-term impacts of child sexual abuse. *Future Child, 4*(2), 54–69.

Briere, J., & Runtz, M. (1987). Post sexual abuse trauma: Data and implications for clinical practice.*Journal of Interpersonal Violence, 2*(4), 367–379.

Briere, J., & Runtz, M. (1988a). Multivariate correlates of childhood psychological and physical maltreatment among university women. *Child Abuse and Neglect, 12*(3), 331–341.

Briere, J., & Runtz, M. (1988b). Symptomatology associated with childhood sexual victimization in a nonclinical adult sample. *Child Abuse and Neglect, 12*(1), 51–59.

Briere, J., & Zaidi, L. Y. (1989). Sexual abuse histories and sequelae in female psychiatric emergency room patients. *American Journal of Psychiatry, 146*(12), 1602–1606.

Brown, D., Schleflin, A. W., & Hammond, E. C. (1998). *Memory, trauma, treatment, and the law.* New York: Norton.

Brown, G. R., & Anderson, B. (1991). Psychiatric morbidity in adult inpatients with childhood histories of sexual and physical abuse. *American Journal of Psychiatry, 148*(1), 55–61.

Cameron, P., Coburn, W., Larson, H., Proctor, K., Forde, N., & Cameron, K. (1986). Child molestation and homosexuality. *Psychological Reports, 58,* 327–337.

Cannell, J., Hudson, J. I., & Pope, H. G. (2001). Standards for informed consent in recovered memory therapy. *Journal of the American Academy of Psychiatry and the Law, 29*(2), 138–147.

Civil Rights Act of 1871, 42 U.S.C. (§ 1983).

Conder, J. B. (2004). Liability of church or religious society for sexual misconduct of clergy. *American Law Reports, 5,* 530.

Conte, J. R., & Schuerman, J. R. (1987). Factors associated with an increased impact of child sexual abuse. *Child Abuse and Neglect, 11*(2), 201–211.

Corbett, K., Gentry, C. S., & Pearson, W. (1993). Sexual harassment in high school. *Youth and Society, 25*(1), 93–103.

Dansky, B. S., & Kilpatrick, D. G. (1997). Effects of sexual harassment. In W. O'Donohue (Ed.), *Sexual harassment: Theory, research, and treatment* (pp. 152–174). Boston: Allyn & Bacon.

DePrince, A. P., Allard, C. B., Oh, H., & Freyd, J. J. (2004). What's in a name for memory errors? Implications and ethical issues arising from the use of the term "false memory" for errors in memory for details. *Ethics and Behavior, 14*(3), 201–233.

Destefano v. Grabrian, 763 P.2d 275 (Colo. 1988).

Dhaliwal, G. K., Gauzas, L., Antonowicz, D. H., & Ross, R. R. (1996). Adult male survivors of childhood sexual abuse: Prevalence, sexual abuse characteristics, and long-term effects. *Clinical Psychology Review, 16*(7), 619–639.

Dimock, P. T. (1988). Male sexual abuse: An underreported problem. *Journal of Interpersonal Violence, 3*(2), 203–221.

Disch, E., & Avery, N. (2001). Sex in the consulting room, the examining room, and sacristy: Survivors of sexual abuse by professionals. *American Journal of Orthopsychiatry, 71*(2), 204–217.

Doe v. Redeemer Lutheran Church, 531 N.W.2d 897 (Minn. Ct. App. 1995).

Doyle, T. P. (2003). Roman Catholic clericalism, religious duress, and clergy sexual abuse. *Pastoral Psychology, 51*(3), 189–231.

Dutton, D. G., & Painter, S. (1993a). The battered woman syndrome: Effects of severity and intermittency of abuse. *American Journal of Orthopsychiatry, 63*(4), 614–622.

Dutton, D. G., & Painter, S. (1993b). Emotional attachments in abusive relationships: A test of traumatic bonding theory. *Violence and Victims, 8*(2), 105–120.

Elliott, D. M., & Briere, J. (1994). Forensic sexual abuse evaluations of older children: Disclosures and symptomatology. *Behavioral Sciences and the Law, 12*(3), 261–277.

Elhai, J. D., Naifeh, J. A., Zucker, I. S., Gold, S. N., Deitsch, S. E., & Frueh, B. C. (2004). Discriminating malingered from genuine civilian posttraumatic stress disorder: A validation of three MMPI-2 infrequency scales (F, Fp, and Fptsd). *Assessment, 11*(2), 139–144.

Evan F. v. Hughson United Methodist Church, 8 Cal. App. 4th 828 3rd Dist. (1992).

F. G. v. McDonell, 696 A.2d 697 (NJ 1997).

Farmer, A., Harris, T., Redman, K., Sadler, S., Mahmood, A., & McGuffin, P. (2000). Cardiff Depression Study: A sib-pair study of life events and familiality in major depression. *British Journal of Psychiatry, 176*(2), 150–155.

Finkelhor, D. (1979). What's wrong with sex between adults and children? Ethics and the problem of sexual abuse. *American Journal of Orthopsychiatry, 49*(4), 692–697.

Finkelhor, D. (1984). *Child sexual abuse: New theory and research.* New York: Macmillan.

Finkelhor, D. (1990). Early and long-term effects of child sexual abuse: An update. *Professional Psychology: Research and Practice, 21*(5), 325–330.

Finkelhor, D., Hotaling, G., Lewis, I. A., & Smith, C. (1990). Sexual abuse in a national survey of adult men and women: Prevalence, characteristics, and risk factors. *Child Abuse and Neglect, 14*(1), 19–28.

Foote, W. E. (2002, August). *The Inuit project: Forensic evaluation of a large group of sex abuse survivors.* Paper presented at the meeting of the American Psychological Association, Chicago.

Foote, W. E., & Goodman-Delahunty, J. (2005). *Evaluating sexual harassment: Psychological, social, and legal considerations in forensic examinations.* Washington, DC: American Psychological Association.

Fritz, G. S., Stoll, K., & Wagner, N. N. (1981). A comparison of males and females who were sexually molested as children. *Journal of Sex and Marital Therapy, 7*(1), 54–59.

Fromuth, M. E., & Burkhart, B. R. (1987). Childhood sexual victimization among college men: Definitional and methodological issues. *Violence and Victims, 2*(4), 241–253.

Fromuth, M. E., & Burkhart, B. R. (1989). Long-term psychological correlates of childhood sexual abuse in two samples of college men. *Child Abuse and Neglect, 13*(4), 533–542.

Gerber, P. N. (1990). Victims becoming offenders: A study of ambiguities. In M. Hunter (Ed.), *The sexually abused male: Vol. 1. Prevalence, impact, and treatment* (pp. 153–175). Lexington, MA: Lexington Books/D. C. Heath.

Golding, J. M., Cooper, M. L., & George, L. K. (1997). Sexual assault history and health perception: Seven general population studies. *Health Psychology, 16*(5), 417–425.

Gonsiorek, J. C. (1994). Assessment of and treatment planning and individual psychotherapy for sexually abused adolescent males. In J. C. Gonsiorek, W. H. Bera, & D. LeTourneau (Eds.), *Male sexual abuse: A trilogy of intervention strategies* (pp. 3–112). Thousand Oaks, CA: Sage.

Gonsiorek, J. C. (1999). *Forensic psychological evaluations in clergy abuse: Bless me Father for I have sinned—Perspectives on sexual abuse committed by Roman Catholic priests.* Westport, CT: Praeger Publishers/Greenwood.

Goodman-Delahunty, J., & Foote, W. E. (1995). Compensation for pain, suffering, and other psychological injuries: The impact of *Daubert* on employment discrimination claims. *Behavioral Sciences and the Law, 13*(2), 183–206.

Gordon, J. D. (1998). Admissibility of repressed memory evidence by therapists in sexual abuse cases. *Psychology, Public Policy, and Law, 4*(4), 1198–1225.

Grauerholz, L. (2000). An ecological approach to understanding sexual revictimization: Linking personal, interpersonal, and sociocultural factors and processes. *Child Maltreatment: Journal of the American Professional Society on the Abuse of Children, 5*(1), 5–17.

Greene, B. L., & Kaltman, S. I. (1995). Recent research findings on the diagnosis of posttraumatic stress disorder. In R. I. Simon (Ed.), *Posttraumatic stress disorder in litigation* (pp. 13–29). Washington, DC: American Psychiatric Press.

Guriel, J., & Fremouw, W. (2003). Assessing malingered posttraumatic stress disorder: A critical review. *Clinical Psychology Review, 23*(7), 881–904.

Gutheil, T. G., Bursztajn, H., Brodsky, A., & Strasburger, L. H. (2000). Preventing "critogenic" harms: Minimizing emotional injury from civil litigation. *Journal of Psychiatry and Law, 28*(1), 5–18.

Haller, L. H. (2002). The forensic evaluation and court testimony. *Child and Adolescent Psychiatric Clinics of North America, 11*(4), 689–704.

Hamilton, M. J. (1989). A comparison of psychological symptoms of treated and non-treated incestuous male perpetrators. *Dissertation Abstracts International, 50*(2-B), 748–749.

Harper, F. W. K., & Arias, I. (2004). The role of shame in predicting adult anger and depressive symptoms among victims of child psychological maltreatment. *Journal of Family Violence, 19*(6), 367–375.

Harris, M. (1990). *Unholy orders: Tragedy at Mount Cashel.* Ontario, Canada: Penguin.

Heilbrun, K., Rosenfeld, B., Warren, J. I., & Collins, S. (1994). The use of third-party information in forensic assessments: A two state comparison. *Bulletin of the American Academy of Psychiatry and Law, 22*(3), 399–406.

Hendrie, C., & Drummond, S. (Eds.). (1998). A trust betrayal: Sexual abuse by teachers. *Education Week,* December 2, 9, & 16.

Hendrie, C., & Drummond, S. (Eds.). (2003). Trust betrayed; Update on sexual misconduct in schools. *Education Week,* , April 30, May 7.

Herman, J. L. (1992). *Trauma and recovery.* New York: Basic Books.

Hickey v. Askren, 403 S.E.2d 225 (Ga. Ct. App. 1991).

Humphrey, J. A., & White, J. W. (2000). Women's vulnerability to sexual assault from adolescence to young adulthood. *Journal of Adolescent Health, 27*(6), 419–424.

Hunter, J. A. (1991). A comparison of the psychosocial maladjustment of adult males and females sexually molested as children. *Journal of Interpersonal Violence, 6*(2), 205–217.

Jacobson, A., & Herald, C. (1990). The relevance of childhood sexual abuse to adult psychiatric inpatient care. *Hospital and Community Psychiatry, 41*(2), 154–158.

John R. v. Oakland Unified School District, 769 P.2d 948. (1989).

Jones, L., & Finkelhor, D. (2001, January). The decline in child sexual abuse cases. *OJJDP Bulletin.* Washington, DC: U.S. Department of Justice, Office of Justice Programs, Office of Juvenile Justice and Delinquency Prevention. http://www.ncjrs.org/html/ojjdp/jjbul2001_1_1/contents.html.

Jumper, S. A. (1995). A meta-analysis of the relationship of child sexual abuse to adult psychological adjustment. *Child Abuse and Neglect, 19*(6), 715–728.

Kendall-Tackett, K. A., & Simon, A. F. (1992). A comparison of the abuse experiences of male and female adults molested as children. *Journal of Family Violence, 7*(1), 57–62.

Kendall-Tackett, K. A., Williams, L. M., & Finkelhor, D. (1993). Impact of sexual abuse on children: A review and synthesis of recent empirical studies. *Psychological Bulletin, 113*(1), 164–180.

Ketring, S. A., & Feinaur, L. L. (1999). Perpetrator-victim relationship: Long term effects of sexual abuse for men and for women. *American Journal of Family Therapy, 27,* 109–120.

Kilpatrick, D. L., Saunders, B. E., Amick-McMullan, A., Best, C. L., Veronen, L. J., & Resnick, H. S. (1989). Victim and crime factors associated with the development of posttraumatic stress disorder. *Behaviour Therapy, 20,* 199–214.

Kuenhle, K. (2003). Child sexual abuse evaluations. In I. B. Weiner (Series Ed.) & A. M. Goldstein (Vol. Ed.), *Comprehensive handbook of psychology: Vol. 11. Forensic psychology* (pp. 437–462). Hoboken, NJ: Wiley.

Langevin, R., Curnoe, S., & Bain, J. (2000). A study of clerics who commit sexual offenses: Are they different from other sex offenders? *Child Abuse and Neglect, 24*(4), 535–545.

Lawson, L., & Chaffin, M. (1992). False negatives in sexual abuse disclosure interviews: Incidence and influence of caretaker's belief in abuse in cases of accidental abuse discovery by diagnosis of STD. *Journal of Interpersonal Violence, 7*(4), 532–542.

Leavitt, F. (2001). Iatrogenic recovered memories: Examining the empirical evidence. *American Journal of Forensic Psychology, 19*(2), 21–32.

Lees-Haley, P. R., Williams, C. W., Zasler, N. D., Margulies, S., English, L. T., & Stevens, K. B. (1997). Response bias in plaintiffs' histories. *Brain Injury, 11*(11), 791–799.

Levitan, R. D., Parikh, S. V., Lesage, A. D., Hegadoren, K. M., Adams, M., Kennedy, S. H., et al. (1998). Major depression in individuals with a history of childhood physical or sexual abuse: Relationship to neurovegetative features, mania, and gender. *American Journal of Psychiatry, 155*(12), 1746–1752.

Little, L., & Hamby, S. L. (1999). Gender differences in sexual abuse outcomes and recovery experiences: A survey of therapist: Survivors. *Professional Psychology: Research and Practice, 30*(4), 378–385.

Loftus, E. F. (1996). The myth of repressed memory and the realities of science. *Clinical Psychology: Science and Practice, 3*(4), 356–362.

Loftus, E. F., & Bernstein, D. M. (2005). Rich false memories: The royal road to success. In A. F. Healy (Ed.), *Experimental cognitive psychology and its applications* (pp. 101–113). Washington, DC: American Psychological Association.

Loftus, E. F., & Polage, D. C. (1999). Repressed memories: When are they real? How are they false? *Psychiatric Clinics of North America, 22*(1), 61–70.

Los Angeles Archdiocese. (2001). *Statement on settlement.* Available from http://www.the-tidings.com/2001/0824/statement.htm.

Maker, A. H., Kemmelmeier, M., & Peterson, C. (2001). Child sexual abuse, peer sexual abuse, and sexual assault in adulthood: A multi-risk model of revictimization. *Journal of Traumatic Stress, 14*(2), 351–368.

Malicki v. Doe, 101 A.L.R. 5th 655 (Fl. 2002).

Mart, E. G. (2004). Victims of Abuse by Priests: Some Preliminary Observations. *Pastoral Psychology, 52*(6), 465–472.

Martelli, M. F., Zasler, N. D., Bender, M. C., & Nicholson, K. (2004). Psychological, Neuropsychological, and Medical Considerations in Assessment and Management of Pain. *Journal of Head Trauma Rehabilitation, 19*(1), 10–28.

McKee, D. D. (2003). Liability of school districts under common law tort theories for the sexual molestation of a student by a teacher. *American Jurisprudence Proof of Facts, 3d, 31,* 31–64.

Meiser-Stedman, R. (2005). Recovered memories: Seeking the middle ground. *Behavioural and Cognitive Psychotherapy, 33*(1), 120–122.

Mendel, M. P. (1995). *The male survivor: The impact of sexual abuse.* Thousand Oaks, CA: Sage.

Merrill, L. L., Thomsen, C. J., Sinclair, B. B., Gold, S. R., & Milner, J. S. (2001). Predicting the impact of child sexual abuse on women: The role of abuse severity, parental support, and coping strategies. *Journal of Consulting and Clinical Psychology, 69*(6), 992–1006.

Metcalfe, M., Oppenheimer, R., Dignon, A., & Palmer, R. L. (1990). Childhood sexual experiences reported by male psychiatric patients. *Psychological Medicine, 20*(4), 925–929.

Meyers, J. E., & Volbrecht, M. E. (2003). A validation of multiple malingering detection methods in a large clinical sample. *Archives of clinical Neuropsychology, 18*(3), 261–276.

Minnesota Department of Children, Families and Learning. (2001). *Minnesota Student Survey: Key trends through 2001.* Roseville, MN: Author.

Moses v. Diocese of Colorado, 863 P.2d 310 (Colo. 1993).

Mullen, P. E., Romans-Clarkson, S. E., Walton, V. A., & Herbison, G. P. (1988). Impact of sexual and physical abuse on women's mental health. *Lancet, 1,* 842–845.

Neumann, D. A., Houskamp, B. M., Pollock, V. E., & Briere, J. (1996). The long-term sequelae of childhood sexual abuse in women: A meta-analytic review. *Child Maltreatment: Journal of the American Professional Society on the Abuse of Children, 1*(1), 6–16.

O'Connor, T. G., McGuire, S., Reiss, D., Hetherington, E. M., & Plomin, R. (1998). Co-occurrence of depressive symptoms and antisocial behavior in adolescence: A common genetic liability. *Journal of Abnormal Psychology, 107*(1), 27–37.

Ornstein, P. A., Ceci, S. J., & Loftus, E. F. (1998). More on the repressed memory debate: A reply to Alpert, Brown, and Courtois. *Psychology, Public Policy, and Law, 4*(4), 1068–1078.

Paolucci, E. O., Genuis, M. L., & Violato, C. (2001). A meta-analysis of the published research on the effects of child sexual abuse. *Journal of Psychology, 135*(1), 17–36.

Paris, J., Zweig-Frank, H., & Guzder, J. (1994). Risk factors for borderline personality in male outpatients. *Journal of Nervous and Mental Diseases, 182*(7), 375–380.

Partlett, D. F., & Nurcombe, B. (1998). Recovered memories of child sexual abuse and liability: Society, science, and the law in a comparative setting. *Psychology, Public Policy, and Law, 4*(4), 1253–1306.

Polusny, M. A., & Follette, V. M. (1995). Long-term correlates of child sexual abuse: Theory and review of the empirical literature. *Applied and Preventive Psychology, 4*(3), 143–166.

Pribor, E. F., & Dinwiddie, S. H. (1992). Psychiatric correlates of incest in childhood. *American Journal of Psychiatry, 149*(1), 52–56.

Rennison, C. M. (2001). *Criminal victimization 2000: Changes 1999–2000.* Bulletin, Department of Justice, Office of Justice Programs.

Rind, B., Bauserman, R., & Tromovitch, P. (1998). A meta-analytic examination of assumed properties of child sexual abuse using college samples. *Psychological Bulletin, 124*(1), 22–53.

Rind, B., & Tromovitch, P. (1997). A meta-analytic review of findings from national samples on psychological correlates of child sexual abuse. *Journal of Sex Research, 34*(3), 237–255.

Roesler, T. A., & McKenzie, N. (1994). Effects of childhood trauma on psychological functioning in adults sexually abused as children. *Journal of Nervous and Mental Diseases, 182*(3), 145–150.

Rogers, R. (1997). *Clinical assessment of malingering and deception* (2nd ed.). New York: Guilford Press.

Rogers, R., & Bender, S. D. (2003). Evaluation of malingering and deception. In I. B. Weiner (Series Ed.) & A. M. Goldstein (Vol. Ed.), *Comprehensive handbook of psychology: Vol. 11. Forensic psychology* (pp. 437–462). Hoboken, NJ: Wiley.

Rohsenow, D. J., Corbett, R., & Devine, D. (1988). Molested as children: A hidden contribution to substance abuse. *Journal of Substance Abuse Treatment, 5,* 13–18.

Romano, E., & De Luca, R. V. (2001). Male sexual abuse: A review of effects, abuse characteristics, and links with later psychological functioning. *Aggression and Violent Behavior, 6*(1), 55–78.

Rosen, G. M. (2004). Litigation and reported rates of posttraumatic stress disorder. *Personality and Individual Differences, 36*(6), 1291–1294.

Rossetti, S. J. (1995). The impact of child sexual abuse on attitudes toward God and the Catholic Church. *Child Abuse and Neglect, 19*(12), 1469–1481.

Rossetti, S. J. (1996). The effects of priest-perpetration of child sexual abuse on the trust of Catholics in priesthood, church, and God. *Journal of Psychology and Christianity, 16*(3), 197–209.

Rowland, D. L., Zabin, L. S., & Emerson, M. (2000). Household risk and child sexual abuse in a low income, urban sample of women. *Adolescent and Family Health, 1*(1), 29–39.

Roy v. Hartogs, 366 N.Y. S.2d 297 Civ. Ct. (1975).

Runtz, M., & Briere, J. (1986). Adolescent "acting out" and childhood history of sexual abuse. *Journal of Interpersonal Violence, 1*(3), 326–334.

Runtz, M. G., & Schallow, J. R. (1997). Social support and coping strategies as mediators of adult adjustment following childhood maltreatment. *Child Abuse and Neglect, 21*(2), 211–226.

Russell, D. E. H. (1986). *The secret trauma: Incest in the lives of girls and women* (Rev. ed.). New York: Basic Books.

Sachs-Ericsson, N., Blazer, D., Plant, E. A., & Arnow, B. (2005). Childhood sexual and physical abuse and the 1-year prevalence of medical problems in the national comorbidity survey. *Health Psychology, 24*(1), 32–40.

Sandberg, D. A., Matorin, A. I., & Lynn, S. J. (1999). Dissociation, posttraumatic symptomatology and sexual revictimization: A prospective examination of mediator and moderator effects. *Journal of Traumatic Stress, 12*(1), 127–138.

Sarwer, D. B., Crawford, I., & Durlak, J. A. (1997). The relationship between childhood sexual abuse and adult male sexual dysfunction. *Child Abuse and Neglect, 21*(7), 649–655.

Saunders, B. E., Villeponteaux, L. A., Lipovsky, J. A., & Kilpatrick, D. G. (1992). Child sexual assault as a risk factor for mental disorders among women: A community survey. *Journal of Interpersonal Violence, 7*(2), 189–204.

Schoener, G. R., Milgrom, J. H., Gonsiorek, J. C., Luepker, E. T., & Conroe, R. M. (1990). *Psychotherapists' sexual involvement with clients: Intervention and prevention.* Minneapolis, MN: Walk-in Counseling Center.

Sedney, M. A., & Brooks, B. (1984). Factors associated with a history of childhood sexual experience in a nonclinical female population. *Journal of the American Academy of Child Psychiatry, 23*(2), 215–218.

Seidner, A. L., & Calhoun, K. S. (1984, August). *Childhood sexual abuse: Factors related to differential adult adjustment.* Paper presented at the second National Conference for Family Violence Researchers, Durham, NC.

Shields, M. (2004). Liability of church or religious organization for negligent hiring, retention, or supervision of priest, minister, or other clergy based on sexual misconduct. *American Law Reporter, 5*(101), 1–37.

Silk, K. R., Lee, S., Hill, E. M., & Lohr, N. E. (1995). Borderline personality disorder symptoms and severity of sexual abuse. *American Journal of Psychiatry, 152*(7), 1059–1064.

Simari, C. G., & Baskin, D. (1982). Incestuous experiences with homosexual populations: A preliminary study. *Archives of Sexual Behavior, 11,* 329–344.

Simon, R. I., & Shuman, D. W. (2003). *Retrospective assessment of mental states in litigation: Predicting the past.* Washington, DC: American Psychiatric Association.

Slovenko, R. (2004). The watering down of PTSD in criminal law. *Journal of Psychiatry and Law, 32*(3), 411–437.

Smith, J. C., Runyan, D. K., & Fredrickson, D. D. (1994). The Little Rascals Day Care Center case: A perspective on medical testimony in a prominent public trial. *Journal of Child Sexual Abuse, 3*(2), 89–97.

Shakeshaft, C. (2003). Educator sexual abuse. *Hofstra Horizons,* 10–14.

Stein, J. A., Golding, J. M., Siegel, J. M., Burnam, M. A., & Sorenson, S. B. (1988). Long-term psychological sequelae of child sexual abuse: The Los Angeles Epidemiologic Catchment Area Study. In G. E. E. Wyatt & G. J. Powell (Eds.), *Lasting effects of child sexual abuse* (pp. 135–154). Newbury Park, CA: Sage.

Stein, M. B., Walker, J. R., Anderson, G., Hazen, A. L., Ross, C. A., Eldridge, G., et al. (1996). Childhood physical and sexual abuse in patients with anxiety disorders and in a community sample. *American Journal of Psychiatry, 153*(2), 275–277.

Stein, N. D., Marshall, N. L., & Tropp, L. R. (1993). *Secrets in public: Sexual harassment in our schools.* Wellesley, MA: Wellesley Centers for Women.

Sullivan, K., & Richer, C. (2002). Malingering on subjective complaint tasks: An exploration of the deterrent effects of warning. *Archives of Clinical Neuropsychology, 17*(7), 691–708.

Texas Civil Practice and Remedies Code Vol. 81.009 (1993).

Urquiza, A. J., & Capra, M. (1990). The impact of sexual abuse: Initial and long-term effects. In M. E. Hunter (Ed.), *The sexually abused male: Vol. 1. Prevalence, impact, and treatment* (pp. 105–135). Lexington, MA: Lexington Books/D. C. Heath.

U.S. Conference of Bishops. (2004). *The nature and scope of sexual abuse of minors by Catholic priests and deacons in the United States 1950–2002.* Washington, DC: Author.

U.S. Department of Education. (2004). *Educator sexual misconduct: A synthesis of existing literature.* Washington, DC: Author.

Ustad, K. L., & Rogers, R. (1996). Malingering and deception: Conceptual and clinical issues in forensic practice. In L. B. Schlesinger (Ed.), *Explorations in criminal psychopathology: Clinical syndromes with forensic implications* (pp. 300–319). Springfield, IL: Charles C. Thomas.

Walton v. Alexander, 20 F.3d 1350 5th Cir. (1994).

Weaver, T. L., & Clum, G. A. (1993). Early family environments and traumatic experiences associated with borderline personality disorder. *Journal of Consulting and Clinical Psychology, 61*(6), 1068–1075.

Wenzel, T. (2002). Forensic evaluation of sequels to torture. *Current Opinion in Psychiatry, 15*(6), 611–615.

Whiffen, V. E., & MacIntosh, H. B. (2005). Mediators of the link between childhood sexual abuse and emotional distress: A critical review. *Trauma, Violence, and Abuse, 6*(1), 24–39.

Wilson, A. E., Calhoun, K. S., & Bernat, J. A. (1999). Risk recognition and trauma-related symptoms among sexually revictimized women. *Journal of Consulting and Clinical Psychology, 67*(5), 705–710.

Wurtele, S. K., Kaplan, G. M., & Keairnes, M. (1990). Childhood sexual abuse among chronic pain patients. *Clinical Journal of Pain, 6,* 110–113.

CHAPTER 23

Correctional Psychology: Law, Ethics, and Practice

Joel A. Dvoskin, Erin M. Spiers, and Stanley L. Brodsky

America's response to crime has traditionally been summarized with one word: corrections. The choice of this word, indicating the ability to ameliorate—that is, to change—human behavior, has long suggested a partnership between these some-times punitive and sometimes rehabilitative institutions we call jails and prisons. In this chapter, we explore the historical, current, and potential interactions between psychology and this aspect of the American criminal justice system. This chapter considers only jails and prisons serving primarily adult offenders and excludes community correctional programs such as probation and parole.

THE DIFFERENCE BETWEEN JAILS AND PRISONS

Though both fall under the rubric of corrections, jails and prisons are distinct institutions, with different functions, auspices, stressors, and roles for psychologists.

Jails in the United States are generally run by municipalities or counties, often under the jurisdiction of an elected sheriff. Their residents consist primarily of two classes of people: (1) pretrial felony or misdemeanor detainees, for whom the jail's primary responsibility is to ensure that they do not escape and that they are safely held until release or trial; and (2) persons who have been convicted and are serving sentences typically for less than 1 year, most often for misdemeanors. Many of the sentences for the latter group are short, and jails generally do not place emphasis on changing how inmates behave following release. There are exceptions, such as special jail-based alcohol treatment programs for those convicted of driving while intoxicated and domestic violence programs that seek to reduce the likelihood of repeated family violence. In general, however, jails spend little time and energy on altering behavior; instead, they focus on safely managing people. They are generally regarded as "people processing institutions." In contrast, prisons generally provide long-term (i.e., more than 1 year) confinement of persons convicted of felonies. At least in theory, prisons have traditionally regarded themselves as "people-changing institutions," with the goal of rehabilitating criminals and reducing crime. There is no consensus that this goal has ever been effectively achieved. We believe that this problem has been due in part to the failure of academic and professional psychologists to provide leadership in the area they know best: helping people to change their behavior.

A BRIEF HISTORY OF CORRECTIONAL PSYCHOLOGY

Over time, the roles of psychologists in jails and prisons have evolved, from the relatively narrow role of intake assessment to the many varied roles that exist today. This section discusses the developmental course of psychologists' roles within jails and prisons.

The Testing Psychologist

In one of the earliest reports about prison psychology, Donald Powell Wilson (1951) described his 3 years in the early 1930s working as a U.S. Public Health Service psychologist at Ft. Leavenworth, Kansas. He drew extensively on employing prisoners as clinical and research assistants; thus the title of his book, *My Six Convicts,* with a popular film of the same title following in 1952. Wilson described professional activities in which he conducted light therapy and hypnosis, sometimes with men on the "psychopathic ward"; he also conducted drug research. However, his primary role was supervision of testing by his inmate assistants. Wilson was severely critical of the utility of paper-and-pencil personality tests with prisoners, observing, "They throw little light on the vast problem of personality" (p. 158). Some 15 years after Wilson's tour of duty, in the late 1940s, Raymond Corsini was employed as a psychologist at Auburn Prison in New York. Corsini (1989) described what he believed "was the most successful and elegant psychotherapy I have ever done" (p. 3). An inmate reported, " 'You told me I had a high IQ.' With one sentence of five words I had (inadvertently) changed this person's life" (p. 4). What is important for our purposes is that Wilson and Corsini alike had been locked into the typical role of the prison psychologist of the early to mid-twentieth century, as the administrators of psychological tests given to entering prisoners for purposes of ascertaining intelligence, vocational skills, and personality patterns.

Psychotherapeutic Treatment of Criminal Behavior

Not all psychologists in the early days of prison psychology were committed to testing. In his books *Rebel without a Cause* (1944) and *The Fifty-Minute Hour* (1954), Robert Lindner sought to apply psychoanalytic principles and methods to understanding and treating offenders. In *Rebel without a Cause,* Lindner published the transcriptions of 46 hour-long hypnotherapy sessions with a single offender, designed to show that criminal psychopathology grew out of repressed, painful experiences. In *The Fifty-Minute Hour,* Lindner described his work at a federal penitentiary with a psychopathic "gutter-fuhrer" inmate who was having blackout spells. Lindner introduced the latter case study by describing the individual psychiatric interviews conducted with all inmates and describing his bulky files on this particular inmate, encompassing psychological tests and complete social, educational, criminal, and personal histories. These full evaluations and extensive utilization of mental health data were more typical of federal prisons than state prisons, as, indeed, they are to the present time.

Early on, prison mental health professionals operated under the assumption that criminal behavior was explicitly determined by psychopathological deficits. The logical and needed remedy was psychotherapeutic treatment to correct these deficits. The treatment of choice at the time was the same as the treatment of choice in free society, namely, psychoanalytically based approaches. As mental health treatments broadened, so did treatment approaches in prisons.

In his best-selling 1966 book *The Crime of Punishment,* psychiatrist Karl Menninger galvanized attention to the harm caused by prisons and the resultant need for change. He described prisons as obsolete, inhumane systems, and he wrote that psychiatrists were caught up in dependence on empty and meaningless jargon. After identifying the unconscious determinants of criminal behaviors, Menninger stated that virtually no treatment is offered to offenders and that effective treatment should be made available for violent offenders. He went on to assert that the majority of offenders are curable:

> It will surely have to begin with motivating or stimulating or arousing in a cornered individual the wish and hope and intention to change his methods of dealing with the realities of life. Can this be done by education, medication, counseling, and training? I would answer *yes*. It can be done successfully in a majority of cases, if undertaken in time. (p. 257)

Among the efforts that reflected the passion of the Menninger polemic was treatment at the Patuxent Institute in Maryland. A "defective delinquent" law had instituted a treatment regime in which release and improvement in living conditions were contingent on therapeutic and behavior gains in a part-behavioral, part-psychodynamic program (Zenoff & Courtless, 1977). The inmates were confined with indeterminate sentences, with length of confinement decided, in large part, by psychological gains. This therapeutic experiment ran from 1955 to 1977 and was criticized for poor diagnostic judgments and ineffectiveness in reducing recidivism (Sidley, 1974). On the other hand, other observers believed the Patuxent experiment to be effective and useful (Rappeport, 1975). These positions were followed by the assertion of Robert Martinson (1974), who declared that "nothing works." Martinson elicited dismay from some psychologists and righteous indignation from others who claimed that treatment was effective. Of greater significance was the resultant commitment to studying which elements of offender therapies did work, for whom, and under what circumstances.

Toward Ethics and Graduate Preparation

In the early 1970s, three major forces influenced mental health services in prisons. In 1971, a major conference with follow-up meetings was held at Lake Wales, Florida. This conference had the ambitious goal of redefining the practice of psychology in the criminal justice system, particularly in corrections (S. L. Brodsky, 1973). Judge David Bazelon was a speaker and participant at the conference, and he urged psychologists working in corrections to do good for prisoners instead of doing well for themselves. The conference report stated that psychologists needed to sort out their alliances to institutions and clients, to rethink their roles, and to move toward a better synthesis of research and treatment.

The issue of role definition was clarified when Monahan (1980) edited an influential book, *Who Is the Client?* Monahan and the contributors to the book identified the nature of loyalty and legal obligations for psychologists in the criminal justice system, including those employed in corrections. In the labyrinthine muddle of competing responsibilities, Monahan clarified how to think about one's role when acting as a mental health professional in corrections. To the present day, major books on ethics in psychology include sections devoted to the issue of the psychologist faced with competing responsibilities to institutions and to offender clients (e.g., Bersoff, 2003).

At the same time this conference was held, the University of Alabama and Florida State University developed the first graduate education programs in correctional-clinical psychology (S. L. Brodsky, 1973; Fowler & Brodsky, 1978). Until the initiation of these programs, correctional and legal psychology was an unwelcome and stigmatized stepchild of mainstream clinical psychology graduate studies. Graduate students who were interested in working with offenders were considered odd. These clinical-correctional psychology PhD concentrations legitimized a research-practitioner model to prepare psychologists for understanding correctional institutions.

Class Action Suits

The third major influence from the 1960s was the success of class action suits addressing the living conditions and medical and mental health needs of prisoners. As described in another section of this chapter, a path opened to legitimate and ready access to the courts to seek redress of deprivation of constitutional rights in areas of 8th Amendment litigation. These efforts were not always successful because of institutional resistance to court orders (S. L. Brodsky, 1986; S. L. Brodsky & Miller, 1981; Yackle, 1989). On the other hand, Metzner (2002a, 2002b) concluded that such class action suits and subsequent court orders greatly improved the quality of prison mental health care.

What had begun with the judiciary expressing the power to intervene in the administration of prisons on behalf of constitutional rights of inmates in the 1960s and 1970s was severely curtailed in the mid-1990s. After 30 years of litigation to improve prison conditions, including the delivery of mental health, the passage of the Prison Litigation Reform Act (PLRA) of 1995 was explicitly intended to shift the playing field to make such suits more difficult. The legal rights and ability of prisoners to file litigation were diminished as these cases were portrayed as "nuisance suits." They were, in fact, often substantive in nature. As Chen (2004) pointed out, it was about the legal ability and resources of prisoners to file meritorious actions for basic aspects of safety and health. Despite the PLRA, such litigation continued, resulting in important cases such as *Coleman v. Wilson* (1995) and *Madrid v. Gomez* (1995), which together resulted in 10s of millions of additional health and mental heath care dollars being funneled into California's prison system.

Professional Organizations and Journals

The role of psychologists in corrections is reflected in the history of the organizations formed to support and promote the field. In their comprehensive discussion of the history of the American Association of Correctional Psychology (AACP), Bartol and Freeman (2005) noted the AACP's difficulty in maintaining continuity. In the American Psychological Association, the criminal justice section of the Division of Psychologists in Public Service has been a home for correctional psychologists. More recently, the British Psychological Society has established its own

Division of Forensic Psychology. Despite the name "forensic" in the title of the division, members are predominantly psychologists working in prisons, probation services, and secure hospitals. The Division has begun a series of books for correctional psychologists, including *Psychology in Prisons* (Towl, 2003), a book series that identifies roles and responsibilities of psychologists who work with offenders and institutional staff.

The professional or scholarly journal serves as a marker of professional respectability. When the journal *Criminal Justice and Behavior* was established in 1974, it reflected a clear commitment to correctional psychology to attain that respectability. Furthermore, correctional psychology articles have become a routine part of other mainstream clinical psychology journals.

The Human Element

Psychologists working in state correctional systems during the early through mid-1900s were often employed at the discretion of the warden. Many psychologists were expected to report the content of therapy sessions to custodial staff. Some were assigned desks in prison corridors, with minimal privacy. At large institutions in Michigan and other states, a single psychologist was expected to test all newly admitted prisoners and write reports, which sometimes meant evaluating as many as 200 prisoners a week. The quality of such assessments was understandably questionable. When psychologists advocated for treatment of prisoners or responded to outside inquiries or reporters, their position could be terminated immediately. Psychologists working in corrections at that time were often frustrated by the institutional controls and disappointed at how little difference they could make.

Five related events changed the occupational toxicity of prison psychology. First, legal and legislative actions legitimized and sometimes mandated the importance of psychological services. Second, civil service positions protected psychologists from arbitrary actions by administrators. Third, psychologists rose to administrative positions, often as associate wardens for treatment, and thus became invested in maintaining a good environment for other psychologists. Fourth, standards of practice were developed in corrections that encompassed mental health care. Fifth, payoffs from research foundations and graduate education began to filter into the correctional setting. Evidence-based treatments and better trained/prepared psychologists made an impact and were more welcome. Some things have not changed: the variability is enormous in how valued and effective psychologists are in different federal and state institutions; ethical conflicts continue to be demanding and difficult; and the milieu influences practice, with overcrowded, understaffed, and unsafe prisons impeding the delivery of mental health services.

THE LEGAL LANDSCAPE

As noted above, correctional psychology has been massively influenced by predominantly constitutional litigation. This section includes a brief history of these developments and a summary of the current status of inmates' rights to mental health treatment.

Constitutional Law

For centuries, Anglo-American common law has required that the government or agency that incarcerates a person is responsible for provision of that person's "necessaries," or those minimally essential goods and services that prisoners are unable to obtain on their own. This "necessaries doctrine" is applied to food, shelter, clothing, and medical care.

The basic tenets of constitutional correctional mental health law can be traced back to the landmark case of *Estelle v. Gamble* (1976). This case, based on the 8th Amendment's prohibition against cruel and unusual punishment, held that states are prohibited from being "deliberately indifferent to the serious medical needs" (p. 103) of the people they incarcerate. One year later, *Bowring v. Godwin* (1977) explicitly included psychiatric need as subject to the requirements of *Gamble*. Although clearly articulating a constitutional duty to provide *some* level of medical and mental health care for inmates, these two cases were vague in defining serious medical or psychiatric need and listing the nature of the services that would be required. In declining to define deliberate indifference, the *Gamble* Court made it clear that the standard promised to inmates was a low one. For example, "Medical malpractice does not become a constitutional violation merely because the victim is a prisoner," nor is deliberate indifference created by "poor judgment, inadvertence or failure to follow the acceptable norms for practice in a particular geographic area" (p. 104–106). According to F. Cohen and Dvoskin (1992, p. 342), "Looked at another way, deliberate indifference requires greater culpability than malpractice, but need not reach the more demanding [criterion] for intentional conduct; that is, consciously acting to achieve a preconceived result."

In 1980, *Ruiz v. Estelle* helped to delineate a prison's responsibilities by articulating six principles that are mandatory to prison mental health:

1. There must be a systematic program for screening and evaluating inmates to identify those who require mental health treatment.

2. Treatment must entail more than segregation and close supervision of the inmate patients.

3. Treatment requires the participation of trained mental health professionals, who must be employed in sufficient numbers to identify and treat, in an individualized manner, those treatable inmates suffering from serious mental disorders.

4. Accurate, complete, and confidential records of the mental health treatment process must be maintained.

5. Prescription and administration of behavior-altering medications in dangerous amounts, by dangerous methods, or without appropriate supervision and periodic evaluations is an unacceptable method of treatment.

6. A basic program for the identification, treatment, and supervision of inmates with suicidal tendencies is a necessary component of any mental health treatment program.

Any consideration of the duties of the government to provide care within its institutions must also include *Youngberg v. Romeo* (1982), which established the principle that "reasonable professional judgments" are presumptively constitutional. Professional judgment occurs when a person with *appropriate* education, training, experience, and/or licensure:

- Addresses the appropriate question.
- Makes a reasonable effort to seek relevant information.
- Makes a decision that falls within the reasonable choices that persons of similar and appropriate education, training, experience, and/or licensure might make.
- Acts on that decision.

Perhaps most important, there is no constitutional requirement that such judgments be "right." The language of *Youngberg* is instructive:

> The decision, if made by a professional, is presumptively valid; liability may be imposed only when the decision by the professional is such a substantial departure from accepted professional judgment, practice, or standards as to demonstrate that the person responsible actually did not base the decision on such a judgment. In an action for damages against a professional in his individual capacity, however, the professional will not be liable if he was unable to satisfy his normal professional standards because of budgetary constraints; in such a situation, good-faith immunity would bar liability. (p. 323)

In 1989, *Langley v. Coughlin* combined these principles and explicitly applied the "professional judgment" standard to an analysis of deliberate indifference with regard to prison mental health care. The magistrate explained that although "isolated and inadvertent errors" would not violate the 8th Amendment, "serious failure to provide needed medical attention when the defendants are fully aware of that need could well constitute deliberate indifference, even if they did not act with punitive intent" (p. 537). In addition, *Langley* articulated a list of specific allegations that would, if proven, indicate constitutionally inadequate care of inmates with serious mental illness, including:

- Failure to take and maintain complete and adequate psychiatric records.
- Failure to respond to inmates' prior psychiatric history.
- Failure to at least observe inmates suffering a mental health crisis.
- Failure to properly diagnose mental conditions.
- Failure to properly prescribe medications.
- Failure to provide meaningful treatment other than drugs.
- Failure to explain treatment refusals, diagnosis, and ending of treatment.
- Seemingly cavalier refusals to consider bizarre behavior as mental illness even when a prior diagnosis existed.
- Personnel doing things for which they are not trained.

The 8th Amendment applies only to convicted prisoners and is not applicable to the pretrial detainees who constitute the majority of residents of local jails. However, courts have consistently held that convicted inmates, if anything, are less deserving of rights and privileges than other institutionalized persons (e.g., pretrial detainees and civilly committed psychiatric patients) who are presumed to be innocent. These courts follow the logic of *Bell v. Wolfish* (1979), which guarantees the same rights to pretrial detainees under the 14th Amendment that are afforded to convicted felons under the 8th.

Nonconstitutional Claims

It is likely that the Americans with Disabilities Act (ADA, 1990) will become the subject of correctional mental health litigation. The ADA, which prohibits discrimination against persons with disabilities, also entitles them to "reasonable accommodations" for those disabilities. An individual can be identified as disabled in three ways: (1) The individual has a physical or mental impairment that substantially limits one or more major life activities; (2) the individual has a record of such impairment; or (3) the individual is perceived or regarded as having such impairment.

Jails and prisons are public entities subject to the ADA because they are agencies or instrumentalities of state or local governments (Stone, 1997). Therefore, inmates cannot be denied participation in any program, service, or activity based solely on the fact that they have a disability, and accommodations for inmates with disabilities must be made by the correctional agency and/or its contractors (Morton & Anderson, 1996). After finding that the California Department of Corrections was violating the ADA and the Rehabilitation Act, the 9th Circuit Court of Appeals issued an injunction to improve access to prison programs for prisoners with physical disabilities at all of California's prisons and parole facilities (*Armstrong v. Wilson,* 1997; *Clark v. California,* 1997). To comply with the ADA, policies and practices must be modified to ensure equal access and to ensure that inmates, including those who are mentally disordered, have access to treatment and rehabilitation programs.

Segregated inmates present a particular concern, given that segregation inherently results in lack of access to a variety of programs. Moreover, given the scarcity of resources in many correctional settings, programs are often reserved for those inmates who are thought to be most likely to benefit (Stone, 1997). Administrators and program officials must take care that this premise does not result in the categorical exclusion of inmates with mental disorders. The U.S. Supreme Court held in a unanimous opinion that the ADA applies to state prisoners (*Pennsylvania Dept. of Corrections v. Yeskey,* 1998).[1]

Prisoners' litigation is not, of course, limited to constitutional or federal statutory claims. Like anyone else, a prisoner might file suit under available laws related to intentional or negligent torts. However, most states have low statutory limitations on the amount that one can recover from the state. Further, inmates may be

---

[1] See also *United States v. Georgia,* 2006 WL 43973, _____ U.S. _____ (January 10, 2006).

met with a hostile reception from state court juries, where the stigma of incarceration—even against those pretrial detainees who are supposed to be presumed innocent as a matter of law—is strongest. It must also be remembered that tort plaintiffs are often represented by attorneys who have accepted cases based on contingency fees. When the defendant is the state and the plaintiff is an inmate, attorneys may be reticent to accept such fee arrangements. Because many inmates are indigent and cannot hire attorneys, such claims are often presented with the inmate acting *pro se.* For this reason, it is rare to see large, successful inmate claims for simple malpractice, or even serious torts such as wrongful death claims. On the other hand, when there is a colorable claim of deliberate indifference, suits may be filed under section 1983 of the Civil Rights Act (1983), which allows a prevailing plaintiff's attorney, even one who is ostensibly acting *pro bono,* a full recovery of fees billed on an hourly basis. (For an excellent and thorough discussion of the rights of inmates with mental disorders, see F. Cohen's, 1998, *The Mentally Disordered Inmate and the Law.*)

The Costs of Failure

There was a time when states chose to ignore their constitutional obligations to provide mental health care to prisoners, or because of inadequate resources, correctional administrators were forced to choose between mental health treatment and institutional safety. Because institutional civil rights actions were rare, some states chose to wait for litigation and take their chances in court. This shortsighted approach had a number of significant negative consequences. First, losing or settling a systemwide class action, in addition to the actual costs of care, carries with it the expensive costs of monitoring the remedy, whether by a court expert, monitor, special master, or federal receiver. Systemwide litigation also creates a negative public image that can affect the system's ability to garner legislative appropriations, to recruit qualified staff, and to collaborate with universities and medical schools. Even other state agencies, such as those addressing mental health, mental retardation, education, and vocational rehabilitation, may not wish to be associated with the negative publicity that comes with losing a lawsuit. Morale can also be severely compromised when plaintiffs' counsel and court monitors become frequent and judgmental visitors to a prison.

Finally, undertreated or untreated mental illness can endanger the lives of the disordered inmates themselves, other inmates, and the staff who work with them. Mental illness per se may contribute relatively little to the risk of violence in the community (see, e.g., Monahan et al., 2001), but leaving symptoms untreated in a closed, crowded, and hostile environment such as a jail or prison is a quite different situation. A person in the community who is experiencing acute mania but lives alone might not bother his or her neighbors. In prison, when that same person prevents dozens of inmates with violent histories from sleeping, the likelihood of violence can escalate dramatically. Even when they are not the targets of such violence, staff are put in danger when forced to intervene.

Lawsuits alleging inadequate mental health care are often directed at wardens and other correctional administrators; ironically, however, correctional professionals are often among the most enthusiastic advocates of improved mental health care for their inmates. They express frustration over the fact that they are forced to provide mental health care under circumstances that are less than therapeutic, in many cases without the assistance of the local mental health authority, for example, a community mental health center. When forced to choose between hiring correctional officers to keep institutions safe and hiring additional mental health staff, correctional administrators make the reasonable decision that without safety, adequate care is impossible. In our view, administrators should not be forced to make such decisions. Security and treatment programs are both essential and constitutional components of any correctional system.

Documentation, Liability, and Risk Management

Documentation is essential in providing mental health care in any setting, including corrections. In underserved settings, clinicians may complain that they are too busy providing care to document it. Some see documentation as an exercise in liability prevention designed only to protect the system from litigation and contributing nothing to the inmates' care. In our opinion, correctional systems frequently require that care be provided by a variety of different mental health practitioners. This requirement makes continuity of care a significantly more difficult challenge. Although treatment plans do not necessarily have to resemble those found in psychiatric hospitals, they are essential to coordinating the efforts of various treatment providers. Equally important, legible progress notes convey important information about each inmate's clinical condition and treatment received, which provides continuity between providers, between shifts, and between institutions. Documentation also plays an important role in preventing unnecessary liability and in protecting the professional licenses and reputations of the mental health providers who serve in correctional settings. Several years may have passed before lawsuits come to trial, and relying on one's memory about the treatment received by a particular patient is ill advised. Documentation can demonstrate that reasonable professional judgment was exercised.

It is important not only to document the decision that was made, but also to briefly document options that were not chosen. For example, in assessing whether or not to place an inmate on suicide watch, a clinician might write the following:

> Despite his earlier threat of suicide, after reviewing his mental health record, consultation with a counselor and several correctional officers, and based on Mr. Jones's improved mood, future orientation, and excitement over a planned visit by his fiancée, it was my professional judgment that he did not require placement on suicide watch. I approved the inmate for return to the general population, and scheduled a follow-up visit in 3 days.
>
> —Michael Jordan, PhD, Licensed Psychologist

This note conveys three important components of professional judgment: The clinician clearly states his credentials to make the judgment; he has clearly considered the possibility of a suicide watch, gathered data from several sources, including direct observation of the inmate, and rendered a reasonable opinion; and he has also taken steps to implement the decision. It is important to understand that, as a matter of law, the opinion does not have to be correct to be constitutionally adequate. *Youngberg* (1982) stands for the proposition that clinicians, when operating competently and in good faith, have a "right to be wrong." Assuming that clinicians ask the correct questions, consider reasonable alternatives, seek relevant information, render an opinion or judgment, and implement that judgment, even in the face of a negative outcome there is likely to be no finding of constitutional liability. In the absence of adequate documentation, however, there is no way to demonstrate the quality of the clinician's decision-making process, leaving the system and the clinician vulnerable to retrospective criticism.

There is one other important benefit to adequate documentation. Systems of care require organized and routine quality management. Because it is not possible to directly observe all or even most of the care that is delivered, quality improvement teams and managers must rely on assessment of documentation to ensure that care is delivered with adequate quantity, quality, timeliness, appropriateness, and competence. Among the many uses of such quality management data, requests for budget increases are far more likely to be granted when accompanied by reliable data that demonstrate efficient management of the resources that are already in place. The American Psychiatric Association (2000) and the National Commission on Correctional Health Care (2003) have produced the most widely referenced guidelines and standards for correctional health care. Each presents straightforward and user-friendly guidelines, detailing the essential features of mental health care in corrections. The guidelines include definitions of credentials necessary to perform each component of care. These sources can be of particular utility in terms of outlining the mechanism of service delivery and for maximizing the efficient movement of inmates through a given system and toward the level of service best suited to address their needs.

Investigation, Mortality Review, and Psychological Autopsy

Sadly, management of quality in providing mental health care also requires reliable and timely investigation of tragedies. Once again, liability prevention is only one of many reasons for this task, and it is clearly not the most important reason. In the event of a death that is related to mental illness, such as suicide, the most important consideration is to identify any conditions or circumstances that created or increased the risk that the death would occur. This allows the institution to quickly revise practices and to minimize the possibility of a similar occurrence.

Mortality reviews and psychological autopsies are organized efforts to examine all of the known facts that preceded a death, leading to recommendations that will reduce the risk of any further deaths from the same causes. Adequate investigation of a suicide might include mental health providers, chaplains, physicians, nurses, correctional officers, teachers, and anyone else with knowledge about the precursors of the death and/or authority to make changes in policies and practices.

These investigations and incident reviews should result in clear, unambiguous recommendations aimed at reducing risk. They must be documented so that correctional managers can verify whether or not they have been implemented successfully. A failure to document recommendations in order to reduce the likelihood of a successful lawsuit is unacceptable and may suggest that an institution is more interested in protecting itself than the inmates for whom it is responsible.

What does it all mean for correctional psychologists? The rules of engagement for correctional mental health in the United States have become relatively clear, and protecting oneself from liability has become a straightforward proposition. To that end, we offer the following suggestions:

- Make sure that a system is in place that screens each newly arriving inmate or detainee for the risk of suicide and for the likelihood that he or she will be in need of treatment for serious mental illness or psychiatric crisis.

- Make certain that every inmate who is screened positive receives at least a brief follow-up evaluation by a qualified mental health professional.

- Make sure that each inmate or detainee with a serious mental illness receives at least a simple but useful, individualized treatment plan.

- Any treatment plan should reflect reasonable professional judgment, and its recommendations should be implemented.

- Make certain that the institution has a sensible and comprehensive suicide prevention plan, which includes screening, referral, policies, and procedures. The plan should also include cross training between correctional and mental health staff aimed at identifying the signs and symptoms of depression and suicidality, as well as the policies, procedures, and post orders related to suicide prevention once an inmate is identified as being at risk.

- Make sure that all of the preceding are clearly and legibly documented.

THE ROLES OF PSYCHOLOGISTS IN CORRECTIONAL MENTAL HEALTH

Historically, the practice of correctional psychology was limited to the treatment and management of mentally ill inmates, with an emphasis on containing potentially disruptive behavior in the institution. This narrow view of the role of a correctional psychologist was both unfortunate and inadequate. In fact, there are several mechanisms by which mental health professionals, like correctional staff, can make important and cost-effective contributions (Spiers, Dvoskin, & Pitt, 2003). Assessment and treatment will always be a fundamental part of correctional mental health care, but to be effective and valued, psychologists in corrections must expand the scope of their practice to include a variety of therapeutic, managerial, and consultative interventions (Spiers et al., 2003).

Treatment of Serious Mental Illness

As previously asserted, the U.S. Constitution requires treatment of serious mental health needs of inmates of correctional institutions. Because of this clear mandate, and because an active plaintiff bar has increasingly sought to vindicate this right in correctional systems across the country, the lion's share of mental health resources has gone to meet this need. Unfortunately, one relatively inexpensive way to treat mental illness, at least in the short run, is with psychotropic medication. Just as in the community, the need to provide care at the lowest possible cost has led to a heavy reliance on medication alone as the predominant treatment modality. As is also the case in the community, this focus on medication has often meant that nurses and psychiatrists are viewed as the most essential members of the treatment team.

However, in the community, there has been a dramatic change in the way organized systems of care are learning to treat the most serious mental illnesses. Medication alone is increasingly viewed as inadequate for most patients. Serious mental illness impairs lives in three important ways: (1) the creation of unwanted psychological experiences and behaviors that interfere with the person's functioning (i.e., symptoms), (2) deficits in essential life skills, and (3) social disconnectedness. Generally, medication alone helps with only the first group of problems, and it is not always the treatment of choice even for them. For example, many knowledgeable consumers may choose to engage in cognitive-behavioral psychotherapy for depression or anxiety disorders instead of or in addition to medication. Moreover, many consumers may reject psychotropic medication for psychotic illnesses because they find the side effects intolerable. More important, psychiatric rehabilitation has offered consumers a successful and user-friendly pathway to a more successful life (Anthony, 1982; Anthony, Cohen, & Kennard, 1990; M. Cohen, 1989; M. Cohen & Anthony, 1988). To the extent that psychoeducational and cognitive-behavioral approaches to the treatment of serious mental illness become the standard of care in the free world, they will also become expected treatments for clients in prison. When they do, psychologists will have an opportunity to once again provide leadership in the correctional environment and to create additional jobs for psychologists.

Initial Assessments: Reception and Initial Classification

Especially in prisons, at the front door of the system, psychologists have traditionally been involved in assessment and initial classification. This may have included psychological testing, interviews, and consultation with reception center staff. In many systems, a battery of psychological tests is administered to each newly admitted inmate; however, it is often unclear to what extent these batteries affect the course of the person's incarceration. Especially in light of the staff time devoted to such assessments, and the fact that constitutionally mandated treatment for serious mental illnesses may be inadequate, it is important to limit these batteries to questions or to individuals for whom the data will matter. For example, if the inmate's initial security classification status is based exclusively or primarily on the person's crime or sentence, psychological testing may not have a great deal of utility toward that decision. To take another example, if the decision to refer inmates for psychological assessment is based on prior history of mental illness and a previously administered screening instrument, then it is difficult to understand the logic behind a full battery of psychological testing of *all* inmates. On the other hand, if the test results are relevant, valid, reliable, and *utilized,* psychological testing at the prison's front door may represent sound policy. For example, if prisons take program assignments seriously, they may rely heavily on intelligence and achievement testing in deciding whether an inmate will be steered toward academic (e.g., General Education Diploma or college courses) or vocational programming.

Intake Screening

Because of the well-documented problem of correctional suicide, especially in jails, no correctional institution should fail to provide intake screening for each newly admitted inmate or detainee. Thanks to recent advances, screening that was once aimed solely at suicide prevention now is equally effective in identifying those inmates who are likely to require psychological or psychiatric services during their incarceration (Steadman, Scott, Osher, Agnese, & Clark Robbins, 2005). In a well-run jail screening system, approximately 25% to 33% of inmates and detainees will screen positive at the front door, and about half of those will require and accept mental health services. These numbers do not include those detainees whose sole or predominant psychological problem is drug abuse or addiction (Peters, Matthews, & Dvoskin, 2005), nor do they include those inmates without serious mental illness but whose habits, personalities, and behaviors suggest the need for help, such as anger management or assertiveness training.

Intelligence tests and personality inventories such as the Minnesota Multiphasic Personality Inventory (MMPI and MMPI-2) have long been used by many state correctional institutions as part of an initial test battery at the time of intake (Gallaghar, Somwaru, & Ben-Porath, 1999; Megargee, 1994; Megargee, Mercer, & Carbonell, 1999). Generally, these tests are used to assist in assigning inmates to security levels and to educational, vocational, and work programs. They alert prison systems to special needs or concerns relative to each inmate, including the need for mental health treatment. The psychometric portion of initial classification is typically performed by and/or under the supervision of psychologists. However, the continuation and utility of this practice depends on two factors. First, the test results must *matter*. That is, the assignments that inmates receive must differ as test results differ, or the tests themselves will be viewed as an expensive waste of resources. Second, academic psychologists must continue to team with their prison counterparts to develop new instruments that keep pace with the ever-changing nature of criminals. This will require attention to reliability and validity of psychometric instruments, which must in turn be normed and renormed as prison populations change.

Assessment of Positive Screens

Inmates and detainees who screen positive are not necessarily mentally ill or in need of services. However, because they have been identified as being at risk, the institution has a responsibility to provide a brief hands-on assessment by a mental health professional. In many cases, this duty will be performed or supervised by a psychologist. This is not intended to be a comprehensive psychological evaluation; its sole purpose is to decide whether or not the person is to be referred for mental health services or managed in some specific way, such as being placed on a suicide watch.

Assignment to Service

As a result of these assessments, inmates and detainees will either be cleared for the general population or referred for appropriate services or special management. For those inmates with a history or current evidence of serious mental illness, including those who claim to be on psychotropic medication at the time of their arrest, this will likely result in a referral to a psychiatrist (or psychiatric nurse practitioner), who will complete the assessment and draw up an initial treatment plan. All other inmates who appear to be in potential need of services or suicide watch will likely be evaluated by a mental health professional. This service is often provided or supervised by a psychologist.

Referral Mechanisms

Assignment to service through intake and/or screening is the most obvious mechanism of referral for mental health care. However, screens, by definition, have gaps that may result in some inmates remaining unidentified at the initial screening stage. Other inmates will conceal their psychological problems or treatment histories, and still others will develop mental illnesses or emotional crises only after they have been admitted to the facility. For this reason, in addition to screening, it is necessary to have a well-publicized, timely, responsive, and competent system for referral of inmates who want or appear to need services.

Referrals should be able to originate from a wide variety of sources, including inmates themselves, other inmates, correctional and program staff, volunteers, family, and friends. Although written referrals are always preferred, verbal referrals can signal equally important or emergent situations and must receive a timely response, preferably with subsequent documentation. Regardless of the referral mechanism, mental health professionals working in a correctional setting must ensure that all members of the institutional community feel safe and comfortable conveying information to them. At times, the concerns expressed will be inconsequential. However, the potential for heading off a crisis through simple communication is profound.

Suicide Prevention and Crisis Services

Inmates and detainees who appear to be suffering acute exacerbations of serious mental illness or who are in emotional or psychological crisis, whether identified via screening or subsequent referral, must be evaluated by a mental health professional as soon as possible. Once such an emergency referral has been made, the facility should take reasonable steps to keep the person safe.

Often, the evaluation and the response to the crisis are identical. By providing the inmate with reliable information about what he or she can expect, arranging for emergency medication, or moving the inmate to a physically or psychologically safer housing area, it is often possible to reduce fear, anxiety, and anger. These "outpatient" interventions may successfully resolve the crisis so that the inmate can remain in general population housing. Like any closed community, inmates often rely on rumors for a great deal of their information. In many cases, the simple provision of accurate information can avert a potential crisis. In other cases, especially exacerbation of serious mental illness, the crisis is not so easily resolved, and it may be necessary to house the person in special mental health housing for some period of time. Often, the crisis involves serious suicidal ideation and intent, and the person must be watched closely. These crisis settings are typically intended to be short term, only for the period of time deemed clinically necessary.

There is no more pressing duty for a correctional administrator than to keep inmates and staff alive and safe. Because of the well-known danger of inmate suicide, especially in jails, suicide prevention is of the utmost importance. A complete discussion of correctional suicide prevention is beyond the scope of this chapter, but some basic principles are the subject of wide agreement among correctional mental health experts.

First, suicide is the leading cause of death in U.S. jails. The risk of suicide in prison is considerably lower than in jail but remains elevated significantly above the base rate in the community. As a result, every correctional institution should have a reasonable and comprehensive suicide prevention plan that includes the components found in this section (Hayes, 1995).

Second, every newly admitted inmate should receive a brief screening designed to identify those who are at heightened risk of suicide or likely to require mental health interventions in the near future. There are a number of different screening instruments that have been used, and none has yet clearly emerged as the standard of care. However, there is widespread agreement as to many of the items that should be addressed at the front door. There is virtually unanimous agreement that one or two broad, vague questions about "psychiatric problems" or "suicidality" will not suffice (see, e.g., Burnaby, Cox, & Morschauser, 1997; Nicholls, Roesch, Olley, Ogloff, & Hemphill, 2005; Steadman et al., 2005). These screening instruments should be simple, and the people who administer them (usually nurses or correctional or detention officers) must be trained in how to do so. The results must be documented in clear, legible, and straightforward language, and every positive screen must be referred to a mental health professional for (at least) a brief follow-up assessment.

There are no firm rules about how many people should screen positive, but in jails, our experience suggests that an effective screen will result in about 25% to 33% of inmates screening positive, of which about half will be referred for treatment, special management, or both. (Note that some will competently decline services.) In other words, the screen is designed to have many false positives and relatively few false-negative findings.

Third, it is impossible to completely eliminate false-negative results; that is, some inmates with serious psychological needs will falsely report no need for mental health services and no suicidal intent and deny any history of mental illness. For this reason, the referral system described earlier is a crucial and essential element of every correctional suicide prevention program.

Fourth, for those inmates who screen positive on the basis of suicide-related issues, and who are deemed to pose a high risk of suicide upon follow-up evaluation by a mental health professional, the plan must include efficient procedures for making it as difficult as possible for the inmate or detainee to take his or her life until the assessed risk has abated. This includes special management procedures such as various levels of suicide watch. Currently, the most common type of suicide watch in U.S. jails requires personal observation of the inmate at least once every 15 minutes. However, in our opinion, 15-minute watches may not be adequate to protect those inmates at the highest risk of suicide. We recommend that watches presumptively occur at least once every five minutes, however, the suicide watch procedure for a particular inmate should be individually determined by a clinician. In some cases, the risk will be so great that the situation requires constant observation of the inmate for a period of time. We also recommend reconsideration of the usual assumption that every suicidal inmate must be housed alone. For some inmates, segregated housing can increase the feelings of depression that led to the suicidal ideation in the first place. In New York's prison mental health system, unless they are deemed to be a danger to others, suicidal inmates are housed in a 6 to 12 bed dormitory, where they can be effectively and cost-efficiently observed by one officer.

Managerial, Administrative, and Educational Roles

Until the 1970s, there was only one career path that led to the running of a prison. One started as a correctional officer and eventually sought promotion to sergeant, lieutenant, and so on, one day rising to the level of warden. Many of these wardens continued their education during their careers, achieving college or advanced degrees, although degrees were not a requirement for the position. Jails, though ostensibly run in many jurisdictions by elected sheriffs, had similar career paths for the leadership positions within the jail itself. The 1970s and 1980s saw a distinct change in this practice, as many systems began to require advanced degrees as a prerequisite for managerial positions within corrections. This professionalization of the field was seen as a way of responding to highly publicized disturbances and riots, which were, in part, thought to have resulted from abuses of power by prison administrators. Early on, this change was a double-edged sword, as highly educated wardens often lacked the experience in corrections that is vital to credibility and good leadership. Over time, however, the two career paths converged, so that today's wardens often have an adult lifetime of experience in corrections and an advanced education that preceded and/or continued during their correctional service.

This preference for leaders with advanced degrees provided another opportunity for psychologists. Increasingly, psychologists became assistant wardens, wardens, and even commissioners and directors of departments of corrections. This new career ladder was especially visible in the federal Bureau of Prisons (BOP; Kathleen Hawke, who began her career as a prison psychologist, became first a warden and ultimately director of the federal BOP, perhaps the most visible leader in U.S. corrections).

In addition to serving as correctional administrators at the highest levels, in their formal role as correctional psychologists, psychologists were often asked to serve on various administrative committees, such as classification and disciplinary boards that are part of the prison's administrative structure. Psychologists can and should play an active role in the totality of the correctional community. Areas including, but not limited to, case management, unit teams, program development and evaluation, and staff screening and selection are all appropriate and important venues for the application of psychological principles (Spiers et al., 2003).

Administratively Oriented Psychological Evaluations

From time to time, jail and prison psychologists are asked to serve as members of administrative boards within the institution, such as classification and disciplinary committees. In addition to membership on these committees, psychologists may be asked to provide consultation and, on occasion, psychological evaluations for them. To such boards, informal consultation can be invaluable. A psychologist or other mental health professional might offer suggestions as to the kind of setting or cellmate that would better suit an inmate, and steps that correctional staff can take to supervise inmates more effectively. Carefully considering whether a given inmate will be capable of negotiating the demands of a given institution, and how to best intervene, can go a long way toward preventing difficulty down the line (Spiers et al., 2003).

Less clear is the value of formal psychological evaluations, especially for disciplinary boards or committees. Certainly, it seems both fair and sensible that inmates should not be punished for behaviors that are symptomatic of severe mental illness. Dvoskin, Petrila, and Stark-Riemer (1995) have argued that formal, quasi-forensic evaluations have a number of downsides and should not be required, a position taken by at least one court (*Powell v. Coughlin,* 1991). Formal evaluations take valuable time away from treatment duties and provide an incentive for inmates to feign mental illness for the purposes of avoiding the consequences of their violations. Formal evaluations also place the prison psychologist squarely and publicly in the crossfire between inmates and staff, whose interests in such hearings may directly conflict. Instead, Dvoskin and his colleagues recommend informal consultation between disciplinary boards and mental health professionals to allow mental illness to be taken into consideration before these committees make decisions about guilt and punishment over allegations of prison rule violations.

In many jurisdictions, psychologists have also served as forensic evaluators for various outside agencies. For many years, parole boards would routinely seek psychological evaluations of prospective parolees, in spite of the fact that there was virtually no evidence at the time of an ability on the part of mental health professionals to predict future crimes. In jails, similar evaluations have been requested by probation agencies, pretrial services, and others.

Sex offender commitment laws have created an additional need for psychological evaluations (*Kansas v. Crane,* 2002; *Kansas v. Hendricks,* 1997). Because the U.S. Supreme Court in *Hendricks* decided to treat these commitments as analogous to civil commitment of persons with serious mental illness, mental health professionals have been drawn into service providing the courts with evaluations, especially in regard to a potential committee's "mental condition."

Consultation, Communication, and Training

Traditionally, consultation between mental health and security staff was predominantly related to the management of inmates and detainees (C. M. Brodsky & Epstein, 1982). Open lines of communication across disciplines are critical for any system to be successful (Dvoskin & Spiers, 2004). Mutual distrust between mental health and correctional professions has been cited as one of the most significant barriers to effective offender care (Roskes & Feldman, 1999). At first glance, the competing demands of security and mental health appear to be polarized and to foster an undercurrent of competition. In fact, the goals of custody and treatment staff are, and should be, remarkably similar: (a) ensure safety, (b) prevent escape, (c) minimize human suffering (in and out of prison), (d) maximize morale, and (e) help to maintain systemic operations (Dvoskin & Spiers, 2004).

Correctional personnel who learn to trust and respect their mental health staff are far more likely to value their advice and respond accordingly. However, for this to be accomplished, mental health professionals in corrections must take steps to *earn* the trust of security staff. In assessing an inmate or a system, mental health staff would be well served to solicit the wisdom of seasoned correctional personnel (Dvoskin, Spiers, & Pitt, 2002). All too often, however, there has been little reason for line staff to believe that their opinions or observations were welcomed and valued. In our experience, far too many mental health professionals discount correctional officers as lacking in expertise and, as a result, treat their inmate patients without critical data from line staff (Dvoskin & Spiers, 2004).

Mentally ill offenders present a unique set of concerns in the correctional setting, and management difficulties may arise when training of correctional staff regarding mental health issues is absent or insufficient (Veysey, Steadman, Morrissey, & Johnsen, 1997). Whereas clinicians spend only a brief amount of time with inmates, correctional officers essentially live with the inmates: at work, at recreation, and in their housing units. As a result, typically the first person to notice a change in an inmate's routine or mental status is a correctional officer (Applebaum, Hickey, & Packer, 2001). If the wealth of information held by correctional staff is to be shared with mental health staff, mental health staff must first demonstrate that they are open and interested. However, correctional staff must also be armed with the fundamental information necessary to first recognize mental health problems and then convey their observations. Research indicates that many correctional officers are highly motivated to obtain additional training related to mentally ill offenders (Kropp, Cox, Roesch, & Eaves, 1989). Correctional mental health staff should be proactive participants in the training of new staff and providing in-services for veteran staff. Recognizing the signs and symptoms of mental illness, suicide risk, and intervention/referral are obviously some of the most critical content areas in which security personnel must be trained. Mental health professionals can also be helpful in developing curricula in diverse training areas, such as communications, interpersonal skills, conflict resolution, crisis/hostage negotiation, hostage survival skills, sexual assault prevention, and intervention (Harowski, 2003). In addition to the obvious benefit of teaching critical information, training programs increase service delivery across disciplines and allow a forum for mental health professionals to demonstrate sensitivity to security concerns (Dvoskin & Spiers, 2004).

CORRECTIONAL MENTAL HEALTH PROGRAMS

Mental health care in the community is offered in varying degrees of intensity, depending on the acuity and individual needs of the client. To cost effectively provide all of the services required, but only the services required, correctional mental health programs must also offer a variety of services analogous to those available in the community.

Clinic Services

Even the most mentally healthy inmates may find themselves in need of psychological services from time to time. Often, brief therapeutic contact will be sufficient to address the situational stressors encountered in the correctional setting. This level of service can be readily accomplished by case managers or social workers, who can provide support, information, and assistance managing the daily demands of incarceration. Often, the type of therapy most helpful to inmates is provided by staff who lack formal training but have an ability to listen to others and to treat them with dignity and respect (Dvoskin, Spiers, Metzner, & Pitt, 2002). For cases in which a more sophisticated level of intervention is necessary, correctional psychologists may engage in a (relatively) long-term treatment relationship with an inmate. Individual therapy will likely mirror free-world treatment, with the caveat that correctional psychologists are mindful of the impact of context on the presenting complaints and selection of intervention strategy.

Group therapy is clearly the most cost-effective treatment modality in corrections (Metzner, Cohen, Grossman, & Wettstein, 1998), as it allows provision of service to a large number of inmates even when resources are limited. Groups can be run by an individual or can be cofacilitated by mental health staff with various credentials. Creative thinking and thoughtful consideration when matching staff expertise with group subject matter can be of great benefit (Dvoskin, Spiers, Metzner, et al., 2002). For example, it may be helpful to include a psychiatric nurse as a facilitator of medication education or life skills groups, whereas a social worker or case manager may be the ideal collaborator for groups focused on discharge planning or managing institutional life, respectively. Group therapy can be particularly effective when the topics are focused, practical, and applied (e.g., stress management, anger management).

Of course, there are potential pitfalls to group therapy that must be addressed. Confidentiality is always a challenge in the group setting. As in the free world, group members must be cautioned from the outset about maintaining the confidentiality of therapeutic communications yet warned that confidentially cannot be guaranteed. In a correctional setting, security issues and the potential for violence must also be carefully considered.

Residential Treatment

Inmates with serious mental illnesses, and those who are psychologically fragile, often have difficulty coping with the stressful environment of the general inmate population. Fears of bullying, physical and sexual assault, and extortion, both real and imagined, can have a profound and negative effect on psychological well-being, especially of inexperienced prisoners. As such, jails and prisons should also have the ability to place psychologically fragile or mentally ill inmates in residential treatment settings (see, e.g., Condelli, Dvoskin, & Holanchock, 1994). These units should maximize the amount of time that the inmate is allowed out of cell, depending of course on the security routines of the institution. Programming is intended to create a reasonably therapeutic environment, which is a constant challenge in a correctional environment. Treatment modalities might include groups or individual supportive counseling.

Typically, there are three different types of inmates housed in such residential treatment units. Some are "halfway in," inmates who require a housing change designed to remove the need for transfer to a crisis bed or inpatient hospital. A second group is those who are "halfway out" of a more intensive placement (i.e., crisis or inpatient bed) and who require a transition period prior to returning to the general population. Finally, some inmates will never be able to survive the stress of the general population, though it is not possible to know this in advance. Typically, in residential treatment, efforts are made to teach inmates the skills and resilience needed to successfully live in the general population, even if, in some cases, those efforts never succeed.

Discharge Planning and Prerelease

Historically, jails and prisons have viewed their responsibilities for inmate health care as beginning and ending at the jailhouse door. *DeShaney v. Winnebago County* (1989) held that the obligation of government actors was based on the taking of custody of the person. Thus, it was reasoned, inmates' release from confinement ended any governmental responsibility for care. However, because systemic malpractice can be grounds for a finding of deliberate indifference (*Estelle v. Gamble,* 1976), it can be argued that abandoning patients, even in the face of known serious dangers to their lives, may have constitutional implications. In *Wakefield v. Thompson* (1999), the court held:

> It is a matter of common sense, however, that a prisoner's ability to secure medication "on his own behalf" is not necessarily restored the minute he walks through the prison gates and into the civilian world. Although many patients must take their medication one or more times a day, it may take a number of days, or possibly even weeks, for a recently released prisoner to find a doctor, schedule an examination, obtain a diagnosis, and have a prescription filled [footnote omitted]. Accordingly, the period of time during which prisoners are unable to secure medication "on their own behalf" may extend beyond the period of actual incarceration. Under the reasoning of Estelle and DeShaney, the state's responsibility to provide a temporary supply of medication to prisoners in such cases extends beyond that period as well.
>
> We therefore hold that the state must provide an outgoing prisoner who is receiving and continues to require medication with a supply sufficient to ensure that he has that medication available during the period of time reasonably necessary to permit him to consult a doctor and obtain a new supply. A state's failure to provide medication sufficient to cover this transitional period amounts to an abdication of its responsibility to provide medical care to those, who by reason of incarceration are unable to provide for their own medical needs.

Linking recently released inmates or detainees with services in the community should not require a legal mandate; basic professional ethics and human compassion should suffice. Mental health systems have long been aware of the critical need for continuity of care and wraparound service provision. Social support, both prior to and after release from prison, has been consistently, significantly, and positively associated with a wide range of quality of life outcomes (Jacoby & Kozie-Peak, 1997). Case management is perhaps the most important, and unfortunately underutilized, solution to the problem of ongoing service delivery and support. Ventura, Cassel, Jacoby, and Huang (1998) found a significant association between quality jail-to-community case management and a reduction in recidivism. Although findings related to recidivism may be mixed, there is no question about the impact of continued care on quality of life.

SPECIAL PROBLEMS AND ROLES FOR PSYCHOLOGISTS

Providing mental health care in a correctional setting is a daunting task in and of itself, but this challenge can be compounded when working with special populations.

Providing quality care to all inmates is, or should be, the aim of anyone working in a correctional setting.

Women

The prevalence of serious mental illness among female detainees is approximately twice that of males (Teplin, 1994). Interestingly, however, this is not true of disorders such as manic-depressive illness and Schizophrenia, which are increasingly thought of as having genetic or biological etiology. Rather, the entire difference appears attributable to depression, anxiety, and trauma spectrum disorders (Teplin, 1994; Teplin, Abram, & McClelland, 1996).

The effects of trauma can be especially hard on female inmates, for whom the circumstances of their confinement can resurrect images of their maltreatment as children. Even when correctional staff are appropriately and professionally performing their duties, realities such as being controlled by men (i.e., male correctional officers) or physically restrained or segregated can cause relapses of serious trauma spectrum disorders such as Posttraumatic Stress Disorder (PTSD). As Veysey (1998) described, the majority of female inmates suffer from problems including, but not limited to, substance abuse/dependence, physical illness, history of childhood and/or adult physical or sexual abuse, and self-esteem issues; they may also have vocational/educational needs and needs associated with pregnancy and/or primary responsibility for minor children. Psychologists can provide valuable aid to such women. Perhaps most important, psychological treatments such as dialectical behavior therapy can help women inmates control and manage their affect, thereby increasing the degree of control they can exert over their circumstances. For example, by learning to avoid losing one's temper, the likelihood of physical restraint by staff can drop dramatically.

Ethnic and Cultural Minorities

For ethnic minorities and non-English-speaking inmates, jails and prisons can be even more frightening. Anxiety stemming from absent or inaccurate information is one of the most easily rectified and often overlooked origins of crisis in a correctional setting. An inmate is further disadvantaged when he or she is forced to confront the complexities of prison life without a command of the language and/or customs of the majority. Toch, Adams, and Greene (1987) found a number of ethnic differences in prison infractions and concluded that psychological and subcultural predispositions may converge to create prison adjustment problems.

Cultural diversity is a significant factor in mental health care, both in custody and in the free world. For example, Blacks and Hispanics have historically been underserved by the mental health system, in and out of prison (Steadman, Holobean, & Dvoskin, 1991). This phenomenon may be secondary to an unwillingness to seek help from predominantly White providers, but may also reflect subtle and/or unintentional racism among those same providers (Dvoskin, Spiers, Metzner, et al., 2002). In the free world, an individual may have the opportunity to exercise some autonomy in terms of selecting his or her care provider(s). In a correctional setting, this is rarely the case. While correctional mental health administrators should make every effort to recruit a diverse professional staff, it is also imperative that all mental health professionals recognize the potential challenges inherent in working with multicultural inmates. Clearly, no psychologist can aspire to be proficient in treating individuals from every possible background and culture; still, it is incumbent upon those working in a correctional setting to make, at a minimum, a concerted effort to approach each case with an appreciation of cultural context (see, e.g., *Guidelines for Multicultural Education, Training, Research, Practice, and Organizational Change for Psychologists,* American Psychological Association, 2002).

Combat Veterans

Some U.S. combat veterans have reported significant difficulties returning to life at home. There is a great deal of controversy about the percentage of Vietnam veterans who ended up in U.S. prisons. However, whether the number is small or large, at least some combat veterans in prisons and jails suffer from PTSD, in some cases in addition to other serious mental disorders or addictions. Treatment that does not address the symptoms of traumatic stress is likely to fail, and psychologists, especially at Veterans Administration facilities, have provided some of the best research on PTSD and its treatment (Keane & Kaloupek, 1996). As these treatments find their way into prison settings, psychologists have an opportunity to provide a valuable service to the correctional system and its prisoners.

"Manipulative" Inmates

It is common to hear inmates referred to dismissively as "manipulative" or "malingering," as if this insult precludes a finding of mental illness. Such a view is misguided for several reasons. First, how can one be manipulative in a situation in which the people one is allegedly manipulating control virtually all of the circumstances and reinforcers in one's environment? Second, the fact that one exaggerates or feigns symptoms of mental illness does not mean that one does not have other or milder symptoms of mental illness. If inmates perceive themselves as falling below the threshold of admissibility into treatment yet are suffering, there is an understandable temptation to gild the lily. Third, some of the behaviors that lead to these characterizations, such as self-injurious behavior, existed long before the person was incarcerated.

It is difficult to imagine how a person confined to a 5′ by 8′ cell, with no property, nothing to do, no television to watch or books to read, could be credibly assumed to have selected this circumstance on purpose. There are certainly times when inmates may have viewed a segregated cell as their least negative alternative, for example, when they believe their life to be in danger in the general population. But even in that case, even if there is objectively no credible threat to the inmate, the fear that leads them to such a choice is undoubtedly legitimate. As Dvoskin (1997) wrote, the power to diagnose people can affect their lives for better and for worse. Dismissing an inmate as manipulative or as a management problem should never relieve psychologists of the responsibility to help troubled inmates better adapt to jail or prison and to help correctional officials deal with their most challenging inmates.

The Special Problems of Segregation

Few correctional issues arouse as much controversy as the use of long-term segregation. Proponents argue that the prevalence of illegal and violent gang activity requires strong measures, and that long-term segregation of gang leaders has reduced violence throughout the correctional system. Critics respond that there are long-term negative psychological effects that apply to most or some inmates. Although controlled research is extremely difficult to conduct on this question, it is generally agreed that at least *some* inmates will demonstrate a psychologically toxic response to long-term segregation, and the most vulnerable inmates in this regard are those with preexisting severe mental disorders.

Advocates argue that the only appropriate response to these circumstances is to ban the use of short- or long-term segregation for any inmate with a mental illness. But this position has some difficult challenges. For example, would mild depression qualify for this exclusion? If so, it is not unreasonable to think that almost any inmate could avoid being housed in segregation by complaining of symptoms for which there is virtually no reliable way to rule out malingering. Even inmates with serious mental illnesses such as Schizophrenia or manic-depressive illness are not necessarily symptomatic at any given time, and some offenses may reflect greed, anger, or sexual desires that have literally nothing to do with the inmate's mental illness. As suggested earlier, formal forensic evaluations in these situations would likely cause more harm than good. Nevertheless, correctional psychologists can be helpful to correctional administrators in resolving this dilemma by providing informal consultation on several questions:

- Is there evidence to suggest that the infraction is largely the result of symptoms of a serious mental illness?

- Is there history or evidence to suggest that the inmate will not be able to safely tolerate segregation due to mental illness?

- If segregation is necessary or appropriate, what mental health services will the inmate require while there?

- Are there alternative sanctions that would provide appropriate consequences for institutional misbehavior without causing an exacerbation of a serious mental illness?

Other Special Needs Groups

Other groups, such as geriatric inmates and those with physical disabilities, present unique challenges for those entrusted with their care. Generally speaking, the offender population is likely to have conducted their lives in a manner less than conducive to good health, thereby lowering the threshold for common ailments associated with aging (Dvoskin, Spiers, Metzner, et al., 2002). Moreover, inmates are more likely to have histories of poor health care and traumatic injury. With this in mind, it has been suggested that age 50 (as opposed to 65, as in the general population) can be used as a useful criterion for identifying geriatric inmates (American Psychiatric Association, 2000). As the correctional population continues to increase, so, too, will the number of elderly persons behind bars. An elderly inmate is subjected to all of the routine stressors of aging. However, these stressors are exacerbated by context-specific factors such as physical vulnerability to other inmates, estrangement/isolation, and the prospect of dying in prison (Dvoskin, Spiers, Metzner, et al., 2002).

Regardless of age, inmates enter the criminal justice system with myriad medical and physical disabilities. Even given legally mandated accommodations for disabled inmates, this population can be especially vulnerable in a correctional setting. Mental health providers must approach care bearing in mind that traditional intervention strategies may be ineffective. Here again, the usual stressors of incarceration are compounded. Inmates who are deaf, blind, or physically disabled face, in addition to risk from predatory peers, a greater likelihood of limitation in their ability to engage in traditional coping strategies such as exercise and recreation.

CONCLUSION

The role of psychology in corrections has evolved over many decades, yet psychologists still are often unable to provide valuable services to the people who need them most. The current state of criminal justice and correctional policy in the United States is at a crossroads for psychology. For those inmates with a constitutional right to treatment of serious mental illness, some of the best and most cost-effective treatments are psychological. For society, the wisdom gained from a century of social science about how to help people behave differently has no more appropriate target than those men and women whose behaviors have been so unacceptable that they have been incarcerated. Psychologists have enormous potential value to America's prisons and jails. The criminal justice system needs help to make better decisions about who can return to society and when. Our communities need help so that children can be safer. These activities, in these settings, promise to save the productive lives of prisoners and their otherwise future victims. For psychologists, whose most valuable expertise is positive behavior change, there is no more deserving or rewarding area for study and practice.

REFERENCES

American Psychiatric Association. (2000). *Psychiatric services in jails and prisons* (2nd ed.). Washington, DC: Author.

American Psychological Association. (2002). *Guidelines on multicultural education, training, research, practice, and organizational change for psychologists.* Washington, DC: Author.

Americans with Disabilities Act of 1990, 104 Stat. 328 42 U.S.C.

Anthony, W. A. (1982). Explaining "psychiatric rehabilitation" by an analogy to "physical rehabilitation." *Psychosocial Rehabilitation Journal, 5,* 61–65.

Anthony, W. A., Cohen, M., & Kennard, W. (1990). Understanding the current facts and principles of mental health systems planning. *American Psychologist, 45,* 1249–1252.

Applebaum, K. L., Hickey, J. M., & Packer, I. (2001). The role of correctional officers in multidisciplinary mental health care in prisons. *Psychiatric Services, 52,* 1343–1347.

Armstrong v. Wilson, 942 F. Supp. 1252 (N. D. Cal. 1996) aff'd 124 F.3d 1019 (9th Cir. 1997).

Bartol, C. R., & Freeman, N. J. (2005). History of the American Association for Correctional Psychology. *Criminal Justice and Behavior, 32,* 123–142.

Bell v. Wolfish, 441 U.S. 520 (1979).

Bersoff, D. N. (Ed.). (2003). *Ethical conflicts in psychology* (3rd ed.). Washington, DC: American Psychological Association.

Bowring v. Goodwin, 551 F.2d 44 (1977).

Brodsky, C. M., & Epstein, L. J. (1982). Psychiatric consultation through continuing education in correctional institutions. *Comprehensive Psychiatry, 23,* 582–589.

Brodsky, S. L. (1973). *Psychologists in the criminal justice system.* Urbana: University of Illinois Press.

Brodsky, S. L. (1986). Civil action and empirical assessment. In G. Melton (Ed.), *Nebraska Symposium on Motivation: Psychology and law* (pp. 213–227). Lincoln: University of Nebraska Press.

Brodsky, S. L., & Miller, K. S. (1981). Coercing change in prisons and mental hospitals: The social scientist and class action suit. In J. M. Joffe & G. W. Albee (Eds.), *Prevention through political action and social change* (pp. 208–227). Hanover, NH: University Press of New England.

Burnaby, B. C., Cox, J. F., & Morschauser, P. C. (1997). A solution to the problem of jail suicide. *Crisis, 18,* 178–184.

Chen, C. (2004). The Prison Litigation Reform Act of 1995: Doing away with more than just crunchy peanut butter. *St. John's Law Review, 78,* 203–232.

Civil Rights Act, 42 U.S.C. § 1983.

Clark v. California, 123 F.3d 1267 (9th Cir. 1997).

Cohen, F. (1998). *The mentally disordered inmate and the law.* Kingston, NJ: Civic Research Institute.

Cohen, F., & Dvoskin, J. (1992). Inmates with mental disorders: A guide to law and practice. *Mental and Physical Disability Law Reporter, 16,* 339–346.

Cohen, M. (1989). Integrating psychiatric rehabilitation into mental health systems. In M. Farkas & W. Anthony (Eds.), *Psychiatric rehabilitation programs: Putting theory into practice.* Baltimore: Johns Hopkins University Press.

Cohen, M., & Anthony, W. A. (1988). A commentary on planning a service system for persons who are severely mentally ill: Avoiding the pitfalls of the past. *Psychosocial Rehabilitation Journal, 12,* 69–72.

Coleman v. Wilson, 912 F. Supp. 1282 (E.D. Cal. 1995).

Condelli, W. S., Dvoskin, J. A., & Holanchock, H. (1994). Intermediate care programs for inmates with psychiatric disorders. *Bulletin of the American Academy of Psychiatry and the Law, 22,* 63–70.

Corsini, R. J. (1989). Introduction. In R. J. Corsini & D. Wedding (Eds.), *Current psychotherapies* (4th ed., pp. 1–16). Itasca, IL: F. E. Peacock.

DeShaney v. Winnebago County Soc. Servs. Dept., 489 U.S. 189 (1989).

Dvoskin, J. A. (1997). Sticks and stones: The abuse of psychiatric diagnosis in prisons. *Journal of the California Alliance for the Mentally Ill, 8,* 20–21.

Dvoskin, J. A., Petrila, J., & Stark-Riemer, S. (1995). Application of the professional judgment rule to prison mental health. *Mental and Physical Disability Law Reporter, 19,* 108–114.

Dvoskin, J. A., & Spiers, E. M. (2004). On the role of correctional officers in prison mental health care. *Psychiatric Quarterly, 75,* 41–59.

Dvoskin, J. A., Spiers, E. M., Metzner, J. L., & Pitt, S. E. (2002). The structure of correctional mental health services. In R. Rosner (Ed.), *Principles and practice of forensic psychiatry* (pp. 489–504). London: Arnold.

Dvoskin, J. A., Spiers, E. M., & Pitt, S. E. (2002). Mental health professionals as institutional consultants and problem solvers. In T. J. Fagan & R. K. Ax (Eds.), *Correctional mental health handbook* (pp. 251–271). Thousand Oaks, CA: Sage.

Estelle v. Gamble, 429 U.S. 97 (1976).

Fowler, R. D., & Brodsky, S. L. (1978). Development of a correctional-clinical psychology program. *Professional Psychology: Research and Practice, 9,* 440–447.

Gallaghar, R. W., Somwaru, D. P., & Ben-Porath, Y. S. (1999). Current usage of psychological tests in state correctional settings. *National Journal for Corrections, The Corrections Compendium, 24,* 1–3.

Harowski, K. J. (2003). Staff training: Multiple roles for mental health professionals. In T. J. Fagan & R. K. Ax (Eds.), *Correctional mental health handbook* (pp. 237–249). Thousand Oaks, CA: Sage.

Hayes, L. M. (1995). Prison suicide: An overview and guide to prevention. *Prison Journal, 75,* 431–457.

Jacoby, J. E., & Kozie-Peak, B. (1997). The benefits of social support for mentally ill offenders: Prison-to-community transitions. *Behavioral Sciences and the Law, 15,* 483–501.

Kansas v. Crane, 70 U.S.L.W. 4117 (2002).

Kansas v. Hendricks, 521 U.S. 346 (1997).

Keane, T. M., & Kaloupek, D. G. (1996). Cognitive behavior therapy in the treatment of posttraumatic stress disorder. *Clinical Psychologist, 49*(1), 7–8.

Kropp, R., Cox, D., Roesch, R., & Eaves, D. (1989). The perceptions of correctional officers toward mentally disordered offenders. *International Journal of Law and Psychiatry, 12,* 181–188.

Langley v. Coughlin, F. Supp. 522 538 540-541 (S.D.N.Y. 1989) aff'd, 888 F.2d 252 (2nd Cir. 1989).

Lindner, R. (1944). *Rebel without a cause.* New York: Grune & Stratton.

Lindner, R. (1954). *The fifty-minute hour: A collection of true psychoanalytic tales.* New York: Holt, Rinehart and Winston.

Madrid v. Gomez, 889 F. Supp. 1146 (N. D. Cal. 1995).

Martinson, R. (1974, Spring). What works? Questions and answers about prison reform. *Public Interest,* 22–54.

Megargee, E. I. (1994). Using the Megargee MMPI-based classification system with MMPI-2s of male prison inmates. *Psychological Assessment, 6,* 337–344.

Megargee, E. I., Mercer, S. J., & Carbonell, J. L. (1999). MMPI-2 with male and female state and federal prison inmates. *Psychological Assessment, 11,* 177–185.

Menninger, K. (1966). *The crime of punishment.* New York: Viking.

Metzner, J. L. (2002a). Class action litigation in correctional psychiatry. *Journal of the American Academy of Psychiatry and the Law, 30,* 19–29.

Metzner, J. L. (2002b). Prison litigation in the USA. *Journal of Forensic Psychiatry, 13,* 240–244.

Metzner, J. L., Cohen, F., Grossman, L. S., & Wettstein, R. M. (1998). Treatment in jails and prisons. In R. M. Wettstein (Ed.), *Treatment of offenders with mental disorders* (pp. 211–265). New York: Guilford Press.

Monahan, J. (Ed.). (1980). *Who is the client? The ethics of psychological intervention in the criminal justice system.* Washington, DC: American Psychological Association.

Monahan, J., Steadman, H., Silver, E., Appelbaum, P., Robbins, P., Mulvey, E., et al. (2001). *Rethinking risk assessment: The MacArthur Study of Mental Disorder and Violence.* New York: Oxford University Press.

Morton, J. B., & Anderson, J. C. (1996). Implementing the Americans with Disabilities Act for inmates. *Corrections Today, 58,* 86–91.

National Commission on Correctional Mental Health Care. (2003). *Correctional mental health care.* Chicago: Author.

Nicholls, T. L., Roesch, R., Olley, M. C., Ogloff, J. R. P., & Hemphill, L. F. (2005). *Jail screening assessment tool: Guidelines for mental health screening in jails.* Burnaby, British Columbia, Canada: Simon Fraser University, Mental Health Law, Policy, and Training Institute.

Pennsylvania Dept. of Corrections v. Yeskey, 524 U.S. 206 (1998).

Peters, R. H., Matthews, C. O., & Dvoskin, J. A. (2005). Treatment in prisons and jails. In J. H. Lowinson, P. Ruiz, R. B. Millman, & J. G. Langrod (Eds.), *Substance abuse: A comprehensive textbook* (4th ed., pp. 707–722). Baltimore: Williams & Wilkins.

Powell v. Coughlin, 953 F.2d 744 (2d Cir. 1991).

Rappeport, J. R. (1974). Patuxent revisited. *Bulletin of the American Academy of Psychiatry and the Law, 3,* 10–16.

Roskes, E., & Feldman, R. (1999). A collaborative community-based treatment program for offenders with mental illness. *Psychiatric Services, 50,* 1614–1619.

Ruiz v. Estelle, 53 F. Supp. 1265 (1980).

Sidley, N. T. (1974). The evaluation of prison treatment and preventive detention programs: Some problems faced by the Patuxent Institution. *Bulletin of the American Academy of Psychiatry and the Law, 2,* 73–95.

Spiers, E. M., Dvoskin, J. A., & Pitt, S. E. (2003). Mental health professionals as institutional consultants and problem-solvers. In T. Fagan & R. Ax (Eds.), *Correctional mental health handbook* (pp. 252–272). Thousand Oaks, CA: Sage Publications.

Steadman, H. J., Holobean, E., & Dvoskin, J. A. (1991). Estimating mental health need and service utilization among prison inmates. *Bulletin of the American Academy of Psychiatry and the Law, 19,* 297–307.

Steadman, H. J., Scott, J. E., Osher, F., Agnese, T. K., & Robbins, B. A. (2005). Validation of the brief jail mental health screen. *Psychiatry Services, 56,* 816–822.

Stone, T. H. (1997). Therapeutic implications of incarceration for persons with severe mental disorders: Searching for rational health policy. *American Journal of Criminal Law, 24,* 283–358.

Teplin, L. A. (1994). Psychiatric and substance abuse disorders among male urban jail detainees. *American Journal of Public Health, 84*(2), 290–293.

Teplin, L. A., Abram, K. M., & McClelland, G. M. (1996). Prevalence of psychiatric disorders among incarcerated women. *Archives of General Psychiatry, 53,* 505–512.

Toch, H., Adams, K., & Greene, R. (1987). Ethnicity, disruptiveness, and emotional disorder among prison inmates. *Criminal Justice and Behavior, 14,* 93–109.

Towl, G. (Ed.). (2003). *Psychology in prisons.* Malden, MA: Blackwell.

Ventura, L. A., Cassel, C. A., Jacoby, J. E., & Huang, B. (1998). Case management and recidivism of mentally ill persons released from jail. *Psychiatric Services, 49,* 1330–1337.

Veysey, B. M. (1998). The specific needs of women diagnosed with mental illness in U.S. jails. In B. L. Levin, A. K. Blanch, & A. Jennings (Eds.), *Women's mental health services: A public health perspective.* Thousand Oaks, CA: Sage.

Veysey, B. M., Steadman, H. J., Morrissey, J. P., & Johnsen, M. J. (1997). In search of missing linkages: Continuity of care in U.S. jails. *Behavioral Sciences and the Law, 15,* 383–397.

Wakefield v. Thompson, 177 F.3d 1164 (9th Cir. 1999).

Wilson, D. P. (1951). *My six convicts: A psychologist's 3 years in Fort Leavenworth.* New York: Rinehart & Company.

Yackle, L. W. (1989). *Reform and regret: The story of federal judicial involvement in the Alabama prison system.* New York: Oxford University Press.

Youngberg v. Romeo, 457 U.S. 307 (1982).

Zenoff, E. H., & Courtless, T. F. (1977). Autopsy of an experiment: The Patuxent experience. *Journal of Psychiatry and Law, 5,* 531–550.

CHAPTER 24

Evaluating the Psychological Sequelae of Elder Abuse

Beth N. Rom-Rymer

> *Idle old man,*
> *That still would manage those authorities*
> *That he hath given away!—Now, by my life,*
> *Old fools are babes again; and must be used*
> *With checks as flatteries, when they are seen*
> *Abused.*
>
> —William Shakespeare, *King Lear*

EPIDEMIOLOGY

Elder abuse may be as old as the history of the human family, but in today's gray-ing society, with its exponential growth of institutionalized care facilities for the elderly, elder abuse has increasingly become a focus of the law, the clinician, and the social scientist.

The Administration on Aging (Greenberg, 2003, p. 2) notes that since 1900:

> The percentage of Americans 65 and older has tripled (from 4.1% in 1900 to 12.3% in 2002) and the number has increased 11 times (from 3.1 million to 35.6 million). The older population itself is getting older. In 2002, the 65 to 75 year age group (18.3 million) was 8 times larger than in 1900, but the 75 to 84 group (12.7 million) was more than 16 times larger and the 85+ group (4.6 million) was almost 38 times larger. There were 50,364 persons age 100 or more in 2002 (0.02% of the total population). This is a 35% increase from the 1990 figure of 37,306.

Moskowitz writes that by 2010, the elderly population will increase to more than 40.1 million, or 13.3% of the population (Levine, 1996, cited by Moskowitz, 2003, p. 593); by 2020, the elderly population will increase to 17.7% of the population; and by 2050, the elderly population will increase to 22% of the population (U.S. Senate Special Committee, 1990, cited by Moskowitz, 2003, p. 593). The United Nations (Daly, 2002, cited by Moskowitz, 2003, p. 593) has estimated that by 2050, one in five people (approximately 2 billion) will be 60 years of age or older. Around the world, as in the United States, people 80 and older are the fastest growing age group in the world (Daly, 2002, cited by Moskowitz, 2003, p. 593).

In testimony before the U.S. Senate Committee on Finance on June 18, 2002, Dr. Catherine Hawes (2002, p. 1) of the Department of Health Policy and Management, School of Rural Public Health at Texas A&M University, stated, "On any given day, approximately 1.6 million people live in approximately 17,000 licensed nursing homes and an estimated 900,000 to one million persons live in approximately 45,000 residential care facilities." From 1996 to 2001, according to the National Ombudsmen Reporting System (2002), there was a 16% increase in board and care facilities and a 43% increase in the number of board and care beds. And these numbers are steadily rising. The U.S. Census Bureau projects that by the year 2050, there will be nearly 21 million Americans over the age of 85 (Federal Interagency Forum on Aging-Related Statistics, 2004), and 4.8 million of those may be living in nursing homes (Chairman of Subcommittee on Health and Long-Term Care, 1991).

What is particularly alarming about these numbers is that as the elderly population is growing, caregivers are not ready for their roles. The middle-aged children of the elderly are often psychologically and financially ill prepared and not trained to effectively manage the complex demands of their elder parents who reside in the community. In nursing homes, certified nursing assistants (CNAs) overwhelmingly outnumber licensed practical nurses (LPNs) and registered nurses (RNs) and do the lion's share of the very tough work of managing the frail, yet often combative, nursing home resident. Further, the turnover rate for CNAs (at more than 90%) is nearly twice the rate for RNs and LPNs (American Health Care Association, 1999); staff-to-patient ratios are typically well below the levels mandated by the government; when criminal and employment background checks on staff are conducted, they are often inadequately done; CNAs are poorly educated, poorly trained, poorly supervised, and poorly paid (Hawes, 2003). Thus, the normative and pathological aging process of the elder, with cognitive and physiological decline, the onset or worsening of psychological disturbance with concomitant behavioral agitation, and the onset of chronic and/or life-threatening disease processes, increases a multidimensional dependency on others, heightening a vulnerability to exploitation, neglect, and physical, sexual, and psychological abuse.

The National Center on Elder Abuse (1998, pp. 3-2, 3-3) defines *physical abuse* as

> the use of physical force that may result in bodily injury, physical pain, or impairment. Physical abuse may include but is not limited to such acts of violence as striking (with or without an object), hitting, beating, pushing, shoving, shaking, slapping, kicking, pinching, and burning. . . . The unwarranted administration of drugs and physical restraints, force-feeding, and physical punishment of any kind also are examples of physical abuse.

The same organization defines *sexual abuse* as

> nonconsensual sexual contact of any kind with an elderly person. Sexual contact with any person incapable of giving consent also is considered sexual abuse; it includes but is not limited to unwanted touching, all types of sexual assault or battery such as rape, sodomy, coerced nudity, and sexually explicit photographing. (p. 3-3)

Emotional or *psychological abuse* is defined as

> the infliction of anguish, emotional pain, or distress. Emotional or psychological abuse includes but is not limited to verbal assaults, insults, threats, intimidation, humiliation, and

harassment. In addition, treating an older person like an infant; isolating an elderly person from family, friends, or regular activities; giving an older person a "silent treatment" . . . [or] enforced social isolation. (p. 3-3)

Neglect is defined as

the refusal or failure to fulfill any part of a person's obligations or duties to an elder. Neglect may also include a refusal or failure by a person who has fiduciary responsibilities to provide care for an elder. Neglect typically means the refusal or failure to provide an elderly person with such life necessities as food, water, clothing, shelter, personal hygiene, medicine, comfort, personal safety, and other essentials included as a responsibility or an agreement. (p. 3-3)

The most prudent national estimate is that a total of 449,924 elderly persons, age 60 and over, experienced abuse and/or neglect in domestic settings in 1996 (*The National Elder Abuse Incidence Study,* National Center on Elder Abuse, 1998). The total number of nursing home complaints in 2000 numbered 186,000, and the total for all reported abuse cases rose from 13,469 in 1996 to 15,501 in 1998, and declined to 15,010 in 2000 (Office of Inspector General, 2003). The collection of data on abuse complaints is not uniform, and most investigators and social scientists agree that elder abuse is underreported. Many cognitively compromised elders cannot accurately perceive or adequately communicate having been abused. Hawes (2003) notes that "fear of retaliation," lack of awareness of how to make a complaint, and a sense of powerlessness contribute to nursing home residents' underreporting. The National Center on Elder Abuse (1998), citing the isolation of the elderly in the community, observed that reported elder abuse is only the "tip of the iceberg": five times as many new incidents of abuse were unreported as reported.

In 2003, older women outnumbered older men in the United States, and the proportion that is female increases with age. In 2003, women accounted for 58% of the population age 65 and over and for 69% of the population age 85 and over (Federal Interagency Forum, 2004). Women are overrepresented (any percentage over 58% is an overrepresentation) as victims of maltreatment. The percentage of women who are victims of neglect is 60%; the percentage of women who are victims of emotional and psychological abuse is 76.3%; the percentage of women who are victims of financial/material exploitation is 63%; and the percentage of women who are victims of physical/sexual abuse is 71.4%. Men are overrepresented as victims of abandonment (62.2%; National Center on Elder Abuse, 1998).

Nationwide, in domestic abuse cases in 1996 among those 60 and older, 84% were White, 8.3% Black, 5.1% Hispanic, 2.1% were Asian or Pacific Islanders, and 0.4% were American Indian or Alaskan Natives. In general, elders from the non-White and non-Black ethnic and racial categories were underrepresented. White elders accounted for 79.0% of the victims of neglect; Black elders accounted for 17.2% and were overrepresented. Among victims of emotional/psychological abuse, 82.8% were White; 14.1% were Black and overrepresented. White elders represented 86.0% of victims of physical abuse, and Black elders constituted approximately 9.0%. The proportion of White elders who were victims of financial/material exploitation was 83.0%; Black elders were 15.4% of victims of

Table 24.1   States Whose Statutes Have Specific Language Pertaining to Criminal Procedures and Penalties for Elder Abuse

Alabama	Maryland	Oregon
Alaska	Michigan	Pennsylvania
Arizona	Minnesota	South Carolina
California	Montana	South Dakota
Connecticut	Mississippi	Tennessee
Georgia	Nevada	Texas
Idaho	New Hampshire	Utah
Indiana	New Jersey	Virginia
Iowa	New York	West Virginia
Kentucky	North Carolina	

exploitation. Abandonment accounted for only 3.6% of all victims of elder abuse. However, 41.3% of abandonment victims were White (an underrepresentation), whereas Blacks were significantly overrepresented, with 57.3% suffering from this type of abuse (National Center on Elder Abuse, 1998).

ELDER ABUSE STATUTES[1]

Just as child abuse became an issue that seared the consciousness of the world and legislative, political, and social activists (Chairman of Subcommittee on Health and Long-Term Care, 1991; Holder, 2005), the growing awareness of elder abuse has spawned civil and/or criminal legislation in every state of the Union. The laws vary in scope but typically include remedies and/or sanctions for abuse, neglect, financial exploitation, and professional malpractice in the context of working with elders (Buchwalter, 2003).

As can be seen in Tables 24.1 through 24.4, a majority of states (29) have elder abuse statutes with specific language pertaining to criminal procedures and penalties. Twenty-three states have elder abuse statutes with specific language pertaining to civil procedures, and eight additional states have specific language pertaining to civil procedures with specific civil penalties; 39 states have broadly inclusive mandatory reporting rules.

What is most interesting to this writer is the anomalous states. Eight states (see Table 24.5) have bare-bones language for elder abuse protections. Illinois, one of the first states, in 1988, to pass protective legislation (2005) for elders, has no specific language in its statute in reference to special civil and criminal procedures and penalties for elder abuse. Kansas (2004) recently repealed its civil statute, the Mentally Ill, Incapacitated, and Dependent Persons Act, thereby taking the state out of an administrative obligation to specifically care for its elderly and other dependent persons, but includes language encouraging "private cause of action." Louisiana (2004) also appears to take a minimal administrative role in the issue by simply offering "to make available" any state documentation "following an investigation or conviction of a person . . . of elderly abuse."

---

[1] I would like to thank Melissa Wurtzel, Esq., attorney-at-law, Pretzel and Stouffer, Chartered, for her legal research assistance.

Table 24.2   States Whose Statutes Have Specific Language Pertaining to Civil Procedures but Not Civil Penalties for Elder Abuse

Alaska	Idaho	Ohio
Arkansas	Maryland	Oklahoma
California	Massachusetts	Pennsylvania
Colorado	Michigan	Vermont
Connecticut	Mississippi	Virginia
Georgia	Nevada	Washington
Hawaii	New Mexico	Utah
Indiana	North Carolina	

Whereas states such as California (2003), Idaho (2005), Maryland (2005), Michigan (2005), Mississippi (2005), New York (2005), North Carolina (2005), Pennsylvania (2004), and Rhode Island (2004) (Table 24.1) have strong criminal sanctions in their penal codes for elder abuse, Louisiana (2004) has none. Further, Louisiana is one of only seven states that does not have any form of elder abuse reporting clause (see Table 24.6).

Arkansas's statute was amended in April 2005, but although it explicitly provides for civil procedural remedies, it does not have a reporting clause and cites no specific criminal procedures or sanctions. Florida (2004), with one of the highest per capita elderly populations in the country, recently removed strong statutory language that allowed for high levels of punitive damages to elder plaintiffs. Yet, Florida is working hard to enforce its strong criminal elder abuse code.

Seven states (see Table 24.7) call for only voluntary reporting of elder abuse. New York has strong criminal sanctions for elder abuse, but its statute contains voluntary reporting language. The Wisconsin statute (2005) is one of the weakest in the country, containing no explicit statement of civil or criminal procedures; its only provision is for voluntary reporting. Interestingly, Illinois mandates reporting for law enforcement, all health professionals, Christian Science practitioners, and human services administrators and personnel, and, for good measure, adds voluntary reporting for "any person." North Dakota (2003) and Colorado (2005) have generally weaker statutory language.

One of the strongest statutes in language and the state that takes the strongest stance in practice against elder abuse is California. One element that makes the California statute so powerful is the California Welfare and Institutions Code, the Elder Abuse and Dependent Adult Civil Protection Act (§ 15600), which allows for

Table 24.3   States Whose Statutes Have Specific Language Pertaining to Civil Procedures and Civil Penalties for Elder Abuse

Delaware	Oregon
Florida	South Carolina
Iowa	Tennessee
Maine	

Table 24.4   States Whose Statutes Have Mandatory Reporting of Elder Abuse

Alabama	Kansas	North Carolina
Alaska	Kentucky	Ohio
California	Maine	Oklahoma
Connecticut	Maryland	Oregon
Delaware	Massachusetts	Rhode Island
District of Columbia	Michigan	South Carolina
Florida	Mississippi	Texas
Georgia	Missouri	Utah
Hawaii	Montana	Virginia
Idaho	Nebraska	Washington
Illinois	New Hampshire	West Virginia
Indiana	New Jersey	Wyoming
Iowa	New Mexico	

Note: Mandatory reporters include all health care providers, police officers, nursing home administrators, and staff employees of the Department of Health and Human Services.

Alabama slightly narrows its mandatory reporting clause to "physicians and other practitioners of the healing arts or any caregiver."

enhanced or additional remedies in civil actions. Not surprisingly, the preponderance of case law in elder abuse is found in California. Some of the most interesting cases are summarized in the next section of this chapter.

CASE LAW DEVELOPMENTS

To date, there have been no elder abuse cases, either civil or criminal, that have been decided by the U.S. Supreme Court. However, *Covenant Care, Inc. v. Superior Court* (2004) was heard in the California Supreme Court; *Matter of Guardianship/Conservatorship of Denton* (1997) was heard by the Arizona Supreme Court; *Vallery v. State of Nevada* (2002) was heard by the Nevada Supreme Court; and *Conner v. State of Florida* (1999) was heard in the Florida Supreme Court. In *Matter of Guardianship,* the Arizona Supreme Court noted the recency of the Elder Abuse Act and reviewed the case to specifically set state precedent.

Civil Suits

Numerous civil suits have been filed that have tested and defined elder abuse case law.

Table 24.5   States Whose Statutes Have Neither Civil nor Criminal Procedural Language regarding Elder Abuse Except for a Reporting Clause

District of Columbia	North Dakota
Illinois	Rhode Island
Kansas	Wisconsin
Louisiana	Wyoming

Note: Louisiana's statute has no reporting clause.

Table 24.6   States Whose Statutes Have No Reporting Language regarding Elder Abuse

Arkansas	Minnesota
Arizona	Nevada
Louisiana	Vermont

Statute of Limitations

Wilson v. Berkeley Long-Term Care (2004) affirms the California trial court's judgment dismissing late filed claims. Wilson's initial complaint alleged that his father had died in 1999 due to defendants' failure "to provide necessary medical attention, medical advice." However, in this current case, Wilson was seeking compensation for loss of "comfort, society, and affection" as a "survivor" of a victimized elder. Although the court cited the 1991 Elder Abuse Act which "was designed to protect elderly and dependent persons from abuse, neglect, or abandonment," (slip opinion at p. 2) the current cause of action was barred by the statute of limitations because it is a "survival" cause of action (slip opinion at p. 2) and does not relate back to the original wrongful death complaint.

In a 2001 case, *Alcott Rehabilitation Hospital v. Superior Court,* the skilled nursing facility's petition to mandate a partial summary judgment was denied because the court ruled that the patient's "insanity tolled 1 year statute of limitations" (pp. 94, 807). The patient, a 70-year-old catastrophic stroke victim, had alleged that the nursing facility had committed elder abuse and neglect and medical malpractice. The court defined insanity as stated in the California Code of Civil Procedure (§ 352) as "incapable of caring for her property or transacting business, or understanding the nature or effects of her acts."

Kennedy v. Closson (2001) denied review of a case because it asserted that the plaintiff, the adult son of the decedent, had not petitioned the court to "maintain" a civil action for elder abuse following the death of the elder. The court noted that the California Welfare and Institutions Code (§ 15657.3(d)) provides that "upon petition, after the death of the elder or dependent adult, the right to maintain an action

Table 24.7   States Whose Statutes Have Voluntary rather than Mandatory Reporting Clause regarding Elder Abuse

Colorado	Pennsylvania
Illinois	South Dakota
New York	Wisconsin
North Dakota	

Note: Illinois's statute includes reporting for "any person."

[for elder abuse] shall be transferred to the personal representative of the decedent" (slip opinion at p. 7).

Procedural Protections

In *Covenant v. Superior Court* (2004), the decedent's children sued the care facility for elder abuse under the Elder Abuse and Dependent Adult Civil Protection Act and moved for leave to claim punitive damages. The Superior Court of California granted the motion. On appeal, the court of appeals denied the petition, but the California Supreme Court granted review and, indeed, held that, under the California Elder Abuse Act, when "egregious acts of misconduct" are committed (p. 773, 290, 222), physicians do not "enjoy" the procedural protections they are generally afforded when they are sued for negligence in their professional health care practice.

Trial Preference

Kraig v. Superior Court (2002) held that an 84-year-old female plaintiff in an elder abuse action, whose doctor stated that there was "substantial medical doubt of her surviving more than 6 months" (slip opinion at p. 1), was entitled to a trial date preference under the California Code of Civil Procedure (§ 36(a)), which mandated a preference on the petition of a party to a civil action who is over age 70, who has a substantial interest in the litigated matter, and who would necessarily be prejudiced because of ill health if the preference was not granted.

Level of Negligence Required to Recover in an Action for Elder Abuse

Grant v. Oh (2003) reversed the judgment following the granting of summary adjudication for a defendant physician as to the plaintiff's elder abuse cause of action. The California court maintained that there was a "triable issue of material fact" (slip opinion at p. 3) that could be resolved by the trier of fact. For example, there was conflicting evidence as to whether the defendant physician subjected the decedent to prolonged periods of deprivation of food she could ingest; whether he failed to properly monitor her food intake and weight to prevent starvation; whether he failed to prevent bedsores and the worsening of existing bedsores, which resulted in the amputation of her leg; and whether he abandoned his patient when she was transferred to another hospital, failing to provide the new hospital with the information necessary for her continued treatment. Plaintiff's expert had offered the opinion that "this was one of the worst cases of elder abuse she had encountered" (slip opinion at p. 4), whereas the defendant's expert had offered the opinion that "the defendant's treatment complied with the standard of care applicable to physicians rendering care and treatment to patients at skilled nursing facilities in this locality and that treatment was not a substantial factor in causing any pain, suffering, or death" (slip opinion at p. 4).

Intrieri v. Superior Court (2004) ruled that there were triable questions of fact regarding the "reckless neglect" element of a cause of action for elder abuse under the Elder Abuse and Dependent Adults Act, thereby precluding a summary judgment. There was reasonable evidence that a non-Alzheimer's patient who was known to have a confused and hostile mental state entered the purportedly locked

Alzheimer's Unit and injured an Alzheimer's patient without intervention by nursing home staff. There was a "reasonable inference that Guardian consciously disregarded the safety" (pp. 85, 108) of the Alzheimer's patients because the code for the lock on the Alzheimer's Unit was posted over the keypad.

Causal Link between Misconduct and Harm

Rodriguez v. Care with Dignity Health Care Inc. (2002) affirmed in part and reversed in part, with directions. The California court affirmed a verdict for the defendants on claims of elder abuse and wrongful death. The jury found that although the nursing home was negligent, the jury did not believe that the negligence caused the victim's injury or death. The plaintiffs appealed on the grounds that the jury's instructions had been given in error. The court concluded that the survivors were not prejudiced by the failure of the trial court to give the jury negligence per se instructions. The court did reverse the jury's verdict for breach of contract for the plaintiffs and did find that the damages awarded for the patient's mental suffering and emotional distress were permissible in a breach of contract action.

Emotional Injuries

Moon v. Guardian Postacute Services, Inc. (2002) rejected a son-in-law's claim for relief following the death of his mother-in-law in a nursing home. The court ruled that the son-in-law was not "closely related" and thus could not establish a "bystander claim" for the negligent infliction of emotional distress and further rejected his argument that he was a "direct victim" of the abuse. The court explained that the Elder Abuse Act could not be used to expand claims for negligent infliction of emotional distress to members of an extended family who have a relative residing in an extended care facility. Citing the Supreme Court in *Elden v. Sheldon* (1988), the court stated, "To do so would result in the unreasonable extension of the scope of liability of a negligent actor" (*Moon,* 2002, p. 1011, 223). In exploring the claim of the "direct victim," the court refuted the argument that because the son-in-law had signed his mother-in-law into the facility and had received assurances from the facility that it would provide proper care, these assurances sufficiently created a legal duty of care. The court cited a case (*Schwarz v. Regents of University of California,* 1990) in which that court had rejected a father's claim of direct victim status in a suit against a psychotherapist who had treated his son. The father had hired the therapist and participated in some counseling sessions with the therapist. "The father in Schwarz had a stronger preexisting relationship with the therapist than Ken [the plaintiff] had with Guardian" (*Moon,* 2002, p. 1015, 225). The therapist's agreement with the father to provide care for the child, however, was not sufficient to impose a duty of care toward the parent.

Pain and Suffering

In *Matter of Guardianship/Conservatorship of Denton* (1997), the court held that the husband could recover damages for the wife's pain and suffering under the elder abuse statute, Arizona Revised Statutes Annotated (§ 46-455). The court held that the husband could recover damages even though his wife had died while the complaint was pending. The Arizona Superior Court granted the motion to the defendants for partial judgment. When the husband filed for a petition for special action in the court of appeals, it declined to accept jurisdiction. The husband then filed for review with the Arizona Supreme Court, which was granted, "as elder abuse statute was relatively new [1997] . . . advancing age of petitioner . . . and claim for pain and suffering would often be most significant element of damages in elder abuse cases" (p. 152, 1283). In granting relief, the court explained that the elder abuse statute "expressly provides to victims of elder abuse and their representatives the right to recover damages for pain and suffering, even after the death of the abused victim" (pp. 154–155, 1285–1286), and that this right is not limited by the survival statute, Arizona Revised Statutes Annotated (§ 14-3110), which generally prevents recovery of pain and suffering damages after the victim's death.

Punitive Damages

Community Care and Rehabilitation Center v. Superior Court (2000) clarified when plaintiffs could seek punitive damages in a medical malpractice action brought under the Elder Abuse Act. The court stated that a motion must be brought that establishes a "substantial probability" of prevailing on the punitive damages claim on the merits of the case and discouraged plaintiffs' "meritless" claims made for "tactical" reasons (p. 791, 345). The court emphasized that the California Code of Civil Procedures (§ 425.13) does not prohibit the recovery of punitive damages but does demand that it be proven that the defendant acted with "recklessness, oppression, fraud, or malice" (p. 792, 346) in claims for medical malpractice made under the Elder Abuse Act.

Criminal Prosecutions for Elder Abuse

Concomitant with the growth of civil litigation in elder abuse law is the surge in criminal prosecutions. Taken together, the litigation is creating an acute awareness of the serious consequences of elder abuse.

Actual Knowledge Requirement

In *Vallery v. State of Nevada* (2002), reviewed by the Nevada Supreme Court, the defendant was convicted on one count of elder neglect, having caused substantial bodily harm, and two counts of elder neglect causing death, arising from her failure to take action to prevent the neglect of elderly persons residing in the group care facilities that she administered. The district court's decisions were affirmed in part, reversed in part, and remanded. The court remanded a new trial on the charge of neglect causing substantial bodily harm. The remand was based on the court's incorrectly instructing the jury to the 1995 Nevada elder abuse statute rather than the prevailing 1993 elder abuse statute. Whereas the 1993 statute required the defendant to take action to protect the elderly if she had "actual knowledge" that the older person was likely to suffer pain or mental suffering, the 1995 statute did not require actual knowledge of the danger to an older person in order to take protective measures, requiring only "that the individual knew or should have known" (p. 360, 69) that harm could have been done.

Care or Custody of Elder Victim Defined

In *Peterson v. State of Florida* (2000), the circuit court convicted the defendant of aggravated manslaughter of an elderly or disabled person. The district court of appeals upheld the conviction. The Florida court held that the defendant had a legal duty under common law and under the aggravated manslaughter of elderly or disabled person statute to care for his elderly mother himself, or to protect her from abuse and neglect by his brother. The defendant owned and shared the home with his mother and brother. The brother had agreed to be the primary caregiver for their mother. However, because the mother and son were co-owners of the property and the mother lived with her sons, the son had a legal obligation to ensure that proper and humane care was provided to her.

Hearsay Evidence of Abuse

The court in *People v. Tatum* (2003) held that the assault victim's out-of-court statement was admissible at trial, following the victim's death by natural causes, pursuant to the elder abuse and dependent adults hearsay exception (California Evidence Code, § 1380). In this Code, the State of California established that an elder victim's out-of-court statement was admissible if the victim was competent to be a witness and had personal knowledge of the events to which he or she testified. The videotape of the interview established that the victim was able to articulate facts so as to be understood and had the capacity both to perceive and to recollect; the victim had no apparent reason to fabricate and had several reasons not to do so; and the victim's statement was corroborated by forensic evidence.

In *Conner v. State of Florida* (1999), the Florida Supreme Court held that a hearsay exception under Florida Statutes Annotated (§ 90.803(24)), for statements by elderly persons or disabled adults describing abuse, violated the defendant's federal and state constitutional right to confront witnesses, guaranteed by the U.S. Code Annotated Constitutional Amendment VI and the Florida Constitutional Article I, § 16(a), and was not "supported by the competing policy interests present in the child abuse context" (p. 960).

EVALUATING THE PSYCHOLOGICAL SEQUELAE OF ELDER ABUSE

In conducting a forensic evaluation of physical, sexual, and/or emotional/psychological abuse with an elderly litigant, the forensic mental health expert confronts some interesting complexities that markedly distinguish this evaluation from the assessments of other populations of litigants (Rom-Rymer, 2001).

Consent

Because of cognitive compromise, many elders are not legally competent to consent to the forensic evaluation, which includes, but is not limited to, interview, testing, full review of records, and interviews with collateral individuals as needed. When incompetence has been adjudicated, the expert secures the consent of the guardian who has received power of attorney for the elder. Adjunctively, or as an alternative, the forensic psychologist elicits a judicial order for the assessment. If the elder is competent to provide informed consent, it is incumbent upon the forensic expert to inform him or her that if the expert finds that the evaluee continues to be at risk or is a risk to others, then family members, other professionals, and state agencies may have to be notified without his or her consent (American Psychological Association, 1998).

Lengthy Medical Records

Prior to an allegation of abuse and because of the inherent status of being "vulnerable," the elderly litigant will typically have had a long medical history. This history should be thoroughly reviewed and will include, but is not be limited to, a history of surgeries, accidental traumas (falls, automobile accidents, athletic injuries), intentional traumas (criminal attacks), emergency room visits, history of disease and recoveries, current acute and chronic illnesses, history of prescribed medications, current prescribed medications, history of mental health treatment, history of smoking, alcohol use and abuse, and illicit drug use and abuse.

Nursing Home Records and/or Medical Records of an In-Home Caregiver

Well-maintained nursing home records and medical records of an in-home caregiver are valuable for evaluating affect, cognitive status, disease process, and behavior— before, during, and after the alleged episode(s). Specifically, the forensic expert should review the verbal and nonverbal expression of healthy and pathological symptomatology. These symptoms include, but are not be limited to, anxiety, depression, tremors, anger outbursts, agitation, crying, problematic sleep patterns, evidence of sleep disturbance, nightmares or night terrors, cognitive awareness and decline, disease processes (stability, deterioration, improvement), levels of physical and psychological engagement in routine social, familial, "therapeutic," and recreational activities, eating behavior, food intake, liquid intake, continence, incontinence, bathing behavior, self-care, and verbal and nonverbal reactions to medical professionals, caregivers, roommates, and other people with whom the elder comes into contact on a regular basis. Unfortunately, nursing home records are often not properly maintained. However, such records are important in the litigation process, and the forensic expert should thoroughly review them to retrieve as much data as possible about the individual's functioning.

Legal Documents

A thorough review of police reports, victim, caregiver, and family statements, depositions, grand jury indictments, criminal proceedings transcripts, and emergency room records gives firsthand information from victims, witnesses, and official sources that serve to clarify and, at times, correct later versions of the event narrative.

Environmental Assessment

Experiencing firsthand the venue in which the alleged abuse occurred contextualizes the data. Questions can be asked and answered about the visibility of the elder's room from the nursing station in a nursing home, the tidiness of a home, the number of elders sitting in wheelchairs in the halls of a nursing home, the manner in which an elder is given assistance with meals or with ambulation, presence of the odor of urine or excrement in an elder's living environment, the level and tenor of sounds (i.e., continual screams for help or pleasant music), the nature of the inter-actions between the caregivers and the elders, photographs on the walls, and the amount of sunlight entering through the windows.

Other environmental factors should also be noted: staff-patient/resident ratios, total number of residents in the nursing home, staff absentee levels, staff turnover rates (particularly CNA turnover), ratio of male staff to female staff, the home's formal and informal rules about male staff members caring for residents without a female staff member present, ratio of agency or contractual staff to regular staff, screening interviews and background checks during the hiring process, and the his-tory of regulatory violations by staff and nursing facility and the sanctions received.

The Forensic Interview

It is not unusual for elderly litigants to be severely neuropsychologically compro-mised or for litigants to have predeceased the evaluation. When the elder is severely neuropsychologically compromised and cannot be fully or even partially responsive to testing, the forensic interview becomes a formal, behavioral assessment of func-tional capacity. Observations are made of verbal ability, sensory capacity, and physical mobility.

When the elder litigant has predeceased the evaluation, recent videos of the elder, taken by family and/or by state investigators, may exist. Reviewing those videos becomes a part of the evaluation, providing the forensic expert with an op-portunity to observe the elder. Although viewing the video may limit the breadth of the expert's opinions, it can provide a data point that should be included.

The Social History

If the forensic expert has the opportunity to conduct an in-person interview with the elderly litigant, the person whom the expert sees in front of him or her may not resemble, physically, cognitively, or emotionally, the person he or she was prior to becoming a frail elder. Yet, to fully comprehend the response to the trauma or, con-versely, to be able to ascertain if an abusive episode in fact occurred, the forensic expert must understand the social belief system, psychological status, emotional re-sponse style, and behavioral patterns of the elder.

Assessing Neuropsychological and Psychological Status

Because neuropsychological compromise can affect the experience and the expression of trauma or the allegation of a trauma, neuropsychological testing must have a firm place, alongside the psychological testing, in the forensic evaluation. (See Chapter 6 for a description of neuropsychological assessment and methodology in forensic cases.) When the elder can meaningfully engage in testing, various assessment instru-ments can be used. The test norms must be age and education appropriate, and sensory and physical impairments and a slowed response style must be taken into account.

The assessment instruments that are used, from the more specific levels of dis-criminative analysis for higher cognitive functioning elders to grosser levels of analysis for lower cognitive functioning elders, include, but are not limited to, the tests listed in Table 24.8.

Table 24.8   Assessment Instruments for Elders

Wechsler Adult Intelligence Scale-IV
Wechsler Memory Scale-III
Minnesota Multiphasic Personality Inventory-2
Millon Clinical Multiaxial Inventory-III
Rorschach Psychodiagnostic Test
Wahler Physical Symptoms Inventory
Posttraumatic Stress Disorder Scale
Beck Depression Inventory
Spielberger State-Trait Anxiety Inventory
Rey Complex Figure Test
Wide Range Achievement Test-III
American New Adult Reading Test
Hopkins Verbal Learning Test
California Verbal Learning Test
Brief Visual Memory Test
Repeatable Battery for the Assessment of Neuropsychological Status
Stroop Color-Word Test
Trail Making Test
Boston Naming Test
Wisconsin Card Sorting Test
Victoria Symptom Validity Test
Anosognosia Questionnaire-Dementia, Patient Form
Draw-a-Clock Test
Dementia Rating Scale
Geriatric Depression Scale

Assessing Pain and Suffering in an Elder Who Is Diagnosed with Late-Stage Dementia

It is not unusual for forensic questions to be raised about the perception of pain in the elder who may be unable to verbally communicate the pain. Locatell (2001) and Harkins (2001) assert that pain accelerates morbidity and mortality. As further clarification, Harkins reports that although an elder may not have the experience of chronic pain because of severe memory impairment, he or she may have an ongoing experience of acute pain, which could be excruciating. The wise forensic expert follows Harkins's recommendations to look for nonverbal expressions of pain when an elder can no longer communicate verbally. He recommends monitoring and documenting facial grimaces, body language, and sounds, even if unintelligible (S. W. Harkins, personal communication, April 26, 2001).

Other Components of the Forensic Evaluation

Several other components are often overlooked but can yield compelling data points. We will discuss them next.

Diaries and Calendars

Contemporaneous family/caregiver diaries, journals, and calendars may reveal details that otherwise remain undocumented by the treating professionals and paraprofessionals and that may be forgotten or mischaracterized months later.

Job Records

If available, employment records may be relevant in providing a historical context for claims of current psychological and behavioral problems.

Financial Records

If available and relevant, such records may provide a context for understanding premorbid functioning and current claims of disability.

Interviews

Interviews, observation sessions, and family visits with the elder that have been video- or audiotaped often provide valuable data on victim functioning and familial relationships. Much of the time, these taped sessions are unrehearsed and even spontaneous, thus enhancing case histories, derived initially from the written record.

Interviews with family members, all health professionals, caregivers, friends, and neighbors, as relevant, should be conducted. Third-party interviews add a significant perspective to the victim self-report. (See Chapter 8 for a discussion of the importance of third-party interviews in forensic evaluations.)

ESTABLISHING A CAUSAL LINK BETWEEN IMPAIRMENTS AND THE ALLEGED ABUSE EPISODE

The greatest challenge in establishing the causal link between impairments and the alleged episode of abuse in the elderly is distinguishing among the following elements: the pre- and postmorbid disease processes, a specific response to a medication, the normative aging process, and the specific response(s) to the alleged abuse episode. An acute depressive reaction to an episode of trauma may be masked by a preexisting dementia, a chronic depressive disorder, a history of Posttraumatic Stress Disorder, a lethargic response to a recently prescribed anxiolytic, a recently diagnosed hypothalamic disorder, and/or a normative response to an increased activity level. The key to establishing the causal link is to understand the baseline functioning of the elder, to rule out pathological responses to prescribed medications and normative responses to the environment, to verify the specific elements of the alleged traumatic episode(s), to learn of the caregivers' response to the outcry, and to carefully assess the elder's initial and latent responses to the alleged trauma.

Expert Testimony, Standards of Practice, and Ethical Issues

For the causal link to be established, the forensic psychological evaluation of an elder's emotional disturbance, proximal to the traumatic event(s), necessarily includes the multiple sources of data described previously (also see Chapter 8). It is understood that each case is evaluated on an individual basis, that all of the data may not be available, and that the appropriate informed consent has been received from all parties interviewed. Embedded in the consent for a forensic evaluation are the explicit statements that the psychologist is performing the function of a forensic examiner, not that of a clinician, and that there is no doctor-patient privilege.

Neuropsychological and psychological tests must meet the *Daubert* (*Daubert v. Merrell Dow Pharmaceuticals,* 1993) or *Frye* (*Frye v. United States Court of Appeals of the District of Columbia,* 1923) standards. The tests must be valid and reliable. They should have been subjected to peer review and publication, and, under *Daubert,* they must have an acceptable known or potential error rate. When data are limited, the forensic psychologist discusses these limitations and the resultant limitations of the opinions. Testimony can speak to the issue of a litigant's "dramatic," "frail," "intact," or "impaired" responses and behavior. Testimony can speak to the litigant's history and lifelong patterns. Professional judgment, jurisdictional statutes and case law, and circumstance will determine if the ultimate issue is directly addressed. Testimony should not address whether the litigant is telling the truth or not. Reasonable alternative hypotheses are articulated, with explanations for exclusion. Conclusions emerge from the weight of the data, and the testimony is provided concisely and clearly, with a humble erudition.

-------------------------------- **Illustrative Case** --------------------------------

Mary Shaw, a 70-year-old African American woman living in Baltimore, was referred for forensic examination by her attorneys pursuant to a lawsuit claiming that she had been subjected to medical malpractice by a hospital internist, Dr. Jones, and a nursing home medical director, Dr. Wright, who, in addition to his administrative duties, had also been Ms. Shaw's attending physician at the nursing home. In addition, the lawsuit claimed that the nursing home staff had been negligent in their care of Ms. Shaw and, further, that Ms. Shaw had been sexually abused while at the nursing home. (All identifying information has been altered.)

More specifically, the medical malpractice complaint stated that the hospital internist had miswritten a prescription for phenobarbital. From subsequent statements, Dr. Jones had admitted that although she had intended to write a prescription for 30 mg of phenobarbital bid (twice a day), she had mistakenly written a prescription for 100 mg bid. Compounding the error, when Dr. Wright performed a cursory physical exam upon Ms. Shaw's admission and reviewed her medications, he rewrote the prescription for phenobarbital at 100 mg bid.

The referral questions are:

- What are the psychological sequelae, if any, of the phenobarbital overdose?
- What are the psychological sequelae, if any, of the alleged sexual abuse by a staff member at the Grazing Pastures Nursing and Rehabilitation Center?

Behavioral Observations

On the occasions of the several meetings at her home between this writer and the evaluee, Mary Shaw appeared older than her 70 years but was neatly and appropriately dressed. She made an excellent effort to respond to interview and test questions. Although initially uncertain of the process and uncomfortable with its ambiguities, Ms. Shaw became increasingly relaxed and displayed a wide range of affect (including expressions of attachment) and a sense of humor. When asked to talk about some of the painful events in her history and the alleged sexual abuse at Grazing Pastures, Ms. Shaw initially became anxious and irritable, saying, "I hate all this. . . . I'm frightened of what happened to me; it keeps coming back in my head." However, she continued to actively participate in the process.

Ms. Shaw would become fatigued during the interview and testing sessions and would ask to be excused to take a nap after an hour to an hour and a half of the questioning. Therefore, the evaluation was conducted in discrete hour-and-a-half segments. At lunchtime, this writer observed Ms. Shaw's niece, Ms. Corbin, with whom Ms. Shaw lived, bringing a meal to her. Although often not very hungry, Ms. Shaw was observed to eat her food and drink her beverages without difficulty. Ms. Shaw asked for and received assistance from Ms. Corbin in transferring from her wheelchair into her bed.

Psychosocial History

Mary Shaw was the middle child in a family of eight children. Along with the rest of the children, she was born in the Deep South, near Jackson, Mississippi. Soon after the birth of the youngest child, Ms. Shaw's mother died at the age of 42. Ms. Shaw was 10 years old at the time. After Mrs. Shaw's death, several relatives moved north and the Shaw family followed. The six surviving children and their children and grandchildren currently live in and around the Baltimore area.

Family Medical and Social History

Ms. Shaw has a very large family of siblings, nieces, nephews, great-nieces, and great-nephews. Along with the joys of a large family come the typical diseases of aging: cancer, stroke, emphysema, glaucoma, Parkinson's disease, heart disease, and pulmonary disease.

As a young woman, Mary Shaw fell in love with a young man but lost him when he was killed in the war. At the age of 35, Ms. Shaw married, but her husband left her after a few months to "pursue a lifetime dream" of working on the oil pipeline in the Alaska wilderness. Their marriage was annulled.

Ms. Shaw reports that, in school, she was a "slow learner," and she ruefully acknowledges that she has also been a slow learner in life. But she reports that she now has her "brains back" and tries to make better decisions about how she can take care of herself.

Ms. Shaw graduated from Baltimore High School at the age of 19 years. She explains that she was older than the usual graduate because she had worked part time at the munitions factory during the war and the postwar period to help the family pay its bills. After graduation, she held several jobs in "cleaning shops" and as a saleswoman in retail shops. She also was employed with the navy as a nurse's aide and in the navy shipyards. Ms. Shaw lived and worked in Virginia for several years. For some of those years, she lived as a tenant in the home of the owner of an apartment complex. She did the gentleman's housekeeping, cooking, cleaning, and yard work and helped to manage the apartment complex. In 1980, she returned to Baltimore to attend classes for certification as a licensed practical nurse. She reports that she graduated from that program in 1981.

Medical History

Ms. Shaw has a complex medical history. She has a history of heavy smoking and moderate caffeine intake, both patterns with probable onset in late adolescence and continuing to the present. She also has a history of chronic alcoholism, beginning in her early 20s and documented in medical records through 1989. Ms. Corbin reports that her husband tried for many years to persuade Ms. Shaw to attend AA meetings, but that her aunt resisted those efforts. Ms. Shaw's history of chronic obstructive pulmonary disease and osteoarthritis date from at least February 1981, the date on which the current record review began.

In September 1981, Ms. Shaw was found in a stuporous condition, drifting in and out of coma, inside the home of a friend, for whom she was house-sitting. She had apparently fallen and had lain there, unattended, for 3 days. She was diagnosed with a large left subdural hemorrhage with a shift of the midline structures toward the right. A left frontoparietal craniotomy was performed with evacuation of the hematoma at Johns Hopkins Hospital. There was residual right hemiparesis and impaired mentation. Ms. Shaw was referred for inpatient physical, occupational, and speech rehabilitation therapy at the University of Maryland Hospital, where some improvement was noted. However, her performance in physical and occupational therapy deteriorated, and she was becoming more lethargic. A CT scan showed a probable reaccumulation of blood in the left hemisphere, and a second left craniotomy was performed. A 1 cm hematoma was found and evacuated. Progress following this second brain surgery was reported as "almost miraculous." There was rapid improvement noted in her physical, occupational, and speech therapy, with the achievement of full independence. Mentation was seen as appropriate and spontaneous. Discharge to her niece's home occurred 2 months later.

About a year later, Ms. Shaw was diagnosed with mild scoliosis, for which she wears a brace support. She was also diagnosed with arthritis and emphysema.

Ms. Shaw asked her doctor for "a slip" not to take Antabuse. She apparently had a severe alcoholic episode in December 1982 and was advised to take Antabuse. The doctor refused to give her the note and wrote that he discussed her alcoholism with her and advised her not to drink.

In July 1983, Ms. Shaw was given a neurological evaluation. An EEG, conducted in October 1982, had shown left frontotemporal seizure discharges indicative of a lowered seizure threshold. The examining physician found left optic nerve damage; higher cortical deficits, primarily affecting memory; and frequent dizzy spells with blackouts.

Notes indicate that Ms. Shaw had been in the emergency room with alcoholic DTs and seizures in August 1983 and was given a CAT scan, which was negative, and Dilantin IV. Valium and Dalmane were prescribed. It was noted that she was denying anxiety at this time and stating that she was much better.

In April 1986, Ms. Shaw was brought to the emergency room of the University of Maryland Hospital by ambulance after having experienced a tonic clonic episode of the right side of her body associated with unconsciousness, followed by confusion. There was associated incontinence of urine and stool. The seizure was witnessed by her nephew. Ms. Shaw was admitted to the hospital and discharged 4 days later with diagnoses of seizure disorder secondary to subdural hematoma sustained in 1981; chronic obstructive pulmonary disease by history; congenital heart murmur by history; and otitis media.

In July 1989, Ms. Shaw was referred for ataxia and posttraumatic neurologic deficits, including a seizure disorder. Her Dilantin level was found to be toxic, and she had a history of vulnerability to Dilantin toxicity. Ms. Corbin, who accompanied Ms. Shaw to the evaluation, stated to the physician that her aunt's weight had been decreasing to a recent low of 100 pounds. The notes state that Ms. Shaw has been suffering from hypertension and that the fall, which resulted in her subdural hematoma, had occurred while she was intoxicated; an abrasion, present on her left forehead, was the result of a recent fall. On neurological exam, she performed poorly. Her CT brain scan revealed "a very striking degree of generalized atrophy with minor residua of her left-sided brain injury," most likely the consequence of her Dilantin toxicity. "If her contention is correct that she takes the medication as prescribed, she may be metabolizing it unusually slowly." The physician also concluded that "multiple neurologic stigmata of alcoholism are present. These include her initial subdural hematoma, the diffuse cerebral atrophy apparent on scan and the memory impairment. Weight loss and some portion of her ataxia may also be consequences."

In April 1994, Ms. Shaw saw her doctor after a fall. He diagnosed tenderness about the right lateral ribs with no evidence of complications. In May 1994, he diagnosed a small torres fracture from an X-ray report, after Ms. Shaw fell on her left wrist. In December 1994, Ms. Shaw fell at home. She presented with a lump on her head and complaining of a "lightheadedness." The physician noted that he must continue to monitor Dilantin levels for toxicity.

In March 1995, Ms. Shaw underwent an extended right colectomy because a "fairly large" lesion had been found on her colon. The pathology on the lesion was that it was a colonic cancer that had invaded the bowel wall. She initially experienced problems eating postsurgery, as she experienced nausea whenever she tried to eat. She was discharged 2 weeks later to home, with outpatient follow-up within 2 days.

In July 1996, Ms. Shaw was given an extracranial carotid artery duplex examination by a neurologist. He found a moderate degree of plaquing in the proximal segments of the internal carotid arteries, but without definite flow-limiting disease.

In September 1997, her doctor noted that Ms. Shaw's seizure disorder was currently stable and that she was not experiencing either seizures or side effects of the Dilantin. He stated that Ms. Shaw's blood pressure was under questionable control and that he would check her BP more frequently.

In January 1998, Ms. Shaw fell from her bed, the third time in 3 weeks. Her family called for an ambulance and told the paramedics that Ms. Shaw was dehydrated and that they wanted her to be taken to Baltimore General Hospital. She was admitted under the care of Dr. Roberta Jones.

Baltimore General Hospital (First Admission)

On January 28, 1998, Dr. Lee is requested by Dr. Jones to give a consult on Ms. Shaw. Dr. Lee notes that she has urgency incontinence that has been present for the past 6 months and has lost 10 pounds in the past 30 days. He notes that she is alert, her blood pressure is high at 210/110, she is traumatic for ecchymoses around the left orbital rim, and has some left wall chest pain. Dr. Lee reports that her mentation and speech are normal, her strength is fair in the arms, and she has proximal weakness in the legs. Heel-to-shin suggest some dysmetria. Gait cannot be tested because Ms. Shaw is feeling too weak. Dr. Lee is unable to explain Ms. Shaw's weight loss and proximal weakness. Dr. Lee prescribes 30 mg phenobarbital bid, in addition to the Dilantin dosage of 100 mg bid. There is a recommendation from Dr. Jones for Ms. Shaw to be discharged to a skilled nursing facility for physical therapy. As part of her discharge orders, Dr. Jones prescribes 100 mg phenobarbital bid, making an error in this dosage. Ms. Shaw is discharged to Grazing Pastures Nursing and Rehabilitation Center on January 31, 1998.

Grazing Pastures Nursing and Rehabilitation Center

Ms. Shaw is admitted to Grazing Pastures on January 31, 1998, and is emergently discharged on February 19, 1998, at the insistence of Mr. and Mrs. Corbin. The express purpose of this purported temporary stay is for Ms. Shaw to adjust to her changed medication regimen; to receive gait, strength, and continence training; to receive dietary and nutritional attention; and to recuperate from her multiple episodes of loss of consciousness and falls. Instead, Ms. Shaw's health precipitously declines. Within the first several days, her facial muscles begin to droop. She develops dysphagia; her speech becomes barely intelligible; her thinking becomes confused; and she becomes completely incontinent. The staff calls Dr. Wright, the attending physician, but he tells the nurses, without examining her, to continue monitoring with no changes in treatment. During the 2nd week, Dr. Wright goes on vacation, and the doctor on call, without personally examining Ms. Shaw, diagnoses her as having had a stroke and orders the addition of a daily aspirin to her medication regimen. Ms. Corbin and several of her aunts, uncles, brothers, and sisters visit Ms. Shaw and insist that dramatic action needs to be taken to staunch the decline. The staff impatiently explain that Ms. Shaw is old and very sick and that there is little that can be done to improve her condition.

In the midst of this crisis, Ms. Shaw whispers to Ms. Corbin that one of the male nurse's aides has touched her sexually.

In the 3rd week, the family is demanding that the staff call an ambulance to take Ms. Shaw back to the hospital. When the staff refuses, her family calls the ambulance and Ms. Shaw returns to the hospital.

The allegations against Grazing Pastures Nursing and Rehabilitation Center include, but are not limited to, physician and staff error and negligence, specifically in the failure to recognize the symptoms of Ms. Shaw's phenobarbital toxicity and the failure to properly treat those symptoms by rectifying the medication dosage error; physician and staff negligence in failure to adequately address the issues of staff misconduct, including allegations of the sexual molestation of Ms. Shaw, Ms. Shaw's falls, equipment failure, failure to provide adequate assistance, failure to provide adequate access to food and drink, documentation falsification and discrepancies, and inadequate care plan documentation.

Baltimore General Hospital (Second Admission)

At the emergency room, Dr. Roberta Jones is on call and is the first doctor whom the family sees when Ms. Shaw arrives. Upon examination, Dr. Jones immediately recognizes signs of phenobarbital toxicity and tells the family that she had made the prescription-writing error. On February 20, 1998, Ms. Shaw is admitted with diagnoses of phenobarbital toxicity, dysphagia, receptive and expressive aphasia, bilateral nystagmus, ataxia, and urinary tract infection. On CT scan, there is indication of a cerebrovascular accident or stroke with moderately severe cerebral atrophy. She must endure surgery to have a PEG tube inserted for feeding. She is incontinent for both bowel and bladder. She has poor strength in all tests. It is noted in her medical record that Ms. Shaw "needs frequent reassurance and emotional support, that she calls frequently for someone to be in the room. She calls frequently for a bedpan then does not need it." On February 25, 1998, Ms. Shaw is noted to "complain of severe abdominal pain." In addition to the medications that she has been habituated to taking for her chronic disorders, she is prescribed Haldol for agitation, subsequent to her severe discomfort with the feeding tube; Demerol for pain, subsequent to her severe discomfort with the feeding tube; and Restoril for sedation. Each of these medications creates additional side effects with which Ms. Shaw must cope. She is discharged to Collins Rehabilitation Center for continued skilled nursing care on February 27, 1998.

Brooke Senior Center

Ms. Shaw experiences several medical emergencies during her stay at Collins Rehabilitation Center, but on July 17, 1998, she is discharged from Collins as physically independent enough to return to live at Ms. Corbin's home with daily outpatient treatment, physical therapy, and elder activities at the Brooke Senior Center. Although the records reveal that Ms. Shaw has had moderate to severe symptoms of depression, a formal diagnosis of depression was withdrawn from the care plan on July 14, 1999. This writer noticed, however, when she observed Ms. Shaw at the Senior Center, and the staff concurred, that depression as of March 13, 2000, continues to be a condition with which Ms. Shaw struggles. Other particular issues include her memories of her poor treatment at Grazing Pastures and her anger at not being able to do the things that she wants to do. She has consistently refused to speak with a treating psychologist and, as of April 2000, refuses antidepressant medication.

Ms. Shaw continues to make progress at the Senior Center with all of her activities of daily living. Prior to a recent acute hospitalization and nursing home stay, she had been elected resident council president in November 1999, a position for which she had campaigned. During Thanksgiving, she had become rather weak, fatigued, and withdrawn. During her recent stay at a nursing home, she had been isolative. Since she has been living at home, again her progress has accelerated, although at a slower pace than before this most recent hospitalization. She could not walk at all when she was initially admitted to Brooke Senior Center, but she can now walk with a gait belt around her waist. She is also practicing her squats on the parallel bars. Progress is reported in toileting, eating, and socialization activities, as well. Ms. Shaw becomes fearful when she is alone. She appears to feel comfortable in the familiar and supportive environment of the Senior Center.

Forensic Interviews with Ms. Shaw and Ms. Corbin

Ms. Shaw was able to converse with this writer, although fatigue shortened the duration of each period and increased the number of sessions. When asked about the episode of sexual abuse, Ms. Shaw was not able to provide specific details. She simply repeated that she had been sexually touched and that she had been scared and that she is still bothered by frightening thoughts and nightmares about being helpless and unable to tell anybody.

Ms. Corbin noted that Ms. Shaw had leaned over to her during one of the daily nursing home visits and had whispered in her ear that a male nurse's aide had sexually touched her. In fact, Ms. Shaw had shown her niece that there was a red pressure mark on her upper thigh. When Ms. Corbin told the staff, they said that no male staff had been alone with Ms. Shaw and that no other staff member had witnessed any sexual misconduct.

Ms. Shaw did recount a narrative of how she had fallen in September 1981. She told this writer that she had been walking home, carrying groceries, and some young boys had followed her. As she walked in the door, the boys knocked her down, took her groceries, and ran out. When asked if she had told her family and her doctors what had happened, she replied that she had told her doctors in the facility and had told her family when she returned home from the rehabilitative facility in November 1981.

When this writer asked Ms. Corbin about the narrative, Ms. Corbin reported that she indeed knew about the assault allegation, but no evidence had ever been found of an actual assault. When Ms. Shaw was found unconscious in her friend's home, the doors had been locked; there did not appear to have been any forced entry; and the emergency medical technicians with the ambulance service had not noticed any evidence of an assault. Moreover, the groceries had been lying on the floor, the milk spoiled and the ice cream melting.

Forensic Testing

Neuropsychological tests and psychological tests were administered to assess Ms. Shaw's level of cognitive impairment and her psychosocial functioning.

Testing consisted of the following instruments:

Dementia Rating Scale.

Repeatable Battery for the Assessment of Neuropsychological Status, Form A.

American New Adult Reading Test.

Wide Range Achievement Test 3.

Hopkins Verbal Learning Test.

Brief Visual Memory Test.

Boston Naming Test.

Verbal Fluency Test.

Stroop Color Word Test.

Trailmaking Test, Parts A and B.

Wisconsin Card Sorting Test.

Rorschach Psychodiagnostic Test.

Geriatric Depression Scale.

Beck Depression Inventory.

State-Trait Anxiety Inventory.

Anosognosia Questionnaire-Dementia, Patient Form.

Testing Results and Summary

The current testing indicates that Ms. Mary Shaw is functioning in the mildly impaired intellectual range, when compared to her premorbid intellectual capability in the low-average range. She demonstrated an impaired ability to encode information, but, once learned, she was able to retain that (small amount of) information at the low-average range of performance. Cued recall scores were substantially higher than free recall scores, falling into the normative range. Attentional scores were in the mildly to moderately impaired range. Executive skills were in the moderately to severely impaired range. Because there appeared to be a cognitive awareness of the rules of one of the tests (Wisconsin Card Sort Test) but an inability to perform according to those rules, a dissociation of knowledge from action was demonstrated.

Results of the current evaluation are significant for problems initiating mental activity, learning new information, attending to tasks, and problem solving. Retrieval-based problems are evident in naming capacity but less conspicuous in the delayed memory performance. A baseline low level of functioning, a history of serious medical illness, and a significantly depressed mood with mild to moderate levels of anxiety can contribute to a picture that appears more seriously deteriorated than the actual current data show. This pattern of learning problems is generally indicative of a mild dementia of likely vascular etiology.

Psychiatric Diagnosis

Axis I: 296.3   Major Depressive Disorder, Recurrent, with Melancholic Features
           309.81 History of Posttraumatic Stress Disorder
           309.28 Adjustment Disorder with Mixed Anxiety and Depressed Mood
           305.10 Nicotine Dependence
           303.90 History of Alcohol Dependence
           304.10 History of Sedative, Hypnotic, or Anxiolytic Abuse
           294.1   Dementia Due to Head Trauma
           291.2   Alcohol-Induced Persisting Dementia
           290.43 Vascular Dementia with Depressed Mood

Axis II: Deferred
Axis III: List of Diagnoses Noted Extensively under Medical History
Axis IV: Severe, Life-Threatening Health Problems
Axis V: GAF = 55 (as of April 2000)

Formulation

The diagnosis of Major Depressive Episode, recurrent, with melancholic features, is attributable to a lifelong, persistent history of depression. She was a very young child, just 10, when her mother died. She was reported to be the most fragile child in the family and the one that appeared to have been the most vulnerable to the chaotic changes that her mother's death brought upon the family. Her depression, with periods of isolation from family members and friends, seemed to worsen once she, her father, and her brothers and sisters moved to Baltimore; the urban lifestyle was a radical change from the rural life she had known in the South. Not feeling particularly successful in school, she had hoped that finding a husband and getting a job would relieve her anxieties about "not fitting in." But when Ms. Shaw was still in high school, the young man whom she loved was killed in the war, and the friends she found in the workplace persuaded her to become one of them by smoking and drinking alcohol. Her only marriage, later in life, was brief and disappointing. Medical records are replete with doctors' warnings about the dangers of her continuing to drink and smoke. Ms. Shaw's niece, Ms. Corbin, shared her home and tried hard to make her feel comfortable and loved. Coping with the aftermath of her devastating, life-threatening brain injury made it more difficult for Ms. Shaw to conquer her addictions.

At the age of 70, Ms. Shaw's health was rapidly deteriorating. Although she was known in the family as a kind and loving person and had tried to retain her humor through her most difficult times, this already frail woman knew that she was failing and needed to find an effective strategy for alleviating some of her health crises. During an acute stay at Baltimore General Hospital, she and her family were told that she would have to enter a skilled nursing home for short-term physical rehabilitation. As much as she did not want to be alone, confined in an unfamiliar environment, she agreed to the plan, hoping that she might gain another chance at independence. However, her optimistic plans went seriously awry. Within the 1st week of her admission to the nursing home, Ms. Shaw had lost even more control of her bodily functions. She could hardly speak; she was not being taken to the bathroom in time for her to avoid wetting and soiling her clothes and her bed; she was drooling; she was becoming physically weaker and weaker; her calls to the staff for help were not heeded; and she lost the ability to swallow. Ms. Shaw was terrified. The more she tried to eat and drink, the more humiliated she became at seeing her food splattered all over her nightgown. The more she tried to ask her family members what was happening to her, the more difficult it became for her to communicate.

Once discharged from the Grazing Pastures Nursing and Rehabilitation Center, Ms. Shaw realized that she would have to climb an even steeper road to recovery. Eating and drinking by mouth were still not possible; tube feeding continued to be her only option. She began to have nightmares about her experiences at Grazing

Pastures and began to feel as if she was never going to get better. At the same time she was trying to recover from the stress of her phenobarbital toxicity, her other chronic conditions continued to worsen. Therefore, the diagnosis of Posttraumatic Stress Disorder fits Ms. Shaw's response to her experiences at Grazing Pastures, 1 month after the time that she left the nursing home, through the period of time (January 1999) at Brooke Senior Center, when she began to feel physically stronger, emotionally safe, comfortable, and motivated to work through her many physical limitations. Currently, Ms. Shaw continues to have health setbacks, and with these setbacks come the fears and the loneliness of her all too familiar Major Depressive Episodes and the memories of her traumatic experience at Grazing Pastures. Her current diagnosis is that of Adjustment Disorder with Mixed Anxiety and Depressed Mood.

It is clear from the cognitive testing that Ms. Shaw has some deficits. She appears to have a mild cognitive dementia that makes it difficult for her to learn new tasks and remember events. Her recounting of the assault from 1981 appears to have been a tale that she created to deny her own level of alcoholism. It appears to be an account that was made long after the episode of the September 1981 fall and after her two brain surgeries. Her allegation of having been sexually abused in Grazing Pastures has not been substantiated and bears a resemblance to the fantasized assault episode of 20 years ago and appears to represent an attempt to explain an overwhelming problem. In this current instance, there was no clear physical evidence and there were no witnesses to this event. Moreover, Ms. Shaw's mentation was severely clouded by the toxicity that was overwhelming her system. This writer believes that there is a low probability that sexual abuse occurred and that there are any psychological sequelae from the alleged event.

Ms. Shaw's life has never been easy. But for her experiences at the Grazing Pastures Nursing and Rehabilitation Center, she could have taken some small steps forward in her efforts to regain some vital time in her life.

Ultimately, the lawsuit was resolved in favor of plaintiff with findings of negligence against the nursing home and findings of medical malpractice against the emergency room physician and the attending nursing home physician. Because the emergency room physician admitted her mistake as soon as she was re-presented with her patient upon the patient's transfer from the nursing home to the hospital, the financial damages that she was ordered to pay were significantly smaller than the financial damages that the attending nursing home physician was required to pay. The sexual abuse complaint was not founded and was excluded from the final lawsuit resolution.

CONCLUSION

William Shakespeare well understood the miseries of old age. Although we might like to rejoice at the prospect of a longer life, unfortunately we, like Shakespeare, are too much aware of the loneliness, despair, and violations in our own homes and by our own trusted caregivers that old age can bring. Social and legislative activists have been working for nearly 2 decades to give our elders recourse in the courts for criminal and civil actions against allegations of abuse. Although several states, including California, Nevada, Arizona, and Florida, are working hard, with both civil and criminal statutes, to put some teeth into their elder abuse laws, the reality is that legal and administrative changes are not occurring as quickly as the growing vulnerability of our aging baby boomers.

When abuse and neglect are alleged, forensic experts are called on to assess the probabilities of the abuse and to assess the psychological damages. The facets of a forensic evaluation are many. They include extensive record review, neuropsychological and psychological testing, and interviews with family, friends, and health professionals. Depression often mimics dementia. Bad dreams sound like psychotic hallucinations, and delusions may be caused by drug toxicity. Only with a comprehensive understanding of the history and the physical, cognitive, and emotional status of the alleged victim can the forensic expert determine the psychological sequelae of the proximal event.

REFERENCES

Alcott Rehabilitation Hospital v. Superior Court, 93 California Appellate Court 4th 94, 112 California Reporter. 2d 807 (2d Dist. 2001).

American Health Care Association. (1999). *Facts and trends: Nursing facility sourcebook.* Washington, DC: Author.

American Psychological Association Presidential Task Force on the Assessment of Age-Consistent Memory Decline and Dementia. (1998). Guidelines for the evaluation of dementia and age-related cognitive decline. *American Psychologist, 53*(12), 1298–1303.

Arizona Revised Statutes Annotated § 14-3110 (2005).

Arizona Revised Statutes Annotated § 46-455(F)(4) (2005).

Arkansas Acts 1811 (2005).

Buchwalter, J. L. (2003). Annotation: Validity, construction, and application of state civil and criminal elder abuse laws. *American Law Reports, 113,* 431–477.

California Code of Civil Procedure § 36(a).

California Code of Civil Procedure § 352.

California Code of Civil Procedure § 425.13.

California Evidence Code § 1380.

California Welfare and Institutions Code, the Elder Abuse and Dependent Adult Civil Protection Act §§ 15600 *et seq.* (2003).

California Welfare and Institutions Code § 15657.3(d).

Chairman of Subcommittee on Health and Long-Term Care, House Select Committee on Aging. (1991). *Protecting Americans' abused elderly: The need for congressional action* (102nd Congress, 1st Session). Washington, DC: U.S. Government Printing Office.

Colorado Revised Statutes § 26-3.1-101, *et seq.* (2005).

Community Care and Rehabilitation Center v. Superior Court, 79 Cal. App. 4th 787, 94 Cal. Rptr. 2d 343 (4th Dist. 2000).

Conner v. State of Florida, 748 So. 2d 950 (Florida 1999).

Covenant Care, Inc. v. Superior Court, 32 Cal.4th 771 86 P.3d 290 11 Cal. Rptr. 3d 222 (California 2004).

Daly, E. (2002, April 9). U.S. says elderly will soon outnumber young for first time. *New York Times,* A6.

Daubert v. Merrell Dow Pharmaceuticals, 509 U.S. 579 (1993).

Elden v. Sheldon, 46 Cal. 3d 275, 250 Cal. Rptr. 254, 758 P.2d 582 (1988).

Federal Interagency Forum on Aging-Related Statistics. (2004, November). *Older Americans 2004: Key indicators of well-being: Federal Interagency Forum on Aging-Related Statistics*. Washington, DC. Available on the Federal Interagency Forum website: http://www.agingstats.gov.

Florida Constitutional Article I § 16(a).

Florida Statutes Annotated § 90.803(24) (2004).

Florida Statutes Annotated § 415.101, *et seq.* (2004).

Frye v. United States Court of Appeals of the District of Columbia, 293 F. 2d 1073 (D.C. Cir. 1923).

Grant v. Oh, W.L. 1194106 (California Appellate Court 2d Dist. 2003).

Greenberg, S. (2003). *A profile of older Americans: 2003*. Washington, DC: U.S. Department of Health and Human Services, Administration on Aging.

Harkins, S. W. (2001, August). *Pain plus failure to assess and treat equal suffering*. Paper presented at the symposium Understanding Trauma in the Elderly: Assessment and Treatment (Abstract), Beth N. Rom-Rymer, PhD (Chair), APA Annual Convention, San Francisco.

Hawes, C. (2002). *Elder abuse in residential long-term care facilities: What is known about prevalence, causes, and prevention*. Testimony of Catherine Hawes before the U.S. Senate Committee on Finance. Washington, DC: U.S. Government Printing Office.

Hawes, C. (2003, November 23). *Preventing abuse and neglect in nursing homes: The role of staffing and training*. Paper presentation at the meeting of the Gerontological Society of America, San Diego, CA.

Holder, E. (2005, April 29). *Long-term care living: The nation's challenge*. Opening keynote address, Mini White House Conference on Aging (pp. 1–10). Washington, DC: U.S. Government Printing Office.

Idaho Code § 18-1505, *et seq.* (2005).

Illinois Elder Abuse & Neglect Act, 320 ILCS 20/1 (2005).

Intrieri v. Superior Court, 117 Cal. App. 4th 72, 12 Cal. Rptr. 3d 97 (6th Dist. 2004).

Kansas Statutes Annotated § 39-1431, *et seq.* (2004).

Kansas Statutes Annotated § 50-679, *et seq.* (2004).

Kennedy v. Closson, W.L. 1338476 (Cal. App. 2d Dist. 2001).

Kraig v. Superior Court, 2002 W.L. 1303405 (Cal. App. 2d Dist. 2004).

Levine, S. (1996, May 21). Aging baby boomers pose challenge: Preparations needed for coming strain on services, census report says. *Washington Post*, A9.

Locatell, K. (2001, August). *When pain is caused by elder abuse: A treatment protocol*. Paper presented at the symposium Understanding Trauma in the Elderly: Assessment and Treatment, Beth N. Rom-Rymer (Chair), PhD, APA Annual Convention, San Francisco.

Louisiana Revised Statutes Title 46 § 61, *et seq.* (2004).

Maryland Code Annotated [Abuse or Neglect of Vulnerable Adult] § 3-604, *et. seq.* (2005).

Maryland Code Annotated § 14-101, *et seq.* (2005).

Matter of Guardianship/Conservatorship of Denton, 190 Ariz. 152, 945, P.2d 1283 (1997).

Michigan Compiled Laws § 400.11b, *et seq.* (2005).

Michigan Compiled Laws § 750.145m, *et seq.* (2005).

Mississippi Code Annotated § 43-47-1, *et seq.* (2005).

Moon v. Guardian Postacute Services, Inc., 95 Cal. App. 4th 1005, 116 Cal. Rptr. 2d 218, 98 A.L.R. 5th 767 (1st Dist. 2002).

Moskowitz, S. (2003, Winter). Honor thy mother and father: Symposium on the legal aspects of elder abuse. In Golden age in the golden state: Contemporary legal developments in elder abuse and neglect. *Loyola of Los Angeles Law Review, 35,* 589–666.

National Center on Elder Abuse at the American Public Human Services Association in Collaboration with Westat, Inc. (1998). *The National Elder Abuse Incidence Study* (Prepared for the Administration for Children and Families and the Administration on Aging). Washington, DC: U.S. Department of Health and Human Services.

National Ombudsmen Reporting System. (2002). *Preliminary FY 2001 data*. Washington, DC: Administration on Aging, U.S. Department of Health and Human Services.

New York Laws § 260.32, *et seq.* (2005).

New York Laws § 473, *et seq.* (2005).

North Carolina General Statutes § 14-32.3, *et seq.* (2005).

North Carolina General Statutes § 108A-99, *et seq.* (2005).

North Dakota Century Code § 60-25.2-03, *et seq.* (2003).

Office of Inspector General. (2003). *State ombudsman data: Nursing home complaints.* Washington, DC: U.S. Department of Health and Human Services.

Pennsylvania Consolidated Statutes Annotated § 9717, *et seq.* (2004).

Pennsylvania Consolidated Statutes Annotated § 10225.101, *et seq.* (2004).

People v. Tatum, 133 Cal. Rptr. 2d 267 (App. 2d Dist. 2003).

Peterson v. State of Florida, 765 So. 2d 861 (Fla. Dist. Ct. App. 5th Dist. 2000).

Rhode Island General Laws § 42-66-1, *et seq.* (2004).

Rodriguez v. Care with Dignity Health Care Inc., W.L. 59621 (Cal. App. 4th Dist. 2002).

Rom-Rymer, B. N. (2001). Demonstrating trauma: Effects of sexual abuse on the elderly. In R. J. Krisztal (Ed.), *Nursing home litigation: Pretrial practice and trials* (pp. 37–53). Arizona: Lawyers & Judges Publishing Co.

Schwarz v. Regents of University of California, 226 Cal. App. 3d 149, 276 Cal. Rptr. 470 (1990).

Shakespeare, W. (1605). *King Lear* (S. Orgel, Ed.). New York: Penguin Putnam.

U.S. Code, Annotated, Constitutional Amendment VI.

U.S. Senate Special Committee on Aging. (1990). *Aging America: Trends and projections* (101st Congress, annotated). Washington, DC: U.S. Government Printing Office.

Vallery v. State of Nevada, 46 P.3d 66 (Nev. 2002).

Wilson v. Berkeley Long-Term Care, W.L. 625792 (Cal. App. 1st Dist. 2004).

Wisconsin Statutes Annotated § 46.90, *et seq.* (2005).

CHAPTER 25

Forensic Issues at the End of Life

Barry Rosenfeld and Colleen McClain Jacobson

The high-profile case of Terry Schiavo catapulted the issues of physician-assisted suicide and the right to refuse or terminate life-sustaining treatments back into American households. With the case of Terry Schiavo publicized around the clock on national television, dinner conversations, ethical debates, and clinical attention around advanced directives and end-of-life decision making increased dramatically. A decade earlier, Dr. Jack Kevorkian, a retired pathologist who acknowledged assisting in the deaths of more than 100 people, helped bring the issues of physician-assisted suicide and euthanasia into the mainstream of public discussion. But although the general public has focused on the practical and ethical, psychologists and other mental health professionals have increasingly identified a wide array of important psycholegal issues that arise at the end of life. This chapter reviews many of the most important and most common issues that arise at the end of life and outlines a process for conducting clinical evaluations in this context.

The case of Terry Schiavo was, in many ways, a common and relatively straightforward scenario. After losing consciousness, she was kept alive in a persistent vegetative state for 15 years with the use of a feeding tube (Quill, 2005). During that time she was unable to speak, move, or relate to others. Her husband maintained that it would have been his wife's wish to be allowed to die peacefully rather than be kept alive by a life-sustaining intervention. Yet, Schiavo's parents and siblings insisted that she was still, in some sense, aware of her surroundings and able to communicate with them, and therefore should be kept alive. During the decade that her parents and husband were at odds with one another, her feeding tube was removed and inserted several times as the courts tried to make a final determination about her right to die. Although many aspects of the Schiavo case were clear, such as her inability to articulate decisions on her own behalf, other aspects were far less so, such as who had the right to make decisions on her behalf and on what basis such decisions were to be made.

Much as the Schiavo case captivated the attention of the media, legal analysts, and ethicists, Jack Kevorkian's case attracted similar attention nearly a decade earlier. Dr. Kevorkian's actions, however, raised a number of different and arguably more complex issues regarding how to respond to a patient's request for aid in dying. After admitting to assisting more than 100 people in committing suicide, and several acquittals attributed to jury nullification, Kevorkian was convicted of second-degree murder in 1998 following the televised administration of a lethal injection to a 52-year-old man who was suffering from amyotrophic lateral sclerosis (Werth, 2001). The debates that followed from Kevorkian's actions centered on how clinicians should respond to a medically ill or terminally ill patient's request to hasten his or her death.

Whereas the media and policymakers have focused primarily on the issues related to the appropriateness or legality of hastened death, a number of important clinical issues have emerged from these scenarios that require special expertise. These issues are particularly complex for the mental health expert who may be faced with the daunting task of evaluating a patient's request to terminate life-sustaining treatment or to seek a hastened death through a lethal medication. Yet, despite the obvious importance of end-of-life mental health issues (literally life-or-death decisions), very few mental health professionals who work in forensic or consultation-liaison settings are trained or experienced in dealing with these situations.

This chapter provides an introduction to the myriad issues that arise in clinical/forensic consultation at the end of life. The specific goals of this chapter are to outline the range of forensic issues that arise for people who are close to death, review the relevant laws governing termination of life support and physician-assisted suicide in the United States, and provide guidance for evaluators faced with questions about an individual's capacity to make end-of-life decisions.

A number of different but equally important and equally difficult clinical-legal issues arise at the end of life and warrant a brief summary here (these issues are discussed in more depth in Rosenfeld, 2004). Perhaps the most hotly debated issues are those implicated in the actions of Dr. Kevorkian: physician-assisted suicide (PAS) and euthanasia. Although both of these terms refer to actions that lead directly to the death of a medically ill individual, they differ on the basis of the clinician's actions. In PAS, the clinician provides assistance, typically in the form of a prescription for a medication that will be used by the patient, if and when he or she so chooses, to end his or her life. Euthanasia, on the other hand, refers to the administration of a lethal medication *by the clinician* for the sole purpose of ending the patient's life (as opposed to medication intended for other purposes, such as symptom control, that might have the unintended but foreseeable effect of hastening death). Both of these interventions have the same ultimate outcome, which is bringing about the patient's death sooner than might otherwise occur. However, most of the legal and clinical attention in the United States has focused on PAS, which is legal in Oregon, whereas euthanasia is not legal anywhere in this country but is used much more often (and is legal) in the Netherlands and Belgium (euthanasia and PAS were legalized briefly in the Northwest Territories of Australia in the late 1990s, but were subsequently banned again).

Although a number of other end-of-life interventions also hasten death, they differ from PAS and euthanasia in that they involve the refusal or withdrawal of life-sustaining interventions rather than the administration of a life-ending substance. Removal of mechanical ventilation, refusal of renal dialysis, termination of artificial nutrition and hydration (as occurred in the Schiavo case), and do-not-resuscitate (DNR) orders are all forms of treatment refusal that have the effect of hastening death that might otherwise be delayed for weeks, months, or even years.

Another important issue that arises at the end of life, and was central to the case of Terry Schiavo, is the nature and role of advance directives. Several different mechanisms fall under the rubric of advanced directives, including DNR orders (i.e., an advance directive specifically intended to prevent cardiopulmonary resuscitation in the case of heart failure), living wills (written instructions or guidelines in case of subsequent incapacity to make treatment decisions), and health care proxy and durable power of attorney (legal mechanisms to appoint another person to make treatment decisions on one's behalf, again in case of future incapacity). Each of these advance directives provides a mechanism for individuals to protect their freedom to make the treatment decisions that are best for themselves. These mechanisms, however, are typically dormant until the patient loses the capacity to make treatment decisions, a determination that can often be quite contentious and challenging for the mental health expert.

HISTORICAL ROOTS OF THE RIGHT TO DIE

Although the right to die has been a topic of debate among physicians, politicians, and ethicists since at least the time of Plato and Hippocrates, in the past 30 years there has been a resurgence of interest in this topic in the United States and other developed countries. The emerging case law has clarified the parameters that surround many of the end-of-life issues that arise in mental health consultation, whether carried out in a medical setting (e.g., a consultation-liaison psychology or psychiatry service) or a legal setting (e.g., as an expert consultant or ethics review panel). Historically, decisions around termination of life support and physician-assisted suicide have been governed by case law. However, in the past 20 years, a number of states have adopted statutes specifically intended to clarify the legality of different practices (see Gorsuch, 2000, for review).

The modern history of end-of-life decision making began with the case of Karen Ann Quinlan (*In re Quinlan,* 1976). This case, which reached the New Jersey Supreme Court but was never heard by the U.S. Supreme Court, was the first major legal battle in the United States over termination of life-sustaining interventions. In 1975, Karen Quinlan, a 21-year-old woman, lost consciousness and suffered severe brain damage due to loss of oxygen, and subsequently fell into a persistent vegetative state with no apparent chance of regaining consciousness. Her parents requested that the life support be removed and that their daughter be allowed to die. However, the hospital staff refused to fulfill the Quinlans' request as they considered the patient to be still alive according to the law and existing medical standards. The Quinlans argued their case to the New Jersey Superior Court, requesting that they be given legal guardianship of Karen and be allowed to request the termination of life support for their daughter. Their request was based on several constitutional rights, including the right to privacy, protection against cruel and unusual punishment, and freedom of religion. After their plea was rejected by the New Jersey Superior Court, the New Jersey Supreme Court ruled in favor of the Quinlans' arguments, citing the right to privacy as the justification for refusal of unwanted medical treatment and noting that this right outweighed the state's interest in preserving the lives of its citizens.

Following the Quinlan case, many states adopted statutes that specified the parameters of end-of-life decision making (Angell, 1998). Legislation and case law pertaining to advance directives, surrogate decision making, and DNR orders have gradually emerged in all states and in most developed nations, although other issues, such as the legality (or illegality) of physician-assisted suicide and the termination of life-sustaining interventions have also been common topics in these legislative debates. The Quinlan case may have focused attention on the issues surrounding end-of-life decision making; however, this case had relatively little legal impact because it was decided at the state level. The first "right-to-die" case to reach the U.S. Supreme Court, *Cruzan v. Director, Missouri Dept. of Health* (1990), galvanized the attention of the general public and lawmakers and spurred even more legislative response.

Similar to Karen Quinlan's case, the Cruzan case also involved a young woman, Nancy Cruzan, who suffered severe brain damage, fell into a persistent vegetative state, and required a feeding tube (which was inserted at the request of her husband) to stay alive. After her condition remained unchanged for 4 years, her parents requested that the feeding tube be removed and she be allowed to die. However, the hospital refused to remove the tube and Nancy's parents sued the Missouri Department of Health. The county court ruled that Nancy's "right to liberty" outweighed the state's interest in preserving life and authorized the removal of the tube. A powerful factor in that decision was the testimony of a friend who asserted that Nancy had stated that she would not want to be kept alive by life support if she were nonresponsive. The case was subsequently appealed to the Missouri Supreme Court and overturned, ruling that the testimony by her friend did not constitute "clear and convincing evidence" that the removal of the feeding tube would have been Nancy's wish. The U.S. Supreme Court agreed to hear the case and rule, in part, on the appropriateness of Missouri's requirement of clear and convincing evidence for making decisions on the behalf of a person deemed incompetent. Although the Court ultimately ruled in favor of the state, rejecting Cruzan's request for termination of feeding, the Court's opinion upheld the right of a competent person to refuse life-sustaining medical interventions. However, the Court left decisions as to what standards to apply (e.g., clear and convincing evidence versus other, more or less rigorous legal thresholds), as well as the nature of evidence that can be considered, to the individual states to decide for themselves. As a result, states differ somewhat in the specifics of their end-of-life legislation, and practitioners must investigate the specific case law in their jurisdiction (a review of which is beyond the scope of this chapter) before offering opinions as to who is authorized to make surrogate decisions and how these decisions should be made.

More relevant for the debate over euthanasia and PAS are the cases of *Washington v. Glucksberg* (1997) and *Vacco v. Quill* (1997). Both of these cases, which were heard simultaneously by the U.S. Supreme Court, involved challenges to state laws (Washington and New York, respectively) prohibiting physician-assisted suicide. Although the specific legal challenges differed slightly in the two cases, plaintiffs in both cases essentially argued that allowing terminally ill patients to end life by terminating life-sustaining treatment (e.g., the *Cruzan* decision) but refusing to allow other terminally ill patients the right to hasten death (i.e., those who do not require life-sustaining medical interventions) was in violation of the due process and equal protection clauses of the 14th Amendment. In both cases, the U.S. Court of Appeals (the 9th and 2nd Circuits, respectively) had deemed the state laws prohibiting PAS to be unconstitutional. The Supreme Court, while reaffirming the right to refuse life-sustaining treatments articulated in *Cruzan,* overturned both of these appellate court decisions, making a distinction between refusal of life-sustaining treatment and active interventions to hasten death. Perhaps equally important, though, was the text of the Court's opinions, which has been interpreted as generally supportive of the right of individual states to make independent determinations as to the legality of PAS.

Almost immediately after these rulings, Oregon became the first, and thus far the only, state in the United States to legalize PAS. Although Oregon's Death with Dignity Act (ODDA) had been passed several years earlier, it was not enacted until October 1997. Under the guidelines of the ODDA, an Oregon resident who is 18 years of age or older, has a terminal illness with a life expectancy of less than 6 months, and is capable of making a "reasoned judgment" (an issue discussed at length later in the chapter) may request a prescription for a medication that, if taken, will result in the person's death. The request for PAS must be made at least twice, at least once in written form, and must come from the patient himself or herself. At the receipt of a request for PAS, the physician is required to confirm the terminal diagnosis and seek consultation with another physician to reaffirm the prognosis. The physician is also instructed to encourage the patient to inform family members of the request, but this is not required (Werth, Benjamin, & Farrenkopf, 2000). Finally, in one of the more controversial aspects of the ODDA, treating physicians are charged with making the determination as to whether any mental disorder exists that has impaired the patient's judgment and, if so, mandating mental health consultation and/or treatment. Thus, Oregon's legislation relies on treating physicians to make determinations as to their patients' mental state. Although perhaps logical, this reliance has been hotly debated in mental health circles, where concerns about the failure to adequately assess depression or cognitive impairment are balanced against the discomfort of placing mental health professionals in the gatekeeper role, effectively deciding whether or not a patient can end his or her life (e.g., Sullivan, Ganzini, & Youngner, 1998).

Despite the discomfort associated with the gatekeeper role, a growing number of mental health experts have been called on to make decisions regarding the capacity of an individual to make end-of-life decisions. The three types of cases in which such consultation typically arises are (a) requests for assisted suicide or euthanasia where it is legal (i.e., in Oregon, the Netherlands, and Belgium); (b) decisions to withdraw or withhold life-sustaining medical interventions; and (c) determinations as to when a surrogate decision maker is needed.

Prevailing Legal Standards

Perhaps the most critical aspect of any forensic evaluation to address an end-of-life issue, as with any other type of assessment conducted in, and in service of, a legal context, is an awareness of the specific laws and legal standards that apply in a given jurisdiction. Although a complete review of the existing state and international standards for the various end-of-life decisions would require an entire chapter itself, a number of factors can be considered overarching principles that pertain to virtually all such evaluations. In addition to understanding the construct of competence, which is described in more detail later in the chapter, there are several other critical issues that impact substantially on patient care and decision making at the end of life. For example, once a determination of incompetence has been reached, whether by a legal fact finder or de facto by a treating clinician, there are important variations in how different jurisdictions make determinations as to what the patient would have wished. This process is, in theory, simplified when advance directives (ADs) exist to document the patient's wishes; in actuality, the help provided by ADs is often far less than is hoped for. Because ADs often present information in vague terms (e.g., "when the prognosis for recovery or posttreatment quality of life is extremely poor"), it can be quite difficult to determine whether an AD actually applies in a given situation. When a health care proxy does not exist, debates can often center on which of several possible family members (or an intimate partner who is not legally related to the incompetent patient) has the authority to make decisions on the patient's behalf (i.e., surrogate decision making). Different jurisdictions also apply different models to guide surrogate decision making. In particular, the "best interest" standard, in which the patient's best interest is presumed to guide surrogate decision making, differs substantially from the "substitute judgment" standard, in which the surrogate is expected to replicate, to the best of his or her abilities, the decision the patient would make if competent. Finally, many jurisdictions utilize definitions of medical futility to guide decision making as to what treatments may be appropriate (i.e., when patients or family members request more aggressive interventions than the physician deems reasonable).

Although complexities abound in each of these scenarios, the responsibility for making determinations as to who should act as surrogate decision maker and what information should guide his or her decisions does not lie with the treating or evaluating clinician but, rather, rests with the courts and hospital ethics committees. Likewise, although a mental health professional might be asked to opine as to a patient's level of cognitive functioning, the issue of whether a patient's condition is "medically futile" is typically the domain of the medical team, not the forensic mental health evaluator. The central focus for most mental health evaluations pertains to questions of competence, with the primary issues being whether a patient is capable of making an informed decision to either terminate life-sustaining treatment or, where applicable, request assisted suicide or euthanasia. A related set of issues pertains to ADs, for which the mental health expert may be asked to help determine whether a patient has lost the capacity to make treatment decisions that do not involve hastened death.

WHAT IS COMPETENCE?

The lynchpin for most end-of-life decision scenarios is the construct of competence. The boundaries of competence to make treatment decisions have been clearly articulated by numerous physicians, bioethicists, and legal scholars and are discussed in the context of treatment decision making more generally in another chapter in Chapter 11. However, the importance of end-of-life decisions and the particular issues that arise in this context require a somewhat more specialized focus than do most medical treatment decisions. Incompetent refusals of life-sustaining interventions can deprive an individual of weeks, months, or even years of life that might otherwise be enjoyed by the individual and his or her family and friends. On the other hand, forcing a terminally ill person to continue suffering because he or she was unjustifiably deprived of the right to refuse life-sustaining treatments can be both a painful and unnecessarily cruel infringement on the individual's autonomy. In short, mistaken outcomes about end-of-life decision making are often unable to be rectified because the individual's death has occurred.

Given the importance of these issues, a clarification of the terms used to discuss decision making is necessary. Many writers confound the term "competence," which refers to a legal determination as to whether one is legally authorized to make decisions for oneself, with broader terms such as decision making "capacity" or "abilities." The latter are descriptive terms used to characterize the person's cognitive functioning but do not necessarily have any direct legal relevance. Although there is often an obvious correspondence among these terms, it is not uncommon for someone with substantial decisional impairments to nevertheless be deemed competent to make a particular decision. On the other hand, some individuals may be declared incompetent despite substantial decision-making abilities (e.g., because of differences in the nature of the decision, the specific types of impairments, or the opinions of family, mental health experts, or a judicial decision maker). The correct use of terminology in one's opinion or report is an important aspect of any forensic evaluation of decision-making capacity.

A number of writers have offered definitions of competence, typically grounded in case law and scholarly legal writings. Roth, Meisel, and Lidz (1977) described five different ways in which competence has typically been conceptualized (i.e., competency standards), ranging from the most simplistic, such as whether the individual can articulate a preference or recall some of the information about the decision that has been disclosed (e.g., paraphrase information from an informed consent form), to more complex standards, such as whether the individual can offer rational reasons for the decision, can appreciate the nature of the decision, and can rationally weigh the risks and benefits in a manner that is consistent with his or her personal values. Although we are unaware of any case law that dictates which standard should apply in any particular situation, most writers suggest that more rigorous standards of competence apply to clinical decisions in which the potential risks are substantial (e.g., death).

Although many evaluators equate incompetence with irrationality, such a simplistic formulation of decision-making ability has significant ramifications for assessing end-of-life decisions. Indeed, the impairments common among terminally ill individuals are quite different from those of the typical psychiatric patient, where psychotic symptoms can preclude any awareness or appreciation of the situation. Terminally ill individuals, on the other hand, are much more likely to have subtle impairments, such as mild cognitive deficits or nonpsychotic depression. But even when rational thinking is intact, these symptoms may impact end-of-life decision making by constraining individuals' ability to generate alternative solutions to their difficulties or engender a feeling of hopelessness about the likelihood of improvement in their condition. Even a relatively mild depression can increase a patient's skepticism about the efficacy of pain or symptom control, or engender a nihilistic view of one's remaining time. These seemingly modest impairments may lead a patient to request PAS or refuse life-sustaining interventions, despite long-standing moral or personal objections to hastened death. Perhaps most important, such patients may be thankful that their request was not fulfilled once their symptoms have remitted. Although this argument may lead some clinicians to believe that no request for hastened death should ever be fulfilled, this presumption is clearly inappropriate for any evaluator charged with objectively assessing the patient's decision-making capacity, as it is unlikely that such an evaluator would opine that a patient's request for hastened death is a rational one. Rather, it highlights the importance of using a thorough approach to the assessment of end-of-life decision-making capacity so that symptoms are identified and their impact is disentangled, as best possible, from the patient's decision.

Unfortunately, although some clarity about possible legal standards for competence exists, translating these standards into a clinical decision is far more complex. Cases at either extreme are obviously quite simple, such as when individuals have completely intact cognitive functioning and can provide a sophisticated explanation for their decision, or when patients are so grossly impaired as to be unable to provide any relevant information. Cases that fall between these two extremes can be far more challenging. Yet, much of the guidance offered to experts is grounded in research focusing on psychiatric patients, where gross impairments in appreciation and rational thinking are relatively common. With patients approaching the end of life, the most common sources of decisional impairments may simply be the result of advanced age, dementia, or transient cognitive impairments (e.g., delirium). These disorders typically include varying degrees of memory impairment that makes simply recalling or paraphrasing the relevant information more difficult, yet may leave actual reasoning processes relatively intact. On the other hand, some types of cognitive deficits can impair individuals' ability to conceptualize or articulate alternative solutions to their difficulties (e.g., because of impaired executive functioning and problem-solving skills). Such individuals may be able to provide plausible justifications for their decision yet not be capable of explaining the underlying basis for their thinking. Without a careful exploration of the patient's rationale, these more subtle impairments may be overlooked.

The law presumes every adult to be competent to make autonomous decisions. Likewise, the vast majority of patients facing important medical decisions are presumed competent by their physicians, and there is no involvement of a mental health expert. However, once a physician questions a patient's competence, the role of the mental health consultant becomes important as this is the expert who will conduct a competency evaluation and make a recommendation as to whether the person is capable of autonomous decision making. Unfortunately, whether or not a physician questions the patient's decision-making competence often hinges more on the decision made than on the patient's decision-making capacity, as physicians are much more prone to challenge a refusal of treatment, whereas acquiescence, even by a grossly incapacitated patient, is much less likely to be questioned. Thus, although many psychological evaluations at the end of life involve the refusal of recommended treatments or requests that will lead to a hastened death, there arguably are a great many patients who accept recommended treatments or experimental interventions who may not fully understand the potential risks, benefits, and implications of the decisions they have made.

Regardless of the particular decision that has spurred a competency evaluation, the principal goal of such an evaluation is to determine if a person has sufficient capacity to provide informed consent to accept or refuse a recommended procedure. It should be noted that, despite the important differences between a legal determination of competence and an expert's assessment of decision-making capacity, many courts and legal decision makers rely heavily, if not entirely, on the opinion of the mental health evaluator (Grisso & Appelbaum, 1998). Thus, although important differences exist between a forensic evaluation of decision-making capacity and a legal determination of decision-making competence, the two are highly interdependent.

Empirical Research on Decision-Making Capacity

A growing body of research has focused on the nature and extent to which psychological factors such as depression, psychosis, and cognitive impairment influence treatment decision making. Most of this research has focused on psychiatric patients, typically those with psychotic disorders such as Schizophrenia (e.g., Grisso & Appelbaum, 1995; Palmer, Dunn, Appelbaum, & Jeste, 2004; Rosenfeld & Turkheimer, 1995). However, though important for clinicians working in psychiatric settings, this literature offers little guidance for clinicians working with terminally ill patients, a setting in which psychotic disorders are quite rare. Instead, factors that are more likely to compromise the decision making of terminally ill adults are cognitive deterioration and depression. Yet, the literature on these factors is relatively modest and has rarely focused specifically on end-of-life decisions.

Depression and Decision Making

Ganzini, Lee, and their colleagues (Ganzini, Lee, Heintz, Bloom, & Fenn, 1994; Lee & Ganzini, 1992; Lee, Smith, Fenn, & Ganzini, 1998) conducted some of the few studies to date that have systematically addressed the impact of psychological factors on end-of-life decisions. In their first study, the authors compared depressed and nondepressed elderly adults' preferences for life-sustaining interventions in a series of hypothetical illness scenarios (Lee & Ganzini, 1992). Using a methodology similar to many ADs, they asked participants which of several possible life-sustaining interventions they would want if they were to experience various medical illnesses. Although there were few across-the-board differences in the preferences expressed by depressed and nondepressed patients, some differences emerged in scenarios in which the prognosis for recovery was good. In these "good prognosis" scenarios, depressed patients were less likely to desire life-sustaining interventions than were nondepressed patients, presumably reflecting a greater cynicism or feelings of hopelessness about future quality of life. The authors interpreted these findings as a type of "fatalism" that often marks the decision-making process of depressed patients (e.g., Bursztajn, Harding, Gutheil, & Brodsky, 1991).

A second study conducted by Ganzini et al. (1994) used a longitudinal methodology to determine whether depression influenced treatment decisions. They assessed preferences for life-sustaining medical therapies in a sample of 43 elderly patients who had been hospitalized for treatment of depression. Twenty-four of these patients were reassessed after their depression was considered to be in remission, and their preferences while depressed were compared to those expressed when in remission. Twenty-five percent of the patients available at follow-up (6 of 24) expressed different opinions regarding life-sustaining interventions after successful treatment for depression. However, contrary to commonsense expectations that the alleviation of depression would result in more interest in life-sustaining interventions, their results were somewhat more complex. Roughly equal numbers of patients expressed a desire for life-sustaining interventions that they had previously declined as did those who declined interventions that they had previously wanted. Moreover, the finding that 25% of patients changed their opinions after treatment is roughly comparable to the rate of changes in ADs among the general public (Gready et al., 2000). Thus, although depression may have influenced some patients to either seek or decline end-of-life interventions, the specific impact of depression may vary in different individuals. However, the authors noted that the subgroup of patients who were the most severely depressed were also those most likely to change their opinions toward desiring life-sustaining interventions that they had previously declined.

Although a handful of other studies have investigated the association between depression and decision-making capacity, these studies have typically used physically healthy psychiatric patients (e.g., Appelbaum, Grisso, Frank, O'Donnell, & Kupfer, 1999; Grisso & Appelbaum, 1995; Lapid, Rummans, Pankratz, & Appelbaum, 2004). Several studies using the MacArthur Competency Assessment Tool for Treatment (MacCAT-T, discussed further later in the chapter; Grisso & Appelbaum, 1998) have found far less influence of depression on decision making when compared to other disorders, such as psychosis and dementia. Nonetheless, rates of impairment have ranged from 10% to 25%, depending on the cutoff score used to determine impairment and the severity of the depression (i.e., inpatients versus outpatients).

In one of the few studies using the MacCAT-T with elderly depressed individuals, Lapid et al. (2004) assessed the decision-making capacity of patients referred for electroconvulsive therapy. The authors found a greater degree of decision-making impairment among the elderly patients compared to nonelderly patients, but the group differences were not large and the extent of impairment was quite modest for both groups (despite substantial levels of depression). Unfortunately, this report did not disclose the proportion of patients who were likely to be impaired based on their MacCAT-T performance, although their published data suggested that a number of individuals were likely to be considered impaired on one or more of the individual MacCAT-T subscales. Interestingly, they found that MacCAT-T scores increased substantially for both elderly and nonelderly patients after a brief educational intervention focused on the informed consent material. These results suggest that although gross impairments in decision-making capacity (as measured by the MacCAT-T) are not rare among patients with depression, they are also not the norm. However, because the presence of cognitive impairment resulted in exclusion from this study, it is not possible to extrapolate these results to actual end-of-life decision evaluations in which a combination of depression and cognitive impairment is quite likely.

But the literature on depression and decisional capacity may have only limited bearing on the real-world assessment of end-of-life decision making. Studies of decision-making capacity in general, and those using the MacCAT-T in particular, focus heavily on the cognitive aspects of decision making, with little ability to disentangle the decision-making process (Breden & Vollmann, 2004). Thus, one could continue to be rational in expressing a desire to terminate life-sustaining interventions (and indeed, such requests are rarely irrational on the surface) but nevertheless be expressing a request that is clearly driven by feelings of hopelessness and pessimism regarding the future.

Breden and Vollmann (2004) suggest that measures such as the MacCAT-T, despite its sophistication and robust psychometric properties, contain an inherent "cognitive bias" that emphasizes cognitive or intellectual capacities rather than decision-making processes. Arguably, this focus allows the assessment of decision making to be "value-free" (i.e., the decision rendered does not necessarily influence the assessment of one's capacity), but it ignores the possibility that a psychological disorder might influence the type of decision one makes and yet leave the ability to articulate or justify the decision relatively intact. Breden and Vollmann argue that this cognitive focus deviates from the actual manner in which decisions are made, in which "emotions, values, or intuitive factors that are not or at least not totally conscious to the decision maker" (p. 276) play a central role. Without an integration of the patient's values, it is not possible to truly assess the extent to which changes in psychological functioning have influenced decision making (see also Chapter 11 for a discussion of the role of personal values in the assessment of the right to refuse and consent to treatment). This issue is discussed further in the context of forensic assessments of end-of-life decisions.

Despite the limited association between depression and decision-making abilities in the published literature, clinicians appear to take a relatively paternalistic approach when considering end-of-life decisions. In a survey of forensic psychiatrists' attitudes toward end-of-life decision-making assessments, Ganzini, Leong, Fenn, Silva, and Weinstock (2000) found that 58% of the respondents believed that a diagnosis of Major Depression should automatically lead to a finding of incompetence, regardless of the extent to which a connection could be seen between the depressive symptoms and the decision at hand. Even more surprisingly, 38% of those surveyed indicated that a diagnosis of Adjustment Disorder or Dysthymia should automatically result in a determination of incompetence. Thus, despite the literature showing a weak association with depression, forensic mental health clinicians may have personal beliefs and biases that fuel their expert opinions about decision-making capacity, leading to higher rates of incompetence than might otherwise be justified. Whenever possible, such beliefs should be clearly articulated such that the fact finder (e.g., a judge or administrator) can differentiate clinical findings from opinions and inferences.

Cognitive Impairment and Decision Making

Studies of cognitive impairment and decision-making capacity in the elderly or medically ill have been somewhat more common than those of depression, perhaps because of the heavy emphasis on cognitive functions in measures such as the Mac-CAT-T. Marson, Ingram, Cody, and Harrell (1995) conducted several studies of cognitive impairment and decision making using an instrument they designed to tap multiple aspects of decision making. They compared elderly individuals who were cognitively intact to patients with mild and moderate dementia using five different legal standards: ability to communicate choice, to make a reasonable choice, to appreciate consequences of choice, to communicate rational reasons, and to understand the choice. They found that even the presence of mild dementia resulted in significantly more impaired decision-making abilities when compared to the cognitively intact comparison group. The differences between the comparison group and those with moderate dementia were even greater.

A more recent study conducted by Kim, Caine, Currier, Leibovichi, and Ryan (2001) using the Clinical Research version of the MacCAT (MacCAT-CR) replicated the findings of Marson et al. (1995). They compared elderly patients with mild or moderate Alzheimer's dementia to a group of healthy elderly adults. Patients in the two Alzheimer's groups revealed significantly greater impairment in decision-making ability compared to the healthy elderly sample. Only one-third of the Alzheimer patients scored in the intact range on the Understanding subscale, although more than half scored in the intact range on the Appreciation and Reasoning subscales of the MacCAT-CR. This result is particularly noteworthy as it highlights the possibility that appreciation and rational thinking may be intact even among individuals who have difficulty articulating a definition or paraphrasing information relevant to the decision. Interestingly, many of those patients who were classified as impaired by the MacCAT-CR were considered competent to make treatment decisions by their treating clinicians, a finding that has been replicated by others (e.g., Breden & Vollmann, 2004). It is unclear, however, whether this discrepancy suggests that the MacArthur instruments (the MacCAT-T and MacCAT-CR) overestimate impairment, that clinicians fail to recognize impairment that genuinely exists, or some combination of the two.

Rosenfeld, White, and Passik (1997) attempted to evaluate the effect of cognitive impairment on treatment decision making among a group of patients with HIV. In their study, participants were presented with hypothetical information about different medications to treat HIV, including traditional, experimental, and alternative medication. Participants were asked to make a series of dichotomous preferences (choosing which of two different medications they would prefer), including some choices where the alternative was to refuse medication altogether. When consistency of participants' decisions was used as an indicator of decision-making ability, patients with more advanced HIV-dementia displayed greater decision-making impairment. However, unlike the more purely cognitive measures of decision making such as the MacCAT-T, this methodology allowed for an analysis of the relative importance placed on different aspects of treatment (i.e., decision-making processes). The authors found no relationship between these relative weights and either the extent of cognitive impairment or psychological distress (measures of depression and anxiety).

In summary, the growing research that has addressed cognitive functioning and decision making has been quite consistent in demonstrating that cognitive impairment, even at mild levels, negatively impacts decision-making ability. These findings highlight the importance of a careful assessment of cognitive functioning as part of any assessment of decision-making capacity, particularly around end-of-life decisions.

THE FORENSIC EVALUATION OF COMPETENCE

Despite the importance of competency evaluations with patients nearing the end of life, there are no standardized approaches to the assessment of competence for either medical decision-making ability in general or capacity to request PAS in particular (Appelbaum & Grisso, 1998; Rosenfeld, 2004). Indeed, the standardized assessment techniques that do exist, and are reviewed further here, are of questionable appropriateness for end-of-life settings. For example, Werth et al. (2000) recommended using the MacCAT-T to assess requests for PAS, but others have criticized this approach as being overly restrictive (e.g., Breden & Vollmann, 2004). Indeed, it is far from clear whether a cognitively based measure can accurately assess the impact of psychological factors such as depression or anxiety on decision making in the absence of severe or psychotic levels of symptomatology. Although there may be a place for such measures as an adjunct to a more thorough evaluation, sole reliance on any formal measure of decision making is inadequate. As a result of the lack of established methods, experts have been left to develop their own techniques, often with little or no guidance as to how such assessments should be conducted.

Despite variability in the approaches used by different evaluators, courts and fact finders are usually quite deferential to the opinions of an expert evaluator. Thus, the outcome of a competency assessment is likely to hinge solely on the clinical judgment of the evaluator. Therefore, it is incumbent upon the expert to provide careful documentation of all the relevant issues and considerations that form the basis of his or her opinion. Although it should not be considered either prescriptive or exhaustive, the following highlights many of the important elements of a decision-making capacity evaluation in patients nearing the end of life.

The structure of a clinical evaluation at the end of life typically follows the same general principles of most competency evaluations, but with a number of important deviations. Like any evaluation of decision-making capacity, the central element of any forensic opinion hinges on the mental status examination. However, whereas many clinicians conceptualize the term "mental status examination" narrowly, as an assessment only of the patient's cognitive functioning (e.g., orientation, memory, attention) and severe psychiatric symptoms (e.g., psychosis, confusion), we consider this term much more broadly, as including a full diagnostic evaluation. The interpretation of the patient's expressions may differ markedly depending on diagnostic considerations, such as whether the patient is depressed or highly anxious, even when cognitive functioning is not grossly impaired. Thus, any forensic evaluation of decision-making capacity must begin with a thorough diagnostic evaluation as well as an assessment of the patient's higher cognitive functioning.

The second critical element of any assessment of decision-making capacity involves a careful analysis of the specific decision at hand. Of course, doing so requires that the evaluator have a general understanding of the relevant medical issues, typically based on the report of the treating physician. The expert must be aware of the underlying medical condition and the nature and purpose of any available treatments, including but not limited to the intervention proposed. For example, in the case of a terminally ill individual, the evaluator should have a clear understanding of the patient's illness and prognosis, the extent of current physical symptoms and palliative care treatments, and what additional interventions may be available to either treat the underlying medical illness or alleviate distressing physical (and psychological) symptoms. The last information is particularly important given the possibility that decisions to hasten death may be fueled, in part, by untreated or undertreated physical symptoms. The relationship between physical and psychological symptoms and interest in hastened death is now widely recognized, and disentangling these various influences is a critical element of any assessment of decision making for patients nearing the end of life.

But, although the assessment of mental status and medical condition may seem sufficient for many assessments of treatment decision making, decisions in which life and death hang in the balance require additional care and inquiry. As noted earlier, the connection between an individual's current decision and his or her previously expressed preferences and values is an integral part of an assessment of end-of-life decision making. Therefore, a review of any living wills or other ADs, as well as interviews with family, friends, or health care providers, may provide important information about the patient's values and preferences that predate the current clinical condition. These sources of information provide the backdrop for analyzing the patient's logic and rationale offered for the current decision. Moreover, family or friends may reveal important information that the physician is unaware of that has shaped the patient's decision, such as alternative interventions that the patient is considering (e.g., when rejecting an ostensibly life-sustaining intervention) or past treatment experiences that have impeded the patient's quality of life more than the physician may realize. It is critical to acknowledge that there is rarely a single indicator of competence or incompetence, other than in cases where depression or dementia is so extreme as to overwhelm the patient's ability to think rationally. Rather, most cases involve a careful weighing of the patient's expressed preference against his or her past decisions and the accuracy of his or her assessment of the current situation.

A common step in this process is to ask patients about the reasons behind their choice. In this context, the central mechanism for assessing the "legitimacy" of a patient's wishes is to compare that decision to previously expressed values and preferences. A thorough exploration of the basis of the patient's request should include a discussion of how this decision fits with previously expressed preferences and long-standing values. Of course, patients have the right to change their opinion as to what treatments they might want and how much they value things like physical functioning and physical comfort, and such changes may be even more common among patients who are nearing death. However, most patients who have changed their perspective will be cognizant that their opinions have evolved and hopefully can articulate the basis for these changes. Moreover, exploring the reasons decisions have changed can help elucidate additional influences on the patient's decisions that were not initially acknowledged (e.g., physical symptom distress, negative expectations about potentially viable palliative care interventions).

Of course, simply because patients cannot readily articulate a clear reason for their decision does not necessarily mean they are either irrational or unrealistic in their decision. For example, many patients suffering from depression will cite physical or prognostic reasons as the basis for a request for hastened death, yet after successful treatment for depression they may acknowledge that their decision was heavily influenced by depression rather than intolerable symptoms or a rational assessment of future quality of life. Depression may engender a feeling of hopelessness about the future that is not necessarily accurate, yet nevertheless leads to a request for hastened death; a decision might be rejected once treatment has been provided (and a growing literature has documented the ability to treat depression even among the terminally ill; Rosenfeld, Abbey, & Pessin, 2005). Patients with mild cognitive impairments may also have difficulty articulating clear answers to questions about treatment decision making, yet with sufficient time and inquiry will be able to offer information that demonstrates both the rationality of the decision and the consistency of their choice with past values and preferences. It is critical for experts to avoid taking an overly paternalistic stance toward end-of-life decision-making assessments, such that any degree of impairment is taken as evidence of incompetence. Many patients retain the ability to think logically and express preferences that are logically consistent with their values and goals, despite limitations in their ability to readily articulate these decisions.

Perhaps the most extreme example of limitations in articulation concerns patients who are intubated and therefore unable to speak. In one case, referred to one of the authors, an elderly, terminally ill patient had repeatedly gestured with her hands toward her throat, seemingly in a slashing motion. When asked by her treating clinician whether she wanted to have the ventilator removed, and whether she understood that the removal would almost invariably result in her death, she repeatedly nodded yes. However, when seen for a psychological consultation, the woman was asked a number of other questions, such as whether she was in a department store (she nodded yes) and whether she was expecting to be returned home (again, nodding yes). Further evaluation made it clear that the woman was quite confused and had been simply nodding yes indiscriminately. In many other cases, however, this approach will reveal a consistent pattern of responses, despite patients' inability to spontaneously articulate the reasons for a decision. Thus, the evaluator must be careful not to uncritically accept simple yes and no answers, but must conceptualize questions that will illuminate patients' wishes without leading them to a predetermined decision outcome.

When significant impairment is detected, the expert should also consider the possibility that the impairment is temporary. Delirium, a transient state of confusion, is quite common in terminally ill patients and may resolve with time, medical stabilization, or psychiatric treatment (e.g., small doses of antipsychotic medications). Premature conclusions that a patient's impairment is permanent may result in unwarranted restrictions on the individual's autonomy. Indeed, repeating the decision-making assessment on at least a second occasion is strongly recommended, both because of the transient nature of many forms of impairment and to allow for a more thorough exploration of the basis for the patient's stated decision. Repeated assessments enable the expert to assess the stability of patients' preferences as well as the consistency of their explanation for the decision. Some incompetent patients are able to offer a plausible explanation for a decision but change their mind repeatedly or offer wholly different explanations at different times, indicating that their decision is not necessarily as clear and consistent as it might appear at first glance.

Other relevant issues that should be considered in any assessment of end-of-life decision making is the possible impact of cultural, religious, and spiritual factors. An exploration of patients' personal, cultural, or religious beliefs can help elucidate the values that underlie their decisions, either helping to bolster their decision or highlighting the discrepancy between a decision rendered and long-standing values and beliefs. Likewise, integration of the family into the evaluation process, when appropriate and acceptable to the patient, can have beneficial effects by helping family members understand the basis for their relative's decision. King, Kim, and Conwell (2000) suggest that this process can "create a supportive atmosphere that will enhance family communication and decision-making" (p. 444). An inclusive approach to the decision-making assessment can also help minimize the risk that families will disagree with the patient's request and seek legal or administrative intervention.

One of the most important considerations for experts assessing end-of-life decision making concerns the potential influence of the evaluator's biases and assumptions. The impact of an evaluator's biases can have a marked impact on the conclusions reached, at times completely overwhelming the actual data provided by the patient. For example, experts who believe that all terminally ill individuals are necessarily sad, anxious, and generally distressed may overlook indications of severe depression because of the belief that such reactions are "normal." Evaluators who find hastened death morally oppositional, or simply believe that all such requests are irrational, may presume that only a depressed, suicidal individual would request hastened death and equate a request to terminate life-sustaining interventions as a form of suicide that requires mental health intervention. In reality, of course, these extreme positions are often inaccurate and highlight the importance of an objective assessment of the patient's decision making.

Despite concerns raised by some critics, many clinicians opt to supplement their interview with formal assessment tools such as the MacCAT-T. These instruments, though emphasizing cognitive processes at the expense of other influences (e.g., emotional or unconscious factors), can help bolster the objectivity of the forensic assessment by providing objective data. One of the most common methods of evaluating cognitive functioning that is frequently used in medical settings is the Mini-Mental State Examination (Folstein, Folstein, & McHugh, 1975). This scale provides a crude assessment of orientation, memory, and concentration and is frequently used in research and consultation, but does not address decision making per se. A somewhat more focused instrument is the Hopkins Competency Assessment Test (HCAT; Janofsky, McCarthy, & Folstein, 1992). This brief measure provides the patient with a description of informed consent and durable power of attorney and measures the patient's short-term recall of this information. Although still broad in scope, the HCAT focuses on information relevant to the process of informed consent in general. One of the only measures that specifically focuses on the decision at hand is the MacCAT-T (Grisso & Appelbaum, 1998). The MacCAT-T enables the expert to structure the information relevant to the decision and uses a systematic method to assess four aspects of decision-making competence: (1) the ability to render a decision, (2) the ability to understand relevant information, (3) the ability to appreciate the significance of that evaluation, and (4) the ability to rationally weigh the risks and benefits of available alternatives. Although the Mac-CAT-T does not specify a cutoff score that is necessary for identifying an individual as unable to make rational decisions, it does enable the expert to more precisely assess and quantify the patient's abilities and limitations.

The final aspect of any decision-making assessment is the expert's documentation of his or her opinion. Thorough documentation is critical both for any legal or administrative review that might follow from the forensic evaluation and may assist the current and future evaluators in identifying changes in mental state that might signal changes in the patient's decision-making capacity. Of course, experts must be clear as to not only the methodology used to evaluate decision making, but the nature of their opinion (both diagnostic and related to decisional abilities and impairments) and the scope of their opinion and expertise. For example, experts may unwittingly confuse their role as authorizing the determination of who is best suited or most appropriate to act as surrogate decision maker, when these determinations are dictated by statute and/or case law and are not the domain of the mental health consultant. On the other hand, recommendations as to what treatments might be available to reduce any impairment observed and the likelihood that improvement will occur with this treatment are often helpful for those charged with determining how to proceed with a particular case (e.g., whether to require treatment or acquiesce to the patient's request).

Framing one's forensic conclusions can also require a tenuous balancing act. Ryan (1996) advocated the use of a three-part classification system for differentiating levels of decision-making capacity. He argues that patients who meet the minimum standards of understanding and rationality should be classified as fully capable. Patients who fail to meet more rigorous standards for competency (e.g., ability to rationally weigh the risks and benefits) but who are capable of expressing a choice consistent with their long-standing values would be classified as partially capable. Those who lack any coherent decision-making abilities would be classified as fully impaired. However, this recommendation does not help clarify where lines should be drawn between these levels (i.e., how much ability constitutes "fully capable"). This inherent limitation further supports the need to document the nature of the patient's decisional abilities and impairments because determinations as to how much ability is necessary for competence is the domain of the judge or administrator charged with making such decisions, not the forensic evaluator.

CONCLUSION

Evaluations of end-of-life decision making are extremely challenging even for the experienced mental health expert. There are few simple answers to the dilemmas that arise when a patient requests termination of life-sustaining treatment or seeks a prescription for use in ending his or her life. Although cases of extreme confusion or depression are quite easily assessed, those presenting with relatively subtle symptoms are far more complex, as no clear guidelines exist as to how much impairment is required to render an individual incapable of making a decision to end his or her life. Some evaluators respond to this ambiguity by relying excessively on their own biases or beliefs, maintaining an extremely low or unrealistically high threshold for labeling an individual's decisions a reflection of a psychological disorder. Although it might seem desirable for this chapter to advocate for a specific approach, such decisions are not necessarily within the domain of the mental health expert, but rather rest with the hospital administration, ethics committee, or judge (if cases ultimately reach the stage of litigation). Moreover, many potential conflicts can be managed by involving family members early on in the evaluation process. Nevertheless, some conflicts are inevitable whenever divergent moral and religious beliefs clash.

Hence, although many referring clinicians may wish to delegate the authority for making ultimate decisions of competence to the mental health expert, we recommend avoiding such ultimate issue determinations. Instead, a thorough analysis of the strengths and limitations in the individual's decision-making abilities, as well as the possible contribution, if any, of psychological factors such as depression, anxiety, or confusion, is far more appropriate and enables those individuals charged with making decisions to understand the strengths and limitations of a particular patient's decision-making abilities. Perhaps most important, a thorough methodology for assessing decision making can help all the parties involved identify the source of the patient's decision, understand (or identify the flaws in) the patient's logic that underlies the decision, and develop appropriate intervention strategies, whether acquiescing to a request for hastened death or recommending more aggressive palliative care. Several studies have demonstrated that a large proportion of patients who request hastened death or assistance in dying rescind their request when more aggressive palliative care is provided (e.g., Ganzini et al., 2000). Although we would not suggest that all requests for hastened death represent a "cry for help," certainly some subset of requests are just that. Differentiating those requests that reflect a genuine desire for death from those that represent a cry for help is a critical aspect of any evaluation of a patient's request for hastened death and is most likely to be accomplished with a thorough evaluation process.

REFERENCES

Angell, M. (1998). Helping desperately ill people to die. In L. L. Emanuel (Ed.), *Regulating how we die: The ethical, medical, and legal issues surrounding physician-assisted suicide* (pp. 2–20). Cambridge, MA: Harvard University Press.

Appelbaum, P. S., & Grisso, T. (1998). Assessing patients' capacities to consent to treatment. *New England Journal of Medicine, 319,* 1635–1638.

Applebaum, P. S., Grisso, T., Frank, E., O' Donnell, S., & Kupfer, D. J. (1999). Competence of depressed patients for consent to research. *American Journal of Psychiatry, 156,* 1380–1384.

Breden, T. M., & Vollmann, J. (2004). The cognitive based approach of capacity assessment in psychiatry: A philosophical critique of the MacCAT-T. *Health Care Analysis, 12,* 273–283.

Bursztajn, H. J., Harding, H. P., Gutheil, T. G., & Brodsky, A. (1991). Beyond cognition: The role of disordered affective states in impaired competence to consent to treatment. *Bulletin of the American Academy of Psychiatry and Law, 19,* 383–388.

Cruzan v. Director, Missouri Dept. of Health, 497 U.S. 261, 110 S. Ct. 2841 (1990).

Folstein, M. F., Folstein, S. E., & McHugh, P. R. (1975). "Mini-mental state": A practical method for grading the cognitive state of patients for the clinician. *Journal of Psychiatric Research, 12,* 189–198.

Ganzini, L., Lee, M. A., Heintz, R. T., Bloom, J. D., & Fenn, D. S. (1994). The effect of depression treatment on elderly patients' preferences for life-sustaining medical therapy. *American Journal of Psychiatry, 51,* 1631–1636.

Ganzini, L., Leong, G. B., Fenn, D. S., Silva, J. A., & Weinstock, R. (2000). Evaluation of competence to consent to assisted suicide: View of forensic psychiatrists. *American Journal of Psychiatry, 157,* 595–600.

Gorsuch, N. M. (2000). The right to assisted suicide and euthanasia. *Harvard Journal of Law and Public Policy, 23,* 599–645.

Gready, R. M., Ditto, P. H., Danks, J. H., Coppola, K. M., Lockhart, L. K., & Smucker, W. D. (2000). Actual and perceived stability of preferences for life-sustaining treatment. *Journal of Clinical Ethics, 11,* 334–346.

Grisso, T., & Appelbaum, P. S. (1995). The MacArthur Treatment Competence Study III: Abilities of patients to consent to psychiatric and medical treatments. *Law and Human Behavior, 19,* 149–174.

Grisso, T., & Appelbaum, P. S. (1998). *Assessing competence to consent to treatment: A guide for physicians and other health professionals.* New York: Oxford University Press.

In re Quinlan, 355 A. 2d 647 (N.J. 1976), *cert. denied,* 429 U.S. 922 (1976).

Janofsky, J. S., McCarthy, R. J., & Folstein, M. F. (1992). The Hopkins Competency Assessment Test: A brief method for evaluating patients' capacity to give informed consent. *Hospital and Community Psychiatry, 43,* 132–136.

Kim, S. Y. H., Caine, E. D., Currier, G. W., Leibovichi, A., & Ryan, J. M. (2001). Assessing the competence of persons with Alzheimer's disease in providing informed consent for participation in research. *American Journal of Psychiatry, 158,* 712–717.

King, D. A., Kim, Y. H., & Conwell, Y. (2000). Family matters: A social systems perspective on physician-assisted suicide and older adults. *Psychology, Public Policy, and Law, 6,* 434–451.

Lapid, M. I., Rummans, T. A., Pankratz, V. S., & Appelbaum, P. S. (2004). Decisional capacity of depressed elderly to consent to electroconvulsive therapy. *Journal of Geriatric Psychiatry and Neurology, 17,* 42–46.

Lee, M. A., & Ganzini, L. (1992). Depression in the elderly: Effect on patient attitudes toward life-sustaining therapy. *Journal of the Geriatric Society, 40,* 983–988.

Lee, M. A., Smith, D. A., Fenn, D. S., & Ganzini, L. (1998). Do patients' treatment decisions match advance statements of their preferences? *Journal of Clinical Ethics, 9,* 258–262.

Marson, D. C., Ingram, K. K., Cody, H. A., & Harrell, L. E. (1995). Assessing the competency of patients with Alzheimer's disease under different legal standards. *Archives of Neurology, 52,* 949–954.

Oregon Death with Dignity Act, Or. Rev. Stat. 13 (1996).

Palmer, B. W., Dunn, L. B., Appelbaum, P. S., & Jeste, D. V. (2004). Correlates of treatment-related decision-making capacity among middle-aged and older patients with schizophrenia. *Archives of General Psychiatry, 61,* 230–236.

Quill, T. E. (2005). Terry Schiavo: A tragedy compounded. *New England Journal of Medicine, 352,* 1630–1633.

Rosenfeld, B. (2004). *Assisted suicide and the right to die: The interface of social science, public policy and medical ethics.* Washington, DC: American Psychological Association.

Rosenfeld, B., Abbey, J. G., & Pessin, H. (2005). Depression and hopelessness at the end of life: Assessment and treatment. In J. L. Werth Jr. & D. Blevins (Eds.), *Psychosocial issues near the end of life: A resource for professional care providers* (pp. 163–182). Washington, DC: American Psychological Association.

Rosenfeld, B., & Turkheimer, E. (1995). Modeling psychiatric patients' treatment decision-making. *Law and Human Behavior, 19,* 389–405.

Rosenfeld, B. D., White, M., & Passik, S. D. (1997). Making treatment decisions with HIV infection: A pilot study of patient preferences. *Medical Decision Making, 17,* 308–314.

Roth, L. H., Meisel, A., & Lidz, C. W. (1977). Tests of competency to consent to treatment. *American Journal of Psychiatry, 134,* 279–284.

Ryan, S. P. (1996). Competence and the elderly patient with cognitive impairments. *Australian and New Zealand Journal of Psychiatry, 30,* 768–773.

Sullivan, M. D., Ganzini, L., & Youngner, S. J. (1998). Should psychiatrists serve as gatekeepers for physician-assisted suicide? *Hastings Center Report, 28,* 24–31.

Vacco v. Quill, 117 S. Ct. 2293 (1997).

Washington v. Glucksberg, 117 S. Ct. 2258 (1997).

Werth, J. L. (2001). Using the Youk-Kevorkian case to teach about euthanasia and end-of-life issues. *Death Studies, 25,* 151–177.

Werth, J. L., Benjamin, G. A., & Farrenkopf, T. (2000). Requests for physician-assisted death: Guidelines for assessing mental capacity and impaired judgment. *Psychology, Public Policy, and the Law, 6,* 348–372.

PART IX

Special Topics in Forensic Practice

CHAPTER 26

Judicial Decision Making about Forensic Mental Health Evidence

Richard E. Redding and Daniel C. Murrie

Over the past 30 years, jury decision making has received considerable attention in the field of law and psychology. But recently, researchers have also turned their attention to judicial decision making. Juries are almost always the finders of fact in criminal cases, but judges must make evidentiary rulings, including decisions about whether to admit mental health evidence and testimony, and often it is the judge who determines the sentence to be imposed. In juvenile court, where trials are held without a jury and the judge determines the disposition in addition to adjudicating the case, judges have considerable decision-making power. In civil cases such as child custody and civil commitment, it also is the judge who makes the decision.

Judges, therefore, play a central decision-making role in the justice system. In this chapter, we review current empirical research on judicial decision making in criminal, juvenile, and civil cases. We discuss judges' decision making about forensic mental health evidence introduced in these cases, judicial receptivity to various kinds of mental health evidence and experts, and judges' understanding of clinical and scientific evidence and the ways they make evidentiary rulings about such evidence. We focus on judicial decision making at the trial court level, in those arenas that are most relevant to the forensic mental health practitioner who is called on to provide testimony for the courts. We begin with a brief description of the successes and failures of psychologists' attempts to influence the courts.

PSYCHOLOGISTS' ATTEMPTS TO INFLUENCE THE COURTS

As Judge Wisdom (1975) observed, "Judicial decision making represents social science in action" (p. 148). Ever since *Brown v. Board of Education* (1954), the legal system has seen a variety of psycholegal research studies and advocacy efforts aimed at informing the law about legally relevant psychological issues, including the accuracy of eyewitness testimony, clinical predictions of dangerousness, the parental fitness of lesbians and gays (Redding, 1998, 1999; Redding & Reppucci, 1999), children's competency to consent to medical treatment, the culpability of juvenile offenders, and jury decision making, to name some of the more prominent research areas. The American Psychological Association (APA) has submitted to the

U.S. Supreme Court *amicus curiae* ("friend of the court") briefs that summarize social science research findings and advocate policy on a wide variety of issues (Wrightsman, 1999). The APA has also been an advocate in state trial and appellate courts, as have other mental health professional organizations, such as the American Psychiatric Association, the American Academy of Child and Adolescent Psychiatry, and the National Association of Social Workers (see Redding, 1998).

At times, psychology's influence on the courts has been substantial. For example, in two recent U.S. Supreme Court cases (*Atkins v. Virginia,* 2002; *Roper v. Simmons,* 2005), the majority opinion relied heavily on psychological research findings presented to the Court in amicus briefs submitted by the APA. But although clinical testimony is embraced by courts, commentators (e.g., Bersoff & Glass, 1995; Ogloff, 2000; Redding, 1998, 1999; Tanford, 1990) have noted that relevant psychological research is all too frequently ignored or dismissed by courts and that psychology's efforts to influence the law have not been as successful as psychologists had expected.

Why do courts ignore relevant social science research evidence? Tanford (1990) reviews various theories suggested over the years: (a) Judges are conservative, whereas social scientists are liberal; (b) judges do not believe they need help from social science; (c) judges are threatened by social science; (d) judges do not understand social science; (e) it is human nature to think unscientifically; and (f) law and social science have competing systems of reasoning. Fradella, Fogarty, and O'Neill's (2003,) analysis of federal judicial opinions between 1987 and 2000 involving social science evidence found that the federal courts "have clearly become more hostile towards social science evidence [since 1987]" (p. 165). Their study suggests additional reasons for the "judicial hostility to social science" (p. 168): (a) Judges distrust statistical analyses; (b) social scientists are seen as nonobjective researchers driven by sociopolitical agendas; (c) social scientists' deterministic view of human behavior conflicts with the law's assumption of free will; (d) social scientists provide excuses for criminal behavior; and (e) it is impractical to accept social science research findings when they suggest the need for systemic legal reforms.

Judicial Biases

In addition, jurists may be disinclined to accept social science research on hot-button sociopolitical issues because the research often refutes the law's traditional or "commonsense" assumptions about human behavior (Redding, 1998, 1999). To test this theory, Redding and Reppucci (1999) experimentally examined whether judges' sociopolitical attitudes affected their judgments about the legal relevance of social science research introduced in court cases. State court judges completed a questionnaire that presented vignette summaries of two U.S. Supreme Court death penalty cases along with descriptions of the social science evidence contained in the Court opinions, with the evidence manipulated to either support or not support the death penalty. After reading each vignette, participants rated the legal relevance, admissibility, and dispositive weight of the social science evidence. They then were asked about their own attitudes about the death penalty, science and social science background, and attitudes about social science. Participants rated the evidence higher when it matched their own beliefs about the death penalty as compared to when it did not conform to their beliefs. Participants' level of science background neither moderated nor mediated the bias effects. There was, however, a relationship between evidentiary ratings and attitudes about the use of social science in law, with those having positive attitudes more likely to rate the social science evidence as relevant and admissible and to give it greater weight. (This finding was recently replicated in a study of law students' interest in learning about forensic mental health issues; Redding, 2004.)

Many of the participants' written explanations for their evidentiary ratings reflected a distrust of social science and particularly of experts who testify in court cases. Moreover, some participants in the Redding and Reppucci (1999) study did not appreciate the value of research evidence, believing instead that nomothetic research had no bearing on individual cases. These findings are consistent with scholarly commentary (e.g., Bersoff & Glass, 1995; Redding, 1998; Tanford, 1990) that judges and lawyers tend to be skeptical about the validity, reliability, and relevance of social science and statistical evidence, finding it to be malleable and susceptible to varying interpretations. It also is consistent with research documenting how judges and jurors often are skeptical about the reliability of expert witnesses who testify in court cases, believing that one can find an expert to testify in support of any position. Indeed, a recent survey of federal trial judges found that their chief complaint about expert witnesses was that litigants rely excessively on paid experts, who fail to be objective by becoming advocates for the party that retained them (Krafka, Dunn, Johnson, Cecil, & Miletich, 2002). Some judges have gone so far as to label mental health experts who testified at trial as "hired guns," "whores," and "prostitutes" (Mossman, 1999).

JUDICIAL DECISION MAKING ABOUT MENTAL HEALTH AND SOCIAL SCIENCE EVIDENCE

In the next sections, we discuss the extant research on judges' perceptions of mental health evidence and experts and how they decide whether to admit such evidence, and the implications for experts who testify in court.

Judicial Perceptions of Mental Health Evidence and Experts

Only a few studies have examined judicial perceptions of mental health evidence and experts. The most recent study, by Redding, Floyd, and Hawk (2001), used vignette survey methodology to compare the preferences of Virginia judges for different types of forensic mental health evidence and experts in a hypothetical insanity case. Judges preferred that forensic evaluations be conducted by psychiatrists. This preference was followed by a preference for doctoral-level psychologists, with master's-level psychologists and social workers being far less preferred. This replicates the earlier findings of Poythress (1983), whose survey of Michigan judges found that the preference for psychiatrists was greatest when the defendant's sanity or competency was at issue. Similarly, LaFortune and Nicholson (1995) found the same pattern of preferences among attorneys and judges, though the preference for psychiatrists over doctoral-level clinical psychologists was slight.

The preference for psychiatrists is likely due to the law's historical preference for medical experts and comfort with the medical model (Melton, Petrila, Poythress, & Slobogin, 1997). Yet, when blind to the discipline of the evaluator, legal experts rate the forensic reports of doctoral-level clinical psychologists as being of higher quality (i.e., more thorough and legally relevant) than those prepared by psychiatrists (Petrella & Poythress, 1983), probably because psychologists have specialized expertise in psychological assessment. Similarly, large-scale studies of several thousand forensic evaluations in Virginia revealed that psychiatrists were no more thorough in conducting legal sanity evaluations than were psychologists (Warren, Murrie, Chahuan, Dietz, & Morris, 2004), and in evaluations of trial competence, psychologists tended to perform more thorough and labor-intensive evaluations than did psychiatrists (Warren & Murrie, 2005). Currently, only 11 states still require that forensic evaluations be conducted by psychiatrists or that psychologists work with psychiatrists in conducting evaluations (Frost, deCamara, & Earl, in press).

The second major finding from the Redding et al. (2001) study was that although judges were receptive to most types of testimony that mental health experts could provide, they were primarily interested in the clinical diagnosis, followed by an opinion as to whether the diagnosis met the legal threshold for an insanity plea. They also were very interested in hearing an ultimate opinion on the legal question of sanity, despite Virginia and federal evidentiary rules prohibiting mental health professionals from testifying about the ultimate issue and the view of many mental health professionals that they should not provide such opinions (Melton et al., 1997). Judges, however, were much less interested in testimony about relevant statistical or actuarial data (e.g., data on diagnostic reliability, crime data related to diagnosis) that could provide important contextual or "social framework" evidence (Monahan & Walker, 1998) for interpreting the relevance and reliability of the clinical testimony.

Indeed, judges are more likely to exclude mental health testimony when it is research evidence rather than clinical evidence (Slobogin, 1998). Research on the fallibility of eyewitness testimony, for example, is frequently excluded because it does not speak directly to the accuracy of the witness in question (Slobogin, 1998). Likewise, studies have found that clinical testimony is more persuasive to jurors than actuarial testimony, even with respect to violence prediction (Krauss & Sales, 2001), where actuarial prediction clearly has superior accuracy (Quinsey, Harris, Rice, & Cormier, 1998). However, Krauss, Lieberman, and Olson's (2004) recent study indicates that people find actuarial evidence to be more persuasive after being primed to engage in a more rational-analytic mode of information processing. Perhaps mental health experts can foster this mode of thinking in judges (and juries) by testifying about the scientific and analytic nature of actuarial evidence (Krauss et al., 2004).

Thus, judges value clinical and ultimate issue testimony, but they view research data and statistical information as less helpful, apparently because they do not understand the relevance of nomothetic data for adjudicating individual cases. Mental health experts may need to be explicit in explaining to lawyers and courts precisely *why* and *how* research findings can provide useful social framework evidence

(Monahan & Walker, 2002). In addition, mental health professionals ought to consider how to educate judges about the utility of scientific data, the dangers inherent in relying on the conclusory testimony of experts, and why the historical preference for medical experts is outmoded in view of psychologists' expertise in forensic assessment.

Daubert and the Admissibility of Mental Health Evidence

Just like any other evidence proffered by litigants, trial judges must make evidentiary rulings on whether to admit scientific evidence. For many years, the federal courts and most state courts followed the *Frye* test (*Frye v. United States,* 1923). Under *Frye,* scientific evidence is admissible if it is "generally accepted" in the scientific community. But much changed when the U.S. Supreme Court decided *Daubert v. Merrell Dow Pharmaceuticals* (1993), which set a new standard for the admissibility of scientific testimony in the federal courts (*Daubert* or a variant thereof has since been adopted by fewer than half the states). *Daubert* requires trial judges to act as evidentiary "gatekeepers" to determine whether proffered "scientific, technical, or specialized knowledge" is scientifically "reliable." (*Daubert* uses "reliability" to mean scientific accuracy and validity.) *Daubert* sets forth four factors to be considered by the judge: (1) Has the research been subjected to empirical testing? (2) What are the error rates of the scientific techniques or tests used? (3) Has it been subjected to peer review and publication? and (4) Has the research been generally accepted in the scientific community? The fourth factor incorporates the *Frye* test, which many states still follow.

Following *Daubert,* the U.S. Supreme Court decided *Kumho Tire Co. v. Patrick Carmichael* (1999), which extended *Daubert* to all expert testimony. (However, judges apparently have greater latitude in assessing nonscientific expert evidence, as *Kumho* directs them to apply only those *Daubert* factors that are relevant for assessing the reliability of such evidence.) Clinical testimony, therefore, also must satisfy the *Daubert* standards. In relying on the *Diagnostic and Statistical Manual of Mental Disorders,* fourth edition, text revision (*DSM-IV-TR;* American Psychiatric Association, 2000) or psychological testing in making a diagnosis, clinicians' opinions are derived ultimately from research, because psychological tests and the *DSM-IV-TR* diagnostic schemes are based on a foundation of empirical research. But *Daubert* cannot be applied in circumstances where there is no scientific research available on the issue that is the subject of the clinical testimony. Under such circumstances, the admissibility determination must rest on "judging the qualifications of the experts and the acceptability of that testimony to other similar practitioners, resulting in nearly identical pre- and post-*Daubert* admissibility decisions" (Shuman & Sales, 1999, p. 10).

Though hundreds of scholarly articles have been published on *Daubert* (Caudill & Redding, 2000), there are only a few empirical studies of its impact on judicial decision making. These studies indicate that *Daubert*'s impact on psychological and psychiatric evidence has been minimal. Dahir, Richardson, Ginsburg, Gatowski, and Dobbin (2005) observe, "One reason that psychology is still considered part of the 'soft sciences' is that judges seldom hold the discipline to the same rigorous methodological standards as the 'hard sciences,' " (p. 78) and *Daubert* will not have an impact until judges do so. A national survey of state trial court judges found that 38% considered clinical testimony from psychologists to be scientific evidence, whereas 64% considered testimony about psychological research studies to be scientific evidence (economic evidence, in contrast, was considered scientific by only 17% of judges; Gatowski et al., 2001).

In criminal cases particularly, *Daubert* has had little impact. An analysis of all published federal criminal cases between 1993 and 2000 found only 75 cases of *Daubert* challenges to the admissibility of behavioral science testimony. There were, for example, only two cases dealing with competence to stand trial and only four with criminal responsibility issues (Fradella et al., 2003). The percentage of federal civil cases in which judges conducted a reliability assessment of proffered social and behavioral science evidence increased substantially between 1991 and 1993 (when *Daubert* was decided) and 1999, as did the percentage of cases in which such evidence was found to be unreliable and thus inadmissible (Dixon & Gill, 2002; Krafka et al., 2002). Yet, in most cases, federal judges did not apply *Daubert* in judging the admissibility of scientific evidence, but rather, most often excluded evidence on the basis of its relevance and helpfulness or the expert's qualifications (Krafka et al., 2002).

If *Daubert* has had an appreciable impact on the admissibility of mental health evidence, it should be most apparent vis-à-vis syndromal evidence, which often is novel and rests on a shaky scientific foundation (Dahir et al., 2005). However, Dahir et al. found that *Daubert*'s impact was "negligible" in this area, and that state trial judges instead tended to rely on the expert's qualifications and the *Frye* general acceptance standard. Judges reported that they usually admitted syndrome evidence, and that evidence about Posttraumatic Stress Disorder, Battered Woman Syndrome, and Child Sex Abuse Accommodation Syndrome was the most frequent type of syndromal testimony heard.

In addition to the *Daubert* factors, many judges consider the clarity and coherence of the expert's evidence to be an important consideration in assessing its reliability (Dixon & Gill, 2002). According to Dixon and Gill's study of federal civil cases, in some cases judges found evidence unreliable even when it was generally accepted in the scientific community (and thus would have been admitted under the *Frye* test), but lack of general acceptance frequently resulted in findings of inadmissibility. Other studies, whether based on vignette methodology (Dahir et al., 2005) or a review of case opinions (Fradella et al., 2003), have also found that judges put great weight on whether the proffered science has been "generally accepted in the scientific community," with publication in peer-reviewed journals relevant to this question (Fradella et al., 2003).

"Brave New World": Judicial Application of *Daubert*

In the wake of *Daubert,* judges expressed concern about their ability to function as gatekeepers for scientific evidence. After the U.S. Supreme Court remanded *Daubert* back to the 9th Circuit Court of Appeals, in a section of the opinion titled "Brave New World," Judge Kozinski noted:

> Though we are largely untrained in science and certainly no match for any of the witnesses whose testimony we are reviewing, it is our responsibility to determine whether those ex-

perts' proposed testimony amounts to "scientific knowledge," constitutes "good science," and was "derived by the scientific method" . . . we take a deep breath and proceed with this heady task. (*Daubert v. Merrell Dow Pharmaceuticals,* 1995, pp. 1315–1316).

Gatowski and colleagues' (2001) national survey of state trial court judges has become the seminal assessment of judges' understanding of how to apply *Daubert.* The study found that only 4% to 5% of judges understood the meaning of the scientific concepts of falsifiability and error rates or how to determine these factors, though most well understood the concepts of general acceptance and peer-reviewed publication. Judges emphasized the general acceptance factor when making admissibility decisions, suggesting that they still continued to conduct a *Frye*-type analysis of admissibility. "The extent to which judges understand and can properly apply the [*Daubert*] criteria when assessing the validity and reliability of proffered scientific evidence was questionable at best," suggesting serious "limitations in the judiciary's understanding of science" (pp. 452–453). Only about half of the judges believed that they had adequate knowledge about scientific methodology and evidence.

Indeed, judges generally have little or no training in science (Redding & Reppucci, 1998), and few judges understand even basic statistical concepts (Manuto & O'Rourke, 1991). Kovera and McAuliff (2000) examined judges' ability to ascertain the methodological quality of proffered social psychological research. They used vignette methodology to vary whether the research had been subjected to peer review and whether it had serious methodological flaws (i.e., no control group, a confound, use of a nonblind confederate). Judges' evaluations of the quality of the studies did not vary as a function of whether the studies contained such flaws or had been published in peer-reviewed journals, nor did their judgments about whether to admit the studies into evidence.

Taken together, the clear implication from these studies is that judges need education in scientific reasoning and methodology, perhaps through judicial training and continuing legal education programs (Merlino, Dillehay, Dahir, & Maxwell, 2003). The Federal Judicial Center's (2000) *Reference Manual on Scientific Evidence* and other publications designed for judges (e.g., Dobbin & Gatowski, 1999) also play an important educational function.

Calling *Daubert* "the dawn of law's scientific age," Faigman and Monahan (2005, p. 631) observe that "*Daubert* unequivocally endorses empirically validated" assessment, diagnostic, and treatment approaches and evidence-based practices. "Whatever clinical value invalidated psychological assessment or treatment techniques may or may not have for patients, *Daubert* makes plain that testimony employing such techniques has no place on the witness stand" (p. 656). Yet it seems that judges have not fully responded to *Daubert*'s clarion call. Clinical testimony rarely is subjected to *Daubert*'s demand for scientifically valid evidence (Shuman & Sales, 1999; Slobogin, 1998), despite the questions one could ask about its scientific foundation: Does research support the clinician's conclusions? Did he or she use standardized and validated testing instruments for the purposes for which they were designed? What are the error rates for such instruments and for the type of diagnoses provided (Shuman & Sales, 1999)? Some commentators have suggested that a rigorous application of *Daubert* would exclude much clinical testimony due to a lack of reliability. Slobogin (1998), for example, points to research showing the relative unreliability of psychiatric diagnoses (with an interclinician agreement of only 50% for mood disorders, 41% for Schizophrenia, 37% for organic disorders, and 1% to 49% for personality disorders).

Implications for Expert Testimony

Sometimes, judges fail to listen to relevant scientific evidence or to distinguish between expert testimony that is scientifically versus non-scientifically based (A. M. Goldstein, Thomson, Redding, & Osman, 2003), and they tend not to scrutinize mental health testimony to the same extent as other kinds of expert evidence (Dahir et al., 2005). Judges do, however, conduct more searching reviews when attorneys vigorously challenge the admissibility of the evidence (Dixon & Gill, 2002; Krafka et al., 2002). What can experts and litigants do to encourage judges to properly fulfill their gatekeeping role under *Daubert*?

First, experts should bring to the court's attention the underlying scientific foundation (or lack thereof) of proffered testimony. Urge the court to examine whether the expert's conclusions reliably follow from the underlying science and methodology (Caudill & Redding, 2000). Ensure that the court requires the opposing expert to reveal the basis for his or her opinions, including whether or not any data or research were relied on, as required by most states' evidentiary rules and the Federal Rule of Civil Procedure 26 (1)(2) (2005). Second, because many judges fail to appreciate the scientific nature of clinical testimony and psychological or psychiatric research generally, believing instead that it is overly subjective and not "true science" (Gatowski et al., 2001; Redding & Reppucci, 1999), it is helpful to detail the ways the proffered evidence or the science underlying it conforms to the criteria of good science: how it represents the scientific method. Third, although *Daubert* contemplates that judges routinely will apply the *Daubert* test each time they make decisions about whether to admit scientific evidence, in practice judges may not conduct a *Daubert* review unless a litigant explicitly raises a "*Daubert* challenge" to the proffered evidence. This is particularly true in criminal cases and with clinical testimony, in which litigants rarely raise *Daubert* challenges. Fourth, experts should establish the scientific reliability and validity of their testimony by describing the proffered evidence in relation to each of the four *Daubert* factors.

JUDICIAL DECISION MAKING IN CRIMINAL CASES

In criminal cases, juries are almost always the finders of fact. But, in addition to making important evidentiary rulings, trial court judges make determinations about defendants' competency to stand trial and often determine the sentence to be imposed.

Competency to Stand Trial Determinations

With about 600,000 evaluations performed each year (Bonnie & Grisso, 2000), competency to stand trial (CST) evaluations are the most common forensic evaluations considered by criminal court judges. The available research suggests that forensic mental health professionals exert tremendous influence on judges' CST determinations. The determination of trial competence is a legal rather than a clinical decision, and the court is not obliged to concur with the evaluating clinician. Nonetheless, courts usually defer to the experts. Recently, Zapf, Hubbard, Galloway, Cox, and Ronan (2004) reported that in all but one of 328 Alabama cases, the court accepted the mental health professional's opinion (a 99.6% agreement rate between courts and experts). Other estimates of expert-court agreement show that judges' decisions concur with the clinical assessment in at least 90% of cases (Cruise & Rogers, 1998; Hart & Hare, 1992).

Such agreement or deference raises concern among some commentators. Winick (1995) argues that CST determinations are too rarely a legal decision and too often "a highly discretionary exercise in clinical judgment" (p. 620). He cautions that "decision-making . . . is effectively delegated to clinical evaluators making low-visibility and essentially unreviewed decisions pursuant to a vague, open-textured standard" (p. 620). Zapf and colleagues (2004) warned that the courts rely too heavily on expert opinions and that such reliance demands the highest standards of practice from clinicians who conduct these evaluations. Judges and attorneys complain that competency evaluations often fail to provide sufficient information about the factual basis for the evaluator's findings and opinions, and do not provide enough information about the defendant's functional capacities to understand the legal proceedings and consult with his or her attorney (LaFortune & Nicholson, 1995).

Sentencing Decisions

Summarizing the extant research, Melton et al. (1997) concluded:

> The impact of clinical opinion is insignificant in many cases. . . . Although a high concordance rate between psychiatric recommendations and court disposition has been found in many studies, it seems to reflect the influence of nonclinical factors on the clinician rather than the effect of *clinical* factors on the judge. Further, a second group of studies that focused on the effect of clinical factors found a relatively low concordance rate. (p. 269)

A decade later, little has changed. If anything, forensic opinion is even less influential on sentencing decisions in an era of offense-based determinate sentencing as well as punitive "get tough" policies toward offenders. (For a discussion of the role of forensic health experts in federal sentencing assessments, see Chapter 14.)

The seriousness of the offense and prior criminal history are the strongest predictors of sentencing decisions, as these factors are relied on to gauge the offender's level of responsibility and likelihood of recidivism. But judges' sentencing goals and philosophy also appear to strongly influence sentencing decisions, which may account for the documented wide disparities between judges' sentencing decisions in actual as well as simulated cases (Lurigio, Carroll, & Stalans, 1994). A judge's sentencing philosophy is, in turn, driven by his or her attitudes toward punishment, rehabilitation, and the causes of crime (Lurigio et al., 1994; McFatter, 1978), with politically conservative judges tending to impose lengthier sentences (Huang, Finn, Ruback, & Friedmann, 1996).

Drawing on empirical and theoretical research, Lurigio et al. (1994) suggest that judges decide cases by constructing a narrative of the case, and that their story construction is driven by attempts to fit case facts into their preexisting conceptualizations of typical offense and offender characteristics:

> Differences [in sentences] result from variations in the kinds of stories judges prefer: retribution-oriented judges may concern themselves with the story of the crime, and perhaps proceed to construct a narrative about the offender's criminal history, but they are unlikely to construct a story of the offender's life as a rehabilitation oriented judge would be likely to do. (p. 107)

Consider, for example, Palys and Divorski's (1984) study of Canadian magistrates' sentencing decisions in a hypothetical case:

> At one extreme, we have those who saw a belligerent drunk who, without provocation, initiated an assault and caused permanent injury to his innocent victim. Protection of the public and general deterrence were salient legal objectives, and a substantial incarceration was warranted. But, at the other extreme we have a second group of judges who saw an employed individual, one with no prior record and pitiable social background, who got involved in a fight in a bar. . . . The legal objectives must be supervision and rehabilitation, and they should be accomplished without causing the offender to lose a job. (p. 339, quoted in Lurigio et al., 1994, p. 101)

McFatter's (1978) experimental study demonstrated that a retributive approach to sentencing produces more severe sentences than a rehabilitative orientation. Moreover, attributing criminal behavior to offenders' stable, internal traits results in more severe sentences than attributions based on external or transient factors (Ewart & Pennington, 1987).

JUDICIAL DECISION MAKING IN JUVENILE COURT

Judicial decision making is particularly significant in the juvenile court, where judges adjudicate "guilt" or innocence and have wide discretion in determining the disposition. In many states, juvenile court judges also decide, in particular cases, whether a serious or violent juvenile offender will be transferred from the juvenile court for trial and sentencing in adult criminal court (Redding & Mrozoski, 2005).

Dispositional Decisions

Research shows that the seriousness of the offense, prior record, and age of the offender are among the strongest factors influencing the severity of the disposition imposed (Campbell & Schmidt, 2000; Elrod & Ryder, 1999; Hoge, Andrews, & Leschied, 1995). Other important factors considered by judges include whether the parents will supervise the juvenile and participate in his or her rehabilitation, the level of family dysfunction, and whether the juvenile is attending school (Campbell & Schmidt, 2000; Horwitz & Wasserman, 1980; Sanborn, 1996).

One recent study investigated the ways that juvenile defendant characteristics described in a psychological evaluation influence judicial decisions (McCoy, Murrie, & Cornell, 2005). Juvenile court judges were sent a mock psychological evaluation that described a young defendant facing assault charges under ambiguous circumstances. Multiple versions of the evaluation vignette allowed for experimental manipulations that varied the youth's (a) history of antisocial behaviors (minimal versus substantial), (b) personality characteristics (psychopathy-like or not psychopathy-like), and (c) diagnostic label (psychopathy, conduct disorder, or no diagnosis). The 143 participating judges then responded to questions regarding the sanctions they would impose and their expectations about the youth's future behavior. Participants were most influenced by whether the defendant demonstrated a substantial, versus minimal, history of antisocial behavior. Antisocial behavior history influenced 5 of the 10 outcome variables and yielded more substantial effects than did the other experimentally manipulated variables. The impact of psychopathic personality traits—such as dishonesty, remorselessness, and manipulativeness—appeared less substantial, influencing only a few of the outcome variables. Finally, diagnostic labels appeared to exert very little influence on judicial decisions, except that judges rated youth diagnosed with Conduct Disorder, as opposed to youth with no diagnosis or a psychopathy diagnosis, as more likely to be a criminal when an adult. The results suggest that when judges make sentencing decisions or form opinions about a youth's future behavior, they are more likely to be influenced by that youth's prior behavior, particularly documented criminal behavior. They appear less influenced by those factors commonly addressed in mental health evaluations, such as personality descriptions and clinical diagnostic labels (McCoy et al., 2005).

These findings are consistent with several other studies suggesting that many juvenile court judges give little weight to mental health factors in fashioning dispositions, but rather focus on the seriousness of the offense and the juvenile's offending history and dangerousness (Brannen et al., 2005; Campbell & Schmidt, 2000). This indicates that more needs to be done to educate judges and juvenile justice personnel about the role of mental disorders as risk factors for delinquency and their amenability to treatment.

In addition, judges' dispositional decision making is likely influenced by judicial philosophies toward juvenile offenders and the availability of local resources. This is illustrated by Mulvey and Reppucci's (1988) study, which found that mental health and juvenile court workers' judgments about juvenile offenders' amenability to treatment, and the likely effectiveness of those treatments, varied according to the level of resources locally available.

Transfer Decisions

Transfer laws, which allow the transfer of juveniles from the juvenile court for trial and sentencing in adult criminal court, exist in every state. In many states, juveniles of a minimum age who commit certain offenses are, by statute, automatically tried as adults, but in these states as well, judges have discretion (under so-called judicial transfer statutes) to decide whether to transfer the juvenile to criminal court (Redding & Mrozoski, 2005). Judicial transfer statutes typically list a number of factors for the judge to consider: (a) the offender's treatment needs and amenability, (b) risk assessment of the likelihood of future offending, (c) offender's sophistication-maturity, (d) presence of mental retardation or mental illness, and (e) offense characteristics. (See Grisso, 2003, for a thorough discussion of evaluating juveniles for transfer to the adult court.)

Studies have consistently found that the juvenile's age, the seriousness of the offense, the prior record, and the number of prior property offenses are the most significant predictors of judicial transfer decisions (Redding & Mrozoski, 2005).

Brannen et al. (2005) surveyed 361 juvenile court judges using a hypothetical case that varied the juvenile's treatment amenability, maturity, and level of dangerousness. Dangerousness and maturity significantly affected judges transfer decisions, but treatment amenability had no effect.

In another recent study, Hensl and Redding (2005) used vignette methodology and an attitudinal questionnaire to examine juvenile court judges' transfer decisions as a function of their attitudes about transfer, deterrence, and rehabilitation and juvenile offender characteristics (immature juvenile offender, socialized juvenile offender, and mature delinquent juvenile offender; see DiCataldo & Grisso, 1995). As expected, judges were more likely to transfer the mature delinquent juvenile offender (characterized by autonomous and adultlike traits, prior court contacts, minimal motivations, and less amenability to treatment) than the immature or socialized offender. But more experienced judges and those who were knowledgeable about the ineffectiveness of transfer as a deterrent were significantly less likely to recommend transfer. (Not surprisingly, politically conservative judges were more likely to have positive attitudes toward transfer and negative attitudes toward rehabilitation.) These findings suggest that educating judges about the counterdeterrent effects of transfer may reduce the number of cases transferred to adult court.

JUDICIAL DECISION MAKING IN CIVIL CASES

Researchers have explored those factors that influence judicial decisions in several types of civil cases, including civil commitment to psychiatric hospitals (e.g., Bursztajn, Hamm, & Gutheil, 1997) and sexual harassment litigation (e.g., Kulik, Perry, & Pepper, 2003). Scholars have also speculated about the potential for judicial bias in many types of civil cases, such as termination of parental rights (e.g., Azar & Benjet, 1994). However, most of the research in civil contexts has examined judicial decision making in child custody cases.

Child Custody

Even when examining idiosyncratic cases, judges make their decisions in the context of broader legal doctrines and an even broader sociocultural context. These macrolevel influences on judicial decision making have been particularly clear in child custody cases.

Evolution of Legal Standards

Throughout the 1700s and much of the 1800s, judges routinely awarded custody of children to their father, given that children were considered to be property and property rights were limited to males (Mason, 1994; Mercer, 1997; Otto, Buffington-Vollum, & Edens, 2003; Sorenson & Goldman, 1990). By the late 1880s, after most legal standards allowed women to own property, courts began to award custody to mothers in what became known as the "tender years doctrine." According to this doctrine, preadolescent children were best served by mothers, who were presumed to be more naturally suited to provide nurturing support

(Hall, Pulver, & Cooley, 1996; Mason & Quirk, 1997; O'Donahue & Bradley, 1999; Sorenson & Goldman, 1990).

During the 1960s and 1970s, the tender years presumption waned in influence as courts increasingly adopted the best interests of the child standard, which emphasized the need for a case-specific analysis of parent capacities and child needs (Mason & Quirk, 1997). Although some current standards still allow for some maternal preference in the case of very young children (Hall et al., 1996) or in cases wherein parents appear equal in all respects other than sex, most states have explicitly rejected any default assumption in favor of the mother (Mason & Quirk, 1997). However, some observers argue that a de facto maternal preference remains influential even if a de jure maternal preference does not. Some scholars emphasize that sole paternal custody is rarely awarded (< 10% of cases) because most judges act on an implicit bias in favor of mothers (Jennison, 1991). Survey research (Stamps, 2002) also suggests that at least some judges maintain default assumptions that favor mothers over fathers as caretakers.

Although the best interests standard dates back to the mid-1920s (*Finlay v. Finlay*, 1925), it gained widespread influence only 5 to 6 decades later. In books that "profoundly affected legal decision making" (Weisz, 1999, p. 330), J. Goldstein and colleagues (e.g., J. Goldstein, Freud, & Solnit, 1973; see J. Goldstein, Solnit, Goldstein, & Freud, 1996, for a compilation) popularized several principles for identifying the child's best interests during decisions about child custody and placement. The first concept was the "psychological parent," or parent with whom the child had the strongest emotional connection; presumably, a continued relationship with the psychological parent would provide the greatest stability and best serve the child's interest. Later work emphasized the concept of the "least detrimental alternative," a concession that although neither parent may be considered the "best" for the child, one option was probably better than the other.

Although the best interests standard has clearly been influential on state statutes and the practice of judges (Hall et al., 1996), more recent scholars have argued that the standard is so ambiguous and free of any clear empirical basis (Mercer, 1997; O'Donahue & Bradley, 1999; Weisz, 1999) that it leaves considerable room for the idiosyncrasies or biases of individual judges to intrude. Chambers (1984) summarized, "The concept of 'children's best interests,' unlike such concepts as distance and mass, has no objective content. Whenever the word 'best' is used, one must always ask 'according to whom?'" (p. 488). Because the best interests standard offers judges substantial discretion, with minimal concrete guidance, it becomes important to examine systematically what factors influence judicial decision making in child custody cases.

Contemporary Judicial Decision Making

Of the divorces that involve children, relatively few are contested in court (Mason, 1994; Reppucci, 1984). However, these contested cases are high-stakes proceedings in which judges must consider the complex interplay of factors involving several individuals and arrive at a decision that will significantly affect the lives of each of them. Research has consistently identified several factors that appear to most influence judges as they make these weighty decisions.

Child preferences are one of the factors most consistently identified as influential to judges. Several early studies suggested a positive relationship between a child's age and the likelihood that a judge would seek and consider the child's wishes regarding the custody decision (Lombard, 1984; Scott, Reppucci, & Aber, 1988; Settle & Lowery, 1982). As Crosby-Currie (1996) summarized, "Overall, the literature suggests that at about 6 to 8 years of age, children are sometimes involved, and at about 12 to 14 years of age, children are almost always involved" (p. 292). Crosby-Currie surveyed 105 judges to ask specifically about child involvement in custody decisions. Although results varied some by jurisdiction, it was clear that judges rarely sought the input of very young (under age 8) children but routinely sought input from teenagers. Similarly, in an earlier study, virtually all of the participating judges reported soliciting information from children over age 14, but fewer solicited input from younger children (Scott et al., 1988).

Not only do judges seek input from children, but they apparently tend to decide cases in a manner congruent with such input. Kunin, Ebbesen, and Konecni (1992) reviewed court records from 282 disputed child custody cases near San Diego, California. After generating statistical models for the data, they reported that the child's stated preference was one of two broad factors that influenced most of the judicial decisions.

More recently, Wallace and Koerner (2003) conducted one of the only studies that employed direct face-to-face interviews with judges to investigate the factors they consider when deciding child custody cases. Researchers used a semistructured interview procedure to query 18 family court judges in Arizona; the researchers then summarized judges' responses using a content analysis procedure. Nearly all judges in the study cited a child's age or developmental level as a key factor in making custody decisions about that child. In terms of *how* they considered age, most judges reported that the older the child, the more they allowed the child's preferences to influence their decisions about custody and visitation arrangements. Similarly, almost all (99%) of the judges in the Crosby-Currie (1996) survey reported that the degree of weight they assigned to a child's preferences depended on that child's apparent maturity.

Overall, results of judicial surveys, as well as post hoc analysis of case files, suggest that child preferences, at least as expressed by older children, are one of the more influential factors for judges hearing contested custody cases.

Parental factors would certainly seem relevant to most custody decisions, and research demonstrates these are influential to judges, at least to some extent. In the Wallace and Koerner (2003) study, judges described considering certain parental factors in their custody decisions. Half of the judges reported some attempts to gauge the parent's potential to meet the child's needs, a process one judge described as examining whether a parent "is in tune with the child's emotional well-being" (p. 184). Half of the participating judges also described examining parental alienation—a pattern of one parent limiting a child's opportunity for relationship with the other parent—and leaning toward awarding custody to the alienated parent in such cases.

Not surprisingly, judges who participated in the interviews (Wallace & Koerner, 2003) also described a strong interest in "parental fitness," that is, restricting the custody rights of parents who manifested clear impairment (e.g., substance abuse) or grossly harmful parenting (e.g., physical abuse or neglect). On the other hand, this finding does not seem to hold true for all judges. When Sorenson and colleagues (1997) studied 60 Florida cases, they reported a few parental factors that, to their surprise, appeared not to influence judges' decisions. Neither parental substance abuse nor substantial parental conflict appeared to play any role in judicial decisions. That is, neither factor made a parent less likely to receive custody of the child, despite the likely implications these factors may have for child development. Although quantifiable data are less readily available, at least one qualitative survey suggested that judges may be influenced by a parent's sexual orientation, leaving lesbian mothers at a disadvantage in child custody proceedings (Duran-Aydintug & Causey, 1996).

Though not a parental factor per se, some judges appear to consider how well a parent can provide stability to the child. In one study (Wallace & Koerner, 2003), most (11 of 18) judges described stability as a key factor in their decisions. They described attempts to preserve as much consistency as possible in terms of the child's living arrangements, school attendance, and contact with siblings.

Allegations of child maltreatment often emerge in contested child custody cases. How do such allegations influence judicial decisions? Sorenson et al. (1995) examined 60 contested custody cases in Florida courts to investigate whether allegations of maltreatment or substance abuse may influence the custody decisions judges made. The authors collected data via guardian ad litem workers, volunteers assigned to advocate for children during court proceedings. The study examined the presence or absence of substantiated or unsubstantiated reports of alcohol or drug abuse, spousal abuse (physical or emotional), child abuse (physical, emotional, or sexual), and child neglect. The authors classified a parent as "unfit" if there were substantiated reports of child abuse or neglect or spousal abuse. Parents were classified as "suspected unfit" if there were only unsubstantiated allegations of such behaviors.

Although allegations of abuse were fairly common, occurring in 83% of cases (Sorenson et al., 1995), the data were not sufficient to compare the relative impact of different types of allegations (e.g., child sexual abuse versus child neglect versus spousal abuse) on judicial decision making. One fairly clear-cut finding did emerge, however. Judges much more often awarded primary physical custody to the parent against whom no allegations had been levied. But when allegations had been made against both parties of a divorce proceeding, the court tended to assign primary physical custody at approximately equal rates between mothers (48%) and fathers (52%). Also, in contrast to the findings regarding primary physical residence, there was no discernable relationship between suspected parental unfitness and the decision to award joint legal custody versus sole legal custody. Results of the Sorenson et al. study should be interpreted with caution, given that they are based on only 60 custody cases, all drawn from a single state. Nevertheless, the results are noteworthy as they suggest that judges who are making decisions about a child's residence tend to be at least somewhat responsive to allegations of abuse, *even when such allegations have not been substantiated,* and that the influence of abuse allegations appeared limited to decisions about primary physical residence and did not extend to decisions about sole legal custody versus joint custody.

Mental health evaluations in child custody cases have become increasingly common (Bow & Quinnell, 2001; Mason & Quirk, 1997), and several studies have provided data on the ways judges use these evaluations in their decision making. For example, in their review of 282 disputed child custody cases, Kunin et al. (1992) analyzed predictors of judicial decisions and found that of only two factors that influenced judicial decisions, one was the recommendation of a court-appointed counselor (the other, as described previously, was the child's stated preference regarding placement).

Almost all (17 of 18) of the participant judges in Wallace and Koerner's (2003) interviews reported that they considered, and could be influenced by, a report produced by a mental health expert or guardian ad litem. They appreciated the integrated information regarding a child's background, home life, and relationships with parents, and they valued a presumably objective third-party opinion that might verify or refute allegations by parents. Yet most of these judges also emphasized that they did not reflexively accept all opinions in these third-party reports. Rather, they gave weight to these reports depending on the apparent quality and thoroughness of the evaluation, including whether the evaluator had directly spoken with the children.

Similarly, in one study of 97 midwestern judges (Waller & Daniel, 2004), respondents tended to endorse, with moderate support, statements indicating that mental health evaluations were useful or influential in their decision making. However, as in other studies (Felner, Rowlison, Farber, Primavera, & Bishop, 1987; Pearson & Ring, 1982), it appeared that judges were active consumers of evaluation reports and that the extent to which they were influenced was related to report quality.

What else does research reveal about judicial use of child custody evaluations? Judges clearly consider more influential those evaluations that involved all relevant parties, including both parents and all affected children (Waller & Daniel, 2004). Similarly, judges place more confidence in those evaluations conducted by a court-appointed evaluator (or an evaluator that both opposing attorneys choose cooperatively) as compared to evaluators retained by one side only (Reidy, Silver, & Carlson, 1989). Indeed, at least some judges appear to view skeptically any evaluator retained by only one side and expect such an evaluator to offer only a biased, partisan opinion (Waller & Daniel, 2004).

Judges appear to be fairly savvy consumers of psychological reports, in that they express preferences that are similar to practice standards among mental health professionals (e.g., Ackerman & Ackerman, 1997; American Academy of Child and Adolescent Psychiatry, 1997; APA, 1994). For example, judges rated as desirable standard evaluation components such as child, parent, and collateral interviews; assessment of the parent-child relationship; and a parenting skills assessment (Waller & Daniel, 2004). Similarly, judges expect evaluators to have observed the children in question, reviewed their records (school, medical, and mental health), performed psychological testing, and consulted with the appropriate guardian ad litem (Ackerman, 2002).

When do judges actively pursue input from a mental health professional to aid decision making? In the study of Missouri judges (Waller & Daniel, 2004), respondents reported that they were particularly inclined to request a mental health evaluation in cases that involved allegations of physical abuse, sexual abuse, or neglect. They were also inclined to seek evaluations when issues of parental fitness (i.e., parental illness, alcoholism, unstable lifestyle) arose. Of course, in some cases, a mental health evaluation serves less to inform or influence judicial decisions than as a bargaining chip that facilitates a resolution before proceedings progress to the point of litigation (see Ash & Guyer, 1986, for a description of this model).

Finally, although judges report giving some consideration to expert testimony in child custody cases, there is less evidence to suggest that judges explicitly consider the social science research related to parenting or divorce that (presumably) underlies the expert testimony. Some early survey research (Felner et al., 1987) revealed that very few judges or attorneys considered social science data as relevant to their on-the-job decisions. In their comprehensive review of appellate cases, Mason and Quirk (1997) noted that despite the "outpouring of psychological research" between 1960 and 1995, they could locate no cases during this period in which a judge "referred to a social science or psychological study per se as a basis for a custody decision" (p. 234).

The absence of social science research in judges' written opinions suggests some ambiguity regarding how much weight expert testimony offered in child custody cases actually carries. A skeptical perspective regarding the impact of expert testimony on judicial decision making might argue that, despite the frequent use of experts, surveyed judges rarely identify expert testimony as *the deciding factor* in a case, and empirical comparisons reveal little difference in outcomes when comparing those cases with, versus those cases without, experts (Mason & Quirk, 1997). Nevertheless, it is clear that mental health professionals continue to play a substantive role in many child custody disputes (Mason & Quirk, 1997).

In summary, the research on judicial decision making in child custody cases suggests that most judges are likely to integrate several key factors in making their decisions. Judges apparently consider the expressed preferences of the children involved in the divorce, and they weight these preferences according to the age and apparent maturity of the children. Not surprisingly, judges also consider factors related to the parents. Many make efforts to identify whether a parent is obviously unfit, and some judges also appear to gauge more subtle factors, such as the degree to which a parent can provide stability and tend to a child's emotional needs. Some research suggests that even unsubstantiated allegations related to these parental factors may influence judicial decisions. Finally, most judges appear to consider input from mental health professionals, usually in the form of written evaluations or expert testimony. However, few judges admitted to reflexively following the evaluator's advice. Instead, judges report that they are active consumers of mental health testimony, gauging the quality of such input and comparing it with other available data.

Temporary Placement of Children

Of course, judges make decisions about child placement not only in the context of divorce litigation, but in cases where physical danger or harmful parenting practices may warrant alternative living arrangements for children, regardless of the parental relationship. Far less research has explored how judges approach these decisions relative to child custody decisions in divorce cases.

In making custody decisions for abused or neglected children, one factor that appears to strongly influence judicial decisions is whether or not parents comply with court directives intended to remediate poor parenting practices. For example, in a 4-year prospective study of 206 severely maltreated Boston children (Jellinek et al., 1992), a judge terminated parental custody in 97% of the cases in which parents failed to comply with court recommendations. On the other hand, in 67% of the cases in which parents complied, the court returned the children to the parents.

Do judges consider child placement decisions in a manner similar to other professionals? Britner and Mossler (2002) surveyed various professional groups, including judges, asking them to rate the influence of several different factors in their decision about placement for an abused child. Even when considering the same hypothetical case, different professional groups demonstrated different patterns of prioritizing and acting on case information. Mental health professionals tended to focus on the severity or nature of abuse, services offered in the past, and parental response to services. In contrast, judges tended to consider a child's ability to recount the abuse and focused heavily on estimates of the likelihood of recurring abuse. Overall, when selecting from a list of potentially relevant variables, judges reported considering fewer of these variables to be important. Compared to mental health professionals, judges were less likely to consider parents' cognitive abilities or the duration of abuse.

In a very different approach to researching the same topic, Ballou et al. (2001) conducted focus-group research with judges to identify areas in which they need assistance in decision making. Two family and probate judges identified a need for a set of guidelines to think through, under intense time pressure, emergency placement decisions for maltreated children. Through "action-oriented research"—a process of considering empirical literature, input from key professionals and focus groups, and repeated revisions—the interdisciplinary group developed a list of six critical domains that judges should consider in determining whether a child should be placed outside the immediate family in emergency placement situations: (1) caretaker's history of behavior with child(ren) in question, (2) caretaker's history of violence and criminality, (3) presence of substance abuse, (4) presence of mental illness, (5) caretaker's coping skills and parenting ability, and (6) other concerns, including child's school adjustment and child's wishes. The study authors emphasized that these were not necessarily normative factors that judges currently *do* consider. Rather, the list generated by multiple experts and stakeholders identified these as factors that judges *should* consider in making decisions.

Civil Commitment

All states have civil commitment laws allowing, under certain circumstances, involuntary hospitalization of mentally disordered individuals (see Chapter 10). Yet mental disorder and a clear need for treatment are not, by themselves, sufficient to warrant involuntary hospitalization (*O'Connor v. Donaldson,* 1975). Rather, civil commitment is defensible only for those whose mental disorder leaves them so impaired as to be a danger to themselves or others or unable to adequately care for themselves; they must need treatment that is unavailable in settings less restrictive than a psychiatric hospital (Murrie & Redding, in press).

Scholars (e.g., Parry, 1994) have described a number of perspectives that can shape case-level and policy-level decisions about civil commitment. Some (Bursztajn, Gutheil, Mills, Hamm, & Brodsky, 1986; Bursztajn et al., 1997; see Chapter 10) have examined judicial decision making about civil commitment as falling along a spectrum ranging from a "police powers" doctrine (i.e., intervening for public safety through preventive detention of those who are potentially dangerous) to a *parens patriae* perspective (intervening for the well-being of those who are incapable of looking after their own best interests). The very limited research available suggests that judges' decisions in civil commitment cases are based on a rationale that is more consistent with a parens patriae as opposed to a police powers perspective.

One early study (Bursztajn et al., 1986) relied on five Massachusetts judges who completed a questionnaire after each civil commitment case they handled, for a total of 35 questionnaires. Based on judge's responses to the 26-topic questionnaire, the authors summarized, "In general, factors having to do with compliance were more influential than those having to do with dangerousness, despite the centrality of dangerousness in the legal code" (pp. 171–172). That is, judges reported considering some practical issues that were not explicitly delineated in the statute, such as whether the patient would reliably adhere to outpatient services. The authors also emphasized the findings that nearly all proceedings resulted in commitments; in no cases did a judge directly deny a psychiatrist's petition for commitment (although judges granted continuances in a few cases). Thus, the authors speculated that either judges were highly influenced by psychiatrists' recommendations, that psychiatrists were highly conservative in petitioning only clear-cut cases that they anticipated the judge would support, or some combination thereof.

In a follow-up study employing a different methodology (Bursztajn et al., 1997), the authors studied only one judge. To compare parens patriae versus police powers considerations, they asked this judge to rate the importance of 26 features in his decision making on 26 civil commitment cases. However, the authors also compared these self-ratings to a statistical model using the same variables to predict the judge's decision, and again found that parens patriae (e.g., a patient's inability to care for self or the patient's propensity for suicide) were more influential than dangerousness-related considerations. The participating judge also rated as influential several factors that were not explicitly defined by statute: the apparent credibility of the psychiatric expert witness, the wishes of the patient's family, and the patient's apparent competence, predictability, and reliability as an outpatient.

Overall, given the extremely small and nonrepresentative samples—five Massachusetts judges in the Bursztajn et al. (1986) study; one Colorado judge in the Bursztajn et al. (1997) study—results from these studies are best considered anecdotal. However, they suggest that "judges use many factors in their decision-making process rather than limiting themselves to the explicit statutory variables (the 'black letter of the law')" (Bursztajn et al., 1997, p. 80).

More recently, Monahan and Silver (2003) surveyed 26 judges about the level of risk at which they would decide to commit someone based on the danger to others standard for civil commitment. On average, judges chose a risk level representing a .26 likelihood of committing a violent act (Level 3 in the MacArthur Violence Risk

Assessment Study) as the decision threshold for ordering short-term civil commitment. There was, however, considerable variability among judges.

Despite these studies examining judicial decision making in hypothetical cases, judicial decisions in actual cases often amount to little more than a rubber stamp of the expert's commitment recommendation, with judges deferring almost entirely to the opinion of mental health professionals. Civil commitment hearings are frequently conducted in a perfunctory manner, and seldom do hearings result in a disposition other than commitment (Bursztajn et al., 1986; Redding, 1993; Schopp, Scalora, & Pearce, 1999).

CONCLUSION

Although there is a substantial body of research on jury decision making, there is a dearth of research on judicial decision making, despite the key role judges play in deciding a variety of issues in criminal and civil cases. If "judicial decision making represents social science in action" (Wisdom, 1975, p. 148), then we must pay far more attention to the psychology of judicial decision making. In particular, research is needed on how mental health experts can most effectively communicate relevant research and clinical-forensic evidence to courts in ways that will maximize effective judicial gatekeeping under *Daubert*. We need research on how judges use and evaluate mental health evidence in criminal sentencing, as well as in dispositional and transfer decision making in the juvenile court. In the civil context, research is needed on how judges consider mental health evidence in child custody and placement decision making, but even more so with respect to guardianship, conservatorship, and competency to consent to medical treatment, areas wholly lacking empirical research.

The limited extant research does, however, indicate the need for judicial education on scientific methodology, and in particular, the potential relevance and value of nomothetic research as social framework evidence in adjudicating individual cases. Moreover, studies suggest that *Daubert* has had little impact on judges' decisions about the admissibility of mental health and social science evidence and that judges apparently do not scrutinize mental health evidence to the same extent as other types of scientific evidence. Some have argued that courts should "hold [psychology] to the same rigorous methodological standards as the 'hard sciences'" (Dahir et al., 2005, p. 78). In any case, experts should take care to convey to judges the scientific foundations of their testimony and opinions, or the lack thereof in opposing testimony. It is clear that mental health professionals must, "in the dawn of law's scientific age" (Faigman & Monahan, 2005, p. 631), contend with a brave new world in which judges determine whether their testimony is scientifically valid and reliable. This alone should provide the impetus for further research on the psychology of judicial decision making about forensic mental health evidence.

REFERENCES

Ackerman, M. J. (2002). Child custody evaluations: Comparing psychologists' practices with judges' and lawyers expectations. In L. Vandecreek & T. L. Jackson (Eds.), *Innovations in clinical practice: A sourcebook* (pp. 443–459). Sarasota, FL: Professional Resource Press.

Ackerman, M. J., & Ackerman, M. C. (1997). Custody evaluation practices: A survey of experienced professionals (revisited). *Professional Psychology: Research and Practice, 28,* 137–144.

American Academy of Child and Adolescent Psychiatry. (1997). Guidelines for child custody evaluations. *Journal of the American Academy of Child and Adolescent Psychiatry, 36,* 17–84.

American Psychiatric Association. (2000). *Diagnostic and statistical manual of mental disorders* (4th ed., text rev.). Washington, DC: Author.

American Psychological Association. (1994). Guidelines for child custody evaluations in divorce proceedings. *American Psychologist, 49,* 677–680.

Ash, P., & Guyer, M. (1986). The functions of psychiatric evaluation in contested child custody cases. *Journal of the American Academy of Child Psychiatry, 25,* 544–561.

Atkins v. Virginia, 536 U.S. 304 (2002).

Azar, S. T., & Benjet, C. L. (1994). A cognitive perspective on ethnicity, race, and termination of parental rights. *Law and Human Behavior, 18,* 249–268.

Ballou, M., Barry, J., Billingham, K., Boorstein, B. W., Butler, C., Gershberg, R., et al. (2001). Psychological model for judicial decision making in emergency or temporary child placement. *American Journal of Orthopsychiatry, 71,* 416–425.

Bersoff, D. N., & Glass, D. J. (1995). The not-so *Weisman:* Supreme Court's continuing misuse of social science research. *University of Chicago Law School Roundtable, 2*(1), 279–302.

Bonnie, R. J., & Grisso, T. (2000). Adjudicative competence and youthful offenders. In T. Grisso & R. G. Schwartz (Eds.), *Youth on trial: A developmental perspective on juvenile justice* (pp. 73–103). Chicago: University of Chicago Press.

Bow, J. N., & Quinnell, F. A. (2001). Psychologists' current practices and procedures in child custody evaluations: Five years after American Psychological Association guidelines. *Professional Psychology: Research and Practice, 32,* 261–268.

Brannen, D. N., Salekin, R. T., Zapf, P. A., Salekin. K. L., Kubak, F. A., & DeCoster, J. (2006). *Transfer of youth to adult courts: How do judges weigh pertinent factors and is there a need to codify a national standard?* Manuscript submitted for publication.

Britner, P. B., & Mossler, D. G. (2002). Professionals' decision-making about out-of-home placements following instances of child abuse. *Child Abuse and Neglect, 26,* 317–332.

Brown v. Board of Education of Topeka (Kansas), 347 U.S. 483 (1954).

Bursztajn, H., Gutheil, T. G., Mills, M., Hamm, R. M., & Brodsky, A. (1986). Process analysis of judges' commitment decisions: A preliminary empirical study. *American Journal of Psychiatry, 143,* 170–174.

Bursztajn, H., Hamm, R. M., & Gutheil, T. G. (1997). Beyond the black letter of the law: An empirical study of an individual judge's decision process for civil commitment hearings. *Journal of the American Academy of Psychiatry and the Law, 25,* 79–94.

Campbell, M. A., & Schmidt, F. (2000). Comparison of mental health and legal factors in the disposition of young offenders. *Criminal Justice and Behavior, 27,* 688–715.

Caudill, D. S., & Redding, R. E. (2000). Junk *philosophy* of science? The paradox of expertise and interdisciplinarity in federal courts. *Washington and Lee Law Review, 57,* 685–766.

Chambers, D. L. (1984). Rethinking the substantive rules for custody disputes in divorce. *Michigan Law Review, 83,* 477–489.

Crosby-Currie, C. A. (1996). Children's involvement in contested custody cases: Practices and experiences of legal and mental health professionals. *Law and Human Behavior, 20,* 289–311.

Cruise, K. R., & Rogers, R. (1998). An analysis of competency to stand trial: An integration of case law and clinical knowledge. *Behavioral Sciences and the Law, 16,* 35–50.

Dahir, V. B., Richardson, J. T., Ginsburg, G. P., Gatowski, S. I., & Dobbin, S. A. (2005). Judicial application of *Daubert* to psychological syndrome and profile evidence: A research note. *Psychology, Public Policy, and Law, 11,* 62–82.

Daubert v. Merrell Dow Pharmaceuticals, Inc., 509 U.S. 579 (1993).

Daubert v. Merrell Dow Pharmaceuticals, Inc., 43 F.3d 1311 (9th Cir. 1995).

DiCataldo, F., & Grisso, T. (1995). A typology of juvenile offenders based on the judgments of juvenile courts professionals. *Criminal Justice and Behavior, 22,* 246–262.

Dixon, L., & Gill, B. (2002). Changes in the standards for admitting expert evidence in federal civil cases since the *Daubert* decision. *Psychology, Public Policy, and Law, 8,* 251–308.

Dobbin, S. A., & Gatowski, S. I. (1999). *A judge's deskbook on the basic philosophies and methods of science.* Reno: University of Nevada, State Justice Institute.

Duran-Aydintug, C., & Causey, K. A. (1996). Child custody determination: Implications for lesbian mothers. *Journal of Divorce and Remarriage, 25,* 55–74.

Elrod, P., & Ryder, R. S. (1999). *Juvenile justice: A social, historical, and legal perspective.* Gaithersburg, MD: Aspen.

Ewart, B., & Pennington, D. C. (1987). An attributional approach to explaining sentencing disparity. In D. C. Pennington & S. Lloyd-Bostock (Eds.), *The psychology of sentencing* (pp. 181–192). Oxford, England: Centre for Socio-Legal Studies.

Faigman, D. L., & Monahan, J. (2005). Psychological evidence at the dawn of the law's scientific age. *Annual Review of Psychology, 56,* 631–659.

Federal Judicial Center. (2000). *Reference manual on scientific evidence.* Washington, DC: Author.

Federal Judicial Procedure and Rules. (2005).

Felner, R. D., Rowlison, R. T., Farber, S. S., Primavera, J., & Bishop, T. A. (1987). Child custody resolution: A study of social science involvement and impact. *Professional Psychology: Research and Practice, 18,* 468–474.

Finlay v. Finlay, 148 N.E. 624 (1925).

Fradella, H. F., Fogarty, A., & O'Neill, L. (2003). The impact of *Daubert* on the admissibility of behavioral science testimony. *Pepperdine Law Review, 30,* 403–444.

Frost, L. E., deCamara, R. L., & Earl, T. R. (in press). Training, certification, and regulation of forensic evaluators. *Journal of Forensic Psychology Practice.*

Frye v. United States, 293 F. 1013 (D.C. Cir. 1923).

Gatowski, S. I., Dobbin, S. A., Richardson, J. T., Ginsburg, G. P., Merlino, M. L., & Dahir, V. (2001). Asking the gatekeepers: A national survey of judges on judging expert evidence in a post-*Daubert* world. *Law and Human Behavior, 25,* 433–458.

Goldstein, A. M., Thomson, M. R., Redding, R. E., & Osman, D. (2003). The role of research in forensic psychological testimony: Do judges listen? *Journal of Forensic Psychology Practice, 3,* 89–101.

Goldstein, J., Freud, A., & Solnit, A. J. (1973). *Beyond the best interests of the child.* New York: Free Press.

Goldstein, J., Solnit, A. J., Goldstein, S., & Freud, A. (1996). *The best interests of the child: The least detrimental alternative.* New York: Free Press.

Grisso, T. (2003). Forensic evaluation in delinquency cases. In I. B. Weiner (Series Ed.) & A. M. Goldstein (Vol. Ed.), *Comprehensive handbook of psychology: Vol. 11. Forensic psychology* (pp. 315–334). Hoboken, NJ: Wiley.

Hall, A. S., Pulver, C. A., & Cooley, M. J. (1996). Psychology of the best interest standard: Fifty state statutes and their theoretical antecedents. *American Journal of Family Therapy, 24,* 171–180.

Hart, S. D., & Hare, R. D. (1992). Predicting fitness to stand trial: The relative power of demographic, criminal, and clinical variables. *Forensic Reports, 5,* 53–65.

Hensl, K. B., & Redding, R. E. (2005, March). *The relationship among juvenile court judges' personal characteristics and attitudes, juvenile offender characteristics, and judicial transfer decisions.* Paper presented at the American Psychology-Law Society annual conference, La Jolla, CA.

Hoge, R. D., Andrews, D. A., & Leschied, A. (1995). Investigation of variables associated with probation and custody dispositions in a sample of juveniles. *Journal of Clinical Child Psychology, 24,* 279–286.

Horwitz, A., & Wasserman, M. (1980). Formal rationality, substantive justice, and discrimination. *Law and Human Behavior, 4,* 103–115.

Huang, M. S. W., Finn, M. A., Ruback, R. B., & Friedmann, R. R. (1996). Individual and contextual influences on sentence lengths: Examining political conservatism. *Prison Journal, 76,* 398–419.

Jellinek, M. S., Murphy, M., Poitrast, F., Quinn, D., Bishop, S. J., & Goshko, M. (1992). Serious child mistreatment in Massachusetts: The course of 206 children through the courts. *Child Abuse and Neglect, 16,* 179–185.

Jennison, J. B. (1991). The search for equality in a woman's world: Fathers' rights to child custody. *Rutgers Law Review, 43,* 1141–1185.

Kovera, M. B., & McAuliff, B. D. (2000). The effects of peer review and evidence quality on judges' evaluations of psychological science: Are judges effective gatekeepers? *Journal of Applied Psychology, 85,* 574–586.

Krafka, C., Dunn, M. A., Johnson, M. T., Cecil, J. S., & Miletich, D. (2002). Judge and attorney experiences, practices, and concerns regarding expert testimony in federal civil trials. *Psychology, Public Policy, and Law, 8,* 309–332.

Krauss, D. A., Lieberman, J. D., & Olson, J. (2004). The effects of rational and experiential information processing of expert testimony in death penalty cases. *Behavioral Sciences and the Law, 22,* 801–822.

Krauss, D., & Sales, B. (2001). The effects of clinical and scientific expert testimony on juror decision making in capital sentencing. *Psychology, Public Policy, and Law, 7,* 267–310.

Kulik, C. T., Perry, E. L., & Pepper, M. B. (2003). Here comes the judge: The influence of judge personal characteristics on federal sexual harassment case outcomes. *Law and Human Behavior, 27,* 69–86.

Kumho Tire Co. v. Patrick Carmichael, 526 U.S. 137 (1999).

Kunin, C. C., Ebbesen, E. B., & Konecni, V. J. (1992). An archival study of decision making in child custody disputes. *Journal of Clinical Psychology, 48,* 564–573.

LaFortune, K. A., & Nicholson, R. A. (1995, Summer). How adequate are Oklahoma's mental health evaluations for determining competency in criminal proceedings? The bench and the bar respond. *Journal of Psychiatry and Law,* 231–262.

Lombard, F. (1984). Judicial interviewing of children in custody cases: An empirical and analytical study. *University of California-Davis Law Review, 17,* 807–851.

Lurigio, A. J., Carroll, J. S., & Stalans, L. J. (1994). Understanding judges' sentencing decisions: Attributions of responsibility and story construction. In L. Heath (Ed.), *Applications of heuristics and biases to social issues* (pp. 91–115). New York: Plenum Press.

Manuto, R., & O'Rourke, S. P. (1991). Federal judges' perceptions of social research in judicial decision making. *Communication Reports, 4,* 103–106.

Mason, M. A. (1994). *From father's property to children's rights: The history of child custody in the United States.* New York: Columbia University Press.

Mason, M. A., & Quirk, A. (1997). Are mothers losing custody? Read my lips: Trends in judicial decision-making in custody disputes—1920, 1960, 1990, and 1995. *Family Law Quarterly, 31,* 215–236.

McCoy, W., Murrie, D. C., & Cornell, D. G. (2005, March). Do youth psychopathy and conduct disorder findings influence juvenile court judges? In D. C. Murrie (Chair), *Psychopathy in legal decision making.* Symposium presented at the meeting of the American Psychology-Law Society, La Jolla, California.

McFatter, R. M. (1978). Sentencing strategies and justice: Effects of punishment philosophy on sentencing decisions. *Journal of Personality and Social Psychology, 36,* 1490–1500.

Melton, G. B., Petrila, J., Poythress, N. G., & Slobogin, C. (1997). *Psychological evaluations for the courts* (2nd ed.). New York: Guilford Press.

Mercer, K. L. (1997). The ethics of judicial decision making regarding the custody of minor children: Looking at the "best interests of the child" and the "primary caretaker" standards as utility rules. *Idaho Law Review, 33,* 389–391.

Merlino, M. L., Dillehay, R. D., Dahir, V., & Maxwell, D. (2003). Science education for judges: What, where, and by whom? *Judicature, 86*(4), 210–213.

Monahan, J., & Silver, E. (2003). Judicial decision thresholds for violence risk management. *International Journal of Forensic Mental Health, 2,* 1–6.

Monahan, J., & Walker, L. (1998). *Social science in law: Cases and materials* (4th ed.). Westbury, NY: Foundation Press.

Monahan, J., & Walker, L. (2002). *Social science in law: Cases and materials* (5th ed.). Westbury, NY: Foundation Press.

Mossman, D. (1999). "Hired guns," "whores," and "prostitutes": Case law references to clinicians of ill repute. *Journal of the American Academy of Psychiatry and the Law, 27,* 414–425.

Mulvey, E. P., & Reppucci, N. D. (1988). The context of clinical judgment: The effect of resource availability on judgments of amenability to treatment in juvenile offenders. *American Journal of Community Psychology, 16,* 525–545.

Murrie, D. C., & Redding, R. E. (in press). Mental disorders and the law. In D. S. Clark (Ed.), *Encyclopedia of law and society: American and global perspectives.* New York: Sage.

O'Conner v. Donaldson, 422 U.S. 563 (1975).

O'Donahue, W., & Bradley, A. R. (1999). Conceptual and empirical issues in child custody evaluations. *Clinical Psychology: Science and Practice, 6,* 310–322.

Ogloff, J. R. P. (2000). Two steps forward and one step backward: The law and psychology movement(s) in the twentieth century. *Law and Human Behavior, 24,* 457–483.

Otto, R. K., Buffington-Vollum, J. K., & Edens, J. F. (2003). Child custody evaluation. In I. B. Weiner (Series Ed.) & A. M. Goldstein (Vol. Ed.), *Comprehensive handbook of psychology: Vol. 11. Forensic psychology* (pp. 179–208). Hoboken, NJ: Wiley.

Palys, T. S., & Divorski, S. (1984). Judicial decision making: An examination of sentencing disparity among Canadian provincial court judges. In D. J. Muller, D. E. Blackman, & A. J. Chapman (Eds.), *Psychology and law* (pp. 333–344). New York: Wiley.

Parry, J. (1994). Involuntary civil commitment in the 1990s: A constitutional perspective. *Mental and Physical Disability Law Reporter, 18,* 320–336.

Pearson, J., & Ring, M. A. (1982). Judicial decision making in contested custody cases. *Journal of Family Law, 21,* 703–724.

Petrella, R., & Poythress, N. G. (1983). The quality of forensic examinations: An interdisciplinary study. *Journal of Consulting and Clinical Psychology, 51,* 76–85.

Poythress, N. G. (1983). Psychological issues in criminal proceedings: Judicial preference regarding expert testimony. *Criminal Justice and Behavior, 10,* 175–194.

Quinsey, V., Harris, G., Rice, M., & Cormier, C. (1998). *Violent offenders: Appraising and managing risk.* Washington, DC: American Psychological Association.

Redding, R. E. (1993). Children's competence to provide informed consent to mental health treatment. *Washington and Lee Law Review, 50,* 695–753.

Redding, R. E. (1998). How common sense psychology can inform law and psycholegal research. *University of Chicago Law School Roundtable, 5,* 107–142.

Redding, R. E. (1999). Reconstructing science through law. *Southern Illinois Law Journal, 23,* 585–610.

Redding, R. E. (2004). Why it is essential to teach about mental health issues in criminal law (and a primer on how to do it). *Washington University Journal of Law and Policy, 14,* 407–440.

Redding, R. E., Floyd, M. Y., & Hawk, G. L. (2001). What do judges and lawyers think about the testimony of mental health experts? A survey of the courts and bar. *Behavioral Sciences and the Law, 19,* 583–594.

Redding, R. E., & Mrozoski, B. (2005). Adjudicatory and dispositional decision making in juvenile justice. In K. Heilbrun, N. Goldstein, & R. Redding (Eds.), *Juvenile delinquency: Assessment, prevention, and intervention* (pp. 232–256). New York: Oxford University Press.

Redding, R. E., & Reppucci, N. D. (1999). Effects of lawyers' sociopolitical attitudes on their judgments of social science in legal decision making. *Law and Human Behavior, 23,* 31–54.

Reidy, T. J., Silver, R. M., & Carlson, A. (1989). Child custody decisions: A survey of judges. *Family Law Quarterly, 23,* 75–87.

Reppucci, N. D. (1984). The wisdom of Solomon: Issues in child custody determinations. In N. D. Reppucci, L. A. Weithorn, E. P. Mulvey, & J. Monahan (Eds.), *Mental health, law, and children* (pp. 59–77). Beverly Hills, CA: Sage.

Roper v. Simmons, 125 S. Ct. 1183 (2005).

Sanborn, J. B. (1996). Factors perceived to affect delinquent dispositions in juvenile court: Putting the sentencing decision into context. *Crime and Delinquency, 42,* 99–113.

Schopp, R. F., Scalora, M. J., & Pearce, M. (1999). Expert testimony and professional judgment: Psychological expertise and commitment as a sexual predator after *Hendricks. Psychology, Public Policy, and Law, 5,* 120–174.

Scott, E. S., Reppucci, N. D., & Aber, M. (1988). Children's preference in adjudicated custody decisions. *University of Georgia Law Review, 22,* 1035–1078.

Settle, S. A., & Lowery, C. R. (1982). Child custody decisions: Content analysis of a judicial survey. *Journal of Divorce, 6,* 125–138.

Shuman, D. W., & Sales, B. D. (1999). The impact of *Daubert* and its progeny on the admissibility of behavioral and social science evidence. *Psychology, Public Policy, and Law, 5,* 3–15.

Slobogin, C. (1998). Psychiatric evidence in criminal trials: To junk or not to junk? *William and Mary Law Review, 40,* 1–56.

Sorenson, E., & Goldman, J. (1990). Custody determinations and child development: A review of the current literature. *Journal of Divorce, 13,* 53–67.

Sorenson, E., Goldman, J., Sheeber, L., Albanese, I., Ward, M., Williamson, L., et al. (1997). Judges' reliance on psychological, sociological, and legal variables in contested custody decisions. *Journal of Divorce and Remarriage, 27,* 39–53.

Sorenson, E., Goldman, J., Ward, M., Albanese, I., Graves, L., & Chamberlin, C. (1995). Judicial decision-making in contested custody cases: The influence of reported child abuse, spouse abuse, and parental substance abuse. *Child Abuse and Neglect, 19,* 251–260.

Stamps, L. E. (2002). Maternal preference in child custody decisions. *Journal of Divorce and Remarriage, 37,* 1–11.

Tanford, J. A. (1990). The limits of a scientific jurisprudence: The Supreme Court and psychology. *Indiana Law Journal, 66,* 137–173.

Wallace, S. R., & Koerner, S. S. (2003). Influence of child and family factors on judicial decisions in contested custody cases. *Family Relations, 52,* 180–188.

Waller, E. M., & Daniel, A. E. (2004). Purpose and utility of child custody evaluations: From the perspective of judges. *Journal of Psychiatry and the Law, 32,* 5–27.

Warren, J. I., & Murrie, D. C. (2005, August). *Opinion formation in 8,000 evaluations of competence to stand trial.* Paper presented at the annual meeting of the American Psychological Association, Washington, DC.

Warren, J. I., Murrie, D. C., Chahuan, P., Dietz, P. E., & Morris, J. (2004). Opinion formation in evaluating sanity at time of offense: An examination of 5,175 pretrial evaluations. *Behavioral Sciences and the Law, 22,* 171–187.

Weisz, V. G. (1999). Commentary on "Conceptual and empirical issues in child custody evaluations." *Clinical Psychology: Science and Practice, 6,* 328–331.

Winick, B. J. (1995). Reforming incompetency to stand trial and plead guilty: A restated proposal and response to Professor Bonnie. *Journal of Criminal Law and Criminology, 85,* 571–624.

Wisdom, J. M. (1975). Random remarks on the role of social sciences in the judicial decision-making process in school desegregation cases. *Law and Contemporary Problems, 39,* 134–149.

Wrightsman, L. S. (1999). *Judicial decision making: Is psychology relevant?* New York: Kluwer Press.

Zapf, P. A., Hubbard, K. L., Galloway, V. A., Cox, M., & Ronan, K. A. (2004). Have the courts abdicated their responsibility for determinations of competency to stand trial to clinicians? *Journal of Forensic Psychology Practice, 4,* 27–44.

CHAPTER 27

Psychopathology of Homicide

Louis B. Schlesinger

The involvement of a forensic mental health professional (MHP) in a homicide case typically entails addressing a specific legal issue such as trial competency, a defendant's state of mind at the time of the crime, or perhaps capital mitigation. For the forensic expert's findings to have legal relevance, a mental disorder must first be established, followed by an opinion as to whether the disorder is severe enough to have affected the defendant's behavior in relation to a specific legal standard. Accordingly, much of the training forensic practitioners receive focuses on various laws and legal standards since it is assumed that MHPs already have adequate knowledge of mental disorders. However, an MHP's knowledge of mental disorders may have little connection with the relationship between mental disorders and criminal behavior. A review of many of the leading books in the field (e.g., Blau, 1998; Cooke, 1980; Goldstein, 2003; Hess & Weiner, 1999; Melton, Petrila, Poythress, & Slobogin, 1997; Rosner, 2003) suggests that most of the emphasis in forensic training is on various legal issues and standards, less on forensic assessment, and even less on criminal psychopathology, psychopathological disorders associated with crime, and the conditions and psychodynamics that cause various crimes such as homicide.

Homicide is not a homogeneous phenomenon, but a complex set of behaviors with distinct and varying etiologies, clinical courses, and prognoses. A psychiatric diagnosis per se cannot explain the vast majority of homicides, except for those committed by individuals laboring under the influence of a psychotic (usually paranoid) process or the rare cases of murder as a direct outgrowth of an organic or toxic confusional state (Revitch & Schlesinger, 1981). In fact, criminal behavior, in general, is rarely a direct result of a mental disorder (Pallone & Hennessey, 1994).

Just as the psychiatric diagnosis cannot explain most homicides, the various legal standards do not explain the offense but are measures with which to assign moral culpability and prescribe punishment. Thus, a first-degree murderer will receive a lengthy prison term regardless of the motivational aspects and dangerousness of the defendant. But an individual who commits an assault or burglary will receive a much shorter sentence, even if he had been harboring dangerous homicidal fantasies with a compulsion to kill. Moreover, the psychiatric nomenclature and the legal classification of homicide are virtually useless as prognostic indicators. Unfortunately, these are the approaches that structure and guide many MHPs' evaluations of homicidal offenders.

The purpose of this chapter is to offer a complementary approach to the assessment of murder that will assist MHPs in gaining an increased understanding of the psychopathology of homicide. This system is useful to MHPs not only in formulating a psycholegal opinion but also in making a prognostic assessment of dangerousness, which is so important to the court, parole boards, and other individuals and agencies responsible for the management and disposition of homicidal offenders. The model of classification is based on the motivational dynamics of the antisocial act, as derived from crime scene behavior analysis, and offers a variety of typologies and profiles of offenders. But because this method of classification is based primarily on what offenders actually did rather than on what they said they did, a detailed look at the distinctions between a forensic and a clinical assessment is necessary first, as this is the methodology that serves as the foundation of MHPs' conclusions.

CLINICAL VERSUS FORENSIC ASSESSMENT

Mental health practitioners who routinely conduct assessments in hospitals, mental health centers, and private offices evaluate their patients by interviewing them, administering psychological or neurodiagnostic tests, and sometimes establishing supplemental contacts with family members and friends. Frequently, they request hospital and school records and perhaps reports from prior therapists. After an evaluation, MHPs formulate a diagnosis and develop a treatment plan. Mental health professionals listen to their patients and generally believe what they say. If, for example, patients report that they feel depressed, anxious, or agitated or that they are contemplating suicide, MHPs usually accept these symptom descriptions and intentions as valid unless there is a specific reason not to. In general clinical practice, patients usually seek treatment for help with their problems, and, more times than not, they are fairly straightforward because they want to receive assistance. Certainly patients may deny, minimize, or perhaps exaggerate symptoms and behaviors; although lying, deception, and malingering do occur in clinical practice, the main emphasis is on diagnosis based on the patient's self-report, followed by treatment.

A forensic assessment, however, cannot follow the typical clinical approach because forensic cases do not originate with a person seeking help but are usually referred by an attorney, the court, or another third party. Accordingly, the traditional clinical method of relying on an individual's self-report and arriving at a psychiatric diagnosis is inadequate. In a forensic case, the evaluation must begin with an analysis of the facts of the case—that is, what the offender actually did, rather than what the offender claims he or she did.

Melton et al. (1997) describe several differences between a forensic and a clinical (or what they refer to as a therapeutic) assessment. They note differences in the scope of the evaluation, the client's perspective, voluntariness, autonomy, threats to validity, relationship and dynamics, and pace and setting. In addition to these factors, a fundamental distinction between a forensic and a clinical assessment is that in forensic cases, the likelihood is high that defendants are not being truthful, as they have an obvious motive to lie, exaggerate, or distort symptoms and events. Thus, the traditional approach and methodology used in arriving at a diagnosis in clinical practice cannot be used in forensic practice. Forensic psychology and psychiatry are not simply the practice of clinical psychology or general psychiatry in a forensic setting (Schlesinger, 2003a, 2003b). A forensic psychological or psychiatric assessment requires a significant modification of the traditional clinical approach. Unfortunately, the necessity and specifics of modifying the traditional clinical methodology are not stressed enough, and they frequently become evident only when many MHPs enter the forensic arena.

An MHP must corroborate a criminal defendant's version of events. Therefore, a review of the facts of the case is fundamental to a forensic assessment and should serve as a starting point even before the MHP meets with the offender. Early forensic psychiatrists (Davidson, 1965; Sadoff, 1975) stressed the importance of corroborative information; unfortunately, many contemporary MHPs who practice in forensic settings do not follow this recommended procedure. In their study of forensic assessments, for instance, Heilbrun, Rosenfeld, Warren, and Collins (1994) found that most of the evaluators questioned reported that they did "incorporate" third-party information, but they did not explain how or whether they made use of this information in the process of arriving at conclusions and opinions. To the extent that the evaluators relied largely on defendants' self-reports, as they would their patients' reports of problems, the validity of their conclusions can be seriously called into question. The following case, involving a defendant who claimed to lack criminal responsibility in a homicide, is illustrative.

--- **Illustrative Case 1** ---

While fishing after school, two adolescents detected several partially wrapped packages that had washed ashore. After opening one, the youngsters immediately realized that it contained the torso of a human, and the other packages contained an arm, legs, and a head. The medical examiner determined that the deceased was a woman in her 50s with a deformed left hand, the result of a birth defect. The authorities released this information to the media, hoping that the deformity could help to identify the victim.

After hearing the story on the evening news, a friend of the deceased called the authorities. On the basis of the information the friend supplied, the victim's 66-year-old common law husband (A. A.) was arrested. He gave a detailed statement to the police, explaining that he got into a fight with the victim, stabbed her two or three times with a kitchen knife, cut her up, put the pieces in plastic bags, and stored them in his refrigerator. Over the next week, he threw the packages off a bridge, hoping that the body parts would wash out to sea. He then moved out of the apartment after cleaning and painting it, disposed of all the victim's clothes, and changed his name.

The defense attorney retained a general psychiatrist, one who had conducted a number of forensic evaluations, to examine the offender. He conducted his evaluation just as if he were examining a patient who was admitted to a psychiatric hospital. In his report, he noted that A. A. did not know whether he killed the woman, and he appeared to be confused and suffering memory loss. The psychiatrist concluded that A. A. had an organic brain syndrome (to explain the memory deficit) and gave the following opinions and recommendations:

> A. A. is very credible in his replies inasmuch as he frankly stated he did not know whether he killed the victim or not. He has no recollection of it. This examiner is of the opinion that he certainly falls within the purview of the M'Naghten Rule in that he did not know the nature and quality of his acts by reason of brain disease.

Here, the defense expert completely disregarded the facts of the case and relied totally on the defendant's self-report. He ignored A. A.'s statements to the police, which detailed how and when he had killed the victim, disposed of the body parts, cleaned the crime scene, painted it, changed his name, and moved. When evaluated by the prosecution expert, A. A. was uncooperative, unpleasant, and hostile. He denied having a criminal history, even when the expert pointed out that records revealed he had been arrested previously for armed robbery. He again said he did not remember murdering anyone and also claimed he never heard of the victim, whom he had in fact lived with for 8 to 10 years. He insisted that he did not recall disposing of the evidence, moving to a new location, changing his name, and telling those who inquired that the victim had gone to a nursing home.

Comment

The defense psychiatrist's reasoning provides a good illustration of what MHPs should not do in conducting a forensic assessment. Not only was the diagnosis of brain impairment (based solely on self-report and observation) incorrect, but the psychiatrist's opinion also demonstrates a commonly held view that the explanation of a homicide lies primarily in a diagnosis. Even if A. A. had some level of organicity, it would not have accounted for the murder and subsequent cover-up. The jury quickly rejected the defense expert's analysis and conclusions.

CLASSIFYING HOMICIDES

Without classification, naturally occurring events would appear random, unrelated, and chaotic. Classification is certainly the approach that medicine has taken since Hippocrates' initial grouping of diseases. And psychiatry has always valued classification, especially since the operationalized approach of the *Diagnostic and Statistical Manual of Mental Disorders,* third edition (*DSM-III;* American Psychiatric Association, 1980), which listed specific criteria for the various mental disorders. However, rigid boundaries are difficult to establish; borderline cases are frequent, especially as one deviates from the nuclear condition. In other words, diagnoses of severe cases of Schizophrenia often exhibit a great deal of agreement, but as the symptom picture becomes less typical, disagreement often results. Thus, highly competent MHPs can view the same individual as schizophrenic, schizoaffective, borderline, bipolar, and the like.

A *DSM*, fourth edition, text revision (*DSM-IV-TR;* American Psychiatric Association, 2000) diagnosis is almost always necessary in a legal proceeding, particularly if mental disease or defect needs to be established. However, the psychiatric nosology is inadequate as a basis for classifying crime in general, and homicide in particular, because only homicides committed under the influence of an overt psychosis (most notably, paranoid delusions or hallucinations) and the occasional violence resulting from organic and toxic confusional states are diagnostically relevant to satisfy the legal standard (Revitch & Schlesinger, 1981). Psychoanalytic penetration into deeper personality levels is often too theoretical, esoteric, and limited to one orientation. And the legal criteria, although useful to determine extent of responsibility, moral guilt, and degree of punishment, do not explain the criminal act and do not offer a guide for prognostication.

Since the mid-1950s, researchers and practitioners have developed various approaches to classifying homicide, independent of psychiatric diagnosis. For example, Brancale (1955) proposed a simple method of separating homicides into two basic groups: administrative and psychiatric. Offenders who are psychotic, mentally deficient, or have major psychopathological symptoms are placed in the psychiatric group and would be handled in specialized settings. All others, a much larger number, fall into the administrative group and would be managed correctionally. In another classification scheme, Bromberg (1961) divided murderers into those whom he deemed "normal" (i.e., not suffering from any mental disorder) and a much smaller group of offenders whom he labeled "psychopathic" (i.e., exhibiting some type of overt disturbance). Tanay (1969) differentiated egosyntonic homicides (those compatible with the offender's conscious wishes) from both egodystonic homicides (those involving a dissociative or altered state of consciousness) and homicides that result from an overt psychosis. And Halleck (1971) distinguished an "adaptive" category of offenders from a much smaller, "maladaptive" group.

These approaches to classification all have merit, but they do not help MHPs in arriving at an opinion regarding an offender's future dangerousness, which is important to the court, parole board, and others involved in the disposition and subsequent release of murderers. Accordingly, Revitch (1977) and Revitch and Schlesinger (1978, 1981, 1989) developed, and Schlesinger (2004b) modified and elaborated, a system not only for classifying crime and homicide but also for predicting future violence based on an analysis of the motivational dynamics of the antisocial act already committed. Offenses that result from a primary psychiatric/neurological disorder form a group of their own apart from the classification model.

HOMICIDE AS THE RESULT OF A PSYCHIATRIC/NEUROLOGICAL DISORDER

The primary psychiatric category covers murders that result from an organic, toxic, or paranoid disorder. For many years, researchers found a relationship between various organic disorders, such as brain injuries, brain infections, brain tumors, and subsequent violence (Mark & Ervin, 1970; Mark & Southgate, 1971; Raine, 1993; Weiger & Bear, 1988). However, a close examination of many of these cases uncovers a strong psychogenic factor, which could also account for the violent behavior (Pincus & Tucker, 1985). Thus, in most cases involving brain infections, injuries, tumors, or other organic conditions, such as epilepsy, the organicity serves to weaken inhibitory controls and indirectly contributes to violence and homicide (Revitch & Schlesinger, 1981).

The most common substance associated with homicide is alcohol (Auerhahn & Parker, 1999). The results of Wolfgang's (1958) classic criminological study of 588 cases of homicide in Philadelphia, which found that 54% of offenders and 53% of victims were under the influence of alcohol at the time of the offense, are still valid today according to statistics in the FBI's (2004) *Uniform Crime Reports*. Alcohol, in a different way than organicity, also reduces inhibitory controls and can contribute to violent explosions (Pernanen, 1991). Other drugs, such as cocaine, amphetamines, and inhalants, can act to increase violence because of their disinhibiting properties, whereas drugs such as opiates can decrease aggressive behavior because of their sedating effects (Friedman, 1998; Parker & Auerhahn, 1999). Psychedelics such as LSD have been connected with homicides; in these cases, the offenders responded to psychotic manifestations induced by the substance (Reich & Hepps, 1972).

Most of the psychotic disorders associated with murder involve various aspects of paranoia, which has a much more complex relationship to violence and homicide than do organic and toxic conditions. Paranoid delusions and paranoid jealousy have been linked as a direct cause of homicide (Lanzkron, 1963; Silva, Harry, Leong, & Weinstock, 1996; Wilcox, 1985). Revitch (1979) found that most patients who kill their physicians are paranoid; Hempel, Meloy, and Richards (1999) found that many mass murderers have strong paranoid traits, as do many political assassins (Lewis, 1987). (Perhaps the most typical example of a homicidal act motivated directly by delusions of persecution was the murder committed by Daniel M'Naghten, from which the legal test of insanity arose.)

In the following case, a young man with bizarre disorganizing psychotic delusions killed his father as a direct response to his paranoid delusional thinking. Here, an analysis of the crime scene information, statements given to the police by the offender immediately after his arrest, and clinical evaluations supported by psychological testing all led to the diagnosis of Schizophrenia, as well as to his meeting the legal standard for insanity.

--------------------------------- **Illustrative Case 2** ---------------------------------

A 19-year-old college student (B. B.) killed his sleeping father with a Samurai sword, stabbing him 11 times in the chest area; he then dropped the sword in the hallway outside his father's bedroom and left the house. Police arrested B. B. the next day while he was walking in the street. He appeared depressed, emotional, and confused. When first questioned, he stated, "I did it 'cause I was scared the guy was gonna come shoot me. Because there was this guy who was gonna come shoot me. He shot my friend, and then he was gonna come shoot me." While he was in the county jail, the treating staff documented multiple psychotic symptoms, including ideas of reference, paranoia, auditory hallucinations, and general confusion. These symptoms corroborated a long-standing diagnosis of Schizoaffective Disorder. Notwithstanding B. B.'s superficial improvement after about a month, he made an almost fatal suicide attempt in jail. B. B. was then transferred to a forensic hospital, where additional symptoms pathognomonic of Schizophrenia, including thought broadcasting, thought insertion, and auditory hallucinations, along with flat and inappropriate affect, were well documented.

About a week prior to the homicide, B. B. had spoken to several police officers and told them about a gang that he believed was trying to kill him and his friends. On the evening of the homicide, B. B. developed an idea that he had a tapeworm in his rectum. He spoke to his mother about this, and he wanted to call his aunt, a nurse, to obtain her help. The offender's mother and father both reassured B. B., promising to take him to a doctor in the morning. About an hour later, B. B. called the police and rescue squad, explaining that he needed assistance for "a worm up my butt." When the rescue squad arrived, his parents became embarrassed, apologized, and told the staffers that they would take their son to the doctor in the morning. After being reassured again, B. B. agreed that the matter could wait until the next day. Several hours later, he killed his father with a decorative sword that had been hanging in his room for the past several years.

For a number of reasons, malingering and deception were ruled out, and the diagnosis of Schizophrenia was substantiated. First, there was no evidence that B. B. had a motive to kill his father, independent of any delusional symptomatology. In fact, according to sources, he had a good relationship with his father, much better than that with his mother, who was the disciplinarian. Second, B. B.'s several descriptions of auditory hallucinations and delusions were consistent with each other. When asked what would have happened if he did not obey his command hallucinations and delusional ideation, he gave a clear answer: "I guess my parents and brother would get killed." Third, many defendants who malinger symptoms do not typically reveal delusional ideation during the arrest process but volunteer it months later, once they have had a chance to speak to other inmates and a legal defense is being planned. In this case, B. B. told the police some of the content of his delusions, specifically that "the guy was gonna come shoot me," when he gave them a brief statement immediately following his arrest. Fourth, the administration of the Structured Interview of Reported Symptoms (Rogers, 1992) and the Minnesota Multiphasic Personality Inventory (Butcher, Graham, Ben-Porath, Tellegen, & Dahlstrom, 2001) did not indicate evidence of malingering. In fact, the results of the tests showed no evidence of exaggeration or feigning. The only severe symptoms that the defendant endorsed were those he reported to other examiners. Fifth, typically a defendant's leaving the crime scene suggests consciousness of guilt, awareness of wrongdoing, and an attempt to avoid apprehension. In this case, however, the defendant left the crime scene because his delusional ideas directed him to do so. When asked specifically whether he did anything to avoid arrest, B. B. responded, "Nothing really; I just kept walking. I thought someone was going to catch up to me and kill me."

Comment

This case serves as a good example of a homicide that was a direct outgrowth of a psychosis. Crime scene evidence, witness statements, and comments B. B. made to the police upon arrest all indicated that he was truly responding to overt psychotic symptoms. If an individual commits a homicide as a direct result of a primary psychiatric/neurological condition, such as in response to hallucinations or delusions, the likelihood of recommitting the offense is reduced if the offender is relieved of these symptoms.

THE MOTIVATIONAL SPECTRUM IN THE CLASSIFICATION OF HOMICIDE

Revitch and Schlesinger (1978, 1981, 1989) and Schlesinger (2004b) based their system of classification of crime and homicide on the motivational dynamics of the antisocial act itself rather than on the psychiatric diagnosis or the legal system's concept of degree of intent. The motivational stimuli leading to a homicide can be conceived of as falling on a spectrum. On one end of the continuum are homicides that are a result of external (sociogenic) factors, and on the opposite end of the scale are homicides that are a result of internal (psychogenic) factors. Offenses are divided into environmental, situational, impulsive, catathymic, and compulsive (see Figure 27.1). External (environmental) factors play less and less

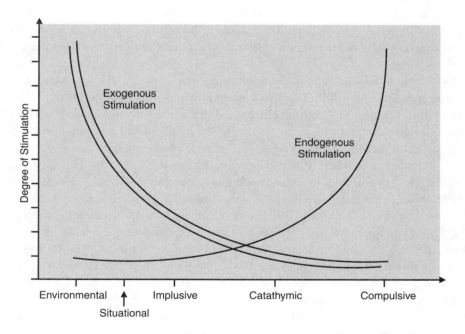

Figure 27.1   The motivational spectrum. *Source:* From *Sexual Murder: Catathymic and Compulsive Homicides* (p. 91), by L. B. Schlesinger, 2004b, Boca Raton, FL: CRC Press. Reproduced by permission of Routledge/Taylor & Francis Group, LLC.

of a role as one approaches the extreme opposite end of the spectrum occupied by the compulsive offenses, which are determined almost entirely by internal (psychogenic) elements. Conversely, psychogenic factors play a minimal role in the environmentally stimulated offenses, where sociogenic influences dominate. And, as indicated, the organic, toxic, and paranoid cases form a group of their own, separate from the motivational spectrum.

The question sometimes arises as to whether we should evaluate the perpetrator or the act. In essence, the act itself forms the basis of classification on the motivational spectrum because what offenders did, not necessarily what they claimed they did (or the makeup of their personality), is most important in understanding their behavior. However, this assessment must include an evaluation of the offender, especially as one moves away from environmentally and situationally stimulated homicides and toward the more purely psychogenically determined acts. The motivational spectrum can be applied to any crime; however, each category is illustrated in this chapter by cases of homicide.

Environmentally Stimulated Homicides

Because all behavior takes places within a social context, and to a large degree is influenced by it, one must take environmental and social factors into account when evaluating homicidal and antisocial conduct. Thus, the environmentally stimulated homicide is a result primarily of the external, social, and environmental pressures and influences, including a weakening of social controls, to which the individual is exposed. Sutherland and Cressey's (1939) theory of differential association (i.e., criminal behavior learned in interaction with others) generally applies to this group of offenders. Most individuals who commit environmentally stimulated homicides are not psychotic and often have reasonably intact personality structures.

Numerous historical examples indicate an increase in antisocial conduct, including murder, when social controls are removed, as illustrated by the surge in mass killings, rapes, and "ethnic cleansing" in the Balkan countries following the Soviet Union's breakup in 1990. In the 1930s and 1940s, those who committed Nazi atrocities acted largely as a result of social, environmental, and subgroup influences rather than because of psychopathology (Arendt, 1966; Lifton, 1986), as psychological evaluations of Nazi leaders demonstrated (Gilbert, 1947; Ritzler, 1978). In cult murders, such as those perpetrated by Charles Manson's infamous "family" (Bugliosi & Gentry, 1975), social pressure within the cult itself influenced many of its members to kill. And some experimental evidence (e.g., Milgram, 1963; Zimbardo, 1973) indicates that nondisturbed college students can easily be influenced to engage in aggressive conduct if the context or environment lends support for such behavior. Homicides committed by amateur, semiprofessional, and professional contract killers are yet another example of murders that are an outgrowth primarily of subculturally stimulated influences (Schlesinger, 2001a). The following case involves an individual who killed more than 100 people for profit.

--------------------------------- **Illustrative Case 3** ---------------------------------

A 52-year-old male (C. C.) had a 30-year career of contract murder as part of a crime network. He used traditional methods of killing, such as shooting, choking, and knifing, as well as more sophisticated techniques, including cyanide poisoning. He planned his murders in a methodical manner and often used elaborate methods of staging to elude law enforcement and avoid arrest. Eventually, the offender was apprehended, not for contract murder but for killing several associates who, he believed, could implicate him in other criminal acts. C. C. had been married for over 25 years, had three children, and led a fairly stable middle-class life, keeping his family members totally insulated from his criminal activities.

C. C.'s personality included traits of orderliness, a need for control, hypervigilance, and the capacity to rationalize actions and encapsulate emotions so that his feelings would not interfere with his homicidal acts. Although he had only average intelligence, C. C. had superior ability in practical reasoning and social judgment, two skills necessary to avoid detection.

Comment

The main motivation for C. C.'s crimes was simply profit, and his decision to seek profit through killing was determined mainly by his living in a subculture in which violence and murder were condoned as being consistent with the crime network's goals. Extensive psychological assessment found no Axis I mental disorder, but there was a finding of Antisocial Personality Disorder on Axis II. However, antisocial personality cannot, by itself, explain such criminal conduct; in fact, most individuals with Antisocial Personality Disorder never commit a murder (Meloy, 1988; Revitch & Schlesinger, 1981).

Situational Homicides

Situational homicides occur because a particular set of circumstances present at a given time creates powerful feelings of stress, especially in susceptible or vulnerable individuals (Pallone & Hennessey, 1994; Schlesinger & Revitch, 1980). Feelings of despair, helplessness, depression, fear, and anger are highly stressful, especially when chronic, and can trigger murders under the right set of conditions. Situational murders include a wide range of offenses, such as many domestic and felony homicides committed during arguments, some of which are premeditated and others of which are spontaneous. A review of the FBI's (2004) *Uniform Crime Reports* over the past 40 years indicates that about 70% to 75% of all murders are basically of a situational nature. The overall recidivism rate for situational homicides is low; consequently, the overall recidivism rate for murder is low since most murders are of this type.

The following case of a domestic homicide triggered by an angry quarrel over money is typical of a situational murder. Here, in an effort to direct the investigation away from himself, the offender attempted to stage the crime scene to make it appear to be a sexual murder.

Illustrative Case 4

A 58-year-old male (D. D.) had been unemployed for 2 years after being laid off from a fairly lucrative job as a computer analyst. His wife continued to work as an administrative assistant, but marital difficulties developed, primarily as a result of financial stress. D. D. reported that several days before the homicide, there was a change in his wife's demeanor and attitude: "Her personality changed. She wasn't interested in me or the house. She had a look of hatred. I wanted to discuss problems with our budget. I needed [information] and I wanted to talk, but she wouldn't contribute money from her raise."

The following day, the couple got into an argument that escalated. The offender grabbed a knife, stabbed his wife multiple times, and killed her. Although D. D. denied remembering subsequent events, a typical claim in such cases, the crime scene evidence indicated that he disposed of the murder weapon, wrapped his wife's body in a tarpaulin, and took her body to the woods adjacent to their home. The victim's pants and underwear had been pulled down below her hips, and her shirt had been pulled up to her neck, exposing her breasts. Mrs. D.'s clothing was drenched in blood, but the lack of blood on the ground directly beneath her indicated that she had not been killed in the location where the body was found. Notwithstanding his attempt to make the crime appear to be a sexual murder, when confronted, D. D. quickly confessed and led the police directly to the body.

Comment

This is a typical case of a situationally stimulated domestic homicide with staging. D. D. had no psychiatric history or current psychiatric diagnosis. The main motivation was anger, stemming from an argument that escalated out of control. He had never behaved violently before, and, absent similar circumstances, the likelihood of future violent conduct is remote.

Impulsive Offenders Who Commit Homicide

Impulsive offenders are distinguished primarily by their lifestyle, involving lack of direction, randomness of action, and general unpredictability. They can be differentiated from situational murderers by the multiplicity of minor antisocial acts in their background (Revitch & Schlesinger, 1981; Schlesinger, 2004b). Such individuals are often passive, easily led, and overly influenced by circumstances. The personalities of impulsive offenders are poorly integrated; they have difficulty seeing life in perspective; and they discharge inner tension through action because of their difficulty with modulating their emotions. The offenses they commit, whether homicides or other crimes, are generally poorly structured and are only partially, if at all, premeditated.

Such individuals are not driven to commit an offense; they simply overreact to circumstances. Thus, the recidivism rate for impulsive offenders is rather high. In fact, prisons are filled with nonhomicidal impulsive offenders, who distinguish themselves by being unreliable and typically more disturbed than those incarcerated for murder, as most murders are generally a situational, one-time offense. The following case of an impulsive offender who killed a woman with whom he was living is illustrative.

---------------------------------- **Illustrative Case 5** ----------------------------------

A 20-year-old male, E. E., who had a learning disability and experienced peer ridicule in school (which eventually led to his dropping out in the 10th grade), was involved in repetitive minor antisocial acts throughout most of his life. After he spent several years unemployed and idle, his mother asked a friend whether E. E. could stay with her for a time, and she agreed in order to give E. E.'s mother "a break." The woman reasoned that E. E. might be able to help her by doing chores, making minor repairs, and the like.

E. E. became involved in a telephone party line, where he met a 15-year-old girl who lived about 70 miles away. After they spent some time together, the adolescent no longer wanted to be with him. But before breaking up with E. E., she decided to spend a weekend with the future offender "one last time." Without telling her parents where she was going, she took a train to where E. E. was staying.

The youngster provided a vivid description of the unplanned murder of the 35-year-old woman with whom E. E. had been residing. E. E. and the victim got into an argument, and he killed her by bludgeoning her head with a club. This act resulted in extensive amounts of blood splattered all over the apartment. The offender disposed of the body, spent 2 days cleaning and repainting the apartment "to get rid of evidence," and was eventually apprehended in an attempt to flee to a different state.

Notwithstanding the 15-year-old witness's vivid description, which was consistent with crime scene evidence, E. E. gave the MHPs who evaluated him a different account of events. He claimed that his 15-year-old girlfriend was pregnant (which was untrue) and that it was her idea to have him kill the victim:

> I did it because of her. They got into a sexual argument. She [the victim] was a lesbian and came on to her. She said she didn't want her around. So I got a knife, went to her room, stabbed her in the back, and hit her with a billy club. I stabbed her three more times so she died.

Strong feelings of inadequacy, self-deprecation, and self-loathing just poured out of this offender when evaluated. In fact, he had shoulder-length hair that he combed over his face because he was so self-conscious of the way he looked. The day before his murder trial was to begin, E. E. stabbed himself in the eye with a pen, which resulted in his death.

Comment

E. E. falls in the impulsive offender category, not primarily because of the explosive nature of the homicide, as many homicides are sudden and unplanned, but because of his behavior pattern: his history of multiple minor antisocial acts; his lifestyle, characterized by lack of direction and unpredictability; and his history of developmental disabilities and strong feelings of inadequacy, chronic hostility, and a nonspecific need for revenge, which dominated his thinking (Schlesinger, 2004b). This offender was chronically depressed and had a severe personality disorder, but these problems had little direct relevance in explaining the homicide and would have had no significant bearing on his future dangerousness.

Catathymic Homicides

The term *catathymia* was introduced by Swiss psychiatrist Hans W. Maier (1912) and is best defined, according to Feyerabend's (1969) Greek dictionary, as meaning "in accordance with emotions." Maier used the concept to explain the development of the content of delusions. He believed that only those delusions rooted in an underlying "complex" are catathymic. Delusions resulting from organicity or intoxication are not considered catathymic because they arise from a change in brain functions rather than from psychogenesis.

Wertham (1937) borrowed Maier's concept as an explanation for what he considered to be (quasi-delusional) changes in thinking that result in extreme acts of violence, including homicide. He defined catathymic crisis as "the transformation of the stream of thought as the result of certain complexes of ideas that are charged with a strong affect—usually a wish, a fear, or an ambivalent striving" (p. 975). Thus, an individual comes to believe that the only solution to an internal conflict is a violent act, and this idea becomes fixed and intractable. Following the outburst, the actor often feels a sense of relief, a removal of the preceding state of tension, along with an almost complete change in thinking, which previously was fixed and rigid. Over the past 50 years, many authors (e.g., Gayral, Millet, Moron, & Turnin, 1956; Meloy, 1988, 1992, 2000; Revitch, 1964; Satten, Menninger, & Mayman, 1960; Schlesinger, 1996a), as well as the *DSM-III* (American Psychiatric Association, 1980), have used catathymia as a descriptive label for various types of explosive outbursts.

Revitch and Schlesinger (1978, 1981) were influenced not only by Wertham's concept of catathymic crisis, which involves a long-term, protracted relationship with the future victim, but also by Satten et al.'s (1960) conception of catathymia as a sudden aggressive act triggered by an individual whom the perpetrator has just met. Accordingly, Revitch and Schlesinger updated Wertham's initial concept and considered catathymia not a clinical diagnosis (as did Wertham) but rather a psychodynamic, or what Meloy (1992) has referred to as a motivational, process with an acute and chronic form (see Table 27.1).

Table 27.1   Differentiating Characteristics of Chronic and Acute Catathymic Processes

	Chronic	Acute
Activation of process	Triggered by a sudden, overwhelming emotion attached to underlying sexual conflicts of symbolic significance.	Triggered by a buildup of tension, a feeling of frustration, helplessness, and inadequacy; sometimes extending into the sexual area.
Relationship to the victim	Usually a stranger.	Usually a close relation, such as a current or former intimate partner.
Victim symbolization	Often a displaced matricide.	Rarely a displaced matricide, but victim may have symbolic significance.
Incubation period	Several seconds.	One day to a year; may involve stalking.
Level of planning	Unplanned.	Planned, frequently in the form of an obsessive rumination.
Method of attack	Sudden, violent; often overkill.	Violent but not sudden.
Crime scene	Very disorganized, reflecting a complete lack of planning.	Less disorganized.
Sexual activity	Occasional sexual activity just before attack; impotency common.	Sexual activity rare at time of homicide.
Postmortem behavior	Sometimes necrophilia and occasionally dismemberment.	Rarely necrophilia or dismemberment.
Feeling following the attack	Usually a flattening of emotions.	Usually a feeling of relief.
Memory of event	Usually poor.	Usually preserved.

Source: From *Sexual Murder: Catathymic and Compulsive Homicides* (p. 162), by L. B. Schlesinger, 2004b, Boca Raton, FL: CRC Press. Reprinted with permission.

Acute Catathymic Homicides

The acute catathymic homicide is different from situational acts of violence triggered by anger, fear, or jealousy or violence perpetrated under the influence of substances. Catathymic dynamics tap deeper sources of emotional conflict, almost always involving strong feelings of inadequacy extending into the sexual area, which, when released, overwhelm the offender's controls and result in a violent outburst. Frequently, the repressed conflict has symbolic significance for the victim. In some cases, offenders cannot provide a logical explanation for their behavior; in other cases, they may only partially recall its having occurred.

Diagnostic difficulties sometimes occur in differentiating catathymic homicides, which are a result of deeper and more complex psychological factors, from severe violence that is simply a result of anger and loss of control. The conclusion that an individual experienced an acute catathymic explosion can be reached only after careful evaluation of the offender and the offense, so that the depth of the individual's inner conflict and the triggering event can be fully understood. Many individuals who have committed an acute catathymic homicide were evaluated by MHPs prior to the explosion; however, the seriousness of their disturbance was either well masked or was not understood by the examining clinician. Thus, a full understanding of the catathymic process is valuable not only for forensic MHPs, but also for nonforensic MHPs who might be able to prevent some tragedies. The following case of an acute catathymic homicide is illustrative.

––––––––––––––––––––––––––––– **Illustrative Case 6** –––––––––––––––––––––––––––––

An 18-year-high school student, F. F., who worked part time as a gas station attendant, strangled a 22-year-old female nightclub entertainer with a rubber hose. While F. F. was working in the gas station, the future victim asked to borrow a dime for a telephone call. Following her call, the defendant claimed she pulled up her dress and invited the young man to have sexual relations with her. Unable to maintain an erection (possibly as a result of the victim's assertiveness and his own immaturity), F. F. was taunted by the woman, who said, "Go back to your mother." Following this comment, he grabbed a rubber hose, approached the victim, and strangled her. He put the body in the trunk of his car and dumped it in a local field.

That evening, F. F. recalled that he slept fairly well, and when he awoke the next morning, he thought that what he had done was a dream. Here, the defense mechanism of denial became operative as his behavior was totally antithetical to his prior conduct and his values. During the next day, while he was at school, fragments of the event began to enter F. F.'s consciousness. He became anxious and began to suspect that what he dreamed actually occurred. When he went to the field where he had dumped the body, the police were there, and he turned himself in. The victim's taunt, "Go back to your mother," had activated underlying emotionally charged sexual conflicts, which he had been secretly struggling with for years but had never revealed to others.

Comment

Sudden loss of control resulting in an explosive homicide has obvious psycholegal implications. Mental health professionals retained to assess a defendant's mental state at the time of the crime are required to supply a traditional *DSM* diagnosis as a condition for a legal defense. Catathymic process, particularly an acute catathymic process, can be helpful in supplementing a traditional *DSM* diagnosis, especially where the motive is unclear (Schlesinger, 1996b). Thus, having MHPs explain the basics of an acute catathymic homicide can often enable the court to gain insight into the complexity of such a case, as well as into how it is different from common acts of impulsive aggression; this information is necessary for reaching an informed opinion regarding guilt as well as sentencing.

Chronic Catathymic Homicides

Revitch and Schlesinger's (1978, 1981, 1989) chronic form of the catathymic process, an updated and simplified version of Wertham's (1937) catathymic crisis, involves three stages: incubation, the violent act, and relief. The incubation stage may last from several days to over a year, during which time the future offender becomes obsessively preoccupied with the future victim. He or she eventually develops a fixed idea that violence is the only solution to an internal conflict that has created enormous inner tension. This conflict also usually involves strong feelings of inadequacy extending into the sexual area (Schlesinger, 2004b). At times, suicidal thoughts may become intermingled with homicidal thoughts, and, in many cases, suicide follows the murder if the catathymic tension is not completely released by the violence.

Chronic catathymic homicides frequently occur within the framework of an intimate or former intimate relationship. Thus, it is often found in cases of stalking (Meloy, 1992, 1998). The interpersonal relationship itself, in these instances, disrupts the offender's psychological stability. In stalking cases, the fixed idea to kill often reflects the offender's inability to contain inner conflicts surrounding an obsession with the future victim (Schlesinger, 2002). Frequently, authorities try to supply a logical motive for the homicide and suggest that the offender reacted in a violent manner simply because the victim pulled away or tried to end the relationship. Such incorrect and simplistic explanations are unfortunately too common. The following case is a typical chronic catathymic homicide involving an individual who killed his wife.

——————————————— **Illustrative Case 7** ———————————————

As their marital difficulties increased, 29-year-old G. G. and his wife sought counseling at a mental health center. The marital therapy ended when Mrs. G. decided to file for divorce. Over the next 9 months, G. G. continued in individual therapy, although his depression deepened and suicidal thoughts emerged. He developed a vague idea of killing his wife. At first, this idea seemed distant and unreal. After toying with the thought for several weeks, he decided to tell his psychiatrist, who dismissed the notion as insignificant. However, the idea of killing his wife increased in intensity and eventually, according to G. G., "no longer seemed crazy."

As the holiday season approached, G. G. became increasingly more depressed because "people were happy but I wasn't happy. On Christmas Eve, I decided to go to Midnight Mass to see my wife. I took my gun because I felt weak." While he drove to the church with his gun in the car, G. G. experienced feelings of depersonalization. "Things didn't look real to me. The trees didn't look real. I actually saw myself driving. It was weird." After Mass, G. G. followed Mrs. G. and her parents into their driveway. He took out his gun and shot his wife several times in the head, kissing her and expressing his love for her while she was dying. The parents were able to run into their house and call the police, and G. G. was quickly arrested. When evaluated in the county jail, G. G. showed no signs of any psychotic process, although he was found to be significantly depressed.

In this case, the incubation phase of the catathymic process was accompanied by depression with suicidal preoccupation, which was later mixed with, and finally dominated by, homicidal thoughts. At first, the idea of killing his wife seemed vague and far off, but it slowly built to the point where the idea became intractable and an obsession and the only way G. G. thought he could solve his problem. Unfortunately, G. G.'s psychiatrist dismissed his revelation about killing the victim. The defendant's kissing his wife after shooting her in the head illustrates his ambivalent feelings for her.

G. G. explained that he felt his wife had left him because he was unable to satisfy her sexually. "She did not say this exactly, but you could tell it was true." As the catathymic tension built, G. G. believed he could reduce it only by eliminating the source of the conflict either by homicide or by removing himself through suicide. The motive cited by the authorities, that the offender was angry because of the impending divorce, is simplistic and does not validly reflect the depth of this offender's conflicts, nor does it explain all of the levels of his motivation. It was not the offender's anger that caused the homicide but the emergence of an intractable idea to kill, with an accompanying pressure to act.

Comment

The chronic catathymic process has been recognized as a clinical entity for almost a half century (Meloy, 1992, 2000; Schlesinger, 1996a). However, its value in forensic practice has not been fully appreciated. Pleas of insanity, such as in Case 7, are usually rejected by the jury for essentially three reasons: (1) There is no clear-cut psychosis, a necessary condition to establish mental disease; (2) the jury does not fully appreciate the significance of the accompanying dissociative state; and (3) the jury often equates obsessive rumination with premeditation. Sentencing options, capacity for rehabilitation, and the potential for repetition if the underlying complex is not adequately addressed are additional important points for the court and the parole board.

Compulsive Homicides

The term *compulsion* is derived from Latin *compellere,* which means "to compel, force, urge, or drive on." The compulsion to kill stems from a fusion of sex and aggression so that the aggressive act is sexually stimulating and, in essence, is a part of the offender's sexual arousal pattern (Schlesinger, 2004b). These homicides do not necessarily involve rape or an overt manifestation of genitality, as the murder itself is sexually arousing and sufficient.

The compulsive, repetitive, sexually motivated murderer is by no means a modern or even an American phenomenon. In fact, history records many examples of such homicides. For instance, fifteenth-century French nobleman Gilles de Rais managed to kidnap, torture, sexually molest, and kill at least 150 children (Benedetti, 1972). In sixteenth-century Germany, Peter Stubbe raped, tortured, and committed 15 sexual murders that involved cannibalism (Hill & Williams, 1967). Perhaps one of the most notorious premodern cases of compulsive homicide was that of Jack the Ripper, who terrorized Victorian England in the late 1800s (Begg, Fido, & Skinner, 1991). He supposedly sent letters to the press proclaiming, "I am down on whores and shan't quit ripping them until I do get buckled." At the same time Jack the Ripper was active, Richard von Krafft-Ebing (1886) began the first scientific study of sexual homicide, chronicled in his classic text *Psychopathia Sexualis*. A careful reading of Krafft-Ebing's book demonstrates that much of what is currently known about the compulsive sexually motivated murderer was first described by him at the end of the nineteenth century.

Compulsive sexually motivated murders did not receive a great deal of attention from researchers until the late 1970s, when members of law enforcement, specifically the FBI, became interested in this group of criminals, mostly from an investigative perspective. Their interest resulted in a comprehensive study of 36 sexual murderers (Ressler, Burgess, & Douglas, 1988), which ultimately led to refinement of an investigative technique commonly referred to as criminal, investigative, or psychological profiling. The process had first been elaborated by psychiatrist James Brussell (1968) during his consultation on the New York case of the "Mad Bomber," an individual who eluded law enforcement for about 17 years. Brussell stressed the importance of crime scene behavior rather than psychological concepts that had been stressed by MHPs.

Compulsive murderers can be envisioned as falling on a continuum. On one end are offenders who plan their crimes in exceptional detail and discharge their compulsion with such care that they often go undetected for long periods of time. On the other end are individuals who also harbor an internal compulsion to kill but who act out in an unplanned, spontaneous fashion. They leave considerable evidence at the crime scene and are, therefore, relatively quickly apprehended.

Planned Compulsive Homicides

Compulsive offenders who plan their crimes in detail often engage in repetitive, ritualistic behavior at the crime scene, sometimes referred to as "personation" or "signature" (Douglas, Burgess, Burgess, & Ressler, 1992). Here, the offender injects his personality into the crime scene by way of body positioning, mutilation, items left, or other symbolic acts. These ritualistic behaviors, an outgrowth of the offender's long-standing deviant fantasies, help the individual achieve psychosexual gratification, which the murder alone does not fully accomplish (Keppel, 1995; MacCulloch, Snowden, Wood, & Mills, 1983; Warren, Hazelwood, & Dietz, 1996). The following case of an individual who committed a series of planned compulsive-repetitive murders is typical.

———————————————— **Illustrative Case 8** ————————————————

A 30-year-old male, H. H., killed a 25-year-old woman and subsequently murdered a 26-year-old woman and her two young children, ages 6 and 8. (He also confessed to killing two other women, ages 62 and 40, but was never indicted.) The offender killed all victims by manual strangulation after hog-tying them, raping them anally and vaginally, and making numerous small knife cuts (which purposefully caused bleeding and pain) all over their bodies. He brought a "murder kit" with him that contained various objects he believed he would need to carry out his acts.

All H. H.'s crime scenes shared a common denominator: an absence of physical evidence. H. H. had read detective magazines and studied books on criminal investigation so that he could avoid detection by not leaving behind any evidence. Accordingly, he shaved his entire body and entered the homes naked, except for sneakers with several socks pulled over them. In addition, he poured alcohol into the vaginas and rectums of the victims (after raping them), believing that alcohol would remove any trace of his DNA. H. H. explained that he got this idea from the movie *Presumed Innocent,* whose subplot involved the use of a spermicide. Unbeknown to H. H., however, alcohol preserves rather than destroys semen, and a perfect DNA match was made, leading to his confession.

This offender's early life was marked by a fascination with knives, occasional use of marijuana, and by the torture and killing of cats. After graduating from high school, H. H. joined the military but was discharged because he intimidated, manipulated, and stole from subordinates. He was described by his army friends as "tremendously self-centered." H. H. demonstrated a strong need for power and control not only in his crimes but also in his general interpersonal relationships. Nevertheless, he had no difficulty attracting women and was living with one throughout the time of all of the murders.

Comment

The defense-retained experts relied solely on what the defendant had told them in their interviews; H. H. painted a picture for them of being a mild-mannered, sensitive individual who had psychological problems because he was unable to achieve all his life's goals. These examiners ignored the sadistic aspects of the crimes, specifically placing little significance on the fact that the victims were hog-tied and that numerous small torture marks were evident all over their bodies. This type of ritualistic behavior is sexually motivated and is a major indication that the homicide was a result of an internal drive, or compulsion, to kill. The ominous significance of such conduct is evident.

Unplanned Compulsive Homicides

The offender's personality is an intervening variable between the compulsion to kill and how the crime is carried out (Schlesinger, 2004b). In other words, compulsive offenders who commit *planned* sexual murders typically have psychopathic, sociopathic, narcissistic, antisocial, and other personality disorders that do not disorganize their thinking, conduct, and ability to plan their crimes (Dietz, Hazelwood, & Warren, 1990; Porter, Woodworth, Earle, Drugge, & Boer, 2003). They are manipulative and deceptive but are not distracted by interfering overt psychopathological symptoms such as hallucinations or delusions. Compulsive murderers who act in an *unplanned,* spontaneous manner do not have different under-lying motivational elements, but they have more overt psychopathological distur-bances, which usually fall within the borderline, schizotypal, or schizoid spectrum of personality disorders, or even more severe forms of mental illness such as Schizophrenia (Schlesinger, 2004b). Their disorganized personalities obstruct careful thought and planning.

Thus, an individual's personality is totally independent of the underlying com-pulsion; instead, it greatly influences how the crime is carried out. Accordingly, of-fenders with more intact personalities are likely to plan their offenses and elude law enforcement; they are obviously very dangerous as they can victimize many people in serial fashion. Offenders with more psychopathology act in a sponta-neous, unplanned way, leaving evidence at the crime scene, and are usually quickly arrested. Hazelwood and Warren (2000) note that such offenders do not ordinarily seek out a particular type of victim; their fantasies are undifferentiated, and their actions are sometimes so spontaneous that they may attack a random stranger while committing another crime simply because the victim is present. The following case of an individual whose compulsion was spontaneously released by the victim's promiscuous behavior is illustrative.

--------- **Illustrative Case 9** ---------

A 25-year-old male, I. I. met a 17-year-old female at an amusement park. After speaking with her briefly, he took her to a motel; they quickly undressed and had intercourse and oral sex. The offender remarked, "I couldn't stand it that she would have sex with me without even knowing me." I. I. killed her by placing his belt around her neck and then took the body to a remote area, where "I continued to beat her and kick her." The next day, he confessed to a friend who then called the police.

In addition to antisocial and severe borderline personality traits, and tremen-dous rage directed toward everyone, I. I. had an impulse-control disorder. He claimed that he initially did not have any thought of killing the victim but wanted only a sexual encounter. However, because of her promiscuity, which he connected to his biological mother, his anger escalated. He explained that he was unable to control himself. (As an adolescent, he tried to discuss his disturbing sexually ag-gressive fantasies with several therapists but, according to I. I., they were disinter-ested as "they never took notes.")

Comment

The unplanned, disorganized, brutal nature of this crime is typical of an offender whose underlying compulsion is released by circumstances. Here, the trigger was the victim's willingness to engage in sexual activity with a person she had just met. The offender's impulse control disorder and personality disorder did not cause the sexual murder but determined how the murder was carried out. I. I. stated clearly that if he were released from prison, he would definitely kill again under similar conditions.

PREDICTION AND THE MOTIVATIONAL SPECTRUM

Mental health professionals are frequently asked to make predictions regarding the likelihood of future violence in individuals they evaluate (Monahan, 2003). The ability of MHPs to make such predictions has generated an enormous amount of research, theory, and debate since the early 1970s (Monahan, 1996, 2003). Initially, most researchers were pessimistic about the ability of MHPs to predict future violence (Ennis & Litwack, 1974). However, research and thinking on dangerousness predictions have evolved, and the current consensus is that some types of predictions can, in fact, be made under some circumstances (Litwack, 2001; Litwack & Schlesinger, 1987, 1999). The concept of the motivational spectrum can be of great practical assistance to forensic MHPs in offering a prognostic assessment of homicide in particular and of antisocial behavior in general.

The future violent conduct of environmentally stimulated homicidal offenders depends largely on the setting in which they live and the interpersonal connections they establish following the commission of the crime or following incarceration. For example, individuals who have committed contract, cult, or gang-related homicides will behave similarly if returned to the same environmental influences or to circumstances similar to those that affected them previously. Most situational offenses, which constitute the majority of all homicides and have the best prognosis for repetition, stem largely from domestic disputes or arguments, and the chance that the murderer will kill again is rather low (Revitch & Schlesinger, 1981). The impulsive offender's lifestyle, characterized by unpredictability, spontaneity, and multiple prior antisocial acts, leads to a poorer prognosis than that for the environmentally or situationally stimulated offender. In most cases, impulsive offenders will not commit another homicide, but they are likely to continue in diverse criminal activities (Schlesinger, 2004a).

Individuals who have already committed a sexual homicide involving either catathymic or compulsive motivational dynamics have a much higher potential for repetition than do the environmental, situational, or impulsive offenders (Revitch & Schlesinger, 1989). Although most catathymic homicides are one-time events, some catathymic offenders, even after many years of incarceration, commit another catathymic murder when similar, unresolved conflicts are again ignited (Schlesinger, 1996a, 1996b). Acute catathymic homicides generally cannot be prevented; however, individuals who struggle with pronounced feelings of inadequacy extending into the sexual area should be red-flagged as having a potential risk factor, especially if they reveal that they believe violence is a solution to an internal problem (Schlesinger, 2002). Such individuals must be questioned with the same level of thoroughness practitioners generally use in assessing individuals whom they suspect of being suicidal.

The offender who has already committed a compulsive homicide, particularly one involving ritualistic, signature behavior, has the worst prognosis for repetitiveness (Revitch & Schlesinger, 1981, 1989; Schlesinger, 2004b). Such individuals do not kill in response to psychotic symptoms, social influence, situational pressure, or even the triggering of unresolved conflicts that may overwhelm and disrupt their psychological integration. Instead, compulsive offenders have an inner pressure that drives them to seek out victims to kill. Accordingly, they are the most dangerous and present the highest risk for repetition (Meloy, 2000; Schlesinger, 2004b).

Of greater importance than a history of psychosis or a history of the usual sex crimes in the prediction of sexually motivated compulsive murder are the following 10 signs, especially when seen in combination (Schlesinger, 2001b): a history of childhood abuse (Ressler et al., 1988); inappropriate maternal sexual conduct (Brittain, 1970; Liebert, 1985); pathological lying and manipulation (Ressler et al., 1988); sadistic fantasy with a compulsion to act (Burgess, Hartman, Ressler, Douglas, & McCormack, 1986); animal cruelty, particularly against cats (Felthous & Keller, 1987); a need to control and dominate others (MacCulloch et al., 1983); repetitive fire setting (Myers, Burgess, & Nelson, 1998); voyeurism, fetishism, and sexually motivated burglary (Schlesinger & Revitch, 1999); unprovoked attacks on females in connection with generalized misogynous emotions (Revitch, 1980); and evidence of ritualistic (signature) behavior (Douglas et al., 1992). As a practical matter, these signs provide guidance for MHPs, who are routinely asked to offer judgments regarding the dangerousness of this population of offenders or potential offenders.

CONCLUSION

The number of homicides per year in the United States (approximately 20,000, according to the FBI's, 2004, *Uniform Crime Reports*) is approaching the number of suicides (approximately 30,000; Insel & Charney, 2003), making homicide a major public health problem, especially for young men 25 to 35 years old. The prevention of homicide, as well as the proper management and disposition of offenders, necessitates an in-depth study of the problem beyond trying to fit homicidal behavior into a Procrustean bed of psychiatric disorders and legal standards. Accordingly, MHPs need to refocus and expand their approach to evaluating and understanding criminal and homicidal offenders.

This chapter described a method of classification that can be helpful to MHPs, in a complementary way, in formulating psycholegal opinions, providing assessments of dangerousness, and conceptualizing the complexity of many homicide cases. Although a *DSM* diagnosis is necessary in most legal proceedings, and the law is the standard to which opinions are formulated, neither the offender's psychiatric diagnosis nor his or her degree of legal culpability is particularly helpful in solving prognostic and dispositional issues. The management of homicidal offenders, specifically with regard to their dangerousness, is often more important for the protection of society than the length of time served or the location (i.e., prison versus hospital) of the incarceration. MHPs' opinions need to be based on a careful analysis of what the offender did rather than simply on the offender's own statements (to the authorities or to MHPs), which are too often self-serving and inaccurate. Therefore, an understanding of the psychopathology, psychodynamics, and various types of homicide, as well as prognostic indicators, is necessary in arriving at accurate and useful opinions for the court, members of law enforcement, governmental agencies, and others who are involved in the management of such potentially dangerous individuals.

REFERENCES

American Psychiatric Association. (1980). *Diagnostic and statistical manual of mental disorders* (3rd ed.). Washington, DC: Author.

American Psychiatric Association. (2000). *Diagnostic and statistical manual of mental disorders* (4th ed., text rev.). Washington, DC: Author.

Arendt, H. (1966). *Eichmann in Jerusalem: A report on the banality of evil.* New York: Viking Press.

Auerhahn, K., & Parker, R. N. (1999). Drugs, alcohol, and homicide. In M. D. Smith & M. A. Zahn (Eds.), *Studying and preventing homicide* (pp. 97–114). Thousand Oaks, CA: Sage.

Begg, P., Fido, M., & Skinner, K. (1991). *Jack the Ripper A–Z.* London: Headline.

Benedetti, J. (1972). *Gilles de Rais.* New York: Stein & Day.

Blau, T. H. (1998). *The psychologist as expert witness* (2nd ed.). New York: Wiley.

Brancale, R. (1955). Problems of classification. *National Probation and Parole Association Journal, 1,* 118–125.

Brittain, R. (1970). The sadistic murderer. *Medicine, Science, and Law, 10,* 198–207.

Bromberg, W. (1961). *The mold of murder: A psychiatric study of homicide.* New York: Grune & Stratton.

Brussell, J. S. (1968). *Casebook of a crime psychiatrist.* New York: Grove Press.

Bugliosi, V., & Gentry, C. (1975). *Helter skelter.* New York: Bantam Books.

Burgess, A. W., Hartman, C. R., Ressler, R. K., Douglas, J. E., & McCormack, A. (1986). Sexual homicide: A motivational model. *Journal of Interpersonal Violence, 1,* 151–272.

Butcher, J. N., Graham, J. R., Ben-Porath, Y. S., Tellegen, A., & Dahlstrom, W. G. (2001). *MMPI-2 manual for administration, scoring, and interpretation.* Minneapolis: University of Minnesota Press.

Cooke, G. (1980). *The role of the forensic psychologist in criminal and civil law.* Springfield, IL: Thomas.

Davidson, H. (1965). *Forensic psychiatry* (2nd ed.). New York: Ronald Press.

Dietz, P. E., Hazelwood, R. R., & Warren, J. (1990). The sexually sadistic criminal and his offenses. *Bulletin of the American Academy of Psychiatry and Law, 18,* 163–178.

Douglas, J. E., Burgess, A. W., Burgess, A. G., & Ressler, R. K. (1992). *Crime classification manual.* San Francisco: Jossey-Bass.

Ennis, B. J., & Litwack, T. R. (1974). Psychiatry and the presumption of expertise: Flipping coins in the courtroom. *California Law Review, 62,* 693–752.

Federal Bureau of Investigation. (2004). *Crime in the United States: Uniform crime reports.* Washington, DC: U.S. Department of Justice.

Felthous, A. R., & Keller, S. R. (1987). Childhood cruelty to animals and later aggression against people: A review. *American Journal of Psychiatry, 144,* 710–717.

Feyerabend, K. (1969). *Pocket Greek dictionary.* New York: McGraw-Hill.

Friedman, A. (1998). Substance use/abuse as a predictor of illegal and violent behavior: A review of the relevant literature. *Aggression and Violent Behavior, 3,* 339–355.

Gayral, L., Millet, G., Moron, P., & Turnin, J. (1956). Crises et paroxysmes catathymiques [Crises and catathymic paroxysms]. *Annales Médico Psychologiques, 114,* 25–50.

Gilbert, G. M. (1947). *Nuremberg diary.* New York: Farrar, Straus.

Goldstein, A. M. (Ed.). (2003). *Comprehensive handbook of psychology: Vol. 11. Forensic psychology.* Hoboken, NJ: Wiley.

Halleck, S. (1971). *Psychiatry and the dilemmas of crime.* Los Angeles: University of California Press.

Hazelwood, R. R., & Warren, J. I. (2000). The sexually violent offender: Impulsive or ritualistic? *Aggression and Violent Behavior, 5,* 267–279.

Heilbrun, K., Rosenfeld, B., Warren, J., & Collins, S. (1994). The use of third party information in forensic assessments: A two state comparison. *Bulletin of the American Academy of Psychiatry and Law, 22,* 399–406.

Hempel, A. G., Meloy, J. R., & Richards, T. C. (1999). Offender and offense characteristics of a nonrandom sample of mass murderers. *Journal of the American Academy of Psychiatry and Law, 27,* 213–225.

Hess, A. K., & Weiner, I. B. (Eds.). (1999). *Handbook of forensic psychology* (2nd ed.). New York: Wiley.

Hill, D., & Williams, P. (1967). *The supernatural.* New York: Signet.

Insel, T. R., & Charney, D. S. (2003). Research on major depression: Strategies and priorities. *Journal of the American Medical Association, 289,* 3167–3168.

Keppel, R. (1995). Signature murders: A report of several related cases. *Journal of Forensic Sciences, 40,* 670–674.

Krafft-Ebing, R. von. (1886). *Psychopathia sexualis* (C. G. Chaddock, Trans.). Philadelphia: F. A. Davis.

Lanzkron, J. (1963). Murder and insanity. *American Journal of Psychiatry, 119,* 754–758.

Lewis, B. (1987). *The assassins.* New York: Oxford University Press.

Liebert, J. A. (1985). Contributions of psychiatric consultation in the investigation of serial murder. *International Journal of Offender Therapy and Comparative Criminology, 28,* 187–200.

Lifton, R. J. (1986). *Nazi doctors: Medical killing and the psychology of genocide.* New York: Basic Books.

Litwack, T. R. (2001). Actuarial versus clinical assessments of dangerousness. *Psychology, Public Policy, and Law, 7,* 409–443.

Litwack, T. R., & Schlesinger, L. B. (1987). Assessing and predicting violence: Research, law, and applications. In I. B. Weiner & A. K. Hess (Eds.), *Handbook of forensic psychology* (pp. 205–257). New York: Wiley.

Litwack, T. R., & Schlesinger, L. B. (1999). Dangerousness risk assessments: Research, legal, and clinical considerations. In A. K. Hess & I. B. Weiner (Eds.), *Handbook of forensic psychology* (2nd ed., pp. 171–217). New York: Wiley.

MacCulloch, M. J., Snowden, P. R., Wood, P. J., & Mills, H. E. (1983). Sadistic fantasy, sadistic behavior, and offending. *British Journal of Psychiatry, 143,* 20–29.

Maier, H. W. (1912). Katathyme Wahnbildung und Paranoia [On the subject of catathymic delusions and paranoia]. *Zeitschrift für die Gesamte Neurologie und Psychiatrie, 13,* 555–610.

Mark, V. M., & Ervin, F. R. (1970). *Violence and the brain.* New York: Harper & Row.

Mark, V. M., & Southgate, T. M. (1971). Violence and brain disease. *Journal of the American Medical Association, 216,* 1025–1034.

Meloy, J. R. (1988). *The psychopathic mind: Origins, dynamics and treatment.* Northvale, NJ: Aronson.

Meloy, J. R. (1992). *Violent attachments.* Northvale, NJ: Aronson.

Meloy, J. R. (Ed.). (1998). *The psychology of stalking.* New York: Academic Press.

Meloy, J. R. (2000). The nature and dynamics of sexual homicide: An integrative review. *Aggression and Violent Behavior, 5,* 1–22.

Melton, G. B., Petrila, J., Poythress, N. G., & Slobogin, C. (1997). *Psychological evaluations for the courts* (2nd ed.). New York: Guilford Press.

Milgram, S. (1963). Behavioral study of obedience. *Journal of Abnormal and Social Psychology, 67,* 371–378.

Monahan, J. (1996). Violence prediction: The past 20 years and the next 20 years. *Criminal Justice and Behavior, 23,* 107–130.

Monahan, J. (2003). Violence risk assessment. In I. B. Weiner (Series Ed.) & A. M. Goldstein (Vol. Ed.), *Comprehensive handbook of psychology: Vol. 11. Forensic psychology* (pp. 527–540). Hoboken, NJ: Wiley.

Myers, W. C., Burgess, A. W., & Nelson, J. A. (1998). Criminal and behavioral aspects of juvenile sexual homicide. *Journal of Forensic Sciences, 43,* 340–347.

Pallone, N. J., & Hennessey, J. J. (1994). *Criminal behavior: A process psychology analysis.* New Brunswick, NJ: Transaction.

Parker, R. N., & Auerhahn, K. (1999). Drugs, alcohol and homicide: Issues in theory and research. In M. D. Smith & M. A. Zahn (Eds.), *Homicide: A sourcebook of social research* (pp. 176–191). Thousand Oaks, CA: Sage.

Pernanen, K. (1991). *Alcohol in human violence.* New York: Guilford Press.

Pincus, J. N., & Tucker, G. J. (1985). *Behavioral neurology* (3rd ed.). New York: Oxford University Press.

Porter, S., Woodworth, M., Earle, J., Drugge, J., & Boer, D. (2003). Characteristics of sexual homicides committed by psychopathic and non-psychopathic offenders. *Law and Human Behavior, 27,* 459–470.

Raine, A. (1993). *The psychopathology of crime: Criminal behavior as a clinical disorder.* New York: Academic Press.

Reich, P., & Hepps, R. B. (1972). Homicide during a psychosis induced by LSD. *Journal of the American Medical Association, 219,* 869–871.

Ressler, R. K., Burgess, A. W., & Douglas, J. E. (1988). *Sexual homicide: Patterns and motives.* New York: Free Press.

Revitch, E. (1964). Paroxysmal manifestations of non-epileptic origin: Catathymic attacks. *Diseases of the Nervous System, 25,* 662–670.

Revitch, E. (1977). Classification of offenders for prognostic and disposition evaluation. *Bulletin of the American Academy of Psychiatry and Law, 5,* 41–50.

Revitch, E. (1979). Patients who kill their physician. *Journal of the Medical Society of New Jersey, 76,* 429–431.

Revitch, E. (1980). Gynocide and unprovoked attacks on women. *Corrective and Social Psychiatry, 26,* 6–11.

Revitch, E., & Schlesinger, L. B. (1978). Murder: Evaluation, classification, and prediction. In I. L. Kutash, S. B. Kutash, & L. B. Schlesinger (Eds.), *Violence: Perspectives on murder and aggression* (pp. 138–164). San Francisco: Jossey-Bass.

Revitch, E., & Schlesinger, L. B. (1981). *Psychopathology of homicide.* Springfield, IL: Thomas.

Revitch, E., & Schlesinger, L. B. (1989). *Sex murder and sex aggression.* Springfield, IL: Thomas.

Ritzler, B. (1978). The Nuremberg mind revisited: A quantitative approach to Nazi Rorschachs. *Journal of Personality Assessment, 42,* 344–353.

Rogers, R. (1992). *Structured Interview of Reported Symptoms.* Odessa, FL: Psychological Assessment Resources.

Rosner, R. (Ed.). (2003). *Principles and practice of forensic psychiatry* (2nd ed.). London: Arnold.

Sadoff, R. L. (1975). *Forensic psychiatry: A practical guide for lawyers and psychiatrists.* Springfield, IL: Thomas.

Satten, J., Menninger, K., & Mayman, M. (1960). Murder without apparent motive: A study in personality disintegration. *American Journal of Psychiatry, 117,* 48–53.

Schlesinger, L. B. (1996a). The catathymic crisis, 1912–present: A clinical study. *Aggression and Violent Behavior, 1,* 307–316.

Schlesinger, L. B. (1996b). The catathymic process: Psychopathology and psychodynamics of extreme aggression. In L. B. Schlesinger (Ed.), *Explorations in criminal psychopathology: Clinical syndromes with forensic implications* (pp. 121–141). Springfield, IL: Thomas.

Schlesinger, L. B. (2001a). The contract murderer: Patterns, characteristics, and dynamics. *Journal of Forensic Sciences, 46,* 1119–1123.

Schlesinger, L. B. (2001b). The potential sex murderer: Ominous signs, risk assessment. *Journal of Threat Assessment, 1,* 47–72.

Schlesinger, L. B. (2002). Stalking, homicide and catathymic process: A case study. *International Journal of Offender Therapy and Comparative Criminology, 46,* 64–74.

Schlesinger, L. B. (2003a). A case study involving competency to stand trial: Incompetent defendant, incompetent examiner, or "malingering by proxy"? *Psychology, Public Policy and Law, 9,* 381–399.

Schlesinger, L. B. (2003b). Forensic psychology. In S. H. James & J. J. Nordby (Eds.), *Forensic science: An introduction to scientific and investigative techniques* (pp. 489–507). Boca Raton, FL: CRC Press.

Schlesinger, L. B. (2004a). Classification of antisocial behavior for prognostic purposes: Study the motivation not the crime. *Journal of Psychiatry and Law, 32,* 191–219.

Schlesinger, L. B. (2004b). *Sexual murder: Catathymic and compulsive homicides.* Boca Raton, FL: CRC Press.

Schlesinger, L. B., & Revitch, E. (1980). Stress, violence, and crime. In I. L. Kutash & L. B. Schlesinger (Eds.), *Handbook on stress and anxiety* (pp. 134–188). San Francisco: Jossey-Bass.

Schlesinger, L. B., & Revitch, E. (1999). Sexual burglaries and sexual homicide: Clinical, forensic, and investigative considerations. *Journal of the American Academy of Psychiatry and Law, 27,* 227–238.

Silva, J. A., Harry, B. E., Leong, G. B., & Weinstock, R. (1996). Dangerous delusional misidentification and homicide. *Journal of Forensic Sciences, 41,* 641–644.

Sutherland, E. H., & Cressey, D. R. (1939). *Principles of criminology.* Philadelphia: Lippincott.

Tanay, E. (1969). Psychiatric study of homicide. *American Journal of Psychiatry, 125,* 1252–1258.

Warren, J. I., Hazelwood, R. R., & Dietz, P. E. (1996). The sexually sadistic serial killer. *Journal of Forensic Sciences, 41,* 970–974.

Weiger, B., & Bear, D. (1988). An approach to the neurology of aggression. *Journal of Psychiatric Research, 22,* 85–89.

Wertham, F. (1937). The catathymic crisis: A clinical entity. *Archives of Neurology and Psychiatry, 37,* 974–977.

Wilcox, D. E. (1985). The relationship of mental illness to homicide. *American Journal of Forensic Psychiatry, 6,* 3–15.

Wolfgang, M. E. (1958). *Patterns of criminal homicide.* Philadelphia: University of Pennsylvania Press.

Zimbardo, P. (1973). Interpersonal dynamics in a simulated prison. *International Journal of Criminology and Penology, 1,* 69–97.

CHAPTER 28

Forensic Hypnosis

Susan C. Knight and Robert G. Meyer

Now that mesmerism under its new name of Hypnotism has been divested of the charlatanry which for so long obscured the subject, and its principles are being scientifically investigated and discussed, jurisprudence may afford to pay some attention to it.

—Brodie-Innes (1891, quoted in Alexander & Scheflin, 1998, p. 72)

Throughout the centuries, a variety of primitive forms akin to the modern-day hypnotic phenomena have existed as ancient practices associated with spirituality and healing. However, hypnosis as it is conceptualized today realized its modern beginnings with the work of Franz Anton Mesmer (1734–1815) on animal magnetism in the eighteenth century (Gravitz, 2004). From the time of Mesmer, the practice of hypnosis has evolved into a clinical tool frequently used for therapeutic purposes. In addition, a large body of hypnosis research continues to build, informing and refining the limits and potential of the technique. Nash (2000) reported that more than 7,000 articles in more than 150 journals have been published on hypnosis since 1966: "No contemporary therapeutic intervention has a longer history of empirical examination, and very few psychotherapy literatures can match the sheer bulk of research" (p. 108).

The U.S. judicial system has also played a role in refining and defining the limits of hypnotic techniques, resulting in a protracted history in the courts (Meyer & Weaver, in press-b; Sales & Shuman, 2005). Hypnosis was first used for contemporary forensic purposes in 1845, to refresh an eyewitness's memory for details of a crime; the earliest noted instance of allowing hypnotically refreshed testimony in a U.S. courtroom occurred in 1846 (Gravitz, 1995). This early instance of admitting hypnotically refreshed testimony proved a false start, as hypnosis was stricken from the courtroom in *People v. Ebanks* (1897, p. 1053): "The law of the United States does not recognize hypnotism. It would be an illegal defense, and I [the Court] cannot admit it." With these authoritative words, the Supreme Court of California effectively banned hypnosis from courtrooms for almost 70 years (Scheflin & Frischholz, 1999).

It was not until the early 1960s that hypnosis reemerged and began advancing through the court system. In *Cornell v. Superior Court of San Diego County* (1959), the rule of "open admissibility" of hypnotically obtained evidence was affirmed. The *Cornell* decision occurred in a period of unprecedented acceptance of hypnosis in scientific circles. In 1958, the American Medical Association recognized hypnosis as a legitimate treatment technique in medicine and dentistry. The national psychological and psychiatric associations were not far behind in their public acceptance of hypnosis, with the American Psychological Association endorsing hypnosis as a legitimate treatment modality in 1960 (Scheflin & Frischholz, 1999). As clinical hypnosis was gaining national recognition for its therapeutic potential, it had also begun its foray back into the courtroom, revitalized after the *Ebanks* decision. Since that time, forensic hypnosis has gained recognition within the legal system and carved out a specialty niche situated within the nexus of psychology, clinical hypnosis, and the legal arena (Meyer & Weaver, in press-b).

In this chapter, we provide an overview of the relevant issues pertaining to forensic hypnosis, commencing with definitional concerns and the distinction between clinical and forensic hypnosis. Empirical research pertaining to the validity of hypnotically refreshed memories is reviewed, including arguments for and against admissibility in the courtroom. The use of hypnosis with criminal defendants, in conjunction with the role of deception, is considered, using the Hillside Strangler case (*State v. Bianchi,* 1979). The role of coercion and a discussion of hypnosis and law enforcement is also presented. Regulating hypnosis in the courtroom is discussed, with relevant case law accompanying a discussion of each method of legal regulation. In conclusion, we review guidelines for ethical practice, including qualification and training, and methods to minimize legal risks when practicing forensic hypnosis.

WHAT IS HYPNOSIS?

Throughout the years, it has been notoriously difficult for the field to reach consensus on a universally accepted definition of hypnosis (Krippner, 2005). Numerous explanations of hypnotic phenomena have been offered, encompassing distinct theoretical explanations, including the dissociative, altered state views versus the nonstate, sociological explanations (Hilgard, 1992; Spanos & Coe, 1992). Yet, despite a proliferation of research and scholarly contributions, definitive parameters have proven elusive, as hypnosis "does not exist as a palpable, definable phenomenon; *it can be almost anything, everything, or nothing*" (Coe, 1992, p. 232). This ambiguity has presented challenges for hypnosis in court as it is difficult to implement ethical or legal regulation of a methodology with indeterminate properties (Sales & Shuman, 2005).

In response to this challenge, some have argued that if hypnosis-like procedures were used under the guise of an alternative label (e.g., relaxation, imagery), the legal controversy might be resolved. This strategy would combat stigma and prevent the contentious-laden term "hypnosis" from generating such restrictive legal policy (e.g., *per se* exclusion rule), as well as "escape the law" (Karle, 1991, p. 194). For example, a cognitive strategy labeled "focused breathing meditation" has been shown to produce a hypnotic-like state without formal induction and has been researched in forensic settings for memory facilitation (Wagstaff et al., 2004). Others have argued, however, that the "only obvious advantage [to the alternative labeling] seems to be that the word hypnosis would no longer have to be mentioned in court" (Naish, 1988, p. 355). Semantics aside, hypnosis is still prominent in the courts under its maiden name and thus subject to legal control.

The Court's Definition

As the field itself is in some disarray regarding a consensual definition, the court has attempted to simplify the issue by using a definition of hypnosis that depends on more objective criteria, such as the use of an induction procedure. In the court's view, if a formal induction is employed, hypnosis has taken place (Scheflin & Shapiro, 1989). Using this definition, phenomena akin to Wagstaff et al.'s (2004) focused breathing meditation would not be subject to exclusionary legal policy because there is no formal induction procedure. One panel of experts believed this legal definition to be problematic because it does not account for level of hypnotizability achieved (Hammond et al., 1995). This committee of experts stated, "It should be demonstrated that both a hypnotic induction was administered, and that the subject was responsive to such a procedure" (p. 3).

Once the procedure has been admitted into court as hypnosis, opposing sides use experts to further cloud the issue of definition (Scheflin & Shapiro, 1989). As for the clinician in court, Scheflin and Shapiro advised defining hypnosis in forensic settings using "primarily the variable of concentration of attention" (p. 133). Noted as the "most relevant and least problematic" definition, they suggested that the expert define hypnosis used for forensic purposes as the following:

> Hypnosis is an altered state of consciousness, characterized by intensified concentration of awareness on certain suggested themes, along with a diminished interest in competing perceptions. Subjects who are hypnotized experience perceptual and sensory distortions and enhanced abilities to utilize normally unconscious mental mechanisms. (p. 134)

Clinical versus Forensic Hypnosis

Hypnosis is used in many clinical arenas for a variety of purposes: as a pain management technique, for stress management and sleep disorders, to enhance athletic performance, as an aid in smoking cessation and weight control, to alleviate test anxiety and sexual dysfunction, and with dermatological and gastrointestinal disorders (Spiegel & Spiegel, 2004). In a clinically therapeutic context, hypnosis is used to enhance memory recall for historical, and frequently traumatic, events.

The distinction between clinical hypnosis and forensic hypnosis is primarily one of context and purpose (Eimer & Gravitz, 2002). Whereas forensic hypnosis assumes all properties of its clinical counterpart, the distinction lies in its use to further legal, not clinical, objectives. Objectives include using hypnosis to generate investigative leads in criminal investigations and refreshing the memory of eyewitnesses and victims too traumatized to recall critical details of crimes. It is also used with defendants who claim amnesia for their crimes, as in the notorious Hillside Strangler case (*State v. Bianchi,* 1979; see Meyer, in press), and has been used, albeit rarely, to obtain confessions from defendants (*People v. Leyra,* 1951). Although clinicians may deliberately choose to practice forensic hypnosis, their practice of clinical hypnosis may also intersect with the legal system, thereby thrusting their work into the forensic arena (Sales & Shuman, 2005).

AN ISSUE OF VALIDITY: HYPNOTICALLY REFRESHED MEMORIES

A central issue in forensic hypnosis is whether hypnotically refreshed memories meet acceptable reliability and validity thresholds for admissibility as evidence in court.

Underlying the debate surrounding hypnosis and memory is the current scientific consensus that memory processes are reconstructive in nature, and thus vulnerable to error and inaccuracies during recall (Dowd, 2002; Haber & Haber, 2000; Mollon, 2002). These inherent inaccuracies associated with memory can be heightened through the use of various memory-retrieval techniques, including hypnosis (Lynn, Lock, Loftus, Krackow, & Lilienfeld, 2003).

Three Fundamental Areas: Suggestibility, Reliability, and Believability

Three areas are fundamental in considering the validity of hypnotically refreshed memories in the forensic context: (1) the suggestibility of the subject, (2) the reliability of the recall, and (3) the believability of the recall (Scheflin, 1996). The hypnotized subject experiences a state of heightened suggestibility and is thereby more vulnerable to the inadvertent or deliberate influence of the hypnotist. In this state of heightened suggestibility, subjects may act in accordance with perceived situational demand characteristics by providing responses they believe will satisfy the hypnotist (Kassin, 2005). This state of increased suggestibility calls into question the reliability of subsequent recall due to increased vulnerability to confabulation, distortion, and fabrication of information when filling in memory gaps. Often, subjects will not know if a memory is false or real, or at what point in time it occurred, a phenomenon referred to as *source amnesia*. Level of hypnotizability or suggestibility has been found to have an adverse impact on memory reconstructive processes, in that higher levels of suggestibility are associated with increased incidence of inaccuracies in recall, including pseudomemories (Barnier & McConkey, 1993; Barnier, McConkey, & Wright, 2004; Cox & Barnier, 2003; Drivdahl & Zaragoza, 2001; Farvolden & Woody, 2004; Labelle, Laurence, Nadon, & Perry, 1990; Sheehan, Statham, & Jamieson, 1991).

In addition to experiencing a state of heightened suggestibility, hypnotized subjects can frequently experience increased confidence in the veracity of their hypnotically refreshed recall. Such confidence effects have been consistently supported throughout the experimental literature (Neuschatz, Lynn, Benoit, & Fite, 2003; Pettinati, 1988; Steblay & Bothwell, 1994). Even under cross-examination and direct contradiction, subjects will defend what they believe to be the accuracy of their hypnotically refreshed memories (Laurence & Perry, 1983). In addition, just as is the case with eyewitness testimony, juries are more apt to be persuaded by a witness who believes strongly in the truth of his or her statements. A subject's increased confidence in hypnotically enhanced memories can have an adverse impact in a jury trial, as "the United States Supreme Court continues to hold that juries should be instructed to consider the confidence of witnesses in weighing the evidence" (Karlin, 1997, p. 33).

Furthermore, there is the believability factor. When confronted with hypnotically refreshed memories in the courtroom, juries are prone to believe in their accuracy (Coleman, Stevens, & Reeder, 2001). This is due in part to heightened confidence on the part of the subject and to the readily accepted and widespread myth that hypnosis, acting as a truth serum, can produce accurate recall (Knight, 2005). Without expert testimony, juries might lack awareness that hypnosis can enhance memory distortion, that subjects can be purposefully deceptive while in trance, and that the hypnotic state can be faked (Sales & Shuman, 2005).

Hypnotic Hypermnesia

All of these concerns are weighed against the possibility that hypnosis may generate enhanced recall that could prove valuable in a forensic setting, as in the oft-cited Chowchilla kidnapping incident, in which a busload of children was abducted and buried alive. The bus driver managed to escape and underwent hypnosis, which yielded the clue used to solve the case: a license plate number of the van driven by the perpetrators (Kroger & Douce, 1979).

As illustrated by this case, hypnosis is often used to refresh the memories of forensic populations, such as victims, witnesses, and offenders, with the ultimate objective of *hypermnesia,* the enhancement of normal memory through repeated retrieval attempts. This phenomenon occurs in various memory recovery procedures and is not unique to hypnosis (Dinges et al., 1992; Register & Kihlstrom, 1987; Whitehouse, Dinges, Orne, & Orne, 1988). It has been demonstrated, however, that hypnotically enhanced recall can be associated with distortions and inaccuracies. For example, a second license plate number recalled during the Chowchilla investigation was completely wrong (Erdelyi, 1994; Kebbell & Wagstaff, 1998; E. C. Orne, Whitehouse, Dinges, & Orne, 1996; Yapko, 2003). There is some question, however, whether the use of hypnosis produces significantly more memory errors than other types of suggestive techniques (e.g., guided imagery, leading questions; Scheflin, Spiegel, & Spiegel, 1999) or more errors than those inherent in general memory processes (Neuschatz et al., 2003).

In addition, when hypnosis appears to have resulted in hypermnesia, there is no definitive way to distinguish honestly confabulated memories from purposeful deception. Therefore, what appears to be enhanced recall could be the result of deceptive strategy on the part of the forensic subject (Boyd, McLearen, Meyer, & Denney, in press; Perlini, Haley, & Buczel, 1998).

Hypnosis and Pseudomemories

Hypnosis is used not only to enhance recall of forensic information related to a crime, it is also frequently used in a therapeutic context to uncover repressed memories of abuse (Lynn et al., 2003). Employing hypnosis for this purpose has been a common catalyst for propelling clinical hypnosis into the forensic spotlight, where "the nature of recovered memories has profoundly different meanings for legal as opposed to therapeutic settings" (Sheehan, 1997, p. 35). Hypnosis used for this purpose can potentially yield false memories or *pseudomemories,* sometimes resulting in the unjust prosecution of the accused (Loftus, 1998).

Research has demonstrated the successful implantation of pseudomemories into a subject's memory (Mazzoni & Memon, 2003; Wade, Garry, Read, & Lindsay, 2002), particularly with eyewitnesses (Haber & Haber, 2000; Loftus, 1979; Ochi, 2002). Studies have demonstrated that eyewitness memory is easily distorted by stress or even a simple suggestion of a false detail after witnessing an event (Deffenbacher, Bornstein, Penrod, & McGorty, 2004; Roebers & McConkey, 2003). Researchers have also been successful in implanting pseudomemories in hypnotized subjects (Labelle, Laurence, et al., 1990; Laurence & Perry, 1983; M. T. Orne, 1979). Level of hypnotizability clearly emerged as the determining factor for subject acceptance of pseudomemories as true memories (McConkey & Sheehan, 1995).

Other research has supported the theory that hypnotic pseudomemories reflected contextually driven reporting biases rather than genuine memory distortions (Lynn, Rhue, Meyers, & Weeks, 1994). Thus, demand characteristics—what subjects ascertained was expected of them—appeared to play a role in the reporting of pseudomemories (Spanos, 1992). The effect was reversible to some extent, as subjects who were financially rewarded for differentiating false memories from real occurrences reported fewer pseudomemories (Murrey, Cross, & Whipple, 1992). In the forensic arena, if the hypnotized subject believes that he or she is expected to remember more of an event under hypnosis or will receive a reward for a certain answer, these variables may affect what is reported.

Pseudomemories are particularly problematic in the forensic context, where the legitimacy of recall is of primary importance. Thus, independent verification is necessary to validate these memories (Kihlstrom, 1994). However, such corroboration may be nearly impossible in cases of childhood abuse, in which time has eroded memory for incriminating circumstances. This leaves the court (and the forensic expert) with the difficult task of differentiating pseudomemories from authentic recall. Due to the difficulties inherent in this process of discerning fact from fiction, some continually warn against the use of suggestive techniques, such as hypnosis, for memory enhancement (Loftus, 1998, 2003). However, Scheflin (1997) reiterated that hypnosis, by itself, does not inherently create false allegations. He contended that accusations can be falsely made for any number of reasons (i.e., revenge, financial gain, distorted memory, bad therapy) and that "most cases of false allegations of childhood sexual abuse have not involved hypnosis" (p. 212).

The Effect of Leading Questions on Hypnotically Enhanced Memories

Although contraindicated, leading and misleading questions are an unfortunate reality in investigative interviewing with or without the use of hypnosis (Sandoval, 2003). However, a hypnotized subject's memory is particularly vulnerable to inaccuracies when the investigative hypnotist uses leading questions or inadvertently presents misinformation during questioning (Lynn & Nash, 1994; Sanders & Simmons, 1983; Sheehan, Grigg, & McCann, 1984; Sheehan & Tilden, 1986; Steblay & Bothwell, 1994).

In more recent research, Scoboria, Mazzoni, Kirsch, and Milling (2002) compared the effects of hypnosis and of using misleading questions on memory during investigative interviews. They asserted that although misleading questions can yield inaccurate memories, witnesses exposed to these questions in interviews are not barred from offering testimony:

> Although both hypnosis and misleading questions appear to have negative effects on the accuracy of memory reports, their status in court is quite different . . . witnesses are not barred from testifying on matters about which they have previously been asked leading questions. (p. 26)

The authors found that although both techniques led to incorrect responses, the use of misleading questions yielded significantly more memory errors than when hypnosis was used as a memory retrieval technique. When the techniques were used together, they produced more errors than either technique alone, yielding an additive effect (Scoboria et al., 2002). Therefore, it is a well-documented recommendation that the forensic hypnotist initially use an open-ended and unstructured approach (free recall), followed by direct questioning based on the initial recall. This approach should help prevent the contamination of memory from misleading information (Hilgard & Loftus, 1979).

Borawick v. Shay

A pivotal case analyzing the admissibility of hypnotically refreshed memories, *Borawick v. Shay* (1995) placed on trial recovered memories of childhood abuse and the method used to recover those memories: hypnosis. Comprehensively analyzed by Karlin and Orne (1996) and Scheflin (1996, 1997), this case served as a battleground for dissecting arguments for and against the admissibility of hypnotically refreshed memories.

The plaintiff, Borawick, sought compensatory damages for incestuous, satanic childhood abuse allegedly perpetrated by family members almost 30 years prior to her initial recall. Memories of the abusive incidents were initially elicited by a lay hypnotist, and she was given instructions while under hypnosis to remain amnesic for the memories, due to their traumatic content. Therefore, several months elapsed between her final hypnosis session and when she initially began to remember a detailed account of the abuse. Subsequent to her recall, she attempted to admit her memories as evidence in a trial against the accused. However, the hypnotically elicited recall was suppressed by the court on the following grounds: (a) hypersuggestibility of the subject during hypnosis, (b) high incidence of confabulation during hypnotic sessions, (c) heightened (unwarranted) confidence in memories as a result of hypnosis, (d) inability to distinguish accurate from inaccurate detail, and (e) the insertion of postevent material into the narrative (Karlin & Orne, 1996). The hypnotically refreshed testimony was also excluded due to the hypnotist lacking adequate credentials and the absence of any formal audio or video recording of the hypnosis sessions (Scheflin, 1996).

Using the "totality of circumstances" approach, the Court of Appeals for the 2nd District upheld the district court's decision to bar Borawick's hypnotically refreshed testimony. Although the U.S. Supreme Court was asked to review the decisions rendered in *Borawick v. Shay* (Scheflin, 1996), a writ of certiorari was denied. In opposition to the ruling, Scheflin maintained:

The *Borawick* judges failed to see that if memory is always in the process of reconstruction, then it is distorted or inaccurate even when hypnosis is not used. Thus the problem lies with memory, not with hypnosis used to facilitate retrieval. (p. 37)

A FIELD DIVIDED

Conflicting research findings in this area reflect a profession divided regarding the extent to which hypnosis contaminates recall, and whether to allow these memories as testimony into the courtroom (Kassin, Ellsworth, & Smith, 1989; Knight, 2005). Few issues have generated such a contentious divide in the field.

The Case for Admission

On one side of the division, proponents defend the position that hypnosis has the potential to yield untainted, accurate memories under certain circumstances, especially with eyewitnesses (Boggs, 1993; Diamond, 1980; Kroger & Douce, 1979; Scheflin, 1994; Spiegel, 1980). Colwick (1995) asserted that banning hypnosis from the courtroom denies the "survivor of sexual abuse the opportunity to testify about memories recalled by means of hypnosis and forces him or her to forgo either an effective means of treatment or judicial recourse" (p. 198). In addition, the American Society for Clinical Hypnosis believes that hypnosis can be a valuable tool in forensic work and should be allowed in the courtroom (Karlin, 1997). Proponents also contend that research demonstrating the fallibility of hypnotically refreshed recall is hard-pressed to simulate the emotionally charged atmosphere, increased motivation level, and real-life trauma to which eyewitnesses and victims are subjected (Tayloe, 1995; Yuille & Cutshall, 1986).

Those in favor of admission cite research demonstrating that memory inaccuracies are present regardless of the use of hypnosis, and that hypnosis does not necessarily increase inaccuracies beyond those inherent in general memory processes (Lynn & Kirsch, 1996; Neuschatz et al., 2003). Singling out hypnosis for exclusionary treatment, while allowing for the admittance of alternative suggestive procedures that have also been proven to yield unreliable information, is questioned with respect to fairness. Inaccuracies and unreliability are inherent in other forensic practices, such as lineups, eyewitness testimonies, police interrogations, and confessions. However, a per se exclusion rule has been "rejected by the law" for all of those practices, and "only hypnosis has been singled out for such harsh treatment" (Scheflin, 1997, p. 272).

The Case against Admission

In opposition are those who believe that accurate memory recall is rarely possible under hypnosis and that most memories are confabulated or biased, if not completely distorted. Unfortunately for the advocates, the bulk of the evidentiary research weighs in on this side of the debate. Prominent organizations, such as the American Medical Association (1985, 1994), have spoken out against the admissibility of hypnotically refreshed memories in the courtroom and endorsed its use only for investigative purposes. The American Psychological Association (1995;

Courtois, 2001) has also cautioned against the use of hypnosis for uncovering re-pressed memories of abuse. Proponents of this position have strongly supported the per se exclusion standard for hypnotically refreshed testimony (Karlin & Orne, 1996, 1997). As justification, they contend that hypnosis creates a suspended belief state, influenced by demand characteristics that can lead to distorted reality recall and misplaced confidence in the resulting memories.

As each side is weighed with consideration, the field is reminded:

> It is not our role to comment on whether recovered memory evidence should be admissible in the courtroom. . . . Rather, our role as psychological researchers is to provide the relevant scientific information to legal decision-makers to assist them in policy and case decisions. (Porter, Campbell, Birt, & Woodworth, 2003, p. 213)

HYPNOSIS WITH DEFENDANTS

Although the use of forensic hypnosis to refresh the memory of victims and eyewit-nesses occurs with more regularity than with defendants, hypnosis with the latter population is often conducted for different purposes and is somewhat more contro-versial. Hypnosis can be used with defendants for a variety of purposes, such as probing for investigative leads in cases in which the defendant's memory is not fully intact (due to faked or real amnesia), to gain exculpatory statements for the defense, and to obtain confessions to crimes (Niehaus, 1999). Hypnosis has also been utilized when there is a question that the defendant suffers from (or is feign-ing) Dissociative Identity Disorder, as in the Hillside Strangler case (*State v. Bianchi,* 1979).

Generating Investigative Leads

A primary purpose involves hypnotizing the defendant to engender investigative leads or to obtain exculpatory information. In these cases, hypnosis is typically used to refresh the defendant's memory for details that might result in exonera-tion. Courts have ruled that the defendant has the legal right to undergo hypnosis to expose possible exculpatory information. Using hypnosis in this manner gener-ates the least amount of legal debate, as the statements obtained under hypnosis are not intended for the purpose of admissible evidence. Courts have set prece-dence for this use of hypnosis in *Cornell v. Superior Court of San Diego County* (1959): "The reliability of the defendant's statements under hypnosis was not an issue because the defendant did not seek to admit those statements in court" (Nardi, 1984, p. 1001).

With respect to allowing criminal defendants to testify after undergoing hypno-sis, *Rock v. Arkansas* (1987) remains the critical ruling on this topic and the first U.S. Supreme Court ruling on the issue of the admissibility of hypnotically re-freshed testimony. The decision allowed previously hypnotized defendants to tes-tify on their own behalf as the Court ruled it would be unconstitutional to prohibit the use of such statements as a defense. (See M. T. Orne, Dinges, & Orne, 1990, for a comprehensive review of this case.)

Obtaining Confessions to Crimes

A less frequent and more controversial use of hypnosis with defendants involves obtaining confessions to crimes. Hypnosis plays a problematic role in eliciting confessions due to increased levels of subject suggestibility and compliance. As might be expected, forensic hypnosis has also been linked to obtaining false confessions from criminal suspects (Yapko, 2003). Although hypnosis "cannot compel a guilty defendant to confess if he is determined not to do so," hypnotic suggestions do have the suggestive power to "convince a defendant that it is to his advantage to confess because he is morally guilty, or because he will feel better, or because somehow it will help him" (Udolf, 1983, pp. 103–104). Because involuntary confessions are inadmissible in court (*Leyra v. Denno,*1954), whichever party wishes to use the confession inherits the burden of proving that it was procured under voluntary circumstances. Not only must the defendant voluntarily consent to the use of hypnosis, but no coercion or suggestion should be employed during hypnosis to obtain the confession. In addition, before admissibility, efforts must be made at independent verification of the confession (Nardi, 1984). Due to the complications involved and adherence to the protection of the constitutional rights of defendants, hypnotically elicited confessions (or spontaneous confessions while under hypnosis) are very difficult to admit as evidence in court.

Defendants and Amnesia: *State v. Bianchi*

A more prevalent reason hypnosis is employed with defendants arises when the accused perpetrator claims no memory for the alleged crime. Although amnesia for traumatic events is clinically rare (Karlin & Orne, 1997), defendants sometimes claim amnesia to reduce their level of criminal responsibility. The most infamous case using hypnosis with a criminal defendant claiming amnesia is the Hillside Strangler case, *State v. Bianchi* (1979). Bianchi's trial was fraught with controversy surrounding the validity of his psychiatric diagnosis, then referred to as Multiple Personality Disorder (MPD). Bianchi was eventually convicted and is currently serving multiple life sentences (Allison, 1984), but the path to his conviction raised key issues related to using hypnosis with defendants and the possibility of deception on the part of the subject.

The most relevant of these issues is whether or not Bianchi was ever truly hypnotized. This is particularly important because his diagnosis of MPD partially arose out of symptoms displayed while under hypnosis. Bianchi was evaluated by both defense and prosecution experts, resulting in extensive hypnosis sessions, which produced a dichotomy of opinion as to whether or not Bianchi was presenting as one who had been genuinely hypnotized. The defense retained Dr. John Watkins, an internationally recognized expert on hypnosis, who concluded that Bianchi had been successfully hypnotized and suffered from MPD (see Watkins, 1984, for a review of his findings). Subsequently, a plea of not guilty by reason of insanity was entered by the defense. The prosecution retained Dr. Martin Orne, also a renowned expert in the area of hypnosis. He came to the opposite conclusion, that Bianchi was faking hypnosis and thus did not warrant a diagnosis of MPD.

Orne drew on his extensive background and experience in hypnosis and compared Bianchi's hypnotic performance with established patterns of hypnotic behavior. In addition, Orne suggested to Bianchi that those with true MPD typically have a third personality (at a point when Bianchi had produced only two). Orne's logic was that if Bianchi was faking, "the production of the additional personality would be an instrumental act to convince the interviewer of the authenticity of his disorder" (M. T. Orne, Soskis, Dinges, & Orne, 1984, p. 142). Bianchi took the bait and promptly produced another personality the very next day, a move that eventually led to the discontinuation of his insanity defense. Bianchi later appealed his conviction based on the grounds that his confession was coerced, as it was obtained under hypnosis (*Bianchi v. Blodgett,* 1994), but his appeal was unsuccessful. (The reader is referred to M. T. Orne et al., 1984, for a complete account of Orne's hypnosis sessions with Bianchi.)

HYPNOSIS AND DECEPTION

As is illustrated by the *Bianchi* case, forensic hypnosis should be carefully assessed for the possibility of deception (Boyd et al., in press). This deception can assume several different forms: self-deception, compliance with demand characteristics, and purposeful deceit. The first of these involves subjects deceiving themselves about their own subjective experience. Spiegel (1980) coined the term "honest liar" to describe the hypnotized subject who believes implanted memories to the point of vigorously defending their authenticity. In the forensic setting, Scheflin and Shapiro (1989) claimed that such honest liars would make effective witnesses in the courtroom as they would be resistant to the pressures of cross-examination and would have heightened confidence in the "truth" of their memories. The second type of deception is related to compliance, expectancies, and demand characteristics. The subject may simply be complying with the procedure in order to pose as a "good" subject, acting on preconceived notions of what he or she believes hypnosis entails (Spanos, 1986).

The third type of deception is that of conscious deception by the hypnotized subject. Purposeful deceit can result in secondary gains, such as achieving a certain diagnosis for an insanity plea, feigning amnesia to escape culpability, or creating seemingly accurate details of a crime to mislead investigators. It is critical for the forensic hypnosis expert to determine the level of veracity of the hypnotic experience (Boyd et al., in press; Newman & Thompson, 2001).

Research Designs Evaluating Hypnosis and Deception

M. T. Orne's (1971) real-simulating model has been one of the prominent research paradigms used to examine hypnosis and deception. Research with this model has been effective in generating successful methods of discriminating "reals" and simulators. The research has also demonstrated, however, that even the most seasoned of experts can be fooled, as Orne discovered when he assumed the role of the blind experimenter. He found that he was "incapable of distinguishing between the two groups" (M. T. Orne, 1979, p. 535).

Whereas Orne's model used a single-session design, Blum and Graef (1971) used six sessions based on Orne's real-simulating model. This longitudinal design was more instrumental in accumulating evidence and indicative behaviors that successfully discriminated the two groups. This design provided support that the hypnotist should be exposed to the client over multiple sessions to assess for the possibility of deception.

A later research paradigm used to study the simulation of hypnosis is the surreptitious observer design (Kirsch, Silva, Carone, Johnston, & Simon, 1989). In this design, simulators and reals were left alone while the experimenter surreptitiously observed their activities by way of a hidden camera or one-way mirror. Those subjects instructed to simulate displayed significantly more role-inappropriate behaviors when they thought they were alone than did the highly hypnotizable subjects (Perugini et al., 1998; Spanos, Burgess, Roncon, Wallace-Capretta, & Cross, 1993).

The literature has yielded certain behavioral cues to consider when trying to detect deception in the hypnotized subject. Perhaps the most consistent finding is that of exaggerated responses. Subjects instructed to simulate hypnosis have been consistently observed to overact their hypnotic behavior in an effort to convince the hypnotist of the authenticity of their experience. However, a potential problem with using exaggerated responses as a marker of deception in hypnosis involves subjects who are extremely hypnotizable. Also known as "hypnotic virtuosos," these subjects tend to enter into a very deep trance and thus display behaviors that may appear to be exaggerated. Approximately 5% to 15% of the population are capable of this deep trance state (Meyer, 1992). Therefore, prior to judging exaggerated responding, the client should be assessed on susceptibility measures to determine capacity for deep trance.

The Hypnotic Simulation Index

A self-report measure that has been successful in discriminating truly hypnotized subjects versus those subjects who have been instructed to simulate hypnosis is the Hypnotic Simulation Index (HSI; Martin & Lynn, 1996). The HSI is a 31-item, self-report scale of subjective experiences based on the premise that "simulators would over-endorse, exaggerate, overplay questions, but that real participants would fail to endorse subjective experiences that are not directly suggested to them" (p. 341). The HSI was found to correctly classify 94% of participants into two groups (simulating versus real participants). Although this measure appears promising based on preliminary results, further research is needed to bolster Martin and Lynn's initial findings.

Physiological Measures

There is a small body of research that has attempted to rely on the traditional nonverbal cues of deception to discriminate between hypnotic simulators and those under trance (Kennedy & Coe, 1990, 1994; Sheehan & McConkey, 1988; Sheehan & Statham, 1988). Such research has not typically proven successful in discriminating between the two groups. Other researchers have used the polygraph in conjunction with hypnosis to aid in deception detection (Gravitz, 2002; Kinnunen,

Zamansky, & Block, 1994; Kinnunen, Zamansky, & Nordstrom, 2001). Based on the electrodermal skin conductance response (used in general deception research as a reliable and effective indicator of deception), this research found that it is possible for hypnotized subjects to consciously lie while under hypnosis.

Recommendations for Detecting Deception in Hypnotized Subjects

Nardi's (1984) early statement that "experts do not use hypnosis for the purpose of guaranteeing the truthfulness of hypnotically-induced statements" (p. 1004) still holds true. Hence, the practice of detecting deception in hypnosis remains a difficult and complex task. The following are recommendations that forensic hypnotists may employ in their attempts to detect deception in the hypnotic state (Boyd et al., in press; M. T. Orne et al., 1984; Yapko, 2003):

- Be familiar with the research literature examining deception and hypnosis, and appreciate that even the expert clinician can be deceived.
- Engage in multiple hypnosis sessions to obtain a longitudinal sampling of behaviors to assess for inconsistencies in responding.
- Consider utilizing tests of hypnosis such as the double hallucination test, circle-touch test, single hallucination test, source amnesia, and the presence of trance logic.
- Allow hypnotized clients to believe they are not being watched and surreptitiously observe their behaviors; simulators will often forgo the deception.
- Consider administration of the HSI after further research has been conducted to validate the measure on individual subjects.
- Consider, with caution, using the polygraph after hypnosis to assess the veracity of the hypnotic experience.
- Be vigilant for exaggerated responding during hypnosis.
- Consider the use of psychological tests designed to assess for malingering.

HYPNOSIS AND COERCION

Hypnosis has historically borne the mystique of possessing coercive powers (the "Svengali effect"), rendering subjects vulnerable to the control of the hypnotist. Intentional misuses of hypnosis, such as using hypnosis to coerce others into committing criminal acts or to facilitate sexual abuse, have raised ethical and legal issues (Stanley, 1994).

Historical arguments purported that a subject's failure to submit to the hypnotic coercion must be an indication of inadequate hypnosis. Others argued that submission simply indicated advantageous license on the part of the subject to act on intrinsic urges (Perry, 1979). Early research in this area demonstrated that hypnotized subjects could be coerced to engage in aversive, antisocial behavior (e.g., handling venomous snakes, throwing toxic acid on others, selling heroin; Coe, 1977; Coe, Kobayashi, & Howard, 1972, 1973). Other research, however, debunked coercion of at least some types of antisocial behavior by demonstrating that *both* simulating and hypnotized subjects engaged in the "coerced" activity (Gibson, 1991; M. T. Orne & Evans, 1965). Due to prevailing ethical standards, additional research attempting to definitely prove coercion of antisocial acts is nearly impossible to conduct in today's laboratories. However, contemporary studies have examined mock jurors' *perception* of hypnotic coercion. Research indicated that more naive jurors (with respect to hypnosis) were more likely to accept a defense of hypnotic automatism, that is, that the defendant's criminal behavior was not under voluntary control due to a hypnotic state. In contrast, jurors with personal experience of hypnosis, especially those who had a history of achieving deeper hypnotic depth, were more likely to reject the defense that the accused committed the offense due to the coercive powers of hypnosis (Roberts & Wagstaff, 1996; Wagstaff, Green, & Somers, 1997).

Currently, professional opinion has all but relinquished the idea that hypnosis coerces compliance to illegal or antisocial acts and holds that subjects will not engage in activity under trance that conflicts with their moral code. More contemporary explanations of seemingly coerced behavior include compliance with demand characteristics within what subjects know to be the secure context of the experimental environment (Laurence & Perry, 1988; Lynn, 1990). However, to accept these contemporary explanations without some degree of healthy skepticism may be too narrow in theoretical scope. As noted by Scheflin and Shapiro (1989):

> It would seem simple to conclude that hypnotists have no power to get people to do things that violate their morals. However, hypnosis may not be that benign. It is theoretically possible to distort subjects' perceptions in a trance to the extent that they believe a particular situation prevails. Their behavior may be very appropriate under that imagined situation and very inappropriate in the actual current situation. (p. 136)

The public is clearly reluctant to accept these contemporary explanations, especially given the exaggeration of the phenomenon exhibited in stage hypnosis shows (Heap, 2000). Combine the acceptance of this Svengali myth with an ill-intentioned hypnotist, and hypnosis may result in what appears to be coerced behavior. As with other positions of authority and influence, "a malevolent hypnotist can take advantage of a trusting subject in much the same way that any influential or charismatic individual can deceive and fool a person" (Scheflin & Shapiro, 1989, p. 136). Such circumstance can result in the sexual abuse of the subject by the hypnotist (*People v. Sorscher,* 1986). When abuse does occur under hypnosis, judicial recourse may be scant, particularly when the hypnotherapist is not professionally qualified or affiliated with a professional hypnosis organization (Karle, 1991).

In sum, primarily due to the difficulties of conducting rigorous scientific examination in this area, there is no definitive answer to one of the most fundamental issues surrounding forensic hypnosis. That is, what degree of coercion is possible under trance, both with respect to the abuse of a hypnotized subject and coerced behavior outside of an experimental setting.

HYPNOSIS AND LAW ENFORCEMENT

Hypnosis first appeared in police journals in the 1940s as a method of interrogation in criminal investigations. In 1976, Martin Reiser (1983) founded the Law

Enforcement Hypnosis Institute, which offered the prototype course to train police officers in hypnotic techniques. With Reiser's newly established Institute, the 1980s saw a dramatic increase in police officers trained to conduct hypnosis. However, the majority of hypnosis societies expressed strong opposition. Many in the field do not believe law enforcement personnel are qualified to adequately and safely conduct the hypnosis session and instead recommend trained psychologists or psychiatrists (Knight, 2005; Meyer & Weaver, in press-b; Yapko, 2003).

Several reasons account for the strong opposition to police officers conducting investigative hypnosis. Traumatic material is often resurrected through hypnosis, and the hypnotist must have the proper mental health training to deal with any trauma-related reaction (Meyer & Weaver, in press-a). Another reason involves the objectivity of the hypnotist. An outside clinician is better able to maintain distance from information pertaining to the crime, thus insulating the interview from leading information and questions; a police hypnotist may be too intimate with the details of the case to conduct an objective interview (Naish, 1988). Furthermore, objectivity might be compromised by a strong desire to successfully solve the case, as M. T. Orne, Soskis, Dinges, Orne, and Tonry (1985) stated: "While they [clinicians] may be working *with* a victim or witness, they [police hypnotists] are working *on* a case, and it is their progress in solving this case that determines their professional success or failure" (p. 32). Law enforcement personnel have argued, however, that psychologists lack the "craft of policemanship in evidence collection" and are not properly skilled in interrogative or investigative techniques (Naish, 1988, p. 353).

There has been little research comparing police hypnotists to licensed, trained clinicians. Yuille and Kim (1987) conducted a rare study that retrospectively examined the use of hypnosis by police hypnotists in real forensic cases. Using transcripts of the hypnotic sessions, the authors analyzed statements made under hypnosis by the eyewitnesses and victims, as well as statements made outside of hypnosis. They compared the statements to verifiable knowledge specific to the crime, which was provided by the police department. They found that the hypnotic interviews, on average, "almost tripled (177%) the amount of total information" (p. 423). Of those details that could be compared to forensic evidence (16.65%), the authors found an 82% accuracy rate for the information provided under hypnosis. However, the value of verifiable details was challenged. In fact, the police officers involved in the cases rated the average usefulness of hypnosis in solving the crimes a 2.5 on a scale of 1 to 5.

LEGAL CONTROLS: REGULATING HYPNOSIS IN THE COURTROOM

"Three judicial approaches to the question of admissibility of hypnotically-refreshed testimony have developed. None command a majority. *The law is in a state of flux*" (Sies & Wester, 1985, p. 78; emphasis added). There are now four different legal criteria to be used as gatekeepers of hypnotically refreshed testimony: (1) the per se exclusion rule; (2) the open admissibility rule; (3) the totality of circumstances rule; and (4) strict adherence to specific criteria, such as the "Orne criteria." Jurisdiction, legal precedent, and the particulars of each case determine which control is implemented. As the tide of judicial leniency ebbs and flows, so does the popularity of each control.

Per se Exclusion

The most restrictive of the legal controls is the per se exclusion rule, which strictly prohibits hypnotically refreshed memories as admissible evidence. Such restrictive legal policy has arisen from research demonstrating that hypnosis can result in the confabulation of information, distortion, and implantation of false memories, as well as a heightened confidence in these memories as fact. Those in favor of this control argue that it is often an impossible task to reliably differentiate between memory fact and fiction, and any increase in actual, verifiable knowledge through the use of hypnosis is often scant and trivial.

The origins of this control extend to the nineteenth century from *People v. Ebanks* (1897), in which the trial judge proclaimed the use of hypnotically elicited testimony an "illegal defense" (Laurence & Perry, 1983, p. 274). In 1979, Orne expressed his support for the per se exclusion rule (Scheflin & Frischholz, 1999), and court cases followed suit. For example, *State v. Mack* (1980) upheld the per se ideal by being the first case of the twentieth century to impose this rule. In the *Mack* case, hypnotized witnesses were prohibited from testifying about memories gathered during an investigative interview. Yet, the police were allowed to use the information as investigative leads to form a case against the defendant (Perry, Orne, London, & Orne, 1996). The authors also noted that "most American state supreme courts that have heard cases involving hypnosis have either adopted *Mack* or a variant of this decision" (p. 67). *People v. Shirley* (1982) and *People v. Guerra* (1984) both followed in this tradition by excluding all testimony from the time hypnosis commenced due to the concern about memory contamination (Beahrs, 1988).

The *Shirley* court is particularly noteworthy in its harsh language, referring to hypnosis as "pretense," which could not be used "without injecting undue delay and confusion into the judicial process" (quoted in Sies & Wester, 1985, p. 107). The *Shirley* court initially ruled that hypnotized witnesses could not testify to any information remembered or recorded *before* hypnosis, as any recall after hypnosis could be tainted. However, the court did amend that "testimony on a topic *wholly unrelated* to the events that were the subject of the hypnotic session would not be rendered inadmissible by the ruling" (quoted in Adelman & Howard, 1984, p. 9). The *Shirley* court also modified its inadmissibility stance by opening up admissibility to defendants testifying in their own behalf, based on constitutional grounds.

Another line of reasoning used for implementation of the per se exclusion rule involves the difficulties associated with the cross-examination of hypnotically elicited testimony. According to Adelman and Howard (1984), the primary constitutional argument used to bar hypnotically refreshed testimony from the courtroom is that "such testimony bars effective cross-examination, in violation of the Sixth Amendment confrontation clause" (p. 11). *State v. Mena* (1981) upheld this view by contending that "cross examination is a right so essential to criminal defendants that, until the general scientific reliability of hypnosis has been established, the confrontation clause prohibits the admission of hypnotically-tainted testimony"

(Adelman & Howard, 1984, p. 11). This was later overturned by *People v. Boudin* (1983), in which the court rejected the defense's motion to suppress hypnotically refreshed testimony and asserted that it was the jury's responsibility to evaluate the veracity of the testimony (Adelman & Howard, 1984).

One issue of concern with the per se exclusion rule involves the preclusion of victim testimony to prosecute the accused. Hypnosis in therapy may preclude a client from being able to use the recovered memories to prosecute the alleged perpetrator, but to forgo hypnosis may prevent a client from obtaining access to abusive memories as well as a potential healing method for traumatic experiences (Boggs, 1993; Scheflin, 1994). In addition, a client sexually abused under hypnosis may not testify to that abuse if a strict interpretation of the per se exclusion is implemented. For these reasons, Perry et al. (1996) noted a resurgent interest in the early 1990s among clinicians seeking to disband this restrictive legal control. Due to the sweeping prohibitive nature of this rule, it has drawn outspoken disfavor within the profession. For example, some scholars have referred to this rule as a "draconian device that effectively renders a previously hypnotized witness incompetent" (Sies & Wester, 1985, p. 103).

Those in opposition to the per se rule might find support from the *Daubert* decision (*Daubert v. Merrell Dow Pharmaceuticals, Inc.,* 1993). Perry et al. (1996) alluded to the possible erosion of the per se exclusion rule with the U.S. Supreme Court embracing the more lenient *Daubert* decision in lieu of the *Frye* rule of admissibility (*Frye v. United States,* 1923). According to Alexander and Scheflin (1998), "Several federal courts have interpreted *Daubert* as mandating a flexible approach to the admission of expert testimony that prohibits the use of *per se* exclusion rules" (p. 313). This more "flexible approach" is due, in part, to the responsibility for evidence reliability being shifted to the trial judge who makes the ultimate determination of reliability and relevancy in a particular case. As Alexander and Scheflin noted, "A *per se* exclusion rule prohibits a judge from performing these tasks and is therefore indefensible under *Daubert*" (p. 314). An early case appeared to support this conclusion (*Rowland v. Commonwealth,* 1995); however, it is too soon to decide the fate of hypnosis under *Daubert,* and some are skeptical that *Daubert* will result in a more hypnosis-friendly legal environment (Scheflin et al., 1999; for a comprehensive review of arguments against the admission of hypnotically refreshed testimony, see Diamond, 1980; M. T. Orne, 1979).

Open Admissibility

The open admissibility rule operates under the principle of allowing into evidence *any* hypnotically refreshed recall, "no matter how well or poorly the hypnosis was conducted" (Scheflin & Frischholz, 1999, p. 89). Under this rule, hypnosis is viewed as is any other memory retrieval technique, posing no unique threats to the integrity of courtroom proceedings. Proponents of this option believe that the right to evaluate the validity of evidence lies with the fact finder, the judge or jury. Under this rule, hypnotically elicited testimony is "subject to the right of the adversary to discredit it by cross-examination or with contrary expert testimony," the same as with any other (forensic) evidence (Scheflin, 1994, p. 27).

Harding v. State (1968) held that previously hypnotized witnesses were permitted to testify to information elicited during hypnosis. In this case, the jury had the responsibility to evaluate the credibility of such testimony and how much weight to assign it. Sies and Wester (1985) underscored the importance of the *Harding* ruling: "Skillful cross-examination of the previously hypnotized witness would act as a safeguard and assist the trier of fact to evaluate the reliability of the hypnotized witness's testimony" (p. 91).

Because research has not succeeded in divesting hypnosis of its potentially distorting influence, proponents of this control suggest that a statement be issued to the jury emphasizing the possible fallibility of hypnotically refreshed testimony. Odgers (1988) indicated that such a statement should include an acknowledgment of the sometimes unreliable nature of hypnotically enhanced recall and the possibility of purposeful deception while under hypnosis. However, he also stated that such a statement does not "ensure that a correct assessment of the value of the testimony be made" (p. 96).

Open admissibility enjoyed a period of popularity until the early 1980s, at which time the legal tide turned toward the more restrictive approach, with the ushering in of the per se exclusion rule by way of the *Mack* and *Shirley* courts. Due to research uncovering problems with confabulation and distortion in hypnotically refreshed recall, the popularity of open admissibility has waned, and it is currently honored in only a few states.

Totality of Circumstances Rule versus Adherence to *Hurd* Guidelines

Flanked on either side by its restrictive and permissive counterparts, the totality of circumstances rule offers a compromise. Although sometimes confused or considered indistinguishable, the totality of circumstances rule is not analogous to evaluating adherence to the *Hurd* or "Orne" criteria (described in this section). It is instead an approach that considers all aspects of the case, including adherence to specific guidelines to determine admissibility (Karlin, 1997).

This approach allows for the use of hypnotically elicited testimony only after the trial judge examines all of the circumstances surrounding the hypnotic interview and determines if it was properly employed. A primary consideration can include determining the degree of adherence to recommended safeguards, known as the "Orne criteria." Although first introduced by Orne in *California v. Quaglino* (1978), *State v. Hurd* (1981) is the landmark case associated with the requirement of specific procedural steps involved in the hypnotic process. As described by Sies and Wester (1985), the *Hurd* court employed a two-stage process for evaluating the possibility of admitting hypnotically refreshed testimony. First, the side that proposed the use of hypnotically refreshed testimony must inform opposing counsel of the intention and provide them with a record of the hypnotic interview. The judge then conducts a hearing to determine the appropriateness of using hypnosis by considering the details of the case. The second step involves evaluating the hypnotic session to determine if certain safeguards were followed to produce a more reliable interview. In addition to following these guidelines, the *Hurd* court also held that the state would then have the *additional* burden of proving that "there was no impermissibly suggestive or coercive conduct by the hypnotist and law enforcement personnel connected with the hypnotic exercise" (*State v. Hurd,* 1981, p. 306). The standard of proof in admitting hypnotically refreshed memories under *Hurd* is "clear and convincing evidence," with the burden resting on the party who proposes use of the testimony (Lynn, Neuschatz, & Fite, 2002; the Orne criteria are presented in the following section).

Although it seems a promising compromise, some have noted problems with the totality of circumstances approach. For example, the *Mack* court opined: "A case-by-case decision on the admissibility question would be prohibitively expensive, and reveals the difficulty of getting experts qualified to testify about hypnosis as an investigative rather than a therapeutic tool" (quoted in Perry, 1997, p. 268).

GUIDELINES FOR USE AND ETHICAL PRACTICE

In addition to the legal controls developed by the courts, the field has generated its own set of controls in the form of guidelines. The key to the ethical practice of forensic hypnosis lies in the expert's strict adherence to these established and accepted guidelines. Although no guarantee, the guidelines are also a prophylactic measure for protecting oneself against litigation, which is potentially more prevalent in forensic work. Almost every hypnosis organization has established guidelines concerning the use of hypnosis in memory enhancement, and some have generated guidelines specific to forensic hypnosis. Individual authors have also provided guidelines for use (Annon, 1989; Bloom, 1994; Brown, 1995; Knapp & VandeCreek, 1996; Timm, 1981; Yapko, 2003).

The Orne Criteria or *Hurd* Guidelines

The most widely recognized set of guidelines was firmly established by legal precedent in *State v. Hurd* (1981). Strongly influenced by Orne, the *Hurd* court adopted the following procedural safeguards:

- The hypnotic session should be conducted by a licensed psychiatrist or psychologist trained in the use of hypnosis.

- The qualified professional conducting the hypnotic session should be independent of and not responsible to the prosecutor, investigator, or defense.

- Any information given to the hypnotist by law enforcement personnel prior to the hypnotic session must be in written form so that subsequently the extent of the information the subject received from the hypnotist may be determined.

- Before induction of hypnosis, the hypnotist should obtain from the subject a detailed description of the facts as the subject remembers them, carefully avoiding adding any new elements to the witness's description of the events.

- All contacts between the hypnotist and the subject should be audio-recorded (if written today, videotaping would most likely be required) so that a permanent record is available for comparison and study to establish that the witness has not received information or suggestion that might later be reported as having been first described by the subject during hypnosis.

- Only the hypnotist and the subject should be present during any phase of the hypnotic session, including the prehypnotic testing and posthypnotic interview.

American Society for Clinical Hypnosis Guidelines

The guidelines recommended by the American Society for Clinical Hypnosis (ASCH) are perhaps the most comprehensive for forensic hypnosis, but they have yet to be tested in court, as there have been "few or no" court cases evaluating their legal impact (Lynn et al., 2002, p. 300).

American Society for Clinical Hypnosis (ASCH) provides general recommendations for clinicians who use hypnosis for memory retrieval, especially with abuse victims, and more specific recommendations for conducting forensic hypnosis. The reader is referred to Hammond et al. (1995) for guidelines specific to memory and hypnosis. Among ASCH's 11 recommended ethical guidelines for the practice of forensic hypnosis as set forth in Hammond et al. (1995, pp. 39–47) are the following:

- The clinician should have a working knowledge of the literature on hypnosis and memory; procure the necessary qualifications, training, and competency in the area of hypnosis; and know when the use of forensic hypnosis is contraindicated.
- The clinician should obtain a comprehensive informed consent.
- A videotaped psychological evaluation of the subject should take place prior to the hypnotic interview, and free recall questioning should take place before hypnosis, as well as preparing the subject for the possibility that memories obtained under hypnosis may or may not be accurate.
- *Consider* utilizing standardized hypnotizability scales to test the subject's hypnotizability potential.
- Assess for the possibility of spontaneous trance in highly hypnotizable persons.
- Use free recall as the first line of questioning, and have the subject repeat new information obtained during the hypnotic session after hypnosis has been terminated.
- If the subject verbalizes self-incriminating statements during the hypnotic session, the clinician should terminate the session immediately so that the subject can be read his or her rights by the investigators.
- Avoid using any leading questions that may contaminate memory.
- Subsequent to the hypnotic session, the clinician should discuss with investigative personnel the quality of the interview and any limitations that were present.

Other Guidelines

The Federal Bureau of Investigation has issued guidelines for their practice of forensic hypnosis (Ault, 1979; Garver, 1987). One notable difference in the FBI's guidelines from others lies in the fact that the "hypnosis coordinator" (often an FBI agent), as well as the mental health professional, are both allowed to question the subject during the investigative session. However, law enforcement personnel do not conduct the initial induction or the termination (dehypnotization) of the interview.

In addition to the FBI, ASCH, and *Hurd* guidelines, individual practitioners (e.g., Knapp & VandeCreek, 1996; London, 1997) have offered recommendations for practice. With regard to the practice of hypnosis in forensic settings, Annon (1989) and McConkey and Sheehan (1995) both provide useful, comprehensive guidelines that the practitioner may find helpful. The reader is also referred to

Brown (1995) for suggested recommendations when using hypnosis for memory enhancement. In addition, as forensic hypnosis cannot be extrapolated from clinical hypnosis, the clinician should also be knowledgeable regarding guidelines pertaining to the ethical practice of clinical hypnosis (Grisso & Vincent, 2005; Hambleton, 2002).

QUALIFICATIONS AND TRAINING TO PRACTICE FORENSIC HYPNOSIS

In addition to adhering to guidelines, it is essential for the clinician to be properly qualified and trained to practice forensic hypnosis. Scheflin (1997) highlighted the importance of hypnotist qualifications when he noted that the most oft-cited cases used to justify the per se exclusion rule involved the use of lay hypnotists (e.g., *Borawick v. Shay,* 1995; *People v. Kempinski,* 1980; *People v. Shirley,* 1982). However, the field may underestimate the need for more in-depth training in forensic hypnosis. Elkins and Hammond (1998) surveyed professionals practicing in the area of clinical hypnosis as to what specific training topics should be emphasized (time in minutes) in hypnosis training. With regard to the topic, "Doing Forensic and Investigative Hypnosis," the sample suggested an average of only 28 minutes.

In research conducted by Knight (2005), more than 200 hypnosis practitioners were surveyed. Participants were asked who they believed was qualified (as defined by degree) to conduct hypnosis for forensic purposes versus who was qualified to conduct hypnosis as part of clinical treatment. The sample believed the clinician should be more qualified to conduct hypnosis for forensic purposes versus clinical purposes. For example, approximately 90% of the sample believed that PhDs and MDs were qualified to conduct both. However, only 51% of the sample believed that licensed clinical social workers were qualified to conduct forensic hypnosis, as opposed to 80% of the sample who believed social workers were qualified to conduct clinical hypnosis. Only 47% of the sample believed that master's-level clinicians were qualified to conduct forensic hypnosis, as opposed to 72% of the sample endorsing the competence of master's-level clinicians to conduct clinical hypnosis. Only 15% of the sample believed that a trained police hypnotist was qualified to conduct forensic hypnosis. Overall, these findings suggest that many hypnosis practitioners believe that a doctoral degree is a necessary prerequisite for conducting forensic hypnosis as opposed to conducting clinical hypnosis.

In other research, Yapko's (1994) survey of more than 800 psychotherapists evidenced the fact that many who conduct hypnosis subscribe to dangerous myths regarding hypnosis and/or do not possess the necessary qualifications. For example, approximately half of Yapko's sample affirmed the following statement: "Psychotherapists can have greater faith in details of a traumatic event when obtained hypnotically than otherwise" (p. 167). Such affirmation of myths is due in part to improper training and lack of education regarding contemporary hypnosis research. The perpetuation of such myths underscores the need for properly qualified and trained professionals.

MINIMIZING THE LEGAL RISKS IN PRACTICING FORENSIC HYPNOSIS

Clinicians should employ techniques to reduce the risk of liability when practicing forensic hypnosis (Hambleton, 2002). Vulnerabilities include lawsuits by alleged perpetrators (which could also include legal action taken by "injured" or surviving family members) and lawsuits by the patients themselves, should they eventually recant their memories of the abusive incidents. London (1997) described the legal risks clinicians incur when practicing forensic hypnosis and suggested the need to maintain a heightened awareness of high-risk situations. He advised the clinician to conduct his or her practice as if there were three involved parties: the patient, the hypnosis professional, and the "potential" attorneys. In addition, he suggested that the practitioner possess specialty training in forensics and hypnosis, decide if hypnosis is advised with each patient, and determine whether there are forensic implications or the potential for forensic concerns throughout the course of treatment.

Often, the choice to use hypnosis must be judicious, as hypnotically refreshed testimony can fall prey to the per se exclusion rule, depriving the patient of pursuing legal retribution. London (1997) also advised that even though hypnosis can be the treatment of choice, in some clinical situations circumstances pose such a substantial legal risk for the clinician or the patient that alternative forms of treatment may be indicated. In addition, McConkey (1995) cautioned about unintentional risks of a legal and ethical nature: "In conducting a forensic hypnosis session, for instance, the actions of the hypnotist may inadvertently harm the witness, the investigation, or *the ultimate pursuit of justice*" (p. 6).

Informed Consent

Informed consent can minimize risk and safeguard against potential legal action (Cannell, Hudson, & Pope, 2001). The clinician must decide whether to inform patients that undergoing hypnosis may prevent them from entering future testimony concerning the material that emerges during hypnosis. Using a comprehensive informed consent strategy is recommended, including informing the patient of all possible legal consequences (McConkey & Sheehan, 1992; see Hammond et al., 1995, p. 50, for a sample informed consent form specific to the practice of forensic hypnosis).

ISSUES RELATED TO TESTIMONY

Clinicians practicing in this area must be prepared to provide testimony regarding forensic hypnosis: "The member of our society who goes ill-prepared and uncritical into the witness box to testify in court in the area of hypnosis is a likely source of anguish, embarrassment and anxiety to his or her colleagues" (Burrows, Dennerstein, & Frenader, 1983, p. 83). Odgers (1988) discussed the role the expert witness plays when called to testify about hypnotically refreshed testimony. He emphasized that the expert will most likely not be asked to speak to the reliability or veracity of the particular statements provided by the witness. Reasons for this include lack of consensus in the field regarding the use of hypnosis for memory enhancement, courts' reluctance in accepting a scientific basis for the technique of hypnosis, and allowing the jury to decide the veracity of the statements. Instead of validating the memories, the expert may explain the technique of hypnosis to the jury, including the hypnotic process and scientific standing of hypnosis (Labelle, Lamarche, & Laurence, 1990). This proactive intervention could serve to temper the typical juror's belief that hypnosis acts as a truth serum (Boyd et al., in press).

McConkey and Sheehan (1992, p. 151) differentiated between two potential positions that may be held by expert witnesses as related to forensic hypnosis: the "well-established knowledge" position and the "best available evidence" position. The former insists that the expert express only those views that are scientifically well established; the latter allows the expert to provide arguments based on the data that are "available in conducting and evaluating forensic hypnosis sessions" (p. 151). If hypnosis experts adhere to the well-established knowledge position, then "an expert would appear to have to argue against the forensic use of hypnosis" due to the variability in the available research findings on issues inherent in forensic hypnosis (p. 151). Therefore, before taking the stand, each expert must decide his or her position with regard to conflictual research findings and strategize how best to defend that position. (See Scheflin & Shapiro, 1989, for a mock cross-examination on issues related to forensic hypnosis.)

CONCLUSION

Forensic hypnosis is a controversial and challenging area in which to practice. The specialty remains under continual scrutiny from the courts and the scientific community, as research reflects inherent risks to truth in a context where truth is paramount. These risks include the proven fallibility of hypnotically refreshed memories and the possibility of deception under trance. Despite these challenges, hypnosis continues to be used for forensic purposes, as there are also data to suggest that it can facilitate recall and provide a valuable tool in forensic and investigative work.

To facilitate ethical practice, the expert must maintain awareness and understanding of contemporary research findings regarding the use of hypnosis with forensic populations. Such awareness will facilitate competent application of a technique in need of knowledgeable, skillful practitioners. Finally, as a requisite before practice, clinicians should obtain proper training and maintain strict adherence to procedural guidelines and ethical standards.

REFERENCES

Adelman, R. M., & Howard, A. (1984). Expert testimony on malingering: The admissibility of clinical procedures of the detection of deception. *Behavioral Sciences and the Law, 2,* 5–19.

Alexander, G. J., & Scheflin, A. W. (1998). *Law and mental disorder.* Durham, NC: Carolina Academic Press.

Allison, R. B. (1984). Difficulties diagnosing the multiple personality syndrome in a death penalty case. *International Journal of Clinical and Experimental Hypnosis, 32,* 102–117.

American Medical Association, Council on Scientific Affairs. (1985). Scientific status of refreshing recollection by the use of hypnosis. *Journal of the American Medical Association, 253,* 1918–1923.

American Medical Association, Council on Scientific Affairs. (1994). Memories of childhood abuse (CSA Report 5-A-94). Reprinted in *International Journal of Clinical and Experimental Hypnosis, 43,* 114–115.

American Psychological Association, Division 17 Committee on Women, Division 42 Trauma and Gender Issues Committee. (1995). *Psychotherapy guidelines for working with clients who may have an abuse or trauma history.* Washington, DC: Author.

Annon, J. S. (1989). Use of hypnosis in a forensic setting: A cautionary note. *American Journal of Forensic Psychology, 7,* 37–48.

Ault, R. L. (1979). FBI guidelines for the use of hypnosis. *International Journal of Clinical and Experimental Hypnosis, 2,* 449–451.

Barnier, A. J., & McConkey, K. M. (1993). Reports of real and repressed memories: The relevance of hypnosis, hypnotizability, and test context. *Journal of Abnormal Psychology, 101,* 521–528.

Barnier, A. J., McConkey, K. M., & Wright, J. (2004). Posthypnotic amnesia for autobiographical episodes: Influencing memory accessibility and quality. *International Journal of Clinical and Experimental Hypnosis, 52,* 260–279.

Beahrs, J. O. (1988). Hypnosis can not be fully nor reliably excluded from the courtroom. *American Journal of Clinical Hypnosis, 31,* 18–27.

Bianchi v. Blodgett, No. 93-35524 (U.S. Ct. of Appeals for the 9th Ct., May 1994).

Bloom, P. (1994). Clinical guidelines in using hypnosis in uncovering memories of sexual abuse: A master class commentary. *International Journal of Clinical and Experimental Hypnosis, 62,* 173–178.

Blum, G. S., & Graef, J. R. (1971). The detection over time of subjects simulating hypnosis. *International Journal of Clinical and Experimental Hypnosis, 19,* 211–224.

Boggs, B. C. (1993). Rethinking the ban on hypnotically enhanced testimony. *IL Bar Journal, 81,* 136–137.

Borawick v. Shay, 68 F. 3rd 597 (2nd Cir. 1995).

Boyd, A., McLearen, A., Meyer, R., & Denney, J. (in press). *The assessment of deception.* Sarasota, FL: Professional Resource Press.

Brodie-Innes, J. W. (1891). Legal aspects of hypnotism. *Judicial Review, 3,* 51–61.

Brown, D. (1995). Pseudomemories: The standard of science and the standard of care in trauma treatment. *American Journal of Clinical Hypnosis, 37,* 1–24.

Burrows, G. D., Dennerstein, L., & Frenader, G. (1983). A note on hypnosis and the law. *Australian Journal of Clinical and Experimental Hypnosis, 11,* 83–88.

California v. Quaglino, 439 U.S. 875, 99 S. Ct. 212, 58 L.Ed.2d 189 (1978).

Cannell, J., Hudson, J. I., & Pope, H. G., Jr. (2001). Standards for informed consent in recovered memory therapy. *Journal of the American Academy of Psychiatry and Law, 29,* 138–147.

Coe, W. C. (1977). The problem of relevance versus ethics in researching hypnosis and antisocial conduct. *Annals of the New York Academy of Sciences,* 90–104.

Coe, W. C. (1992). Hypnosis: Wherefore art thou? *International Journal of Clinical and Experimental Hypnosis, 40,* 219–237.

Coe, W. C., Kobayashi, K., & Howard, M. D. (1972). An approach toward isolating factors that influence antisocial conduct in hypnosis. *International Journal of Clinical and Experimental Hypnosis, 20,* 118–131.

Coe, W. C., Kobayashi, K., & Howard, M. D. (1973). Experimental and ethical problems of evaluating the influence of hypnosis in antisocial conduct. *Journal of Abnormal Psychology, 82,* 472–482.

Coleman, B. L., Stevens, M. J., & Reeder, G. D. (2001). What makes recovered-memory testimony compelling to jurors? *Law and Human Behavior, 2,* 317–338.

Colwick, E. (1995). Hypnotically recalled testimony: Issues facing courts in their determination of its admissibility in civil sexual abuse cases. *Law and Psychology Review, 19,* 183–201.

Cornell v. Superior Court of San Diego County, 52 Cal. 2d 99, 338 P.2d 447 (1959).

Courtois, C. A. (2001). Implications of the memory controversy for clinical practice: An overview of treatment recommendations and guidelines. *Journal of Child Sexual Abuse, 9,* 183–210.

Cox, R. E., & Barnier, A. J. (2003). Posthypnotic amnesia for a first romantic relationship: Forgetting the entire relationship versus forgetting selected events. *Memory, 11,* 307–318.

Daubert v. Merrell Dow Pharmaceuticals, Inc., 125 L.Ed.2d 469 (1993).

Deffenbacher, K. A., Bornstein, B. H., Penrod, S. D., & McGorty, E. K. (2004). A meta-analytic review of the effects of high stress on eyewitness memory. *Law and Human Behavior, 28,* 687–706.

Diamond, B. L. (1980). Inherent problems in the use of pretrial hypnosis on a prospective witness. *California Law Review, 68,* 313–349.

Dinges, D. F., Whitehouse, W. G., Orne, E. C., Powell, J. W., Orne, M. T., & Erdelyi, M. H. (1992). Evaluating hypnotic memory enhancement (hypermnesia and reminiscence) using multiple forced recall. *Journal of Experimental Psychology: Learning, Memory, and Cognition, 18,* 1139–1147.

Dowd, T. E. (2002). Memory processes in psychotherapy: Implications for integration. *Journal of Psychotherapy Integration, 12,* 233–246.

Drivdahl, S. B., & Zaragoza, M. S. (2001). The role of perceptual elaboration and individual differences in the creation of false memories for suggested events. *Applied Cognitive Psychology, 15,* 265–281.

Eimer, B. N., & Gravitz, M. A. (2002). Clinical and forensic hypnosis. In F. Dattilio & R. Sadoff (Eds.), *Mental health experts: Roles and qualifications for court* (pp. 147–162). Mechanicsburg, PA: Pennsylvania Bar Institute.

Elkins, G. R., & Hammond, D. C. (1998). Standards of training in clinical hypnosis: Preparing professionals for the twenty-first century. *American Journal of Clinical Hypnosis, 41,* 55–64.

Erdelyi, M. H. (1994). Hypnotic hypermnesia: The empty set of hypermnesia. *International Journal of Clinical and Experimental Hypnosis, 42,* 379–390.

Farvolden, P., & Woody, E. Z. (2004). Hypnosis, memory and frontal executive functioning. *International Journal of Clinical and Experimental Hypnosis, 52,* 3–26.

Frye v. United States, 293 F. 1013 34 A.L.R. 145 (D.C. Cir. 1923).

Garver, R. B. (1987). Investigative hypnosis. In W. C. Wester (Ed.), *Clinical hypnosis: A case management approach* (pp. 213–225). Cincinnati, OH: Behavioral Science Center.

Gibson, H. B. (1991). Can hypnosis compel people to commit harmful, immoral and criminal acts? A review of the literature. *Contemporary Hypnosis: Journal of the British Society of Experimental and Clinical Hypnosis, 8,* 129–140.

Gravitz, M. A. (1995). First admission (1846) of hypnotic testimony in court. *American Journal of Clinical Hypnosis, 37,* 326–330.

Gravitz, M. A. (2002). Hypnosis as a counter-measure against the polygraph test of deception. *Polygraph Journal, 31,* 293–297.

Gravitz, M. A. (2004). The historical role of hypnosis in the theoretical origins of transference. *International Journal of Clinical and Experimental Hypnosis, 52,* 113–131.

Grisso, T., & Vincent, G. M. (2005). The empirical limits of forensic mental health assessment. *Law and Human Behavior, 29,* 1–5.

Haber, R. N., & Haber, L. (2000). Experiencing, remembering, and reporting events. *Psychology, Public Policy, and Law, 6,* 1057–1097.

Hambleton, R. W. (2002). *Practising safe hypnosis: A risk management guide.* Norwalk, CT: Crown House Publishing.

Hammond, D. C., Garver, R. B., Mutter, C. B., Crasilneck, H. B., Frischholz, E. J., Gravitz, M. A., et al. (1995). *Clinical hypnosis and memory: Guidelines for clinicians and for forensic hypnosis.* Seattle, WA: American Society of Clinical Hypnosis.

Harding v. State, 5 Md. App. 230, 246 A.2d 302 *cert. denied,* 395 U.S. 949, 89 S. Ct. 2030; 23, L.Ed.2d 468 (1968).

Heap, M. (2000). The alleged dangers of stage hypnosis. *Contemporary Hypnosis, 17,* 117–126.

Hilgard, E. R. (1992). Dissociation and theories of hypnosis. In E. Fromm & M. R. Nash (Eds.), *Contemporary hypnosis research* (pp. 69–101). New York: Guilford Press.

Hilgard, E. R., & Loftus, E. F. (1979). Effective interrogation of the eyewitness. *International Journal of Clinical and Experimental Hypnosis, 27,* 342–357.

Karle, H. W. A. (1991). Professional and ethical issues. In M. Heap & W. Dryden (Eds.), *Hypnotherapy: A handbook—Psychotherapy handbook series* (pp. 184–199). Philadelphia: Open University Press.

Karlin, R. A. (1997). Illusory safeguards: Legitimizing distorting recall with guidelines for forensic hypnosis: Two case reports. *International Journal of Clinical and Experimental Hypnosis, 45,* 18–40.

Karlin, R. A., & Orne, M. T. (1996). Commentary on *Borawick v. Shay:* Hypnosis, social influence, incestuous child abuse, and satanic ritual abuse—The iatrogenic creation of horrific memories of the remote past. *Cultic Studies Journal, 31,* 42–91.

Karlin, R. A., & Orne, M. T. (1997). Hypnosis and the iatrogenic creation of memory: On the need for a *per se* exclusion of testimony based on hypnotically influenced recall. *Cultic Studies Journal, 14,* 172–206.

Kassin, S. M. (2005). On the psychology of confessions. *American Psychologist, 60,* 215–229.

Kassin, S. M., Ellsworth, P. C., & Smith, V. L. (1989). The "general acceptance" of psychological research on eyewitness testimony: A survey of the experts. *American Psychologist, 44,* 1089–1098.

Kebbell, M. R., & Wagstaff, G. F. (1998). Hypnotic interviewing: The best way to interview eyewitnesses? *Behavioral Sciences and the Law, 16,* 115–129.

Kennedy, J., & Coe, W. C. (1990, August). *Breaching posthypnotic amnesia: Deception or self-deception?* Paper presented at the 98th annual convention of the American Psychological Association, Boston.

Kennedy, J., & Coe, W. C. (1994). Nonverbal signs of deception during posthypnotic amnesia: A brief communication. *International Journal of Clinical and Experimental Hypnosis, 42,* 13–19.

Kilhstrom, J. F. (1994). Hypnosis, delayed recall, and the principles of memory. *International Journal of Clinical and Experimental Hypnosis, 42,* 337–345.

Kinnunen, T., Zamansky, H. S., & Block, M. (1994). Is the hypnotized subject lying? *Journal of Abnormal Psychology, 103,* 184–191.

Kinnunen, T., Zamansky, H. S., & Nordstrom, B. L. (2001). Is the hypnotized subject complying? *International Journal of Clinical and Experimental Hypnosis, 49,* 83–94.

Kirsch, I., Silva, C. E., Carone, J. E., Johnston, J. D., & Simon, B. (1989). The surreptitious observation design: An experimental paradigm for distinguishing artifact from essence in hypnosis. *Journal of Abnormal Psychology, 98,* 132–136.

Knapp, S., & VandeCreek, L. (1996). Risk management for psychologists: Treating patients who recover lost memories of childhood abuse. *Professional Psychology Research and Practice, 27,* 452–459.

Knight, S. (2005). Beliefs toward forensic hypnosis: An expert sample versus an undergraduate sample with an educational lecture manipulation. *Dissertation Abstracts International, 65,* 4292B. (UMI No. AAI3144725)

Krippner, S. (2005). Trance and the trickster: Hypnosis as a liminal phenomenon. *International Journal of Clinical and Experimental Hypnosis, 53,* 97–118.

Kroger, W., & Douce, R. (1979). Hypnosis in criminal investigation. *International Journal of Clinical and Experimental Hypnosis, 27,* 358–374.

Labelle, L., Lamarche, M., & Laurence, J. (1990). Potential jurors' opinions on the effects of hypnosis on eyewitness identification: A brief communication. *International Journal of Clinical and Experimental Hypnosis, 38,* 315–319.

Labelle, L., Laurence, J. R., Nadon, R., & Perry, C. W. (1990). Hypnotizability preference for an imagic cognitive style, and memory creation in hypnosis. *Journal of Abnormal Psychology, 99,* 222–228.

Laurence, J. R., & Perry, C. (1983). Hypnotically created memory among highly hypnotizable subjects. *Science, 222,* 523–524.

Laurence, J. R., & Perry, C. (1988). *Hypnosis, will, and memory: A psycho-legal history.* New York: Guilford Press.

Leyra v. Denno, 347 U.S. 556, 74 S. Ct. 716, 98 L.Ed.948 (1954).

Loftus, E. F. (1979). *Eyewitness testimony.* Cambridge, MA: Harvard University Press.

Loftus, E. F. (1998). The price of bad memories. *Skeptical Inquirer, 22,* 23–24.

Loftus, E. F. (2003). Our changeable memories: Legal and practical implications. *Nature Reviews: Neuroscience, 4,* 231–234.

London, R. W. (1997). Forensic and legal implications in clinical practice: A master class commentary. *International Journal of Clinical and Experimental Hypnosis, 65,* 6–17.

Lynn, S. J. (1990). "Some conditions of compliance and resistance among hypnotic subjects": Comment: Is hypnotic influence coercive? *American Journal of Clinical Hypnosis, 32,* 239–241.

Lynn, S. J., & Kirsch, I. (1996). Alleged alien abductions: False memories, hypnosis and fantasy proneness. *Psychological Inquiry, 7,* 151–155.

Lynn, S. J., Lock, T., Loftus, E., Krackow, E., & Lilienfeld, S. O. (2003). The remembrance of things past: Problematic memory recovery techniques in psychotherapy. In S. O. Lilienfeld & S. J. Lynn (Eds.), *Science and pseudoscience in clinical psychology* (pp. 205–239). New York: Guilford Press.

Lynn, S. J., & Nash, M. R. (1994). Truth in memory: Ramifications for psychotherapy and hypnotherapy. *American Journal of Clinical Hypnosis, 36,* 194–208.

Lynn, S. J., Neuschatz, J., & Fite, R. (2002). Hypnosis and memory: Implications for the courtroom and psychotherapy. In M. L. Eisen (Ed.), *Memory and suggestibility in the forensic interview* (pp. 287–307). Mahwah, NJ: Erlbaum.

Lynn, S. J., Rhue, J. W., Meyers, B. P., & Weeks, J. R. (1994). Pseudomemory in hypnotized and simulating subjects. *International Journal of Clinical and Experimental Hypnosis, 42,* 118–129.

Martin, D. J., & Lynn, S. J. (1996). The hypnotic simulation index: Successful discrimination of real versus simulating participants. *International Journal of Clinical and Experimental Hypnosis, 44,* 338–353.

Mazzoni, G., & Memon, A. (2003). Imagination can create false autobiographical memories. *Psychological Science, 14,* 186–188.

McConkey, K. M. (1995). Hypnosis, memory, and the ethics of uncertainty. *Australian Psychologist, 30,* 1–10.

McConkey, K. M., & Sheehan, P. (1992). Ethical issues in forensic hypnosis. *Australian Psychologist, 27,* 150–153.

McConkey, K. M., & Sheehan, P. W. (1995). *Hypnosis, memory and behavior in criminal investigation.* New York: Guilford Press.

Meyer, R. (1992). *Practical clinical hypnosis: Techniques and applications.* New York: Lexington Books.

Meyer, R. (in press). *Case studies in abnormal behavior* (7th ed.). Boston: Allyn & Bacon.

Meyer, R., & Weaver, C. (in press-a). *The clinician's handbook* (5th ed.). Manuscript in preparation.

Meyer, R., & Weaver, C. (in press-b). *Law and mental health.* New York: Guilford Press.

Mollon, P. (2002). *Remembering trauma: A psychotherapist's guide to memory and illusion* (2nd ed.). London: Whurr.

Murrey, G. J., Cross, H. J., & Whipple, J. (1992). Hypnotically created pseudomemories: Further investigation into the "memory distortion or response bias" question. *Journal of Abnormal Psychology, 101,* 75–77.

Naish, P. (1988). Forensic hypnosis: An overview. In M. Heap (Ed.), *Hypnosis: Current clinical, experimental and forensic practices* (pp. 351–356). New York: Croom Helm.

Nardi, C. (1984). Hypnosis of the accused: Defendant's choice. *Journal of Criminal Law and Criminology, 75,* 995–1019.

Nash, M. R. (2000). The status of hypnosis as an empirically validated clinical intervention: A preamble to the special issue. *International Journal of Clinical and Experimental Hypnosis, 48,* 107–112.

Neuschatz, J. S., Lynn, S. J., Benoit, G. E., & Fite, R. (2003). Hypnosis and memory illusions: An investigation using the Deese/Roediger and McDermott paradigm. *Imagination, Cognition, and Personality, 22,* 3–12.

Newman, A. W., & Thompson, J. W. (2001). The rise and fall of forensic hypnosis in criminal investigation. *Journal of the American Academy of Psychiatry and Law, 29,* 75–84.

Niehaus, J. (1999). *Investigative forensic hypnosis.* Boca Raton, FL: CRC Press.

Ochi, K. (2002). Use of hypnosis to enhance eyewitness memory. *Japanese Journal of Hypnosis, 47,* 23–30.

Odgers, S. J. (1988). Evidence law and previously hypnotized witnesses. *Australian Journal of Clinical and Experimental Hypnosis, 16,* 91–102.

Orne, E. C., Whitehouse, W. G., Dinges, D. F., & Orne, M. T. (1996). Memory liabilities associated with hypnosis: Does low hypnotizability confer immunity? *International Journal of Clinical and Experimental Hypnosis, 44,* 354–369.

Orne, M. T. (1971). The simulation of hypnosis: Why, how, and what it means. *International Journal of Clinical and Experimental Hypnosis, 19,* 183–210.

Orne, M. T. (1979). The use and misuse of hypnosis in court. *International Journal of Clinical and Experimental Hypnosis, 27,* 311–341.

Orne, M. T., Dinges, D. E., & Orne, E. C. (1990). *Rock v. Arkansas:* Hypnosis, the defendants' privilege. *International Journal of Clinical and Experimental Hypnosis, 38,* 250–265.

Orne, M. T., & Evans, F. J. (1965). Social control in the psychological experiment: Antisocial behavior and hypnosis. *Journal of Personality and Social Psychology, 1,* 198–200.

Orne, M. T., Soskis, D. A., Dinges, D. F., & Orne, E. C. (1984). Hypnotically induced testimony. In G. L. Wells & E. F. Loftus (Eds.), *Eyewitness testimony: Psychological perspectives* (pp. 171–215). New York: Cambridge University Press.

Orne, M. T., Soskis, D. A., Dinges, D. F., Orne, E. C., & Tonry, M. H. (1985). Hypnotically refreshed testimony: Enhanced memory or tampering with evidence. In National Institute of Justice (Ed.), *Issues and practices in criminal justice* (pp. 41–49). Washington, DC: National Institute of Justice.

People v. Boudin, 460 N.Y. S. 2d 879, 884 (1983).

People v. Ebanks, 117 Cal. 652, 49 P. 1049, 40 L.R.A. 269 (1897).

People v. Guerra, 37 Cal. 3d 385 (1984).

People v. Kempinski, No. W8OCF 352 (Cir. Ct., 12th Dist. Will County, October 21, 1980, unreported, 1980).

People v. Leyra, 302 N.Y. 353 98 N.E.2d 553 (1951).

People v. Shirley, 31 Cal. 3d 18 723 P.2d 1354 181 Cal. Rptr. 243 (1982).

People v. Sorscher, 151 Mich. App.122 391 N.W. (1986).

Perlini, A. H., Haley, A., & Buczel, A. (1998). Hypnosis and reporting biases: Telling the truth. *Journal of Research in Personality, 32,* 13–32.

Perry, C. (1979). Hypnotic coercion and compliance to it: A review of evidence presented in a legal case. *International Journal of Clinical and Experimental Hypnosis, 27,* 187–218.

Perry, C. (1997). Admissibility and *per se* exclusion of hypnotically elicited recall in American courts of law. *International Journal of Clinical and Experimental Hypnosis, 55,* 266–279.

Perry, C., Orne, M. T., London, R. W., & Orne, E. C. (1996). Rethinking *per se* exclusions of hypnotically-elicited recall as legal testimony. *International Journal of Clinical and Experimental Hypnosis, 44,* 66–81.

Perugini, E. M., Kirsch, I., Allen, S. T., Coldwell, E., Meredith, J. M., Montgomery, G. H., et al. (1998). Surreptitious observation of responses to hypnotically suggested hallucinations: A test of the compliance hypothesis. *International Journal of Clinical and Experimental Hypnosis, 46,* 191–203.

Pettinati, H. M. (1988). Measuring hypnotizability in psychotic patients. *International Journal of Clinical and Experimental Hypnosis, 30,* 404–416.

Porter, S., Campbell, M., Birt, A., & Woodworth, M. (2003). We said, she said: A response to Loftus. *Canadian Psychology, 44,* 213–215.

Register, P. A., & Kilhstrom, J. F. (1987). Hypnotic effects on hypermnesia. *International Journal of Clinical and Experimental Hypnosis, 35,* 155–170.

Reiser, M. (1983). LAPD: The police behavioral scientist. *American Journal of Forensic Psychology, 3,* 28–32.

Roberts, K., & Wagstaff, G. F. (1996). The effects of beliefs and information about hypnosis on the legal defense of automatism through hypnosis. *Psychology, Crime, and Law, 2,* 259–268.

Rock v. Arkansas, 483 U.S. 44 (1987).

Roebers, C. M., & McConkey, K. M. (2003). Mental reinstatement of the misinformation context and the misinformation effect in children and adults. *Applied Cognitive Psychology, 17,* 477–493.

Rowland v. Commonwealth, 901 S.W.2d 871 (Ky. S. Ct. 1995).

Sales, B. D., & Shuman, D. W. (2005). *Experts in court: Reconciling law, science, and professional knowledge.* Washington, DC: American Psychological Association.

Sanders, G. S., & Simmons, W. L. (1983). Use of hypnosis to enhance eyewitness accuracy: Does it work? *Journal of Applied Psychology, 68,* 70–77.

Sandoval, V. A. (2003). Strategies to avoid interview contamination. *Federal Bureau of Investigation Law Enforcement Bulletin, 72,* 1–12.

Scheflin, A. W. (1994). Forensic hypnosis: Unanswered questions. *Australian Journal of Clinical and Experimental Hypnosis, 22,* 25–37.

Scheflin, A. W. (1996). A commentary on *Borawick v. Shay:* The fate of hypnotically retrieved memories. *Cultic Studies Journal, 13,* 26–41.

Scheflin, A. W. (1997). False memory and Buridan's ass: A response to Karlin and Orne. *Cultic Studies Journal, 14,* 207–289.

Scheflin, A. W., & Frischholz, E. J. (1999). Significant dates in the history of forensic hypnosis. *American Journal of Clinical Hypnosis, 42,* 85–107.

Scheflin, A. W., & Shapiro, J. L. (1989). *Trance on trial.* New York: Guilford Press.

Scheflin, A. W., Spiegel, H., & Spiegel, D. (1999). Forensic uses of hypnosis. In A. K. Hess & I. B. Weiner (Eds.), *Handbook of forensic psychology* (pp. 474–500). New York: Wiley.

Scoboria, A., Mazzoni, G., Kirsch, I., & Milling, L. (2002). Immediate and persisting effects of misleading questions and hypnosis on memory reports. *Journal of Experimental Psychology: Applied, 8,* 26–32.

Sheehan, P. (1997). Recovered memories: Some clinical and experimental challenges. *Australian Journal of Clinical and Experimental Hypnosis, 25,* 18–39.

Sheehan, P. W., Grigg, L., & McCann, T. (1984). Memory distortion following exposure to false information in hypnosis. *Journal of Abnormal Psychology, 93,* 259–265.

Sheehan, P. W., & McConkey, K. M. (1988). Lying in hypnosis: A conceptual analysis of the possibilities. *Australian Journal of Clinical and Experimental Hypnosis, 16,* 1–9.

Sheehan, P. W., & Statham, D. (1988). Associations between lying and hypnosis: An empirical study. *British Journal of Experimental and Clinical Hypnosis, 5,* 87–94.

Sheehan, P. W., Statham, D., & Jamieson, G. A. (1991). Pseudomemory effects and their relationship to level of susceptibility to hypnosis and state instruction. *Journal of Personality and Social Psychology, 60,* 130–137.

Sheehan, P. W., & Tilden, J. (1986). The consistency of occurrences of memory distortion following hypnotic induction. *International Journal of Clinical and Experimental Hypnosis, 24,* 122–137.

Sies, D. E., & Wester, W. C. (1985). Judicial approaches to the question of hypnotically refreshed testimony: A history and analysis. *Depaul Law Review, 35,* 77–124.

Spanos, N. P. (1986). Hypnotic Behavior: A social-psychological interpretation of amnesia, analgesia, and "trance logic." *Behavioral and Brain Sciences, 9,* 449–467.

Spanos, N. P. (1992). Compliance and reinterpretation in hypnotic responding. *Contemporary Hypnosis, 9,* 7–15.

Spanos, N. P., Burgess, C. A., Roncon, V., Wallace-Capretta, S., & Cross, P. (1993). Surreptitiously observed hypnotic responding in simulators and in skill-trained and untrained high hypnotizables. *Journal of Personality and Social Psychology, 65,* 391–398.

Spanos, N. P., & Coe, W. C. (1992). A social-psychological approach to hypnosis. In E. Fromm & M. R. Nash (Eds.), *Contemporary hypnosis research* (pp. 102–130). New York: Guilford Press.

Spiegel, H. (1980). Hypnosis and evidence: Help or hindrance? *Annals of the New York Academy of Sciences, 347,* 73–85.

Spiegel, H., & Spiegel, D. (2004). *Trance and treatment: Clinical uses of hypnosis* (2nd ed.). Washington, DC: American Psychiatric Association.

Stanley, R. O. (1994). The protection of the professional use of hypnosis: The need for legal controls. *Australian Journal of Clinical and Experimental Hypnosis, 22,* 39–51.

State v. Bianchi, No. 79-10116 (Wash. Super. Ct. October 19, 1979).

State v. Hurd, 414 A.2d 291 (N.J. 1981).

State v. Mack, 292 N.W.2d (Minn. 1980).

State v. Mena, No. 502-6-R (Ariz. 1981).

Steblay, N. M., & Bothwell, R. K. (1994). Evidence for hypnotically refreshed testimony. *Law and Human Behavior, 18,* 635–651.

Tayloe, D. R. (1995). The validity of repressed memories and the accuracy of their recall through hypnosis: A case study from the courtroom. *American Journal of Clinical Hypnosis, 37,* 25–31.

Timm, H. W. (1981). The effect of forensic hypnosis techniques on eyewitness recall and recognition. *Journal of Police Science and Administration, 9,* 188.

Udolf, R. (1983). *Forensic hypnosis.* Lexington, MA: Heath.

Wade, K. A., Garry, M., Read, J. D., & Lindsay, S. A. (2002). A picture is worth a thousand lies. *Psychonomic Bulletin Review, 9,* 597–603.

Wagstaff, G. F., Brunas-Wagstaff, J., Cole, J., Knapton, L., Winterbottom, J., Rean, V., et al. (2004). Facilitating memory with hypnosis, focused meditation, and eye closure. *International Journal of Clinical and Experimental Hypnosis, 52,* 434–455.

Wagstaff, G. F., Green, K., & Somers, E. (1997). The effects of the experience of hypnosis, and hypnotic depth, on jurors' decisions regarding the defense of hypnotic automatism. *Legal and Criminological Psychology, 2,* 65–74.

Watkins, J. G. (1984). The Bianchi (L.A. Hillside Strangler) case: Sociopath or multiple personality disorder? *International Journal of Clinical and Experimental Hypnosis, 32,* 67–101.

Whitehouse, W., Dinges, D., Orne, E. C., & Orne, M. T. (1988). Hypnotic hypermnesia: Enhanced memory accessibility or report bias? *Journal of Abnormal Psychology, 97,* 289–295.

Yapko, M. (1994). Suggestibility and repressed memories of abuse: A survey of psychotherapists' beliefs. *American Journal of Clinical Hypnosis, 36,* 163–171.

Yapko, M. (2003). *Trancework.* New York: Taylor & Francis.

Yuille, J. C., & Cutshall, J. L. (1986). A case study of eyewitness memory of a crime. *Journal of Applied Psychology, 71,* 291–301.

Yuille, J. C., & Kim, C. K. (1987). A field study of the forensic use of hypnosis. *Canadian Journal of Behavioural Science, 19,* 418–429.

Author Index

Subject Index